Property Law: Cases and Materials

Property Law
Cases and Materials

Sixth Edition

Roger J. Smith

Fellow and Tutor in Law,
Magdalen College, Oxford

PEARSON

Harlow, England • London • New York • Boston • San Francisco • Toronto • Sydney
Auckland • Singapore • Hong Kong • Tokyo • Seoul • Taipei • New Delhi
Cape Town • São Paulo • Mexico City • Madrid • Amsterdam • Munich • Paris • Milan

Pearson Education Limited
Edinburgh Gate
Harlow CM20 2JE
United Kingdom
Tel: +44 (0)1279 623623
Web: www.pearson.com/uk

First published in 2000 (print)
Second edition published 2003 (print)
Third edition published 2006 (print)
Fourth edition published 2009 (print)
Fifth edition published 2012 (print and electronic)
Sixth edition published 2015 (print and electronic)

ISBN: 978–1–292–07852–6 (print)
      978–1–292–07854–0 (PDF)
      978–1–292–07853–3 (eText)
      978–1–292–07855–7 (ePub)

British Library Cataloguing-in-Publication Data
A catalogue record for the print edition is available from the British Library

Library of Congress Cataloging-in-Publication Data
Smith, Roger J. (Roger John), 1948- author
   Property law : cases and materials / Roger J. Smith. -- Sixth Edition.
      pages cm
   ISBN 978-1-292-07852-6
   1. Real property--England. I. Title.
   KD829.S643 2015
   346.4104'3--dc23

                                        2015001802

10 9 8 7 6 5 4 3 2 1
19 18 17 16 15

Print edition typeset in 10/12pt Minion Pro by 35
Print edition printed and bound in Malaysia (CTP-PJB)

NOTE THAT ANY PAGE CROSS REFERENCES REFER TO THE PRINT EDITION

Brief contents

Contents in detail

Preface

The years since the previous edition have seen a steady stream of cases and these have been duly incorporated in this new edition. Two areas stand out. Unsurprisingly, human rights cases have continued to flow. Particular mention may be made of *Malik* v *Fassenfelt* and *McDonald* v *McDonald* on the horizontal effect of Article 8 (respect for home, etc.) and *Sims* v *Dacorum BC* (Supreme Court) on the termination of joint periodic tenancies. However, it is registration of title that has seen the most interesting developments. Leaving aside the perennially litigated area of overriding interests (on which, see *Chaudhary* v *Yavuz*), forgery has provided the basis for much modern analysis. This was investigated in *Fitzwilliam* v *Richall Holdings Services Ltd* and *Swift 1st Ltd* v *Chief Land Registrar*, the latter case also dealing with indemnity. Whether rectification can affect successors in title (to the proprietor involved in the 'mistake' triggering rectification) has attracted much attention in the past few years. We now have a full and authoritative Court of Appeal analysis in *Gold Harp Properties Ltd* v *Macleod*.

Although there have been no cases on the family home of the importance of *Stack* v *Dowden* and *Jones* v *Kernott*, there has been some guidance as to how the post-*Stack* principles operate. This chapter has been substantially re-ordered and rewritten, adopting the structure in the eighth edition of *Property Law*.

Acknowledgements

We are grateful to the following for permission to reproduce copyright material:

Figures

Figure 10.1 from Land Registry, Official copy of register of title, title number CS705289, Edition date 19.11.2008. © Crown copyright 2011 HMLR. Reproduced with kind permission of Land Registry; Figure 10.2 from Land Registry, Official copy of title plan, title number CS705289, Ordnance Survey map reference TL2467SW. © Crown copyright 2011 HMLR. Reproduced with kind permission of Land Registry.

Text

Extract 1.1.1 from 'Before we begin' by Peter Birks (footnotes omitted) in *Land Law: Themes and Perspectives*, 1st ed., Oxford University Press (Bright, S. and Dewar, J. (eds.) 1998) pp. 457–63, 467–8, 470–3, 476–86, by permission of Oxford University Press; Extract 1.1.2 from 'The idea of property in land' by Kevin Gray and Susan Francis Gray (footnotes omitted) in *Land Law: Themes and Perspectives*, 1st ed., Oxford University Press (Bright, S. and Dewar, J. (eds.) 1998) pp. 15–6, 18–21, 27–31, 35–40, 51, by permission of Oxford University Press; Extract 1.2.1 from *Property and Justice (some footnotes omitted)*, 3rd ed., Oxford University Press (Harris, J. W. 1996) pp. 149–51, by permission of Oxford University Press; Extract 1.3.2 from *Baker* v *Archer-Shee* [1927] AC 844; Extract 2.2.1 from *X* v *Y* (2004) ICR 1634; Extract 2.3.1 from *Manchester City Council* v *Pinnock* [2010] 3 WLR 1441 (SC); Extract 3.1.1 from *The Law of Property*, 3rd ed., Oxford University Press (Lawson, F. H. and Rudden, B. 2002) pp. 77–80, 90, by permission of Oxford University Press; Extract 3.1.2 from *Lord Bernstein of Leigh* v *Skyviews & General Ltd* [1978] QB 479; Extract 3.1.3 from *Bocardo SA* v *Star Energy UK Onshore Ltd* [2011] 1 AC 380; Extract 3.1.4 from *Re Moore* (1888) 39 Ch D 116; Extract 3.1.5 from *Re Wilkinson* [1926] Ch 842; Extract 3.1.6 from *Re Macleay* (1875) LR 20 Eq 186; Extract 3.1.7 from *Re Rosher* (1884) 26 Ch D 801; Extract 3.1.11 from *Blathwayt* v *Baron Cawley* [1976] AC 397; Extract 3.1.12 from *Re Tuck's Settlement Trusts* [1978] Ch 49; Extract 3.1.13 from *Doherty* v *Allman* (1878) 3 App Cas 709; Extract 3.1.16 from *Re Cartwright* (1889) 41 Ch D 532; Extract 3.1.18 from *National Provincial Bank Ltd* v *Ainsworth* [1965] AC 1175; Extract 3.2.2 from *Manchester Trust* v *Furness* [1895] 2 QB 539; Extract 4.1.3 from *Moffatt* v *Kazana* [1969] 2 QB 152; Extract 4.1.5 from *Hibbert* v *McKiernan* [1948] 2 KB 142; Extract 4.1.7 from *Parker* v *British Airways Board* [1982] QB 1004; Extract 4.1.8 from *Waverley BC* v *Fletcher* [1996] QB 334; Extract 4.1.10 from *Elwes* v *Brigg Gas Company* (1886) 33 Ch D 562; Extract 4.2.2 from *JA Pye Oxford* v *Graham* [2000] Ch 676; Extracts 4.2.5, 4.2.8 from *Buckinghamshire CC* v *Moran* [1990] Ch 623; Extracts 4.2.10, 4.2.13 from *J A Pye (Oxford) Ltd* v *Graham* [2003] 1 AC 419; Extract 4.2.11 from *George Wimpey & Co Ltd* v *Sohn*

[1967] Ch 487; Extract 4.2.14 from *Hyde* v *Pearce* [1982] 1 WLR 560; Extract 4.2.16 from *Colchester BC* v *Smith* [1992] Ch 421; Extract 4.2.20 from *Asher* v *Whitlock* (1865) LR 1 QB 1; Extract 4.2.21 from *St Marylebone Property Co Ltd* v *Fairweather* [1963] AC 510; Extract 4.3.1 from *Elitestone Ltd* v *Morris* [1997] 1 WLR 687; Extract 4.3.2 from *Holland* v *Hodgson* (1872) LR 7 CP 328; Extract 4.3.4 from *D'Eyncourt* v *Gregory* (1866) LR 3 EQ 382; Extract 4.3.5 from *Re De Falbe* [1901] 1 Ch 523; Extract 4.3.7 from *TSB Bank plc* v *Botham* [1996] EGCS 149, *Estates Gazette Case Summaries*, Reed Business Information; Extracts 4.3.8, 4.3.12 from *Hobson* v *Gorringe* [1897] 1 Ch 182; Extract 4.3.9 from *Melluish* v *BMI (No 3) Ltd* [1996] AC 454; Extract 4.3.11 from *Gough* v *Wood & Co* [1894] 1 QB 713; Extract 4.3.13 from *Re Samuel Allen & Sons Ltd* [1907] 1 Ch 575; Extract 5.1.2 from *HSBC Trust Company (UK) Limited* v *Quinn* [2007] EWHC (Ch) 1543; Extract 5.1.3 from *Alan Estates Ltd* v *WG Stores Ltd* [1982] Ch 511; Extract 5.2.1 from *Tiverton Estates Ltd* v *Wearwell Ltd* [1975] Ch 146; Extract 5.2.2 from *Pitt* v *PHH Asset Management Ltd* [1994] 1 WLR 327; Extract 5.2.4 from *Firstpost Homes Ltd* v *Johnson* [1995] 1 WLR 1567; Extract 5.2.5 from *Spiro* v *Glencrown Properties Ltd* [1991] Ch 537; Extract 5.2.8 from *North Eastern Properties Ltd* v *Coleman* [2010] 1 WLR 2715; Extract 5.2.9 from *Commission for the New Towns* v *Cooper (Great Britain) Ltd* [1995] Ch 259; Extract 5.2.12 from *McCausland* v *Duncan Lawrie Ltd* [1997] 1 WLR 38; Extract 5.2.13 from *Yaxley* v *Gotts* [2000] Ch 162; Extract 5.2.14 from *Kinane* v *Mackie-Conteh* [2005] WTLR 345, *Wills and Trusts Law Report*, [22-4], [26-9], [32], [39-41], [44-9], [51], Headnotes reprinted with permission from Legalease Limited; Extract 5.2.15 from *Cobbe* v *Yeoman's Row Management Ltd* [2008] 1 WLR 1752; Extract 5.3.4 from *Long* v *Tower Hamlets LBC* [1998] Ch 197; Extract 5.4.2 from *Standing* v *Bowring* (1885) 31 Ch D 282; Extract 5.4.3 from *Dewar* v *Dewar* [1975] 1 WLR 1532; Extract 5.4.4 from *Cochrane* v *Moore* (1890) 25 QBD 57; Extract 5.4.6 from *Re Wasserberg* [1915] 1 Ch 195; Extract 5.4.8 from *Re Cole* [1964] Ch 175; Extract 5.4.9 from *Re Stoneham* [1919] 1 Ch 149; Extract 5.4.10 from *Thomas* v *Times Book Co Ltd* [1966] 1 WLR 911; Extract 5.5.1 from *Trendtex Trading Corporation* v *Crédit Suisse* [1982] AC 679; Extract 5.5.4 from *Government of Newfoundland* v *Newfoundland Railway Co* (1888) 13 App Cas 199; Extract 5.5.5 from *Stoddart* v *Union Trust Ltd* [1912] 1 KB 181; Extract on page 155 from *Gorringe* v *Irwell India Rubber & Gutta Percha Works* (1886) 34 Ch D 128; Extract 5.5.6 from *Holt* v *Heatherfield Trust Ltd* [1942] 2 KB 1; Extract 5.5.7 from *Ward* v *Duncombe* [1893] AC 369; Extract 5.6.1 from *Re Cozens* [1913] 2 Ch 478; Extract 5.6.2 from *Jones* v *Lock* (1865) LR 1 Ch App 25; Extract 5.6.3 from *Richards* v *Delbridge* (1874) LR 18 Eq 11; Extract 5.6.4 from *Paul* v *Constance* [1977] 1 WLR 527; Extract 5.6.5 from *Re Bowden* [1936] Ch 71; Extract 5.6.8 from *Grey* v *IRC* [1960] AC 1; Extract 5.6.10 from *Vandervell* v *IRC* [1967] 2 AC 291; Extract 5.6.11 from *Neville* v *Wilson* [1997] Ch 144; Extract 6.2.1 from *Westdeutsche Landesbank Girozentrale* v *Islington LBC* [1996] AC 669; Extract 6.2.2 from *Air Jamaica* v *Charlton* [1999] 1 WLR 1399; Extract 6.2.3 from *Pettitt* v *Pettitt* [1970] AC 777; Extract 6.2.4 from *Sekhon* v *Alissa* [1989] 2 FLR 94, © Jordan Publishing Ltd; Extract 6.2.5 from *Jones* v *Maynard* [1951] Ch 572; Extract 6.2.7 from *Tinsley* v *Milligan* [1994] 1 AC 340; Extract 6.2.8 from *Bannister* v *Bannister* [1948] 2 All ER 133, reproduced by permission of Reed Elsevier (UK) Limited, trading as Lexis Nexis; Extract 6.2.9 from *Hodgson* v *Marks* [1971] Ch 892; Extract 6.2.10 from *Binions* v *Evans* [1972] Ch 359; Extract 6.2.11 from *Ashburn Anstalt* v *Arnold* [1989] Ch 1; Extract 7.1.1 from *Taylors Fashions Ltd* v *Liverpool Victoria Trustees Co Ltd* [1982] QB 133; Extracts 7.1.2, 7.2.2 from *Crabb* v *Arun DC* [1976] Ch 179; Extract 7.1.3 from *Gillett* v *Holt* [2001] Ch 210; Extract 7.1.4 from *Cobbe* v *Yeoman's Row Management Ltd* [2008]

1 WLR 1752; Extract 7.1.5 from *Thorner* v *Major* [2009] 1 WLR 776; Extract 7.1.6 from *Greasley* v *Cooke* [1980] 1 WLR 1306; Extract 7.1.7 from *Coombes* v *Smith* [1986] 1 WLR 808; Extract 7.2.3 from *Pascoe* v *Turner* [1979] 1 WLR 431; Extract 7.2.4 from *Baker* v *Baker & Baker* [1993] 2 FLR 247, © Jordan Publishing Ltd; Extract 7.4.1 from *ER Ives Investment Ltd* v *High* [1967] 2 QB 379; Extract 7.4.2 from *Halsall* v *Brizell* [1957] Ch 169; Extract 7.4.3 from *Rhone* v *Stephens* [1994] 2 AC 310; Extract 7.4.7 from *Re Rose* [1949] Ch 78; Extract 7.4.8 from *Pennington* v *Waine* [2002] 1 WLR 2075; Extract 7.4.9 from *Re Goodchild Deceased* [1997] 1 WLR 1216; Extract 7.4.10 from *Re Innes* [1910] 1 Ch 188; Extract on page 226 from *Re Stewart* [1908] 2 Ch 251; Extract 7.4.11 from *Sen* v *Headley* [1991] Ch 425; Extract 8.1.1 from *Goodman* v *Gallant* [1986] Fam 106; Extracts 8.2.1, 8.6.1 from *Oxley* v *Hiscock* [2005] Fam 211; Extracts 8.2.2, 8.3.1, 8.4.1, 8.5.5, 8.6.2, 12.2.7 from *Stack* v *Dowden* [2007] 2 AC 432; Extracts 8.2.3, 8.3.2, 8.4.3, 8.5.7, 8.6.3, 8.7.1 from *Jones* v *Kernott* [2012] 1 AC 776; Extract 8.4.2 from *Fowler* v *Barron* [2008] 2 FLR 831, reproduced by permission of Reed Elsevier (UK) Limited, trading as Lexis Nexis; Extract 8.5.1 from *Gissing* v *Gissing* [1971] AC 886; Extract 8.5.2 from *Burns* v *Burns* [1984] Ch 317; Extract 8.5.3 from *Lloyds Bank plc* v *Rosset* [1991] 1 AC 107; Extracts 8.5.4, 8.9.1 from *Grant* v *Edwards* [1986] Ch 638; Extract on page 266 from *Bernard* v *Josephs* [1982] Ch 391; Extract 8.7.2 from *Jansen* v *Jansen* [1965] P 478; Extract 8.7.3 from *Pettitt* v *Pettitt* [1970] AC 777; Extract 8.8.1 from *Hammond* v *Mitchell* [1991] 1 WLR 1127; Extract on page 271 from *Stack* v *Dowden* [2005] 2 FLR 254, © Jordan Publishing Ltd; Extract 8.9.2 from *Stokes* v *Anderson* [1991] 1 FLR 391, © Jordan Publishing Ltd; Extract 9.1.2 from *Walker* v *Linom* [1907] 2 Ch 104; Extract 9.2.9 from *Hunt* v *Luck* [1902] 1 Ch 428; Extract 9.2.7 from *Caunce* v *Caunce* [1969] 1 WLR 286; Extract 9.2.8 from *Wilkes* v *Spooner* [1911] 2 KB 473; Extract 9.5.1 from *Abbey National BS* v *Cann* [1991] 1 AC 56; Extract 9.6.4 from *Oak Co-operative Building Society* v *Blackburn* [1968] Ch 730; Extract 10.4.3 from *Swift 1st Ltd* v *Chief Land Registrar* [2014] All ER (D) 12 (Feb), reproduced by permission of Reed Elsevier (UK) Limited, trading as Lexis Nexis; Extract 10.2.16 from *Lyus* v *Prowsa Developments Ltd* [1982] 1 WLR 1044; Extract on page 329 from *Webb* v *Pollmount Ltd* [1966] Ch 584; Extracts 10.2.19, 10.2.28 from *Williams & Glyn's Bank Ltd* v *Boland* [1981] AC 487; Extract 10.2.20 from *National Provincial Bank Ltd* v *Ainsworth* [1964] Ch 665; Extracts 10.2.22, 10.2.37 from *Malory Enterprises Ltd* v *Cheshire Homes (UK) Ltd* [2002] Ch 216; Extracts 10.2.23, 12.4.3 from *City of London BS* v *Flegg* [1988] AC 54; Extract 10.2.24 from *Bristol & West BS* v *Henning* [1985] 1 WLR 778; Extract 10.2.27 from *Hodgson* v *Marks* [1971] Ch 892; Extract 10.2.29 from *Lloyds Bank plc* v *Rosset* [1989] Ch 350; Extracts 10.2.30, 10.2.38 from *Abbey National BS* v *Cann* [1991] 1 AC 56; Extract 10.2.32 from *Strand Securities Ltd* v *Caswell* [1965] Ch 958; Extract 10.2.33 from *Kingsnorth Finance Co Ltd* v *Tizard* [1986] 1 WLR 783; Extract 10.2.35 from *Epps* v *Esso Petroleum Co Ltd* [1973] 1 WLR 1071; Extract 11.1.2 from *Re Bate* [1947] 2 All ER 418, reproduced by permission of Reed Elsevier (UK) Limited, trading as Lexis Nexis; Extract on page 369 from *Hickman* v *Peacey* [1945] AC 304; Extract 11.2.1 from *Robertson* v *Fraser* (1871) LR 6 Ch App 696; Extract 11.2.2 from *Malayan Credit Ltd* v *Jack Chia-MPH Ltd* [1986] AC 549; Extract 11.2.3 from *Re Jackson* (1887) 34 Ch D 732; Extract 11.3.3 from *Nielson-Jones* v *Fedden* [1975] Ch 222; Extract 11.3.4 from *Burgess* v *Rawnsley* [1975] Ch 429; Extract 11.3.6 from *Harris* v *Goddard* [1983] 1 WLR 1203; Extract 11.3.8 from *Kinch* v *Bullard* [1999] 1 WLR 423; Extract 11.3.9 from *Re K* [1985] Ch 85; Extract 12.1.2 from *Hammersmith and Fulham London Borough Council* v *Alexander-David* [2010] Ch 272; Extract 12.1.5 from *Bull* v *Bull* [1955] 1 QB 234; Extract 12.2.2 from *Chan* v *Leung* [2003]

1 FLR 23, © Jordan Publishing Ltd; Extract 12.2.4 from *Rodway* v *Landy* [2001] Ch 703; Extract 12.2.8 from *Murphy* v *Gooch* [2007] 2 FLR 934, © Jordan Publishing Ltd; Extract 12.2.9 from *French* v *Barcham* [2009] 1 WLR 1124; Extract 12.2.10 from *Suttill* v *Graham* [1977] 1 WLR 819; Extract 12.2.12 from *Leake* v *Bruzzi* [1974] 1 WLR 1528; Extract 12.3.4 from *Tempest* v *Lord Camoys* (1882) 21 Ch D 571; Extract 12.3.7 from *Jones* v *Challenger* [1961] 1 QB 176; Extract 12.3.8 from *Bedson* v *Bedson* [1965] 2 QB 666; Extract 12.3.9 from *Re Evers' Trust* [1980] 1 WLR 1327; Extract 12.3.11 from *Williams* v *Williams* [1976] Ch 278; Extract 12.3.13 from *Re Citro* [1991] Ch 142; Extract 12.3.14 from *Re Bailey* [1977] 1 WLR 278; Extract 12.3.17 from *Barca* v *Mears* [2005] 2 FLR 1, © Jordan Publishing Ltd; Extract 12.3.19 from *Abbey National plc* v *Moss* [1994] 1 FLR 307, © Jordan Publishing Ltd; Extract 12.3.20 from *Mortgage Corpn* v *Shaire* [2001] Ch 743; Extract 12.3.21 from *Edwards* v *Lloyds TSB Bank plc* [2005] 1 FCR 139, reproduced by permission of Reed Elsevier (UK) Limited, trading as Lexis Nexis; Extract 12.4.2 from *State Bank of India* v *Sood* [1997] Ch 276; Extract 12.4.5 from Harpum [1990] CLJ 277, © Cambridge University Press 1990; Extracts 14.1.1 from *Ashburn Anstalt* v *Arnold* [1989] Ch 1; Extract on page 461 from *King's Motors (Oxford) Ltd* v *Lax* [1970] 1 WLR 426; Extract 14.1.4 from *Harvey* v *Pratt* [1965] 1 WLR 1025; Extract 14.1.5 from *Prudential Assurance Co Ltd* v *London Residuary Body* [1992] 2 AC 386; Extract 14.1.6 from *Mexfield Housing Co-operative Ltd* v *Berrisford* [2012] 1 AC 955; Extract 14.1.8 from *Street* v *Mountford* [1985] AC 809; Extract on page 476 from *Snook* v *London & West Riding Investments Ltd* [1967] 2 QB 786; Extracts 14.1.10, 14.1.22 from *AG Securities* v *Vaughan* [1990] 1 AC 417; Extract 14.1.11 from *Aslan* v *Murphy* [1990] 1 WLR 766; Extract 14.1.14 from *Westminster City Council* v *Clarke* [1992] 2 AC 288; Extracts on page 482, 14.2.13, 15.1.6 from Bruton v London & Quadrant Housing Trust [2000] 1 AC 406; Extract 14.1.17 from *Hilton* v *Plustitle Ltd* [1989] 1 WLR 149; Extract on page 485 from *Belvedere Court Management Ltd* v *Frogmore Developments Ltd* [1997] QB 858; Extract 14.1.18 from *Ramnarace* v *Lutchman* [2001] 1 WLR 1651; Extract 14.1.20 from *Norris* v *Checksfield* [1991] 1 WLR 1241; Extract 14.1.21 from *Colchester BC* v *Smith* [1991] Ch 448; Extract 14.1.23 from *Mikeover Ltd* v *Brady* [1989] 3 All ER 618, reproduced by permission of Reed Elsevier (UK) Limited, trading as Lexis Nexis; Extract 14.2.1 from *Hammersmith and Fulham LBC* v *Monk* [1992] 1 AC 478; Extract 14.2.3 from *Javad* v *Aqil* [1991] 1 WLR 1007; Extract on page 499 from *Adler* v *Blackman* [1953] 1 QB 146; Extract 14.2.4 from *Martin* v *Smith* (1874) LR 9 Ex 50; Extract 14.2.5 from *Queen's Club Gardens Estates Ltd* v *Bignell* [1924] 1 KB 117; Extract 14.2.6 from *Wheeler* v *Mercer* [1957] AC 416; Extract 14.2.7 from *Errington* v *Errington* [1952] 1 KB 290; Extract 14.2.8 from *Walsh* v *Lonsdale* (1882) 21 Ch D 9; Extract 14.2.9 from *Manchester Brewery Co* v *Coombs* [1901] 2 Ch 608; Extract on page 504 from *Tinsley* v *Milligan* [1994] 1 AC 340; Extract 14.2.12 from *Industrial Properties (Barton Hill) Ltd* v *AEI Ltd* [1977] QB 580; Extract 14.2.16 from *Caerphilly Concrete Products Ltd* v *Owen* [1972] 1 WLR 372; Extract 15.1.1 from *Liverpool City Council* v *Irwin* [1977] AC 239; Extract 15.1.2 from *National Carriers Ltd* v *Panalpina (Northern) Ltd* [1981] AC 675; Extract 15.1.7 from *Kay* v *Lambeth LBC* [2006] 2 AC 465; Extract 15.2.1 from *Southwark LBC* v *Mills* [2001] 1 AC 1; Extract 15.2.2 from *Drane* v *Evangelou* [1978] 1 WLR 455; Extract 15.2.6 from *Harmer* v *Jumbil (Nigeria) Tin Areas Ltd* [1921] 1 Ch 200; Extract 15.2.7 from *Birmingham, Dudley & District Banking Company* v *Ross* (1888) 38 Ch D 295; Extract 15.3.1 from *Duke of Westminster* v *Guild* [1985] QB 688; Extract 15.3.2 from *Barrett* v *Lounova (1982) Ltd* [1990] 1 QB 348; Extract 15.3.4 from *Warren* v *Keen* [1954] 1 QB 15; Extract 15.3.7 from *Sarson* v *Roberts* [1895] 2 QB 395; Extract 15.3.9 from

Ravenseft Properties Ltd v *Davstone (Holdings) Ltd* [1980] QB 12; Extract 15.3.10 from *Quick* v *Taff Ely BC* [1986] QB 809; Extract 15.3.12 from *O'Brien* v *Robinson* [1973] AC 912; Extract 15.3.13 from *Jeune* v *Queens Cross Properties Ltd* [1974] Ch 97; Extract 15.3.14 from *Rainbow Estates Ltd* v *Tokenhold Ltd* [1998] 3 WLR 980; Extract 15.3.15 from *British Anzani (Felixstowe) Ltd* v *International Marine Management (UK) Ltd* [1980] QB 137; Extracts 15.4.1, 15.4.16, 15.4.19 from *Billson* v *Residential Apartments Ltd* [1992] 1 AC 494; Extract 15.4.5 from *Central Estates (Belgravia) Ltd* v *Woolgar (No 2)* [1972] 1 WLR 1048; Extract 15.4.6 from *Re A Debtor* [1995] 1 WLR 1127; Extract 15.4.9 from *Gill* v *Lewis* [1956] 2 QB 1; Extract 15.4.10 from *Bland* v *Ingrams Estates Ltd (No 2)* [2002] Ch 177; Extract 15.4.12 from *Rugby School (Governors)* v *Tannahill* [1935] 1 KB 87; Extract 15.4.13 from *Glass* v *Kencakes Ltd* [1966] 1 QB 611; Extract 15.4.14 from *Expert Clothing Service & Sales Ltd* v *Hillgate House Ltd* [1986] Ch 340; Extract 15.4.17 from *Escalus Properties Ltd* v *Robinson* [1996] QB 231; Extract 15.4.20 from *Chatham Empire Theatre (1955) Ltd* v *Ultrans Ltd* [1961] 1 WLR 817; Extract 15.4.21 from *Ewart* v *Fryer* [1901] 1 Ch 499; Extract 15.4.23 from *Sidnell* v *Wilson* [1966] 2 QB 67; Extract 15.4.24 from *SEDAC Investments Ltd* v *Tanner* [1982] 1 WLR 1342; Extract 15.4.25 from *Jervis* v *Harris* [1996] Ch 195; Extract 16.1.1 from *City of London Corporation* v *Fell* [1994] 1 AC 458; Extract 16.1.2 from *St Marylebone Property Co Ltd* v *Fairweather* [1963] AC 510; Extract 16.1.3 from *Barrett* v *Morgan* [2000] 2 AC 264; Extract 16.2.1 from *Milmo* v *Carreras* [1946] KB 306; Extract 16.2.2 from *Old Grovebury Manor Farm Ltd* v *W Seymour Plant Sales & Hire Ltd* [1979] 1 WLR 1397; Extract 16.2.6 from *Go West Ltd* v *Spigarolo* [2003] QB 1140; Extract 16.2.7 from *International Drilling Fluids Ltd* v *Louisville Investments (Uxbridge) Ltd* [1986] Ch 513; Extract 16.2.8 from *Bromley Park Garden Estates Ltd* v *Moss* [1982] 1 WLR 1019; Extract on page 579 from *West Layton Ltd* v *Ford* [1979] QB 593; Extract 16.2.9 from *Ashworth Frazer Ltd* v *Gloucester CC* [2001] 1 WLR 2180; Extract 16.3.5 from *BHP Petroleum Great Britain Ltd* v *Chesterfield Ltd* [2002] Ch 194; Extract 16.3.7 from *P & A Swift Investments* v *Combined English Stores Group plc* [1989] AC 632; Extract 16.3.8 from *Caerns Motor Services Ltd* v *Texaco Ltd* [1994] 1 WLR 1249; Extract 16.3.9 from *Kumar* v *Dunning* [1989] QB 193; Extract on page 587 from *Woodall* v *Clifton* [1905] 2 Ch 257; Extract 16.3.12 from *Friends' Provident Life Office* v *British Railways Board* [1996] 1 All ER 336, reproduced by permission of Reed Elsevier (UK) Limited, trading as Lexis Nexis; Extract 16.3.18 from *London Diocesan Fund* v *Phithwa* [2005] 1 WLR 3956; Extract on page 598 from *Granada Theatres Ltd* v *Freehold Investment (Leytonstone) Ltd* [1959] Ch 592; Extract 16.3.21 from *Re King* [1963] Ch 459; Extract 16.3.22 from *City & Metropolitan Properties Ltd* v *Greycroft Ltd* [1987] 1 WLR 1085; Extract 16.3.23 from *Purchase* v *Lichfield Brewery Co* [1915] 1 KB 184; Extract 16.3.24 from *Boyer* v *Warbey* [1953] 1 QB 234; Extract 16.4.1 from *Hall* v *Ewin* (1887) 37 Ch D 74; Extracts 18.1.1, 18.1.4 from *Hurst* v *Picture Theatres Ltd* [1915] 1 KB 1; Extract 18.1.2 from *Tanner* v *Tanner* [1975] 1 WLR 1346; Extract 18.1.6 from *Hounslow LBC* v *Twickenham Garden Developments Ltd* [1971] Ch 233; Extract 18.1.3 from *Hardwick* v *Johnson* [1978] 1 WLR 683; Extract 18.1.8 from *Errington* v *Errington* [1952] 1 KB 290; Extract 18.1.9 from *National Provincial Bank Ltd* v *Ainsworth* [1965] AC 1175; Extract 18.1.10 from *Ashburn Anstalt* v *Arnold* [1989] Ch 1; Extract 18.1.11 from *Binions* v *Evans* [1972] Ch 359; Extract 18.1.13 from *Maharaj* v *Chand* [1986] AC 898; Extract 18.1.14 from *Lloyds Bank plc* v *Carrick* [1996] 4 All ER 630, reproduced by permission of Reed Elsevier (UK) Limited, trading as Lexis Nexis; Extract 18.1.15 from *Esso Petroleum Co Ltd* v *Kingswood Motors (Addlestone) Ltd* [1974] QB 142; Extract 18.3.1 from *Manchester Airport plc* v *Dutton* [2000] QB 133; Extract 18.3.2 from *Hunter* v *Canary Wharf Ltd* [1997] AC 655;

Extract 19.1.1 from *Lord Chesterfield* v *Harris* [1908] 2 Ch 397; Extract 19.1.2 from *Re Ellenborough Park* [1956] Ch 131; Extract on page 649 from *Attorney-Gen of Southern Nigeria* v *John Holt & Co (Liverpool) Ltd* [1915] AC 599; Extract 19.1.4 from *Moody* v *Steggles* (1879) 12 Ch D 261; Extract 19.1.5 from *Crow* v *Wood* [1971] 1 QB 77; Extract 19.1.7 from *Phipps* v *Pears* [1965] 1 QB 76; Extract 19.1.8 from *Copeland* v *Greenhalf* [1952] Ch 488; Extract 19.1.9 from *Miller* v *Emcer Products Ltd* [1956] Ch 304; Extracts 19.1.10, 19.2.8 from *Ward* v *Kirkland* [1967] Ch 194; Extract 19.1.11 from *Moncrieff* v *Jamieson* [2007] 1 WLR 2620; Extracts 19.2.1, 19.2.2, 19.2.6 from *Wheeldon* v *Burrows* (1879) 12 Ch D 31; Extract 19.2.3 from *Nickerson* v *Barraclough* [1981] Ch 426; Extract 19.2.4 from *Union Lighterage Co* v *London Graving Dock Co* [1902] 2 Ch 557; Extract 19.2.5 from *Wong* v *Beaumont Property Trust Ltd* [1965] 1 QB 173; Extract 19.2.7 from *Borman* v *Griffith* [1930] 1 Ch 493; Extract 19.2.9 from *Wheeler* v *JJ Saunders Ltd* [1996] Ch 19; Extract 19.2.12 from *International Tea Stores Co* v *Hobbs* [1903] 2 Ch 165; Extracts 19.2.13, 19.2.15 from *Green* v *Ashco Horticultural Ltd* [1966] 1 WLR 889; Extract 19.2.14 from *Goldberg* v *Edwards* [1950] Ch 247; Extract 19.2.17 from *Clark* v *Barnes* [1929] 2 Ch 368; Extract 19.2.18 from *Long* v *Gowlett* [1923] 2 Ch 177; Extract on page 678 from *Sovmots Investments Ltd* v *SSE* [1979] AC 144; Extract 19.2.19 from *Kent* v *Kavanagh* [2007] Ch 1; Extracts 19.2.22, 19.2.29 from *Simmons* v *Dobson* [1991] 1 WLR 720; Extract 19.2.23 from *Davies* v *Du Paver* [1953] 1 QB 184; Extract 19.2.24 from *R (Lewis)* v *Redcar and Cleveland BC (No 2)* [2010] 2 AC 70; Extract 19.2.25 from *Sturges* v *Bridgman* (1879) 11 Ch D 852; Extract 19.2.26 from *Hollins* v *Verney* (1884) 13 Ch D 304; Extract on page 686 from *Earl de la Warr* v *Miles* (1881) 17 Ch D 535; Extract 19.2.28 from *Mills* v *Silver* [1991] Ch 271; Extract 19.3.1 from *White* v *Grand Hotel, Eastbourne Ltd* [1913] 1 Ch 113; Extract 19.3.4 from *Bracewell* v *Appleby* [1975] Ch 408; Extract 19.3.5 from *Allen* v *Greenwood* [1980] Ch 119; Extract 19.4.1 from *Wall* v *Collins* [2007] Ch 390; Extract 19.4.3 from *Cook* v *Mayor & Corporation of Bath* (1868) LR 6 Eq 177; Extract 20.1.2 from *Smith and Snipes Hall Farm Ltd* v *River Douglas Catchment Board* [1949] 2 KB 500; Extract 20.1.4 from *Amsprop Trading Ltd* v *Harris Distribution Ltd* [1997] 1 WLR 1025; Extract 20.2.2 from *Rhone* v *Stephens* [1994] 2 AC 310; Extracts on page 709, 20.2.6 from *Shepherd Homes Ltd* v *Sandham (No 2)* [1971] 1 WLR 1062; Extract 20.2.3 from *London CC* v *Allen* [1914] 3 KB 642; Extract 20.2.4 from *Wrotham Park Estate Co Ltd* v *Parkside Homes Ltd* [1974] 1 WLR 798; Extract 20.2.5 from *Cosmichome Ltd* v *Southampton City Council* [2013] 1 WLR 2436; Extract 20.2.8 from *University of East London* v *Barking and Dagenham LBC* [2005] Ch 354; Extract on page 714 *Rogers* v *Hosegood* [1900] 2 Ch 388; Extract 20.2.8 from *Federated Homes Ltd* v *Mill Lodge Properties Ltd* [1980] 1 WLR 594; Extract 20.2.10 from *Crest Nicholson Residential (South) Ltd* v *McAllister* [2004] 1 WLR 2409; Extract 20.2.11 from *Re Union of London & Smith's Bank Ltd's Conveyance, Miles* v *Easter* [1933] Ch 611; Extract 20.2.12 from *Roake* v *Chadha* [1984] 1 WLR 40; Extract 20.2.13 from *Elliston* v *Reacher* [1908] 2 Ch 374; Extract 20.2.14 from *Baxter* v *Four Oaks Properties Ltd* [1965] Ch 816; Extract on page 724 from *Brunner* v *Greenslade* [1971] Ch 993; Extract 20.2.15 from *Texaco Antilles Ltd* v *Kernochan* [1973] AC 609; Extract 20.3.1 from *Lawrence* v *Fen Tigers Ltd* [2014] WLR 433; Extract 20.3.2 from *Jaggard* v *Sawyer* [1995] 1 WLR 269; Extract 21.2.1 from *Grangeside Properties Ltd* v *Collingwoods Securities Ltd* [1964] 1 WLR 139; Extract 21.2.2 from *United Bank of Kuwait plc* v *Sahib* [1997] Ch 107; Extract 21.3.1 from *Barclays Bank plc* v *O'Brien* [1994] 1 AC 180; Extract 21.3.2 from *Royal Bank of Scotland plc* v *Etridge (No 2)* [2002] 2 AC 773; Extract 21.3.3 from *Credit Lyonnais Bank Nederland NV* v *Burch* [1997] 1 All ER 144, reproduced by permission of Reed Elsevier (UK) Limited, trading as Lexis Nexis;

Extract 21.3.4 from *Yorkshire Bank plc* v *Tinsley* [2004] 1 WLR 2380; Extract 21.4.1 from *Knightsbridge Estates Trust Ltd* v *Byrne* [1939] Ch 441; Extract 21.4.2 from *Fairclough* v *Swan Brewery Co Ltd* [1912] AC 565; Extract 21.4.3 from *Samuel* v *Jarrah Timber & Wood Paving Corporation Ltd* [1904] AC 323; Extract 21.4.4 from *Lewis* v *Frank Love Ltd* [1961] 1 WLR 261; Extract 21.4.5 from *Biggs* v *Hoddinott* [1898] 2 Ch 307; Extract 21.4.6 from *Santley* v *Wilde* [1899] 2 Ch 474; Extract 21.4.7 from *Noakes & Co Ltd* v *Rice* [1902] AC 24; Extract 21.4.8 from *Bradley* v *Carritt* [1903] AC 253; Extract 21.4.9 from *Kreglinger* v *New Patagonia Meat and Cold Storage Co Ltd* [1914] AC 25; Extract 21.4.11 from *Esso Petroleum Co Ltd* v *Harper's Garage (Stourport) Ltd* [1968] AC 269; Extract 21.4.12 from *Multiservice Bookbinding Ltd* v *Marden* [1979] Ch 84; Extract 21.4.15 from *Campbell* v *Holyland* (1877) 7 Ch D 166; Extract 21.4.16 from *Esso Petroleum Co Ltd* v *Alstonbridge Properties Ltd* [1975] 1 WLR 1474; Extract 21.4.17 from *Birmingham Citizens Permanent BS* v *Caunt* [1962] Ch 883; Extract 21.4.18 from *Quennell* v *Maltby* [1979] 1 WLR 318; Extract on page 774 from *Ropaigelach* v *Barclays Bank* [2000] QB 263; Extracts 21.4.21, 21.4.22 from *Habib Bank Ltd* v *Tailor* [1982] 1 WLR 1218; Extract 21.4.23 from *Western Bank Ltd* v *Schindler* [1977] Ch 1; Extract 21.4.24 from *Cheltenham & Gloucester BS* v *Norgan* [1996] 1 WLR 343; Extract 21.4.25 from *First National Bank plc* v *Syed* [1991] 2 All ER 250, reproduced by permission of Reed Elsevier (UK) Limited, trading as Lexis Nexis; Extract 21.4.28 from *Cheltenham & Gloucester BS plc* v *Booker* [1997] 1 FLR 311, © Jordan Publishing Ltd; Extract 21.4.30 from *White* v *City of London Brewery Co* (1889) 42 Ch D 237; Extract on page 788 from *Selwyn* v *Garfit* (1888) 38 Ch D 273; Extract 21.4.33 from *Horsham Properties Group Ltd* v *Clark* [2009] 1 WLR 1255; Extract 21.4.35 from *Waring* v *London & Manchester Assurance Co Ltd* [1935] Ch 311; Extract 21.4.36 from *Cuckmere Brick Co Ltd* v *Mutual Finance Ltd* [1971] Ch 949; Extract 21.4.37 from *Parker-Tweedale* v *Dunbar Bank plc* [1991] Ch 12; Extract 21.4.38 from *Downsview Nominees Ltd* v *First City Corporation Ltd* [1993] AC 295; Extract 21.4.39 from *Silven Properties Ltd* v *Royal Bank of Scotland plc* [2004] 1 WLR 997; Extract on page 795 from *Farrar* v *Farrars Ltd* (1888) 40 Ch D 395; Extract 21.4.42 from *Palk* v *Mortgage Services Funding plc* [1993] Ch 330; Extract 21.4.43 from *Cheltenham & Gloucester plc* v *Krausz* [1997] 1 WLR 1558.

Table of cases

Page numbers in **bold** refer to pages where the cases are extracted

Table of statutes

Page numbers in **bold** refer to pages where the cases are extracted

Other jurisdictions

Australia

Table of statutory instruments

Page numbers in **bold** refer to pages where the Statutory Instruments are extracted

Part I
Introductory matters

1

Basic property principles

In this chapter, we will consider some of the basic principles and distinctions to be observed in property law. Most of them will be further developed in later chapters and, as in many subjects, the basic principles may be more readily comprehended once some of the more detailed material has been considered.

1. General principles

We will investigate ideas of property through two contributions to the literature. These relate specifically to land, though many of the principles apply to all forms of property.

Extract 1.1.1

Peter Birks, 'Before We Begin: Five Keys to Land Law', in *Land Law: Themes and Perspectives* (eds Bright and Dewar) pp 457–463, 467–468, 470–473, 476–486 (footnotes omitted)

Land Law is a complex subject. It is not in the end a very difficult one. It is less unstable than other areas of the law. Yet it is hard to get into. The purpose of this chapter is to make access easier. It is impossible to improve access to a completely unknown quantity. The first section, therefore, asks what kind of category we are trying to understand.

WHAT KIND OF CATEGORY?

The name 'land law' suggests a simple contextual category: all the law about land. The law does use many such categories, ordered only by the alphabet: all the law about aviation, banks, commerce, dogs, education, and so on. They take as their subject some aspect of life, just as a non-lawyer would identify it. But in this case things are not quite so straightforward. By the end of this section we will have formulated a more complex proposition: land law, as generally understood, is a contextual subset of a legal-conceptual category.

. . .

The core of land law

A target has a centre. Taking land law as a simple contextual category, we can identify at least five topics . . . Four of these must on reflection be located in the second or third circles, just outside the bull's-eye at which we are aiming. They matter, but they do not relieve us of the intellectual necessity of mastering the core. Two belong largely in public law. One of these comprises the social control essential if the environment is to be protected. The other is the housing law which applies to local government tenancies. Within private law, a third unit lies in the law of civil wrongs and deals with the duties imposed by the law for regulating the behaviour of neighbours towards each other, especially through the torts of nuisance and trespass to land. Fourthly, there is the structuring of mega-wealth, the mission of the old Lincoln's Inn conveyancers. That is breaking away, not specifically land law any longer but wealth manage-ment. Its principal vehicle is the trust, often enough offshore, in which land becomes just one kind of asset in a rolling fund. Fifthly and last of all, there is the unit at the very centre of the target. When lawyers speak of land law, it is usually to this core that they refer.

Every business needs premises, every factory needs a site. For most of us as private individuals our home is the centre of our lives. Functionally, this core of land law has the task of providing the structure within which people and businesses can safely acquire and exploit land for daily use, to live and to work. To discharge that function, it has to have its own con-ceptual apparatus. The proper content of this fifth unit thus becomes the nature, creation, and protection of interests in land. Those interests and their implications are the conceptual appa-ratus of our land law.

The word 'interests' is slightly evasive. The law recognizes different kinds of rights, among them property rights. By 'interest' we mean 'property right'. The category of all property rights (or, in other words and more simply, 'the law of property') is a legal-conceptual category. It differs from, say, the law of dogs in that its subject is a legal concept, the concept of a proprietary right. The core of land law is the subset formed when the conceptual category of 'property right' is confined to one context: the law relating to property rights in land. To focus on that core is neither to downgrade the importance of the units in the next circles nor to forget that in real life all the units which we have identified, and others, cohere together.

Land law in this core sense is, therefore, a contextual subset of a legal-conceptual category. There is a recurrent problem. Property rights in land have roots a millennium deep in a pre-commercial society in which land and wealth were virtually synonymous. The structuring of landed wealth, and the power that went with it, was then land law's principal mission. The subject of land law – the law, that is, of the recognized proprietary interests in land – is therefore intellectually entangled in a history not always obviously relevant to its contemporary function.

THE FIVE KEYS

The five keys have one-word tags: Time, Space, Reality, Duality, and Formality. There is a per-vasive theme which has its own label: Facilitation. This might be said to be the string on which the five keys hang. There is also a complication. All five keys have to be turned together. Exposition is easiest when each point has a natural priority. Here there is no natural priority, and no expository device to achieve what King Arthur intended when he seated his knights at a round table.

Facilitation

Some areas of law are primarily concerned to inhibit undesirable conduct. This is most obviously true of the law relating to wrongs, whether criminal or civil. Even there, behind the inhibition, lies a facilitative goal – namely, to allow civilized life to be conducted free from the fear of harm. The wrong of nuisance facilitates the enjoyment of land, but primarily by inhibiting unreasonable interference. By contrast, other areas are primarily facilitative. The law of contract, for example, helps people do something which by and large they want to be able to do – namely, to make reliable agreements.

Like contract, land law is primarily facilitative. Each of the five keys, though some more obvi-ously than others, can be seen as facilitating the achievement of goals which people routinely want to achieve. . . .

A landowner may be willing to pay a large sum for a permanent proprietary right to prevent building on the neighbouring land. The first instinct is to facilitate, but there are arguments the other way. Should he be able to sterilize the economic use of that land? In fact the law does allow such a right to be created. Restrictive covenants, as property rights, are a relatively new invention. . . .

TIME

Although bits do occasionally wash away or slip into the sea, land is in general permanent. For most human purposes we have to regard it as lasting for ever. There is a powerful urge to deal in slices of time. It is not confined to land. The institution of the trust makes it relatively easy to turn all kinds of wealth into an enduring fund, and that facility in turn excites and to a degree gratifies the urge to deal in slices of time. However, it is the natural permanence of land which makes slices of time a dominant feature of land law.

Two motivations

Why do people want to deal in slices of time? It is an urge which has been fed from at least two sources. One is essentially commercial, the other not.

The commercial motivation

Commercial motivation means, in plain words, the desire to get money out of land. There are all sorts of ways of getting money out of land. For instance, one can farm the land and sell the produce. The most extreme method of all is to sell one's whole interest in the land. That means selling the whole slice of time over which one has control. The largest interest in land – the greatest slice of time – is 'for ever'. In everyday conversation I tend to say 'my house' or 'the house I own'. In all probability, what I actually have in my house is 'for ever', a slice of time measured by the length of time the land will last. There is no harm in calling that ownership. That is what in effect it is. But in the technical language of the law that huge slice of time mea-sured by the life of the land itself is called a fee simple. The fee simple in the land on which my house stands is worth about £200,000. I could mortgage it or sell it. But there is another pos-sibility. I could keep 'for ever' and deal instead in a shorter slice of time.

The commercial motivation for dealing in lesser slices of time is to realize in money some of the value of the land without giving up one's whole interest. The lease is the proprietary interest which most obviously facilitates this. I might let my land for a fixed number of years, say for ten years. . . .

The family motivation

The primary non-commercial motivation for dealing in slices of time is concern for one's family. In obsolescent aristocratic terms this might be restated as a dynastic motivation. The idea of benefiting the different generations of one's family is perfectly natural. . . .

The evolution of the doctrine of estates

In ordinary language the sentence 'Mr Smith has an estate in Suffolk' suggests a goodish patch of Constable landscape of which Mr Smith is the owner. But in land law an estate is a slice of time. The doctrine of estates is the learning which tells you what slices of time the law allows or has allowed a landowner to deal in. A 'life estate' was a recognized estate at common law.

. . .

SPACE

Mention of a piece of land by name – as, for example, Lord's Cricket Ground or Wembley Stadium – brings to mind an image of the surface of the land. But the surface is merely a cross-section of a space which, in a flat-earthish sort of way, we still think of as stretching infinitely up and down. Modern cosmology requires modification of the image of that space, but some of the mind's worst problems in comprehending its true shape have been overtaken by much humbler science. First balloons and then aeroplanes necessitated a rethink. The tube in which estates subsist has had to be cut off in order to deprive the surface-owner of exclusive control of the upper air. . . .

REALITY

In the technical language of the law 'real' never denotes the opposite of 'illusory' or 'fake'. It is usually an anglicization of the adjective from *res*, which is Latin for 'thing'. Hence, 'real' always indicates that something has some quality of or relation to a thing. If a creditor, about to lend money, asks for real security, he means that he wants to be able to turn against a thing for the purpose of obtaining what is due to him. That contrasts with personal security. A guarantee will allow the creditor an extra recourse, against the person of the guarantor. We could talk about 'thing-security' and 'person-security'. We do not. We distinguish instead between real and personal security.

A lawyer cannot be frightened of technical meanings. It helps, however, if each word pressed into technical service has just one technical meaning. Here there is more than one. The law uses 'real' to mean 'in some significant way thing-related', but the nature of the relation is not always the same. Very importantly, there is a difference between the 'reality' which is indicated in the contrast between real and personal property and the 'reality' indicated in the contrast between real and personal rights. Though the distinction between real and personal property is ancient and venerable, it is nowadays far less important than the distinction between real and personal rights.

Realty and personalty

There is an almost perfect match between the category of real property and land. If a lay person hears 'real property', or 'real estate', or 'realty', what will come to mind will be an image of land. For most lawyers the effect will be the same. Some lawyers may just manage to remind themselves that they should be thinking more abstractly, not of the land itself, but of interests in land. 'Personal property' or 'personalty' similarly evoke cars, cows, televisions, crockery, pictures, money, and a host of other moveable things. In fact the correlation is not quite perfect. A lease of land, however long, is technically personalty, and some moveable things are heirlooms and fall within the category of realty. The right to call a parson to the freehold in a church, called an advowson, was always realty.

In what sense is realty 'thing-related' and in what sense are personal things like cars not 'thing-related'?. . .

. . . In some actions you could recover the thing itself. Those actions came to be called 'real actions', 'real' meaning 'thing-related' in the simple sense that the person claiming would recover the very thing claimed. . . . It is almost a perfect truth that the category of specific recoverability extended no further than land. Hence the near-perfect correlation between realty and land.

Real rights and personal rights

We move now to the kind of 'reality' or 'thing-relatedness' which matters in the modern law. The key proposition is that land law is, centrally, the law of real rights in land. The slice of time which we call a lease, or, less commonly, a 'term of years', is for historical reasons personalty or personal property, but it is indisputably a real right in land and as such central to land law. A fee simple is similarly a real right in land, the greatest of all.

People's wealth – their 'property' in the widest sense of that slippery word – consists in rights of two kinds, real rights and personal rights. It is important to say at once that there are different ways of expressing this distinction. 'Real' and 'personal' here anglicize the Latin labels *in rem* and *in personam*. Many people prefer to use the Latin labels. The Latin tells us that a right *in rem* is a right in or against a thing, while a right *in personam* is a right in or against a person.

One can change to different language. A right *in personam* can be called an obligation. A right *in personam* and an obligation are one and the same thing, but looked at from different ends. I have an overdraft. I owe my bank £1,000. The bank has a right *in personam*, the person here being me. I have an obligation to pay. The relationship can be named from either end, and in practice we usually name it from the liability end. Hence we very frequently speak, not of the law of personal rights or of rights *in personam*, but of obligations. As for rights *in rem*, if we drop both the Latin and the latinate English, they usually become 'property rights' or 'proprietary rights'. We sometimes use 'property' loosely to mean 'wealth'. In that loose sense 'property' wobbles. Sometimes 'my property' evokes and is intended to evoke specific things, such as cars and clothes and cottages. Sometimes, and rather more technically, 'my property' denotes mere rights vested in me, such as a fee simple, a lease, ownership, or the obligations of my debtors. Whichever the focus, the loose notion of property as wealth is too broad to be useful in analysis. To think clearly the law has to draw a bright line between two classes of right, both of which can fall within the loose notion of wealth.

The bright line distinguishes between property and obligations. When that line is drawn, property clearly has a narrower and much more technical sense. Within wealth, taken as including all assets, the law of obligations is the law of rights *in personam* and the law of property is the law of rights *in rem*. Hence a 'property right' or 'proprietary right' is a real right, is a right *rem*. The law of property is the law of all known real rights, and land law is the law of real rights in land.

What is the difference? The practical difference bears on this question. Against whom can the right be demanded? 'Demandability' is intelligible but not really English. But another word for 'to demand' is 'to exact', which gives us 'exigible' and 'exigibility'. A right *in rem* is a right the exigibility of which is defined by the location of the thing. The exigibility of a right *in personam* is defined by the location of the person. Where I have a right *in personam* the notional chain in my hand is tied round that person's neck. Where I have a right *in rem*, the notional chain in my hand is tied around a thing. Between me and the car which I own there is such a chain.

. . .

DUALITY

There is duality where a proposition is true in one conceptual dimension but is falsified or heavily modified in another. Our land law is shot through by instances. There is one of ubiquitous and fundamental importance – namely, the duality between law and equity. There is another, now of fading significance, which emanates from tenure. A third consists in the difference between beneficial interests and security interests. A fourth, perhaps inessential at the point of access to the subject, turns on the relativity of title.

Law and equity

Proprietary rights in land can be legal or equitable. The mind can cope with the proposition that English law is different from Scots law. It is more difficult to accept the existence within English law itself of two legal systems with different answers to many questions. Yet for centuries that was the position. The courts of common law administered common law, and the court of chancery administered its own law, called equity. And on many issues the court of chancery took a position different from that of the courts of common law. The institutional duality was abolished more than a century ago. Modern courts administer both law and equity, and the conflicts' rule laid down by statute is that, where law and equity differ, equity prevails. The conceptual duality continues. In some areas it has weakened and will weaken further. But, wherever the law of trusts has a role to play, the duality is here to stay. Where there is a trust, the law says *A* is owner but equity disagrees and prefers *B*. Or we might put it the other way about: wherever equity thinks *B* should be owner, even though the common law takes a different view, there is a trust. *A*, the owner at common law, becomes a trustee for *B*.

The law of trusts was equity's principal creation, and trusts have become the distinctive feature of the Anglo–American law of property. [Trusts are considered later in this chapter.]

Tenure

Tenure was once co-equal in importance with estates. After the Conquest all land was vested in the king. The king made grants to tenants in chief in return for military and other services. The tenants in chief subinfeudated to others, and so on, creating the characteristic feudal pyramid. Tenure was the service by which one held one's estate. Different tenures carried different incidents. In 1290 Edward I forbade further subinfeudation of freeholds. Alienation thenceforth could only be by substitution. An alienor had to step out of the pyramid and put the buyer into his place.

We need not follow out the rest of the story. We are interested only in the vestiges of tenure which survive in the modern law. There are only two points which matter. The most obvious is that all land is still technically held of the Crown, so that, in the tenurial dimension, it remains technically true that only the Crown owns the land. Every fee simple is held of the Crown by a notional tenure involving no services at all. The other is the duality between freehold and leasehold. . . .

Beneficial interests and security interests

This can be dealt with very shortly, though security is an immensely important subject. The vast majority of purchases of land are made at least in part with borrowed money, secured on the land which is acquired or on other land. This is common knowledge. . . . The word 'mortgage' covers a variety of differently structured securities. Nowadays the commonest kind is unequivocal, for the mortgagee acquires a right which can only be security interest, 'a charge by way of legal mortgage'. But it is possible for the same estate to be either a beneficial or a security interest. Historically, the lender-mortgagee took the fee simple. But the proposition that he was tenant in fee simple was heavily qualified by the fact that he held that estate as a security interest, not as a beneficial interest. His fee simple was held subject to the borrower's right to redeem. Since 1925 mortgagors no longer transfer the fee simple. . . .

Relativity of title

The interest one holds has to be distinguished from the title by which one holds it. Suppose you are unlucky enough to take a conveyance of a fee simple from someone who is merely a squatter. You go into possession of the land. *Nemo dat quod non habet.* The maxim suggests that you have nothing. You took a conveyance from someone who had nothing to give. However, you do have something. The reason lies in relativity of title. The law will protect a good title against a bad one, and a bad one against a worse one. . . .

FORMALITY

Formal requirements oblige people to do things in particular ways, usually ways which put them to some slight extra trouble. It might be, for example, that the law would treat a promise as binding only if you made it meekly kneeling upon your knees. In practice writing and registration are the formalities usually insisted upon. There can be lighter and heavier versions of both.

. . .

What does formality facilitate? What ends does it serve? Even though it lies outside the land law, it is convenient to answer by reference to the best-known formality of all. Everyone knows that a last will has to be made in writing and signed before witnesses. It is no use just scribbling it on the back of an envelope or whispering it to one's best friend. There are huge advantages in this formal requirement. It helps the person making the will think hard about the job to be done. Later, it goes a long way towards eliminating doubt and argument at a juncture in human affairs at which strife is all too near the surface. All hell would break out if a deceased's last will were a matter of proving by general evidence, and in the absence of the only person who could really know, what the last wishes really were. The formal will settles the matter.

It is much the same in land law. There is an extra reason too. It derives from the invisibility of real rights. Just as one cannot see a fee simple, so one cannot see an easement or a restrictive covenant. A neighbour's right to pass over a field does not reveal itself in a pink line, nor will even an infra-red camera disclose his right to restrict or forbid building. . . .

CONCLUSION

The purpose has been to introduce five aspects of land law, with a view to making access to it easier. It was said at the beginning that none of the five has any natural priority. This conclusion summarizes in slightly different order.

(1) It is the business of land law to say what property rights can exist in land. A property right is a real right, a right *in rem*. It has special characteristics, which distinguish it from a personal right, a right *in personam*. It is not exigible solely against the person against whom it arose.

(2) English law has an inheritance of duality. There are dualities implicit in tenure, in the difference between security interests and beneficial interests, and in the relativity of title. But above all there is the duality between law and equity. The real rights which land law recognizes can be legal or equitable. In a historically unitary system, equitable rights might be called 'weak' proprietary rights. Equitable proprietary rights are more vulnerable than legal rights. That is the price of equity's more relaxed attitude to 'reality'.

(3) The value of legal certainty, which the equitable jurisdiction seems on occasion to undermine, is in general reinforced by insistence on the rigour of formality, especially as against strangers who have given value. Formality has meant writing in one form or another, but nowadays it means above all the public registration of real rights in land. The legislator, in providing that some interests override the register, has attempted to foresee the cases in which, even against strangers, the destruction of unregistered interests would give rise to screams of pain.

(4) The surface of a piece of land is a cross-section of a space. Every space has the potential for multiple uses. The law goes some way towards allowing those uses to be split up and dealt with strand by strand. Proprietary facilitation of that goal has to be kept within limits. The sometimes obscure nature of those limits is a stumbling block.

(5) Time and slices of time have been the dominant theme. Land law continues to facilitate dealing in slices of time, most obviously through the lease. But the rise of the managed fund of wealth has brought it about that the long fight over tying up the land itself is no longer fought. The law has seen to it that, behind a trust, such future interests can in general be detached from the land to become interests in a fund. A residual facility remains to meet the accommodation needs of the family through a trust of land. The days have gone when land law's principal mission was to structure wealth and power. Institutions and individuals alike, if they have wealth worth planning, managing, and tying up, prefer trust funds with mixed portfolios.

Extract 1.1.2

Kevin Gray and Susan Francis Gray, 'The Idea of Property in Land', in *Land Law: Themes and Perspectives* (eds Bright and Dewar) pp 15–16, 18–21, 27–31, 35–40, 51 (footnotes omitted)

It is just over a century since, in a paper still regarded as seminal, Oliver Wendell Holmes observed that the trouble with law was not that there had been too much theory but rather that there had not been enough. We must, therefore, begin with some conceptualization about property.

A BRIEF INTRODUCTION TO THE JURISPRUDENCE OF PROPERTY

Few concepts are quite so fragile, so elusive and so often misused as the idea of property. Most everyday references to property are unreflective, naïve and relatively meaningless. Frequently the lay person (and even the lawyer) falls into the trap of supposing the term 'property' to connote the *thing* which is the object of 'ownership'. But the beginning of truth about property is the realization that property is not a *thing* but rather a *relationship* which one has with a thing. It is infinitely more accurate, therefore, to say that one has property *in* a thing than to declare that the thing is one's property.

To claim 'property' in a resource is, in effect, to assert a strategically important degree of control over that resource; and to conflate or confuse this relationship of control with the actual thing controlled may often prove to be an analytical error of some substance. 'Property' is, rather, the word used to describe particular concentrations of power *over* things and resources. The term 'property' is simply an abbreviated reference to a quantum of socially permissible power exercised in respect of a socially valued resource. Used in this way, the word 'property' reflects its semantically correct root by identifying the condition of a particular resource as being 'proper' to a particular person. In this deeper sense, as we shall see later, the language of 'property' may have more in common with 'propriety' than with entitlement; and the notion of a 'property right' may ultimately have more to do with perceptions of 'rightness' than with any understanding of enforceable exclusory title.

It may be noted, furthermore, that the power relationship implicit in property is not absolute but relative: there may well be gradations of 'property' in a resource. . . . Far from being a monolithic notion of standard content and invariable intensity, 'property' thus turns out to have an almost infinitely gradable quality. And it follows, moreover, that to have 'property' in a resource may often be entirely consistent with the acquisition or retention by others of 'property' in the same resource. It is, in fact, the complex interrelation of these myriad gradations of 'property' which comprises the stuff of modern land law.

. . .

AMBIVALENT CONCEPTUAL MODELS OF PROPERTY

The task of the present chapter is to outline the various ways in which English law – and perhaps, more generally, common law jurisprudence – handles the idea of property in land. It will be argued that our dominant models of property in land fluctuate inconsistently between three rather different perspectives. It will be suggested that this doctrinal uncertainty – this deep structural indeterminacy – explains the intractable nature of some of land law's classic dilemmas, whilst simultaneously impeding constructive responses to the more immediately pressing challenges of twenty-first century land law. The common law world has never really resolved whether property in land is to be understood in terms of empirical facts, artificially defined rights, or duty-laden allocations of social utility. Although these three perspectives sometimes interact and overlap, it remains ultimately unclear whether the substance of property resides in the raw data of human conduct or in essentially positive claims of abstract entitlement or in the socially directed control of land use. In short, the idea of property in land oscillates ambivalently between the behavioural, the conceptual, and the obligational, between competing models of property as a *fact*, property as a *right*, and property as a *responsibility*.

Property as a fact

Much of the genius of the common law derives from a rough-and-ready grasp of the empirical realities of life. According to this perspective, the identification of property in land is an earthily pragmatic affair. There is a deeply anti-intellectual streak in the common law tradition which cares little for grand or abstract theories of ownership, preferring to fasten instead upon the raw organic facts of human behaviour. . . .

Throughout the history of English land law the operative concept has been *possession* rather than *ownership*: the common lawyer's overwhelming concern has been with the externally verifiable modalities of possessory control. Indeed, the property of estate ownership is ultimately a derivative of 'exclusive possession', a phrase used in English law to denote not merely an exclusive factual presence upon land but also some inner assumption as to the power relationships generated by such presence. Correspondingly, the absence of estate ownership is epitomized in the 'property deficit' inherent, for instance, in the status of the mere 'lodger'. The lodger, unlike the tenant, is subject to the supervisory authority of the owner, who at all times 'retains his character of master of the house, and . . . retains the general control and dominion over the whole house'. . . .

Property as a right

The foregoing analysis of the law of real property has concentrated on property in land as a perception of socially constituted fact. A rather different – and not entirely consistent – focus is provided by the competing assessment of property in land as comprising various assortments of artificially defined jural right. On this view, the law of real property becomes distanced from the physical reality of land and enters a world of conceptual – indeed some would say virtually mathematical – abstraction. In sharp contrast to the crudely empirical foundations of property as a fact, the vision of property as a right rests upon a complex calculus of carefully calibrated 'estates' and 'interests' in land, all underpinned by the political theory implicit in the doctrine of tenure. All property relationships with land are, accordingly, analysed at one remove – through the intermediacy of an estate or interest in land. No citizen can claim that he or she owns the physical *solum*, merely that he or she owns some unitary jural right in or over that *solum*. One has 'property' in an abstract right rather than 'property' in a physical thing.

. . . The Crown's radical title is, in truth, no proprietary title at all, but merely an expression of the *Realpolitik* which served historically to hold together the theory of tenure. Under the tenurial system of tiered or hierarchical landholding, all land in England (save unalienated Crown land) was held, in relationships of reciprocal obligation, either mediately or immediately of the Crown. It remains the case even today that no subject can own lands allodially – that is, outside the tenurial scheme of things – although all tenures have now been commuted to a uniform 'socage tenure' directly from the Crown.

It was left to the doctrine of estates to quantify the grades of abstract entitlement which might be enjoyed by any particular tenant (or landholder) within the tenurial framework. This doctrine spelt out a rich taxonomy of 'estates' in the land, each estate representing an artificial proprietary construct interposed between the tenant and the physical object of his tenure. Each tenant owned (and still owns) not land but an *estate* in land. The precise nature of the estate was graded by its temporal duration and by the possible attachment of variegated conditions precedent or subsequent. Each common law estate – whether the fee simple, the fee tail, or the life estate – comprised a time-related segment of the bundle of rights and powers exercisable over land; and the doctrine of estates effectively provided diverse ways in which three-dimensional realty might be carved up in a fourth dimension of time.

In the form of the common law estates, English land law thus comprised, from the earliest times, a field of highly manipulable abstract constructs which conferred enormous flexibility in the management of wealth. . . .

Today the taxonomy of the common law estates is still largely preserved in the property legislation of 1925, although with necessary modifications and additions. The fee simple absolute in possession remains as the primary estate in English law and is now joined as a legal estate by the term of years absolute. . . . Thus the 1925 legislation seeks to maintain consistently the dogma that landownership and use are mediated by the distribution, not of land as such, but of intangible jural entitlements interposed between persons and land. The perspective embraced by the statutory schema is of property as a right, precisely on the footing that the only property one can have is *in* a right.

Yet English land law remains inevitably a curious blend of the conceptual and the pragmatic, the cerebral and the material. Certainly, the conceptual purity of systematically ordered estates and interests provides an intellectual base for the rational manipulation of axiomatic truths and for the multiple applications of propositional dogma so familiar to the student. But even the austere regime of the 1925 property legislation contains its share of mongrelized ideas, convenient adaptations, and internal contradictions. English land law reveals, for instance, an intermittent tendency to conflate property as fact with property as right, as evidenced by the way in which statutory definitions of 'land' are expressly fashioned to include 'an easement, right, privilege, or benefit in, over, or derived from land'. This reification of intangible entitlement – a frequent feature of the common law mind-set – brings about the result that appurtenant easements become notionally affixed to their dominant tenement rather as fixtures become annexed to realty, their benefit passing with any subsequent conveyance or transfer of the relevant land.

. . .

Other, less obvious but not less significant, implications have gathered around the conceptualization of property as a *right* rather than as a *fact*. During the twentieth century a preoccupation with the supposedly crystalline essence of property rights has conduced to a wholly mistaken theory as to the potential significance of property for third parties. Common lawyers, having once conceived of property in terms of artificially pre-packaged commodities of tightly defined right, found it easy to embrace the seductive fallacy which still pervades the common law understanding of property. 'Property' appeared to comprise those rights which were sufficiently hard-edged and durable to be commerciable and, no less perversely, it seemed to follow that only those rights which could be bought and sold could ever constitute 'property'. In other words, the crisp definitional quality which facilitates the commercial trading of identifiable assets began – in a wholly illusory relationship of cause and effect – to make alienability or transmissibility appear as essential qualifying characteristics or hallmarks of 'property' itself.

Nor did the fallacy stop there. In a closely associated *non sequitur*, it came to be believed that, in order to enjoy 'proprietary' as distinct from merely 'personal' quality, rights must be capable of an even more general third-party impact. Not only must rights of property be capable of conferring benefits on third parties through onward sale; their proprietary character was, in turn, reinforced by their potential to impose enforceable burdens on other strangers. Beguiled again by the heavily formative pragmatics of the nineteenth century market place, the common lawyer fell into the lazy confusion that something was 'property' if sufficiently identifiable to burden third parties and, conversely, that the only rights which could adversely affect third parties were rights sufficiently clear-cut and durable to constitute 'property'. Hence emerged the convenient, but wholly mendacious, proposition that asset entitlements comprised 'property' if enforceable against strangers; and such entitlements were, of course, enforceable against strangers provided that they were 'proprietary'.

The absurd circularity of this concentration on assignability of benefit and enforceability of burden is almost too embarrassing to recount, yet its influence has infiltrated even the most exalted levels of common law decision-making. In so far as proprietary character is made to depend upon some supposed quality of 'permanence' or 'stability' – to use the terms adopted by Lord Wilberforce in *National Provincial Bank Ltd* v *Ainsworth* – the definition of 'property' becomes patently self-fulfilling. Quite often – as, for instance, with the 'deserted wife's equity' in dispute in *Ainsworth* itself – the reason for asking whether a particular right is *proprietary* is precisely in order to determine whether the right is capable of binding third parties and thereby attaining the relevantly critical qualities of 'permanence' and 'stability'. Proprietary character cannot be credibly or satisfactorily predicated in terms of tautological consequence, although this is exactly the trap induced by the common lawyer's ready disposition to see property as discrete blocks of conceptual entitlement. The initial judgment whether a particular claim is sufficiently hard-edged and durable to rank as property has tended, quite irrationally, to predetermine the question of binding impact on strangers.

Lord Wilberforce's proprietary criteria of alienability and enduring impact have often served to stultify emerging, and important, developments in the law – another example coming to the fore in the contemporary recognition of traditional land rights in Australia. Once again it was, significantly, the conceptualization of property in terms of abstract right rather than empirical fact which, for two centuries, disabled the common law from recognizing the proprietary nature of Australian native title. . . .

Property as a responsibility

A third model of property in land is provided by an alternative – less widely acknowledged – perspective which views property, not in terms of an abstract estate or interest, but in terms of each of the isolable strands of utility or use power which combine variously as the constituent elements of any land interest. By a process sometimes known as 'conceptual severance', this approach separates and identifies the many elements of utility which can characterize relationships with land, and then concedes the label 'property' to each individual element in turn.

Land may, of course, be turned to advantage in many overlapping ways; it may generate utilities of occupancy, enjoyment, consumption, investment, exploitation, exchange, endowment, aesthetic appreciation, and so on. These elements of utility all require to be held in some sort of balance, and our third model of property in land focuses on the way in which the precise balance or mix of utilities inherent in any particular landholding is subjected, through state intervention, to an overarching criterion of publicly defined responsibility. It follows, moreover, that, when there is any addition to, or subtraction from, the bundle of utilities enjoyed by any person, it can be suggested that a movement or transaction of 'property' has occurred – a proposition not only of venerable authority in English law, but also of huge contemporary relevance to the jurisprudence of environmental regulation and just compensation.

On the present analysis, property comprises not so much a bundle of rights as a bundle of individuated elements of land-based utility. The modern governmental role in regulating all land use is now so pervasive that these elements of utility are best seen as dispensed in various combinations by the state, subject only to occasional alteration either by private bargain or in accordance with supervening considerations of community policy. A plethora of regulatory controls, over matters ranging from urban planning to the conservation of natural resources, testifies to the constant engagement of the modern state in the constraint of land user for purposes of public amenity and welfare. Estate ownership is thus constantly stripped back to a bare residuum of socially permitted power over land resources, and the regime of property in land comprises simply a distribution – on a vast scale – of diverse patterns of state-approved usufruct, each heavily conditioned by the public interest. In effect, property in land is constituted by those publicly endorsed user forms which the state, at its discretion, allows individuals to enjoy consonantly with large strategies of public policy and social design. Property is no more than a defeasible privilege for the citizen.

. . .

CONCLUSION

This chapter has attempted to highlight three ways in which common law jurisprudence characteristically conceives of property in land. The chapter has also adumbrated some of the difficulties and challenges implicit in each of these divergent approaches. At different times and in many different contexts our notion of property has resonated with a varying sense that property emerges as a self-constituting fact or derives from some abstract jural entitlement or even emanates from the state control of socially responsible land use. The truth is, of course, that these alternative models of property do not exist in resolute opposition, for they are bound together in a creative tension which is part of the richness of our land law. Relativities of time and place certainly constrain the applicability of each of these modes of perception, and this chapter has pointed to some of the problems generated by the mismatching of sense and context. Each analysis nevertheless provides, in its own way, an important focus upon the essentially human institution of property, whilst reminding us of the ultimately elusive quality which still attaches to the core of the phenomenon.

Comment

(1) In what ways do these perceptions of land law – and property law generally – differ?

(2) The paper by the Grays is highly critical of the role of third parties being bound in defining property rights.[1] What is this role? Is the criticism convincing? What approach would Birks take?

Perhaps the real point is that there is no clearly defined 'land law' or 'property law': the labels can be used for whatever content a course, or an author, chooses. This book is based upon interests which bind purchasers: the heart of most courses on property law. As Birks stresses, there are other important and challenging questions, but they are less central to most lawyers' notions of property.

One element of property which may be worth considering further is the power of exclusion: if I own a car, I can stop others from interfering with it. We recognise property rights outside physical assets: copyright in a book and patents provide examples, where others cannot exploit the words or processes involved. This has led to attempts to develop further property claims, in order to provide protection for some right or expectation. By and large, the courts are reluctant to extend property notions in response to such invitations.

Extract 1.1.3

Victoria Park Racing & Recreation Grounds Co Ltd v *Taylor* (1937) 58 CLR 479

The defendant broadcast the plaintiff's racing activities from premises which overlooked their racecourse. The plaintiff sought to restrain this.

LATHAM CJ: . . . It has been argued that by the expenditure of money the plaintiff has created a spectacle and that it therefore has what is described as a quasi-property in the spectacle which the law will protect. The vagueness of this proposition is apparent upon its face. What it really means is that there is some principle (apart from contract or confidential relationship) which prevents people in some circumstances from opening their eyes and seeing something and then describing what they see. The court has not been referred to any authority in English law which supports the general contention that if a person chooses to organize an entertainment or to do anything else which other persons are able to see he has a right to obtain from a court an order that they shall not describe to anybody what they see. . . .

I find difficulty in attaching any precise meaning to the phrase 'property in a spectacle'. A 'spectacle' cannot be 'owned' in any ordinary sense of that word. Even if there were any legal principle which prevented one person from gaining an advantage for himself or causing damage to another by describing a spectacle produced by that other person, the rights of the latter person could be described as property only in a metaphorical sense. Any appropriateness in the metaphor would depend upon the existence of the legal principle. The principle cannot itself be based upon such a metaphor.

Even if, on the other hand, a spectacle could be said to exist as a subject matter of property, it would still be necessary, in order to provide the plaintiff in this case with a remedy, to show

---

[1] See also Dixon in Tee (ed.), *Land Law: Issues, Debates, Policy*, pp 16–18.

that the description of such property is wrongful or that such description is wrongful when it is widely disseminated. No authority has been cited to support such a proposition.

DIXON J: . . . So far as freedom from view or inspection is a natural or acquired physical characteristic of the site, giving it value for the purpose of the business or pursuit which the plaintiff conducts, it is a characteristic which is not a legally protected interest. It is not a natural right for breach of which a legal remedy is given, either by an action in the nature of nuisance or otherwise. The fact is that the substance of the plaintiff's complaint goes to interference, not with its enjoyment of the land, but with the profitable conduct of its business. If English law had followed the course of development that has recently taken place in the United States, the 'broadcasting rights' in respect of the races might have been protected as part of the quasi-property created by the enterprise, organization and labour of the plaintiff in establishing and equipping a racecourse and doing all that is necessary to conduct race meetings. But courts of equity have not in British jurisdictions thrown the protection of an injunction around all the intangible elements of value, that is, value in exchange, which may flow from the exercise by an individual of his powers or resources whether in the organization of a business or undertaking or the use of ingenuity, knowledge, skill or labour. . . .

In dissenting from a judgment of the Supreme Court of the United States by which the organized collection of news by a news service was held to give it in equity a quasi-property protected against appropriation by rival news agencies, Brandeis J gave reasons which substantially represent the English view and he supported his opinion by a citation of much English authority (*International News Service* v *Associated Press*). His judgment appears to me to contain an adequate answer both upon principle and authority to the suggestion that the defendants are misappropriating or abstracting something which the plaintiff has created and alone is entitled to turn to value. Briefly, the answer is that it is not because the individual has by his efforts put himself in a position to obtain value for what he can give that his right to give it becomes protected by law and so assumes the exclusiveness of property, but because the intangible or incorporeal right he claims falls within a recognized category to which legal or equitable protection attaches . . .

In my opinion, the right to exclude the defendants from broadcasting a description of the occurrences they can see upon the plaintiff's land is not given by law. It is not an interest falling within any category which is protected at law or in equity . . .

Comment

(1) This is one of a number of arguments advanced by the plaintiff; all were unsuccessful. The central argument was based upon the tort of nuisance. Why was the notion of property significant?

(2) Is the development of property concepts an appropriate way to develop legal protection against invasions of privacy?

2. The new property

In recent decades, property terminology has been used to advance the protection of claims which have not been traditionally considered as property. The label 'new property' has been applied in this setting.

Extract 1.2.1

Harris, *Property and Justice* pp 149–151 (some footnotes omitted)

. . . When the boundaries of the concept of property are discussed in modern Anglo–American theory, reference is frequently made to an article written by Charles Reich, published in 1964, which is entitled 'The New Property'.[i] Reich seeks to show that the wealth-allocation function of property institutions is, in modern societies, of diminishing relative importance because of the growth of 'government largesse'. Wealth is increasingly allocated through welfare benefits, government jobs, occupational licences, State franchises, contracts, and subsidies, and access to State-owned resources and to governmental services. Allocation takes place in accordance with the assessment by various governmental agencies of what would best serve the public interest. In the past, Reich contends, holdings of wealth in the form of private property had the great merit of securing independence from the State. However, it also had the great demerit that holders of wealth were increasingly able to dominate the lives of others, especially as wealth became consolidated in the form of large corporate holdings. The 'public-interest State' has evolved as a counter to this domination-potential of private property holdings, as well as a vehicle for performing many functions which modern societies expect their governments to discharge. But with it has come the loss of independence which private property once secured.

The discretionary power to award, withhold, or terminate largesse introduces new dangers of illegitimate domination . . .

Reich disavows any suggestion that the remedy for the independence-threatening aspects of the public-interest State is to turn the clock back to a time when wealth was distributed via agglomerated private holdings. Government largesse we must have. He advocates measures which will, so far as possible, ensure that the wealth which results from government largesse confers upon its recipients an independence equivalent to that which private property provides. Discretionary receipts should be replaced, where possible, with entitlements held as of right. Substantive restraints should be imposed so that discretion cannot be exercised on improper grounds – especially so as to prevent rights guaranteed by the constitution being indirectly infringed. All withholding or cancellation of government largesse should be subjected to procedural due process.

That independence is one of the instrumental justifications for property institutions, and that domination-potential counts as an important disjustification, are matters considered later in this book. For the moment we are only concerned with the question whether Reich's important diagnosis entails an expansion in the concept of property beyond the conventional understanding which the stipulation at the beginning of this Chapter seeks to capture. Some commentators have taken it for granted that it does: that, according to the diagnosis, welfare benefits, government jobs, subsidies, and other categories of largesse simply are, or should be thought of as being, 'property'.[ii] Consider, however, the following three claims which emerge from Reich's article: (1) property used to secure independence; (2) the terms on which government largesse is available today threaten independence; (3) we ought to change the terms on which largesse is allocated so that it accords an independence similar to that which property once afforded. None of these claims warrants any shift in what property means. If the article had been entitled '[t]he need for a property substitute', and if it had not ended with the clarion call: '[w]e must create a new property', there would have been no doubt about it. No expansive definition would have been proposed. As it is, the article can be understood as calling for an extension in the concept of property beyond its conventional use in the service of a justificatory analogy. Property is justified by its instrumental advantages in securing citizen independence against the all-encroaching public-interest State. The recommended reforms in the way largesse is distributed are justified because they too would secure independence. Therefore, they should also be called 'property'.

Note, however, that it is the reformed largesse, not the present array of discretionary welfare benefits and the rest, to which the extended label is to be applied. As Reich says: '[g]overnment largesse is plainly "wealth", but it is not necessarily "property".' Different concept-expansion arguments, not advanced by Reich, can be put forward for insisting that discretionary access to wealth already is property. . . . It can be argued that if they are given the property label, then they can be subsumed under constitutional provisions which protect 'property'; or that announcing the label will serve as part of a political rhetoric which will induce people to accord them greater respect.

Reich's justificatory-analogy argument raises many problems. What if one disagrees with his contention that independence was a justification for property institutions whilst agreeing with his proposed reforms for largesse? What if one supposes that reformed largesse cannot or should not be modelled on property-substitutes? What if one considers that claims to largesse should indeed become entitlements as of right, but that, unlike cashable rights, they should not be freely tradable or fall within the purview of bankruptcy law? In all these cases, calling reformed largesse 'property' serves only to confuse. 'The New Property' was a catchy title for an article which highlighted important dangers of the modern wealth-allocating State. But it is possible to support any or all of Reich's remedial proposals without any expansion in the concept of property.

[i] Charles A Reich, 'The New Property' (1964) 73 YLJ 733.
[ii] See, e.g., Bruce A Ackerman, *Private Property and the Constitution* (Yale UP, 1977), 165, n. 115. C B MacPherson, 'Capitalism and the Changing Concept of Property', in E Kamenka and R S Neale, *Feudalism, Capitalism and Beyond* (Edward Arnold, 1975), 115.

Comment

(1) What is the new property?

(2) Do these highly sceptical comments mean that property lawyers can and should decry new property analyses?

3. Trusts and equitable interests

As Professor Birks observes,[2] equity (and in particular the trust) has played a central role in the development of English property law. Later chapters will consider particular aspects of trusts and equitable interests, but we must first note some general principles. The essential nature of the trust is that the settlor gives property to the trustee to hold for the benefit of the beneficiary; in some respects the trustee can be seen as a sort of manager of the property.

Extract 1.3.1

Maitland, *Equity* (2nd ed) pp 23, 30–31, 117, 129, 139, 147–149, 153 (footnotes omitted) by permission of Cambridge University Press

Of all the exploits of Equity the largest and the most important is the invention and development of the Trust.

It is an 'institute' of great elasticity and generality; as elastic, as general as contract.

This perhaps forms the most distinctive achievement of English lawyers. It seems to us almost essential to civilization, and yet there is nothing quite like it in foreign law. Take up for instance the Bürgerliches Gesetzbuch – the Civil Code of Germany; where is trust? Nowhere. This in the eyes of an English practitioner is a big hole.

Foreigners don't see that there is any hole. 'I can't understand your trust', said Gierke to me. We must ask why this is so. Well, the trust does not fit easily into what they regard as the necessary scheme of jurisprudence.

Let me explain a little; for this will be of service in practical consideration of the nature of equitable rights.

---

[2] See Extract 1.1.1, p 3 above.

Jurists have long tried to make a dichotomy of Private Rights: they are either *in rem* or *in personam*. The types of these two classes are, of the former, *dominium*, ownership; of the latter the benefit of contract – a debt.

Now under which head does trust – the right of *cestui que trust*[i] – fall? Not easily under either. It seems to be a little of both . . .

The best answer may be that in history, and probably in ultimate analysis, it is *jus in personam*; but that it is so treated (and this for many important purposes) that it is very like *jus in rem*. A right primarily good against *certa persona*, viz. the trustee, but so treated as to be almost equivalent to a right good against all – a *dominium*, ownership, which however exists only in equity. And this is so from a remote time.

. . .

Did the Chancellor ask himself what sort of right he was giving, whether *in rem* or *in personam*; did he ask himself under what rubric this new chapter would stand? Probably not. As between the feoffor (*cestui que use*) and the original feoffees the case is plain – it is scandalous dishonesty if the feoffees disregard the trust.

It might have been regarded as a breach of contract. But this was not done, perhaps because breach of contract was a matter for the common law. At any rate the language of contract was not used – there was no formal promise exacted from the feoffees, no '*obligo me*', etc. It seems to be felt from the first that contract is not what is wanted – that contract won't do.

There is one strong reason against treating it as a contract, the feoffor (who is *cestui que use*) has then a chose in action and this would be inalienable. But our landowner did not mean to exchange ownership of land for the (inalienable) benefit of a promise.

No, there is no 'obligatory' language: all is done under cover of 'use'; a little later of 'confidence' and 'trust'.

Secondly, we see this at an early time: the remedy is given not to the trustor but to the *destinatory*. In the earliest instances the trustor and the *cestui que trust* (or use) are the same person – still it is as destinatory, not as 'author of the trust' that he has the remedy. This marks it off from contract. Refer to John of Gaunt's will; consider the disposition in favour of the Beauforts – it would not do to give the remedy to John of Gaunt's heir: he is the very person who is interested in breaking the will.

This principle runs through our law of equity to the present day – the destinatory, beneficiary, *cestui que trust* has the remedy. (It is an unfortunate term, '*cestui que trust*', with an obscure history. It suggests a falsehood at this point.)

Thirdly, as regards estates and interests the common law of land is to be the model. . . . The new class of rights is made to look as much like rights *in rem* (estates in land) as the Chancellor can make them look . . .

But (fourthly) the Chancellor can not create new rights *in rem*. So to do would be not to supplement but to overrule the common law . . .

Equitable estates and interests are rights *in personam* but they have a misleading resemblance to rights *in rem*. This resemblance has been brought about in the following way. The trust will be enforced not only against the trustee who has accepted it and his representatives and volunteers claiming through or under him, but also against persons who acquire legal rights through or under him with knowledge of the trust – nor is that all; it will be enforced against persons who acquire legal rights through or under him if they ought to have known of the trust . . .

Here then again we get a distinction between legal and equitable rights, and this is quite intelligible, for legal estates are proprietary rights, ownership or fractions of ownership, equitable rights are not. Negligence will not deprive one of ownership. It is excessively negligent for one to leave one's purse on the counter of a shop, but one shall not for that reason lose ownership. Fraud or connivance at fraud is a different matter. But as between merely equitable claimants, the Court can consider the moral merits of the parties – *qui prior est tempore potior est jure* is a natural rule where merits are equal, but negligence may be a ground for postponing an older to a younger equity.

. . .

By this time we shall have convinced ourselves, if we required conviction, that it is practically unsafe to regard equitable estates and interests as rights *in rem*, as ownership or fractions of ownership. As to what I may call the theoretic question, the question of appropriate classification, I will say one word more. I do not for one minute think that it should be part of our conception of a right *in rem*, that the person who has that right can never be deprived of it save by his own act . . .

And now a few words as to the general relation between Equity and Law. A few years ago there was, if I may so speak, a visible distinction. If it was impossible to explain the distinction without a long historical discourse, still it was possible to point to the distinction as a visible matter of fact – to say to the inquirer 'Go to Westminster Hall and you will there see courts administering Common Law; then go to Lincoln's Inn and you will there see courts administering Equity.' The existence of the distinction was made emphatic in every sort of way. In the Courts of Common Law were judges hearing 'actions' begun by 'writ', carried on by 'declaration' and 'plea' with a system of procedure of which trial by jury was the central fact. In the Court of Chancery were the Chancellor, Master of the Rolls, and Vice-Chancellors hearing 'suits' begun by 'bill' with a system of procedure which made no use of a jury and differed at almost every possible point from the procedure of the Common Law . . .

And now all this has passed away; one can no longer say 'Here is a Court which administers nothing but common law, and there a Court which administers nothing but equity.' The task of the student is really all the harder. Let us look at the matter a little.

In the first place let us guard ourselves against the fallacy of supposing that the Chancery Division of the new High Court is the Court of Chancery under a new name, or that the old courts of common law are now called the Queen's Bench Division. This would be a great error. It is true that actions of certain kinds have been assigned to one division, actions of certain other kinds to the other, though in many cases the plaintiff has a choice. This is a convenient division of labour – the trying with a jury is done in one division, the other has a machinery adapted for taking accounts. But a rule of court might alter this assignment, and an Order in Council might abolish the existing 'divisions' – the Common Pleas Division and the Exchequer Division were thus merged in the Queen's Bench Division. And, to come to a more important point, every judge in whatever division he may be sitting is bound to apply every rule whether of common law or of equity that is applicable to the case before him. He cannot stop short and say that is a question of common law which I am incompetent to decide, or, that is a merely equitable right and I can take no notice of it.

But if this be so, if the two bodies of rules have to be administered together, have not the terms law and equity lost their meaning? Well, as terms, they are merely historical terms, and such they have been for centuries past; but they will endure for a long time yet, for they do express distinctions of the utmost importance – distinctions among the rules of substantive law – and if we had not inherited this pair of terms we should be obliged to invent others to serve the same purpose.

For the Judicature Act did not alter the substantive law – save in a few points to be hereafter mentioned – did not change the nature of rights or even give new remedies. It only made a thorough change in procedure – introducing a new procedural code, partly borrowed from that of the common law, partly borrowed from that of equity, and in part newly invented.

A few points of substantive law were expressly dealt with by section 25 . . . then follows the 11th [sub-section] to which I wish to draw attention. 'Generally in all matters not herein-before particularly mentioned in which there is any conflict or variance between the rules of equity and the rules of the common law with reference to the same matter, the rules of equity shall prevail.'

Now what did this sub-section do? Did it turn equitable estates into legal estates, acting like a second Statute of Uses? Of course it did not. There was no conflict or variance here between common law and equity. The statement that T is owner but is a trustee for E is not self-contradictory. It is no more self-contradictory than the statement that A is the owner of goods but owes more debts than he can pay. Austin, we have seen, speaking of the position of one who has agreed to buy land but had not yet obtained a conveyance, talks of the conflict between law and equity, of how equity held that the contract passed a *jus in rem*. To speak thus is to take a very superficial view of the case – the right that the purchaser gets by the contract is no right *in rem*, and there is no conflict between law and equity.

. . .

The Judicature Act 1873, s 25, sub-s 11, speaks, we have seen, of cases in which there is a conflict or variance between the rules of the common law and the rules of equity. We have seen, however, that normally the relation between equity and law has not been one of conflict. How could it have been otherwise? After all, for centuries past this country has been decently governed and reasonably peaceful, and this would not have been so if we had really had two conflicting systems of law in full operation. 'The courts of common law said that the trustee was the owner, but the Court of Chancery said that the *cestui que trust* was the owner' – if we take this crude statement literally it is an invitation to civil war. No, we ought to think of the relation between common law and equity not as that between two conflicting systems, but as that between code and supplement, that between text and gloss. And we should further remember this, that equity was not a self-sufficient system – it was hardly a system at all – but rather a collection of additional rules. Common law was, we may say, a complete system – if the equitable jurisdiction of the Chancery had been destroyed, there still would have been law for every case, somewhat rude law it may be, and law imperfectly adapted to the needs of our time, but still law for every case. On the other hand, if the common law had been abolished equity must have disappeared also, for at every point it presupposed a great body of common law.

[i] [The beneficiary under a trust.]

Comment

(1) Maitland's analysis that equitable interests are not rights *in rem* is not generally accepted today. Nevertheless, the stress on the trust as involving obligations owed by the trustee is faithful to equitable analyses past and present; it is always worth remembering.

(2) How does the trust differ from contractual analyses?

(3) How can one tell whether an interest is equitable or legal?

(4) Why does not the merger of the courts of law and equity by the Judicature Acts 1873–75 spell the end of the distinction between legal and equitable interests? A broader view of the Acts may have been taken by Jessel MR in *Walsh v Lonsdale*.[3]

(5) It will be seen in the following chapter that the property legislation of 1925 has made significant changes in the division between legal and equitable interests and also in the effect of equitable interests.

Only rarely is it necessary for the courts to consider the nature of the rights of a beneficiary under a trust. When the question does arise, it can be very difficult.

---

[3] (1882) 21 Ch D 9 (Extract 14.2.8 below), explained by Maitland in Extract 14.2.10.

Extract 1.3.2

Baker v Archer-Shee **[1927] AC 844**

For taxation purposes, it was crucial to determine whether Lady Archer-Shee, a beneficiary entitled to the income, was entitled to the dividends received by the trustees, or merely to the income handed over by the trustees to her.

LORD WRENBURY: . . . My Lords, the question is not what the trustees have thought proper to hand over and have handed over (which is question of fact) but what under the will Lady Archer-Shee is entitled to (which is question of law). The trustees, of course, have a first charge upon the trust funds for their costs, charges and expenses, and American income tax will be a tax which they would have to bear and which would fall upon the beneficiary. But this does not reduce the right of property of the beneficiary to a right only to a balance sum after deducting these. If an owner of shares deposits them with his banker by way of security for a loan he is not reduced to being the owner of a balance sum being the difference between the dividends on the shares and the interest on the loan. He is the owner of the equity of redemption of the whole fund. If a landowner employs an agent to collect his rents and authorizes him to deduct a commission he does not cease to be owner of the rents. Under Mr Pell's will Lady Archer-Shee (if American law is the same as English law) is, in my opinion, as matter of construction of the will, entitled in equity specifically during her life to the dividends upon the stocks.

LORD CARSON: . . . in my opinion the Master of the Rolls correctly stated the law when he said[i] 'that in considering sums which are placed in the hands of trustees for the purpose of paying income to beneficiaries, for the purposes of the Income Tax Acts, you may eliminate the trustees. The income is the income of the beneficiaries; the income does not belong to the trustees.'

LORD BLANESBURGH (dissenting): My Lords, her position from an English point of view, could not, I think, be better put than it is by Rowlatt J in his judgment.[ii] 'What this lady enjoys,' he says, 'is not the stocks, shares and rents or other property constituting the trust fund under the will; what she has is the right to call upon the trustees, and, if necessary, to compel the trustees, to administer this property during her life so as to give her the income arising there from according to the provisions of the trust. Her interest is merely an equitable one, and it is not an interest in the specific stocks and shares constituting the trust fund at all. There is no doubt about the correctness of that proposition.'

[i] [1927] 1 KB 123.
[ii] [1927] 1 KB 116.

Comment

(1) The House of Lords split 3:2 in deciding that there was entitlement to the dividends.

(2) What would Maitland have made of the question? The decision has always been controversial: is it consistent with equitable principles?

(3) Lord Hoffmann has said:[4] 'But a trustee in English law is not an agent for his beneficiary. He contracts in his own name with a right of indemnity against the beneficiary for the liabilities he has incurred.' How far is this consistent with the majority in *Baker v Archer-Shee*?

---

[4] *Ingram* v *IRC* [2000] 1 AC 293 at p 395.

A. Equitable interests and equities

So far, much of our stress has been on trusts, which constitute the most significant contribution of equity to property law. However, equity also developed new forms of interests. Three major examples are the mortgage, the estate contract and restrictive covenants. For mortgages, equity developed the principle that the borrower is always able to recover the property on which the loan is secured (the equitable right to redeem, or equity of redemption). Estate contracts include the everyday contract to buy land, together with options. Because equity is willing to grant specific performance of such contracts and 'equity treats as done what ought to be done', the purchaser is treated as having an equitable interest from the outset. Restrictive covenants, a relative newcomer as a mid nineteenth-century development, enable one landowner to restrict the use of his or her land for the benefit of neighbouring land. All these will be considered in detail later on.

Equities constitute a more dubious category. The label is used to cover two rather different types of rights, both less definitive than equitable interests. The existence, content and significance of the equity category are all controversial. They differ from equitable interests as regards when they will bind purchasers. This last point today applies only to unregistered land; it is considered in Chapter 9.[5]

<hr>

Extract 1.3.3

<hr>

Latec Investments Ltd v Hotel Terrigal Pty Ltd (in liquidation) (1965) 113 CLR 265

<hr>

KITTO J: . . . It is the case of a suit 'where there are circumstances that give rise to an equity as distinguished from an equitable estate – as, for example, an equity to set aside a deed for fraud, or to correct it for mistake'.[i] . . . each of the illustrations Lord Westbury chose [in *Phillips* v *Phillips*[ii]] was also a case where the equity was accompanied by an equitable interest which might constitute an equitable estate. So much had been shown by decisions of most eminent judges, at least twice in the ten years before his Lordship spoke: see *Stump* v *Gaby*;[iii] *Gresley* v *Mousley*,[iv] and Lord Westbury's judgment gives every indication of an intention to state systematically the effect of previous decisions, and not to depart from them in any degree. The illustrations therefore make it clear, it seems to me, that the cases to which his Lordship was referring were not only those in which there is an assertion of an equity unaccompanied by an equitable interest . . . – indeed he may not have had them in mind at all – but those in which an equity is asserted which must be made good before an equitable interest can be held to exist. In the latter class of cases the equity is distinct from, because logically antecedent to, the equitable interest . . .

[i] (1861) 4 De GF&J, at p 218 [45 ER, at p 1167].
[ii] (1861) 4 De GF&J 208 [45 ER 1164].
[iii] (1852) 2 De GM&G 623 [42 ER 1015].
[iv] (1859) 4 De G&J 78 [45 ER 31].

Comment

(1) Kitto J refers to an equity 'accompanied by an equitable interest'. How does this apply to cases where the claim is one to set a conveyance aside? In *Latec*, the claim was that what appeared to be an absolute conveyance was in fact a mortgage.

<hr>

[5] See pp 291–292.

(2) Further extracts from *Latec*, relating to the effect of equities on purchasers, will be found later.[6]

Cases where the equity does not depend upon an equitable remedy linked to an equitable interest are more controversial. It has sometimes been argued that the availability of any equitable remedy gives rise to an equity which can bind a purchaser, but this argument became untenable after *National Provincial Bank Ltd* v *Ainsworth*.[7] Lord Upjohn was quite clear: 'a mere "equity" naked and alone is, in my opinion, incapable of binding successors in title even with notice; it is personal to the parties'. Nevertheless, it remains the case that some rights, of which estoppel probably provides the best example, are commonly described as equities. This may indicate no more than a reluctance to use the more definite language of equitable interests. Can it be argued that equities provide a useful and flexible tool for use in developing proprietary interests?

Extract 1.3.4

Land Registration Act 2002, s 116

116.—It is hereby declared for the avoidance of doubt that, in relation to registered land, . . .
  (b) a mere equity,
has effect from the time the equity arises as an interest capable of binding successors in title (subject to the rules about the effect of dispositions on priority).

Extract 1.3.5

Law Commission No 271: Land Registration for the Twenty First Century: A Conveyancing Revolution (footnotes omitted)

5.36 The effect of the Bill is as follows.
(1) It declares for the avoidance of doubt that, in relation to registered land, a mere equity has effect from the time when the equity arises as an interest capable of binding successors in title (subject to the rules about the effect of dispositions on priority). In one sense this is, of course, no more than declaratory of the present law, because it is not disputed that a mere equity is a proprietary right of some kind.

Explanatory Notes, 512. In relation to 'mere equities' the Bill clarifies the present law. A 'mere equity' is difficult to define with any clarity. The term is used to denote a claim to discretionary equitable relief in relation to property, such as a right to set aside a transfer for fraud or undue influence, a right to rectify an instrument for mistake, or a right to seek relief against the forfeiture of a lease after a landlord has peaceably re-entered.

Comment

(1) What is a mere equity (it has no statutory definition)? Is it satisfactory to use this term in legislation when it is 'difficult to define'?

(2) In the light of the material earlier discussed, is it correct to assert that a mere equity was already a proprietary right?

(3) How is s 116 most likely to be interpreted?

---

[6] See Extract 9.4.1.
[7] [1965] AC 1175 at p 1238; see also Extract 18.1.9 below.

Further reading

Baker (1977) 93 LQR 529: The future of equity.

Everton (1976) 40 Conv (NS) 209: 'Equitable interests' and 'equities' – in search of a pattern.

Hargreaves, E (2011) 25 Trust Law International 163: The nature of beneficiaries' rights under trusts.

Harris, J W (1987) 'Legal doctrine and interests in land', in *Oxford Essays in Jurisprudence*, Third Series, eds J M Eekelaar and J Bell, Chapter 8.

Honoré, A M (1961) 'Ownership' in *Oxford Essays in Jurisprudence*, First Series, ed. A G Guest, Chapter 5.

Reich, C A (1964) 73 Yale LJ 733: The new property.

2
Human rights

As we are interested in the impact of human rights principles on property law, this is not an appropriate book in which to provide detailed treatment of these principles. This chapter will include a little of the basic material: cases raising human rights issues in specific property areas will be considered in the relevant chapters.

1. The Convention rights

Extract 2.1.1

Human Rights Act 1998, ss 3, 6; Articles 6, 8; First Protocol, Article 1

3.—(1) So far as it is possible to do so, primary legislation and subordinate legislation must be read and given effect in a way which is compatible with the Convention rights.

6.—(1) It is unlawful for a public authority to act in a way which is incompatible with a Convention right.
  (2)   Subsection (1) does not apply to an act if—
    (a)   as the result of one or more provisions of primary legislation, the authority could not have acted differently; or
    (b)   in the case of one or more provisions of, or made under, primary legislation which cannot be read or given effect in a way which is compatible with the Convention rights, the authority was acting so as to give effect to or enforce those provisions.
  (3)   In this section 'public authority' includes—
    (a)   a court or tribunal, and
    (b)   any person certain of whose functions are functions of a public nature, but does not include either House of Parliament or a person exercising functions in connection with proceedings in Parliament . . .

Article 6   1.   In the determination of his civil rights and obligations or of any criminal charge against him, everyone is entitled to a fair and public hearing within a reasonable time by an independent and impartial tribunal established by law.

Article 8   1.   Everyone has the right to respect for his private and family life, his home and his correspondence.
  2.   There shall be no interference by a public authority with the exercise of this right except such as is in accordance with the law and is necessary in a democratic society in the interests of national security, public safety or the economic well-being of the country, for the prevention of disorder or crime, for the protection of health or morals, or for the protection of the rights and freedoms of others.

First Protocol, Article 1 Every natural or legal person is entitled to the peaceful enjoyment of his possessions. No one shall be deprived of his possessions except in the public interest and subject to the conditions provided for by law and by the general principles of international law.

The preceding provisions shall not, however, in any way impair the right of a State to enforce such laws as it deems necessary to control the use of property in accordance with the general interest or to secure the payment of taxes or other contributions or penalties.

Extract 2.1.2

JA Pye (Oxford) Ltd v *United Kingdom* (2007) 46 EHHR 1083 (footnotes omitted)

The applicant argued that the rules relating to adverse possession of registered land (whereby ownership may be lost if another person adversely possessed the land for 12 years) contravened Article 1.

EUROPEAN COURT OF HUMAN RIGHTS (GRAND CHAMBER): 43. The Government . . . considered, in the first place, that the matter should be determined by reference to Art 6 of the Convention, and not Art 1 of Protocol No 1. Unlike in previous cases, the Government in this case had not appropriated property to its own use, and had not introduced legislation for the involuntary transfer of private property from one person to another in pursuit of a social policy objective. The only interference with the applicant companies' land came about through the actions of private individuals, the squatters, who obtained adverse possession in 1983–1984. The outcome of the proceedings was dictated by the applicant companies' own inaction. It contended that the application to the present facts of the conventional case law as to the necessity, in principle, for compensation to be paid in respect of deprivations of property confirmed the logic of analysing the case by reference to Art 6: the purpose of a limitation period is to deprive a claimant, at the end of the relevant time period, of any opportunity of enforcing his rights through the courts. That objective would be frustrated if a limitation provision could only be compatible with the Convention if the claimant was provided with compensation against the very person against whom his claim was barred.

45. Under Art 1 of Protocol No 1, the Government considered that the provision was not engaged, because the applicant companies acquired the disputed land subject to the risk of losing it pursuant to the provisions of the 1925 and 1980 Acts. That risk had to be viewed as an incident of their property. . . .

53. In order to be compatible with the general rule set forth in the first sentence of the first paragraph of Art 1, an interference with the right to the peaceful enjoyment of possessions must strike a 'fair balance' between the demands of the general interest of the community and the requirements of the protection of the individual's fundamental rights.

54. A taking of property under the second sentence of the first paragraph of Art 1 without payment of an amount reasonably related to its value will normally constitute a disproportionate interference that cannot be justified under Art 1. The provision does not, however, guarantee a right to full compensation in all circumstances, since legitimate objectives of 'public interest' may call for less than reimbursement of the full market value.

55. In respect of interferences which fall under the second paragraph of Art 1 of Protocol No 1, with its specific reference to '[T]he right of a State to enforce such laws as it deems necessary to control the use of property in accordance with the general interest . . .', there must also exist a reasonable relationship of proportionality between the means employed and the aim sought to be realised. In this respect, States enjoy a wide margin of appreciation with regard both to choosing the means of enforcement and to ascertaining whether the consequences of enforcement are justified in the general interest for the purpose of achieving the object of the law in question.

60. The Court finds nothing in its case law to suggest that the present case should be dealt with only under Art 6 of the Convention, and indeed, given the different content of the two rights, it would be unusual if the Court were to decline to deal with a complaint under one head

solely because it were capable of raising different issues under a separate Article. The Court agrees with the Chamber that there is nothing in principle to preclude the examination of a claim under Art 1 of Protocol No 1 where the complaint is directed against legislation concerning property rights.

65.   The applicant companies did not lose their land because of a legislative provision which permitted the State to transfer ownership in particular circumstances, or because of a social policy of transfer of ownership, but rather as the result of the operation of the generally applicable rules on limitation periods for actions for recovery of land. Those rules provided that at the end of the limitation period, the paper owner's title to unregistered land was extinguished. In the case of registered land, the position was amended to take into account the fact that until the register was rectified, the former owner continued to appear as registered proprietor . . .

66.   The statutory provisions which resulted in the applicant companies' loss of beneficial ownership were thus not intended to deprive paper owners of their ownership, but rather to regulate questions of title in a system in which, historically, 12 years' adverse possession was sufficient to extinguish the former owner's right to re-enter or to recover possession, and the new title depended on the principle that unchallenged lengthy possession gave a title. The provisions of the 1925 and 1980 Acts which were applied to the applicant companies were part of the general land law, and were concerned to regulate, amongst other things, limitation periods in the context of the use and ownership of land as between individuals. The applicant companies were therefore affected, not by a 'deprivation of possessions' within the meaning of the second sentence of the first paragraph of Art 1, but rather by a 'control of use' of land within the meaning of the second paragraph of the provision.

Comment

(1) Was there any merit in seeking to apply Article 6 rather than Article 1 of Protocol 1? Does the decision herald a wide scope for human rights?

(2) Why was it important that there was a control of use rather than deprivation of possessions?

(3) The majority of the Court went on to hold that there was no breach of Article 1: Extract 4.2.3 below.

A rather different point is that much of property law operates by implying terms into agreements. Thus in a mortgage it is implied that the lender can sell the land if there is default by the borrower. We shall see that *Horsham Properties Group Ltd* v *Clark*[1] establishes that there is no breach of Article 1 in such situations. This may constitute a significant limit on human rights arguments in some areas of property law.

2. Enforcement of Convention rights

Extract 2.2.1

X v *Y* **[2004] ICR 1634**

MUMMERY LJ: 43.   The HRA . . . has generated more legal literature than litigation on the disputed question whether it applies as between private individuals.

---

[1] [2009] 1 WLR 1255, Extract 21.4.33 below.

44.   The terminology of vertical effect (state/citizen) and horizontal effect (citizen/citizen), which is familiar in European Community law, has been used in the debate on the applicability of the HRA to disputes between private citizens. In the year 2000 a wide range of views was published in the Law Quarterly Review. Sir William Wade (whose writings have been of immense influence in the development of English law over the last 40 years and whose death a few weeks ago was a great loss to legal scholarship) argued that the HRA has horizontal effects between individuals: 'Horizons of Horizontality' (2000) 116 LQR 217. He was responding to Sir Richard Buxton, who argued that the HRA only has vertical effect between public authorities and individuals: 'The Human Rights Act and Private Law' (2000) 116 LQR 48. Lord Lester of Herne Hill and Mr David Pannick suggested that the HRA did not 'confer complete or automatic horizontality' and that Convention rights will significantly influence private law in a more sophisticated way than is indicated by a simple horizontal effect: 'The impact of the Human Rights Act on Private Law: The Knight's Move' (2000) 116 LQR 380. Other writers have put the arguments for 'indirect horizontality' of the HRA. . . .

DYSON LJ: 66.   In my view, however, the interpretative duty imposed by section 3 applies to the same degree in legislation applying between private parties as it does in legislation which applies between public authorities and individuals. There is nothing in the HRA which, either expressly or by necessary implication, indicates a contrary intention. If the position were otherwise, the same statutory provision would require different interpretations depending on whether the defendant was a public authority or a private individual. I acknowledge that Parliament could, without perversity, have intended such a distinction. After all, public authorities are, but private entities are not, subject to sections 6 and 7 of the HRA, and yet the dividing line between public authorities and private entities is sometimes very fine, and can lead to distinctions which may appear to lead to somewhat arbitrary results. Nevertheless, sections 6 and 7 show that Parliament was alive to the distinction between public authorities and private entities, and yet drew no distinction when it came to enacting section 3. In my judgment, the language of section 3(1) is plain: it should be accorded its clear and unqualified meaning.

Comment

(1) What is meant by 'horizontal effect'? Much of the argument is based on the court's status as a public authority which must act compatibly with Convention rights. How important is horizontal effect for property law?

(2) Recent cases on horizontal effect are considered in the following section.

3. Convention rights in the Courts

A. Human rights in the exercise of proprietary rights

There has been much controversy and litigation concerning the exercise by a public authority of normal proprietary rights. The principal question has been how far Article 8 (respect for home) is relevant when a local authority seeks possession, relying on its rights as owner or landlord.

Extract 2.3.1

Manchester City Council v *Pinnock* [2011] 2 AC 104

LORD NEUBERGER OF ABBOTSBURY MR: 21.   This appeal gives rise to four main issues, of increasing specificity. The first is whether the jurisprudence of the European Court of Human Rights ('the European court') requires that, before making an order for possession of property which consists of a person's home pursuant to a claim made by a local authority (or other public authority), a domestic court should be able to consider the proportionality of evicting that person from his home under article 8 and, in the process of doing so, to resolve any relevant factual disputes between the parties. We deal with that question in paras 22–54 below and answer it in the affirmative. The second issue (paras 55–64 below) is what this conclusion means in practice in relation to claims for possession, and related claims, in relation to residential property. The third issue (paras 65–107 below) is whether the demoted tenancy regime in the 1985, 1996 and 2003 Acts can properly be interpreted so as to comply with the requirements of article 8, or whether at least some aspects of that regime are incompatible with the occupiers' article 8 Convention rights. The fourth issue (paras 108–132 below), which requires a fuller consideration of the facts of this case, is how the appeal should be disposed of in the light of the answers on the first three issues.

First issue: what does the Convention require of the courts?

The nature of the issue

23. The argument on behalf of Mr Pinnock is as follows. (a) At any rate where the person seeking possession is a 'public authority', a court invited to make an order for possession of a person's home must be satisfied that article 8 is complied with. . . . (c) Article 8, when read together with article 6, required the judge, as the relevant independent tribunal, to be satisfied that the order for possession (i) would be 'in accordance with the law' and (ii) would be 'necessary in a democratic society'—ie, that it would be proportionate. (d) The order for possession was 'in accordance with the law' since it was made pursuant to the provisions relating to demoted tenancies in the 1985 and 1996 Acts, which are in principle unobjectionable under article 8. (e) However, Mr Pinnock was not given the opportunity to raise with the court the question whether the order for possession was, in all the circumstances of this case, proportionate. Therefore article 8 was violated. (f) Further, in order to determine proportionality, the court should have had power to resolve for itself any issues of fact between the council and Mr Pinnock, and to form its own view of proportionality, rather than adopting the traditional judicial review approach taken by the judge. . . .

The House of Lords cases

25. In three relatively recent cases the House of Lords held that it was not open to a residential occupier, against whom possession was being sought by a local authority, to raise a proportionality argument under article 8. In other words, the House rejected points (e) and (f) in the outline of the argument for Mr Pinnock in para 23 above. Point (g) therefore did not arise.

26. The three decisions of the House of Lords are: *Harrow London Borough Council v Qazi* [2004] 1 AC 983, *Kay v Lambeth London Borough Council* [2006] 2 AC 465, and *Doherty v Birmingham City Council (Secretary of State for Communities and Local Government intervening)* [2009] AC 367. In each of them the defendants were residential occupiers of properties owned by a local authority but, for one reason or another, they were not secure tenants and, having had any right to continue to occupy the respective properties brought to an end in accordance with domestic law, they were trespassers. So, in accordance with domestic law, the defendants could raise no defence to the local authority's claim for possession. In each case, however, the defendants contended that they should be able to rely on the argument that, even though they were trespassers with no defence to a claim for possession under domestic law, they had the right to have the proportionality of the loss of their home taken into account by virtue of their article 8 Convention rights. No disrespect is intended to the impressive and careful reasoning in those three decisions when we say that, for present purposes, it is unnecessary to consider them in any detail.

27.   In *Harrow London Borough Council* v *Qazi* [2004] 1 AC 983 and in *Kay* v *Lambeth London Borough Council* [2006] 2 AC 465, albeit in each case by a bare majority, the House decided that 'a defence which does not challenge the law under which the possession order is sought as being incompatible with article 8 but is based only on the occupier's personal circumstances should be struck out': *Kay* v *Lambeth London Borough Council* [2006] 2 AC 465, 516–517, para 110, per Lord Hope of Craighead, with whom Lord Scott of Foscote, Baroness Hale of Richmond and Lord Brown of Eaton-under-Heywood agreed. This observation applied to claims against trespassers, just as much as to claims against current or former tenants or licensees. At the end of the same paragraph Lord Hope explained that, following *Wandsworth London Borough Council* v *Winder* [1985] AC 461, in principle, it would be open to a defendant 'to challenge the decision of a local authority to recover possession as an improper exercise of its powers at common law' on the traditional judicial review ground 'that it was a decision that no reasonable person would consider justifiable'.

28.   In *Doherty* v *Birmingham City Council* [2009] AC 367 the law as stated in para 110 of *Kay* v *Lambeth London Borough Council* was substantially reaffirmed. . . . Nevertheless, in the light of the developments in the Strasbourg jurisprudence which we describe below, the House developed the law by acknowledging that the traditional approach to judicial review would have to be expanded, particularly to permit the court to make its own assessment of the relevant facts: [2009] AC 367, especially at para 68, per Lord Scott, and at para 138, per Lord Mance.

29.   In both *Harrow London Borough Council* v *Qazi* [2004] 1 AC 983 and *Kay* v *Lambeth London Borough Council* [2006] 2 AC 465, Lord Bingham of Cornhill (dissenting along with Lord Steyn in the former case, and with Lord Nicholls of Birkenhead and Lord Walker in the latter) accepted that it should be open, as a matter of principle, to a residential occupier, against whom a local authority is seeking possession, to raise an article 8 proportionality argument based on the facts of the particular case. However, in *Harrow London Borough Council* v *Qazi* [2004] 1 AC 983, para 25 Lord Bingham said that, if this was right, 'the occasions on which a court would be justified in declining to make a possession order would be very highly exceptional'. He effectively repeated this view in *Kay* v *Lambeth London Borough Council* [2006] 2 AC 465, para 29, where he suggested that only in 'rare and exceptional cases' would an article 8 proportionality challenge 'not be futile'.

The Strasbourg jurisprudence

30.   Mr Pinnock contends that, exceptionally, it is appropriate for this nine-judge court to depart from the majority view in these cases because there is now a consistent series of decisions of the European court which unambiguously supports the minority view in the earlier House of Lords decisions, and there is no good reason not to follow that series of decisions. We must therefore examine them.

31.   In *Connors* v *United Kingdom* (2004) 40 EHRR 189, gipsies had initially been permitted to locate their caravan on a piece of land owned by a local authority but their right of occupation was brought to an end because the local authority considered that they were committing a nuisance. The local authority then successfully brought summary proceedings for possession on the ground that they were trespassers and had no right to remain in occupation of the land. Before the First Section of the European court the gipsies successfully contended that the proceedings violated their rights under article 8.

33.   In a passage, at paras 81–83, which has often been quoted verbatim in subsequent decisions, the European court said:

> '81.   An interference will be considered 'necessary in a democratic society' for a legitimate aim if it answers a 'pressing social need' and, in particular, if it is proportionate to the legitimate aim pursued. While it is for the national authorities to make the initial assessment of necessity, the final evaluation as to whether the reasons cited for the interference are

relevant and sufficient remains subject to review by the court for conformity with the requirements of the Convention.

'82.   In this regard, a margin of appreciation must, inevitably, be left to the national authorities . . . This margin will vary according to the nature of the Convention right in issue, its importance for the individual and the nature of the activities restricted, as well as the nature of the aim pursued by the restrictions . . . Where general social and economic policy considerations have arisen in the context of article 8 itself, the scope of the margin of appreciation depends on the context of the case, with particular significance attaching to the extent of the intrusion into the personal sphere of the applicant.

'83.   The procedural safeguards available to the individual will be especially material in determining whether the respondent state has, when fixing the regulatory framework, remained within its margin of appreciation. In particular, the court must examine whether the decision-making process leading to measures of interference was fair and such as to afford due respect to the interests safeguarded to the individual by article 8.'

35.   In *McCann* v *United Kingdom* (2008) 47 EHRR 913 the county court made an order for possession against a man who occupied his home as a joint tenant with his estranged wife, on the ground that the tenancy had been determined by a notice to quit which she had served at the request of the local authority landlord and without reference to her husband. The European court (Fourth Section) rejected the contention that the reasoning in *Connors* v *United Kingdom* 40 EHRR 189, paras 81–83, was 'confined only to cases involving the eviction of gipsies or cases where the applicant sought to challenge the law itself rather than its application in his particular case': 47 EHRR 913, para 50. The court continued:

'The loss of one's home is the most extreme form of interference with the right for respect for the home. Any person at risk of an interference of this magnitude should in principle be able to have the proportionality of the measure determined by an independent tribunal in the light of the relevant principles under [article 8], notwithstanding that, under domestic law, his right of occupation has come to an end.'

36.   At para 54, the European court considered and rejected the contention that 'the grant of the right to the occupier to raise an issue under article 8 would have serious consequences for the functioning of the system or for the domestic law of landlord and tenant', citing and confirming the view of Lord Bingham in *Kay* v *Lambeth London Borough Council* [2006] 2 AC 465, para 29 to the effect that 'only in very exceptional cases' could 'an applicant . . . succeed in raising an arguable case which would require a court to examine the issue'. The court also said that 'in the great majority of cases, an order for possession could continue to be made in summary proceedings.'

41.   Finally, there is *Kay* v *United Kingdom* (Application No 37341/06) given 21 September 2010; . . . . In that case the application was made to the Strasbourg court by the unsuccessful appellants in *Kay* v *Lambeth London Borough Council* [2006] 2 AC 465. They had no security of tenure in their homes and their defences to claims for possession brought by the local authority—based on the contention that it was disproportionate to deprive them of their homes in the light of article 8—had been struck out. After carefully considering the various views expressed in the House of Lords in *Kay* v *Lambeth London Borough Council* [2006] 2 AC 465 and *Doherty* v *Birmingham City Council* [2009] AC 367, and the relevant decisions of the Court of Appeal, the European court stated, at paras 65–68, that the principles laid down in *Connors* v *United Kingdom* 40 EHRR 189 and *McCann* v *United Kingdom* 47 EHRR 913 applied.

42.   The European court then stated, at para 73:

'The court welcomes the increasing tendency of the domestic courts to develop and expand conventional judicial review grounds in the light of article 8. A number of their Lordships in *Doherty* alluded to the possibility for challenges on conventional judicial review grounds in cases such as the applicants' to encompass more than just traditional *Wednesbury* grounds (see Lord Hope, at para 55; Lord Scott, at paras 70 and 84 to 85; and Lord Mance, at paras 133 to 135 of the House of Lords judgment). However, notwithstanding these developments, the court considers that at the time that the applicants' cases were considered by the domestic courts, there was an important distinction between the majority and minority approaches in the House of Lords, as demonstrated by the opinions in *Kay* itself. In *McCann*, the court agreed with the minority approach [in *Kay* v *Lambeth London Borough Council* [2006] 2 AC 465] although it noted that, in the great majority of cases, an order for possession could continue to be made in summary proceedings and that it would be only in very exceptional cases that an applicant would succeed in raising an arguable case which would require a court to examine the issue.'

43.   Accordingly, in the next paragraph of its judgment, the European court concluded:

'In conclusion, the *Kay* applicants' challenge to the decision to strike out their article 8 defences failed because it was not possible at that time to challenge the decision of a local authority to seek a possession order on the basis of the alleged disproportionality of that decision in light of personal circumstances. Accordingly, for the reasons given in *McCann*, the court concludes that the decision by the county court to strike out the applicant's article 8 defences meant that the procedural safeguards required by article 8 for the assessment of the proportionality of the interference were not observed. As a result, the applicants were dispossessed of their homes without any possibility to have the proportionality of the measure determined by an independent tribunal. It follows that there has been a violation of article 8 of the Convention in the instant case.'

Conclusion on the first issue

45.   From these cases, it is clear that the following propositions are now well established in the jurisprudence of the European court: (a) Any person at risk of being dispossessed of his home at the suit of a local authority should in principle have the right to raise the question of the proportionality of the measure, and to have it determined by an independent tribunal in the light of article 8, even if his right of occupation under domestic law has come to an end: *McCann* v *United Kingdom* 47 EHRR 913, para 50; *Ćosić* v *Croatia* given 15 January 2009, para 22; *Zehentner* v *Austria* given 16 July 2009, para 59; *Paulić* v *Croatia* given 22 October 2009, para 43; and *Kay* v *United Kingdom* given 21 September 2010, paras 73–74. (b) A judicial procedure which is limited to addressing the proportionality of the measure through the medium of traditional judicial review (ie, one which does not permit the court to make its own assessment of the facts in an appropriate case) is inadequate as it is not appropriate for resolving sensitive factual issues: *Connors* v *United Kingdom* 40 EHRR 189, para 92; *McCann* v *United Kingdom* 47 EHRR 913, para 53; *Kay* v *United Kingdom*, paras 72–73. (c) Where the measure includes proceedings involving more than one stage, it is the proceedings as a whole which must be considered in order to see if article 8 has been complied with: *Zehentner* v *Austria*, para 54. (d) If the court concludes that it would be disproportionate to evict a person from his home notwithstanding the fact that he has no domestic right to remain there, it would be unlawful to evict him so long as the conclusion obtains—for example, for a specified period, or until a specified event occurs, or a particular condition is satisfied. Although it cannot be described as a point of principle, it seems that the European court has also franked the view that it will only be in exceptional cases that article 8 proportionality would even arguably give a right to continued possession where the applicant has no right under domestic law to remain: *McCann* v *United Kingdom* 47 EHRR 913, para 54; *Kay* v *United Kingdom*, para 73.

46.   We have referred in a little detail to the European court jurisprudence. This is because it is important for the court to emphasise what is now the unambiguous and consistent approach of

the European court, when we have to consider whether it is appropriate for this court to depart from the three decisions of the House of Lords.

47.   As we have already explained, the House of Lords decisions have to be seen against the backdrop of the evolving Strasbourg jurisprudence. . . . Importantly, the judgments in *Ćosić* v *Croatia* given 15 January 2009, *Zehentner* v *Austria* given 16 July 2009, *Paulić* v *Croatia* given 22 October 2009 and *Kay* v *United Kingdom* The Times, 18 October 2010 were all given after the last of the three House of Lords decisions.

48.   This court is not bound to follow every decision of the European court. Not only would it be impractical to do so: it would sometimes be inappropriate, as it would destroy the ability of the court to engage in the constructive dialogue with the European court which is of value to the development of Convention law: see eg *R v Horncastle* [2010] 2 WLR 47. Of course, we should usually follow a clear and constant line of decisions by the European court: *R (Ullah)* v *Special Adjudicator* [2004] 2 AC 323. But we are not actually bound to do so or (in theory, at least) to follow a decision of the Grand Chamber. As Lord Mance pointed out in *Doherty* v *Birmingham City Council* [2009] AC 367, para 126, section 2 of the 1998 Act requires our courts to 'take into account' European court decisions, not necessarily to follow them. Where, however, there is a clear and constant line of decisions whose effect is not inconsistent with some fundamental substantive or procedural aspect of our law, and whose reasoning does not appear to overlook or misunderstand some argument or point of principle, we consider that it would be wrong for this court not to follow that line.

49.   In the present case there is no question of the jurisprudence of the European court failing to take into account some principle or cutting across our domestic substantive or procedural law in some fundamental way. . . . Even before the decision in *Kay* v *United Kingdom* The Times, 18 October 2010, we would, in any event, have been of the opinion that this court should now accept and apply the minority view of the House of Lords in those cases. In the light of *Kay* v *United Kingdom* that is clearly the right conclusion. Therefore, if our law is to be compatible with article 8, where a court is asked to make an order for possession of a person's home at the suit of a local authority, the court must have the power to assess the proportionality of making the order, and, in making that assessment, to resolve any relevant dispute of fact.

50.   We emphasise that this conclusion relates to possession proceedings brought by local authorities. As we pointed out, at para 4 above, nothing which we say is intended to bear on cases where the person seeking the order for possession is a private landowner. Conflicting views have been expressed both domestically and in Strasbourg on that situation. In *Harrow London Borough Council* v *Qazi* [2004] 1 AC 983 the views of Lord Bingham and Lord Steyn, at paras 23 and 26, can be contrasted with the view of Lord Hope, at para 52. In *Belchikova* v *Russia* (Application No 2408/06) (unreported) given 25 March 2010 the application was held to be inadmissible, but the European court (First Section) seems to have considered that article 8 was relevant, even when the person seeking possession was a private sector landowner. Presumably, this was on the basis that the court making the order was itself a public authority. But it is not clear whether the point was in contention. In the rather older admissibility decision of *Di Palma* v *United Kingdom* (1986) 10 EHRR 149, 155–156, the European Human Rights Commission seems to have taken a different view, but the point was only very briefly discussed. No doubt, in such cases article 1 of the First Protocol to the Convention will have a part to play, but it is preferable for this court to express no view on the issue until it arises and has to be determined.

Exceptionality

51.   It is necessary to address the proposition that it will only be in 'very highly exceptional cases' that it will be appropriate for the court to consider a proportionality argument. Such a proposition undoubtedly derives support from the views expressed by Lord Bingham, and has been referred to with apparent approval by the European court in more than one case.

Nevertheless, it seems to us to be both unsafe and unhelpful to invoke exceptionality as a guide. It is unhelpful because, as Baroness Hale of Richmond JSC pointed out in argument, exceptionality is an outcome and not a guide. It is unsafe because, as Lord Walker observed in *Doherty* v *Birmingham City Council* [2009] AC 367, para 122, there may be more cases than the European court or Lord Bingham supposed where article 8 could reasonably be invoked by a residential tenant.

52.   We would prefer to express the position slightly differently. The question is always whether the eviction is a proportionate means of achieving a legitimate aim. Where a person has no right in domestic law to remain in occupation of his home, the proportionality of making an order for possession at the suit of the local authority will be supported not merely by the fact that it would serve to vindicate the authority's ownership rights. It will also, at least normally, be supported by the fact that it would enable the authority to comply with its duties in relation to the distribution and management of its housing stock, including, for example, the fair allocation of its housing, the redevelopment of the site, the refurbishing of sub-standard accommodation, the need to move people who are in accommodation that now exceeds their needs, and the need to move vulnerable people into sheltered or warden-assisted housing. Furthermore, in many cases (such as this appeal) other cogent reasons, such as the need to remove a source of nuisance to neighbours, may support the proportionality of dispossessing the occupiers.

53.   ... the fact that the authority is entitled to possession and should, in the absence of cogent evidence to the contrary, be assumed to be acting in accordance with its duties, will be a strong factor in support of the proportionality of making an order for possession. But, in a particular case, the authority may have what it believes to be particularly strong or unusual reasons for wanting possession-for example, that the property is the only occupied part of a site intended for immediate development for community housing. The authority could rely on that factor, but would have to plead it and adduce evidence to support it.

54.   Unencumbered property rights, even where they are enjoyed by a public body such as a local authority, are of real weight when it comes to proportionality. So, too, is the right—indeed the obligation—of a local authority to decide who should occupy its residential property. As Lord Bingham said in *Harrow London Borough Council* v *Qazi* [2004] 1 AC 983, 997, para 25:

> 'the administration of public housing under various statutory schemes is entrusted to local housing authorities. It is not for the court to second-guess allocation decisions. The Strasbourg authorities have adopted a very pragmatic and realistic approach to the issue of justification.'

Therefore, in virtually every case where a residential occupier has no contractual or statutory protection, and the local authority is entitled to possession as a matter of domestic law, there will be a very strong case for saying that making an order for possession would be proportionate. However, in some cases there may be factors which would tell the other way.

Second issue: the application of this conclusion in general

57.   The implications of article 8 being potentially in play are much more significant where a local authority is seeking possession of a person's home in circumstances in which domestic law imposes no requirement of reasonableness and gives an unqualified right to an order for possession. In such a case the court's obligation under article 8(2), to consider the proportionality of making the order sought, does represent a potential new obstacle to the making of an order for possession. The wide implications of this obligation will have to be worked out. As in many situations, that is best left to the good sense and experience of judges sitting in the county court.

60.   Nevertheless, certain general points can be made, even at this stage.

61.   First, it is only where a person's 'home' is under threat that article 8 comes into play. .... Secondly, as a general rule, article 8 need only be considered by the court if it is raised in the proceedings by or on behalf of the residential occupier. Thirdly, if an article 8 point is raised, the

court should initially consider it summarily, and if, as will no doubt often be the case, the court is satisfied that, even if the facts relied on are made out, the point would not succeed, it should be dismissed. Only if the court is satisfied that it could affect the order that the court might make should the point be further entertained.

62.   Fourthly, if domestic law justifies an outright order for possession, the effect of article 8 may, albeit in exceptional cases, justify (in ascending order of effect) granting an extended period for possession, suspending the order for possession on the happening of an event, or even refusing an order altogether.

Third issue: the application of this conclusion to demoted tenancies
72.   Rightly, in our view, it is common ground that a court has jurisdiction, under normal judicial review principles, to satisfy itself that the local authority and panel have indeed acted reasonably and have investigated the relevant facts fairly, when deciding to bring possession proceedings. From this it must follow that any decision by the local authority to continue possession proceedings is similarly susceptible to judicial review. . . .

73.   In our judgment, once it is accepted that it is open to a demoted tenant to seek judicial review of a landlord's decision to bring and continue possession proceedings, then it inevitably follows that, as a generality, it is open to a tenant to challenge that decision on the ground that it would be disproportionate and therefore contrary to article 8. Further, as we saw at paras 31 to 43 above, the European court jurisprudence requires the court considering such a challenge to have the power to make its own assessment of any relevant facts which are in dispute. . . . In these circumstances we are satisfied that, wherever possible, the traditional review powers of the court should be expanded so as to permit it to carry out that exercise.

74.   In summary: where it is required in order to give effect to an occupier's article 8 Convention rights, the court's powers of review can, in an appropriate case, extend to reconsidering for itself the facts found by a local authority, or indeed to considering facts which have arisen since the issue of proceedings, by hearing evidence and forming its own view.

Comment

(1) Lord Neuberger delivered the judgment of a nine-judge court. It was decided that (on undisputed facts) there was no reasonable prospect of possession being refused, so the human rights defence failed.[2]

(2) It is unusual, to put it mildly, for three recent House of Lords decisions to be overruled. Why was this done?

(3) Earlier cases had expressed the fear that the Strasbourg approach would preclude the speedy resolution of possession claims. Is this fear justified following the Supreme Court decision?

(4) Prior to *Pinnock*, the courts placed great emphasis on widening judicial review as a way of defending English law from Article 8 claims. What is the role of judicial review within the approach adopted by the Supreme Court?

(5) Where the court has a statutory discretion whether or not to make an order, how will this impact on Article 8 arguments?[3] In *Hounslow LBC v Powell*,[4] the Supreme Court considered the application of *Pinnock* to other forms of public sector tenancies. This was designed to establish the form and content of the required proportionality review.

---

[2] Technically, the Supreme Court ruled on proportionality and ordered possession (subsequent proceedings in the Supreme Court, reported [2011] 2 AC 104).
[3] See *National Westminster Bank plc v Rushmer* [2010] 2 FLR 362 at [50] (trusts of land).
[4] [2011] 2 AC 186.

The ease with which courts can be persuaded of an Article 8 argument may illustrated by the following Court of Appeal dicta.

Corby BC v Scott,[5] Lord Neuberger MR:

25.   The only other fact relied on by the Judge was that the rent arrears were cleared the day before the hearing. I do not think that that is an impressive point at all. . . . In the absence of extraordinary facts, it seems to me fanciful to suggest that a residential occupier should be able to pray in aid the fact that she has paid the landlord money which she owed him, as a significant factor, which enables her to cross the high threshold identified in the two Supreme Court cases, when invoking Article 8.

Birmingham CC v Lloyd,[6] Lord Neuberger MR:

18.   It would, I accept, be wrong to say that it could never be right for the court to permit a person, who had never been more than a trespasser, to invoke Article 8 as a defence against an order for possession. But such a person seeking to raise an Article 8 argument would face a very uphill task indeed, and, while exceptionality is rarely a helpful test, it seems to me that it would be require the most extraordinarily exceptional circumstances.

20.   The fact that Mr Lloyd suffered from depression and that his depression might get worse if he was evicted was not supported by that evidence, and it was apparent that his depression was in abeyance. It is sad, but not exceptional. The fact that he would encounter difficulty in finding other accommodation slightly misses the point of Article 8, whose purpose in this connection is respect for a person's current home: it does not involve any duty to ensure that a person has a home. . . .

Thurrock BC v West,[7] Etherton LJ:

31.   . . . even where an Article 8 defence is established, in a case where the defendant would otherwise have no legal right to remain in the property, it is difficult to imagine circumstances in which the defence could operate to give the defendant an unlimited and unconditional right to remain: comp. *Pinnock* at [52]. That might be the effect of a simple refusal of possession without any qualification. It is particularly difficult to imagine how that could possibly be appropriate in a case where the defendant has never been a tenant or licensee of the local authority. . . .

33.   . . . There is, however, nothing exceptional in this context about the housing needs of a couple who have limited financial means and are the parents of a young child. Indeed, such a family unit is entirely typical of those with a need for social housing. . . .

36.   Sympathy for the predicament of the respondent and his family, which is entirely under-standable, cannot obscure the remarkable effect of the District Judge's decision. . . . In effect, the Court has assumed for itself the power Parliament has conferred on the Council to select the most suitable property for the numerous and various persons who have a legal right to social housing. This has been done without any knowledge on the Court's part as to who are those other people who have an equal, or possibly better, claim to be housed. . . .

Fareham BC v Miller,[8] Patten LJ:

36.   . . . The decision to seek possession is driven by the need to control the effect on neighbours of what has occurred at the Flat. To say, as Mr Miller [the tenant] does, that he is not responsible for that conduct [of those he allowed to live there] does not lessen that imperative. At most it

---

[5] [2012] EWCA Civ 276; [2012] HLR 366.
[6] [2012] EWCA Civ 969; [2012] HLR 681.
[7] [2012] EWCA Civ 1435; [2013] 1 P&CR 175.
[8] [2013] EWCA Civ 159; [2013] HLR 282.

provides a factor for the Council to consider when deciding whether the need to obtain possession outweighs any adverse impacts on Mr Miller.

37.   Although his personal circumstances [heroin addiction coupled with persistent offending and imprisonment] need to be seriously considered, my own view is that they do not raise a sufficiently compelling case as to require a full-blown proportionality review.

For a decision in favour of an occupier, see *Southend-on-Sea BC v Armour*,[9] Lewison LJ:

17.   The first point raised by this appeal concerns the function of the appeal court. . . . the test which the courts must apply, whether described as proportionality or as deciding whether eviction is 'necessary in a democratic society' is not, in my judgment, a bright line test. It is more in the nature of a value judgment. . . . In my judgment, this is the kind of decision in which an appeal court should be reluctant to reverse the value judgment of the trial judge.

30.   . . . Where, as here, the tenant under an introductory tenancy gets off to a shaky start, but mends his ways for almost all of the one year period, I consider that that improvement in behaviour is capable of being a factor in deciding whether it is disproportionate for the landlord to continue to insist on recovering possession. What weight to give it is a question for the trial judge. . . . Other judges might have come to a different conclusion, but that does not mean that the Recorder's conclusion in our case was wrong.

It may be noted that the first four decisions reversed trial judges applying Article 8, though the fact situations were often in favour of the possession order. Is *Armour* consistent with the earlier cases?

B. Horizontal effect following *Pinnock*

Extract 2.3.2

Malik v Fassenfelt [2013] EWCA Civ 798; [2013] 3 EGLR 99

McPhail v Persons Unknown[10] allows an owner to get an immediate possession order against trespassers.

SIR ALAN WARD:
The next issue: how does this development of the Article 8 argument impinge on the claim for possession by a private landowner: is McPhail *still good law?*

25.   That question arose on an application for permission to appeal in *Boyland & Son Ltd v Rand* [2006] EWCA Civ 1860 where Neuberger LJ said . . . :

. . .

'13.   Finally, there is a suggestion, which was dealt with very clearly by the judge below, that the decision in *McPhail* may be inconsistent with the European Court on Human Rights jurisprudence on Article 8, in a case such as this, where the trespasser is occupying as his home. It is fair to say that some support for that view is to be found in the speech of Lord Bingham of Cornhill in the *Kay* case (see paragraph 37). However, Lord Bingham was in a minority in that case. It seems to me quite clear from the passages I [have] identified in the speeches of the four members in the majority in that case that they came to a contrary view.'

As this was decided before the developments I have been describing above had taken place, I would not place much reliance on these observations made on an application for permission to appeal.

---

[9] [2014] EWCA Civ 231; [2014] HLR 362.
[10] [1973] Ch 447.

26.   Mr Jan Luba QC, who now appears for the appellants though he did not appear below, submits that, in the light of the developments of the law following the decisions in Strasbourg after *Kay*, it is time to acknowledge, as the Supreme Court did in *Pinnock* and *Powell*, that the minority view of Lord Bingham, Lord Nicholls and Lord Walker should prevail over the majority. . . . I am now satisfied that *McPhail* can no longer be regarded as good law. I come to that conclusion for these reasons:

- i) It is rightly common ground that the squatters have established a home on the land by reason of the existence of a 'sufficient and continuous link with a specific place' which is the autonomous test in European jurisprudence. . . .
- ii) Even if Article 8 has no direct application between a private landowner and the trespassers on his land, the Court as a public authority is obliged by section 6 of the Human Rights Act 1998 to act in a way which is compatible with that Convention right. . . .
- iv) Proportionality is, therefore, in issue. The rule in *McPhail* that the court has no jurisdiction to extend time to a trespasser can no longer stand against a requirement that proportionality may demand, albeit most exceptionally, that a trespasser can be given some time before being required to vacate. . . .

28.   I conclude that the court must approach the claim made by a private landowner against a trespasser in a similar way to that adopted to claims of various sorts made by a local authority as set out in the cases to which I have referred. Thus the test is whether the eviction is a proportionate means of achieving a legitimate aim. The fact that the landowner has a legal right to possession is a very strong factor in support of proportionality: it speaks for itself and needs no further explanation or justification. Thus, even if the defendants have established a home on the land but where they have otherwise no legal right to remain there, it is difficult to imagine circumstances which would give the defendant an unlimited and unconditional right to remain. The circumstances would have to be exceptional.

LORD TOULSON: 42.   I do not think that it would be right in these circumstances [there being no appeal on the applicability of Article 8] to decide whether the judge was correct about the availability of article 8 as a potential defence to the claim. . . . Sir Alan Ward has reviewed the development of the law in relation to public authority landowners, but the courts have been careful to emphasise that nothing in them was intended to bear on claims by private landowners: see *Manchester City Council* v *Pinnock* at [4] and [50], cited by Sir Alan Ward at [16].

44.   The primary obligations imposed by article 8 are negative: the state is not to interfere with a person's private life or home, etc, except on limited grounds. It has been long recognised that the article also imposes some implied positive obligations, but the Convention jurisprudence does not provide a universal formula or touchstone for determining the incidence or extent of such obligations. The Convention imposes obligations on states, not private citizens, but in some instances the Strasbourg court has held there to be an obligation on the part of states to take measures to protect a person's private life from interference by another private person or private enterprise – in particular, by criminal acts (*X & Y* v *Netherlands* (1985) 8 EHRR 235 paragraph 23, *MC* v *Bulgaria* (2003) 15 BHRC 627 paragraph 153) or by the intrusive and harassing activities of paparazzi (*Von Hannover* v *Germany* (2005) 40 EHRR 1 paragraph 57). However, these are striking and unusual cases in which the applicants were victims of particularly objectionable conduct which seriously impaired their ability to lead a normal life. Article 8 does not ordinarily apply to regulate conduct in the private sector.

45.   It would be a considerable expansion of the law to hold that article 8 imposes a positive obligation on the state, through the courts, to prevent or delay a private citizen from recovering possession of land belonging to him which has been unlawfully occupied by another. There would also be a weighty argument that for the state to interfere in that way with a private

owner's right to possession of his property would be contrary to a long standing principle of the common law, which finds echo in article 1 to protocol 1. . . .

Comment

(1) Lloyd LJ agreed with Lord Toulson. All the judges agreed that any proportionality requirement was satisfied, so that the Article 8 claim failed.

(2) Pelling QC followed Sir Alan Ward in *Manchester Ship Canal Developments Ltd* v *Persons Unknown.*[11]

Extract 2.3.3

McDonald v *McDonald* [2014] EWCA 1049; [2014] 2 P&CR 377

Article 8 was argued when a private landlord terminated an assured shorthold tenancy.

ARDEN LJ: 16.   What is in dispute is whether the proportionality test applies where a person can contend that it would be disproportionate under Article 8(2) to make a PO [possession order] against him as the tenant of a private landlord. This point does not matter in a case where the court must be satisfied as to the reasonableness of making a PO. But it does matter where the landlord relies on a mandatory ground for making a possession order, as in section 21 of the HA 1988.

19.   In my judgment, . . . Miss McDonald's claim that the PO should be set aside because it violates her Article 8 right must be rejected for the following reasons, which are amplified later in this judgment:

- i) There is no 'clear and constant' jurisprudence of the Strasbourg court that the proportionality test implied into Article 8(2) applies where there is a private landlord.
- ii) Even if the proportionality test had applied in this case, the court would still have made a possession order.
- iii) In any event, this court is bound by *Poplar Housing and Regeneration Community Association Ltd* v *Donoghue* [2002] QB 48 to hold that section 21 of the HA 1988 is compatible with the Convention. That precludes this court from holding that the proportionality test applies.

33.   In none of these [European Court of Human Rights] cases was there any decision that the proportionality test applied to a case involving a private landlord or co-owner. It was simply assumed to be the case that the proportionality test applied as if the landlord (or co-owner) was in the public sector. In my judgment, that is not enough to make it a clear and constant line of decisions if there are other indications that there is a countervailing principle.

35.   It is remarkable that there is little discussion of the impact of the fact that the private landowner has rights as well as the tenant. However, there is some material in the form of the decision in *Di Palma* v *United Kingdom* (1986) 10 E.H.R.R. 149 and in the separate opinion by Judge De Gaetano in the recent case of *Buckland* [App No. 40060/08].

41.   None of the cases on which Miss Bretherton [for the tenant] relies is a decision of the Grand Chamber of the Strasbourg court. Normally cases are heard by Chambers of judges in Strasbourg, but, if there is a serious point or one which would require an extension of the case law, the case may be referred to or, if already heard, reheard by a larger constitution of judges known as the Grand Chamber (see Article 43 of the Convention). To apply the proportionality

---

[11] [2014] EWHC 645 (Ch); as in *Malik*, the Article 8 argument failed on the facts.

test when a tenant relies on Article 8 in the context of a private dispute would raise substantial issues. The absence of a Grand Chamber decision requiring Article 8(2) to be applied in these circumstances confirms the conclusion that I have already reached.

CONCLUSIONS FROM THE CASE LAW

42. As stated, I do not consider that the cases cited by Miss Bretherton can be regarded as a clear and constant line of decisions that the proportionality test applies when Article 8 is raised in a dispute between a tenant and a private landlord. If there was an unbroken line of decisions since the new Court was established, then it was broken by Judge Gaetano's separate opinion in *Buckland*. He did not consider that the law was settled. The fact that in *Buckland*, *Brezec*, *Belchikova* and *Zrilic* the Strasbourg court was content to proceed on the basis that there was a public sector tenancy does not necessarily prove otherwise because in some of those cases there were reasons why the court should wish to treat them as public authorities and in none of the cases was there any argument on this point. Moreover, in none of these cases is there any suggestion that there was a contractual term which would be breached if the proportionality test applied.

CONCLUSION ON THE ARTICLE 8 GROUND

57. I bear in mind that Ward LJ considered that the proportionality test under Article 8(2) applied where squatters had acquired a home for Convention purposes on privately owned land on which they had encamped: *Malik* v *Fassenfelt* [2013] EWCA Civ 798. He went on to apply the same weight in the proportionality exercise to the owner's rights as the Supreme Court had done to the local housing authority's rights in *Pinnock*. However, this was not the view of the other members of the court. In any event, the context on this appeal is different and the authorities relevant to this case were not cited.

Comment

(1) Is the treatment of the European Court of Human Rights cases convincing?

(2) Does Arden LJ adequately counter the arguments raised by Sir Alan Ward in *Malik*?

(3) Does the different context of *McDonald* (noting the dicta in [57]) mean that its authority is limited?

C. The impact of human rights on property principles

So far as Article 8 is concerned, it would be extremely important if were to have horizontal impact – something denied by *McDonald*. Nevertheless, it is still likely to have a significant role whenever a court has a discretion as to whether to exclude an occupier – though the significance of a home would often be taken into account anyway. One example is provided by dicta of Strauss QC[12] regarding sale on bankruptcy. Both Article 8 and other provisions could be used to attack existing rules and principles. Although it is easy to think of property rules and principles which could be challenged on human rights grounds, it is more difficult to be confident as to when the challenge will succeed. The application of human rights will be considered in the specific contexts in which there has been litigation. So far, the impact of human rights on property law has been limited. The most high profile issue (leaving aside *Pinnock*) has been the attack on adverse possession in *Pye*, but this eventually failed.

---

[12] *Barca* v *Mears* [2005] 2 FLR 1 (Extract 12.3.17 below).

Further reading

Buxton, R (2000) 116 LQR 48: The Human Rights Act and private law.

Goymour, A (2011) Chapter 12 in *The Impact of the UK Human Rights Act on Private Law* (ed Hoffman).

Nield, S [2013] King's LJ 147: Article 8 respect for the home: a human property right?

Phillipson, G and Williams, A (2011) 74 MLR 878: Horizontal effect and the constitutional restraint.

Thompson, M P [2011] Conv 421: Possession actions and human rights.

Wade, H W R (2000) 116 LQR 217: Horizons of horizontality.

3

Property interests

In this chapter, the main property interests will be considered. Many of them will be studied in detail in subsequent chapters, so this chapter sets out to establish the general picture and to provide detail on some topics which are not fully covered later. Interests in land have been developed to a much more sophisticated level than interests in other forms of property and accordingly they form the main emphasis of this chapter. Their status as legal or equitable interests was affected by the property legislation of 1925 and this is also considered.

1. Land

A. Tenures and estates

Extract 3.1.1

Lawson and Rudden, *The Law of Property* (3rd ed) pp 90, 77–80 (footnotes omitted)

One of the greatest difficulties encountered by students of property law comes from the English habit of splitting what may in a general way be called ownership into its component parts and making each of them an abstract entity. The estate concept developed for realty . . . is a strong and persistent example of this type of approach.

. . .

TENURE

The institution of tenure is of little practical importance today. It must be briefly mentioned, however, since it gave rise to a number of concepts and technical terms which are still in use throughout the common-law world – even in the USA, which broke with the monarchy long ago. The word itself means 'holding' (Latin *tenere*, French *tenir*) and is found in such forms as 'tenancy' and 'tenant'. The Middle Ages used these forms where nowadays we would say 'own' and 'owner'.

In relation to land, tenure is historically a product of the feudal system which reached its strongest form in England after 1066. In a society short of the precious metals and unable to pay for services in money, land was the most convenient medium with which the monarch could both reward his chief supporters and at the same time bind them to provide further services. Politically, the most important of such services were military. The king therefore granted parcels of land to men of substance or status (so-called tenants-in-chief) upon the terms that they would provide a certain number of knights to serve for forty days a year. The tenants-in-chief would procure the services of the knights by giving each a portion of the land to hold by the service of serving in the army. A knight might replicate the process by granting some of the land which he held of his lord to the Church in return for the provision of religious services. Economically, the most important services were agricultural, performed at the lower levels of society. This is only the core of what was a most complicated pyramid of landholding but it gives sufficient information to explain what is meant by tenure.

. . . As a means of organizing the economy, the system itself died out long ago, leaving a few picturesque and some profitable relics, a number of legal terms, and certain entrenched ways of thought.

The student needs to be aware of the notion, for a number of reasons. First of all the Crown still holds some land – for instance, the foreshore – as sovereign, as lord paramount, by an entitlement which is at the root of property relations in land. The technical term for this Crown (i.e. State) property is 'demesne land'. . . . Secondly, something very similar to the old notion of tenure operates nowadays, not in its old terrain of freehold land but in the law of leases, where the words 'tenancy' and 'tenant' are part of ordinary English. A modern [example] might be the firm which leases one office from the person who has a sub-lease of the whole floor from the company which has a lease of the whole office block whose landlord is the freeholder.

The third reason for having some grasp of the old notion of tenure is that it was not applied to movables, thus causing a sharp difference in treatment between realty and other property. Goods and cattle seem to have always been the object of direct and absolute ownership . . .

THE 'ESTATE CONCEPT'

A final reason to remember tenure is that it gave rise to the habit of classifying entitlement to land in terms of the time for which it could be enjoyed. Where land was given in return for the performance of personal services, it might well be granted only for the life of the tenant, so that on his death possession reverted to his lord: the tenant's entitlement came to be called a 'life estate', the word being a version of *status*. If land is given to endow a family, it could be granted for the tenant's life and that of his children, grandchildren, and so on. Finally it could be granted so as to be inheritable by the person who was heir (not necessarily lineal heir) on the death of the current holder. Each of these latter two entitlements was called a 'fee' (from the word *feodum*) to denote that it was inheritable. If the range of permitted heirs was limited to lineal descendants, there was a 'fee tail' from the French word '*tailler*' meaning to cut (or to tailor). If the land could descend to any heir, the fee was 'simple', that is not limited in any way.

. . .

Thus English lawyers have always been accustomed to classifying interests in land in terms of the time for which they could endure. Leases were easily fitted into this perception, although they grew up outside the feudal system. Furthermore, the co-existence of these estates was common. Land might be let on a yearly farming lease by A who was entitled to the land for his life; on his death B or B's lineal descendants might be entitled to the land while the family line endured; and when it died out, C or his successor would be entitled. Thus four people had at the same time an interest in the land. It is very difficult to say that any one of them *owns* the land, and the common law instead said that each holds an estate in the land (respectively a lease, a life estate, a fee tail (entail), and a fee simple). These estates co-exist, but each can be treated as the object of property, since each can be sold, mortgaged, given away, reached by creditors, and so on. Indeed at the present time, where title to land is registered and guaranteed by the State, if you buy a house you will be registered as proprietor, not of the land, but of the 'fee simple absolute in possession' if it is freehold and of a 'legal term of years absolute' if it is leasehold.

Comment

(1) What is tenure? Why was it important?

(2) Does tenure have any significance today? Could it be abolished?

(3) What are estates? In what ways do estates differ from ownership of chattels, such as cars?

B. Freehold estates

The nature of the estate determines the length of time for which the land can be enjoyed. The two basic forms today are the life estate and the fee simple. These estates may be in possession (denoting their present enjoyment) or in remainder (denoting that they will come into enjoyment on the determination of a prior interest). They are said to be in reversion if the remainder reverts (goes back) to the grantor. Interests can also be contingent: they will come into possession if some uncertain event occurs, an example being 'To Brenda, if she obtains a First Class degree'.

This question of length will be studied in some detail in this section, but first the physical extent of enjoyment should be considered.

Extract 3.1.2

Lord Bernstein of Leigh v Skyviews & General Ltd [1978] QB 479

The defendants flew over the plaintiff's land, taking photographs of his house. The plaintiff sued in trespass.

GRIFFITHS J: . . . The plaintiff claims that as owner of the land he is also owner of the air space above the land, or at least has the right to exclude any entry into the air space above his land. He relies upon the old Latin maxim, *cujus est solum ejus est usque ad coelum et ad inferos* ['the owner of land owns everything up to the sky and down to the centre of the earth'], a colourful phrase often upon the lips of lawyers since it was first coined by Accursius in Bologna in the 13th century. There are a number of cases in which the maxim has been used by English judges, but an examination of those cases shows that they have all been concerned with structures attached to the adjoining land, such as overhanging buildings, signs or telegraph wires, and for their solution it has not been necessary for the judge to cast his eyes towards the heavens; he has been concerned with the rights of the owner in the air space immediately adjacent to the surface of the land.

. . .

. . . The point that the judge [in *Kelsen* v *Imperial Tobacco Co (of Great Britain and Ireland) Ltd* [1957] 2 QB 334] was considering was whether the sign was a trespass or a nuisance at the very low level at which it projected. This to my mind is clearly indicated by his reference to *Winfield on Tort*, 6th ed (1954) in which the text reads, at p 380: 'it is submitted that trespass will be committed by [aircraft] to the air space if they fly so low as to come within the area of ordinary user'. The author in that passage is careful to limit the trespass to the height at which it is contemplated an owner might be expected to make use of the air space as a natural incident of the user of his land. . . .

I do not wish to cast any doubts upon the correctness of the decision upon its own particular facts. It may be a sound and practical rule to regard any incursion into the air space at a height which may interfere with the ordinary user of the land as a trespass rather than a nuisance. Adjoining owners then know where they stand; they have no right to erect structures overhanging or passing over their neighbours' land and there is no room for argument whether they are thereby causing damage or annoyance to their neighbours about which there may be much room for argument and uncertainty. But wholly different considerations arise when considering the passage of aircraft at a height which in no way affects the user of the land.

There is no direct authority on this question, but as long ago as 1815 Lord Ellenborough in *Pickering* v *Rudd* expressed the view that it would not be a trespass to pass over a man's land in a balloon . . .

I can find no support in authority for the view that a landowner's rights in the air space above his property extend to an unlimited height. In *Wandsworth Board of Works* v *United Telephone Co Ltd*, 13 QBD 904 Bowen LJ described the maxim, *usque ad coelum*, as a fanciful phrase, to which I would add that if applied literally it is a fanciful notion leading to the absurdity of a trespass at common law being committed by a satellite every time it passes over a suburban garden. The academic writers speak with one voice in rejecting the uncritical and literal application of the maxim . . . I accept their collective approach as correct. The problem is to balance the rights of an owner to enjoy the use of his land against the rights of the general public to take advantage of all that science now offers in the use of air space. This balance is in my judgment best struck in our present society by restricting the rights of an owner in the air space above his land to such height as is necessary for the ordinary use and enjoyment of his land and the structures upon it, and declaring that above that height he has no greater rights in the air space than any other member of the public.

Applying this test to the facts of this case, I find that the defendants' aircraft did not infringe any rights in the plaintiff's air space, and thus no trespass was committed.

Comment

(1) Is the estate owner adequately protected by this decision?

(2) It is possible to split land horizontally. Thus the first floor of a house, or minerals in the ground, may become owned by different persons than the surface owner. What problems may arise from severing land horizontally?

Extract 3.1.3

Bocardo SA v *Star Energy UK Onshore Ltd* [2011] 1 AC 380

Trespass was alleged as regards pipelines which passed 800 feet under the claimant's land.

LORD HOPE: 26.   In my opinion the brocard [*cuius est solum, eius est usque ad coelum et ad inferos*] still has value in English law as encapsulating, in simple language, a proposition of law which has commanded general acceptance. It is an imperfect guide, as it has ceased to apply to the use of airspace above a height which may interfere with the ordinary user of land: *Baron Bernstein of Leigh* v *Skyviews & General Ltd* [1978] QB 479 . . . But I think that the reasons for holding that the brocard has no place in the modern world as regards what goes on below the surface, even in England, are not by any means as compelling as they are in relation to the use of airspace. In *United States* v *Causby* 328 US 256 the United States Supreme Court regarded the airspace as a public highway to which only the public had a just claim. The same cannot be said of the strata below the surface. As Aikens LJ said in the Court of Appeal [2010] Ch 100, para 61, it is not helpful to try to make analogies between the rights of an owner of land with regard to the airspace above it and his rights with regard to the strata beneath the surface. Although modern technology has found new ways of making use of it in the public interest, there is no question of it having become a public highway. The test applied in *Chance* v *BP Chemicals Inc* 670 NE 2d 985, that some type of physical damage or interference with the use of the land must be shown, would lead to much uncertainty. It overlooks the point that, at least so far as corporeal elements such as land and the strata beneath it are concerned, the question is essentially one about ownership. As a general rule anything that can be touched or worked must be taken to belong to someone.

27.   The better view, as the Court of Appeal recognised [2010] Ch 100, para 59, is to hold that the owner of the surface is the owner of the strata beneath it, including the minerals that are to be found there, unless there has been an alienation of it by a conveyance, at common law or by statute to someone else . . .

Comment

(1) On what principle are rights above and below ground distinguished?

(2) The calculation of damages was the most controversial issue; a majority of the Supreme Court agreed with the Court of Appeal that damages should be limited to £1,000.

(i) The fee simple

The fee simple is, in essence, a perpetual right to the land. It does not terminate on the holder's death, but will pass under the holder's will. If there is no will (so that the holder dies intestate), the intestacy rules operate on all forms of property.[1] Failure to make reasonable financial provision, whether by will or on intestacy, for certain family members or dependants may be challenged under the Inheritance (Provision for Family and Dependants) Act 1975.

Our concern is principally with the distinction between absolute and qualified interests. Absolute interests are indeed perpetual: the fee simple absolute in possession is as close to ownership as makes no difference. On the other hand, a qualified interest is one which, though it might be perpetual, may also be cut short. An example would be 'To Andrew, on condition that he never smokes'. The fee simple of a squatter can be defeated by the true owner. Does this mean that it is not absolute?[2]

(a) Conditional and determinable fees

An immensely complicating factor is that there are two forms of qualified fees: the conditional fee and the determinable fee (the latter sometimes described as a limitation). The essence of a conditional fee is that the fee is conferred on the grantee, but then some qualification is imposed upon it which may later terminate it. In a determinable fee, the grant is qualified right from the outset: conceptually there is no idea of taking anything away from the grantee. The same qualifications can also be imposed on life estates. It is important to note that the rules applying to conditional and determinable fees differ markedly, despite the fact that any qualification can be effective as a conditional fee or as a determinable fee provided that the appropriate words are used.

Extract 3.1.4

Re Moore (1888) 39 Ch D 116

The case involved a payment to the testator's sister 'while so living apart from her husband'.[3] Such encouragement for spouses to live apart is contrary to public policy.

COTTON LJ: . . . According to English law if a condition subsequent which is to defeat an estate, is against the policy of the law, the gift is absolute, but if the illegal condition is precedent there is no gift. In the Civil Law a distinction is taken between what is *malum in se* and what is only *malum prohibitum*, but in the view I take of this case we need not consider within which of these two classes the restriction in the present case falls. Are the words relating to living separate a condition? In my opinion they are not a condition, but a part of the limitation, and although in some respects a condition and a limitation may have the same effect, yet in English law there is a great distinction between them. Here if you give effect to the Appellant's contention [that

---

[1] Administration of Estates Act 1925, s 46, amended by Inheritance and Trustees' Powers Act 2014.
[2] See *Turner v Chief Land Registrar* [2013] 2 P&CR 223.
[3] Technically, it was not a qualified fee, but a qualified interest under a trust: the same rules apply.

there was an effective gift, free of the condition], you give her what the testator never intended to give her, an annuity during the whole of her life if the son is so long under age. It is wrong to give to an expression a forced construction in order to prevent a particular result that follows from the natural construction . . . Many authorities have been cited, but it has not been laid down in any of them that a gift in this form is to be treated as a gift upon condition.

Comment

The court held there to be a determinable estate (limitation), which was wholly void.

Extract 3.1.5

Re Wilkinson [1926] Ch 842

TOMLIN J: . . . It is said by Mrs Page that on the true construction of the clause in the will dealing with the bequest of 7000*l*, there is a gift which is cut down by a subsequent condition, and that this subsequent condition is void either as being contrary to public policy, because it tends in restraint of marriage, or as being too uncertain, and that, in those circumstances, the gift goes to her free from the conditions . . .

The first question which I have to determine is, whether on the true construction of the gift it is made to her by way of limitation until the happening of certain events, or is made to her for her life, but subject to a condition subsequent determining it on the happening of the same events. I think it is plain that the gift is in the form of a limitation, and that a limitation until the happening of some event, which if it were expressed in the form of a condition subsequent might be bad as being in restraint of marriage, will not be bad. Of course a question may always arise in cases of this kind whether the whole gift is bad as being against public policy. Thus in *In re Moore*[i] there was a gift which was held to be bad, because it tended to produce future separation between the spouses. On the other hand, if, on its true construction, a gift is not in the form of a limitation until the happening of an event, but is a gift subject to a condition subsequent, which would operate to cut the gift down upon the happening of the event, then if the condition is bad on the ground of public policy, the condition goes and the gift stands unaffected by it.

[i] 39 Ch D 116.

Comment

(1) In each of these cases, the court held there to be a determinable estate. In each, a conditional fee would have given an absolute estate to the grantee. *Re Moore* resulted in there being no gift at all, whereas *Re Wilkinson* resulted in a valid determinable estate. Why are the results different?

(2) How do we tell whether there is a conditional or determinable fee?

(3) In what way do the results vary according to the type of qualified fee? Why do they vary?

(b) The validity of determining events (including conditions subsequent)

Extract 3.1.6

Re Macleay (1875) LR 20 Eq 186

Property was given 'on condition that he never sells out of the family'.

JESSEL MR: . . . It has been suggested, however, that it is void as being repugnant to the quality of the estate, that is to say, that you cannot restrict the right of an owner in fee of alienating in any way in which he may think fit. If that were the law, the condition would be plainly void. But, with the exception of one authority, a case decided by my immediate predecessor, I am not aware that the law has ever been laid down in that way.

The law on the subject is very old, and I do not think it can be better stated than it is in *Coke* upon *Littleton*, in *Sheppard's* Touchstone, and other books of that kind, which treat it in the same way. *Littleton* says:[i] 'If a feoffment be made upon this condition, that the feoffee shall not alien the land to any, this condition is void, because when a man is enfeoffed of lands or tenements he hath power to alien them to any person by the law. For if such a condition should be good, then the condition should oust him of all the power which the law gives him, which should be against reason, and therefore such a condition is void.' Then he says:[ii] 'But if the condition be such that the feoffee shall not alien to such a one, naming his name, or to any of his heirs or of the issues of such a one, or the like, which conditions do not take away all power of alienation from the feoffee, then such condition is good.' So that, according to *Littleton*, the test is, does it take away all power of alienation? I think it is fair to make one remark, which is made in the case of *Muschamp* v *Bluet*,[iii] cited in *Jarman* on Wills,[iv] and adopted by Lord *Romilly* in the case I am going to refer to, of *Attwater* v *Attwater*[v] – that it must not, in fact, take away all power, because, if you say that he shall not alien except to *AB*, who you know will not or cannot purchase, that would be in effect restraining him from all alienation . . .

Now, you may restrict alienation in many ways. You may restrict alienation by prohibiting a particular class of alienation, or you may restrict alienation by prohibiting it to a particular class of individuals, or you may restrict alienation by restricting it to a particular time. In all those ways you may limit it, and it appears to me that in two ways, at all events, this condition is limited. First, it is limited as to the mode of alienation, because the only prohibition is against selling. There are various modes of alienation besides sale; a person may lease, or he may mortgage, or he may settle; therefore it is a mere limited restriction on alienation in that way. Then, again, it is limited as regards class; he is never to sell it out of the family, but he may sell it to any one member of the family. It is not, therefore, limited in the sense of there being only one person to buy; the will shews there were a great many members of the family when she made her will; a great many are named in it; therefore you have a class which probably was large, and was certainly not small . . . So that this is strictly a limited restraint on alienation, and unless *Coke* upon *Littleton* has been overruled or is not good law, this is a good condition.

[i] Page 222 a.
[ii] Page 223 a.
[iii] Bridgm 137.
[iv] 3rd Ed vol ii p 17.
[v] 18 Beav 330.

Extract 3.1.7

Re Rosher (1884) 26 Ch D 801

PEARSON J: . . . What am I to say is the principle? Is it that there may be a condition that, if you alienate, you must alienate to a member of your own family, or that you must look to the number of the individuals to whom the alienation is permitted, or when there are a number of individuals (not knowing at the present moment what that number may be), am I to inquire whether they are able, or likely to be willing, to purchase the property to which the condition is attached? If they are able and willing to purchase the property, am I to say that the condition is good, and if from their poverty they are unable, or from other circumstances are unwilling, am I to say that the condition is bad? It seems to me that the adoption of any such rule as that would produce the greatest uncertainty and confusion; in fact it would be absolutely impossible for any Judge to apply such a rule to any case which might come before him, unless the facts of the case were absolutely identical with those of some previously decided case.

. . . With all deference to Sir *G Jessel* [in *Re Macleay*], I do not find in *Coke* upon *Littleton* that which he seems to have found, . . . I may say that, if any one will take the trouble to read two or three passages in *Sheppard's* Touchstone, he will find that the learned professors of the law are perpetually at loggerheads as to what is a good condition, and the reason is that they have departed from the first principle, that a condition which is repugnant to a gift is a void condition, and the exceptions have been made without any principle at all, and it is therefore perfectly impossible to say by any rule what exceptions are good and what are bad.

I should be very sorry to do Sir *George Jessel* any injustice, and I must honestly say that in attempting to criticise so able and learned a Judge I am always afraid of falling into some error myself, and I am not quite certain that I understand correctly the extent to which in those passages he means to go. If he means to assert that, provided you give a power to mortgage or lease, you may restrain the power to sell, all I can say is, that I most respectfully differ from him, and I cannot understand how, after he had cited the maxim from *Coke* which he had quoted, he should have tried to lay down any such doctrine.

Comment

(1) Although Jessel MR identifies the essence of the test, its application to the facts of *Re Macleay* is commonly criticised. Is it possible to say what sorts of restrictions upon alienation should be allowed?

(2) If the restraint is invalid, what happens to the gift?

It is important to note that the results in these two cases do not apply to determinable fees,[4] something already seen in *Re Wilkinson* in the slightly different context of a restraint on marriage. Why is this? It is in fact quite common to create determinable interests designed to prevent alienation. The protective trust provides a statutory example as regards life interests.[5]

Extract 3.1.8

Trustee Act 1925, s 33

33.—(1) Where any income, including an annuity or other periodical income payment, is directed to be held on protective trusts for the benefit of any person (in this section called 'the principal beneficiary') for the period of his life or for any less period, then, during that period (in this section called the 'trust period') the said income shall, without prejudice to any prior interest, be held on the following trusts, namely:—

(i) Upon trust for the principal beneficiary during the trust period or until he, whether before or after the termination of any prior interest, does or attempts to do or suffers any act or thing, or until any event happens, other than an advance under any statutory or express power, whereby, if the said income were payable during the trust period to the principal beneficiary absolutely during that period, he would be deprived of the right to receive the same or any part thereof, in any of which cases, as well as on the termination of the trust period, whichever first happens, this trust of the said income shall fail or determine;

(ii) If the trust aforesaid fails or determines during the subsistence of the trust period, then, during the residue of that period, the said income shall be held upon trust for the application

---

[4] *Brandon* v *Robinson* (1811) 18 Ves 429 (34 ER 379).

[5] *Brandon* v *Robinson* (1811) 18 Ves 429 (34 ER 379) shows that the rules relating to restraints on alienation apply to both fees simple and life estates.

thereof for the maintenance or support, or otherwise for the benefit, of all or any one or more exclusively of the other or others of the following persons (that is to say)—

(a) the principal beneficiary and his or her spouse or civil partner, if any, and his or her children or more remote issue, if any; or

. . .

as the trustees in their absolute discretion, without being liable to account for the exercise of such discretion, think fit.

Comment

Why would a settlor employ a protective trust? What happens if the life interest determines?

The role of public policy is assessed in the following case.

Extract 3.1.9

Re King's Trusts (1892) 29 LR Ir 401

An annuity was payable until the marriage of a nephew of the testatrix. The nephew had married.

PORTER MR: . . . I think I am bound, on the whole clause, to hold that the words are words of mere limitation. I confess I should have been better pleased could I have arrived at the opposite conclusion; for it is a hard case that the nephew, who knew nothing of the will, and did not consciously violate the wishes of testatrix, should lose the benefit she meant for him without having any option in the matter. But, on the other hand, there can be no doubt that her intentions are best carried out by the construction I am driven to adopt.

The case is an instance of the very unsatisfactory state of the law on this question. It is little short of disgraceful to our jurisprudence that in reference to a rule professedly founded on considerations of public policy, a gift of an annuity to A B for life, coupled with a proviso that if he married the annuity should cease, whether there be a gift over or not, gives A B a life estate, whether he marries or not; while a gift to C D until he marries or dies, with a gift over, is at an end if C D should marry. The distinction is intelligible to a lawyer; but no testator except a lawyer could be expected to understand it, much less to have regard to it in framing his will. We must, however, take the law as we find it.

Comment

(1) In *Morley* v *Rennoldson*,[6] Wigram V-C had explained the law as follows:

> . . . But, until I heard the argument of this case, I had certainly understood that, without doubt, where property was limited to a person until she married, and when she married then over, the limitation was good. It is difficult to understand how this could be otherwise, for in such a case there is nothing to give an interest beyond the marriage. If you suppose the case of a gift of a certain interest, and that interest sought to be abridged by a condition, you may strike out the condition, and leave the original gift in operation; but if the gift is until marriage, and no longer, there is nothing to carry the gift beyond the marriage . . .

How does this stand up to the criticisms of Porter MR? Might it be said that many things are unintelligible to a layman and yet not 'little short of disgraceful'?

(2) *Re Moore* (Extract 3.1.4 above) shows that some infringements of public policy are so heinous that the provision is void even in a determinable fee. What is then the result?

---

[6] (1843) 2 Hare 570 at pp 579–580 (67 ER 235 at p 239).

(c) Certainty requirements

While it is not surprising that certainty is required, a particularly strict regime has been applied to conditional interests.

Extract 3.1.10

Clavering v *Ellison* (1859) 7 HLC 707 (11 ER 282)

LORD CRANWORTH: . . . And I consider that, from the earliest times, one of the cardinal rules on the subject has been this: that where a vested estate is to be defeated by a condition on a contingency that is to happen afterwards, that condition must be such that the Court can see from the beginning, precisely and distinctly, upon the happening of what event it was that the preceding vested estate was to determine.

. . . I think that, looking at the language here used, it is far too indefinite and uncertain to enable the Court to say what it was that the testator meant should be the event on which the estate was to determine. It was to go over in case one or more of such children should be educated abroad. What does that mean? No two minds would agree upon the question when education begins. Suppose the child was born abroad, and he was brought over to England before he could speak, of course you could not say that he had been educated abroad, though it is said that more ideas are taken in during the first two years of life than in all the years afterwards of the very longest life. If that would not have been a breach of the condition, would it be a breach if the child came back at the age of seven, or if he came back at the age of ten? If he remained abroad all his minority, you would certainly say in that case that he was educated abroad. But the question is, not whether in the particular case he was educated abroad, but whether you can predicate on reading the will, what it was that was to defeat the vested estate? I concur in Lord Eldon's observations about an estate being defeated by a person not living and residing in a particular house, which he thought too remote; and I think that this is far more remote than that.

Comment

(1) In what ways is this test stricter than normal certainty requirements? Why is it imposed?

(2) Would you expect a similar test to be applied to determinable interests?

Extract 3.1.11

Blathwayt v *Baron Cawley* [1976] AC 397

LORD WILBERFORCE: . . . On the question whether the forfeiture clause, in so far as it relates to being or becoming a Roman Catholic, is void for uncertainty, I am clearly of opinion that it is not. Clauses relating in one way or another to the Roman Catholic Church, or faith, have been known and recognised for too many years both in Acts of Parliament (e.g., the Bill of Rights and the Act of Settlement ('Popish religion') and Roman Catholic Relief Acts of 1791 and 1829) and in wills and settlements for it now to be possible to avoid them on this ground. I am of course aware that the present clause is a condition subsequent (or resolutive condition) and I need not quarrel with the accepted doctrine of English law derived from Lord Cranworth's words in *Clavering* v *Ellison* (1859) 7 HLCas 707, 725 which requires a greater degree of certainty in advance as to the scope of such conditions than is needed when the condition is precedent (or suspensive). I can respect this distinction for the purposes of this case without renouncing the right, which I conceive judges have, to judge the degree of certainty with some measure of common sense and knowledge and without excessive astuteness to discover ambiguities . . . The balance of authority is strongly in favour of validity and the contrary would be barely arguable but for the views expressed in this House in *Clayton* v *Ramsden* [1943] AC 320. The condition there was composite 'not of Jewish parentage and of the Jewish faith'. It was held by all members of the House that the first limb (and therefore on this ground the whole condition) was void for uncertainty and by four of their Lordships that the second limb was void on the same ground. Lord Wright took the opposite view on the second limb, as had Lord Greene MR delivering the judgment of the Court of Appeal.

My Lords, I have no wish to whittle away decisions of this House by fine distinctions; but accepting, as I fully do, the opinions of the majority of their Lordships as regards the religious part of this condition, I do not consider myself obliged, or, indeed justified, in extending the conclusion there reached, as to uncertainty, to other clauses relating to other religions or branches of religions . . . The absence of any reference to [the earlier cases] in the speeches in this House refutes any suggestion that a new general principle was being laid down as to the invalidity on ground of uncertainty of all subsequent conditions whatsoever relating to all varieties of religious belief. It confirms that the decision in *Clayton* v *Ramsden* [1943] AC 320 was a particular decision on a condition expressed in a particular way about one kind of religious belief or profession. I do not think it right to apply it to Roman Catholicism.

Comment

Does this decision indicate a weakening of the traditional approach?

Extract 3.1.12

Re Tuck's Settlement Trusts [1978] Ch 49

LORD DENNING MR: . . . In addition to those troubles, there is another distinction to be found in the cases. It is between condition precedent and condition subsequent. Conceptual uncertainty may avoid a condition subsequent, but not a condition precedent. I fail to see the logic of this distinction. Treating the problem as one of construction of words, there is no sense in it. If the words are conceptually uncertain – so as to avoid a condition subsequent – they are just as conceptually uncertain in a condition precedent – and should avoid it also. But it is a distinction authorised by this court in *In re Allen, decd* [1953] Ch 810, and acknowledged by Lord Wilberforce in *Blathwayt* v *Baron Cawley* [1976] AC 397, 424–425.

I deplore both these dichotomies, for a simple reason and a good reason. They serve in every case to defeat the intention of the testator or settlor.

Comment

Though this criticism has not been accepted, is it justified?

Few would defend the rules on determining events in their present form. How should the law be reformed, and which of the rules should be retained?

(ii) The fee tail

This is mentioned for sake of completeness, though no new fees tail can be created since the Trusts of Land and Appointment of Trustees Act 1996. Like the fee simple, the fee tail can survive the grantee; it passes to the lineal descendants of the grantee. Accordingly (and unlike the fee simple), it lasts only so long as there are descendants of the initial grantee; it is liable to terminate in the future. Complications are multiplied by the ability, in certain circumstances, to convert the fee tail into a fee simple, thus defeating the fee simple in remainder. Although suitable for family dynasties of the eighteenth and nineteenth centuries, the fee tail was increasingly foreign to twentieth-century ideas of landholding and had become increasingly uncommon.

(iii) Life estates

Life estates may exist in possession or remainder and may exist as qualified interests in the same way as the fee simple. However, the single topic we will consider is that of waste: the liability of the life interest holder for the state of the premises. The rules apply to both life interest holders and (subject to statutory repairing obligations) tenants under leases.

Waste is commonly divided into four categories. The first, ameliorating waste, improves the premises.

Extract 3.1.13

Doherty v *Allman* (1878) 3 App Cas 709

LORD O'HAGAN: . . . In the case of *Mollineux* v *Powell*,[i] which contains perhaps the clearest dictum we have upon the matter, two conditions as to the exercise of jurisdiction in cases of waste have been very clearly pointed out, and one at least of those conditions is expressly recognised afterwards in the Irish case of *Coppinger* v *Gubbins*.[ii] Those conditions are that the waste with which a Court of Equity, or your Lordships acting as a Court of Equity, ought to interfere, should be not ameliorating waste, nor trivial waste. It must be waste of an injurious character – it must be waste of not only an injurious character, but of a substantially injurious character, and if either the waste be really ameliorating waste – that is a proceeding which results in benefit and not in injury – the Court of Equity, and your Lordships acting as a Court of Equity, ought not to interfere to prevent it . . .

. . . We have most conclusive evidence that the change will be beneficial. We have the most clear evidence that, as the matter stands, this old dilapidated store has become useless, I presume, to any human being. Circumstances have changed; the necessity for a store of that kind has ceased, and the result has been that the store, if it be allowed to continue in its present condition – because the parties are compelled to leave it in its present condition – till the end of this term of 999 years, the whole premises will be utterly valueless; whereas, upon the other side, if you substitute for this store the houses which are contemplated you double, you treble the security of the landlord, and give him, or whoever may live at the end of the term of 999 years, certainly not an injured property but an improved one. Therefore, inasmuch as the waste, if waste there be, is ameliorating waste, and the injury to the property produced by the waste is not merely trivial but absolutely non-existent, it appears to me that upon that ground the judgment of the Court below may very fairly be maintained.

[i] 3 P Wms 268, n (F).
[ii] 3 J&Lat 411.

Voluntary waste involves doing something which damages the premises: it is clear that liability results. The cases offer useful guidance, however, as to what can properly be taken from the land.

Extract 3.1.14

Pardoe v *Pardoe* (1900) 82 LT 547

STIRLING J: . . . Jessel, MR [in *Honywood* v *Honywood* (1874) LR 18 Eq 306] says: 'Once arrive at the fact of what is timber, the tenant for life impeachable for waste, cannot cut it down. That I take to be the clear law, with one single exception, which has been established principally by modern authorities in favour of the owners of timber estates – that is, estates which are cultivated merely for the produce of saleable timber, and where the timber is cut periodically. The reason of the distinction is this, that as cutting the timber is the mode of cultivation, the timber is not to be kept as part of the inheritance, but part, so to say, of the annual fruits of the land, and in these cases the same kind of cultivation may be carried on by the tenant for life that has been carried on by the settlor of the estate, and the timber so cut down periodically in due course is looked upon as the annual profits of the estate, and therefore goes to the tenant for life.' And the principle on which this is based is explained more fully in *Dashwood v Magniac* [[1891] 3 Ch 306] both by Chitty, J in the court of first instance and by Lindley, MR in his judgment in the Court of Appeal. I shall content myself with reading what was said by Chitty, J. On what principle this is allowed he refers to the case which is well established, that it is not waste to work an open mine, and he asks 'on what principle?' and says: 'The acts of the settlor show an irresistible indication of his intention that the mines should be dealt with as he dealt with them, and that the mineral extracted should be deemed to be profits by all who take under his settlement. It is in vain to say that being owner he may do what he likes with his own.'. . .

It is quite common for the settlor to exclude liability for voluntary waste. We must now consider whether this removes all control over what the life interest holder can do.

Extract 3.1.15

Turner v *Wright* (1860) 2 De GF&J 234 (45 ER 612)

LORD CAMPBELL LC: . . . The waste which intervenes between what is denominated legal waste [voluntary waste] and what is denominated malicious waste, viz, equitable waste, may admit of a different consideration. But equitable waste is that which a prudent man would not do in the management of his own property. This Court may interfere where a man unconscientiously exercises a legal right to the prejudice of another – and an act may in some sense be regarded as unconscientious if it be contrary to the dictates of prudence and reason, although the actor, from his peculiar frame of mind, does the act without any malicious motive. The prevention of acts amounting to equitable waste may well be considered as in furtherance of the intention of the testator, who, no doubt, wished that the property should come to the devisee over in the condition in which he, the testator, left it at his death; the first taker having had the reasonable enjoyment of it, and having managed it as a man of ordinary prudence would manage such property were it absolutely his own . . .

Comment

What is the difference between voluntary and equitable waste? What is the role of equitable waste?

Rather different is the question whether there is liability for not preventing the premises from deteriorating: permissive waste. Another way of putting the question is whether there is a duty to repair.

Extract 3.1.16

Re Cartwright (1889) 41 Ch D 532

KAY J: . . . The result appears to be this: Sir *James Mansfield* was clearly of opinion that an action for permissive waste would not lie even against a tenant for years. That is clearly shewn in the case of *Gibson v Wells*[i] . . . [Lord Cranworth LC in *Powys v Blagrave*[ii]] decided most certainly that in equity no interference whatever would be made on the ground of permissive waste by a tenant for life. Now, in that state of the authorities, this consideration is to be added. Since the Statutes of *Marlbridge* and of *Gloucester* there must have been hundreds of thousands of tenants for life who have died leaving their estates in a condition of great dilapidation. Not once, so far as legal records go, have damages been recovered against the estate of a tenant for life on that ground. To ask me in that state of the authorities to hold that a tenant for life is liable for permissive waste to a remainderman is to my mind a proposition altogether startling. I should not think of coming to such a decision without direct authority upon the point. Such authority as there is seems to me to be against the contention . . .

ⁱ 1 B&P NR 290.
ⁱⁱ 4 D M&G 458.

Waste rules are little referred to today. The land is more likely to be controlled by trustees, who are likely to have more onerous duties. However, the life interest holder may be allowed into possession and then the rules may well be relevant.

(iv) Words of limitation

This is the technical term used to describe the words necessary to create particular estates. Originally, a fee simple could be created only by the phrase 'and his heirs', though this was relaxed over time.

Extract 3.1.17

Law of Property Act 1925, s 60

60.—(1)   A conveyance of freehold land to any person without words of limitation, or any equivalent expression, shall pass to the grantee the fee simple or other the whole interest which the grantor had power to convey in such land, unless a contrary intention appears in the conveyance.

C. Other interests

A wide range of legal and equitable interests is recognised today, ranging from leases to easements and mortgages. Equitable interests include estate contracts (the right of a person who has agreed to buy land, or has an option to buy) and restrictive covenants (restricting the use of land for the benefit of a neighbour). Both legal and equitable interests will be considered in detail in subsequent chapters.

What is of greatest interest is the question why we have a fixed list of interests. Our investigation of licences (see Chapter 18) will illustrate the present boundaries of property rights and the courts' reactions to attempts to extend them. The general approach may be seen from the following extract.

Extract 3.1.18

National Provincial Bank Ltd v Ainsworth **[1965] AC 1175**

A deserted wife has a right against her husband to occupy the former matrimonial home. Is this a property right capable of binding purchasers?

LORD WILBERFORCE: . . . The conclusion emerges to my mind very clearly from this that the wife's rights, as regards the occupation of her husband's property, are essentially of a personal kind: personal in the sense that a decision can only be reached on the basis of considerations essentially dependent on the mutual claims of husband and wife as spouses and as the result of a broad weighing of circumstances and merit. Moreover, these rights are at no time definitive, they are provisional and subject to review at any time according as changes take place in the material circumstances and conduct of the parties.

On any division, then, which is to be made between property rights on the one hand, and personal rights on the other hand, however broad or penumbral the separating band between these two kinds of rights may be, there can be little doubt where the wife's rights fall. Before a right or an interest can be admitted into the category of property, or of a right affecting property, it must be definable, identifiable by third parties, capable in its nature of assumption by third parties, and have some degree of permanence or stability. The wife's right has none of these qualities, it is characterised by the reverse of them.

. . .

Let us look at the claim of a 'deserted wife' through the eyes of a prospective purchaser or mortgagee. Mrs X is living in the house: she claims that she has been 'deserted'. But Mr X denies this. Perhaps he claims that he is living elsewhere for business reasons, or to care for his aged parents . . . Not every case, nor necessarily the majority of cases, are such as the present where the desertion is clear and incontestable: yet where it is not, how can a third party, seeking to take a title to the property, be expected to involve himself in these matrimonial complications? . . .

Comment

(1) Why is it necessary to limit the range of proprietary interests? Would it really cause such great problems if there were no limit?

(2) We have seen that some authors are critical of the analysis used by Lord Wilberforce to define proprietary rights: Extract 1.1.2 above.

(3) Since 1967, spouses (also, today, civil partners) have had statutory rights to possess which, if registered, can bind purchasers: see now the Family Law Act 1996, ss 30–31.

Extract 3.1.19

Law of Property Act 1925, s 4

4.—(1)   Interests in land validly created or arising after the commencement of this Act, which are not capable of subsisting as legal estates, shall take effect as equitable interests . . .

Provided that, after the commencement of this Act (and save as hereinafter expressly enacted), an equitable interest in land shall only be capable of being validly created in any case in which an equivalent equitable interest in property real or personal could have been validly created before such commencement.

Comment

It is the proviso to s 4(1) which is of interest. Does it prevent the courts from developing new equitable interests?[7] If not, how is it to be explained?

D. The role of legislation and registration

It is important to appreciate that legislation plays a significant role throughout modern land law. Although most of the basic concepts are based in the common law, their very age has required extensive statutory amendment. This has been true for centuries, though the amount of legislation grew rapidly in the late nineteenth century.

---

[7] It will be seen below that legal interests are restricted to those listed in the Law of Property Act 1925, s 1. This unequivocally prevents new legal interests from being developed.

(i) 1925 legislation

The property legislation of 1925 is of prime importance. Much was done to tidy up the previous law and consolidate the nineteenth-century reforms. We will study most of the important provisions in later chapters, but at this stage we need to investigate the adjustment of the boundaries between legal and equitable interests, together with the reasons for such changes.

Extract 3.1.20

Law of Property Act 1925, ss 1, 7

1.—(1) The only estates in land which are capable of subsisting or of being conveyed or created at law are—
  (a) An estate in fee simple absolute in possession;
  (b) A term of years absolute.
 (2) The only interests or charges in or over land which are capable of subsisting or of being conveyed or created at law are—
  (a) An easement, right, or privilege in or over land for an interest equivalent to an estate in fee simple absolute in possession or a term of years absolute;
  (b) A rentcharge in possession issuing out of or charged on land being either perpetual or for a term of years absolute;
  (c) A charge by way of legal mortgage;
  (d) Rights of entry exercisable over or in respect of a legal term of years absolute, or annexed, for any purpose, to a legal rentcharge.
 (3) All other estates, interests, and charges in or over land take effect as equitable interests.

7.—(1) . . . a fee simple subject to a legal or equitable right of entry or re-entry is for the purposes of this Act a fee simple absolute.

Comment

(1) Section 1 obviously restricts the number of legal estates and interests recognised today. Their legal status means that a purchaser of unregistered land[8] has to ensure that they are discovered: they will be binding whether or not the purchaser knows about them.

(2) The significance of s 7 is that conditional fees can be legal estates, despite not being absolute. The reason for this is historical and obsolescent. It used to be conveyancing practice in some areas (especially around Manchester) to create a rentcharge (an annual payment) on selling land,[9] together with a right of entry to secure the payment. This was a standard commercial arrangement, for which the rules applying to equitable interests were inappropriate.

(3) Remember that the interests listed in s 1 are not necessarily legal. They will be equitable if, for example, not created by deed (a deed is essential for most legal interests) or if they are created under a trust.

(4) The fact that there will always be a fee simple absolute in possession goes far to establish a notion of ownership in English law, something which was more difficult when there could be numerous legal estates.

---

[8] Even in registered land, several of these rights will, as overriding interests, bind purchasers.
[9] Since the Rentcharges Act 1977, it is no longer possible to create rentcharges of the type described.

Limiting the number of legal estates would achieve relatively little by itself to ease the purchase of land: the doctrine of notice means that purchasers have to take care to discover equitable interests. However, most equitable interests are subject to one of two regimes today; in neither case is there scope for notice. So far as the former legal estates (commonly called *family interests*) are concerned, they are subject to the doctrine of overreaching.[10] This means that the trustees can sell the land and the purchaser is unaffected by the interest. The interest takes effect against the proceeds of sale. Thus a life interest in Blackacre is converted on sale for £250,000 to a life interest in £250,000 (or shares purchased with the proceeds). (This is investigated more fully in Chapter 12.)

So far as other (*commercial*) equitable interests are concerned, they usually have to be registered in order to bind a purchaser. Thus it may be seen that equitable status is an indication of overreaching or registrability: it has little to do with historical status or the doctrine of notice. However, land registration (which applies to 95% of titles today) requires many legal estates and interests, as well as equitable interests, to be registered. Even here, nevertheless, legal status remains significant. Interests which are registered, rather than merely protected, are guaranteed to exist and it is generally only legal interests which can be registered. (These matters are further considered in Chapters 9 and 10.)

(ii) Other legislation

Some parts of the 1925 legislation have been re-enacted in more recent years. One example is the Trusts of Land and Appointment of Trustees Act 1996, which regulates trusts of land. Such trusts operate where there are successive family interests, as discussed above, or where two or more people hold land concurrently (such as a couple owning their house). This legislation deals with the rights of the parties (to occupy, for example), the powers of the trustees and court resolution of disputes (see Chapter 12). Land registration is today regulated by the Land Registration Act 2002.

Other statutes go beyond the scope of the 1925 legislation. Two examples are the regulation of the running of covenants in leases by the Landlord and Tenant (Covenants) Act 1995 (see Chapter 16) and the introduction of commonhold, a new form of landholding for flats and other interdependent properties, by the Commonhold and Leasehold Reform Act 2002 (see Chapter 17).

2. Chattels

The law relating to chattels is far less developed. Quite apart from the fact that the doctrine of tenure has no application, the law does not recognise as wide a range of interests as for land. Why might this be?

However, bailment (where one person possesses by agreement with the owner) is a recognised interest. This covers a person who borrows or hires an object, as well as (for example) a shop undertaking a repair to a television in their workshop. Bailment can also underpin security transactions with chattels, such as pledge.[11]

Bailment is often important in establishing the liability of the bailee, especially in establishing a duty to take care of the property so as to prevent theft. It is also important as a

---

[10] Overreaching is not limited to family interests. One example concerns sales by mortgagees: the mortgagor (borrower) loses the land and receives the purchase money less the amount owing.

[11] There can also be a mortgage of chattels, whereby the ownership is held by the lender as security.

basis for actions by the bailee against third parties. This is unsurprising given English law's stress on possession rather than ownership as the root of most actions.[12]

Extract 3.2.1

The Winkfield [1902] P 42

Can a bailee sue for the entire value of a chattel lost or damaged?

COLLINS MR: . . . Therefore, as I said at the outset, and as I think I have now shewn by authority, the root principle of the whole discussion is that, as against a wrongdoer, possession is title. The chattel that has been converted or damaged is deemed to be the chattel of the possessor and of no other, and therefore its loss or deterioration is his loss, and to him, if he demands it, it must be recouped. His obligation to account to the bailor is really not *ad rem* in the discussion. It only comes in after he has carried his legal position to its logical consequence against a wrongdoer, and serves to soothe a mind disconcerted by the notion that a person who is not himself the complete owner should be entitled to receive back the full value of the chattel converted or destroyed. There is no inconsistency between the two positions; the one is the complement of the other. As between bailee and stranger possession gives title – that is, not a limited interest, but absolute and complete ownership, and he is entitled to receive back a complete equivalent for the whole loss or deterioration of the thing itself. As between bailor and bailee the real interests of each must be inquired into, and, as the bailee has to account for the thing bailed, so he must account for that which has become its equivalent and now represents it. What he has received above his own interest he has received to the use of his bailor. The wrongdoer, having once paid full damages to the bailee, has an answer to any action by the bailor.

Comment

(1) Does this produce a rational result?

(2) A claim can be brought by the bailor, but it has been explained that is limited to loss actually suffered and does not apply if the bailee has compensated the bailor: *HSBC Rail (UK) Ltd* v *Network Rail Infrastructure Ltd* [2006] 1 WLR 643.

The development of equitable interests in chattels is urged from time to time. The attitude of the courts has usually been hostile.

Extract 3.2.2

Manchester Trust v Furness [1895] 2 QB 539

LINDLEY MR: . . . What is wanted in this case is to say that by reason of the reference to the charterparty the holder of the bill of lading and the person who takes it in the ordinary course of business are to be treated as having notice of all the contents of the charterparty. There is no doctrine that goes to anything like that extent; and as regards the extension of the equitable doctrines of constructive notice to commercial transactions, the Courts have always set their faces resolutely against it. The equitable doctrines of constructive notice are common enough in dealing with land and estates, with which the Court is familiar; but there have been repeated protests against the introduction into commercial transactions of anything like an extension of those doctrines, and the protest is founded on perfect good sense. In dealing with estates in land title is everything, and it can be leisurely investigated; in commercial transactions possession

---

[12] See Chapter 4, especially p 63 below.

is everything, and there is no time to investigate title; and if we were to extend the doctrine of constructive notice to commercial transactions we should be doing infinite mischief and paralyzing the trade of the country.

Comment

(1) A bill of lading is a document provided by a shipper: transfer of the document is treated as the same as transfer of the goods.

(2) This approach has frequently been followed.[13] Is it justified?

(3) It should not be thought that no equitable interests can be created in chattels: one can for example create a trust of chattels. Indeed, the role of equity in commercial transactions has expanded considerably in recent years.[14] The point is rather that the courts are reluctant to interpret a commercial dealing as giving rise to equitable rights at odds with normal commercial expectations.

Further reading

Fox, D [2006] CLJ 330: Relativity of title at law and in equity.

Harris, D (1986) 'Ownership of land in English Law', in *The Legal Mind: Essays in Honour of Tony Honoré*, eds N MacCormick and P Birks, Chapter 9.

Millett, P J (1998) 114 LQR 214: Equity's place in the law of commerce.

Nugee, E (2008) 124 LQR 586: The feudal system and the Land Registration Acts.

Rudden, B (1994) 14 OxJLS 81: Things as things and things as wealth.

---

[13] See, e.g., *Polly Peck International plc v Nadir (No 2)* [1992] 4 All ER 769 at p 782.
[14] Millett (1998) 114 LQR 214.

Part II

General principles: how property interests arise and purchasers

4

Original acquisition of property interests

As a mode of acquisition, original acquisition is the exception rather than the rule. The huge majority of property interests are acquired by transfer from an existing holder: sale and gift are obvious examples. This chapter considers three examples of original acquisition: finding, adverse possession and fixtures.

1. Finding

Finding illustrates the relativity of titles recognised by English law. Virtually all the cases involve property lost, but not abandoned, by an original owner whose identity is unknown. Litigation is generally between the finder and somebody who has taken, or claims, a superior right to the property. The person claiming a superior right may be the occupier of land where the object has been found, somebody with a superior right to the land (such as a landlord) or the finder's employer. It matters not that none of the parties to the litigation could prevail against the original owner of the lost property: the *jus tertii* principle is that it is no defence to show that a third party has a better title than the claimant. In this section, we will investigate the law by looking at the various relationships involved. First, however, it is important to note a modern statutory restriction upon the *jus tertii* principle.

Extract 4.1.1

Torts (Interference with Goods) Act 1977, s 8

8.—(1) The defendant in an action for wrongful interference shall be entitled to show, in accordance with rules of court, that a third party has a better right than the plaintiff as respects all or any part of the interest claimed by the plaintiff, or in right of which he sues, and any rule of law (sometimes called jus tertii) to the contrary is abolished.

Extract 4.1.2

Battersby [1992] Conv 100 at p 102 (footnotes omitted)

The principal effect of section 8 on the *jus tertii* principle is twofold: (1) to require the plaintiff to identify any person who, to his knowledge, has or claims an interest in the property, and (2) to permit the defendant to join as a party to the action any person who is alleged by the defendant to have a better title than the plaintiff. The purpose of the exercise is to provide that, as far as possible, the one set of proceedings shall be used in order to determine all competing claims by having all competing claimants before the court and thus bound by the ultimate order which the court makes . . . It follows that, in all cases where, for whatever reason, neither the plaintiff nor the defendant can (or will) identify a person with a superior title, the old *jus tertii* principle will continue to apply, *i.e.* the plaintiff will win against the defendant if the plaintiff has a title superior to the defendant's, even though it is clear that some third party has a better title than either of them. Thus, none of the classic finding cases would be affected by section 8 . . . Putting the matter another way, it is clear that, when section 8(1) states that the common law *jus tertii* principle 'is abolished', the meaning is that it is abolished only to the extent necessary to make room for the new machinery; where that machinery cannot operate, because the *tertius* cannot be identified, the common law will continue to govern . . .

Comment

The finder will also succeed if the owner is identified, but fails to appear.[1]

A. Things found on, in or under land

(i) Finder – true owner disputes

Extract 4.1.3

Moffatt v *Kazana* [1969] 2 QB 152

It was proved that the deceased (Mr Russell) had hidden a biscuit tin containing cash in the roof of his house. He had forgotten about it when he sold the house to the defendant. Some three years later, the defendant discovered the tin . . . Could the deceased's estate claim the money?

WRANGHAM J: [In] the existing authorities there is an implication at least from the language in which the judgments are expressed that the true owner of a chattel found on land has a title superior to that of anybody else . . . Abandonment is not suggested. One does not abandon property merely because one has forgotten where one put it. Gift is not suggested.

There remains only sale. That sale can only be the conveyance of No 19 Northcliffe Avenue and Mr Heald was obliged at the outset of his argument boldly to face the difficulty that section 62 of the Law of Property Act, 1925, provides in effect that a conveyance of land does not include a conveyance of chattels. In this conveyance there is no reference to chattels, so it would appear on the face of it that that section wholly excludes any possible argument based upon the conveyance.

. . . If Mr Russell never got rid of the notes, that is to say, never got rid of the ownership of the notes, he continued to be the owner of them and, if he continued to be the owner of them, he had a title to those notes which nobody else, whether the owner of the land in which they were found, or the finders, or anybody else would have.

Comment

(1) The effect of sale is considered further below, in the context where the seller is not the true owner.[2]

(2) Limitation rules prevent any claim by the true owner after six years, but only from the time the object is demanded from the finder.[3] How far do they act as a real constraint on the true owner's rights?

---

[1] *Civil Procedure 2012 (White Book), Vol 1*, Rule 19.5A.
[2] See pp 72–73.
[3] Limitation Act 1980, s 2; sale by the finder might well be a conversion causing time to run (Marshall (1984) 2 CLP 68 at p 70).

(ii) Finder–dispossessor disputes

Extract 4.1.4

Armory v *Delamirie* (1722) 1 Strange 505 (93 ER 664)

The plaintiff being a chimney sweeper's boy found a jewel and carried it to the defendant's shop (who was a goldsmith) to know what it was, and delivered it into the hands of the apprentice, who under pretence of weighing it, took out the stones, . . . the apprentice delivered him back the socket without the stones. And now in trover against the master these points were ruled:

1. That the finder of a jewel, though he does not by such finding acquire an absolute property or ownership, yet he has such a property as will enable him to keep it against all but the rightful owner, and consequently may maintain trover.

Comment

(1) The defendant was liable for the value of the finest jewel that would fit the socket.

(2) Why should the law protect the finder?

(3) If the finder is a trespasser or thief, should this make any difference?[4]

(iii) Finder–occupier disputes

Does occupation of land give rights to chattels found there, regardless of who finds them? This question may sometimes be avoided by more specific circumstances, such as an agreement between finder and occupier which expressly or impliedly regulates the position. Before we consider more general issues in finder–occupier disputes, two other specific possibilities will be mentioned.

(a) Wrongdoers

Extract 4.1.5

Hibbert v *McKiernan* [1948] 2 KB 142

The accused took lost golf balls from a golf course with the intention of selling them.

LORD GODDARD CJ: . . . We are here dealing with a charge of larceny; with a thief who took the balls *animo furandi*; not with a honest man who, finding an article on the land of another, proclaims that fact with a view to discovering the owner if he can, and when no owner comes forward, asserts a possessory title against the owner of the land on which it was found. We need not be troubled with nice questions relating to *animus domini*, *corpus possessionis*, *de facto* control, or the like. Every householder or occupier of land means or intends to exclude thieves and wrongdoers from the property occupied by him, and this confers on him a special property in goods found on his land sufficient to support an indictment if the goods are taken therefrom, not under a claim of right, but with a felonious intent.

---

[4] See *Costello* v *Derbyshire Chief Constable* [2001] 1 WLR 1437 and *Webb* v *Merseyside Chief Constable* [2000] QB 427.

Comment

(1) What principle emerges from *Hibbert*?

(2) Would the golf club have a good title to the golf balls in a civil action? How can it be that the occupier's property rights depend upon the *mens rea* of the finder?

(3) Suppose I visit a neighbour to return a book I borrowed. I pick up a gold ring (now believed to have been taken and dropped by a magpie) from a rose bed a couple of feet from the path to the front door. Does *Hibbert* apply?

(b) Employees and agents

Although there is virtually no direct English authority,[5] it seems clearly recognised that employers are entitled to objects found by employees.

Extract 4.1.6

M'Dowell v *Ulster Bank* (1899) 33 ILT 225

A bank porter discovered a sum of money on the floor, probably dropped by a customer.

PALLES LCB: . . . I decide [this case] on the ground of the relation of master and servant, and that it was by reason of the existence of that relationship and in the performance of the duties of that service that the plaintiff acquired possession of this property. I conceive that it is the duty of the porter of the Bank, who acts as caretaker, to pick up matters of this description, and to hand them over to the Bank. I hold that the possession of the servant of the Bank was the possession of the Bank itself, and that, therefore, the element is wanting which would give the title to the servant as against the master . . .

Comment

(1) The cases support the extension of this principle to employees other than porters and to lost objects generally. Is this justified?

(2) Should an employer have a right to goods found by an employee on somebody else's premises?[6]

(c) The general question

Extract 4.1.7

Parker v *British Airways Board* [1982] QB 1004

The plaintiff found a gold bracelet in an airport lounge and handed it over to the defendants. He stated that he did so only to allow the owner to be discovered.

DONALDSON LJ: . . . The plaintiff's claim is founded upon the ancient common law rule that the act of finding a chattel which has been lost and taking control of it gives the finder rights with respect to that chattel . . . [The defendants] must and do claim on the basis that they had rights in relation to the bracelet immediately *before* the plaintiff found it and that these rights are superior to the plaintiff's. The defendants' claim is based upon the proposition that at common

---

[5] Closest probably is *City of London Corporation* v *Appleyard* [1963] 1 WLR 982 at p 988; see also *Parker* v *British Airways Board* [1982] QB 1004 at pp 1014, 1017.

[6] *Byrne* v *Hoare* [1965] QdR 135 and *Crinion* v *Minister for Justice* [1959] Ir Jur Rep 15 reached contrasting conclusions as regards police officers.

law an occupier of land has such rights over all lost chattels which are on that land, whether or not the occupier knows of their existence.

The common law right asserted by the plaintiff has been recognised for centuries . . . The rule as stated by Pratt CJ [in *Armory* v *Delamirie*] must be right as a general proposition, for otherwise lost property would be subject to a free-for-all in which the physically weakest would go to the wall.

. . .

Some qualification has also to be made in the case of the trespassing finder. The person *vis à vis* whom he is a trespasser has a better title. The fundamental basis of this is clearly public policy. Wrongdoers should not benefit from their wrongdoing. This requirement would be met if the trespassing finder acquired no rights. That would, however, produce the free-for-all situation to which I have already referred, in that anyone could take the article from the trespassing finder. Accordingly, the common law has been obliged to give rights to someone else, the owner ex hypothesi being unknown. The obvious candidate is the occupier of the property upon which the finder was trespassing.

. . .

I must now return to the respective claims of the plaintiff and the defendants. Mr Brown, for the plaintiff, relies heavily upon . . . *Bridges* v *Hawkesworth* (1851) 21 LJQB 75; 15 Jur 1079 . . . Mr Bridges was a commercial traveller and in the course of his business he called upon the defendant at his shop. As he was leaving the shop, he picked up a small parcel which was lying on the floor, showed it to the shopman and, upon opening it in his presence, found that it contained £65 in notes . . .

Patteson J gave the judgment of the court . . . I take the text of the report in the Jurist, 15 Jur 1079, 1082 but refer to the Law Journal version, 21 LJQB 75, 77–78, in square brackets where they differ. It reads:

'. . . The general right of the finder to any article which has been lost, as against all the world, except the true owner, was established in . . . *Armory* v *Delamirie*, 1 Stra 505, which has never been disputed. This right would clearly have accrued to the plaintiff had the notes been picked up by him outside the shop of the defendant . . . The case, therefore, resolves itself into the single point on which it appears that the learned judge decided it, namely, whether the circumstance of the notes being found inside [word emphasised in *Law Journal*] the defendant's shop gives him, the defendant, the right to have them as against the plaintiff, who found them. There is no authority in our law to be found directly in point . . . It was well asked, on the argument, if the defendant has the right, *when* did it accrue to him? If at all, it must have been antecedent to the finding by the plaintiff, for that finding could not give the defendant any right. If the notes had been accidentally kicked into the shop ["the street" in *Law Journal*, which must be right], and there found by someone passing by, could it be contended that the defendant was entitled to them from the mere fact of their being originally dropped in his shop? If the discovery had never ["not"] been communicated to the defendant, could the real owner have had any cause of action against him because they were found in his house? Certainly not. The notes never were in the custody of the defendant, nor within the protection of his house, before they were found, as they would have been had they been intentionally deposited there . . . We find, therefore, no circumstances in this case to take it out of the general rule of law, that the finder of a lost article is entitled to it as against all persons except the real owner . . .'

The ratio of this decision seems to me to be solely that the unknown presence of the notes on the premises occupied by Mr Hawkesworth could not, without more, give him any rights or impose any duty upon him in relation to the notes.

Mr Desch, for the defendants, submits that *Bridges* v *Hawkesworth*, 15 Jur 1079, can be distinguished and he referred us to the judgment of Lord Russell of Killowen CJ, with which

Wills J agreed, in *South Staffordshire Water Co* v *Sharman* [1896] 2 QB 44. *Sharman's* case itself is readily distinguishable, either upon the ground that the rings were in the mud and thus part of the realty or upon the ground that the finders were employed by the plaintiff to remove the mud and had a clear right to direct how the mud and anything in it should be disposed of, or upon both grounds. However, Lord Russell of Killowen CJ in distinguishing *Bridges* v *Hawkesworth* expressed views which, in Mr Desch's submission, point to the defendants having a superior claim to that of the plaintiff on the facts of the instant case. Lord Russell of Killowen CJ said, at pp 46–47:

> 'The principle on which this case must be decided, and the distinction which must be drawn between this case and that of *Bridges* v *Hawkesworth*, is to be found in a passage in *Pollock and Wright*, . . . *Possession in the Common Law*, p 41: "The possession of land carries with it in general, by our law, possession of everything which is attached to or under that land, and, in the absence of a better title elsewhere, the right to possess it also. And it makes no difference that the possessor is not aware of the thing's existence . . . [It] seems preferable to say that the legal possession rests on a real de facto possession, constituted by the occupier's general power and intent to exclude unauthorised interference." That is the ground on which I prefer to base my judgment . . . *Bridges* v *Hawkesworth* stands by itself, and on special grounds; and on those grounds it seems to me that the decision in that case was right . . . The shop was open to the public, and they were invited to come there . . . the ground of the decision being, as was pointed out by Patteson J, that the notes, being dropped in the public part of the shop, were never in the custody of the shopkeeper, or "within the protection of his house". It is somewhat strange that there is no more direct authority on the question; but the general principle seems to me to be that where a person has possession of house or land, with a manifest intention to exercise control over it and the things which may be upon or in it, then, if something is found on that land, whether by an employee of the owner or by a stranger, the presumption is that the possession of that thing is in the owner of the locus in quo.'

For my part, I can find no trace in the report of *Bridges* v *Hawkesworth*, 21 LJQB 75, of any reliance by Patteson J upon the fact that the notes were found in what may be described as the public part of the shop . . .

However, I would accept Lord Russell of Killowen CJ's statement of the general principle in *South Staffordshire Water Co* v *Sharman* [1896] 2 QB 44, 46–47, provided that the occupier's intention to exercise control over anything which might be on the premises was manifest. But it is impossible to go further and to hold that the mere right of an occupier to exercise such control is sufficient to give him rights in relation to lost property on his premises without overruling *Bridges* v *Hawkesworth*, 21 LJQB 75. Mr Hawkesworth undoubtedly had a right to exercise such control, but his defence failed.

. . .

One of the great merits of the common law is that it is usually sufficiently flexible to take account of the changing needs of a continually changing society. Accordingly, Mr Desch rightly directed our attention to the need to have common law rules which will facilitate rather than hinder the ascertainment of the true owner of a lost chattel and a reunion between the two. In his submission the law should confer rights upon the occupier of the land where a lost chattel was found which were superior to those of the finder, since the loser is more likely to make inquiries at the place of loss. I see the force of this submission. However, I think that it is also true that if this were the rule and finders had no prospect of any reward, they would be tempted to pass by without taking any action or to become concealed keepers of articles which they found.

. . .

Rights and obligations of the finder

1.   The finder of a chattel acquires no rights over it unless (a) it has been abandoned or lost and (b) he takes it into his care and control.

2.   The finder of a chattel acquires very limited rights over it if he takes it into his care and control with dishonest intent or in the course of trespassing.

3.   Subject to the foregoing and to point 4 below, a finder of a chattel, whilst not acquiring any absolute property or ownership in the chattel, acquires a right to keep it against all but the true owner or those in a position to claim through the true owner or one who can assert a prior right to keep the chattel which was subsisting at the time when the finder took the chattel into his care and control.

4.   Unless otherwise agreed, any servant or agent who finds a chattel in the course of his employment or agency and not wholly incidentally or collaterally thereto and who takes it into his care and control does so on behalf of his employer or principal who acquires a finder's rights to the exclusion of those of the actual finder.

5.   A person having a finder's rights has an obligation to take such measures as in all the circumstances are reasonable to acquaint the true owner of the finding and present whereabouts of the chattel and to care for it meanwhile.

Rights and liabilities of an occupier

1.   An occupier of land has rights superior to those of a finder over chattels in or attached to that land . . .

2.   An occupier of a building has rights superior to those of a finder over chattels upon or in, but not attached to, that building if, but only if, before the chattel is found, he has manifested an intention to exercise control over the building and the things which may be upon it or in it.

3.   An occupier [within 2] is under an obligation to take such measures as in all the circumstances are reasonable to ensure that lost chattels are found and, upon their being found, whether by him or by a third party, to acquaint the true owner of the finding and to care for the chattels meanwhile . . .

It was suggested in argument that in some circumstances the intention of the occupier to assert control over articles lost on his premises speaks for itself. I think that this is right. If a bank manager saw fit to show me round a vault containing safe deposits and I found a gold bracelet on the floor, I should have no doubt that the bank had a better title than I, and the reason is the manifest intention to exercise a very high degree of control. At the other extreme is the park to which the public has unrestricted access during daylight hours. During those hours there is no manifest intention to exercise any such control. In between these extremes are the forecourts of petrol filling stations, unfenced front gardens of private houses, the public parts of shops and supermarkets as part of an almost infinite variety of land, premises and circumstances.

This lounge is in the middle band and in my judgment, on the evidence available, there was no sufficient manifestation of any intention to exercise control over lost property before it was found such as would give the defendants a right superior to that of the plaintiff or indeed any right over the bracelet. As the true owner has never come forward, it is a case of 'finders keepers'.

Comment

(1) What are the differences between the views expressed in *Bridges*, *Sharman* and Pollock and Wright?

(2) Before *Parker*, *Bridges* was perceived as having been convincingly criticised. Is it rehabilitated by *Parker*?

(3) Central to *Parker* is the notion of manifesting an intention to exercise control. Is this a safe criterion upon which to rest this area of law? What does it mean? In *Sharman*, it was stressed that the notes in *Bridges* were dropped in a public part of the shop. Does this distinction survive in the modern law?

(4) Leaving the authorities on one side, are there arguments from principle or policy that would support the occupier of land?

Things *in* or *under* land have proved less troublesome.

Extract 4.1.8

Waverley BC v *Fletcher* [1996] QB 334

The defendant, while using a metal detector, found a mediaeval gold brooch nine inches below the surface of the plaintiff's public park.

AULD LJ: . . . As to articles found in or attached to land, the foundation of the modern rule is *Elwes* v *Brigg Gas Co* (1886) 33 Ch D 562, in which Chitty J clearly regarded ownership or lawful possession of the land as determinative and the legal status of the object in dispute as immaterial. He held that a tenant for life as lessor of land was entitled against its lessee to ownership of a prehistoric boat embedded six feet below the surface in the demised land. In so holding, he said, at pp 568–569, that it was unnecessary to determine whether the boat was a mineral, part of the soil in which it was embedded or a chattel because:

> 'he was in possession of the ground, not merely of the surface, but of everything that lay beneath the surface down to the centre of the earth, and consequently in possession of the boat . . . The plaintiff then, being thus in possession of the chattel, it follows that the property in the chattel was vested in him. Obviously the right of the original owner could not be established; . . .'

> . . .

The test of possession, in its most abstract form, may have a constant meaning whether applied to objects in or unattached and on land. But it is clear from Pollock and Wright's statement, citing *Elwes* v *Brigg Gas Co*, 33 Ch D 562, that they regarded its application to objects in land to be free from the uncertainties inherent in disputes about entitlement to unattached objects found on land. Their proposition was that in practice possession of land should generally be taken as carrying with it an intent to possession of objects in or attached to it. To the extent that Lord Russell of Killowen CJ's words in the *Sharman* case [1896] 2 QB 44 may be construed as ignoring that distinction, they go beyond Pollock and Wright's test for objects in or attached to land and beyond what was necessary for the decision. That is certainly how A L Goodhart viewed it in his article in 3 CLJ 195, 206–207 . . .

Donaldson LJ in his review of the authorities and statement of the principles that he derived from them in *Parker* v *British Airways Board* [1982] QB 1004, appears to have been of the same view. As to objects found in or attached to land, he said, at p 1010:

> '. . . The rationale of this rule is probably either that the chattel is to be treated as an integral part of the realty as against all but the true owner and so incapable of being lost or that the "finder" has to do something to the realty in order to get at or detach the chattel and, if he is not thereby to become a trespasser, will have to justify his actions by reference to some form of licence from the occupier. In all likely circumstances that licence will give the occupier a superior right to that of the finder . . .'

. . .

Mr Munby . . . argued that it is against commonsense that it should make all the difference whether an object is just under or on the surface . . . Mr Munby gave as one of a number of examples in support of his argument, a lost watch on a muddy path which might within a day or two become covered by a thin coating of mud. Why, he asked, should the landowner's claim be different and stronger when the watch finally, but only just, disappears from sight?

In my view, the authorities reveal a number of sound and practical reasons for the distinction.

First, as Donaldson LJ said in *Parker* v *British Airways Board* [1982] QB 1004, 1010, an object in land 'is to be treated as an integral part of the realty as against all but the true owner' or that the finder in detaching the object would, in the absence of licence to do so, become a trespasser. Mr Munby suggested that this is wrong because if an object is treated as part of the realty the true owner cannot have priority. However, the English law of ownership and possession, unlike that of Roman Law, is not a system of identifying absolute entitlement but of priority of entitlement, and Donaldson LJ's rationale is consistent with that . . .

Second, removal of an object in or attached to land would normally involve interference with the land and may damage it . . .

Third, putting aside the borderline case of a recently lost article which has worked its way just under the surface, in the case of an object in the ground its original owner is unlikely in most cases to be there to claim it. The law, therefore, looks for a substitute owner, the owner or possessor of the land in which it is lodged. Whereas in the case of an unattached object on the surface, it is likely in most cases to have been recently lost, and the true owner may well claim it.

Comment

(1) Auld LJ went on to deny that the public nature of the park made any difference.

(2) Is the distinction between objects in or under the land, as opposed to on it, justified by (i) authority and (ii) principle?

(3) If the occupier is neither aware of the object nor manifests an intention to exercise control, why should the occupier succeed? Is the answer a dislike of metal detectors?

(4) Counsel argued that if the object was really treated as 'an integral part of the realty', then it was inexplicable that the rights of the true owner remain. Is counsel's argument adequately answered by Auld LJ?

(iv) Finder–predecessor in title disputes

Suppose the occupier, in circumstances where the occupier would have a good claim, is unaware of the object and sells the land to a purchaser who finds it. Does the seller have a better claim than the finder? What does *Moffatt* v *Kazana*[7] tell us about this situation? Is it materially different because the seller was the true owner?

Extract 4.1.9

Hoath [1992] Conv 348 at pp 350–351 (footnotes partly omitted)

. . . However, even though the object in question has not become a fixture, and even though section 62 cannot operate in this context, the purchaser of the land may still be able to take over his predecessors' rights to claim objects found on or in the land, where they are found after the conveyance or transfer to him. Where the previous owner of the land was not the 'true owner' of the object, then he will never have acquired any 'absolute property or ownership'[i] in

---

[7] Extract 4.1.3 above.

it; he will merely have had a right to claim a limited title to the object if found during his own period of ownership and occupation of the land. It is submitted that this limited right will pass to the purchaser (quite independently of section 62) as an ordinary common law incident of land ownership, unless the conveyance or transfer expressly provides to the contrary . . .

[i] *Per* Donaldson LJ in *Parker* v *British Airways Board* [1982] 1 All ER 834, 843, CA.

Comment

(1) Is this argument based upon principle or convenience?

(2) *Merry* v *Green*,[8] Extract 4.1.11 below, is admitted to be a contrary authority.

What happens if the finder is a tenant and the predecessor in title is the landlord?

Extract 4.1.10

Elwes v *Brigg Gas Company* (1886) 33 Ch D 562

A tenant discovered a prehistoric boat when excavating the leased land as part of building works.

CHITTY J: . . . The boat did not pass to them by the mere demise; a lease being only a contract for the possession and profits of the land . . . As against the lessors the permission [to excavate and remove the soil] ought not to be carried beyond what may be reasonably inferred to have been the intention of the parties . . . The implied permission to remove and dispose ought then to extend to what the parties might fairly be deemed to have contemplated would be found in making the excavations; but beyond this point it ought not to be carried. The existence of the boat was unknown and its discovery was not contemplated. In my opinion, then, the license to remove and dispose extended to the clay and ordinary soil likely to be found in pursuing the license to excavate, but it did not extend to what was unknown and not contemplated, and therefore did not comprise the boat.

Comment

Should the length of the lease make any difference? Should lessees be better or worse off than purchasers?

B. Things found in chattels

Extract 4.1.11

Merry v *Green* (1841) 7 M&W 623 (151 ER 916)

The plaintiff, having bought a bureau ('secretary') at auction, discovered a purse containing money in a hidden compartment.

PARKE B: . . . It was contended that there was a delivery of the secretary, and the money in it, to the plaintiff as his own property, which gave him a lawful possession, and that his subsequent misappropriation did not constitute a felony. But it seems to us, that though there was a delivery of the secretary, and a lawful property in it thereby vested in the plaintiff, there was no delivery so as to give a lawful possession of the purse and money. The vendor had no intention to deliver it, nor the vendee to receive it; both were ignorant of its existence . . .

[8] (1841) 7 M&W 623 (151 ER 916).

Comment

It appears that the vendor was not the true owner of the purse. If so, is there any justification for the vendor's having a better claim than the plaintiff? How does it fit Hoath's analysis (Extract 4.1.9 above)?

C. Treasure

Extract 4.1.12

Treasure Act 1996

1.—(1) Treasure is—
- (a) any object at least 300 years old when found which—
    - (i) is not a coin but has metallic content of which at least 10% by weight is precious metal;
    - (ii) when found, is one of at least two coins in the same find which are at least 300 years old at that time and have that percentage of precious metal; or
    - (iii) when found, is one of at least ten coins in the same find which are at least 300 years old at that time;
- (b) any object at least 200 years old when found which belongs to a class designated under section 2(1);

. . .

- (d) any object which, when found, is part of the same find as—
    - (i) an object within paragraph (a), (b) or (c) found at the same time or earlier; or
    - (ii) an object found earlier which would be within paragraph (a) or (b) if it had been found at the same time.

2.—(1) The Secretary of State may by order, for the purposes of section 1(1)(b), designate any class of object which he considers to be of outstanding historical, archaeological or cultural importance.

3.—(3) 'Precious metal' means gold or silver.

4.—(1) When treasure is found, it vests, subject to prior interests and rights—
- (a) in the franchisee, if there is one;
- (b) otherwise, in the Crown.

6.—(4) If the Crown's title is disclaimed, the treasure—
- (a) is deemed not to have vested in the Crown under this Act, and
- (b) without prejudice to the interests or rights of others, may be delivered to any person in accordance with the code published under section 11.

8.—(1) A person who finds an object which he believes or has reasonable grounds for believing is treasure must notify the coroner for the district in which the object was found before the end of the notice period.

(3) Any person who fails to comply with subsection (1) is guilty of an offence . . .

10.—(1) This section applies if treasure—
- (a) has vested in the Crown under section 4; and
- (b) is to be transferred to a museum.

(2) The Secretary of State must determine whether a reward is to be paid by the museum before the transfer.

(6) Payment of the reward is not enforceable against a museum or the Secretary of State.

(7) In a determination under this section, the Secretary of State must take into account anything relevant in the code of practice issued under section 11.

Extract 4.1.13

Treasure Act 1996: Code of Practice (revised)

II. Guidelines for the payment of rewards where the finder is searching for artefacts

72.   Those eligible to receive rewards are the finder(s), landowner and/or occupier. Where the finder has a valid permission from the occupier or landowner to be on the land where he made his find in order to search for and remove artefacts he will receive his full share of the reward. The burden of proof as to whether he has permission will rest with the finder. It is normal practice to divide rewards equally between the finder and landowner on a 50:50 basis unless another form of agreement has been reached between them . . .

79.   Finders may expect to receive no rewards at all or abated rewards under the following circumstances:

(i)   where the finder has committed an offence under section 8 of the Act by failing to report treasure within 14 days of making the find . . . ;

(vii) where there are reasonable grounds for believing that the finder was trespassing;

(viii) where significant damage has been done deliberately or recklessly . . . ;

. . .

It will be within the discretion of the Secretary of State to decide by how much the reward to the finder is to be abated in such circumstances or whether no reward will be payable at all to the finder.

80.   In such circumstances the occupier or the landowner will be eligible for the whole of the balance of the reward in such proportion as the Secretary of State may determine, according to the principles laid down in paragraph 74,[i] provided that there is no evidence that they have been a party to wrong behaviour on the part of the finder . . .

III. Guidelines for the payment of rewards where the finder was not searching for artefacts

82.   Where the finder, who has not been searching for artefacts, makes a chance find and where he clearly has permission to be where he made his find and where he has reported his find according to the law, then the reward will be divided in whatever proportions the Secretary of State thinks fit, taking account of the circumstances of each case. In most cases the finder or finders may expect to receive half of the reward . . .

83.   Where the finder has not been searching for artefacts and there are reasonable grounds for believing that the finder did not have permission to be where he made the find, then it may be appropriate for the reward to be divided between the finder, the occupier and the landowner, the Secretary of State being able to use discretion according to the individual circumstances of the case.

[i] [Substantially, 'the person who would have been entitled to give permission to enter the land to search for treasure'.]

Comment

(1) One of the principal purposes of the legislation is to ensure that significant archaeological finds are reported and available to the public. How far does the legislation advance these objectives?

(2) Do the guidelines regarding rewards reflect normal finding principles?

2. Adverse possession

Most legal systems discourage stale claims. In this section, we will concentrate on claims to land. We shall see that the Land Registration Act 2002 (hereafter LRA, or 2002 Act) has changed the area almost beyond recognition for registered titles.

Nourse LJ described the traditional principles as follows:[9]

> Under most systems of law a squatter who has been in long possession of land can acquire title to it in the place of the true owner. The Scots and continental systems, more faithful to the Roman law, have opted for prescription, a doctrine founded on the fiction that the land has been granted to the squatter. In England, prescription, although a shoot well favoured by the common law, was stunted in its lateral growth by the statutes of limitation . . . Limitation, so far from being founded on some fictional grant, extinguishes the right of the true owner to recover the land, so that the squatter's possession becomes impregnable, giving him a title superior to all others.
>
> The essential difference between prescription and limitation is that in the former case title can be acquired only by possession as of right. That is the antithesis of what is required for limitation, which perhaps can be described as possession as of wrong . . . But with limitation it is the intention of the squatter which is decisive. He must intend to possess the land to the exclusion of all the world, including the true owner, while the intention of the latter is, with one exception, entirely beside the point.

Comment

Why is it significant whether there is a system of prescription or limitation?

A. Can adverse possession be justified today?

Extract 4.2.1

Law Commission No 271: Land Registration for the Twenty First Century: A Conveyancing Revolution (footnotes omitted)

2.71 The reasons why there is a doctrine of adverse possession are well known and often stated, but they need to be tested. For example, it is frequently said that the doctrine is an embodiment of the policy that defendants should be protected from stale claims and that claimants should not sleep on their rights. However, it is possible for a squatter to acquire title by adverse possession without the owner realising it. This may be because the adverse possession is either clandestine or not readily apparent. It may be because the owner has more land than he or she can realistically police. Many public bodies fall into this category. A local authority, for example, cannot in practice keep an eye on every single piece of land that it owns to ensure that no one is encroaching on it. But the owner may not even realise that a person is encroaching on his or her land. He or she may think that someone is there with permission and it may take an expensive journey to the Court of Appeal to discover whether or not this is so. In none of these examples is a person in any true sense sleeping on his or her rights. Furthermore, even if a landowner does realise that someone – typically a neighbour – is encroaching on his or her land, he or she may be reluctant to take issue over the incursion, particularly if it is comparatively slight. He or she may not wish to sour relations with the neighbour and is, perhaps, afraid of the consequences of so doing. It may not only affect relations with the neighbour but may also bring opprobrium upon him or her in the neighbourhood. In any event, even if the

---

[9] *Buckinghamshire CC v Moran* [1990] Ch 623 at p 644.

policy against allowing stale claims is sound, the consequences of it under the present law – the loss for ever of a person's land – can be extremely harsh and have been judicially described as disproportionate.

2.72 There are other grounds for the doctrine of adverse possession that have greater weight. Land is a precious resource and should be kept in use and in commerce. A person may be in adverse possession where the true owner has disappeared and there is no other claimant for the land. Or he or she may have acquired the land informally so that the legal ownership is not a reflection of the practical reality. A person may have innocently entered land, quite reasonably believing that he or she owned it, perhaps because of uncertainties as to the boundaries.

2.73 In relation to land with unregistered title, there are cogent legal reasons for the doctrine. The principles of adverse possession do in fact presuppose unregistered title and make sense in relation to it. This is because the basis of title to unregistered land is ultimately possession. The person best entitled to the land is the person with the best right to possession of it. As we explain below, the investigation of title to unregistered land is facilitated (and therefore costs less) because earlier rights to possess can be extinguished by adverse possession. However, where title is registered, the basis of title is primarily the fact of registration rather than possession. It is the fact of registration that vests the legal title in the registered proprietor. This is so, even if the transfer to the proprietor was a nullity as, for example, where it was a forgery. The ownership of land is therefore apparent from the register and only a change in the register can take that title away. It is noteworthy that, in many Commonwealth states which have systems of title registration, these considerations have led to changes in the law governing acquisition of title by adverse possession. In some states it has been abolished altogether. In others, it has been modified. As we have indicated above, the doctrine of adverse possession does have benefits and we do not therefore favour outright abolition in relation to registered land. However, we consider that the balance between landowner and squatter needs to be adjusted to overcome some of the deficiencies outlined above, while maintaining the advantages it can offer. We have therefore devised a modified scheme of adverse possession that attempts to achieve that balance and is at the same time appropriate to the principles of registered title.

Comment

(1) How convincing are the justifications for adverse possession? Do they justify a system of limitation rather than prescription?

(2) How far do these justifications extend to registered land?

(3) Note that there is no requirement of good faith for adverse possession. Would such a requirement improve the law?

(4) In some instances, statute has made squatting a crime. Would you expect this to act as a bar to adverse possession?[10]

Extract 4.2.2

JA Pye (Oxford) Ltd v Graham **[2000] Ch 676**

An adverse possession claim was brought 15 years after the termination of a licence. In this Extract, we are interested in the broader ramifications of adverse possession claims and the human rights implications.

---

[10] See *R (Best)* v *Chief Land Registrar* [2015] EWCA Civ 17.

NEUBERGER J: A frequent justification for limitation periods generally is that people should not be able to sit on their rights indefinitely, and that is a proposition to which at least in general nobody could take exception. However, if as in the present case the owner of land has no immediate use for it and is content to let another person trespass on the land for the time being, it is hard to see what principle of justice entitles the trespasser to acquire the land for nothing from the owner simply because he has been permitted to remain there for 12 years. To say that in such circumstances the owner who has sat on his rights should therefore be deprived of his land appears to me to be illogical and disproportionate. Illogical because the only reason that the owner can be said to have sat on his rights is because of the existence of the 12-year limitation period in the first place; if no limitation period existed he would be entitled to claim possession whenever he actually wanted the land. Of course one can well see the justification for saying that the owner should not be entitled to recover damages for trespass going back more than six years; that involves rather different considerations. I believe that the result is disproportionate because, particularly in a climate of increasing awareness of human rights including the right to enjoy one's own property, it does seem draconian to the owner and a windfall for the squatter that, just because the owner has taken no steps to evict a squatter for 12 years, the owner should lose 25 hectares of land to the squatter with no compensation whatsoever.

Comment

The human rights aspects were not pursued in the House of Lords[11] because the legislation had not been in force at the time of the hearing before Neuberger J. The House of Lords held that the adverse possession claim succeeded, though Lords Bingham and Hope expressed unease with the operation of the adverse possession rules. The case then went to the European Court of Human Rights. Although the Chamber held in favour of Pye,[12] the case was then heard by the Grand Chamber – the subject of the following extract.

Extract 4.2.3

JA Pye (Oxford) Ltd v *United Kingdom* (2007) 46 EHRR 1083

EUROPEAN COURT OF HUMAN RIGHTS: 68.   The Court has considered limitation periods as such in the context of Art 6 of the Convention in the case of *Stubbings* v *United Kingdom*. It held as follows:

> 'It is noteworthy that limitation periods in personal injury cases are a common feature of the domestic legal systems of the Contracting States. They serve several important purposes, namely to ensure legal certainty and finality, protect potential defendants from stale claims which might be difficult to counter and prevent the injustice which might arise if courts were required to decide upon events which took place in the distant past on the basis of evidence which might have become unreliable and incomplete because of the passage of time.'

69.   Although that statement referred to limitation periods in personal injury cases in the context of Art 6, the Court considers that it can also be applied to the situation where limitation periods in actions for recovery of land are being assessed in the light of Art 1 of Protocol No 1. Indeed, the parties do not suggest that limitation periods for actions for recovery of land do not pursue a legitimate aim in the general interest.

---

[11] [2003] 1 AC 419 at [65], [73].
[12] *JA Pye (Oxford) Ltd* v *United Kingdom* (2005) 43 EHRR 43 (4:3 majority). The first instance decision in *Beaulane Properties Ltd* v *Palmer* [2006] Ch 79 had likewise found adverse possession of registered land inconsistent with human rights.

70.   The Court finds that the existence of a 12-year limitation period for actions for recovery of land as such pursues a legitimate aim in the general interest.

71.   As to the existence, over and above the general interest in the limitation period, of a specific general interest in the extinguishment of title and the attribution of new title at the end of the limitation period, the Court recalls that in discussing the public interest present in the case of *Jahn*, in the context of a deprivation of property, it stated that:

> '[F]inding it natural that the margin of appreciation available to the legislature in implementing social and economic policies should be a wide one [the Court] will respect the legislature's judgment as to what is "in the public interest" unless that judgment is manifestly without reasonable foundation.'

This is particularly true in cases such as the present one where what is at stake is a longstanding and complex area of law which regulates private law matters between individuals.

72.   It is plain from the comparative material submitted by the parties that a large number of Member States possesses some form of mechanism for transferring title in accordance with principles similar to adverse possession in the common law systems, and that such transfer is effected without the payment of compensation to the original owner.

73.   The Court further notes, as did the Chamber, that the amendments to the system of adverse possession contained in the Land Registration Act 2002 did not abolish the relevant provisions of the 1925 and the 1980 Acts. Parliament thus confirmed the domestic view that the traditional general interest remained valid.

74.   It is a characteristic of property that different countries regulate its use and transfer in a variety of ways. The relevant rules reflect social policies against the background of the local conception of the importance and role of property. Even where title to real property is registered, it must be open to the legislature to attach more weight to lengthy, unchallenged possession than to the formal fact of registration. The Court accepts that to extinguish title where the former owner is prevented, as a consequence of the application of the law, from recovering possession of land cannot be said to be manifestly without reasonable foundation. There existed therefore a general interest in both the limitation period itself and the extinguishment of title at the end of the period.

5 Whether there was a fair balance

75.   The second paragraph of Art 1 is to be construed in the light of the general principle enunciated in the opening sentence. There must, in respect of a 'control of use', also exist a reasonable relationship of proportionality between the means employed and the aim sought to be realised. In other words, the Court must determine whether a fair balance has been struck between the demands of the general interest and the interest of the individuals concerned. In determining whether a fair balance exists, the Court recognises that the State enjoys a wide margin of appreciation, with regard both to choosing the means of enforcement and to ascertaining whether the consequences of enforcement are justified in the general interest for the purpose of achieving the object of the law in question. In spheres such as housing, the Court will respect the legislature's judgment as to what is in the general interest unless that judgment is manifestly without reasonable foundation.

76.   The Chamber found that the relevant provisions – s 75 of the 1925 Act in particular – went further than merely precluding the applicant companies from invoking the assistance of the courts to recover possession of their property. The Court recalls that the Court of Appeal in the present case was of the view that the Grahams had not established the requisite intention to possess the land, so that time had not started to run against the applicant companies. It nevertheless considered that the extinguishment of title at the end of the limitation period of an

action for recovery of land was a logical and pragmatic consequence of the barring of the right to bring an action after the expiration of the limitation period. The House of Lords disavowed the Court of Appeal's interpretation of the law on intention to possess, but did not comment on the suggestion that to terminate title at the end of the limitation period was 'logical and pragmatic'. Even though the general position in English law is that the expiry of a limitation period bars the remedy but not the right, the Court accepts that where an action for recovery of land is statute-barred, termination of the title of the paper owner does little more than regularise the respective positions, namely to confirm that the person who has acquired title by 12 years' adverse possession is the owner. Moreover, the law reflected the aim of the land registration legislation, which was to replicate the pre-registration law so far as practicable. As already noted above, such a regime cannot be considered as 'manifestly without reasonable foundation'.

77. . . . The fact that the rules contained in both the 1925 and the 1980 Acts had been in force for many years before the first applicant even acquired the land is nevertheless relevant to an assessment of the overall proportionality of the legislation. In particular, it is not open to the applicant companies to say that they were not aware of the legislation, or that its application to the facts of the present case came as a surprise to them. Indeed, although the case proceeded domestically as far as the House of Lords, the applicant companies do not suggest that the conclusions of the domestic courts were unreasonable or unforeseeable, in the light of the legislation.

79. The Chamber and the applicant companies emphasised the absence of compensation for what they both perceived as a deprivation of the applicant companies' possessions. The Court has found that the interference with the applicant companies' possessions was a control of use, rather than a deprivation of possessions, such that the case law on compensation for deprivations is not directly applicable. Further, in the cases in which a situation was analysed as a control of use, even though the applicant had lost possessions, no mention was made of a right to compensation. The Court would note, in agreement with the Government, that a requirement of compensation for the situation brought about by a party failing to observe a limitation period would sit uneasily alongside the very concept of limitation periods, whose aim is to further legal certainty by preventing a party from pursuing an action after a certain date. . . .

81. It is true that since the entry into force of the Land Registration Act 2002, the paper owner of registered land against whom time has been running is in a better position than were the applicant companies at the relevant time. . . . In any event, legislative changes in complex areas such as land law take time to bring about, and judicial criticism of legislation cannot of itself affect the conformity of the earlier provisions with the Convention.

82. The Government contended that it could not be the role of Art 1 of Protocol No 1 to protect commercial operators against their own failings. The Court regards this suggestion as related to those aspects of the Court's case law which underline that the Court is not in theory required to settle disputes of a private nature, in respect of which states enjoy a wide margin of appreciation. In a case such as the present, where the Court is considering, principally, the statutory regime by which title is extinguished at the end of the limitation period, rather than the specific facts of the case, the relevance of the individual applicant's conduct is correspondingly restricted.

83. The applicant companies contended that their loss was so great, and the windfall to the Grahams so significant, that the fair balance required by Art 1 of Protocol No 1 was upset . . . In the present case . . . , whilst it would be strained to talk of the 'acquired rights' of an adverse possessor during the currency of the limitation period, it must be recalled that the registered land regime in the United Kingdom is a reflection of a long-established system in which a term of years' possession gave sufficient title to sell. Such arrangements fall within the state's margin of appreciation, unless they give rise to results which are so anomalous as to render the legislation unacceptable. The acquisition of unassailable rights by the adverse possessor must go hand in hand with a corresponding loss of property rights for the former owner . . .

DISSENTING OPINION: O-I9. . . . We find much force in the view of Lord Bingham in the present case, endorsed by Judge Loucaides in his dissenting opinion, that where land is registered, it is difficult to see any justification for a legal rule which compels such an apparently unjust result as to deprive the owner of his beneficial title in favour of an adverse possessor. However, not only is the taking of property as a result of adverse possession a feature common to many legal systems, including other common law systems, but, despite the important changes to the system of adverse possession made by the Act of 2002 in the case of registered land, the system itself has not been abolished. In these circumstances, we share the view of the majority that the extinction of the beneficial ownership of the registered title-holder following the expiry of 12 years of adverse possession cannot be said to be manifestly without reasonable foundation and that the system, as applied in the case of the present applicants, may therefore be said to have served a legitimate aim in the general interest.

O-I10.   The central question remains whether the rules of adverse possession applicable to registered land and applied in the present case struck a fair balance between the rights of the registered owners and the general interest served by that system or whether, as the applicant companies argue, they were required to bear 'an individual and excessive burden'. It is primarily on this point that we part company with the majority of the Court.

O-I11.   The striking feature of the manner in which the rules on adverse possession applied in the present case is the contrast between the gravity of the interference with the owners' property rights and the justification provided for that interference.

O-I15.   While we can accept that, where land is abandoned, it may be in the general interest that it should be acquired by someone who would put it to effective use, we are unable to accept that the general interest would extend to depriving a registered landowner of his beneficial title to the land except by a proper process of compulsory acquisition for fair compensation.

O-I18.   While the general interest served by the law of adverse possession in the case of registered land was thus in our view of limited weight, the impact of the law on the registered landowner was exceptionally serious, as is graphically illustrated by the facts of the present case. Although the case falls to be examined under Art 1 of the Protocol as one concerning the control of use of land, in judging the proportionality of the measures it is in our view a highly material factor that the relevant legislative provisions went further than merely precluding the registered landowners from invoking the assistance of the courts to recover possession of their land, by depriving them of their beneficial ownership of it.

O-I21.   While the absence of compensation cannot thus of itself be regarded as rendering the control of use disproportionate, the fact that the landowner received no compensation made the loss of beneficial ownership the more serious and required, in our view, particularly strong measures of protection of the registered owner's property rights if a fair balance was to be preserved.

O-I23.   . . . no form of notification was required to be given to the owner during the currency of that period [the 12-year period] to alert him to the risk of losing his title to the land. What was lacking were effective safeguards to protect a registered landlord from losing beneficial ownership of land through oversight or inadvertence. Such safeguards were provided by the Land Registration Act 2002 . . .

O-I25.   . . . the amendments made by the 2002 Act represented more than a natural evolution in the law of adverse possession as it affected registered land; they marked a major change in the existing system which had been recognised, both by the Law Commission and judicially, as leading to unfairness and as having a disproportionate effect on the rights of the registered owner.

Comment

(1) The decision was reached on a ten to seven majority. The quoted dissenting opinion is that of five judges. See also Extract 2.1.2 above.

(2) On what basis did the judges disagree? Which arguments are the stronger?

(3) The case clearly closes the door on the question,[13] though the challenge to adverse possession was relevant only to registered land pre-2002. Is the decision likely to impact on human rights challenges to other areas of property law?

B. Adverse possession against registered estates

LRA, s 96 disapplies for registered land the existing statutory provisions which give effect to adverse possession. Schedule 6 to the Act provides details as to how adverse possession will operate in future.

(i) Applying for registration

Extract 4.2.4

Land Registration Act 2002, Sched 6, paras 1–2; s 98

1 (1)   A person may apply to the registrar to be registered as the proprietor of a registered estate in land if he has been in adverse possession of the estate for the period of ten years ending on the date of the application.

(2)   A person may also apply to the registrar to be registered as the proprietor of a registered estate in land if—

(a) he has in the period of six months ending on the date of the application ceased to be in adverse possession of the estate because of eviction by the registered proprietor, or a person claiming under the registered proprietor,

(b) on the day before his eviction he was entitled to make an application under sub-paragraph (1), and

(c) the eviction was not pursuant to a judgment for possession.

(3)   However, a person may not make an application under this paragraph if—

(a) he is a defendant in proceedings which involve asserting a right to possession of the land, or

(b) judgment for possession of the land has been given against him in the last two years.

(4)   For the purposes of sub-paragraph (1), the estate need not have been registered throughout the period of adverse possession.

2 (1)   The registrar must give notice of an application under paragraph 1 to—

(a) the proprietor of the estate to which the application relates,

(b) the proprietor of any registered charge on the estate,

(c) where the estate is leasehold, the proprietor of any superior registered estate,

(d) any person who is registered in accordance with rules as a person to be notified under this paragraph, and

(e) such other persons as rules may provide.

98.—(1)   A person has a defence to an action for possession of land if—

(a) on the day immediately preceding that on which the action was brought he was entitled to make an application under paragraph 1 of Schedule 6 to be registered as the proprietor of an estate in the land, and

(b) had he made such an application on that day, the condition in paragraph 5(4) of that Schedule would have been satisfied.

---

[13] Confirmed by *Ofulue v Bossert* [2009] Ch 1 (not challenged in the House of Lords: [2009] AC 990 at [73]).

(2)   A judgment for possession of land ceases to be enforceable at the end of the period of two years beginning with the date of the judgment if the proceedings in which the judgment is given were commenced against a person who was at that time entitled to make an application under paragraph 1 of Schedule 6.

(5)   Where in any proceedings a court determines that—

(a)   a person is entitled to a defence under this section, or

. . .

the court must order the registrar to register him as the proprietor of the estate in relation to which he is entitled to make an application under Schedule 6.

Comment

(1) A para 1 application is the first stage in the procedure: it certainly does not mean that the adverse possession claim will succeed.

(2) Note that the period is ten years – to be contrasted with the normal 12-year period for adverse possession in unregistered land. The Law Commission has proposed reducing this 12-year period to ten years.[14]

(3) In unregistered land it does not matter that adverse possession has ceased after the 12-year period has been completed. By contrast, under para 1(1) adverse possession must be for the period immediately before the application: the logic is that the passing of time no longer by itself terminates the paper title. Paragraph 1(2) protects those who have been out of possession for up to six months. Why does this relaxation exist?

(4) Paragraph 1(3) and s 98 establish the interrelationship between the new rules and court proceedings. The fundamental principles are that (i) the holder of the paper title (O) can take court proceedings and these will usually defeat any Sched 6 rights (note that any court order ceases to be effective after two years); (ii) but in those rare cases where the adverse possession claim will succeed despite opposition by the owner (O) (see the cross-reference in s 98 to para 5(4): Extract 4.2.5 below) those court proceedings will fail; (iii) otherwise, the court has no jurisdiction to determine adverse possession claims.[15]

(ii) Resolution of objections

Extract 4.2.5

Land Registration Act 2002, Sched 6, paras 3–5

3   (1)   A person given notice under paragraph 2 may require that the application to which the notice relates be dealt with under paragraph 5.

(2)   The right under this paragraph is exercisable by notice to the registrar given before the end of such period as rules may provide.

4   If an application under paragraph 1 is not required to be dealt with under paragraph 5, the applicant is entitled to be entered in the register as the new proprietor of the estate.

5   (1)   If an application under paragraph 1 is required to be dealt with under this paragraph, the applicant is only entitled to be registered as the new proprietor of the estate if any of the following conditions is met.

---

[14] Law Com No 270, para 4.130.
[15] *Swan Housing Association Ltd* v *Gill* [2013] 1 WLR 1253 (a result of LRA, s 96).

(2) The first condition is that—
  (a) it would be unconscionable because of an equity by estoppel for the registered pro-
       prietor to seek to dispossess the applicant, and
  (b) the circumstances are such that the applicant ought to be registered as the proprietor.
(3) The second condition is that the applicant is for some other reason entitled to be
registered as the proprietor of the estate.
(4) The third condition is that—
  (a) the land to which the application relates is adjacent to land belonging to the applicant,
  (b) the exact line of the boundary between the two has not been determined under rules
       under section 60,
  (c) for at least ten years of the period of adverse possession ending on the date of the
       application, the applicant (or any predecessor in title) reasonably believed that the land
       to which the application relates belonged to him, and
  (d) the estate to which the application relates was registered more than one year prior
       to the date of the application.
(5) In relation to an application under paragraph 1(2), this paragraph has effect as if the
reference in sub-paragraph (4)(c) to the date of the application were to the day before the date
of the applicant's eviction.

Comment

(1) Paragraph 4 provides that the applicant squatter (S) is entitled to be registered if O fails
to object. What policy objectives does this satisfy? The notice will be sent to O's address as
held by the land registry. What problems might this give rise to? If no objection is lodged,
can the registration of S ever be attacked?[16]

(2) If O does object, then the squatter (S) will succeed only if one of the three conditions in
para 5 is satisfied. Paragraph 5(2) and (3) apply where S has a separate claim to ownership
– S has no need to rely on adverse possession. Why, then, should they be brought within
Sched 6?

(3) Paragraph 5(4) provides the single example where a contested adverse possession claim
will be successful today. Why does it exist? How commonly is it likely to apply? When
looking at old claims to adverse possession later in this chapter, it is worth considering
whether they would today fall within para 5(4).

(4) Must the reasonable belief in para 5(4)(c) be for the *last* ten years?[17]

(iii) Further applications for registration

Extract 4.2.6

Land Registration Act 2002, Sched 6, paras 6–7

6 (1) Where a person's application under paragraph 1 is rejected, he may make a further
application to be registered as the proprietor of the estate if he is in adverse possession of the
estate from the date of the application until the last day of the period of two years beginning
with the date of its rejection.

---

[16] See *Baxter* v *Mannion* [2011] 1 WLR 1594 (no adverse possession for the required period).
[17] See *IAM Group plc* v *Chowdery* [2013] 2 P&CR 282 at [30] and *Zarb* v *Parry* [2012] 1 WLR 1240 at [17]; neither
     case indicates that the burden on S is unduly heavy.

(2) However, a person may not make an application under this paragraph if—
    (a) he is a defendant in proceedings which involve asserting a right to possession of the land,
    (b) judgment for possession of the land has been given against him in the last two years, or
    (c) he has been evicted from the land pursuant to a judgment for possession.

7 If a person makes an application under paragraph 6, he is entitled to be entered in the register as the new proprietor of the estate.

Comment

(1) Why should such a further application be permitted? What is its effect?

(2) Paragraph 6(2) makes provision for court proceedings, in a similar manner to para 1. They are especially important in this context, as it is expected that O will take steps to evict S after objecting under para 3(1). Section 98(3) protects S against court proceedings after S has become entitled to make a para 6 application.

(iv) Successive adverse possessors

We are here considering situations where S evicts O but S then either transfers his or her rights to S^2 or is evicted by S^2.

Extract 4.2.7

Land Registration Act 2002, Sched 6, para 11

11 (2) A person is also to be regarded for those purposes as having been in adverse possession of an estate in land—
    (a) where he is the successor in title to an estate in the land, during any period of adverse possession by a predecessor in title to that estate, or
    (b) during any period of adverse possession by another person which comes between, and is continuous with, periods of adverse possession of his own.

Comment

(1) Suppose that S has been there for four years and S^2 for seven years. How do the Sched 6 rules apply? Would it be different if either of them had been there for, say, 12 years?

(2) These rules are not identical to those applying to unregistered land.[18] What justification is there for them?

C. Requirements for adverse possession

(i) Possession; *animus possidendi*

Factual possession and intention to possess are two separate requirements. However, they are closely related in the cases. The same rules apply for both registered and unregistered land.[19]

---

[18] See p 96 below. In unregistered land, S^2 can count S's period of adverse possession even if S had been dispossessed by S^2.

[19] See LRA, Sched 6, para 11(1): 'A person is in adverse possession of an estate in land for the purposes of this Schedule if, but for section 96, a period of limitation under section 15 of the Limitation Act 1980 (c. 58) would run in his favour in relation to the estate.'

Extract 4.2.8

Buckinghamshire CC v Moran [1990] Ch 623

A person claiming adverse possession had incorporated council owned land (for which it had no immediate use) into part of his garden.

SLADE LJ: . . . It is clear that, under the Act of 1980 as under the previous law, the person claiming a possessory title must show either (1) discontinuance by the paper owner followed by possession, or (2) dispossession (or, as it is sometimes called 'ouster') of the paper owner . . .

In the present case the judge found that the council had never discontinued its possession of the plot, and this finding is not challenged on this appeal. The defendant's claim is that the council had been dispossessed of the plot by him more than 12 years before it instituted its proceedings.

. . .

[After noting that the Limitation Act 1980 had abrogated a doctrine whereby an owner with no present use for the land was treated as impliedly licensing the possession, which therefore could not be adverse:] However, Mr Douglas, on behalf of the council, while accepting that the implied licence doctrine is now abrogated, nevertheless submits that paragraph 8(1) [of Schedule 1] (I quote from his skeleton argument):

'leaves intact the special rule formulated by Bramwell LJ in *Leigh* v *Jack* (1879) 5 Ex D 264 and Sir John Pennycuick in *Treloar* v *Nute* [1976] 1 WLR 1295 that where land is acquired or retained by the owner for a specific future purpose, then acts of trespass which are not inconsistent with such purpose do not amount to dispossession.'

The origin of the suggested 'special rule' is said to be the often cited statement of Bramwell LJ in *Leigh* v *Jack*, 5 Ex D 264, 273, where he said:

'in order to defeat a title by dispossessing the former owner, acts must be done which are inconsistent with his enjoyment of the soil for the purposes for which he intended to use it: that is not the case here, where the intention of the plaintiff and her predecessors in title was not either to build upon or to cultivate the land, but to devote it at some future time to public purposes.'

. . .

On any footing, it must, in my judgment, be too broad a proposition to suggest that an owner who retains a piece of land with a view to its utilisation for a specific purpose in the future can never be treated as dispossessed, however firm and obvious the intention to dispossess, and however drastic the acts of dispossession of the person seeking to dispossess him may be. Furthermore, while it may well be correct to say that the implied licence doctrine (so long as it survived) itself involved the 'adaptation' of the literal application of the statutory provisions 'to meet one special type of case', I do not think it correct to suggest that the decisions in *Leigh* v *Jack*, 5 Ex D 264, or *Williams Brothers Direct Supply Ltd* v *Raftery* [1958] 1 QB 159 (or indeed any other decisions prior to *Wallis's* case [1975] QB 94) authorise or justify an application of the statutory provisions otherwise than in accordance with their ordinary and natural meaning.

In the course of my judgment in *Powell* v *McFarlane*, 38 P&CR 452, 472–474, I considered in some detail the decisions in *Leigh* v *Jack* and *Williams Brothers Direct Supply Ltd* v *Raftery* and *Tecbild Ltd* v *Chamberlain* (1969) 20 P&CR 633 . . . :

'I incline to the view that the ratio decidendi of all the various judgments in cases such as *Leigh* v *Jack*, the *Williams* case and *Tecbild Ltd* v *Chamberlain* was either (a) that the necessary animus possidendi had not been shown or (b) that the acts relied on had been too trivial to amount to the taking of actual possession; some members of each court seem to have relied on the first ground and others on the second. I venture to think that all these three decisions are readily explicable, not so much on the basis of any imputed licence, but merely on the grounds that in circumstances where an owner has no present use for his land but has future plans for its use (for example by development or by dedication to the public as a highway), then the court will, on the facts, readily treat a trespasser, whose acts have not been inconsistent with such future plans, as having not manifested the requisite animus possidendi or alternatively, as not having acquired a sufficient degree of exclusive occupation to constitute possession.'

On re-reading the relevant authorities, the view to which I then inclined has become a firm one . . . If in any given case the land in dispute is unbuilt land and the squatter is aware that the owner, while having no present use for it, has a purpose in mind for its use in the future, the court is likely to require very clear evidence before it can be satisfied that the squatter who claims a possessory title has not only established factual possession of the land, but also the requisite intention to exclude the world at large, including the owner with the paper title, so far as is reasonably practicable and so far as the processes of the law will allow. In the absence of clear evidence of this nature, the court is likely to infer that the squatter neither had had nor had claimed any intention of asserting a right to the possession of the land.

. . .

I turn then to consider the first of the two requisite elements of possession. First, as at 28 October 1973 did the defendant have factual possession of the plot? I venture to repeat what I said in *Powell* v *McFarlane*, 38 P&CR 452, 470–471:

'Factual possession signifies an appropriate degree of physical control. It must be a single and [exclusive] possession . . . Thus an owner of land and a person intruding on that land without his consent cannot both be in possession of the land at the same time. The question what acts constitute a sufficient degree of exclusive physical control must depend on the circumstances, in particular the nature of the land and the manner in which land of that nature is commonly used or enjoyed.'

On the evidence it would appear clear that by 28 October 1973 the defendant had acquired complete and exclusive physical control of the plot. He had secured a complete enclosure of the plot and its annexation to Dolphin Place . . . The defendant had put a new lock and chain on the gate and had fastened it . . . They had incorporated it into the garden of Dolphin Place. They had planted bulbs and daffodils in the grass. They had maintained it as part of that garden and had trimmed the hedges. I cannot accept Mr Douglas's submission that the defendant's acts of possession were trivial. It is hard to see what more he could have done to acquire complete physical control of the plot by October 1983. In my judgment, he had plainly acquired factual possession of the plot by that time.

However, as the judge said, the more difficult question is whether the defendant had the necessary animus possidendi. As to this, Mr Douglas accepted the correctness of the following statement (so far as it went) which I made in *Powell* v *McFarlane*, 38 P&CR 452, 471–472:

'the animus possidendi involves the intention, in one's own name and on one's own behalf, to exclude the world at large, including the owner with the paper title if he be not himself the possessor, so far as is reasonably practicable and so far as the process of the law will allow.'

. . .

As a number of authorities indicate, enclosure by itself prima facie indicates the requisite animus possidendi. As Cockburn CJ said in *Seddon* v *Smith* (1877) 36 LT 168, 169: 'Enclosure is the strongest possible evidence of adverse possession.'. . .

Mr Douglas, however, submitted that even if enclosure had occurred, the defendant's intention must be assessed in the light of the particular circumstances of this case . . .

If the defendant had stopped short of placing a new lock and chain on the gate, I might perhaps have felt able to accept these submissions . . . In my judgment, however, the placing of the new lock and chain and gate did amount to a final unequivocal demonstration of the defendant's intention to possess the land . . .

The other main point which Mr Douglas has argued in support of this appeal has caused me slightly more difficulty. In his submission there can be no sufficient animus possidendi to constitute adverse possession for the purpose of the Act of 1980 unless there exists the intention to exclude the owner with the paper title in *all* future circumstances . . .

There are some dicta in the authorities which might be read as suggesting that an intention to *own* the land is required . . .

Nevertheless, I agree with the judge that 'what is required for this purpose is not an intention to own or even an intention to acquire ownership but an intention to possess' – that is to say, an intention for the time being to possess the land to the exclusion of all other persons, including the owner with the paper title. No authorities cited to us establish the contrary proposition.

Comment

(1) Deliberate adverse possession has long troubled the courts. How does Slade LJ accommodate the earlier cases?

(2) What are the rival views as to what is required for *animus possidendi*? Once we exclude any need for intention to own, does it add anything significant?

(3) The claimant must intend 'to possess the land to the exclusion of all other persons, including the owner'. Is it consistent with this to accept adverse possession where the claimant readily admits that the land will be given up if the owner brings a claim?[20]

Extract 4.2.9

Powell v McFarlane (1977) 38 P&CR 452

A 14-year-old boy began in 1956 to make use of vacant land for looking after a cow. Had adverse possession commenced by 1959?

SLADE J: . . . In the case of open land, absolute physical control is normally impracticable, if only because it is generally impossible to secure every part of a boundary so as to prevent intrusion . . . Everything must depend on the particular circumstances, but broadly, I think what must be shown as constituting factual possession is that the alleged possessor has been dealing with the land in question as an occupying owner might have been expected to deal with it and that no-one else has done so.

. . .

The question of *animus possidendi* is, in my judgment, one of crucial importance in the present case. An owner or other person with the right to possession of land will be readily assumed to have the requisite intention to possess, unless the contrary is clearly proved. This, in my judgment, is why the slightest acts done by or on behalf of an owner in possession will be found to negative discontinuance of possession. The position, however, is quite different from a case where the question is whether a trespasser has acquired possession. In such a situation the courts will, in my judgment, require clear and affirmative evidence that the trespasser, claiming that he has acquired possession, not only had the requisite intention to possess, but made such intention clear to the world . . .

In summary the plaintiff's activities on the land in 1956 and 1957 were the following: He cut and took the hay crop; he did some rough and ready, but quite widespread repairs to the

---

[20] As in *Ocean Estates Ltd v Pinder* [1969] 2 AC 19 at p 24 (PC).

boundary fences, to the extent required to make them stock-proof; he cut back a fair quantity of brambles and other growth, including the remaining 50 or so Christmas trees, with a view to increasing the hay area for the future; he put the family cow and goat (or subsequently two or three cows) in the field to pasture; he connected some sort of water supply to the land; he also did a bit of shooting on it.

. . .

There are a few acts which by their very nature are so drastic as to point unquestionably, in the absence of evidence to the contrary, to an intention on the part of the doer to appropriate the land concerned. The ploughing up and cultivation of agricultural land is one such act: compare *Seddon* v *Smith*.[i] . . . The placing of a notice on land warning intruders to keep out, coupled with the actual enforcement of such notice, is another such act. So too is the locking or blocking of the only means of access. The plaintiff, however, did none of these things in 1956 or 1957. The acts done by him were of a far less drastic and irremediable nature. What he did, in effect, was to take various profits from the land . . . These activities, done, as they were, by a 14-year-old boy who himself owned no land in the neighbourhood, were in my judgment equivocal within the meaning of the authorities in the sense that they were not necessarily refer-able to an intention on the part of the plaintiff to dispossess Mr McFarlane and to occupy the land wholly as his own property. At first, surely, any objective informed observer might probably have inferred that the plaintiff was using the land simply for the benefit of his family's cow or cows, during such periods as the absent owner took no steps to stop him, without any intention to appropriate the land as his own.

. . .

. . . Very probably by 1962, when he was older and had established his own business and had already been using the land for several years, his intentions had hardened, just as his activities (for example his parking of vehicles and lorries and the erecting of a sign board) had become more unequivocally those of a person asserting ownership. It is, I think, quite possible that he did effectively take possession of the land in 1962 by sufficient acts and manifestations of *animus possidendi* . . .

[i] (1877) 36 LT 168, CA.

Comment

(1) Other aspects of Slade J's analysis appear from *Moran*.

(2) What does the judgment tell us about the relationship between factual possession and *animus possidendi*? Why did the claim in *Powell* fail?

(3) Was the occupier's age relevant?

(4) Slade J states that the intention to possess must be made 'clear to the world'. In *Wretham* v *Ross* [2005] EWHC 1259 (Ch) at [32] it was held that:

> in the light of the decision in *Pye* v *Graham*, [protection of O] is not achieved by the application of a test which requires consideration of what would be obvious to the paper owner visiting the property. It is achieved by consideration objectively whether the squatter was in factual possession and whether he had shown the necessary intention to possess the property.

Is this likely to cause significant prejudice to O?

As Slade J indicated in *Powell*, the nature of the land can be material. In *Red House Farms (Thorndon) Ltd* v *Catchpole*[21] a change in the course of a river had formed an island. The bridge providing access to the island collapsed and this, coupled with the marshy land,

[21] [1977] 2 EGLR 125.

rendered it of no agricultural value. Cairns LJ upheld an adverse possession claim based upon shooting as 'the only profitable use of the land was for shooting'.

Powell and *Moran* were approved in the following leading modern authority.

Extract 4.2.10

JA Pye (Oxford) Ltd v Graham [2003] 1 AC 419

LORD BROWNE-WILKINSON: 31. . . . In a remarkable judgment at first instance, *Powell* v *McFarlane* (1977) 38 P&CR 452, Slade J traced his way successfully through a number of Court of Appeal judgments which were binding on him so as to restore a degree of order to the subject and to state clearly the relevant principles. Although there are one or two minor points on which (unlike Slade J) your Lordships are not bound by authority and can therefore make necessary adjustments, for the most part the principles set out by Slade J as subsequently approved by the Court of Appeal in *Buckinghamshire County Council v Moran* [1990] Ch 623 cannot be improved upon. Hereafter I adopt them without specific recognition beyond marking with inverted commas those passages which I have quoted verbatim.

40. . . . there has always, both in Roman law and in common law, been a requirement to show an intention to possess in addition to objective acts of physical possession. Such intention may be, and frequently is, deduced from the physical acts themselves. But there is no doubt in my judgment that there are two separate elements in legal possession. So far as English law is concerned intention as a separate element is obviously necessary. Suppose a case where A is found to be in occupation of a locked house. He may be there as a squatter, as an overnight trespasser, or as a friend looking after the house of the paper owner during his absence on holiday. The acts done by A in any given period do not tell you whether there is legal possession. If A is there as a squatter he intends to stay as long as he can for his own benefit: his intention is an intention to possess. But if he only intends to trespass for the night or has expressly agreed to look after the house for his friend he does not have possession. It is not the nature of the acts which A does but the intention with which he does them which determines whether or not he is in possession.

43. . . . Slade J reformulated the requirement [of intention to possess] (to my mind correctly) as requiring an 'intention, in one's own name and on one's own behalf, to exclude the world at large, including the owner with the paper title if he be not himself the possessor, so far as is reasonably practicable and so far as the processes of the law will allow'.

Comment

(1) Further parts of this case are quoted below, see Extract 4.2.13.

(2) Intention is not mentioned in the Limitation Act 1980. Why is it part of the law? Its Germanic origins are explored by Radley-Gardner (2005) 25 OxJLS 727.

Most cases involve acts which are, as described in *Powell*, equivocal. However, sometimes apparently unequivocal acts can be explained on grounds fatal to adverse possession.

Extract 4.2.11

George Wimpey & Co Ltd v Sohn [1967] Ch 487

The Montpelier Hotel shared an easement with other local residents to use an area as a garden. It was tacitly agreed between the dominant owners that the hotel should have exclusive rights to that part of the area closest to it (the 'blue land'). It then enclosed the blue land.

RUSSELL LJ: . . . Ordinarily, of course, enclosure is the most cogent evidence of adverse possession and of dispossession of the true owner . . . But there seems to have grown up over the years what might be described as a tacit partition of the easement in common among the Sillwood Place householders, by processes of enclosure which would, of course, also usefully serve to keep out the general public, the private roadway being in fact open to the public in Sillwood Street. The enclosure being perhaps referable to an informal partition of the easement in common, it is, as the judge said, equivocal; it can be referred to an intention to continue the easement but excluding the public and excluding the exercise by other householders of their easement over that particular land. When against that equivocal background there is found on various occasions, not assertion by the owners of the Montpelier Hotel property of an exclusive right as owners to possession of the blue land, but on the contrary distinct reference to an easement over it, I am unable to hold that it established that the occupation by the predecessors of the vendors of the blue land was animo possidendi in the sense of owning the land as distinct from exercising an easement to use it as a garden. I remark that there is, of course, no suggestion in evidence that the paper-title freeholder ever sought entry through the locked gate, or a key, and was denied it.

Comment

Is the decision rather harsh on the hotel? What more could have been done to establish adverse possession?

In *Chambers* v *Havering LBC*,[22] Etherton LJ stated:

In some cases, [fencing] will be cogent evidence, perhaps the most cogent evidence, of adverse possession where its effect is wholly to exclude the paper owner, even if it was erected to keep animals inside rather than to exclude people, including the paper owner. In other cases, when considered in the context of the evidence as a whole, fencing may be not be inconsistent with the absence of actual possession and of an intention to possess on the defendant's part, even where the fencing physically excludes the paper owner.

Might this qualify *Wimpey*, especially bearing in mind that *Wimpey* predated *Pye*?

(ii) The possession must be adverse

Extract 4.2.12

Limitation Act 1980, Sched 1, paras 8, 5

8. (1) No right of action to recover land shall be treated as accruing unless the land is in the possession of some person in whose favour the period of limitation can run (referred to below in this paragraph as 'adverse possession') . . .

(2) Where a right of action to recover land has accrued and after its accrual, before the right is barred, the land ceases to be in adverse possession, the right of action shall no longer be treated as having accrued and no fresh right of action shall be treated as accruing unless and until the land is again taken into adverse possession.

(3) For the purposes of this paragraph—

. . .

(b) receipt of rent under a lease by a person wrongfully claiming to be entitled to the land in reversion immediately expectant on the determination of the lease shall be treated as adverse possession of the land.

[22] [2011] EWCA Civ 1576 at [40]; [2012] 1 P&CR 373. Lewison LJ places greater stress on the effect of fencing: see especially [65]–[69].

(4)   For the purpose of determining whether a person occupying any land is in adverse possession of the land it shall not be assumed by implication of law that his occupation is by permission of the person entitled to the land merely by virtue of the fact that his occupation is not inconsistent with the latter's present or future enjoyment of the land.

This provision shall not be taken as prejudicing a finding to the effect that a person's occupation of any land is by implied permission of the person entitled to the land in any case where such a finding is justified on the actual facts of the case.

5.   (1)   Subject to sub-paragraph (2) below, a tenancy from year to year or other period, without a lease in writing, shall for the purposes of this Act be treated as being determined at the expiration of the first year or other period; and accordingly the right of action of the person entitled to the land subject to the tenancy shall be treated as having accrued at the date on which in accordance with this sub-paragraph the tenancy is determined.

(2)   Where any rent has subsequently been received in respect of the tenancy, the right of action shall be treated as having accrued on the date of the last receipt of rent.

As Slade LJ observed in *Moran*:[23]

> Possession is never 'adverse' within the meaning of the Act of 1980 if it is enjoyed under a lawful title. If, therefore, a person occupies or uses land by licence of the owner with the paper title and his licence has not been duly determined, he cannot be treated as having been in 'adverse possession' as against the owner with the paper title.

Suppose a registered proprietor's title is mistaken and is successfully challenged in rectification proceedings. Can that proprietor claim adverse possession prior to the rectification?[24]

It was seen in *Moran* that the courts had developed a doctrine whereby an owner with no present use for the land would be treated as impliedly licensing the possession, so that it would not be adverse. Paragraph 8(4) abrogates this doctrine. What scope is there for implied licences today?[25] Paragraph 8(4), coupled with the interpretation of *animus possidendi* in *Moran*, revitalised adverse possession. Its impact is likely to be greatest as regards the intentional, rather than mistaken, adverse possessor. In the light of the Land Registration Act 2002 and the human rights arguments, was this a wrong turning?

The House of Lords has considered the 'adverse' requirement, in a context where the possessor's licence had expired and the possessor expected the licence to be extended.

Extract 4.2.13

JA Pye (Oxford) Ltd v *Graham* [2003] 1 AC 419

LORD BROWNE-WILKINSON: 35. . . . In my judgment the references to 'adverse possession' in the 1939 and 1980 Acts did not reintroduce by a side wind after over 100 years the old notions of adverse possession in force before 1833 . . . Although it is convenient to refer to possession by a squatter without the consent of the true owner as being 'adverse possession' the convenience of this must not be allowed to re-introduce by the back door that which for so long has not formed part of the law.

36.   Many of the difficulties with these sections which I will have to consider are due to a conscious or subconscious feeling that in order for a squatter to gain title by lapse of time he has to act adversely to the paper title owner. It is said that he has to 'oust' the true owner in order

---

[23] [1990] Ch 623 at p 636.
[24] See *Parshall* v *Hackney* [2013] Ch 568 (two people inconsistently each registered as proprietor).
[25] Modern cases include *Batsford Estates (1983) Co Ltd* v *Taylor* [2006] 2 P&CR 64 and *Hicks Developments Ltd* v *Chaplin* [2007] 1 EGLR 1.

to dispossess him; that he has to intend to exclude the whole world including the true owner; that the squatter's use of the land has to be inconsistent with any present or future use by the true owner. In my judgment much confusion and complication would be avoided if reference to adverse possession were to be avoided so far as possible and effect given to the clear words of the Acts. The question is simply whether the defendant squatter has dispossessed the paper owner by going into ordinary possession of the land for the requisite period without the consent of the owner.

37.   It is clearly established that the taking or continuation of possession by a squatter with the actual consent of the paper title owner does not constitute dispossession or possession by the squatter for the purposes of the Act. Beyond that, as Slade J said, the words possess and dispossess are to be given their ordinary meaning.

38.   It is sometimes said that ouster by the squatter is necessary to constitute dispossession: see for example per Fry J in *Rains* v *Buxton* (1880) 14 Ch D 537 at p 539. The word 'ouster' is derived from the old law of adverse possession and has overtones of confrontational, knowing removal of the true owner from possession. Such an approach is quite incorrect. There will be a 'dispossession' of the paper owner in any case where (there being no discontinuance of possession by the paper owner) a squatter assumes possession in the ordinary sense of the word. Except in the case of joint possessors, possession is single and exclusive. Therefore if the squatter is in possession the paper owner cannot be. If the paper owner was at one stage in possession of the land but the squatter's subsequent occupation of it in law constitutes possession the squatter must have 'dispossessed' the true owner . . .

45.   . . . The highest it can be put is that, if the squatter is aware of a special purpose for which the paper owner uses or intends to use the land and the use made by the squatter does not conflict with that use, that may provide some support for a finding as a question of fact that the squatter had no intention to possess the land in the ordinary sense but only an intention to occupy it until needed by the paper owner. For myself I think there will be few occasions in which such inference could be properly drawn in cases where the true owner has been physically excluded from the land. But it remains a possible, if improbable, inference in some cases.

Comment

(1) See also Extract 4.2.10 above. The House of Lords held that there was adverse possession on the facts.

(2) How do these dicta develop the law?

(3) How readily will adverse possession be recognised where O has no current use for the land? Does it make any difference if S is aware of this?

(4) Suppose S wrongly believes that O has given consent. Should this preclude adverse possession?[26]

One specific problem concerns the effect of taking possession when a purchase is never completed. Even if there is no express permission, Rix LJ[27] has approved the proposition that it is 'natural to draw an inference of permission where a person is in possession pending negotiations for the grant of an interest in that land'. But for how long will this permission operate?

---

[26] See *J Alston & Sons Limited* v *BOCM Pauls Ltd* [2008] EWHC 3310 (Ch), [2009] 1 EGLR 93, not following *Clowes Developments (UK) Ltd* v *Walters* [2006] 1 P&CR 1.

[27] *Colin Dawson Windows Ltd* v *Howard* [2005] 2 P&CR 333.

Extract 4.2.14

Hyde v *Pearce* [1982] 1 WLR 560

The plaintiff entered land following a contract to purchase it. The sale stalled because of a dispute, yet the plaintiff remained there for 16 years after a request for him to leave.

TEMPLEMAN LJ: . . . For my part, in the peculiar circumstances of this case, it seems to me that it is not sufficient to show that a right of action had accrued. The plaintiff must show some further quality, namely, adverse possession. The plaintiff was allowed into possession as a purchaser pending completion; and he was allowed to stay there because he was a purchaser. If he had been a mere trespasser no doubt the vendors would have brought proceedings. But the vendors, in all the circumstances of the case, seem to have decided by accident or design to allow matters to drift on . . .

For my part, not only can I see no date by which the vendors ought to have realised the changed status of the plaintiff but, in addition, it seems to me that, having entered the property under a claim of right, albeit on the terms of the undertaking, and then having continued in possession ostensibly and as far as he himself was saying at the time, or implying by his conduct at the time, as a purchaser pending completion, if he was to throw off that capacity and appear in the full light as a person in adverse possession acquiring a title, it was at least necessary that he should have repudiated the contract, thus marking his change of status.

In the event, he never did change his status and, as I have indicated, at the end of the day he is really seeking to have the best of both worlds. He was able to stay there because of the contract; now he says, in effect, he was there the whole of the time in spite of the contract. I do not think he has shown that he was in adverse possession . . .

Comment

(1) Once the plaintiff had been told to leave, why was he not in adverse possession?

(2) In *Sandhu* v *Farooqui*,[28] Chadwick LJ said: 'What is essential, in my view, is that there should be some mutual communication from which the objective observer could deduce that each would appreciate that the transaction is no longer proceeding.' How does this fit with *Hyde*?

(3) In *Bridges* v *Mees*,[29] a purchaser who had paid the purchase price but had not taken a conveyance was held to be in adverse possession. How is this explicable?

(iii) Stopping time running

The one clear rule for unregistered land is that issuing legal proceedings is effective. As Dillon LJ has stated:[30]

> . . . if an action to recover land is brought within the 12 years and judgment for possession is given in that action, albeit after the expiration of the 12 years, it would be idle to suppose that the judgment for possession could, because of the expiration of the 12 years, never be enforced. The judgment must be enforceable if the action was started in due time . . .

On the other hand, *Mount Carmel Investments Ltd* v *Peter Thurlow Ltd*[31] confirms that simply telling the adverse possessor to leave does not suffice.

---

[28] [2004] 1 P&CR 19 at [25].
[29] [1957] Ch 475.
[30] *BP Properties Ltd* v *Buckler* (1987) 55 P&CR 337 at p 344.
[31] [1988] 1 WLR 1078.

For registered land, the running of time by itself is not determinative. One aspect of this is that bringing proceedings does not stop time running (LRA, Sched 6, para 11(3)). However, we have seen that paras 1 and 6 disallow applications when there are pending or recent court proceedings.

Bringing proceedings is not the only way for O to stop time running. The Limitation Act 1980, Sched 1, para 8(2), establishes that time ceases to run if the possession ceases to be adverse.

Extract 4.2.15

BP Properties Ltd v *Buckler* (1987) 55 P&CR 337

The owner, choosing not to enforce an order for possession, told the possessor that she had a licence to occupy.

DILLON LJ: . . . It is said for BP Properties Ltd that under the letters Mrs Buckler became a licensee for life of the farmhouse and garden. Therefore she was no longer in adverse possession and time ceased to run in her favour . . . In so far as it is urged for the other side that Mrs Buckler's possession continued to be adverse before and after the receipt of the letters, without any change, and was referable to her own expressed belief that she was the owner of the land because of her grandfather's title, it is said for BP Properties Ltd that there is a rule that 'possession is never adverse if it can be referred to a lawful title', and reference is made to the judgment of Harman LJ in *Hughes* v *Griffin*.[i]

The claim that a unilateral licence can stop time running is a new one. It may be of some general importance in that it would enable a person who is not prepared to incur the obloquy of bringing proceedings for possession, or of enforcing a possession order, to keep his title alive for very many years until it suits him to evict. It might be thought that for title to be kept alive in this way was contrary to the policy of the statute . . .

So far as the facts are concerned, it would in my judgment be artificial to say that Mrs Buckler 'accepted' the terms set out in the two letters; BP Properties Ltd neither sought nor waited for her acceptance. It would be equally artificial to say that there was any consideration in law for those terms.

It may be that the result would have been different if Mrs Buckler had, as soon as she learned of the letters, plainly told BP Properties Ltd that she did not accept the letters, and maintained her claims to be already the owner of the property; she did not however do that . . . In essence she was not asserting during the time from the receipt of the letters until after December 11, 1974 – or indeed thereafter – any claim to ownership of the farmhouse and garden, or any intention to exclude the owner of the paper title.

Whether BP Properties Ltd could or could not in law, in the absence of consideration, have sought to determine in her lifetime the licence granted to Mrs Buckler by the two letters, they did not in fact seek to do so. Had they sought to do so, they would in the absence of any repudiation of the letters by Mrs Buckler have had to give Mrs Buckler a reasonable time to quit as with any licensee.

The nature of Mrs Buckler's possession after receipt of the letters cannot be decided just by looking at what was locked up in her own mind. It must depend even more, on this aspect of the case, on the position as seen from the standpoint of the person with the paper title. What could that person have done? The rule that possession is not adverse if it can be referred to a lawful title applies even if the person in possession did not know of the lawful title; the lawful title would still preclude the person with the paper title from evicting the person in possession. So far as Mrs Buckler was concerned, even though she did not 'accept' the terms of the letters, BP Properties Ltd would, in the absence of any repudiation by her of the two letters, have been bound to treat her as in possession as licensee on the terms of the letters. They could not have evicted her (if they could have done so at all) without determining the licence.

I can see no escape therefore from the conclusion that, whether she liked it or not, from the time of her receipt of the letters, Mrs Buckler was in possession of the farmhouse and garden by the licence of BP Properties Ltd, and her possession was no longer adverse within the meaning of section 10 of the 1939 Act.

[i] [1969] 1 WLR 23 at p 27; 20 P&CR 113 at p 119.

Comment

(1) If the possessor had not 'accepted' the licence, why should the possession cease being adverse? Can the holder of the paper title unilaterally create a lawful title so that the possession ceases to be adverse?

(2) Is the decision consistent with the stress on the need for proceedings to be issued to stop time running (for unregistered land)?

(3) Sections 29 and 30 of the Limitation Act 1980 provide that a *written* acknowledgement by the adverse possessor of the owner's title will stop time running. How does this fit with *Buckler*?

(4) What significance does *Buckler* have for the operation of adverse possession in registered land?

Once the 12 years have run, then in unregistered land it is of course too late to talk about stopping time running: no licence or acknowledgement can obscure the fact that the original title has been extinguished. But is it open to the parties to agree otherwise?

Extract 4.2.16

Colchester BC v *Smith* [1992] Ch 421

As adverse possession was disputed, the possessor agreed to acknowledge the plaintiff's title and in return obtained a lease. Could the plaintiff obtain possession on the expiry of the lease?

BUTLER-SLOSS LJ: . . . Where parties to a dispute reach a compromise which brings that dispute to an end and avoids the need for litigation or further litigation, such a compromise is a valuable part of the resolution of disputes within the machinery of the administration of justice. The compromise has to be genuine, entered into freely by all parties to it without concealment of essential information or undue advantage taken by one party of another party, and preferably with the assistance of lawyers. Consequently, an agreement to compromise an action or a dispute which may lead to litigation is binding and is enforceable against the party seeking subsequently to repudiate it.

Comment

(1) Can it be argued that this is an impermissible contracting out of the legislation?[32]

(2) What would be the effect of such an agreement if title were registered?

(iv) Twelve years

It follows from the Limitation Act 1980, Sched 1, para 8(2) (Extract 4.2.12 above), that the owner succeeds if adverse possession ceases during the 12 years. But what happens if possession is taken by a second squatter? It is clear that the initial squatter can transfer his

---

[32] See Dixon [1991] CLJ 234; [1992] CLJ 420.

or her rights: adverse possession is completed 12 years after adverse possession first commenced (whatever the date of the transfer). The same principle applies in registered land: LRA, Sched 6, para 11(2) (Extract 4.2.7 above).

More difficult is the situation where the initial squatter is dispossessed by the second. For unregistered land, the later squatter can add the period the initial squatter was there.[33] We have seen that this rule does not apply to registered land (Extract 4.2.7 above). Why is there such a difference? Is either solution doctrinally superior to the other?

Special rules apply to future interests.

Extract 4.2.17

Limitation Act 1980, s 15(2)

15.—(2) . . . where—
- (a) the estate or interest claimed was an estate or interest in reversion or remainder or any other future estate or interest and the right of action to recover the land accrued on the date on which the estate or interest fell into possession by the determination of the preceding estate or interest; and
- (b) the person entitled to the preceding estate or interest (not being a term of years absolute) was not in possession of the land on that date;

no action shall be brought by the person entitled to the succeeding estate or interest after the expiration of twelve years from the date on which the right of action accrued to the person entitled to the preceding estate or interest or six years from the date on which the right of action accrued to the person entitled to the succeeding estate or interest, whichever period last expires.

Comment

(1) *St Marylebone Property Co Ltd v Fairweather*[34] is authority for the proposition that the landlord's reversion on a lease counts as a future interest.

(2) Suppose adverse possession commences 15 years before a lease terminates. When will (i) the tenant and (ii) the landlord be debarred from asserting title? What if it commences nine years before termination?

(3) These rules do not apply to registered land: if S wishes to institute an adverse possession claim against the landlord, then there will need to be ten years' adverse possession after the end of the lease. Note that LRA, Sched 6, para 1(1) requires adverse possession of the registered estate in respect of which the application is made.

D. The effect of adverse possession

(i) General principles: unregistered land

Extract 4.2.18

Limitation Act 1980, ss 15, 17

15.—(1) No action shall be brought by any person to recover any land after the expiration of twelve years from the date on which the right of action accrued to him, or if it first accrued to some person through whom he claims, to that person.

---

[33] *Willis* v *Earl Howe* [1893] 2 Ch 545 at pp 553–554.
[34] [1963] AC 510 at pp 536, 544.

17. . . . at the expiration of the period prescribed by this Act for any person to bring an action to recover land (including a redemption action) the title of that person to the land shall be extinguished.

The squatter remains bound by other claims to the land, such as easements and restrictive covenants. The major dispute has been as to whether there is a statutory transfer of title to the squatter. This is particularly important where there has been adverse possession against a tenant.

Extract 4.2.19

Tichborne v *Weir* (1892) 67 LT 735

Did the squatter step into the shoes of the lessee so as to be liable on the leasehold covenants?

BOWEN LJ: . . . I think that the statute makes no transfer of any kind. The section in question says that, at the determination of the period limited by the Act . . . the right and title of such person to the land . . . shall be extinguished. It is argued that the extinguishment of the title must have the effect of transferring the term to the man in possession, although there is no mention in the statute of any transfer . . . It is true that the effect of the statute is not only to bar the remedy, but also to extinguish the title of the person out of possession, and in that sense the person in possession holds by virtue of the Act, but not by a fiction of a transfer of title . . . The most that can be said is, that he acquired an absolute title to the land as against everybody but the landlord . . . The landlord has his rights against [the tenant] on his covenants, but not against the [squatter] . . .

Comment

This is a fundamental aspect of thinking about adverse possession in unregistered land. While it certainly fits with the legislative structure for unregistered land, is it the most sensible way of approaching the effect of adverse possession?

(ii) General principles: registered land

The idea of a statutory transfer of the estate is accepted for registered land. This follows from the wording of LRA, Sched 6, paras 4 and 7 (Extracts 4.2.5 and 4.2.6 above). Its principal significance is where there is adverse possession against a tenant. The position is summarised by the Law Commission in the following words:[35]

> When a squatter's application for registration is successful for any of the reasons explained above, the registrar will register him or her as the new proprietor of the estate against which he or she adversely possessed. The squatter will, therefore, be the successor in title to the previous registered proprietor.

(iii) Before the adverse possession is completed

Extract 4.2.20

Asher v *Whitlock* (1865) LR 1 QB 1

The plaintiff had been in adverse possession, though the limitation period had not expired. Could the plaintiff sue another person (not the true owner) who was now in possession?

---

[35] Law Com No 271, para 14.71, footnotes omitted.

COCKBURN CJ: . . . Mr Merewether was obliged to contend that possession acquired, as this was, against a rightful owner, would not be sufficient to keep out every other person but the rightful owner. But I take it as clearly established, that possession is good against all the world except the person who can shew a good title; and it would be mischievous to change this established doctrine. In *Doe* v *Dyeball*[i] one year's possession by the plaintiff was held good against a person who came and turned him out; and there are other authorities to the same effect. Suppose the person who originally inclosed the land had been expelled by the defendant, or the defendant had obtained possession without force, by simply walking in at the open door in the absence of the then possessor, and were to say to him, 'You have no more title than I have, my possession is as good as yours', surely ejectment could have been maintained by the original possessor against the defendant . . . On the simple ground that possession is good title against all but the true owner, I think the plaintiffs entitled to succeed . . .

MELLOR J: . . . The fact of possession is prima facie evidence of seisin in fee . . .

[i] Mood & M 346.

Comment

(1) Why should the plaintiff prevail over the defendant?

(2) It is important to note that the plaintiff is treated as having a claim to a fee simple. In essence there are two fees simple: one held by the true owner and one by the plaintiff. How can this be explained? How does it fit with the finding cases?

(3) Similar principles apply to registered land. Under the previous legislation, O held on trust for S once adverse possession was complete. Since LRA 2002, we are happy to accept that both O and S can have legal fees simple (though O will win in all but a few cases).

(iv) Adverse possession against tenants: unregistered land

A few points have already been noted. First, the title of the landlord will not normally be extinguished until six years after the lease expires. Next, it has been seen from *Tichborne* v *Weir* that the squatter does not acquire the lease and so is not liable on the covenants. On the other hand, failure by the squatter to comply with the covenants is likely to enable the landlord to forfeit the lease and claim possession immediately. A highly controversial question has been whether the tenant, whose title has been extinguished by s 17, can surrender the lease to the landlord so that the landlord can seek possession. If so, the rights of the squatter are precarious indeed.

Extract 4.2.21

St Marylebone Property Co Ltd v *Fairweather* [1963] AC 510

LORD RADCLIFFE: . . . One branch of [the appellant squatter's] argument is to say that the lessee had lost any right or title to possession of the shed, because his title was extinguished . . . and he had nothing, therefore, in this respect that he could transfer to the landlord; the other branch involves the proposition that until 1992 [the end of the lease] the landlord could only claim a present right to possession through the lessee and, if the lessee himself had no right to possession against the squatter, the landlord claiming through him could be in no better position.

   . . . After some hesitation . . . I have come to the conclusion that the appellant's arguments are vitiated by the fact that their reasoning contains an engaging but considerable fallacy. It seeks to revive in an elegant new form the rejected proposition that a squatter becomes in some way the successor to the title of the dispossessed owner.

It is necessary to start, I think, by recalling the principle that defines a squatter's rights. He is not at any stage of his possession a successor to the title of the man he has dispossessed. He comes in and remains in always by right of possession, which in due course becomes incapable of disturbance as time exhausts the one or more periods allowed by statute for successful intervention. His title, therefore, is never derived through but arises always in spite of the dispossessed owner . . . The point was fully considered by the members of the court [in *Tichborne* v *Weir*[1]] . . .

If this principle is applied, as it must be, to the appellant's situation, it appears that the adverse possession completed in 1932 against the lessee of No 315 did not transfer to him either the lessee's term or his rights against or his obligations to the landlord who held the reversion. The appellant claims to be entitled to keep the landlord at bay until the expiration of the term by effluxion of time in 1992: but, if he is, it cannot be because he is the transferee or holder of the term which was granted to the lessee. He is in possession by his own right, so far as it is a right: and it is a right so far as the statutes of limitation which govern the matter pre-scribe both when the rights to dispossess him are to be treated as accruing and when, having accrued, they are thereafter to be treated as barred . . .

In the ordinary way one would regard a lease or tenancy as being determinable by effluxion of time, by notice, by forfeiture on breach of condition or by surrender. Ostensibly the lease of No 315, including the site of the shed, was determined by the surrender in December, 1959, and upon that event, one would say the fee simple owner's right to possession of the demised property accrued. According to the appellant's argument, however, the surrender was ineffective in law to determine the lease so far as it extended to the site of the shed because . . . the lessee's right and title to that part of the demised premises was 'extinguished' upon the barring of his right to dispossess the squatter: and, if his right and title had been thus extinguished in 1932, he had nothing by way of title that he could pass to the landlord by his ostensible surrender. Nemo dat quod non habet . . .

On one view, which seems not an implausible one having regard to the structure of the respective sections, the right or title extinguished is coterminous with the right of action the barring of which is the occasion of the extinguishment. This would mean that, when a squatter dispossesses a lessee for the statutory period, it is the lessee's right and title as against the squatter that is finally destroyed but not his right or title as against persons who are not or do not take through the adverse possessor. On the other view, that upon which the appellant's case depends, the lessee's right and title to the premises becomes extinguished for all pur-poses and in all relations, so that as between himself and the lessor, for instance, he has there-after no estate or interest in the land demised.

My Lords, I think that even at first impression I should have been inclined to favour the former of these two possible interpretations as being more consistent with the apparent purpose of the Limitation Acts. But the major difficulty that I see in considering the adoption of the second alternative is that its logical application is very far-reaching indeed, much more far-reaching than is convenient for the appellant's argument, and would produce situations that would seem to me neither reasonable nor just. First, if the lessee's estate or right or title or interest – I do not believe that there is any useful distinction between these words in this connection – is really extinguished as against his landlord, I see no escape from the conclusion that the landlord's right to possession against the squatter accrues upon that event. The squatter has not got the lessee's term or estate and there is nothing between the fee simple owner and the man in possession . . .

. . .

Then there is the question of forfeiture. The appellant's argument, I think, included the proposition that, if he does not take the incautious step of accepting a surrender, the landlord could achieve a forfeiture on breach of condition and under it enter on the squatter's land. But I have not been able to see how this can be. A condition, the breach of which justifies a forfeiture or re-entry, must be attached to the estate the grant of which imposes the condition; and if a statute has itself wiped out or destroyed the estate, so that the squatter is in possession by a different title derived aliunde, I cannot see how the landlord can any longer rely upon the condition or forfeit an interest which has ceased to exist.

I think, therefore, that it is a false approach to the provisions of the Limitation Acts to regard the 'extinguishment of title' as extinguishing more than the title of the dispossessed against the dispossessor. Where the person dispossessed is a lessee, I do not think it right to try to build legal conclusions on the assumption that the nexus between him and his lessor has been destroyed; or, consequently, that, once adverse possession has been completed, he ceases to hold the term of years and estate in it granted to him by his lessor . . .

I conclude, therefore, that the effect of the 'extinguishment' sections of the Limitation Acts is not to destroy the lessee's estate as between himself and the lessor; and that it would be incorrect to say that if he offers a surrender to the lessor he has nothing to surrender to him in respect of the land in the possession of the squatter. Nemo dat quod non habet, and I daresay that he does not, but, as Pearson LJ indicated in the Court of Appeal,[ii] the question here is not whether there are any exceptions from that general principle but whether, as a principle, it is relevant to the situation that we have here. In my opinion it is not.

[i] (1892) 67 LT 735; 8 TLR 713, CA.
[ii] [1962] 1 QB 498, 530.

Comment

(1) Lord Morris dissented.

(2) Does Lord Radcliffe demonstrate conclusively that the lease cannot wholly be extinguished by the adverse possession?

(3) The decision has received much criticism. Professor Wade[36] has noted that the squatter and landlord can, by collusion, achieve what neither could alone: this is the essence of the *nemo dat quod non habet* (nobody can give what they do not have) argument. Does Lord Radcliffe deal adequately with this point?

(4) The squatter receives a fee simple, though it must give way to the landlord's fee simple on the termination of the lease. Does the result demonstrate that the statutory transfer theory is preferable?

(v) Adverse possession against tenants: registered land

We have seen that Sched 6 enables (in the few cases where adverse possession operates) S to be registered as proprietor of the relevant estate: the lease in the context we are considering. It follows that the lease is vested in S and there is no possibility of the original tenant surrendering it.[37] Paragraph 9(1) provides as follows:

> Where a person is registered as the proprietor of an estate in land in pursuance of an application under this Schedule, the title by virtue of adverse possession which he had at the time of the application is extinguished.

In the context of adverse possession against a tenant, what title is held by S by virtue of adverse possession before registration? Is it the same as will result from registration?

[36] (1962) 78 LQR 541.
[37] *Spectrum Investment Co v Holmes* [1981] 1 WLR 221.

What is the position before S is registered as proprietor? Prior to the 2002 Act, *Central London Commercial Estates Ltd* v *Kato Kagaku Co Ltd*[38] held that the statutory trust imposed on the tenant precluded surrender. The 2002 Act drops the statutory trust. Does this mean that the original tenant can surrender the lease as permitted by *Fairweather*?

3. Fixtures

How does the law treat an object attached to land?[39] Take, for example, the building of a house. The bricks cease to possess an identity of their own and become subsumed within the house and, thereby, the land. It is irrelevant whether the bricks belonged to the builder or to somebody else, though the builder may of course incur liability in the latter case.

One common problem area is where a tenant (either under a lease or as tenant for life under a settlement) affixes objects to the land. The law is reluctant to hold that a gift is being made to the landlord or remainderman and accordingly confers a right to remove certain fixtures, as we will see later in this section. There has been some confusion as to whether there is no fixture in the first place or a right to remove an object that has become a fixture.

Extract 4.3.1

Elitestone Ltd v *Morris and another* **[1997] 1 WLR 687**

LORD LLOYD: . . . The term fixture is apt to be a source of misunderstanding owing to the existence of the category of so called 'tenants' fixtures' (a term used to cover both trade fixtures and ornamental fixtures), which are fixtures in the full sense of the word (and therefore part of the realty) but which may nevertheless be removed by the tenant in the course of or at the end of his tenancy. Such fixtures are sometimes confused with chattels which have never become fixtures at all. Indeed the confusion arose in this very case . . .

For my part I find it better in the present case to avoid the traditional twofold distinction between chattels and fixtures, and to adopt the threefold classification set out in *Woodfall, Landlord and Tenant* (looseleaf ed), vol 1, para 13.131:

'An object which is brought onto land may be classified under one of three broad heads. It may be (a) a chattel; (b) a fixture; or (c) part and parcel of the land itself. Objects in categories (b) and (c) are treated as being part of the land.'

Comment

(1) In many cases, it does not matter whether an object never becomes part of the land or the tenant has a right to remove it. However, the right to remove may be lost in certain cases and there may be differences if a third party claims a right to the land.

(2) What merits are there in the threefold classification?

---

[38] [1998] 4 All ER 948 (Sedley J).
[39] Similar points arise when one object is attached to another, though this rarely arises in litigation.

A. General principles

Extract 4.3.2

***Holland* v *Hodgson* (1872) LR 7 CP 328**

Looms were nailed to the floor of a factory. Did they pass to mortgagees of the factory as fixtures?

BLACKBURN J: . . . There is no doubt that the general maxim of the law is, that what is annexed to the land becomes part of the land; but it is very difficult, if not impossible, to say with precision what constitutes an annexation sufficient for this purpose. It is a question which must depend on the circumstances of each case, and mainly on two circumstances, as indicating the intention, viz, the degree of annexation and the object of the annexation. When the article in question is no further attached to the land, than by its own weight it is generally to be considered a mere chattel; see *Wiltshear* v *Cottrell*,[i] and the cases there cited. But even in such a case, if the intention is apparent to make the articles part of the land, they do become part of the land: see *D'Eyncourt* v *Gregory*.[ii] Thus blocks of stone placed one on the top of another without any mortar or cement for the purpose of forming a dry stone wall would become part of the land, though the same stones, if deposited in a builder's yard and for convenience sake stacked on the top of each other in the form of a wall, would remain chattels. On the other hand, an article may be very firmly fixed to the land, and yet the circumstances may be such as to shew that it was never intended to be part of the land, and then it does not become part of the land. The anchor of a large ship must be very firmly fixed in the ground in order to bear the strain of the cable, yet no one could suppose that it became part of the land, even though it should chance that the shipowner was also the owner of the fee of the spot where the anchor was dropped. An anchor similarly fixed in the soil for the purpose of bearing the strain of the chain of a suspension bridge would be part of the land. Perhaps the true rule is, that articles not otherwise attached to the land than by their own weight are not to be considered as part of the land, unless the circumstances are such as to shew that they were intended to be part of the land, the onus of shewing that they were so intended lying on those who assert that they have ceased to be chattels, and that, on the contrary, an article which is affixed to the land even slightly is to be considered as part of the land, unless the circumstances are such as to shew that it was intended all along to continue a chattel, the onus lying on those who contend that it is a chattel . . . In some cases, such as the anchor of the ship or the ordinary instance given of a carpet nailed to the floor of a room, the nature of the thing sufficiently shews it is only fastened as a chattel temporarily, and not affixed permanently as part of the land. But ordinary trade or tenant fixtures which are put up with the intention that they should be removed by the tenant (and so are put up for a purpose in one sense only temporary, and certainly not for the purpose of improving the reversionary interest of the landlord) have always been considered as part of the land, though severable by the tenant. In most, if not all, of such cases the reason why the articles are considered fixtures is probably that indicated by Wood, VC, in *Boyd* v *Shorrock*,[iii] that the tenant indicates by the mode in which he puts them up that he regards them as attached to the property during his interest in the property . . .

The words 'merely for a temporary purpose' must be understood as applying to such a case as we have supposed, of the anchor dropped for the temporary purpose of mooring the ship, or the instance immediately afterwards given by Parke, B, of the carpet tacked to the floor for the purpose of keeping it stretched whilst it was there used, and not to a case such as that of a tenant who, for example, affixes a shop counter for the purpose (in one sense temporary) of more effectually enjoying the shop whilst he continues to sell his wares there . . . *Walmsley* v *Milne*[iv] . . . and . . . *Wiltshear* v *Cotterill*[v] seem authorities for this principle, that where an article is affixed by the owner of the fee, though only affixed by bolts and screws, it is to be considered as part of the land, at all events where the object of setting up the articles is to enhance the value of the premises to which it is annexed for the purposes to which those premises are applied. The threshing machine in *Wiltshear* v *Cotterill* was affixed by the owner of the fee to the barn as an adjunct to the barn, in much the same sense as the hay-cutter in *Walmsley* v *Milne* was affixed to the stable as an adjunct to it, and to improve its usefulness as a stable . . . If, therefore, the matter were to be decided on principle, without reference to what has since been done on the faith of the decisions, we should be much inclined . . . to hold that the looms now in question were, as a matter of fact, part of the land.

[i] 1 E&B 674; 22 LJ (QB) 177.
[ii] Law Rep 3 Eq 382.
[iii] Law Rep 5 Eq at p 78.
[iv] 7 CB (NS) 115; 29 LJ (CP) 97.
[v] 1 E&B 674; 22 LJ (QB) 177.

Comment

(1) Blackburn J went on to stress that the cases also pointed towards the looms being fixtures.

(2) This leading case establishes that physical annexation (or its absence) is not conclusive. Determining when intention will overthrow the effect of physical annexation is difficult: it is revealing that relatively minor annexation in *Holland* itself was the crucial element.

(3) A test employed in this and later cases is whether the annexation was intended to increase the value of the land or for the better enjoyment of the object in question. If a loom is nailed to the floor of a factory, is it meaningful to ask whether this is to benefit the factory as opposed to the better enjoyment of the loom?

Cases involving no physical annexation are unusual, but two examples will be considered.

Extract 4.3.3

Elitestone Ltd v *Morris and another* [1997] 1 WLR 687

A wooden bungalow rested on its own weight on concrete pillars.

LORD LLOYD: . . . The materials out of which the bungalow was constructed, that is to say, the timber frame walls, the feather boarding, the suspended timber floors, the chipboard ceilings, and so on, were all, of course, chattels when they were brought onto the site. Did they cease to be chattels when they were built into the composite structure? The answer to the question, as Blackburn J pointed out in *Holland* v *Hodgson* (1872) LR 7 CP 328, depends on the circumstances of each case, but mainly on two factors, the degree of annexation to the land, and the object of the annexation.

Purpose of annexation

Many different tests have been suggested, such as whether the object which has been fixed to the property has been so fixed for the better enjoyment of the object as a chattel, or whether it has been fixed with a view to effecting a permanent improvement of the freehold. This and similar tests are useful when one is considering an object such as a tapestry, which may or may not be fixed to a house so as to become part of the freehold: see *Leigh* v *Taylor* [1902] AC 157. These tests are less useful when one is considering the house itself. In the case of the house the answer is as much a matter of common sense as precise analysis. A house which is constructed in such a way so as to be removable, whether as a unit, or in sections, may well remain a chattel, even though it is connected temporarily to mains services such as water and electricity.

But a house which is constructed in such a way that it cannot be removed at all, save by destruction, cannot have been intended to remain as a chattel. It must have been intended to form part of the realty . . . Applying [the dry stone wall] analogy to the present case, I do not doubt that when Mr Morris's bungalow was built, and as each of the timber frame walls were placed in position, they all became part of the structure, which was itself part and parcel of the land. The object of bringing the individual bits of wood onto the site seems to be so clear that the absence of any attachment to the soil (save by gravity) becomes an irrelevance.

Comment

Why was this structure a fixture? How would cases involving, say, sheds and greenhouses be resolved? Or a houseboat resting on a wooden frame?[40]

Our second example involves ornamental fixtures, some (but not all) of which were physically annexed.

Extract 4.3.4

D'Eyncourt v *Gregory* (1866) LR 3 Eq 382

LORD ROMILLY MR: . . . The first of these which I think proper to mention is the tapestry which was put up by the testator, *Gregory Gregory*, himself. It is clear that the testator could not have disposed of paper affixed to the walls, nor, if he had used silk instead of paper for lining the walls, could he, in my opinion, have removed the silk. So, if the testator had covered the walls of the house with panelling, he could not, in my opinion, have removed the panelling, and have left the walls bare. If he caused them to be painted in fresco, he could not have removed the paintings, and I think if he had caused the panels to be painted he could not have removed the painting any more than if he had put in panels already painted, and fixed them close to the wall. In all these cases I think they must be considered to be fixtures not removable by the tenant for life.

Upon considering the case of the tapestries already fixed at the death of *Gregory Gregory*, I have come to the conclusion that these fall within the description of such matters as those I have just enumerated, and that they could not be removed; in other words, that the testator himself could not have been allowed to remove them . . . In the same class with these tapestries is the portrait of Lady *Williams* . . . The observation that 'the painting and gilt frame may be removed easily and without damage, and if the painting were removed, and the framework were filled in with figured satin in the same manner as all the other panels in the room', is, in my opinion, very pregnant. Both the painting and the tapestries could be removed unquestionably in this sense, that they could be taken down, and the space left or filled with satin . . . : but, in my opinion, in all these cases, whether it is the paper, or the satin, or the panels, or the tapestry, they are all part of the wall itself, and they are fixtures not to be removed. In all these cases the question is not whether the thing itself is easily removable, but whether it is essentially a part of the building itself from which it is proposed to remove it, as in the familiar instance of the grinding-stone of a flour-mill, which is easily removable, but which is nevertheless a part of the mill itself, and goes to the heir, and not to the legal personal representative . . .

With respect to the carved kneeling figures on the staircase in the great hall, and the sculptured marble vases in the hall, they appear to me to come within the category of articles that cannot be removed. I think it does not depend on whether any cement is used for fixing these articles, or whether they rest by their own weight, but upon this – whether they are strictly and properly part of the architectural design for the hall and staircase itself, and put in there as

---

[40]   *Tristmire Ltd* v *Mew* [2012] 1 WLR 852.

such, as distinguished from mere ornaments to be afterwards added. There may be mansions in *England* on which statues may be placed in order to complete the architectural design as distinguished from mere ornament; and when they are so placed, as, for instance, they are in the cathedral of *Milan*, I should consider that they could not properly be removed, although they were fixed without cement or without brackets, and stand by their own weight alone . . . In the present case I have thought the articles which I have mentioned are not removable, relying upon the evidence given and the drawings laid before me. The same rule will apply to the lions at the head of the flight of steps in the garden, and the sixteen stone garden-seats in the garden itself.

Comment

(1) How convincing is the reasoning from wallpaper to tapestries?

(2) When considering objects which are not physically annexed, does a useful test emerge as to when they are fixtures?

<hr>

Extract 4.3.5

<hr>

Re De Falbe [1901] 1 Ch 523

RIGBY LJ: . . . As regards *D'Eyncourt* v *Gregory*,[i] I do not hesitate to say that I feel great diffi-culty, owing in part to what seems to me the very inconclusive reasoning of Lord Romilly MR in support of his decision. He speaks of paper and panelling and other such matters as if they concluded the case. Paper, he says, is part of the wall, and so no doubt it is, and he says it cannot be taken away by a tenant for life. That I question entirely. If there be on a wall a paper which the tenant for life does not like, I conceive that he has a right to take it away and to sub-stitute another . . . As regards panelling, I am by no means satisfied that the law has changed since Lord Hardwicke in *Lawton* v *Lawton*[ii] laid it down in 1743 that, whatever might have been the rule originally, at the time at which he was speaking wainscot fixed with screws to the wall had become recognised as removable. Another instance which was referred to by Lord Romilly, namely, the upper grindstone of a mill, does not appear to me to be at all applicable. In my opinion the ruling as to the tapestries in that case cannot be maintained, unless it should turn out that there was some proof (of which I can find no trace in the report) that the house was fitted to the tapestry rather than the tapestry to the house, and in that way (although I do not say that even then it would be clear) it might be possible to support the decision, on the ground that the tenant for life who affixed the tapestry had shewn a plain intention to add it irrevocably and permanently to the house. At any rate, I think that the decision in *D'Eyncourt* v *Gregory* is not right if it would apply to such a case as the present, and for the purpose of this judgment, and so far as may be necessary, I must hold that the decision ought not to be followed.

[i] LR 3 Eq 382.
[ii] 3 Atk 13.

Comment

(1) *Re De Falbe* was upheld by the House of Lords.[41]

(2) Is *D'Eyncourt* criticised on the basis that there should have been no fixture, or that the tenant had a right to remove the fixture? Does anything survive from it?

We now turn to two more recent cases, which illustrate the operation of these principles to fixtures in houses.

[41] Sub nom *Leigh* v *Taylor* [1902] AC 157.

Extract 4.3.6

Berkley v Poulett [1977] 1 EGLR 86

Could a vendor remove paintings and other items?

SCARMAN LJ: . . . The answer today to the question whether objects which were originally chattels have become fixtures, that is to say part of the freehold, depends upon the application of two tests: (1) the method and degree of annexation; (2) the object and purpose of the annexation . . .

Since *Leigh* v *Taylor* [1902] AC 157 the question is really one of fact. The two tests were explained in that case by the Lord Chancellor (see the report at pp 158 and 159), who commented that not the law but our mode of life has changed over the years; that what has changed is 'the degree in which certain things have seemed susceptible of being put up as mere ornaments whereas at our earlier period the mere construction rendered it impossible sometimes to sever the thing which was put up from the realty'. In other words, a degree of annexation which in earlier times the law would have treated as conclusive may now prove nothing. If the purpose of the annexation be for the better enjoyment of the object itself, it may remain a chattel, notwithstanding a high degree of physical annexation. Clearly, however, it remains significant to discover the extent of physical disturbance of the building or the land involved in the removal of the object. If an object cannot be removed without serious damage to, or destruction of, some part of the realty, the case for its having become a fixture is a strong one. The relationship of the two tests to each other requires consideration. If there is no physical annexation there is no fixture. *Quicquid plantatur solo solo cedit*. Nevertheless an object, resting on the ground by its own weight alone, can be a fixture, if it be so heavy that there is no need to tie it into a foundation, and if it were put in place to improve the realty . . .

. . . It is enough to say that the pictures were firmly fixed and that their removal needed skill and experience if it were to be done without damage to the wall and panelling. Certainly they were firmly enough fixed to become fixtures if that was the object and purpose of their affixing . . . The decisive question is therefore as to the object and purpose of their affixing. Pictures had hung in the two rooms for centuries. 'The Return' had been in the ante-room for a very long time – perhaps ever since it was painted. The 7th Earl decided in the early part of the 20th century to install in the two rooms the panelling and so designed it that there were recesses for pictures. It is this feature which lends plausibility to the suggestion that the pictures, fitted into the recesses left for them, were not to be enjoyed as objects in themselves but as part of the grand architectural design of the two rooms. The Vice-Chancellor rejected this view. So do I. When the panelling was installed in the two rooms the design was either panelled walls with recesses for pictures to be enjoyed as pictures, or rooms having walls which were a composite of panelling and pictures: in other words, the pictures were to be part of a composite mural. I think the former was the truth . . . They were put in place on the wall to be enjoyed as pictures . . .

The statue and the sundial give rise in my judgment to no difficulty. Neither was at the time of the sale physically attached to the realty. The sundial was a small object and, once the Earl had detached it (as he did many years earlier) from its pedestal, it ceased to be part of the realty. The statue was heavy. It weighed 10 cwt and stood 5 ft 7 in high on its plinth. There is an issue as to whether it was cemented into the plinth or rested on its own weight. The question is not decisive, for, even if it was attached by a cement bond, it was (as events proved) easily removable . . . The best argument for the statue being a fixture was its careful siting in the West Lawn so as to form an integral part of the architectural design of the west elevation of the house. The design point is a good one so far as it goes: it explains the siting of the plinth, which undoubtedly was a fixture. But what was put upon the plinth was very much a matter for the taste of the occupier of the house for the time being. We know that at one time the object on the plinth had been a sundial . . . Sundial or statue – it did not matter to the design, so long as it was in the right place – a result ensured by the plinth which was firmly fixed into the ground. Being, as I think, unattached, the statue was, *prima facie*, not a fixture, but, even if it were attached, the application of the second test would lead to the same conclusion.

Comment

(1) Goff LJ dissented.

(2) Does this result fit easily with the cases on industrial premises, such as *Holland* v *Hodgson*?

Our second recent case concerns more everyday objects on a sale of a house.

Extract 4.3.7

TSB Bank plc v *Botham* [1996] EGCS 149[42]

ROCH LJ: . . . If the item, viewed objectively, is intended to be permanent and to afford a lasting improvement to the building, the thing will have become a fixture. If the attachment is temporary and is no more than is necessary for the item to be used and enjoyed, then it will remain a chattel. Some indicators can be identified. For example, if the item is ornamental and the attachment is simply to enable the item to be displayed and enjoyed as an adornment that will often indicate that this item is a chattel. Obvious examples are pictures. But this will not be the result in every case; for example ornamental tiles on the walls of kitchens and bathrooms. The ability to remove an item or its attachment from the building without damaging the fabric of the building is another indicator. The same item may in some areas be a chattel and in others a fixture. For example a cooker will, if free standing and connected to the building only by an electric flex, be a chattel. But it may be otherwise if the cooker is a split level cooker with the hob set into a work surface and the oven forming part of one of the cabinets in the kitchen . . .

I have no hesitation in agreeing with the judge that . . . the bathroom fittings namely the taps, plugs and showerhead together with the towel rails, soap dishes and lavatory roll holders which are all the items listed under the heading 'Ironmongery' in the schedule of disputed items helpfully prepared by Mr Chapman, the Bank's counsel for the purpose of this appeal, are fixtures.

Those items are attached to the building in such a way as to demonstrate a significant connection with the building, and are of a type consistent with the bathroom fittings such as the basins, baths, bidets and lavatories, as to demonstrate an intention to effect a permanent improvement to the flat. They are items necessary for a room which is used as a bathroom. They are not there, on the evidence which was before the judge and which is before us, to be enjoyed for themselves, but they are there as accessories which enable the room to be used and enjoyed as a bathroom. Viewed objectively, they were intended to be permanent and to afford a lasting improvement to the property.

The third group about which I have no doubt is . . . the kitchen units, including the sink . . . Again in my judgment the degree of annexation, the fact that between the working surfaces and the underside of the wall cupboards of the wall units there is tiling, demonstrates both a degree of annexation and an intention to effect a permanent improvement to the kitchen of the flat so as to make those units fixtures . . .

I would allow the appeal with regard to the fitted carpets and the curtains and blinds . . . These items, although made or cut to fit the particular floor or window concerned, are attached to the building in an insubstantial manner . . . In my opinion, the method of keeping fitted carpets

---

[42] Text taken from New Law Online.

in place and keeping curtains hung are no more than is required for enjoyment of those items as curtains and carpets . . .

This leaves . . . the white goods [hob, oven, freezer, refrigerator, washing machine etc] in the kitchen . . .

The judge . . . found that they were manufactured to standard sizes, they were fitted into standard sized holes and that they were removable. They were very probably expensive items, although he had no direct evidence of their value. He held them to be fixtures because:

> 'They were there as part of the overall kitchen. If one were taking a flat on a lease one would expect them to be there. They were put in to be part of the kitchen as it stood. They were all physically fixed in, not only resting on their own weight, but being plumbed in, wired in and in most cases aligned with and perhaps to some extent abutted to, so that they could not be too easily removed, the remaining parts of the fitted kitchen. A fitted kitchen is a whole.'

I differ from the judge on this group of items on the slender facts in this case . . . Here the judge should have reminded himself that the degree of annexation was slight: no more than that which was needed for these items to be used for their normal purposes. In fact these items remain in position by their own weight and not by virtue of the links between them and the building. All these items can be bought separately, and are often acquired on an instalment payment basis, when ownership does not pass to the householder immediately. Many of these items are designed to last for a limited period of time and will require replacing after a relatively short number of years. The degree of annexation is therefore slight. Disconnection can be done without damage to the fabric of the building and normally without difficulty. The purpose of such links as there were to the building was to enable these machines to be used to wash clothes or dishes or preserve or cook food.

Comment

How well do these solutions fit (i) the principles relating to fixtures; (ii) the expectations of sellers and buyers of houses?

Roch LJ places some stress on the fact that certain objects are commonly bought on hire purchase and remain in the ownership of the finance company. This leads to a more general question as to the nature of the intention.

Extract 4.3.8

Hobson v *Gorringe* [1897] 1 Ch 182

It was argued that the fact that the object was subject to a hire purchase agreement showed that there was no intention that it become a fixture.

A L SMITH LJ: . . . Now, in *Holland* v *Hodgson*,[i] Lord Blackburn, when dealing with the 'circumstances to shew intention', was contemplating and referring to circumstances which shewed the degree of annexation and the object of such annexation which were patent for all to see, and not to the circumstances of a chance agreement that might or might not exist between an owner of a chattel and a hirer thereof. This is made clear by the examples that Lord Blackburn alludes to to shew his meaning . . . In each of these instances it will be seen that the circumstance to shew intention is the degree and object of the annexation which is in itself apparent, and thus manifested the intention. Lord Blackburn in his proposed rule was not contemplating a hire and purchase agreement between the owner of a chattel and a hirer or any other agreement unknown to either a vendee or mortgagee in fee of land, and the argument that such a consideration was to be entertained, in our judgment, is not well founded.

[i] LR 7 CP 328.

Extract 4.3.9

Melluish v BMI (No 3) Ltd [1996] AC 454

LORD BROWNE-WILKINSON: . . . The equipment in these cases was attached to the land in such a manner that, to all outward appearance, it formed part of the land and was intended so to do. Such fixtures are, in law, owned by the owner of the land. It was suggested in argument that this result did not follow if it could be demonstrated that, as between the owner of the land and the person fixing the chattel to it, there was a common intention that the chattel should not belong to the owner of the land . . .

    Hobson v *Gorringe* [1897] 1 Ch 182 . . . (which was approved by this House in *Reynolds* v *Ashby & Son* [1904] AC 466) demonstrates that the intention of the parties as to the ownership of the chattel fixed to the land is only material so far as such intention can be presumed from the degree and object of the annexation. The terms expressly or implicitly agreed between the fixer of the chattel and the owner of the land cannot affect the determination of the question whether, in law, the chattel has become a fixture and therefore in law belongs to the owner of the soil: see pp 192–193. The terms of such agreement will regulate the contractual rights to sever the chattel from the land as between the parties to that contract and, where an equitable right is conferred by the contract, as against certain third parties. But such agreement cannot prevent the chattel, once fixed, becoming in law part of the land and as such owned by the owner of the land so long as it remains fixed.

Comment

(1) In what way is intention to be taken into account?

(2) This approach, coupled with the stress[43] that tenants' fixtures depend on separate principles, may indicate a somewhat reduced role for intention. Is this to be seen as a good or bad thing?

B. Removable fixtures

Extract 4.3.10

Elwes v Maw (1802) 3 East 38 (102 ER 510)

LORD ELLENBOROUGH CJ: . . . But the general rule on this subject is that . . . where a lessee, having annexed any thing to the freehold during his term, afterwards takes it away, it is waste. But this rule at a very early period had several exceptions attempted to be engrafted upon it, and which were at last effectually engrafted upon it, in favour of trade and of those vessels and utensils which are immediately subservient to the purposes of trade . . . However in process of time the rule in favour of the right in the tenant to remove utensils set up in relation to trade became fully established: and accordingly, we find Lord Holt, in *Poole's case*, Salk 368, laying down, (in the instance of a soap-boiler, an under tenant, whose vats, coppers, &c fixed had been taken in execution, and on which account the first lessee had brought an action against the sheriff,) that during the term the soap-boiler might well remove the vats he set up in relation to trade; and that he might do it by the common law, and not by virtue of any special custom, in favour of trade, and to encourage industry; but that after the term they became a gift in law to him in reversion, and were not removeable . . . The indulgence in favour of the tenant for years

---

[43] See p 101 above.

during the term has been since carried still further, and he has been allowed to carry away matters of ornament, as ornamental marble chimney-pieces, pier glasses, hangings, wainscot fixed only by screws, and the like . . .

Comment

(1) This applies to tenants for life as well as tenants under leases.

(2) What types of fixtures can and cannot be removed?

One complicating factor is that some fixtures (even if otherwise trade fixtures) may, to quote Willes J,[44] 'be made so completely a part of the land, as being essential to its convenient use, that even a tenant could not remove them. An example of this class of chattel may be found in doors or windows.' Thus the object may be a landlord's fixture and irremovable, a removable fixture or a chattel. How does this fit with the threefold categorisation advocated in *Elitestone Ltd* v *Morris*?[45]

C. Is a right to remove fixtures a property interest?

A person who lends goods (or sells goods on credit) frequently reserves a right to remove them should they be affixed to land. The term can readily be enforced as a matter of contract, but can rights to remove bind purchasers (most commonly mortgagees) of the land? Three routes, whereby removal may operate, may be identified. The first is that it is clear that the tenant's right to remove affects any third party bound by the lease.[46] The second is to treat the mortgagee as authorising the removal. The third is to treat the right to remove as a proprietary interest binding the mortgagee. This last analysis can work only if the mortgage post-dates the fixture, for otherwise the mortgage must have priority as the first in time.

Extract 4.3.11

Gough v *Wood & Co* [1894] 1 QB 713

The second route described above (authorising removal) was argued.

LINDLEY LJ: . . . By leaving the mortgagor in possession the mortgagee impliedly authorized him to carry on his business and to sell and remove the plants, trees, and shrubs which, though fixed to the soil, constituted his stock-in-trade. This implied authority can hardly be confined to such things, but may fairly be regarded, and I think ought to be regarded, as authorizing the mortgagor whilst in possession to hire and bring and fix other fixtures necessary for his business, and to agree with their owner that he shall be at liberty to remove them at the end of the time for which they are hired. Unless this be so, persons dealing bona fide with mortgagors in possession will be exposed to very unreasonable risks; and honest business with them will be seriously impeded.

---

[44] *Climie* v *Wood* (1869) LR 4 Ex 328 at p 329.
[45] [1997] 1 WLR 687; Extract 4.3.1 above.
[46] *Sanders* v *Davis* (1885) 15 QBD 218.

Extract 4.3.12

Hobson v Gorringe [1897] 1 Ch 182

A L SMITH LJ: This case . . . raises a considerable question, which is whether a mortgagee of land in fee, when he enters upon the mortgaged premises, can take possession of an engine which is attached to the soil thereof by means of bolts and screws, although the engine did not and never had belonged to the mortgagor, but to a third party.

    . . . The case of *Gough* v *Wood & Co*,[i] decided in this court, in no way assists the plaintiff [the third party owner of the engine], and has no application to the present case. That case was decided solely upon the ground that the mortgagee had acquiesced in the removal by the mortgagor during his tenancy of trade fixtures. For additional confirmation of the ratio decidendi of this case what was said by Lindley LJ and by Kay LJ in the case of the *Huddersfield Banking Co* v *Henry Lister & Son*[ii] may be referred to. Even if in the present case a licence had been granted by Gorringe [mortgagee] to King [mortgagor] to remove the gas engine during the continuance of a term, neither of which conditions in fact existed, Gorringe, by entering and taking possession of the land and engine, would have determined such licence.

[i] [1894] 1 QB 713.
[ii] [1895] 2 Ch 273, 282, 286.

Comment

(1) The *Huddersfield* case suggests that *Gough* is limited to cases where the removal is in the normal course of trade and therefore inapplicable where the purpose of removal is to prevent the mortgagee from taking the fixture. How significant would this restriction be?

(2) The cases combine to ensure that *Gough* 'depended on the special circumstances of the case, and I do not think it has ever been cited except to be distinguished'.[47]

(3) Is it good legal policy to disallow the removal of fixtures which post-date the mortgage?[48]

Where the right to remove pre-dates a mortgage, it may be possible to argue that it constitutes a proprietary right binding the mortgagee.

Extract 4.3.13

Re Samuel Allen & Sons Ltd [1907] 1 Ch 575

PARKER J: . . . It appears, however, in the judgment of A L Smith LJ in *Hobson v Gorringe*[i] that he conceived that the result might have been different if when the mortgagee took his mortgage he had had notice of the interest of the owner of the chattels under the hiring agreement . . . What A L Smith LJ says is: '. . . Neither could the right be enforced in equity against any purchaser of the land without notice of the right, and the defendant Gorringe is such a purchaser' – Gorringe being the mortgagee who had the legal estate.

    Now, for what it is worth, I think that passage is in favour of Mr Cave's contention, and seems to shew that A L Smith LJ thought that, in the particular case he was dealing with, if the legal mortgagee had had notice of the hiring agreement, the decision would have been otherwise than it was . . . The point, therefore, though not covered by authority, is more or less affected by the dicta of the judges who have decided the cases cited to me. On the other hand, it is said that the hiring agreement is of such a nature that it creates a purely personal right . . .

---

[47] *Ellis* v *Glover & Hobson Ltd* [1908] 1 KB 388 at p 401.
[48] Goode, *Hire Purchase Law and Practice* (2nd ed), pp 740–741.

Now I do not think I should be right if I were to hold that an agreement of this sort was of a purely personal nature. These agreements are very common and very useful, and, of course, it is open to a mortgagee, when he takes his mortgage, to make what inquiries he likes as to whether there are any agreements affecting the fixtures upon the property.

ⁱ [1897] 1 Ch 192.

Comment

(1) The decision was soon approved by the Court of Appeal[49] and clearly represents the present state of the law.

(2) Does the recognition that the right to remove is a proprietary interest fit our perceptions as to when new proprietary interests will be permitted?

Further reading

Finding

Goodhart, A L (1929) 3 CLJ 195: Three cases on possession.

Marshall (1949) 2 CLP 68: The problem of finding.

Adverse possession

Cobb and Fox (2007) 27 LS 236: Living outside the system? The (im)morality of urban squatting after the Land Registration Act 2002.

Dockray, M [1985] Conv 272: Why do we need adverse possession?

Radley-Gardner, O (2005) 25 OxJLS 727: Civilized squatting.

Wade, H W R (1962) 78 LQR 541: Landlord, tenant and squatter.

Fixtures

Guest, A and Lever, J (1963) 27 Conv 30: Hire-purchase, equipment leases and fixtures.

Luther, P (2004) 24 OxJLS 597: Fixtures and chattels: a question of more or less . . .

---

[49] *Re Morrison, Jones & Taylor Ltd* [1914] 1 Ch 50.

5

The transfer and creation of property interests

This chapter considers ways in which interests in all forms of property can be transferred and created. For example, we will study how the holder of a fee simple in land can transfer the fee simple to a purchaser or create a lease.

As will be seen, different forms of property involve different rules. Occasionally, an expression of intention is sufficient, as with declarations of trust and sale of personalty. Sometimes the law recognises transfer of possession, as with gifts of personalty. Particularly as regards land, statutory rules often require writing and registration. These writing requirements were introduced in order to promote certainty and to avoid the fraudulent assertion of rights that in fact do not exist, but they can lead to unfair results if advantage is taken of failure to observe the necessary formalities. (These problems with formality requirements are considered in Chapters 6 and 7.)

1. Deeds

Before looking at the rules applicable to different forms of property, we must first consider deeds – a type of document. Deeds provide a particularly formal type of writing. As will be seen below, their importance lies in two contexts. First, certain transactions require a deed to be effective: this is true of the transfer and creation of most legal interests in land. Next, a deed is a powerful instrument. It enables the unilateral[1] transfer or creation of virtually any interest in virtually any property and is effective regardless of whether there is consideration.

What is a deed? The old requirements that a deed must be 'signed, sealed and delivered' have been modified by legislation.

Extract 5.1.1

Law of Property (Miscellaneous Provisions) Act 1989, s 1

1.—(1) Any rule of law which—
    (a) restricts the substances on which a deed may be written;
    (b) requires a seal for the valid execution of an instrument as a deed by an individual; . . .
is abolished.
  (2) An instrument shall not be a deed unless—
    (a) it makes it clear on its face that it is intended to be a deed by the person making it or, as the case may be, by the parties to it (whether by describing itself as a deed or expressing itself to be executed or signed as a deed or otherwise); and

---

[1] In the sense that only the transferor or creator need sign the deed. The person in whom the interest is created can disclaim it: *Standing* v *Bowring* (1885) 31 Ch D 282.

    (b) it is validly executed as a deed—
        (i) by that person or a person authorised to execute it in the name or on behalf of that person, or
        (ii) by one or more of those parties or a person authorised to execute it in the name or on behalf of one or more of those parties.

  (2A) For the purposes of subsection (2)(a) above, an instrument shall not be taken to make it clear on its face that it is intended to be a deed merely because it is executed under seal.

  (3) An instrument is validly executed as a deed by an individual if, and only if—
    (a) it is signed—
        (i) by him in the presence of a witness who attests the signature; or
        (ii) at his direction and in his presence and the presence of two witnesses who each attest the signature; and
    (b) it is delivered as a deed.

Comment

(1) The requirement of witnesses is a new one. Does s 1 create risks which those executing deeds need to take into account?

(2) If there is some irregularity, but on its face the document appears to satisfy s 1, does this present a danger to those relying on the deed?[2]

(3) Execution of deeds by companies is dealt with by the Companies Act 2006, s 46. There is no witness requirement and, subject to contrary intention, delivery is presumed on execution.

Section 1 deals with the requirements for there to be a deed, but is not explicit as to how we tell whether a document is a deed. The previous law required a seal and this avoided any such difficulty.

Extract 5.1.2

HSBC Trust Company (UK) Ltd v *Quinn* [2007] EWHC 1543 (Ch)

NUGEE QC: 51. Mr Schmitz relies on a number of factors as indicating that the parties intended it to be a deed. First, the language is appropriate to a formal document . . . ; second the parties have given their full names and addresses; and third, that care was taken to see that the signatures were witnessed and the witnesses gave their names and addresses. I fully accept that these are all indications that the document was intended to be a formal one and no doubt intended to have formal legal effect. But I do not regard any of them, singly or together, as any indication that the parties intended it to take effect as a deed, let alone as making it clear on the face of the document that they did. All that they show is that the parties intended it to be legally binding, and in my judgment this is plainly not enough; what is needed is something showing that the parties intended the document to have the extra status of being a deed. It is perhaps unlikely that a document drawn up by non-lawyers would happen to do this . . .

Comment

Is this an unduly restrictive approach, at least as regards those who are not legally advised?

It remains a requirement that the deed is 'delivered'.

---

[2] See *Shah* v *Shah* [2002] QB 35.

Extract 5.1.3

Alan Estates Ltd v *WG Stores Ltd* [1982] Ch 511 (Court of Appeal)

SIR DENYS BUCKLEY: . . . 'Delivery' for this purpose is not to be confused with any form of exchange of documents or of physical delivery of the instrument to someone other than the maker.

. . .

The maker of the deed may retain it physically in his own possession and yet 'deliver' it so long as he makes clear that he intends it as his deed presently binding on him. Anything which shows that he treats the instrument as his deed will suffice: *Tupper* v *Foulkes* (1861) 9 CBNS 797, 809, *per* William J. If, however, an instrument intended to take effect as a deed be delivered with the intention that it shall operate only at some future time or on the happening of a specified event, or upon condition that it shall not be operative until some condition is performed, it is said to be delivered as an escrow.

. . .

Again no special form of words is necessary to constitute delivery of an instrument delivery as an escrow: it is a question of intention, however that intention may be displayed. After the happening of the event or the performance of the condition upon which the delivery of an escrow was made, the instrument operates as a deed without any further delivery.

. . .

I am much disposed to think that the effect of delivery upon a deed is the same as the effect of delivery upon an escrow. Each renders the delivered instrument inescapably binding upon the deliverer. The difference between a deed and an escrow lies not in the binding quality of the instrument but in the time and circumstances at and in which the obligation can be enforced.

Comment

(1) Does delivery mean anything?

(2) What is an escrow? Is there any real difference between an undelivered deed and an escrow?

(3) Is it likely that the maker 'intends it as his deed presently binding on him' if negotiations are still continuing? See *Bolton MBC* v *Torkington* [2004] Ch 66.

2. Contracts for sales and dispositions of interests in land

It is common for the transfer or creation of interests to be preceded by a contract. At least for land, the contract does not itself pass the interest in question,[3] but enables each party to insist on completion of the transaction by a subsequent transfer. However, such contracts relating to land (estate contracts) do more than this: they confer an immediate equitable interest on the purchaser (though not giving any right to immediate enjoyment of the land). Most common is the contract to sell the fee simple. The remainder of this section will be devoted to such contracts, although the same principles apply to contracts for the transfer or creation of any interest in land. Contracts for forms of property other than land rarely raise equivalent issues.

When a buyer of land is found, it is not usual for contracts to be entered into immediately. A delay is likely while the buyer makes enquiries to ensure that the property is suitable for his or her purposes (these may include a survey and checks made of the seller) and that

---

[3] For sales of goods, title may pass under the contract of sale. Surprisingly, the Supreme Court in *Scott* v *Southern Pacific Mortgages Ltd* [2014] 3 WLR 1163 stated that the holder of an estate contract can create only personal rights.

funds are available. In addition, purchasers often need to sell their existing houses before committing themselves. The law recognises these needs.

Extract 5.2.1

Tiverton Estates Ltd v *Wearwell Ltd* [1975] Ch 146

LORD DENNING MR: On April 10, 1973, this court decided *Law* v *Jones* [1974] Ch 112. It caused consternation amongst the solicitors in this country. They had always understood that, on a sale of land, they could protect their clients by writing their letters 'subject to contract.' *Law* v *Jones* shattered this belief . . .

Law v *Jones* has sounded an alarm bell in the offices of every solicitor in the land. And no wonder. It is everyday practice for a solicitor, who is instructed in a sale of land, to start the correspondence with a letter 'subject to contract' setting out the terms or enclosing a draft. He does it in the confidence that it protects his client. It means that the client is not bound by what has taken place in conversation. The reason is that, for over a hundred years, the courts have held that the effect of the words 'subject to contract' is that the matter remains in negotiation until a formal contract is executed: see *Eccles* v *Bryant and Pollock* [1948] Ch 93. But *Law* v *Jones* has taken away all protection from the client . . .

[After considering other authorities] I would, therefore, hold here and now that *Law* v *Jones* was wrongly decided, and should be overruled. The writing here, being expressly 'subject to contract', was not sufficient to satisfy the statute. There is no enforceable contract between the parties.

Agreements subject to contract bring their own problems. As either party can withdraw, neither can be confident that the transaction will go ahead.

Extract 5.2.2

Pitt v *PHH Asset Management Ltd* [1994] 1 WLR 327

SIR THOMAS BINGHAM MR: . . . For very many people their first and closest contact with the law is when they come to buy or sell a house. They frequently find it a profoundly depressing and frustrating experience. The vendor puts his house on the market. He receives an offer which is probably less than his asking price. He agonises over whether to accept or hold out for more. He decides to accept, perhaps after negotiating some increase. A deal is struck. Hands are shaken. The vendor celebrates, relaxes, makes plans for his own move and takes his house off the market. Then he hears that the purchaser who was formerly pleading with him to accept his offer has decided not to proceed. No explanation is given, no apology made. The vendor has to embark on the whole dreary process of putting his house on the market all over again.

For the purchaser the process is, if anything, worse. After a series of futile visits to unsuitable houses he eventually finds the house of his dreams. He makes an offer, perhaps at the asking price, perhaps at what the agent tells him the vendor is likely to accept. The offer is accepted. A deal is done. The purchaser instructs solicitors to act. He perhaps commissions an architect to plan alterations. He makes arrangements to borrow money. He puts his own house on the market. He makes arrangements to move. He then learns that the vendor has decided to sell to someone else, perhaps for the price already offered and accepted, perhaps for an increased price achieved by a covert, unofficial auction. Again, no explanation, no apology. The vendor is able to indulge his self-interest, even his whims, without exposing himself to any legal penalty.

This practice of 'gazumping' can be restricted if (for example) the seller contracts not to negotiate with anybody else for a specified period.

PETER GIBSON LJ: . . . It seems to me that what was agreed was a lock-out agreement. In *Walford* v *Miles* [1992] 2 AC 128, 139, Lord Ackner said:

> 'There is clearly no reason in the English contract law why A, for good consideration, should not achieve an enforceable agreement whereby B agrees for a specified period of time, not to negotiate with anyone except A in relation to the sale of his property.'

He identified that negative element in such an agreement as being the characteristic of a lock-out agreement:

> '. . . B, by agreeing not to negotiate for this fixed period with a third party, locks himself out of such negotiations. He has in no legal sense locked himself into negotiations with A. What A has achieved is an exclusive opportunity, for a fixed period, to try and come to terms with B, an opportunity for which he has, unless he makes his agreement under seal, to give good consideration.'

Comment

(1) The lock-out agreement was held not to require writing (unlike contracts to sell land).

(2) How useful are such agreements likely to be for buyers and sellers of land?

A. Writing requirements

Leaving the above considerations on one side, the most significant element of estate contracts is the requirement of writing. This has existed for centuries (being re-enacted by the Law of Property Act 1925 (hereafter LPA), s 40), but was significantly modified in 1989. Both the old law and, sadly, the new law have given rise to much litigation.

Extract 5.2.3

Law of Property (Miscellaneous Provisions) Act 1989, s 2

2.—(1) A contract for the sale or other disposition of an interest in land can only be made in writing and only by incorporating all the terms which the parties have expressly agreed in one document or, where contracts are exchanged, in each.

(2) The terms may be incorporated in a document either by being set out in it or by reference to some other document.

(3) The document incorporating the terms or, where contracts are exchanged, one of the documents incorporating them (but not necessarily the same one) must be signed by or on behalf of each party to the contract.

(5) This section does not apply in relation to—

(a) a contract to grant such a lease as is mentioned in section 54(2) of the Law of Property Act 1925 (short leases);

(b) a contract made in the course of a public auction; . . .

and nothing in this section affects the creation or operation of resulting, implied or constructive trusts.

(6) In this section—

'disposition' has the same meaning as in the Law of Property Act 1925; 'interest in land' means any estate, interest or charge in or over land or in or over the proceeds of sale of land.

Comment

(1) Disposition (see s 2(1), (6)) is defined by LPA, s 205(1)(ii) so as to include mortgages, charges and leases. This makes it clear that contracts for leases, for example, are within the 1989 Act; contracts for the transfer of existing leases are covered by the plain wording of s 2(1).

(2) For the application of s 2 to mortgages by deposit of title deeds, see *United Bank of Kuwait plc* v *Sahib*.[4]

(3) These rules will become obsolete if electronic conveyancing is introduced. This topic is considered later in this chapter in the section on Land.

Extract 5.2.4

***Firstpost Homes Ltd* v *Johnson* [1995] 1 WLR 1567**

PETER GIBSON LJ: Section 2 brought about a markedly different regime from that which obtained hitherto. Whereas under section 40 contracts which did not comply with its requirements were not void but were merely unenforceable by action, contracts which do not comply with section 2 are ineffective: a contract for the sale of an interest in land can only be made in writing and in conformity with the other provisions of section 2. Whereas an oral contract was allowed and enforceable provided that it was evidenced in writing and the memorandum or the note thereof was signed by or on behalf of the party against whom it was sought to be enforced, oral contracts are now of no effect and all contracts must be signed by or on behalf of all the parties. Whereas the contract or the memorandum or note evidencing the contract previously could be contained in more than one document, only one document is now allowed, save where contracts are exchanged, although reference to another document may be permitted in the circumstances laid down in subsections (2) and (3). Whereas the memorandum or note needed for section 40 did not have to contain every term of the contract, all the terms must now be contained in the document in question . . .

Comment

(1) The old cases must be viewed with some suspicion, as it cannot be assumed that they will survive the stricter regime introduced in 1989, even where they were not specifically reversed.

(2) The 1989 changes greatly reduce the need for 'subject to contract' clauses.

(i) What transactions are included?

The scope of the section is made fairly clear by its express provisions. It might be noted that contracts for both legal and equitable interests are included, as are contracts relating to the proceeds of sale of land. Is there any reason why contracts relating to proceeds of sale should have to be in writing? One example of uncertainty concerning the scope of the legislation has arisen as regards options to purchase. Options involve two stages: the grant of the option and the full contract of sale which arises on the exercise of the option.

---

[4] [1997] Ch 107; see Extract 21.2.2 below.

Extract 5.2.5

Spiro v *Glencrown Properties Ltd* [1991] Ch 537

HOFFMANN J: . . . Apart from authority, it seems to me plain enough that section 2 was intended to apply to the agreement which created the option and not to the notice by which it was exercised. Section 2, which replaced section 40 of the Law of Property Act 1925, was intended to prevent disputes over whether the parties had entered into a binding agreement or over what terms they had agreed. It prescribes the formalities for recording their mutual consent. But only the grant of the option depends upon consent. The exercise of the option is a unilateral act. It would destroy the very purpose of the option if the purchaser had to obtain the vendor's countersignature to the notice by which it was exercised . . .

The language of section 2 places no obstacle in the way of construing the grant of the option as the relevant contract. An option to buy land can properly be described as a contract for the sale of that land conditional on the exercise of the option. A number of eminent judges have so described it . . .

The purchaser, however, submits that I am constrained by authority to characterise an option as an irrevocable offer which does not become a contract for the sale of land until it has been accepted by the notice which exercises the option . . .

But the concept of an offer is of course normally used as part of the technique for ascertaining whether the parties have reached that mutual consent which is a necessary element in the formation of a contract. In this primary sense, it is of the essence of an offer that by itself it gives rise to no legal obligations. It was for this reason that Diplock LJ said in *Varty* v *British South Africa Co* [1965] Ch 508, 523:

'To speak of an enforceable option as an "irrevocable offer" is juristically a contradiction in terms, for the adjective "irrevocable" connotes the existence of an obligation on the part of the offeror, while the noun "offer" connotes the absence of any obligation until the offer has been accepted.'

This does not mean that in Lord Diplock's opinion, Lord Herschell LC and Lord Watson in *Helby* v *Matthews* [1895] AC 471 were speaking nonsense. They were not using 'offer' in its primary sense but, as often happens in legal reasoning, by way of metaphor or analogy. Such metaphors can be vivid and illuminating but prove a trap for the unwary if pressed beyond their original context . . .

[T]he analogy of an irrevocable offer is, as I have said, a useful way of describing the position of the purchaser between the grant and exercise of the option. Thus in *J Sainsbury Plc* v *O'Connor* [1990] STC 516 Millett J used it to explain why the grantee of an option to buy shares did not become the beneficial owner until he had exercised the option.

But the irrevocable offer metaphor has much less explanatory power in relation to the position of the vendor. The effect of the 'offer' which the vendor has made is, from his point of view, so different from that of an offer in its primary sense that the metaphor is of little assistance . . .

Thus in explaining the vendor's position, the analogy to which the courts usually appeal is that of a conditional contract. This analogy might also be said to be imperfect, because one generally thinks of a conditional contract as one in which the contingency does not lie within the sole power of one of the parties to the contract . . .

The purchaser's argument requires me to say that 'irrevocable offer' and 'conditional contract' are mutually inconsistent concepts and that I must range myself under one or other banner and declare the other to be heretical. I hope that I have demonstrated this to be a misconception about the nature of legal reasoning. An option is not strictly speaking either an offer or a conditional contract. It does not have all the incidents of the standard form of either of these concepts. To that extent it is a relationship sui generis. But there are ways in which it resembles each of them. Each analogy is in the proper context a valid way of characterising the situation created by an option. The question in this case is not whether one analogy is true and the other false, but which is appropriate to be used in the construction of section 2 of the Law of Property (Miscellaneous Provisions) Act 1989.

. . .

In my judgment there is nothing in the authorities which prevents me from giving section 2 of the Act of 1989 the meaning which I consider to have been the clear intention of the legislature . . . It follows that in my view the grant of the option was the only 'contract for the sale or other disposition of an interest in land' within the meaning of the section and the contract duly complied with the statutory requirements.

Comment

While it is plain that the result in *Spiro* is desirable, is it readily justified by the wording of s 2?

A rather similar sort of right is a right of pre-emption: a right to buy if the seller wishes to sell. Today,[5] the Land Registration Act 2002, s 115(1) provides:

A right of pre-emption in relation to registered land has effect from the time of creation as an interest capable of binding successors in title (subject to the rules about the effect of dispositions on priority).

Very different are agreements whereby land will be sold to a third party.

Extract 5.2.6

Nweze v Nwoko [2004] 2 P&CR 667

A compromise provided that land should be marketed, with the proceeds of sale going to the Nwezes.

WALLER LJ: 24.   It may be that in a situation such as existed in the *Jelson* case [*Jelson Ltd* v *Derby County Council* [1999] 39 EG 149] where A and B (the local authority) made a contract under which B can call for property to be transferred to a nominated buyer C (its housing association) on terms provided for in the schedule to the contract, that would be a contract to which Section 2 would apply, because it is a contract for the sale or disposition of an interest in land rather as an option to purchase is such a contract . . .
26.   Under the oral compromise, without the marketing of the property there can be no sale, or disposition, and it would simply be a misuse of language in my view to say that the compromise is a contract for sale or disposition of an interest in land . . . [For section 2 to apply, it would have to be shown that] the Nwezes were intended to gain an interest in the legal or equitable sense.

Comment

If A (the owner) and B agree that there should be a sale to C, does either policy or the wording of s 2 indicate that C should sign the contract?[6]

Different again is an agreement relating to the line of a disputed boundary.

---

[5] Previously, proprietary status had (controversially) been denied by *Pritchard v Briggs* [1980] Ch 338.
[6] See *RG Kensington Management Co Ltd v Hutchinson IDH Ltd* [2003] 2 P&CR 195 at [57].

Extract 5.2.7

Joyce v *Rigolli* [2004] EWCA Civ 79

Neighbours agreed the line of an uncertain boundary, involving a slight but deliberate change.

ARDEN LJ: 32. . . . the land would also be quite difficult to define without the disproportionate expense of a survey. Further, to make the validity of a boundary agreement dependent on the preparation and execution of a written contract would be contrary to the important public policy in upholding boundary agreements so powerfully identified by Megarry J in *Neilson* v *Poole* [(1969) 20 P&CR 909]. In those circumstances, I do not consider that Parliament, which after all enacted section 2 against the background of *Neilson* v *Poole*, could have intended section 2 to apply to transfers of land pursuant to boundary agreements of Megarry J's latter type ('demarcating' agreements) simply because a trivial transfer or transfers of land were consciously involved.

34. . . . In interpreting legislation it is a well-established part of the court's role to see whether a situation has arisen in which the mischief against which Parliament has legislated does not apply or is outweighed by other policy considerations of the law, and if so, whether an acceptable way of dealing with that problem can be found. As Megarry J put it, a boundary agreement is 'an act of peace, quieting strife and averting litigation'. If section 2(1) applies where trivial transfers of land are consciously involved, the expense to the parties will also be disproportionate to the value of the land involved. Accordingly, in my judgment, it can in this case properly be concluded that section 2 does not apply to trivial dispositions of land consciously made pursuant to an informal boundary agreement of the 'demarcating' kind.

Comment

(1) Can s 2 be interpreted in the way Arden LJ desires? Does it represent good policy?

(2) What happens if there is a boundary agreement when the boundary is not disputed? See *Nata Lee Ltd* v *Abid* [2014] EWCA Civ 1652.

Prosser QC has said this about the amount of land involved:[7]

> The applicants submit that this interpretation of section 2(1) does not apply where more than a trivial amount of land is disposed of. I do not agree. As we have seen, the Court of Appeal in *Joyce's* case [2004] EWCA Civ 79 applied the reasoning of Megarry J in *Neilson* v *Poole* 20 P & CR 909, and it was no part of Megarry J's reasoning that a contract to demarcate which has a disposing effect is a contract to convey where more than a trivial amount of land is disposed of. . . . In my view, therefore, Arden LJ was of the opinion that a demarcation agreement which has a disposing effect does not fall foul of section 2(1) unless it has a disposing purpose *and* more than a trivial amount of land is disposed of.

(ii) The requirement of writing; terms of the contract

It has been seen that the contract, including all its terms, must be in writing. It is easy to appreciate that the parties may fail to include an agreed term in the written contract. Prima facie, s 2 is not satisfied. Is the result that there is no contract, or that those terms which are written can be enforced?

The courts have recognised that there may be a collateral contract. Thus the buyer might say to the seller 'I will sign the contract of purchase if you agree to replace the lounge window,

---

[7] *Yeates* v *Line* [2012] EWHC 3085 (Ch) at [30]; [2013] Ch 363.

the wood of which is rotten.' *Record* v *Bell*[8] accepts that such a collateral contract is a separate agreement which need not satisfy s 2. In *Record* v *Bell* itself, the collateral promise was as to the state of the title. Is this a proper application of the collateral contract principle?[9]

Extract 5.2.8

North Eastern Properties Ltd v *Coleman* [2010] 1 WLR 2715 (Court of Appeal)

The buyer and seller of 11 properties agreed that a 'finder's fee' of 2% should be payable to the purchaser, but should not appear in the contract. The contract stated: 'This agreement contains the entire agreement between the parties.'

BRIGGS J: 42.   None the less, it does not seem to me that anything in the differences between section 2(1) of the 1989 Act and its ancestor in the Bill proposed by the Law Commission comes anywhere near to making it inappropriate to conclude, as I do, that it was no part of Parliament's intention by enacting section 2 of the 1989 Act to make it easier for people who have genuinely contracted to escape their contractual obligations.

43.   Even more unfortunately, the reported cases in which the courts have sought to interpret and apply section 2(1) of the 1989 Act demonstrate that, because of the rigorous discipline which it imposes upon parties to land contracts, it does indeed enable persons who have genuinely contracted to do just that. It enables parties to land contracts who have changed their minds to look around for expressly agreed terms which have not found their way into the final form of land contract which they signed, for the precise purpose of avoiding their obligations, on the ground that the lack of discipline of their counterparty, or even their own lack of discipline, has rendered the contract void. As Judge Behrens noted in the present case, the exclusion of the 2% finder's fee from each of the 11 contracts occurred at the express request, and to serve the commercial purposes of, the defendant purchasers. Mr Holland did not on their behalf attempt to suggest that a successful outcome for his clients on the section 2 issue would do otherwise than to provide a wholly unmerited escape from genuine obligations deliberately entered into.

44.   It is not uncommon to find a statutory provision which, in seeking to remedy one mischief, unexpectedly creates another, which cannot be undone by any purposive approach to construction. In the present case, the undeserved escape route which, on Mr Holland's submissions, would be afforded to his clients by succeeding on the section 2 issue would give rise to an injustice of a type which it was an express purpose of the 1989 Act to mitigate or prevent.

45.   Although I am mindful of the need to avoid treating an apparent parliamentary purpose as the basis simply for disapplying a statutory provision in a case in which its application would otherwise give rise to injustice, I consider it legitimate to approach the interpretation and application to the unusual facts of this case of section 2(1) of the 1989 Act upon the basis that if it can be construed so as to prevent or mitigate the injustice of enabling genuine contracting parties to escape from their obligations, it ought to be.

46.   A party seeking to avoid a land contract under section 2 must identify a term which the parties have expressly agreed, which is not to be found in the single, or exchanged, signed document. It is not sufficient merely to show that the land contract formed part of a larger transaction which was subject to other expressly agreed terms which are absent from the land contract. The expressly agreed term must, if it is required by section 2 to be included in the single document, be a term of the sale of the land, rather than a term of some simultaneous contract (whether for the sale of a chattel or the provision of a service) which happens to take place at the same time as the land contract, and to form part of one commercial transaction.

---

[8] [1991] 1 WLR 853; foreshadowed by Law Com No 164, para 5.7.
[9] An attempt to put part of the purchase price into a collateral contract failed in *Sukhlall* v *Bansoodeb* [2013] EWHC 952 (Ch).

Section 2(1) does not prohibit parties from structuring a transaction, for example, for the sale of the whole of a company's assets, in such a way that the land sale is dealt with in a different document from the sale of stock, work in progress or goodwill, unless the sale of the land is conditional upon the sale of the other assets. For an illustration of this point, see *Grossman* v *Hooper* [2001] 2 EGLR 82, paras 19–22, per Chadwick LJ.

47.   A more difficult problem, to which the authorities do not provide a harmonious response, is the question whether a deliberate choice by the parties to exclude expressly agreed terms from the signed document (as occurred in the present case) affects the issue whether those excluded terms actually form part of the land contract. In *Tootal Clothing Ltd* v *Guinea Properties Management Ltd* (1992) 64 P& CR 452, 456 Scott LJ said:

> 'If parties choose to hive off part of the terms of their composite bargain into a separate contract distinct from the written land contract that incorporates the rest of the terms, I can see nothing in section 2 that provides an answer to an action for enforcement of the land contract, on the one hand, or of the separate contract on the other hand. Each has become, by the contractual choice of the parties, a separate contract.'

54.   In my judgment, the apparent disharmony constituted by the dicta on this point may be reconciled as follows: (i) Nothing in section 2 of the 1989 Act is designed to prevent parties to a composite transaction which includes a land contract from structuring their bargain so that the land contract is genuinely separated from the rest of the transaction in the sense that its performance is not made conditional upon the performance of some other expressly agreed part of the bargain. Thus, in Chadwick LJ's example in *Grossman* v *Hooper* [2001] 2 EGLR 82, parties may agree to the sale and purchase both of a house and of its curtains and carpets in a single composite transaction. None the less it is open to them to agree either (a) that completion of the purchase of the house is dependent upon the sale of the carpets and curtains or (b) that it is not. They are free to separate the terms of a transaction of type (b) into two separate documents (one for the house and the other for the carpets and curtains) without falling foul of section 2. They may also agree to structure a transaction which includes the sale of two or more parcels of land by way of separate contracts for each, so that none of the land contracts is conditional upon the performance of any of the others. (ii) By contrast, the parties to a composite transaction are not free to separate into a separate document expressly agreed terms, for example as to the sale of chattels or the provision of services, if upon the true construction of the whole of the agreement, performance of the land sale is conditional upon the chattel sale or service provision. That would, albeit for reasons which seem to me to frustrate rather than serve the purposes for which the 1989 Act was passed, fall foul of section 2(1), however purposively construed. So would a series of separate contracts for the sale of separate parcels of land, if each was conditional upon the performance of the other. (iii) Since the splitting into separate contracts of parts of a composite transaction is inherently likely to give rise to uncertainties as to whether performance of the one is conditional upon performance of the other, the parties are free, and in my opinion should positively be encouraged, to make plain by express terms whether or not that conditionality exists. To do so serves rather than evades or frustrates the purposes of section 2, an important part of which is to encourage clarity rather than uncertainty in land transactions.

55.   An obvious way of providing expressly that performance of the terms of a separate contract are not to operate as a condition for the performance of the land contract where they form parts of a composite transaction, is for the parties to insert an appropriately worded entire agreement clause in the land contract . . .

58.   I turn therefore to the application of section 2, thus interpreted, to the unusual facts of the present case. It is in my judgment clear that the 2% finder's fee agreement was part of a composite transaction which also included originally 12 land contracts, but which had been altered so as to include only 11 land contracts by the time of exchange. It is equally clear in my

judgment that performance of the land contracts was not conditional upon performance of the finder's fee agreement. If there had been any doubt about that, it is in my view laid firmly to rest by the entire agreement clause in each of the 11 contracts . . .

Comment

(1) Would the result have been the same if there had been no entire agreement clause?

(2) Is the analysis different from that in *Record* v *Bell*?

The Law Commission[10] contemplated that it might be possible to rectify the written contract so as to insert a term omitted by mistake.

Extract 5.2.9

Francis v *F Berndes Ltd* [2011] EWHC 3377 (Ch); [2012] 1 EGLR 117

Counsel relied on rectification as the parties had overlooked inserting a term in the contract.

HENDERSON J: 39.   In my judgment these submissions betray a fundamental misunderstanding of the nature of the remedy of rectification. The function of rectification is to correct a common mistake (or, in limited circumstances, a unilateral mistake) in the way in which a transaction has been reduced to writing . . .

41.   The question whether rectification could be used to cure a failure to comply with section 2 was carefully considered by Morgan J in *Oun* v *Ahmad* [2008] EWHC 545 (Ch) at [24] to [55]. The passage is too long to quote in full, but it repays study, and I respectfully agree with it. In short, Morgan J distinguished between cases where rectification is sought on conventional grounds, to correct a mistake in the drafting of a document, and cases where it is sought in order to make a document compliant with section 2 by inserting an express term which the parties agreed to exclude from the document. He held that rectification of the first kind is contemplated by the 1989 Act. . . . On the other hand, he held that rectification of the second kind is not available, because to allow it would make an unjustifiable inroad into the policy of the 1989 Act.

43.   It is true that the case considered by Morgan J was in one respect more extreme than the present case, because it concerned a term which the parties had expressly agreed to exclude from the written agreement. It seems to me, however, that the same result should follow whatever the explanation for the omission of an express term may be, unless of course the circumstances are such that rectification on conventional grounds is available. Ignorance of the 1989 Act, or a misapprehension about its operation, cannot in my view suffice, because the policy which underpins section 2 is the need for certainty in contracts for the sale of land and the avoidance of disputes about what the parties have agreed which can be resolved only by recourse to extrinsic evidence. The general law of rectification makes a limited inroad into this policy, which Parliament clearly regarded as acceptable; but to allow rectification of the second kind would in my judgment subvert the statutory purpose in a way that Parliament could never have intended.

Comment

How useful is rectification likely to be?

A quite different point concerns the position after the land transfer has been completed.

---

[10]   Law Com No 164, para 5.6.

Extract 5.2.10

***Keay v Morris Homes (West Midlands) Ltd* [2012] EWCA Civ 900; [2012] 1 WLR 2855**

Counsel argued that 'once all the *land* elements of the original sale agreement . . . were performed on completion' other obligations under the void agreement became enforceable.

RIMER LJ: 36.   [This submission] may appear to be a surprising one. Indeed, but for the fact that he claims that the submission is supported by this court's decision in *Tootal* [*Tootal Clothing Ltd* v *Guinea Properties Ltd* (1992) 64 P&CR 452], I doubt whether Mr Cousins would have had the nerve to advance it. If the supplemental agreement was, from the outset, a nullity and the works obligation can at best be regarded as part of that nullity, it is not easy to see how the performance of some of the purported terms of the nullity can have had the effect of breathing life into the others sufficient to enable them to be the subject of a claim at law. . . .

44.   I set out in [40] above Lewison J's understanding [in *Kilcarne Holdings Ltd* v *Targetfollow (Birmingham) Ltd* [2005] 2 P&CR 105] of the ratio decidendi of *Tootal*. He deduced from *Tootal* a principle to the effect that, in a case in which the parties have purportedly made a section 2 contract, but have in fact created a nullity because not all the terms of the sale were included in it, then once the land elements of the purported contract have been completed, either side can then enforce any non-land terms that either were or should have been also included in it, even though, by reason of the non-compliance with section 2, they have no contractual force.

45.   With respect, I disagree with that summary of what *Tootal* decided. Had this court made a decision to that effect in *Tootal*, it would, I consider, have been fairly remarkable. Moreover, any such decision would have required careful explanation, whereas none is to be found in the judgments. In my view, neither Scott LJ nor Parker LJ reached their respective conclusions on the basis of any such principle. . . .

47.   . . . The proposition that a void contract can, by acts in the nature of part performance, mature into a valid one is contrary to principle and wrong. . . .

Comment

There were other dicta supporting the other view, but is it appropriate to conclude that this is an obviously correct conclusion?

(iii) The one document rule

Section 2(1) requires one document; it is not sufficient that there are two signed documents, each of which incorporates some of the terms. The normal practice on the sale of land is that two copies of the contract are drawn up (in identical terms, of course), each party signing one copy. When the lawyers are satisfied that all outstanding issues have been cleared up, the two copies are exchanged and the contract is effective. Section 2(3) recognises the continuing validity of this, despite there not being a single document signed by both parties.

Extract 5.2.11

***Commission for the New Towns* v *Cooper (Great Britain) Ltd* [1995] Ch 259**

It was argued that a contract by exchange of letters satisfies s 2(3).

STUART-SMITH LJ: . . . Although the judge did not have such extensive argument on the point as we have, he rejected [the defendant's] submission. He held that the expression 'exchange of contracts' was one that was familiar to all property lawyers and had long borne a technical meaning. What the section had done was to extend the concept, which usually involves lawyers, to those where there were none, and the transaction was conducted solely by laymen.

At the conclusion of the argument, and in the absence of authority to the contrary, I had reached the clear conclusion that the judge was right. In my opinion, the authorities show that, even if the expression 'exchange of contracts' is not a term of art, it is a well-recognised concept understood both by lawyers and laymen which has the following features.

1. Each party draws up or is given a document which incorporates all the terms which they have agreed, and which is intended to record their proposed contract. The terms that have been agreed may have been agreed either orally or in writing or partly orally or partly in writing.

2. The documents are referred to as 'contracts' or 'parts of contract', although they need not be so entitled. They are intended to take effect as formal documents of title and must be capable on their face of being fairly described as contracts having that effect.

3. Each party signs his part in the expectation that the other party has also executed or will execute a corresponding part incorporating the same terms.

4. At the time of execution neither party is bound by the terms of the document which he has executed, it being their mutual intention that neither will be bound until the executed parts are exchanged.

5. The act of exchange is a formal delivery by each party of its part into the actual or constructive possession of the other with the intention that the parties will become actually bound when exchange occurs, but not before.

6. The manner of exchange may be agreed and determined by the parties. The traditional method was by mutual exchange across the table, both parties or their solicitors being present. It also commonly takes place by post, especially where the parties or their solicitors are at a distance . . . Exchange can also take place by telephone . . .

Comment

(1) The Law Commission (Law Com No 164, para 4.15) had suggested that exchanges of letters should suffice, but the legislation is materially different from what they had proposed.

(2) Is there a good policy reason why a contract by correspondence should not constitute a valid contract?

(iv) Subsequent variation and rescission

Extract 5.2.12

McCausland v Duncan Lawrie Ltd [1997] 1 WLR 38

Subsequent to the contract, there was a variation of the completion date. The variation was not in a document signed by both parties.

NEILL LJ: . . . The law in this regard is made plain in the speech of Lord Parmoor in *Morris* v *Baron & Co* [1918] AC 1, 39 where he referred with approval to the following passage in the judgment of Shearman J in *Williams* v *Moss' Empires Ltd* [1915] 3 KB 242, 246–247:

> 'The principle . . . is where there is alleged to have been a variation of a written contract by a new parol contract, which incorporates some of the terms in the old contract, the new contract must be looked at in its entirety, and if the terms of the new contract when thus considered are such that by reason of the Statute of Frauds it cannot be given in evidence unless in writing, then being an unenforceable contract it cannot operate to effect a variation of the original contract . . . whenever parties vary a material term of an existing contract they are in effect entering into a new contract, the terms of which must be looked at in their entirety, and if the new contract is one which is required to be in writing but is not in writing, then it must be wholly disregarded and the parties are relegated to their rights under the original contract.'

. . . Furthermore, there are other passages in the speeches in *Morris* v *Baron & Co* which show that if a contract is required to be in writing variations which are not in writing cannot be relied upon . . .

Comment

(1) If the agreement to vary is signed by both parties, does this mean that s 2 is satisfied? Would it be possible (expressly or impliedly) to incorporate the original agreement into the variation agreement?

(2) *Morris* v *Baron* held that rescission does not require writing, and in *McCausland* Morritt LJ observed that a rescission 'may well be capable of being done otherwise than in writing'. Are there satisfactory reasons for distinguishing between variation and rescission?

(3) If a variation is agreed but does not satisfy s 2, is it possible to argue that the original agreement should be treated as rescinded rather than being enforceable in its original form?

B. Enforcing agreements that do not comply with the 1989 Act

It has already been seen that collateral contracts and rectification may cure some apparent defects. In the past, a claimant who acted on an oral contract was able to bring an action by virtue of the doctrine of part performance. Part performance was not explicitly abolished by the 1989 Act,[11] but the general assumption is that making the contract void rather than merely enforceable precludes the operation of part performance. This was confirmed by *United Bank of Kuwait plc* v *Sahib*.[12]

Sahib also shows, as foreshadowed by the Law Commission, that it might be possible to rely on estoppel in at least some cases where part performance used to be available.[13] The role of estoppel and constructive trusts is explored in the following extracts, against the background that s 2(5) of the 1989 Act exempts constructive trusts from its application, but makes no reference to estoppel.

Extract 5.2.13

Yaxley v *Gotts* [2000] Ch 162

ROBERT WALKER LJ: . . . I have no hesitation in agreeing. . . that the doctrine of estoppel may operate to modify (and sometimes perhaps even counteract) the effect of section 2 of the Act of 1989. The circumstances in which section 2 has to be complied with are so various, and the scope of the doctrine of estoppel is so flexible, that any general assertion of section 2 as a 'no-go area' for estoppel would be unsustainable. Nevertheless the impact of the public policy principle to which Sir John Balcombe drew attention in *Godden* v *Merthyr Tydfil Housing Association* does call for serious consideration. It is not concerned with illegality (some confusion may have arisen from the inadequate report or note shown to this court in *Bankers Trust Co* v *Namdar*) but with what Viscount Radcliffe in *Kok Hoong* v *Leong Cheong Kweng Mines Ltd* [1964] AC 993, 1016, called a principle of general social policy,

---

[11] LPA, s 40(2), which preserved it in 1925, was repealed by the 1989 Act.

[12] [1997] Ch 107; see also *Yaxley* v *Gotts* [2000] Ch 162 at p 172.

[13] It was held that, on the facts, estoppel could not be relied upon as estoppels do not bind successors in title. This is controversial: see p 215 below.

'to ask whether the law that confronts the estoppel can be seen to represent a social policy to which the court must give effect in the interests of the public generally or some section of the public, despite any rules of evidence as between themselves that the parties may have created by their conduct or otherwise.'

In this case that principle must of course be applied consistently with the terms in which section 2 of the Act of 1989 has been enacted, including the saving at the end of section 2(5).

Parliament's requirement that any contract for the disposition of an interest in land must be made in a particular documentary form, and will otherwise be void, does not have such an obviously social aim as statutory provisions relating to contracts by or with moneylenders, infants, or protected tenants. Nevertheless it can be seen as embodying Parliament's conclusion, in the general public interest, that the need for certainty as to the formation of contracts of this type must in general outweigh the disappointment of those who make informal bargains in ignorance of the statutory requirement. If an estoppel would have the effect of enforcing a void contract and subverting Parliament's purpose it may have to yield to the statutory law which confronts it, except so far as the statute's saving for a constructive trust provides a means of reconciliation of the apparent conflict.

. . .

In inquiring whether the parliamentary purpose is frustrated it is necessary to note the wide range of relief which may be granted where a claim to proprietary estoppel is established . . .

. . . The report and the working paper are invaluable guides to the old law and to the problems which constituted the 'mischief' at which section 2 of the Act of 1989 is directed, but they cannot be conclusive as to how section 2, as enacted, is to be construed and applied.

Proprietary estoppel and constructive trusts

. . .

The overlap between estoppel and the constructive trust was less fully covered in counsel's submissions but seems to me to be of central importance to the determination of this appeal . . .

. . . Those findings [justifying a proprietary estoppel] do in my judgment equally provide the basis for the conclusion that Mr Yaxley was entitled to such an interest under a constructive trust . . .

To recapitulate briefly: the species of constructive trust based on 'common intention' is established by what Lord Bridge in *Lloyds Bank Plc v Rosset* [1991] 1 AC 107, 132, called an 'agreement, arrangement or understanding' actually reached between the parties, and relied on and acted on by the claimant. A constructive trust of that sort is closely akin to, if not indistinguishable from, proprietary estoppel. Equity enforces it because it would be unconscionable for the other party to disregard the claimant's rights. Section 2(5) expressly saves the creation and operation of a constructive trust.

I cannot accept that the saving should be construed and applied as narrowly as Mr Laurence contends. To give it what I take to be its natural meaning, comparable to that of section 53(2) of the Law of Property Act 1925 in relation to section 53(1), would not create a huge and unexpected gap in section 2. It would allow a limited exception, expressly contemplated by Parliament, for those cases in which a supposed bargain has been so fully performed by one side, and the general circumstances of the matter are such, that it would be inequitable to disregard the claimant's expectations, and insufficient to grant him no more than a restitutionary remedy.

CLARKE LJ: . . . The Act of 1989 expressly refers to resulting, implied or constructive trusts but it does not expressly refer to proprietary estoppel, in so far as its principles are different from those relating to constructive trusts. The Act neither expressly saves the operation of the doctrine of proprietary estoppel nor expressly provides that it should have no application. Whether the principles of proprietary (or indeed other classes of estoppel) can be invoked will no doubt depend upon the principle which Robert Walker LJ has quoted from *Halsbury's Laws of England*, 4th ed reissue, vol 16, pp 849–850, para 962, namely that the doctrine of estoppel may not be invoked to render valid a transaction which the legislature, on grounds of general public policy, has enacted is to be invalid or void.

It seems to me that in considering whether a particular estoppel relied upon would offend the public policy behind a statute it is necessary to consider the mischief at which the statute is directed. Where a statute has been enacted as a result of the recommendations of the Law Commission, it is, as I see it, both appropriate and permissible for the court to consider those recommendations in order to help to identify both the mischief which the Act is designed to cure and the public policy underlying it. Indeed, although I agree with Robert Walker LJ that they cannot be conclusive as to how a particular provision should be construed, I entirely agree with Beldam LJ that the policy behind section 2 of the Act of 1989 can clearly be seen from the Law Commission Report to which he refers. In my opinion the contents of that report will be of the greatest assistance in deciding whether or not the principles of particular types of estoppel should be held to be contrary to the public policy underlying the Act. In this regard it seems to me that the answer is likely to depend upon the facts of the particular case. So, for example, an attempt to apply the principles of estoppel by convention is likely to fail, as in *Godden* v *Merthyr Tydfil Housing Association* [1997] NPC 1; Court of Appeal (Civil Division) Transcript No 370 of 1997, whereas an attempt to apply the principles of proprietary estoppel might well succeed, depending upon the facts of the particular case.

BELDAM LJ: . . . In the present case the policy behind the Commission's proposals was as clearly stated as its intention that the proposal should not affect the power of the court to give effect in equity to the principles of proprietary estoppel and constructive trusts. Even if the use to be made of the Commission's report is to be confined to identifying the defect in the law which the proposals were intended to correct, in a case such as the present it is unrealistic to divorce the defect in the law from the policy adopted to correct it. The Commission's report makes it clear that in proposing legislation to exclude the uncertainty and complexities introduced into unregistered conveyancing by the doctrine of part performance, it did not intend to affect the availability of the equitable remedies to which it referred.

The general principle that a party cannot rely on an estoppel in the face of a statute depends upon the nature of the enactment, the purpose of the provision and the social policy behind it. This was not a provision aimed at prohibiting or outlawing agreements of a specific kind, though it had the effect of making agreements which did not comply with the required formalities void. This by itself is insufficient to raise such a significant public interest that an estoppel would be excluded. . . .

Quite apart from the views expressed by the Commission, it was well recognised that circumstances in which equity is prepared to draw the inference that a party is entitled to a beneficial interest in land held by another may frequently also give rise to a proprietary estoppel . . .

For my part I cannot see that there is any reason to qualify the plain words of section 2(5). They were included to preserve the equitable remedies to which the Commission had referred. I do not think it inherent in a social policy of simplifying conveyancing by requiring the certainty of a written document that unconscionable conduct or equitable fraud should be allowed to prevail.

In my view the provision that nothing in section 2 of the Act of 1989 is to affect the creation or operation of resulting, implied or constructive trusts effectively excludes from the operation of the section cases in which an interest in land might equally well be claimed by relying on constructive trust or proprietary estoppel.

Comment

(1) All three judges held in favour of the purchaser. Are their analyses the same?

(2) Why should part performance be abolished when estoppel (or the constructive trust) is recognised? It may be noted that part performance had developed detailed rules. In some respects, these rules were more relaxed than the modern rules,[14] but they required conduct which pointed to the existence of a contract, a requirement seemingly absent today.

Extract 5.2.14

***Kinane* v *Mackie-Conteh* [2005] WTLR 345**

ARDEN LJ: 22.   Mr Macpherson submits that the security agreement contained an agreement to execute a legal charge. Mr Kinane would not have made the loan without security, and accordingly that it would be unconscionable for Mr Mackie-Conteh now to contend the security agreement is unenforceable: see *Yaxley* v *Gotts*.

23.   Mr Jack submits that the only representation upon which Mr Kinane can rely is that arising out of the unenforceable security agreement itself and that that is insufficient. In *Actionstrength Ltd* v *International Glass Engineering SpA* [2003] 2 AC 541, the House of Lords held that where a guarantee was not in writing as required by section 4 of the Statute of Frauds Act 1677 ('the 1677 statute') the beneficiary of the invalid guarantee could not set up an estoppel simply on the basis of the giving of the guarantee. The *Actionstrength* case shows that the courts will not allow the statutory policy to be undermined. The effect of allowing Mr Kinane to rely on a constructive trust is to undermine section 2(1) of the 1989 Act. In this case there was a misunderstanding as to whether the agreement was enforceable or not. Moreover, Mr Kinane knew that he had not got the mortgage for which he had stipulated. Furthermore, the making of the loan was a 'one-off' act of reliance, not a series of acts as in the *Yaxley* case.

26.   In *Yaxley* v *Gotts* this court recognised that the doctrine of estoppel may not be invoked to render valid a transaction which the legislature has, on the grounds of general public policy, enacted is to be invalid. However, it held that that principle was not violated where the circumstances giving rise to proprietary estoppel also gave rise to a constructive trust as the legislature has specifically made a saving for constructive trusts in section 2(5) of the 1989 Act.

27.   Mr Jack submits that where a party relies on proprietary estoppel he may not rely on the agreement which is invalidated by section 2(1) of the 1989 Act. For this proposition, he relies on the *Actionstrength* case referred to above. However, there is no saving in the 1677 statute which is comparable with section 2(5) of the 1989 Act . . .

28.   In my judgment, therefore, a party seeking to rely on proprietary estoppel as a basis for disapplying section 2(1) of the 1989 Act is not prevented from relying in support of his case on the agreement which section 2(1) would otherwise render invalid. Thus, the requirement that the defendant encouraged (or allowed) the claimant to believe that he would acquire an interest in land may (depending on the facts) consist in the defendant encouraging the claimant (by words or conduct) to believe that the agreement for the disposition of an interest in land (here a security interest) was valid and binding . . .

29.   It is to be noted that, even on this scenario, reliance on the unenforceable agreement only takes the claimant part of the way: he must still prove all the other components of proprietary estoppel. In particular, the requirement that the defendant encouraged or permitted the claimant in his erroneous belief is not satisfied simply by the admission of the invalid agreement in evidence. In this sort of case, the claimant has to show that the defendant represented to the

---

[14] The reliance did not need to be detrimental; there was no trace of the discretion seen in determining the remedy (p 206 below).

claimant, by his words or conduct, including conduct in the provision or delivery of the agreement, that the agreement created an enforceable obligation. The cause of action in proprietary estoppel is thus not founded on the unenforceable agreement but upon the defendant's conduct which, when viewed in all relevant respects, is unconscionable.

32.   As I see it, the policy of section 2(1) of the 1989 Act is to protect the public by preventing parties from being bound by a contract for the disposition of an interest in land unless it has been fully documented in writing. However, in section 2(5) Parliament has acknowledged that under section 2(1) there is a risk that one party will seek to take advantage of the sanction provided by that subsection when it is unconscionable for him so to do. To that extent, section 2(5) plays a role similar to that of part performance, although it operates more flexibly than that doctrine. Unconscionability on the part of the party seeking to rely on subsection (1) is the touchstone giving rise to a constructive trust. It will arise where a party led another party to believe that he would obtain an interest in property from another and then stands by while that other party acts to his detriment in reliance on that promise. The knowledge of the disadvantaged party is of less significance . . .

33.   In proprietary estoppel, the court awards a remedy appropriate to satisfy the expectations that the defendant has indeed. This need not be an interest in land. However, in my judgment, that is the appropriate remedy in this case and neither counsel has suggested otherwise.

NEUBERGER LJ: 39.   In these circumstances, it appears to me that the only real question in the present case is whether, in the light of the facts found by the judge, it can be said that a 'constructive trust', within the meaning of section 2(5) of the 1989 Act, was created.

40.   When considering that question, one must, I think, avoid regarding the subsection as an automatically available statutory escape route from the rigours of section 2(1) of the 1989 Act, simply because fairness appears to demand it. A provision such as section 2 of the 1989 Act was enacted for policy reasons which, no doubt, appeared sensible to the legislature. Accordingly, just as with section 4 of the 1677 Act, the Court should not allow its desire to avoid what might appear a rather harsh result in a particular case to undermine the statutory policy.

41.   Accordingly, when considering whether section 2(5) is engaged, the court should consider whether, on the particular facts, it can fairly be said that a resulting, implied or constructive trust has been created. It would be contrary to legal principle, and inconsistent with the statutory purpose, if the court were to hold that a particular set of facts fell within section 2(5) if, as a matter of extra-statutory law, the facts could not properly be said to give rise to 'the creation or operation of [a] resulting implied or constructive trust'. In other words, in my view, it would be wrong to give an artificially wide (or indeed an artificially narrow) meaning to the words of section 2(5) of the 1989 Act.

44.   In those circumstances it seems to me that the classic requirements for some sort of equitable right in favour of Mr Kinane are established. There was a common understanding between the parties that a certain relationship existed between them (namely that of mortgagor and mortgagee), payment of money by the assumed mortgagee in faith of the existence of that relationship, and receipt of the money on the part of the assumed mortgagor, who must have appreciated that the money would not have been forthcoming unless the assumed mortgagee had believed that the relationship existed.

45.   The other question is whether Mr Mackie-Conteh can contend that the equity is satisfied by a mere estoppel, or whether as Mr Kinane contends, it is an estoppel which can also properly be said to amount to a constructive trust. If it is merely a proprietary estoppel, then section 2(5) may well not assist Mr Kinane, and his case would run into the same difficulties as that of the party seeking to enforce the guarantee in *Actionstrength*.

46.   There are observations in the speeches of Robert Walker and Beldam LJJ (with both of whom Clarke LJ agreed) in *Yaxley v Gotts* [2000] Ch 174, to the effect that facts giving rise to an estoppel, could be sufficient (even if they do not give rise to a trust) to enable a claimant to

avoid the rigours of Section 2(1) of the 1989 Act: see at 174F–G and 188F–9G. It is unnecessary to decide in this case whether those observations can survive in light of the reasoning of the House of Lords in *Actionstrength*. For the purposes of this appeal, I am content to assume, in favour of Mr Mackie-Conteh, that it would not be open to Mr Kinane to avoid the consequences of Section 2(1) of the 1989 Act if he could only establish a proprietary estoppel, and not a trust.

47. There are clearly circumstances which can give rise to an estoppel, but not a trust. This point was made clear by Robert Walker LJ in *Yaxley* at 176D where he said this of 'estoppel and the constructive trust': 'Plainly there are large areas where the two concepts do not overlap: when a landowner stands by while his neighbour mistakenly builds on the former's land the situation is far removed (except for the element of unconscionable conduct) from that of a fiduciary who derives an improper advantage from his client.' He then went on to explain at 176E that, in light of cases such as *Gissing* v *Gissing* [1971] AC 886, it was well established that 'the two concepts coincide' 'in the area of a joint enterprise for the acquisition of land'.

48. It initially appeared to me well arguable that the nature of the estoppel which could be established by Mr Kinane may not be such as to amount to a constructive trust. There is obviously a conceptual similarity between a person building on another's land in the false belief that he owns it, thereby conferring a benefit on the true owner, and a person who lends money to the owner of land, in the false belief that he has a mortgage over the land. In each case, the true owner of the land receives a benefit at the expense of a person who has spent money in the mistaken belief that he has an interest in the land.

49. However, I am persuaded that the reasoning, and the authorities cited, in *Yaxley* do lead to the conclusion that a constructive trust was created in the present case. [He cites Sir Nicolas Browne-Wilkinson V-C in *Grant* v *Edwards* [1986] Ch 638 at 656 and Robert Walker LJ in *Yaxley*.]

Comment

(1) Can one give a clear answer to the question whether estoppels survive the 1989 Act? Are the analyses of Arden and Neuberger LJJ the same?

(2) Note the argument of McFarlane:[15]

> The decision in *Actionstrength* has no relevance at all to proprietary estoppel . . . Two very different forms of estoppel are at stake. In *Actionstrength*, the alleged estoppel was not a cause of action, rather it was a means of allowing B to bring a contractual claim . . . However, a proprietary estoppel claim does not seek to prevent [the denial of] the contractual enforceability of an agreement . . . The crucial point . . . is that proprietary estoppel is a claim in its own right.

Is this argument, which leads to a wide scope for proprietary estoppel, convincing? How does it affect the *Kinane* analyses?

(3) When will a constructive trust arise? *Kinane* involved a security agreement. If money is lent, will this virtually always suffice to give rise to a trust?

(4) The overlap between estoppel and constructive trusts will be investigated in Chapter 8, where further dicta of Neuberger LJ will be quoted. It will be seen that Lord Walker in *Stack* v *Dowden*[16] doubted whether there is such a strong link between estoppels and constructive trusts as he had suggested in *Yaxley*. What effect may this have as regards s 2?

---

[15] [2005] Conv 501 at p 514.
[16] [2007] 2 AC 432 at [37]; Extract 8.9.3 below.

Extract 5.2.15

Cobbe v *Yeoman's Row Management Ltd* **[2008] 1 WLR 1752**

LORD SCOTT: 29.   There is one further point regarding proprietary estoppel to which I should refer. Section 2 of the 1989 Act declares to be void any agreement for the acquisition of an interest in land that does not comply with the requisite formalities prescribed by the section. Subsection (5) expressly makes an exception for resulting, implied or constructive trusts. These may validly come into existence without compliance with the prescribed formalities. Proprietary estoppel does not have the benefit of this exception. The question arises, therefore, whether a complete agreement for the acquisition of an interest in land that does not comply with the section 2 prescribed formalities, but would be specifically enforceable if it did, can become enforceable via the route of proprietary estoppel. It is not necessary in the present case to answer this question, for the second agreement was not a complete agreement and, for that reason, would not have been specifically enforceable so long as it remained incomplete. My present view, however, is that proprietary estoppel cannot be prayed in aid in order to render enforceable an agreement that statute has declared to be void. The proposition that an owner of land can be estopped from asserting that an agreement is void for want of compliance with the requirements of section 2 is, in my opinion, unacceptable. The assertion is no more than the statute provides. Equity can surely not contradict the statute. As I have said, however, statute provides an express exception for constructive trusts . . .

Comment

(1) As Lord Scott states, the point was obiter. Lord Walker chose not to express any opinion on the point, but all the other Law Lords agreed with Lord Scott generally.

(2) Does it make any practical difference if estoppel cannot be relied upon?

Arden LJ has considered when a claim will succeed after *Cobbe* (as a constructive trust, it appears):[17]

> In my judgment, there is a common thread running through the speeches of Lord Scott and Lord Walker. Applying what Lord Walker said in relation to proprietary estoppel also to constructive trust, that common thread is that, if the parties intend to make a formal agreement setting out the terms on which one or more of the parties is to acquire an interest in property, or, if further terms for that acquisition remain to be agreed between them so that the interest in property is not clearly identified, or if the parties did not expect their agreement to be immediately binding, neither party can rely on constructive trust as a means of enforcing their original agreement. In other words, at least in those situations, if their agreement (which does not comply with section 2(1)) is incomplete, they cannot utilise the doctrine of proprietary estoppel or the doctrine of constructive trust to make their agreement binding on the other party by virtue of section 2(5) of the 1989 Act.

It appears to follow that a claim will quite readily be accepted if a certain and final agreement has been reached. Is this consistent with the statutory policy?

3. Land

We can now turn to the rules applicable to the transfer and creation of interests in differing forms of property, starting with land.

---

[17] *Herbert* v *Doyle* [2011] 1 EGLR 119 at [57]. For the facts of *Cobbe*, see Extract 7.1.4 below. For first instance analyses as to the effect of *Cobbe*, see *Hutchison* v *B & DF Ltd* [2008] EWHC 2286 (Ch) at [68] and *Whittaker* v *Kinnear* [2011] EWHC 1479 (QB).

A. Transfer

Extract 5.3.1

Law of Property Act 1925, ss 51, 52

51.—(1)   All lands and all interests therein lie in grant and are incapable of being conveyed by livery or livery and seisin, or by feoffment, or by bargain and sale . . .

52.—(1)   All conveyances of land or of any interest therein are void for the purpose of conveying or creating a legal estate unless made by deed.
  (2)   This section does not apply to—
    (a)   assents by a personal representative; . . .

Comment

Section 51 deals with the old forms of transfer.[18]

Two further observations may be made. The first is that s 53(1)(a) (Extract 5.3.3 below) requires transfers of equitable interests in land to be in writing. Next, a transfer of a legal estate other than by deed may be construed as a contract for a transfer and thereby give the transferee an equitable interest under an estate contract.

Extract 5.3.2

Parker v *Taswell* (1858) 2 De G&J 559 (44 ER 1106)

LORD CHELMSFORD LC: . . . The better course will be to consider first the objection to the claim of the Plaintiff for specific performance, on the ground of there being no agreement which the law will recognize. This objection is founded on the 8 & 9 Vict c 106, s 3, which provides that a lease of any tenements or hereditaments shall be void at law, unless made by deed. On the part of the Defendant it is insisted that this document was intended for a lease, and that therefore if it is void for that purpose, it cannot be used as an agreement . . .
 . . . [Y]et there is nothing, in the Act to prevent its being used as an agreement, though void as a lease because not under seal.
  The Legislature appears to have been very cautious and guarded in language, for it uses the expression 'shall be void at law' – that is as a lease. If the Legislature had intended to deprive such a document of all efficacy, it would have said that the instrument should be 'void to all intents and purposes'. There are no such words in the Act. I think it would be too strong to say that because it is void at law as a lease, it cannot be used as an agreement enforceable in equity, the intention of the parties having been that there should be a lease, and the aid of equity being only invoked to carry that intention into effect.

Comment

(1) This analysis is in the context of a grant of a lease, but could equally apply to sales of the fee simple. Virtually all transfers of the fee simple are preceded by a contract, so there is no need for one to be implied by equity.

---

[18] Until the Statute of Frauds 1677, writing was not required; a deed was made mandatory by the Real Property Act 1845 (8 & 9 Vict c 106), s 3.

(2) Remember that s 2 of the Law of Property (Miscellaneous Provisions) Act 1989 requires the contract (whether an express contract or in the form of an ineffective transfer) to be in writing signed by both parties.

(3) The analysis in *Parker* does not apply to gifts.

B. Creation of interests

Extract 5.3.3

Law of Property Act 1925, ss 53–55

53.—(1)   Subject to the provisions hereinafter contained with respect to the creation of interests in land by parol—
  (a)   no interest in land can be created or disposed of except by writing signed by the person creating or conveying the same, or by his agent thereunto lawfully authorised in writing, or by will, or by operation of law;
  (b)   a declaration of trust respecting any land or any interest therein must be manifested and proved by some writing signed by some person who is able to declare such trust or by his will;
      . . .

(2)   This section does not affect the creation or operation of resulting, implied or constructive trusts.

54.—(2)   Nothing in the foregoing provisions of this Part of this Act shall affect the creation by parol of leases taking effect in possession for a term not exceeding three years (whether or not the lessee is given power to extend the term) at the best rent which can be reasonably obtained without taking a fine.

55.—Nothing in the last two foregoing sections shall—
  (a)   invalidate dispositions by will; or
  (b)   affect any interest validly created before the commencement of this Act; or
  (c)   affect the right to acquire an interest in land by virtue of taking possession; or
  (d)   affect the operation of the law relating to part performance.

Comment

(1) It will be noted that trusts of land require writing, though trusts generally do not.

(2) Remember that the creation of legal interests requires a deed: LPA, s 52. The principal effect of s 53 is to require writing for equitable interests. Is this distinction justifiable in the modern law of property?

(3) Section 53(2) exempts resulting, implied and constructive trusts. This is extremely important, as such trusts of the family home are very common. (They are considered in Chapter 8.)

The exception in s 54(2) for short leases is worth considering. Short leases are commonly created informally, and of particular importance is the periodic tenancy: a form of tenancy often implied by the courts from the payment of rent.[19] Do these factors provide sufficiently strong reasons for the exception? Can a short lease be assigned orally?[20]

---

[19] See p 494 below.
[20] *Crago* v *Julian* [1992] 1 WLR 372.

Extract 5.3.4

Long v Tower Hamlets LBC **[1998] Ch 197**

A tenancy document was executed on 8 September 1975. The tenancy was to commence on 29 September 1975 and the tenant had no right to take possession until then.

JAMES MUNBY QC: [As] appears from a comparison of section 54(2) of the Law of Property Act 1925 with section 2 of the Statute of Frauds, section 54(2) did make two changes . . . The second, which is crucial to Mr Walter's argument, was to substitute for the reference in the Statute of Frauds to a lease not exceeding three years 'from the making thereof' reference in section 54(2) to a lease 'taking effect in possession' for a term not exceeding three years.

. . .

However, submits Mr Walter, the tenancy did not 'tak[e] effect in possession' and the tenancy document was therefore not, as required by section 54(2), a 'lease taking effect in possession' . . . Therefore, says Mr Walter, it took effect, if at all, as a reversionary lease. Whatever may have been the position at common law or prior to 1925, he says, the inclusion in section 54(2) of the words 'taking effect in possession' has the effect of excluding altogether from the ambit of section 54(2) reversionary leases conferring no immediate right to take possession. Thus, he submits, a reversionary lease can only take effect if made by deed . . .

Miss Hargreaves, on the other hand, disputes that reversionary leases were excluded from the exception in section 2 of the Statute of Frauds or that they are excluded from the ambit of section 54(2) . . . The fundamental principle, common both to section 2 of the Statute of Frauds and to section 54(2), she says, is this: the term, whether it is to commence immediately or at some date in the future, must take effect in possession within three years from the date of the parol grant and must not extend beyond three years from the date of the parol grant. So long as it satisfies this condition it matters not, she submits, whether the term takes effect in possession at the date of the parol grant. It is implicit in this argument that the words 'taking effect in possession' in section 54(2) are descriptive only of the quality of the lease at the date when the term commences and not of the quality of the lease at the date of the parol grant. She suggests that the restrictions on the grant of reversionary leases are to be found in section 149 of the Law of Property Act 1925, and not in section 54(2).

(a) The Statute of Frauds

[After considering the authorities:] It follows, in my judgment, that prior to the coming into force of the Law of Property Act 1925 Mr Walter's argument would have failed . . .

(b) Section 54(2) of the Law of Property Act 1925

As I have already mentioned, the words 'taking effect in possession' which appear in section 54(2) of the Law of Property Act 1925 were not to be found in section 2 of the Statute of Frauds. There appears to be no judicial authority as to the effect (if any) of this change; certainly I was referred to none. The question is canvassed by some of the commentators . . .

The preponderance of the commentaries therefore supports Mr Walter. That fact though suggestive can hardly be decisive. There are, however, in my judgment three reasons why Mr Walter's argument is indeed correct.

In the first place, the words 'in possession', when used as part of the phrase 'taking effect in possession for a term not exceeding three years', in my judgment have their normal legal meaning. They connote an estate or interest in the land which is vested 'in possession' rather than merely vested 'in interest'. This reading is powerfully reinforced by the distinction drawn in section 205(1)(xxvii) of the Law of Property Act 1925 between a 'term of years taking effect in possession' and a 'term of years taking effect in reversion'. The words 'taking effect in possession' in section 54(2) are, in my judgment, used in the same sense in which those words are used in section 205(1)(xxvii) and thus, and this is the critical point, in distinction to the words 'taking effect in reversion'. This, as it seems to me, demonstrates that, as Mr Walter submits, reversionary leases were not intended to come within the ambit of section 54(2) . . .

Secondly, it is very difficult, if Miss Hargreaves's argument is correct, to see what was the purpose of including the words 'in possession' in section 54(2) at all . . .

The third reason is, in my judgment, decisive. It will be remembered that those leases which fell within the exception in section 2 of the Statute of Frauds were defined, so far as is material for present purposes, as being 'leases not exceeding the term of three years from the making thereof'. In contrast, those leases which fall within the exception in section 54(2) are defined, so far as is material for present purposes, as being 'leases taking effect in possession for a term not exceeding three years'. It will be seen that the three-year period referred to in section 2 of the Statute of Frauds is not the same as the three-year period referred to in section 54(2). Under the Statute of Frauds the three-year period was the period 'from the making' of the lease, in other words the period of three years from the date of the parol grant . . . Under section 54(2), on the other hand, the three-year period is the period of the term comprised in the lease. Moreover, there has been omitted from section 54(2) any express reference to the date of 'the making' of the lease. Thus, if Miss Hargreaves's argument is correct, there is no limit expressed in section 54(2) to the period which may elapse before the lease 'tak[es] effect in possession', the only requirement being that the lease, when eventually it does 'tak[e] effect in possession', must be 'for a term not exceeding three years'. On this footing the only limit to the period which might elapse before the term 'tak[es] effect in possession' would be the period of 21 years specified in section 149(3) of the Law of Property Act 1925.

Comment

(1) *Long* involved an adverse possession claim, for which purposes it was material whether there was a legal lease.

(2) Was the result inevitable given the wording of s 54(2)?[21] Are reversionary short leases common?

(3) Agreements for short leases, to be entered into in the future, do not require writing,[22] provided that the short lease will take effect in possession when entered into. Consider the following cases. A orally agrees with B in August to grant a lease on 1 October, the lease to be for two years from 1 October (contract route). D orally enters into a lease with E in August whereby E is to have possession from 1 October for two years (grant route). Is there good reason for legislating such that only the first is valid? How easy will it be for the courts to determine which route has been employed?

(4) Remember that the 'best rent' must be payable, not merely what the parties have chosen to agree.[23]

It is important to distinguish between dispositions (and declarations of trusts) caught by these provisions and the rules relating to contracts (which are often contracts for such dispositions). This was recently stressed by Lord Neuberger MR:[24]

> Mr Helden's case on section 2 is hopeless. It proceeds on a fundamental misunderstanding of the reach and purpose of that section, a misunderstanding, it is fair to say, which appears to be not

---

[21] Bright [1998] Conv 229 observes that *Long* is inconsistent with much previous thinking.
[22] Law of Property (Miscellaneous Provisions) Act 1989, s 2(5); Extract 5.2.3 above.
[23] *Fitzkriston LLP* v *Panayi* [2008] L&TR 412.
[24] *Helden* v *Strathmore Ltd* [2011] HLR 635 at [27].

uncommon. Section 2 is concerned with contracts for the creation or sale of legal estates or interests in land, not with documents which actually create or transfer such estates or interests. So a contract to transfer a freehold or a lease in the future, a contract to grant a lease in the future, or a contract for a mortgage in the future, are all within the reach of the section, provided of course the ultimate subject matter is land. However, an actual transfer, conveyance or assignment, an actual lease, or an actual mortgage are not within the scope of section 2 at all.

Why does it matter which provision has to be satisfied?

C. Electronic conveyancing

Extract 5.3.5

Law Commission No 271: Land Registration for the Twenty First Century: A Conveyancing Revolution

1.1 . . . The purpose of the Bill is a bold and striking one. It is to create the necessary legal framework in which registered conveyancing can be conducted electronically. The move from a paper-based system of conveyancing to one that is entirely electronic is a very major one and it will transform fundamentally the manner in which the process is conducted. The Bill will bring about an unprecedented conveyancing revolution within a comparatively short time. It will also make other profound changes to the substantive law that governs registered land. These changes, taken together, are likely to be even more far-reaching than the great reforms of property law that were made by the 1925 property legislation. Not only will the Bill introduce a wholly different method of conveyancing, but, as we explain below, it will also alter the way in which title to land is perceived.

1.12 The Bill will create a framework in which it will be possible to transfer and create interests in registered land by electronic means. It is envisaged that, within a comparatively short time, it will be the only method of conducting registered conveyancing. As we have indicated above, an essential feature of the electronic system when it is fully operational is that it will be impossible to create or transfer many rights in or over registered land expressly except by registering them. Investigation of title will be almost entirely online. It is intended that the secure electronic communications network on which the system will be based, will be used to provide information about properties for intending buyers. It will also provide a means of managing a chain of transactions by monitoring them electronically. This will enable the cause of delays in any chain to be identified and remedial action encouraged. It is anticipated that far fewer chains will break in consequence and that transactions will be considerably expedited. Faster conveyancing is also likely to provide the most effective way of curbing gazumping. The process of registration under the electronic system will be initiated by solicitors and licensed conveyancers, though the Land Registry will exercise control over the changes that can be made to the register. Electronic conveyancing will not come into being as soon as the Bill is brought into force. It will be introduced over a number of years, and there will be a time when both the paper and electronic systems co-exist.

Comment

(1) The significance of the proposed changes will be considered later as we study the new rules, as well as land registration more generally (in Chapter 10).

(2) It was always intended that e-conveyancing would require planning (with much of the detail to be in rules, rather than the 2002 Act). However, after many delays, development of e-conveyancing was halted in 2011, against the background of turmoil in conveyancing

following the collapse of the housing market in the preceding years.[25] There will now be indeterminable delay before it will be introduced.

(3) Individual titles have been held in digital form for many years. The problems facing e-conveyancing have not precluded increasing use of electronic means in the present system. For example, around half of all registration applications are now delivered electronically.

One set of proposed changes[26] would enable contracts for sale of land to be entered into electronically. However, we will concentrate on registered dispositions.

Extract 5.3.6

Land Registration Act 2002, ss 91–93

91.—(1) This section applies to a document in electronic form where—
   (a) the document purports to effect a disposition which falls within subsection (2), and
   (b) the conditions in subsection (3) are met.
(2) A disposition falls within this subsection if it is—
   (a) a disposition of a registered estate or charge,
   (b) a disposition of an interest which is the subject of a notice in the register, or
   (c) a disposition which triggers the requirement of registration,
   which is of a kind specified by rules.
(3) The conditions referred to above are that—
   (a) the document makes provision for the time and date when it takes effect,
   (b) the document has the electronic signature of each person by whom it purports to be authenticated,
   (c) each electronic signature is certified, and
   (d) such other conditions as rules may provide are met.
(4) A document to which this section applies is to be regarded as—
   (a) in writing, and
   (b) signed by each individual, and sealed by each corporation, whose electronic signature it has.
(5) A document to which this section applies is to be regarded for the purposes of any enactment as a deed.

92.—(1) The registrar may provide, or arrange for the provision of, an electronic communications network for use for such purposes as he thinks fit relating to registration or the carrying on of transactions which—
   (a) involve registration, and
   (b) are capable of being effected electronically.
(2) Schedule 5 (which makes provision in connection with a network provided under subsection (1) and transactions carried on by means of such a network) has effect.

93.—(1) This section applies to a disposition of—
   (a) a registered estate or charge, or
   (b) an interest which is the subject of a notice in the register, where the disposition is of a description specified by rules.

---

[25] Land Registry Annual Report and Accounts 2010–11, p 26.
[26] Land Registry consultation: E-conveyancing Secondary Legislation Part I (2007).

(2) A disposition to which this section applies, or a contract to make such a disposition, only has effect if it is made by means of a document in electronic form and if, when the document purports to take effect—

    (a) it is electronically communicated to the registrar, and

    (b) the relevant registration requirements are met.

(3) For the purposes of subsection (2)(b), the relevant registration requirements are—

    (a) in the case of a registrable disposition, the requirements under Schedule 2, and

    (b) in the case of any other disposition, or a contract, such requirements as rules may provide.

. . .

Schedule 5

8 Where—

    (a) a person who is authorised under a network access agreement to do so uses the network for the making of a disposition or contract, and

    (b) the document which purports to effect the disposition or to be the contract—

        (i) purports to be authenticated by him as agent, and

        (ii) contains a statement to the effect that he is acting under the authority of his principal,

he shall be deemed, in favour of any other party, to be so acting.

Comment

(1) Section 91 provides for voluntary use of electronic creation of documents: it effectively replaces present formality requirements. It does not apply to either (i) dispositions of unregistered land (unless they require registration) or (ii) contracts. Why is it so limited?

(2) The network referred to by s 92 is a crucial part of the scheme, though the details are beyond the scope of this book. It will ensure that interests are not merely created electronically but, as part of the process of creation, entered on the register. The stages of creating interests and protecting them will thereby be unified. This distinguishes e-conveyancing from simple electronic delivery of applications.

(3) It is expected that electronic signature will, at least initially, be by the legal advisers of the parties.

(4) Compulsion is provided for by s 93 and would represent one of the final stages of the introduction of electronic conveyancing.

(5) Is the scope of s 93 different from that of s 91? What is the result of failure to employ electronic conveyancing? Does the law possess techniques to overcome the operation of s 93 in deserving cases?

It is not expected that every disposition of registered land will have to employ electronic creation. Indeed, we should remember that certain dispositions are currently valid even if unwritten and not entered on the register – it would be grossly unrealistic to expect many of these dispositions to be electronically undertaken.

Extract 5.3.7

Law Commission No 254: Land Registration for the Twenty First Century

11.12 The following would *not* be subject to the requirement of registration explained above, but would have the same effect as they do at present—

(1) *Rights that can arise without any express grant or reservation*. This would include an equity arising by proprietary estoppel, a right to be registered as proprietor as a result of adverse possession, an easement arising by prescription or by implied grant or reservation, or a mere equity (such as a right to set aside a transfer on grounds of fraudulent misrepresentation). . . .

(2) *Dispositions taking effect by operation of law*. Those dispositions that take effect by operation of law, such as the vesting of—

    (a) a deceased's property in his or her executors or in the Public Trustee; or

    (b) an insolvent's property in his or her trustee in bankruptcy;

    would continue to do so. The executor, Public Trustee or trustee in bankruptcy would be able to apply to be registered as proprietor of the land in question.

(3) *Interests under trusts*. . . . The appropriate form of protection – whether to ensure overreaching, stipulate for some consent to any disposition by the trustees, or to indicate some limitation on their powers – would be a restriction. However, a trust of land could be created, as now, without any entry on the register. This is, of course, consistent with the policy of the Land Registration Act 1925 that references to trusts should so far as possible be excluded from the register.

(4) *Leases which were overriding interests*. By definition, those short leases which take effect as overriding interests and cannot be registered would be outside the registration requirements outlined above. The creation of such leases, their assignment, and the creation of any rights in or over them would, as now, be conducted in the same way as if title were unregistered.

Comment

(1) The exceptions would be established by rules. Their significance is primarily for compulsory electronic creation under s 93.

(2) Are these proposed categories justified? How significant are they?

4. Chattels

A. Transfer

Sale constitutes the most obvious transfer of chattels. This very large area of law lies outside the mainstream of this book and we will do no more than consider the principal legislative provisions.

Extract 5.4.1

Sale of Goods Act 1979,[27] ss 16–18

16.—Subject to section 20A, where there is a contract for the sale of unascertained goods no property in the goods is transferred to the buyer unless and until the goods are ascertained.

17.—(1) Where there is a contract for the sale of specific or ascertained goods the property in them is transferred to the buyer at such time as the parties to the contract intend it to be transferred.

18.—Unless a different intention appears, the following are rules for ascertaining the intention of the parties as to the time at which the property in the goods is to pass to the buyer.

---

[27] Consolidating legislation of 1893, which itself codified the common law.

Rule 1.—Where there is an unconditional contract for the sale of specific goods in a deliverable state the property in the goods passes to the buyer when the contract is made, and it is immaterial whether the time of payment or the time of delivery, or both, be postponed.

Rule 2.—Where there is a contract for the sale of specific goods and the seller is bound to do something to the goods for the purpose of putting them into a deliverable state, the property does not pass until the thing is done and the buyer has notice that it has been done.

Rule 3.—Where there is a contract for the sale of specific goods in a deliverable state but the seller is bound to weigh, measure, test, or do some other act or thing with reference to the goods for the purpose of ascertaining the price, the property does not pass until the act or thing is done and the buyer has notice that it has been done.

Rule 4.—When goods are delivered to the buyer on approval or on sale or return or other similar terms the property in the goods passes to the buyer:—

    (a) when he signifies his approval or acceptance to the seller or does any other act adopting the transaction;

    (b) if he does not signify his approval or acceptance to the seller but retains the goods without giving notice of rejection, then, if a time has been fixed for the return of the goods, on the expiration of that time, and, if no time has been fixed, on the expiration of a reasonable time.

Rule 5.—(1)   Where there is a contract for the sale of unascertained or future goods by description, and goods of that description and in a deliverable state are unconditionally appropriated to the contract, either by the seller with the assent of the buyer or by the buyer with the assent of the seller, the property in the goods then passes to the buyer; and the assent may be express or implied, and may be given either before or after the appropriation is made.

Comment

(1) A sale of unascertained goods, where part of a bulk, may result in the bulk being jointly owned (s 20A) or become appropriated when the bulk is reduced to the amount being sold (s 18, Rule 5(3)).

(2) It should be noted that there is no requirement of delivery, nor of payment of the price. Is this surprising?

(3) There are no formality requirements: an oral contract suffices.

The other area to consider is that of gift. Though of limited practical importance, gift will be considered in rather more detail, as it illustrates the role and meaning of possession. First, however, it may be noted that gifts are effective if made by deed.

Extract 5.4.2

Standing v Bowring (1885) 31 Ch D 282

LINDLEY LJ: . . . It was, however, contended before us that the legal title had not passed to the Defendant; that, as he never knew of the transfer or assented to it until after he was requested to retransfer the stock, the gift of it to him was really incomplete, and that the legal title to it was still in the Plaintiff. I am of opinion, however, that this is not the case. An incomplete gift can, of course, be revoked by the donor at any time; and I believe that by the civil law and the laws of some, if not all, foreign countries founded upon it, a gift is incomplete until the donee has assented to it . . . [O]ur own law as to the necessity of assent to gifts seems settled by *Butler and Baker's Case*,[i] *Thompson v Leach*,[ii] in the House of Lords, and *Siggers v Evans*.[iii] The older authorities were carefully examined in this last case by Lord *Campbell*, and I take it now to be settled, that although a donee may dissent from and thereby render null a gift to him, yet that a gift to him of property, whether real or personal, by deed, vests the property in him subject to his dissent.

ⁱ 3 Rep 25 a.
ⁱⁱ 2 Vent 198, 208.
ⁱⁱⁱ 5 E&B 367.

Comment

(1) Is it sensible not to allow the grantor to repudiate the deed before the donee is aware of it? Are there other consequences of the gift's being complete?

(2) This is a case on a chose in action, but the same principles apply to deeds of gift of chattels.

(3) If there is no transfer of possession then the deed may be invalidated by the Bills of Sale legislation unless it has been registered.

Other forms of gift also require some element of acceptance: gifts cannot be forced on people.

Extract 5.4.3

Dewar v Dewar [1975] 1 WLR 1532

A mother gave her son £500 as a gift, the son intending to accept the money as a loan. Following the mother's death, the son claimed that it constituted a valid gift.

GOFF J: [After quoting from *Standing* v *Bowring*:] The passages to which I have referred lead me to the conclusion that where a person intends to make a gift and the donee receives the thing given, knows that he has got it and takes it, the fact that he says: 'Well, I will only accept it as a loan, and you can have it back when you want it' does not prevent it from being an effective gift. Of course, it does not turn it into a loan unless the donor says: 'Very well, let it be a loan.' He could not force the donor to take it back, but the donor, having transferred it to him effectively and completely, intending to make a gift, and he – so far from repudiating it – having kept it, it seems to me that that is an effective gift and accordingly I hold that the defendant has established that the mother's contribution was a gift.

Comment

(1) If the son did not intend a gift, what justification is there for saying that there is a gift?[28]

(2) *Day* v *Harris* [2014] Ch 211 involved the transfer of manuscripts. The Court of Appeal was clear that it was the intention of the transferor alone that determined whether it was a bailment or gift.

(i) Delivery

At the heart of the law relating to gifts of chattels lies the proposition that a gift (other than by deed) is effective only if there is delivery.

---

[28] Roberts (1975) 38 MLR 700; Thornely [1976] CLJ 47; Hill (2001) 117 LQR 127.

Extract 5.4.4

Cochrane v *Moore* (1890) 25 QBD 57

FRY LJ: . . . On these facts, it was argued that there was no delivery and receipt of the one-fourth of the horse, and, consequently, that no property in it passed by the gift. The learned judge has, however, held that delivery is not indispensable to the validity of the gift.

The proposition on which the Lord Justice proceeded may perhaps be stated thus: that where a gift of a chattel capable of delivery is made *per verba de praesenti* by a donor to a donee, and is assented to by the donee, and that assent is communicated to the donor by the donee, there is a perfect gift, which passes the property without delivery of the chattel itself . . .

The proposition adopted by the Lord Justice is in direct contradiction to the decision of the Court of King's Bench in the year 1819 in *Irons* v *Smallpiece*.[i] . . . The case is a very strong one, because a Court consisting of Lord Tenterden, CJ, and Best and Holroyd, JJ, refused a rule nisi, and all held delivery to be necessary. The Chief Justice said: 'I am of opinion that, by the law of England, in order to transfer property by gift there must either be a deed or instrument of gift, or there must be an actual delivery of the thing to the donee', and he went on to refer to the case of *Bunn* v *Markham*[ii] as a strong authority.

These observations of the Chief Justice have created some difficulty. What did he mean by an instrument as contrasted with a deed? If he meant that an instrument in writing not under seal was different from parol in respect of a gift inter vivos, he was probably in error; but if in speaking of the transfer of property by gift, he included gifts by will as well as gifts inter vivos, then by instrument he meant testamentary instrument, and his language was correct.

Holroyd, J, was equally clear on the principal point: 'In order to change the property by a gift of this description' (by which we understand him to mean, a gift inter vivos) 'there must be a change of possession.'

The correctness of the proposition thus laid down has been asserted in many subsequent cases of high authority.

. . .

This review of the authorities leads us to conclude that according to the old law no gift or grant of a chattel was effectual to pass it whether by parol or by deed, and whether with or without consideration unless accompanied by delivery: that on that law two exceptions have been grafted, one in the case of deeds, and the other in that of contracts of sale where the intention of the parties is that the property shall pass before delivery: but that as regards gifts by parol, the old law was in force when *Irons* v *Smallpiece* was decided: that that case therefore correctly declared the existing law . . .

LORD ESHER MR: It is a transaction consisting of two contemporaneous acts, which at once complete the transaction, so that there is nothing more to be done by either party. The act done by the one is that he gives; the act done by the other is that he accepts. These contemporaneous acts being done, neither party has anything more to do. The one cannot give, according to the ordinary meaning of the word, without giving; the other cannot accept then and there such a giving without then and there receiving the thing given . . . I have come to the conclusion that in ordinary English language, and in legal effect, there cannot be a 'gift' without a giving and taking. The giving and taking are the two contemporaneous reciprocal acts which constitute a 'gift'. They are a necessary part of the proposition that there has been a 'gift'. They are not evidence to prove that there has been a gift, but facts to be proved to constitute the proposition that there has been a gift. That being so, the necessity of their existence cannot be altered unless by Act of Parliament.

---

[i] 2 B&A 551.
[ii] 2 Marsh 532.

Comment

(1) There was an elaborate consideration of the relevant authorities. It was held on the facts that there was an effective declaration of trust in favour of the donee.

(2) Authority apart, is there a good reason in principle for insisting upon delivery?

(ii) Actions less than handing over

Delivery operates very easily if I give a friend a box of chocolates as a Christmas present. However, more bulky objects give rise to far greater problems. The same is true of collections of things, such as furniture in a house. Picking each item up and handing it over is scarcely an option.

Extract 5.4.5

Rawlinson v Mort (1905) 93 LT 555

The owner of a church organ 'gave' it to the plaintiff, handing over the receipts. Subsequently, placing his hand on the organ, he repeated that he was giving it.

BRAY J: . . . In *Chaplin* v *Rogers* (1 East, 192), where the question was whether there had been a delivery to satisfy the Statute of Frauds, Lord Kenyon says: 'Where goods are ponderous, and incapable, as here, of being handed over from one to another, there need not be an actual delivery; but it may be done by that which is tantamount, such as the delivery of the key of a warehouse in which the goods are lodged, or by delivery of other indicia of property.' I think delivery of a box can be given by handing over the key. Symbolical delivery may be actual delivery. The key was already in the plaintiff's possession, and I think the handing over of the documents evidencing the owner's title, or, as stated in *Chaplin* v *Rogers*, of the indicia of the property, is symbolical delivery and equivalent to actual delivery, at all events where manual delivery is practically impossible. It was not the intention of the donor or the donee that the organ should be removed from the church, and real manual delivery was impossible under these circumstances. In my opinion, there was a valid completed gift at the plaintiff's rooms. I am, however, of opinion that, if the gift was not completed then, it was completed at the church. I have found that by putting his hand on the organ and using the words (whichever they were) Mr Copelin intended to give delivery, and I think that delivery can be made in this way when manual delivery is impossible. In *Cochrane* v *Moore* the learned judges confined their decision to cases where the article was capable of delivery. If the organ was under the circumstances capable of delivery, I think it was delivered. If it was not, I think there was symbolical delivery which was the nearest approach to delivery that could be made . . .

Comment

The dicta regarding symbolical delivery are viewed with suspicion. Although keys may be a special case, handing over receipts seems unlikely to be sufficient.[29]

Even the position regarding keys is less settled than one might have expected. Most of the cases involve *donationes mortis causa*,[30] a form of gift where rules for delivery are more relaxed than those presently under discussion. The first case, however, involves inter vivos gifts.

---

[29] Diamond (1964) 27 MLR 357 at p 360.
[30] See p 227 below.

Extract 5.4.6

Re Wasserberg [1915] 1 Ch 195

A husband took his wife with him to his bank, where he placed bonds in an envelope bearing his wife's name in a locked box. Subsequently, he gave the key to the box to her. The husband died shortly afterwards.

SARGANT J: . . . As regards the incident at the bank the case of *Cochrane* v *Moore*[i] shows that mere words of gift are not in themselves sufficient, but there must be delivery. If the testator had actually given the parcel to his wife and she had handed it back to him for the purpose of safe custody, that would probably have been enough; but as the facts are I think that the testator did not at any time during that incident part with the custody of the bonds. Again as regards the subsequent delivery of the key I cannot think that this was a sufficient delivery to pass the bonds by way of ordinary gift. It would seem that the delivery of a key might be sufficient if the subject-matter of the gift were bulky goods in a warehouse which could not actually be delivered; but here not only was the subject-matter of the gift eminently portable property, but the delivery of the key did not in itself enable the recipient to get at the bonds, since the bank would not (as the testator must have known at any rate after his conversation with Mr Watson) have allowed Mrs Wasserberg to have access to the box without some further authority from the testator.

[i] 25 QBD 57.

Comment

Ought it to be sufficient that the donor has effectively lost control by handing over the only key?[31]

Extract 5.4.7

Woodard v *Woodard* [1995] 3 All ER 980

DILLON LJ: . . . In *Re Craven's Estate* [1937] 3 All ER 33 at 38, [1937] Ch 423 at 428 there is a dictum of Farwell J where he is dealing not with motor cars but with the question of handing over a box, or the key to a box, and he says:

> 'In the case of a box, it is not necessary to hand over the box if the key is handed over, because it is assumed that if the key which unlocks the box is in the possession of the donee, the donor cannot have access to the contents of the box so as to deal with them in any way. I know of no decided case in which the question has arisen whether the handing over of a box and one key, it being proved that there was another key retained by the donor, would be sufficient, but, in the absence of authority, in my judgment, it would probably be held not to be a sufficient parting with dominion over the box, because the donor would have retained dominion over it and its contents by retaining the power to open the box, although it might be in the possession of the donee.'

It seems to me that the question is perhaps not so much one of dominion as of evidence of intention. If there are several keys to a box and the donor retains one, one would naturally ask: 'Why is he retaining it?' and 'Did he intend to make an immediate gift? Did he intend to part with dominion?'

---

[31] *Wrightson* v *McArthur & Hutchisons (1919) Ltd* [1921] 2 KB 807 supports possession in such cases.

Comment

(1) This is a *donatio mortis causa* case. Dillon LJ held that retention of a key to a car was not fatal because, on the facts, the donee had actual possession.

(2) Is it a matter of intention rather than dominion? Is such an approach consistent with *Cochrane* v *Moore*?

Gifts of items in a house, as between those living there, have given rise to considerable difficulty. Gifts of furniture or, for example, substantial collections of china are unlikely to satisfy delivery requirements.

Extract 5.4.8

Re Cole [1964] Ch 175

HARMAN LJ: . . . In December, 1945 . . . the wife came down to London with the other child and the bankrupt met her at the station and took her to the new home. He brought her into the house, took her into a room, put his hands over her eyes and then uncovered them saying 'Look'. He then accompanied her into other rooms on the ground floor where she handled certain of the articles – a silk carpet and an inlaid card table: next she went upstairs by herself and examined the rest of the house. When she came down again the husband said: 'It's all yours.'. . .

Mr Megarry on behalf of the wife boldly put forward an entirely novel proposition to the effect that a perfect gift of chattels is constituted by showing them to the donee and speaking words of gift. It is enough, he says, that the donee should be brought to the chattels rather than the chattels to the donee and that she should be 'near' the chattels (though what degree of proximity is needful remained vague) when the words of gift are spoken. This amounts to a change of possession, says Mr Megarry, particularly if you are dealing with a collection of chattels, a fortiori if the chattels are or come under the physical control of the donee; and the case is strengthened if the donee handles some of the chattels in the donor's presence.

This remarkable submission is unsupported by authority and is in my judgment entirely heterodox. It is, I think, trite law that a gift of chattels is not complete unless accompanied by something which constitutes an act of delivery or a change of possession. The English law of the transfer of property, dominated as it has always been by the doctrine of consideration, has always been chary of the recognition of gifts . . .

If the chattels be many or bulky there may be symbolical delivery, as, for instance, of a chair – *Lock* v *Heath*,[i] or the case about the gift of a church organ – *Rawlinson* v *Mort*,[ii] where the donor put his hand upon it in the presence of the donee and accompanied his gesture with words of gift.

The question, therefore, for our decision is whether there has been anything here which amounts to an act of delivery or a change of possession either preceding or following or coincident with the words of gift so as to make it perfect. The judge dealt with this point very briefly. He assumed that there must be delivery and that words of gift alone are not enough, but he said he could not decide in the trustee's favour without deciding that a husband cannot give his wife the contents of the matrimonial home without executing a deed of gift. He said he did not see what more Mr Cole could have done to put Mrs Cole into the possession of the gift which he thought he was making. It seems to me that this was in fact a reliance on the word or words of gift which was the very thing which the judge said he could not do . . .

Perhaps the strongest case in the wife's favour is *Kilpin* v *Ratley*.[iii] In that case furniture belonging to the husband and in the matrimonial home was purchased by his father-in-law who took an assignment of it by deed. Subsequently the father visited his daughter at the house and standing in one of the rooms orally gave her the furniture and then walked out of the house, leaving it behind him, and this was held to amount to a sufficient delivery to the wife. This furniture, until the time of the gift, was owned by the father and was in the possession of the son-in-law, but the father by pointing the furniture out to his daughter and then leaving the house put her and not her husband in possession of it and there was, therefore, a sufficient change of possession.

I cannot find that there was any change of possession here. It is argued that a wife living in her husband's house, and therefore having control to some extent of the furniture in it, is in possession of it, but this, I think, does not follow. In the ordinary case where a wife lives with her husband in a house owned and furnished by him, she has the use of the furniture by virtue of her position as wife, but that gives her no more possession of it than a servant has who uses the furniture. As to this, see Goddard LJ in *Youngs* v *Youngs*.[iv] It is true that it may be doubtful who is in possession of the furniture and that you must look to the title, as in *Ramsay* v *Margrett*,[v] but in the absence of delivery there is no title in her, as was pointed out by Lord Evershed MR in *Hislop* v *Hislop*.[vi]

PEARSON LJ: [A]n act to constitute delivery must be one which in itself shows an intention of the donor to transfer the chattel to the donee. If the act in itself is equivocal – consistent equally with an intention of the husband to transfer the chattels to his wife or with an intention on his part to retain possession but give to her the use and enjoyment of the chattels as his wife – the act does not constitute delivery.

[i] (1892) 8 TLR 295, DC.
[ii] (1905) 21 TLR 774; 93 LT 555.
[iii] [1892] 1 QB 582; 8 TLR 290, DC.
[iv] [1940] 1 KB 760, 770; [1940] 1 All ER 349, CA.
[v] [1894] 2 QB 18.
[vi] [1950] WN 124, CA.

Comment

(1) It is interesting that *Rawlinson* v *Mort* is approved. Why should we distinguish laying on of hands by the donor (*Rawlinson*) from handling by the donee (*Cole*)?

(2) *Cole* involved a question of ownership when the husband later became bankrupt. Might the court have been influenced by the potential for collusion between donor and donee? Is this a material consideration?

(3) There is a principle that, where possession is unclear, it is taken to be in the legal owner. Why was the wife unable to rely upon it?

(4) How likely is it that acts of delivery will be 'equivocal' in the sense employed by Pearson LJ?

(5) Is the law relating to gifts in a common household in a satisfactory state? What improvements, if any, might be suggested?

(iii) Constructive delivery

So far, we have been considering what constitutes delivery. Constructive delivery involves no physical delivery, but involves possession by the donee in some manner recognised by the law.

(a) Possession before the gift

Extract 5.4.9

Re Stoneham [1919] 1 Ch 149

P O LAWRENCE J: . . . On behalf of the claimant, however, it is contended that the rule thus affirmed by the Court of Appeal [in *Cochrane* v *Moore*] does not involve the proposition that where the chattel the subject-matter of the parol gift is already in the possession of the donee at the time when the gift is made, a further delivery or a change of possession is necessary in order to render the gift effectual. In my judgment this contention of the claimant is sound, and I will now proceed to state my reasons for coming to this conclusion. In *Cochrane* v *Moore*[i] the subject-matter of the gift was never in the possession of the donee, and I cannot find anything in the report to suggest that the Court, in affirming the proposition that delivery was necessary in the case of a parol gift of ordinary chattels, intended to hold that where the chattels had already been delivered to the donee any further delivery was necessary; no argument, so far as I can see, was addressed to the Court as to any distinction between a gift of chattels previously delivered to the donee and then in his possession, and a gift of chattels not in the possession of the donee at the time of the gift; nor in my judgment was the Court considering any such question. From a common-sense point of view it seems to me strange that articles already in the possession of an intended donee could not be effectually given by word of mouth without first removing them from the possession of the intended donee and then handing them back to him.

[i] 25 QBD 57.

Comment

(1) *Re Cole* insists upon delivery where delivery is scarcely practicable. Is there sufficient reason not to require delivery in cases such as *Re Stoneham*?

(2) How well does *Re Stoneham* fit in with the reasons for requiring delivery?

(b) Taking possession after the gift

Extract 5.4.10

Thomas v Times Book Co Ltd [1966] 1 WLR 911

Dylan Thomas told Cleverdon that he could keep a lost manuscript, if it were found.

PLOWMAN J: . . . It is then said on behalf of the plaintiff that even if Dylan Thomas intended to give this manuscript to Cleverdon, he did not succeed in giving effect to that intention because there was no delivery of the subject-matter of it to Cleverdon by Dylan Thomas. I feel bound to reject that argument. The fact is that Cleverdon got possession of this manuscript from the Soho public-house in which it had been left by Dylan Thomas and that he got that possession with the consent of Dylan Thomas. That, in my judgment, is sufficient delivery to perfect a gift in Cleverdon's favour. I can see nothing in *In re Cole, A Bankrupt*[i] which was relied upon by Mr Sparrow, which precludes me from taking what appears to me to be the common-sense view of the matter, and concluding that when Cleverdon got possession of the manuscript with the consent of Dylan Thomas, the gift was perfected.

[i] [1964] Ch 175; [1963] 3 WLR 621; [1963] 3 All ER 433, CA.

Comment

Is this case easier or more difficult to justify than *Re Stoneham*?

(c) Possession held by bailee

If a third party holds goods as a bailee, how is delivery to take place?

Extract 5.4.11

Elmore v *Stone* (1809) 1 Taunt 458; 127 ER 912

Two horses were sold by a keeper of a livery stable, who agreed to hold them at livery for the defendant purchaser. Under the law as it then stood, delivery was essential for the action for the purchase price to succeed.

MANSFIELD CJ: ... It was afterwards argued that this was not a sufficient delivery, but upon consideration we think that the horses were completely the horses of the Defendant, and that when they stood at the Plaintiff's stables, they were in effect in the Defendant's possession ... A common case is that of goods at a wharf, or in a warehouse, where the usual practice is, that the key of the warehouse is delivered, or a note is given addressed to the wharfinger, who in consequence makes a new entry of the goods in the name of the vendee, although no transfer of the local situation or actual possession takes place. Thus in the present case, after the Defendant had said that the horses must stand at livery, and the Plaintiff had accepted the order, it made no difference whether they stood at livery at the vendor's stable, or whether they had been taken away and put in some other stable. The Plaintiff possessed them from that time, not as owner of the horses, but as any other livery stable keeper might have them to keep ...

Comment

(1) This extract demonstrates that the principle is well recognised where a third party holds the goods as a bailee. However, a mere authority to the bailee to deliver the goods to the donee or purchaser does not suffice: it is necessary for the bailee to agree to hold for the donee or purchaser.

(2) In cases of third party bailees, how well does this fit in with the normal principles applicable to gifts?

(3) *Elmore* extends the principle to the transferor holding as bailee. Is this an extension too far? Should *Elmore* be applied where the transferor is not (for example) a livery stable keeper, but simply agrees to hold as bailee for the donee?[32]

B. Creation of interests

It is less usual to carve interests out of ownership of chattels, save for bailment (possession). Bailment is created by delivery. It seems that other interests, for example charges, can be created by delivery, contract or deed. It is also, of course, possible to create trusts of chattels. No formalities are required.

---

[32] Cf *Marvin* v *Wallis* (1856) 6 El&Bl 726 (119 ER 1035); *Michael Gerson (Leasing) Ltd* v *Wilkinson* [2001] QB 514.

5. Choses in action

A. Transfer

Suppose A owes B £100. It is possible for B to assign the benefit of this debt to C, so that C can sue A. It should be noted that we are dealing with the benefit of an obligation, not the burden. It is not possible for A to assign the burden to D: this would require a fresh agreement between D and B (or C). The burden can pass only where the contract constitutes a recognised proprietary interest in property affected by it, such as an estate contract over land.

(i) Assignable rights

Not every chose in action can be assigned, although the courts have been less inclined to impose limits in recent decades. It is clear that personal rights cannot be assigned. If I contract to paint R's portrait, I cannot assign the benefit of the contract (though I would be able to assign the right to the price after the painting has been completed). Assignment of a contractual right will not be permitted where the contract precludes assignment.[33]

<hr>

Extract 5.5.1

Trendtex Trading Corporation v *Crédit Suisse* **[1982] AC 679**

LORD ROSKILL: . . . My Lords, one of the reasons why equity would not permit the assignment of what became known as a bare cause of action, whether legal or equitable, was because it savoured of maintenance [the support of another person's litigation]. If one reads the well-known judgment of Parker J in *Glegg* v *Bromley* [1912] 3 KB 474, 490, one can see how the relevant law has developed. Though in general choses in action were assignable, yet causes of action which were essentially personal in their character, such as claims for defamation or personal injury, were incapable of assignment for the reason already given. But even so, no objection was raised to assignments of the proceeds of an action for defamation as in *Glegg* v *Bromley*, for such an assignment would in no way give the assignee the right to intervene in the action and so be contrary to public policy: see Fletcher Moulton LJ, at pp 488–489.

My Lords, just as the law became more liberal in its approach to what was *lawful* maintenance, so it became more liberal in its approach to the circumstances in which it would recognise the validity of an assignment of a cause of action and not strike down such an assignment as one only of a bare cause of action. Where the assignee has by the assignment acquired a property right and the cause of action was incidental to that right, the assignment was held effective . . . My Lords, I am afraid that, with respect, I cannot agree with the learned Master of the Rolls [1980] QB 629, 657 when he said in the instant case that 'The old saying that you cannot assign a "bare right to litigate" is gone.' I venture to think that that still remains a fundamental principle of our law. But it is today true to say that in English law an assignee who can show that he has a genuine commercial interest in the enforcement of the claim of another and to that extent takes an assignment of that claim to himself is entitled to enforce that assignment unless by the terms of that assignment he falls foul of our law of champerty, which, as has often been said, is a branch of our law of maintenance.

Comment

What sorts of causes of action remain incapable of assignment?

<hr>

[33] *Linden Gardens Trust Ltd* v *Lenesta Sludge Disposals Ltd* [1994] 1 AC 85.

(ii) Statutory assignments

Extract 5.5.2

Law of Property Act 1925, s 136

136.—(1)   Any absolute assignment by writing under the hand of the assignor (not purporting to be by way of charge only) of any debt or other legal thing in action, of which express notice in writing has been given to the debtor, trustee or other person from whom the assignor would have been entitled to claim such debt or thing in action, is effectual in law (subject to equities having priority over the right of the assignee) to pass and transfer from the date of such notice—

   (a)   the legal right to such debt or thing in action;
   (b)   all legal and other remedies for the same; and
   (c)   the power to give a good discharge for the same without the concurrence of the assignor . . .

Comment

Before statutory assignments were introduced by the Judicature Act 1873, equity recognised assignments. However, the assignee had to join the assignor in an action against the debtor.

Section 136 applies only to absolute assignments and therefore excludes assignments by way of charge or of part of a debt, as well as conditional assignments. Why does s 136 require an absolute assignment, when equitable assignments do not?

   What constitutes an assignment (for both equitable and statutory assignments)?

Extract 5.5.3

Curran v Newpark Cinemas Ltd [1951] 1 All ER 295

JENKINS LJ: . . . Counsel for the judgment creditor, on the other hand, contended that s 136(1) only applied where there was a document amounting to an absolute assignment and that the document here in question, being in form not an assignment but merely a direction to the garnishees to pay a third party (i.e., the bank), could only answer that description if and when communicated to the bank, as, until so communicated, it was revocable by the judgment debtors at any time and, therefore, not absolute . . . We are disposed to think counsel for the judgment creditor right on this part of the argument. It is, no doubt, true that s 136(1) does not require any particular form of assignment, or that the notice given to the debtor should necessarily have been given by the assignee. The sub-section does, however, clearly postulate that, whatever its form, there should be a document amounting to an absolute assignment by writing under the hand of the assignor. Given such an assignment, and given the requisite notice to the debtor, the assignment (to put it shortly) is to operate as a legal assignment of the debt in question. Section 136(1), however, does not provide that a document which would not, independently of the sub-section or its predecessor (Supreme Court of Judicature Act, 1873, s 25(6)), have operated as an absolute assignment at law or in equity is to have the force of an absolute assignment for the purposes of the sub-section. The document here relied on is the direction and authority, which in point of form is not an assignment to the bank of the debt in question but merely a direction to the garnishees to pay the debt in question to the bank . . .

Comment

It is clear that notice to the assignee is crucial.[34] Why should this be?

(iii) Claims by the debtor (equities)

Whether the assignment be statutory or equitable, in certain cases the assignee may be subject to claims the debtor could have deployed against the assignor. In considering the cases, three questions must be borne in mind. First, does the claim arise before or after the assignment? Second, is the claim for liquidated damages, that is, for a specific sum of money? Third, is the claim closely connected with the chose in action?

Extract 5.5.4

Government of Newfoundland v *Newfoundland Railway Co* (1888) 13 App Cas 199

PRIVY COUNCIL: . . . The true principle is shewn by Bovill, CJ,[i] in the following terms: – 'No case has been cited to us where equity has allowed against the equitable chose in action a set-off of a debt arising between the original parties subsequently to the notice of assignment, out of matters not connected with the debt claimed, nor in any way referring to it.'

. . .

But then it is said that the rule of law deducible from the authorities is, that when a debt or claim under a contract has been assigned and notice given to the debtor, which may be assumed to have been done in this case, the debt or claim is so severed from the rest of the contract that the assignee may hold it free from any counter-claim in respect of other terms of the same contract . . .

It certainly cannot be said that the claim by the Government for non-construction of the railway arises out of matters not connected with the payment of the subsidy. On the contrary, the obligation to construct the whole is so intimately connected with the obligation to pay for a portion, as to give rise to a forcible argument that one is a condition precedent to the other; so intimately that their Lordships have serious difficulty in disengaging them, and can only do so by modifying the language of part of the contract.

. . .

The present case is entirely different from any of those cited by the plaintiffs' counsel. The two claims under consideration have their origin in the same portion of the same contract, where the obligations which gave rise to them are intertwined in the closest manner. The claim of the Government does not arise from any fresh transaction freely entered into by it after notice of assignment by the company. It was utterly powerless to prevent the company from inflicting injury on it by breaking the contract. It would be a lamentable thing if it were found to be the law that a party to a contract may assign a portion of it, perhaps a beneficial portion, so that the assignee shall take the benefit, wholly discharged of any counter-claim by the other party in respect of the rest of the contract, which may be burdensome. There is no universal rule that claims arising out of the same contract may be set against one another in all circumstances. But their Lordships have no hesitation in saying that in this contract the claims for subsidy and for non-construction ought to be set against one another.

. . . Unliquidated damages may now be set off as between the original parties, and also against an assignee if flowing out of and inseparably connected with the dealings and transactions which also give rise to the subject of the assignment.

[i In *Watson* v *Mid-Wales Railway Co* (1867) LR 2 CP 593.]

---

[34] *Morrell* v *Wootten* (1852) 16 Beav 197 (51 ER 753); questioned by Hill (2001) 117 LQR 127 at p 137.

Comment

(1) This decision concerns claims arising after notice of the assignment. It shows that such claims, whether or not liquidated, may be recognised if closely connected to the contract.

(2) Why should the law recognise such claims as affecting the assignee? Does it adequately recognise the needs of assignees to have confidence in what is being assigned?

(3) Note that post-notice claims, unless closely connected with the contract, are not recognised even if based on pre-notice obligations.[35] Why should the law not recognise such claims?

Extract 5.5.5

Stoddart v Union Trust Ltd [1912] 1 KB 181

The debtor claimed that the assignor was liable in damages for a fraudulent misrepresentation which induced the contract.

VAUGHAN WILLIAMS LJ: . . . In equity he was allowed to sue in his own name, and in such a suit the defendant was allowed to set up some of the defences which would have been available to him as against the assignor, but a Court of Equity would not allow him to set up any defence or set-off arising as between him and the assignor subsequently to the notice of the assignment out of matters not connected with the chose in action assigned. It appears to me that, although the words of s 25, sub-s 6,[i] 'subject to all equities', &c, may not, perhaps, be very happily chosen, the result is that an assignee of a debt could not, under the circumstances of this case, have been restrained in equity from proceeding to enforce the debt, if he were an assignee of it for value and without notice of any fraud. That seems to me to be the result of the authorities . . . It would not be true upon the authorities, I think, to say that in a Court of Equity the debtor could never in such cases set up against the assignee of a debt a defence based upon fraud of the assignor by which he, the debtor, was induced to enter into the contract which gave rise to the debt assigned. I think that a debtor sued by the assignee of a debt might set up the defence that the contract under which the debt arose ought to be set aside and cancelled on the ground of fraud, but whether that could have been done in the present case is immaterial, for the defendants have not sought to do that, for the reason that they have so acted with regard to the subject-matter the sale of which was the consideration for the debt that they could not repudiate the contract. The question is whether, under these circumstances, the defendants here are in such a position that they cannot rely on the fraud of the assignor, and I am of opinion that they cannot. I come to that conclusion with some reluctance, because I doubt whether it is entirely consistent with justice that an assignee of a chose in action, even if innocent, should be allowed under such circumstances as these to recover without regard to the fraud of the assignor. The decisions in cases like *Young v Kitchin*[ii] and *Government of Newfoundland v Newfoundland Ry Co*,[iii] which were cases where a contract involved the performance of work by one of the parties to it in the future, and the consideration for the sum to be paid under it was the performance of that work in accordance with the contract, shew that matters flowing out of, and inseparably connected with, the contract which gave rise to the chose in action assigned may be set up by way of defence as against an assignee suing in respect thereof. I come, however, with some regret to the conclusion that the principle of those decisions cannot be applied in the present case.

[i The predecessor of s 136.]

[ii] 3 Ex D 127.

[iii] 13 App Cas 199.

---

[35] *Watson v Mid-Wales Railway Co* (1867) LR 2 CP 593.

Comment

(1) A claim to rescind the contract would fall within the test of 'matters flowing out of, and inseparably connected with' the contract. Why did the claim in *Stoddart* fall outside that test?

(2) How readily can assignees discover whether they will be bound by pre-notice claims?

It has been said that:[36]

> If the debt sought to be set off in an action brought on behalf of the assignee of a debt had existed at the time of the transfer, equity would not interfere to restrain the legal set-off which the parties had.

Why was this principle not applied in *Stoddart*?

(iv) Equitable assignments

Unlike statutory assignments, there are no requirements of writing and written notice to the debtor is unnecessary for equitable assignments (nor need they be absolute). However, if notice is not given to the debtor the assignee runs (i) the risk of payment being made to the assignor; (ii) further 'equities' arising which may affect him (equities were considered above); and (iii) dangers from other competing assignments of the same chose in action.

Thus in *Gorringe* v *Irwell India Rubber & Gutta Percha Works*,[37] Cotton LJ said as regards equitable assignments:

> It is contended that in order to make an assignment of a *chose in action*, such as a debt, a complete charge, notice must be given to the debtor. It is true that there must be such a notice to enable the title of the assignee to prevail against a subsequent assignee. That is established by *Dearle* v *Hall*, but there is no authority for holding this rule to apply as against the assignor of the debt. Though there is no notice to the debtor the title of the assignee is complete as against the assignor.

What is the effect of the assignment's being 'complete' before notice? *Dearle* v *Hall* is considered below.[38]

The major controversy concerns the need for consideration.[39] Consideration is not required for statutory assignments, but non-absolute assignments cannot be statutory. In particular, a part of a debt cannot be assigned under the statute. Arguments from principle are finely balanced. On the one hand, equity does not normally come to the aid of volunteers unless there is a completely constituted trust.[40] On the other hand, equity will intervene if a donor has done all in his power to perfect a gift.[41]

---

[36] Montague Smith J in *Watson* v *Mid-Wales Railway Co* (1867) LR 2 CP 593 at p 600.
[37] (1886) 34 Ch D 128.
[38] See p 157 below.
[39] Treitel, *The Law of Contract* (13th ed), pp 723–730; Hall [1959] CLJ 99; Megarry (1943) 59 LQR 58; Sheridan (1955) 33 Can BR 284.
[40] *Milroy* v *Lord* (1862) 4 De GF&J 264 (45 ER 1185) (see p 160 below).
[41] See p 221 below. Would it be fatal today if the assignment were unwritten? See *German* v *Yates* (1915) 32 TLR 52.

Extract 5.5.6

Holt v Heatherfield Trust Ltd [1942] 2 KB 1

The assignee could not rely on a statutory assignment as notice had not been given to the debtor at the relevant time.

ATKINSON J: . . . The next point is more difficult. It is said that the assignment was ineffective inasmuch as notice of it had not been given before the service of the garnishee order, so that at the date of the service of the garnishee order it was merely an equitable assignment and depended for its efficacy on proof of valuable consideration, and no consideration had been given for it. The mere existence of an antecedent debt is not valuable consideration, but forbearance to sue may be . . . I need not determine the difficult question of consideration, because I am satisfied that the validity of the assignment did not depend on its having been given for valuable consideration.

. . .

   The precise point was dealt with by Sargant J in *In re Westerton.*[i] . . . Obviously, there was no consideration, and notice had not been given. Sargant J held that Mrs Gray's title was good . . . In his judgment Sargant J said: '. . . It seems to me, though I am not sure that it was completely admitted by Mr Gover, that apart from [LPA, s 136], the want of consideration would have been fatal to Mrs Gray's claim . . . The third case which is in some respects similar to the present is *In re Williams,*[ii] where it was held that the alleged assignment was bad as being conditional and future. It is to be noticed however that the assignment in that case was an assignment without consideration, and if the question of consideration was essential there was a very simple means of arriving at the conclusion at which the Court of Appeal arrived without the necessity of going through the difficult questions arising in that case as to the real meaning of the documents. It appears to me that the Court of Appeal really assumed in that case – without, I agree, actually deciding the point – that the voluntary character of the assignment was not fatal to its efficacy.'

[i] [1919] 2 Ch 104.
[ii] [1917] 1 Ch 1.

Comment

(1) This remains the latest case on the question. While it holds that consideration is not essential, it should be remembered that there are other cases which are less supportive of voluntary assignments.

(2) What is *Re Westerton* authority for?

(3) Atkinson J left open whether there is consideration if an assignment is in satisfaction of an existing debt, but it seems clear that this is good consideration for assignment purposes.[42]

A rather different point relating to consideration is that it is clearly required for future choses in action, which cannot be the subject matter of an immediate assignment. Thus if I wish to assign debts which will be due to my business in the future, consideration is essential (no statutory assignment is possible) and the assignment will operate on the chose in action when it comes into existence.[43] Does this approach to future choses mean that the obligation must be enforceable at the time of the assignment? If X owes me £100 in a month's time, is this a future chose?

---

[42] Hollond (1943) 59 LQR 129; Megarry (1943) 59 LQR 208.
[43] *Tailby* v *Official Receiver* (1888) 13 App Cas 523. Expectancies, such as rights under the will of a living person, similarly cannot be assigned until the person dies: *Meek* v *Kettlewell* (1843) 1 Ph 342 (41 ER 662).

It has been seen that equitable assignments do not require notice to the debtor but that the assignee may be disadvantaged if notice is not given. One specific aspect of this concerns the priority of two competing assignees of the same chose in action. On normal priority principles, one would expect the first assignment to have priority. The rules are based on dealings with trust interests and the following case is from that context.

Extract 5.5.7

Ward v *Duncombe* [1893] AC 369

LORD HERSCHELL LC: . . . The doctrine that where a fund is legally vested in trustees, an assignee or incumbrancer who gives notice to the trustees has a better title in equity than an assignee or incumbrancer of earlier date who has not given such notice, is of comparatively recent origin. It was so decided for the first time in the cases of *Dearle* v *Hall* and *Loveridge* v *Cooper*.[i] The Master of the Rolls (Sir T Plumer), before whom these cases came in the first instance, pointed out that where a contract was made behind the back of those in whom the legal estate was vested, it was necessary, if the security was intended to attach to the thing itself, to lay hold of that thing in the manner in which its nature permits it to be laid hold of; that is, by giving notice of the contract to those in whom the legal interest is . . . The learned judge then dwelt on the consideration that the assignee or incumbrancer who has not given notice has been guilty of neglect, that the consequence of such neglect is to cause the cestui que trust to appear to be the real owner and so to enable him to commit a fraud, and that this must be considered as foreseen by those who omit to give notice.

LORD MACNAGHTEN: . . . In defence of the rule in *Dearle* v *Hall*, it has been said that notice is necessary in order to 'perfect' the title of the assignee – in order to 'complete' his title. Those expressions have frequently been used; but they are, I venture to think, little more than mere phrases. Notice does not render the title perfect. Notice was not even a step in the title until it was made so by the decision in *Foster* v *Cockerell*.[ii] Apart from the rule in *Dearle* v *Hall*, an assignee of an equitable interest from a person capable of disposing of it has a perfect equitable title, though the title is no doubt subject to the infirmity which attaches to all equitable titles. And that infirmity is not and cannot be wholly cured or removed by notice to the trustees.

. . .

I am inclined to think that the rule in *Dearle* v *Hall* has on the whole produced at least as much injustice as it has prevented. It was argued in *Dearle* v *Hall* that notice to the trustees necessarily prevents fraud on the part of the assignor . . . But it is founded, I think, upon rather loose notions as to the duties of trustees which no doubt were prevalent at one time . . .

My Lords, I have made these observations, not for the purpose of impugning the authority of the rule in *Dearle* v *Hall*. The rule is settled law. But it seems to me that when your Lordships are asked to extend the rule to a case not already covered by authority, it is proper to inquire into the principles upon which the rule is said to be founded.

[i] 3 Russ 1.
[ii] 3 Cl&F 456.

Comment

(1) Is there good sense in the priority rule established by *Dearle* v *Hall*?

(2) The priority rule has been applied to assignments of choses in action.[44] Given the doubts expressed in *Ward* v *Duncombe*, was this sensible?

[44] *Marchant* v *Morton, Down & Co* [1901] 2 KB 829.

B. Creation of interests

Charges, for example, may be created by assignment. However, such assignments are not absolute and so cannot be statutory; they can only be equitable. A trust of a chose in action can be created. Thus it is common for a trust to comprise shares and bank accounts. Save where LPA s 53 applies, no formalities are required.

6. Declarations of trust and equitable interests

A. Declaration of trust

Trusts are most commonly set up by transferring property to trustees, but it has long been possible to declare oneself a trustee. This form of creation of interests is exceptional: it is effective despite being unilateral, informal[45] and not involving any dealing (such as delivery) with the property. Not surprisingly, the courts are cautious in finding that a trust has been declared.

Extract 5.6.1

Re Cozens [1913] 2 Ch 478

The alleged declaration was based upon pencil entries in Cozens' accounts (he had subsequently died).

NEVILLE J: . . . It is somewhat startling to find, if that indeed be the case, that a man can declare a trust in the secrecy of his chamber, uncommunicated to any living creature . . .

The questions in this and similar cases are after all mainly decisions on questions of fact, and it must be borne in mind that in each case where a declaration of trust is relied on the Court must be satisfied that a present irrevocable declaration of trust has been made . . .

In my opinion the absence of communication raises a strong inference against an intention to make an appropriation irrevocable. In the absence of evidence to the contrary I think the inference is that silence was intended to enable the declarant to adhere to or abandon the declaration as best served his advantage for the time being.

Comment

Should the law insist on some form of corroboration of such declarations of trust?

Most problems concern some dealing between purported trustee and beneficiary.

Extract 5.6.2

Jones v *Lock* (1865) LR 1 Ch App 25

A father gave a cheque to his nine-month-old son, saying 'I give this to baby for himself.'

LORD CRANWORTH LC: . . . [W]hen there has been a declaration of trust, then it will be enforced, whether there has been consideration or not. Therefore the question in each case is one of fact; has there been a gift or not, or has there been a declaration of trust or not? I should have every inclination to sustain this gift, but unfortunately I am unable to do so; the case turns

---

[45] But trusts of land do require writing: LPA, s 53(1)(b) (Extract 5.3.3 above).

on the very short question whether Jones intended to make a declaration that he held the property in trust for the child; and I cannot come to any other conclusion than that he did not. I think it would be of very dangerous example if loose conversations of this sort, in important transactions of this kind, should have the effect of declarations of trust.

Extract 5.6.3

Richards v *Delbridge* (1874) LR 18 Eq 11

A voluntary assignment of a lease to a child failed because it was not by deed.

JESSEL MR: . . . It is true he need not use the words, 'I declare myself a trustee', but he must do something which is equivalent to it, and use expressions which have that meaning; for, however anxious the Court may be to carry out a man's intention, it is not at liberty to construe words otherwise than according to their proper meaning.

. . .

The true distinction appears to me to be plain, and beyond dispute: for a man to make himself a trustee there must be an expression of intention to become a trustee, whereas words of present gift shew an intention to give over property to another, and not retain it in the donor's own hands for any purpose, fiduciary or otherwise.

In *Milroy* v *Lord*,[i] Lord Justice *Turner*, after referring to the two modes of making a voluntary settlement valid and effectual, adds these words: 'The cases, I think, go further, to this extent, that if the settlement is intended to be effectuated by one of the modes to which I have referred, the Court will not give effect to it by applying another of those modes. If it is intended to take effect by transfer, the Court will not hold the intended transfer to operate as a declaration of trust, for then every imperfect instrument would be made effectual by being converted into a perfect trust.'

. . . It appears to me that these cases of voluntary gifts should not be confounded with another class of cases in which words of present transfer for valuable consideration are held to be evidence of a contract which the Court will enforce.

[i] 4 DF&J 264, 274.

The point was forcefully stated by Maitland[46] in the following words:

> . . . The two intentions are very different – the giver means to get rid of his rights, the man who is intending to make himself a trustee intends to retain his rights but to come under an onerous obligation. The latter intention is far rarer than the former. Men often mean to give things to their kinsfolk, they do not often mean to constitute themselves trustees. An imperfect gift is no declaration of trust . . .

Comment

One can appreciate that a declaration of trust is not the same as an outright transfer, but can it be replied that a declaration of trust in these cases would be more faithful to the donor's underlying intention than total failure of any form of gift? Could some of these cases be distinguished on the basis that the informality makes it difficult to prove an intention of making a gift?

---

[46] *Equity* (2nd ed), p 72.

Extract 5.6.4

Paul v *Constance* [1977] 1 WLR 527

Mr Constance, now deceased, obtained damages in a personal injuries action, the money being placed in a bank deposit account. It was claimed that he had declared a trust of the money in favour of the woman he had been living with for some years. Counsel argued that the evidence must show 'an intention to dispose of a property or a fund so that somebody else to the exclusion of the disponent acquires the beneficial interest in it'.

SCARMAN LJ: . . . When one looks at the detailed evidence to see whether it goes as far as that – and I think that the evidence does have to go as far as that – one finds that from the time that the deceased received his damages right up to his death he was saying, on occasions, that the money was as much the plaintiff's as his. When they discussed the damages, how to invest them or what to do with them and when they discussed the bank account, he would say to her: 'The money is as much yours as mine.'

The judge, rightly treating the basic problem in the case as a question of fact, reached this conclusion. He said:

'I have read through my notes and I am quite satisfied that it was the intention of Mrs Paul and Mr Constance to create a trust in which both of them were interested.'

. . . When one bears in mind the unsophisticated character of the deceased and his relationship with the plaintiff during the last few years of his life, Mr Wilson submits that the words that he did use on more than one occasion, 'This money is as much yours as mine', convey clearly a present declaration that the existing fund was as much the plaintiff's as his own. The judge accepted that conclusion. I think that he was well justified in doing so and, indeed, I think that he was right to do so . . .

Comment

(1) This is a good example of a trust's being found without there being any formal words of trust.

(2) *Jones* v *Lock* and *Richards* v *Delbridge* were distinguished on the basis that 'There is no suggestion of a gift by transfer in the present case.' Is this convincing? If Mr Constance said that it was as much hers as his, does this not indicate a purported transfer of the chose in action?

Reluctance to find a trust is also encountered where there is an ineffective transfer to trustees on trust for a third party. *Milroy* v *Lord*,[47] relied upon in *Richards* v *Delbridge*, is emphatic that the transaction is wholly ineffective and there is no trust. Is there a convincing argument that a trust really is intended (though admittedly not one binding the transferor) and therefore finding a declaration of trust is justified? After all, a transferor who does not wish to have the burdens of trusteeship can always appoint further trustees and then retire as trustee.

Lastly, an ineffective transfer on trust may be rendered valid by a subsequent transfer of property to the trustee. Just as delivery may follow words of gift for gifts of chattels, so transfer of property may follow a declaration of trust.

---

[47] (1862) 4 De GF&J 264 (45 ER 1185).

Extract 5.6.5

Re Bowden [1936] Ch 71

A settlor sought to recover property obtained by the trustees.

BENNETT J: . . . As regards the second subject which the settlor purported to assign she had only a spes successionis and no property capable of assignment by law: but in addition to purporting to assign her expectation under her father's will or intestacy she appointed the trustees of the settlement her agents to receive her share of whatever might come to her under her father's will . . .

The settlor's father died on November 18, 1869, . . . and in due course of time these trustees as the settlor's agents received from the executors of the will substantial sums, and from the time when they were received those sums have been held by the original and subsequent trustees on the trusts of the voluntary settlement.

Counsel for the settlor . . . contended that the settlement, being a voluntary settlement, was void and altogether unenforceable . . . All that was decided in *Meek* v *Kettlewell*[i] was that where the assistance of the court of equity is needed to enable the trustees of a voluntary settlement to obtain possession of property subjected to the trusts of the voluntary settlement, the property not having been vested in the trustees, a court of equity will render no assistance to the plaintiff.

But here nobody is seeking the assistance of the court of equity to enforce the voluntary settlement. Under a valid authority, unrevoked, the persons appointed trustees under the settlement received the settlor's interest under her father's will, and, immediately after it had been received by them, as a result of her own act and her own declaration, contained in the voluntary settlement, it became impressed with the trusts contained in the settlement.

[i] 1 Ha 464.

Comment

What would have been the result if, before they received the money, the settlor had told the trustees that she had changed her mind and wished the money to be held for herself?

B. Transfer of equitable interests

These interests provide one specific form of choses in action (they fall within LPA, s 136), but they attracted slightly different assignment rules. An equitable assignee never needed to join the assignor in an action: given that an equitable right was involved, equity had no need to respect the existence of a legal right in the assignor.

Extract 5.6.6

Kekewich v *Manning* (1851) 1 De GM&G 176 (42 ER 519)

KNIGHT BRUCE LJ: . . . For as, upon one hand, it is, on legal and equitable principles, we apprehend, clear that a person *sui juris*, acting freely, fairly and with sufficient knowledge, ought to have and has it in his power to make, in a binding and effectual manner, a voluntary gift of any part of his property, whether capable or incapable of manual delivery, whether in possession or reversionary, and howsoever circumstanced, so, on the other, it is as clear generally, if not universally, that a gratuitously expressed intention, a promise merely voluntary, or, to use a familiar phrase, *nudum pactum*, does not (the matter resting there) bind legally or equitably. I have been speaking of transactions without any sealed writing. But though it is true that in cases where such an intention, such a promise, is expressed in a deed, it may bind generally at law as a covenant by reason of the light in which the particular kind of instrument called a deed is regarded at law, yet in equity, where at least the covenantor is living, or where specific performance of such a covenant is sought, it stands scarcely, or not at all, on a better footing than if it were contained in an instrument unsealed . . . To state, however, a simple case: – Suppose stock or money to be legally vested in A as a trustee for B for life, and, subject to B's life interest, for C absolutely; surely it must be competent to C in B's lifetime, with or without the consent of A, to make an effectual gift of C's interest to D by way of mere bounty, leaving the legal interest and legal title unchanged and untouched. Surely it would not be consistent with natural equity or with reason or expediency to hold the contrary, C being *sui juris*, and acting freely, fairly and with sufficient advice and knowledge. If so, can C do this better or more effectually than by executing an assignment to D? . . .

Comment

This shows that, whatever the position for legal choses in action, consideration is not required. Is there adequate justification for any difference in this respect? Why do we not apply the rule that equity does not assist volunteers?

However, formality rules provide the main reason for studying equitable interests separately.

Extract 5.6.7

Law of Property Act 1925, s 53

53.—(1) Subject to the provisions hereinafter contained with respect to the creation of interests in land by parol—

    (a) a disposition of an equitable interest or trust subsisting at the time of the disposition, must be in writing signed by the person disposing of the same, or by his agent thereunto lawfully authorised in writing or by will.

    (2) This section does not affect the creation or operation of resulting, implied or constructive trusts.

It is obvious that an assignment of an equitable interest falls within para (c), but what other transactions are caught?

Extract 5.6.8

Grey v IRC [1960] AC 1

Hunter, for whom shares were held on trust, instructed the trustees to hold the shares for specified persons.

VISCOUNT SIMONDS: . . . If the word 'disposition' is given its natural meaning, it cannot, I think, be denied that a direction given by Mr Hunter, whereby the beneficial interest in the shares theretofore vested in him became vested in another or others, is a disposition. But it is contended by the appellants that the word 'disposition' is to be given a narrower meaning and (so far as relates to inter vivos transactions) be read as if it were synonymous with 'grants and assignments' and that, given this meaning, it does not cover such a direction as was given in this case. As I am clearly of the opinion, which I understand to be shared by your Lordships, that there is no justification for giving the word 'disposition' a narrower meaning than it ordinarily bears, it will be unnecessary to discuss the interesting problem that would otherwise arise . . . My Lords, the argument for narrowing the meaning of 'disposition' was that the Law of Property Act, 1925, was a consolidating Act, that among the Acts which it consolidated was the Statute of Frauds (29 Car 2, c 3), s 9, that that section enacted that 'all grants and assignments of any trust or confidence shall likewise be in writing . . .' and that therefore the word 'disposition' in section 53(1)(c) of the Act of 1925 is to be given the same meaning as would be given to 'grants and assignments' in section 9 of the Statute of Frauds.

[After investigating the history of LPA 1925.] But I have said enough to show that the Act of 1925, though in a sense a consolidating Act, in fact consolidated Acts which themselves were amending Acts.

Comment

Now that 'disposition' is to be given its natural meaning, what does it mean? Does it cover disclaimers[48] or surrenders?[49] Is it limited to forms of transfers of interests, or might it extend to the creation of subordinate rights (such as the creation of a life interest in an equitable interest)?

Other transactions involving trusts have given rise to difficulty. What happens if a beneficiary declares himself or herself a trustee of his or her beneficial interest? A declaration of trust does not normally require writing, but is this declaration a disposition of the equitable interest?

Extract 5.6.9

Nelson v *Greening & Sykes (Builders) Ltd* [2008] EGLR 59

LAWRENCE COLLINS LJ: 55.   It is true that under the rule in *Saunders* v *Vautier* [(1841) 4 Beav 115] a beneficiary with a vested and indefeasible interest can require a trustee to transfer trust property to the beneficiary.

56.   It is also true that in *Grey* v *IRC* [1958] Ch 690 (affirmed [1960] AC 1) at 715, Lord Evershed MR (dissenting, but not on this point) said that where a person who is the owner beneficially of property (and the legal estate is vested in another as trustee for him) makes a declaration of trust the practical effect would seem, in common sense, to amount, or be capable of amounting, to the 'getting rid of' a trust or equitable interest then subsisting. It is said in Snell, *Equity* (31st ed. McGhee, 2005), para 19–11 that 'where property is transferred to T "on trust for B absolutely". . . [i]f B in turn becomes a bare trustee of his equitable interest for C, T will hold directly in trust for C . . .', citing *Head* v *Lord Teynham* (1783) 1 Cox Eq. 57 (which only holds that where trustees and the beneficiary are before the court, an intermediate trustee of the equitable interest need not be made a party).

57.   These authorities do not bind this court to hold that as a matter of law an intermediate trustee ceases to be a trustee. I accept the submission for G&S that saying (as Lord Evershed MR said) that the practical effect would seem to amount to or be capable of amounting to the 'getting rid' of the trust of the equitable interest then subsisting, is not the same as saying that as a matter of law it does get rid of the intermediate trust. What he was saying was that in the case of a trust and sub-trust of personal property the trustees may decide that as a matter of practicality it is more convenient to deal directly with the beneficiary of the sub-trust.

Comment

(1) This runs counter to much previous thinking.[50] Is it justified?

(2) *Greening* was not a case on formalities. What is its effect on formalities issues?

A very different question exists if the beneficiary directs the trustees to transfer the legal estate.

---

[48] *Re Paradise Motor Co* Ltd [1968] 1 WLR 1125.
[49] *IRC* v *Buchanan* [1958] Ch 289.
[50] In addition to the cases cited in *Greening*, see *Grainge* v *Wilberforce* (1889) 5 TLR 436.

Extract 5.6.10

Vandervell v IRC [1967] 2 AC 291

Vandervell, the beneficiary, directed the trustees to transfer the legal title to the Royal College of Surgeons. They did so.

LORD UPJOHN: . . . The question is whether . . . the absence of writing prevented any equitable or beneficial interest in the shares passing to the college so that contrary to his wishes and understanding they remained bare trustees for him. This depends entirely upon the true construction of section 53(1)(c) of the Law of Property Act, 1925, which the Crown maintain makes writing necessary to pass the beneficial interest . . .

[Quoting LPA, s 53(1)(c):] Those words were applied in *Grey*[i] and *Oughtred*[ii] to cases where the legal estate remained outstanding in a trustee and the beneficial owner was dealing and dealing only with the equitable estate. That is understandable; the object of the section, as was the object of the old Statute of Frauds, is to prevent hidden oral transactions in equitable interests in fraud of those truly entitled, and making it difficult, if not impossible, for the trustees to ascertain who are in truth his beneficiaries. But when the beneficial owner owns the whole beneficial estate and is in a position to give directions to his bare trustee with regard to the legal as well as the equitable estate there can be no possible ground for invoking the section where the beneficial owner wants to deal with the legal estate as well as the equitable estate.

I cannot agree with Diplock LJ[iii] that prima facie a transfer of the legal estate carries with it the absolute beneficial interest in the property transferred; this plainly is not so, e.g., the transfer may be on a change of trustee; it is a matter of intention in each case. But if the intention of the beneficial owner in directing the trustee to transfer the legal estate to X is that X should be the beneficial owner I can see no reason for any further document or further words in the document assigning the legal estate also expressly transferring the beneficial interest; the greater includes the less.

LORD DONOVAN: [Section 53(1)(c)] clearly refers to the disposition of an equitable interest as such. If, owning the entire estate, legal and beneficial, in a piece of property, and desiring to transfer that entire estate to another, I do so by means of a disposition which ex facie deals only with the legal estate, it would be ridiculous to argue that section 53(1)(c) has not been complied with, and that therefore the legal estate alone has passed.

The present case, it is true, is different in its facts in that the legal and equitable estates in the shares were in separate ownership; but when Mr Vandervell, being competent to do so, instructed the bank to transfer the shares to the college, and made it abundantly clear that he wanted to pass, by means of that transfer, his own beneficial, or equitable, interest, plus the bank's legal interest, he achieved the same result as if there had been no separation of the interests. The transfer thus made pursuant to his intentions and instructions was a disposition not of the equitable interest alone, but of the entire estate in the shares. In such a case I see no room for the operation of section 53(1)(c).

LORD WILBERFORCE: . . . The case should then be regarded as one in which the appellant himself has, with the intention to make a gift, put the college in a position to become the legal owner of the shares, which the college in fact became. If the appellant had died before the college had obtained registration, it is clear on the principle of *In re Rose*[iv] that the gift would have been complete, on the basis that he had done everything in his power to transfer the legal interest, with an intention to give, to the college. No separate transfer, therefore, of the equitable interest ever came to or needed to be made and there is no room for the operation of the subsection.

---

[i] [1960] AC 1.
[ii] [1960] AC 206.
[iii] [1966] Ch 261, 287.
[iv] [1949] Ch 78; [1948] 2 All ER 971 [see Extract 7.4.7 below].

Comment

(1) Is Lord Upjohn's distinguishing of *Grey* satisfactory? Where a person holds the entire beneficial interest, why should we distinguish between (i) telling the trustees to hold for X and (ii) telling the trustees to transfer to X?

(2) Lord Donovan relies, as does Lord Upjohn in a passage not quoted, upon the ability of the legal and beneficial owner to transfer without writing. This is obvious, as with the every-day gift of chattels. However, can we extrapolate from that setting to that of *Vandervell*?

(3) Lord Wilberforce's analysis is based upon the fact that Vandervell handed a transfer signed by the trustees to the college. Is it convincing?

(4) Is there anything to be said for Diplock LJ's analysis in the Court of Appeal?

Section 53(2) exempts resulting, implied and constructive trusts. This has a fairly limited impact on s 53(1)(c), save for one very controversial question: can a contract to sell a beneficial interest give rise to a constructive trust, similar to a contract to sell an interest in land giving rise to an estate contract? If A agrees to sell his equitable interest to B, the argument is that, as a contract, this does not require writing.[51] Equity will enforce this contract by way of constructive trust,[52] with the practical effect that equity will treat the beneficial interest as being in B.

Extract 5.6.11

Neville v Wilson [1997] Ch 144

In *Oughtred* v *IRC*,[53] the facts had been similar to the example above, but A subsequently executed a transfer of the equitable interest and it was held that this was the operative transfer. In *Neville* there was no such transfer, but dicta in *Oughtred* on this situation had to be considered.

NOURSE LJ (delivering the judgment of the court): The views of their Lordships as to the effect of section 53 can be summarised as follows. Lord Radcliffe, agreeing with Upjohn J, thought that subsection (2) applied. He gave reasons for that view. Lord Cohen and Lord Denning thought that it did not. Although neither of them gave reasons, they may be taken to have accepted the submissions of Mr Wilberforce at pp 220–222. Lord Keith and Lord Jenkins expressed no view either way . . .

We do not think that there is anything in the speeches in the House of Lords which prevents us from holding that the effect of each individual agreement was to constitute the shareholder an implied or constructive trustee for the other shareholders. In this respect we are of the opinion that the analysis of Lord Radcliffe, based on the proposition that a specifically enforceable agreement to assign an interest in property creates an equitable interest in the assignee, was unquestionably correct; cf *London and South Western Railway Co* v *Gomm* (1882) 20 Ch D 562, 581, *per* Sir George Jessel MR. A greater difficulty is caused by Lord Denning's outright rejection of the application of section 53(2), with which Lord Cohen appears to have agreed.

So far as it is material to the present case, what subsection (2) says is that subsection (1)(c) does not affect the creation or operation of implied or constructive trusts. Just as in *Oughtred* v *Inland Revenue Commissioners* [1960] AC 206 the son's oral agreement created a constructive trust in favour of the mother, so here each shareholder's oral or implied agreement created

---

[51] Unlike a contract to sell an interest in land.
[52] Applying the maxim that equity treats as done what ought to be done.
[53] [1960] AC 206.

an implied or constructive trust in favour of the other shareholders. Why then should subsection (2) not apply? No convincing reason was suggested in argument and none has occurred to us since. Moreover, to deny its application in this case would be to restrict the effect of general words when no restriction is called for, and to lay the ground for fine distinctions in the future.

Comment

In the light of what is said in *Oughtred*, is this result surprising? How well does it fit with principle and with the policy behind the statutory provisions?

By way of conclusion, the formality requirements for equitable interests can be seen as being complex and scarcely satisfactory. Does it make sense to single out dispositions of equitable interests as requiring writing? When should writing be required?

7. Wills

So far we have concentrated upon lifetime (inter vivos) transfers. Obviously, property is often left by will on death. The essence of a will is that it takes effect on death: it is this factor which distinguishes it from inter vivos transfers. If I declare myself a trustee of specific property in favour of myself for life, remainder to Rachel, is this a will?

Special provisions, relating particularly to formalities, have long applied to wills.

Extract 5.7.1

Wills Act 1837

7.—No will made by any person under the age of eighteen years shall be valid.

9.—No will shall be valid unless—
    (a) it is in writing, and signed by the testator, or by some other person in his presence and by his direction; and
    (b) it appears that the testator intended by his signature to give effect to the will; and
    (c) the signature is made or acknowledged by the testator in the presence of two or more witnesses present at the same time; and
    (d) each witness either—
        (i) attests and signs the will; or
        (ii) acknowledges his signature,
          in the presence of the testator (but not necessarily in the presence of any other witness),
    but no form of attestation shall be necessary.

11.—Provided always, that any soldier being in actual military service, or any mariner or seaman being at sea, may dispose of his personal estate as he might have done before the making of this Act.

15.—If any person shall attest the execution of any will to whom or to whose wife or husband any beneficial devise, legacy, . . . shall be thereby given or made, such devise, legacy . . . shall, so far only as concerns such person attesting the execution of such will, or the wife or husband of such person, or any person claiming under such person or wife or husband, be utterly null and void . . .

18.—(1) Subject to subsections (2) to (4) below, a will shall be revoked by the testator's marriage.

(3)   Where it appears from a will that at the time it was made the testator was expecting to be married to a particular person and that he intended that the will should not be revoked by the marriage, the will shall not be revoked by his marriage to that person.

18A.—(1)   Where, after a testator has made a will, a decree of a court of civil jurisdiction in England and Wales dissolves or annuls his marriage . . .
    (b)   any property which, or an interest in which, is devised or bequeathed to the former spouse shall pass as if the former spouse had died on that date, except in so far as a contrary intention appears by the will.

Comment

Sections 18 and 18A are extended to civil partnerships (see p 399 below) by ss 18B, 18C.

Wills constitute a large topic and we can do no more than sketch the major outlines. Care must be taken in executing the will, particularly as regards witnesses and the need for them both to be present when the will is signed (or the signature acknowledged). Also, of course, legacies to witnesses are ineffective.[54]

Generally, a will can be revoked only by a document satisfying s 9. Sections 18 and 18A show the effect of marriage and divorce. Section 20 provides for revocation 'by the burning, tearing, or otherwise destroying the same by the testator . . . , with the intention of revoking the same'.

What happens if a will is known to have been executed but cannot be found?

Extract 5.7.2

Sugden v Lord St Leonards (1876) 1 PD 154

COCKBURN CJ: . . . The only conclusion I can arrive at is, not that he destroyed it, but that it was clandestinely got at by somebody and surreptitiously taken away; who that somebody is, is one of those mysteries which time may possibly solve, but which at present it would defy human ingenuity to say.

When the idea of Lord St Leonards having himself destroyed the will is disposed of, the next question which presents itself is, whether, the will having been lost, secondary evidence can be given of its contents. Now, that matter is disposed of by the authority of *Brown v Brown,*[i] which, I think, has been recognised as perfectly sound. There Lord Campbell says, 'Parol evidence of the contents of the lost instrument may be received as much when it is a will as if it were any other document', and in that I, for one, most entirely concur. The consequence of a contrary ruling would be in the highest degree mischievous, it would enable any person who desired, from some sinister motive, to frustrate the testamentary disposition of a dead man, by merely getting possession of the will to prevent the possibility of the will of the deceased being carried into execution . . .

As regards the only remaining question, namely, whether, assuming that we have not before us all the contents of the lost will, probate should be allowed of that which we have, so long as we are satisfied that we have the substantial parts of the will made out, I cannot bring myself to entertain a doubt. If part of a will were accidentally burnt, or if a portion of it were torn out designedly by a wrongdoer, it would nevertheless, in my opinion, be the duty of a Court of Probate to give effect to the will of the testator as far as it could be ascertained.

[i]   8 E&B 876; 27 LJ (QB) 173.

---

[54]   Save sometimes for the rare case where there are more than two witnesses: Wills Act 1968, s 1.

Comment

(1) Is the case for giving effect to lost wills unanswerable?

(2) How difficult is it likely to be to discover the text of lost wills?

8. Restrictions upon transfers

There are several statutory provisions which limit the efficacy of transfers, usually transfers designed to frustrate bankruptcy rules. If a person about to become bankrupt could give his or her property away, this would plainly be unfair on the creditors. In this book, we can do no more than outline the most important restrictions.

Extract 5.8.1

Insolvency Act 1986, ss 339, 340, 423

339.—(1) Subject as follows in this section and sections 341 and 342, where an individual is adjudged bankrupt and he has at a relevant time (defined in section 341) entered into a transaction with any person at an undervalue, the trustee of the bankrupt's estate may apply to the court for an order under this section.

(2) The court shall, on such an application, make such order as it thinks fit for restoring the position to what it would have been if that individual had not entered into that transaction.

(3) For the purposes of this section and sections 341 and 342, an individual enters into a transaction with a person at an undervalue if—

    (a) he makes a gift to that person or he otherwise enters into a transaction with that person on terms that provide for him to receive no consideration,

    (b) he enters into a transaction with that person in consideration of marriage, or

    (c) he enters into a transaction with that person for a consideration the value of which, in money or money's worth, is significantly less than the value, in money or money's worth, of the consideration provided by the individual.

340.—(1) Subject as follows in this and the next two sections, where an individual is adjudged bankrupt and he has at a relevant time (defined in section 341) given a preference to any person, the trustee of the bankrupt's estate may apply to the court for an order under this section.

(2) The court shall, on such an application, make such order as it thinks fit for restoring the position to what it would have been if that individual had not given that preference.

(3) For the purposes of this and the next two sections, an individual gives a preference to a person if—

    (a) that person is one of the individual's creditors or a surety or guarantor for any of his debts or other liabilities, and

    (b) the individual does anything or suffers anything to be done which (in either case) has the effect of putting that person into a position which, in the event of the individual's bankruptcy, will be better than the position he would have been in if that thing had not been done.

(4) The court shall not make an order under this section in respect of a preference given to any person unless the individual who gave the preference was influenced in deciding to give it by a desire to produce in relation to that person the effect mentioned in subsection (3)(b) above.

423.—(1) This section relates to transactions entered into at an undervalue . . .

(2) Where a person has entered into such a transaction, the court may, if satisfied under the next subsection, make such order as it thinks fit for—

(a) restoring the position to what it would have been if the transaction had not been entered into, and

(b) protecting the interests of persons who are victims of the transaction.

(3)   In the case of a person entering into such a transaction, an order shall only be made if the court is satisfied that it was entered into by him for the purpose—

(a) of putting assets beyond the reach of a person who is making, or may at some time make, a claim against him, or

(b) of otherwise prejudicing the interests of such a person in relation to the claim which he is making or may make.

Comment

The relevant time for ss 339 and 340 varies between five years (undervalue) and six months (no undervalue, not in favour of an associate). Unless there is undervalue and it is within two years of bankruptcy, the bankrupt must be insolvent at the time of the transaction. For s 423, there is no time limit and no requirement of insolvency at the time of transfer.[55]

Bankruptcy is not the only setting for such restrictions. For example, s 37(2) of the Matrimonial Causes Act 1973 enables the court to set aside dispositions made with the intention of defeating spouses' claims for financial relief. Purchasers in good faith are protected.

Further reading

Hall J C [1959] CLJ 99: Gift of part of a debt.

Harpum, C (2001) 'Property in an electronic age', in *Modern Studies in Property Law*, Vol 1, ed. E. Cooke, Chapter 1.

Pettit, P [1989] Conv 431: Farewell section 40.

Tettenborn, A [1987] Conv 358: Fraud, cross-claims and the assignment of choses in action.

Thornely, J W A [1953] CLJ 355: Transfer of choses in possession between members of a common household.

---

[55] *Midland Bank plc* v *Wyatt* [1995] 1 FLR 696.

6

Formalities: rationale and trusts

Formality requirements are quite frequently overlooked, especially in the family context where people are likely to be aware neither of categories of proprietary interests nor of formalities rules. The following two chapters will consider ways in which the courts enforce transfers and arrangements despite failure to comply with formality requirements. Most of the cases under discussion involve oral arrangements relating to land; other forms of property are less likely to require writing. Without a deed, even writing is not enough for most claims to legal rights in land, though consideration may result in a contract and thereby a good equitable interest.[1]

The principal focus of this chapter will be upon the use of resulting and constructive trusts. An important point to grasp is that these trusts are more important than merely getting around formality rules:[2] they can be the source of rights to property. Take the resulting trust as an example. If A transfers property to B on trust for C for life, then the law presumes that B holds on resulting trust for A once C's life interest terminates. Here we see the resulting trust fulfilling two roles. First, it ensures that A rather than B has a good claim to the property on C's death. Second, the fact that there is a resulting trust means that lack of writing is irrelevant – this is important if land is the subject matter of the trust.

1. The role of formality requirements

Before considering resulting and constructive trusts, it is important to assess the reasons for having formality rules.

Extract 6.1.1

Moriarty (1984) 100 LQR 376 at pp 398–401 (footnotes omitted)

1. Functional objections to informality

For over 300 years now, since the Statute of Frauds 1677, the law has thought it important to require formality in the creation of proprietary rights to land. The precise details of the present requirements need not concern us here; but what we must be clear about, in order to assess the functional objections to the proprietary licence, are the reasons for their existence. A requirement of formality, it is suggested, can fulfil a three-fold purpose: it can have a forensic function, an evidentiary function, and a protective function. The forensic function needs little explanation as it is the purpose which has most commonly been associated with a requirement of formality since the Statute of Frauds 1677 was given that name. Land is such an attractive

---

[1] See p 134 above.
[2] Law of Property Act 1925 (hereafter LPA), s 53(2) exempts them from writing requirements.

commodity, it is said, that there is always the risk that a rogue might try to get it on the cheap by fraudulently alleging a non-existent agreement to transfer him some. The risk might be slight, but it can be avoided altogether by requiring all agreements to be evidenced in writing and signed. Formality, therefore, performs a forensic function in providing simple yet conclusive evidence of the fact of agreement.

The evidentiary function, by contrast, is concerned with the role of writing in evidencing not the fact of agreement, but rather its content. A further consequence of the social and economic importance of land, all apart from its potential to attract rogues, is the variety of uses to which it can be put; and this variety is reflected in the many different kinds of interest in land which the law has come to provide. There are a whole host of interests like the fee simple, the lease, the covenant, the easement, the profit, the mortgage, the rentcharge; some of which may then, through the doctrine of estates, be divided up temporally, or, as joint interests, be divided up concurrently. Some agreements, therefore, can be quite complex if they involve a number of such interests in land. Other agreements can involve a factual situation which can look like several different interests, although each may have slightly different consequences. In either circumstance, it can be of crucial importance to define the terms of the agreement with precision. Writing, therefore, performs a useful evidentiary function, both in encouraging such precision at the outset, and then recording the result for posterity.

Finally, there is the protective function. For most people, land will be the single most important asset they will ever own; yet, in moments of rashness, they make promises in respect of it which they soon live to regret. A present owner of land may, on the spur of the moment, promise rights to it which, on later reflection, he wishes he had not. A potential purchaser of land may promise to buy a property without, for example, first having it surveyed or ensuring that he can finance its acquisition, and then find he has made a costly mistake. Nothing, of course, can totally protect people from the consequences of their own folly; but a requirement of formality can, at least, minimise the chances of such a mistake being made. Writing performs a protective function, therefore, by giving people a chance to think again if the agreement is no more than oral. Only written agreements will be irrevocable; and they will have been made with greater deliberation, and usually with the advice of a lawyer.

The point, then, is that if a requirement of formality fulfils such important forensic, evidentiary, and protective functions in land law, each policy would seem to argue strongly against a doctrine that dispenses with the need for writing at all. It is suggested, however, that these arguments are by no means conclusive. The forensic argument, in fact, need hardly detain us at all. The risk of fraud and perjury may have been a real one in 1677; especially when, because of the common law rule that prevented parties to a dispute from giving evidence themselves, the evidence of a few corrupt witnesses could be decisive. But . . . it is difficult to believe that there is a horde of potential perjurers just awaiting a relaxation in the requirement of writing in order to get their hands on some land . . .

The evidentiary argument for formality, however, must be taken more seriously. Agreements concerning land *can* sometimes be complex; and, even when they are simple, writing may still be important in evidencing precisely what was intended . . . we should note two qualifications.

First; true as it is that some agreements about land can be complicated, and that it can be of particular importance to record the details of their terms in writing, it is equally true that other agreements can be very simple indeed. There is nothing complex, for example, about the transaction in *Pascoe* v *Turner*. The gift of the house was as simple as the gift of its contents; and the law did not require writing for that . . .

Comment

Are our formality requirements justified by the functions described by Moriarty? This is crucial when considering how far the courts are justified in circumventing the requirements (as described in this and the following chapter).

2. Resulting and constructive trusts

These forms of trusts have long been recognised. In some cases (at least as regards constructive trusts) they are imposed regardless of intentions. Thus a trustee who makes a profit out of his or her position is likely to hold that profit on a constructive trust for the original beneficiaries. This rule has nothing to do with formalities; requiring writing would frustrate justice.

A. Presumption of resulting trust

Sometimes the law presumes a gift in family situations: transfers to wives and certain transfers to children. However, this presumption of advancement was abolished by s 199 of the Equality Act 2010 (not yet in force). Absent advancement, there is a presumption of resulting trust, so that the transferor retains beneficial ownership.

Extract 6.2.1

Westdeutsche Landesbank Girozentrale v *Islington LBC* **[1996] AC 669**

LORD BROWNE-WILKINSON: . . . Under existing law a resulting trust arises in two sets of circumstances: (A) where A makes a voluntary payment to B or pays (wholly or in part) for the purchase of property which is vested either in B alone or in the joint names of A and B, there is a presumption that A did not intend to make a gift to B: the money or property is held on trust for A (if he is the sole provider of the money) or in the case of a joint purchase by A and B in shares proportionate to their contributions. It is important to stress that this is only a *presumption*, which presumption is easily rebutted either by the counter-presumption of advancement or by direct evidence of A's intention to make an outright transfer: see *Underhill and Hayton, Law of Trusts and Trustees*, pp 317 et seq; *Vandervell* v *Inland Revenue Commissioners* [1967] 2 AC 291, 312 et seq; *In re Vandervell's Trusts (No 2)* [1974] Ch 269, 288 et seq. (B) Where A transfers property to B on express trusts, but the trusts declared do not exhaust the whole beneficial interest: *ibid* and *Quistclose Investments Ltd* v *Rolls Razor Ltd (In Liquidation)* [1970] AC 567. Both types of resulting trust are traditionally regarded as examples of trusts giving effect to the common intention of the parties. A resulting trust is not imposed by law against the intentions of the trustee (as is a constructive trust) but gives effect to his presumed intention. Megarry J in *In re Vandervell's Trusts (No 2)* suggests that a resulting trust of type (B) does not depend on intention but operates automatically. I am not convinced that this is right. If the settlor has expressly, or by necessary implication, abandoned any beneficial interest in the trust property, there is in my view no resulting trust: the undisposed-of equitable interest vests in the Crown as bona vacantia: see *In re West Sussex Constabulary's Widows, Children and Benevolent (1930) Fund Trusts* [1971] Ch 1.

Extract 6.2.2

Air Jamaica Ltd v *Charlton* **[1999] 1 WLR 1399 (Privy Council)**

LORD MILLETT: . . . Like a constructive trust, a resulting trust arises by operation of law, though unlike a constructive trust it gives effect to intention. But it arises whether or not the transferor intended to retain a beneficial interest – he almost always does not – since it responds to the absence of any intention on his part to pass a beneficial interest to the recipient. It may arise even where the transferor positively wished to part with the beneficial interest, as in *Vandervell* v *Inland Revenue Commissioners* [1967] 2 AC 291. In that case the retention of a beneficial interest by the transferor destroyed the effectiveness of a tax avoidance scheme which the transferor was seeking to implement. The House of Lords affirmed the principle that a resulting trust is not defeated by evidence that the transferor intended to part with the beneficial interest if he has not in fact succeeded in doing so. As Plowman J had said in the same case at first instance [1966] Ch 261, 275: 'As I see it, a man does not cease to own property simply by saying "I don't want it." If he tries to give it away the question must always be, has he succeeded in doing so or not?' Lord Upjohn [1967] 2 AC 291, 314 expressly approved this.

Comment

Is this analysis compatible with that of Lord Browne-Wilkinson in *Westdeutsche*? Where does it leave the 'automatic' resulting trust?

The following Extract considers the strength of the presumption.

Extract 6.2.3

Pettitt v Pettitt [1970] AC 777

LORD DIPLOCK: . . . A similar technique is applied in imputing an intention to a person wherever the intention with which an act is done affects its legal consequences and the evidence does not disclose what was the actual intention with which he did it. This situation commonly occurs when the actor is deceased. When the act is of a kind to which this technique has frequently to be applied by the courts the imputed intention may acquire the description of a 'presumption' – but presumptions of this type are not immutable. A presumption of fact is no more than a consensus of judicial opinion disclosed by reported cases as to the most likely inference of fact to be drawn in the absence of any evidence to the contrary – for example, presumptions of legitimacy, of death, or survival and the like. But the most likely inference as to a person's intention in the transactions of his everyday life depends upon the social environment in which he lives and the common habits of thought of those who live in it. The consensus of judicial opinion which gave rise to the presumptions of 'advancement' and 'resulting trust' in transactions between husband and wife is to be found in cases relating to the propertied classes of the nineteenth century and the first quarter of the twentieth century among whom marriage settlements were common, and it was unusual for the wife to contribute by her earnings to the family income. It was not until after World War II that the courts were required to consider the proprietary rights in family assets of a different social class. The advent of legal aid, the wider employment of married women in industry, commerce and the professions and the emergence of a property-owning, particularly a real-property-mortgaged-to-a-building-society-owning, democracy has compelled the courts to direct their attention to this during the last 20 years. It would, in my view, be an abuse of the legal technique for ascertaining or imputing intention to apply to trans-actions between the post-war generation of married couples 'presumptions' which are based upon inferences of fact which an earlier generation of judges drew as to the most likely intentions of earlier generations of spouses belonging to the propertied classes of a different social era.

Comment

(1) All the judges recognised that the role for the presumption will today be small. How likely is it that there will be no evidence as to intention?

(2) We will see later that the presumption of resulting trust has dropped out of favour as regards the family home (see Chapter 8).

If A transfers property to B, without any evidence as to the motive for the transfer, the law requires some starting point, some presumption. As has been seen, the basic presumption is that of resulting trust: that there is no gift. It is quite frequently observed that this is an odd stance for the law to adopt. There is much to be said for such criticism, though it is very rare for resulting trusts, after taking account of any evidence of actual intentions, to produce strange results. In certain situations, a presumption of a gift would seem odd. Examples would be transfers to trustees or other fiduciaries, such as the transferor's solicitor. Even within a family setting, a very substantial transfer may not look like a gift, as the following case demonstrates.

Extract 6.2.4

Sekhon v *Alissa* [1989] 2 FLR 94

A mother contributed approximately 60% of the cost of a house purchased by her daughter (one of her three children). This contribution virtually exhausted the mother's savings.

HOFFMANN J: . . . In my judgment neither of the parties thought that the mother's contribution was really a gift. First, it would have meant that she had parted irrevocably with almost the whole of her savings. Secondly, on the only occasion on which there is any suggestion that she spoke of the money as a gift, she said that this was the 'official' version. I construe this to mean that it was not a gift at all. Thirdly, no other member of the family thought that there was any question of the money having been a gift. The mother herself said that she regarded the purchase as a commercial venture which would not only help the daughter but also give her a better return on her money than the building society . . . Fourthly, all the purposes for which the daughter said the house had been bought – to provide her with income, to give her a capital asset, to use her mortgage-raising capacity, to improve her marriage prospects – did not necessarily require that the mother's contribution should have been a gift . . .

The daughter's own interpretation of the transaction distinguished between what she regarded as its legal effect, which was to vest the whole beneficial interest in her absolutely, and her moral obligation to repay her mother, which she has never attempted to deny. Most of the conduct which I have mentioned as evidence that the payment was not a gift was in her view explicable as a recognition of purely moral obligations. But the law does not readily accept that the parties intended to distinguish between legal and moral obligations. The parties may of course expressly agree that obligations which would ordinarily be legally enforceable are to be binding only in honour. Normally, however, the object of equitable institutions such as a resulting trust is to give the force of law to moral obligations. In my judgment, whatever the parties may have intended the outward form of the transaction to be, they did not as between themselves intend to distinguish between legal and moral obligations.

The next question is whether the mother's contribution was to be an unsecured loan or to give her a beneficial interest. In my judgment the law presumes a resulting trust in her favour and that presumption has to be rebutted by evidence that she intended a personal loan without acquiring any interest in the property. I am not satisfied on the evidence that a loan was agreed.

Comment

(1) The case is a good example of how it is possible to find evidence from the facts, rather than simply relying upon presumptions.

(2) When will it be appropriate to find a loan rather than a resulting trust?[3] Why is the distinction important?

---

[3] See also *Hussey* v *Palmer* [1972] 1 WLR 1286.

(3) The presumptions come into play whenever property is transferred. However, as illustrated by *Sekhon*, their main impact is that if one person provides another with part of the purchase money for property, then that property will be held on resulting trust.

It remains to consider two more specific situations. As regards land, LPA, s 60(3) provides that 'In a voluntary conveyance a resulting trust for the grantor shall not be implied merely by reason that the property is not expressed to be conveyed for the use or benefit of the grantee.' Although intended to deal with technical changes in conveyancing practice following the 1925 legislation, it seems arguable that it reverses the presumption of resulting trust.[4] Nicholas Strauss QC at first instance in *Lohia* v *Lohia*[5] came to this conclusion, but the Court of Appeal regarded the issue as being open. In any event, its scope is limited, as it applies only to the grantor in a conveyance. Nearly all modern cases arise from the provision of money rather than the transfer of land by the claimant.

The second situation concerns joint bank accounts, which are common for spouses and those living together. The question of ownership of funds in these accounts is important by itself, but its greatest significance lies in ownership of assets (particularly the family home) funded from the account.

Extract 6.2.5

Jones v *Maynard* [1951] Ch 572

VAISEY J: . . . In my judgment, when there is a joint account between husband and wife, and a common pool into which they put all their resources, it is not consistent with that conception that the account should thereafter (in this case in the event of a divorce) be picked apart, and divided up proportionately to the respective contributions of husband and wife, the husband being credited with the whole of his earnings and the wife with the whole of her dividends. I do not believe that, when once the joint pool has been formed, it ought to be, and can be, dissected in any such manner. In my view a husband's earnings or salary, when the spouses have a common purse, and pool their resources, are earnings made on behalf of both; and the idea that years afterwards the contents of the pool can be dissected by taking an elaborate account as to how much was paid in by the husband or the wife, is quite inconsistent with the original fundamental idea of a joint purse or a common pool.

. . .

That being my view, it follows that investments paid for out of the joint account, although made in the name of the husband, were in fact made by him in his own name as a trustee as to a moiety for his wife.

Comment

(1) Where one person's capital simply passes through the account (perhaps a wife sells a block of shares and purchases further shares with the proceeds), then the courts are not inclined to say that the capital (or its proceeds) is jointly owned.[6]

(2) There are many difficult cases involving ownership of the family home (as will be seen in Chapter 8). It is interesting that few of these involve funding (and especially mortgage instalment funding) from a joint account.

---

[4] *Tinsley* v *Milligan* [1994] 1 AC 340 at p 371 (Extract 6.2.7 below).
[5] [2001] WTLR 101; [2001] EWCA Civ 1691 at [24], [25]. In *Ali* v *Khan* (2002) 5 ITELR 127 at [24], the Court of Appeal cited the views of Strauss QC with apparent approval; the Court of Appeal decision in *Lohia* was not cited.
[6] *Jansen* v *Jansen* [1965] P 478; *Drake* v *Whipp* [1996] 1 FLR 826.

B. Transfers for fraudulent purposes

The fraud which is being considered in this section consists of executing a transfer which is intended to mislead third parties. The best example is where the transferor fears bankruptcy and transfers property to, say, his wife. If he becomes bankrupt, the trustee in bankruptcy will be told that the wife owns the property so that the creditors have no claim to it.[7] If bankruptcy does not occur, the husband and wife intend that the husband should be entitled to the property.

Extract 6.2.6

Tinker v *Tinker* [1970] P 136

LORD DENNING MR: . . . So it is plain that the husband had the house put into his wife's name so as to avoid any risk of it being taken by his creditors in case his business was not a success. What is the result in law? In *Gascoigne* v *Gascoigne* [1918] 1 KB 223, it was held that when a husband put a house in his wife's name so as to avoid it being taken by his creditors the house belonged to the wife. The husband could not be heard to say that it belonged to him, because he could not be allowed to take advantage of his own dishonesty. That case was applied in *In re Emery's Investment Trusts* [1959] Ch 410; and also in *McEvoy* v *Belfast Banking Co Ltd* [1934] NI 67. We were invited by Mr Wheatley to overrule those decisions. But in my opinion they are good law.

Then Mr Wheatley said that *Gascoigne* v *Gascoigne* is distinguishable, because there the husband was dishonest, whereas here the registrar has found that the husband was honest . . .

Accepting that in the present case the defendant was honest – he acted, he said, on the advice of his solicitor – nevertheless I do not think he can claim that the house belongs to him . . .

. . . I am quite clear that the husband cannot have it both ways. So he is on the horns of a dilemma. He cannot say that the house is his own and, at one and the same time, say that it is his wife's. As against his wife, he wants to say that it belongs to him. As against his creditors, that it belongs to her. That simply will not do. Either it was conveyed to her for her own use absolutely: or it was conveyed to her as trustee for her husband. It must be one or other. The presumption is that it was conveyed to her for her own use: and he does not rebut that presumption by saying that he only did it to defeat his creditors. I think it belongs to her.

Extract 6.2.7

Tinsley v *Milligan* [1994] 1 AC 340

Miss Milligan and her lover, Miss Tinsley, bought a house jointly, but placed it in Miss Tinsley's name so that Miss Milligan could claim social security benefits.

LORD BROWNE-WILKINSON: . . . In the present case, Miss Milligan claims under a resulting or implied trust. The court below have found, and it is not now disputed, that apart from the question of illegality Miss Milligan would have been entitled in equity to a half share in the house in accordance with the principles exemplified in *Gissing* v *Gissing* [1971] AC 886; *Grant* v *Edwards* [1986] Ch 638 and *Lloyds Bank Plc* v *Rosset* [1991] 1 AC 107. The creation of such an equitable interest does not depend upon a contractual obligation but on a common intention acted upon by the parties to their detriment. It is a development of the old law of resulting trust under which, where two parties have provided the purchase money to buy a property which is

---

[7] Subject to the rules protecting creditors, summarised in Chapter 5, p 168.

conveyed into the name of one of them alone, the latter is presumed to hold the property on a resulting trust for both parties in shares proportionate to their contributions to the purchase price. In arguments, no distinction was drawn between strict resulting trusts and a *Gissing* v *Gissing* type of trust.

. . . The presumption of a resulting trust is, in my view, crucial in considering the authorities. On that presumption (and on the contrary presumption of advancement) hinges the answer to the crucial question 'does a plaintiff claiming under a resulting trust have to rely on the under-lying illegality?' Where the presumption of resulting trust applies, the plaintiff does not have to rely on the illegality. If he proves that the property is vested in the defendant alone but that the plaintiff provided part of the purchase money, or voluntarily transferred the property to the defendant, the plaintiff establishes his claim under a resulting trust unless either the contrary presumption of advancement displaces the presumption of resulting trust or the defendant leads evidence to rebut the presumption of resulting trust. Therefore . . . a plaintiff can establish his equitable interest in the property without relying in any way on the underlying illegal transaction . . .

Comment

(1) This is an important decision on illegality. The quoted passages are limited to the role of the presumptions. Illegality is considered by Law Com No 320 (2010).

(2) In the family home context, the House of Lords has denied any role for a resulting trust analysis.[8] What effect may this have on *Tinsley*? See *O'Kelly* v *Davies* [2014] EWCA Civ 1606, especially [29].

(3) Subject to that last point, it follows from *Tinsley* that the transferor will nearly always be able to recover the property. If the fraudulent purpose materialises (bankruptcy etc. actually results), it will be unusual for it to be in either party's interest to claim a trust in favour of the transferor. Cases such as *Tinsley* involve dishonest transferors (those who deliberately vest title in another to give a false impression of beneficial rights). How well do the results fit with the position of the honest transferor in *Tinker*? Is it possible for the transferor both to intend to retain ownership and to be honest?[9]

C. Constructive trusts: an oral promise by a transferee to hold on trust for the transferor

Extract 6.2.8

Bannister v *Bannister* [1948] 2 All ER 133

The plaintiff transferred a house to the defendant, her brother-in-law, on the oral understanding that she was to have a life interest.

SCOTT LJ: . . . Secondly, it was said that, even if the terms of the oral undertaking were such as to amount to a promise that the defendant should retain a life interest in No 30, a tenancy at will free of rent was, nevertheless, the greatest interest she could claim in view of the absence of writing and the provisions of ss 53 and 54 of the Law of Property Act, 1925. Thirdly, it was said that a constructive trust in favour of the defendant (which the absence of writing admittedly

---

[8] *Stack* v *Dowden* [2007] 2 AC 432 (primarily as regards transfers into joint names): see Extracts 8.2.2 and 8.4.1 below and Piska (2008) 71 MLR 120 at p 130.
[9] See *Lowson* v *Coombes* [1999] Ch 373.

would not defeat) could only be raised by findings to the effect that there was actual fraud on the part of the plaintiff and that the property was sold and conveyed to him on the faith of an express oral declaration of trust which it would be fraudulent in him to deny . . .

As will be seen from what is said below, the second objection (based on want of writing) in effect stands or falls with the third, and it will, therefore, be convenient to deal with that next. It is, we think, clearly a mistake to suppose that the equitable principle on which a constructive trust is raised against a person who insists on the absolute character of a conveyance to himself for the purpose of defeating a beneficial interest, which, according to the true bargain, was to belong to another, is confined to cases in which the conveyance itself was fraudulently obtained. The fraud which brings the principle into play arises as soon as the absolute character of the conveyance is set up for the purpose of defeating the beneficial interest, and that is the fraud to cover which the Statute of Frauds or the corresponding provisions of the Law of Property Act, 1925, cannot be called in aid in cases in which no written evidence of the real bargain is available. Nor is it, in our opinion, necessary that the bargain on which the absolute conveyance is made should include any express stipulation that the grantee is in so many words to hold as trustee. It is enough that the bargain should have included a stipulation under which some sufficiently defined beneficial interest in the property was to be taken by another. The above propositions are, we think, clearly borne out by the cases to which we were referred of *Booth v Turle*,[i] *Chattock v Muller*,[ii] *Re Duke of Marlborough*,[iii] and *Rochefoucauld v Boustead*.[iv] We see no distinction in principle between a case in which property is conveyed to a purchaser on terms that the entire beneficial interest in some part of it is to be retained by the vendor (as in *Booth v Turle*) and a case, like the present, in which property is conveyed to a purchaser on terms that a limited beneficial interest in some part of it is to be retained by the vendor . . . The failure of the third ground of objection necessarily also destroys the second objection based on want of writing and the provisions of ss 53 and 54 of the Law of Property Act, 1925.

[i] *Booth v Turle* (1873) LR 16 Eq 182; 37 JP 710; 43 Digest 556, *75*.
[ii] *Chattock v Muller* (1878) 8 Ch Div 177; 42 Digest 459, *286*.
[iii] *Re Marlborough (Duke)*, *Davis v Whitehead* [1894] 2 Ch 133; 63 LJ Ch 471; 70 LT 314; 43 Digest 555, *62*.
[iv] *Rochefoucauld v Boustead* [1897] 1 Ch 196; 66 LJ Ch 74; 75 LT 502; 43 Digest 558, *87*.

Extract 6.2.9

Hodgson v Marks [1971] Ch 892

The plaintiff transferred her house to her lodger, in circumstances where it was clearly not intended that the lodger should be beneficial owner. The lodger then sold the house to the defendant.

RUSSELL LJ: . . . I turn next to the question whether section 53(1) of the Law of Property Act 1925 prevents the assertion by the plaintiff of her entitlement in equity to the house. Let me first assume that, contrary to the view expressed by the judge, Mr Marks is not debarred from relying upon the section, and the express oral arrangement or declaration of trust between the plaintiff and Mr Evans found by the judge was not effective as such. Nevertheless, the evidence is clear that the transfer was not intended to operate as a gift, and, in those circumstances, I do not see why there was not a resulting trust of the beneficial interest to the plaintiff, which would not, of course, be affected by section 53(1). It was argued that a resulting trust is based upon implied intention, and that where there is an express trust for the transferor intended and declared – albeit ineffectively – there is no room for such an implication. I do not accept that. If an attempted express trust fails, that seems to me just the occasion for implication of a resulting trust, whether the failure be due to uncertainty, or perpetuity, or lack of form. It would be a strange outcome if the plaintiff were to lose her beneficial interest because her evidence had not been confined to negativing a gift but had additionally moved into a field forbidden by section 53(1) for lack of writing . . . The accepted evidence is that this was not intended as a gift, notwithstanding the reference to love and affection in the transfer, and section 53(1) does not exclude that evidence.

. . .

On the above footing it matters not whether Mr Marks was or was not debarred from relying upon section 53(1) by the principle that the section is not to be used as an instrument for fraud. Mr Marks was in fact ignorant of the plaintiff's interest and it is forcefully argued that there is nothing fraudulent in his taking advantage of the section.

Comment

(1) Are there differences in the analyses employed in *Bannister* and *Hodgson*?

(2) Russell LJ refers to the principle that a statute cannot be used as an instrument of fraud. This has been used to enforce such trusts as express trusts: *Rochefoucauld* v *Boustead*.[10] Does it make any difference which analysis is employed?

(3) Suppose the transferee gives effect to what he has orally agreed. Is there a binding trust in such cases? If the transferee is in fact complying with the terms of the trust, does it matter whether there is a binding trust?

D. Constructive trusts: an oral promise by a transferee to recognise the rights of a third party

It is just as fraudulent for the transferee to deny third party rights as to deny rights of the transferor: in each case the transferee has obtained the property on the basis of an undertaking and has then sought to resile from that undertaking. However, real problems have arisen regarding a number of issues.

(i) Agreement to hold for the third party

How do we decide whether the transferee has agreed to hold for the third party? Of course, no problem arises if the transferee explicitly agrees to hold on trust, but such clarity is frequently absent. Equally obviously, the courts look at the substance of the situation: the absence of an explicit declaration of trust is certainly not fatal.[11]

Extract 6.2.10

Binions v *Evans* [1972] Ch 359

LORD DENNING MR: . . . Suppose, however, that the defendant did not have an equitable interest at the outset, nevertheless it is quite plain that she obtained one afterwards when the Tredegar Estate sold the cottage. They stipulated with the plaintiffs that they were to take the house 'subject to' the defendant's rights under the agreement. They supplied the plaintiffs with a copy of the contract: and the plaintiffs paid less because of her right to stay there. In these circumstances, this court will impose on the plaintiffs a constructive trust for her benefit: for the simple reason that it would be utterly inequitable for the plaintiffs to turn the defendant out contrary to the stipulation subject to which they took the premises. That seems to me clear from the important decision of *Bannister* v *Bannister* [1948] 2 All ER 133, which was applied by the judge, and which I gladly follow.

---

[10] [1897] 1 Ch 196.
[11] *Cochrane* v *Moore* (1890) 25 QBD 57 (third party would be 'all right'); *Paul* v *Constance* [1977] 1 WLR 527 (a two-party case): see Extract 5.6.4 above.

This imposing of a constructive trust is entirely in accord with the precepts of equity. As Cardozo J once put it: 'A constructive trust is the formula through which the conscience of equity finds expression', see *Beatty* v *Guggenheim Exploration Co* (1919) 225 NY 380, 386: or, as Lord Diplock put it quite recently in *Gissing* v *Gissing* [1971] AC 886, 905, a constructive trust is created 'whenever the trustee has so conducted himself that it would be inequitable to allow him to deny to the cestui que trust a beneficial interest in the land acquired'.

. . . Whenever the owner sells the land to a purchaser, and at the same time stipulates that he shall take it 'subject to' a contractual licence, I think it plain that a court of equity will impose on the purchaser a constructive trust in favour of the beneficiary. It is true that the stipulation (that the purchaser shall take it subject to the rights of the licensee) is a stipulation for the benefit of one who is not a party to the contract of sale; but, as Lord Upjohn said in *Beswick* v *Beswick* [1968] AC 58, 98, that is just the very case in which equity will 'come to the aid of the common law'. It does so by imposing a constructive trust on the purchaser. It would be utterly inequitable that the purchaser should be able to turn out the beneficiary . . .

In many of these cases the purchaser takes *expressly* 'subject to' the rights of the licensee. Obviously the purchaser then holds the land on an imputed trust for the licensee. But, even if he does not take expressly 'subject to' the rights of the licensee, he may do so *impliedly*. At any rate when the licensee is in actual occupation of the land, so that the purchaser must know he is there, and of the rights which he has: see *Hodgson* v *Marks* [1971] Ch 892. Whenever the purchaser takes the land impliedly subject to the rights of the contractual licensee, a court of equity will impose a constructive trust for the beneficiary.

Comment

The use of the constructive trust in the licences context gives rise to particular problems. These are considered later, together with the question whether the constructive trust affects subsequent purchasers (see Chapter 18).

Extract 6.2.11

Ashburn Anstalt v Arnold [1989] Ch 1

FOX LJ: [T]he finding on appropriate facts of a constructive trust may well be regarded as a beneficial adaptation of old rules to new situations.

The constructive trust principle, to which we now turn, has been long established and has proved to be highly flexible in practice. It covers a wide variety of cases from that of a trustee who makes a profit out of his trust or a stranger who knowingly deals with trust properties, to the many cases where the courts have held that a person who directly or indirectly contributes to the acquisition of a dwelling house purchased in the name of and conveyed to another has some beneficial interest in the property. The test, for the present purposes, is whether the owner of the property has so conducted himself that it would be inequitable to allow him to deny the claimant an interest in the property: see *Gissing* v *Gissing* [1971] AC 886, 905, *per* Lord Diplock.

. . .

In *Lyus* v *Prowsa Developments Ltd* [1982] 1 WLR 1044, the plaintiffs contracted to buy a plot of registered land which was part of an estate being developed by the vendor company. A house was to be built which would then be occupied by the plaintiffs. The plaintiffs paid a deposit to the company, which afterwards became insolvent before the house was built. The company's bank held a legal charge, granted before the plaintiffs' contract, over the whole estate. The bank was under no liability to complete the plaintiffs' contract. The bank, as mortgagee, sold the land to the first defendant. By the contract of sale it was provided that the land was sold subject to and with the benefit of the plaintiffs' contract. Subsequently, the first defendant contracted to sell the plot to the second defendant. The contract provided that the land was sold subject to the plaintiffs' contract so far, if at all, as it might be enforceable against the first defendant. The contract was duly completed. In the action the plaintiffs sought a declaration that their contract was binding on the defendants and an order for specific performance. The action succeeded. This again seems to us to be a case where a constructive trust could justifiably be imposed. The bank were selling as mortgagees under a charge prior in date to the contract. They were therefore not bound by the contract and on any view could give a title which was free from it. There was, therefore, no point in making the conveyance subject to the contract unless the parties intended the purchaser to give effect to the contract . . . How far any constructive trust so arising was on the facts of that case enforceable by the plaintiffs against owners for the time being of the land we do not need to consider.

. . .

We come to the present case. It is said that when a person sells land and stipulates that the sale should be 'subject to' a contractual licence, the court will impose a constructive trust upon the purchaser to give effect to the licence: see *Binions* v *Evans* [1972] Ch 359, 368, *per* Lord Denning MR. We do not feel able to accept that as a general proposition. We agree with the observations of Dillon J in *Lyus* v *Prowsa Developments Ltd* [1982] 1 WLR 1044, 1051:

'By contrast, there are many cases in which land is expressly conveyed subject to possible incumbrances when there is no thought at all of conferring any fresh rights on third parties who may be entitled to the benefit of the incumbrances. The land is expressed to be sold subject to incumbrances to satisfy the vendor's duty to disclose all possible incumbrances known to him, and to protect the vendor against any possible claim by the purchaser . . . So, for instance, land may be contracted to be sold and may be expressed to be conveyed subject to the restrictive covenants contained in a conveyance some 60 or 90 years old. No one would suggest that by accepting such a form of contract or conveyance a purchaser is assuming a new liability in favour of third parties to observe the covenants if there was for any reason before the contract or conveyance no one who could make out a title as against the purchaser to the benefit of the covenants.'

The court will not impose a constructive trust unless it is satisfied that the conscience of the estate owner is affected. The mere fact that that land is expressed to be conveyed 'subject to' a contract does not necessarily imply that the grantee is to be under an obligation, not otherwise existing, to give effect to the provisions of the contract. The fact that the conveyance is expressed to be subject to the contract may often, for the reasons indicated by Dillon J, be at least as consistent with an intention merely to protect the grantor against claims by the grantee as an intention to impose an obligation on the grantee. The words 'subject to' will, of course, impose notice. But notice is not enough to impose on somebody an obligation to give effect to a contract into which he did not enter. Thus, mere notice of a restrictive covenant is not enough to impose upon the estate owner an obligation or equity to give effect to it: *London County Council* v *Allen* [1914] 3 KB 642.

Comment

(1) The case is also an important authority on contractual licences (see Chapter 18).

(2) What is required before a constructive trust will be found?

(3) What survives from *Binions* v *Evans*? Is the approach of Fox LJ to be preferred to that of Lord Denning MR? Both cases stress inequitable (or unconscionable) conduct. How useful is this as a basis for liability?

(4) What different interpretations may be given to a promise to purchase 'subject to' a third party claim? Which will suffice for a constructive trust?

(5) Does the Contracts (Rights of Third Parties) Act 1999[12] provide an alternative and preferable approach? Is it likely to produce identical results?

(6) Is it conclusive in favour of a trust that the purchaser pays less than the market value of the land (valued assuming there is no third party)? Is it conclusive against a trust that the purchaser pays the full market value of the land?[13]

The operation of the constructive trust has recently been reviewed by the Court of Appeal in *Chaudhary* v *Yavuz*,[14] with particular reference to the registration context (see Extract 10.2.17 below).

(ii) Who can enforce the trust?

Binions v *Evans* shows that the third party can enforce the trust, though some commentators have challenged this.[15] Would it be possible (and preferable) to reverse the fraud on the part of the transferee without permitting third party enforcement?

(iii) The nature of the trust

These cases avowedly employ constructive trusts. In so far as there is a trust of land, it must be constructive in order not to be ensnared by writing requirements.[16] However, *Binions* v *Evans* and *Ashburn Anstalt* (as well as *Lyus* v *Prowsa*, discussed in *Ashburn Anstalt*) both involved promises in writing. Why then did the courts not rely on there being express trusts? If the court is saying that the transferee promised to hold for the third party, is this not a clear case of an express trust? If no such promise can be found, is there any basis for finding that the transferee has acted in an unconscionable manner?

Further reading

Bright, S [2000] Conv 398: The third party's conscience in land law.

Gulliver, A G and Tilson, C J (1941) 51 Yale LJ 1: Classification of gratuitous transfers.

Hopkins, N (2006) 26 LS 475: Conscience, discretion and the creation of property rights.

McFarlane, B (2004) 120 LQR 667: Constructive trusts arising on a receipt of property *sub conditione*.

Mee, J [2012] Conv 307: Resulting trusts and voluntary conveyances of land.

Swadling, W J (2008) 124 LQR 72: Explaining resulting trusts.

Youdan, T G [1984] CLJ 306: Formalities for trusts of land, and the doctrine in *Rochefoucauld* v *Boustead*.

---

[12] Extract 20.1.5 below.
[13] As occurred in *Lyus* v *Prowsa Developments Ltd* [1982] 1 WLR 1044.
[14] [2013] Ch 249. Another unsuccessful recent attempt to argue a constructive trust is *Groveholt Ltd* v *Hughes* [2013] 1 P&CR 342.
[15] Feltham [1987] Conv 246. See also Ford and Lee, *Principles of the Law of Trusts* (3rd ed), paras 6090–6100.
[16] LPA, s 53(1)(b).

7

Formalities: estoppel

At the heart of estoppel lies the following proposition. A person who has made a representation or allowed another to labour under a misapprehension should not be allowed unconscionably to deny that which has been represented or misapprehended. Unconscionability will usually be shown by the other person's acting to their detriment. It matters not that there is no contractual or other enforceable obligation, nor that formality requirements have not been satisfied. A further aspect of estoppel is that it may protect expectations which are not proprietary in nature. (This aspect will be considered in Chapter 18 on licences.)

Most readers will be aware of the promissory estoppel developed in the *High Trees* case,[1] though conventional analysis does not allow this estoppel to be used as the basis of a cause of action.[2] The proprietary estoppel discussed in this chapter appears both to give rise to a cause of action (resulting in the transfer of the fee simple at one extreme) and to bind purchasers.

1. When will an estoppel arise?

Proprietary estoppel has been much litigated over the last half century, though it is rooted in nineteenth-century authorities.

Extract 7.1.1

Taylors Fashions Ltd v Liverpool Victoria Trustees Co Ltd [1982] QB 133

Options to renew leases had become unenforceable because they were not registered. Tenants expended money on the premises in the expectation of exercising the options, nobody being aware of the registration problem.

OLIVER J: . . . The starting point of both Mr Scott's and Mr Essayan's arguments on estoppel is the same and was expressed by Mr Essayan in the following proposition: if A under an expectation created or encouraged by B that A shall have a certain interest in land, thereafter, on the faith of such expectation and with the knowledge of B and without objection by him, acts to his detriment in connection with such land, a Court of Equity will compel B to give effect to such expectation. This is a formulation which Mr Millett accepts but subject to one important qualification, namely that at the time when he created and encouraged the expectation and (I think that he would also say) at the time when he permitted the detriment to be incurred (if those two points of time are different) B not only knows of A's expectation but must be aware of his true rights and that he was under no existing obligation to grant the interest.

---

[1] *Central London Property Trust Ltd v High Trees House Ltd* [1947] KB 130.
[2] *Combe v Combe* [1951] 2 KB 215.

This is the principal point upon which the parties divide. Mr Scott and Mr Essayan contend that what the court has to look at in relation to the party alleged to be estopped is only his conduct and its result, and not – or, at any rate, not necessarily – his state of mind. It then has to ask whether what that party is now seeking to do is unconscionable. Mr Millett contends that it is an essential feature of this particular equitable doctrine that the party alleged to be estopped must, before the assertion of his strict rights can be considered unconscionable, be aware both of what his strict rights were and of the fact that the other party is acting in the belief that they will not be enforced against him.

The point is a critical one in the instant case and it is one upon which the authorities appear at first sight to be divided. The starting point is *Ramsden* v *Dyson* (1866) LR 1 HL 129 where a tenant under a tenancy at will had built upon the land in the belief that he would be entitled to demand a long lease. The majority in the House of Lords held that he would not, but Lord Kingsdown dissented on the facts. There was no – or certainly no overt – disagreement between their Lordships as to the applicable principle, but it was stated differently by Lord Cranworth LC and Lord Kingsdown and the real question is how far Lord Cranworth was purporting to make an exhaustive exposition of principle and how far what he stated as the appropriate conditions for its application are to be treated, as it were, as being subsumed sub silentio in the speech of Lord Kingsdown. Lord Cranworth expressed it thus, at pp 140–141:

> 'If a stranger begins to build on my land supposing it to be his own, and I, perceiving his mistake, abstain from setting him right, and leave him to persevere in his error, a court of equity will not allow me afterwards to assert my title to the land on which he had expended money on the supposition that the land was his own . . . But it will be observed that to raise such an equity two things are required, first, that the person expending the money supposes himself to be building on his own land; and, secondly, that the real owner at the time of the expenditure knows that the land belongs to him and not to the person expending the money in the belief that he is the owner. For if a stranger builds on my land knowing it to be mine, there is no principle of equity which would prevent my claiming the land with the benefit of all the expenditure made on it. There would be nothing in my conduct, active or passive, making it inequitable in me to assert my legal rights.'

So here, clearly stated, is the criterion upon which Mr Millett relies. Lord Kingsdown stated the matter differently and rather more broadly although in the narrower context of landlord and tenant. He says, at p 170:

> 'The rule of law applicable to the case appears to me to be this: If a man, under a verbal agreement with a landlord for a certain interest in land, or, what amounts to the same thing, under an expectation, created or encouraged by the landlord, that he shall have a certain interest, takes possession of such land, with the consent of the landlord, and upon the faith of such promise or expectation, with the knowledge of the landlord, and without objection by him, lays out money upon the land, a court of equity will compel the landlord to give effect to such promise or expectation. This was the principle of the decision in *Gregory* v *Mighell* (1811) 18 Ves Jun 328, and as I conceive, is open to no doubt.'

So here, there is no specific requirement, at any rate in terms, that the landlord should know or intend that the expectation which he has created or encouraged is one to which he is under no obligation to give effect.

Mr Millett does not – nor could he in the light of the authorities – dispute the principle. What he contends is that even if (which he contests) this is a case where the defendants could be said to have encouraged the plaintiffs' expectations – and that it is not necessarily the same as having encouraged or acquiesced in the expenditure – the principle has no application to a case where, at the time when the expectation was encouraged, both parties were acting under a mistake of law as to their rights.

There is, he submits, a clear distinction between cases of proprietary estoppel or estoppel by acquiescence on the one hand and promissory estoppel or estoppel by representation (whether express or by conduct) on the other. In the latter case, the court looks at the knowledge of the party who has acted and the effect upon him of his having acted. The state of mind of the promissor or representor (except to the extent of knowing, either actually or inferentially, that his promise or representation is likely to be acted upon) is largely irrelevant. In the former case, however, it is essential, Mr Millett submits, to show that the party alleged to have encouraged or acquiesced in the other party's belief himself knew the true position, for if he did not there can be nothing unconscionable in his subsequently seeking to rely upon it. Mr Millett concedes that there may be cases which straddle this convenient dichotomy – cases which can be put either as cases of encouragement or proprietary estoppel on Lord Kingsdown's principle or as estoppel by representation, express or implied . . .

So far as proprietary estoppel or estoppel by acquiescence is concerned, he supports his submission by reference to the frequently cited judgment of Fry J in *Willmott* v *Barber* (1880) 15 Ch D 96 which contains what are described as the five 'probanda'. The actual case was one where what was alleged was a waiver by acquiescence . . . The sublessee built on the land and the head landlord was aware that he was in possession and was expending money. It was, however, proved that he did not then know that his consent was required to a sub-letting or assignment . . . It having been found as a fact that the landlord did not, at the time of the plaintiff's expenditure, know about the covenant against assignment and that there was nothing in what had passed between them to suggest either that the landlord was aware that the plaintiff was labouring under the belief that no consent was necessary or to encourage that belief, Fry J dismissed the plaintiff's claim. It has to be borne in mind, however, in reading the judgment, that this was a pure acquiescence case where what was relied on was a waiver of the landlord's rights by standing by without protest. It was a case of mere silence where what had to be established by the plaintiff was some duty in the landlord to speak. The passage from the judgment in *Willmott* v *Barber*, 15 Ch D 96 most frequently cited is where Fry J says, at pp 105–106:

'A man is not to be deprived of his legal rights unless he has acted in such a way as would make it fraudulent for him to set up those rights. What, then, are the elements or requisites necessary to constitute fraud of that description? In the first place the plaintiff must have made a mistake as to his legal rights. Secondly, the plaintiff must have expended some money or must have done some act (not necessarily upon the defendant's land) on the faith of his mistaken belief. Thirdly, the defendant, the possessor of the legal right, must know of the existence of his own right which is inconsistent with the right claimed by the plaintiff. If he does not know of it he is in the same position as the plaintiff, and the doctrine of acquiescence is founded upon conduct with a knowledge of your legal rights. Fourthly, the defendant, the possessor of the legal right, must know of the plaintiff's mistaken belief of his rights. If he does not, there is nothing which calls upon him to assert his own rights. Lastly, the defendant, the possessor of the legal right, must have encouraged the plaintiff in his expenditure of money or in the other acts which he has done, either directly or by abstaining from asserting his legal right. Where all these elements exist, there is fraud of such a nature as will entitle the court to restrain the possessor of the legal right from exercising it, but, in my judgment, nothing short of this will do.'

Mr Millett's submission is that when one applies these five probanda to the facts of the instant case it will readily be seen that they are not all complied with. In particular, Mr Millett submits, the fourth probandum involves two essential elements, viz, (i) knowledge by the possessor of the legal right of the other party's belief; and (ii) knowledge that that belief is mistaken. In the instant case the defendants were not aware of their inconsistent right to treat the option as void and equally they could not, thus, have been aware that the plaintiffs' belief in the validity of the option was a mistaken belief. The alternative approach via estoppel by representation is not, he submits, open to the plaintiffs in this case because so far as Taylors were concerned the defendants made no representation to them at all and so far as Olds were concerned the representation of the continuing validity of the option, if there was one at all, was a representation of law.

Now, convenient and attractive as I find Mr Millett's submissions as a matter of argument, I am not at all sure that so orderly and tidy a theory is really deducible from the authorities – certainly from the more recent authorities, which seem to me to support a much wider equitable jurisdiction to interfere in cases where the assertion of strict legal rights is found by the court to be unconscionable. It may well be (although I think that this must now be considered open to doubt) that the strict *Willmott v Barber*, 15 Ch D 96 probanda are applicable as necessary requirements in those cases where all that has happened is that the party alleged to be estopped has stood by without protest while his rights have been infringed. It is suggested in *Spencer Bower and Turner, Estoppel by Representation*, 3rd ed (1977), para 290 that acquiescence, in its strict sense, is merely an instance of estoppel by representation and this derives some support from the judgment of the Court of Appeal in *De Bussche v Alt* (1878) 8 Ch D 286, 314. If that is a correct analysis then, in a case of mere passivity, it is readily intelligible that there must be shown a duty to speak, protest or interfere which cannot normally arise in the absence of knowledge or at least a suspicion of the true position. Thus for a landowner to stand by while a neighbour lays drains in land which the landowner does not believe that he owns (*Armstrong v Sheppard & Short Ltd* [1959] 2 QB 384) or for a remainderman not to protest at a lease by a tenant for life which he believes he has no right to challenge (*Svenson v Payne* (1945) 71 CLR 531) does not create an estoppel. Again, where what is relied on is a waiver by acquiescence, as in *Willmott v Barber* itself, the five probanda are no doubt appropriate. There is, however, no doubt that there are judicial pronouncements of high authority which appear to support as essential the application of all the five probanda over the broader field covering all cases generally classified as estoppel by 'encouragement' or 'acquiescence': see, for instance, the speech of Lord Diplock in *Kammins Ballrooms Co Ltd v Zenith Investments (Torquay) Ltd* [1971] AC 850, 884.

Mr Scott submits, however, that it is historically wrong to treat these probanda as holy writ and to restrict equitable interference only to those cases which can be confined within the strait-jacket of some fixed rule governing the circumstances in which, and in which alone, the court will find that a party is behaving unconscionably. Whilst accepting that the five probanda may form an appropriate test in cases of silent acquiescence, he submits that the authorities do not support the absolute necessity for compliance with all five probanda, and, in particular, the requirement of knowledge on the part of the party estopped that the other party's belief is a mistaken belief, in cases where the conduct relied on has gone beyond mere silence and amounts to active encouragement. In Lord Kingsdown's example in *Ramsden v Dyson*, LR 1 HL 129, for instance, there is no room for the literal application of the probanda, for the circumstances there postulated do not presuppose a 'mistake' on anybody's part, but merely the fostering of an expectation in the minds of *both* parties at the time but from which, once it has been acted upon, it would be unconscionable to permit the landlord to depart. As Scarman LJ pointed out in *Crabb v Arun District Council* [1976] Ch 179, the 'fraud' in these cases is not to be found in the transaction itself but in the subsequent attempt to go back upon the basic assumptions which underlay it.

Certainly it is not clear from the early cases that the courts considered it in all cases an essential element of the estoppel that the party estopped, although he must have known of the other party's belief, necessarily knew that that belief was mistaken. Thus in *Stiles v Cowper* (1748) 3 Atk 692 a remainderman was held to be estopped from setting up the invalidity of a lease granted by the life tenant in excess of his powers after he had accepted rent for some years and allowed the tenant to lay out money on building . . . There is no suggestion in the report that at the time of the expenditure and the receipt of rent the remainderman knew that the lease was invalid. Indeed the statement in the report that he 'thought it proper' to receive rent rather suggests the contrary.

. . .

In *Gregory* v *Mighell*, 18 Ves Jun 328, the case relied on by Lord Kingsdown in formulating his proposition, the defendant was estopped from claiming that the plaintiff's possession was non-consensual so as to render it unavailable as an act of part performance. Here again this does not seem to have been a unilateral misapprehension as to what the legal position was when possession was taken. Nor, in my judgment, is any such essential condition deducible from the cases following *Ramsden* v *Dyson*, LR 1 HL 129 and particularly from the more modern authorities. The fact is that acquiescence or encouragement may take a variety of forms. It may take the form of standing by in silence whilst one party unwittingly infringes another's legal rights. It may take the form of passive or active encouragement of expenditure or alteration of legal position upon the footing of some unilateral or shared legal or factual supposition. Or it may, for example, take the form of stimulating, or not objecting to, some change of legal position on the faith of a unilateral or a shared assumption as to the future conduct of one or other party. I am not at all convinced that it is desirable or possible to lay down hard and fast rules which seek to dictate, in every combination of circumstances, the considerations which will persuade the court that a departure by the acquiescing party from the previously supposed state of law or fact is so unconscionable that a court of equity will interfere. Nor, in my judgment, do the authorities support so inflexible an approach, and that is particularly so in cases in which the decision has been based on the principle stated by Lord Kingsdown. . . .

Mr Millett's dichotomy does, it is fair to say, derive some small support from the judgment of Evershed MR in *Hopgood* v *Brown* [1955] 1 WLR 213, 223 where he refers to Fry J's formulation of the requisites of estoppel in *Willmott* v *Barber*, 15 Ch D 96 as addressed and limited to cases of estoppel by acquiescence and as not intended as a comprehensive formulation of the necessary requisites of estoppel by representation. That, however, does not necessarily imply his acceptance of the proposition that all the probanda are applicable to every case of estoppel by acquiescence and it seems clear from his earlier pronouncement in *Electrolux Ltd* v *Electrix Ltd* (1953) 71 RPC 23, 33 that that was not, indeed, his view.

Furthermore the more recent cases indicate, in my judgment, that the application of the *Ramsden* v *Dyson*, LR 1 HL 129 principle – whether you call it proprietary estoppel, estoppel by acquiescence or estoppel by encouragement is really immaterial – requires a very much broader approach which is directed rather at ascertaining whether, in particular individual circumstances, it would be unconscionable for a party to be permitted to deny that which, knowingly, or unknowingly, he has allowed or encouraged another to assume to his detriment than to inquiring whether the circumstances can be fitted within the confines of some preconceived formula serving as a universal yardstick for every form of unconscionable behaviour.

So regarded, knowledge of the true position by the party alleged to be estopped, becomes merely one of the relevant factors – it may even be a determining factor in certain cases – in the overall inquiry. This approach, so it seems to me, appears very clearly from the authorities to which I am about to refer. In *Inwards* v *Baker* [1965] 2 QB 29 there was no mistaken belief on either side. Each knew the state of the title, but the defendant had been led to expect that he would get an interest in the land on which he had built and, indeed, the overwhelming probability is that that was indeed the father's intention at the time. But it was not mere promissory estoppel, which could merely be used as a defence, for, as Lord Denning MR said, at p 37, 'it is for the court to say in what way the equity can be satisfied'. The principle was expressed very broadly both by Lord Denning MR and by Danckwerts LJ. Lord Denning said at p 37:

'But it seems to me, from *Plimmer's* case, 9 App Cas 699, 713–714 in particular, that the equity arising from the expenditure on land need not fail "merely on the ground that the interest to be secured has not been expressly indicated . . . the court must look at the circumstances in each case to decide in what way the equity can be satisfied".'

And a little further down he said:

'All that is necessary is that the licensee should, at the request or with the encouragement of the landlord, have spent the money in the expectation of being allowed to stay there. If so, the court will not allow that expectation to be defeated where it would be inequitable so to do.'

. . .

An even more striking example is *ER Ives Investment Ltd* v *High* [1967] 2 QB 379. Here again, there does not appear to have been any question of the persons who had acquiesced in the defendant's expenditure having known that his belief that he had an enforceable right of way was mistaken. Indeed, at the stage when the expenditure took place, both sides seem to have shared the belief that the agreement between them created effective rights. Nevertheless the successor in title to the acquiescing party was held to be estopped . . .

More nearly in point is *Crabb* v *Arun District Council* [1976] Ch 179 where the plaintiff had altered his legal position in the expectation, encouraged by the defendants, that he would have a certain access to a road. Now there was no mistake here. Each party knew that the road was vested in the defendants and each knew that no formal grant had been made. Indeed I cannot see why in considering whether the defendants were behaving unconscionably, it should have made the slightest difference to the result if, at the time when the plaintiff was encouraged to open his access to the road, the defendants had thought that they were bound to grant it. The fact was that he had been encouraged to alter his position irrevocably to his detriment on the faith of a belief, which was known to and encouraged by the defendants, that he was going to be given a particular right of access – a belief which, for all that appears, the defendants probably shared at that time.

The particularly interesting features of the case in the context of the present dispute are, first, the virtual equation of promissory estoppel and proprietary estoppel or estoppel by acqui-escence as mere facets of the same principle and secondly the very broad approach of both Lord Denning MR and Scarman LJ, both of whom emphasised the flexibility of the equitable doctrine. It is, however, worth noting that Scarman LJ adopted and applied the five probanda in *Willmott* v *Barber*, 15 Ch D 96 which he described as 'a valuable guide'. He considered that those probanda were satisfied and it is particularly relevant here to note again the fourth one – namely that the defendant, the possessor of the legal right, must know of the plaintiff's mistaken belief. If Scarman LJ had interpreted this as meaning – as Mr Millett submits that it does mean – that the defendant must know not only of the plaintiff's belief but also that it was mistaken, then he could not, I think, have come to the conclusion that this probandum was satisfied, for it seems clear from Lord Denning's recital of the facts that, up to the critical moment when the plaintiff acted, *both* parties thought that there *was* a firm assurance of access. The defendants had, indeed, even erected a gate at their own expense to give effect to it. What gave rise to the necessity for the court to intervene was the defendants' attempt to go back on this subsequently when they fell out with the plaintiff. I infer therefore that Scarman LJ must have construed this probandum in the sense which Mr Scott and Mr Essayan urge upon me, namely that the defendant must know merely of the plaintiff's belief which, in the event, turns out to be mistaken.

. . .

The inquiry which I have to make therefore, as it seems to me, is simply whether, in all the circumstances of this case, it was unconscionable for the defendants to seek to take advantage of the mistake which, at the material time, everybody shared, and, in approaching that, I must consider the cases of the two plaintiffs separately because it may be that quite different considerations apply to each.

Comment

(1) On the facts, one of two estoppel claims was recognised. One claim depended upon installing a lift; this was rejected as 'So far as acquiescence pure and simple is concerned, the defendants could not lawfully object to the work and could be under no duty to Taylors to communicate that which they did not know themselves . . .' On the facts, the work had not been encouraged by the defendants. Further, undertaking the work could be explained by the fact that the lease still had 18 years to run. However, the second and successful claim involved expanding the premises upon the basis that the option was valid, this basis being apparent to the defendants. Indeed, the defendants (from whom additional premises were leased) encouraged both the belief that the option was valid and the expenditure. Do these conclusions fit well with the legal principles enunciated by Oliver J?

(2) *Taylors Fashions* is, of course, a first instance decision. However, it has received approval from higher courts on numerous occasions.[3]

(3) Why was the controversy regarding the role of the five probanda important in *Taylors Fashions*? What role, if any, do the probanda play in the modern law?

(4) What is the significance of the distinction between estoppel by acquiescence and estoppel by representation?

A. Representation or assurance

The language of acquiescence points towards the claimant (C) having made a mistake concerning his or her legal position. Such a mistake is difficult to establish when the estoppel is based upon a promise made by the owner (O). Therefore, an initial and important question concerns the extent to which estoppel can have the effect of enforcing promises.

Extract 7.1.2

Crabb v Arun DC [1976] Ch 179

The parties reached a non-binding agreement for a right of way over the defendant's land. Subsequently, the plaintiff sold off part of his land, leaving the remainder landlocked save for the right of way over the defendant's land. The defendant repudiated the agreement.

SCARMAN LJ: . . . I think it is now well settled law that the court, having analysed and assessed the conduct and relationship of the parties, has to answer three questions. First, is there an equity established? Secondly, what is the extent of the equity, if one is established? And, thirdly, what is the relief appropriate to satisfy the equity? See *Duke of Beaufort* v *Patrick* (1853) 17 Beav 60; *Plimmer* v *Wellington Corporation*, 9 App Cas 699 and *Inwards* v *Baker* [1965] 2 QB 29, a decision of this court, and particularly the observations of Lord Denning MR at p 37. Such therefore I believe to be the nature of the inquiry that the courts have to conduct in a case of this sort. In pursuit of that inquiry I do not find helpful the distinction between promissory and proprietary estoppel. This distinction may indeed be valuable to those who have to teach or expound the law; but I do not think that, in solving the particular problem raised by a particular case, putting the law into categories is of the slightest assistance.

. . .

---

[3] *Habib Bank Ltd* v *Habib Bank AG Zurich* [1981] 1 WLR 1265; *Nationwide Anglia BS* v *Ahmed & Balakrishnan* (1995) 70 P&CR 381; *Lloyds Bank plc* v *Carrick* [1996] 4 All ER 630; *Gillett* v *Holt* [1998] 3 All ER 917. See also Robert Goff J at first instance in *Amalgamated Investment & Property Co Ltd* v *Texas Commerce International Bank Ltd* [1982] QB 84 and *Cobbe* v *Yeoman's Row Management Ltd* [2008] 1 WLR 1752 (Extract 7.1.4 below).

I come now to consider the first of the three questions which I think in a case such as this the court have to consider. What is needed to establish an equity? In the course of an interesting addition to his submissions this morning, Mr Lightman cited *Ramsden* v *Dyson*, LR 1 HL 129, 142, to support his proposition that in order to establish an equity by estoppel there must be a belief by the plaintiff in the existence of a right created or encouraged by the words or actions of the defendant. With respect, I do not think that that is today a correct statement of the law. I think the law has developed so that today it is to be considered as correctly stated by Lord Kingsdown in his dissenting speech in *Ramsden* v *Dyson*. Like Lord Denning MR, I think that the point of dissent in *Ramsden* v *Dyson* was not on the law but on the facts. Lord Kingsdown's speech, in so far as it dealt with propositions of law, has been often considered, and recently followed by this court in *Inwards* v *Baker* [1965] 2 QB 29 . . .

While *Ramsden* v *Dyson* may properly be considered as the modern starting-point of the law of equitable estoppel, it was analysed and spelt out in a judgment of Fry J in 1880 in *Willmott* v *Barber* (1880) 15 Ch D 96, a decision to which Pennycuick V-C referred in his judgment. I agree with Pennycuick V-C in thinking that the passage from Fry J's judgment, from p 105, is a valuable guide as to the matters of fact which have to be established in order that a plaintiff may establish this particular equity . . .

Mr Lightman, in the course of an interesting and vigorous submission, drew the attention of the court to the necessity of finding something akin to fraud before the equity sought by the plaintiff could be established. 'Fraud' was a word often in the mouths of those robust judges who adorned the bench in the 19th century. It is less often in the mouths of the more wary judicial spirits today who sit upon the bench. But it is clear that whether one uses the word 'fraud' or not, the plaintiff has to establish as a fact that the defendant, by setting up his right, is taking advantage of him in a way which is unconscionable, inequitable or unjust. It is to be observed from the passage that I have quoted from the judgment of Fry J, that the fraud or injustice alleged does not take place during the course of negotiation, but only when the defendant decides to refuse to allow the plaintiff to set up his claim against the defendants' undoubted right. The fraud, if it be such, arises after the event, when the defendant seeks by relying on his right to defeat the expectation which he by his conduct encouraged the plaintiff to have. There need not be anything fraudulent or unjust in the conduct of the actual negotiations – the conduct of the transaction by the defendants.

The court therefore cannot find an equity established unless it is prepared to go as far as to say that it would be unconscionable and unjust to allow the defendants to set up their undoubted rights against the claim being made by the plaintiff. In order to reach a conclusion upon that matter the court does have to consider the history of the negotiations under the five headings to which Fry J referred. I need not at this stage weary anyone with an elaborate state-ment of the facts. I have no doubt upon the facts of this case that the first four elements referred to by Fry J exist. The question before the judge and now in this court is whether the fifth element is present: have the defendants, as possessor of the legal right, encouraged the plaintiff in the expenditure of money or in the other acts which he has done, either directly or by abstaining from asserting their legal rights? . . .

Clearly the plaintiff and Mr Alford came away from that meeting [in July 1967] in the confident expectation that a right would in due course be accorded to the plaintiff. Mr Alford did foresee 'further processes'. Of course, there would be further processes. The nature of the legal right to be granted had to be determined. It might be given by way of licence. It might be granted by way of easement. Conditions might be imposed. Payment of a sum of money might be required . . . The confident expectation with which the plaintiff and Mr Alford left the meeting in July remained remarkably undisturbed by the meeting of January 1968. Indeed it was reinforced because there on the ground, plain for all to see, was a fence with gaps which accorded exactly with the agreement in principle reached in the previous July. Ten days later the defendants ordered gates, and by March the gates were installed. I ask myself: as at March 1968 had these defendants encouraged the plaintiff to think that he had or was going to be given a right? To use the language of Fry J, had they done it directly or had they done it by abstaining from asserting a legal right? Their encouragement of the belief in the mind of the plaintiff and Mr Alford was both direct and indirect. It was direct because of what they had done on the ground. It was indirect because ever since the July meeting they had abstained from giving the plaintiff or his architect any indication that they were standing on their rights, or had it in mind to go back, as, of course, they were entitled at that stage to go back, upon the agreement in principle reached at that meeting . . . In September 1968, without telling the defendants or giving them any notice, so far as I am aware, the plaintiff entered into a contract to sell the northern piece of land without reservation over that land of any right of way. This was the act which was detrimental to the interests of the plaintiff. He did it in the belief that he had or could enforce a right of way and access at point B in the southern land.

One of the points taken by Mr Lightman is that the defendants had no notice of the sale, and therefore no opportunity to correct what on his case was a false belief in the mind of the plaintiff. Mr Millett in the course of his submissions conceded that he had not found in the books any case in which the sort of estoppel which we are here considering had arisen when the fact known to the defendants was an intention and not the realisation of that intention . . . I can conceive of cases in which it would be absolutely appropriate for a defendant to say: 'But you should not have acted to your detriment until you had had a word with me and I could have put you right.' But there are cases in which it is far too late for a defendant to get himself out of his pickle by putting upon the plaintiff that sort of duty; and this, in my judgment, is one of those cases . . . It is for those reasons – the passage of time, the abstention and the gates – that I think the defendants cannot rely upon the fact that the plaintiff acted, without referring to the defendants, on his intention – an intention of which they had had notice ever since their agent was informed of it at the meeting in July 1967. I think therefore an equity is established.

Comment

(1) The remedy given will be considered later in this chapter: Extract 7.2.2.

(2) How well does the enforcement of such agreements (or of unilateral promises) fit within estoppel principles? Is the rejection of any distinction between promissory and proprietary estoppels justified?

One difficult type of case is where C asserts an expectation of inheriting O's assets on O's death.

Extract 7.1.3

Gillett v *Holt* [2001] Ch 210

Gillett worked for Holt for about 40 years, 30 as farm manager. In many respects, he was treated as a family member. There were clear and repeated assurances that he would inherit under Holt's will, but eventually the two men fell out.

ROBERT WALKER LJ: . . . it is important to note at the outset that the doctrine of proprietary estoppel cannot be treated as subdivided into three or four watertight compartments. Both sides are agreed on that, and in the course of the oral argument in this court it repeatedly became apparent that the quality of the relevant assurances may influence the issue of reliance, that reliance and detriment are often intertwined, and that whether there is a distinct need for a 'mutual understanding' may depend on how the other elements are formulated and understood. Moreover the fundamental principle that equity is concerned to prevent unconscionable conduct permeates all the elements of the doctrine. In the end the court must look at the matter in the round.

In his discussion of the law the judge took as his starting point the decision of Mr Edward Nugee QC in *In re Basham decd* [1986] 1 WLR 1498. In that case the claimant and her husband had helped her mother and her stepfather in all sorts of ways throughout the claimant's adult life. She received no remuneration but understood that she would inherit her stepfather's property when he died. After her mother's death in 1976, and until her stepfather's death in 1982, she and her husband lived near the cottage to which her stepfather had moved (but never lived in the cottage). The claimant was told by her stepfather that 'she would lose nothing' by her help and (a few days before his death) that she was to have the cottage. The deputy judge held that she was entitled, by proprietary estoppel, to the whole of the estate of her stepfather (who died intestate). He rejected the submission that the principle could not extend beyond cases where the claimant already had enjoyment of an identified item of property: see pp 1509–1510. In that context he referred to the well known judgment of Oliver J in *Taylors Fashions Ltd v Liverpool Victoria Trustees Co Ltd (Note) (1979)* [1982] QB 133 . . .

Irrevocability of assurances

The judge referred to these authorities [two Court of Appeal cases referred to *In re Basham*] and then to the decision of Judge Weeks QC in *Taylor v Dickens* [1998] 1 FLR 806 (which has since been compromised on appeal). That was the case of the elderly lady who said that she would leave her estate to the gardener and did so, but then changed her mind (without telling him) after he had stopped charging her for his help with gardening and odd jobs. Judge Weeks rejected the claim and, at p 821, criticised *In re Basham* in two respects. The first criticism was that Mr Nugee's judgment omitted the requirement of unconscionability. That criticism seems misplaced: see [1986] 1 WLR 1498, 1504a–b and 1509A–c. The second criticism was [1998] 1 FLR 806, 821:

> 'it is not sufficient for A to believe that he is going to be given a right over B's property if he knows that B has reserved the right to change his mind. In that case, A must show that B created or encouraged a belief on A's part that B would not exercise that right.'

For that proposition Judge Weeks referred to the decision of the Privy Council in *Attorney General of Hong Kong v Humphreys Estate (Queen's Gardens) Ltd* [1987] AC 114.

Taylor v Dickens has itself attracted a good deal of criticism: see, for instance, Professor M P Thompson, 'Emasculating Estoppel' [1998] Conv 210, and William Swadling [1998] RLR 220; but compare the contrary view in M Dixon, 'Estoppel: A panacea for all wills?' [1999] Conv 39, 46. Mr Swadling's comment is short and pithy:

> 'This decision is clearly wrong, for the judge seems to have forgotten that the whole point of estoppel claims is that they concern promises which, since they are unsupported by consideration, are initially revocable. What later makes them binding, and therefore irrevocable, is the promisee's detrimental reliance on them. Once that occurs, there is simply no question of the promisor changing his or her mind.'

Mr McDonnell has added his voice to the criticism. In his skeleton argument he has submitted that *Taylor v Dickens* is 'simply wrong'. Mr Martin, while reminding the court that it is not hearing an appeal in *Taylor v Dickens*, has not given the case whole-hearted support. He has been inclined to concede that Judge Weeks should have focused on the promise which was made and whether it was of an irrevocable character, instead of looking for a second promise not to revoke a testamentary disposition.

In my judgment these criticisms of *Taylor v Dickens* are well founded. The actual result in the case may be justified on the other ground on which it was put (no unconscionability on the facts); or (as Mr Swadling suggests later in his note) the gardener's unremunerated services might have merited some modest restitutionary relief. But the inherent revocability of testamentary dispositions (even if well understood by the parties, as Mr Gillett candidly accepted that it was by him) is irrelevant to a promise or assurance that 'all this will be yours' . . . Even when the promise or assurance is in terms linked to the making of a will . . . the circumstances may make clear that the assurance is more than a mere statement of present (revocable) intention, and is tantamount to a promise. *Attorney General of Hong Kong* v *Humphreys Estate (Queen's Gardens) Ltd* [1987] AC 114, on which Judge Weeks relied, is essentially an example of a purchaser taking the risk, with his eyes open, of going into possession and spending money while his purchase remains expressly subject to contract. Carnwath J observed that the advice to the claimant in *Taylor* v *Dickens* 'not to count his chickens before they were hatched' is [1998] 3 All ER 917, 929:

> 'an apt statement of how, in normal circumstances, and in the absence of a specific promise, any reasonable person would regard – and should be expected by the law to regard – a representation by a living person as to his intentions for his will.'

In the generality of cases that is no doubt correct, and it is notorious that some elderly persons of means derive enjoyment from the possession of testamentary power, and from dropping hints as to their intentions, without any question of an estoppel arising. But in this case Mr Holt's assurances were repeated over a long period, usually before the assembled company on special family occasions, and some of them (such as 'it was all going to be ours anyway' . . .) were completely unambiguous . . . Mr Gillett, after discussing the matter with his wife and his parents, decided to rely on Mr Holt's assurances because 'Ken was a man of his word'. Plainly the assurances given on this occasion were intended to be relied on, and were in fact relied on. In any event reliance would be presumed: see *Greasley* v *Cooke* [1980] 1 WLR 1306; Mr Martin accepted that, while challenging the suggestion that that case also supported any presumption of detriment.

. . .

Mutual understandings and reliance

The judge's approach seems also to have been influenced by the need to find what he called, at p 929:

> 'a mutual understanding – which may be express or inferred from conduct – between promisor and promisee, both as to the content of the promise and as to what the promisee is doing, or may be expected to do, in reliance on it.'

Similarly he set out his view that, at p 932, 'the *In re Basham* principle requires some mutual "understanding" as to the quid pro quo' – i.e. the consideration – 'for the promise . . .'
 Here again I think that the judge may have been too influenced by the cases on mutual wills in which a definite agreement is an essential part of the doctrine. There is of course a kernel of truth, indeed a considerable nugget of truth in this approach, because (as Balcombe LJ said in *Wayling* v *Jones* (1993) 69 P&CR 170, and other distinguished judges said in the earlier cases which he cited) there must be a sufficient link between the promises relied on and the conduct which constitutes the detriment. In cases where the detriment involves the claimant moving house (as in *Watts* v *Storey* (unreported), 14 July 1983; Court of Appeal (Civil Division) Transcript No 319 of 1983), or otherwise taking some particular course of action at the other party's request, the link is, in the nature of things, going to have some resemblance to the process of offer and acceptance leading to a mutual understanding. But in other cases well within the mainstream of proprietary estoppel, such as *Inwards* v *Baker* [1965] 2 QB 29 and the 19th century decisions which this court applied in that case, there is nothing like a bargain as to what particular interest is to be granted, or when it is to be granted, or by what type of disposition it is to be granted. The link is provided by the bare fact of A encouraging B to incur expenditure on A's land.

. . .

Detriment

It is therefore necessary to go on to consider detriment. The judge would have decided the case against Mr Gillett on this point also, as he indicated at the end of his judgment in the main action [1998] 3 All ER 917, 932–936. The judge devoted almost all of this part of his judgment to an analysis of whether Mr Gillett was substantially underpaid between 1965 and 1995. He dealt with the other matters relied on as detriment in a manner which Mr McDonnell has described as perfunctory.

. . . The overwhelming weight of authority shows that detriment is required. But the authorities also show that it is not a narrow or technical concept. The detriment need not consist of the expenditure of money or other quantifiable financial detriment, so long as it is something substantial. The requirement must be approached as part of a broad inquiry as to whether repudiation of an assurance is or is not unconscionable in all the circumstances.

. . . Although the judge's view, after seeing and hearing Mr and Mrs Gillett, was that detriment was not established, I find myself driven to the conclusion that it was amply established. I think that the judge must have taken too narrowly financial a view of the requirement for detriment, as his reference [1998] 3 All ER 917, 936 to 'the balance of advantage and disadvantage' suggests. Mr Gillett and his wife devoted the best years of their lives to working for Mr Holt and his company, showing loyalty and devotion to his business interests, his social life and his personal wishes, on the strength of clear and repeated assurances of testamentary benefits.

Comment

Why do such claims on death cause so much difficulty? Does the law go too far if it recognises expectancies in cases such as *Gillett*?

It must not be thought that the judges are an easy touch when it comes to estoppel claims. Although *Crabb* shows that certainty is not essential, a vague expectation that all will be well does not suffice.[4] Two House of Lords decisions in recent years now form the basis for this area.

Extract 7.1.4

Cobbe v Yeoman's Row Management Ltd [2008] 1 WLR 1752

LORD SCOTT: 2. The essence of the problem to be resolved in this case can be quite shortly stated. A is the owner of land with potential for residential development and enters into negotiations with B for the sale of the land to B. They reach an oral 'agreement in principle' on the core terms of the sale but no written contract, or even a draft contract for discussion, is produced. There remain some terms still to be agreed. The structure of the agreement in principle that A and B have reached is that B, at his own expense, will make and prosecute an application for the desired residential development and that, if the desired planning permission is obtained, A will sell the land to B, or more probably to a company nominated by B, for an agreed upfront price, £x. B will then, again at his own expense, develop the land in accordance with the planning permission, sell off the residential units, and, when the gross proceeds of sale received by B equals £2x, any further gross proceeds of sale will be divided equally between A and B. Pursuant to this agreement in principle B makes and prosecutes an application for planning permission for the residential development that A and he have agreed upon. B is encouraged by A to do so. In doing so B spends a considerable sum of money as well, of course, as a considerable amount of time. The application is successful and the desired planning permission is obtained. A then seeks to renegotiate the core financial terms of the sale, asking, in particular,

---

[4] *Coombes v Smith* [1986] 1 WLR 808.

for a substantial increase in the sum of money that would represent £x. B is unwilling to commit himself to the proposed new financial terms and A is unwilling to proceed on the basis of the originally agreed financial terms. So B commences legal proceedings. The question for your Lordships is what relief, in the circumstances described, B should be granted, for, I believe, none of your Lordships considers that he would not be entitled to any.

3.   A number of possible bases for the grant of relief to B need to be considered.

(i)   First, there is proprietary estoppel. B has, with the encouragement of A, spent time and money in obtaining the planning permission and has done so, to the knowledge of A, in reliance on the oral agreement in principle and in the expectation that, following the grant of the planning permission, a formal written agreement for the sale of the property, incorporating the core financial terms that had already been agreed and any other terms necessary for or incidental to the implementation of the core terms, would be entered into. In these circumstances, it could be, and has been, argued, A should be held to be estopped from denying that B had acquired a proprietary interest in the property and a court of equity should grant B the relief necessary to reflect B's expectations.

(iv)   Fourthly, there is the question of a *quantum meruit.* B has supplied valuable services to A in obtaining planning permission for the benefit of A's property . . . In these circumstances a *quantum meruit*, taking into account the amount of B's expenditure of time and money and the value of the services, can, it could be argued, be fixed by the court.

  . . .

4.   Two features of these possible remedies are worth noticing. First, both the proprietary estoppel claim and the constructive trust claim are claims to a proprietary interest in the property. . . . Second, a proprietary estoppel claim and a constructive trust claim would constitute, if successful, a means whereby B could obtain a remedy providing him with a benefit more or less equivalent to the benefit he expected to obtain from the oral and inchoate agreement; in effect a benefit based on the value of his non-contractual expectation . . .

7.   The oral agreement in principle that had been reached, i.e. the core terms, did not cover everything that would have been expected in due course to be dealt with in a formal written contract . . . These would not have been expected to have been difficult matters on which to reach agreement but were all matters for future discussion, and the outcome of future negotiations has always an inherent uncertainty.

10.   Etherton J held, on 25 February 2005, that the conditions for proprietary estoppel were satisfied and that the minimum equity to do justice to Mr Cobbe required that he be awarded one-half of the increase in value of the property brought about by the grant of planning permission and that he be granted a lien over the property to secure that interest.

14.   Both the learned judge and the Court of Appeal regarded the relief granted as justified on the basis of proprietary estoppel. I respectfully disagree. The remedy to which, on the facts as found by the judge, Mr Cobbe is entitled can, in my opinion, be described neither as based on an estoppel nor as proprietary in character. There are several important authorities to which I want to refer but I want first to consider as a matter of principle the nature of a proprietary estoppel. An 'estoppel' bars the object of it from asserting some fact or facts, or, sometimes, something that is a mixture of fact and law, that stands in the way of some right claimed by the person entitled to the benefit of the estoppel. The estoppel becomes a 'proprietary' estoppel – a sub-species of a 'promissory' estoppel – if the right claimed is a proprietary right, usually a right to or over land but, in principle, equally available in relation to chattels or choses in action.

15.   . . . The terms that had already been agreed were regarded by the parties as being 'binding in honour', but it follows that the parties knew they were not legally binding. So what is it that the appellant is estopped from asserting or from denying? . . .

16.   . . . My Lords, unconscionability of conduct may well lead to a remedy but, in my opinion, proprietary estoppel cannot be the route to it unless the ingredients for a proprietary estoppel are present. These ingredients should include, in principle, a proprietary claim made by a claimant

and an answer to that claim based on some fact, or some point of mixed fact and law, that the person against whom the claim is made can be estopped from asserting. To treat a 'proprietary estoppel equity' as requiring neither a proprietary claim by the claimant nor an estoppel against the defendant but simply unconscionable behaviour is, in my respectful opinion, a recipe for confusion.

20.   Lord Kingsdown's requirement [in *Ramsden* v *Dyson* (1866) LR 1 HL 129] that there be an expectation of 'a certain interest in land', repeated in the same words by Oliver J in the *Taylors Fashions* case, presents a problem for Mr Cobbe's proprietary estoppel claim. The problem is that when he made the planning application his expectation was, for proprietary estoppel purposes, the wrong sort of expectation. It was not an expectation that he would, if the planning application succeeded, become entitled to 'a certain interest in land'. His expectation was that he and Mrs Lisle-Mainwaring, or their respective legal advisers, would sit down and agree the outstanding contractual terms to be incorporated into the formal written agreement, which he justifiably believed would include the already agreed core financial terms, and that his purchase, and subsequently his development of the property, in accordance with that written agreement would follow. This is not, in my opinion, the sort of expectation of 'a certain interest in land' that Oliver J in the *Taylors Fashions* case or Lord Kingsdown in *Ramsden* v *Dyson* had in mind.

25.   The *Humphreys Estate* case [*Attorney-General of Hong Kong* v *Humphreys Estate (Queen's Gardens) Ltd* [1987] AC 114] was one in which a written agreement, expressed to be 'subject to contract', for the purchase of development property had been signed . . . The Hong Kong government, the intended purchaser, was permitted to take possession of the property and to spend money on it. The owners of the property then decided to withdraw from the transaction and gave notice terminating the government's licence to occupy the property . . . The government lost in the courts in Hong Kong and appealed to the Privy Council but lost there too. Lord Templeman explained why at 127H:

> 'It is possible but unlikely that in circumstances at present unforeseeable a party to negotiations expressed to be "subject to contract" would be able to satisfy the court that the parties had subsequently agreed to convert the document into a contract or that some form of estoppel had arisen to prevent both parties from refusing to proceed with the transaction envisaged by the document. But in the present case the government chose to begin and elected to continue on terms that either party might suffer a change of mind and withdraw.'

The reason why, in a 'subject to contract' case, a proprietary estoppel cannot ordinarily arise is that the would-be purchaser's expectation of acquiring an interest in the property in question is subject to a contingency that is entirely under the control of the other party to the negotiations.

28.   The reality of this case, in my opinion, is that Etherton J and the Court of Appeal regarded their finding that Mrs Lisle-Mainwaring's behaviour in repudiating, and seeking an improvement on, the core financial terms of the second agreement was unconscionable, an evaluation from which I do not in the least dissent, as sufficient to justify the creation of a 'proprietary estoppel equity' . . . But to leap from there to a conclusion that a proprietary estoppel case was made out was not, in my opinion, justified . . . Proprietary estoppel requires, in my opinion, clarity as to what it is that the object of the estoppel is to be estopped from denying, or asserting, and clarity as to the interest in the property in question that that denial, or assertion, would otherwise defeat. If these requirements are not recognised, proprietary estoppel will lose contact with its roots and risk becoming unprincipled and therefore unpredictable, if it has not already become so. This is not, in my opinion, a case in which a remedy can be granted to Mr Cobbe on the basis of proprietary estoppel.

42.   It seems to me plain that Mr Cobbe is entitled to a *quantum meruit* payment for his services in obtaining the planning permission. He did not intend to provide his services gratuitously . . .

LORD WALKER: 59.   [After quoting Oliver J in *Taylors Fashions*] This passage certainly favours a broad or unified approach to equitable estoppel. But it is emphatically not a licence for abandoning careful analysis for unprincipled and subjective judicial opinion. It is worth noting that on this part of the case Oliver J analysed over twenty authorities spanning more than two centuries.

66.   The point that hopes by themselves are not enough is made most clearly in cases with a commercial context, of which *Attorney General of Hong Kong* is the most striking example. It does not appear so often in cases with more of a domestic or family flavour . . . They may not have had a clear idea of the quantum of what they expected to get (in *Grundy* v *Ottey*, unusually, the expected quantum was precisely defined). But in those cases in which an estoppel was established, the claimant believed that the assurance on which he or she relied was binding and irrevocable.

67.   It may possibly be that some of the domestic cases might have been decided differently if the nature of the claimant's belief had been an issue vigorously investigated in cross-examination . . .

68.   . . . In the commercial context, the claimant is typically a business person with access to legal advice and what he or she is expecting to get is a *contract*. In the domestic or family context, the typical claimant is not a business person and is not receiving legal advice. What he or she wants and expects to get is an *interest* in immovable property, often for long-term occupation as a home. The focus is not on intangible legal rights but on the tangible property which he or she expects to get. The typical domestic claimant does not stop to reflect (until disappointed expectations lead to litigation) whether some further legal transaction (such as a grant by deed, or the making of a will or codicil) is necessary to complete the promised title.

79.   *Crabb* v *Arun District Council*, the facts of which are well known, is a difficult case, not least because of different views taken by different members of the Court (Lord Denning MR, and Lawton and Scarman LJJ). The situation was that of a commercial negotiation in which both sides expected formal legal documents to be agreed and executed. The case is best explained, I think, by recognising that the Council's erection of the two sets of gates was an act so unequivocal that it led to Mr Crabb irretrievably altering his position, putting the matter beyond the stage at which it was open to negotiation . . .

81.   In my opinion none of these cases casts any doubt on the general principle laid down by this House in *Ramsden* v *Dyson*, that conscious reliance on honour alone will not give rise to an estoppel. Nor do they cast doubt on the general principle that the court should be very slow to introduce uncertainty into commercial transactions by over-ready use of equitable concepts such as fiduciary obligations and equitable estoppel. That applies to commercial negotiations whether or not they are expressly stated to be subject to contract.

Comment

(1) Lords Hoffmann, Brown and Mance agreed with Lord Scott; Lord Brown also agreed with Lord Walker.

(2) What differences, if any, are there between the analyses of Lord Scott and Lord Walker?

(3) *Haq* v *Island Homes Housing Association*[5] illustrates how difficult it is to rely on estoppel when there is a subject to contract agreement. Permission to enter land and expenditure of around £200,000 were insufficient to establish an estoppel.

(4) What is the role of conscionability today?

The analyses in *Cobbe* caused considerable concern. McFarlane and Robertson observed ([2008] LMCLQ 449 at p 453):

The reasoning of each of Lord Scott and Lord Walker (while differing one from the other) rests on what seems to be a dramatic re-interpretation of proprietary estoppel, as it has come to be

---

[5] [2011] 2 P&CR 277.

commonly understood and applied. Lord Scott's re-interpretation essentially denies the existence of proprietary estoppel as a distinct doctrine. Its effect is that proprietary estoppel does not exist as an independent means by which B can acquire a right against A . . . So, for example, it does not avail B to show that A is estopped from denying that A made a promise to give B a right: the mere fact of such a promise cannot give B a right against A.

Extract 7.1.5

Thorner v *Major* **[2009] 1 WLR 776**

It was alleged that an unusually taciturn farmer had promised that a farm would be inherited by a member of the family, who worked on the farm for very many hours over many years without payment.

LORD WALKER: 29.   My Lords, this appeal is concerned with proprietary estoppel. An academic authority (Simon Gardner, *An Introduction to Land Law* (2007), p 101) has recently commented: 'There is no definition of proprietary estoppel that is both comprehensive and uncontroversial (and many attempts at one have been neither).' Nevertheless most scholars agree that the doctrine is based on three main elements, although they express them in slightly different terms: a representation or assurance made to the claimant; reliance on it by the claimant; and detriment to the claimant in consequence of his (reasonable) reliance: see *Megarry & Wade, The Law of Real Property*, 7th ed (2008), para 16–001; *Gray & Gray, Elements of Land Law*, 5th ed (2009), para 9.2.8; *Snell's Equity*, 31st ed (2005), paras 10–16 to 10–19; *Gardner, An Introduction to Land Law* (2007), para 7.1.1.

31.   I should say at once that the defendants to the appeal did not contend that this House's decision in *Cobbe* v *Yeoman's Row Management Ltd* [2008] 1 WLR 1752 has severely curtailed, or even virtually extinguished, the doctrine of proprietary estoppel (a rather apocalyptic view that has been suggested by some commentators: see for instance Ben McFarlane and Professor Andrew Robertson, 'The Death of Proprietary Estoppel' [2008] LMCLQ 449 and Sir Terence Etherton's extrajudicial observations to the Chancery Bar Association 2009 Conference, paras 27ff.) But *Cobbe's* case is certainly relevant to the second issue. The defendants' case is that in *Cobbe's* case this House reaffirmed the need for certainty of interest which has, it is argued, been part of the law since *Ramsden* v *Dyson* (1866) LR 1 HL 129. The defendants argue that *In re Basham, decd* [1986] 1 WLR 1498 was wrongly decided so far as it extended, not just to the deceased's cottage, but to the whole of his residuary estate.

52.   In this House Mr McDonnell QC based David's appeal primarily on the deputy judge's findings as to the adequacy of the assurances given to David. He submitted that the Court of Appeal erred (in the passage set out in the last paragraph) because the 'clear and unequivocal' test did not apply in proprietary estoppel; and that in any case the test was, if necessary, satisfied . . .

56.   I would prefer to say (while conscious that it is a thoroughly question-begging formulation) that to establish a proprietary estoppel the relevant assurance must be clear enough. What amounts to sufficient clarity, in a case of this sort, is hugely dependent on context. I respectfully concur in the way Hoffmann LJ put it in *Walton* v *Walton* [1994] CA Transcript No 479 (in which the mother's 'stock phrase' to her son, who had worked for low wages on her farm since he left school at 15, was 'You can't have more money and a farm one day'). Hoffmann LJ stated, at para 16:

> 'The promise must be unambiguous and must appear to have been intended to be taken seriously. Taken in its context, it must have been a promise which one might reasonably expect to be relied upon by the person to whom it was made.'

59.   In this case the context, or surrounding circumstances, must be regarded as quite unusual. The deputy judge heard a lot of evidence about two countrymen leading lives that it may be

difficult for many city-dwellers to imagine – taciturn and undemonstrative men committed to a life of hard and unrelenting physical work, by day and sometimes by night, largely unrelieved by recreation or female company. The deputy judge seems to have listened carefully to this evidence and to have been sensitive to the unusual circumstances of the case.

60.   I respectfully consider that the Court of Appeal did not give sufficient weight to the advantage that the trial judge had in seeing and hearing the witnesses . . .

The identity of the farm

61.   In my opinion it is a necessary element of proprietary estoppel that the assurances given to the claimant (expressly or impliedly, or, in standing-by cases, tacitly) should relate to identified property owned (or, perhaps, about to be owned) by the defendant. That is one of the main distinguishing features between the two varieties of equitable estoppel, that is promissory estoppel and proprietary estoppel. The former must be based on an existing legal *relationship* (usually a contract, but not necessarily a contract relating to land). The latter need not be based on an existing legal relationship, but it must relate to *identified property* (usually land) owned (or, perhaps, about to be owned) by the defendant. It is the relation to identified land of the defendant that has enabled proprietary estoppel to develop as a sword, and not merely a shield: see Lord Denning MR in *Crabb* v *Arun District Council* [1976] Ch 179, 187.

63.   The situation is to my mind quite different from a case like *Layton* v *Martin* [1986] 2 FLR 227, in which the deceased made an unspecific promise of 'financial security'. It is also different (so far as concerns the award of the whole of the deceased's residuary estate) from *In re Basham, decd* [1986] 1 WLR 1498. Your Lordships do not need to decide whether *In re Basham* was correctly decided, so far as it extended to the residuary estate, and I would prefer to express no decided view. But on this point the deputy judge in *In re Basham* relied largely on authorities about mutual wills, which are arguably a special case.

64.   Mr Simmonds relied on some observations by my noble and learned friend, Lord Scott of Foscote, in *Cobbe's* case [2008] 1 WLR 1752, paras 18–21, pointing out that in *Ramsden* v *Dyson* LR 1 HL 129, 170, Lord Kingsdown referred to 'a *certain* interest in land' (emphasis supplied). But, as Lord Scott noted, Lord Kingsdown immediately went on to refer to a case where there was uncertainty as to the terms of the contract (or, as it may be better to say, in the assurance) and to point out that relief would be available in that case also. All the 'great judges' to whom Lord Kingsdown referred, at p 171, thought that even where there was some uncertainty an equity could arise and could be satisfied, either by an interest in land or in some other way.

67.   I wish to add a brief postscript as to *Cobbe's* case [2008] 1 WLR 1752. It will be apparent from this opinion that I have some difficulty with Lord Scott's observation (in para 14 of his opinion in that case) that proprietary estoppel is a sub-species of promissory estoppel. But the terminology and taxonomy of this part of the law are, I acknowledge, far from uniform . . .

LORD NEUBERGER: 68.   My Lords, I have had the benefit of reading in draft the opinion of my noble and learned friend, Lord Walker of Gestingthorpe. For the reasons he gives, I too would allow this appeal. However, partly because the issues are of some importance, and partly out of deference to the excellent written and oral arguments presented on behalf of the defendants, I shall give my views in my own words.

84.   It should be emphasised that I am not seeking to cast doubt on the proposition, heavily relied on by the Court of Appeal (eg paras 71 and 74), that there must be some sort of an assurance which is 'clear and unequivocal' before it can be relied on to found an estoppel. However, that proposition must be read as subject to three qualifications. First, it does not detract from the normal principle, so well articulated in this case by Lord Walker, that the effect of words or actions must be assessed in their context. Just as a sentence can have one meaning in one context and a very different meaning in another context, so can a sentence, which would be ambiguous or unclear in one context, be a clear and unambiguous assurance in another context.

Indeed, as Lord Walker says, the point is underlined by the fact that perhaps the classic example of proprietary estoppel is based on silence and inaction, rather than any statement or action: see per Lord Eldon LC ('knowingly, though but passively') in *Dann* v *Spurrier* (1802) 7 Ves 231, 235–236 and per Lord Kingsdown ('with the knowledge . . . and without objection') in *Ramsden* v *Dyson* (1866) LR 1 HL 129, 170.

85.   Secondly, it would be quite wrong to be unrealistically rigorous when applying the 'clear and unambiguous' test. The court should not search for ambiguity or uncertainty, but should assess the question of clarity and certainty practically and sensibly, as well as contextually. Again, this point is underlined by the authorities, namely those cases I have referred to in para 78 above, which support the proposition that, at least normally, it is sufficient for the person invoking the estoppel to establish that he reasonably understood the statement or action to be an assurance on which he could rely.

86.   Thirdly, as pointed out in argument by my noble and learned friend, Lord Rodger of Earlsferry, there may be cases where the statement relied on to found an estoppel could amount to an assurance which could reasonably be understood as having more than one possible meaning. In such a case, if the facts otherwise satisfy all the requirements of an estoppel, it seems to me that, at least normally, the ambiguity should not deprive a person who reasonably relied on the assurance of all relief: it may well be right, however, that he should be accorded relief on the basis of the interpretation least beneficial to him.

92.   In *Cobbe's* case [2008] 1 WLR 1752, Mr Cobbe devoted considerable time, effort, and expertise to obtaining planning permission for land owned by Yeoman's Row . . . As I see it, Mr Cobbe's claim failed because he was effectively seeking to invoke proprietary estoppel to give effect to a contract which the parties had intentionally and consciously not entered into, and because he was simply seeking a remedy for the unconscionable behaviour of Yeoman's Row.

93.   In the context of a case such as *Cobbe's* case [2008] 1 WLR 1752, it is readily understandable why Lord Scott considered the question of certainty was so significant. The parties had intentionally not entered into any legally binding arrangement while Mr Cobbe sought to obtain planning permission: they had left matters on a speculative basis, each knowing full well that neither was legally bound–see para 27. There was not even an agreement to agree (which would have been unenforceable), but, as Lord Scott pointed out, merely an expectation that there would be negotiations. And, as he said, at para 18, an 'expectation dependent upon the conclusion of a successful negotiation is not an expectation of an interest having [sufficient] certainty'.

94.   There are two fundamental differences between that case and this case. First, the nature of the uncertainty in the two cases is entirely different. It is well encapsulated by Lord Walker's distinction between 'intangible legal rights' and 'the tangible property which he or she expects to get', in *Cobbe's* case [2008] 1 WLR 1752, para 68. In that case, there was no doubt about the physical identity of the property. However, there was total uncertainty as to the nature or terms of any benefit (property interest, contractual right, or money), and, if a property interest, as to the nature of that interest (freehold, leasehold, or charge), to be accorded to Mr Cobbe.

95.   In this case, the extent of the farm might change, but, on the deputy judge's analysis, there is, as I see it, no doubt as to what was the subject of the assurance, namely the farm as it existed from time to time. Accordingly, the nature of the interest to be received by David was clear: it was the farm as it existed on Peter's death. As in the case of a very different equitable concept, namely a floating charge, the property the subject of the equity could be conceptually identified from the moment the equity came into existence, but its precise extent fell to be determined when the equity crystallised, namely on Peter's death.

96.   Secondly, the analysis of the law in *Cobbe's* case [2008] 1 WLR 1752 was against the background of very different facts. The relationship between the parties in that case was entirely arm's length and commercial, and the person raising the estoppel was a highly experienced businessman. The circumstances were such that the parties could well have been expected to

enter into a contract, however, although they discussed contractual terms, they had consciously chosen not to do so. They had intentionally left their legal relationship to be negotiated, and each of them knew that neither of them was legally bound. . . .

97. In this case, by contrast, the relationship between Peter and David was familial and personal, and neither of them, least of all David, had much commercial experience. Further, at no time had either of them even started to contemplate entering into a formal contract as to the ownership of the farm after Peter's death. Nor could such a contract have been reasonably expected even to be discussed between them. On the deputy judge's findings, it was a relatively straightforward case: Peter made what were, in the circumstances, clear and unambiguous assurances that he would leave his farm to David, and David reasonably relied on, and reasonably acted to his detriment on the basis of, those assurances, over a long period.

98. In these circumstances, I see nothing in the reasoning of Lord Scott in *Cobbe's* case [2008] 1 WLR 1752 which assists the defendants in this case. It would represent a regrettable and substantial emasculation of the beneficial principle of proprietary estoppel if it were artificially fettered so as to require the precise extent of the property the subject of the alleged estoppel to be strictly defined in every case. Concentrating on the perceived morality of the parties' behaviour can lead to an unacceptable degree of uncertainty of outcome, and hence I welcome the decision in *Cobbe's* case [2008] 1 WLR 1752. However, it is equally true that focussing on technicalities can lead to a degree of strictness inconsistent with the fundamental aims of equity.

Comment

(1) Lord Hoffmann delivered a short concurring judgment and Lord Rodger agreed with Lord Walker. Lord Scott preferred a constructive trust analysis, an indication that his views on estoppel are not shared by the other judges.

(2) What is the role of certainty after the two decisions? Is it ever relevant as regards (a) the property subject to the claim; or (b) the interest to be obtained?[6]

(3) Is it easy or desirable to distinguish commercial from domestic claims? Arden LJ has found a claim to be commercial on the basis that 'the parties were dealing at arm's length, and they had ready access to the services of lawyers had they wished to use them'.

(4) Is anything of significance left from *Cobbe*?

Lord Neuberger has, since *Thorner*, observed extra-judicially:[7]

> Ben Macfarlane and Andrew Robertson have suggested that *Cobbe* represented 'the death of proprietary estoppel,' not so much because the decision was wrong but because the reasoning precluded a proprietary estoppel claim unless the claimant believed that he had a legally enforceable claim. I agree – and, at least in a commercial context, what's wrong with it? In the original cases such as *Dann* v *Spurrier*, *Ramsden* v *Dyson* and *Rochdale Canal Co* v *King*, the basis of the estoppel claim was the plaintiff's mistaken belief that he was legally entitled to a property interest. Why should it be any different where the claimant believes he will receive a property interest? There is no reason to think that an estoppel claim should necessarily extend to some sort of moral right, which is unenforceable in law – especially in the light of what Lord Cranworth said.

---

[6] *Herbert* v *Doyle* [2011] 1 EGLR 119 at [56].
[7] [2009] CLJ 537 at p 543. Yet the courts appear to be content to apply estoppel (or a constructive trust) in a commercial setting: *Herbert* v *Doyle* [2011] 1 EGLR 119 at [56].

B. Reliance

Extract 7.1.6

Greasley v Cooke [1980] 1 WLR 1306

C had originally arrived as a maid, but lived with a member of a family (Kenneth) for nearly 30 years. During this period she had been assured by the family that she could stay in the house for her life; she looked after the house and a mentally ill family member.

LORD DENNING MR: . . . The first point is on the burden of proof. Mr Weeks referred us to many cases, such as *Reynell v Sprye* (1852) 1 De GM&G 660, 708; *Smith v Chadwick* (1882) 20 Ch D 27, 44 and *Brikom Investments Ltd v Carr* [1979] QB 467, 482–483 where I said that when a person makes a representation intending that another should act on it:

> 'It is no answer for the maker to say: "You would have gone on with the transaction anyway." That must be mere speculation. No one can be sure what he would, or would not, have done in a hypothetical state of affairs which never took place . . . Once it is shown that a representation was calculated to influence the judgment of a reasonable man, the presumption is that he was so influenced.'

So here. These statements to Miss Cooke were calculated to influence her – so as to put her mind at rest – so that she should not worry about being turned out. No one can say what she would have done if Kenneth and Hedley had not made those statements. It is quite possible that she would have said to herself:

> 'I am not married to Kenneth. I am on my own. What will happen to me if anything happens to him? I had better look out for another job now: rather than stay here where I have no security.'

So, instead of looking for another job, she stayed on in the house looking after Kenneth and Clarice. There is a presumption that she did so, relying on the assurances given to her by Kenneth and Hedley. The burden is not on her, but on them, to prove that she did not rely on their assurances. They did not prove it, nor did their representatives. So she is presumed to have relied on them. So on the burden of proof it seems to me that the judge was in error.

The second point is about the need for some expenditure of money – some detriment – before a person can acquire any interest in a house or any right to stay in it as long as he wishes. It so happens that in many of these cases of proprietary estoppel there has been expenditure of money. But that is not a necessary element. I see that in *Snell's Principles of Equity*, 27th ed (1973), p 565, it is said: 'A must have incurred expenditure or otherwise have prejudiced himself.' But I do not think that that is necessary. It is sufficient if the party, to whom the assurance is given, acts on the faith of it – in such circumstances that it would be unjust and inequitable for the party making the assurance to go back on it: see *Moorgate Mercantile Co Ltd v Twitchings* [1976] QB 225 and *Crabb v Arun District Council* [1976] Ch 179, 188. Applying those principles here it can be seen that the assurances given by Kenneth and Hedley to Doris Cooke – leading her to believe that she would be allowed to stay in the house as long as she wished – raised an equity in her favour. There was no need for her to prove that she acted on the faith of those assurances. It is to be presumed that she did so. There is no need for her to prove that she acted to her detriment or to her prejudice. Suffice it that she stayed on [sic] the house – looking after Kenneth and Clarice – when otherwise she might have left and got a job elsewhere . . .

Comment

(1) The presumption of reliance is a very important weapon for C. It has been accepted in subsequent cases,[8] though in *Coombes* v *Smith* (Extract 7.1.7 below) the presumption was rebutted. Both *Coombes* and *Greasley* are examples of how detriment and reliance issues are intertwined.

(2) Note that Lord Denning MR appears to accept acting on the assurance rather than requiring detriment. However, Dunn LJ adopted a more conventional analysis and other cases (including *Coombes*) use the language of detriment. Was there clear detriment in *Greasley*?[9]

(3) It sometimes happens that C voluntarily embarks on a course of conduct that benefits O: care services provide one example. O then makes a promise to C, who continues with the benefiting conduct. Should this be sufficient to establish an estoppel?[10]

C. Detriment

Some detriment is essential to an estoppel claim. Although improvement of the land is a feature of many cases, *Crabb* (sale of adjoining land) shows that this is by no means necessary.

Extract 7.1.7

Coombes v *Smith* [1986] 1 WLR 808

C claimed a right to live in a house as long as she wished.

JONATHAN PARKER QC: . . . The second element or requisite is that the plaintiff must have expended money, or otherwise prejudiced himself or acted to his detriment, on the faith of his mistaken belief in his legal rights . . .

The first point to make in this connection is that this is not, as Mr Nield acknowledged, a case in which expenditure of money on the property can be relied upon as creating the equity. The only relevant expenditure (on the installation of central heating) was incurred long after the issue of the writ and without the knowledge of the defendant. The acts of detriment relied upon are those which I listed earlier in this judgment. I take them in turn. Two questions have, it seems to me, to be asked in relation to each of them: (1) was it done in reliance on the defendant's assurances or, in other words, on the faith of the plaintiff's mistaken belief, the existence of which I have, for present purposes, to assume? and (2) by doing it, did the plaintiff prejudice herself or otherwise act to her detriment? The first act relied on by the plaintiff is allowing herself to become pregnant by the defendant. In my judgment, it would be wholly unreal, to put it mildly, to find on the evidence adduced before me that the plaintiff allowed herself to become pregnant by the defendant in reliance on some mistaken belief as to her legal rights. She allowed herself to become pregnant because she wished to live with the defendant and to bear his child. The second question accordingly does not arise, but I would in any event have been unable to treat the act of the plaintiff in allowing herself to become pregnant as constituting detriment in the context of the doctrine of proprietary estoppel.

[8] One example is *Wayling* v *Jones* (1993) 69 P&CR 170.
[9] See *Bostock* v *Bryant* (1990) 61 P&CR 23.
[10] *Wayling* v *Jones* (1993) 69 P&CR 170; *Grundy* v *Ottey* [2003] WTLR 1253.

The second act relied on as detriment was the plaintiff's act in leaving her husband and moving to 67, Bulwark Road. As I have already said, I know nothing about the plaintiff's marriage save that it was not a happy one, and that it was never consummated. In his closing speech, Mr Nield suggested that by moving to 67, Bulwark Road the plaintiff was giving up the chance that her marriage might survive. But I cannot conjecture, let alone making any finding about, what the chances may have been of the plaintiff's marriage becoming a happy and successful one. The reality is that the plaintiff decided to move to 67, Bulwark Road because she preferred to have a relationship with, and a child by, the defendant rather than continuing to live with her husband. It seems to me to have been as simple as that. There is no evidence that she left her husband in reliance on the defendant's assurance that he would provide for her if and when their relationship came to an end: the idea of detriment or prejudice is only introduced ex post facto.

The third act relied on is giving birth to Clare. I take that to be no more in effect than a repetition of the first act relied upon and I make the same observations in relation to it.

The fourth act relied on is not an isolated one but a course of conduct on the part of the plaintiff in looking after 33, Stanway Road, being ready for the defendant's visits, and looking after Clare. But these things were done by the plaintiff as occupier of the property, as the defendant's mistress, and as Clare's mother, in the context of a continuing relationship with the defendant. Even if the plaintiff held the requisite mistaken belief and did these things on the faith of that belief, I cannot see how any question of prejudice or detriment arises from them. The same observations apply to the fifth act, or category of acts, relied on, namely, redecorating the property and installing the decorative beams which I have mentioned.

Lastly, it is pleaded that in reliance on the defendant's alleged assurances, the plaintiff took no other steps to provide for herself and Clare, i.e., she did not look for a job. Apart from the fact that there was no evidence that she forebore to look for a job on the faith of a belief that she was legally entitled to security of tenure, I cannot regard her omission to look for a job as a detriment. The contrary would seem to be more readily arguable, in view of the fact that until things went wrong between them the defendant was content to pay all the bills and to pay an allowance to the plaintiff for herself and Clare.

In my judgment, therefore, even assuming the existence of the requisite mistaken belief, it has not been established that she acted to her detriment on the faith of that belief so as to give rise to an equity in her favour to remain at the property . . .

Comment

(1) The conduct here is typical of many relationships. If estoppel had been proved, it would mean that representations would almost invariably become enforceable as between persons living together. Even allowing for this, is the decision justified? *Southwell v Blackburn* [2014] EWCA Civ 1347 reveals a more generous approach.

(2) O had no objection to C's living in the house until the daughter reached 17, so can it be argued that C got a good deal (even if short of her mistaken belief)?

(3) Sir Nicolas Browne-Wilkinson V-C in *Grant v Edwards*[11] appears to support 'Setting up house together, having a baby, making payments to general housekeeping expenses . . .' as detriment. Is this consistent with *Coombes v Smith*?

(4) See also the detriment analysis in *Gillett v Holt* (Extract 7.1.3 above). Does this cast doubt on *Coombes v Smith*?

(5) On the facts, it was found that C had no mistaken belief and so an estoppel could not in any event be made out.

[11] [1986] Ch 638 at p 657.

2. The effect of the estoppel

A. Use as a sword

Extract 7.2.1

Dillwyn v Llewelyn (1862) 4 De GF&J 517 (45 ER 1285)

LORD WESTBURY LC: ... Subsequently the father and mother became desirous that the Plaintiff, their son, should reside in their immediate neighbourhood, and accordingly they selected a small estate and determined to give it to the son in order that he might build a proper dwelling-house for his residence thereon ...

... The Plaintiff was put in possession of the estate and immediately proceeded to build a dwelling-house thereon, and laid out, as it is stated, a sum of no less than £14,000. This expenditure took place in the lifetime of the father, and with his assent and approbation. No alteration was made by the father in his will, and he died in the month of August 1855. The question now arises, what estate the Plaintiff has in the property so given to him, and which was made the site of his dwelling-house ...

About the rules of the Court there can be no controversy. A voluntary agreement will not be completed or assisted by a Court of Equity, in cases of mere gift. If anything be wanting to complete the title of the donee, a Court of Equity will not assist him in obtaining it; for a mere donee can have no right to claim more than he has received. But the subsequent acts of the donor may give the donee that right or ground of claim which he did not acquire from the original gift. Thus, if A gives a house to B, but makes no formal conveyance, and the house is afterwards, on the marriage of B, included, with the knowledge of A, in the marriage settlement of B, A would be bound to complete the title of the parties claiming under that settlement. So if A puts B in possession of a piece of land, and tells him, 'I give it to you that you may build a house on it', and B on the strength of that promise, with the knowledge of A, expends a large sum of money in building a house accordingly, I cannot doubt that the donee acquires a right from the subsequent transaction to call on the donor to perform that contract and complete the imperfect donation which was made. The case is somewhat analogous to that of verbal agreement not binding originally for the want of the memorandum in writing signed by the party to be charged, but which becomes binding by virtue of the subsequent part performance. The early case of *Foxcroft v Lester* (2 Vern 456), decided by the House of Lords, is an example nearly approaching to the terms of the present case.

Comment

(1) Although estoppel may sometimes operate as a shield, doing no more than denying O's claim to possession, *Dillwyn* is an excellent early example of its acting as a sword. This has been confirmed in large numbers of more recent cases, from *Crabb* to *Thorner*. How compelling is the analogy of part performance?

(2) Can its acting as a sword be justified when promissory estoppel has no such effect? Might the answer lie in the acquiescence origins of much of proprietary estoppel?

(3) It will be seen below that the remedy is not simply the enforcement of the promise, but involves some element of discretion. Australian analyses explain the circumvention of contractual rules (especially consideration requirements) by employing a restitutionary basis for estoppel.[12]

---

[12] *Waltons Stores (Interstate) Ltd* v *Maher* (1988) 164 CLR 387; *Commonwealth* v *Verwayen* (1990) 170 CLR 394; Spence (1991) 107 LQR 221.

B. The remedy

An important aspect of estoppel decisions over the past two or three decades has concerned the remedy.

Extract 7.2.2

Crabb v *Arun DC* [1976] Ch 179

SCARMAN LJ: . . . I turn now to the other two questions – the extent of the equity and the relief needed to satisfy it. There being no grant, no enforceable contract, no licence, I would analyse the minimum equity to do justice to the plaintiff as a right either to an easement or to a licence upon terms to be agreed . . . It is interesting that there has been some doubt amongst distinguished lawyers in the past as to whether the court can so proceed. Lord Kingsdown refers in fact to those doubts in a passage, which I need not quote, in *Ramsden* v *Dyson*, LR 1 HL 129, 171. Lord Thurlow clearly thought that the court did have this power. Other lawyers of that time did not. But there can be no doubt that since *Ramsden* v *Dyson* the courts have acted upon the basis that they have to determine not only the extent of the equity, but also the conditions necessary to satisfy it, and they have done so in a great number and variety of cases. I need refer only to the interesting collection of cases enumerated in *Snell's Principles of Equity*, 27th ed (1973), at pp 567–568, para 2 (b).

In the present case the court does have to consider what is necessary now in order to satisfy the plaintiff's equity. Had matters taken a different turn, I would without hesitation have said that the plaintiff should be put upon terms to be agreed if possible with the defendants, and, if not agreed, settled by the court. But, as already mentioned by Lord Denning MR and Lawton LJ, there has been a history of delay, and indeed high-handedness, which it is impossible to disregard. . . . I am not disposed to consider whether or not the defendants are to be blamed in moral terms for what they did. I just do not know. But the effect of their action has been to sterilise the plaintiff's land; and for the reasons which I have endeavoured to give, such action was an infringement of an equitable right possessed by the plaintiff. It has involved him in loss, which has not been measured; but, since it amounted to sterilisation of an industrial estate for a very considerable period of time, it must surpass any sort of sum of money which the plaintiff ought reasonably, before it was done, to have paid the defendants in order to obtain an enforceable legal right. I think therefore that nothing should now be paid by the plaintiff and that he should receive at the hands of the court the belated protection of the equity that he has established. Reasonable terms, other than money payment, should be agreed: or, if not agreed, determined by the court.

The 'minimum equity to do justice' or, as stated earlier in the judgment, 'the relief appropriate to satisfy the equity' test has been quoted and applied in very many subsequent cases. The question for consideration is how far the court possesses a discretion as to what remedy to give, going beyond the discretion inherent in every equitable remedy. More specifically, we need to consider whether (and how far) the 'equity' is based upon C's expectation or C's detriment.

Extract 7.2.3

Pascoe v *Turner* [1979] 1 WLR 431

On the breakdown of a relationship, O purported to transfer a house to C. However, the absence of writing (let alone a deed) rendered C no more than a licensee.

CUMMING-BRUCE LJ: . . . On the judge's findings the defendant, having been told that the house was hers, set about improving it within and without. Outside she did not do much: a little work on the roof and an improvement which covered the way from the outside toilet to the rest of the house, putting in a new door there, and Snowcem to protect the toilet. Inside she did a good deal more. She installed gas in the kitchen with a cooker, improved the plumbing in the kitchen and put in a new sink. She got new gas fires, putting a gas fire in the lounge. She redecorated four rooms. The fitted carpets she put in the bedrooms, the stair carpeting, and the curtains and the furniture that she bought are not part of the realty, and it is not clear how much she spent on those items. But they are part of the whole circumstances. There she was, on her own after he left her in 1973. She had £1,000 left of her capital, and a pension of some kind. Having as she thought been given the house, she set about it as described. On the repairs and improvement to the realty and its fixtures she spent about £230. She had £300 of her capital left by the date of the trial, but she did not establish in evidence how much had been expended on refurbishing the house with carpets, curtains and furniture. We would describe the work done in and about the house as substantial in the sense that that adjective is used in the context of estoppel. All the while the plaintiff not only stood by and watched but encouraged and advised, without a word to suggest that she was putting her money and her personal labour into his house. What is the effect in equity?

. . .

In *Crabb v Arun District Council* [1976] Ch 179 this court had to consider the principles upon which the court should give effect to the equity: [Scarman LJ is quoted]. So the principle to be applied is that the court should consider all the circumstances, and the counterclaimant having at law no perfected gift or licence other than a licence revocable at will, the court must decide what is the minimum equity to do justice to her having regard to the way in which she changed her position for the worse by reason of the acquiescence and encouragement of the legal owner. The defendant submits that the only appropriate way in which the equity can here be satisfied is by perfecting the imperfect gift as was done in *Dillwyn v Llewelyn*.

. . .

We are satisfied that the problem of remedy on the facts resolves itself into a choice between two alternatives: should the equity be satisfied by a licence to the defendant to occupy the house for her lifetime, or should there be a transfer to her of the fee simple?

The main consideration pointing to a licence for her lifetime is that she did not by her case at the hearing seek to establish that she had spent more money or done more work on the house than she would have done had she believed that she had only a licence to live there for her lifetime. But the court must be cautious about drawing any inference from what she did not give in evidence as the hypothesis put is one that manifestly never occurred to her. Then it may reasonably be held that her expenditure and effort can hardly be regarded as comparable to the change of position of those who have constructed buildings on land over which they had no legal rights.

This court appreciates that the moneys laid out by the defendant were much less than in some of the cases in the books. But the court has to look at all the circumstances. When the plaintiff left her she was, we were told, a widow in her middle fifties . . . Compared to her, on the evidence the plaintiff is a rich man. He might not regard an expenditure of a few hundred pounds as a very grave loss. But the court has to regard her change of position over the years 1973 to 1976.

We take the view that the equity cannot here be satisfied without granting a remedy which assures to the defendant security of tenure, quiet enjoyment, and freedom of action in respect of repairs and improvements without interference from the plaintiff. The history of the conduct of the plaintiff since April 9, 1976, in relation to these proceedings leads to an irresistible inference that he is determined to pursue his purpose of evicting her from the house by any legal means at his disposal with a ruthless disregard of the obligations binding upon conscience. The court must grant a remedy effective to protect her against the future manifestations of his ruthlessness. It was conceded that if she is granted a licence, such a licence cannot be registered as a land charge, so that she may find herself ousted by a purchaser for value without notice . . .

Weighing such considerations this court concludes that the equity to which the facts in this case give rise can only be satisfied by compelling the plaintiff to give effect to his promise and her expectations. He has so acted that he must now perfect the gift.

Comment

(1) Does this support giving effect to the expectation or the detriment?

(2) The cynic might observe that the defendant did remarkably well out of the expenditure of a few hundred pounds. Should the remedy be regarded as being over the top?

Extract 7.2.4

Baker v *Baker & Baker* [1993] 2 FLR 247

DILLON LJ: . . . The purchase of the property was duly completed with the use of Edward Baker's money [£33,950] and a mortgage . . . , and Edward Baker moved in in October 1987, giving up his council house in Finchley. His 'granny room' in the property was a bed-sitting room on the ground floor with French windows to the garden . . .

On 13 June 1988, however, the arrangement came to an abrupt end because Peter Baker accused Edward Baker of sexually molesting Mr and Mrs Baker's young daughter . . . It is accepted that Peter Baker honestly believed that his accusation was true but the judge's finding indicates not only that the accusation was unfounded but also that Peter Baker, even though he believed it to be true, had no reasonable grounds for making it.

The predictable consequence was that Edward Baker was deeply hurt, highly offended and furious. The sharing arrangement obviously could not continue, and Edward Baker left the property that day . . .

[It was conceded that the facts gave rise to an estoppel.]

It is common ground that in this field of law the court must look at the circumstances in each case to decide in what way the equity can be satisfied – *Plimmer* v *Wellington Corporation* (1884) 9 App Cas 699. It is equally common ground that in this particular case the only way in which the equity can be satisfied is by a payment of money by Mr and Mrs Peter Baker to Edward Baker. The dispute is over how much that payment should be. The judge held, as I have indicated, that this should be £33,950 . . .

The general rule is stated in *Snell's Equity* (29th ed), at p 576 as follows:

'The extent of the equity is to have made good, so far as may fairly be done between the parties, the expectations of A which O has encouraged. A's expectation or belief is the maximum extent of the equity.'

In support of the latter part of that statement reference is made to *Dodsworth* v *Dodsworth* (1973) 228 EG 1115 where Russell LJ in giving the judgment of the court said:

'We do not think that it can be right to satisfy such an equity by conferring upon the defendants a greater interest in the property than was envisaged by the parties.'

In the present case the greatest interest in the property that the parties envisaged Edward Baker having was the right, living as part of the family, to occupy the granny room rent-free for the rest of his life making the contributions to household expenses which I have indicated.

What he was deprived of was that right – and no more – as from 13 June 1988 when owing to a false accusation he had to leave the property. Therefore what he is entitled to in satisfaction of that equity should not, in my judgment, be more than the value of that right as at 13 June 1988 with interest from that date.

That approach of Russell LJ is consistent, in my judgment, with a telling phrase used by Scarman LJ in *Crabb* v *Arun District Council* [1976] 1 Ch 179 at p 198G–H, where, referring to the extent of the equity, he said that it should be 'the minimum equity to do justice to the plaintiff'.
. . .

In some cases of equitable estoppel, the course taken by the court to satisfy the equity has been to order the defendant to repay the plaintiff's expenditure. That was the course adopted in *Dodsworth* v *Dodsworth* and the course considered in *Chalmers* v *Pardoe* [1963] 1 WLR 677. It is the course the judge followed in a sense in the present case. He considered that there was no distinction of any particular importance between the loss that he thought Edward Baker had suffered, and the loss of that which he had been promised, and he concluded that what Edward Baker had lost was the gift – of the £33,950 – that he made to Mr and Mrs Peter Baker in reliance on the understanding that he would be able to live in the property for the rest of his life.

But the gift in the present case was directed to achieving two aims – the provision of a family home for Mr and Mrs Peter Baker and their children, as well as the rent-free occupation of the granny room for life by Edward Baker. In *Dodsworth* v *Dodsworth* the expenditure had the one aim only of adapting the property in question for shared occupation by the original owner and the party who incurred the expenditure and in whose favour the equity arose. In the present case the correct appreciation is, in my judgment, that what Edward Baker has lost is not the whole £33,950 but merely the right to rent-free occupation of the granny room in a family home from 13 June 1988 for the rest of his life.

Comment

(1) Dillon LJ dissented on the calculation of the value of the right, but this does not affect the passage quoted.

(2) What principles emerge from the analysis in *Baker*?

(3) Is the stress on the value of the expectation consistent with the result in *Crabb*, where C must have expected to pay for the right of access and yet was awarded access without payment?

Extract 7.2.5

Jennings v *Rice* [2003] 1 P&CR 100

O was an elderly woman for whom C provided extensive care services. There was no precise agreement, but O led C to believe that he would get at least the house and furniture (valued at £435,000) and possibly the entire estate (close to £1.3 million). C's counsel, Mr Warner, argued that the expectation should be satisfied.

ALDOUS LJ: 22. Against that background I turn to consider the crucial question in this case, namely how to give effect to the estoppel. Mr Warner took us back to cases decided in the last century. For my part, I believe it is appropriate to start with the *Crabb* case, decided in 1976. In that case the dispute concerned a right of access that had been promised by the defendants. The court held that the plaintiff had acted upon that promise to his detriment in circumstances where an equity was raised in his favour and that equity was satisfied by the grant free of charge of an easement. The award exceeded the expectation, but it was the proportionate response as appears from the judgment of Scarman LJ . . .
26. [*Pascoe* v *Turner* [1979] 1 WLR 431] was a case where the award equalled the expectation, but the court did not come to that conclusion because the award had to equal the expectation. The court looked at all the circumstances (see page 438 F), including the financial position of the parties. This case does not support Mr Warner's submission.
29. [*Sledmore* v *Dalby* (1996) 72 P&CR 196] is another case where the court did not merely conclude that the award should satisfy the expectation. All the members of the court took

account of the material circumstances. The need for proportionality was at the heart of the judgments.

30.   I do not believe it is necessary to examine any of the Australian authorities which appear to lean towards the view that the award should compensate the detriment. In so far as they differ from the law stated by Mason CJ in *Verwayen*, which was cited by Hobhouse LJ in *Sledmore*, they do not reflect the law of this country.

36.   Both the result and the reasoning of the judgment in [*Campbell v Griffin* [2001] WTLR 981] are inconsistent with Mr Warner's submission. There is a clear line of authority from at least *Crabb* to the present day which establishes that once the elements of proprietary estoppel are established an equity arises. The value of that equity will depend upon all the circumstances including the expectation and the detriment. The task of the court is to do justice. The most essential requirement is that there must be proportionality between the expectation and the detriment.

39.   I have read the judgment of Robert Walker LJ in draft and agree with it.

ROBERT WALKER LJ: 42.   This court was referred to two recent articles which contain a full and illuminating discussion of this area: *Estoppel and the Protection of Expectations* by Elizabeth Cooke [1997] 17 LS 258 and *The Remedial Discretion in Proprietary Estoppel* by Simon Gardner (1999) 115 LQR 438. Those articles could with advantage have been cited in *Gillett v Holt* [2001] Ch 210. Both are concerned with whether the fundamental aim of this form of estoppel is to fulfil the claimant's expectations, or to compensate him for his detrimental reliance on the defendant's non-contractual assurances, or is some intermediate objective; and (following on from the identification of the correct principle) the nature of the discretion which the court exercises in granting a remedy to the claimant. The articles amply demonstrate that the range of English authorities provides some support for both theories and for a variety of intermediate positions; and that recent Australian authority (especially the decision of the High Court in *Commonwealth v Verwayen* (1990) 170 CLR 394) has moved in favour of the reliance loss theory.

43.   It cannot be doubted that in this as in every other area of the law, the court must take a principled approach, and cannot exercise a completely unfettered discretion according to the individual judge's notion of what is fair in any particular case. Dr Gardner's fourth hypothesis ('the approach is for the court to adopt whatever style and measure of relief it thinks fit, for whatever reason it thinks fit') cannot be right. I do not think that the judgment of Hobhouse LJ in *Sledmore v Dalby* (1996) 72 P&CR 196 (to which I shall return) can possibly be regarded as adopting or advocating an unfettered judicial discretion.

44.   The need to search for the right principles cannot be avoided. But it is unlikely to be a short or simple search, because (as appears from both the English and the Australian authorities) proprietary estoppel can apply in a wide variety of factual situations, and any summary formula is likely to prove to be an over-simplification. The cases show a wide range of variation in both of the main elements, that is the quality of the assurances which give rise to the claimant's expectations and the extent of the claimant's detrimental reliance on the assurances. The doctrine applies only if these elements, in combination, make it unconscionable for the person giving the assurances (whom I will call the benefactor, although that may not always be an appropriate label) to go back on them.

45.   Sometimes the assurances, and the claimant's reliance on them, have a consensual character falling not far short of an enforceable contract (if the only bar to the formation of a contract is non-compliance with section 2 of the Law of Property (Miscellaneous Provisions) Act 1989, the proprietary estoppel may become indistinguishable from a constructive trust: *Yaxley v Gotts* [2000] Ch 162). In a case of that sort both the claimant's expectations and the element of detriment to the claimant will have been defined with reasonable clarity. A typical case would be an elderly benefactor who reaches a clear understanding with the claimant (who may be a relative, a friend, or a remunerated companion or carer) that if the claimant resides

with and cares for the benefactor, the claimant will inherit the benefactor's house (or will have a home for life). In a case like that the consensual element of what has happened suggests that the claimant and the benefactor probably regarded the expected benefit and the accepted detriment as being (in a general, imprecise way) equivalent, or at any rate not obviously disproportionate. Cases of that sort, if free from other complications, fit fairly comfortably into Dr Gardner's first or second hypothesis (both of which aim to vindicate the claimant's expectations as far as possible, and if possible by providing the claimant with the specific property which the benefactor has promised).

46.   However the claimant's expectations may not be focused on any specific property. In *Re Basham* [1986] 1 WLR 1498 the deputy judge (Mr Edward Nugee QC) rejected the submission that there must be some clearly identified piece of property, and that decision has been approved more than once in this court. Moreover (as the judge's findings in this case vividly illustrate) the claimant's expectations may have been formed on the basis of vague and inconsistent assurances . . .

47.   If the claimant's expectations are uncertain (as will be the case with many honest claimants) then their specific vindication cannot be the appropriate test. A similar problem arises if the court, although satisfied that the claimant has a genuine claim, is not satisfied that the high level of the claimant's expectations is fairly derived from his deceased patron's assurances, which may have justified only a lower level of expectation. In such cases the court may still take the claimant's expectations (or the upper end of any range of expectations) as a starting point, but unless constrained by authority I would regard it as no more than a starting point.

48.   I do not see that approach as being inconsistent with authority. On the contrary, I think it is supported by a substantial body of English authority. Scarman LJ's well-known reference to 'the minimum equity to do justice to the plaintiff' (*Crabb* v *Arun District Council* [1976] Ch 179, 198) must no doubt be read in the context of the rather unusual facts of that case, but it does not stand alone . . . Scarman LJ's reference to the minimum does not require the court to be constitutionally parsimonious, but it does implicitly recognise that the court must also do justice to the defendant.

49.   It is no coincidence that these statements of principle refer to satisfying the equity (rather than satisfying, or vindicating, the claimant's expectations). The equity arises not from the claimant's expectations alone, but from the combination of expectations, detrimental reliance, and the unconscionableness of allowing the benefactor (or the deceased benefactor's estate) to go back on the assurances . . .

50.   To recapitulate: there is a category of case in which the benefactor and the claimant have reached a mutual understanding which is in reasonably clear terms but does not amount to a contract. I have already referred to the typical case of a carer who has the expectation of coming into the benefactor's house, either outright or for life. In such a case the court's natural response is to fulfil the claimant's expectations. But if the claimant's expectations are uncertain, or extravagant, or out of all proportion to the detriment which the claimant has suffered, the court can and should recognise that the claimant's equity should be satisfied in another (and generally more limited) way.

51.   But that does not mean that the court should in such a case abandon expectations completely, and look to the detriment suffered by the claimant as defining the appropriate measure of relief. Indeed in many cases the detriment may be even more difficult to quantify, in financial terms, than the claimant's expectations. Detriment can be quantified with reasonable precision if it consists solely of expenditure on improvements to another person's house, and in some cases of that sort an equitable charge for the expenditure may be sufficient to satisfy the equity (see *Snell's Equity* 30th ed para 39–21 and the authorities mentioned in that paragraph). But the detriment of an ever-increasing burden of care for an elderly person, and of having to be subservient to his or her moods and wishes, is very difficult to quantify in money terms. Moreover the claimant may not be motivated solely by reliance on the benefactor's assurances, and may

receive some countervailing benefits (such as free bed and board). In such circumstances the court has to exercise a wide judgmental discretion.

52.   It would be unwise to attempt any comprehensive enumeration of the factors relevant to the exercise of the court's discretion, or to suggest any hierarchy of factors. In my view they include, but are not limited to, the factors mentioned in Dr Gardner's third hypothesis (misconduct of the claimant as in *J Willis & Son* v *Willis* [[1986] 1 EGLR 62] or particularly oppressive conduct on the part of the defendant, as in *Crabb* v *Arun District Council* or *Pascoe* v *Turner* [1979] 1 WLR 431). To these can safely be added the court's recognition that it cannot compel people who have fallen out to live peaceably together, so that there may be a need for a clean break; alterations in the benefactor's assets and circumstances, especially where the benefactor's assurances have been given, and the claimant's detriment has been suffered, over a long period of years; the likely effect of taxation; and (to a limited degree) the other claims (legal or moral) on the benefactor or his or her estate. No doubt there are many other factors which it may be right for the court to take into account in particular factual situations.

54.   . . . In my view it would rarely if ever be appropriate to go into detailed inquiries as to hours and hourly rates where the claim was based on proprietary estoppel (rather than a restitutionary claim for services which were not gratuitous). But the going rate for live-in carers can provide a useful cross-check in the exercise of the court's discretion.

55.   I have made some references to the general trend of Australian jurisprudence in this area. It is unnecessary to attempt any detailed study of the different views expressed by the High Court in the *Verwayen* case (which was concerned with estoppel in the very different context of litigation arising out of personal injuries suffered in a collision between two warships) or of Australian cases since then.

56.   However I respectfully agree with the view expressed by Hobhouse LJ in *Sledmore* v *Dalby* (1996) 72 P&CR 196, that the principle of proportionality (between remedy and detriment), emphasised by Mason CJ in *Verwayen*, is relevant in England also. As Hobhouse LJ observed at p 209, to recognise the need for proportionality

'. . . is to say little more than that the end result must be a just one having regard to the assumption made by the party asserting the estoppel and the detriment which he has experienced.'

The essence of the doctrine of proprietary estoppel is to do what is necessary to avoid an unconscionable result, and a disproportionate remedy cannot be the right way of going about that . . .

Comment

(1) The judge's award of £200,000 was upheld. This was the same as the cost of full-time nursing care. If the value of the work is much less than what has been promised, would it be a fair result to award double the value of the work?[13]

(2) The result illustrates a growing willingness to award a monetary, as opposed to proprietary, remedy. This is investigated by Bright and McFarlane [2005] CLJ 449.

(3) How do we balance (i) giving effect to intentions and (ii) recognising the detriment incurred by C? To what extent does the court exercise a discretion in awarding a remedy?

(4) How useful is the distinction drawn by Robert Walker LJ as regards different types of case?[14] Is the 'claimant's expectations are uncertain' category viable after *Cobbe* (see

---

[13] The remedy (obiter) in *Murphy* v *Burrows* [2004] EWHC 1900 (Ch); (2004) 7 ITELR 116.
[14] See the criticism by Gardner (2006) 122 LQR 492, recognised in *Powell* v *Benney* [2007] EWCA Civ 1283 at [21].

Extract 7.1.4 above). On which side of the line do the facts in *Jennings* fall? *Grundy* v *Ottey*[15] applied a proportionality test to all cases and required an 'appropriate remedy in respect of the unconscionable conduct'. Does this help the resolution of cases?

(5) Suppose that O agrees to leave property worth £250,000 in his will to C if C provides care services. These services are valued at £50,000 per annum (cost of commercial provision). What would be the appropriate remedy if O dies after (i) one month; (ii) one year; (iii) three years; (iv) 15 years?

(6) Is it now possible to state what the court is setting out to achieve in awarding estoppel remedies?

Extract 7.2.6

Suggitt v *Suggitt* [2012] EWCA Civ 1140; [2012] WTLR 1607

A father promised that his son would inherit a farm. There was limited reliance, though the son structured his life around that expectation. The father concluded that he was not fit to run the farm and left it to his daughter.

ARDEN LJ: 44.   In my judgment, this principle [in *Jennings* v *Rice*] does not mean that there has to be a relationship of proportionality between the level of detriment and the relief awarded. What Walker LJ holds in this paragraph is that if the expectations are extravagant or 'out of all proportion to the detriment which the claimant has suffered', the court can and should recognise that the claimant's equity should be satisfied in another and generally more limited way. So the question is: was the relief that the judge granted 'out of all proportion to the detriment' suffered?

45.   In my judgment, this particular question is again a question of evaluation and judgment. That judgment was exercised by the judge in favour of John in his award of the farmland and indeed of Wellfield; I will deal with Wellfield in a moment. I do not, however, consider that in principle, we can interfere with the exercise by the judge of his evaluation of what was out of all proportion unless it is shown to have been clearly wrong. Since the promise was that John should have the farmland unconditionally, I do not consider that to grant him the farmland, whatever that means, could be said to be out of all proportion.

50.   I have taken into account both the farmland and Wellfield are very valuable. Their aggregate value was said to be some £3.3 million. Wellfield alone was said to be worth some £760,000. However, the fact is that, on the judge's findings, the assurances were made and the values only reflect the assurances.

Comment

Does this move the law towards giving effect to the expectation in virtually all cases? To what extent is it consistent with the outcome in *Jennings*?

The Court of Appeal in *Cobbe* v *Yeoman's Row Management Ltd*[16] undertook a full discussion of the remedy. It may be recalled that C obtained planning permission, which greatly increased the value of O's land. C relied upon an informal agreement to buy the land, seeking a financial remedy equivalent to the value of the contract. The value of the expectation and the increase in the value of O's land both hugely exceeded the value of C's

---

[15] [2003] WTLR 1253 at [58], [61].
[16] [2006] 1 WLR 2964.

work. The court allowed C the value of his expectation, largely on the basis that otherwise O would be 'disproportionately advantaged'. Two further points are of interest. The first is that court found the cases difficult to reconcile, Dyson LJ observing that 'the two approaches [expectation and detriment] are fundamentally different. The cases are replete with examples, but short on analysis of the reason why one approach is adopted rather than another.'[17] The second point is that the court appeared to assume that either expectation or detriment should be chosen, rather than any compromise between them.

When *Cobbe* went to the House of Lords,[18] it was held no estoppel existed, so there was no need to consider estoppel remedies. However, C claimed an unjust enrichment remedy, based upon the increase in the value of the land. Lord Scott stated:[19]

> Since the planning permission was obtained at the expense of Mr Cobbe it is very easy to conclude that the appellant has been enriched at his expense and, in the circumstances that I need not again rehearse, unjustly enriched . . . But what is the extent of the unjust enrichment? It is not, in my opinion, the difference in market value between the property without the planning permission and the property with it. The planning permission did not create the development potential of the property; it unlocked it. The appellant was unjustly enriched because it obtained the value of Mr Cobbe's services without having to pay for them.

Does this provide any clues as to what the House of Lords would have held if an estoppel had been proved?

We shall see that purchasers from O may be bound by the estoppel: how far is a separate discretion exercised as regards the purchaser? This was considered by the Privy Council in *Henry* v *Henry*:[20]

> Nor, in the opinion of the Board, is there any substance in Miss Stacey's submission that the issue of proprietary estoppel has to be considered afresh in relation to the position of Theresa Henry as a third party purchaser. The Board does not rule out the possibility that cases may arise in which the particular circumstances surrounding a third party purchase may . . . require the court to reassess the extent of the claimant's equity in the property. However, in the instant case that issue simply does not arise since the Defence . . . contains no plea to that effect . . .

In what circumstances might it be necessary to consider the position of the purchaser?

Lastly, two points may be noted relating to C's conduct. Where that conduct pre-dates the court's giving a remedy, it appears that it can be considered by the court.[21] On the other hand, misconduct at a later date will not affect a remedy (even if equitable) already ordered.[22]

3. The proprietary status of the estoppel

So far, we have been concentrating upon the liability of O, the person who has undertaken the encouragement or acquiescence. This section looks at successors in title to that person.

---

[17] *Ibid*, at [121].
[18] [2008] 1 WLR 1752.
[19] [2008] 1 WLR 1752 at [40]–[41].
[20] [2010] 1 All ER 988 at [56].
[21] *J Willis & Son* v *Willis* [1986] 1 EGLR 62; similarly, O's conduct was considered in each of *Crabb* and *Pascoe*.
[22] *Williams* v *Staite* [1979] Ch 291.

In order for successors in title to be bound, the right must of course be more than purely personal. Most authors (and the Law Commission) make a distinction as to whether the remedy has been decided at the time of the disposition to the successor in title, though McFarlane[23] has argued that, in assessing proprietary status, there should be no difference as regards timing.

A. The status of the estoppel before a remedy has been given

Why is there a problem in these cases? If C has a right to a particular remedy then it is easy to appreciate an argument that there is an equitable right to a fee simple, easement or whatever expectation the case involves. Yet cases such as *Jennings* v *Rice* show that there are difficulties in arguing that C has a right to a particular remedy: it is more a right to the exercise of the court's discretion. In addition, difficulties arise both because the expectation may constitute a licence (not capable on conventional principles of binding successors) and because the remedy may be a monetary one.[24] In any event, there is a real problem for successors in title (particularly purchasers) in discovering what it is that they might be bound by.

There are some difficult and controversial questions of principle to be asked in this area. Is the discretion as to remedy sufficient to show that there is such a lack of certainty as to be inconsistent with proprietary status? Is it a satisfactory reply to say that what binds the purchaser is the equity arising from the detrimental reliance, or (to put it another way) the right to the exercise of the court's discretion? We should consider whether uncertainty as to remedy really is a problem for purchasers. In this regard, what is the likely response of an intending purchaser who becomes aware of an estoppel claim? Does *Baker* v *Baker & Baker* provide adequate protection to a purchaser who is prepared to proceed with the purchase?

When we turn to the cases, we find that there are numerous cases holding that estoppels do in fact bind purchasers and other successors in title. It is a fair comment that many of them pre-date *Crabb* v *Arun DC* and the modern prominence of the discretion as regards the remedy, but there are more recent cases taking exactly the same approach. It is also fair to say that the point is often assumed or else baldly asserted, yet some cases go out of their way to consider it.[25] Although some doubts had been expressed,[26] the proprietary effect of estoppels continued to be asserted.[27]

---

[23] [2003] CLJ 661; see p 634 below.
[24] See Bright and McFarlane [2005] CLJ 449. There may be a charge on the land to secure it, though it is unclear when there will be such a charge.
[25] Examples are *Inwards* v *Baker* [1965] 2 QB 29 at p 37; *ER Ives Investment Ltd* v *High* [1967] 2 QB 379; *Voyce* v *Voyce* (1991) 62 P&CR 290.
[26] See especially *United Bank of Kuwait plc* v *Sahib* [1997] Ch 107 at p 142; also Hayton [1990] Conv 370; Sir Nicolas Browne-Wilkinson, Presidential Address to the Holdsworth Club, 1990–91, reprinted (1996) 10 *Trust Law International* 98.
[27] *Lloyds Bank plc* v *Carrick* [1996] 4 All ER 630 at p 642; *Locabail (UK) Ltd* v *Bayfield Properties Ltd* [1999] The Times, 31 March; *Bhullar* v *McArdle* (2001) 82 P&CR 481 at [50]; *Sweet* v *Sommer* [2005] EWCA Civ 227; *Vehicles and Supplies Ltd* v *Financial Institutions Services Ltd* [2005] UKPC 24 at [24].

Extract 7.3.1

Land Registration Act 2002, s 116

116.—It is hereby declared for the avoidance of doubt that, in relation to registered land, each of the following—

    (a)   an equity by estoppel, and

. . .

has effect from the time the equity arises as an interest capable of binding successors in title (subject to the rules about the effect of dispositions on priority).

Comment

(1) This is intended to clarify that estoppel claims do bind purchasers of registered land. Is there any ambiguity in its wording? Is it conclusive against the views of McFarlane (p 215 above), as regards registered land?

(2) Might s 116 have an effect upon the position in unregistered land?

(3) Whether or not s 116 represents the previous law, does it represent good legal policy?

B. The status of the estoppel after a remedy has been given

Most court orders confer a conventional property right (or an entitlement to such a right) or a monetary remedy in favour of C. From that time onwards, there is no difficulty in seeing that the conventional property right (which may be equitable)[28] binds successors in title on normal priority principles; a monetary remedy is inherently personal. The single problem area is the exceptional case where the court order is for something other than a conventional property right, a licence being the best example.[29] This is considered in our discussion on licences (see Chapter 18).[30] In registered land, are such estoppel remedies within s 116 so as to be accorded proprietary status?

In fact there are very few cases involving post-remedy disputes. Commonly, the dispute is sparked off by the transferee's denial of C's claim, so that the question is whether a remedy should be ordered against the successor, not whether an existing remedy binds the successor.

C. Can the claimant transfer the benefit of an estoppel?

There is little clear guidance from the cases as to whether the benefit of estoppels can be transferred. However, in the family context the nature of many promises is such that they will be personal to C. This is especially the case where there is an understanding that C can live in a property as long as he or she wishes. Would you expect that, apart from these family cases, the benefit can be transferred? Relevant cases to consider include *Crabb* v *Arun District Council*[31] and *Taylors Fashions Ltd* v *Liverpool Victoria Trustees Co Ltd.*[32] What does the transferability of the benefit tell us about the proprietary nature of estoppels?

---

[28] If, for example, an order for the transfer of the fee simple has not yet been complied with.
[29] Rather more common may be orders for monetary compensation, but it is very difficult to see how such orders could affect subsequent purchasers unless charged on the land.
[30] See p 634 below.
[31] [1976] Ch 179; Extract 7.1.2 above.
[32] [1982] QB 133; Extract 7.1.1 above.

4. Other means of getting round formality requirements

A. Mutual benefit and burden

The idea that a person cannot take advantage of one part of an agreement without accepting a correlative obligation within that agreement is entirely natural. It is illustrated by several cases over the past half century and expressed in the following dicta of Evershed MR:[33]

> There was, therefore, something in the nature of mutual licences; and it seems to me, as a matter of plain justice and of law, that a person who is enjoying one part of such reciprocal licences cannot at the same time purport to revoke the other part which imposes a burden on him. In other words, so long as the defendant was taking the water from the plaintiff's land, or was liable to take it, through his drain under his land, the plaintiff was not entitled to revoke, or to purport to revoke, the licence which the defendant had to discharge into the manhole of the plaintiff . . .

Extract 7.4.1

ER Ives Investment Ltd v *High* [1967] 2 QB 379

High agreed with the claimant's predecessor in title that foundations of the claimant's flats might remain on High's land. In return, High (whose access to the rear of his house was compromised by the building line of the flats) could get access to his garage at the rear of his house by crossing the claimant's land at the back of the flats. The claimant sought to prevent such access, arguing that any equitable easement had not been registered as a land charge.

LORD DENNING MR: . . . The right arises out of the agreement of November 2, 1949, and the subsequent action taken on it: on the principle that 'he who takes the benefit must accept the burden'. When adjoining owners of land make an agreement to secure continuing rights and benefits for each of them in or over the land of the other, neither of them can take the benefit of the agreement and throw over the burden of it. This applies not only to the original parties, but also to their successors. The successor who takes the continuing benefit must take it subject to the continuing burden. This principle has been applied to neighbours who send their water into a common drainage system: see *Hopgood* v *Brown*;[i] and to purchasers of houses on a building estate who had the benefit of using the roads and were subject to the burden of contributing to the upkeep: see *Halsall* v *Brizell*.[ii] The principle clearly applies in the present case. The owners of the block of flats have the benefit of having their foundations in Mr High's land. So long as they take that benefit, they must shoulder the burden. They must observe the condition on which the benefit was granted, namely, they must allow Mr High and his successors to have access over their yard: cf *May* v *Belleville*.[iii] Conversely, so long as Mr High takes the benefit of the access, he must permit the block of flats to keep their foundations in his land.

[i] [1955] 1 WLR 213; [1955] 1 All ER 550, CA.
[ii] [1957] Ch 169; [1957] 2 WLR 123; [1957] 1 All ER 371.
[iii] [1905] 2 Ch 605.

Comment

(1) The case also involved an estoppel claim based upon expense undertaken by High (in resurfacing the rear access) in reliance upon this access. Does this estoppel claim possess the same characteristics as the benefit and burden claim?

---

[33] *Hopgood* v *Brown* [1955] 1 WLR 213 at p 226.

(2) Would it have been different if the claimant's predecessor (the owner of the flats) had enjoyed a once and for all benefit?[34] An example might be entry on to High's land to gain access for building the flats.

(3) Suppose the access land had been sold to the claimants but not the flats, or that the claimants had sold the flats and retained the access land. Would the result have been the same?

One particular use of the benefit and burden doctrine has been to allow positive covenants to bind purchasers from the covenantor. Positive covenants, not being proprietary interests, do not normally have this effect. However, the covenant may be reciprocal to a right which the purchaser from the covenantor wishes to enforce.

Extract 7.4.2

Halsall v Brizell [1957] Ch 169

A deed granted rights to use roads and drains on a housing estate, with obligations to pay a proper proportion of the expenses. A dispute arose concerning payment of the expenses.

UPJOHN J: . . . But it is conceded that it is ancient law that a man cannot take benefit under a deed without subscribing to the obligations thereunder. If authority is required for that proposition, I need but refer to one sentence during the argument in _Elliston v Reacher_,[i] where Lord Cozens-Hardy MR observed: 'It is laid down in Co Litt 230b, that a man who takes the benefit of a deed is bound by a condition contained in it, though he does not execute it.' If the defendants did not desire to take the benefit of this deed, for the reasons I have given, they could not be under any liability to pay the obligations thereunder. But, of course, they do desire to take the benefit of this deed . . . Therefore, it seems to me that the defendants here cannot, if they desire to use this house, as they do, take advantage of the trusts concerning the user of the roads contained in the deed and the other benefits created by it without undertaking the obligations thereunder. Upon that principle it seems to me that they are bound by this deed, if they desire to take its benefits.

[i] [1908] 2 Ch 665, 669.

Comment

Would you expect that the obligations should be registered before the benefit and burden principle can bind a purchaser? See _Elwood v Goodman_ [2014] Ch 442 at [34]–[36].

Extract 7.4.3

Rhone v Stephens [1994] 2 AC 310

The roof of a house extended over the adjoining cottage. It was argued that an obligation on the owner of the house to maintain the roof was a burden linked with the benefit of rights of support from the cottage.

LORD TEMPLEMAN: . . . Mr Munby also sought to persuade your Lordships that the effect of the decision in the _Austerberry_ case had been blunted by the 'pure principle of benefit and burden' distilled by Sir Robert Megarry V-C from the authorities in _Tito v Waddell (No 2)_ [1977]

---

[34] See _Tito v Waddell (No 2)_ [1977] Ch 106 at p 308; Aughterson [1985] Conv 12.

1 Ch 106, 301 et seq. I am not prepared to recognise the 'pure principle' that any party deriving any benefit from a conveyance must accept any burden in the same conveyance. Sir Robert Megarry V-C relied on the decision of Upjohn J in *Halsall* v *Brizell* [1957] Ch 169. . . . Conditions can be attached to the exercise of a power in express terms or by implication. *Halsall* v *Brizell* was just such a case and I have no difficulty in wholeheartedly agreeing with the decision. It does not follow that any condition can be rendered enforceable by attaching it to a right nor does it follow that every burden imposed by a conveyance may be enforced by depriving the covenantor's successor in title of every benefit which he enjoyed thereunder. The condition must be relevant to the exercise of the right. In *Halsall* v *Brizell* there were reciprocal benefits and burdens enjoyed by the users of the roads and sewers. In the present case clause 2 of the 1960 conveyance imposes reciprocal benefits and burdens of support but clause 3 which imposed an obligation to repair the roof is an independent provision. In *Halsall* v *Brizell* the defendant could, at least in theory, choose between enjoying the right and paying his proportion of the cost or alternatively giving up the right and saving his money. In the present case the owners of Walford House could not in theory or in practice be deprived of the benefit of the mutual rights of support if they failed to repair the roof.

Comment

(1) What is the 'pure principle' of benefit and burden? How does it differ from benefit and burden as recognised by Lord Templeman?

(2) In many cases (but not *Rhone*), the covenant will be imposed on a person who is purchasing land. Can a successor in title to such a purchaser keep the land and still deny liability under the covenant?

Extract 7.4.4

Thamesmead Town Ltd v *Allotey* (1998) 79 P&CR 557

As in *Halsall*, a conveyance imposed an obligation to contribute towards road repairs, landscaping, etc. Did the obligation extend to facilities that the defendant was not actively making use of?

PETER GIBSON LJ: . . . The reasoning of Lord Templeman [in *Rhone* v *Stephens*] suggests that there are two requirements for the enforceability of a positive covenant against a successor in title to the covenantor. The first is that the condition of discharging the burden must be relevant to the exercise of the rights which enable the benefit to be obtained. In *Rhone* v *Stephens* the mutual obligation of support was unrelated to and independent of the covenant to maintain the roof. The second is that the successors in title must have the opportunity to choose whether to take the benefit or having taken it to renounce it, even if only in theory, and thereby to escape the burden and that the successors in title can be deprived of the benefit if they fail to assume the burden. On both those grounds *Halsall* v *Brizell* was distinguished. Although Lord Templeman expressed his wholehearted agreement with the decision by Upjohn J, Lord Templeman's description of that decision was limited to the defendant being unable to exercise the rights to use the estate roads and to use the sewers without paying his costs of ensuring that they could be exercised. Nothing was expressly said about the cost of maintaining the sea wall or promenade and it is a little difficult to see how, consistently with Lord Templeman's reasoning and, in particular, the second requirement for the enforceability of a positive covenant, the cost of maintaining the sea wall would fall within the relevant principle.

. . . Mr Routley submitted that where the burden of a positive covenant is conditional upon a reciprocal or a relevant benefit, it will be enforced. He pointed out that this is not restricted to the benefit of rights granted by a deed. That is true. An oral agreement or arrangement will suffice, as was held in *ER Ives Investment Ltd* v *High* [1967] 2 QB 379. But that is irrelevant, as here the plaintiff has only the transfer on which it can rely. Mr Routley also pointed out that the benefits need not be expressly related to a corresponding burden but can be related by implication. That is not in dispute. He drew attention to the fact that Lord Templeman did not use the language of benefit throughout but also referred to rights and power. He submitted that this meant that Lord Templeman was deliberately distinguishing a right or power, upon which a positive covenant might be made conditional, from the benefit of a covenant. This led him to submit that the communal areas could be used or enjoyed without the defendant walking on them and that their mere existence was sufficient to confer a relevant benefit . . .

I have no hesitation in rejecting this argument. Mr Routley seems to me to read far more into Lord Templeman's words than could possibly have been intended. Lord Templeman was plainly seeking to restrict, not enlarge, the scope of the exception from the rule that positive covenants affecting freehold land are not directly enforceable except against the original covenantor. Lord Templeman treated *Halsall* v *Brizell* as a case where the right to use the estate roads and sewers was conditional on a payment of a due proportion of the maintenance expenses for those facilities. Whilst agreeing with the decision, Lord Templeman made clear that for a burden to be enforceable it must be relevant to the benefit. He said that simply to attach a right to a condition for payment would not render that condition enforceable. Similarly, it is not possible to enforce every burden in a conveyance by depriving the covenantor's successors in title of every benefit which he enjoyed under the conveyance. There must be a correlation between the burden and the benefit which the successor has chosen to take. Lord Templeman plainly rejected the notion that taking a benefit under a conveyance was sufficient to make every burden of the conveyance enforceable. Further, there is no authority to suggest that any benefit obtained by a successor in title, once the property has been transferred to him, to enable the enforcement of a burden under the conveyance is sufficient, even if that benefit was not conferred as of right by the conveyance . . .

Comment

Why did *Halsall* not apply? Did the result inevitably follow from *Rhone*? How convenient is it?

Extract 7.4.5

Wilkinson v *Kerdene Ltd* [2013] EWCA Civ 44; [2013] 2 EGLR 163

Under sale agreements, developers of a holiday village were obliged to maintain various aspects of it. Purchasers of bungalows were required to pay a fixed annual sum (inflation adjusted).

PATTEN LJ: 30.   In [*Thamesmead Town Ltd* v *Allotey*] it was possible to apportion the amount claimed for repairs between the various facilities on the estate just as in a conventional service charge for a block of flats. Insofar as the defendants had no rights to use the communal areas, they could not be compelled to pay that part of the bill. But it has always been accepted in this case that the payment of a fixed annual amount increased by reference to an index of inflation rather than the actual cost incurred is not capable of being apportioned in that way. . . .
31.   [Counsel's] submission was that the consequence of this is that the burden of the fixed sum does not correlate with the exercise of the rights . . .
32.   But that, with respect to him, is a *non sequitur*. In the . . . conveyances the payment is due . . . for the purpose of maintaining the roads, car parks, pleasure grounds and other recreational facilities . . .
33.   . . . Although the continued exercise of the rights is not made expressly conditional upon payment (any more than it was in *Halsall* v *Brizell* or in *Thamesmead Town Ltd* v *Allotey*) the payment is intended to ensure that the rights remain capable of being exercised. The authorities require one to look beyond the express terms of the conveyance and consider what in

substance the covenantor is paying for. Here, as in *Halsall* v *Brizell*, the payment, at least in substantial part, is intended to provide a contribution to the cost of maintaining the roads and other facilities over which the owners of the bungalows are granted rights. None of them has ceased to use the roads nor wishes to do so.

Comment

(1) The purchasers of bungalows complained that some of the required maintenance was not being undertaken, or that they did not benefit from it. How and why was *Thamesmead* distinguished?

(2) Should one feel sympathy for the purchasers when not all the required work had been undertaken?

B. Donor doing all in his power

Extract 7.4.6

Milroy v *Lord* (1862) 4 De GF&J 264 (45 ER 1185)

TURNER LJ: . . . I take the law of this Court to be well settled, that, in order to render a voluntary settlement valid and effectual, the settler must have done everything which, according to the nature of the property comprised in the settlement, was necessary to be done in order to transfer the property and render the settlement binding upon him. He may of course do this by actually transferring the property to the persons for whom he intends to provide, and the provision will then be effectual, and it will be equally effectual if he transfers the property to a trustee for the purposes of the settlement, or declares that he himself holds it in trust for those purposes; and if the property be personal, the trust may, as I apprehend, be declared either in writing or by parol; but, in order to render the settlement binding, one or other of these modes must, as I understand the law of this Court, be resorted to, for there is no equity in this Court to perfect an imperfect gift . . .

Comment

This is the leading authority for the proposition that equity will not enforce failed gifts. However, it contains the seed of an exception.

Extract 7.4.7

Re Rose [1949] Ch 78

JENKINS J: . . . It is argued on behalf of the residuary legatee that the testator's transfer of the 5,000 preference shares to Mr Hook, owing to the fact that the transfer was not registered in his lifetime, was at the time of the testator's death in the state of being an incomplete or inchoate gift. I was referred on that to the well-known case of *Milroy* v *Lord*,[i] and also to the recent case of *In re Fry*.[ii] Those cases, as I understand them, turn on the fact that the deceased donor had not done all in his power, according to the nature of the property given, to vest the legal interest in the property in the donee. In such circumstances it is, of course, well settled that there is no equity to complete the imperfect gift. If any act remained to be done by the donor to complete the gift at the date of the donor's death the court will not compel his personal representatives to do that act and the gift remains incomplete and fails.

. . . In this case, as I understand it, the testator had done everything in his power to divest himself of the shares in question to Mr Hook. He had executed a transfer. It is not suggested that the transfer was not in accordance with the company's regulations. He had handed that transfer together with the certificates to Mr Hook. There was nothing else the testator could do. It is true that Mr Hook's legal title would not be perfected until the directors passed the transfer for registration, but that was not an act which the testator had to do, it was an act which depended on the discretion of the directors. Therefore it seems to me that the present case is not in pari materia with the two cases to which I have been referred.

[i] 4 De GF&J 264.
[ii] [1946] Ch 312.

Comment

(1) *Re Rose* involved the construction of a will. However, the Court of Appeal in a different case also called *Re Rose*[35] approved Jenkins J and stressed that the analysis means that the donee has a full equitable interest.

(2) The principle obviously applies to the transfer of shares. When else might it apply? Is it obvious that donors should not be allowed to change their minds before their gifts are complete? Note that in most cases the gift has subsequently been completed at law: the question is usually whether the equitable title passed at an earlier time.

(3) It is clear that the principle operates even if an act remains to be done, provided it can be undertaken by the transferee.[36]

Extract 7.4.8

Pennington v *Waine* [2002] 1 WLR 2075

The question arose as to whether a share assignment was valid in equity without delivery of the share transfer to the transferee (the transferor had died).

ARDEN LJ: 52.   This appeal raises the question of what is necessary for the purposes of a valid equitable assignment of shares by way of gift. If the transaction had been for value, a contract to assign the shares would have been sufficient: neither the execution nor the delivery of an instrument of transfer would have been required. However, where the transaction was purely voluntary, the principle that equity will not assist a volunteer must be applied and respected. This principle is to be found in *Milroy* v *Lord* and other cases on which Mr Weatherill relies, such as *Jones* v *Lock*, *Warriner* v *Rogers* and *Richards* v *Delbridge*: see in particular the citation from the judgment of Turner LJ set out above. Accordingly the gift must be perfected, or 'completely constituted'.

54.   Thus explained, the principle that equity will not assist a volunteer at first sight looks like a hard-edged rule of law not permitting much argument or exception. Historically the emergence of the principle may have been due to the need for equity to follow the law rather than an intuitive development of equity. The principle against imperfectly constituted gifts led to harsh and seemingly paradoxical results. Before long, equity had tempered the wind to the shorn lamb (i.e. the donee). It did so on more than one occasion and in more than one way.

55.   Firstly it was held that an incompletely constituted gift could be upheld if the gift had been completed to such an extent that the donee could enforce his right to the shares as against third parties without forcing the donor to take any further step . . .

[35] [1952] Ch 499.
[36] *Mascall* v *Mascall* (1984) 50 P&CR 119 (application for registration of a transfer of land).

56.   That exception was extended in *Re Rose*, *Rose* v *IRC* and other cases by holding that for this exception to apply it was not necessary that the donor should have done all that it was necessary to be done to complete the gift, short of registration of the transfer. On the contrary it was sufficient if the donor had done all that it was necessary for him or her to do.

59.   Secondly equity has tempered the wind (of the principle that equity will not assist a volunteer) to the shorn lamb (the donee) by utilising the constructive trust. This does not constitute a declaration of trust and thus does not fall foul of the principle (see *Milroy* v *Lord* and *Jones* v *Lock*, above) that an imperfectly constituted gift is not saved by being treated as a declaration of trust . . .

60.   Thirdly equity has tempered the wind to the shorn lamb by applying a benevolent construction to words of gift. As explained above an imperfect gift is not saved by being treated as a declaration of trust. But where a court of equity is satisfied that the donor had an intention to make an immediate gift, the court will construe the words which the donor used as words effecting a gift or declaring a trust if they can fairly bear that meaning and otherwise the gift will fail . . .

62.   The cases to which Counsel have referred us do not reveal any, or any consistent single policy consideration behind the rule that the court will not perfect an imperfect gift. The objectives of the rule obviously include ensuring that donors do not by acting voluntarily act unwisely in a way that they may subsequently regret . . . There must also be, in the interests of legal certainty, a clearly ascertainable point in time at which it can be said that the gift was completed, and this point in time must be arrived at on a principled basis.

63.   There are countervailing policy considerations which would militate in favour of holding a gift to be completely constituted. These would include effectuating, rather than frustrating, the clear and continuing intention of the donor, and preventing the donor from acting in a manner which is unconscionable . . .

64.   If one proceeds on the basis that a principle which animates the answer to the question whether an apparently incomplete gift is to be treated as completely constituted is that a donor will not be permitted to change his or her mind if it would be unconscionable, in the eyes of equity, vis à vis the donee to do so, what is the position here? There can be no comprehensive list of factors which makes it unconscionable for the donor to change his or her mind: it must depend on the court's evaluation of all the relevant considerations. What then are the relevant facts here? Ada made the gift of her own free will: there is no finding that she was not competent to do this. She not only told Harold about the gift and signed a form of transfer which she delivered to Mr Pennington for him to secure registration: her agent also told Harold that he need take no action. In addition Harold agreed to become a director of the Company without limit of time . . .

65.   There is next the pure question of law: was it necessary for Ada [to] deliver the form of transfer to Harold? I have referred above to the difference of view between Evershed MR and Jenkins LJ. In *Re Rose*, *Rose* v *IRC* the issue was whether the gift was perfected by 10 April 1943, by which date the donor had executed the declarations of gift and delivered the share transfers to reflect the gifts to the transferees. Argument was not therefore directed to the question whether a beneficial interest in the shares passed on the dates of the declarations of trust or on the date on which the share transfers were handed over. For my own part I do not consider that it was necessary to the conclusions of Evershed MR that the gift should have taken effect before the transfers were delivered to the transferees. Indeed for him so to hold would not in my view be consistent with the second sentence cited from the relevant part of his judgment (set out above) or with the fact that he went on to approve as a correct statement of the law the decision of Jenkins J in *Re Rose*, *Midland Bank* v *Rose* (where, the share transfers having been delivered to the donee, the gift was held to be perfect because there was nothing else the donor could do) or with the fact that Morris LJ agreed with both judgments. Moreover if this were the view of Evershed MR it seems to me that it would not in my view be possible to reconcile it with *Milroy* v *Lord*, and in particular with the principle that the court will not convert

an imperfect gift into a declaration of trust. There could not be a constructive trust until the gift was perfected. The conclusion of Jenkins LJ was predicated on the basis that delivery of the transfer to the donee was necessary and had occurred. Likewise the decision of this court in *Mascall* v *Mascall* and of the Privy Council in *Pehrsson* v *von Greyerz* were predicated on the same basis. I have summarised those cases earlier in this judgment. Accordingly the ratio of *Re Rose, Rose* v *IRC* was as I read it that the gifts of shares in that case were completely constituted when the donor executed share transfers and delivered them to the transferees even though they were not registered in the register of members of the company until a later date.

66.   However, that conclusion as to the ratio in *Re Rose, Rose* v *IRC* does not mean that [this gift was ineffective]. Even if I am correct in my view that the Court of Appeal took the view in *Re Rose, Rose* v *IRC* that delivery of the share transfers was there required, it does not follow that delivery cannot in some circumstances be dispensed with. Here, there was a clear finding that Ada intended to make an immediate gift. Harold was informed of it. Moreover, I have already expressed the view that a stage was reached when it would have been unconscionable for Ada to recall the gift. It follows that it would also have been unconscionable for her personal representatives to refuse to hand over the share transfer to Harold after her death. In those circumstances, in my judgment, delivery of the share transfer before her death was unnecessary so far as perfection of the gift was concerned.

Comment

(1) Is delivery essential for the principle in *Re Rose* to operate?

(2) What is the role of unconscionability? Why did it apply in *Pennington*?

(3) Do the earlier cases support the conclusion in *Pennington*?[37]

(4) Briggs J has observed[38] that he had no 'great comfort that the existing rules about the circumstances when equity will and will not perfect an apparently imperfect gift of shares serve any clearly identifiable or rational policy objective'. Is that justified?

C. Rules relating to death

The Wills Act 1837 lays down quite strict rules for the validity of wills. This, together with the occasionally unwelcome publicity of wills, has led to attempts to make gifts on death other than by will. Although statutory policy points against their recognition, a number of exceptions have been accepted. It has already been seen that estoppel may occasionally be used to enforce promises to leave property by will.

(i) Secret trusts

Although they have limited practical application, secret trusts involve difficult issues relating to principle and policy. Property may be given to a person by will, that person promising (either before or after the will) to hold the property on trust for another. The courts are prepared to enforce the promise to hold on trust, despite the fact that it does not satisfy the Wills Act requirements. It is easy to see that it would be fraudulent for the legatee to take the property beneficially: it is not unlike the constructive trust in cases such as *Ashburn Anstalt* v *Arnold*.[39] An alternative analysis is that the trust takes effect outside the will and

---

[37] In *Zeital* v *Kaye* [2010] WTLR 913, the Court of Appeal appeared to take formality requirements more seriously.
[38] *Curtis* v *Pulbrook* [2011] 1 BCLC 638 at [47]; no gift, where no reliance by intended donee.
[39] [1989] Ch 1 (Extract 6.2.11 above).

therefore is not affected by the formality requirements. How well does such an analysis fit with trusts principles? When would the trust take effect?[40]

This principle is extended to half-secret trusts: the legatee (who has agreed to hold for the beneficiary) is appointed a trustee by the will, but the will does not declare the beneficial interests. Does the rationale for enforcing fully secret trusts apply as readily to half-secret trusts? A special rule for half-secret trusts is that the communication of the beneficial interests to the legatee has to pre-date the will;[41] there is no such rule for fully secret trusts. Can this difference be justified?

(ii) Mutual wills

Two people sometimes make wills leaving property to each other and, should the other be dead, to the same third party. If it is agreed that the survivor will enjoy the other's property, but that all should end up with the agreed third party, then the law recognises this. It may mean that the survivor is obliged to leave the property received under the will to the agreed person (less what is required during the survivor's lifetime) and also to leave his or her own separate property to that person.

Extract 7.4.9

Re Goodchild Dec'd **[1997] 1 WLR 1216**

LEGGATT LJ: . . . Two wills may be in the same form as each other. Each testator may leave his or her estate to the other with a view to the survivor leaving both estates to their heir. But there is no presumption that a present plan will be immutable in future. A key feature of the concept of mutual wills is the irrevocability of the mutual intentions. Not only must they be binding when made, but the testators must have undertaken, and so must be bound, not to change their intentions after the death of the first testator . . .

MORRITT LJ: . . . The doctrine of mutual wills is anomalous. The bequest of his entire estate by a husband to his wife absolutely and beneficially with a gift over of whatever was left at her death could not take effect in accordance with its terms. Either the interest taken by the wife would be limited or the gift over would be void as repugnant to the absolute and beneficial nature of the gift. Similarly the bare promise of the wife to leave her property by will in a particular manner would be unenforceable for any will she then made would be revocable under the Wills Act 1837. In my judgment, if these principles are to be excluded in the case of mutual wills it is essential that there should be a contract to that effect. In my view that is what both principle and the authorities require.

Comment

Is this reluctance to apply mutual wills save in very clear cases necessary in order to accord with trusts and wills principles? Does it represent good legal policy?

(iii) The rule in *Strong* v *Bird*

This curious rule applies where a gift is ineffective, but the donee is made the executor of the donor's will.

---

[40] *Re Gardner* [1923] 2 Ch 230 employs an analysis that the trust arises before death (beneficiary under secret trust predeceased testatrix: the trust was effective despite the normal rule that gifts by will lapse if a legatee predeceases).

[41] *Re Keen* [1937] Ch 236 at p 246.

Extract 7.4.10

Re Innes **[1910] 1 Ch 188**

PARKER J: . . . It has been held in the case of *Strong v Bird*[i] that where a testator has attempted to forgive a debt by telling his debtor that the debt is forgiven, though that cannot at law operate as a release, yet there is a present intention of giving, which, if the debt is subsequently released, may be effectual, and that the appointment of the debtor subsequently as an executor is a sufficient release at law to give validity to the gift which was otherwise imperfect. That is a decision of Sir George Jessel in 1874, and it has been acted upon, I think, ever since, and recently has been somewhat extended by a decision of Neville J in *In re Stewart*.[ii] The way in which the principle enunciated by Sir George Jessel has been extended is that it has been made, according to Neville J's decision, applicable not only to the release of a debt, but in order to perfect an imperfect gift of specific property . . .

It is attempted here to extend the doctrine of those cases still further. In the first place it is attempted to extend it to what, if there was a gift at all, was a gift of money without that money being identified, or sufficiently identified to enable it to be separated from the rest of the estate of the testator; and in the second place it is attempted to extend the principle of the earlier cases not only to an actual attempted gift which as a matter of fact is imperfect, and therefore will not take effect unless it is subsequently perfected, but to a mere promise to give on a future occasion.

In my opinion the principle of *Strong v Bird* and *In re Stewart* and other similar cases ought not to be so extended. What is wanted in order to make that principle applicable is certain definite property which a donor has attempted to give to a donee, but has not succeeded. There must be in every case a present intention of giving, the gift being imperfect for some reason at law, and then a subsequent perfection of that gift by the appointment of the donee to be executor of the donor, so that he takes the legal estate by virtue of the executorship conferred upon him. It seems to me that it would be exceedingly dangerous to try to give effect by the appointment of an executor to what is at most an announcement of what a man intends to do in the future, and is not intended by him as a gift in the present which though failing on technical considerations may be subsequently perfected.

[i] LR 18 Eq 315.
[ii] [1908] 2 Ch 251.

Neville J in *In re Stewart* had explained the rule as follows:

> The reasoning by which the conclusion is reached is of a double character – first, that the vesting of the property in the executor at the testator's death completes the imperfect gift made in the lifetime, and, secondly, that the intention of the testator to give the beneficial interest to the executor is sufficient to countervail the equity of beneficiaries under the will, the testator having vested the legal estate in the executor.

Comment

(1) Are the reasons for recognising these gifts convincing?

(2) The principle has been extended[42] to those appointed as administrators by the court (when there is no effective appointment of personal representatives by will). How well does this accord with principle?

(3) The intention of making a gift must be unchanged up to death.

---

[42] *Re James* [1935] Ch 449, questioned in *Re Gonin* [1979] Ch 16.

(iv) *Donationes mortis causa*

These 'amphibious'[43] gifts combine elements of inter vivos gifts and gifts by will. There is a delivery, but the gift is to be effective only on death.

Extract 7.4.11

Sen v Headley [1991] Ch 425

NOURSE LJ: [T]hree general requirements for such a gift may be stated very much as they are stated in *Snell's Equity*, 29th ed (1990), pp 380–383. First, the gift must be made in contemplation, although not necessarily in expectation, of impending death. Secondly, the gift must be made upon the condition that it is to be absolute and perfected only on the donor's death, being revocable until that event occurs and ineffective if it does not. Thirdly, there must be a delivery of the subject matter of the gift, or the essential indicia of title thereto, which amounts to a parting with dominion and not mere physical possession over the subject matter of the gift . . .

Let it be agreed that the doctrine is anomalous. Anomalies do not justify anomalous exceptions. If due account is taken of the present state of the law in regard to mortgages and choses in action, it is apparent that to make a distinction in the case of land would be to make just such an exception. A donatio mortis causa of land is neither more nor less anomalous than any other. Every such gift is a circumvention of the Wills Act 1837. Why should the additional statutory formalities for the creation and transmission of interests in land be regarded as some larger obstacle? . . .

. . . Finally, while we certainly agree that the policy of the law in regard to the formalities for the creation and transmission of interests in land should be upheld, we have to acknowledge that that policy has been substantially modified by the developments to which we have referred.

Comment

(1) It should be noted that, as well as not having to satisfy the Wills Act, these gifts do not have to satisfy strictly the normal rules for inter vivos transfers. In particular, transfer of indicia of title, such as the title deeds in *Sen*, will suffice and the delivery rules are relaxed.

(2) *Sen* recognises the anomalous nature of these gifts but declines to restrict their scope. Does this represent good policy?

Further reading

Bright, S and McFarlane, B [2005] CLJ 449: Proprietary estoppel and property rights.

Davis, C J [1998] CLJ 522: The principle of benefit and burden.

Dixon, M (2010) 30 LS 408: Confining and defining proprietary estoppel: the role of unconscionability.

Gardner, S (2006) 122 LQR 492: The remedial discretion in proprietary estoppel – again.

Handley, K R [2008] Conv 382: Unconscionability in estoppel by conduct: a triable issue or underlying principle?

Mee, J (2008) 'The role of expectation in the determination of proprietary estoppel remedies', in *Modern Studies in Property Law*, Vol 5, ed. Cooke, Chapter 16.

Neuberger, Lord [2009] CLJ 537: The stuffing of Minerva's owl? Taxonomy and taxidermy in equity.

Piska, N (2009) 72 MLR 998: Hopes, expectations and revocable promises in proprietary estoppel.

Robertson, A [2008] Conv 295: The reliance basis of proprietary estoppel remedies.

---

[43]   *Re Beaumont* [1902] 1 Ch 889 at p 892.

8
The family home

The large numbers of cases on this topic, stretching over several decades, demonstrate great difficulty and uncertainty in identifying and applying legal principles. A number of factors combine to make the area particularly fraught. The family home is a very important and valuable asset: the principles under discussion can apply to different assets, but the cases concentrate almost exclusively upon the home. In addition, the nature of family relationships is such that not only will there be informality, but the parties are unlikely to have articulated their intentions at all clearly (even if they have formed intentions in the first place).

In some countries, these factors are recognised by according spouses and (in defined cases) other partners rights to a share in the family home and other assets. English law has not developed such rights. However, there is a wide discretion to vary property rights on marriage breakdown[1] and virtually all ownership disputes between husband and wife are decided under this discretion. But two very large areas lie outside this jurisdiction. The discretion does not affect creditors' rights: mortgagees can be affected by rights under a trust, but not by a future exercise of the discretion. Second, the discretion does not extend to unmarried couples (unless civil partners), so their disputes regarding ownership of the family home continue to be resolved on trusts principles.

In this chapter we will observe that the law is dominated by two pairs of cases: 45 years ago, the basic structure of the law was established by the House of Lords in *Pettitt* v *Pettitt*[2] and, 15 months later, *Gissing* v *Gissing*.[3] These employed a trust based upon common intention, declining to develop specific family assets principles. More recently, *Stack* v *Dowden*[4] in the House of Lords and *Jones* v *Kernott*[5] in the Supreme Court have developed the principles to take account of the requirements of modern society, establishing that the trust works as a common intention constructive trust. Considerable flexibility was introduced, countering stricter rules introduced 20 years earlier by the House of Lords in *Lloyds Bank plc* v *Rosset*.[6] These cases, especially the two most recent ones, will be considered in some detail in this chapter.

A final feature of the cases in the past two decades is the recognition of two stages.[7] At the first stage, we set out to decide whether there is a common intention either to share the property at all, or to vary the prima facie shares. The second stage is to establish the exact size of the shares. We shall see that different criteria operate at these two stages.

---

[1] Matrimonial Causes Act 1973, s 24: Extract 12.3.10 below. This extends to civil partners.
[2] [1970] AC 777.
[3] [1971] AC 886.
[4] [2007] 2 AC 432.
[5] [2012] 1 AC 776.
[6] [1991] 1 AC 107.
[7] Resulting from *Oxley* v *Hiscock* [2005] Fam 211 and developed in *Jones* v *Kernott*.

1. Declaring the beneficial interests

Extract 8.1.1

Goodman v *Gallant* [1986] Fam 106

The defendant shared the beneficial interest in a house with her husband. On the breakdown of the marriage, the defendant and plaintiff (her new partner) bought out the husband's half share. The transfer of the legal title to the plaintiff and defendant declared them to be joint tenants in equity.

SLADE LJ: . . . If, however, the relevant conveyance contains an express declaration of trust which comprehensively declares the beneficial interests in the property or its proceeds of sale, there is no room for the application of the doctrine of resulting implied or constructive trusts unless and until the conveyance is set aside or rectified; until that event the declaration contained in the document speaks for itself.

We have prefaced any consideration of the decided cases with these observations because in the light of certain judicial observations we seek to make two points clear. First, in our judgment, sections 34 to 36 of the Law of Property Act 1925 do not enable or assist a person to establish a beneficial interest in land or its proceeds of sale greater than or different in nature from the interest which he would have enjoyed if those sections had not been enacted . . . Secondly, the many decisions which deal with the situation where the legal estate in land has been conveyed to persons as joint tenants without any declaration of the beneficial interest are, in our opinion, clearly distinguishable from cases where an express declaration of the beneficial interests has been made.

. . .

Lord Diplock in *Gissing* v *Gissing* [1971] AC 886, 905, reaffirmed the general principle:

'where the trust is expressly declared in the instrument by which the legal estate is transferred to the trustee or by a written declaration of trust by the trustee, the court must give effect to it.'

However, the reference by Lord Upjohn in *Pettitt* v *Pettitt* [1970] AC 777, 813, to the possibility of 'fraud or mistake at the time of the transaction' illustrates that there is one (though we think only one) qualification to this principle. The declaration of trust will no longer be binding if the court is satisfied by appropriate evidence either that the relevant document ought to be rectified (as was Buckley J in a case also named *Wilson* v *Wilson* [1969] 1 WLR 1470) or that it ought to be rescinded on the grounds of fraud or mistake.

. . .

In these circumstances the overwhelming preponderance of authority, including the three decisions of this court in *Wilson* v *Wilson* [1963] 1 WLR 601, *Leake (formerly Bruzzi)* v *Bruzzi* [1974] 1 WLR 1528 and *Pink* v *Lawrence*, 36 P&CR 98, in our judgment both entitle and oblige us to hold that, in the absence of any claim for rectification or rescission, the provision in the conveyance declaring that the plaintiff and the defendant were to hold the proceeds of sale of the property 'upon trust for themselves as joint tenants' concludes the question of the respective beneficial interests of the two parties in so far as that declaration of trust, on its true construction, exhaustively declares the beneficial interests.

Comment

(1) Given that the defendant had a half share before the purchase from the husband, was there merit in her claim to a three-quarters share?

(2) The approach in *Goodman* was approved by the House of Lords in *Stack* v *Dowden*,[8] which also confirms that stating that the survivor can give a good receipt does not trigger *Goodman*.

(3) We shall see that *Jones* v *Kernott*[9] shows that an initial common intention can later be varied. That case did not involve an express declaration of beneficial interests, but could such a variation circumvent *Goodman*?[10]

2. Resulting or constructive trust

Where the beneficial interests are not declared, the original legal analysis was probably that of a resulting trust, based on financial contributions to the purchase. However, this is immediately complicated by the fact that the purchase of most homes is funded by a mortgage loan representing nearly all the cost of the property. More fundamentally, it fails to recognise non-financial contributions, in particular caring for children, and fails to give effect to the expectations of many couples.

In *Gissing* v *Gissing*,[11] Lord Diplock left the nature of the trust open: 'A resulting, implied or constructive trust – and it is unnecessary for present purposes to distinguish between these three classes of trust . . .'. More recently, it has become apparent that the constructive trust provides greater flexibility, both as regards finding a common intention and determining the shares.

Extract 8.2.1

Oxley v Hiscock [2007] 2 AC 432

CHADWICK LJ: 24. The first question on this appeal, therefore, is whether the judge was required, by the decision of this court in *Springette* v *Defoe*, to find that, in the absence of some 'shared intention [as to the proportions in which they should be entitled] communicated between them and made manifest at the time of the transaction itself', the property was held upon a resulting trust for Mr Hiscock and Mrs Oxley in beneficial shares proportionate to the respective financial contributions which they had made to the acquisition cost. Or was the judge entitled and required – as she plainly thought – to follow the approach adopted by this court in *Midland Bank plc* v *Cooke* [1995] 4 All ER 562.

The decision in *Midland Bank plc* v *Cooke*

53. . . . The issue in [*Cooke*] – as to the extent of the wife's beneficial interest in the former matrimonial home – arose in proceedings brought by the bank to enforce a charge given by the husband to secure a business loan. The property had been purchased with the assistance of a mortgage advance (£6,450); the balance being found out of a wedding gift from the husband's parents (£1,100) and the husband's own moneys (£1,000 or thereabouts). The property was conveyed into the husband's sole name. There had been no discussion or agreement between husband and wife at the time of the acquisition as to the basis upon which the property was

---

[8] [2007] 2 AC 432. *Pankhania* v *Chandegra* [2013] 1 P&CR 238 confirms that this is unaffected by *Jones* v *Kernott* [2012] 1 AC 776.
[9] [2012] 1 AC 776.
[10] See *Clarke* v *Meadus* [2013] WTLR 199 at [46], [53], [83].
[11] [1971] AC 886 at p 905.

held by the husband, or as to the extent of their respective beneficial interests. Treating the wedding gift as made to husband and wife equally, it had been held in the county court that the wife was entitled to a beneficial interest on the basis of her contribution to the purchase price. But, following the approach in *Springette* v *Defoe*, the judge had held that the extent of that beneficial interest was limited to the proportion (6.47%) which her contribution (equal to one half of the wedding gift) bore to the whole. This court (Stuart-Smith, Waite and Schiemann LJJ) took a different view, holding that the wife was entitled to a half share in the property.

55.   After referring to the observations of Dillon LJ in *Springette* v *Defoe*, at p 393d–h, which I have already set out earlier in this judgment, and having compared the approach of the same judge in *McHardy & Sons* v *Warren* [1994] 2 FLR 338, 340 – in which Dillon LJ had said:

> 'To my mind it is irresistible conclusion that where a parent pays the deposit, either directly to the solicitors or to the bride and groom, it matters not which, on the purchase of their first matrimonial home, it is the intention of all three of them that the bride and groom should have equal interests in the matrimonial home, not interests measured by reference to the percentage half the deposit [bears] to the full price . . .'

– Waite LJ went on to observe [1995] 4 All ER 562, 572:

> 'I confess that I find the differences of approach in these two cases mystifying. In the one a strict resulting trust geared to mathematical calculation of the proportion of the purchase price provided by cash contribution is treated as virtually immutable in the absence of express agreement: in the other a displacement of the cash-related trust by inferred agreement is not only permitted but treated as obligatory.'

57.   Waite LJ . . . continued, at 574:

> 'The general principle to be derived from *Gissing* v *Gissing* and *Grant* v *Edwards* can in my judgment be summarised in this way. When the court is proceeding, in cases like the present where the partner without legal title has successfully asserted an equitable interest through direct contribution, to determine (in the absence of express evidence of intention) what proportions the parties must be assumed to have intended for their beneficial ownership, the duty of the judge is to undertake a survey of the whole course of dealing between the parties relevant to their ownership and occupation of the property and their sharing of its burdens and advantages. That scrutiny will not confine itself to the limited range of acts of direct contribution of the sort that are needed to found a beneficial interest in the first place. It will take into consideration all conduct which throws light on the question what shares were intended. Only if that search proves inconclusive does the court fall back on the maxim that "equality is equity".'

58.   [He concluded that] the court is not bound to deal with the matter on the strict basis of the trust resulting from the cash contribution to the purchase price, and is free to attribute to the parties an intention to share the beneficial interest in some different proportions . . .

60.   I return, therefore, to the first question on this appeal – whether the judge was required by the decision of this court in *Springette* v *Defoe* [1992] 2 FLR 388 to find that, in the absence of some shared intention as to the proportions in which they should be entitled to the property communicated between them at the time of the purchase, the property was held upon a resulting trust for Mr Hiscock and Mrs Oxley in beneficial shares proportionate to the respective financial contributions which they had made to the acquisition cost. In my view the judge was not so required. For my part, I doubt whether the observations in *Springette* v *Defoe* upon which the defendant relies did, in truth, reflect the state of the law at the time when that appeal was decided. Be that as it may, they have not done so since the decision of this court in *Midland Bank plc* v *Cooke* [1995] 4 All ER 562. I reject the submission, in so far as it was pursued in argument, that *Midland Bank plc* v *Cooke* was wrongly decided . . .

Extract 8.2.2

Stack v *Dowden* [2007] 2 AC 432

LADY HALE: 60. The presumption of resulting trust is not a rule of law. According to Lord Diplock in *Pettitt* v *Pettitt* [1970] AC 777, 823h, the equitable presumptions of intention are 'no more than a consensus of judicial opinion disclosed by reported cases as to the most likely inference of fact to be drawn in the absence of any evidence to the contrary'. Equity, being concerned with commercial realities, presumed against gifts and other windfalls (such as survivorship). But even equity was prepared to presume a gift where the recipient was the provider's wife or child. These days, the importance to be attached to who paid for what in a domestic context may be very different from its importance in other contexts or long ago. As Kevin Gray and Susan Francis Gray, in *Elements of Land Law*, 4th ed (2005), point out, at p 864, para 10.21:

> 'In recent decades a new pragmatism has become apparent in the law of trusts. English courts have eventually conceded that the classical theory of resulting trusts, with its fixation on intentions presumed to have been formulated contemporaneously with the acquisition of title, has substantially broken down . . . Simultaneously the balance of emphasis in the law of trusts has transferred from crude factors of money contribution (which are pre-eminent in the resulting trust) towards more subtle factors of intentional bargain (which are the foundational premise of the constructive trust) . . . But the undoubted consequence is that the doctrine of resulting trust has conceded much of its field of application to the constructive trust, which is nowadays fast becoming the primary phenomenon in the area of implied trusts.'

Extract 8.2.3

Jones v *Kernott* [2012] 1 AC 776

LORD WALKER and LADY HALE: 25. The time has come to make it clear, in line with *Stack* v *Dowden* (see also *Abbott* v *Abbott* [2007] UKPC 53 . . .), that in the case of the purchase of a house or flat in joint names for joint occupation by a married or unmarried couple, where both are responsible for any mortgage, there is no presumption of a resulting trust arising from their having contributed to the deposit (or indeed the rest of the purchase) in unequal shares. The presumption is that the parties intended a joint tenancy both in law and in equity. But that presumption can of course be rebutted by evidence of a contrary intention, which may more readily be shown where the parties did not share their financial resources.

Comment

(1) The preceding paragraph in *Jones*, supported by dicta in *Stack* and *Abbott*, indicates that the resulting trust is equally inappropriate for single name transfers.

(2) How convincing are the arguments in these cases in favour of the constructive trust analysis?

(3) How far would you expect these cases to apply to other family relationships?[12]

(4) These cases centre on joint names transfers and the quantification of the shares. They are studied further in those contexts (Extracts 8.4.1 and 8.4.3; 8.6.1–8.6.3.)

---

[12] See *Adekunle* v *Ritchie* [2007] WTLR 1505; *Laskar* v *Laskar* [2008] 1 WLR 2695; *Chaudhary* v *Chaudhary* [2013] 2 FLR 1526 (all parents and children); *Gallarotti* v *Sebastianelli* [2012] 2FLR 1231 (friends).

3. Inferring and imputing intentions

The common intention that is at the heart of the constructive trust is relatively rarely explicitly agreed by the parties. Explicit agreement is likely to be accompanied by an express declaration of interests. Instead, the court finds the common intention from the circumstances. As the following extracts show, the debate is whether the court is finding what the parties really intended (inferred intention) or what the court considers to be a sensible intention or outcome (imputed intention).

Extract 8.3.1

Stack v Dowden [2007] 2 AC 432

LORD WALKER: 20.   Lord Diplock [in *Gissing*] then proceeded to explain the circumstances in which the court would find a 'resulting, implied or constructive trust', and in particular when the court would 'infer [the parties'] common intention from their conduct': p 906b. The very important passage which follows, at pp 906b–910a, uses the word 'infer' (in various parts of speech) at least 23 times. But for the substitution of the word 'infer' for 'impute' the substance of the reasoning is, it seems to me, essentially the same (although worked out in a good deal more detail) as Lord Diplock's reasoning in *Pettitt* v *Pettitt* [1970] AC 777, when he was in the minority.

21.   . . . The whole problem is very helpfully discussed in chapter 10 of *Gray & Gray, Elements of Land Law*, 4th ed (2005), especially (as to the lack of reality of the bargain requirement) paras 10.92 to 10.99. Your Lordships may think that only a judge of Lord Diplock's stature could have achieved such a remarkable reversal of the tidal flow of authority as has followed on his speech in *Gissing* v *Gissing* [1971] AC 886. But it might have been better for the long-term development of the law if this House's rejection of 'imputation' in *Pettitt* v *Pettitt* [1970] AC 777 had been openly departed from (under the statement as to judicial precedent made by the Lord Chancellor in 1966) rather than being circumvented by the rather ambiguous (and perhaps deliberately ambiguous) language of 'inference.'

LORD NEUBERGER: 125.   While an intention may be inferred as well as express, it may not, at least in my opinion, be imputed. That appears to me to be consistent both with normal principles and with the majority view of this House in *Pettitt* v *Pettitt* [1970] AC 777, as accepted by all but Lord Reid in *Gissing* v *Gissing* [1971] AC 886, 897h, 898b–d, 900e–g, 901b–d, 904e–f, and reiterated by the Court of Appeal in *Grant* v *Edwards* [1986] Ch 638, 651f–653a. The distinction between inference and imputation may appear a fine one (and in *Gissing* v *Gissing* [1971] AC 886, 902g–h, Lord Pearson, who, on a fair reading I think rejected imputation, seems to have equated it with inference), but it is important.

126.   An inferred intention is one which is objectively deduced to be the subjective actual intention of the parties, in the light of their actions and statements. An imputed intention is one which is attributed to the parties, even though no such actual intention can be deduced from their actions and statements, and even though they had no such intention. Imputation involves concluding what the parties would have intended, whereas inference involves concluding what they did intend.

127.   To impute an intention would not only be wrong in principle and a departure from two decisions of your Lordships' House in this very area, but it also would involve a judge in an exercise which was difficult, subjective and uncertain. (Hence the advantage of the resulting trust presumption). It would be difficult because the judge would be constructing an intention where none existed at the time, and where the parties may well not have been able to agree. It would be subjective for obvious reasons. It would be uncertain because it is unclear whether one considers a hypothetical negotiation between the actual parties, or what reasonable parties would have agreed . . .

Comment

Lord Neuberger was in a minority in his reasoning in *Stack*, though the remaining judges say less about this issue. Baroness Hale states (without elaboration): 'The search is to ascertain the parties' shared intentions, actual, inferred or imputed . . .'[13]

Extract 8.3.2

Jones v *Kernott* [2012] 1 AC 776

LORD WALKER and LADY HALE:

Inference or imputation?

29. [After discussion of *Gissing*] This sort of constructive intention (or any other constructive state of mind), and the difficulties that they raise, are familiar in many branches of the law. Whenever a judge concludes that an individual 'intended, or must be taken to have intended,' or 'knew, or must be taken to have known,' there is an elision between what the judge can find as a fact (usually by inference) on consideration of the admissible evidence, and what the law may supply (to fill the evidential gap) by way of a presumption. The presumption of a resulting trust is a clear example of a rule by which the law *does* impute an intention, the rule being based on a very broad generalisation about human motivation . . .

31. In deference to the comments of Lord Neuberger and Rimer LJ, we accept that the search is primarily to ascertain the parties' actual shared intentions, whether expressed or to be inferred from their conduct. However, there are at least two exceptions. The first, which is not this case, is where the classic resulting trust presumption applies. Indeed, this would be rare in a domestic context, but might perhaps arise where domestic partners were also business partners: see *Stack* v *Dowden*, para 32. The second, which for reasons which will appear later is in our view also not this case but will arise much more frequently, is where it is clear that the beneficial interests are to be shared, but it is impossible to divine a common intention as to the proportions in which they are to be shared. In those two situations, the court is driven to impute an intention to the parties which they may never have had.

34. However, while the conceptual difference between inferring and imputing is clear, the difference in practice may not be so great. In this area, as in many others, the scope for inference is wide. The law recognizes that a legitimate inference may not correspond to an individual's subjective state of mind . . .

LORD COLLINS: 65. [I]t is my view that in the present context the difference between inference and imputation will hardly ever matter (as Lord Walker and Lady Hale recognise at para 34), and that what is one person's inference will be another person's imputation . . .

66. Nor will it matter in practice that at the first stage, of ascertaining the common intention as to the beneficial ownership, the search is not, at least in theory, for what is fair. It would be difficult (and, perhaps, absurd) to imagine a scenario involving circumstances from which, in the absence of express agreement, the court will infer a shared or common intention which is unfair. The courts are courts of law, but they are also courts of justice.

LORD KERR: 67. I agree that this appeal should be allowed. There are differences of some significance in the reasoning that underlies the joint judgment of Lord Walker and Lady Hale and that contained in Lord Wilson's judgment. I agree with Lord Collins that these are both terminological and conceptual. I am less inclined to agree, however, that the divergence in reasoning is unlikely to make a difference in practice. While it may well be that the outcome in many cases will be the same, whether one infers an intention or imputes it, that does not mean that the

---

[13] At [60]. That statement is adopted in *Abbott* v *Abbott* [2008] 1 FLR 1451 at [6] (PC).

process by which the result is arrived at is more or less the same. Indeed, it seems to me that a markedly and obviously different mode of analysis will generally be required . . .

73.   In this context, it is important to understand what is meant by 'imputing an intention'. There are reasons to question the appropriateness of the notion of imputation in this area but, if it is correct to use this as a concept, I strongly favour the way in which it was described by Lord Neuberger in *Stack* v *Dowden* [2007] 2 AC 432 para 126, where he said that an imputed intention was one which was attributed to the parties, even though no such actual intention could be deduced from their actions and statements, and even though they had no such intention. This exposition draws the necessary strong demarcation line between attributing an intention to the parties and inferring what their intention was in fact.

74.   The reason that I question the aptness of the notion of imputing an intention is that, in the final analysis, the exercise is wholly unrelated to ascertainment of the parties' views. It involves the court deciding what is fair in light of the whole course of dealing with the property. That decision has nothing to do with what the parties intended, or what might be supposed would have been their intention had they addressed that question. In many ways, it would be preferable to have a stark choice between deciding whether it is possible to deduce what their intention was and, where it is not, deciding what is fair, without elliptical references to what their intention might have – or should have – been. But imputing intention has entered the lexicon of this area of law and it is probably impossible to discard it now.

LORD WILSON: 78.   In the light of the continued failure of Parliament to confer upon the courts limited redistributive powers in relation to the property of each party upon the breakdown of a non-marital relationship, I warmly applaud the development of the law of equity, spear-headed by Baroness Hale of Richmond and Lord Walker of Gestingthorpe in their speeches in *Stack* v *Dowden* [2007] 2 AC 432, and reiterated in their judgment in the present appeal, that the common intention which impresses a constructive trust upon the legal ownership of the family home can be imputed to the parties to the relationship.

89.   Lord Walker and Lady Hale observe, at para 34 above, that in practice the difference between inferring and imputing a common intention to the parties may not be great. I consider that, as a generalisation, their observation goes too far – at least if the court is to take (as in my view it should) an ordinarily rigorous approach to the task of inference . . .

Comment

(1) These dicta must be read together with the fuller quotations in Extract 8.6.3, dealing with how imputing works in quantifying shares.

(2) Is there a significant difference between imputed intentions and inferred intentions?

(3) What arguments are there for and against imputing intentions?

In *Geary* v *Rankine*,[14] the Court of Appeal stated:

Whether the beneficial interests are to be shared at all is still a question of a party's actual shared intentions. An imputed intention only arises where the court is satisfied that the parties' actual common intention, express or inferred, was that the beneficial interest would be shared, but cannot make a finding about the proportions in which they were to be shared.

Is it rational to distinguish between the two stages? Are there any indications to the contrary in *Jones* v *Kernott*?

---

[14] [2012] EWCA Civ 555 at [19]; [2012] 2 FLR 1409.

4. Transfer into joint names

Where the parties are married, it is worth noting that it is common today for the family home to be put in joint names. Modern land transfer forms provide for the beneficial interests to be stated, but in *Stack* Baroness Hale explains that this does not guarantee compliance. The number of cases involving transfer into joint names had been relatively small before *Stack*, but they remain troublesome.

Extract 8.4.1

Stack v Dowden [2007] 2 AC 432

An unmarried couple bought a house in their joint names. Apart from the house, they kept their finances separate. They lived together for 27 years and had four children. The woman clearly contributed more financially to the purchase of the house and repayment of the mortgage. Calculating what each had contributed was difficult, but the man's share of the contributions was at most 35%. The Court of Appeal held him entitled to 35%, but he argued for a 50% share.

BARONESS HALE: 53.   . . . In what circumstances should it be expected that, independently of the information required by the Land Registry forms, joint transferees would execute a declaration of trust? Is it when they intend that the beneficial interests should be the same as the legal interests or when they intend that they should be different?

54.   At first blush, the answer appears obvious. It should only be expected that joint transferees would have spelt out their beneficial interests when they intended them to be different from their legal interests. Otherwise, it should be assumed that equity follows the law and that the beneficial interests reflect the legal interests in the property. I do not think that this proposition is controversial, even in old fashioned unregistered conveyancing. It has even more force in registered conveyancing in the consumer context.

55.   Of course, it is something of an over-simplification. All joint legal owners must hold the land on trust . . . Section 53(1)(b) of the Law of Property Act 1925 requires that a declaration of trust respecting any land or any interest therein be manifested and proved by signed writing; but section 53(2) provides that this 'does not affect the creation or operation of resulting, implied or constructive trusts'. The question is, therefore, what are the trusts to be deduced in the circumstances?

56.   Just as the starting point where there is sole legal ownership is sole beneficial ownership, the starting point where there is joint legal ownership is joint beneficial ownership. The onus is upon the person seeking to show that the beneficial ownership is different from the legal ownership. So in sole ownership cases it is upon the non-owner to show that he has any interest at all. In joint ownership cases, it is upon the joint owner who claims to have other than a joint beneficial interest.

58.   The issue as it has been framed before us is whether a conveyance into joint names indicates only that each party is intended to have some beneficial interest but says nothing about the nature and extent of that beneficial interest, or whether a conveyance into joint names establishes a prime facie case of joint and equal beneficial interests until the contrary is shown. For the reasons already stated, at least in the domestic consumer context, a conveyance into joint names indicates both legal and beneficial joint tenancy, unless and until the contrary is proved.

59.   The question is, how, if at all, is the contrary to be proved? Is the starting point the presumption of resulting trust, under which shares are held in proportion to the parties' financial contributions to the acquisition of the property, unless the contributor or contributors can be shown to have had a contrary intention? Or is it that the contrary can be proved by looking at all the relevant circumstances in order to discern the parties' common intention?

66.   . . . But the questions in a joint names case are not simply 'what is the extent of the parties' beneficial interests?' but 'did the parties intend their beneficial interests to be different from their legal interests?' and 'if they did, in what way and to what extent?' There are differences between sole and joint names cases when trying to divine the common intentions or understanding between the parties. I know of no case in which a sole legal owner (there being no declaration of trust) has been held to hold the property on a beneficial joint tenancy. But a court may well hold that joint legal owners (there being no declaration of trust) are also beneficial joint tenants. Another difference is that it will almost always have been a conscious decision to put the house into joint names. Even if the parties have not executed the transfer, they will usually, if not invariably, have executed the contract which precedes it. Committing oneself to spend large sums of money on a place to live is not normally done by accident or without giving it a moment's thought.

67.   This is not to say that the parties invariably have a full understanding of the legal effects of their choice: there is recent empirical evidence from a small scale qualitative study to confirm that they do not: see Gillian Douglas, Julia Pearce and Hilary Woodward, 'Dealing with Property Issues on Cohabitation Breakdown' [2007] Fam Law 36. But that is so whether or not there is an express declaration of trust and no-one thinks that such a declaration can be overturned, except in cases of fraud or mistake: see para 49 above. Nor do they always have a completely free choice in the matter. Mortgagees used to insist upon the home being put in the name of the person whom they assumed would be the main breadwinner. Nowadays, they tend to think that it is in their best interests that the home be jointly owned and both parties assume joint and several liability for the mortgage. (It is, of course, a matter of indifference to the mortgagees where the beneficial interests lie.) Here again, this factor does not invalidate the parties' choice if there is an express declaration of trust, nor should it automatically count against it where there is none.

68.   The burden will therefore be on the person seeking to show that the parties did intend their beneficial interests to be different from their legal interests, and in what way. This is not a task to be lightly embarked upon. In family disputes, strong feelings are aroused when couples split up. These often lead the parties, honestly but mistakenly, to reinterpret the past in self-exculpatory or vengeful terms. They also lead people to spend far more on the legal battle than is warranted by the sums actually at stake. A full examination of the facts is likely to involve disproportionate costs. In joint names cases it is also unlikely to lead to a different result unless the facts are very unusual. Nor may disputes be confined to the parties themselves. People with an interest in the deceased's estate may well wish to assert that he had a beneficial tenancy in common. It cannot be the case that all the hundreds of thousands, if not millions, of transfers into joint names using the old forms are vulnerable to challenge in the courts simply because it is likely that the owners contributed unequally to their purchase.

69.   In law, 'context is everything' and the domestic context is very different from the commercial world. Each case will turn on its own facts. Many more factors than financial contributions may be relevant to divining the parties' true intentions. These include: any advice or discussions at the time of the transfer which cast light upon their intentions then; the reasons why the home was acquired in their joint names; the reasons why (if it be the case) the survivor was authorised to give a receipt for the capital moneys; the purpose for which the home was acquired; the nature of the parties' relationship; whether they had children for whom they both had responsibility to provide a home; how the purchase was financed, both initially and subsequently; how the parties arranged their finances, whether separately or together or a bit of both; how they discharged the outgoings on the property and their other household expenses. When a couple are joint owners of the home and jointly liable for the mortgage, the inferences to be drawn from who pays for what may be very different from the inferences to be drawn when only one is owner of the home. The arithmetical calculation of how much was paid by each is also likely to be less important. It will be easier to draw the inference that they intended that each

should contribute as much to the household as they reasonably could and that they would share the eventual benefit or burden equally. The parties' individual characters and personalities may also be a factor in deciding where their true intentions lay. In the cohabitation context, mercenary considerations may be more to the fore than they would be in marriage, but it should not be assumed that they always take pride of place over natural love and affection. At the end of the day, having taken all this into account, cases in which the joint legal owners are to be taken to have intended that their beneficial interests should be different from their legal interests will be very unusual.

92.   This is, therefore, a very unusual case. There cannot be many unmarried couples who have lived together for as long as this, who have had four children together, and whose affairs have been kept as rigidly separate as this couple's affairs were kept. This is all strongly indicative that they did not intend their shares, even in the property which was put into both their names, to be equal (still less that they intended a beneficial joint tenancy with the right of survivorship should one of them die before it was severed). Before the Court of Appeal, Ms Dowden contended for a 65% share and in my view she has made good her case for that.

LORD NEUBERGER (dissenting on the reasoning): 101.   The determination of the ownership of the beneficial interest in a property held in joint names primarily engages the law of contract, land and equity. The relevant principles in those areas of law have been established and applied over hundreds of years, and have had to be applied in all sorts of circumstances. While both the nature and the characteristics of the particular relationship must be taken into account when applying the principles, the court should be very careful before altering those principles when it comes to a particular type of relationship. After all, these principles are not static and develop as the needs and values of society change. Thus, the presumption of advancement, as between man and wife, which was so important in the 18th and 19th centuries, has now become much weakened, although not quite to the point of disappearance.

102.   However, that does not mean that a change in the principles should be easy or frequent. A change in the law, however sensible and just it seems, always carries a real risk of new and unforeseen uncertainties and unfairnesses. That is a particular danger when the change is effected by the court rather than the legislature, as the change is influenced by, indeed normally based on, the facts of a particular case, there is little room for public consultation, and there is no input from the democratically elected legislature.

106.   In my judgment, it is therefore inappropriate for the law when applied to cases of this sort to depart from the well-established principles laid down over the years. It also seems to me that the law of resulting and constructive trusts is flexible enough to deal with problems such as those thrown up by cases such as this, and it would be a disservice to the important causes of certainty and consistency if we were to hold otherwise. I note that the Court of Appeal's recent decisions in this case and in *Oxley v Hiscock* [2005] Fam 211 (both of which were rightly decided) produced an outcome which would be dictated by a resulting trust solution.

107.   Accordingly, while the domestic context can give rise to very different factual considerations from the commercial context, I am unconvinced that this justifies a different approach in principle to the issue of the ownership of the beneficial interest in property held in joint names. In the absence of statutory provisions to the contrary, the same principles should apply to assess the apportionment of the beneficial interest as between legal co-owners, whether in a sexual, platonic, familial, amicable or commercial relationship. In each type of case, one is concerned with the issue of the ownership of the beneficial interest in property held in the names of two people, who have contributed to its acquisition, retention or value.

114.   There is also an important point about consistency of approach with a case where the purchase of a home is in the name of one of the parties. As Baroness Hale observes, where there is no evidence of contributions, joint legal ownership is reflected in a presumption of joint beneficial ownership just as sole legal ownership is reflected in a presumption of sole beneficial ownership . . . The resulting trust presumption arises because it is assumed that neither party

intended a gift of any part of his own contribution to the other party. That would seem to me to apply to contributions irrespective of the name or names in which the property concerned is acquired and held, as a matter of both principle and logic.

115.   It may be asked why the bigger contributor agreed to the property being taken in joint names, unless he intended joint beneficial ownership. There are four answers to that. The first is that the question sets out to justify what it assumes, namely that, in the absence of any discussion, the parties must have assumed an equal split. Secondly, if the other party was a contributor, he would often want to be a co-owner, and the only way real property can be held in law by two persons is as joint owners. Thirdly, the converse point can be made where a property is acquired in the name of one party: if the other party has contributed to the purchase, his absence from the title is not evidence that he was not intended to have an interest. (In this connection, it seems to me that, where a home is taken in the name of only one party, this is almost as likely to have been a conscious decision as where it is acquired in joint names: where both have contributed to the purchase, it is unlikely that either will have been unaware of the fact that the home was being acquired in the name of only one of them). Fourthly, there are the practical considerations to which I have already alluded.

Comment

(1) Lords Hoffmann, Hope and Walker agreed with Baroness Hale. Further extracts from the case appear later in this chapter, especially in the context of its role in transfer into the name of just one of a couple. Ultimately, all the dicta need to be considered together, as they may be relevant whether there is a transfer into joint or single names.

(2) A resulting trust had been employed for centuries where there is unequal contribution. Does Baroness Hale provide convincing reasons for departing from this practice?

(3) Were the facts in *Stack* really exceptional, so as to justify departing from the principle the majority established?[15]

Extract 8.4.2

Fowler v Barron [2008] 2 FLR 831

An unmarried couple lived together for 22 years. The house was in joint names (with a joint mortgage), though all capital and mortgage payments (and other costs such as council tax) were paid by the man.

ARDEN LJ: 33.   The starting point is of course that the transfer of the property was into the joint names of Mr Barron and Miss Fowler. Whatever Mr Barron's motive was for doing this, it was a deliberate choice. As a matter of law, a presumption of joint beneficial ownership arose from the fact that they were joint legal owners: see *Stack* at [58] per Baroness Hale. It was open to Mr Barron to rebut this presumption. There was no direct evidence of the parties' intentions, and accordingly the only evidence was circumstantial.

41.   Mr Barron also places reliance on the fact that Miss Fowler made no contribution to the cost of acquiring the property (whether directly or by paying off the mortgage). But the decision in *Stack* shows that the critical factor is not necessarily the amount of the parties' contributions: the court has to have regard to all the circumstances which may throw light on the parties' intentions as respects ownership of the property. In this case, the judge found that Miss Fowler paid a number of expenses . . . The reality was that she spent much of her income and the child benefits principally on herself and her children and meeting what the judge termed 'optional

---

[15] See Probert [2007] Fam Law 924.

expenditure' such as gifts, school clubs and trips, personal clothing, holidays and special occasions. In my judgment, the proper inference is that, with the exception of clothing for herself, these payments were her contributions to household expenses for which both parties were responsible . . .

44.   This requires some analysis as to the basis on which Ms Dowden was able to rebut the presumption of equal shares in *Stack* and successfully assert that the parties' shares in the property should reflect their contributions to the purchase price in cash payments towards the price or the mortgage payments made in respect of it or the premiums on the endowment policies supporting the mortgage. At [87] to [92], Baroness Hale identified a number of points arising out of the facts in that case: the fact that Ms Dowden paid much more of the purchase price, the fact that she paid the greater part of the lump sums required to redeem the mortgage, the fact that Mr Stack's payments in respect of the mortgage were to service the interest payments due and to pay premiums on one of the endowment policies supporting it, the fact that the parties intended to reduce the mortgage as soon as they could, the fact that the parties kept their financial affairs 'rigidly separate' and did not pool their resources 'even notionally' for the common good, and the fact that Ms Dowden paid all the other household expenses. Baroness Hale considered that the case was very unusual with regard to the way the parties maintained their affairs separately.

46.   The facts in this case are different in many respects. For instance, the evidence as to mutual wills is not replicated in *Stack*. . . . Miss Fowler made no direct contribution to paying for the property . . . The way that she used her own income indicates that the parties largely treated their incomes and assets as one pool from which household expenses will be paid . . .

47.   This result can be criticised because it may leave Miss Fowler better off than the case of a cohabitee who contributes (say) 20% of the purchase price. But that would only be the case where the court found that the parties' shared intention was that they should share the beneficial interest in their home in proportion to the amount of their financial contributions to the cost. But the reason why the result in that case may be different is because that is what the court infers to be the parties' intention . . .

Comment

Might the man in *Fowler* be thought to have a much stronger case than the woman in *Stack*? Was his problem the difficulty in finding any basis for giving the woman in *Fowler* anything other than nothing or half?

Extract 8.4.3

Jones v *Kernott* [2012] 1 AC 776

LORD WALKER and LADY HALE: 2.   The decision in *Stack* v *Dowden* has also attracted a good deal of comment from legal scholars . . . But counsel have not argued that *Stack* v *Dowden* was wrongly decided or that this court should now depart from the principles which it laid down. This appeal provides an opportunity for some clarification.

19.   The presumption of a beneficial joint tenancy is not based on a mantra as to 'equity following the law' (though many non-lawyers would find it hard to understand the notion that equity might do anything else). There are two much more substantial reasons (which overlap) why a challenge to the presumption of beneficial joint tenancy is not to be lightly embarked on. The first is implicit in the nature of the enterprise. If a couple in an intimate relationship (whether married or unmarried) decide to buy a house or flat in which to live together, almost always with the help of a mortgage for which they are jointly and severally liable, that is on the face of things a strong indication of emotional and economic commitment to a joint enterprise. That is so even if the parties, for whatever reason, fail to make that clear by any overt declaration or agreement.

   . . .

22. The notion that in a trusting personal relationship the parties do not hold each other to account financially is underpinned by the practical difficulty, in many cases, of taking any such account, perhaps after 20 years or more of the ups and downs of living together as an unmarried couple. That is the second reason for caution before going to law in order to displace the presumption of beneficial joint tenancy.

47. In a case such as this, where the parties already share the beneficial interest, and the question is what their interests are and whether their interests have changed, the court will try to deduce what their actual intentions were at the relevant time. It cannot impose a solution upon them which is contrary to what the evidence shows that they actually intended. But if it cannot deduce exactly what shares were intended, it may have no alternative but to ask what their intentions as reasonable and just people would have been had they thought about it at the time. This is a fallback position which some courts may not welcome, but the court has a duty to come to a conclusion on the dispute put before it.

Conclusion

51. In summary, therefore, the following are the principles applicable in a case such as this, where a family home is bought in the joint names of a cohabiting couple who are both responsible for any mortgage, but without any express declaration of their beneficial interests.

(1) The starting point is that equity follows the law and they are joint tenants both in law and in equity.

(2) That presumption can be displaced by showing (a) that the parties had a different common intention at the time when they acquired the home, or (b) that they later formed the common intention that their respective shares would change.

(3) Their common intention is to be deduced objectively from their conduct: 'the relevant intention of each party is the intention which was reasonably understood by the other party to be manifested by that party's words and conduct notwithstanding that he did not consciously formulate that intention in his own mind or even acted with some different intention which he did not communicate to the other party' (Lord Diplock in *Gissing* v *Gissing* [1971] AC 886, 906). Examples of the sort of evidence which might be relevant to drawing such inferences are given in *Stack* v *Dowden*, at para 69.

(4) In those cases where it is clear either (a) that the parties did not intend joint tenancy at the outset, or (b) had changed their original intention, but it is not possible to ascertain by direct evidence or by inference what their actual intention was as to the shares in which they would own the property, 'the answer is that each is entitled to that share which the court considers fair having regard to the whole course of dealing between them in relation to the property': Chadwick LJ in *Oxley* v *Hiscock* [2005] Fam 211, para 69. In our judgment, 'the whole course of dealing . . . in relation to the property' should be given a broad meaning, enabling a similar range of factors to be taken into account as may be relevant to ascertaining the parties' actual intentions.

(5) Each case will turn on its own facts. Financial contributions are relevant but there are many other factors which may enable the court to decide what shares were either intended (as in case (3)) or fair (as in case (4)).

Comment

(1) More detailed analyses as to how inferring and imputing intentions operate in quantifying shares are found in Extract 8.6.3. The judges disagreed as to this.

(2) The court goes out of its way to endorse *Stack* v *Dowden*. Even though counsel had not argued that it should be reconsidered, it is clearly strengthened by this decision. The resulting trust as an alternative analysis is rejected (see Extract 8.2.3 above).

5. Transfer into a single name

A. Early developments: *Pettitt* and *Gissing*

Problems in applying simple resulting trust analyses to the family home led to a number of approaches being developed in the 1950s and 1960s. These were designed to widen entitlements to property rights, often based upon some element of court discretion. However, we need look no further back than the House of Lords decisions in *Pettitt* v *Pettitt*[16] and *Gissing* v *Gissing*.[17] Although *Pettitt* was important in rejecting some earlier misconceptions, subsequent analyses were dominated by *Gissing* – at least, until *Stack* and *Jones* v *Kernott*.

Extract 8.5.1

Gissing v *Gissing* [1971] AC 886

LORD DIPLOCK: . . . It concerns a claim by a former wife to a proprietary interest in real property of which the legal estate in fee simple is vested in her former husband subject to a mortgage to a building society which has not yet been fully paid off . . . She founds her claim upon the contention that she contributed substantially, though indirectly, to the payment by her husband of the original deposit and the subsequent instalments payable under the mortgage which enabled him to acquire the fee simple in the house.

The actual decision of your Lordships' House in *Pettitt* v *Pettitt* is thus not directly in point . . . Your Lordships decided unanimously, first, that section 17 of the Married Women's Property Act, 1882, was procedural only and did not entitle the court to vary the existing proprietary rights of the parties; and, secondly, that upon the facts disclosed by the evidence it was not possible to infer any common intention of the parties that the husband by doing work and expending money on materials for the improvement of the house should acquire any beneficial proprietary interest in real property in which the whole legal and beneficial interest had previously been vested in the wife.

But although, as a matter of decision, *Pettitt* v *Pettitt* does not govern the instant appeal, it entailed for the first time a survey by your Lordships of numerous decisions of the Court of Appeal during the past 20 years in which the beneficial interests of spouses in a former matrimonial home had been the subject of consideration not only in applications under section 17 of the Married Women's Property Act, 1882, but also in other kinds of proceedings. In the cases examined the practice had developed of using the expression 'family asset' to describe the kind of property about which disputes arose between spouses as to their respective beneficial interests in it. . . . I did, however, differ from the majority of the members of your Lordships' House who were parties to the decision in *Pettitt* v *Pettitt* in that I saw no reason in law why the fact that the spouses had not applied their minds at all to the question of how the beneficial interest in a family asset should be held at the time when it was acquired should prevent the court from giving effect to a common intention on this matter which it was satisfied that they would have formed as reasonable persons if they had actually thought about it at that time. I must now accept the majority decision that, put in this form at any rate, this is not the law.

. . .

Any claim to a beneficial interest in land by a person, whether spouse or stranger, in whom the legal estate in the land is not vested must be based upon the proposition that the person in whom the legal estate is vested holds it as trustee upon trust to give effect to the beneficial interest of the claimant as cestui que trust. The legal principles applicable to the claim are those

---

[16] [1970] AC 777.
[17] [1971] AC 886.

of the English law of trusts and in particular, in the kind of dispute between spouses that comes before the courts, the law relating to the creation and operation of 'resulting, implied or constructive trusts'. . . . But to constitute a valid declaration of trust by way of gift of a beneficial interest in land to a cestui que trust the declaration is required by section 53(1) of the Law of Property Act, 1925, to be in writing. If it is not in writing it can only take effect as a resulting, implied or constructive trust to which that section has no application.

A resulting, implied or constructive trust – and it is unnecessary for present purposes to distinguish between these three classes of trust – is created by a transaction between the trustee and the cestui que trust in connection with the acquisition by the trustee of a legal estate in land, whenever the trustee has so conducted himself that it would be inequitable to allow him to deny to the cestui que trust a beneficial interest in the land acquired. And he will be held so to have conducted himself if by his words or conduct he has induced the cestui que trust to act to his own detriment in the reasonable belief that by so acting he was acquiring a beneficial interest in the land.

. . .

An express agreement between spouses as to their respective beneficial interests in land conveyed into the name of one of them obviates the need for showing that the conduct of the spouse into whose name the land was conveyed was intended to induce the other spouse to act to his or her detriment upon the faith of the promise of a specified beneficial interest in the land and that the other spouse so acted with the intention of acquiring that beneficial interest. The agreement itself discloses the common intention required to create a resulting, implied or constructive trust.

But parties to a transaction in connection with the acquisition of land may well have formed a common intention that the beneficial interest in the land shall be vested in them jointly without having used express words to communicate this intention to one another; or their recollections of the words used may be imperfect or conflicting by the time any dispute arises. In such a case – a common one where the parties are spouses whose marriage has broken down – it may be possible to infer their common intention from their conduct.

As in so many branches of English law in which legal rights and obligations depend upon the intentions of the parties to a transaction, the relevant intention of each party is the intention which was reasonably understood by the other party to be manifested by that party's words or conduct notwithstanding that he did not consciously formulate that intention in his own mind or even acted with some different intention which he did not communicate to the other party. On the other hand, he is not bound by any inference which the other party draws as to his intention unless that inference is one which can reasonably be drawn from his words or conduct. It is in this sense that in the branch of English law relating to constructive, implied or resulting trusts effect is given to the inferences as to the intentions of parties to a transaction which a reasonable man would draw from their words or conduct and not to any subjective intention or absence of intention which was not made manifest at the time of the transaction itself. It is for the court to determine what those inferences are.

. . . But it would in my view be unreasonably legalistic to treat the relevant transaction involved in the acquisition of a matrimonial home as restricted to the actual conveyance of the fee simple into the name of one or other spouse. Their common intention is more likely to have been concerned with the economic realities of the transaction than with the unfamiliar technicalities of the English law of legal and equitable interests in land. The economic reality which lies behind the conveyance of the fee simple to a purchaser in return for a purchase price the greater part of which is advanced to the purchaser upon a mortgage repayable by instalments over a number of years, is that the new freeholder is purchasing the matrimonial home upon credit and that the purchase price is represented by the instalments by which the mortgage is repaid in addition to the initial payment in cash. The conduct of the spouses in relation to the payment of the mortgage instalments may be no less relevant to their common intention as to the beneficial interests in a matrimonial home acquired in this way than their conduct in relation to the payment of the cash deposit.

It is this feature of the transaction by means of which most matrimonial homes have been acquired in recent years that makes difficult the task of the court in inferring from the conduct of the spouses a common intention as to how the beneficial interest in it should be held. Each case must depend upon its own facts but there are a number of factual situations which often recur in the cases.

Where a matrimonial home has been purchased outright without the aid of an advance on mortgage it is not difficult to ascertain what part, if any, of the purchase price has been provided by each spouse . . . [T]he prima facie inference is that their common intention was that the contributing spouse should acquire a share in the beneficial interest in the land in the same proportion as the sum contributed bore to the total purchase price . . .

Similarly when a matrimonial home is not purchased outright but partly out of moneys advanced on mortgage repayable by instalments, and the land is conveyed into the name of the husband alone, the fact that the wife made a cash contribution to the deposit and legal charges not borrowed on mortgage gives rise, in the absence of evidence which makes some other explanation more probable, to the inference that their common intention was that she should share in the beneficial interest in the land conveyed. But it would not be reasonable to infer a common intention as to what her share should be without taking account also of the sources from which the mortgage instalments were provided. If the wife also makes a substantial direct contribution to the mortgage instalments out of her own earnings or unearned income this would be prima facie inconsistent with a common intention that her share in the beneficial interest should be determined by the proportion which her original cash contribution bore either to the total amount of the deposit and legal charges or to the full purchase price. The more likely inference is that her contributions to the mortgage instalments were intended by the spouses to have some effect upon her share.

Where there has been an initial contribution by the wife to the cash deposit and legal charges which points to a common intention at the time of the conveyance that she should have a beneficial interest in the land conveyed to her husband, it would be unrealistic to regard the wife's subsequent contributions to the mortgage instalments as without significance unless she pays them directly herself. It may be no more than a matter of convenience which spouse pays particular household accounts, particularly when both are earning, and if the wife goes out to work and devotes part of her earnings or uses her private income to meet joint expenses of the household which would otherwise be met by the husband, so as to enable him to pay the mortgage instalments out of his moneys this would be consistent with and might be corroborative of an original common intention that she should share in the beneficial interest in the matrimonial home and that her payments of other household expenses were intended by both spouses to be treated as including a contribution by the wife to the purchase price of the matrimonial home.

Even where there has been no initial contribution by the wife to the cash deposit and legal charges but she makes a regular and substantial direct contribution to the mortgage instalments it may be reasonable to infer a common intention of the spouses from the outset that she should share in the beneficial interest or to infer a fresh agreement reached after the original conveyance that she should acquire a share. But it is unlikely that the mere fact that the wife made direct contributions to the mortgage instalments would be the only evidence available to assist the court in ascertaining the common intention of the spouses.

. . .

The relative size of their respective contributions to the instalments . . . may make it a more probable inference that the wife's share in the beneficial interest was intended to be in some proportion other than one-half. And there is nothing inherently improbable in their acting on the understanding that the wife should be entitled to a share which was not to be quantified immediately upon the acquisition of the home but should be left to be determined when the mortgage was repaid or the property disposed of, on the basis of what would be fair having regard to the total contributions, direct or indirect, which each spouse had made by that date . . .

Where the wife has made no initial contribution to the cash deposit and legal charges and no direct contribution to the mortgage instalments nor any adjustment to her contribution to other expenses of the household which it can be inferred was referable to the acquisition of the house, there is in the absence of evidence of an express agreement between the parties no material to justify the court in inferring that it was the common intention of the parties that she should have any beneficial interest in a matrimonial home conveyed into the sole name of the husband, merely because she continued to contribute out of her own earnings or private income to other expenses of the household.

Comment

(1) The wife had purchased some furniture, a cooker and a refrigerator at the time of purchase and paid for her own clothes out of her earnings. There was no joint bank account. On this evidence, Lord Diplock found it impossible to discover a common intention for her to have a beneficial share in the house.

(2) This was not the only speech in *Gissing*, but it has been the most influential. It is important to note that the idea of 'family assets' was rejected: property rights must follow from normal equitable principles.[18]

(3) The quantification of shares has to be considered in the light of *Jones* v *Kernott*.[19]

B. The development of common intention prior to *Stack*: inferring intentions

Though many consider that *Stack* v *Dowden* and *Jones* v *Kernott* form the basis of the modern law, the two traditional routes to finding a common intention were inference from contributions and evidence of an actual common intention agreed between the parties. For several decades following *Gissing*, the major stress was upon contributions. It is plain beyond argument that contributions to the initial purchase cost and significant sharing of mortgage instalments suffice: this was made clear by Lord Diplock.

One very important question is whether the courts will take account of non-financial contributions. It is obvious that, in many relationships, one of the parties (almost invariably the woman) will be at home looking after the children or, less commonly today, the home. Simply because this person is not working, there is usually no opportunity to contribute in cash towards the cost of the purchase or the mortgage. Yet that person is undertaking a very important role in the relationship and may justifiably feel aggrieved if the home is owned entirely by the other party on a breakdown of the relationship.

Extract 8.5.2

Burns v Burns [1984] Ch 317

The parties lived together, unmarried, for 19 years. They had two children and the woman did not work for the first 14 years of the relationship. The house was bought in the man's name.

---

[18] The statutory power to allocate property on marriage breakdown post-dates *Gissing*.
[19] Extract 8.6.3 below.

FOX LJ: . . . It seems to me that at the time of the acquisition of the house nothing occurred between the parties to raise an equity which would prevent the defendant denying the plaintiff's claim. She provided no money for the purchase; she assumed no liability in respect of the mortgage; there was no understanding or arrangement that the plaintiff would go out to work to assist with the family finances; the defendant did nothing to lead her to change her position in the belief that she would have an interest in the house. It is true that she contemplated living with the defendant in the house and, no doubt, that she would do housekeeping and look after the children. But those facts do not carry with them any implication of a common intention that the plaintiff should have an interest in the house. Taken by themselves they are simply not strong enough to bear such an implication.

. . . What is needed, I think, is evidence of a payment or payments by the plaintiff which it can be inferred was referable to the acquisition of the house . . . If there is a substantial contribution by the woman to family expenses, and the house was purchased on a mortgage, her contribution is, indirectly, referable to the acquisition of the house since, in one way or another, it enables the family to pay the mortgage instalments. Thus, a payment could be said to be referable to the acquisition of the house if, for example, the payer either (a) pays part of the purchase price or (b) contributes regularly to the mortgage instalments or (c) pays off part of the mortgage or (d) makes a substantial financial contribution to the family expenses so as to enable the mortgage instalments to be paid.

. . .

There remains the question of housekeeping and domestic duties. So far as housekeeping expenses are concerned, I do not doubt that (the house being bought in the man's name) if the woman goes out to work in order to provide money for the family expenses, as a result of which she spends her earnings on the housekeeping and the man is thus able to pay the mortgage instalments and other expenses out of his earnings, it can be inferred that there was a common intention that the woman should have an interest in the house – since she will have made an indirect financial contribution to the mortgage instalments. But that is not this case.

During the greater part of the period when the plaintiff and the defendant were living together she was not in employment or, if she was, she was not earning amounts of any consequence and provided no money towards the family expenses. Nor is it suggested that the defendant ever asked her to. He provided, and was always ready to provide, all the money that she wanted for housekeeping. The house was not bought in the contemplation that the plaintiff would, at some time, contribute to the cost of its acquisition. She worked to suit herself. And if towards the very end of the relationship she had money to spare she spent it entirely as she chose. It was in no sense 'joint' money. It was her own; she was not expected and was not asked to spend it on the household.

I think it would be quite unreal to say that, overall, she made a substantial financial contribution towards the family expenses. That is not in any way a criticism of her; it is simply the factual position.

But, one asks, can the fact that the plaintiff performed domestic duties in the house and looked after the children be taken into account? . . . The house was bought by the defendant in his own name and, prima facie, he is the absolute beneficial owner. If the plaintiff, or anybody else, claims to take it from him, it must be proved the claimant has, by some process of law, acquired an interest in the house. What is asserted here is the creation of a trust arising by common intention of the parties. That common intention may be inferred where there has been a financial contribution, direct or indirect, to the acquisition of the house. But the mere fact that parties live together and do the ordinary domestic tasks is, in my view, no indication at all that they thereby intended to alter the existing property rights of either of them . . . The assertion that they do alter property rights seems to me to be, in substance, reverting to the idea of the 'family asset' which was rejected by the House of Lords in *Pettitt* v *Pettitt* [1970] AC 777. The decision in *Gissing* v *Gissing* [1971] AC 886 itself is really inconsistent with the contrary view since the parties lived together for ten years after the house was bought.

Comment

(1) Simon P said extra-judicially,[20] 'The cock can feather the nest because he does not have to spend most of his time sitting on it.' Does *Burns* adequately reflect this insight? Does *Burns* follow from *Gissing*?

(2) *Burns* will be reassessed in the light of *Stack* v *Dowden* (p 258 below).

Given the stress on financial contributions, a very important question is whether indirect contributions will suffice. These are discussed in *Burns*, as well as by Lord Diplock in *Gissing*. The claimant may spend money on, for example, clothes and housekeeping so that the legal owner can pay off the mortgage. It may be merely a matter of convenience as to whose money pays which debts. Both cases support the recognition of such contributions, though not where the claimant's expenditure represents extra 'luxury' expenditure which is not essential. In such cases, it cannot be said either that the legal owner's payment of the mortgage is a matter of convenience or that the claimant's expenditure is essential in order that the mortgage instalments can be paid. However, firm authority for indirect contributions was curiously lacking (statements in cases being either obiter dicta or based on counsel's concessions) and their role was doubted by the Court of Appeal in *Grant* v *Edwards*.[21]

Extract 8.5.3

Lloyds Bank plc v Rosset [1991] 1 AC 107

A derelict house was bought as the future matrimonial home. Builders were employed to renovate it.

LORD BRIDGE: . . . It is clear . . . that the judge based his inference of a common intention that Mrs Rosset should have a beneficial interest in the property under a constructive trust essentially on what Mrs Rosset did in and about assisting in the renovation of the property between the beginning of November 1982 and the date of completion on 17 December 1982. Yet by itself this activity, it seems to me, could not possibly justify any such inference. It was common ground that Mrs Rosset was extremely anxious that the new matrimonial home should be ready for occupation before Christmas if possible. In these circumstances it would seem the most natural thing in the world for any wife, in the absence of her husband abroad, to spend all the time she could spare and to employ any skills she might have, such as the ability to decorate a room, in doing all she could to accelerate progress of the work quite irrespective of any expectation she might have of enjoying a beneficial interest in the property. The judge's view that some of this work was work 'upon which she could not reasonably have been expected to embark unless she was to have an interest in the house' seems to me, with respect, quite untenable . . .

On any view the monetary value of Mrs Rosset's work expressed as a contribution to a property acquired at a cost exceeding £70,000 must have been so trifling as to be almost de minimis. I should myself have had considerable doubt whether Mrs Rosset's contribution to the work of renovation was sufficient to support a claim to a constructive trust in the absence of writing to satisfy the requirements of section 51 of the Law of Property Act 1925 even if her husband's intention to make a gift to her of half or any other share in the equity of the property had been clearly established or if he had clearly represented to her that that was what he intended. . . .

---

[20] Quoted by Lord Hodson in *Pettitt* v *Pettitt* [1970] AC 777 at p 811.
[21] [1986] Ch 638.

The first and fundamental question which must always be resolved is whether, independently of any inference to be drawn from the conduct of the parties in the course of sharing the house as their home and managing their joint affairs, there has at any time prior to acquisition, or exceptionally at some later date, been any agreement, arrangement or understanding reached between them that the property is to be shared beneficially. The finding of an agreement or arrangement to share in this sense can only, I think, be based on evidence of express discussions between the partners, however imperfectly remembered and however imprecise their terms may have been. Once a finding to this effect is made it will only be necessary for the partner asserting a claim to a beneficial interest against the partner entitled to the legal estate to show that he or she has acted to his or her detriment or significantly altered his or her position in reliance on the agreement in order to give rise to a constructive trust or a proprietary estoppel.

In sharp contrast with this situation is the very different one where there is no evidence to support a finding of an agreement or arrangement to share, however reasonable it might have been for the parties to reach such an arrangement if they had applied their minds to the question, and where the court must rely entirely on the conduct of the parties both as the basis from which to infer a common intention to share the property beneficially and as the conduct relied on to give rise to a constructive trust. In this situation direct contributions to the purchase price by the partner who is not the legal owner, whether initially or by payment of mortgage instalments, will readily justify the inference necessary to the creation of a constructive trust. But, as I read the authorities, it is at least extremely doubtful whether anything less will do.

Comment

Rosset is a relatively unusual example of a modern case involving husband and wife. The matrimonial discretion was unavailable because the litigation concerned the rights of a mortgagee of the legal title.

It is interesting that *Rosset* rejects indirect contributions ('it is at least extremely doubtful whether anything less [than direct contributions] will do') with minimal consideration of the authorities. This led to much criticism. Indirect contributions were accepted by Nicholas Mostyn QC, deciding *Le Foe* v *Le Foe*,[22] encouraged by the Law Commission and are almost certainly recognised following *Stack* v *Dowden* (Extract 8.5.5 below).[23]

C. The development of common intention prior to *Stack*: express common intentions

The extract from *Rosset* demonstrated that an express common intention can be relied upon where it can be proved from 'express discussions between the partners, however imperfectly remembered and however imprecise their terms may have been'. This had not received much attention in earlier cases, save for *Eves* v *Eves* and *Grant* v *Edwards*.

Extract 8.5.4

Grant v *Edwards* [1986] Ch 638

NOURSE LJ: . . . There is another and rarer class of case, of which the present may be one, where, although there has been no writing, the parties have orally declared themselves in such a way as to make their common intention plain. Here the court does not have to look for conduct from which the intention can be inferred, but only for conduct which amounts to an

---

[22] [2001] 2 FLR 970 (Ch D).
[23] Law Com No 278 (Extract 8.8.3 below).

acting upon it by the claimant. And although that conduct can undoubtedly be the incurring of expenditure which is referable to the acquisition of the house, it need not necessarily be so.

The clearest example of this rarer class of case is *Eves* v *Eves* [1975] 1 WLR 1338. That was a case of an unmarried couple where the conveyance of the house was taken in the name of the man alone. At the time of the purchase he told the woman that if she had been 21 years of age, he would have put the house into their joint names, because it was to be their joint home. He admitted in evidence that that was an excuse for not putting the house into their joint names, and this court inferred that there was an understanding between them, or a common intention, that the woman was to have some sort of proprietary interest in it; otherwise no excuse would have been needed. After they had moved in, the woman did extensive decorative work to the downstairs rooms and generally cleaned the whole house. She painted the brickwork of the front of the house. She also broke up with a 14-lb sledge hammer the concrete surface which covered the whole of the front garden and disposed of the rubble into a skip, worked in the back garden and, together with the man, demolished a shed there and put up a new shed. She also prepared the front garden for turfing. Pennycuick V-C at first instance, being unable to find any link between the common intention and the woman's activities after the purchase, held that she had not acquired a beneficial interest in the house. On an appeal to this court the decision was unanimously reversed, by Lord Denning MR on a ground which I respectfully think was at variance with the principles stated in *Gissing* v *Gissing* [1971] AC 886 and by Browne LJ and Brightman J on a ground which was stated by Brightman J [1975] 1 WLR 1338, 1345:

> 'The defendant clearly led the plaintiff to believe that she was to have some undefined interest in the property, and that her name was only omitted from the conveyance because of her age. This, of course, is not enough by itself to create a beneficial interest in her favour; there would at best be a mere "voluntary declaration of trust" which would be "unenforceable for want of writing": per Lord Diplock in *Gissing* v *Gissing* [1971] AC 886, 905. If, however, it was part of the bargain between the parties, expressed or to be implied, that the plaintiff should contribute her labour towards the reparation of a house in which she was to have some beneficial interest, then I think that the arrangement becomes one to which the law can give effect. This seems to be consistent with the reasoning of the speeches in *Gissing* v *Gissing*.'

. . .

About that case the following observations may be made. First, as Brightman J himself observed, if the work had not been done the common intention would not have been enough. Secondly, if the common intention had not been orally made plain, the work would not have been conduct from which it could be inferred. That, I think, is the effect of the actual decision in *Pettitt* v *Pettitt* [1970] AC 777. Thirdly, and on the other hand, the work was conduct which amounted to an acting upon the common intention by the woman.

. . . There remains this difficult question: what is the quality of conduct required for the latter purpose [acting upon the common intention]? . . . the law is not so cynical as to infer that a woman will only go to live with a man to whom she is not married if she understands that she is to have an interest in their home. So what sort of conduct is required? In my judgment it must be conduct on which the woman could not reasonably have been expected to embark unless she was to have an interest in the house. If she was not to have such an interest, she could reasonably be expected to go and live with her lover, but not, for example, to wield a 14-lb sledge hammer in the front garden. In adopting the latter kind of conduct she is seen to act to her detriment on the faith of the common intention.

[In the present case] The defendant told the plaintiff that her name was not going onto the title because it would cause some prejudice in the matrimonial proceedings between her and her husband. The defendant never had any real intention of replacing his brother with the plaintiff when those proceedings were at an end. Just as in *Eves* v *Eves* [1975] 1 WLR 1338, these facts appear to me to raise a clear inference that there was an understanding between the plaintiff and the defendant, or a common intention, that the plaintiff was to have some sort of proprietary interest in the house; otherwise no excuse for not putting her name onto the title would have been needed.

Comment

(1) The court regarded indirect contributions to mortgage instalments as acting to the claimant's detriment. In *Rosset*, the wife supervised (and assisted) the restoration work. Lord Bridge doubted whether this would suffice as detriment; is this unduly harsh?

(2) Gardner[24] argues that detriment is no longer required, as it is not mentioned in *Stack* v *Dowden*.[25] Is this a likely outcome, at least if intentions to share ownership cannot be imputed? There is quite a large body of recent cases assuming that detriment remains essential, though they do not explicitly consider whether *Stack* may have changed the law.[26]

Though *Rosset* quotes them with approval, *Eves* and *Grant* are controversial cases because they do not involve explicit agreements for the claimant to have a share. Rather, they each involve excuses why she was not given one. It is, of course, irrelevant that one party possesses a subjective intention that no interest should be given: we look for an objective intention.[27] However, it may be dangerous to argue that there is a common intention merely because an excuse has been given.[28] Lawrence Collins J has said this point 'accords with commonsense, and if the matter were free from authority, I would have preferred a proprietary estoppel approach in "excuse" cases'.[29] Is it a reasonable defence of the cases that an excuse would not have been necessary unless there had been an initial understanding that the claimant should have a share?

The context in which detriment has most often been discussed is that of estoppel claims.[30] One problem is that it is difficult to distinguish normal family activity (*Rosset*) from exceptional conduct (*Eves*). It may be objected that the courts have indulged in gender stereotyping in their attitude, for example, to the woman's work with a sledgehammer in *Eves*.[31] Is this a fair criticism?

The strictness of the contribution rules after *Rosset* led to more cases being argued on the basis of a common intention.[32] Waite LJ[33] in particular was very critical of the extent to which conversations over many years have to be raked over to see whether an express common intention can be found. Although it seems right that a clear statement of a common intention should be given effect to, is the search for an express common intention anything other than a haphazard exercise, or else a cloak for the court's imposing what it regards as a fair result? Will use of the express common intention trust diminish following *Stack* v *Dowden*?

---

[24] (2008) 124 LQR 422 at p 424; supported by Etherton [2008] CLJ 265 at p 277.
[25] [2007] 2 AC 432.
[26] *Parris* v *Williams* [2009] 1 P&CR 169; *Qayyum* v *Hameed* [2009] 2 FLR 962 (Etherton LJ); *Thomson* v *Humphrey* [2010] 2 FLR 107; *De Bruyne* v *De Bruyne* [2010] 2 FCR 1240; *Smith* v *Bottomley* [2014] 1 FLR 626 at [31]; *Agarwala* v *Agarwala* [2014] 2 FLR 1069 (plus several first instance decisions).
[27] *Gissing* v *Gissing* [1971] AC 886 at p 906.
[28] Gardner (1993) 109 LQR 263 at p 265.
[29] *Van Laethem* v *Brooker* [2006] 2 FLR 495 at [67].
[30] See pp 203 above and 276 below. In the common intention context, see *Cox* v *Jones* [2004] 2 FLR 1010.
[31] Lawson (1996) 16 LS 218, especially pp 224–231.
[32] *Stokes* v *Anderson* [1991] 1 FLR 391; *Hammond* v *Mitchell* [1991] 1 WLR 1127; *Midland Bank plc* v *Cooke* [1995] 4 All ER 562; *Hyett* v *Stanley* [2004] 1 FLR 394; *Cox* v *Jones* [2004] 2 FLR 1010.
[33] See *Midland Bank plc* v *Cooke* [1995] 4 All ER 562 and *Hammond* v *Mitchell* [1991] 1 WLR 1127 (Extract 8.8.1 below).

D. *Stack* v *Dowden*

Extract 8.5.5

Stack v *Dowden* [2007] 2 AC 432

LORD HOPE: 4.   The cases can be broken down into those where there is a single legal ownership and those where there is joint legal ownership. There must be consistency of approach between these two cases, a point to which my noble and learned friend, Lord Neuberger of Abbotsbury, has drawn our attention. I think that consistency is to be found by deciding where the onus lies if a party wishes to show that the beneficial ownership is different from the legal ownership. I agree with Baroness Hale that this is achieved by taking sole beneficial ownership as the starting point in the first case and by taking joint beneficial ownership as the starting point in the other . . .

5.   The advantage of this approach is that everyone will know where they stand with regard to the property when they enter into their relationship. Parties are, of course, free to enter into whatever bargain they wish and, so long as it is clearly expressed and can be proved, the court will give effect to it. But for the rest the state of the legal title will determine the right starting point. The onus is then on the party who contends that the beneficial interests are divided between them otherwise than as the title shows to demonstrate this on the facts.

LORD WALKER: 26.   Lord Bridge's extreme doubt 'whether anything less will do' was certainly consistent with many first-instance and Court of Appeal decisions, but I respectfully doubt whether it took full account of the views (conflicting though they were) expressed in *Gissing* v *Gissing* [1971] AC 886 (see especially Lord Reid, at pp 896g–897b, and Lord Diplock, at p 909d–h). It has attracted some trenchant criticism from scholars as potentially productive of injustice: see *Gray & Gray, Elements of Land Law*, 4th ed, paras 10.132–10.137, the last paragraph being headed 'A More Optimistic Future'. Whether or not Lord Bridge's observation was justified in 1990, in my opinion the law has moved on, and your Lordships should move it a little more in the same direction, while bearing in mind that the Law Commission may soon come forward with proposals which, if enacted by Parliament, may recast the law in this area.

BARONESS HALE: 42.   Another development has been the recognition in the courts that, to put it at its lowest, the interpretation to be put on the behaviour of people living together in an intimate relationship may be different from the interpretation to be put upon similar behaviour between commercial men. To put it at its highest, an outcome which might seem just in a purely commercial transaction may appear highly unjust in a transaction between husband and wife or cohabitant and cohabitant. This recognition developed in a series of cases between separating spouses, beginning with *In re Rogers's Question* [1948] 1 All ER 328; *Newgrosh* v *Newgrosh* (1950) 100 LJ 525; *Jones* v *Maynard* [1951] Ch 572 and *Rimmer* v *Rimmer* [1953] 1 QB 63 . . . That section 17 conferred any discretion to interfere with established titles was firmly rejected by this House in *Pettitt* v *Pettitt* [1970] AC 777. Nevertheless, the opinions in that case and in *Gissing* v *Gissing* [1971] AC 886 contain vivid illustrations of how difficult it is to apply simple assumptions to the complicated, interdependent and often-changing arrangements made between married couples. As Lord Reid famously put it in *Gissing* v *Gissing*, at p 897a, 'It cannot surely depend on who signs which cheques'.

44.   Inter vivos disputes between unmarried cohabiting couples are still governed by the ordinary law. These disputes have become increasingly visible in recent years as more and more couples live together without marrying. The full picture has recently been painted by the Law Commission in Cohabitation: The Financial Consequences of Relationship Breakdown – A Consultation Paper, (2006) Consultation Paper No 179, Part 2, and its overview paper, paras 2.3–2.11. For example, the 2001 Census recorded over 10m married couples in England and

Wales, with over 7.5m dependent children; but it also recorded over 2m cohabiting couples, with over 1.25m children dependent upon them. This was a 67% increase in cohabitation over the previous ten years and a doubling of the numbers of such households with dependent children. The Government Actuaries Department predicts that the proportion of couples co-habiting will continue to grow, from the present one in six of all couples to one in four by 2031.

45. Cohabitation comes in many different shapes and sizes. People embarking on their first serious relationship more commonly cohabit than marry. Many of these relationships may be quite short-lived and childless. But most people these days cohabit before marriage – in 2003, 78.7% of spouses gave identical addresses before marriage, and the figures are even higher for second marriages. So many couples are cohabiting with a view to marriage at some later date – as long ago as 1998 the British Household Panel Survey found that 75% of current cohabi-tants expected to marry, although only a third had firm plans: John Ermisch, Personal Relationships and Marriage Expectations (2000) Working Papers of the Institute of Social and Economic Research: Paper 2000–27. Cohabitation is much more likely to end in separation than is marriage, and cohabitations which end in separation tend to last for a shorter time than mar-riages which end in divorce. But increasing numbers of couples cohabit for long periods without marrying and their reasons for doing so vary from conscious rejection of marriage as a legal institution to regarding themselves 'as good as married' anyway: Law Commission, Consultation Paper No 179, Part 2, para 2.45. There is evidence of a wide-spread myth of the 'common law marriage' in which unmarried couples acquire the same rights as married after a period of cohabitation: Anne Barlow, et al, 'Just a Piece of Paper? Marriage and Cohabitation', in Alison Park, et al (eds), *British Social Attitudes: Public policy, social ties. The 18th Report*, (2001), pp 29–57. There is also evidence that 'the legal implications of marriage are a long way down the list of most couples' considerations when deciding whether to marry': Law Commission, Consultation Paper No 179, Part 5, para 5.10.

46. . . . In 2002, however, the commission published Sharing Homes, A Discussion Paper (2002) (Law Com No 278). Unlike most Law Commission publications, this did not contain even provisional, let alone final, proposals for reform. Its principal conclusion was that:

> 'It is quite simply not possible to devise a statutory scheme for the ascertainment and quan-tification of beneficial interests in the shared home which can operate fairly and evenly across the diversity of domestic circumstances which are now to be encountered.' (Para 1.31.)

While this conclusion is not surprising, its importance for us is that the evolution of the law of property to take account of changing social and economic circumstances will have to come from the courts rather than Parliament.

60. . . . There is no need for me to rehearse all the developments in the case law since *Pettitt v Pettitt* [1970] AC 777 and *Gissing v Gissing* [1971] AC 886, discussed over more than 70 pages following the quoted passage, by Chadwick LJ in *Oxley v Hiscock* [2005] Fam 211, and most importantly by my noble and learned friend, Lord Walker of Gestingthorpe, in his opinion, which make good that proposition. The law has indeed moved on in response to changing social and economic conditions. The search is to ascertain the parties' shared intentions, actual, inferred or imputed, with respect to the property in the light of their whole course of conduct in relation to it.

63. We are not in this case concerned with the first hurdle [proving a common intention as to shared beneficial ownership]. There is undoubtedly an argument for saying, as did the Law Commission in Sharing Homes, A Discussion Paper, para 4.23 that the observations, which were strictly obiter dicta, of Lord Bridge of Harwich in *Lloyds Bank plc v Rosset* [1991] 1 AC 107 have set that hurdle rather too high in certain respects. But that does not concern us now. It is common ground that a conveyance into joint names is sufficient, at least in the vast majority of cases, to surmount the first hurdle. The question is whether, that hurdle surmounted, the approach to quantification should be the same.

69.   In law, 'context is everything' and the domestic context is very different from the commercial world. Each case will turn on its own facts. Many more factors than financial contributions may be relevant to divining the parties' true intentions. These include: any advice or
discussions at the time of the transfer which cast light upon their intentions then; the reasons
why the home was acquired in their joint names; the reasons why (if it be the case) the survivor
was authorised to give a receipt for the capital moneys; the purpose for which the home was
acquired; the nature of the parties' relationship; whether they had children for whom they both
had responsibility to provide a home; how the purchase was financed, both initially and subsequently; how the parties arranged their finances, whether separately or together or a bit of both;
how they discharged the outgoings on the property and their other household expenses. When
a couple are joint owners of the home and jointly liable for the mortgage, the inferences to be
drawn from who pays for what may be very different from the inferences to be drawn when only
one is owner of the home. The arithmetical calculation of how much was paid by each is also
likely to be less important. It will be easier to draw the inference that they intended that each
should contribute as much to the household as they reasonably could and that they would
share the eventual benefit or burden equally. The parties' individual characters and personalities
may also be a factor in deciding where their true intentions lay. In the cohabitation context,
mercenary considerations may be more to the fore than they would be in marriage, but it should
not be assumed that they always take pride of place over natural love and affection. At the end
of the day, having taken all this into account, cases in which the joint legal owners are to be
taken to have intended that their beneficial interests should be different from their legal interests
will be very unusual.

Comment

(1) Two basic strands of reasoning appear: that the beneficial rights should follow the legal
title and that *Rosset* provides too strict a test. How can these be reconciled?

(2) It seems clear that *Rosset* must be seen as being too strict today.[34] The question (considered below) is whether the courts will infer a common intention whenever a couple
share the financial and practical aspects of running a joint household, especially where
there are children.

(3) The dicta of Lord Walker indicate that he is contemplating that indirect contributions
(the focus of the relevant dicta in *Gissing*) will suffice. Subsequently, *Webster* v *Webster*[35]
has assumed that indirect contributions are to be allowed.

(4) The House of Lords still applies the core test of common intention. Is this to be
regretted?

E. The application of *Stack* v *Dowden*

An initial point is that imputing intentions has the potential to change the law almost
beyond recognition. However, it has been seen that, apart from quantification of shares,
this is not as yet a result of *Jones* v *Kernott*.[36] Accordingly, this section concentrates on
developments to inferred intentions.

---

[34] Repeated by the Privy Council in *Abbott* v *Abbott* [2008] 1 FLR 1451 at [5].
[35] [2009] 1 FLR 1240 at [33] (County Court).
[36] See p 235 above.

Extract 8.5.6

Sir Terence Etherton [2008] CLJ 265 (footnotes omitted)

The majority in *Stack*, and in particular Lord Walker and Baroness Hale, appear to have attempted to give legitimacy to their approach by introducing the fiction of an actual agreement or common intention, where there was none in fact, and so providing consistency with *Pettitt* and *Gissing*. The use of a fiction in modern times to legitimise legal analysis is unsatisfactory.

. . .

I suggest that the relief in *Stack* was in response to unjust enrichment. There was an enrichment of Mr. Stack, at the expense of Ms. Dowden since he was the joint owner of the property but she contributed financially more than half of the purchase price of the property. On the later approach of Professor Birks, that is to say, all enrichments are unjust unless there is some juristic reason for the retention of the enrichment, the enrichment of Mr Stack was plainly unjust.

. . .

In summary, then, the analysis in a *Stack* type of case of the cause of action for unjust enrichment would be as follows. The starting presumption, in a case where both parties are joint legal owners, is that they intended that they would be joint beneficial owners. If that presumption is not rebutted, no question of unjust enrichment arises. Their rights to joint beneficial ownership would be based on mutual consent. The presumption may be rebutted by evidence that it was not the intention of the partner who made a larger contribution (the claimant) to confer on the other partner (the defendant) a financial benefit on realisation of the value of the home.

Comment

Is this the true basis for *Stack*? How would it apply in transfers into a single name?

Extract 8.5.7

Jones v Kernott [2012] 1 AC 776

LORD WALKER and LADY HALE:

A single regime?
16. In an interesting article by Simon Gardner and Katherine Davidson, 'The Future of *Stack* v *Dowden*' (2011) 127 LQR 13, 15, the authors express the hope that the Supreme Court will 'make clear that constructive trusts of family homes are governed by a single regime, dispelling any impression that different rules apply to "joint names" and "single name" cases'. At a high level of generality, there is of course a single regime: the law of trusts (this is the second of Mustill LJ's propositions in *Grant v Edwards* [1986] Ch 638, 651). To the extent that we recognise that a 'common intention' trust is of central importance to 'joint names' as well as 'single names' cases, we are going some way to meet that hope. Nevertheless it is important to point out that the starting point for analysis is different in the two situations. That is so even though it may be necessary to enquire into the varied circumstances and reasons why a house or flat has been acquired in a single name or in joint names (they range, for instance, from *Lowson v Coombes* [1999] Ch 373, where the property was in the woman's sole name because the man was apprehensive of claims by his separated wife, to *Adekunle v Ritchie* [2007] WTLR 1505, where an enfranchised freehold was in joint names because the elderly tenant could not obtain a mortgage on her own).
17. The starting point is different because the claimant whose name is not on the proprietorship register has the burden of establishing some sort of implied trust, normally what is now

termed a 'common intention' constructive trust. The claimant whose name is on the register starts (in the absence of an express declaration of trust in different terms, and subject to what is said below about resulting trusts) with the presumption (or assumption) of a beneficial joint tenancy.

Comment

Does this encourage or discourage the development of principles in single names cases so as to mirror (even if not completely) those applied in joint names transfers?

Perhaps the most minimal impact of *Stack* would be a limited relaxation of the *Rosset* requirements. Thus recognition of indirect contributions has been seen to be highly likely.[37] However, far more significant changes might arise from a much relaxed approach to inferring common intentions. It is that which is the subject of this section.

Baroness Hale in [69] (see Extract 8.5.5) identifies a very wide range of factors which the court is to take into account; this approach is clearly approved in *Jones* v *Kernott*. One thing to remember is that these dicta were in the context of quantifying shares in joint names transfers; indeed, they overtly recognise that single name transfers may be different. Even though her approach has been applied to quantifying the shares in single name transfers,[38] does it apply to the initial question as to whether there is a common intention that beneficial interests do not follow the legal title? The argument for a broad approach is that common intention is the principle underpinning all issues and it would be artificial to recognise different factors in the various settings. Thus Gardner argues[39] that a broad approach to common intention 'will surely overwhelm such technical objections'.

Turning to the cases since *Stack*, there has been no sustained analysis of its impact in single name cases. The leading cases are joint names cases: *Fowler* v *Baron* and, especially, *Jones* v *Kernott*. Such cases as we have are interesting for quite short dicta on the question, rather than longer analyses which would justify extended extracts. These dicta will be collected into two groups. The first relates to whether the broader range of factors (as expressed by Baroness Hale at [69]) can be considered. The second deals with the question whether, in practice, there is any significant change to when in fact a common intention will be inferred. The two groups are not mutually exclusive: it should be obvious that an analysis rejecting the broader factors will also reject any significant change.

The first group includes the following:

(i) In *Morris* v *Morris*,[40] Sir Peter Gibson said of the dicta in *Stack*:

> Those comments were, of course, directed to what is always regarded as the second question relating to quantification of beneficial entitlement, the first question being whether an agreement arrangement or understanding that the claimant was to acquire a beneficial interest in the land has been shown. The authorities make clear that a common intention constructive trust based only on conduct will only be found in exceptional circumstances.

(ii) By contrast, Etherton J took a different approach in *Bindra* v *Chopra*:[41]

> 86.   The first way in which Jennifer puts this part of her case is on the basis of a common intention constructive trust, as expounded by the House of Lords in *Stack* v *Dowden*. There is some

[37] See p 248 above.
[38] *Abbott* v *Abbott* [2008] 1 FLR 1451; *Holman* v *Howes* [2008] 1 FLR 1217, especially at [28].
[39] (2008) 124 LQR 422 at pp 426–427.
[40] [2008] EWCA Civ 257 at [23].
[41] [2008] 3 FLR 541. The issue was not considered by the Court of Appeal: [2009] 2 FLR 786.

debate about the principles underlying the decision of the majority in that case. In broad terms, where co-habitants have been living together in a property as a couple, one of them may apply to the court to declare that he or she has an interest or a larger interest in the property by virtue of the common intention of the parties, such common intention to be determined by a 'holistic approach', undertaking a survey of the whole course of dealing between the parties and taking account of all conduct which throws light on the question what shares were intended. In the words of Baroness Hale, at para 60: 'The search is to ascertain the parties' shared intentions, actual, inferred or imputed, with respect of the property in light of their whole course of conduct in relation to it.'

(iii) Similarly Black J in *Q* v *Q*[42] (not a normal case involving a couple, though it was a single name transfer) stated:

114.   As Baroness Hale put it in *Stack* v *Dowden* (a case of a cohabiting couple where the family home was conveyed into joint names but their beneficial interests in it were held to be unequal),

'The search is to ascertain the parties' shared intentions, actual, inferred or imputed, with respect to the property in the light of their whole course of conduct in relation to it.'

She made clear that each case turns on its own facts and that many more factors than financial contributions may be relevant in divining the parties' true intentions as to their beneficial interests. The list that she gives in her speech (at paragraph 69) is particularly tailored to the most common situation in which a 'common intention trust' may arise, that of the cohabiting couple, but it does show how widely the net must be cast in order to catch everything that may have a bearing on the issue.

(iv) Patten LJ stated in *de Bruyne* v *de Bruyne*:[43]

42.   This view of the law [*Rosset*] was regarded as outmoded and too narrowly stated by the majority of the House of Lords in *Stack* v *Dowden* [2007] 2 AC 432. Baroness Hale stated in her speech (at paragraph 60) that the search was 'to ascertain the parties' shared intentions, actual, inferred or imputed with respect to the property in the light of their whole course of conduct in relation to it' and in paragraph 69 she set out various factors which might be relevant to this process. This approach is not uncontroversial and has been said by some commentators and practitioners to be unworkable . . .

(v) Though most cases apply the *Stack* dicta, the trial judge in *Re Ali*[44] observed:

98.   The law has been further clarified by the case of *Jones* v *Kernott* [2012] 1 AC 776, in which it was noted that in 'sole name' cases, there were two questions to be asked – namely whether it was intended that the other party have any beneficial interest in the property at all and, if he does, the second issue is what that interest is. In considering the first of the questions there will need to be evidence of an actual agreement, arrangement or understanding between the parties which must 'be based on evidence of express discussions between the partners, however imperfectly remembered and however imprecise their terms may have been' (*Lloyds Bank* v *Rosset and Another* [1991] AC 107, Lord Bridge of Harwich at 132 F-G).
99.   In considering the second of these questions the Court may have regard to the 'whole course of dealing' between the parties, in order to ascertain their intentions, or, if necessary, to impute them.

---

[42] [2009] 1 FLR 935.
[43] [2010] 2 FLR 1240.
[44] [2013] 1 FLR 1061 (not a family home case, though involving family members).

Comment

(1) Does any consistent picture emerge from these dicta? Which best fit what was said in *Stack*?

(2) Is *Re Ali*, in particular the implication in [99], to be viewed as out of line with other cases?

The second group of cases concerns the question as to when, post-*Stack*, a common intention will be inferred.

(i) Evans-Lombe J *Tackaberry* v *Hollis*[45] provides our first dicta:

> 82.   The proper approach of the court in determining whether such an agreement has been established is summarized in the judgment of Lord Justice Mustill in *Grant* v *Edwards* [1986] 1 Ch 638 at page 651 in a case where the Claimant was a female cohabitant who had assisted with work to improve the property in question.
>
> > '(1) The law does not recognise a concept of family property, whereby people who live together in a settled relationship ipso facto share the rights of ownership in the assets acquired and used for the purposes of their life together. Nor does the law acknowledge that by the mere fact of doing work on the asset of one party to the relationship the other party will acquire a beneficial interest in that asset.'
>
> 84.   The decision of the Court of Appeal in *Grant* v *Edwards* has recently been approved and applied in *Stack* v *Dowden* in particular in the speech of Lord Neuberger.

It may be recalled that *Grant* v *Edwards* provided the basis for the analysis in *Rosset*.

(ii) Sir John Chadwick stated in *James* v *Thomas* [2008] 1 FLR 1598 (Extract 8.5.8 below):

> 24.   . . . But . . . in the absence of an express post-acquisition agreement, a court will be slow to infer from conduct alone that parties intended to vary existing beneficial interests established at the time of acquisition.
>
> 27.   . . . it is possible to envisage circumstances in which the fact that one party began to make contributions to capital repayments due under a mortgage might evidence an agreement that that party was to have a share in the property . . .
>
> 38.   . . . As Baroness Hale of Richmond observed in *Stack* v *Dowden* . . . it is not for the court to abandon the search for the result which reflects what the parties must, in the light of their conduct, be taken to have intended in favour of the result which the court itself considers fair.

These dicta could also be fitted in the first group of cases.

(iii) Perhaps most striking is the analysis of Warren J in *Thomson* v *Humphrey*:[46]

> 25.   . . . The leading case in this area is, of course, *Stack* v *Dowden* [2007] 2 AC 542. The present case, unlike *Stack* v *Dowden*, is one where the property, whether the Long Stratton property or Church Farm itself, is vested in one person, the defendant, and where another person, the claimant, claims an interest. Nonetheless, it is clear that the starting point is that the beneficial ownership in a case of sole ownership rests with the sole owner. A person in the situation of the claimant who seeks to establish an interest as against the holder of the legal title has a dual hurdle. She must show that it was intended that she should have some share, and must then establish the extent of that share. Much of what was said in the opinions of *Stack* v *Dowden*, as well as by the Court of Appeal in *Oxley* v *Hiscock* [2005] Fam 211, is directed at the second question.

---

[45]   [2008] WTLR 279.
[46]   [2010] 2 FLR 107.

26. In relation to the first question, it is necessary to go back to *Lloyds Bank* v *Rosset* [1991] 1 AC 107.

29. Accepting that matters have moved on since Lord Bridge's restrictive requirement that there needs to be a direct contribution in terms of the mortgage payments, it is not sensible to attempt to say what will and will not be enough. There will be cases which, on any view, fall from the claimant's point of view on the wrong side of the line, wherever that line is to be drawn. Each case is to be viewed on its facts, but one can obtain a flavour of the correct approach from the reported cases, as in *Burns* v *Burns* [1984] Ch 317, where performance of domestic duties and staying home to look after the children, contribution to rates and certain utility bills and purchase of some fittings and fixtures and domestic chattels was insufficient to give rise to any interest.

Comment

(1) This last quotation from *Thomson* is remarkable on account of its endorsement of *Burns*. If *Stack* is to have a really important impact, it is this area – relating to non-financial contributions – which is likely to be crucial.

(2) If the wider criteria adopted by Baroness Hale at [69] do apply to single names cases, is it justifiable for the second group of cases to turn back to the older cases? It may be noted that the cases in the first group which support the application of the wider criteria do not go on to apply them in a manner inconsistent with cases such as *Rosset* and *Burns* (at least, not beyond indirect financial contributions).

(3) Though it has nothing direct to say about these cases, might *Jones* v *Kernott* lead to an approach which recognises far greater flexibility in finding common intentions?

Some of the discussion in these cases relates to the type of conduct from which an intention can be inferred. But how strict is the law when a party argues that that was an express common intention? In *Ullah* v *Ullah*,[47] Martin QC was clear that this requires express discussions regarding the beneficial interest, applying dicta in *Rosset*. Does this maintain too rigid a line between common intention inferred from conduct and cases where the judge is persuaded that the parties did intend to share ownership? Is it possible that successful claims today should be split into three categories: express agreement between the parties, situations where all the evidence persuades the judge that the parties did so intend and contributions from which inferences are semi-automatically drawn?[48]

Although non-financial and indirect contributions have provided the most difficult and important challenges for the law, other problems can arise. A feature of some cases is that the claimant has worked in the legal owner's business, often without payment.

Extract 8.5.8

James v *Thomas* [2008] 1 FLR 1598 (Court of Appeal)

The parties lived together as man and wife for about 15 years. During that time the woman had helped the man extensively with his business and had then become a partner in it. They carried out extensive works of renovation to the property.

SIR JOHN CHADWICK: 27. Although it is possible to envisage circumstances in which the fact that one party began to make contributions to capital repayments due under a mortgage might

---

[47] [2013] BPIR 928 at [6].

[48] The third category would include financial contributions: *Dibble* v *Pfluger* [2011] 1 FLR 659.

evidence an agreement that that party was to have a share in the property, the circumstances of this case are not of that nature. On the facts found by the judge, the only source of funds to meet Mr Thomas' commitments under the mortgage, as well as all other household and personal expenses, was the receipts of the business. While the parties were living together they were dependent on the success of the business to meet their outgoings. It was not at all surprising that, in the early days of their relationship, Miss James should do what she could to ensure that the business prospered. That is not to undervalue her contribution; which, as Mr Thomas recognised, was substantial. But it is to recognise that what she was doing gives rise to no inference that the parties had agreed (or had reached a common understanding) that she was to have a share in the property: what she was doing was wholly explicable on other grounds.
38.   Miss James will be entitled, as a partner, to a share in the partnership assets after taking accounts. Her interest in the property (if any) must be determined by applying principles of law and equity which (however inadequate to meet the circumstances in which parties live together in the twenty-first century) must now be taken as well-established. Unless she can bring herself within those principles, her claim in the present case must fail. As Baroness Hale of Richmond observed in *Stack v Dowden* [2007] UKHL 17, [61]; [2007] 2 WLR 831, 851 D–E it is not for the court to abandon the search for the result which reflects what the parties must, in the light of their conduct, be taken to have intended in favour of the result which the court itself considers fair.

Comment

(1) Is this analysis consistent with the broader approach taken to common intention in *Stack*?

(2) The house had been purchased before the relationship started. Should this be a significant factor? See also *Williams* v *Lawrence* [2011] WTLR 1455.

6. Quantification of shares

It has been seen that the Court of Appeal adopted a constructive trust in *Oxley* v *Hiscock* (Extract 8.2.1 above). We now need to consider how the court employed the greater flexibility that such an analysis permits.

Extract 8.6.1

Oxley v *Hiscock* [2005] Fam 211

A couple's existing house (Page Close) was sold, with Mr Hiscock being entitled to £25,200 from the proceeds and Mrs Oxley £36,300. A new house (Dickens Close) was bought in Mr Hiscock's name. Dickens Close was sold when the relationship ended ten years later. Mrs Oxley claimed a half share in the proceeds.

CHADWICK LJ: 4.   The purchase price for 35 Dickens Close was £127,000. The purchase was funded (i) by a building society advance of £30,000, (ii) by the net proceeds of sale of 39 Page Close (some £61,500) and (iii), as to the balance, £35,500 or thereabouts, by Mr Hiscock from his own savings.
15.   . . . The effect of the judge's findings, as it seems to me, is that that [sic] Mr Hiscock and Mrs Oxley were in agreement, before the acquisition of 35 Dickens Close, that the property would be shared; but that there was no express agreement as to what their respective shares should be.
16.   . . . the judge held that, notwithstanding that decision, she should follow observations of Waite LJ in *Midland Bank plc* v *Cooke* [1995] 4 All ER 562. Waite LJ had said, at p 575: 'I would therefore hold that positive evidence that the parties neither discussed nor intended any agreement as to the proportions of their beneficial interest does not preclude the court, on

general equitable principles, from inferring one.' In the light of that passage, the judge directed herself, at para 17:

> 'It could not be clearer therefore that the proper approach of a court to a dispute of this nature is that when there is no express agreement between the parties the court must look to the whole course of dealings to infer what the agreement between those parties was.'

19. . . . She expressed her conclusion, at para 31:

> 'from the analysis of the law and the facts in this case, it is clear that the order which the claimant sought in her notice of application is the only one that can properly be made, namely to declare that the claimant is equally entitled, with the defendant, to a half share in the proceeds of sale of the Hartley property . . .'

23. . . . there was no evidence as to how, in fact, the mortgage debt was discharged; and it is (at the least) arguable that, on the judge's findings, the parties should be treated as having contributed equally to the payment-off of that debt. But, making all assumptions in Mrs Oxley's favour, the amount of her share (based on financial contributions) could not exceed 40% – (£36,300 + 1/2 £30,000)/ £127,000.

The law as understood before Midland Bank plc v Cooke

. . .

48. For the reasons which I have sought to explain, I think that the better view is that, in the passage in *Rosset's case* [1991] 1 AC 107, 132f, to which both Dillon LJ and Steyn LJ referred in *Springette* v *Defoe*, Lord Bridge was addressing only the primary question – 'was there a common intention that each should have a beneficial interest in the property?' He was not addressing the secondary question – 'what was the common intention of the parties as to extent of their respective beneficial interests?' As this court had pointed out in *Grant* v *Edwards* and *Stokes* v *Anderson*, the court may well have to supply the answer to that secondary question by inference from their subsequent conduct: see, in particular, the reference in the judgment of Sir Nicolas Browne-Wilkinson V-C in *Grant* v *Edwards* [1986] Ch 638, 657e–f to the passages in the speech of Lord Diplock in *Gissing* v *Gissing* [1971] AC 886, 909a, d–e. And it may be, as Nourse LJ observed in *Stokes* v *Anderson* [1991] 1 FLR 391, 400:

> 'Once you get to that stage . . . there is no practicable alternative to the determination of a fair share. The court must supply the common intention by reference to that which all the material circumstances have shown to be fair.'

Developments since the decision in Midland Bank plc v Cooke

[*Drake* v *Whipp* [1996] 1 FLR 826 is considered, in which a property was bought in Whipp's name, Drake contributing 40%. They undertook extensive building work, to the cost of which Drake contributed 10%.]

62. . . . On the basis of their respective financial contributions, the county court judge held that Mrs Drake was entitled to share to the extent of 19.4% – that being the proportion which her aggregate contributions (£38,000) bore to the whole cost of acquisition and conversion (£195,790). On appeal Mrs Drake contended for a share of 40.1% – that being the proportion which her contribution to the purchase price (£25,000) bore to the cost of acquisition (£61,250). The Court of Appeal held that a 'fair share' would be one third; and varied the county court order accordingly. It is material, in the context of the present appeal, to analyse the reasoning which led the [Court] to that conclusion.

64. As I have indicated, this court in *Drake* v *Whipp* [1996] 1 FLR 826 was in no doubt that it had been the common understanding and intention of the parties, at the time that the property was acquired, that each should have some beneficial interest. In those circumstances – notwithstanding a concession by counsel for Mr Drake that there had been no common

intention – the court held, at p 830, that it would 'be artificial in the extreme to proceed to decide this appeal on the false footing that the parties' shares are to be determined in accordance with the law on resulting trusts'. The case was plainly one of a constructive trust. So it was to be approached on the basis explained by this court in *Grant* v *Edwards* [1986] Ch 638 – the judgments in which Peter Gibson LJ described as 'particularly helpful and illuminating' . . . Peter Gibson LJ went on [1996] 1 FLR 826, 831:

> 'In my judgment the judge's finding on common intention cannot stand in the absence of any evidence that Mrs Drake intended her share to be limited to her direct contributions to the acquisition and conversion costs. I would approach the matter more broadly, looking at the parties' entire course of conduct together. I would take into account not only those direct contributions but also the fact that Mr Whipp and Mrs Drake together purchased the property with the intention that it should be their home, that they both contributed their labour in 70:30% proportions, that they had a joint account out of which the costs of conversion were met, but that that account was largely fed by his earnings, and that she paid for the food and some other household expenses and took care of the housekeeping for them both. I note that whilst it was open to Mrs Drake to argue at the trial for a constructive trust and for a 50% share, she opted to rely solely on a resulting trust and a 40.1% share. In all the circumstances, I would hold that her fair share should be one third.'

65.   It is very difficult, if not impossible, to find anything in the facts in *Drake* v *Whipp* [1996] 1 FLR 826 to suggest that either of the parties ever gave thought to an arrangement under which the property should be shared in the proportions two-thirds and one-third; let alone that that was ever their common intention. Nor do I think that Peter Gibson LJ approached the matter on that basis. As he said, at p 830, 'in constructive trust cases, the court can adopt a broad brush approach to determining the parties' respective shares'. And that is what he did, as he acknowledged in the passage, at p 831, which I have just set out: 'I would approach the matter more broadly, looking at the parties' entire course of conduct together.' . . .

Summary
69.   In those circumstances, the second question to be answered in cases of this nature is: 'what is the extent of the parties' respective beneficial interests in the property?' Again, in many such cases, the answer will be provided by evidence of what they said and did at the time of the acquisition. But, in a case where there is no evidence of any discussion between them as to the amount of the share which each was to have – and even in a case where the evidence is that there was no discussion on that point – the question still requires an answer. It must now be accepted that (at least in this court and below) the answer is that each is entitled to that share which the court considers fair having regard to the whole course of dealing between them in relation to the property. And, in that context, 'the whole course of dealing between them in relation to the property' includes the arrangements which they make from time to time in order to meet the outgoings (for example, mortgage contributions, council tax and utilities, repairs, insurance and housekeeping) which have to be met if they are to live in the property as their home.
70.   As the cases show, the courts have not found it easy to reconcile that final step with a traditional, property-based, approach. It was rejected, in unequivocal terms, by Dillon LJ in *Springette* v *Defoe* [1992] 2 FLR 388, 393 when he said: 'The court does not as yet sit, as under a palm tree, to exercise a general discretion to do what the man in the street, on a general overview of the case, might regard as fair.' Three strands of reasoning can be identified.
    (1)   That suggested by Lord *Diplock* in *Gissing* v *Gissing* [1971] AC 886, 909d and adopted by Nourse LJ in *Stokes* v *Anderson* [1991] 1 FLR 391, 399g, 400b–c. The parties are taken to have agreed at the time of the acquisition of the property that their respective shares are not to be quantified then, but are left to be determined when their relationship comes to an end or the property is sold on the basis of what is then fair having regard to the whole course of dealing

between them. The court steps in to determine what is fair because, when the time came for that determination, the parties were unable to agree.

(2)   That suggested by Waite LJ in *Midland Bank plc* v *Cooke* [1995] 4 All ER 562, 574d–g. The court undertakes a survey of the whole course of dealing between the parties 'relevant to their ownership and occupation of the property and their sharing of its burdens and advantages' in order to determine 'what proportions the parties must be assumed to have intended [from the outset] for their beneficial ownership'. On that basis the court treats what has taken place while the parties have been living together in the property as evidence of what they intended at the time of the acquisition.

(3)   That suggested by Sir Nicolas Browne-Wilkinson V-C in *Grant* v *Edwards* [1986] Ch 638, 656g–h, 657h and approved by Robert Walker LJ in *Yaxley* v *Gotts* [2000] Ch 162, 177c–e. The court makes such order as the circumstances require in order to give effect to the beneficial interest in the property of the one party, the existence of which the other party (having the legal title) is estopped from denying. That, I think, is the analysis which underlies the decision of this court in *Drake* v *Whipp* [1996] 1 FLR 826, 831e–g.

71.   For my part, I find the reasoning adopted by this court in *Midland Bank plc* v *Cooke* to be the least satisfactory of the three strands. It seems to me artificial – and an unnecessary fiction – to attribute to the parties a common intention that the extent of their respective beneficial interests in the property should be fixed as from the time of the acquisition, in circumstances in which all the evidence points to the conclusion that, at the time of the acquisition, they had given no thought to the matter. The same point can be made – although with less force – in relation to the reasoning that, at the time of the acquisition, their common intention was that the amount of the respective shares should be left for later determination. But it can be said that, if it were their common intention that each should have some beneficial interest in the property – which is the hypothesis upon which it becomes necessary to answer the second question – then, in the absence of evidence that they gave any thought to the amount of their respective shares, the necessary inference is that they must have intended that question would be answered later on the basis of what was then seen to be fair. But, as I have said, I think that the time has come to accept that there is no difference in outcome, in cases of this nature, whether the true analysis lies in constructive trust or in proprietary estoppel.

Determination of the present appeal
74.   . . . In my view to declare that the parties were entitled in equal shares would be unfair to Mr Hiscock. It would give insufficient weight to the fact that his direct contribution to the purchase price (£60,700) was substantially greater than that of Mrs Oxley (£36,300). On the basis of the judge's finding that there was in this case 'a classic pooling of resources' and conduct consistent with an intention to share the burden of the property (by which she must, I think, have meant the outgoings referable to ownership and cohabitation), it would be fair to treat them as having made approximately equal contributions to the balance of the purchase price (£30,000). Taking that into account with their direct contributions at the time of the purchase, I would hold that a fair division of the proceeds of sale of the property would be 60% to Mr Hiscock and 40% to Mrs Oxley.

Comment

(1) A resulting trust analysis would have given Mrs Oxley a 40.4% share. What then is the significance of employing a constructive trust? Could the £30,000 mortgage have been allocated to both of them (as the above calculation assumes) without a constructive trust? There was no evidence how the mortgage was paid off, but the judge found a 'classic pooling of resources, even though there was no joint bank account'.

(2) Why is the analysis in *Cooke* rejected? How important is this?

(3) In *Cooke*, a 6.47% contribution led to a 50% share in the property, bearing in mind the nature of the relationship. Though Chadwick LJ stated at [60] that *Cooke* was correctly decided, does it reach an appropriate result?

(4) Note that a finding that the parties intended specific shares obviates any need to assess shares on the *Oxley* basis.

Extract 8.6.2

Stack v *Dowden* [2007] 2 AC 432

BARONESS HALE: 61.   . . . *Oxley* v *Hiscock* has been hailed by *Gray & Gray, Elements of Land Law*, 4th ed, p 931, para 10.138, as 'an important breakthrough'. The passage quoted is very similar to the view of the Law Commission in Sharing Homes, A Discussion Paper, para 4.27 on the quantification of beneficial entitlement:

> 'If the question really is one of the parties' "common intention", we believe that there is much to be said for adopting what has been called a "holistic approach" to quantification, under-taking a survey of the whole course of dealing between the parties and taking account of all conduct which throws light on the question what shares were intended.'

That may be the preferable way of expressing what is essentially the same thought, for two reasons. First, it emphasises that the search is still for the result which reflects what the parties must, in the light of their conduct, be taken to have intended. Second, therefore, it does not enable the court to abandon that search in favour of the result which the court itself considers fair. For the court to impose its own view of what is fair upon the situation in which the parties find themselves would be to return to the days before *Pettitt* v *Pettitt* [1970] AC 777 without even the fig leaf of section 17 of the 1882 Act.

62.   Furthermore, although the parties' intentions may change over the course of time, produc-ing what my noble and learned friend, Lord Hoffmann, referred to in the course of argument as an 'ambulatory' constructive trust, at any one time their interests must be the same for all pur-poses. They cannot at one and the same time intend, for example, a joint tenancy with survivor-ship should one of them die while they are still together, a tenancy in common in equal shares should they separate on amicable terms after the children have grown up, and a tenancy in common in unequal shares should they separate on acrimonious terms while the children are still with them.

Comment

(1) At [65] and [12], Baroness Hale explicitly approves paras [48] and [69] in *Oxley*.

(2) In *Stack* at [69],[49] Baroness Hale articulates a very wide range of criteria, many non-financial in nature, but then observes: 'When a couple are joint owners of the home and jointly liable for the mortgage, the inferences to be drawn from who pays for what may be very different from the inferences to be drawn when only one is owner of the home.'

(3) Should *Stack* be seen as approving the approach in *Cooke*?

---

[49] Extract 8.5.5 above.

Extract 8.6.3

Jones v *Kernott* [2012] 1 AC 776

There was a joint names transfer; it was common ground that the shares were equal at the time of the parties' separation. The novel question was raised whether the fact that the parties had separated for some 15 years affected the value of the shares. During that period, the man had made no contribution to the house; it was occupied by the woman, who had paid the mortgage and other outgoings.

LORD WALKER and LADY HALE: 13. Fourthly, however, if the task [seeking to show that the parties intended their beneficial interests to be different from their legal interests] is embarked upon, it is to ascertain the parties' common intentions as to what their shares in the property would be, in the light of their whole course of conduct in relation to it: Lady Hale, at para 60. It is the way in which this point was made which seems to have caused the most difficulty in the lower courts. The difficulty is well illustrated in Lord Wilson's judgment, at paras 85 to 87, which read the judgment in a way which we would not read it. It matters not which reading is correct. It does matter that any confusion is resolved.

32. Lord Diplock, in *Gissing* v *Gissing* [1971] AC 886, 909, pointed out that, once the court was satisfied that it was the parties' common intention that the beneficial interest was to be shared in some proportion or other, the court might have to give effect to that common intention by determining what in all the circumstances was a fair share. And it is that thought which is picked up in the subsequent cases, culminating in the judgment of Chadwick LJ in *Oxley* v *Hiscock* [2005] Fam 211, paras 65, 66 and 69, . . .

33. Chadwick LJ was not there saying that fairness was the criterion for determining whether or not the property should be shared, but he was saying that the court might have to impute an intention to the parties as to the proportions in which the property would be shared. In deducing what the parties, as reasonable people, would have thought at the relevant time, regard would obviously be had to their whole course of dealing in relation to the property.

Discussion

46. . . . The primary search must always be for what the parties actually intended, to be deduced objectively from their words and their actions. If that can be discovered, then, as Mr Nicholas Strauss QC pointed out in the High Court, it is not open to a court to impose a solution upon them in contradiction to those intentions, merely because the court considers it fair to do so.

47. In a case such as this, where the parties already share the beneficial interest, and the question is what their interests are and whether their interests have changed, the court will try to deduce what their actual intentions were at the relevant time. It cannot impose a solution upon them which is contrary to what the evidence shows that they actually intended. But if it cannot deduce exactly what shares were intended, it may have no alternative but to ask what their intentions as reasonable and just people would have been had they thought about it at the time. This is a fallback position which some courts may not welcome, but the court has a duty to come to a conclusion on the dispute put before it.

48. In this case, there is no need to impute an intention that the parties' beneficial interests would change, because the judge made a finding that the intentions of the parties did in fact change . . . [Following failure to sell after separation] The life insurance policy was cashed in and Mr Kernott was able to buy a new home for himself. He would not have been able to do this had he still had to contribute towards the mortgage, endowment policy and other outgoings on 39 Badger Hall Avenue. The logical inference is that they intended that his interest in Badger Hall Avenue should crystallise then. Just as he would have the sole benefit of any capital gain in his own home, Ms Jones would have the sole benefit of any capital gain in Badger Hall

Avenue. Insofar as the judge did not in so many words infer that this was their intention, it is clearly the intention which reasonable people would have had had they thought about it at the time. But in our view it is an intention which he both could and should have inferred from their conduct.

51. (4) In those cases where it is clear either (a) that the parties did not intend joint tenancy at the outset, or (b) had changed their original intention, but it is not possible to ascertain by direct evidence or by inference what their actual intention was as to the shares in which they would own the property, 'the answer is that each is entitled to that share which the court considers fair having regard to the whole course of dealing between them in relation to the property': Chadwick LJ in *Oxley* v *Hiscock* [2005] Fam 211, para 69. In our judgment, 'the whole course of dealing . . . in relation to the property' should be given a broad meaning, enabling a similar range of factors to be taken into account as may be relevant to ascertaining the parties' actual intentions.

(5) Each case will turn on its own facts. Financial contributions are relevant but there are many other factors which may enable the court to decide what shares were either intended (as in case (3)) or fair (as in case (4)).

52. This case is not concerned with a family home which is put into the name of one party only. The starting point is different. The first issue is whether it was intended that the other party have any beneficial interest in the property at all. If he does, the second issue is what that interest is. There is no presumption of joint beneficial ownership. But their common intention has once again to be deduced objectively from their conduct. If the evidence shows a common intention to share beneficial ownership but does not show what shares were intended, the court will have to proceed as at para 51(4) and (5) above.

LORD KERR: 72. . . . But the conscientious quest to discover the parties' actual intention should cease when it becomes clear either that this is simply not deducible from the evidence or that no common intention exists. It would be unfortunate if the concept of inferring were to be strained so as to avoid the less immediately attractive option of imputation. In summary, therefore, I believe that the court should anxiously examine the circumstances in order, where possible, to ascertain the parties' intention but it should not be reluctant to recognise, when it is appropriate to do so, that inference of an intention is not possible and that imputation of an intention is the only course to follow.

77. . . . Like Lord Wilson, therefore, I would prefer to allow this appeal on the basis that it is impossible to infer that the parties intended that their shares in the property be apportioned as the judge considered they should be but that such an intention should be imputed to them.

LORD WILSON: 87. The problem has lain in Lady Hale's third sentence [her preferred approach 'does not enable the court to abandon that search in favour of the result which the court itself considers fair': *Stack* at [61]]. Where equity is driven to impute the common intention, how can it do so other than by search for the result which the court itself considers fair? The sentence was not obiter dictum so rightly, under our system, judges below the level of this court have been unable to ignore it. Even in these proceedings judges in the courts below have wrestled with it. Mr Strauss observed, at para 31, that it was difficult to see how – at that final stage of the inquiry – the process could work without the court's supply of what it considered to be fair. In his judgment on the second appeal Lord Justice Rimer went so far as to suggest, at para 77, that Lady Hale's third sentence must have meant that, contrary to appearances, she had not intended to recognise a power to impute a common intention at all.

88. I respectfully disagree with Lady Hale's third sentence.

89. . . . I regard it, as did Mr Strauss at [48] and [49] of his judgment, as more realistic, in the light of the evidence before the judge, to conclude that inference is impossible but to proceed to impute to the parties the intention that it should be held on a basis which equates to those proportions. At all events I readily concur in the result which Lord Walker and Lady Hale propose.

Comment

(1) Lord Collins agrees with the approach of Lord Walker and Lady Hale. See also Extracts 8.3.2 (imputing intentions) and 8.4.3 (joint names transfers) above.

(2) What remains of the approach of Baroness Hale in *Stack*? Does it matter that Lords Kerr and Wilson prefer to take an approach which is based upon imputed intention and fairness?

(3) What is meant by fairness? Could it be based on the Law Commission's proposals, considered later (Extract 8.8.4)? Could it enable the outcome in a case similar to *Fowler* v *Barron* to be different?

(4) An intention was imputed in *Thompson* v *Hurst*,[50] so that a man who had contributed very little was awarded 10% in a single name purchase. This was because, financially, he contributed very little to the relationship. Is this harsh given that the parties had intended it to be a joint names transfer, excluding that only in order to make mortgage finance more readily attainable?

7. Common intention after purchase; improvements

We will start this section by considering whether a common intention can be found after the purchase of the property. That subsequent mortgage contributions can suffice has been recognised in a number of cases, including *Gissing* and *Rosset*. This is particularly important where the relationship between the parties commences after one of them has bought the property. However, it is to be noted that to recognise these contributions involves changing existing property rights; the courts exercise considerable caution. Thus Griffiths LJ said:[51]

> It might in exceptional circumstances be inferred that the parties agreed to alter their beneficial interests after the house was bought; an example would be if the man bought the house in the first place and the woman years later used a legacy to build an extra floor to make more room for the children. In such circumstances the obvious inference would be that the parties agreed that the woman should acquire a share in the greatly increased value of the house produced by her money. But this depends upon the court being able to infer an intention to alter the share in which the beneficial interest was previously held . . .

Given that many relationships will arise after the property is bought, it is surprising that there are not more cases to provide guidance.[52]

The cases (in particular *Stack* v *Dowden*) are clear that the common intention can be 'ambulatory' – it may change over the course of the relationship. A specific aspect of this concerns taking into account events between separation of the parties and the court proceedings. Accounting permits the value of the shares to be adjusted; it will be considered in the context of trusts of land, as today it is usually governed by the trusts of land legislation.[53] However, the following extract from *Jones* v *Kernott* identifies disadvantages in using accounting.

---

[50] [2014] 1 FLR 238.
[51] *Bernard* v *Josephs* [1982] Ch 391 at p 404.
[52] See *Kowalczuk* v *Kowalczuk* [1973] 1 WLR 930; *McKenzie* v *McKenzie* [2003] EWHC 601 (Ch) at [82]; *Churchill* v *Roach* [2004] 2 FLR 989 at p 1001; *James* v *Thomas* [2008] 1 FLR 1598 at [24].
[53] See pp 402–407 below.

Extract 8.7.1

Jones v Kernott [2012] 1 AC 776

LORD WALKER and LADY HALE: 50. . . . Had their beneficial interests in the property remained the same, there would have been the possibility of cross-claims: Mr Kernott against Ms Jones for an occupation rent, and Ms Jones against Mr Kernott for his half share in the mortgage interest and endowment premiums which she had paid. It is quite likely, however, that the court would hold that there was no liability to pay an occupation rent, at least while the home was needed for the couple's children, whereas the liability to contribute towards the mortgage and endowment policy would accumulate at compound interest over the years since he ceased to contribute. This exercise has not been done. In a case such as this it would involve a quite disproportionate effort, both to discover the requisite figures (even supposing that they could be discovered) and to make the requisite calculations, let alone to determine what the ground rules should be . . .

Comment

(1) Is there any reason why a similar analysis should not apply if the beneficial shares are expressly declared?

(2) When, if ever, will it be appropriate to employ accounting?

(3) *Gallarotti* v *Sebastianelli*[54] provides a variation on this theme. Rather than a new common intention emerging, the original common intention may cease to apply – in this case because the expected contribution of one of two friends never materialised. Could this have a significant impact where couples are involved, where a common intention is predicated upon the continuing of the relationship?

It should be noted that accounting permits the recognition of a contribution without giving (or increasing) a share in the property. Improvements might provide an example.[55] It may also be useful where the parties have agreed to share the property in a certain way (most obviously by an express statement of beneficial interests), but their relationship breaks down before one of them has made a planned financial contribution. It enables the one who has contributed to be credited with that contribution.[56] Is this preferable to adjusting the percentage shares?

Improvements to the land provide a specific example of post-purchase events that are used to argue that there is a common intention to share ownership – assuming that the improver previously had no interest in the property.

Extract 8.7.2

Jansen v Jansen [1965] P 478

LORD DENNING MR: . . . In the present case it is quite plain that there was a joint enterprise akin to a partnership. The wife supplied the capital in the shape of the house. The husband supplied the labour. By means of their joint efforts a profit was made. If these two were not

---

[54] [2012] 2 FLR 1231.
[55] *Jansen* v *Jansen* [1965] P 478 (Russell LJ). This is unlikely to adjust shares where improvements are made during the relationship: *Wilcox* v *Tait* [2007] 2 FLR 871 (p 406 below).
[56] *Muschinski* v *Dodds* (1984) 62 ALR 429.

husband and wife, the law would readily infer a provision that he should have some part of the profit. So should equity say today, seeing that the marriage has broken up. Their rights have not been determined by agreement. So the court has to do it according to what is fair and just in all the circumstances.

The husband has done a lot of work on the property which has enabled the wife to make large profits. But it must be remembered that he has not had to provide a roof for his wife and child, nor to pay the housekeeping expenses. She has done most of that out of her earnings or out of lettings of her house. He cannot expect to receive a half share of the profit or anything like it. He should give credit for the amount which he would have probably contributed to the household if he had gone out to work. Making all allowances, I think that the registrar's figure of £1,000 is correct.

RUSSELL LJ (dissenting as to this analysis): Admittedly he has done a great deal of work on his wife's property, work which otherwise would have had to be paid for to a builder. On the other hand, he would have otherwise been expected – having abandoned his studies – to have worked to earn an income with which to support his wife and family and in relief of the wife's own income which pro tanto could have been available to pay for the work to be done on her own property for her own exclusive benefit. It was argued before us that the substance of the case is the value to be put upon his work, the registrar having concluded that there was an arrangement that he should do the work for a reward. It was said that there was an agreement, either express or by conduct, that he should do the necessary work of conversion and share equally in the profits; and that the wife recognised this by her conduct in assisting in the preparation of the agreement which the husband rejected. I am bound to say that, on that last point, the inference is that there was no previous agreement such as is suggested.

Extract 8.7.3

Pettitt v Pettitt [1970] AC 777

LORD UPJOHN: . . . My Lords, the facts of this case depend not upon the acquisition of property but upon the expenditure of money and labour by the husband in the way of improvement upon the property of the wife which admittedly is her own beneficial property. Upon this it is quite clearly established that by the law of England the expenditure of money by A upon the property of B stands in quite a different category from the acquisition of property by A and B.

It has been well settled in your Lordships' House (*Ramsden v Dyson* (1865) LR 1 HL 129) that if A expends money on the property of B, prima facie he has no claim on such property. And this, as Sir William Grant MR held as long ago as 1810 in *Campion v Cotton* (1810) 17 Ves 263, is equally applicable as between husband and wife. If by reason of estoppel or because the expenditure was incurred by the encouragement of the owner that such expenditure would be rewarded, the person expending the money may have some claim for monetary reimbursement in a purely monetary sense from the owner or even, if explicitly promised to him by the owner, an interest in the land (see *Plimmer v Wellington Corpn* (1884) 9 App Cas 699). But the respondent's claim here is to a share of the property and his money claim in his plaint is only a qualification of that. Plainly, in the absence of agreement with his wife (and none is suggested) he could have no monetary claim against her and no estoppel or mistake is suggested so, in my opinion, he can have no charge upon or interest in the wife's property.

. . . I prefer to decide this appeal upon the wider ground that in the absence of agreement, and there being no question of any estoppel, one spouse who does work or expends money upon the property of the other has no claim whatever upon the property of the other. *Jansen v Jansen* [1965] P 478 was a very good example of that type of case . . . In those circumstances it seems to me clear that the husband had no claim against the wife even personally and certainly no claim against the property itself either by way of charge or by way of a share in the property. In my opinion *Jansen v Jansen* was wrongly decided.

LORD DIPLOCK: . . . During the four years that the spouses lived together in their new home the husband in his spare time occupied himself, as many husbands do, in laying out the garden with a lawn and patio, putting up a side wall with a gate, and in various jobs of redecoration and the like in the house itself. He claimed that these leisure activities had enhanced the value of the property by £1,000 and that he was entitled to a beneficial interest in it of that amount . . .

It is common enough nowadays for husbands and wives to decorate and to make improvements in the family home themselves, with no other intention than to indulge in what is now a popular hobby, and to make the home pleasanter for their common use and enjoyment. If the husband likes to occupy his leisure by laying a new lawn in the garden or building a fitted wardrobe in the bedroom while the wife does the shopping, cooks the family dinner or bathes the children, I, for my part, find it quite impossible to impute to them as reasonable husband and wife any common intention that these domestic activities or any of them are to have any effect upon the existing proprietary rights in the family home on which they are undertaken. It is only in the bitterness engendered by the break-up of the marriage that so bizarre a notion would enter their heads.

I agree with the Court of Appeal that the present case cannot be distinguished from that of *Appleton* v *Appleton*, but in my view *Appleton* v *Appleton* [[1965] 1 WLR 25] was wrongly decided . . . *Jansen* v *Jansen* [1965] P 478 falls into a different category. There it was not a case of leisure activities of the spouses. The husband, in agreement with his wife, had abandoned his prospects of paid employment in order to work upon her property which, although the family lived in part of it, had been acquired as a commercial venture to which both were contributing. There were circumstances in that case which, in my view, justified the court in imputing to the spouses a common intention that his work should entitle him to a proprietary interest in the property whose value was enhanced by his full-time labours directed to that end.

Comment

(1) After *Pettitt*, what would be the appropriate result in *Jansen*, where the work was such that a contractor would normally be brought in? Note that Lord Reid took a similar approach to Lord Diplock, and Lord Hodson one similar to Lord Upjohn. It may be material that Lords Reid and Diplock took a more welcoming stance towards notions of family property, which stance was subsequently rejected in *Gissing*.

(2) Would it strengthen the claim if there had been contribution to the costs of substantial improvement, as opposed to simply doing the work?

In many cases, claimants can rely on other factors to prove a common intention – the improvements can then be taken into account in assessing the claimant's share.[57] Recent cases present a mixed picture. Perhaps unsurprisingly, substantial work done after the end of a relationship gave rise to a common intention in *Aspden* v *Elvy*.[58] On the other hand, greater reluctance to find a common intention was evident in *Williams* v *Lawrence*[59] and *Re Ali*.[60]

It should be noted that improvements by spouses and civil partners are covered by statute.

---

[57] One example is *Drake* v *Whipp* [1996] 1 FLR 826. See also *Stack* v *Dowden* [2007] 2 AC 432 at [70].
[58] [2012] 2 FLR 807, especially at [123]–[125].
[59] [2011] WTLR 1455, especially at [61].
[60] [2013] 1 FLR 1061 at [100].

Extract 8.7.4

Matrimonial Proceedings and Property Act 1970, s 37[61]

37.   It is hereby declared that where a husband or wife contributes in money or money's worth to the improvement of real or personal property in which or in the proceeds of sale of which either or both of them has or have a beneficial interest, the husband or wife so contributing shall, if the contribution is of a substantial nature and subject to any agreement between them to the contrary express or implied, be treated as having then acquired by virtue of his or her contribution a share or an enlarged share, as the case may be, in that beneficial interest of such an extent as may have been then agreed or, in default of such agreement, as may seem in all the circumstances just to [the] court . . .

Comment

(1) Given the discretion on marriage breakdown, is it a fair observation that this provision operates where a remedy is least needed?

(2) How does this provision work where there has been a conveyance to parties as joint tenants in equity? Is it sensible to vary their shares?[62]

8. Looking to the future

It may be claimed that the law provides neither certainty nor justice for non-property-owning cohabitants, at least those who are unable to go out to work and are thereby unable to make financial contributions.

Extract 8.8.1

Hammond v *Mitchell* **[1991] 1 WLR 1127**

WAITE J: . . . Had they been married, the issue of ownership would scarcely have been relevant, because the law these days when dealing with the financial consequences of divorce adopts a forward-looking perspective in which questions of ownership yield to the higher demands of relating the means of both to the needs of each, the first consideration given to the welfare of children. Since this couple did not marry, none of that flexibility is available to them, except a limited power to direct capital provision for their children. In general, their financial rights have to be worked out according to their strict entitlements in equity, a process which is anything but forward-looking and involves, on the contrary, a painfully detailed retrospect.

   . . . If there have been no such discussions [relating to ownership] . . . the investigation of subsequent events has to take the form of an inferential analysis involving a scrutiny of all events potentially capable of throwing evidential light on the question whether, in the absence of express discussion, a presumed intention can be spelt out of the parties' past course of dealing. This operation was vividly described by Dixon J in Canada as, 'The judicial quest for the fugitive or phantom common intention' (*Pettkus* v *Becker* (1980) 117 DLR (3d) 257), and by Nourse LJ, in *Grant* v *Edwards* [1986] Ch 638, 646, as a 'climb up the familiar ground which slopes down from the twin peaks of *Pettitt* v *Pettitt* [1970] AC 777 and *Gissing* v *Gissing* [1971] AC 886'. The process is detailed, time-consuming and laborious.

---

[61] For civil partners, see the Civil Partnership Act 2004, s 65.

[62] This would necessarily sever the joint tenancy.

. . . The primary emphasis accorded by the law in cases of this kind to express discussions between the parties ('however imperfectly remembered and however imprecise their terms') means that the tenderest exchanges of a common law courtship may assume an unforeseen significance many years later when they are brought under equity's microscope and subjected to an analysis under which many thousands of pounds of value may be liable to turn on fine questions as to whether the relevant words were spoken in earnest or in dalliance and with or without representational intent. This requires that the express discussions to which the court's initial inquiries will be addressed should be pleaded in the greatest detail, both as to language and as to circumstance . . .

Those studying this area may sympathise with the fairly recent comment of Carnwath LJ:[63]

To the detached observer, the result may seem like a witch's brew, into which various esoteric ingredients have been stirred over the years, and in which different ideas bubble to the surface at different times. They include implied trust, constructive trust, resulting trust, presumption of advancement, proprietary estoppel, unjust enrichment, and so on. These ideas are likely to mean nothing to laymen, and often little more to the lawyers who use them.

To what extent do the developments in *Stack* v *Dowden* and *Jones* v *Kernott* answer these concerns?

Extract 8.8.2

Gardner (2008) 124 LQR 422 at pp 431, 433–434, 436–437, 439–441, 443 (footnotes omitted)

A 'materially communal' relationship is one in which C and D in practical terms pool all their material resources (including money, other assets, and labour), rather than keeping separate tallies. The presence of a joint bank account will strongly, almost conclusively, suggest a materially communal relationship, but its absence will not particularly prove the opposite. The parties' having, or not having, a sexual relationship will prove nothing either way; likewise even their having children together, though in this event it is probably commoner for their relationship to be materially communal.

. . .

The jurisdiction's driver
Finally, a deeper-lying difficulty. Even if the thesis just sketched is an accurate portrayal of the way the courts (should) now operate this jurisdiction, it is hard to say what is the jurisdiction's driver: that is, its basis of principle, entailing that cases *should be* decided in the manner described. *Stack* v *Dowden* and *Abbott* v *Abbott* tell us nothing explicit about this (and no more did their predecessors); any answer will have to be gleaned inferentially, from a scrutiny of the set of rules they have established. If no satisfactory answer can be found, we have a problem. It will mean that this jurisdiction lacks a justification; and also that uncertainties and injustices will occur when cases arise at the boundary between this jurisdiction and another.

In the next section, we shall explore some of the drivers that might characterise a jurisdiction addressed at the kind of case under discussion, and compare them with the jurisdiction as it seems to be . . .

SOME POSSIBLE DRIVERS

Four possible drivers will be considered . . .

---

[63] *Stack* v *Dowden* [2006] 1 FLR 254 at [75].

Effectuating intentions

If the owner of property purports intentionally to bestow it on another, the law should in principle recognise him as having done so. This response is driven by very familiar libertarian considerations. So in our situation, if D, being wholly (as in the single name scenario) or partly (as in the joint names scenario) beneficially entitled to property, voluntarily acts to confer some or all of his entitlement on C – as where D and C have a genuine common intention on these lines – the law should give effect to that act.

This analysis plainly cannot explain the normative force that the jurisdiction accords to an invented common intention . . .

Redressing C's reliance loss

If C suffers a loss for which D is to be held responsible, C will look to D to redress that loss. Affording such redress is a proper and familiar driver for a legal claim, and the law does indeed operate a project on these lines, most especially in the form of tort claims.

. . .

More important, however, C cannot claim to have suffered reliance loss unless he genuinely held the belief on which he claims to have relied: there is no room, as there is in our jurisdiction, for an invented intention.

Redressing C's unjust enrichment of D

Unjust enrichment is another well established driver for a legal response. If C enriches D in circumstances rendering it unjust that D should retain the enrichment, D should be obliged to restore it.

The kind of facts with which we are concerned might well disclose a case of unjust enrichment. Suppose that C confers a benefit on D: maybe, by directly or indirectly contributing to the mortgage payments, or by working for D, or by picking up some of D's responsibilities. D is enriched, at C's expense . . .

The fit is patchier, however, when we consider relief. A claim based on unjust enrichment would aim to restore to C the amount by which he enriched D. For example, if C unjustly enriches D by contributing a third of what it costs D to acquire his house, C should get a third of the house's value. According to the argument made above, this should indeed be the outcome under our jurisdiction where the required common intention is imputed rather than genuine, and the parties' relationship is not materially communal: as we have seen, the common intention – and thus the relief it indicates – is then shaped by the parties' relative contributions. But it should be otherwise in the case of an imputed common intention between parties whose relationship is materially communal, where the outcome will be equal shares. It should also be otherwise in the case where the parties have a genuine common intention, where the outcome will be shaped by that intention, rather than by the value of any contributions they may have made . . .

Effectuating the implications of the parties' relationship

In the kind of situation with which we are concerned, C and D will generally be in some sort of family relationship. It may be right to give C an (enlarged) interest because that is what the relationship itself requires.

. . .

How does our jurisdiction compare with such a project? Plainly, there is a very good fit where C and D have no genuine common intention, but do have what we have termed a materially communal relationship. Then, according to the account suggested above, a common intention will be imputed that they should have equal shares (as in *Abbott* v *Abbott*): which is exactly the outcome the present approach would deliver in such cases, though it would not proceed via an imputed common intention. In these terms, too, it is unsurprising that where the parties have a non-materially communal relationship, our jurisdiction should take a different direction, reflecting instead the parties' individual contributions (as in *Stack* v *Dowden*). A non-materially communal relationship is one in which, by definition, the parties stick with separate accounting. Effectuating its implications means respecting that, and therefore applying legal redress, if at all, only on an individualistic basis – as we have seen the law does in such cases, taking what is in effect a restitutionary approach to relief, as it would between strangers. On this view, too, the primacy given to a genuine common intention can be understood, as a facility allowing the parties, even in what would otherwise be a materially communal relationship, to opt out of the treatment the law would otherwise mete out to them on that account – though this does not quite explain why they should then be treated in accordance with their intentions, when as we have seen there is a formality problem with that.

CONCLUSIONS

Lessons
So in two out of its three aspects – those not involving a genuine common intention – our jurisdiction can be seen as in truth well-founded: its effects can be ascribed to the parties' relationship, or to the unjust enrichment significance of their contributions to the acquisition of the house (as modified by a compromise agreement, in some cases). But in proceeding not overtly on the basis of these drivers, but via a fictitious common intention tacitly reflecting them, the jurisdiction is distracted and opaque. By dropping the fiction, the law would escape the difficulties in regard to the meaning of imputation, and the content of the imputed agreement, that we noted earlier.

As regards its third aspect – that concerned with genuine common intentions – however, the jurisdiction lacks a defensible basis, and needs reconsideration. Since effectuation of the common intention is prevented by the want of formality, situations of this kind need to be handled instead, like the other two kinds, with reference to the parties' relationship, where this is materially communal, or otherwise to their respective contributions to the acquisition of the house.

Comment

Is it likely that the courts will abandon their stress on common intention? Should they do so? Note that the Supreme Court of Canada has abandoned the common intention trust (articulated as a resulting trust) in favour of an unjust enrichment-based analysis: *Kerr* v *Brown* (2011) 14 ITELR 171.

Extract 8.8.3

Law Commission No 278: Sharing Homes (footnotes omitted)

2.112. The current requirements for establishing the existence of an interest under a trust are not ideally suited to the typical informality of those sharing a home. We feel that to demand proof of an intention to share the beneficial interest in the home can be somewhat unrealistic, as people do not tend to think about their home in such legalistic terms. The emphasis on financial input towards the acquisition of the home fails to recognise the realities of most cohabiting relationships. Finally, and importantly, the uncertainties in the present law can cause lengthy and costly litigation, wasting court time, public funding and the parties' own resources.

[A scheme for allocating property rights in a wide range of relationships, based on contributions, is considered.]

3.76. The uncompromising rejection of intention, central to the scheme, was ultimately impossible to justify. It may be possible to encourage parties into making express provision, but they cannot be compelled to do so.

3.81.   Real problems would arise where a person lives, rent-free, in the home at the invitation of the legal owner. This may be nothing more than an act of charity or kindness by the legal owner – or the parties may be involved in an intimate relationship. Contributions by the occupier towards the expenses of the home or the household may be made by the claimant out of gratitude for the accommodation provided by the legal owner – or they may be made in the context of the parties 'sharing their lives'. The only distinguishing factor between these factual circumstances would once more be the parties' intentions.

3.87.   However, the proposed scheme would create problems of its own. The proof of contributions would inevitably involve the production and inspection of bank accounts, and oral evidence may well be necessary as the court determines by whom a particular payment has been made. While we have advanced the case for applying a 'broad brush' to issues of quantification, it seems to us naive to assume that the proposed scheme would lead to much by way of savings in court time.

4.24.   While we realise that the application of 'common intention' causes real difficulties to the courts and that it can lead to a highly artificial exercise, it is difficult to present a convincing case for any more effective criteria on which an assessment of beneficial entitlement could be based. Intention is clearly important, as it would be wholly unsatisfactory if a person were to obtain a beneficial interest where it was made extremely clear that a particular contribution, by financial or other contribution, would not be met this way.

Comment

Are convincing reasons given for not making positive proposals? The Report was not well received.[64]

Extract 8.8.4

Law Commission No 307: Cohabitation: The Financial Consequences of Relationship Breakdown

8.1.   We recommend that legislation should create a scheme of general application, whereby cohabiting couples would be entitled to apply for financial relief on separation:
  (1)   provided they satisfy statutory eligibility criteria;
  (2)   but not where they had reached an agreement disapplying the statutory scheme ('an opt-out agreement'), in which case the parties' own financial arrangements (if any) would apply.

8.2.   We recommend that persons should be cohabitants for the purposes of being eligible to apply for financial relief on separation where:
  (1)   they are living as a couple in a joint household; . . .

8.4.   We recommend that:
  (1)   save where cohabitants have a child together, they should not be eligible to apply for financial relief on separation unless they have lived as a couple in a joint household for a duration specified by statute (the 'minimum duration requirement');
  (2)   any such minimum duration requirement should be set by statute within a range of two to five years; . . .

8.9.   We recommend that financial relief on separation should be granted in accordance with a statutory scheme based upon the economic impact of cohabitation, to the following effect.

---

[64] See especially Rotherham [2004] Conv 268.

8.10.   An eligible cohabitant applying for relief following separation ('the applicant') must prove that:

(1)   the respondent has a retained benefit; or

(2)   the applicant has an economic disadvantage

as a result of qualifying contributions the applicant has made.

8.11.   A qualifying contribution is any contribution arising from the cohabiting relationship which is made to the parties' shared lives or to the welfare of members of their families. Contributions are not limited to financial contributions, and include future contributions, in particular to the care of the parties' children following separation.

8.12.   A retained benefit may take the form of capital, income or earning capacity that has been acquired, retained or enhanced.

8.13.   An economic disadvantage is a present or future loss. It may include a diminution in current savings as a result of expenditure or of earnings lost during the relationship, lost future earnings, or the future cost of paid child-care.

8.14.   The court may make an order to adjust the retained benefit, if any, by reversing it in so far as that is reasonable and practicable having regard to the discretionary factors listed below. If, after the reversal of any retained benefit, the applicant would still bear an economic disadvantage, the court may make an order sharing that loss equally between the parties, in so far as it is reasonable and practicable to do so, having regard to the discretionary factors.

8.15.   The discretionary factors are:

(1)   the welfare while a minor of any child of both parties who has not attained the age of eighteen;

(2)   the financial needs and obligations of both parties;

(3)   the extent and nature of the financial resources which each party has or is likely to have in the foreseeable future;

(4)   the welfare of any children who live with, or might reasonably be expected to live with, either party; and

(5)   the conduct of each party, defined restrictively but so as to include cases where a qualifying contribution can be shown to have been made despite the express disagreement of the other party.

Of these discretionary factors, item (1) above shall be the court's first consideration.

Comment

(1) These proposals give financial remedies, rather than property rights. If implemented, what would be the likely impact upon developments regarding property rights?

(2) The core ideas are those of 'retained benefit' or 'economic disadvantage'. The former would apply if a house was put in joint names, but payment is made by one alone. The donee would have a retained benefit.[65] The latter would apply if a woman stayed at home to look after children, but found that on returning to work (a) she could earn less than if she had been continuously employed or (b) she was disadvantaged in terms of pension entitlement.

(3) The proposals (which are very detailed) are unlikely to be implemented soon.[66]

(4) How would these proposals fit the analysis suggested by Gardner (Extract 8.8.2 above)?

---

[65]   *Fowler* v *Barron* [2008] 2 FLR 831 (Extract 8.4.2 above) provides an example.

[66]   It has been announced that it will not be in the present parliament (until 2015, assuming no earlier general election): [2011] NLJ 1264.

9. Constructive trusts and estoppels: the links

It has become apparent that there are distinct similarities between constructive trusts (of the type considered in this chapter)[67] and estoppels. Each involves an expectation (or, for constructive trusts, common intention) and acting to the claimant's detriment in reliance upon that. At a general level, each analysis is designed to prevent unconscionable conduct by the legal owner, but is this criterion too imprecise for much weight to be put upon it? The constructive trust may be said to recognise both actual and inferred (or imputed) common intentions.[68] Which looks most like an estoppel? Are there examples of estoppels which do not look like the constructive trust?

For those constructive trusts and estoppels which do appear very similar, the courts have considered the possible convergence of the rules relating to each.

Extract 8.9.1

Grant v Edwards [1986] Ch 638

SIR NICOLAS BROWNE-WILKINSON V-C: . . . There is little guidance in the authorities on constructive trusts as to what is necessary to prove that the claimant so acted to her detriment. What 'link' has to be shown between the common intention and the actions relied on? . . .

I suggest that in other cases of this kind, useful guidance may in the future be obtained from the principles underlying the law of proprietary estoppel which in my judgment are closely akin to those laid down in *Gissing* v *Gissing* [1971] AC 886. In both, the claimant must to the knowledge of the legal owner have acted in the belief that the claimant has or will obtain an interest in the property. In both, the claimant must have acted to his or her detriment in reliance on such belief. In both, equity acts on the conscience of the legal owner to prevent him from acting in an unconscionable manner by defeating the common intention. The two principles have been developed separately without cross-fertilisation between them: but they rest on the same foundation and have on all other matters reached the same conclusions.

In many cases of the present sort, it is impossible to say whether or not the claimant would have done the acts relied on as a detriment even if she thought she had no interest in the house. Setting up house together, having a baby, making payments to general housekeeping expenses (not strictly necessary to enable the mortgage to be paid) may all be referable to the mutual love and affection of the parties and not specifically referable to the claimant's belief that she has an interest in the house. As at present advised, once it has been shown that there was a common intention that the claimant should have an interest in the house, any act done by her to her detriment relating to the joint lives of the parties is, in my judgment, sufficient detriment to qualify. The acts do not have to be inherently referable to the house: see *Jones (AE)* v *Jones (FW)* [1977] 1 WLR 438 and *Pascoe* v *Turner* [1979] 1 WLR 431. The holding out to the claimant that she had a beneficial interest in the house is an act of such a nature as to be part of the inducement to her to do the acts relied on. Accordingly, in the absence of evidence to the contrary, the right inference is that the claimant acted in reliance on such holding out and the burden lies on the legal owner to show that she did not do so: see *Greasley* v *Cooke* [1980] 1 WLR 1306.

The possible analogy with proprietary estoppel was raised in argument. However, the point was not fully argued and since the case can be decided without relying on such analogy, it is unsafe for me to rest my judgment on that point. I decide the case on the narrow ground already mentioned.

---

[67] Other forms of constructive trusts owe less to the parties' intentions.
[68] *Lloyds Bank plc* v *Rosset* [1991] 1 AC 107; Extract 8.5.3 above.

Stokes v *Anderson* [1991] 1 FLR 391

NOURSE LJ: . . . Before *Grant* v *Edwards* (above), the distinction between the category of case exemplified by that decision and *Eves* v *Eves* [1975] 1 WLR 1338 on the one hand, and that exemplified by *Gissing* v *Gissing* and *Burns* v *Burns* [1984] FLR 216; [1984] Ch 317 on the other, had not been clearly perceived. The distinction has now been authoritatively recognised in the speech of Lord Bridge of Harwich in *Lloyds Bank plc* v *Rosset* [1991] 1 AC 107 at pp 132 and 133; [1990] 2 FLR 155 at pp 163 to 164, a passage which is also notable for two references to conduct giving rise to 'a constructive trust or a proprietary estoppel'. Since it is necessary, in order to decide the extent of Miss Anderson's beneficial interest in Stone Cottage, to ascertain the principle on which such a decision ought to be made, a brief diversion into the burgeoning question of the relationship between the *Gissing* v *Gissing* species of constructive trust and proprietary estoppel is here desirable.

In *Grant* v *Edwards* [1987] 1 FLR 87 at pp 99H and 100E; [1986] Ch 638 at pp 656G and 657H, the Vice-Chancellor suggested that in cases under *Gissing* v *Gissing* the principles underlying the law of proprietary estoppel might provide useful guidance both in regard to the conduct necessary to constitute an acting upon the common intention by the claimant and in regard to the quantification of his or her beneficial interest in the property. In *Austin* v *Keele* [1987] ALJR 605 at p 609; 72 ALR 579 at p 587, Lord Oliver of Aylmerton, in delivering the judgment of the Privy Council, said that in essence the doctrine of *Gissing* v *Gissing* was an application of proprietary estoppel. The Vice-Chancellor's suggestion was echoed by Nicholls LJ in *Lloyds Bank plc* v *Rosset* [1989] 1 FLR 51 at p 72A; [1989] Ch 350 at pp 387A–B, and it has now been adopted and enlarged upon by Professor Hayton; see *Conveyancer and Property Lawyer* [1990] 370. However, it must be emphasised that this question was only touched on in the arguments in this court in *Grant* v *Edwards* and *Lloyds Bank plc* v *Rosset* and both the Vice-Chancellor and Nicholls LJ were careful to base their decisions on conventional *Gissing* v *Gissing* principles.

It is possible that the House of Lords will one day decide to solve the problems presented by these cases, either by assimilating the principles of *Gissing* v *Gissing* and those of proprietary estoppel, or even by following the recent trend in other Commonwealth jurisdictions towards more generalised principles of unconscionability and unjust enrichment. The Vice-Chancellor has identified two areas where the application of *Gissing* v *Gissing* might be enlarged through the influence of proprietary estoppel, and there is no real reason for thinking that their assimilation would be unduly hindered by their separate development out of basically different factual situations. But they have not yet been assimilated and we, in this court, must continue to regard cases such as the present as being governed by the principles of *Gissing* v *Gissing* . . .

Comment

(1) Is it safe to conclude from these cases that the same rules apply to each of constructive trusts and estoppels?

(2) The focus in *Grant* v *Edwards* is principally upon the nature of the reliance and detriment. In this area, can differences in the rules be justified?

(3) It has been seen that some writers have doubted the role of detriment in constructive trusts since *Stack* v *Dowden*.[69] How significant is this for the comparison between constructive trusts and estoppels?

---

[69] See p 250 above.

The Court of Appeal in *Yaxley* v *Gotts*[70] again recognised the links between estoppel and constructive trusts. Robert Walker LJ made the following comments:

> At a high level of generality, there is much common ground between the doctrines of proprietary estoppel and the constructive trust, just as there is between proprietary estoppel and part performance. All are concerned with equity's intervention to provide relief against unconscionable conduct, whether as between neighbouring landowners, or vendor and purchaser, or relatives who make informal arrangements for sharing a home, or a fiduciary and the beneficiary or client to whom he owes a fiduciary obligation . . .
>
> Plainly there are large areas where the two concepts do not overlap: when a landowner stands by while his neighbour mistakenly builds on the former's land the situation is far removed (except for the element of unconscionable conduct) from that of a fiduciary who derives an improper advantage from his client. But in the area of a joint enterprise for the acquisition of land (which may be, but is not necessarily, the matrimonial home) the two concepts coincide.

How significant is it that 'there are large areas where the two concepts do not overlap'?

The earlier cases reveal significant differences regarding remedy, with the discretion seen in estoppel not being replicated in constructive trusts. However, the Court of Appeal in *Oxley* v *Hiscock*[71] held that 'the time has come to accept that there is no difference in outcome, in cases of this nature, whether the true analysis lies in constructive trust or in proprietary estoppel'. The test to be applied is that 'each is entitled to that share which the court considers fair having regard to the whole course of dealing between them in relation to the property', though little was said as to how this fits with the operation of the discretion in estoppel cases. Though the fairness test was criticised in *Stack* v *Dowden*, it may be regarded as being rehabilitated (through imputed intention) by *Jones* v *Kernott* (Extract 8.6.3 above).

Of greater importance may be the approach of Lord Walker in *Stack*.

Extract 8.9.3

Stack v *Dowden* [2007] 2 AC 432

LORD WALKER: 37.   I add a brief comment as to proprietary estoppel. In paras 70 and 71 of his judgment in *Oxley* v *Hiscock* [2005] Fam 211 Chadwick LJ considered the conceptual basis of the developing law in this area, and briefly discussed proprietary estoppel, a suggestion first put forward by Sir Nicolas Browne-Wilkinson V-C in *Grant* v *Edwards* [1986] Ch 638, 656. I have myself given some encouragement to this approach (*Yaxley* v *Gotts* [2000] Ch 162, 177) but I have to say that I am now rather less enthusiastic about the notion that proprietary estoppel and 'common interest' [sic] constructive trusts can or should be completely assimilated. Proprietary estoppel typically consists of asserting an equitable claim against the conscience of the 'true' owner. The claim is a 'mere equity'. It is to be satisfied by the minimum award necessary to do justice (*Crabb* v *Arun District Council* [1976] Ch 179, 198), which may sometimes lead to no more than a monetary award. A 'common intention' constructive trust, by contrast, is identifying the true beneficial owner or owners, and the size of their beneficial interests.

Comment

(1) Why does Lord Walker want to separate estoppel from constructive trusts?

(2) How much damage do these dicta (together with the rejection of the fairness test) do to the movement towards aligning estoppel rules and constructive trust rules?

---

[70] [2000] Ch 162 at p 176; see Extract 5.2.13 above.
[71] [2005] Fam 211 at [71]; Extracts 8.2.1 and 8.6.1 above. Note the criticism of Gardner (2004) 120 LQR 541.

Somewhat similarly, Neuberger LJ said in *Kinane v Mackie-Conteh*:[72]

> As I see it, at least for present purposes, the essential difference between a proprietary estoppel which does not also give rise to a constructive trust, and one that does, is the element of agreement, or at least expression of common understanding, exchanged between the parties, as to the existence, or intended existence, of a proprietary interest, in the latter type of case.

How strong is the argument that common intention usually possesses greater clarity than expectation, as well as involving agreement rather than unilateral promise or representation? If the common intention does possess some such special factors, is this sufficient to justify different rules?[73]

Yet another problem area is overreaching. Beneficial interests under constructive trusts can be overreached; the position for estoppel was raised in our next case.

Extract 8.9.4

Birmingham Midshires Mortgage Services Ltd v *Sabherwal* (1999) 80 P&CR 256

A contributor to a purchase chose to rely on an estoppel rather than a constructive trust. This was in an attempt to avoid the overreaching of her interest.

ROBERT WALKER LJ: 24.   On the facts of this case, Mrs Sabherwal plainly made a substantial financial contribution to all the properties successively owned by the family. She could rely on a resulting trust and had no need to rely on proprietary estoppel (if and so far as the two are, in the context of the family home, distinct doctrines: see the observations of Sir Nicolas Browne-Wilkinson V-C in *Grant v Edwards* [1986] Ch 638, 656). If she had made no financial contribution, but had nevertheless acted to her detriment in reliance on her sons' promises, she might have obtained (through the medium of estoppel rather than through the medium of a trust) equitable rights of a proprietary nature. Her actual occupation of the house would then have promoted those rights into an overriding interest. That, I think, is not conceded by counsel for the respondents but I assume that to be the case. On that basis, it would have been a remarkable result if those more precarious rights were incapable of being overreached, on a sale by trustees, under section 2(1)(ii) of the Law of Property Act 1925.

31.   Similarly, in *Lloyds Bank v Rosset* [1991] 1 AC 107 Lord Bridge (in a very well-known passage at pp 132–133) referred to 'direct contributions to the purchase price by [a party] who is not the legal owner', as readily justifying the creation of a constructive trust. Such a trust, however labelled, does not then leave room for a separate interest by way of equitable estoppel: compare the remarks of Morritt LJ in *Lloyds Bank v Carrick* [1996] 4 All ER 630 at p 639C–E. To do so would cause vast confusion in an area which is already quite difficult enough . . . In this type of family situation, the concepts of trust and equitable estoppel are almost interchangeable, and both are affected in the same way by the statutory mechanism of overreaching, the substance of which is not affected by the 1996 Act.

Comment

(1) One can see why the courts do not wish to allow estoppel to bypass overreaching, but is it consistent with the legislation under which overreaching operates?[74]

---

[72] [2005] WTLR 345 at [51]; see also McFarlane [2005] Conv 501 at pp 517–518.
[73] See Ferguson (1993) 109 LQR 114, criticising Hayton [1990] Conv 370 (see also (1993) 109 LQR 485).
[74] Considered in more detail in Chapter 12: see p 435 below.

(2) Robert Walker LJ distinguishes between family and commercial cases. On what side of the line would *Pascoe* v *Turner*,[75] or claims to licences, fall?

(3) Is *Sabherwal* likely to affect a large proportion of estoppel claims? Is it affected by Lord Walker's revised views expressed in *Stack* v *Dowden* (Extract 8.9.3 above)?

Further reading

Douglas, G, Pearce, J and Woodward, H (2009) 72 MLR 24: Cohabitants property and the law: a study of injustice.

Gardner, S (2008) 124 LQR 422: Family property today.

Gardner, S [2013] CLJ 301: Problems in family property.

Ferguson, P (1993) 109 LQR 114: Constructive trusts – a note of caution.

Hopkins, N (2011) 31 LS 175: The relevance of context in property law: a case for judicial restraint?

Hughes, D, Davis, M and Jacklin, L [2008] Conv 197: 'Come live with me and be my love': a consideration of the 2007 Law Commission proposals on cohabitation breakdown.

Rotherham, C [2004] Conv 268: The property rights of unmarried cohabitees: the case for reform.

---

[75] [1979] 1 WLR 431; Extract 7.2.3 above.

9

Purchasers: general principles and land charges

Simply deciding that a right is proprietary does not mean that it will bind everybody else claiming a right to the land. Most obviously, it is unlikely to affect those whose rights are earlier in time. Take this example: A leases land to B for three years. A immediately afterwards grants C a right of way over the land, but without disclosing that he has leased it to B. Subsequently, A transfers the fee simple to D. C's right of way cannot affect B, for the simple reason that B's lease is prior in time. On the other hand, the right of way may affect D, so that when B's lease expires the right can be exercised against D.

The reasoning in this example illustrates the most basic priority rule: the first in time wins. However, this rule is by no means universal in operation. In the modern land law it is much affected by registration requirements, and very often it is the first interest to be entered upon the register which has priority. However, the details of this last point lie in the realm of registration of title (the subject matter of the next chapter).

Other forms of property also demonstrate modifications of the first in time rule. The law on sale of goods, for example, recognises an exception where a seller retains possession after title has passed to a purchaser. Because leaving the seller in possession gives the impression that the seller can still deal with the property, a later purchaser from the same seller may have priority over the earlier one.[1] However, the most complex analyses have arisen in relation to equitable interests and to land. These areas form the basis of the present chapter, which is limited to unregistered land.

1. Rules for legal interests

A legal interest normally takes priority over all subsequent interests, whether legal or equitable. It follows that a purchaser or mortgagee, for example, must ensure that all earlier legal interests are discovered. This is impossible to guarantee: however much care is taken, there is always a danger that a legal interest will remain undiscovered.

What does the purchaser do in practice? Apart from making enquiries of the seller, the answer is to inspect the land and the title deeds. The title deeds are, in essence, the documents transferring the land from one person to another. As well as demonstrating a chain of title, they are likely to disclose rights such as easements and restrictive covenants which have been created in favour of other people. Other documents, such as leases, should also be produced by the seller, though there is always a danger of the purchaser's being kept in the dark about their existence. It is plainly impracticable to search documents going back for centuries: to do that would clog up sales and impose intolerable expense.

---

[1] Sale of Goods Act 1979, s 24(1).

Extract 9.1.1

Law of Property Act 1925, s 44

44.—(1)　After the commencement of this Act thirty years shall be substituted for forty years as the period of commencement of title which a purchaser of land may require . . .

(2)　Under a contract to grant or assign a term of years, whether derived or to be derived out of freehold or leasehold land, the intended lessee or assign shall not be entitled to call for the title to the freehold.

(4A)　Subsections (2) and (4) of this section do not apply to a contract to grant a term of years if the grant will be an event within section 4(1) of the Land Registration Act 2002 (events which trigger compulsory first registration of title).

(5)　Where by reason of any of subsections (2) to (4) of this section, an intending lessee or assign is not entitled to call for the title to the freehold or to a leasehold reversion, as the case may be, he shall not, where the contract is made after the commencement of this Act, be deemed to be affected with notice of any matter or thing of which, if he had contracted that such title should be furnished, he might have had notice.

(8)　A purchaser shall not be deemed to be or ever to have been affected with notice of any matter or thing of which, if he had investigated the title or made enquiries in regard to matters prior to the period of commencement of title fixed by this Act, or by any other statute, or by any rule of law, he might have had notice, unless he actually makes such investigation or enquiries.

Comment

(1) The period was reduced to 15 years by the Law of Property Act 1969, s 23. If A sold to B in 1930, B to C in 1970 and C made a gift of the land to V in 1997, what documents is a purchaser from V in 2015 entitled to see?

(2) Typically, the purchaser will be entitled to see around two transfers. Why are purchasers content with what is, in the lifetime of property, a short period of 15 years?

(3) The original position was that intending lessees are not entitled to inspect the freehold or the title to a lease. Sub-section (4A) was inserted by the Land Registration Act 2002, with the practical effect that intending tenants under leases for more than seven years can today insist on seeing the deeds. What are the advantages of this change?

(4) Section 44(5) and (8) provide no assistance where the earlier interest is legal: the purchaser is bound automatically. Their effect on earlier equitable interests will be considered below.

It is unusual for a legal interest to be postponed to a later interest, whether legal or equitable. However, it can happen.

Extract 9.1.2

Walker v Linom [1907] 2 Ch 104

Purchasers of land (trustees) failed to obtain the title deeds. This enabled the transferor to create a later mortgage of the land.

PARKER J: . . . The circumstances under which a mortgagee or purchaser with the legal estate is, by reason of some conduct on his part in relation to the title deeds, postponed to some person having only an equitable interest is discussed fully in the case of *Northern Counties of England Fire Insurance Co v Whipp*,[i] in which Fry LJ delivered the considered judgment of the Court of Appeal. The Lord Justice states the question for decision by referring to the rival contentions of the parties. 'It has been contended', he says, 'on the part of the plaintiffs that nothing short of fraud will justify the Court in postponing the legal estate. It has been contended by the defendant that gross negligence is enough.' . . .

The conclusion he ultimately arrives at is that in order to postpone a prior legal to a subsequent equitable estate there must be fraud as apart from negligence, and this conclusion is stated in language wide enough to cover cases of postponement based upon the conduct of the holder of the legal estate in not getting possession of the title deeds as well as cases of postponement based upon the conduct of such holder in dealing with the title deeds after he has got them. It would seem at first sight that the Lord Justice uses the word 'fraud' throughout this judgment as connoting a dishonest intent . . .

. . . There are, however, subsequent cases which suggest that at any rate in cases of postponement, based on no inquiry having been made for the deeds, fraud is not necessary. It is, for example, clear from the case of *Oliver* v *Hinton*[ii] that a purchaser obtaining the legal estate, but making no inquiry for the title deeds, or making inquiry and failing to take reasonable means to verify the truth of the excuse made for not producing them or handing them over, is, although perfectly honest, guilty of such negligence as to make it inequitable for him to rely on his legal estate so as to deprive a prior incumbrancer of his priority . . .

In [two other cases] referred to the question was between a prior equitable and a subsequent legal estate, and I think the later case was actually decided on constructive or imputed notice. But the Master of the Rolls expressly refused to decide *Oliver* v *Hinton* on any such ground. The question, however, arises whether the principle laid down in *Oliver* v *Hinton* is equally applicable between the holder of the legal estate who has omitted to make inquiry for the title deeds and a subsequent equitable estate the creation of which has been rendered possible by such omission. In my opinion any conduct on the part of the holder of the legal estate in relation to the deeds which would make it inequitable for him to rely on his legal estate against a prior equitable estate of which he had no notice ought also to be sufficient to postpone him to a subsequent equitable estate the creation of which has only been rendered possible by the possession of deeds which but for such conduct would have passed into the possession of the owner of the legal estate.

[i] 26 Ch D 482, 486.
[ii] [1899] 2 Ch 264.

Comment

Mortgagees invariably obtain the title deeds: the absence of deeds is a clear warning either that the property is not owned at all, or that there has already been a mortgage. *Walker* was a case on purchasers failing to obtain deeds, but would also apply to mortgagees who fail to obtain deeds.

2. Equitable interests and the doctrine of notice

Extract 9.2.1

Maitland, *Equity* (2nd ed) at pp 113–115, 118–119 (footnotes omitted)
by permission of Cambridge University Press

(v)   A fifth step was taken and this also at an early time. The trust was enforced even against one who purchased the thing from the trustee, if he at the time of the conveyance knew of the trust. What is the ground for this? The old books are clear about it, the ground is fraud or something akin to fraud. It is unconscientious – 'against conscience' – to buy what you know to be held on trust for another. The purchaser in such a case is, we may well say, liable *ex delicto vel quasi*. He has done what is wrong; has been guilty of fraud, or something very like fraud.

(vi)   Having taken this step, another is inevitable. If we stop here purchasers will take care not to know of the trust. To use a phrase used in the old reports, they will shut their eyes. The trust must be enforced against those who would have known of the trust had they behaved as prudent purchasers behave. Thus, to use the term which Holmes has made familiar, an objective standard is set up, a standard of diligence. It is not enough that you should be honest, it is required of you that you should also be diligent. To describe this standard will be my object in another lecture. Here it must be enough that it was and is a high standard – the conduct of a prudent purchaser according to the estimate of equity judges. If a purchaser failed to attain this standard, to make all such investigations of his vendor's title as a prudent purchaser would have made, he was treated as having notice, he was 'affected with notice', of all equitable rights of which he would have had knowledge had he made such investigations: of such rights he had 'implied notice', or 'constructive notice'. We arrive then at this result, equitable rights will hold good even against one who has come to the legal ownership by purchase for value, if when he obtained the legal ownership he had notice express or constructive of those rights.

But here a limit was reached. Against a person who acquires a legal right *bona fide*, for value, without notice express or constructive of the existence of equitable rights those rights are of no avail. I will read one passage in which James LJ stated this in forcible terms. In the case of *Pilcher* v *Rawlins*, LR 7 Ch 259, at page 268, he said this:

> 'I propose simply to apply myself to the case of a purchaser for valuable consideration, without notice, obtaining, upon the occasion of his purchase, and by means of his purchase deed, some legal estate, some legal right, some legal advantage; and according to my view of the established law of this Court, such a purchaser's plea of a purchase for valuable consideration without notice is an absolute, unqualified, unanswerable defence, and an unanswerable plea to the jurisdiction of this Court . . .'

How could it be otherwise? A purchaser in good faith has obtained a legal right. In a court of law that right is his: the law of the land gives it him. On what ground of equity are you going to take it from him? He has not himself undertaken any obligation, he has not succeeded by voluntary (gratuitous) title to any obligation, he has done no wrong, he has acted honestly and with diligence. Equity cannot touch him, because, to use the old phrase, his conscience is unaffected by the trust.

. . .

I have said that the standard of diligence required of purchasers is high, so high that a purchaser without notice of equitable rights is not a very common object of the law courts.

How was this standard fixed? The starting point is here: – Quite apart from any doctrine of equity, a prudent purchaser (or mortgagee) of land will investigate his vendor's (or mortgagor's) title. Further a vendor of land who contracts to sell it, contracts to show a good title. This is a legal contract enforceable at law by an action for damages. If the vendor fail in his part of the contract, the purchaser is not bound to fulfil his part. Rules were evolved as to what title must be shown. For instance as to length of title, it became settled that, in the absence of any bargain to the contrary, the vendor had to show a 60 years title . . . But our present point must be to notice that if there had never been any such thing as equity a prudent purchaser would have investigated his vendor's title – he would have done so in order to see that the vendor had an estate to sell, that there were no legal charges on the land, no legal rent-charges for example, for against such legal rights it would be no defence to say 'I purchased in good faith.' Now equity required of purchasers that they should make that investigation of title which a prudent purchaser would have made and which a purchaser on an open contract (*i.e.* a contract without special terms) would have been entitled to make. The purchaser was deemed to have notice of all equitable rights the existence of which he would have discovered if he had made such an investigation. The standard was high. According to the view taken by equity judges the prudent purchaser of land was one who employed a solicitor – and certainly this view was defensible . . . even with all our modern reforms, the average man could not yet be counselled to carry through a purchase without legal aid. But in reading some of the cases about constructive notice we may be inclined to say that equity demanded not the care of the most prudent father of a family but the care of the most prudent solicitor of a family aided by the skill of the most expert conveyancer.

For some years past indeed there has been a noticeable inclination against extending and even towards contracting the range of constructive notice, and in 1882 Parliament attempted to define the doctrine.

Comment

(1) We have seen that only a 15-year title has to be shown today.

(2) Why did equity develop priority rules different from those applying to legal interests?

The statutory reform mentioned by Maitland is now found in the Law of Property Act 1925.

Extract 9.2.2

Law of Property Act 1925, s 199

199.—(1) A purchaser shall not be prejudicially affected by notice of—

. . .

(ii) any other instrument or matter or any fact or thing unless—
   (a) it is within his own knowledge, or would have come to his knowledge if such inquiries and inspections had been made as ought reasonably to have been made by him; or
   (b) in the same transaction with respect to which a question of notice to the purchaser arises, it has come to the knowledge of his counsel, as such, or of his solicitor or other agent, as such, or would have come to the knowledge of his solicitor or other agent, as such, if such inquiries and inspections had been made as ought reasonably to have been made by the solicitor or other agent.

(3) A purchaser shall not by reason of anything in this section be affected by notice in any case where he would not have been so affected if this section had not been enacted.

Comment

(1) The one clear result of s 199 is to restrict the effect of notice by agents (such as solicitors), when it arises from a different transaction.

(2) Otherwise, it is difficult to pinpoint precise effects of the provision. Perhaps its significance lies primarily in the recognition that not too much should be required of purchasers.

Maitland clearly explains the development of equitable rules and their rationale based upon the conscience of the purchaser. Why should the modern law maintain different rules for legal and equitable interests? Note that, even in the realm of registration, legal interests are more likely to escape the need to register.

We can now turn to the operation of notice.

A. Purchase of legal estate

Extract 9.2.3

Phillips v Phillips (1861) 4 De GF&J 208 (45 ER 1164)

It was argued that a bona fide purchaser of an *equitable* interest took priority over an earlier equitable interest of which there was no notice.

LORD WESTBURY LC: . . . I have permitted the argument to proceed with reference to the general proposition, which was maintained before me with great energy and learning, viz, that the doctrine of a Court of Equity was this, that it would give no relief whatever to any claimant against a purchaser for valuable consideration without notice . . .

I undoubtedly was struck with the novelty and extent of the doctrine that was thus advanced, and in order to deal with the argument it becomes necessary to revert to elementary principles. I take it to be a clear proposition that every conveyance of an equitable interest is an innocent conveyance, that is to say, the grant of a person entitled merely in equity passes only that which he is justly entitled to and no more. If, therefore, a person seised of an equitable estate (the legal estate being outstanding), makes an assurance by way of mortgage or grants an annuity, and afterwards conveys the whole estate to a purchaser, he can grant to the purchaser that which he has, viz, the estate subject to the mortgage or annuity, and no more. The subsequent grantee takes only that which is left in the grantor. Hence grantees and incumbrancers claiming in equity take and are ranked according to the dates of their securities; and the maxim applies, 'Qui prior est tempore potior est jure' [The first in time has the better right] . . .

Comment

Why is a distinction drawn between purchasers of legal and equitable interests? Should it be?

B. Constructive notice: inspecting deeds

This is described by Maitland in Extract 9.2.1.

Extract 9.2.4

Peto v Hammond (1861) 30 Beav 495 (54 ER 981)

ROMILLY MR: . . . Various arguments have been addressed to me, which, if acceded to, would, in my opinion, lead to very dangerous consequences. One was, that conditions of sale may make it unnecessary for a person to inquire into particular circumstances which otherwise he would be bound to do, and that the dispensing with the necessity of so inquiring takes away from a purchaser any charge of negligence, or any imputation of constructive notice. Now, in the first place, a more dangerous doctrine can hardly be conceived, than that two persons may, by means of special conditions of sale, dispose of property in such a manner as to deprive a third person of his rights, and which, without such conditions of sale, they could not effect. It has been usually supposed to be the doctrine of equity and of law, that no two persons could, by their act, deprive another person of his rights, and yet that would be the effect of this doctrine. But in truth when, by a special condition of sale, a purchaser contracts with the vendor that he will not make certain inquiries which he would otherwise be bound to make, the consequence is, that the purchaser takes on himself the risk; and if by that means he takes a bad title, the loss falls upon him . . .

Comment

(1) This is particularly important where the title is based upon adverse possession. If a title cannot be shown for the normal period then neither the initial adverse possessor nor any purchaser will be protected against equitable interests.[2]

(2) Note the rules applicable to tenants in s 44(2)–(5) of the Law of Property Act 1925 (Extract 9.1.1 above). What justification is there for these rules?

---

[2] *Re Nisbet and Potts' Contract* [1906] 1 Ch 386.

C. Constructive notice: inspecting the land

Extract 9.2.5

Barnhart v *Greenshields* (1853) 9 Moo PC 18 (14 ER 204)

RT HON T PEMBERTON LEIGH: . . . With respect to the effect of possession merely, we take the law to be, that if there be a tenant in possession of land, a purchaser is bound by all the equities which the tenant could enforce against the vendor, and that the equity of the tenant extends not only to interests connected with his tenancy, as in *Taylor* v *Stibbert* (2 Ves Jun 437), but also to interests under collateral agreements, as in *Daniels* v *Davison* (16 Ves 249), *Allen* v *Anthony* (1 Mer 282), the principle being the same in both classes of cases; namely, that the possession of the tenant is notice that he has some interest in the land, and that a purchaser having notice of that fact, is bound, according to the ordinary rule, either to inquire what that interest is, or to give effect to it, whatever it may be.

. . .

We now come to the parol evidence of notice. Upon this subject the rule is settled, that a purchaser is not bound to attend to vague rumours – to statements by mere strangers, but that a notice, in order to be binding, must proceed from some person interested in the property.

Comment

What credence should be given to doubts expressed by other people?

Extract 9.2.6

Hunt v *Luck* [1902] 1 Ch 428

Does a tenant's occupation give notice of the *landlord's* rights?

VAUGHAN WILLIAMS LJ: . . . I think that the conclusion of Farwell J was right. In his judgment he, after quoting the older authorities, said:[i] 'The rule established by these two cases may be stated thus: (1) A tenant's occupation is notice of all that tenant's rights, but not of his lessor's title or rights; (2) actual knowledge that the rents are paid by the tenants to some person whose receipt is inconsistent with the title of the vendor is notice of that person's rights.' In the present case I do not understand that any one suggests, and, if it is suggested, in my opinion the suggestion is ill-founded, that there was actual knowledge that the rents were paid by the tenants to some person whose receipt would be inconsistent with the title of the mortgagor, Gilbert. We have, therefore, to apply the first of the rules stated by the learned judge. Now, what does that mean? It means that, if a purchaser or a mortgagee has notice that the vendor or mortgagor is not in possession of the property, he must make inquiries of the person in possession – of the tenant who is in possession – and find out from him what his rights are, and, if he does not choose to do that, then whatever title he acquires as purchaser or mortgagee will be subject to the title or right of the tenant in possession.

. . .

[In relation to the Conveyancing Act 1882, the forerunner of s 199, Law of Property Act 1925.] In my judgment, the only inquiry which ought reasonably to have been made here by the intending mortgagees was an inquiry to protect themselves against any right which the tenant might have in the subject-matter of the mortgage. I do not think that there is, for the purpose of ascertaining the title of the vendor, any obligation on the purchaser to make inquiries of the tenant in reference to anything but protection against the rights of the tenant.

---

[i] [1901] 1 Ch 51.

Comment

This is the most frequently cited case on the duties of purchasers. What is it *not* necessary for the purchaser to do? Are there convincing reasons for the decision?

In more recent years, the centre of attention has been on cases where the claimant to an equitable interest has been living on the premises together with the legal owner. Typically, the legal owner mortgages the property, no enquiry being made of the claimant. Does the mortgagee have notice?

Extract 9.2.7

Caunce v *Caunce* [1969] 1 WLR 286

STAMP J: . . . It is urged – and this is really in the forefront of the plaintiff's argument – that today when so many matrimonial homes are purchased out of moneys provided in part by the wife, a purchaser – by which expression I include a mortgagee – who finds the matrimonial home vested in one of the spouses, more particularly in this case a husband, is put upon inquiry as to whether the other spouse has an equitable interest in the property, and it is urged that, if he does not inquire of the other spouse whether such an interest is claimed, he takes subject to the interest. As a bare proposition of law no authority has been cited for that proposition, and in view of the disinclination of the courts to extend the doctrine of constructive notice (see *Hunt* v *Luck* [1901] 1 Ch 45), I am not persuaded that it ought to be accepted. More particularly is this the case where, as was the fact here, the wife knew almost at the outset that the property was in the sole name of her husband, and had taken no step to assert her rights.

. . .

[In relation to an argument based on the wife's being a customer of the bank.] In this connection I would borrow two passages in the judgment of Farwell J in *Hunt* v *Luck* [1901] 1 Ch 45, to which I have already referred. The first is on p 48 of the report, and runs as follows:

'This doctrine of constructive notice, imputing as it does knowledge which the person affected does not actually possess, is one which the courts of late years have been unwilling to extend. I am not referring to cases where a man wilfully shuts his eyes so as to avoid notice, but to cases like the present, where honest men are to be affected by knowledge which every one admits they did not in fact possess. So far as regards the merits of the case, even assuming both parties to the action to be equally innocent, the man who has been swindled by too great confidence in his own agent has surely less claim to the assistance of a court of equity than a purchaser for value who gets the legal estate, and pays his money without notice. Granted that the vendor has every reason to believe his agent an honest man, still, if he is mistaken and trusts a rogue, he, rather than the purchaser for value without notice who is misled by his having so trusted, ought to bear the burden.'

And so it appears to me, as between a wife who has trusted her husband to have the property vested in his sole name, or who has not taken steps to get it vested in joint names, on the one hand and a mortgagee bank on the other.

The second passage of Farwell J's judgment is at p 52 of the report, and runs as follows:

'Constructive notice is the knowledge which the courts impute to a person upon a presumption so strong of the existence of the knowledge that it cannot be allowed to be rebutted, either from his knowing something which ought to have put him to further inquiry or from his wilfully abstaining from inquiry, to avoid notice. How can I hold that the mortgagees here wilfully neglected to make some inquiry which is usual in cases of mortgages or sales of real estate in order to avoid acquiring some knowledge which they would thereby have obtained.'

The last sentence of that passage appears to be applicable to the facts of the present case. Nor do I find the suggestion that a bank mortgagee should at its peril be bound to conduct an inquiry into the financial relations between husband and wife, before it can advance money on security of property vested in the husband, at all an attractive one, and in my view in this day and age husbands and wives ought to be able to bank at the same bank without having their accounts analysed by the bank in order to find out if one of them is deceiving the other.

The exercise which, it is submitted, ought to have been conducted in the present case would – so it seems to me – have been more appropriate to a police inquiry or that of a detective agency than to a bank manager who often no doubt arranges advances daily in the ordinary course of business . . .

I must now consider a further argument advanced on behalf of the plaintiff. It is contended that an inquiry ought to have been made on the property and that if such an inquiry had been made the plaintiff would have asserted her equitable interest, ergo – so the argument runs – the bank had constructive notice of that interest. Before going on to consider this contention it is, perhaps, convenient that I should remark by way of warning, that section 199 is a section designed not to extend but to limit the doctrine of constructive notice. The section does not operate so as to fix a purchaser with constructive notice of a matter of which he would not have had constructive notice prior to the coming into force of the Law of Property Act. The law, as I understand it, is this: if there be in possession or occupation of the property, contracted to be sold or mortgaged, a person other than the vendor, or, as in this case, other than the mortgagor, and the purchaser makes no inquiry of that person, he takes the property fixed with notice of that person's rights and interests, however that may be. (See the judgment in the Court of Appeal of Vaughan-Williams LJ in *Hunt* v *Luck* [1902] 1 Ch 428, 432.) Here it is said that the plaintiff was in possession or occupation. No inquiry was made of her and therefore the bank is fixed with notice of her equitable interest. In my judgment, it is here that the fallacy arises, for the plaintiff, unlike the deserted wife, was not in apparent occupation or possession. She was there, ostensibly, because she was the wife, and her presence there was wholly consistent with the title offered by the husband to the bank.

. . .

In my judgment, where the vendor or mortgagor is himself in possession and occupation of the property, the purchaser or the mortgagee is not affected with notice of the equitable interests of any other person who may be resident there, and whose presence is wholly consistent with the title offered. If you buy with vacant possession on completion and you know, or find out, that the vendor is himself in possession and occupation of the property, you are, in my judgment, by reason of your failure to make further inquiries on the premises, no more fixed with notice of the equitable interest of the vendor's wife who is living there with him than you would be affected with notice of the equitable interest of any other person who might also be resident on the premises, *e.g.*, the vendor's father, his 'Uncle Harry' or his 'Aunt Matilda', any of whom, be it observed, might have contributed towards the purchase of the property. The reason is that the vendor being in possession, the presence of his wife or guest or lodger implies nothing to negative the title offered. It is otherwise if the vendor is not in occupation and you find another party whose presence demands an explanation and whose presence you ignore at your peril.

. . . Mr Nourse also points out . . . how unworkable and undesirable it would be if the law required such an inquiry – an inquiry, let me add, which would be as embarrassing to the inquirer as it would, in my view, be intolerable to the wife and the husband. Mr Nourse, I think, put it well when, in commenting on the whole of the plaintiff's case, he said it is not in the public interest that bank mortgagees should be snoopers and busybodies in relation to wholly normal transactions of mortgage . . .

Comment

This approach is avowedly designed to benefit purchasers. Does it represent an appropriate balance between claimants and purchasers?

Caunce is but the first of a large number of cases dealing with the problem. However, most relate to the overriding interest of those in actual occupation of registered land; they will be studied in that setting.[3] It will be seen that they contain some criticism of *Caunce*. Today, legislation provides that purchasers of registered land are protected unless the occupation is obvious on a reasonably careful inspection. How would this apply to the facts of *Caunce?*

D. Other considerations

We will consider now the position of a successor in title to a bona fide purchaser without notice. If the successor possesses notice, can the equitable interest revive as against that person?

Extract 9.2.8

Wilkes v *Spooner* [1911] 2 KB 473

VAUGHAN WILLIAMS LJ: . . . It cannot seriously be disputed that the proposition which I quoted from Ashburner's *Principles of Equity*, p 75, is good law. It is as follows: 'A purchaser for valuable consideration without notice can give a good title to a purchaser from him with notice. The only exception is that a trustee who has sold property in breach of trust, or a person who has acquired property by fraud, cannot protect himself by purchasing it from a bona fide purchaser for value without notice.' The learned author cites as authorities for that proposition the cases of *Sweet* v *Southcote*[i] and *Barrow's Case*.[ii] Those cases seem to me to be conclusive authorities for the proposition stated by the author in the text . . . The only exception, and the well-known exception, to the rule which protects a purchaser with notice taking from a purchaser without notice is that which prevents a trustee buying back trust property which he has sold, or a fraudulent man who has acquired property by fraud saying he sold it to a bona fide purchaser without notice, and has got it back again. Those are cases to shew that a person shall not take advantage of his own wrong.

[i] 2 Bro CC 66.
[ii] 14 Ch D 432.

Comment

What justification is there for the successor's not normally being bound?

3. Two competing equitable interests

We have already seen that the second interest cannot take advantage of the bona fide purchaser principle.[4] But is it inevitable that the first interest has priority?

Extract 9.3.1

Rice v *Rice* (1853) 2 Drew 73 (61 ER 646)

KINDERSLEY V-C: . . . What is the rule of a Court of Equity for determining the preference as between persons having adverse equitable interests? The rule is sometimes expressed in this form: – 'As between persons having only equitable interests, *qui prior est tempore potior est jure* [he who is first in time has the strongest claim in law].' This is an incorrect statement of the rule; for that proposition is far from being universally true . . .

[3] See p 336 below.
[4] See Extract 9.2.3.

Another form of stating the rule is this: – 'As between persons having only equitable interests, if their equities are equal, *qui prior est tempore potior est jure.*' This form of stating the rule is not so obviously incorrect as the former. And yet even this enunciation of the rule (when accurately considered) seems to me to involve a contradiction. For when we talk of two persons having equal or unequal equities, in what sense do we use the term 'equity'? For example, when we say that A has a better equity than B, what is meant by that? It means only that, according to those principles of right and justice which a Court of Equity recognizes and acts upon, it will prefer A to B, and will interfere to enforce the rights of A as against B. And therefore it is impossible (strictly speaking) that two persons should have equal equities, except in a case in which a Court of Equity would altogether refuse to lend its assistance to either party as against the other . . . To lay down the rule therefore with perfect accuracy, I think it should be stated in some such form as this: – 'As between persons having only equitable interests, if their equities are *in all other respects* equal, priority of time gives the better equity; or, *qui prior est tempore potior est jure.*'

Comment

Is this an example of judicial hair splitting? What circumstances might disturb the priority of the first in time?

Other cases place greater emphasis upon the time order. This is seen in the extract from *Phillips* v *Phillips*[5] and somewhat more recently in *Barclays Bank Ltd* v *Taylor*.[6]

4. Priority rules for equities

The time order is less conclusive when the first interest is an equity. It will be recalled that many equities are rights to remedies such as rescission or rectification.[7]

Extract 9.4.1

Latec Investments Ltd v *Hotel Terrigal Pty Ltd (in liquidation)* (1965) 113 CLR 265 (High Court of Australia)

TAYLOR J: It cannot, of course, be disputed at the present time that the defence of purchaser for value without notice of a prior equitable interest cannot be generally maintained but it does appear that it has always – that is to say, both before and after *Phillips* v *Phillips*[i] – been allowed to prevail where the person entitled to the earlier interest required the assistance of a court of equity to remove an impediment to his title as a preliminary to asserting his interest. In such cases it seems that the court will not interfere and to me it does not seem to matter much whether it be said that this is because, as Lord *Westbury's* observations suggest, that a plaintiff seeking to set aside a deed for fraud or to reform it for mistake is, at that stage, asserting an equity as distinguished from an equitable estate, or, because a plaintiff in such cases will be denied the assistance of a court of equity to remove the impediment to his title if, before he seeks that assistance, an equitable interest in the subject property has passed to a purchaser for value without notice of the plaintiff's prior interest. I prefer the latter as a more precise statement of the law and, indeed, I think this is the true meaning of Lord *Westbury's* observations.

[i] (1861) 4 De GF&J 208 [45 ER 1164].

---

[5] (1861) 4 De GF&J 208 (45 ER 1164); Extract 9.2.3 above.
[6] [1974] Ch 137.
[7] See p 22 above.

Comment

(1) What are the different approaches identified by Taylor J?

(2) Another different priority rule is that a purchaser is not expected to discover rights of an occupier which are inconsistent with documents under which the occupier holds the land: a purchaser is entitled to assume that the documents are accurate.[8]

Although registered land will be studied in the following chapter, this is an appropriate point at which to note changes introduced by the Land Registration Act 2002. As we have seen,[9] equities are treated as equitable interests by s 116. This means that they are subject to the same statutory priority rules as apply to other interests in registered land. Indeed, there appears little point in maintaining a category of equities. So much seems clear, but two questions may be raised. The first is that we have seen that the courts would postpone an undiscovered equity if it was inconsistent with documents under which the claimant to the equity holds. Is the loss of this rule a harmful reduction in the purchaser's protection? The second point concerns the stress of Taylor J in *Latec* on the effect of discretion in claims to equities. Will this discretion survive now that priority is based on being first in time or, as against a subsequent registered disposition, being entered on the register or an actual occupation overriding interest?

5. The time order

Priorities frequently depend upon the time order of the rival claims. However, often the time order is unclear: two interests may appear to arise at the same time. Suppose that A provides B with £10,000 towards the purchase of a house, in circumstances which would give rise to a resulting trust. Unknown to A, B raises the remaining £90,000 by a mortgage loan from a bank. Both the resulting trust and the mortgage take effect on the conveyance to B. Which comes first? A controversial doctrine – *scintilla temporis* – was developed whereby it was reasoned that B could not mortgage the property to the bank until after the conveyance. The logic was that B had to own the property before being able to grant a mortgage. In the split second before the mortgage took effect, the resulting trust would attach to the land: it would therefore pre-date the mortgage.

Extract 9.5.1

Abbey National BS v *Cann* [1991] 1 AC 56

LORD OLIVER: . . . This is a puzzling problem upon which it is not easy to reconcile the authorities.

The appellants rely upon the decision of the Court of Appeal in *Church of England Building Society* v *Piskor* [1954] Ch 553, a case concerned with unregistered conveyancing . . . The argument of the society was that the conveyance and the charge were in reality one single transaction with the result that the legal estate vested in the purchaser was, from the outset, subject to the society's charge and so could not be available to feed the estoppel free from it. This argument was rejected by the Court of Appeal. It was held that, despite the fact that the two documents were executed contemporaneously, the transaction necessarily involved conveyancing steps which, in contemplation of law, must be regarded as taking place in a defined

---

[8] *Smith* v *Jones* [1954] 1 WLR 1089 (tenant claiming to rectify lease).
[9] See Extract 1.3.4 above.

order, so that there was a 'scintilla temporis' between the purchaser's acquisition of the legal estate and the creation of the society's charge during which the estoppel could be fed . . .

On the other side of the line are *In re Connolly Brothers Ltd (No 2)* [1912] 2 Ch 25 and *Security Trust Co* v *Royal Bank of Canada* [1976] AC 503. In the former, . . . Warrington J held that her charge had priority over the charge created by the debentures and his decision was upheld by the Court of Appeal, Sir Herbert Cozens-Hardy MR remarking, at p 31:

'we should be shutting our eyes to the real transaction if we were to hold that the unencumbered fee simple in the property was ever in the company so that it became subject to the charge of the debenture holders.'

. . . The question in issue was whether the company's legal estate, without the existence of which her charge could never have taken effect, existed at any point of time free from her charge so that the prior interest of the debenture holders could attach. No other analysis of the decision is possible save that the court considered the transaction consisting of the conveyance, the advance and the memorandum of deposit as a single transaction.

The more recent decision of the Privy Council in *Security Trust Co* v *Royal Bank of Canada* [1976] AC 503 is equally capable of analysis only on the 'single transaction' basis . . .

These three authorities were carefully reviewed by Mustill LJ in the course of his judgment in *Lloyds Bank Plc* v *Rosset* [1989] Ch 350, 388–393. He concluded that it was difficult to see how they could live together. I agree. I do not, for my part, consider that they can be reconciled. In neither *In re Connolly* nor the *Security Trust Co* case could the charge which was given priority have been created unless and until the legal estate had been obtained by the chargor. In both cases the chargee had notice of the existence of the charge which failed to achieve priority. Both necessarily rest therefore upon the proposition that, at least where there is a prior agreement to grant the charge on the legal estate when obtained, the transactions of acquiring the legal estate and granting the charge are, in law as in reality, one indivisible transaction . . .

One is therefore presented with a stark choice between them. Of course, as a matter of legal theory, a person cannot charge a legal estate that he does not have, so that there is an attractive legal logic in the ratio in *Piskor's* case. Nevertheless, I cannot help feeling that it flies in the face of reality. The reality is that, in the vast majority of cases, the acquisition of the legal estate and the charge are not only precisely simultaneous but indissolubly bound together. The acquisition of the legal estate is entirely dependent upon the provision of funds which will have been provided before the conveyance can take effect and which are provided only against an agreement that the estate will be charged to secure them. Indeed, in many, if not most, cases of building society mortgages, there will have been, as there was in this case, a formal offer and acceptance of an advance which will ripen into a specifically enforceable agreement immediately the funds are advanced which will normally be a day or more before completion. In many, if not most, cases, the charge itself will have been executed before the execution, let alone the exchange, of the conveyance or transfer of the property . . . The reality is that the purchaser of land who relies upon a building society or bank loan for the completion of his purchase never in fact acquires anything but an equity of redemption, for the land is, from the very inception, charged with the amount of the loan without which it could never have been transferred at all and it was never intended that it should be otherwise. The 'scintilla temporis' is no more than a legal artifice and, for my part, I would adopt the reasoning of the Court of Appeal in *In re Connolly Brothers Ltd (No 2)* [1912] 2 Ch 25 and of Harman J in *Coventry Permanent Economic Building Society* v *Jones* [1951] 1 All ER 901 and hold that *Piskor's* case was wrongly decided.

LORD JAUNCEY: . . . In my view a purchaser who can only complete the transaction by borrowing money for the security of which he is contractually bound to grant a mortgage to the lender *eo instante* with the execution of the conveyance in his favour cannot in reality ever be said to have acquired even for a scintilla temporis the unencumbered fee simple or leasehold interest in land whereby he could grant interests having priority over the mortgage or the estoppel in favour of prior grantees could be fed with similar results. Since no one can grant what he does not have it follows that such a purchaser could never grant an interest which was not subject to the limitations on his own interest.

Comment

(1) Is there any merit in the *scintilla temporis* analysis?

(2) Two specific points in favour of the mortgagee are noted: that there may be an agreement for the mortgage in advance of the purchase (Lord Oliver) and that the mortgage money may be essential in order that the purchase should proceed (Lord Jauncey). How persuasive are these points? Would the result be different if one or both were absent?

(3) *Cann* makes it clear that an acquisition mortgage will normally be treated as being first in time relative to any other interest in the land created by the purchaser. Why should the mortgage have priority over other sources of finance, such as Mrs Cann's contribution of half the cost of purchase in *Cann*?

(4) *Cann* is a case on registered land, but the time order may be of vital importance whether or not title is registered.

(5) As will be seen in the following chapter,[10] this is but one of a battery of arguments available to the acquisition mortgagee, any one of which would guarantee success. Two other arguments, both deployed in *Cann* itself, are that (i) a person who is aware of the need for money to be raised on mortgage to realise his or her objective (purchase, in *Cann*) will be treated as agreeing to the mortgagee's having priority; and (ii) it is unlikely that the mortgagee will have notice or, in registered land, that the claimant will be in actual occupation so as to have an overriding interest binding the mortgagee.

An issue which has arisen in later cases concerns claims by the seller. Does the mortgagee enjoy the same priority over these claims as it enjoys over claims by a third party, such as Mrs Cann? Though a claim based upon undue influence on the part of the purchaser has succeeded,[11] in *Mortgage Business plc v O'Shaughnessy*[12] the Supreme Court applied *Cann* to other claims. *Mortgage Business* involved equity release schemes, in which people sell houses in return for cash and a right to live there for life. Does principle indicate that *Cann* should, or should not, apply?

6. The land charges scheme

Whatever the merits of the priority rules discussed above, they do produce uncertainty. The purchaser is always subject to the risk of an allegation that further enquiries should have been made, so that an equitable interest becomes binding, quite apart from dangers from undiscovered (and perhaps undiscoverable) legal interests. Meanwhile, the holder of an equitable interest may be defeated by a bona fide purchaser of the legal estate.

Registration of interests can remove this uncertainty. Once registered, the interest holder can be confident that a purchaser will be bound, while the purchaser can discover registered interests easily and cheaply and will be protected against interests which have

---

[10] See especially pp 334, 334 below.
[11] *Bank of Scotland* v *Hussain* [2010] EWHC 2812 (Ch) (the claim failed for other reasons).
[12] [2014] 3 WLR 1163.

not been registered. English law has two forms of registration today, mutually exclusive in their operation. In unregistered land, the land charges scheme requires certain interests to be registered. In essence, these comprise a wide range of equitable interests, together with some statutory charges. In registered land, the subject matter of the following chapter, most legal as well as equitable rights have to be registered: it follows that ownership of the fee simple itself is registered. Because registered titles are guaranteed, the purchaser no longer has to spend time looking at the title deeds: the register acts as a substitute for them. Although both systems date back over a century, registered land for many years applied only to certain parts of the country and hence to a small proportion of titles. Today, it applies to approximately 95% of titles and is growing. Land charges, therefore, are of relatively small importance. This section looks at the essentials of the land charges scheme and at some of the problems in its operation. They demonstrate the superiority of land registration.

A. What can be registered?

Extract 9.6.1

Land Charges Act 1972, s 2

2.—(4) A Class C land charge is any of the following (not being a local land charge), namely—
  (i) a puisne mortgage;
  . . .
  (iii) a general equitable charge;
  (iv) an estate contract;
and for this purpose—
  (i) a puisne mortgage is a legal mortgage which is not protected by a deposit of documents relating to the legal estate affected;
  . . .
  (iii) a general equitable charge is any equitable charge which—
    (a) is not secured by a deposit of documents relating to the legal estate affected; and
    (b) does not arise or affect an interest arising under a trust of land or a settlement; and
    . . .
    (d) is not included in any other class of land charge;
  (iv) an estate contract is a contract by an estate owner or by a person entitled at the date of the contract to have a legal estate conveyed to him to convey or create a legal estate, including a contract conferring either expressly or by statutory implication a valid option to purchase, a right of pre-emption or any other like right.
  (5) A Class D land charge is any of the following (not being a local land charge), namely—
  . . .
  (ii) a restrictive covenant;
  (iii) an equitable easement;
and for this purpose—
  . . .
  (ii) a restrictive covenant is a covenant or agreement (other than a covenant or agreement between a lessor and a lessee) restrictive of the user of land and entered into on or after 1st January 1926;
  (iii) an equitable easement is an easement, right or privilege over or affecting land created or arising on or after 1st January 1926, and being merely an equitable interest.
  (7) A Class F land charge is a charge affecting any land by virtue of the Part IV of the Family Law Act 1996.

Comment

(1) The 1972 Act consolidated earlier (very similar) legislation of 1925.

(2) Classes A and B cover various statutory charges; Class E is obsolescent; Class F comprises spouses' and civil partners' statutory rights of occupation.[13] Note that Class C(i) is exceptional in including a legal interest. Why might this be?

(3) The classes have been the subject of extensive litigation, though this detail lies outside the scope of this book.

One point to note is that, although the scheme sets out to cover many equitable interests, it does not include interests under trusts of land. It is intended that purchasers will be protected by overreaching whenever there is a trust of land, rendering registration unnecessary. How valid is this reasoning? There is, furthermore, no principle that all equitable interests are either overreachable or registrable.[14] What interests remain subject to the old doctrine of notice?

B. Registering and searching

Section 3(1) of the Land Charges Act 1972 provides: 'A land charge shall be registered in the name of the estate owner whose estate is intended to be affected.' This simple provision is fundamental: registration is against the name of the owner of the legal estate. This is both a strength and a weakness. It is a strength because it ensures a simple and cheap system, computerised for many years. Unfortunately, errors are very common and loss can frequently be caused as a consequence.

The form of registration determines how searches are made. The purchaser must discover, from the title deeds, the names of the previous owners of the land and search against those names. Searching is almost invariably by an official search. Quite apart from convenience, this has advantages in that it gives protection against new entries between the date of searching and the time of completion.[15] In addition, protection is also given by s 10(4) against entries erroneously overlooked:

> In favour of a purchaser or an intending purchaser, as against persons interested under or in respect of matters or documents entries of which are required or allowed as aforesaid, the certificate, according to its tenor, shall be conclusive, affirmatively or negatively, as the case may be.

C. The effect of registration and of failure to register

Extract 9.6.2

Law of Property Act 1925, s 198

198.—(1) The registration of any instrument or matter in any register kept under the Land Charges Act 1972 or any local land charges register, shall be deemed to constitute actual notice of such instrument or matter, and of the fact of such registration, to all persons and for all purposes connected with the land affected, as from the date of registration or other prescribed date and so long as the registration continues in force.

---

[13] See Extract 12.2.6 below.
[14] *Shiloh Spinners Ltd* v *Harding* [1973] AC 691.
[15] Land Charges Act 1972, s 11(5) (for 15 working days).

Extract 9.6.3

Land Charges Act 1972, s 4; Law of Property Act 1925, s 199

4.—(5) A land charge of Class B and a land charge of Class C (other than an estate contract) created or arising on or after 1st January 1926 shall be void as against a purchaser of the land charged with it, or of any interest in such land, unless the land charge is registered in the appropriate register before the completion of the purchase.

(6) An estate contract and a land charge of Class D created or entered into on or after 1st January 1926 shall be void as against a purchaser for money or money's worth . . . of a legal estate in the land charged with it, unless the land charge is registered in the appropriate register before the completion of the purchase.

199.—(1) A purchaser shall not be prejudicially affected by notice of—
(i) any instrument or matter capable of registration under the provisions of the Land Charges Act 1925, or any enactment which it replaces, which is void or not enforceable as against him under that Act or enactment, by reason of the non-registration thereof;

. . .

As a result, registered interests bind purchasers and unregistered interests fail as against purchasers. An important consequence of s 10(4) of the 1972 Act is that an interest omitted from a search will fail, even if registered. This is particularly important because the computerisation of land charges requires a perfect match between the registration and the search: even the introduction or omission of one of a number of forenames is likely to cause a registration to be overlooked.

Extract 9.6.4

Oak Co-operative Building Society v *Blackburn* [1968] Ch 730

The legal owner was Francis David Blackburn. An interest was registered against the name of *Frank* David Blackburn. Subsequently, the plaintiff mortgagee searched against the name of Francis *Davis* Blackburn; the search certificate omitted the registration. The plaintiff argued that the registration was invalid.

RUSSELL LJ: . . . In the case of a request for an official search, which of course takes place before completion after title examined, we can only think that the name or names referred to in the request should be that or those appearing on the title. A nil certificate here as to Francis Davis *Blackburn* would not have served to override the third defendant's land charge had it been registered in the name Francis David *Blackburn*, though it *could* have been issued.

In most cases of contracts to purchase land nowadays many of the formalities precede exchange of contracts, and indeed those acting for the vendor would have used in the contract the name of the proposed vendor as appearing on the title. But of course there are other cases, such as the present, where the contract is much less formally arrived at, and the purchaser has no ready means of ascertaining the 'title' names of the vendor. It would seem to be a great hardship on a purchaser registering in the name by which the vendor ordinarily passed that his registration should be entirely without operation, which is of course the submission of the plaintiffs in this case . . .

We have come to the conclusion that the registration on this occasion ought not to be regarded as a nullity simply because the formal name of Blackburn was Francis and not Frank, and notwithstanding that Frank as a name is not merely an abbreviation or version of Francis but also a name in its own right, as are also for example Harry and Willie . . . We take a broader view that so far as possible the system should be made to work in favour of those who seek to make use of it in a sensible and practical way. If a proposing purchaser here had requested a search in the correct full names he would have got a clean certificate and a clear title under section 17(3) of the Land Charges Act, 1925,[i] and would have suffered no harm from the fact that the registration was not in such names: and a person registering who is not in a position to satisfy himself what are the correct full names runs that risk. But if there be registration in what may be fairly described as a version of the full names of the vendor, albeit not a version which is bound to be discovered on a search in the correct full names, we would not hold it a nullity against someone who does not search at all, or who (as here) searches in the wrong name.

[i] [Now Land Charges Act 1972, s 10(4).]

Comment

(1) It was treated as clear that searches have to be against the precisely correct name. Why are registrations and searches treated differently?

(2) What 'may be fairly described as a version'?

(3) How well protected is the person who registers in a fair version of the true name?

A variation on this theme concerns the question as to what a person's true name is. Is it the name on the birth certificate, or (if different) the name on the title deeds when the land was conveyed to him?

Extract 9.6.5

Standard Property Investments plc v British Plastics Federation (1985) 53 P&CR 25

WALTON J: . . . There is just one other thing that I would add at this stage, and it is simply this. Quite obviously, the proper names for registration and for search must coincide. Therefore, one would expect to find in the legislation expressly or by implication, some fixed point of reference equally available to both the party registering the charge and to the person effecting the search.

. . .

This suggests, and suggests very strongly, that what is required is some fixed point of reference, equally available to both parties, which is, for this purpose, conclusive as to the name to be used. It cannot possibly be the birth certificate; what use is the birth certificate of 'Winston Spencer Churchill' if he has changed his name, as he is entitled to do, to 'Winston Spencer Attlee?' It will, however, be seen from the examination of this problem subsequently effected in this judgment that there is, indeed, such a fixed point which effectively and conclusively settles the matter for all such purposes.

. . . suppose that registration under the 1972 Act is effected against a person whose name at the time of registration is 'John William Smith'. Afterwards, he changes his surname, so that his name becomes indisputably 'John William Brown'. Perhaps even less surprisingly, 'Jane Mary Foster' may have become 'Jane Mary Brown'. When a person comes to make a search, against what name should he effect the search? It would be ludicrously stupid to search against a subsequent name in either case, for in neither case would there be any possibility of the search revealing what on any footing was perfectly properly registered at the time when it was registered. I need not multiply examples; they readily suggest themselves. Accordingly, one is driven back to the fact that the search, to be effective, must be against the name actually borne by the estate owner at the time when he, or she, acquired the estate. So on this consideration alone, we are already some distance away from being safe if the search is conducted in the true and actual name or, as Mr Barker for the first defendant would have it, the 'full name' which the person against whom the search is made bears.

Now what is the name which was borne by such person at the time when he or she acquired the estate? The first and most obvious answer to that is, the name in which he or she took the conveyance. But Mr Barker would have none of this. He insisted upon the fact that the registration and the search must be in the 'full' name of the estate owner, however much, or little, that differed from the name in which he took the conveyance of the estate . . .

Now there is no limit to the number of Christian names which a man or woman may have, so that there is no obvious and easy way in which a person wishing to register a land charge will have of finding out what the full name of the estate owner in the sense indicated by Mr Barker, is.

. . . by the simple process of considering how the system must be made to work, it appears to me quite inevitable that one ends up with the position that 'the name of the estate owner' is the name as disclosed by the conveyance of that estate to him or her. This is in fact the assumption which to my knowledge has always been made by those who had to do with registration ever since I first came to the bar: and it is correct.

Comment

This does seem to be the only practical answer. Is it likely to favour those registering or those searching?

D. Undiscoverable land charges

As has been seen, the system depends upon purchasers discovering the names of previous owners from the title deeds. Because only one deed older than 15 years will be seen, it will be obvious that the names of many owners since 1925 remain hidden. Although unable to discover land charges registered against these names, the purchaser remains liable: see s 198 of the Law of Property Act 1925. Why does the search certificate, which naturally omits these charges, not provide protection by virtue of s 10(4)?

This flaw again demonstrates the weakness of a name-based system; it necessitated a statutory response.

Extract 9.6.6

Law of Property Act 1969, s 25

25.—(1)   Where a purchaser of any estate or interest in land under a disposition to which this section applies has suffered loss by reason that the estate or interest is affected by a registered land charge, then if—

   (a)   the date of completion was after the commencement of this Act; and

   (b)   on that date the purchaser had no actual knowledge of the charge; and

   (c)   the charge was registered against the name of an owner of an estate in the land who was not as owner of any such estate a party to any transaction, or concerned in any event, comprised in the relevant title;

the purchaser shall be entitled to compensation for the loss.

(2)   For the purposes of subsection (1)(b) above, the question whether any person had actual knowledge of a charge shall be determined without regard to the provisions of section 198 of the Law of Property Act 1925 (under which registration under the Land Charges Act 1925 or any enactment replaced by it is deemed to constitute actual notice).

(4)   Any compensation for loss under this section shall be paid by the Chief Land Registrar . . .

(10)   In this section—

. . .

'relevant title' means—

    (a)   in relation to a disposition made under a contract, the title which the purchaser was, apart from any acceptance by him (by agreement or otherwise) of a shorter or an imperfect title, entitled to require . . .

Comment

(1) Is this a completely satisfactory solution?

(2) Rather surprisingly, there has been just one recorded claim under s 25. Given the millions of names not included in conveyances in the title deeds, why have there not been many more?

Further reading

Megarry (1940) 7 CLJ 243: Priority after 1925 of mortgages of a legal estate in land.

10

Purchasers: registration of title

This chapter must start with a disclaimer. It is possible to study most property topics through the cases, but land registration is a statutory topic and the cases illustrate only certain aspects. The Land Registration Act 2002 (hereafter LRA, or 2002 Act) provided a new and substantially different statutory regime from that which had operated since 1925. Reading a textbook is essential to comprehend the general scheme of the registration system. This chapter will concentrate upon the main statutory provisions and those cases (many predating the 2002 Act) which are likely to provide a guide to their interpretation.

1. The scheme and its objectives

The essence of registration of title is that one source – the register – discloses who owns a particular plot of land and what adverse rights (mortgages, easements etc.) bind it. Instead of having to investigate the title deeds and taking the risk of being bound by undiscovered rights, a purchaser can simply rely on the register.

Registered estates (fees simple, leases) have their own titles on the register, which guarantees that the proprietor holds the relevant estate. This guarantee means that there is no reason to doubt what the register says. Registrable dispositions (sales, leases, mortgages, easements) will defeat earlier but unprotected interests. A very important and controversial exception to the protection of registered dispositions is provided by overriding interests: these bind purchasers despite not being entered on the register. Other interests (examples are options, restrictive covenants and equitable charges) are generally minor interests and bind purchasers if they are entered on the register, but they enjoy no protection against earlier unprotected interests.

Extract 10.1.1

**Ruoff, *An Englishman Looks at the Torrens System* at pp 8–15
(footnotes omitted)**

. . . I suggest that in each particular country or state [registration] succeeds or fails according to the degree with which the local law and the local administration accord, or do not accord, with certain fundamental principles. I will call these:–
  (1) The mirror principle.
  (2) The curtain principle.
  (3) The insurance principle.

The mirror principle involves the proposition that the register of title is a mirror which reflects accurately and completely and beyond all argument the current facts that are material to a man's title. This mirror does not reveal the history of the title, for disused facts are obliterated. It does not show matters (such as trusts) that are incapable of substantive registration. And it does not allow anyone to view and consider facts and events which are capable of being registered and ought to have been registered but which have not in fact been registered. In other words, a title is free from all adverse burdens, rights and qualifications unless they are mentioned on the register . . .

Now in this imperfect world the mirror does not invariably give a completely reliable reflection. I will give a few obvious examples of events that vitiate the picture:–

(a) Fraud, because rights gained by it must never be upheld.

. . .

(c) The existence of certain well-recognised burdens that are matters of common knowledge, or are easily discoverable outside the register although they cannot, or cannot conveniently, be entered on it . . .

The curtain principle is one which provides that the register is the sole source of information for proposing purchasers, who need not and, indeed, must not concern themselves with trusts and equities which lie behind the curtain . . .

The aims of the mirror principle and the curtain principle are to make land transfer simple, and simplicity has an intrinsic virtue . . .

When I meet a registrar or other official from a titles office or land registry in another country I always enquire about the state of his insurance fund. All too often I receive a smug reply to the effect that there has been no successful claim on the fund for ten or twenty, or perhaps thirty years . . . The true principle is this, that the mirror that is the register is deemed to give an absolutely correct reflection of the title but if, through human frailty, a flaw appears, anyone who thereby suffers loss must be put in the same position, so far as money can do it, as if the reflection were a true one. A lost right is converted into hard cash . . .

Comment

(1) Is the best registration scheme one in which the mirror and curtain principles have fewest exceptions?

(2) The success of the English scheme, together with the application of the three principles, needs to be assessed after registration has been studied.

A. What the register looks like

Figures 10.1 and 10.2 on pp 303–306 show a sample official copy of register entries. The three divisions (covering the land, the owner and adverse rights) are intended to make the information more digestible.

We have seen that electronic entries will, if and when implemented, make a radical change to the operation of land registration (see Chapter 5). It is worth observing that the existing registers are already computerised.

Land Registry

Official copy of register of title

Title number CS705289	Edition date 19.11.2008

— This official copy shows the entries in the register of title on 15 January 2009 at 11:50:13.
— This date must be quoted as the "search from date" in any official search application based on this copy.
— The date at the beginning of an entry is the date on which the entry was made in the register.
— Issued on 15 January 2009.
— Under s.67 of the Land Registration Act 2002, this copy is admissible in evidence to the same extent as the original.
— For information about the register of title see Land Registry website www.landregistry.gov.uk or Land Registry Public Guide 1 – *A guide to the information we keep and how you can obtain it.*
— This title is dealt with by Land Registry Maradon office.

A: Property register
The register describes the registered estate comprised in the title.

CORNSHIRE : DEVONBRIDGE

1. (19.12.1989) The Freehold land shown edged with red on the plan of the above Title filed at the Registry and being 13 Augustine Way, Kerwick, (PL14 3JP).

2. (19.12.1989) The land has the benefit of a right of way on foot only over the passageway tinted brown on the filed plan.

3. (19.12.1989) The land has the benefit of the rights granted by but is subject to the rights reserved by the Transfer dated 5 December 1989 referred to in the Charges Register.

4. (19.12.1989) The land has the benefit of a right of drainage through the pipe shown by a blue broken line on the filed plan so far as such pipe lies outside the land in this title.

5. (14.09.2006) The land edged and numbered in green on the title plan has been removed from this title and registered under the title number or numbers shown in green on the said plan.

B: Proprietorship register
This register specifies the class of title and identifies the owner. It contains any entries that affect the right of disposal.

Title absolute

Figure 10.1

Source: Land Registry, Official copy of register of title, title number CS705289, Edition date 19.11.2008. © Crown copyright 2011 HMLR. Reproduced with kind permission of Land Registry.

Title Number CS705289

B: Proprietorship register continued

1. (19.11.2008) PROPRIETOR: PAUL JOHN DAWKINS and ANGELA MARY DAWKINS both of 13 Augustine Way, Kerwick, Maradon, Cornshire PL14 3JP.

2. (19.11.2008) The price stated to have been paid on 12 November 2008 was £325,500.

3. (19.11.2008) No disposition by a sole proprietor of the registered state (except a trust corporation) under which capital money arises is to be registered unless authorised by an order of the court.

4. (19.11.2008) RESTRICTION: No disposition of the registered estate by the proprietor of the registered estate is to be registered without a written consent signed by the proprietor for the time being of the charge dated 12 November 2008 in favour of Weyford Building Society referred to in the charges register or their conveyancer.

C: Charges register
This register contains any charges and other matters that affect the registered estate.

1. (19.12.1989) A Conveyance of the land tinted yellow on the filed plan and other land dated 19 May 1924 made between (1) Allan Ansell (Vendor) and (2) Frances Amelia Moss (Purchaser) contains covenants details of which are set out in the schedule of restrictive covenants hereto.

2. (19.12.1989) A Conveyance of the land tinted pink of the filed plan and other land dated 16 August 1926 made between (1) Edward Philip Green (Vendor) and (2) Peter John Brown and Hannah Sarah Brown contains covenants details of which are set out in the schedule of restrictive covenants hereto.

3. (19.12.1989) A Transfer of the land in this title dated 5 December 1989 made between (1) Freeman Builders Limited and (2) James Michael Pritchard and Molly Carol Pritchard contains restrictive covenants.

   NOTE: Copy filed

4. (19.12.1989) The land is subject to rights of way on foot only over the passageway tinted blue on the filed plan.

5. (19.11.2008) REGISTERED CHARGE dated 12 November 2008.

6. (19.11.2008) PROPRIETOR: WEYFORD BUILDING SOCIETY of Society House, The Avenue, Weyford, Cornshire CN12 4BD.

Schedule of restrictive covenants

1. The following are details of the covenants contained in the Conveyance dated 19 May 1924 referred to in the Charges Register: -

   "And the Purchaser for himself his heirs, executors, administrators, and assigns hereby covenants with the Vendor its heirs and assigns that he will perform and observe the stipulations set out in the first schedule hereto so far as they relate to the hereditaments hereby assured.

   THE FIRST SCHEDULE

Figure 10.1 continued

Title Number CS705289

a) The Purchaser shall within 3 months from the date of his purchase erect (if not already erected) and afterwards maintain in good condition a good and sufficient open pale or other approved fence or hedge on the sides of the plot marked 'T' on the plan within the boundary.

b) No external alterations whatsoever shall be made to the premises without the written consent of the Vendor.

c) The premises shall not be used for the purpose of a public house or hostel or any purpose connected with the sale of intoxicating liquor."

NOTE: The 'T' marks referred to above do not affect the land in this title.

2. The following are details of the covenants contained in the Conveyance dated 16 August 1926 referred to in the Charges Register: -

"And the purchaser for themselves their heirs and executors administrators and assigns hereby covenants

that they would not erect or carry on upon any part said pieces of land delineated on said plan and coloured Green and Pink respectively any Manufactory whatsoever or upon any part of said pieces of land delineated on said plan any Mill Hospital Lunatic Asylum Steam Engine Barracks Beer Shop Gasworks Limeworks Pottery Brickworks or carry or permit or suffer to be carried on any noisome noisy dangerous or offensive trade business or occupation whatsoever.

And would not at any time thereafter uncope or dig for any stone sand or clay or use any stone Quarry Sand Pit or Clay pit for the purpose of selling Stone Sand or Clay in or upon any part of said land and premises or use said land and premises or any part thereof as a cemetery or Burial Ground nor bore for water or sink any well on any part of said land and premises which should require any power beyond manual labour to pump or force up the water or sell any water from off said land and premises.

NOTE: The land coloured pink on the filed plan forms part of the land coloured green and coloured pink referred to in the first paragraph above.

End of register

Figure 10.1 continued

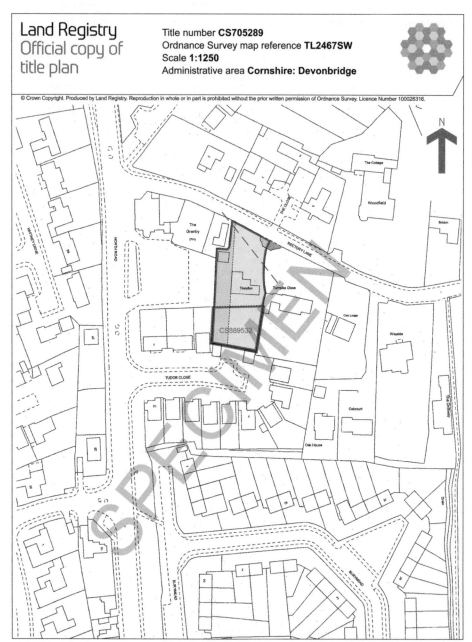

This official copy is issued on 15 January 2009 shows the state of this title plan, on 15 January 2009 at 11:50:13.
It is admissible in evidence to the same extent as the original (s.67 Land Registration Act 2002).
This title plan shows the general position, not the exact line, of the boundaries. It may be subject to distortions in scale.
Measurements scaled from this plan may not match measurements between the same
points on the ground. See Land Registry Public Guide 19 – Title plans and boundaries.
This title is dealt with by Land Registry, Maradon Office.
© Crown Copyright. Produced by Land Registry. Reproduction in whole or in part is prohibited without the prior written
permission of Ordnance Survey. Licence Number 100026316.

Figure 10.2

Source: Land Registry, Official copy of title plan, title number CS705289, Ordnance Survey map reference TL2467SW. © Crown
copyright 2011 HMLR. Reproduced with kind permission of Land Registry.

2. Types of interests

A. Registrable interests: first registration

LRA, ss 2–4 provide that only legal estates can be registered, whether one is considering voluntary or compulsory registration.

(i) The fee simple

Until recently, relatively few registrations were voluntary. Compulsion provided the key to the development of registration.

Extract 10.2.1

Land Registration Act 2002, ss 4, 5

4.—(1) The requirement of registration applies on the occurrence of any of the following events—

(a) the transfer of a qualifying estate—

   (i) for valuable or other consideration, by way of gift or in pursuance of an order of any court,

   (ii) by means of an assent (including a vesting assent); or

   (iii) giving effect to a partition of land subject to a trust of land;

(aa) the transfer of a qualifying estate—

   (i) by a deed that appoints . . . a new trustee

(g) the creation of a protected [i.e., by deposit of title deeds] first legal mortgage of a qualifying estate.

(2) For the purposes of subsection (1), a qualifying estate is an unregistered legal estate which is—

(a) a freehold estate in land, or

. . .

5.—(1) The Lord Chancellor may by order—

(a) amend section 4 so as to add to the events on the occurrence of which the requirement of registration applies such relevant event as he may specify in the order, and

. . .

Comment

(1) In essence, registration is required whenever the legal fee simple changes hands. These 'triggers' for first registration were expanded by the Land Registration Act 1997 into much their present form.

(2) Until 1990, the land had to be in a designated area before compulsory registration operated: the spread of these areas determined the growth of the system. Approximately 95% of titles are now registered.

(3) After a further generation, what land will not be registered? What additional triggers might be introduced under s 5? Additional triggers ((a)(iii) and (aa)) were added in 2008.

(4) Registration must take place within two months: the sanction for failure is the loss of the legal estate (but not the equitable estate): ss 6–8. How significant is this sanction?

(5) A person who fears that they might be prejudiced by registration of another person can enter a *caution against first registration* (ss 15–22). This caution ensures that the cautioner is involved in any future registration. A person claiming ownership of the fee simple cannot enter a caution (s 15(3)). Why should such a caution not be allowed?

(a) Forms of registered titles

Virtually all titles are 'absolute' and we will limit detailed consideration to these. There can also be possessory titles (where there is no documentary title: there is no guarantee in relation to the state of the title at the time of registration) and qualified titles (where there may be some defect in the title: there is no guarantee regarding matters within the qualification).

(b) The effect of first registration

Extract 10.2.2

Land Registration Act 2002, ss 58, 11

58.—(1) If, on the entry of a person in the register as the proprietor of a legal estate, the legal estate would not otherwise be vested in him, it shall be deemed to be vested in him as a result of the registration.

11.—(1) This section is concerned with the registration of a person under this Chapter as the proprietor of a freehold estate.

(2) Registration with absolute title has the effect described in subsections (3) to (5).

(3) The estate is vested in the proprietor together with all interests subsisting for the benefit of the estate.

(4) The estate is vested in the proprietor subject only to the following interests affecting the estate at the time of registration—

    (a) interests which are the subject of an entry in the register in relation to the estate,

    (b) unregistered interests which fall within any of the paragraphs of Schedule 1, and

    (c) interests acquired under the Limitation Act 1980 (c. 58) of which the proprietor has notice.

(5) If the proprietor is not entitled to the estate for his own benefit, or not entitled solely for his own benefit, then, as between himself and the persons beneficially entitled to the estate, the estate is vested in him subject to such of their interests as he has notice of.

Comment

(1) What effect does s 58 have? Is it duplicated by s 11(3)? See also Extract 10.2.6 below.

(2) Schedule 1 interests are overriding interests; they are considered later in this chapter.

(3) Until the 2002 Act, adverse possession claims were overriding interests. They now bind the first registered proprietor only if there is notice. This is a rare application of notice within the 2002 Act.

(4) What is the effect of s 11(5)?

(5) Palk argues[1] that, where the equitable title is in somebody other than the registered proprietor, dicta in *Epps* v *Esso Petroleum Co Ltd*[2] suggest that the previous legislation did not confer the equitable title on the proprietor. It is dubious whether the dicta should be read this way, but is the result consistent with s 11?

---

[1] (1974) 38 Conv 236.
[2] [1973] 1 WLR 1071.

(6) The very essence of guaranteeing the proprietor's title necessitates confiscation (generally for compensation) of other people's interests, should they not be discovered by the registrar. How can this be justified? Is it compatible with human rights principles?[3]

(ii) Leases

Extract 10.2.3

Land Registration Act 2002, s 4

4.—(1) The requirement of registration applies on the occurrence of any of the following events—

  . . .

  (c) the grant out of a qualifying estate of an estate in land—
    (i) for a term of years absolute of more than seven years from the date of the grant, and
    (ii) for valuable or other consideration, by way of gift or in pursuance of an order of any court;
  (d) the grant out of a qualifying estate of an estate in land for a term of years absolute to take effect in possession after the end of the period of three months beginning with the date of the grant.

Comment

(1) This is dealing with the situation where the landlord is not already registered. If the landlord is already registered, then the lease constitutes a registrable disposition (considered below).

(2) Paragraph (d) deals with future leases. These must be registered regardless of their length. What justification is there for this? What is the significance of the exception for those taking effect within three months?

(3) The assignment of leases with more than seven years unexpired also requires registration (there is a transfer of a qualifying estate, as defined by s 4(2)).

(4) The rules (timing; effect of non-compliance) for compulsory registration of leases under s 4 are the same as for fees simple, discussed above.

Leases can be registered with absolute, qualified or possessory titles, as with fees simple (their effect is stated by s 12, in almost identical terms to s 11 for the fee simple). One problem when the landlord is not registered is that, especially in the past, the registrar may not be aware of the details of the freehold title and will not therefore know about rights (charges, easements and restrictive covenants provide examples) that may bind both the freehold and the newly granted lease. Good leasehold title is designed for this situation: the lease is guaranteed subject to obligations deriving from the landlord's title. See LRA, s 12(6):

> Registration with good leasehold title has the same effect as registration with absolute title, except that it does not affect the enforcement of any estate, right or interest affecting, or in derogation of, the title of the lessor to grant the lease.

---

[3] See *Kingsalton Ltd* v *Thames Water Developments Ltd* [2002] 1 P&CR 184 at [45].

B. Registrable dispositions

We have seen that the significance of registrable dispositions is that they defeat earlier but unprotected interests. In this section, we will investigate four topics. The first concerns powers of the registered proprietor (whether of a freehold or leasehold title) to deal with the land. These powers extend beyond registrable dispositions, but are quite straightforward. The second area (looked at alongside the first in the following extract) identifies what are registrable dispositions. The third deals with the registration requirements. Finally, we will consider the effect of registration.

Extract 10.2.4

Land Registration Act 2002, ss 23, 27

23.—(1) Owner's powers in relation to a registered estate consist of—
   (a) power to make a disposition of any kind permitted by the general law in relation to an interest of that description, other than a mortgage by demise or sub-demise, and
   (b) power to charge the estate at law with the payment of money.

27.—(1) If a disposition of a registered estate or registered charge is required to be completed by registration, it does not operate at law until the relevant registration requirements are met.
   (2) In the case of a registered estate, the following are the dispositions which are required to be completed by registration—
   (a) a transfer,
   (b) where the registered estate is an estate in land, the grant of a term of years absolute—
      (i) for a term of more than seven years from the date of the grant,
      (ii) to take effect in possession after the end of the period of three months beginning with the date of the grant,
      (iii) under which the right to possession is discontinuous,
      . . .
   (d) the express grant or reservation of an interest of a kind falling within section 1(2)(a) of the Law of Property Act 1925 (c. 20), other than one which is capable of being registered under the Commons Registration Act 1965 (c. 64),
   (e) the express grant or reservation of an interest of a kind falling within section 1(2)(b) or (e) of the Law of Property Act 1925, and
   (f) the grant of a legal charge.
   (7) In subsection (2)(d), the reference to express grant does not include grant as a result of the operation of section 62 of the Law of Property Act 1925 (c. 20).

Comment

(1) The powers of the proprietor in s 23 are unremarkable. The one point of interest is a provision in s 26 protecting purchasers against limitations upon those powers. This is most likely to apply to trusts of land (it will be studied in Chapter 12).

(2) The principal registrable dispositions are transfers, leases, easements (and profits) and charges. These are interests recognised as legal by s 1 of the Law of Property Act 1925 (hereafter LPA). Why should the registration system accord special status to these interests?

(3) Note that only express easements fall within s 27: easements arising by implication (especially *Wheeldon* v *Burrows*[4]), LPA, s 62 or prescription are excluded. The reason is not to downgrade their status, but to enable them to be overriding interests. Why is this desirable?

Leases deserve particular attention. Section 4 (Extract 10.2.1) applies when the landlord is not registered and s 27 when the landlord is registered. What differences are there between the two forms of compulsory registration?

Prior to the 2002 Act, leases had to exceed 21 years to be registered. Shorter leases have always been overriding interests. The Law Commission explains the change as regards length to seven years (and likely future developments) as follows:[5]

> At present, most business leases – the most common form of commercial dealing with land – are granted for periods of less than 21 years and are therefore incapable of registration. We can see no justification for excluding such leases from the benefits of land registration and, in particular, electronic conveyancing . . . It is likely that, when electronic conveyancing is fully operative, the period will be reduced to include all leases that have to be made by deed – in other words, those granted for more than three years.

This was one of the most controversial parts of the proposals. Are there significant benefits to tenants from reducing the period to seven years? Are there disadvantages? Why is three years the period specified as the likely future minimum period for registration? Note also the extension of compulsory registration to future leases (as for first registration under s 4) and discontinuous leases. The latter category is exemplified by a lease for the first week in May each year for four years. Why should it be registrable? Why is it not subject to compulsory registration under s 4?

Turning to registration requirements for registrable dispositions (our third topic), these are specified in some detail by LRA, Sched 2. If there are two titles (freehold and leasehold for leases; benefited and burdened land for easements), then entry on both is required. The need for registration is emphasised by s 27(1) – legal status is denied unless the requirements are satisfied. Suppose a transfer is not registered. Does principle provide any clue as to the rights of the transferee if (i) there is a sale; (ii) there is a gift?[6]

Extract 10.2.5

Land Registration Act 2002, s 29

29.—(1) If a registrable disposition of a registered estate is made for valuable consideration, completion of the disposition by registration has the effect of postponing to the interest under the disposition any interest affecting the estate immediately before the disposition whose priority is not protected at the time of registration.

(2) For the purposes of subsection (1), the priority of an interest is protected—

    (a) in any case, if the interest—

        (i) is a registered charge or the subject of a notice in the register,

        (ii) falls within any of the paragraphs of Schedule 3, or

        (iii) appears from the register to be excepted from the effect of registration, and

    (b) in the case of a disposition of a leasehold estate, if the burden of the interest is incident to the estate.

---

[4] (1879) 12 Ch D 31; see Extract 19.2.6 below.
[5] Law Com No 271, paras 2.6, 3.17. LRA, s 118 confers powers to amend the seven-year period.
[6] For gifts, see *Mascall* v *Mascall* (1984) 50 P&CR 119.

(4)   Where the grant of a leasehold estate in land out of a registered estate does not involve a registrable disposition, this section has effect as if—
    (a)   the grant involved such a disposition, and
    (b)   the disposition were registered at the time of the grant.

Comment

(1) LRA, s 58 vests the legal estate on transferees in a similar manner to first registration.

(2) In what ways does s 29 differ from s 11 on first registration? Why are there differences?

(3) Schedule 3 contains overriding interests; it is considered in detail later in this chapter. The reference to 'excepted' interests refers to qualified, possessory and good leasehold titles.

(4) Turning to leases, what is the purpose and effect of s 29(2)(b)? Section 29(4) means that an overriding interest lease, even though not registered, defeats unprotected minor interests.[7] Why should it do so?

(5) The position of a purchaser who is actually aware of an unprotected interest has provoked controversy. This is considered separately below.[8]

Forgeries pose a good test of the guarantee provided by the legislation. We might contemplate the following cases, where R is the original registered proprietor:

(i) F forges a transfer to herself and is registered. F sells the land to P, who is unaware of the forgery and is himself registered in due course;

(ii) F forges a transfer in favour of P, who again is unaware of the forgery and is himself registered in due course;

(iii) F forges a transfer in favour of herself and is registered.

The first and third examples can be dealt with quite quickly. In the third, it is quite clear that F cannot rely on her own fraud: R must retain a right to the land. On the other hand, in (i) R's claim is one 'whose priority is not protected'[9] before the transfer to P: it will fail as against P. This is a nice example of how a more secure title can be conferred by land registration. It is the second example that is more troublesome.

Extract 10.2.6

***Fitzwilliam v Richall Holdings Services Ltd* [2013] EWHC 86 (Ch); [2013] 1 P&CR 318**

NEWEY J: 70.   Mr Fitzwilliam bases this part of his case on *Malory Enterprises Ltd* v *Cheshire Homes (UK) Ltd*.

72.   *Malory* pre-dated the Land Registration Act 2002 and so was governed by the Land Registration Act 1925. . . .

73.   In *Malory*, the Court of Appeal concluded that Malory BVI had standing to maintain a claim for trespass against Cheshire even when the latter company was the registered proprietor of the relevant land. The reasoning of Arden LJ, who gave the leading judgment, appears from paragraphs 64 and 65 of her judgment. She said there:

---

[7] Confirmed by *Barclays Bank plc* v *Zaroovabli* [1997] Ch 321 at p 327 in relation to similar previous legislation.
[8] See p 319.
[9] Unless, probably, R is in actual occupation.

'64. Although Malory UK had no title to convey to Cheshire, the position of Cheshire once it is registered as proprietor is governed by section 69 of the [Land Registration Act 1925]. Accordingly, when it became the registered proprietor of the rear land, Cheshire was deemed to have vested in it "the legal estate in fee simple in possession".

65. However, section 69 deals only with the legal estate. Unlike section 5, which deals with first registration, that registered estate is not vested in Cheshire "together with all rights, privileges, and appurtenances". Moreover, since the transfer to Cheshire could not in law be of any effect in itself, in my judgment it cannot constitute a "disposition" of the rear land and accordingly section 20 cannot apply. . . .'

75. This aspect of the *Malory* case has been the subject of a good deal of criticism. Megarry & Wade, *'The Law of Real Property'*, 8th edition, observes that '[t]he reasoning [in *Malory*] is unsatisfactory' (page 221). One of Megarry & Wade's editors, Mr Charles Harpum, has expressed the view that the interpretation of section 69(1) of the Land Registration Act 1925 that was adopted in *Malory* 'undermines . . . the essential structure of land registration without any compensating gains' (see 'Registered Land – A Law Unto Itself?' in Getzler (ed), *'Rationalising Property, Equity and Trusts: Essays in Honour of Edward Burns'*, at page 199). Another of Megarry & Wade's editors, Dr Martin Dixon, has said in a book of which he is the sole author (*'Modern Land Law'*, 8th edition, at page 44):

'Acceptance of the *Malory* approach would be to import principles of unregistered conveyancing into registered land and this would wholly contradict the system of registration of title and the move to e-conveyancing that the LRA 2002 is designed to facilitate'.

Professor Elizabeth Cooke has spoken of the 'heresy' from *Malory* and described the proposition that a void transfer passes only the legal title to the registered estate while leaving the beneficial interest with the former proprietor as 'untenable' (see [2004] Conv, at 485–486). Mr Alexander Hill-Smith has argued that 'the construction put by the Court of Appeal in *Malory* on what constitutes a "disposition" was wrong in the context of the 1925 Act and *Malory* should not be applied to the construction of s.29 of the 2002 Act' (see [2009] Conv, at 135).

76. For what it is worth, I can see considerable force in some of the arguments advanced by *Malory's* critics. Whatever merit the criticisms of *Malory* may have, however, I am bound by the decision. That means that it is not open to me to depart from the Court of Appeal's construction of the Land Registration Act 1925. . . . Further, it is incumbent on me, I think, to construe equivalent provisions in the Land Registration Act 2002 similarly unless there are relevant distinctions between those provisions and their predecessors in the 1925 Act.

77. The key provisions of the 2002 Act in this context are sections 58 and 29, which broadly correspond to sections 69 and 20 of the 1925 Act. . . .

78. Mr Greville Healey, who appeared for Richall, argued that the 2002 Act differs in important respects from that of 1925. Echoing Mr Harpum (see 'Registered Land – A Law Unto Itself?' in Getzler (ed), *'Rationalising Property, Equity and Trusts: Essays in Honour of Edward Burns'*, at pages 201–202), Mr Healey submitted, in particular, that the wording of section 58 of the 2002 Act is significantly different from that of section 69 of the 1925 Act.

79. In this connection, Mr Healey advanced essentially two arguments:
   (i) Section 58(2) of the 2002 Act gives effect to the principle that a registrable disposition operates only in equity until it is completed by registration (see section 27(1) of the Act). It therefore makes no sense to read section 58(1) as meaning that, once the registration requirements have been met, the disposition *ceases* to take effect in equity (having previously done so); and
   (ii) The *legal estates* that are the subject-matter of section 58 include all of the interests, including charges, referred to in sections 1(4) and 205(1)(x) of the Law of Property Act

1925 (see section 132(1) of the 2002 Act). In respect of a charge registered pursuant to a void instrument, it makes no sense to say that the registered proprietor of the charge is its bare legal owner (who would be its equitable owner?), so in this context 'legal estate' cannot be construed consistently as meaning *bare* legal estate.

80.   I am afraid that I do not find either of these arguments convincing. Like Mr Hill-Smith (see [2009] Conv, at 133), I cannot see that section 58 of the 2002 Act differs significantly from section 69 of the 1925 Act.

81.   So far as argument (i) is concerned, . . . Sections 27(1) and 58(2) are . . . concerned with when a disposition is to take effect at law. Neither provision makes any reference to the position in equity, and I do not think it can even be said that the provisions *assume* that a disposition will have effect in equity in advance of registration. They simply do not touch on the equitable implications of a disposition. Further, I cannot see that construing section 58(1) in line with section 69 of the 1925 Act would involve reading it as meaning that a disposition *ceases* to have effect in equity on registration. In *Malory*, the Court of Appeal took the view that section 69 of the 1925 Act dealt only with the legal estate and, hence, that Malory BVI's rights as beneficial owner endured. It was not suggested that section 69 said anything about whether a disposition ceased to have effect in equity when registered.

83.   Mr Healey's fall-back position was that, in the context of section 29 of the 2002 Act, the word 'disposition' should be read as extending to a void transfer. In this respect, he prayed in aid arguments put forward by Mr Hill-Smith (see [2009] Conv, at pages 127–140).

84.   In *Malory*, the Court of Appeal concluded that a transfer that 'could not in law be of any effect in itself' could not constitute a 'disposition' for the purposes of the 1925 Act. Mr Hill-Smith's arguments suggest, not merely that 'disposition' should be given a wider interpretation in the context of the 2002 Act, but that it should have been so construed for the purposes of the 1925 Act. As Mr Hill-Smith states in his article, he contends that 'the construction put by the Court of Appeal in *Malory* on what constitutes a "disposition" was wrong in the context of the 1925 Act' (see [2009] Conv, at 135). As I have already noted, however, I am bound by *Malory*. In the circumstances, I do not think it is open to me to give a wider interpretation to 'disposition' as regards the 2002 Act. The case for taking 'disposition' to include a void transfer was at least as strong in relation to the 1925 Act.

Comment

(1) It might be noted that s 29 protects against 'any interest affecting the estate immediately before the disposition'. Are these words appropriate to describe the claim of a proprietor whose title has been lost following a forgery?[10]

(2) Should a different result have been reached by virtue of s 58?

(3) Is the interpretation of 'disposition' compelling?

(4) Would Newey J have reached the same conclusion if he had not been bound by *Malory*?

Subsequently, Richard Sheldon QC has said in *Swift 1st Ltd v Chief Land Registrar*:[11]

I have no hesitation in declining to accede to the invitation to depart from the decision of Newey J in *Fitzwilliam* (and the later case [*Park Associated Developments Ltd v Kinnear* [2013] EWHC 3617 (Ch)] in which he followed this decision). It is clear from his judgment that the area is a potential legal minefield with wide ramifications. He is an experienced judge with considerable

[10] The previous legislation defeated 'all other estates and interests whatsoever', which appears to give wider protection to purchasers.
[11] [2014] All ER (D) 12 (Feb) at [32].

expertise in this area of the law. The decision is carefully reasoned and, far from being obviously wrong, seems to me to have been dictated by the Court of Appeal decision in *Malory*. . . .

C. Minor interests

Unlike the previous legislation, the 2002 Act does not employ minor interests as a statutory category, though the terminology remains useful. The category covers interests which are not registered (in the sense discussed above) or overriding. We will concentrate first on methods of protecting claims on the register, short of registration.

(i) Methods of protection

Two methods of protection are recognised: notice and restriction. A notice ensures that purchasers are bound, whilst a restriction ensures that an entry on the register will be made only if an appropriate procedure is followed. Most obviously, in a trust of land a restriction may require there to be two trustees in order to comply with the requirements for over-reaching. Some interests may require both protections.[12] First, we will look at notices.

Extract 10.2.7

Land Registration Act 2002, ss 32–36, 77

32.—(1) A notice is an entry in the register in respect of the burden of an interest affecting a registered estate or charge.

(3) The fact that an interest is the subject of a notice does not necessarily mean that the interest is valid, but does mean that the priority of the interest, if valid, is protected for the purposes of sections 29 and 30.

33.—No notice may be entered in the register in respect of any of the following—

    (a) an interest under—
        (i)   a trust of land, or
        (ii) a settlement under the Settled Land Act 1925 (c. 18),
    (b) a leasehold estate in land which—
        (i)   is granted for a term of years of three years or less from the date of the grant, and
        (ii) is not required to be registered,
    (c) a restrictive covenant made between a lessor and lessee, so far as relating to the demised premises, . . .

34.—(1) A person who claims to be entitled to the benefit of an interest affecting a registered estate or charge may, if the interest is not excluded by section 33, apply to the registrar for the entry in the register of a notice in respect of the interest.

(2) Subject to rules, an application under this section may be for—
    (a) an agreed notice, or
    (b) a unilateral notice.

(3) The registrar may only approve an application for an agreed notice if—
    (a) the applicant is the relevant registered proprietor, or a person entitled to be registered as such proprietor,
    (b) the relevant registered proprietor, or a person entitled to be registered as such proprietor, consents to the entry of the notice, or
    (c) the registrar is satisfied as to the validity of the applicant's claim.

. . .

---

[12] Law Com No 271, para 6.44 (in the context of pre-emptions).

35.—(1)   If the registrar enters a notice in the register in pursuance of an application under section 34(2)(b) ('a unilateral notice'), he must give notice of the entry to—

(a)   the proprietor of the registered estate or charge to which it relates, and

(b)   such other persons as rules may provide.

36.—(1)   A person may apply to the registrar for the cancellation of a unilateral notice if he is—

(a)   the registered proprietor of the estate or charge to which the notice relates, or

(b)   a person entitled to be registered as the proprietor of that estate or charge.

(2)   Where an application is made under subsection (1), the registrar must give the beneficiary of the notice notice of the application and of the effect of subsection (3).

(3)   If the beneficiary of the notice does not exercise his right to object to the application before the end of such period as rules may provide, the registrar must cancel the notice.

77.—(1)   A person must not exercise any of the following rights without reasonable cause—

(a)   the right to lodge a caution under section 15,

(b)   the right to apply for the entry of a notice or restriction, and

(c)   the right to object to an application to the registrar.

(2)   The duty under this section is owed to any person who suffers damage in consequence of its breach.

Comment

(1) Most interests can be protected by notice. What reasons are there for the exceptions listed in s 33?

(2) The unilateral notice is designed for situations when a claimed interest in land is disputed. The potential for proprietors to be damaged by its unjustified use explains the need for s 77. How might the proprietor be damaged and what is the consequence of an entry without reasonable cause?

(3) Apart from the right of the proprietor to object, the effect of the unilateral notice is the same as an agreed notice. Any dispute is resolved by the First-tier Tribunal (LRA, s 73).

(4) LRA, ss 37–38 make provision for the registrar to place notices on the register: this is useful as it helps to ensure that the register is as comprehensive as possible.

Let us turn to the effect of notices. The central point is that the interest is protected, so that it binds a later registered disposition: LRA, s 29(2)(a)(i). However, there is no guarantee or priority over earlier interests (see s 32(3)).

Extract 10.2.8

Kitney v MEPC Ltd [1977] 1 WLR 981

An option was protected by notice on first registration, though it had previously been rendered void for non-registration under the land charges scheme.

GOFF LJ: . . . Mr Browne has maintained that the whole essence of the matter is that after the date of first registration it is neither necessary nor permissible to go behind the impenetrable curtain of the register. Lower down on p 70 [*Ruoff & Roper, Registered Conveyancing*, 3rd ed] says: 'Thus landowners are able to obtain an improved title through first registration and, in fact, they often do so.' All that, however, is speaking of the curative effect of registration. Mr Browne is seeking to make it destructive.

. . .

On general principle it seems to me that registration, which is designed to establish the proprietor's title, cannot create rights against him which do not exist, and cannot enable anyone to enforce a right which such person has lost. Nor do I think that the principle is overridden by the fact that section 52 [cf 2002 Act, s 32(3)] says 'if valid' and sections 5 and 20 [2002 Act, ss 11, 29] do not . . .

Comment

(1) The question arose on first registration, but the same principles operate in favour of subsequent purchasers.

(2) The result seems clear given the modern wording: 'does not necessarily mean that the interest is valid'.

The second method of protection is the restriction.

Extract 10.2.9

Land Registration Act 2002, ss 40–41, 43–44

40.—(1)   A restriction is an entry in the register regulating the circumstances in which a disposition of a registered estate or charge may be the subject of an entry in the register.
(2)   A restriction may, in particular—
   (a)   prohibit the making of an entry in respect of any disposition, or a disposition of a kind specified in the restriction;
   (b)   prohibit the making of an entry—
      (i)   indefinitely,
      (ii)   for a period specified in the restriction, or
      (iii)   until the occurrence of an event so specified.
      . . .

41.—(1)   Where a restriction is entered in the register, no entry in respect of a disposition to which the restriction applies may be made in the register otherwise than in accordance with the terms of the restriction, subject to any order under subsection (2).

43.—(2)   Rules may—
   (d)   specify standard forms of restriction.
(3)   If an application under subsection (1) is made for the entry of a restriction which is not in a form specified under subsection (2)(d), the registrar may only approve the application if it appears to him—
   (a)   that the terms of the proposed restriction are reasonable, and
   (b)   that applying the proposed restriction would—
      (i)   be straightforward, and
      (ii)   not place an unreasonable burden on him.

44.—(1)   If the registrar enters two or more persons in the register as the proprietor of a registered estate in land, he must also enter in the register such restrictions as rules may provide for the purpose of securing that interests which are capable of being overreached on a disposition of the estate are overreached.

Comment

(1) The restriction is ideal for requiring two trustees where there is a trust of land. It both protects the beneficiaries and ensures that the purchaser has nothing to worry about if there are two trustees. This explains why the notice is not available for trusts of land.

(2) There are complex provisions (not reproduced) as to when restrictions may be entered by an individual, the registrar and the court. Section 44(1) is one central provision making provision for a restriction where the legal estate is jointly held. Even if it is held beneficially for the legal owners, there will be a trust of land.

(3) Section 45 provides for the equivalent of the unilateral notice – the proprietor can object.

(4) If the terms of a restriction are overlooked or do not bite on the transaction (an overriding interest provides an example), does the interest protected by the restriction bind a purchaser? Note the wording of s 29 (Extract 10.2.5 above).

It is important to note that it is not necessary to have an interest in land before a restriction can be entered. This means that the use of restrictions can be very wide: one traditional example has been protection against a company transferring land in excess of powers under its constitution. However, the registrar retains a significant control over when a restriction can be entered; today this is found in s 43(3). One imaginative use of the restriction is in the context of positive covenants, as the Law Commission has observed:[13]

> Although the use of restrictions to protect interests under trusts is well known, they are also used for a wide variety of other purposes. They can (for example) be used as an indirect means of making positive covenants run with land. A restriction is entered to the effect that no disposition is to be registered unless the transferee of the land enters into a fresh covenant with the covenantee.

(ii) Minor interests and priorities: the general rule

For the first time, the 2002 Act provides a priority rule applying to interests which are not registered.

Extract 10.2.10

Land Registration Act 2002, s 28

28.–(1) Except as provided by sections 29 and 30, the priority of an interest affecting a registered estate or charge is not affected by a disposition of the estate or charge.

(2) It makes no difference for the purposes of this section whether the interest or disposition is registered.

Comment

(1) This establishes a first in time of creation rule. The Law Commission[14] describes it as 'absolute', but is it possible to contemplate situations where the holder of an interest who has failed to protect it will lose priority to a subsequent interest?

(2) Remember that s 29 gives registered dispositions priority over earlier but unprotected interests.

(3) Is it a weakness of the system that a person taking a minor interest will be bound by earlier and often undiscoverable unprotected interests? How would electronic conveyancing impact upon this question?

(4) We have seen[15] that equities are accorded full proprietary status in registered land. This means that they are subject to the priority regime established by s 28.

---

[13] Law Com No 254, para 6.36. See also Law Com No 271, para 6.40, n 144.
[14] Law Com No 271, para 5.4.
[15] See p 23 above.

(iii) Minor interests and priorities: registered dispositions

The basic rules are established by LRA, s 29, discussed above. A minor interest will bind a registered disposition if, but only if, it is protected by notice (or, by virtue of actual occupation, it is an overriding interest). Problems and controversy have arisen in some cases where the minor interest is not protected.

(a) Actual notice and bad faith

Defeating unprotected minor interests has been controversial where the purchaser has actual notice of it or is in bad faith. Under the previous legislation, Graham J in *Peffer* v *Rigg*[16] held that a purchaser had to be in good faith to take advantage of the statutory provisions defeating unprotected minor interests. His analysis depended on provisions which are not repeated in the 2002 Act and it seems clear that there is no longer any basis upon which to import a requirement of actual notice or bad faith. This is the clear intention of the Law Commission.[17] However, the question continues to raise important policy issues, as shown by the following extracts. The first involves the land charges scheme in unregistered land, which (like the 2002 Act) makes no explicit provision relating to actual notice and bad faith.

Extract 10.2.11

Midland Bank Trust Co Ltd v *Green* [1981] AC 513

A husband transferred land to his wife, the purpose appearing to be to readjust the family finances and to defeat an unregistered option granted to their son.

LORD WILBERFORCE: My Lords, I recognise that the inquiring mind may put the question: why should there be an omission of the requirement of good faith in this particular context? I do not think there should be much doubt about the answer. Addition of a requirement that the purchaser should be in good faith would bring with it the necessity of inquiring into the purchaser's motives and state of mind. The present case is a good example of the difficulties which would exist. If the position was simply that the purchaser had notice of the option, and decided nevertheless to buy the land, relying on the absence of notification, nobody could contend that she would be lacking in good faith. She would merely be taking advantage of a situation, which the law has provided, and the addition of a profit motive could not create an absence of good faith. But suppose, and this is the respondents' argument, the purchaser's motive is to defeat the option, does this make any difference? Any advantage to oneself seems necessarily to involve a disadvantage for another: to make the validity of the purchase depend upon which aspect of the transaction was prevalent in the purchaser's mind seems to create distinctions equally difficult to analyse in law as to establish in fact: avarice and malice may be distinct sins, but in human conduct they are liable to be intertwined. The problem becomes even more acute if one supposes a mixture of motives . . . To eliminate the necessity for inquiries of this kind may well have been part of the legislative intention. Certainly there is here no argument for departing – violently – from the wording of the Act.

Comment

What would Lord Wilberforce consider to be bad faith?

[16] [1977] 1 WLR 285.
[17] Law Com No 271, paras 5.16–5.21.

Extract 10.2.12

Battersby (1995) 58 MLR 637 at p 655 (footnotes omitted)

[After supporting the *Peffer* requirement of good faith:] However, it is argued that there is a good case for going further and removing the protection given to purchasers with actual knowledge. The argument might run as follows.

(i)   The present rule excludes from the registration system any ethical element. It deliberately allows a purchaser with actual knowledge to take advantage of an unconscionable dealing and to profit from his own wrong. It deliberately sacrifices a beneficiary who, albeit in ignorance of the legal necessity, has failed to register. The present rule creates a standing temptation to judges to find some way of evading it. The policy would be justified if it could be shown to be necessary for the efficient working of the registration system. However, there is no such necessity. Registration under the Land Charges Act was designed principally to overcome the difficulties created by the doctrine of constructive notice, which depends upon the duty to make reasonable inquiries; this is a shifting and uncertain standard, which works to the disadvantage of both purchaser and beneficiary. But there is no such uncertainty when the purchaser has actual knowledge . . .

Extract 10.2.13

Law Commission No 254: Land Registration for the Twenty First Century

3.44   . . . However, we consider that the matter should be placed beyond doubt by a statement in the Act of the general principle that the doctrine of notice should have no application in dealings with registered land except where the Act expressly provides to the contrary.

3.45   In making this recommendation, we are very conscious that we are going against the view strongly expressed by a number of distinguished academic commentators . . .

3.46   We have the greatest respect for these views and for the concerns that underlie them. However, we have concluded – as the Law Commission has done on two previous occasions – that there should in general be no place for concepts of knowledge or notice in registered land. We have reached this conclusion for the following reasons—

(1)   It was intended that the system of registration under the Land Registration Act 1925 should displace the doctrine of notice.

(2)   There is little evidence of which we are aware that the absence of the doctrine of notice in dealings with registered land has been a cause of injustice in the seventy-two years in which the present system has been operative.

(3)   The ethical argument is weaker than at first sight it appears to be if the issue is considered in relation to those principles which should, in our view, guide the development of land registration. Registration should be regarded as an integral part of the process of creating or transferring interests in registered land, closely akin to the formal requirement of using a deed (or in some cases, writing) in unregistered conveyancing . . . When electronic registration is introduced, it seems probable that many rights will be incapable of being created *except* by registering them.

(4)   In practice, if it were provided that unregistered rights in or over registered land were binding because a purchaser had *actual* knowledge of them, it would be very difficult to prevent the introduction by judicial interpretation of doctrines of *constructive* notice. If actual knowledge sufficed, the question would inevitably be asked: why not wilful blindness as well? In reality the boundary between actual knowledge and constructive notice is unclear and is, in our view, incapable of precise definition.

(5)   The mere fact that a purchaser *could* be bound if he or she had actual knowledge of an unregistered right or interest would inevitably weaken the security of title that registered land at present provides . . .

Comment

(1) There is no explicit statement of the irrelevance of notice in the 2002 Act,[18] though this does not indicate any change in policy on the part of the Law Commission.

(2) Are Battersby's arguments convincingly rebutted by the Law Commission?

(3) How do the arguments differ as regards (i) bad faith, and (ii) actual notice? Which would be the preferable requirement should some limit on purchasers' protection be permitted?

(b) Personal obligations and fraud

It should not be thought, however, that there are no circumstances in which an unprotected interest may affect a registered transferee (or lessee or chargee). Overseas registration systems – especially the Torrens systems in Australia and New Zealand – have long recognised personal obligations. These are obligations accepted by (or imposed upon) purchasers. These obligations have been seen as being quite different from proprietary obligations which automatically bind purchasers. This was recognised by the Law Commission immediately following the extract quoted above.

Extract 10.2.14

Law Commission No 254: Land Registration for the Twenty First Century

3.48   . . . the law provides a wide range of *personal* remedies against those who in some way behave improperly . . .

(1)   If A transfers trust property to B in breach of trust and B knows or (perhaps) has notice of this, B is liable as constructive trustee for 'knowing receipt' of trust property. Liability is personal and not proprietary and the obligation is to make restitution for the loss suffered by the trust. It has been assumed that this form of liability may apply where the trust property transferred is registered land and the rights of the beneficiaries have not been protected, so that as a matter of property law, the transferee takes the land free of the trust.

(2)   If property is transferred by A to B expressly subject to some right of C's which will not in fact bind B, a constructive trust may be imposed upon B if he refuses to give effect to C's right in circumstances in which that refusal is unconscionable . . .

3.49   In each of these cases, a purchaser may acquire the registered land free from the rights of the third party, yet find himself personally liable for the loss suffered by that third party or subject to some personal equity, which enables the transaction to be set aside. This accords with the principle applicable under Torrens systems that indefeasibility of title, 'in no way denies the right of the plaintiff to bring against a registered proprietor a claim in personam, founded in law or in equity, for such relief as a court acting in personam may grant'.

Comment

(1) Is it sufficient to say that we need not worry because the remedy is personal rather than proprietary in nature?[19] What difference is there between personal and proprietary liability?[20] Is the acceptance of this liability consistent with the arguments for not imposing proprietary liability on purchasers with actual notice?

---

[18] Save for s 78, which provides that the registrar is not affected by notice of a trust. This repeats the previous law.

[19] This has received recent attention from commentators: Conaglen and Goymour in *Constructive and Resulting Trusts* (ed Mitchell), Chapter 5 and Smith, *Landmark Cases in Land Law* (ed Gravells), p 148; contrast Dixon [2012] Conv 439.

[20] See also *Halifax plc v Curry Popeck* [2008] EWHC 1692 (Ch).

(2) Note that s 29 protects against 'any [unprotected] interest affecting the estate immediately before the disposition'. Does this wording cover personal claims? See *Lictor Anstalt* v *Mir Steel Ltd* [2014] EWHC 3316 (Ch), [283]–[295].

Personal claims have received more attention in Torrens registration systems, where it has been recognised for some years 'that the imposition of a constructive trust would seem difficult to reconcile with the policy of the Torrens system, at least when the registered owner is sought to be made liable on the basis of constructive notice.'[21]

The issue has recently been considered by the High Court of Australia.

Extract 10.2.15

Farah Constructions Pty Ltd v *Say-Dee Pty Ltd* (2007) 230 CLR 89
(footnotes omitted)

Section 42 of the Real Property Act 1900 (New South Wales) protects purchasers (broadly similar to LRA, s 29, though with an express exception for fraud).

HIGH COURT OF AUSTRALIA: 193. *In personam exception.* An exception operating outside the language of s 42(1) can exist in relation to certain legal or equitable causes of action against the registered proprietor. So far as Say-Dee was relying on *Barnes* v *Addy*, it was certainly alleging a recognised equitable cause of action. In *Macquarie Bank Ltd* v *Sixty-Fourth Throne Pty Ltd* Tadgell JA (Winneke P concurring, Ashley AJA dissenting) held that a claim under *Barnes* v *Addy* was not a personal equity which defeated the equivalent of s 42(1) in Victoria, namely the Transfer of Land Act 1958, s 42(1). Tadgell JA said:

> '[H]ere it is not possible to escape the circumstance that, if there was a "knowing receipt" by the appellant, it was a receipt by virtue of registration under the Transfer of Land Act.'

He continued:

> 'The argument for the respondent appears to assume that the acquisition by a mortgagee, in that capacity, of a proprietary interest following registration of a forged instrument of mortgage in respect of property that is subject to a trust amounts to a receipt by the mortgagee of trust property. If it were so, it might be possible to treat the holder of the registered proprietary interest as a constructive trustee arising from "knowing receipt" of trust property. As it seems to me, however, there is neither room nor the need, in the Torrens system of title, to do so. If registration of the mortgagee's interest is achieved dishonestly then the registration, and with it the interest, are liable to be set aside not because, on registration, the registered holder became a constructive trustee but because s 42(1) recognises that fraud renders the interest defeasible. If, on the other hand, the registration is not achieved by fraud the Act provides, subject to its terms, for an indefeasible interest. Those terms allow, it is true, a claim in personam founded in equity against the holder of a registered interest to be invoked to defeat the interest; and a claim in personam founded in equity may no doubt include a claim to enforce what is called a constructive trust ... [T]o recognise a claim in personam against the holder of a mortgage registered under the Transfer of Land Act, dubbing the holder a constructive trustee by application of a doctrine akin to "knowing receipt" when registration of the mortgage was honestly achieved, would introduce by the back door a means of undermining the doctrine of indefeasibility which the Torrens system establishes. It is to be distinctly understood that, until a forged instrument of mortgage is

---

[21] *White* v *Tomasel* [2004] 2 Qd R 438, McMurdo J at [72].

registered, the mortgagee receives nothing: before registration the instrument is a nullity. As Street J pointed out in *Mayer v Coe* [[1968] 2 NSWR 747] . . . the proprietary rights of a registered mortgagee of Torrens title land derive "from the fact of registration and not from an event antecedent thereto". In truth, I think it is not possible, consistently with the received principle of indefeasibility as it has been understood since *Frazer v Walker* [[1967] 1 AC 569] and *Breskvar v Wall* [(1971) 126 CLR 376], to treat the holder of a registered mortgage over property that is subject to a trust, registration having been honestly obtained, as having received trust property. The argument that the appellant is liable as a constructive trustee because it had "knowingly received" trust property should in my opinion fail.'

194. That reasoning . . . applies here . . .

195. The essential point on which Ashley AJA differed from the majority in *Macquarie Bank Ltd v Sixty-Fourth Throne Pty Ltd* was put thus:

'The proposition that an equity may be recognised and enforced so long as it involves no conflict with the indefeasability [sic] provisions has not prevented the High Court from imposing constructive trusts so as to recognise equities in cases where the transfer of real property was effected at different stages in the course of events giving rise to the equities.'

. . . However, as Pullin J pointed out in *LHK Nominees Pty Ltd v Kenworthy*, in [the cases relied upon by Ashley AJA] 'the defendant was the primary wrongdoer, attempting to ignore an obligation to share or convey the land with or to the plaintiff. In none of those cases was the defendant a party who merely had notice of an earlier interest or notice of third party fraud.' There is no analogy between the constructive trusts involved in those cases and that which can arise from application of the first limb of *Barnes v Addy*.

Comment

(1) The Australian analysis may be coloured by (i) a wider acceptance of recipient-based liability than English law currently recognises (*BCCI (Overseas) Ltd v Akindele* [2001] Ch 437); and (ii) a statutory provision whereby fraud defeats registered disponees. See also Cooke and O'Connor (2004) 120 LQR 640 at pp 660–665.

(2) Does the High Court of Australia see any role for constructive trusts binding registered proprietors?[22]

(3) What lessons should be learned by English law? Should we distinguish between obligations which are accepted by a purchaser and those which are imposed by law?

We can now turn to fraud. The constructive trust identified in Law Com No 254, para 3.48(2) illustrates how the legislation cannot be used to perpetrate a fraud.

Extract 10.2.16

Lyus v Prowsa Developments Ltd [1982] 1 WLR 1044

Land was sold on the basis that the purchaser (the first defendant) would give effect to an estate contract, even though it was not binding on the seller and not entered on the register. It has already been seen[23] that the facts gave rise to a constructive trust.

---

[22] For an argument in favour of a limited view of *Say-Dee*, see Harding (2008) 31 Melb ULR 343.
[23] See p 181 above.

DILLON J: . . . It has been pointed out by Lord Wilberforce in *Midland Bank Trust Co Ltd* v *Green* [1981] AC 513, 531, that it is not fraud to rely on legal rights conferred by Act of Parliament. Under section 20,[i] the effect of the registration of the transferee of a freehold title is to confer an absolute title subject to entries on the register and overriding interests, but, 'free from all other estates and interests whatsoever, including estates and interests of His Majesty . . .' In *Miles* v *Bull (No 2)* [1969] 3 All ER 1585, Bridge J expressed the view that the words which I have quoted embraced, prima facie, not only all kinds of legal interests, but all kinds of equitable interests: see p 1589. He therefore held, at p 1590, as I read his judgment, that actual or constructive notice on the part of a purchaser of an unregistered interest would not have the effect of imposing a constructive trust on him . . . it was not in *Miles* v *Bull (No 2)* a stipulation of the bargain between the vendor and the purchaser that the purchaser should give effect to the rights as against the vendor of the deserted wife. *Miles* v *Bull (No 2)* is thus distinguishable from the facts of the present case as I interpret those facts.

It seems to me that the fraud on the part of the defendants in the present case lies not just in relying on the legal rights conferred by an Act of Parliament, but in the first defendant reneging on a positive stipulation in favour of the plaintiffs in the bargain under which the first defendant acquired the land. That makes, as it seems to me, all the difference. It has long since been held, for instance, in *Rochefoucauld* v *Boustead* [1897] 1 Ch 196, that the provisions of the Statute of Frauds 1677 (29 Car 2 c 3), now incorporated in certain sections of the Law of Property Act 1925, cannot be used as an instrument of fraud, and that it is fraud for a person to whom land is agreed to be conveyed as trustee for another to deny the trust and relying on the terms of the statute to claim the land for himself. *Rochefoucauld* v *Boustead* was one of the authorities on which the judgment in *Bannister* v *Bannister* [1948] 2 All ER 133 was founded.

It seems to me that the same considerations are applicable in relation to the Land Registration Act 1925 . . .

i [See now 2002 Act, s 29, though it is differently worded.]

Comment

(1) How does Dillon J justify holding the purchaser liable? Is it a personal obligation or an exception to the indefeasibility of the registered title?

(2) Is it possible to have examples of fraud that do not amount to personal obligations? Consider forgery as a possible example. Should the law attempt to channel all cases through personal obligations, or are there advantages in recognising fraud as an independent basis for defeating a purchaser?

(3) Sometimes, a fraudulent disposition may operate so that there is no valuable considera-tion, so that LRA, s 29 is inapplicable: *Halifax plc* v *Curry Popeck*.[24] This case also implicitly denies that fraud by itself permits an unprotected interest to survive registration.

(4) Note that Torrens registration systems recognise fraud as a statutory exception to the purchaser's normal protection. What conduct amounts to fraud? Is fraud significantly different from bad faith?

The operation of the constructive trust in registered land has been recently considered by the Court of Appeal.

---

24 [2008] EWHC 1692 (Ch) at [46] (Norris J).

Extract 10.2.17

Chaudhary v *Yavuz* [2011] EWCA Civ 1314; [2013] Ch 249

An equitable easement had not been protected on the register, but the trial judge found a constructive trust based upon the contract.

LLOYD LJ: 58. If this conclusion is right it would have potentially very wide ramifications. The incorporation in a contract for the sale of land of the Standard Conditions of Sale must be a very widespread practice. Thus, most, or at least many, contracts for the sale of land are, by this means, expressed to be subject to incumbrances discoverable by inspection of the property before the contract. . . .

59. With respect to the judge, I do not consider that his conclusion is correct on this point. It does not seem to me that the fact that the contract is subject to such an incumbrance, by virtue of Standard Condition 3.1 being incorporated, satisfies the test laid down in *Lloyd* v *Dugdale* [[2002] 2 P&CR 167]. There is nothing in the contract which seems to me to allow the court to conclude that by this contract the purchaser 'has undertaken a new obligation, not otherwise existing, to give effect to the relevant encumbrance or prior interest'. In my judgment this criterion, laid down in *Lloyd* v *Dugdale*, should be applied in a case of this kind, and if applied to these facts leads to the conclusion that the Defendant's conscience is not bound to give effect to the Claimant's asserted rights.

61. It may be said that, on this basis, *Lyus* v *Prowsa* is a very unusual case, and is not likely to be followed in more than a few others. That is a fair comment, but not a fair criticism. I know of no English case in which the precedent of *Lyus* has been used successfully to make binding on a purchaser an interest which could be but was not protected on the register as against him. . . .

62. . . . in a case such as the present, where the rights asserted are capable of protection on the register and where they are not referred to in the contract in specific but only in general terms, then it seems to me that the registration system is relevant. That is for at least two reasons. One is that, absent a specific reference in the contract, the purchaser may be thought to be entitled to rely on third parties protecting themselves in the manner provided for under the legislation. The other is that the contract provision will more readily be interpreted as intended to protect the vendor against a possible claim by the purchaser than as imposing a new personal obligation on the purchaser towards the third party.

68. In my judgment that approach [in *Lloyd* v *Dugdale*] is even more amply justified under the 2002 Act than it was before. It does not exclude the possibility that the court may find an obligation binding on the registered proprietor personally, by way of, for example, a constructive trust, as a result of which an obligation which is not protected on the register is nevertheless effective. *Lyus* v *Prowsa* is an example of that, and a rare one. The present case is not.

Comment

Would it be fair to conclude that it will be almost impossible to rely on *Lyus* when an interest has not been protected on the register?

(c) Search certificates and priority protection

In order to establish the state of the vendor's title, a purchaser of registered land sees a recent copy of the register. Traditionally this was a paper copy, but this is being overtaken by electronic inspection of the register. How is the purchaser to discover very recent entries on the register? The problem is particularly acute because the registration of the purchase will be some time after completion of the purchase[25] with the consequent danger

---

[25] The crucial date is that of the application: LRA, s 74.

of interests being entered on the register after the purchaser's point of no return. This point is at completion, when the purchase money is paid and the purchaser goes into possession.

Shortly before completion, the purchaser obtains an official search certificate to check that there are no more recent entries. An important benefit of the certificate is that it gives *forward* protection. Thus LRA, s 72(2) provides: 'any entry made in the register during the priority period relating to the application is postponed'. The priority period is 30 working days: the purchaser must apply for registration within that period. This covers the 'registration gap': the inevitable delay between making final checks and then taking a transfer and seeking registration of it.

D. Overriding interests

Overriding interests are those interests which affect the registered proprietor despite not being entered on the register.

Extract 10.2.18

Law Commission No 254: Land Registration for the Twenty First Century

4.4   The orthodox explanation for the existence of overriding interests is that they are—

> various minor liabilities which are not usually, or at any rate not invariably, shown in title-deeds or mentioned in abstracts of title, and as to which, therefore, it is impracticable to form a trustworthy record on the register . . . As to these, persons dealing with registered land must obtain information *aliunde* in the same manner and from the same sources as persons dealing with unregistered land obtain it.[i]

The way in which the law on overriding interests has developed over the last seventy-two years has demonstrated that overriding interests are by no means only 'minor liabilities' . . . Most overriding interests do appear to have one shared characteristic, however, that is related to the orthodox explanation of them, namely that *it is unreasonable to expect the person who has the benefit of the right to register it as a means of securing its protection.* As we shall explain, not every overriding interest can be justified on that basis, and this in itself is a reason for examining such interests in detail. An examination of the list of overriding interests – at least as they have come to be understood in practice – suggests that most of them fall into five tolerably clear categories.

Categories of overriding interests

Those which provide a means of accommodating rights which may be created informally or where the origins of the rights may be obscure
4.5   First, overriding interests provide a means of accommodating rights which can be created (or may arise) informally, and where registration at the time of creation may therefore be unrealistic. These include—
(1)   easements that arise by prescription or by implied grant or reservation;
(2)   the rights of adverse possessors; and
(3)   in the case of persons in actual occupation, rights arising by estoppel or constructive trust.

Rights which it would be inconvenient or pointless to register
4.9   Fourthly, some rights are overriding interests because it would be either inconvenient or even pointless to register them. Leases granted for a term not exceeding 21 years, and rights in coal both fall into this category.

Rights which are otherwise protected

4.10 Finally, there are rights which are otherwise protected and where it may therefore be regarded as otiose to expect them to be registered. An obvious example of this is the category of local land charges which are protected by registration on a register kept by the relevant local authority. More controversially, the rights of those in actual occupation are also explicable on this basis. At common law, the rights over land of a person in occupation – and perhaps in possession as well – were protected by that occupation or possession . . . Whatever the extent of the principle, the idea that an occupier was not required to take any further steps to protect his or her rights in the property was an ancient and deeply engrained one.

[i] Brickdale & Stewart Wallace's *Land Registration Act, 1925* (4th ed 1939) p 190. The substance of the passage is retained in Ruoff & Roper, *Registered Conveyancing*, 6–04.

Comment

How convincing are these justifications for overriding interests? Note that purchasers bound by overriding interests receive no compensation.

Overriding interests are recognised by ss 11 and 12 (first registration) and s 29 (registered dispositions). Schedule 1 lists overriding interests operating on first registration and Sched 3 those operating on registered dispositions. The two schedules are very similar, but Sched 1 takes into account the fact that registration may well take place separately from any disposition of the land. A number of provisions in Sched 3 refer to inspections and inquiries by purchasers. These references are excluded from Sched 1, as there may well be no purchase where Sched 1 applies. Because around 95% of titles are today registered and therefore attract the registered disposition provisions, we will concentrate upon Sched 3.

Paragraph 1: leases

> A leasehold estate in land granted for a term not exceeding seven years from the date of the grant, except for—
> (a) a lease the grant of which falls within section 4(1)(d), (e) or (f);
> (b) a lease the grant of which constitutes a registrable disposition.

Comment

(1) We have already investigated the reason why leases must exceed seven years before they can be registered. The same reasons explain why short leases need not be protected by notice.

(2) *City Permanent BS* v *Miller*[26] established that the equivalent to para 1 in LRA 1925 (s 70(1)(k)) did not apply to equitable leases. Is this result supported by the wording of para 1? Why should equitable leases be excluded?

Paragraph 2: actual occupation

> An interest belonging at the time of the disposition to a person in actual occupation, so far as relating to land of which he is in actual occupation, except for—
> (a) an interest under a settlement under the Settled Land Act 1925 (c. 18);
> (b) an interest of a person of whom inquiry was made before the disposition and who failed to disclose the right when he could reasonably have been expected to do so;

[26] [1952] Ch 840.

(c) an interest—
  (i) which belongs to a person whose occupation would not have been obvious on a reasonably careful inspection of the land at the time of the disposition, and
  (ii) of which the person to whom the disposition is made does not have actual knowledge at that time;
(d) a leasehold estate in land granted to take effect in possession after the end of the period of three months beginning with the date of the grant and which has not taken effect in possession at the time of the disposition.

The interests of those in actual occupation constitute the most controversial and most litigated head of overriding interests. There are several highly significant changes to the pre-2002 law and these must be taken into account when considering older cases.

(i) Application to equitable interests

Under the previous legislation, it was argued that the fact that equitable interests can be protected as minor interests was inconsistent with their being actual occupation overriding interests.

Extract 10.2.19

Williams & Glyn's Bank Ltd v *Boland* [1981] AC 487

Where persons buy a house together jointly, one of them may be the legal owner holding on trust for both of them. Can the beneficial interests of the other person constitute an actual occupation overriding interest?

LORD WILBERFORCE: . . . This brings me to the second question, which is whether such rights as a spouse has under a trust for sale are capable of recognition as overriding interests – a question to my mind of some difficulty. The argument against this is based upon the structure of the Land Registration Act 1925 and upon specific provisions in it.

As to structure, it is said that the Act recognises three things: (a) legal estates, (b) minor interests, which take effect in equity, (c) overriding interests. These are mutually exclusive: an equitable interest, which is a minor interest, is incapable of being at the same time an overriding interest. The wife's interest, existing under or behind a trust for sale, is an equitable interest and nothing more. To give it the protection of an overriding interest would, moreover, contradict the principle according to which such an equitable interest can be overreached by an exercise of the trust for sale . . .

But I can see no reason why, if these interests, or that of any one of them, are or is protected by 'actual occupation' they should remain merely as 'minor interests'. On the contrary, I see every reason why, in that event, they should acquire the status of overriding interests . . .

There are decisions, in relation to other equitable interests than those of tenants in common, which confirm this line of argument. In *Bridges* v *Mees* [1957] Ch 475, Harman J decided that a purchaser of land under a contract for sale, who had paid the price and so was entitled to the land in equity, could acquire an overriding interest by virtue of actual occupation, and a similar position was held by the Court of Appeal to arise in relation to a resulting trust: *Hodgson* v *Marks* [1971] Ch 892. These decisions . . . provide an answer to the argument that there is a firm dividing line, or an unbridgeable gulf, between minor interests and overriding interests, and, on the contrary, confirm that the fact of occupation enables protection of the latter to extend to what without it would be the former. In my opinion, the wives' equitable interests, subsisting in reference to the land, were by the fact of occupation, made into overriding interests, and so protected by section 70(1)(g) [2002 Act, Sched 3, para 2].

Comment

(1) Part of the problem in *Boland* related to the old trust for sale rules. This issue is obsolete following the Trusts of Land and Appointment of Trustees Act 1996 (especially s 3).

(2) There is no longer any statutory category of minor interests. What effect does this have on the issues discussed in *Boland*?

(3) Why should there be an overlap between overriding and minor interests?

(ii) The range of rights protected

An initial point is that the occupier may have a number of interests. Is the overriding interest limited to that interest which is the source of the occupation? In *Webb* v *Pollmount Ltd*,[27] Ungoed-Thomas J said:

> It was suggested for the defendant that 'the right of every person in actual occupation of the land' should be construed as the rights by virtue of which a person is in actual occupation of the land. The short answer to this, it seems to me, is that it does not say so, . . . It is neither, in my view, consistent with the wording of section 70(1)(g) of the Land Registration Act, 1925 [2002 Act, Sched 3, para 2], nor with the authorities from which I have quoted.

What significance does this have for the inquiries which purchasers should make?

Extract 10.2.20

National Provincial Bank Ltd v *Ainsworth* [1964] Ch 665; on appeal [1965] AC 1175

A deserted wife has a right to occupy the matrimonial home. It was held by the House of Lords that this 'deserted wife's equity' is not an interest in land but is merely a personal right against the husband. Could it nevertheless fall within s 70(1)(g) [2002 Act, Sched 3, para 2]?

RUSSELL LJ: . . . It seems to me that section 70 in all its parts is dealing with rights in reference to land which have the quality of being capable of enduring through different ownerships of the land, according to normal conceptions of title to real property. If such a right as is now in question is not of this quality, I would not be prepared as a matter of construction to hold that it is embraced by the language of section 70; the contrary would indeed involve a startling result from a statute designed as a simplification of the processes of making and investigating title to land . . . Nor should the mind be in any way distracted by the fact that the owner of the rights under section 70(1)(g) is identified as a person in actual occupation. It is the rights of such a person which constitute the overriding interest and must be examined, not his occupation.

LORD WILBERFORCE: . . . Lord Denning said[i] of the subsection that it 'is a statutory application to registered land of the well-known rule protecting the rights of persons in occupation'.

I entirely agree with this and (as I shall shortly show) it provides the best argument against the alternative approach adopted by Donovan LJ . . .

Under the general law it is not such a right as affects a purchaser, even one with notice, and all that section 70(1)(g) of the Land Registration Act, 1925, does is to adapt the system of registration, and the modified form of inquiry which is appropriate to that system, to the same kind of right as under the general law would affect a purchaser finding a person in occupation of his land.

---

[27] [1966] Ch 584 at p 598.

This brings me to the more radical argument of Donovan LJ[ii] which involves that any right of an occupier becomes by this subsection binding on a purchaser who does not inquire. The answer to this, in my view, is that provided by Lord Denning in the passage[iii] I have already quoted. This Act is a registration Act concerned (in this instance) to provide that certain rights are to be binding without registration and without the necessity for actual notice. To ascertain what 'rights' come within this provision, one must look outside the Land Registration Act and see what rights affect purchasers under the general law. To suppose that the subsection makes any right, of howsoever a personal character, which a person in occupation may have, an over-riding interest by which a purchaser is bound, would involve two consequences: first that this Act is, in this respect, bringing about a substantive change in real property law by making personal rights bind purchasers; second, that there is a difference *as to the nature of the rights by which a purchaser may be bound* between registered and unregistered land; for purely personal rights including the wife's right to stay in the house (if my analysis of this is correct) cannot affect purchasers of unregistered land even with notice. One may have to accept that there is a difference between unregistered land and registered land as regards what kind of notice binds a purchaser, or what kind of inquiries a purchaser has to make. But there is no warrant in the terms of this paragraph or elsewhere in the Act for supposing that the nature of the rights which are to bind a purchaser is to be different, excluding personal rights in one case, including them in another. The whole frame of section 70, with the list that it gives of interests, or rights, which are overriding, shows that it is made against a background of interests or rights whose nature and whose transmissible character is known, or ascertainable, *aliunde*, i.e., under other statutes or under the common law.

[i] [1964] Ch 665, 689.
[ii] [1964] Ch 665, 692, 693.
[iii] *Ibid.* 689.

Comment

(1) Russell LJ dissented in the Court of Appeal, but was upheld by the House of Lords; the quoted passage was explicitly approved.

(2) What rights fall within para 2? Should para 2 (and title registration generally) influence our thinking as to what rights are capable of binding purchasers?[28]

The adoption of unregistered land categories of interests for para 2 means that the question as to which rights are included is not specific to registered land. However, we have already seen that LRA, ss 115 and 116 clarify that pre-emptions, estoppels and equities constitute proprietary interests in registered land. This means that they can be protected by notice or by actual occupation and thereby bind purchasers. These sections settle some of the most controversial questions in recent years.

One problem that has surfaced in recent years concerns a person who loses title as the result of registration of the wrong person. What proprietary interest can the original owner claim? Not the legal fee simple, as that is vested in the new proprietor. But there are problems in saying that it is an equitable fee simple, as there never was a separate equitable interest prior to the registration.

[28] Tee [1998] CLJ 328 criticises this limitation and argues that all types of claims should fall within para 2.

Extract 10.2.21

Fitzwilliam v *Richall Holdings Services Ltd* [2013] EWHC 86 (Ch); [2013] 1 P&CR 318

A question arose as to whether there could be an overriding interest if a registered proprietor's title was lost as a result of a forgery.

NEWEY J: 89.   Mr Healey's response to this was that the interest for which protection is claimed did not exist in October 2003. Where a person owns a property outright (as Mr Fitzwilliam did until January 2010), no separate equitable interest exists, Mr Healey said. . . .

91.   On the other hand, *Malory* [see also Extract 10.2.22] proceeds on the basis that an absolute owner has 'rights . . . as beneficial owner' which can survive the registration of another person as proprietor. That might be thought to suggest that an absolute owner has pre-existing rights that could qualify for protection under paragraphs 2 and 2A of schedule 3 to the 2002 Act. Further, Mr Healey's submissions, if correct, could produce some unattractive consequences. Even actual occupation would not seem to afford protection to an absolute owner. On Mr Healey's case, no one can have an equitable interest unless and until someone else acquires legal ownership. An absolute owner whose property came to be registered in the name of another person would not therefore have had any equitable interest that could qualify for protection 'at the time of the disposition'. A person absolutely entitled to a property might therefore lack the protection afforded to lesser interests (e.g. a mere equity – see section 116 of the 2002 Act). An absolute owner would, moreover, be less well-placed than either a beneficiary under a bare trust or a co-owner. If X held land on bare trust for Y and Z was registered as proprietor as a result of a fraud, Z should be bound by Y's beneficial interest if Y was in actual occupation. A co-owner in actual occupation would also enjoy protection. It was established in *Williams & Glyn's Bank Ltd* v *Boland* [1981] AC 487 that the rights of a co-owner could constitute overriding interests even though (at the time) they subsisted behind a trust for sale. A husband and wife who owned a property jointly would consequently, as it seems to me, be protected if they were in actual occupation. Yet actual occupation would not protect an absolute owner.

92.   I do not need to arrive at a final conclusion on these matters. As I have already indicated, they do not arise if a void transfer does not constitute a 'disposition' for the purposes of section 29 of the 2002 Act, and it seems to me that I must proceed on that basis.

Comment

(1) The same problem can arise in other circumstances, such as the wrong person being registered as first proprietor.

(2) Is there a compelling argument that there should not be an actual occupation overriding interest in these circumstances?

(3) Could it be argued that there can be two legal fees simple? See Law Com No 254, para 10.27.

Also problematic is the statutory right to rectify (or alter) the register, as this is peculiar to the registration scheme. The operation of the statutory right will be studied later in this chapter.

Extract 10.2.22

Malory Enterprises Ltd v *Cheshire Homes (UK) Ltd* [2002] Ch 216

Malory BVI was the registered proprietor. A transfer in favour of Cheshire was forged by a third party. The Court of Appeal held that Cheshire failed to obtain a good title because of the forgery, but proceeded to consider an overriding interest claim based upon the right to rectify.

ARDEN LJ: 67. Mr Martin submits that the right cannot constitute an overriding interest because it is only discretionary. In my judgment, a distinction is to be drawn between a right to seek rectification and the fulfilment of that right. The exercise by the court of its discretion is necessary for the fulfilment of the right (and if exercised in a manner which is adverse to the holder will result in extinction of the right) but the exercise by the court of its discretion is not necessary to bring the right into existence.

68. In my judgment, the right to seek rectification to reflect a proprietary interest in land fulfils the criteria approved in *Williams & Glyn's* v *Boland*, above, namely that it is a right in reference to land which is capable of transmission through different ownerships of land. There is no reason why the sale by Malory BVI of its beneficial interest in the rear land with any rights attaching thereto should not be effective to vest in the purchaser the right to apply to the court for rectification of the register . . . As respects transmissibility there can be no distinction between the equity of rectification of a document and a claim for rectification under section 82 [2002 Act, Sched 4]. Moreover in this case the right cannot be exercised in isolation from the interest in the land Malory BVI has, and thus in my judgment is a right in reference to land.

69. Nor do I accept the argument that the right to seek rectification comes into existence only after Cheshire is registered. The registration of Cheshire gives rise to the right to seek rectification at the same time as, and as part of, the same transaction. I do not consider that the registration can be treated as pre-dating the right to seek rectification in this way.

Comment

(1) On the facts, Malory BVI had a beneficial right to the land protected by actual occupation. Would a right to rectify constitute an overriding interest if there were no such beneficial right binding the purchaser? When will there be such a 'bare' right to rectify?

(2) After studying the law on alteration and rectification, the question will need to be asked whether such an overriding interest fits well with the principles operating in that area.

These cases establish the types of interests protected by para 2. However, just because an interest *can* bind a purchaser does not mean that it *will always* do so, simply because there is actual occupation.

Extract 10.2.23

City of London BS v *Flegg* [1988] AC 54

Husband and wife held the legal title on trust for themselves and the wife's parents, who were living in the house. Were the parents' interests overreached by a mortgage of the legal estate by husband and wife?

LORD OLIVER: . . . The respondents' submission, which succeeded in the Court of Appeal, is a very simple one. What is said is that the decision of this House in *Boland's* case [1981] AC 487 established the proposition that the interest of a tenant in common in occupation of registered land is, by reason of such occupation, an interest incapable of being overreached by a sale or other disposition of the land, save with the consent of the occupier, that section 70 [2002 Act, Sched 3] makes that interest an overriding one; and that, accordingly, the disposition by the registered proprietors in favour of the appellants takes effect subject to the right of the respondents to remain in occupation of the house indefinitely notwithstanding that (a) the appellants were specifically exonerated from inquiry into the trusts affecting the rents and profits of land pending sale by section 27 of the Law of Property Act 1925, and (b) the capital moneys raised by the registered proprietors were paid to two trustees in accordance with section 27(2). My

Lords, if the first step in this composite proposition be correct, then the remainder follows as a matter of unassailable logic. The Court of Appeal concluded that it was correct by reference to an analysis of the speech of Lord Wilberforce in *Boland's* case. Dillon LJ accepted that Lord Wilberforce's observations were made in the context of a case where the dealing which was claimed as being subject to an overriding interest in the occupying beneficiary was with a single trustee and would not therefore overreach the beneficiary's interest. But in his view the reasoning did not depend upon the fact that in *Boland* there was only one registered proprietor of the land and therefore only one trustee for sale. It concentrated simply on the distinction between a minor interest and an overriding interest, the mere fact of occupation converting what would otherwise be a minor interest into an overriding interest . . .

The fundamental criticism of this advanced by the appellants is that it fails to analyse the incidents of and limitations upon the interest which the court held to override the interest of the appellants. What section 70(1)(g) [2002 Act, Sched 3, para 2] does is to define as an overriding interest the rights (whatever they may be) of every person in actual occupation and to subject the registered land to such overriding interests 'as may be for the time being subsisting in reference thereto'. It does not create or enlarge rights but merely operates, to use the words of Lord Wilberforce in *National Provincial Bank Ltd* v *Hastings Car Mart Ltd* [1965] AC 1175, 1260–1261:

> 'to adapt the system of registration, and the modified form of inquiry which is appropriate to that system, to the same kind of right as under the general law would affect a purchaser finding a person in occupation of his land.'

. . .

With this preliminary caution in mind, therefore, I turn to consider whether, in fact, the decision of this House in *Boland* [1981] AC 487 does lead to the conclusion that the occupying co-owner's interest under the statutory trusts is, by reason of his occupation, one which is incapable of being overreached . . . It is in the light of these arguments [of counsel in *Boland*] that one finds in the judgments of the Court of Appeal [in *Boland*] specific references to the fact that the transactions there in question were transactions in which the capital money was received by one trustee only so that the beneficiaries' rights were not overreached . . . Dillon LJ in the Court of Appeal [in *Flegg*] regarded these references as merely part of the narrative but I am, for my part, unable to agree. They were, as it seems to me, an essential part of the reasoning upon which the judgments were based, for it was a critical feature of the appellants' argument that their interests were not overreached but were kept alive as against the purchaser, by notice in the case of unregistered land or by being overriding interests in the case of registered land. In the argument before your Lordships' House, one finds the same underlying thesis . . . Thus, the only question, it being common ground that there had not, in fact, been any overreaching, was whether the respondents' interests, although capable of being overreached by appropriate machinery and so within the definition of minor interests, could also be overriding interests by reason of the beneficiaries' occupation of the land . . .

. . . I cannot, however, for my part, read Lord Wilberforce's words as applying to a case which was not before the House where the effect of the transaction in question was precisely that to which he himself had alluded in his outline of the legal framework within which the appeals before the House fell to be decided, that is to say a conveyance by two trustees involving the consequence that the purchaser took free from the trusts regardless of notice.

Considered in the context of a transaction complying with the statutory requirements of the Law of Property Act 1925 the question of the effect of section 70(1)(g) of the Land Registration Act 1925 must, in my judgment, be approached by asking first what are the 'rights' of the person in occupation and whether they are, at the material time, subsisting in reference to the land. In the instant case the exercise by the registered proprietors of the powers conferred on trustees for sale by section 28(1) of the Law of Property Act 1925 had the effect of overreaching the interests of the respondents under the statutory trusts upon which depended their right to continue in occupation of the land. The appellants took free from those trusts (section 27) and were not, in any event, concerned to see that the respondents' consent to the transaction was obtained (section 26). If, then, one asks what were the subsisting rights of the respondents referable to their occupation, the answer must, in my judgment, be that they were rights which, *vis-à-vis* the appellants, were, *eo instante* with the creation of the charge, overreached and therefore subsisted only in relation to the equity of redemption. I do not, for my part, find in *Boland's* case [1981] AC 487 anything which compels a contrary conclusion . . . Section 70(1)(g) protects only the rights in reference to the land of the occupier whatever they are at the material time . . . Once the beneficiary's rights have been shifted from the land to capital moneys in the hands of the trustees, there is no longer an interest in the land to which the occupation can be referred or which it can protect. If the trustees sell in accordance with the statutory provisions and so overreach the beneficial interests in reference to the land, nothing remains to which a right of occupation can attach and the same result must, in my judgment, follow *vis-à-vis* a chargee by way of legal mortgage.

Comment

(1) How is Lord Oliver able to reach a result differing from that on the facts of *Boland*?

(2) Could a contrast between registered and unregistered land (as contemplated by Dillon LJ) be justified?

(3) The Law Commission's recommendation[29] that the result in *Flegg* should be reversed has not received government support. In any event, the recommendations relate to the operation of overreaching rather than overriding interests.

A similar point arises when it is alleged that the claimant agreed to the transaction (usually a mortgage).

Extract 10.2.24

Bristol & West BS v Henning [1985] 1 WLR 778

BROWNE-WILKINSON LJ: . . . There is a risk that the common sense answer in this case may get lost in the many different technicalities which can arise. The basic fact is that the mortgage was granted to the society with the full knowledge and approval of Mrs Henning. There was a joint project between her and Mr Henning to buy the villa with the assistance of such mortgage. Without it, the villa could never have been bought. Yet Mrs Henning is alleging that she has the right to stay in the villa in priority to the rights of the society which provided the bulk of the purchase money for it. Although she has unsuccessfully tried to find some way of paying the instalments under the mortgage, the logical result of her argument (if right) is that she is entitled to stay in possession indefinitely without making any payment. That would be a strange result which I would be reluctant to reach.

Mr Lindsay (who did not appear below) has in my judgment provided a short but complete solution to the technical problems raised by the case . . . Since Mr and Mrs Henning did not declare any trust of the villa in writing or reach any express agreement between themselves as to the beneficial interests, the only way in which Mrs Henning can establish either right in the villa would be to show, inter alia, that as between her and Mr Henning there was an express

---

[29] Law Com 188; see Extract 12.4.4 below.

or imputed intention or assumption that she should have such a right . . . Therefore, in order to determine what, on the assumption made, is the nature of Mrs Henning's right in the villa, it is necessary first to determine from the parties' actions what were their express or imputed intentions as to her beneficial interest.

Once that is identified as the relevant question, in my judgment the answer becomes obvious. Mr and Mrs Henning did not contemporaneously express any intention as to the beneficial interests in the property. Therefore such intention if it exists has to be imputed to them from their actions. Mrs Henning knew of and supported the proposal to raise the purchase price of the villa on mortgage. In those circumstances, it is in my judgment impossible to impute to them any common intention other than that she authorised Mr Henning to raise the money by mortgage to the society. In more technical terms, it was the common intention that Mr Henning as trustee should have power to grant the mortgage to the society. Such power to mortgage must have extended to granting to the society a mortgage having priority to any beneficial interests in the property . . .

. . . There was no way in which the villa could have been bought at all without the assistance of the mortgage to the society and the mortgage to the society could not be properly granted without giving the society a charge over the whole legal and equitable interest.

Comment

(1) Does it make economic sense for the wife to have priority over the mortgagee?

(2) Can legal principle adequately explain why the wife does not have priority?

(3) A mortgagee who funds the purchase automatically has priority today: *Abbey National BS* v *Cann*.[30] When might reliance on *Henning* be necessary today?

Extract 10.2.25

Paddington BS v *Mendelsohn* (1985) 50 P&CR 244

A mother contributed to her son's purchase, which she knew required a mortgage. *Henning* had involved unregistered land and it was argued that the actual occupation overriding interest made all the difference where title was registered.

BROWNE-WILKINSON LJ: . . . Section 70(1) deems the registered land to be subject to certain rights which 'override' the rights appearing on the register. The rights referred to in paragraph (g) are 'the rights of every person in occupation'. There is no doubt therefore that the registered land is subject to the rights of such person. But the essential question remains to be answered, 'What are the rights of the person in actual occupation?' If the rights of the person in actual occupation are not under the general law such as to give any priority over the holder of the registered estate, there is nothing in section 70 which changes such rights into different and bigger rights. Say, in the present case, before the acquisition of the flat a trust deed had been executed declaring that the flat was held in trust for the mother but expressly subject to all the rights of the society under the proposed legal charge. The effect of section 70(1)(g) could not in my judgment have been to enlarge the mother's rights so as to give her rights in priority to the society when, under the trust deed, her rights were expressly subject to those of the society. Her rights would be 'overriding interests' in that the society would have to give effect to them, but the inherent quality of the mother's rights would not have been such as to give them priority over the society's rights. So in the present case, once it is established that the imputed intention must be that the mother's rights were to be subject to the mortgage, there is nothing in section 70 of the Land Registration Act 1925 which enlarges those rights into any greater rights.

[30] [1991] 1 AC 56; see Extract 9.5.1 above.

I can see nothing in *Williams & Glyn's Bank Ltd* v *Boland*[i] which conflicts with this view. In the two cases under consideration by the House of Lords, the mortgages had been granted after the purchase of the matrimonial homes and without the knowledge or consent of the wives.

[i] [1981] AC 487; (1980) 40 P&CR 451.

Comment

(1) Why could the mother not rely on an overriding interest?

(2) Is the reasoning related to that in *Flegg*?

(3) What is the likely outcome where the occupier is aware of the proposed mortgage, but gains no benefit (whether financial or the attainment of a desired objective)? For example, suppose the wife in *Boland* had been told about the mortgage in advance and had expressed no objection.

The analysis in these cases appears to be that of agency: the legal owner is expressly or impliedly authorised to enter into the mortgage. However, different analyses have subsequently been employed. The later cases involve licensees or lessees in possession who sign papers confirming that they claim no right.

Extract 10.2.26

Skipton BS v *Clayton* (1993) 66 P&CR 223 (Court of Appeal)

SIR CHRISTOPHER SLADE: . . . Recent authorities such as *Abbey National Building Society* v *Cann* and *Bristol and West Building Society* v *Henning* demonstrate that in a case where A, the holder of the legal estate in land, has executed a mortgage of the land in favour of B, and C, who claims an interest in the land, has so conducted himself as to give B reasonable grounds for believing that C is consenting to the creation by A of a charge over the land in favour of B which will have priority to C's interest, then C will be estopped from asserting that his interest has priority to B's charge . . .

Comment

(1) Is it appropriate to use estoppel when the mortgagee is wholly unaware that there is any occupier?

(2) A similar approach was taken by the Court of Appeal in *Woolwich BS* v *Dickman*.[31] Are there reasons to prefer estoppel over express or implied agency?

(iii) Actual occupation

(a) The meaning of actual occupation

Controversy has raged as to how far actual occupation mirrors the doctrine of notice. In *Caunce* v *Caunce*,[32] Stamp J held that a purchaser had no notice of the rights of a wife living with her husband: her being there was in no way inconsistent with the husband's title. Could a similar analysis be employed in registered land?

---

[31] [1996] 3 All ER 204; see especially p 214.
[32] [1969] 1 WLR 286; Extract 9.2.7 above.

Extract 10.2.27

Hodgson v Marks [1971] Ch 892

Most cases involve a couple living together, but here an old lady transferred title to her lodger. He held on trust for her, but purported to sell as the beneficial owner.

RUSSELL LJ: . . . But the judge then proceeded to attach a different and special meaning to the words 'in actual occupation' in section 70(1)(g) [2002 Act, Sched 3, para 2]. He took as a starting point to justify departure from the ordinary meaning of the words first the fact that every person in actual occupation could not include the vendor himself . . . Having by this means freed himself from the fetters of the golden rule, he then, after considering the circumstances in which in the case of unregistered land a purchaser would be fixed with constructive notice of the rights of persons in occupation of the land sold, concluded that 'actual' should be construed in the sense of 'actual and apparent'. I do not see that this adds to or detracts from the words in the section. In connection with the word 'apparent' I remark on the phrase of the judge that, after the registration of the transfer to Mr Evans, 'to all appearances' the plaintiff continued in actual occupation. I am prepared, for the purposes of this case, to assume (without necessarily accepting) that section 70(1)(g) of the Land Registration Act 1925 is designed only to apply to a case in which the occupation is such, in point of fact, as would in the case of unregistered land affect a purchaser with constructive notice of the rights of the occupier; and it is [to] be observed that the words 'actual occupation' are used in section 14 of the Law of Property Act 1925 and were used in *Barnhart* v *Greenshields* (1853) 9 Moo PCC 18, 34. But, nevertheless, how can it be said that the plaintiff was not in actual occupation of the house? The judge said that in all fairness a purchaser of this house (if unregistered) should not be fixed with notice of the plaintiff's rights. But why not? It is a principle of law (and of the Land Registration Act 1925) that a person in occupation is protected in his rights by that occupation, unless, of course, the rights are such that they require registration if they are to be protected. A purchaser must pay heed to anyone in occupation if he is to be sure of getting a good title. It was argued, on the basis of a quotation from the judgment of Vaughan Williams LJ in *Hunt* v *Luck* [1902] 1 Ch 428, 432 that this does not apply when the vendor is in occupation, and that (as is the fact) there is no reported case of unregistered land where a purchaser was fixed with constructive notice of the rights of any other occupier when the vendor was in occupation, and that any other view would lead to an impossible burden of inquiry on a purchaser and more particularly on a lender of money on mortgage such as the building society . . . I do not think this is a real problem. . . . I do not consider that it is correct in law to say that any rights of a person who is in occupation will be overridden whenever the vendor is, or appears to be, also in occupation.

I do not think it desirable to attempt to lay down a code or catalogue of situations in which a person other than the vendor should be held to be in occupation of unregistered land for the purpose of constructive notice of his rights, or in actual occupation of registered land for the purposes of section 70(1)(g). It must depend on the circumstances, and a wise purchaser or lender will take no risks. Indeed, however wise he may be he may have no ready opportunity of finding out; but, nevertheless, the law will protect the occupier. Reliance upon the untrue ipse dixit of the vendor will not suffice. Take the present case – though the test of occupation must be objective. Mr Evans was only a lodger, and whether in law he was in occupation at all is at least doubtful. But the plaintiff was there for Mr Marks to see and he saw her on two occasions . . .

Comment

How should purchasers seek to discover overriding interests?

Extract 10.2.28

Williams & Glyn's Bank Ltd v *Boland* [1981] AC 487

We have seen that the husband held their home on trust for himself and his wife. Could she, living in the house with her husband, assert actual occupation?

LORD WILBERFORCE: . . . The system of land registration, as it exists in England, which long antedates the Land Registration Act 1925, is designed to simplify and to cheapen conveyancing. It is intended to replace the often complicated and voluminous title deeds of property by a single land certificate, on the strength of which land can be dealt with. In place of the lengthy and often technical investigation of title to which a purchaser was committed, all he has to do is to consult the register; from any burden not entered on the register, with one exception, he takes free. Above all, the system is designed to free the purchaser from the hazards of notice – real or constructive – which, in the case of unregistered land, involved him in enquiries, often quite elaborate, failing which he might be bound by equities. The Law of Property Act 1925 contains provisions limiting the effect of the doctrine of notice, but it still remains a potential source of danger to purchasers. By contrast, the only provisions in the Land Registration Act 1925 with regard to notice are provisions which enable a purchaser to take the estate free from equitable interests or equities whether he has notice or not . . . The only kind of notice recognised is by entry on the register.

The exception just mentioned consists of 'overriding interests' listed in section 70. As to these, all registered land is stated to be deemed to be subject to such of them as may be subsisting in reference to the land, unless the contrary is expressed on the register. The land is so subject regardless of notice actual or constructive. In my opinion therefore, the law as to notice as it may affect purchasers of unregistered land, whether contained in decided cases, or in a statute (the Conveyancing Act 1882, section 3, Law of Property Act, section 199) has no application even by analogy to registered land. Whether a particular right is an overriding interest, and whether it affects a purchaser, is to be decided upon the terms of section 70, and other relevant provisions of the Land Registration Act 1925, and upon nothing else.

In relation to rights connected with occupation, it has been said that the purpose and effect of section 70(1)(g) of the Land Registration Act 1925 [2002 Act, Sched 3, para 2] was to make applicable to registered land the same rule as previously had been held to apply to unregistered land: see *per* Lord Denning MR in *National Provincial Bank Ltd* v *Hastings Car Mart Ltd* [1964] Ch 665, 689, and in this House [1965] AC 1175, 1259.

I adhere to this, but I do not accept the argument which learned counsel for the appellant sought to draw from it. His submission was that, in applying section 70(1)(g), we should have regard to and limit the application of the paragraph in the light of the doctrine of notice. But this would run counter to the whole purpose of the Act. The purpose, in each system, is the same, namely, to safeguard the rights of persons in occupation, but the method used differs. In the case of unregistered land, the purchaser's obligation depends upon what he has notice of – notice actual or constructive. In the case of registered land, it is the fact of occupation that matters. If there is actual occupation, and the occupier has rights, the purchaser takes subject to them. If not, he does not. No further element is material.

I now deal with the first question. Were the wives here in 'actual occupation'? These words are ordinary words of plain English, and should, in my opinion, be interpreted as such . . .

Then, were the wives in actual occupation? I ask: why not? There was physical presence, with all the rights that occupiers have, including the right to exclude all others except those having similar rights. The house was a matrimonial home, intended to be occupied, and in fact occupied by both spouses, both of whom have an interest in it: it would require some special doctrine of law to avoid the result that each is in occupation. Three arguments were used for a contrary conclusion. First, it was said that if the vendor (I use this word to include a mortgagor) is in occupation, that is enough to prevent the application of the paragraph. This seems to be a proposition of general application, not limited to the case of husbands, and no doubt, if correct, would be very convenient for purchasers and intending mortgagees. But the presence of the vendor, with occupation, does not exclude the possibility of occupation of others. There are observations which suggest the contrary in the unregistered land case of *Caunce* v *Caunce* [1969] 1 WLR 286, but I agree with the disapproval of these, and with the assertion of the proposition I have just stated by Russell LJ in *Hodgson* v *Marks* [1971] Ch 892, 934. Then it was suggested that the wife's occupation was nothing but the shadow of the husband's – a version I suppose of the doctrine of unity of husband and wife . . . It somewhat faded from the arguments in the present case and appears to me to be heavily obsolete. The appellant's main and final position became in the end this: that, to come within the paragraph, the occupation in question must be apparently inconsistent with the title of the vendor. This, it was suggested, would exclude the wife of a husband-vendor because her apparent occupation would be satisfactorily accounted for by his. But, apart from the rewriting of the paragraph which this would involve, the suggestion is unacceptable . . . A wife may, and everyone knows this, have rights of her own, particularly, many wives have a share in a matrimonial home. How can it be said that the presence of a wife in the house, as occupier, is consistent or inconsistent with the husband's rights until one knows what rights she has? And if she has rights, why, just because she is a wife (or in the converse case, just because an occupier is the husband), should these rights be denied protection under the paragraph? If one looks beyond the case of husband and wife, the difficulty of all these arguments stands out if one considers the case of a man living with a mistress, or of a man and a woman – or for that matter two persons of the same sex – living in a house in separate or partially shared rooms. Are these cases of apparently consistent occupation, so that the rights of the other person (other than the vendor) can be disregarded? The only solution which is consistent with the Act (section 70(1)(g)) and with common sense is to read the paragraph for what it says. Occupation, existing as a fact, may protect rights if the person in occupation has rights . . .

I would only add, in conclusion, on the appeal as it concerns the wives a brief observation on the conveyancing consequences of dismissing the appeal. . . . What is involved is a departure from an easy-going practice of dispensing with enquiries as to occupation beyond that of the vendor and accepting the risks of doing so. To substitute for this a practice of more careful enquiry as to the fact of occupation, and if necessary, as to the rights of occupiers cannot, in my view of the matter, be considered as unacceptable except at the price of overlooking the widespread development of shared interests of ownership. In the light of section 70 of the Act, I cannot believe that Parliament intended this, though it may be true that in 1925 it did not foresee the full extent of this development.

Comment

(1) *Boland* involved a mortgagee. Are mortgagees more likely than purchasers to be affected by occupiers' overriding interests?

(2) Although some predicted that disruption of conveyancing would occur as a result of *Boland*, the effect of the case on the conveyancing process proved to be minimal. Is protecting the occupier worth some cost in the conveyancing process?

Extract 10.2.29

Lloyds Bank plc v *Rosset* [1989] Ch 350

Husband and wife agreed to purchase a semi-derelict property. In advance of the formal transfer, they commenced renovation. The work was done by builders, supervised much of the time by the wife. The work was completed after the transfer, but was the wife in actual occupation at the time of the transfer so as to have priority over a mortgagee?

NICHOLLS LJ: . . . Lord Wilberforce observed in *Williams & Glyn's Bank Ltd* v *Boland* [1981] AC 487, 504, that the words 'actual occupation' are ordinary words of plain English and that they should be interpreted as such. The bank submitted that in ordinary, every day speech the wife would not have been regarded as being in occupation of Vincent Farmhouse on 17 December. Residential premises are occupied only by those who live in them.

I agree with this submission to the extent that I accept that in ordinary speech one normally does equate occupation in relation to a house with living there. If a person is intending to move into a house but has not yet done so, he would not normally be regarded as having gone into occupation. That is the normal position, with a house which is fit for living in. But that does not provide the answer in the present case, where the house was semi-derelict. In the first place, I do not think that in every day speech actual occupation of a house can never exist short of residence . . . if the words 'actual occupation' are given the rigid, restricted meaning submitted by the bank in relation to residential premises, and that meaning is applied to a house in course of being built or renovated, the result in some cases will be to defeat the purpose intended to be achieved by paragraph (g) of section 70(1) [2002 Act, Sched 3, para 2]. If, day after day, workmen are actively building a house on a plot of land, or actively and substantially renovating a semi-derelict house, it would be contrary to the principle underlying paragraph (g) if a would-be purchaser or mortgagee were entitled to treat that site as currently devoid of an occupant for the purpose of the paragraph . . .

In my view, the test of residence propounded by the bank is too narrow. As the judge observed, what constitutes occupation will depend upon the nature and state of the property in question. I can see no reason, in principle or in practice, why a semi-derelict house such as Vincent Farmhouse should not be capable of actual occupation whilst the works proceed and before anyone has started to live in the building.

The bank further submitted that the presence of the builder and his men in the property could not constitute actual occupation by the defendants. I am unable to agree. I can detect nothing in the context in which the expression 'actual occupation' is used in paragraph (g) to suggest that the physical presence of an employee or agent cannot be regarded as the presence of the employer or principal when determining whether the employer or principal is in actual occupation . . . In [*Strand Securities Ltd* v *Caswell* [1965] Ch 958, 981, 984] both Lord Denning MR and Russell LJ accepted that, if a tenant puts a resident caretaker into a residential flat to look after it, that would be actual occupation by the tenant. . . .

PURCHAS LJ: . . . The provisions of the section clearly were intended to import into the law relating to registered land the equitable concept of constructive notice. Thus, a purchaser or a chargee acquiring the title to or an interest in the land where the vendor was not in actual possession in order to protect his interest had to make appropriate inquiries if he found someone else in occupation of the property. Thus, a tenant in occupation was protected under the old rules as being an owner of an overriding interest and his presence put the purchaser on inquiry . . .

In order for the wife's interest in the property to qualify as an overriding interest under section 70(1)(g) two things must be established: (a) was she in actual occupation? and (b) would appropriate inquiries made by the bank have elicited the fact of her interest? I have found neither of these questions easy to answer . . .

Comment

(1) Mustill LJ dissented on the facts, though his approach is very similar to that of the majority. Is it appropriate to say, as he did, that constructive notice 'gives a flavour' to this overriding interest?

(2) Purchas LJ appears to require that there must be constructive notice as well as actual occupation. Is this compatible with the wording of para 2, or with *Boland*?

(3) On appeal to the House of Lords ([1991] 1 AC 107), the wife was held never to have had any beneficial interest.

Extract 10.2.30

Abbey National BS v *Cann* [1991] 1 AC 56

The claimant was the mother of the legal owner. Her furniture was moved in some 35 minutes before completion (the relevant time for determining actual occupation). Was she in actual occupation so as to have priority over the son's mortgagee?

LORD OLIVER: [Actual occupation] is, of course, essentially a question of fact, but there is the serious question of what, in law, can amount to 'actual occupation' for the purposes of section 70(1)(g). In *Williams & Glyn's Bank Ltd* v *Boland* [1981] AC 487, 504, Lord Wilberforce observed that these words should be interpreted for what they are, that is to say, ordinary words of plain English. But even plain English may contain a variety of shades of meaning. At the date of completion Mrs Cann was not personally even in England, leave alone in personal occupation of the property, and the trial judge held that the acts done by Mr Abraham Cann and Mr George Cann amounted to

> 'no more than the taking of preparatory steps leading to the assumption of actual residential occupation on or after completion, whatever the moment of the day when completion took place . . .'

For my part, I am content to accept this as a finding of fact which was amply justified by the evidence before him . . . It is, perhaps, dangerous to suggest any test for what is essentially a question of fact, for 'occupation' is a concept which may have different connotations according to the nature and purpose of the property which is claimed to be occupied. It does not necessarily, I think, involve the personal presence of the person claiming to occupy. A caretaker or the representative of a company can occupy, I should have thought, on behalf of his employer. On the other hand, it does, in my judgment, involve some degree of permanence and continuity which would rule out mere fleeting presence. A prospective tenant or purchaser who is allowed, as a matter of indulgence, to go into property in order to plan decorations or measure for furnishings would not, in ordinary parlance, be said to be occupying it, even though he might be there for hours at a time. Of course, in the instant case, there was, no doubt, on the part of the persons involved in moving Mrs Cann's belongings, an intention that they would remain there and would render the premises suitable for her ultimate use as a residential occupier. Like the trial judge, however, I am unable to accept that acts of this preparatory character carried out by courtesy of the vendor prior to completion can constitute 'actual occupation' for the purposes of section 70(1)(g).

Comment

(1) Why was there no actual occupation? Is it anything more than reaching a very convenient practical result?

(2) We saw in the previous chapter[33] that the mortgagee would have won even if there had been actual occupation.

All these cases have now to be considered in the light of the protection for purchasers in para 2 as regards the interest of 'a person whose occupation would not have been obvious on a reasonably careful inspection of the land'.

---

[33] See Extract 9.5.1 above.

How will the new provision operate? One vitally important point is that it is the occupation that has to be obvious on a reasonably careful inspection, not the interest.[34] If we consider the facts of *Boland*, the wife's occupation was indeed obvious – the question was primarily as to what inferences should have been drawn from it. In many of the cases, there was some uncertainty as to whether or not there was actual occupation. Quite reasonably, the courts employed issues of discoverability in deciding whether there was actual occupation. Thus Arden LJ stated,[35] in the context of derelict land, 'The requisite physical presence must, as it seems to me, in fairness be such as to put a person inspecting the land on notice that there was some person in occupation.'

How would the inspection provision apply to the facts of *Rosset* and *Cann*? *Thomas* v *Clydesdale Bank plc*[36] involved very similar facts to *Rosset*. Ramsey J held that the occupation was obvious on a reasonably careful inspection:

> In my judgment the concept of inspection strongly suggests that what has to be obvious is the relevant visible signs of occupation upon which a person who asserts an interest by actual occupation relies . . . I find it difficult to read into the objective phrase 'reasonably careful inspection' a requirement that the person inspecting would have any particular knowledge or that, in the absence of any express provision, the term 'inspection' would also require the person inspecting to make reasonable enquiries. On that basis, it is the visible signs of occupation which have to be obvious on inspection.

Is any other approach viable? Is the Ramsey J approach most likely to favour occupiers or purchasers?

The Law Commission is emphatic that the restructuring does not reintroduce the doctrine of notice:[37] 'The test is not one of constructive notice of the occupation. It is the less demanding one (derived from the test applicable to intending buyers of land) that it should be obvious on a reasonably careful inspection of the land.' But is it really different from notice?

Extract 10.2.31

Hypo-Mortgage Services Ltd v *Robinson* [1997] 2 FLR 71

Could infant children claim to be in actual occupation?

NOURSE LJ: . . . I regard it as axiomatic that minor children of the legal owner are not in actual occupation within s 70(1)(g). That seems to have been assumed without discussion by Templeman J in *Bird* v *Syme-Thomson* . . . The minor children are there because their parent is there. They have no right of occupation of their own. As Templeman J put it, they are only there as shadows of occupation of their parent. Moreover, as Mr Marks submits, it cannot have been intended that s 70(1)(g) should operate as the second defendant suggests. No inquiry can be made of minor children or consent obtained from them in the manner contemplated by that provision, especially when they are, as here, of tender years at the material date.

Comment

(1) *Bird* v *Syme-Thomson* was overruled in *Boland* as regards spouses. Was it safe for Nourse LJ to rely upon it?

---

[34] Stressed by Law Com No 271, para 8.62.
[35] *Malory Enterprises Ltd* v *Cheshire Homes (UK) Ltd* [2002] Ch 216 at [81] (on the pre-2002 law).
[36] [2010] EWHC 2755 (QB).
[37] Law Com No 271, para 8.62; see also para 5.21.

(2) Is it relevant whether the children had an independent right to occupy? What conclusions should be drawn from the fact that infant children very rarely will have property interests in the home?

(3) There is, of course, a very real problem as to how enquiries can be made.[38] Can the decision be justified on the wording of para 2?

(b) The application of actual occupation
So far as those living in family homes are concerned, the above cases provide ample guidance. How does actual occupation apply to other situations?

Extract 10.2.32

Strand Securities Ltd v Caswell **[1965] Ch 958**

The claimant allowed his step-daughter to live in a house rent free. Could he claim to be in actual occupation?

RUSSELL LJ: . . . Reference was made to a number of authorities, including cases in the fields of rating, poor law, and landlord and tenant, with a view to showing that possession, and therefore occupation, may be had through the medium of another. Suppose, it was said, that the first defendant employed a resident caretaker to look after the flat in question, would the first defendant not be a person in actual occupation? I think that is correct. Then, it was argued, that is because the caretaker would be his licensee, bound to go at his will, and that was the position of the second defendant. But I think that here is the distinction between occupation by the caretaker as a matter of duty on behalf of the first defendant and the occupation of the second defendant on her own behalf; both were licensees, but the former, by her occupation for which she was employed, was the representative of the first defendant and her occupation may therefore be regarded as his. . . .

Nor, it seems to me, can the presence on the premises of some of the first defendant's furniture, nor the previously mentioned use by him and others of the family of the flat, nor the fact, which I am prepared to assume though it was not proved, that he had a key, nor a combination of those matters, constitute actual occupation by him.

Comment

(1) When can a claimant rely on the occupation of another person? Note that similar points were discussed more recently in *Rosset*.

(2) Until the 2002 Act, receipt of rent counted as actual occupation. This extension of actual occupation was removed by para 2. Are purchasers safe in ignoring payment of rent?

Extract 10.2.33

Kingsnorth Finance Co Ltd v Tizard **[1986] 1 WLR 783 (Ch D)**

Following marriage breakdown, Mrs Tizard stayed with her sister, returning to the matrimonial home to look after the children. Mr Tizard mortgaged the property to the plaintiffs.

JUDGE JOHN FINLAY QC: . . . Mrs Tizard was, in my judgment, in occupation of Willowdown notwithstanding that Mr Tizard was living there also; and notwithstanding the fact that on

---

[38] When a child's consent is required in a trust of land, purchasers are given special protection: Trusts of Land and Appointment of Trustees Act 1996, s 10(3).

numerous occasions she slept elsewhere. The 'physical presence' to which Lord Wilberforce refers does not connote continuous and uninterrupted presence; such a notion would be absurd. Nor, indeed, do I consider that the requisite 'presence' is negatived by regular and repeated absence. I find that Mrs Tizard was in Willowdown virtually every day for some part of the day; that her life and activities were based on her presence, interrupted though it was, in Willowdown; there she prepared herself for work; there she cared for her children; there she looked after the house and the concerns of herself and the children; she went in the morning and returned in the evening to discharge her duties as housewife and mother. It is clear that prior to the time, November 1982, when she ceased always to sleep in the house when her husband was there, she had been in occupation; and, in my judgment, she did not cease to be in occupation simply because she made that change in her habits, significant though the change was.

. . .

Here Mr Marshall carried out his inspection on a Sunday afternoon at a time arranged with Mr Tizard. If the only purpose of such an inspection were to ascertain the physical state of the property, the time at which the inspection is made and whether or not that time is one agreed in advance with the vendor or mortgagor appears to me to be immaterial. Where, however, the object of the inspection (or one of the objects) is to ascertain who is in occupation, I cannot see that an inspection at a time pre-arranged with the vendor will necessarily attain that object. Such a pre-arranged inspection may achieve no more than an inquiry of the vendor or mortgagor and his answer to it. In the case of residential property an appointment for inspection will, in most cases, be essential so far as inspection of the interior is concerned. How then is a purchaser or mortgagee to carry out such inspection 'as ought reasonably to have been made' for the purpose of determining whether the possession and occupation of the property accords with the title offered? What is such an inspection 'as ought reasonably to be made' must, I think, depend on all the circumstances. In the circumstances of the present case I am not satisfied that the pre-arranged inspection on a Sunday afternoon fell within the category of 'such inspections which ought reasonably to have been made', the words in section 199 of the Law of Property Act 1925 . . .

Comment

(1) *Tizard* involved unregistered land. What does it tell us about the relationship between actual occupation and the doctrine of notice? Might the result now be different for registered land, in the light of the requirement for the occupation to be obvious on a reasonably careful inspection?

(2) Is the conduct of inspections more suited to private detectives than surveyors?

The question of when actual occupation terminates is dealt with by the following extract.

Extract 10.2.34

Link Lending Ltd v Bustard [2010] 2 EGLR 55

Psychiatric problems forced an occupier to move into a residential care home. Though she was unable to live in her own home (her visits were brief and supervised), she still hoped to return there.

MUMMERY LJ: 25. The facts are not all one way. Some of the primary facts point against Ms Bustard's actual occupation of the Property at the relevant date: she was not personally present in the Property on 29 February 2008; she had been in a residential care home since January 2007; she was incapable of living safely in the Property; and her visits to the Property were brief and supervised.

26. Some of the primary facts point to Ms Bustard's continuing actual occupation of the Property: it was her furnished home and the only place to which she genuinely wanted to return; she continued to visit the Property because she still considered it her home; those who had taken responsibility for her finances regularly paid the bills, such as the community charge, from her funds; she was in the process of making an application to the Mental Health Review Tribunal in order to be allowed to return home; and no-one took a final and irrevocable decision that she would not eventually be permitted to return home.

27. Whether Ms Bustard was in 'actual occupation' of the Property at the relevant date was an issue on which the trial judge had to make an evaluation based on his findings of primary fact. As for the law he considered the relevant authorities on the concept of a 'person in actual occupation' of land in the earlier Land Registration legislation and now found in the 2002 Act. The construction of the earlier equivalent provisions by the House of Lords is binding on this court. The trend of the cases shows that the courts are reluctant to lay down, or even suggest, a single legal test for determining whether a person is in actual occupation. The decisions on statutory construction identify the factors that have to be weighed by the judge on this issue. The degree of permanence and continuity of presence of the person concerned, the intentions and wishes of that person, the length of absence from the property and the reason for it and the nature of the property and personal circumstances of the person are among the relevant factors.

30. The assistance given in the authorities is in clarifying the legal principles, exploring the range of decisions available to the court and identifying the factors to which weight should be given. It is clear from the citations that Ms Bustard's is not a case of a 'mere fleeting presence', or a case, like *Cann*, of acts preparatory to the assumption of actual occupation . . . In this case the new and special feature is in the psychiatric problems of the person claiming actual occupation. The judge was, in my view, justified in ruling, at the conclusion of a careful and detailed judgment, that Ms Bustard was a person in actual occupation of the Property. His conclusion was supported by evidence of a sufficient degree of continuity and permanence of occupation, of involuntary residence elsewhere, which was satisfactorily explained by objective reasons, and of a persistent intention to return home when possible, as manifested by her regular visits to the Property.

Comment

(1) The 'obvious on a reasonably careful inspection' test was not relied upon by the purchaser. How would it have applied on the facts? Does it provide an adequate response to any concerns that actual occupation is being extended too far?

(2) In *Thompson* v *Foy* [2010] 1 P&CR 308 (approved in *Link Lending*), Lewison J held there would not be actual occupation because the owner did not intend to return. Is it satisfactory that such a subjective factor, also relied upon in *Link Lending*, should be crucial in deciding whether there is actual occupation?

Parking of cars has featured in two cases.

Extract 10.2.35

Epps v Esso Petroleum Co Ltd [1973] 1 WLR 1071

The claimant had an equitable title to a strip of land adjoining his house, but which appeared to be part of the adjoining garage premises. The claimant and his predecessor (Mr Jones) used the strip for car parking.

TEMPLEMAN J: . . . But even if Mr Jones regularly parked his car on the disputed strip I do not consider that this constituted actual occupation of the disputed strip in the circumstances of the present case. I reach this conclusion for the following reasons: first, the parking of a car on a strip 11 feet wide by 80 feet long does not actually occupy the whole, or a substantial, or any defined part of that disputed strip for the whole or any defined time. Secondly, the parking of a car on an unidentified piece of land, apparently comprised in garage premises, is not an assertion of actual occupation of anything.

In addition to these two reasons there are circumstances which show that, not only was Mr Jones not in actual occupation, but on the contrary that the defendants were. First, there is no evidence that Mr Ball or the defendants were ever aware that Mr Jones parked his car on the disputed strip . . . Secondly, the brick wall 4 feet from the house, 4 Darland Avenue, was an assertion that the occupier of Darland Garage occupied land up to that wall, and was just as much in possession of the disputed strip as of any other part of the apparent Darland Garage premises. Thirdly, as appears from the defendants' photographs, there was no method of driving on to the strip from Darland Avenue without trespassing on to the garage premises unless the car in question was bounced up the kerb and steered between a stop sign and a tree . . .

Comment

(1) What would have counted as actual occupation of this strip of land?

(2) How does the decision fit with the provisions in para 2? How do they apply when the occupation is obvious only at certain times of the day (when the car is parked)?

The second car parking case is *Kling* v *Keston Properties Ltd*,[39] though this involved parking in a garage. Vinelott J held in favour of actual occupation 'while he was using it in the ordinary course for the purpose for which the licence was granted, that is, for garaging a car as and when it was convenient for him to do so'. How can *Epps* be distinguished? Might the result be changed by the new requirement for the occupation to be obvious?

This leads to a somewhat related question – can exercise of an easement ever amount to actual occupation?

Extract 10.2.36

Chaudhary v *Yavuz* [2011] EWCA Civ 1314; [2013] Ch 249

Access to a first floor flat was by an exterior metal staircase, attached to the allegedly servient land.

LLOYD LJ: 30.   Mr Gavaghan prayed in aid *Kling* v *Keston Properties Ltd* (1985) 25 P&CR 212 as a stronger case about parking . . . There the use of a garage was held to amount to actual occupation, thereby protecting as an overriding interest a right of pre-emption as regards the garage. However, the use of the garage in that case was under a licence, not an easement, so that case does not assist the Claimant.

31.   In my judgment there was no actual occupation of any part of the metal structure by anyone which could give the Claimant's rights the status of an overriding interest. The judge did not record any findings of fact as to how the metal structure was used at any given time, other than that it was used by the Claimant's tenants to get to and from their flats on the upper floors of number 37 . . . In my judgment such use does not amount to actual occupation. I dare say that no-one else was in occupation of the metal structure either, but not every piece of land is occupied by someone, let alone in someone's actual occupation (as distinct from possession). I do not need to consider the use of the servient land in the case of an easement such as a right to park, where the dominant owner may place a large object on the relevant land and leave it

---

[39] (1984) 49 P&CR 212 at p 219.

there for what may be a substantial time. That issue does not arise on this appeal and I say nothing about it.

Comment

(1) The case illustrates that not everything that is obvious will amount to actual occupation.

(2) As regards *Kling*, why should it matter what right is being claimed over the land in question? Does *Chaudhary* mean that no easement could ever be protected by actual occupation?

Finally in this context, what about derelict land? *Rosset* provides guidance where building work is carried on. Rather more difficult questions are raised by the following case.

Extract 10.2.37

Malory Enterprises Ltd v *Cheshire Homes (UK) Ltd [2002]* Ch 216

ARDEN LJ: 80. That leaves the question whether the judge's finding that Malory BVI was in 'actual occupation' of the rear land is susceptible to review on appeal. The judge's finding involves questions of primary fact and the application of the correct principles to the facts. What constitutes actual occupation of property depends on the nature and state of the property in question, and the judge adopted that approach. If a site is uninhabitable, as the rear land was, residence is not required, but there must be some physical presence, with some degree of permanence and continuity (cf *Strand Securities Ltd* v *Caswell*, above) . . .

82. . . . Nor do I consider that [the judge] was wrong in the circumstances to attach significance to the fencing of the rear land. In this particular case, the fencing cannot be regarded as wholly separate from occupation of the rear land. The fencing was one of the factors relevant to be taken into account. The judge was also right in my judgment to attach significance to the access permitted from the front land. Even though there was another gate, the access from the front land supported the notion that some person connected with the front land claimed a right to be on the rear land. On that basis the question of whether applying those principles there was 'actual occupation' was essentially a question of fact for the judge. At the relevant time, there were derelict buildings on the rear land which meant that it was not possible to occupy it by living in those buildings or by cultivating the land or by using the land for recreation. The judge had to consider other acts denoting occupation such as boarding up the windows of the building and fencing the site (in both cases) to keep vandals and trespassers out, and also using the land for storage. In my judgment, the judge was entitled to draw the conclusion that Malory BVI was in occupation from the facts as found by him, and accordingly, his conclusion cannot be disturbed by this court. Moreover, no-one visiting the rear land at the time of the sale to Cheshire could have drawn the conclusion that the land and buildings on the rear land had been abandoned; the evidence of activity on the site clearly indicated that someone claimed to be entitled to be on it.

Comment

Does this place too much of a burden on purchasers?

A rather different point is that para 2 extends only to the area over which there is actual occupation: this is relevant where there is actual occupation of part only of the land in a title.[40] How does actual occupation operate for extensive properties? Supposing that the owner of a house has never ventured into an orchard forming part of the large garden, how would para 2 apply?

---

[40] See the words 'so far as relating to land of which he is in actual occupation'; this reverses *Ferrishurst Ltd* v *Wallcite Ltd* [1999] Ch 355.

(iv) The time of actual occupation

Must there be actual occupation at the time of completion, or does actual occupation at the time of registration (technically, the time of application to register) suffice? Until e-conveyancing is in effect, there will inevitably be a gap.

The general rule for overriding interests is that they must exist 'at the time of registration'.[41] However, the opening words of para 2 require the occupation to be at the time of the disposition. The reasons for this are found in the following extract based on LRA 1925, which was silent on the point.

Extract 10.2.38

Abbey National BS v Cann **[1991] 1 AC 56**

LORD OLIVER: . . . The case which does give rise to difficulty if the date of registration is the relevant date for determining whether there is a claimant in actual occupation is one in which the sequence of events is that the right, unaccompanied by occupation, is created before completion and before the chargee has advanced his money and then subsequently the claimant enters into actual occupation after completion and remains in occupation up to the date when the registration of the charge is effected. The chargee in that event would have no possibility of discovering the existence of the claimant's interest before advancing his money and taking his charge, but would nevertheless be subject, on registration, to the claimant's prior equitable interest which, ex hypothesi, would not have been subject to the charge at its creation.

Comment

(1) We saw in the previous chapter[42] that acquisition mortgages are protected by the rejection (also in *Cann*) of the *scintilla temporis* doctrine. The effect of this is to rob the time question of much of its significance.

(2) Why is a special rule for para 2 justified? Lord Oliver described taking the registration date as leading to a 'conveyancing absurdity'. Would there be a significant problem for a person buying land?

(3) Would you expect that actual occupation has to be continued up to the time of the litigation?[43]

An unresolved question is whether actual occupation has to exist both at the time of the disposition and the time of registration.

Extract 10.2.39

Thompson v Foy **[2010] 1 P&CR 308**

LEWISON J: 122.   What, to my mind, is less clear is whether, in a case where actual occupation is relied on, there must be actual occupation both at the date of the disposition (April 5 in this case) and also at the date of registration (April 10 in this case). Section 29 contains two requirements:
(i)   The interest must affect the estate immediately before the disposition and
(ii)   The interest must be protected at the time of registration.

---

[41] LRA, ss 11, 12, 29.
[42] See Extract 9.5.1 above.
[43] *See London & Cheshire Insurance Co Ltd* v *Laplagrene Property Co Ltd* [1971] Ch 499.

123.   Where actual occupation is relied on as causing the interest to affect the estate, this suggests that there must be actual occupation both at the date of the disposition and also at the time of registration. Paragraph 2 of Sch 3 begins with the words:

'An interest belonging at the time of the disposition to a person in actual occupation.'

124.   If it had been intended that actual occupation at the time of the disposition was the sole criterion, the phrase would more naturally have read:

'An interest belonging to a person in actual occupation at the time of the disposition.'

125.   As written, the phrase can be read as tying the 'belonging' to the date of the disposition, while leaving at large the date of actual occupation. The relevant date of actual occupation would then be determined by s 29, so that actual occupation at the date of the disposition would be required in order for the right to affect the estate immediately before the disposition; and actual occupation at the date of registration would be required in order for that interest to be protected at the time of registration.

126.   It is fair to say that neither party adopted this construction; and the text books are against it: Ruoff & Roper on *Registered Conveyancing* paras 15.009 and 17.013; Gray & Gray on *Land Law* para 8.2.50. I will therefore leave the point to a case in which it needs to be decided. . . .

Comment

How persuasive is the reasoning of Lewison J?

(v) Statutory protections and exclusions

Purchasers are protected if inquiry is made of the occupier, but the right is not disclosed. This is a crucial provision, as in most cases purchasers can do no more than make inquiries of occupiers. The condition that the occupier 'could reasonably have been expected' to disclose the right is new in the 2002 Act. Is it likely to have a significant effect?

Four statutory exclusions from para 2 should be noted: statutory home possession rights,[44] beneficial interests under old Settled Land Act settlements,[45] future leases and rights to 'overriding leases' (a confusing label) under the Landlord and Tenant (Covenants) Act 1995.[46] Home possession rights and future leases are the most interesting: why are they excluded from para 2?

Para 3: easements

(1)   A legal easement or profit a prendre, except for an easement, or a profit a prendre which is not registered under the Commons Registration Act 1965 (c. 64), which at the time of the disposition—
   (a)   is not within the actual knowledge of the person to whom the disposition is made, and
   (b)   would not have been obvious on a reasonably careful inspection of the land over which the easement or profit is exercisable.

(2)   The exception in sub-paragraph (1) does not apply if the person entitled to the easement or profit proves that it has been exercised in the period of one year ending with the day of the disposition.

---

[44]   Family Law Act 1996, s 31(10).
[45]   There is no equivalent under the trust of land regime in the Trusts of Land and Appointment of Trustees Act 1996.
[46]   Section 20(6) of the 1995 Act.

This provision is markedly different from the pre-2002 law. It clearly excludes equitable easements and profits. This ensures that easements which constitute registrable dispositions have to be entered on the register if they are to bind purchasers of the servient land. Which legal easements are not registrable dispositions (and therefore fall within para 3)? Note that easements pre-dating first registration will also fall within para 3.

The protection of purchasers against easements which are not obvious on a reasonably careful inspection was introduced by the 2002 Act. What sorts of easements is this likely to apply to? Note that the easement will still be protected if exercised within the past year. What benefits and dangers may be expected as a result of these provisions? Schedule 12, para 9 ensures that overriding interest easements pre-dating the 2002 Act fall outside the new rule. How significant is this saving of vested rights?

Reducing overriding interests

We have considered paras 1–3: the most interesting categories. A further seven are listed in Sched 3. The result is a reduction in the numbers of overriding interests – partly a matter of substance (for example, adverse possession ceases to be a separate category) and partly a matter of form (for example, qualified, possessory and good leasehold titles are explicitly provided for in ss 11, 12 and 29). Six other categories (franchises, manorial rights, Crown rents, liability in respect of embankments or sea or river walls, payments in lieu of tithe, chancel repair liability) survived for ten years until 2013, as stipulated in the 2002 Act.

Rather differently, there is a more concerted attempt to bring overriding interests on to the register. Thus those seeking registration are required to disclose overriding interests.[47] The registrar has authority to enter notice of these (and other) interests.

Considering the changes to individual overriding interests and the points mentioned in this section, how justified is the claim of the Law Commission[48] that 'the range of overriding interests will be significantly reduced in their scope'?

3. Alteration

Alteration is the amendment of the register under statutory powers. The 2002 legislation is quite different from the previous law, more so here than in most areas of registration of title.

A. Terminology

In the previous law, this area was known as rectification. Rectification is today a subdivision of alteration. LRA, Sched 4 deals with alteration. Para 1 provides that:

> In this Schedule, references to rectification, in relation to alteration of the register, are to alteration which – (a) involves the correction of a mistake, and (b) prejudicially affects the title of a registered proprietor.

The important point to grasp is that the title must be prejudicially affected for there to be rectification. If the alteration gives effect to existing rights then it is not rectification: this is further explained in Extract 10.3.3 below. Perhaps the most compelling example is where a purchaser is bound by an overriding interest. Giving effect to the overriding interest by

---

[47] Land Registration Rules 2003, rr 28, 57.
[48] Law Com No 271, para 1.14.

an entry on the register will be alteration but not rectification: the purchaser is already bound by the interest and so is not prejudicially affected by the alteration.

We will see that the distinction permeates the provisions both on alteration and indemnity. A general point to consider about alteration is that it has the potential to be an important qualification upon the protection of registered dispositions accorded by the registration scheme. Is this issue relevant to alterations generally or rectification alone?

B. Grounds for alteration

Extract 10.3.1

Land Registration Act 2002, Sched 4, Para 2

2   (1)   The court may make an order for alteration of the register for the purpose of—
   (a)   correcting a mistake,
   (b)   bringing the register up to date, or
   (c)   giving effect to any estate, right or interest excepted from the effect of registration.

Extract 10.3.2

Law Commission No 254: Land Registration for the Twenty First Century

8.38   The yardstick for determining whether there is an error or omission is, in some cases, the position that would have existed had title not been registered. There are a number of objections to this. First, there is the risk that it may bring into play aspects of unregistered land, such as the doctrine of notice and the registration of land charges, which the registered system was meant to supersede. The difficulty with this approach is to know just how much of the unregistered system is brought into play. Secondly, as the great majority of titles are now registered, it is inappropriate, particularly as the principles of unregistered conveyancing are becoming unfamiliar to practitioners. Thirdly, it is unnecessary. The existence of an error or omission can be readily defined according to the principles of registered conveyancing.

8.41   As we have indicated, rectification is an issue where the register is in some way incorrect. We consider that rectification should be confined to that situation.

Extract 10.3.3

Law Commission No 271: Land Registration for the Twenty First Century: A Conveyancing Revolution[49]

3.47   [In relation to a claim by A falling outside the categories in LRA, s 11 which bind C on first registration] A will not be able to seek alteration of the register because C is not bound by her rights and there is, therefore, no mistake in the register that requires rectification.

10.7   The principal differences [relative to the previous law] may be summarised as follows—
(1)   Rectification is confined to cases where a mistake is to be corrected. This will not include every case which is at present treated as rectification. It will not therefore cover cases where the register is altered to give effect to rights that have been acquired over the land since it was registered,[i] or where the register was originally correct, but subsequent events have made it incorrect.[ii] In such cases the court will no longer have any discretion (albeit one that has seldom been exercised) whether or not to give effect to the right so established.
(2)   Not every correction of a mistake will constitute rectification. The correction must be one which prejudicially affects the title of a registered proprietor. Under the 1925 Act, if, in order to

---

[49] Selected footnotes reproduced.

correct a mistake, the register is altered to give effect to an overriding interest, that is regarded as rectification.[iii] However, no indemnity will be payable because the proprietor will suffer no loss in consequence. He or she had taken the land subject to any overriding interests. Rectification in such a case therefore does no more than update the title and the registered proprietor is in no worse position than he or she was before. In other words, there can be rectification under the present law even where an alteration to the register does *not* prejudicially affect the title of the registered proprietor. That will cease to be so under the Bill. The circumstances in which the register is rectified and those in which the proprietor will be entitled to an indemnity will coincide.

[i] As where a court determines that X has acquired an easement by prescription over Y's land subsequent to Y's acquisition of that land as registered proprietor.

[ii] As where A was registered as proprietor, but B subsequently obtains an order setting aside the transfer to A on the grounds that A procured it by fraud on B.

[iii] See *Chowood Ltd v Lyall (No 2)* [1930] 2 Ch 156. In that case the mistake was to register X as proprietor of land when Y had already acquired title to it by adverse possession: see *ibid*, at p 168.

Comment

(1) Powers to alter are conferred by Sched 4, para 2. The registrar is given similar powers by para 5, extending also to the administrative act of removing superfluous entries.

(2) Sub-paragraphs (b) and (c) of para 2 may be seen as essentially administrative acts: plainly no significant change in legal rights is involved.

(3) Most interesting is the correction of mistakes, especially where there is no overriding interest. Could there be correction of a mistake in the following examples (mainly taken from cases on the previous law)?

(a) the wrong person is registered as proprietor;[50]
(b) the transfer to the present proprietor (who is in good faith) was forged;
(c) the transfer to the present proprietor was obtained by undue influence or misrepresentation;
(d) some adverse claim was overlooked on first registration of the land;[51]
(e) a squatter has been registered in circumstances in which the squatter had not been in adverse possession.[52]

(4) It will be recalled that rectification involves the correction of a mistake, where the title of the proprietor is prejudicially affected. It is easy to contemplate cases where correcting a mistake is not rectification – for example, where it gives effect to an overriding interest. Where there can be alteration in the examples considered in (3), would this constitute rectification?

(5) The philosophy of the Law Commission, most clearly seen in Law Com 254, is to move away from unregistered land principles. Is this feasible, whether as regards first registration or registered dispositions? Is it achieved by Sched 4? Contrast the approach of Lady Hale (in a different context) in *Mortgage Business plc v O'Shaughnessy* [2014] 3 WLR 1163 at [96]: 'the system of land registration is merely conveyancing machinery. The underlying law relating to the creation of estates and interests in land remains the same'.

(6) For alteration which is not rectification, the Law Commission makes it clear that alteration should be automatic, without any discretion being exercised. Why should this be?

[50] A disastrous example of this is found in *Parshall v Hackney* [2013] Ch 568 where two people were each (inconsistently) registered as proprietor of the same plot.

[51] This was the substance of a successful claim in *Sainsbury's Supermarkets Ltd v Olympia Homes Ltd* [2006] 1 P&CR 289.

[52] *Baxter v Mannion* [2011] 1 WLR 1594.

C. The proprietor in possession

Extract 10.3.4

Land Registration Act 2002, Sched 4, para 3, s 115

3   (1)   This paragraph applies to the power under paragraph 2, so far as relating to rectification.

(2)   If alteration affects the title of the proprietor of a registered estate in land, no order may be made under paragraph 2 without the proprietor's consent in relation to land in his possession unless—

(a)   he has by fraud or lack of proper care caused or substantially contributed to the mistake, or

(b)   it would for any other reason be unjust for the alteration not to be made.

(3)   If in any proceedings the court has power to make an order under paragraph 2, it must do so, unless there are exceptional circumstances which justify its not doing so.

. . .

115.—(1)   For the purposes of this Act, land is in the possession of the proprietor of a registered estate in land if it is physically in his possession, or in that of a person who is entitled to be registered as the proprietor of the registered estate.

(2)   In the case of the following relationships, land which is (or is treated as being) in the possession of the second-mentioned person is to be treated for the purposes of subsection (1) as in the possession of the first-mentioned person—

(a)   landlord and tenant;

(b)   mortgagor and mortgagee;

(c)   licensor and licensee;

(d)   trustee and beneficiary.

(3)   In subsection (1), the reference to entitlement does not include entitlement under Schedule 6.

Comment

(1) Why should proprietors in possession receive special protection? It should be remembered that whoever loses may be entitled to compensation ('indemnity') under LRA, Sched 8.

(2) Why is the protection limited to cases of rectification?

(3) It has sometimes been suggested that the provision relating to lack of proper care (para 3(2)(a); in its present form since 1977) could require purchasers to make the sorts of enquiries appropriate for unregistered land. This is not borne out by the cases so far, but would it be undesirable?

(4) Why should para 3(3) *require* rectification (absent exceptional circumstances) once there is power to rectify?

(5) The definition of possession is introduced for the first time by the 2002 Act. Why should possession be given the extended meaning in s 115(2)? How many proprietors will not be in possession?

Extract 10.3.5

***Hounslow London Borough Council v Hare* (1992) 24 HLR 9**

A long lease was void under charities legislation but was nevertheless registered. Should the register be rectified to delete the lease?

KNOX J: . . . The other decision which is of assistance is *Epps* v *Esso Petroleum* [1973] 1 WLR 1071 where there was in fact registration twice over, a double registration, and Templeman J discussed the basis upon which he should exercise the discretion that is conferred by this jurisdiction . . . The learned Judge, for reasons that it is quite unnecessary to go into, came to the conclusion that the defendants were in possession and at page 1080 he observed:

> 'There remains the question, under condition (c) of section 82(3) of whether it would be unjust not to rectify against the defendants.'

. . . The conclusion of the learned Judge was that whereas the defendants bought the disputed strip, the plaintiffs bought a law suit, thanks to the fault of their vendor in not taking steps to assert ownership and possession of the disputed strip and thanks to the failure of the plaintiffs to make before completion inquiries which they made immediately after completion. He then dealt with arguments about the availability of compensation and there was a very substantial difference in time between the dates for valuation as between the two paragraphs of section 83(6) which gave that particular distinction more weight, but at the end of the day in the particular circumstances of that case he came to the conclusion that it was not enough to outweigh the considerations going in the opposite direction. In particular he came to the conclusion that the problem facing him could not be solved merely on the question of money. In that case he took into account the fact that the defendants had bought the land for a commercial purpose and that commercial purpose would be prejudiced by the grant of rectification against them and on that basis he declined to order rectification.

The facts, of course, of the case were quite different, but there are certain features of it which do have an echo in this case. In particular there can be no doubt in my mind that Miss Hare was not only an innocent party in the sense that there was no way which I can discern that she could have known that there was the problem that emerged, based on the existence of the charitable trusts in the testatrix's will, either personally or through her solicitor . . .

. . . What I have primarily, as I see it, to look at is whether it is considered that it would be unjust not to rectify the register against Miss Hare and I cannot reach that conclusion. She has been in possession of this property for a very long time . . . just as Templeman J held that money was not the only consideration in the *Epps* v *Esso Petroleum* case so *a fortiori* it seems to me that when one is dealing with a person's home the change from the near equivalent of freehold that a 125 year lease gives to somebody of the age of nearing forty to that of a tenant, assured or not, is one of very considerable significance . . .

Comment

(1) The claim to an overriding interest in *Epps* was considered above.[53]

(2) In each of *Hare* and *Epps*, the rectification claim failed. How strong must a claim be to satisfy para 3(2)(b)?

D. Subsequent dealings and the effect of rectification

If rectification substitutes A for B as proprietor, it is pretty clear what the impact on A and B will be. But what happens if B has mortgaged or leased the land to C? Similar points may arise where B has sold the land to C. This has caused considerable difficulty and controversy in recent years, especially where C is registered.

There are at least two ways in which the problem may be viewed. The first is that we may ask whether there is an independent right to rectify against C. This requires that the

---

[53] See Extract 10.2.35 above.

registration of C must be a 'mistake'. The difficulty is that, at the time of the disposition to C, B was the registered proprietor. Given the powers of the proprietor (LRA, s 23; Extract 10.2.4 above), it is difficult to argue that the registration of C was a mistake.[54] The second argument is that rectification against B opens up the possibility of consequential rectification affecting C – without any independent mistake having to be proved. As we shall see, this appears to be the way forward.

Before considering this further, we should note a pre-2002 decision which involved a situation in which C was not registered. *Freer v Unwins Ltd*[55] involved a restrictive covenant omitted from the register. The proprietor subsequently granted an overriding interest lease. Following rectification of the landlord's title, the question arose as to whether this also affected the tenant. Walton J held, after considering provisions in the legislation which have no direct equivalent in the 2002 Act, that the rectification did not affect the lease. The underlying analysis was that nothing in the legislation gave the entry retrospective effect, as would be necessary to bind earlier interests.

We should now turn to the 2002 Act.

Extract 10.3.6

Land Registration Act 2002, Sched 4, para 8
Law Commission No 271: Land Registration for the Twenty First Century:
A Conveyancing Revolution (footnotes omitted)

8   The powers under this Schedule to alter the register, so far as relating to rectification, extend to changing for the future the priority of any interest affecting the registered estate or charge concerned.

LAW COMMISSION: 10.8   The Bill makes it clear that—
(1)   rectification of the register, whether by order of the court or by the register can (as now) affect derivative interests; but
(2)   any such changes are prospective only, which accords with the manner in which the analogous provisions of the Land Registration Act 1925 have been interpreted.

Comment

This would not have affected *Freer*, given that the rectification did not purport to change the priority of the overriding interest lease. When rectification is ordered, it may well not be known whether there are such interests: the provision is much more likely to be invoked when an interest is either registered or protected by notice.

Extract 10.3.7

Gold Harp Properties Ltd v *Macleod* [2014] EWCA Civ 1084

Rectification was ordered to restore to the register a lease (Lease 1), wrongly removed from the register in the belief that it had been forfeited. The rectification decision provided that Lease 1 should have priority over another lease (Lease 2) registered in the intervening period.

UNDERHILL LJ: 37.   Mr Brown submitted that those passages [in *Freer*] constituted plain statements that rectification under the 1925 Act could not have retrospective effect. However

---

[54] Supported by *Norwich and Peterborough Building Society* v *Steed* [1993] Ch 116 and *Barclays Bank plc* v *Guy* [2008] 2 EGLR 74.
[55] [1976] Ch 288.

they have to be read in the context of the matters in dispute. . . . rectification had already occurred . . . Walton J does in fact contemplate that if the purchasers had had a registered leasehold interest the Court would have had jurisdiction to rectify in such a way that they were bound by the covenant . . .

40.   The reasoning in *Argyle Building Society* v *Hammond* [(1984) 49 P&CR 148] makes it clear that under the 1925 Act, where the proprietor of a registered interest had been mistakenly removed from the Register, the power to rectify extended to the removal of a competing interest which had been duly registered at a time when the first interest did not appear on the Register . . .

42.   . . . The Court [in *Norwich and Peterborough Building Society* v *Steed* [1993] Ch 116] held that the circumstances of the case did not fall within any of the heads of section 82 (1). Scott LJ held that the intention of heads (d)-(h) was 'to enable errors to be corrected' (see p. 134 G-H); but the registration of the charge was not an error because the transfer to the Hammonds was only voidable and had not at the material time been avoided (p. 135 A-C). . . .

50.   . . . Arden LJ [in *Malory Enterprises Ltd* v *Cheshire Homes (UK) Ltd* [2002] Ch 216] expressed the view that the rectification ordered by the Judge was not simply unnecessary, which followed from her primary ratio, but wrong, because the Court had no jurisdiction under section 82 to order rectification with retrospective effect.

51.   Clarke and Schiemann LJJ declined to endorse that part of Arden LJ's reasoning, pointing out that it was not necessary to the disposal of the appeal. . . .

65.   There is nothing in the drafting of the bill or its exposition in the 2001 report to suggest any change from the thinking in the 1998 consultation paper as summarised above, namely that the effect of section 82 (2) should be preserved but on the basis that any changes should be 'prospective only'.

71.   . . . Lord Neuberger MR did say this [in *Barclays Bank plc* v *Guy (No 2)* [2011] 1 WLR 681], at para 35 (p 687 F):

> 'It . . . seems clear that Lloyd LJ's analysis proceeded on the basis that the alleged "mistake" for the purposes of para 2 (1) of schedule 4 to the 2002 Act was the registration of the Charge in the charges registers. However, there are other ways of putting Mr Guy's case, namely (a) that the removal of his name from the proprietorship register was a mistake, and, in order to correct that mistake, the Charge would have to be removed from the charges register, or (b) that the registration of the Charge flowed from the mistake of registering the Transfer, and therefore should be treated as part and parcel of that mistake.'

As will be seen, those potential other ways of analysing the issue have been picked up in the more recent case-law.

The Deputy Adjudicator Decisions

83.   Those cases fall into two groups. Two of them – *Piper Trust* [*Piper Trust Ltd* v *Caruso (UK) Ltd* [2010] EWLandRA 2009/0623] and *DB* [*DB UK Bank Ltd* v *Santander UK plc* [2012] EWLandRA 2011/1169] – are explicitly concerned with the question of priority, and in both the Adjudicators held that they were precluded by the terms of paragraph 8 of Schedule 4 from making an order giving the wrongly de-registered but now reinstated charge priority over a charge created during the period of mistaken de-registration. They are thus closely analogous to the present case and support Mr Brown's submission. The other three – *Ajibade* [*Ajibade* v *Bank of Scotland plc* [2008] EWLandRA 2006/0613], *Stewart* [*Stewart* v *Lancashire Mortgage Corporation* [2010] EWLandRA 2009/86] and *Knights Construction* [*Knights Construction (March) Ltd* v *Roberto Mac Ltd* [2011] 2 EGLR 124] – are all (like *Guy*) concerned with the different question of whether the power to correct the original mistake extends, by one route or another, to correcting the consequences of that mistake by the removal of the later-created interest. They were not concerned with priority between derivative interests. I do not, however, believe that they are for that reason irrelevant, for reasons which I will give in due course.

91.   I have concluded that the Judge was entitled to make the order that he did. My reasons are as follows.

92.   It is useful to start by spelling out the essentials of the situation in which paragraph 8, whatever its effect, is intended to apply. It is a situation in which at the point of rectification there are two competing derivative interests – A and B. Interest A has been mistakenly omitted or removed from the Register, but that mistake is to be corrected by its reinstatement. Subject to the effect of the rectification, interest B would have priority: otherwise the question of changing priorities would not arise. It is important to appreciate that the only reason why that would be so is because interest B was created before (obviously) the restoration of interest A to the Register but after the date of its mistaken omission or removal.

93.   The primary effect of paragraph 8 is to confirm that the power of the Court or Registrar in that situation is not limited to restoring interest A to the Register but 'extends' to changing what would otherwise be the priority as between it and interest B – in other words, to giving it the priority which it should have had but for the mistake. The words 'for the future' no doubt qualify that power – the question being in what way – but that is the context in which they fall to be interpreted.

94.   The Appellant's case has to be, and is, that the effect of the words 'for the future' is that if interest B has been registered after the mistake but before the rectification, and thus would otherwise enjoy priority, that priority cannot be altered: an alteration to a priority which already exists cannot be described as an alteration 'for the future'. But if that is right then their effect is to prevent the Court from changing priorities in the very situation which paragraph 8 is intended to address. There is no problem of competing priorities once the rectification has been achieved. The only priorities that could be changed relate, necessarily, to interests which have already been created.

95.   It is worth recalling that Schedule 4 is concerned with 'correcting' mistakes in the Register, and it is established by the decisions to which I have referred that the power to do so extends to correcting the consequences of such mistakes. It should be noted that that power is in some circumstances a duty: see paragraph 3 (3). The Appellant's construction would mean that in all cases where derivative interests have been created during the period of mistaken de-registration that correction would be less than complete and that in some cases, such as the present, it would be valueless.

96.   Quiet [sic] apart from those points, the Appellant's construction does not correspond to the words actually used in the statute. What paragraph 8 permits (for the future) is 'changing the priority' of an interest. What an interest having priority means is that the owner can exercise the rights which he enjoys by virtue of that interest to the exclusion of any inconsistent rights of the owner of the competing interest. The concept of priority thus bites at the moment that those rights are sought to be enjoyed. Once that is appreciated the effect of the words 'for the future' seems to me straightforward. They mean that the beneficiary of the change in priority – that is, the person whose interest has been restored to the Register – can exercise his rights as owner of that interest, to the exclusion of the rights of the owner of the competing interest, as from the moment that the order is made, but that he cannot be treated as having been entitled to do so up to that point. The distinction can be illustrated by the facts of this case. The effect of the Judge's order is that thenceforward the Claimants were entitled to exercise their rights as leaseholders – primarily, that is, their rights to occupy the roofspace – to the exclusion of Gold Harp. But until that point they had no such right: they could not, for example, claim mesne profits from Gold Harp or its predecessors in respect of any occupation (though in fact there was none) up to that date. . . .

98.   I see no difficulty with this construction on policy grounds. It is true that it means that the indefeasibility of the Register is qualified to a greater extent than would be the case on Mr Brown's construction. But, as all the Law Commission reports acknowledge, the Act was not intended to provide for absolute indefeasibility. Schedule 4 explicitly recognises that the rectification has the potential to prejudice the interests of third parties who have relied in good

faith on the Register. The carefully structured provisions of paragraphs 2 and 3 (and their equivalents in the case of rectification by the Registrar), with the special protection given to a proprietor in possession, allow a fair balance between the competing interests to be struck in any particular case; and Schedule 8 gives the loser the right to an indemnity.

Comment

(1) The tenant of Lease 2 was associated (by family relation and corporate control) with the freeholder who had instigated the wrongful removal of Lease 1. The merits of the dispute seem distinctly to favour Lease 1.

(2) The analysis of *Hammond* is problematic because the 1925 legislation provided a direct right to rectify the competing interest where there has been a void transfer (this is not clearly replicated in the 2002 Act). If so, does this affect the conclusion?

(3) *Steed* is seen as distinguishing between void and voidable transfers (replicating the common law analysis for unregistered land). Does this survive into the 2002 Act? Should it?[56]

(4) Underhill LJ recognises that his analysis differs from that of some (but not all) prominent authors. Should this concern us? Is his interpretation of 'for the future' the most obvious one?

(5) Remember that the intervening registration will often be protected by the provisions favouring a proprietor in possession. Is this an adequate protection for a proprietor who claims that dealing with a registered proprietor should be sufficient to ensure an indefeasible title?

(6) One good consequence of the decision is that it avoids the spectre of an innocent proprietor (whose title has been affected by forgery or other mistake) being unable to seek rectification or indemnity – this was a risk when the loss was caused by the intervening registration, if that registration could not be rectified.[57]

4. Indemnity

Potentially, indemnity is one of the great advantages possessed by registered land. It enables an innocent party to gain compensation if some error is made in the conveyancing process. Registration cannot completely avoid the problem that some innocent parties will lose property rights, but it can offer financial recompense.

A. Rights to indemnity

Extract 10.4.1

Land Registration Act 2002, Sched 8, paras 1, 11

1 (1) A person is entitled to be indemnified by the registrar if he suffers loss by reason of—
    (a) rectification of the register,
    (b) a mistake whose correction would involve rectification of the register,
    (c) a mistake in an official search,
    (d) a mistake in an official copy,
    (e) a mistake in a document kept by the registrar which is not an original and is referred to in the register,

---

[56] Note the doubts expressed by Jacob LJ in *Baxter v Mannion* [2011] 1 WLR 1594 at [31].
[57] Cf Lees (2013) 76 MLR 62.

(f)   the loss or destruction of a document lodged at the registry for inspection or safe custody,

(g)   a mistake in the cautions register, or

(h)   failure by the registrar to perform his duty under section 50.

(2)   For the purposes of sub-paragraph (1)(a)—

(a)   any person who suffers loss by reason of the change of title under section 62 is to be regarded as having suffered loss by reason of rectification of the register, and

(b)   the proprietor of a registered estate or charge claiming in good faith under a forged disposition is, where the register is rectified, to be regarded as having suffered loss by reason of such rectification as if the disposition had not been forged.

(3)   No indemnity under sub-paragraph (1)(b) is payable until a decision has been made about whether to alter the register for the purpose of correcting the mistake; and the loss suffered by reason of the mistake is to be determined in the light of that decision.

11   (1)   For the purposes of this Schedule, references to a mistake in something include anything mistakenly omitted from it as well as anything mistakenly included in it.

(2)   In this Schedule, references to rectification of the register are to alteration of the register which—

(a)   involves the correction of a mistake, and

(b)   prejudicially affects the title of a registered proprietor.

Comment

(1) Grounds (c)–(h) cover various administrative errors and need not be considered further. Most interesting are grounds (a) and (b). They show that the central requirement is that there be a mistake which requires rectification to be corrected. If rectification is ordered, then the affected proprietor is entitled to indemnity. If the rectification claim fails (perhaps because the proprietor is in possession), then the claimant can claim indemnity.

(2) Should the policy of the law be to expand rectification, in order that indemnity is more readily available?

(3) Suppose a purchaser is bound by an overriding interest.[58] What will be the consequences as regards alteration/rectification and indemnity?

(4) Why is indemnity not available for alterations not amounting to rectification?

In the 1980s, the Law Commission proposed[59] compensation for those bound by overriding interests. Given the need for claimants not to be at fault (discussed below), it was unclear just what impact this change would have had. There have now been second thoughts.

Extract 10.4.2

Law Commission No 254: Land Registration for the Twenty First Century

4.19   The [proposal] was that indemnity should be payable when the register is rectified to give effect to an overriding interest. There is undoubtedly a strong case for this proposal. If overriding interests are not discoverable on inspection they can work great hardship on purchasers and the system of registered title – which is supposed to increase the security of title – can be seen to fail them. Nevertheless, this proposal has proved to be the major stumbling block to the acceptance of the Third and Fourth Reports, however desirable many other proposals in those

---

[58] For the previous law (not significantly different), see *Re Chowood's Registered Land* [1933] Ch 574.
[59] Law Com No 158, paras 2.10–2.14.

Reports might be. We consider that, notwithstanding its attractions, it is open to a number of serious practical objections—

(1) It would create an open-ended financial liability. The extent of this liability would be incapable of prediction but it might be considerable. The cost would have to be borne by all users of the Land Registry. It would undoubtedly increase registration fees and thereby detract significantly from the attractiveness of land registration.

(2) The potential liability would never end. There would be no final extinction of overriding interests or prohibition on their creation.

(3) It would mark a significant change in the concept of indemnity. Hitherto indemnity has been paid for those errors in the register which cause loss. Where the register is rectified to give effect to an overriding interest, the change does no more than reflect the reality of the title.

Comment

(1) How convincing are these objections? One relevant factor is that the present annual cost of indemnity is around £8–10 million as compared to fee income of around £350 million.

(2) How well does the third point fit with the purpose of indemnity?

Paragraph 1(2)(b) operates where there has been a forgery. Its operation has raised awkward questions.

Extract 10.4.3

Swift 1st Ltd v *Chief Land Registrar* [2014] All ER (D) 12 (Feb)

RICHARD SHELDON QC: 30.   I now turn to consider . . . the indemnity provisions in Schedule 8 of LRA 2002. The Registrar's argument is that entitlement to an indemnity only arises if there has been a 'rectification' within the meaning of Schedule 8 paragraph 11, namely an alteration which involves the correction of a mistake 'and prejudicially affects the title of a registered proprietor'. If *Malory* and *Fitzwilliam* were to apply, in the case of a forged disposition, the original registered proprietor retains beneficial ownership and the new registered proprietor only acquires the legal estate but without acquiring any beneficial ownership. It would follow that alteration of the register by removal of the entry will 'affect' the title of the new registered proprietor, but not 'prejudicially' so as it merely makes the register correspond with the underlying legal position . . . As Mr Morshead frankly accepted, that would make Schedule 8 paragraph l(2)(b) a dead letter because the innocent person claiming through a forged disposition and registered as proprietor could never claim an indemnity as there would never be a 'rectification' as defined in paragraph 11. It is clear that this was not intended: see paragraph 10.31 of the Proposals. If correct, the position would revert to that found by the Court of Appeal in *Re Odell* ([1906] 2 Ch 47 which was specifically reversed by statute and clearly no further change was intended.

33.   Swift's argument . . . [relies] on the deeming provision in paragraph 1(2)(b) (ie Swift is 'to be regarded as having suffered loss by reason of such rectification as if the disposition had not been forged'). Swift argues that this statutory hypothesis applies for the purposes of paragraph 1(a) ('rectification of the register'), including the issue of whether there has been a 'rectification' within paragraph 1(a) as amplified by paragraph 11(2). On the footing that Swift has 'suffered loss by reason of such rectification as if the disposition had not been forged', the alteration to the register 'prejudicially affects' Swift's title.

34.   However, Mr Morshead points to a number of factors which he suggests shows that Swift's argument is incorrect.

35.   . . . Swift's argument has the merit of achieving one consequence, which was plainly intended when Schedule 8 was enacted, namely of continuing the reversal of the effect of the decision in *Re Odell* (see paragraph 10.31(2) of the Proposals cited above). I also consider that,

whilst the relevant provisions could have been more clearly drafted, in the case of a registered proprietor claiming in good faith under a forged disposition, the concept of a 'prejudicial' effect of an alteration to the register in paragraph 11 (2)(b) cannot be separated from the issue of loss under paragraphs 1(1)(a) and paragraph 1(2)(b) in the manner suggested by the Registrar. . . .

36. The second factor to which Mr Morshead referred as suggesting Swift's argument must be wrong was that it would run counter to the general principle that registration is always subject to overriding interests at the date of the disposition, and that no indemnity is payable where the register is 'altered' to give effect to an overriding interest (see *Re Chowood's Registered Land* [1933] Ch 574). Why, he asks, should there be an exception in the case of a forged disposition? In support of these arguments he relied heavily on the Proposals which I have cited earlier. I would also accept that there is force in this second factor. It seems clear from the Proposals that the existing law, namely that a person could not claim an indemnity when the register was rectified to give effect to an overriding interest, was not intended to be changed.

39. I nevertheless find, though with some doubt, that Swift's position is to be preferred. It is clear from the passages in the Proposals dealing with indemnity that an exception is made in a case where a registered proprietor is claiming in good faith under a forged disposition. Exception is therefore made, at least to some extent, for forged dispositions. It also seems to me that the change in the wording to which I have referred in paragraph 25 above may bear on this point. Under the 1925 LRA, s 83(4), a registered proprietor claiming in good faith under a forged disposition is deemed to have suffered loss by reason of rectification. That leaves open the question of what loss was suffered, and a claim for an indemnity could in such a case, it would appear, be defeated or reduced by an existing overriding interest (*Re Chowood*). The wording of paragraph 1(2)(b) of Schedule 8 of the 2002 adds to the phrase 'is to be regarded as having suffered loss by reason of such rectification' the words 'as if the disposition had not been forged'. Giving effect to these added words, the loss suffered by a registered proprietor claiming in good faith under a forged disposition is now to be determined on the basis that the disposition had not been forged. On that basis, the overriding interests of the purported disponor could not be set up to reduce or defeat the claim.

Comment

(1) Is the drafting of para 1(2)(b) defective? Does the judge respond to the problem in the most appropriate manner?

(2) Does the overriding interest point follow from the wording of para 1(2)(b)? Does it make sense in policy terms?

(3) Is there a sufficient reason for singling out forgery as a special case for protecting proprietors?

(4) Should this make us more or less inclined to accept the *Fitzwilliam* analysis (Extract 10.2.6 above) as to the effect of forgery?

B. Restrictions on indemnity

Extract 10.4.4

Land Registration Act 2002, Sched 8, paras 5–6, 8–10

5 (1) No indemnity is payable under this Schedule on account of any loss suffered by a claimant—

    (a) wholly or partly as a result of his own fraud, or

    (b) wholly as a result of his own lack of proper care.

(2) Where any loss is suffered by a claimant partly as a result of his own lack of proper care, any indemnity payable to him is to be reduced to such extent as is fair having regard to his share in the responsibility for the loss.

(3) For the purposes of this paragraph any fraud or lack of care on the part of a person from whom the claimant derives title (otherwise than under a disposition for valuable consideration which is registered or protected by an entry in the register) is to be treated as if it were fraud or lack of care on the part of the claimant.

6 Where an indemnity is payable in respect of the loss of an estate, interest or charge, the value of the estate, interest or charge for the purposes of the indemnity is to be regarded as not exceeding—

    (a) in the case of an indemnity under paragraph 1(1)(a), its value immediately before rectification of the register (but as if there were to be no rectification), and

    (b) in the case of an indemnity under paragraph 1(1)(b), its value at the time when the mistake which caused the loss was made.

8 For the purposes of the Limitation Act 1980 (c. 58)—

    (a) a liability to pay an indemnity under this Schedule is a simple contract debt, and

    (b) the cause of action arises at the time when the claimant knows, or but for his own default might have known, of the existence of his claim.

9 Rules may make provision about the payment of interest on an indemnity under this Schedule, . . .

10 (1) Where an indemnity under this Schedule is paid to a claimant in respect of any loss, the registrar is entitled (without prejudice to any other rights he may have)—

    (a) to recover the amount paid from any person who caused or substantially contributed to the loss by his fraud, or

    . . .

Two areas are worthy of note. The exclusion of claims by careless claimants is unsurprising, though it nibbles away at the idea of indemnity being a form of insurance. Contributory negligence ideas (para 5(2)) were introduced by the Land Registration Act 1997. Lightman J has said that indemnity will be excluded only if:[60]

> the significance and causative effect of the claimant's lack of proper care was such that the loss should be regarded as wholly the result of that lack of care: section 83(5). For this purpose it will only rarely be sufficient to establish that the Land Registry error would not have caused the loss 'but for' the claimant's lack of care: see *Dean v Dean* [(2000) 80 P&CR 457].

Para 6(b) limits the claim to the value of the land at the time of the error or omission. This means that the claimant is limited to an out of date valuation of land that has been lost by a mistaken registration (assuming no rectification), even though the mistake is undiscoverable.

Extract 10.4.5

Law Commission No 235: Transfer of Land: Land Registration

4.6 At present, in any case in which rectification is not ordered, indemnity is assessed by reference to the value of the land at the time when the error or omission which caused the loss occurred. Formerly this limitation was the cause of some injustice, and in the Third Report it was

---

[60] *Prestige Properties Ltd* v *Scottish Provident Institution* [2003] Ch 1 at [36].

recommended that it should be abolished. If this were implemented, it would mean that indemnity would be assessed on the basis of the value of the land at the time at which the decision not to rectify was made. However, the Land Registry considered that although this would take into account the effects of inflation or deflation, it would not provide an accurate measure of indemnity in all cases. Thus it might be the case that since the error or omission occurred, the value of the land had either increased due to construction work, or decreased because a building was destroyed by fire. It is now the practice of the Registry when settling by agreement claims for indemnity, to include appropriate interest on the sum assessed under section 83(6) . . . This payment of interest does of course compensate for any inflationary increase in the value of land.

4.7   We therefore recommend that there should be no change to the present law.

Comment

Does allowing interest (para 9) meet the problems arising from changes in land values?[61]

C. The significance of indemnity

Extract 10.4.6

Land Registry Annual Report and Accounts 2013/14

Nature of claim	Number of claims	Substantive loss (£)	Costs (£)	Percentage of total
Extent of registered titles	171	480,394	510,879	9
Errors in/omissions from register entries	111	2,090,280	586,192	24
Sundry plans errors	16	42,500	53,348	1
Fraud and forgery	53	6,445,498	764,215	64
Official inspections of the title plans	4	—	929	—
Bankruptcy errors	1	25	—	—
Official Searches	4	—	5,309	—
Official Copies	3	—	1,337	—
Errors in searches of the index map	15	40,100	19,231	1
Errors in filed extracts	165	485	30,892	—
Lost documents/administrative errors	491	29,990	103,321	1
Land charges errors	—	—	—	—
Total	1,034	9,129,272	2,075,653	100
Gross Payment			£11,204,925	
Less sums recovered under Land Registry's statutory right of recourse			£2,155,632	
Net Indemnity			£9,049,293	

[61] Tee [1996] CLJ 241 at p 247.

Comment

(1) The payment of costs is authorised by the LRA, Sched 8, paras 3, 4. It is apparent that many claims result in no loss other than legal costs.

(2) The last decade has shown a distinct growth in claims, especially as regards fraud and forgery.

(3) The number of claims must be viewed against the many millions of first registrations and dealings with registered land (quite apart from ancillary searches etc.). Does the relatively small number of claims reflect well on the system as a whole?

Further reading

Bogusz, B [2014] Conv 27: The relevance of 'Intentions and wishes' to determine actual occupation: a sea change in judicial thinking?

Cooke, E J and O'Connor, P A (2004) 120 LQR 640: Purchaser liability to third parties in the English registration system: a comparative perspective.

Goymour, A [2013] CLJ 617: Mistaken registrations of land: exploding the myth of 'title by registration'.

Harpum, C (2003) 'Registered land: a law unto itself?' in *Rationalizing Property, Equity and Trusts*, ed. J Getzler, Chapter 9.

Hill-Smith, A [2009] Conv 127: Forgery and land registration: the decision in *Malory Investments* v *Cheshire Homes*.

Jackson, N (2003) 119 LQR 660: Title by registration and concealed overriding interests: the cause and effect of antipathy to documentary proof.

O'Connor, P A (2005) 'Registration of invalid dispositions: who gets the property?' in *Modern Studies in Property Law*, Vol 3, ed. E J Cooke, Chapter 3.

Pottage, A [1995] 15 OxJLS 371: The originality of registration.

Thompson, M P [1985] CLJ 280: Registration, fraud and notice.

Part III

Rights to enjoy land: estates and commonhold

11

Concurrent ownership: joint tenancy and tenancy in common

There is concurrent ownership where two or more people are entitled to property at the same time. The most obvious example is where two people buy a house together as their home. The concurrent ownership may be expressed in the documentation or implied (as considered in Chapter 8). The present chapter will concentrate upon concurrent ownership of the fee simple absolute in possession, although there can be concurrent ownership of any interest. Thus a life interest, a lease and a remainder interest can each be held concurrently. Successive interests are found where the people entitled do not enjoy their interests at the same time, but sequentially. An obvious example is 'To Emma for life, remainder to Fiona in fee simple'. (Successive interests are considered in Chapter 13.)

Within concurrent interests there are two principal topics: the different forms of concurrent interests and their legal regulation. Legal regulation covers topics such as rights to sell the land (coupled with protections for purchasers and beneficiaries); occupation rights; and resolution of disagreements. Legal regulation is a large topic, dealt with in the following chapter.

1. Joint tenancy and tenancy in common

Two different forms of co-ownership are recognised today: the joint tenancy and tenancy in common. The crucial difference between them is that the right of survivorship (*jus accrescendi*) operates on the death of a joint tenant. This means that the surviving joint tenants are now the co-owners; the deceased person's estate is entitled to nothing and a purported gift by will is wholly ineffective. The joint tenancy is very commonly used by spouses or partners buying a house together: their intention is that the survivor should be the owner if one of them should die. This result can, of course, be achieved by will but the joint tenancy guards against a will not being made (probable for younger people) and is very simple to administer. It will also be seen in the following chapter that the joint tenancy is very well suited to landholding by trustees: nobody wants a trustee's personal representatives to get involved in running the trust. Of course, survivorship is inappropriate for many situations: business people buying land for investment or for their offices would provide examples. The tenancy in common is then appropriate: it is hedged around with fewer rules and offers the flexibility which is essential in any legal system. It is always possible for a joint tenancy to be converted into a tenancy in common. This is referred to as severance of the joint tenancy: one example is that a tenancy in common results if a joint tenant transfers his or her interest whilst alive.

Turning to the operation of survivorship, what happens where it is uncertain who dies first?

Extract 11.1.1

Law of Property Act 1925, s 184

184.—In all cases where, after the commencement of this Act, two or more persons have died in circumstances rendering it uncertain which of them survived the other or others, such deaths shall (subject to any order of the court), for all purposes affecting the title to property, be presumed to have occurred in order of seniority, and accordingly the younger shall be deemed to have survived the elder.

Extract 11.1.2

Re Bate [1947] 2 All ER 418

JENKINS J: This summons raises the question of the order in which the testator, George Bate, and his wife, Ada Jane Bate, are to be presumed to have died for the purpose of determining the devolution of their estates under the will of George Bate and the intestacy of his wife.

On Jan 8, 1946, at 10 pm, the husband and the wife were found dead in their kitchen, the cause of their deaths being carbon monoxide poisoning . . .

On Jan 10 Dr John Taylor, a distinguished pathologist, carried out a post-mortem on the bodies. He says:

> . . . I am of opinion that in all reasonable probability Ada Jane Bate died first, since the concentration of coal gas in her blood was lower . . .

Further medical evidence, on the other side, is contained in the affidavits of two other eminent pathologists. The first, Dr R D Teare, says:

> When a sample of blood is taken for analysis of its saturation with carbon monoxide errors may arise before the blood reaches the laboratory. These errors depend on the fact that the carbon monoxide in the blood escapes into the surrounding atmosphere, and, consequently, the final analysis gives a lower figure than that which is present at the time of death.

. . .

The question for me is whether on that evidence the circumstances in which the testator and his wife died were such as to render it 'uncertain' which of them died first, within the meaning of the Law of Property Act, 1925, s 184, or whether the circumstances are such that I can find that there is no uncertainty, but that one of them died before the other, *i.e.*, that the wife, although she was the younger, died before her husband. This question must depend on the degree of proof which, on the true construction of s 184, is to be regarded as establishing the certainty of the death of one person before another, or the degree of deficiency of proof, one might say, which amounts, on the true construction of the section, to uncertainty. I have been referred to a number of passages in the speeches in the House of Lords in *Hickman v Peacey*, which dealt with deaths caused by one explosion which destroyed an air raid shelter in which the persons concerned had taken refuge. The questions involved were whether the deaths ought to be held to have taken place simultaneously and whether s 184 of the Law of Property Act, 1925, contemplated simultaneous deaths at all. The question, therefore, was different there from that which I have to decide, because no question of simultaneous deaths arises here . . .

. . . [T]here was something less than unanimity among their Lordships as to the degree of proof of survivorship which, in their view, was necessary to exclude the presumption enacted by s 184, but I think all would have agreed that Lord Simon did not put it too high when he spoke of 'evidence leading to a defined and warranted conclusion'.

Applying that as the test, am I, as a tribunal of fact, on this evidence, warranted in coming to a definite conclusion that the testator survived his wife? To do that, I think, I must be able to do something more than merely conclude that a reasonable explanation of the circumstances was that the testator survived his wife or, indeed, that on the whole the more reasonable conclusion is that he survived her. I think I must be able to come to a conclusion of fact on grounds which so far outweigh any grounds for a contrary conclusion that I can ignore the latter. It seems to me that, on the evidence in this case, I cannot do anything of the kind . . .

Comment

(1) What is the difference, if any, between the test adopted by Jenkins J and the normal test of the balance of probabilities?

(2) Jenkins J quoted from *Hickman* v *Peacey* [1945] AC 304, in which the deceased persons had been killed by a bomb. The House of Lords held by a 3:2 majority that s 184 applied even though it might be thought that they died at the same time. A flavour of the arguments is provided by two brief quotations:

> VISCOUNT SIMON LC (dissenting): A rule of racing which provided that, where the judge was uncertain which of two horses passed the winning post first, the younger horse should take the prize, would not prevent the sharing of the prize in a dead-heat.
> LORD MACMILLAN: I prefer to read the enactment as meaning that where the circumstances are such that it is not possible to say with certainty that one of the victims survived the other there is then uncertainty as to which survived the other. Clearly you cannot say with certainty that one of the victims survived the other if your belief is that both died at the same time, if that be possible.

Where the parties die at the same time, does this really fall within the wording of s 184? If there is no uncertainty because they die at the same time, does this lead to a satisfactory outcome?

2. Joint tenancy or tenancy in common?

How do we tell which form of co-ownership exists? Our starting point is that there is a preference for the joint tenancy. If all its requirements are satisfied, a joint tenancy will follow. However, the parties can always (expressly or impliedly by use of 'words of severance') stipulate for a tenancy in common and, in certain types of cases, equity will prefer a tenancy in common.

First, however, we need to consider the requirements for a joint tenancy. Its nature is that each co-owner owns the entirety of the land. In contrast, a tenant in common is treated as owning an undivided share in the land.[1] This is very much a conceptual difference: it does not affect what the co-owners are entitled to. It does help to explain in analytical terms how survivorship operates. In so far as each owns the whole, the effect of death of one is that there are fewer co-owners entitled to the whole. The idea of each being entitled to the whole finds expression in the requirement that the *four unities* must be present for a joint tenancy.

---

[1] The 1925 legislation frequently refers to tenancies in common as 'undivided shares': see, e.g., Law of Property Act 1925 (hereafter LPA), s 1(6).

A. The four unities

(i) Unity of possession

This is the only unity which is required for the tenancy in common. Its role is to distinguish between separate ownership of different parts of a property and co-ownership of the entire property. Its essence is that each co-owner must be entitled to possession of the property. However, it is perfectly acceptable for the parties to agree that each shall occupy part of it:[2] we are concentrating on rights flowing from the co-ownership rather than any separate agreements. It should be added that rights to possess the land are now regulated by legislation: unity of possession now needs to be considered far more as a right to enjoy the interest than a right to enjoy the land.[3]

(ii) Unity of interest

This is, perhaps, the most interesting unity. For a joint tenancy, the parties must have the same estate (a life interest in one person and fee simple in another, for example, does not suffice) and the same size of interest. This latter point is the most important. If the parties wish to have interests of differing sizes (perhaps reflecting their contributions), they cannot have a joint tenancy. Although the concept of each owning the whole is not readily compatible with differing shares, there may be practical reasons for wanting to have differing shares within a joint tenancy. Thus the size of the shares may be important for taxation reasons, or be intended as the basis for shares should the parties later decide to sever the joint tenancy so as to create a tenancy in common.[4] It is worth considering whether the modern law should continue to require this particular unity (and perhaps any of the unities, other than possession) for joint tenancies.

(iii) Unity of title

This requires that the joint tenants should each derive their interests from the same immediate document. If A transfers land to B and C, this transfer provides the title. However, if C subsequently transfers her interest to D, then D's immediate title (C's transfer) is different from that of B (A's transfer). This is an example of severance; it provides the context in which unity of title is most relevant.

(iv) Unity of time

This requires that the interests must vest at the same time. It is so riddled with exceptions that it is rarely relevant today.

B. Words of severance

It is important to note that a joint tenancy is not imposed against the wishes of the parties. Even though the four unities are satisfied, the parties can stipulate for a tenancy in common. Most interesting is the question as to what words will be taken as implying a desire for a tenancy in common: these are the 'words of severance'.

---

[2] *Malayan Credit Ltd* v *Jack Chia-MPH Ltd* [1986] AC 549.
[3] As would always have been the case for joint tenancies of equitable interests.
[4] The normal rule is that the parties' shares on severance of a joint tenancy are equal, regardless of their contributions: *Goodman* v *Gallant* [1986] Fam 106. Severance is dealt with later in this chapter.

Extract 11.2.1

Robertson v *Fraser* (1871) LR 6 Ch App 696

LORD HATHERLEY LC: . . . I cannot doubt, having regard to the authorities respecting the effect of such words as 'amongst' and 'respectively', that anything which in the slightest degree indicates an intention to divide the property must be held to abrogate the idea of a joint tenancy, and to create a tenancy in common. Perhaps it would have been well if the Courts had held that in bequests, as in partnerships, every community of interest was to be considered a tenancy in common. But that has not been done. However, putting aside such words as 'alike' and 'equally' – for they may be considered more decidedly inconsistent with joint tenancy, inasmuch as the interests of joint tenants are very rarely quite equal, considering the difference that may exist in the ages of the legatees – it does not appear to me that such words as 'amongst' and 'respectively' are at all stronger than 'participate'. I have, therefore, no doubt that the word 'participate' is sufficient to indicate an intention to divide, and to create a tenancy in common.

Comment

(1) Might it be argued that use of such words is likely to be random? Can they be taken as a true indicator of a desired tenancy in common?

(2) Would it not be better to reverse the presumption in favour of joint tenancies? Should one distinguish between (i) joint tenancies arising from a will or settlement, and (ii) those arising on joint purchase of land?

C. Equitable presumptions of tenancy in common

The principles considered above were applied by both courts of law and of equity. However, equity went further in its dislike of the right of survivorship and therefore of joint tenancies.[5] Although the presumption of a joint tenancy has never been challenged, there are three circumstances in which a tenancy in common is preferred. Originally, this was by requiring the joint tenants to hold on trust to give effect to a tenancy in common, but today every concurrent interest involves a trust (as will be seen in the following chapter) and the role of equity is simply to determine the nature of the beneficial interest.

(i) Partners in a business

Extract 11.2.2

Malayan Credit Ltd v *Jack Chia-MPH Ltd* [1986] AC 549 (PC)

The parties took a lease of business premises as joint tenants. They had agreed that each would occupy a specific part of the premises and pay rent and expenses pro rata.

LORD BRIGHTMAN: . . . The argument is that, in the absence of an express agreement, persons who take as joint tenants at law hold as tenants in common in equity only in three classes of case: first, where they have provided the purchase money in unequal shares; in this case they hold the beneficial interest in similar shares: secondly, where the grant consists of a security for a loan and the grantees were equal or unequal contributors to the loan; again they would hold the beneficial interest in the same shares; and thirdly, where they are partners and the subject matter of the grant is partnership property. See for example, *Snell's Principles of Equity*,

---

[5] Described as odious in *R* v *Williams* (1735) Bunb 342 (145 ER 694).

28th ed (1982), pp 37 and 38. The plaintiff contends that the instant case falls into none of these three categories. Therefore it is said that the lessees hold as joint tenants in equity as well as at law, with the result that either party was at liberty to sever the joint tenancy and thus ensure that the beneficial interest was thereafter held in equal shares . . .

. . .

It seems to their Lordships that where premises are held by two persons as joint tenants at law for their several business purposes, it is improbable that they would intend to hold as joint tenants in equity. Suppose that an accountant and an architect take a lease of premises containing four rooms, that the accountant uses two rooms, and that the architect uses two rooms. It is scarcely to be supposed that they intend that if, for example, the accountant dies first without having gone through the formalities of a severance, the beneficial interest in the entire premises is to survive to the architect. Their Lordships do not accept that the cases in which joint tenants at law will be presumed to hold as tenants in common in equity are as rigidly circumscribed as the plaintiff asserts. Such cases are not necessarily limited to purchasers who contribute unequally, to co-mortgagees and to partners. There are other circumstances in which equity may infer that the beneficial interest is intended to be held by the grantees as tenants in common. In the opinion of their Lordships, one such case is where the grantees hold the premises for their several individual business purposes.

Furthermore, there is no fundamental distinction to be drawn for present purposes between joint tenants who acquire a term of years on payment of a premium and at a token rent, and joint tenants who acquire a term of years on the payment of no premium but at a rack rent . . .

There are features in the instant case which appear to their Lordships to point unmistakably towards a tenancy in common in equity, and furthermore towards a tenancy in common in unequal shares: (1) the lease was clearly taken to serve the separate commercial interests of the defendant and the plaintiff. (2) Prior to the grant of the lease the parties had settled between themselves what space they would respectively occupy when the lease came to be granted. This was roughly 62% to the defendant and 38% to the plaintiff. (3) Prior to the grant of the lease, the parties had made meticulous measurements of their respective allotted areas, and divided their liability for the rent and service charge in unequal shares in accordance with the respective areas that they would occupy. (4) Prior to the grant of the lease, the plaintiff was invoiced for its due share of the deposit . . . (5) After the grant of the lease, the defendant and the plaintiff paid the stamp duty and the survey fees in the same unequal shares. (6) As from the grant of the lease, the rent and service charges were paid in the same unequal shares.

Comment

(1) Would there have been a joint tenancy if the parties' contributions had been identical?

(2) Would a proved intention of a joint tenancy prevail?[6]

(ii) Mortgages

We are here dealing with two people who together lend money on mortgage. The commercial setting readily raises an inference of a tenancy in common, but what if (as is common) the mortgage contains a joint account clause, saying that the money is lent from a joint account (in equity as well as at law) so that the survivor can give a receipt for repayment of the loan?

---

[6] One fairly recent case is *Bathurst v Scarborow* [2005] 1 P&CR 58.

Extract 11.2.3

Re Jackson (1887) 34 Ch D 732

NORTH J: . . . It is clear that if the joint account clause had not been inserted in the mortgages, the three sisters would have been tenants in common of the mortgage moneys. That is settled law. The Chief Clerk was of opinion that the joint account clause amounted to a declaration that there was to be a joint tenancy in the money, and that it negatived the presumption in favour of a tenancy in common, which would otherwise have existed. Various circumstances are relied upon as shewing conclusively that there was really a tenancy in common. The fact that the money originally belonged to the three sisters separately, not jointly, is a strong circumstance, as is also the fact that the mortgages were consolidated mortgages, so to speak. It is clear that no specific instructions were given by the ladies when the mortgages were prepared as to the form which they should take, and, on the first occasion on which a mortgage was made in the joint names, the gentleman who acted for the ladies was also the solicitor for the mortgagor, and it would obviously facilitate dealing with the property, in case the mortgage should be paid off, that there should be a joint account clause, so that a receipt for the mortgage money might be given by the survivors or survivor of the mortgagees, without the necessity for the con-currence of the representatives of a deceased mortgagee . . . [We] have this, that the mortgages were prepared in this form, not at the instance of the ladies or their advisers, but apparently because it was the most convenient form for the mortgagor.

Comment

The court concluded that there was a tenancy in common in equity. Would the result have been different if the mortgagor's solicitor had not acted on behalf of the mortgagees?

(iii) Unequal contribution

Extract 11.2.4

Lake v Gibson (1729) 1 Eq Cas Abr 290 (21 ER 1052)

. . . his Honour held, that where Two, or more, purchase Lands, and advance the Money in equal Proportions, and take a Conveyance to them and their Heirs, that this is a Jointenancy, that is, a Purchase by them jointly of the Chance of Survivorship, which may happen to the one of them as well as to the other; but where the Proportions of the Money are not equal, and this appears in the Deed itself, this makes them in the Nature of Partners; and however the legal Estate survive, yet the Survivor shall be considered but as a Trustee for the others, in Proportion to the Sums advanced by each of them . . .

Comment

(1) This principle operates today whether or not the contribution is express on the face of the deed.

(2) Is this really a separate rule, or is it merely a working out of the unity of interest? Remember that equity gives effect to contributions to the purchase of land by means of a resulting trust, regardless of whether the legal estate is conveyed to joint tenants.

(3) In the context of the family home, the House of Lords held in *Stack v Dowden*[7] that the beneficial interests will normally follow the legal estate where there is a transfer

---

[7] [2007] 2 AC 432; Extract 8.4.1 above. For purchase of property as an investment, see *Laskar v Laskar* [2008] 1 WLR 2695 (mother and son).

into joint legal ownership. How great an effect will this have on finding a beneficial joint tenancy?

Suppose that a house is transferred into the name of a single legal owner but that a constructive trust is imposed so that it is held for two cohabitants equally. In *Stack*,[8] Baroness Hale observed, 'I know of no case in which a sole legal owner (there being no declaration of trust) has been held to hold the property on a beneficial joint tenancy.' Does principle point to there being a tenancy in common?

3. Severance of the joint tenancy

Extract 11.3.1

Law of Property Act 1925, s 36(2)

36.—(2) No severance of a joint tenancy of a legal estate, so as to create a tenancy in common in land, shall be permissible, whether by operation of law or otherwise, but this subsection does not affect the right of a joint tenant to release his interest to the other joint tenants, or the right to sever a joint tenancy in an equitable interest whether or not the legal estate is vested in the joint tenants:

Provided that, where a legal estate (not being settled land) is vested in joint tenants beneficially, and any tenant desires to sever the joint tenancy in equity, he shall give to the other joint tenants a notice in writing of such desire or do such other acts or things as would, in the case of personal estate, have been effectual to sever the tenancy in equity, and thereupon the land shall be held in trust on terms which would have been requisite for giving effect to the beneficial interests if there had been an actual severance.

Comment

(1) The bar on the severance of legal joint tenancies ties in with the prohibition on legal tenancies in common (see Extract 12.1.4 below).

(2) What is meant by the requirement in the proviso that the 'legal estate . . . is vested in joint tenants beneficially'? Can other equitable joint tenancies be severed?

(3) The cross-reference to severance of personal estate is odd now that equitable joint tenancies are firmly established as interests in land.[9] However, it has little practical significance as the rules are the same as for realty.

The next extract, commonly cited in modern cases, reveals the content of the severance rules.

Extract 11.3.2

Williams v *Hensman* (1861) 1 J&H 546 (70 ER 862)

PAGE-WOOD V-C: . . . A joint-tenancy may be severed in three ways: in the first place, an act of any one of the persons interested operating upon his own share may create a severance as

---

[8] At [66]. Some contrary indications are found in *Eves* v *Eves* [1975] 1 WLR 1338 at p 1345 and *Supperstone* v *Hurst* [2006] 1 FLR 1245 at [11]–[12], though most cases support Baroness Hale.

[9] Trusts of Land and Appointment of Trustees Act 1996, s 3; there had earlier been an argument that, under a trust for sale, beneficial concurrent interests were to be treated as being in the proceeds of sale.

to that share. The right of each joint-tenant is a right by survivorship only in the event of no severance having taken place of the share which is claimed under the *jus accrescendi*. Each one is at liberty to dispose of his own interest in such manner as to sever it from the joint fund – losing, of course, at the same time, his own right of survivorship. Secondly, a joint-tenancy may be severed by mutual agreement. And, in the third place, there may be a severance by any course of dealing sufficient to intimate that the interests of all were mutually treated as constituting a tenancy in common. When the severance depends on an inference of this kind without any express act of severance, it will not suffice to rely on an intention, with respect to the particular share, declared only behind the backs of the other persons interested. You must find in this class of cases a course of dealing by which the shares of all the parties to the contest have been affected, as happened in the cases of *Wilson v Bell* and *Jackson v Jackson*.

Comment

(1) The first method of severance reflects the old common law rule that destruction of any of the unities shatters the joint tenancy and creates a tenancy in common.[10] By far the most common application of this is where one joint tenant transfers his or her interest. The transferee will have a different immediate title (the transfer) than the other joint tenants and this shatters the unity of title. Necessarily such transfers must be before death: a will is ineffective because survivorship operates on death.

(2) Do (and should) charges and leases also effect severance?[11]

Most controversy surrounds the second and third methods, as is seen from the following two extracts.

Extract 11.3.3

Nielson-Jones v Fedden **[1975] Ch 222**

On the break-up of a marriage, the parties negotiated as to their financial position. It was agreed (by the 'memorandum') that a jointly-owned house should be sold in order to enable the husband to buy a new house, though the judge found that there had been no agreement as to ownership of the proceeds of sale. A purchaser of the house was found, but the husband then died suddenly.

WALTON J: . . . [B]oth of them had made it perfectly plain that they were looking forward to an ending of the joint tenancy in the proceeds of sale of the property. However, there were without prejudice negotiations being carried on between them all the time, which negotiations it is admitted never resulted in any actual agreement . . .

I think that the questions of severance . . . must, to some extent, be dealt with together. Persons can only be joint tenants if the three unities of possession, interest and title are present. It is customary, following Blackstone, to add the unity of time to the commencement of title . . .

In order to effect a severance before the 1925 legislation came into force, it was essential to destroy one of the three unities. Time, being past, could, of course, no longer be affected. Unity of possession was clearly destroyed by a partition, and hence the joint tenancy could be severed in this way. An agreement, or conduct amounting to an agreement for severance, clearly

---

[10] Destruction of the unity of possession creates separate ownerships of the parts. This is called partition and is considered in the next chapter.

[11] See Nield [2001] Conv 462; Fox [2000] Conv 208.

destroys the unity of interest and so does the acquisition of another estate which is capable of merging; and an actual alienation also clearly destroys the unity of title quoad the assignee. All this is carefully explained in *Blackstone's Commentaries* (1813 ed, vol II, pp 177 et seq) . . .

[Section 36(2)] is a rather elliptic method of legislation, but since it is, I think, not in dispute that the methods of severance of a joint tenancy in personal estate before 1926 were precisely the same as the methods of severance of a joint tenancy in real estate (see *Williams on Personal Property*, 18th ed (1926), p 524) the final effect of this subsection is merely to add another method to the ways in which the severance of a joint tenancy in real estate may be effected. Why this highly convenient method of severance was not also extended to personal estate, I am at a loss to understand. This disparity led to a highly ingenious argument on the part of Mr Essayan to the effect that it would be so highly inconvenient if this really is the law – because presumably once the real property has been sold in exercise of the trust for sale it has become converted into personal property – that one must read section 36(2) as really declaratory of the law, so that the same methods were available in all cases. From this he went on to submit that severance in general was much easier than had previously been thought.

Whilst I feel unable to accept Mr Essayan's analysis, he has indeed a very valid point; severance by notice is only possible where a legal estate (not being settled land) is vested in joint tenants beneficially. Once there has been a sale, that condition no longer applies, and the net result would appear to be that severance after sale could not be effected by a notice in writing. This is a highly inconvenient position, obviously.

Leaving that on one side, I now pass to a consideration of the second and third points above mentioned. If, as I have held, the memorandum was not an assignment of Mrs Todd's interest in the proceeds of sale of the house to her husband, can it nevertheless be read as a severance of their joint beneficial interests: an agreement to the effect that each of them thereafter is to be solely entitled to his and her respective one half share in such proceeds? With the best will in the world, I find myself wholly unable to give the memorandum such a construction. I think it is in fact rather easier to read the memorandum as an assignment than it is as a severance, so that as I cannot give it the first construction, almost *a fortiori* I cannot give it the second. It appears to me that the memorandum is dealing solely with the use by Mr Todd of the whole of the proceeds of sale, and that, qua ownership, use is wholly ambiguous: hence, it cannot be implied from the fact that Mr Todd was to have the use of the whole of the money either that the title thereto was assigned to him or that he was entitled to have his own half absolutely, and Mrs Todd her own half share absolutely.

There remains the third point: is it possible from the correspondence, more particularly from the determination therein manifested by both parties that their respective financial affairs were going to be kept separate, whether or not coupled with the fact that they were both negotiating as to what precise share of the proceeds of sale each should take, and whether or not coupled with the actual distributions out of the deposit paid by the purchaser of the Old Rectory, to say either (i) in accordance with the established authorities, that there was a sufficient course of conduct by Mr and Mrs Todd as to lead to the implication of an agreement to sever, and hence a severance? or (ii) to amount to a declaration by one or either of them of their intention to sever, which declaration, submits Mr Essayan, is also an established method of severance?

As to (i), I think I can take the matter very shortly. It appears to me that when parties are negotiating to reach an agreement, and never do reach any final agreement, it is quite impossible to say that they have reached any agreement at all . . .

As to (ii), I shall first of all assume in favour of Mr Essayan that the correspondence does indeed disclose an unequivocal declaration by Mr Todd to the effect that he wishes to sever the joint tenancy so as to make himself master of a one half share of the net proceeds of sale of the property. The question then is, can such a declaration – a unilateral declaration – ever be effective to sever a beneficial joint tenancy? It appears to me that in principle there is no conceivable ground for saying that it can. So far as I can see, such a mere unilateral declaration does not in any way shatter any one of the essential unities. Moreover, if it did, it would appear that a wholly unconscionable amount of time and trouble has been wasted by conveyancers of old in framing elaborate assignments for the purpose of effecting a severance, when all that was required was a simple declaration.

The question, moreover, is not untouched by authority. One may start with *Moyse* v *Gyles* (1700) Prec Ch 124 . . . Again, in *Partriche* v *Powlet* (1740) 2 Atk 54, a decision of Lord Hardwicke LC, the side note is as follows: 'An actual alienation only can sever a joint tenancy; a declaration of one of the parties that it shall be severed, is not sufficient.' It is quite clear from that case that Lord Hardwicke LC regarded severance as only effected (if one leaves out of account the acquisition of a mergeable interest) by either (i) an agreement to that effect or (ii) actual alienation. He would, I think, have regarded the third head, which is often referred to in the cases, namely, a course of conduct, as merely being material from which an agreement is to be inferred. For a modern instance of the adoption of this analysis, see per Hanna J in *Flynn* v *Flynn* [1930] IR 337, 343. The final authority in this line is *In re Wilks, Child* v *Bulmer* [1891] 3 Ch 59, a decision of Stirling J . . .

Accordingly, down to that case I think it is fair to say that the whole current of authority was against severance by means of such a declaration as is now envisaged. However, in *Hawkesley* v *May* [1956] 1 QB 304 Havers J said: . . .

'The first method indicated, namely, an act of any one of the persons interested operating upon his own share, obviously includes a declaration of intention to sever by one party . . .'

With very great respect to Havers J, I think he had, in deciding as he did that the letter written by the sister was a sufficient act on her part to constitute a severance of the joint tenancy, entirely misapprehended the judgment of Page Wood V-C in *Williams* v *Hensman*, 1 John&H 546. The first method of severance of which the Vice-Chancellor was talking was actual alienation, or something equivalent thereto . . .

In *In re Draper's Conveyance* [1969] 1 Ch 486, Plowman J unfortunately applied the dictum of Havers J, to which I have referred above, to a case between husband and wife. . . .

Plowman J after quoting from *Hawkesley* v *May* [1956] 1 QB 304 continued as follows, at p 491:

'So from that case I derive this; a declaration by one of a number of joint tenants of his intention to sever operates as a severance. Mr Cooke also, as I have said, relied upon the notice in writing which under section 36(2) of the Law of Property Act 1925 is allowed in the case of a joint tenancy in land, although not in personalty, and he submits that the summons [by the wife, seeking a determination of the interests of the joint tenants], although not signed, amounted to a notice in writing on the part of the wife that she desired to sever the joint tenancy in equity . . .

Dealing with the matter there, and ignoring for a moment certain matters which were submitted by Mr McCulloch, it seems to me that Mr Cooke's submissions are right whether they are based on the new provision in section 36(2) of the Law of Property Act 1925 or whether they are based on the old law which applied to severing a joint tenancy in the case of a personal estate. It seems to me that that summons, coupled with the affidavit in support of it, clearly evinced an intention on the part of the wife that she wished the property to be sold and the proceeds distributed, a half to her and a half to the husband . . .'

Once again, none of the relevant cases were cited to the judge – *In re Wilks, Child* v *Bulmer* [1891] 3 Ch 59 in particular, should have been drawn to his attention. Since I have already concluded above that Havers J's dictum was wholly unwarranted, I regret that I can place no greater reliance upon it when blandly repeated in *In re Draper's Conveyance*. I am also troubled about the suggestion that the mere issue of the originating summons, coupled with the affidavit in support, could amount to a notice in writing under section 36(2). It appears to me that the reasons so cogently stated by Stirling J in *In re Wilks, Child v Bulmer* apply with equal force: until any order had been made, the wife was *domina litis*, and entitled to withdraw the proceedings entirely. In other words, it appears to me that section 36(2) contemplates an irrevocable notice, and that the issue of proceedings is the very reverse of an irrevocable act. If the proceedings are, indeed, to constitute a severance, it must, I think, follow as a consequence that they themselves become irrevocable, and this I find difficult to appreciate.

. . .

I would finally add on this branch of the case that my misgivings as to the two cases referred to are clearly shared by the writer of a note appearing in 84 *Law Quarterly Review*, p 462, and also that, if they were correct, so far as I can see, section 36(2) of the Law of Property Act 1925 would be wholly otiose, since there was already in existence an even simpler method of severing a joint tenancy. Indeed, on one view, it might even have been restrictive! I find either conclusion impossible to reach.

Extract 11.3.4

Burgess v *Rawnsley* [1975] Ch 429

Two elderly people met. They bought a house as joint tenants, though with misunderstandings as to the nature of their relationship. The man agreed orally to buy out the woman's share. However, the woman withdrew from the arrangement; the man subsequently died.

LORD DENNING MR: . . . The important finding is that there was an agreement that she would sell her share to him for £750. Almost immediately afterwards she went back upon it. Is that conduct sufficient to effect a severance?

Mr Levy submitted that it was not. He relied on the recent decision of Walton J in *Nielson-Jones* v *Fedden* [1975] Ch 222, given subsequently to the judgment of the judge here. Walton J held that no conduct is sufficient to sever a joint tenancy unless it is irrevocable. Mr Levy said that in the present case the agreement was not in writing. It could not be enforced by specific performance. It was revocable and was in fact revoked by Mrs Rawnsley when she went back on it. So there was, he submitted, no severance.

Walton J founded himself on the decision of Stirling J in *In re Wilks, Child v Bulmer* [1891] 3 Ch 59. He criticised *Hawkesley* v *May* [1956] 1 QB 304 and *In re Draper's Conveyance* [1969] 1 Ch 486, and said that they were clearly contrary to the existing well-established law. He went back to *Coke upon Littleton*, 189a, 299b and to *Blackstone's Commentaries*. Those old writers were dealing with legal joint tenancies. *Blackstone* said, 8th ed (1778), vol II, pp 180, 185:

> 'The properties of a joint estate are derived from its unity, which is fourfold; the unity of interest, the unity of title, the unity of time, and the unity of possession: . . . an estate in joint tenancy may be severed and destroyed . . . by destroying any of its constituent unities.'

and he gives instances of how this may be done. Now that is all very well when you are considering how a legal joint tenancy can be severed. But it is of no application today when there can be no severance of a legal joint tenancy; and you are only considering how a beneficial joint tenancy can be severed. The thing to remember today is that equity leans against joint tenants and favours tenancies in common.

Nowadays everyone starts with the judgment of Sir William Page Wood V-C in *Williams* v *Hensman* (1861) 1 John&Hem 546 . . . Page Wood V-C distinguished between severance 'by mutual agreement' and severance by a 'course of dealing'. That shows that a 'course of dealing' need not amount to an agreement, expressed or implied, for severance. It is sufficient if there is a course of dealing in which one party makes clear to the other that he desires that their shares should no longer be held jointly but be held in common. I emphasise that it must be made clear to the other party. That is implicit in the sentence in which Page Wood V-C says:

'it will not suffice to rely on an intention, with respect to the particular share, declared only behind the backs of the other persons interested.'

Similarly it is sufficient if both parties enter on a course of dealing which evinces an intention by both of them that their shares shall henceforth be held in common and not jointly. As appears from the two cases to which Page Wood V-C referred of *Wilson* v *Bell*, 5 Ir Eq R 501 and *Jackson* v *Jackson*, 9 Ves Jun 591.

I come now to the question of notice. Suppose that one party gives a notice in writing to the other saying that he desires to sever the joint tenancy. Is that sufficient to effect a severance? I think it is. It was certainly the view of Sir Benjamin Cherry when he drafted section 36(2) of the Law of Property Act 1925. It says in relation to real estates:

'. . . where a legal estate (not being settled land) is vested in joint tenants beneficially, and any tenant desires to sever the joint tenancy in equity, he shall give to the other joint tenants <u>a notice in writing of such desire or do such other acts or things as would, in the case of personal estate, have been effectual</u> to sever the tenancy in equity . . .'

I have underlined the important words. The word 'other' is most illuminating. It shows quite plainly that, in the case of personal estate one of the things which is effective in equity to sever a joint tenancy is 'a notice in writing' of a desire to sever. So also in regard to real estate.

Taking this view, I find myself in agreement with Havers J in *Hawkesley* v *May* [1956] 1 QB 304; 313–314, and of Plowman J in *In re Draper's Conveyance* [1969] 1 Ch 486. I cannot agree with Walton J [1975] Ch 222, 234–235, that those cases were wrongly decided. It would be absurd that there should be a difference between real estate and personal estate in this respect. Suppose real estate is held on a joint tenancy on a trust for sale and is sold and converted into personal property. Before sale, it is severable by notice in writing. It would be ridiculous if it could not be severed afterwards in like manner. I look upon section 36(2) as declaratory of the law as to severance by notice and not as a new provision confined to real estate. A joint tenancy in personal estate can be severed by notice just as a joint tenancy in real estate.

It remains to consider *Nielson-Jones* v *Fedden* [1975] Ch 222. In my view it was not correctly decided. The husband and wife entered upon a course of dealing sufficient to sever the joint tenancy . . . Furthermore there was disclosed in correspondence a declaration by the husband that he wished to sever the joint tenancy: and this was made clear by the wife. That too was sufficient.

. . .

It remains to apply these principles to the present case. I think there was evidence that Mr Honick and Mrs Rawnsley did come to an agreement that he would buy her share for £750. That agreement was not in writing and it was not specifically enforceable. Yet it was sufficient to effect a severance. Even if there was not any firm agreement but only a course of dealing, it clearly evinced an intention by both parties that the property should henceforth be held in common and not jointly.

BROWNE LJ: . . . Mr Levy conceded, as is clearly right, that if there had been an enforceable agreement by Mrs Rawnsley to sell her share to Mr Honick, that would produce a severance of the joint tenancy; but he says that an oral agreement, unenforceable because of section 40 of the Law of Property Act 1925, is not enough. . . . But here the plaintiff is not seeking to enforce by action the agreement by Mrs Rawnsley to sell her share to Mr Honick. She relies upon it as effecting the severance in equity of the joint tenancy. An agreement to sever can be inferred from a course of dealing (see Lefroy B in *Wilson* v *Bell*, 5 Ir Eq R 501, 507 and Stirling J in *In re Wilks, Child* v *Bulmer* [1891] 3 Ch 59). . . . It seems to me that the point is that the agreement establishes that the parties no longer intend the tenancy to operate as a joint tenancy and that automatically effects a severance . . .

This conclusion makes it unnecessary to consider the important and difficult questions of what the effect of negotiations not resulting in an agreement or of a mere declaration would have been and, in particular, the problem raised by the decision of Plowman J in *In re Draper's Conveyance* [1969] 1 Ch 486, and Walton J in *Nielson-Jones v Fedden* [1975] Ch 222. Further, if the evidence and the conclusion that there was an agreement in this case are rejected, I doubt whether there was enough evidence in this particular case as to a course of dealing to raise the question of the application of Page Wood V-C's third category, 1 John&Hem 546, 557. I therefore prefer not to express any final opinion on these points. Lord Denning MR has dealt with them in his judgment and I have the advantage of knowing what Sir John Pennycuick is going to say about that aspect of the case. I agree with both of them that Page Wood V-C's third category is a separate category from his second category. I agree also that the proviso to section 36(2) of the Law of Property Act 1925 seems to imply that notice in writing would, before 1925, have been effective to sever a joint tenancy in personal property. It is clear that section 36(2), as Sir John Pennycuick is going to point out, made a radical alteration in the previous law by introducing the new method of severance by notice in writing, and that cases before 1925, in particular *In re Wilks, Child v Bulmer* [1891] 3 Ch 59, must now be read in the light of this alteration. I agree that an uncommunicated declaration by one joint tenant cannot operate as a severance.

SIR JOHN PENNYCUICK: . . . It is not in dispute that an agreement for severance between joint tenants effects a severance. This is the rule 2 propounded by Sir William Page Wood V-C in *Williams v Hensman*, 1 John&Hem 546, 557. . . . In the present case the judge found as a fact that Mr Honick and Mrs Rawnsley at the beginning of July 1968 agreed upon the sale by her to him of her share at the price of £750 . . . Once that finding of facts is accepted, the case falls squarely within rule 2 of Page Wood V-C. It is not contended that it is material that the parties by mutual consent did not proceed to carry out the agreement. Rule 2 applies equally, I think, whether the agreement between the two joint tenants is expressly to sever or is to deal with the property in a manner which involves severance. Mr Levy contended that in order that rule 2 should apply, the agreement must be specifically enforceable. I do not see any sufficient reason for importing this qualification. The significance of an agreement is not that it binds the parties; but that it serves as an indication of a common intention to sever, something which it was indisputably within their power to do. It will be observed that Page Wood V-C in his rule 2 makes no mention of specific enforceability. Contrast this position where severance is claimed under his rule 1 by reason of alienation by one joint tenant in favour of a third party . . .

Mr Mummery advanced an alternative argument to the effect that even if there were no agreement by Mr Honick to purchase Mrs Rawnsley's share, nevertheless the mere proposal by Mr Honick to purchase her share would operate as a severance under rule 3 in *Williams v Hensman*, 1 John&Hem 546, 557 . . .

I do not doubt myself that where one tenant negotiates with another for some rearrangement of interest, it may be possible to infer from the particular facts a common intention to sever even though the negotiations break down. Whether such an inference can be drawn must I think depend upon the particular facts. In the present case the negotiations between Mr Honick and Mrs Rawnsley, if they can be properly described as negotiations at all, fall, it seems to me, far short of warranting an inference. One could not ascribe to joint tenants an intention to sever merely because one offers to buy out the other for £X and the other makes a counter-offer of £Y.

. . . I think it may be helpful to state very shortly certain views which I have formed in the light of the authorities.

(1) I do not think rule 3 in Page Wood V-C's statement, 1 John&Hem 546, 557, is a mere sub-heading of rule 2. It covers only acts of the parties, including, it seems to me, negotiations which, although not otherwise resulting in any agreement, indicate a common intention that the joint tenancy should be regarded as severed.

I do not overlook the words which I have read from Page Wood V-C's statement, namely, that you must find a course of dealing by which the shares of all the parties to the contract have been affected. But I do not think those words are sufficient to import a binding agreement.

(2)   Section 36(2) of the Law of Property Act 1925 has radically altered the law in respect of severance by introducing an entirely new method of severance as regards land, namely, notice in writing given by one joint tenant to the other.

(3)   Pre-1925 judicial statements, in particular that of Stirling J in *In re Wilks, Child* v *Bulmer* [1891] 3 Ch 59, must be read in the light of this alteration in the law; and, in particular, I do not see why the commencement of legal proceedings by writ or originating summons or the swearing of an affidavit in those proceedings, should not in appropriate circumstances constitute notice in writing within the meaning of section 36(2). The fact that the plaintiff is not obliged to prosecute the proceedings is I think irrelevant in regard to notice.

(4)   Perhaps in parenthesis because the point does not arise, the language of section 36(2) appears to contemplate that even under the existing law notice in writing would be effective to sever a joint tenancy in personalty: see the words 'such other act or thing'. The authorities to the contrary are rather meagre and I am not sure how far this point was ever really considered in relation to personalty before 1925. If this anomaly does exist, and I am afraid I am not prepared to say positively that it does not exist, the anomaly is quite indefensible and should be put right as soon as possible.

(6)   An uncommunicated declaration by one party to the other or indeed a mere verbal notice by one party to another clearly cannot operate as a severance.

(7)   The policy of the law as it stands today, having regard particularly to section 36(2), is to facilitate severance at the instance of either party, and I do not think the court should be over zealous in drawing a fine distinction from the pre-1925 authorities.

(8)   The foregoing statement of principles involves criticism of certain passages in the judgments of Plowman J and Walton J in the two cases cited. Those cases, like all other cases, depend on their own particular facts, and I do not myself wish to go on to apply these obiter statements of principle to the actual decisions in these cases.

Comment

(1) These cases raise many difficult issues. Do the old common law rules have any significance today?

(2) So far as unilateral declarations are concerned (and leaving s 36(2) written notices on one side), is Walton J supported by the older cases? What does the Court of Appeal say on this point?

(3) In what way, if at all, is the third of Page-Wood VC's methods of severance (course of dealing) wider than the second (agreement)?

(4) Agreements to sell or dispose of an interest in land must be in writing.[12] Is it consistent with the wording or the spirit of this requirement to permit oral agreements to sever?

(5) Turning to written notices under s 36(2), why was there no notice from the correspondence in *Nielson-Jones* v *Fedden*? Are the comments by Walton J convincing? See Prichard [1975] CLJ 28.

(6) Lord Denning was keen to extend s 36(2) notices to personalty, so that this form of severance is widely available. Is this justified on the wording of the section and on principle? What do the other judges say on this question?[13]

---

[12]   Law of Property (Miscellaneous Provisions) Act 1989, s 2 (Extract 5.2.3 above).
[13]   See Hayton [1976] CLJ 20.

Nielson-Jones involved an agreement to sell the jointly owned house. The following extract considers the operation of severance in that context.

Extract 11.3.5

Davis v *Smith* [2011] EWCA Civ 1603; [2012] 1 FLR 1177

The joint tenants agreed to sell the land and divide the proceeds. Proceeds from an insurance policy were divided unequally between them, with the proceeds from the land sale to be adjusted to take account of this. One of them died before sale took place.

LORD NEUBERGER MR: 12. The law relating to severance is largely to be found in the decision of the Court of Appeal in *Burgess* v *Rawnsley* [1975] Ch 429. . . .

14. Applying these principles to this case, it seems to me that there is obvious force in the point advanced by Ms April Plant in her well presented written and oral submissions that neither the proposal nor the agreement to put the house on the market, nor even the acceptance of a subject to contract offer, could have severed the joint tenancy on their own. Even a sale could be said to have been entirely consistent, on the face of it at least, with the joint tenancy continuing and applying to the proceeds of sale. This is consistent with what was said by Mummery LJ in *Marshall* v *Marshall* [1998] EWCA Civ 1467 . . .

15. This is not, however, a case where all that happened was that it was agreed that a jointly owned property would be placed on the market; nor is it even a case where the only relevant fact is that the house was put on the market and a subject to contract offer had been made and accepted. What passed between the parties went further than that.

16. First, there was what was stated in the correspondence and the 22 June meeting. More than once it had been indicated by Mr Smith's solicitor that the house should be sold and that the proceeds of sale would be divided. . . .

18. Thirdly, there was not merely the attitude expressed in relation to the proceeds of the surrender of the policy, but the fact that the policy was actually surrendered and the proceeds distributed unequally between the parties on the clearly agreed basis that a balancing payment was then to be made to Mrs Smith to reflect the fact that she had received less of the proceeds of the surrender of the policy. . . .

21. In my view, therefore, applying the principles laid down in *Burgess*, the Judge reached the right conclusion [that there was severance]. Whether one would reach the same conclusion on the basis of what was said in the correspondence, without any action having been taken in relation to the policy, need not been decided, but I would incline to the view that there was enough in the correspondence taken as a whole to justify the same result. Whether one can go even further, as was postulated during argument, and say that simply by agreeing that the property would be sold in the context of the divorce which was under way, in circumstances where both parties must have appreciated that there would be a fifty-fifty split of proceeds, is not a point that needs to be decided. It may be enough of a reason for distinguishing *Marshall* and giving effect to the intention of the parties; on the other hand, it may be a step too far.

Comment

(1) Why does the law distinguish between agreements to sell the land and agreements to sell a joint tenant's share?

(2) Should an agreement to sell the land suffice to sever? Does it?

Extract 11.3.6

Harris v *Goddard* [1983] 1 WLR 1203

Severance was argued upon the wording of a court application, in divorce proceedings, relating to the land.

LAWTON LJ: . . . Counsel on both sides in this court went through the authorities again, starting with *Blackstone's Commentaries*, 8th ed (1778), vol 2, p 185. I did not find them of much help. The question to be decided in this appeal is the correct construction of the proviso to section 36(2) of the Law of Property Act 1925. Parliament intended this Act to define rights of property. It made radical changes in the law. I can see no good reason for looking behind the words of the Act unless they are capable of more than one meaning or the meaning is obscure.

I start with section 36. It dealt with beneficial joint tenancies, which must mean all joint tenancies, including those held by husbands and wives. The section makes no special provisions by way of giving extra rights or raising presumptions in favour of spouses . . . In reaching this conclusion I have followed what Russell LJ said in *Bedson v Bedson* [1965] 2 QB 666, 689–690 rather than the obiter statement of Lord Denning MR in the same case at p 678. Lord Denning MR said that spouses holding as beneficial joint tenants cannot sever their interests so as to convert them into tenancies in common . . .

In *Williams v Hensman* (1861) 1 Johns&Hem 546, 557, Page-Wood V-C said that a joint tenancy could be severed in three ways, that is, by disposal of one of the interests, by mutual agreement and 'by any course of dealing sufficient to intimate that the interests of all were mutually treated as constituting a tenancy in common'. The words in section 36(2) 'do such other acts or things as would . . . have been effectual to sever the tenancy' put into statutory language the other ways of effecting severance to which Page-Wood V-C referred in *Williams v Hensman*. The words 'and any tenant desires to sever the joint tenancy in equity, he shall give to the other joint tenants a notice in writing of such desire' operate to extend the mutual agreement concept of severance referred to in *Williams v Hensman*. Unilateral action to sever a joint tenancy is now possible. Before 1925 severance by unilateral action was only possible when one joint tenant disposed of his interest to a third party. When a notice in writing of a desire to sever is served pursuant to section 36(2) it takes effect forthwith. It follows that a desire to sever must evince an intention to bring about the wanted result immediately. A notice in writing which expresses a desire to bring about the wanted result at some time in the future is not, in my judgment, a notice in writing within section 36(2) . . . I am unable to accept Mr Berry's submission that a notice in writing which shows no more than a desire to bring the existing interest to an end is a good notice. It must be a desire to sever which is intended to have the statutory consequences. Paragraph 3 of the prayer to the petition does no more than invite the court to consider at some future time whether to exercise its jurisdiction under section 24 of the Act of 1973, and if it does, to do so in one or more of three different ways. Orders under section 24(1) (a) and (b) could bring co-ownership to an end by ways other than by severance. It follows, in my judgment, that paragraph 3 of the prayer of the petition did not operate as a notice in writing to sever the joint tenancy in equity . . .

Perhaps this case should be a cautionary tale for those who draft divorce petitions when the spouses hold property as joint tenants in equity. The decision of Plowman J in *In re Draper's Conveyance* [1969] 1 Ch 486 is an example of how starting legal proceedings can sever a joint tenancy . . . Plowman J adjudged that the summons and the affidavit together effected a severance during the lifetime of the husband. I agree that it did . . . I do not share the doubts about the correctness of this judgment on this point which Walton J expressed in *Nielson-Jones v Fedden* [1975] Ch 222, 236 relying on *In re Wilks* [1891] 3 Ch 59. The fact that the wife in *In re Draper's Conveyance* [1969] 1 Ch 486 could have withdrawn the summons is a factor which could have been taken into account in deciding whether what was done was effectual to sever the joint tenancy in equity. The weight of that factor would have depended upon all the other circumstances and was in that case clearly negligible.

Comment

(1) Does this shed any light on severance other than by a s 36(2) written notice?

(2) Should the law be proud of the way in which a notice of severance is (or is not) found in these cases?

Extract 11.3.7

Gore & Snell v *Carpenter* (1990) 60 P&CR 456 (Ch D)

On marriage breakdown, there were negotiations concerning a separation agreement, which would include severance. During these negotiations, the husband died.

JUDGE BLACKETT-ORD: . . . Then, was there a course of dealing? There were negotiations, as I have said, but negotiations are not the same thing as a course of dealing. A course of dealing is where over the years the parties have dealt with their interests in the property on the footing that they are interests in common and are not joint . . . In the present case there was, of course, . . . negotiation, but I cannot infer from it a common intention to sever, because I do not think that Mrs Carpenter was prepared to commit herself at that stage . . .

It is, in my judgment, a question of intention and this applies also when it is a question of the fourth possible method of severance, namely the service of a notice under section 36(2) of the Law of Property Act. It is argued for the executors that the proposed separation agreement put forward by Mr Carpenter amounted to such a notice. It will be recalled that the paragraph I read expressly refers to severance, but that was only part of the deed and the deed was never accepted. It was put forward by Mr Carpenter, not in isolation but as part of the package of proposals, and was not intended in my judgment and therefore did not take effect as a notice under section 36(2). Later, as I have said, Mr Gore was advising Mr Carpenter to serve a notice or notices under the Act and Mr Carpenter refused to do so. I think that there is nothing in the correspondence which can fairly be called a notice of severance . . .

Comment

Is the judge's conclusion consistent with *Burgess* v *Rawnsley*?

Extract 11.3.8

Kinch v *Bullard* [1999] 1 WLR 423

A wife posted a s 36(2) notice of severance. The husband suffered a heart attack and the wife, realising that survivorship could operate in her favour, destroyed the notice after it had been delivered. The husband died, unaware of the notice; the wife subsequently also died.

NEUBERGER J: . . . In light of the provisions of section 36(2) of the Act of 1925, the question as to whether or not the joint tenancy was severed depends on whether Mrs Johnson 'gave' the notice to Mr Johnson. As a matter of ordinary language, at least on the assumptions I am currently making, the notice was not 'given' to Mr Johnson, because he never received it. In order to justify the contention that the notice was in fact given to Mr Johnson, the plaintiffs rely on section 196 of the Act of 1925 . . . Section 196(3) and (4) is in the following terms:

> (3) Any notice . . . shall be sufficiently served if it is left at the last-known place of abode or business in the United Kingdom of the . . . person to be served . . .'

It appears to me that the natural meaning of section 196(3) is that, if a notice can be shown to have been left at the last-known abode or place of business of the addressee, then that constitutes good service, even if the addressee does not actually receive it . . .

Thirdly, it was contended on behalf of the defendants that the fact that Mrs Johnson changed her mind and no longer 'desired to sever the joint tenancy' by the time that the notice might otherwise have been said to have been 'given' (i.e. by the time that the notice arrived at the property) meant that the notice was ineffective to effect such severance. This argument is based on the language of section 36(2). Assuming that the notice was validly 'given' pursuant to section 196(3), the giving of the notice only occurred when it was actually delivered to the property, and at that time Mrs Johnson no longer 'desired to sever the joint tenancy'. Accordingly, it is said that the statutory precondition for the giving of a valid notice was not, at the date it was given, satisfied, because at that date Mrs Johnson did not have the necessary 'desire'.

In my judgment, this argument is not correct. The function of the relevant part of section 36(2) is to instruct any joint tenant who desires to sever the joint tenancy how to do it: he is to give the appropriate notice (or do such other things as are prescribed by the section). Clear words would be required, in my judgment, before a provision such as section 36(2) could be construed as requiring the court to inquire into the state of mind of the sender of the notice. Once the sender has served the requisite notice, the deed is done and cannot be undone. . . .

I reach this conclusion based on the proper construction of section 36(2). However, it appears to me that it is also correct as a matter of policy. If it were possible for a notice of severance or any other notice to be ineffective because, between the sender putting it in the post and the addressee receiving it, the sender changed his mind, it would be inconvenient and potentially unfair. The addressee would not be able to rely confidently upon a notice after it had been received, because he might subsequently be faced with the argument that the sender had changed his mind after sending it and before its receipt. Further, as I have already mentioned, it is scarcely realistic to think that the legislature intended that the court could be required to inquire into the state of mind of the sender of the notice in order to decide whether the notice was valid.

I am inclined to think that the position would be different if, before the notice was 'given', the sender had informed the addressee that he wished to revoke it. In such a case, it appears to me that the notice would have been withdrawn before it had been 'given' . . .

So far as convenience is concerned, I consider that, if section 196(3) is satisfied once it is shown that the relevant document was bona fide delivered to the last-known place of abode or business of the addressee, then, although it might lead to an unfair result in an exceptional case, the law is at least simple and clear. On the other hand, if the court starts implying exceptions into the clear and simple statutory procedure, confusion and uncertainty could result. Thus, if, by picking up the notice after it was posted through the front door of the property, Mrs Johnson might have prevented the notice being 'served', problems could arise. Would there be a maximum time within which Mrs Johnson would have to pick up the notice before it would be held to be validly served? Would it make any difference if Mr Johnson had seen the envelope containing the notice on the mat? What if Mrs Johnson had picked up the notice and had kept it but not destroyed it? What if she had picked up the notice intending to destroy it but had changed her mind? What if she had picked up the notice and tried to destroy it, but Mr Johnson had seen her doing it, or had seen and read the imperfectly burnt notice?

The defendants also rely on the unusual feature of this case that the person who physically got the notice, and indeed who destroyed it, was the very person who sent it, namely Mrs Johnson. It can be said to be one thing for a sender to be entitled to assume that he has given a notice to the addressee if he serves at the property, even if a third party picked up the notice and filed it away or destroyed it: as between the sender and the addressee, one can see good policy reasons as to why such a risk, like the possibility of the dog eating the notice, should be that of the addressee and not that of the sender. However, there is obviously a powerful argument for saying that the position should surely be different where it is the sender herself who has picked up the notice and filed it away or destroyed it.

It is not so much that the facts of this case cause me concern: if the defendants, as the executors of Mrs Johnson, are effectively 'landed' with the consequences of Mrs Johnson having served the notice, that does not seem to me to be a particularly unfair result, particularly bearing in mind the extent to which equity tends to lean against joint tenancies: see the discussion in *Megarry & Wade, The Law of Real Property*, 5th ed (1984), p 427. However, I am concerned that, if it could be said that the notice in the present case was validly served, unfair advantage could be taken of an addressee by the sender of a notice if the sender (or his agent) had some means of access to the notice after it was served in accordance with section 196 but before the addressee actually saw it, and this resulted in the notice being destroyed or hidden without the addressee ever becoming aware of it . . .

On reflection, however, I think it neither appropriate nor desirable to impose such a further qualification on the plain words of section 196(3). First, as a matter of general principle, the court should be slow to imply qualifications into a statutory provision, particularly when that provision is clear and simple in its effect and is intended to have practical consequences. Secondly, it does not seem to me that a conclusion in favour of the plaintiffs in the present case should lead to any unfair abuse. In the present case, it is Mr Johnson (or, more accurately, his executors) who wish to allege that the notice delivered by Mrs Johnson was validly served in light of section 196(3). There is no potential for abuse in that context. If, however, it was the defendants, the executors of Mrs Johnson, who were seeking to allege that the notice was validly served, then it seems to me that it would be open to the plaintiffs, as executors of Mr Johnson, to contend successfully that, despite the apparent applicability of section 196(3), valid service had not been effected. In my judgment, it would not have been open to the defendants to contend, as against the plaintiffs, that the notice had been validly served on the instant facts, because it cannot be right for a sender of a notice, who had intentionally taken steps to ensure that it did not in fact come to the attention of the addressee, to contend that it was served on him. In other words, whatever section 196 provides, it could not be relied on by the sender of a notice as an engine of fraud. The very purpose of serving a notice is to convey information, with legal consequences, on the addressee: it cannot be right that the sender of a notice can take positive steps to ensure that the notice does not come to the attention of the addressee, after it has been statutorily deemed to have been served, and then fall back on the statute to allege that service has none the less been effected.

Comment

(1) Section 196(4) deals with registered letters: they are deemed served unless returned undelivered.

(2) How strong is the argument that the addressee was not prejudiced by the posting and destruction of the notice and therefore that the notice should not have been effective?

(3) Are there any circumstances in which delivery of a notice of severance will not be conclusive?

A very different form of severance is based on public policy. If one of two joint tenants murders the other, it would plainly be repugnant to public opinion for the murderer to gain the victim's share.

Extract 11.3.9

Re K [1985] Ch 85

VINELOTT J: . . . As I have mentioned the matrimonial home (which is registered land) was vested in the deceased and the widow as joint tenants at law and in equity. Mr Barlow on behalf of the widow accepts that the forfeiture rule unless modified under the Act of 1982 applies in effect to sever the joint tenancy in the proceeds of sale and in the rents and profits until sale. I think that concession is rightly made. There is curiously no reported case on the point in England but it has been held in other jurisdictions where the law was similar to English law before 1925 that where one of two joint tenants murders the other while the entire interest vests in the survivor the law imports a constructive trust of an undivided one-half share for the benefit of the next of kin of the deceased other than the offender: see *Schobelt* v *Barber* (1966) 60 DLR

(2d) 519, and *In re Pechar, decd* [1969] NZLR 574. Under English law since 1925 the result is more simply reached by treating the beneficial interest as vesting in the deceased and the survivor as tenants in common.

Comment

(1) Most issues in this area concern either the types of killing that activate this 'forfeiture' principle or the modification of forfeiture by the Forfeiture Act 1982. These topics were considered on appeal in *Re K*,[14] but lie outside the scope of this book.

(2) Suppose Rachel, Samantha and Terry are joint tenants. If another person, Ursula, murders Terry, then Rachel and Samantha are the surviving joint tenants. According to *Re K*, what happens if it were Samantha who had murdered Terry? How well do these two situations fit together? See *Rasmanis* v *Jurewitsch* (1970) 70 SR NSW 407 and *Cawley* v *Lillis* [2013] WTLR 559 (Ireland); also Law Com No 295, paras 2.27, 3.21–3.24.

Standing back from the detail of the cases, it needs to be considered what attitude ought to be taken to severance today. It is clear from the modern cases that severance (and survivorship) problems arise following the breakdown of relationships, most often marriage. While a joint tenancy was entirely appropriate when the relationship was in good health, it is plainly inappropriate once it has broken down. Accordingly, it is easy to understand a desire to make severance as flexible as possible. On the other hand, this can lead to considerable uncertainty as to property rights. Not only may this result in expensive litigation, but it can place purchasers in a very difficult position. The written notice introduced by s 36(2) avoids most of these problems by virtue of requiring writing. Questions which need to be considered include the following. Should the courts develop severance outside the written notice? Are there circumstances in which the law on written notice fails to provide certainty? How might the statutory provisions be usefully amended?

4. Do we need both the joint tenancy and the tenancy in common?

The above concluding remarks on severance reveal how survivorship within a joint tenancy can provide inappropriate results. Further, the existence of the two forms of co-ownership inevitably complicates the law. If we were to recognise only the tenancy in common then this entire chapter could be excised. It might be noted that a single form of co-ownership would have to be modelled on the tenancy in common. The unity of interest and survivorship inherent within joint tenancies mean that they signally fail to offer the flexibility in co-ownership that any modern society requires. It will be seen in the following chapter that the joint tenancy has an important role to play as the form of landholding appropriate for trustees: every co-ownership today operates under a trust. Insofar as the joint tenancy might be argued to be undesirable, this is limited to beneficial joint tenancies.

---

[14] [1986] Ch 180.

Extract 11.4.1

M P Thompson [1987] Conv 29 at pp 30–35 (footnotes omitted)

THE DRAWBACKS OF BENEFICIAL JOINT TENANCIES

If the conveyance to joint owners contains an express declaration that they are to hold as beneficial joint tenants then in the absence of a claim to rectification, this declaration is conclusive. How these declarations come to be made in the conveyance is not known. One suspects, however, that in the normal case involving cohabiting couples, be they married or not, it stems from them being asked by their solicitor whether it is desired that the other gets the house if one of them dies. If the answer is affirmative then this result is assured by the creation of a beneficial joint tenancy.

The main problem with this is that it can store up trouble for the future if the relationship turns sour. Then, the last thing that may be intended is that the survivor should become sole owner of the house. Instead, it may well be preferred that what is perceived as an individual share should go to other members of the family. Had the prevailing wish at the time of acquisition been effected by a will rather than by using the right of survivorship, this will be known to the parties who can accordingly alter their wills . . .

SEVERANCE

The three methods of severance articulated by Sir William Page-Wood V-C in *Williams* v *Hensman* are well known and hardly need repeating here. Unfortunately, although the methods are familiar, their application continues to prove difficult as is evidenced by the recent spate of litigation on this issue . . .

When a course of conduct is relied upon as having effected severance, difficult problems can also ensue. In these cases one must find a mutual intent to sever, the onus of proof being on the person alleging severance. These cases entail a close examination of the conduct of the parties including any explanation of facts which would ordinarily evince an intention to sever but were not in fact done for that purpose. This must represent a problem for the administrators of a deceased joint tenant's estate. They may well be in a quandary as to whether or not the other joint tenant is entitled by survivorship or whether there had been severance and another person is entitled under the deceased's will or intestacy. This is of some importance, bearing in mind that a mistake as to this can be costly. Similarly, the surviving co-owner may wish, if severance has occurred and he is not entitled on death, to make a claim under the Inheritance (Provision for Family and Dependants) Act 1975. This uncertainty and possible litigation could be avoided had they been tenants in common from the outset.

. . .

THE EFFECT OF SEVERANCE

In *Goodman* v *Gallant* it was held, resolving some earlier doubts, that upon severance of a beneficial joint tenancy, the tenants in common take in equal shares, regardless of the relative size of their contributions to the purchase price. This is certainly correct in principle but may nevertheless represent a trap for the unwary. As indicated previously, a co-owning couple may have become joint tenants as a result of their response to a question as to whether it is intended that the survivor should take the house on the death of one of them. A matter which may not have been addressed is who gets what proportion of the proceeds of sale in the event of a sale following the breakdown of the relationship. A person who has provided the lion's share of the purchase price may be surprised to learn that he is only entitled to a half share in this event. Accordingly, it would seem preferable if this matter was squarely addressed at the outset by the creation of a tenancy in common in whatever shares the parties think appropriate.

CONCLUSIONS

It is hoped to have shown that little of advantage would be lost if joint tenancies were confined to ownership of the legal estate. In fairness, it should be pointed out that the abolition of equitable joint tenancies would carry one drawback. On the death of one of the tenants in common the sole survivor would need to appoint a second trustee to effect a sale of the property. It could not be assumed that the survivor took under the will of the deceased, thereby terminating the co-ownership. While this is a disadvantage, it is suggested that it is outweighed by the advantages.

These advantages can be summarised as including ridding the law of the difficult and technical problem of determining whether severance has occurred and the concomitant possibility that the right of survivorship may operate inappropriately. Instead, the destination of the beneficial interests on death would be determined by each party's will which, one hopes, each would be encouraged to make when the property was acquired. Secondly, potential problems or interpretation of the Forfeiture Act 1982 would be avoided and, finally, each party would be encouraged to agree at the outset what share each would get in the event of a sale.

For these reasons it is hoped that in any reform of co-ownership, consideration will be given to the abolition of beneficial joint tenancies. If, as is suggested, they were to be abolished then it is thought that the scope for much troublesome and expensive litigation will be reduced. In the meantime, however, it is urged that when acting for a couple buying a house together, solicitors should encourage their clients to take as tenants in common, thereby achieving the same result. In this way, when co-ownership arises the parties would be encouraged to work out for themselves their respective rights in the property, rather than having that done for them by law in a manner which may ultimately prove not to be what they would have wanted.

Extract 11.4.2

A M Prichard [1987] Conv 273 at pp 273–275 (footnotes omitted)

In his recent article 'Beneficial Joint Tenancies: A Case for Abolition?' Mr Mark Thompson has reviewed a number of complications that can occur in law where land has been vested in co-owners as beneficial joint tenants. His suggested solution is to leave potential co-owners with just the one form, the tenancy in common, in respect of the beneficial interest in land. He also suggests that until legislation is effected to this end practitioners should urge clients to adopt that form of co-ownership. What he does not seem to make entirely clear is whether spouses and other co-purchasers should adopt a tenancy in equal shares or one according to their contributions, in so far as they may be at the outset calculable.

The mischiefs he envisages as justifying this radical solution are:

(i)   problems when the marriage or other initial arrangement goes sour;
(ii) the uncertainties as to the manners in which severance may be effected;
(iii) the special problems arising when one co-owner is responsible for the death of another; and
(iv) the unpleasant surprise for a severing co-owner that a severance will create equal beneficial shares, not resurrect the original contribution proportions.

Underlying all these mischiefs seems to be a belief that the parties have often, perhaps even usually, opted for joint tenancy without adequate advice. Is there any real evidence that this is so?

If mischief (iv) is a real one, the moral seems to be that couples should make their homes not on a pooling basis, but on 'what's mine remains mine, thank you' basis. Is it fanciful to suspect that this might lead to an increase in mischief (i)? Again, is mischief (iii) so widespread and intractable as not to be curable by minor amendments to the Forfeiture Act 1982? Similarly, could not mischief (ii) be best met by clearer legislation on the means of severance if, *ex hypothesi*, there is to be legislation?

Mischief (i) remains as at least a seemingly major problem. But how often can one categorically say that injustice has been worked by a failure to sever in time? Any more often than might be the cases of a surviving spouse or other co-tenant failing to 'inherit' by absence or failure of testation? And could not the mischief, if mischief it is thought to be, be best solved by legislation allowing severance by will?

Against all this is the clear fact that many people are genuinely attracted to the survival aspects of joint tenancy. Not just married couples in the first romantic flush, wishing to demonstrate the full commitment of their mutual vows, but also unmarried siblings anxious to secure the smooth transmission of ownership as death overtakes each of them in their family home; or the father or mother in business with a child, wishing to effect just such a smooth transmission whether deaths do or do not occur in expected order. Should such people be told by the law that their simple wish should not be attainable in their purchase deed, but should require their immediate execution of a perhaps complex and expensive will as well (especially if licensed conveyancers are acting, who are not trained or empowered to act professionally in respect of wills)? With money and other property they can have the very useful apparatus of joint accounts and joint ownership – how useful, anyone advising a recent widow or widower can readily testify. Or is Mr Thompson suggesting that that apparatus too should be done away with so as to meet the possible desires of soured co-owners?

Mr Thompson admits one drawback, but dismisses it cursorily as outweighed by the advantages he sees in exclusive tenancies in common. This is the need for appointment of a second trustee if the survivor wishes to sell: no longer could the benefits of the Law of Property (Joint Tenants) Act 1964, relating to unregistered land, be relied upon. The second trustee, however, is not the sole drawback. What if the widow or widower wishes to sell at an under-value, to, for instance, a child or other relative? . . .

The fundamental issue, however, remains whether the current option which is, in this writer's experience, often taken up with enthusiasm by co-owners should be denied them. Is it unarguably the case that the unsuccessful partnerships should dictate the apparatus of the law? If a relationship turns sour enough, why should not an aggrieved co-owner effect a severance? And are not the powers of the court to divide property on a break-down of a marriage sufficient? And is not the Inheritance (Provision for Family and Dependants) Act 1975 an adequate protection to cover the hardest cases that might occur through the failure to sever? Especially if the law were changed to allow severance by will?

Comment

(1) Note also the reply by Thompson [1987] Conv 275.

(2) It is estimated that 90% of married co-owners choose a joint tenancy.[15]

(3) Is the case for the abolition of beneficial joint tenancies made out?

Further reading

Butt, P (1982) 9 Syd LR 568: Severance of joint tenancies in matrimonial property.

Luther, P (1995) 15 LS 219: *Williams* v *Hensman* and the uses of history.

McClean, A J (1979) 57 Can BR 1: Severance of joint tenancies.

---

[15] *Administration of Estates – Review of the Statutory Legacy*, pp 31–32 (DCA CP 11/05).

12
Trusts of land

Since 1925, every concurrent and successive interest has taken effect under a trust. Thus there will be a trust whenever a couple buy a house together or if property is left to a widower for life, remainder to his daughter. In this chapter, we are principally concerned with how this trust works, the rights accorded to the beneficiaries and the protection accorded to third parties (especially purchasers) dealing with the trustees. Since 1996, trusts of land have been regulated by the Trusts of Land and Appointment of Trustees Act 1996 (hereafter TLATA or 1996 Act) and it is to this legislation that we must turn for much of our investigation of the law.

Before TLATA, most trusts[1] took the form of a trust for sale and were regulated by the Law of Property Act 1925 (hereafter LPA). There was much litigation on the operation of the trust for sale and, in particular, when sale would be ordered. Despite the nominal stress on sale, the trust almost invariably contained a power to postpone sale (it would be implied) and the courts were able to delay sale until the purpose for which the property had been bought no longer operated. A recurring question in this chapter is the extent to which the pre-TLATA cases can be relied upon today. Many of the principles in those cases have been incorporated into TLATA, and it follows that frequently we can look to the earlier material as a guide to the likely application of TLATA. On the other hand, there are some areas in which the legislation goes much further (or provides more detailed guidance) than the previous law: beneficiaries' rights to occupy provide perhaps the best example.

The legislation does not distinguish between successive and concurrent interests. However, some provisions are especially applicable to successive interests and full consideration of these is postponed to the following chapter. Beyond this, many provisions may have a somewhat different effect according to the nature of the interests. In particular, most concurrent interests will have one or more of the beneficiaries as the trustees, whereas successive interests are more likely to involve independent trustees. This is a vitally important factor in considering both how disagreements are likely to arise and the courts' likely response to them.

How does TLATA apply to trusts for sale? For the future, it remains possible to create trusts for sale expressly. However, whenever statute implies a trust, it is a 'simple' trust of land. Trusts for sale will be considered at the end of this chapter, where it will be seen that they differ from simple trusts of land in only very minor ways. It would be surprising if many new trusts for sale were to be created: there is little point in doing so.

Turning to pre-1996 trusts, after 1925 every concurrent interest involved a trust for sale. There are two separate points to grasp regarding TLATA. The first is that trusts for sale implied by the legislation cease to be trusts for sale, becoming simple trusts of land;[2] express trusts

---

[1] Exceptions were bare trusts (neither successive nor concurrent interests) and, for successive interests, settlements under the Settled Land Act 1925. Settled land is briefly considered in the following chapter.

[2] TLATA, Sched 2.

for sale remain trusts for sale. The second point is that all pre-1996 trusts of land, whether or not trusts for sale, are covered by TLATA and its regulatory regime.[3]

1. When is there a trust of land?

A. Statutory definition

Extract 12.1.1

Trusts of Land and Appointment of Trustees Act 1996, s 1

1.—(1) In this Act—

(a) 'trust of land' means (subject to subsection (3)) any trust of property which consists of or includes land, and

(b) 'trustees of land' means trustees of a trust of land.

(2) The reference in subsection (1)(a) to a trust—

(a) is to any description of trust (whether express, implied, resulting or constructive), including a trust for sale and a bare trust, and

(b) includes a trust created, or arising, before the commencement of this Act.

Comment

(1) Note that this automatically catches successive interests, which can take effect only as equitable interests by virtue of LPA, s 1.

(2) TLATA, Sched 1 ensures that the Act applies to certain other situations, especially grants to infants and family charges. These situations had previously been within the Settled Land Act regime, but that regime applies only to pre-1996 settlements.

(3) The definition covers bare trusts (as where Sheila holds on trust for Tabitha absolutely), which had previously not been subject to any regulatory regime. This is particularly important as regards the protection of purchasers from the trustees.

(4) The stress on trusts raises the question as to whether TLATA might apply to situations where one would not expect the Act's regulatory control to operate. Are trusts of land to be found outside the conventional contexts of concurrent interests, successive interests and bare trusts?

The use of a trust in grants to infants has caused problems where the grant takes the form of a lease. The following Extract considers the question whether a landlord can exercise rights as landlord when the land is held on trust (by the landlord) for an infant tenant.

Extract 12.1.2

Hammersmith and Fulham London Borough Council v *Alexander-David* **[2010] Ch 272**

SULLIVAN LJ: 14.   Miss Bretherton submitted on behalf of the defendant that when the agreement was made on 25 July 2006 the defendant was a minor. She could not hold a legal estate. In entering into its standard form tenancy agreement with the defendant the claimant had

---

[3] TLATA, s 1(2).

nevertheless purported to grant her a legal estate with the consequence that, in accordance with paragraph 1(1) of Schedule 1 to the Trusts of Land and Appointment of Trustees Act 1996 the agreement was not effective to grant her a legal tenancy, and operated as a declaration by the claimant that it held the premises in trust for her. As a trustee holding the premises on behalf of the defendant, the claimant could not, without committing a fundamental breach of trust, serve a notice to quit determining the subject matter of the trust . . .

[After considering the facts and the statutory background applicable to local authorities]

25.   In my judgment, none of these factors, whether considered individually or collectively, is sufficient to displace the obvious inference to be drawn from the fact that the agreement is in the claimant's standard form for creating legal tenancies with its adult tenants.

29.   There is a further difficulty with Mr Rutledge's submission that the claimant granted 'an equitable tenancy' of the premises. 'Equitable tenancy' is a convenient shorthand for a tenancy that is treated as being effective in equity even though it is, for some reason, not effective as a legal estate: eg because a trustee is holding the legal estate on trust for a minor, as in *Prince's* case [1999] LGR 333, or because there is only an agreement for a lease: see the example given in the Law Commission's report, para 5.15.

30.   I am not persuaded that a landlord who has full capacity to grant a legal tenancy, and who grants a tenancy without any express qualification to the effect that something less than a legal tenancy is being granted, can subsequently say that what he granted was not a legal tenancy but an 'equitable tenancy' . . .

35.   In the present case the claimant is, in the absence of any other trustee, in the uncomfortable position of being both lessor and trustee, and in the former capacity of being not merely a party to the breach of trust but the instigator of the breach. In these particular circumstances I con-clude that service of notice to quit only on the minor beneficiary of the trust was not sufficient to terminate the tenancy that was being held by the claimant as trustee on her behalf.

Comment

(1) The application of TLATA would seem difficult to avoid.

(2) The impact of the trust on most transfers of estates will be technical. However, there was a significant effect in the leasehold context of *Alexander-David*. Is this defensible?

B. Concurrent interests

Before the LPA 1925, concurrent interests could be legal: there would be no trust in the great majority of cases. A prime objective of the 1925 legislation was to simplify the sale of land (and also other transactions, such as leases and mortgages). Ease of sale demands that a small and manageable number of owners can sell the land. Why did concurrent interests cause problems before 1925? The answer lay within tenancies in common. Suppose that there were two tenants in common. One might die leaving her share to her five grandchildren. Instead of two co-owners, there are now six. Any purchase would require the participation of all of them. It is obvious that obtaining their agreement would often be difficult and, at best, be time-consuming.

The response was to create a trust and to empower the trustees to sell the land. By the process called overreaching,[4] the beneficial interests are removed from the land on sale and take effect against the proceeds of sale. The 1925 legislation employed a trust for sale, with a maximum of four trustees, to enable overreaching. The overreaching provisions

---

[4] Summarised at p 58 above. For details, see p 435 below.

were amended by TLATA so as to refer to trusts of land, but otherwise remain in much their original form. The existence of a trust of land ensures the operation not only of overreaching, but also of the entire regulatory regime in TLATA, with factors such as occupation rights and court control.

(i) Joint tenancies

Extract 12.1.3

Law of Property Act 1925, s 36

36.—(1)   Where a legal estate (not being settled land) is beneficially limited to or held in trust for any persons as joint tenants, the same shall be held in trust, in like manner as if the persons beneficially entitled were tenants in common, but not so as to sever their joint tenancy in equity.

Comment

The need for overreaching is not so obvious in the case of a joint tenancy, as the death of one joint tenant will reduce (by survivorship) the number of co-owners. Why, then, does the legislation provide that the co-owners hold the legal title on trust for themselves?

(ii) Tenancies in common

Extract 12.1.4

Law of Property Act 1925, ss 1(6), 34

1.—(6)   A legal estate is not capable of subsisting or of being created in an undivided share in land or of being held by an infant.

34.—(1)   An undivided share in land shall not be capable of being created except as provided by the Settled Land Act 1925 or as hereinafter mentioned.

(2)   Where, after the commencement of this Act, land is expressed to be conveyed to any persons in undivided shares and those persons are of full age, the conveyance shall (notwithstanding anything to the contrary in this Act) operate as if the land had been expressed to be conveyed to the grantees, or, if there are more than four grantees, to the four first named in the conveyance, as joint tenants in trust for the persons interested in the land:

. . .

(3)   A devise bequest or testamentary appointment, coming into operation after the commencement of this Act, of land to two or more persons in undivided shares shall operate as a devise bequest or appointment of the land to the personal representatives of the testator, and (but without prejudice to the rights and powers of the personal representatives for purposes of administration) in trust for the persons interested in the land.

(3A)   In subsections (2) and (3) of this section references to the persons interested in the land include persons interested as trustees or personal representatives (as well as persons beneficially interested).

Comment

(1) If land is transferred to A and B as tenants in common, what is the effect of this?

(2) If land is left by will to C and D as tenants in common, what is the effect of this?

Section 34(1) provides that an undivided share in land cannot be created save as provided by the Settled Land Act 1925 or as provided in s 34. It has long been appreciated that many tenancies in common appear to fall outside s 34(2) and (3), as shown by the following Extract, and yet it would be ridiculous for the law to fail to recognise a tenancy in common. Nobody, of course, argues that there can be a legal tenancy in common today: that would not only be inconsistent with the wording of the legislation, but also the overreaching and regulatory principles underpinning it.

Extract 12.1.5

Bull v *Bull* [1955] 1 QB 234

Land was purchased by the plaintiff, with his mother contributing part of the purchase money. These circumstances gave rise to a resulting trust and, as the contributions were unequal, a tenancy in common in equity. This is probably the best example of a tenancy in common which does not naturally fit within the wording of s 34(2): 'land is expressed to be conveyed to any persons in undivided shares'.

DENNING LJ: . . . I realize that since 1925 there has been no such thing as a legal tenancy in common: see section 1(6) of the Law of Property Act, 1925. All tenancies in common now are equitable only and they take effect behind a trust for sale: see section 36(4) of the Settled Land Act, 1925.

Comment

(1) At the time of *Bull* v *Bull*, the courts had to justify not merely a trust, but also a trust for sale. Now that a simple trust is employed by TLATA, this second point is no longer a problem.

(2) It has always been unclear how s 36(4) of the Settled Land Act 1925[5] assists in the resolution of the problem. However, the result of Denning LJ's brief analysis is convenient and has been routinely applied by later courts.

(3) Are there any ways in which s 34 could be interpreted so as to avoid the problem?

2. Occupation

This area is now covered by legislation. Although the courts had recognised before 1996 both that unity of possession involved a right to occupy all the land[6] and that equitable co-owners might have a right to occupy,[7] it is the legislation which must form the focus of our analysis.

---

[5] 'An undivided share in land shall not be capable of being created except under a trust instrument or under the Law of Property Act 1925, and shall then take effect behind a trust of land.' Trust instruments are relevant only to settled land.

[6] *Jacobs* v *Seward* (1872) LR 5 HL 464 (joint tenancy of legal estate).

[7] *Bull* v *Bull* [1955] 1 QB 234; *Williams & Glyn's Bank Ltd* v *Boland* [1981] AC 487; *City of London BS* v *Flegg* [1988] AC 54 (especially Lord Oliver). It has been argued that the old law conferred a universal right to occupy, wider than under TLATA: Barnsley [1998] CLJ 123.

A. Trusts of Land and Appointment of Trustees Act 1996

(i) Rights to occupy

Extract 12.2.1

Trusts of Land and Appointment of Trustees Act 1996, s 12

12.—(1) A beneficiary who is beneficially entitled to an interest in possession in land subject to a trust of land is entitled by reason of his interest to occupy the land at any time if at that time—

(a) the purposes of the trust include making the land available for his occupation (or for the occupation of beneficiaries of a class of which he is a member or of beneficiaries in general), or

(b) the land is held by the trustees so as to be so available.

(2) Subsection (1) does not confer on a beneficiary a right to occupy land if it is either unavailable or unsuitable for occupation by him.

(3) This section is subject to section 13.

Comment

(1) Note that s 12 confers rights to occupy upon beneficiaries with interests in possession. Unless other beneficiaries also have rights to occupy (covered by s 13), the trustees cannot deny such rights and, perhaps, neither can the court.

(2) It is likely that the purposes of the trust (para (a)) will be the most significant factor: this reflects the pre-1996 law. Obviously, houses are usually purchased for occupation, but occupation may not be the purpose of settlements of land (whether inter vivos or by will; whether involving concurrent or successive interests). All will depend upon the particular circumstances.

(3) What is the intended role of s 12(1)(b)?

(4) Limits are imposed by s 12(2). What is meant by 'unavailable'? Is it simply the opposite of 'available', which is the basis for a right to occupy under s 12(1)(b)?

(5) A very difficult question is whether suitability is a continuing requirement or a 'snapshot' requirement when occupation is first claimed. For example, could it be argued that, because a beneficiary has become aged and infirm, a house is no longer suitable for occupation by him? Alternatively, circumstances may have changed such that the purpose of occupation is no longer applicable (s 12(1)(a)). Which interpretation best fits the wording of s 12?

Extract 12.2.2

***Chan v Leung* [2003] 1 FLR 23**

JONATHAN PARKER LJ: 100. Given the judge's finding that one of the purposes of the trust of Hill House was to provide a home for Miss Chan should her relationship with Mr Leung come to an end, the short issue on this aspect of the case is whether Hill House is 'unsuitable for occupation by [Miss Chan]' within the meaning of section 12(1) of the TLATA.

101. There is no statutory definition or guidance as to what is meant by 'unsuitable' in this context, and it would be rash indeed to attempt an exhaustive definition or explanation of its meaning. In the context of the present case it is, I think, enough to say that 'suitability' for this purpose must involve a consideration not only of the general nature and physical characteristics of the particular property but also a consideration of the personal characteristics, circumstances and requirements of the particular beneficiary. This much is, I think, clear from the fact that the

statutory expression is not simply 'unsuitable for occupation' but 'unsuitable for occupation *by him*', that is to say by the particular beneficiary.

102. In the instant case Mr Leung's complaint, in substance, is that Hill House is too large for Miss Chan's needs and too expensive for her to maintain. However, taking into account that Miss Chan's requirement under the terms of the judge's order (which she has not cross-appealed) is for a right of occupation only until Summer 2003, I agree with the judge that Hill House is not 'unsuitable for occupation by [her]' within the meaning of section 12(1). In any event I would have taken some persuading that a property which was on any footing suitable for occupation by Miss Chan and Mr Leung whilst they lived together should be regarded as unsuitable for occupation by her alone once Mr Leung had left.

Comment

(1) It is unusual for the intention to be for use as a home of just one of a couple purchasing a home, but the case involved unusual facts.

(2) When might land be 'unsuitable'?

(3) Do the dicta support a continuing or snapshot approach to the s 12 requirements?

(ii) Regulation of occupation

Extract 12.2.3

Trusts of Land and Appointment of Trustees Act 1996, s 13

13.—(1)   Where two or more beneficiaries are (or apart from this subsection would be) entitled under section 12 to occupy land, the trustees of land may exclude or restrict the entitlement of any one or more (but not all) of them.

(2)   Trustees may not under subsection (1)—

    (a)   unreasonably exclude any beneficiary's entitlement to occupy land, or

    (b)   restrict any such entitlement to an unreasonable extent.

(3)   The trustees of land may from time to time impose reasonable conditions on any beneficiary in relation to his occupation of land by reason of his entitlement under section 12.

(4)   The matters to which trustees are to have regard in exercising the powers conferred by this section include—

    (a)   the intentions of the person or persons (if any) who created the trust,

    (b)   the purposes for which the land is held, and

    (c)   the circumstances and wishes of each of the beneficiaries who is (or apart from any previous exercise by the trustees of those powers would be) entitled to occupy the land under section 12.

(5)   The conditions which may be imposed on a beneficiary under subsection (3) include, in particular, conditions requiring him—

    (a)   to pay any outgoings or expenses in respect of the land, or

    (b)   to assume any other obligation in relation to the land or to any activity which is or is proposed to be conducted there.

(6)   Where the entitlement of any beneficiary to occupy land under section 12 has been excluded or restricted, the conditions which may be imposed on any other beneficiary under subsection (3) include, in particular, conditions requiring him to—

    (a)   make payments by way of compensation to the beneficiary whose entitlement has been excluded or restricted, or

    (b)   forgo any payment or other benefit to which he would otherwise be entitled under the trust so as to benefit that beneficiary.

(7) The powers conferred on trustees by this section may not be exercised—

    (a) so as prevent any person who is in occupation of land (whether or not by reason of an entitlement under section 12) from continuing to occupy the land, or

    (b) in a manner likely to result in any such person ceasing to occupy the land, unless he consents or the court has given approval.

(8) The matters to which the court is to have regard in determining whether to give approval under subsection (7) include the matters mentioned in subsection (4)(a) to (c).

Comment

(1) Under s 13(3), conditions may be imposed upon beneficiaries even where there is a single person entitled to occupy. What is the purpose of this?

(2) Otherwise, the powers are limited to the regulation of multiple rights to occupy. Does this constitute an unfortunate limitation upon the powers of trustees? Remembering that most concurrent interests involve the same persons being trustees and beneficiaries, how useful are the s 13 powers likely to prove in practice?

(3) Note that there are limits on what the trustees can do. For example, they cannot use their powers to evict existing occupiers save with the approval of the court: s 13(7). Does this prevent trustees from evicting beneficiaries who have no entitlement to occupation under s 12?[8]

Extract 12.2.4

Rodway v Landy **[2001] Ch 703**

The parties were medical practitioners who jointly owned a surgery. It was suggested that the building should be split between the two of them, so that each could practise from separate parts of the building.

PETER GIBSON LJ: 31. The main argument of Mr Berry related to section 13 of the 1996 Act. He submitted that the judge erred in concluding that he could make an order excluding or restricting each of the two doctors from a part of the property. This point turns on the construction of the words in parenthesis in section 13(1), '(but not all)' . . .

32. Mr Pearce supported the reasoning and conclusion of the judge. He said that to construe the subsection literally, as Mr Berry urged, would produce an irrational limitation on section 13(1) as it would mean that the trustees can exclude one of two beneficiaries entirely from the occupation of trust property but not limit each of them to occupation of only part of it. Mr Pearce urged that the words 'but not all' mean that the trustees may not exclude or restrict the entitlement of the beneficiaries collectively; after the trustees have exercised their powers the beneficiaries collectively must have rights which are as extensive as those which the beneficiaries collectively had previously. Mr Berry on the other hand submitted that the limitation on the power to exclude or restrict is in terms of the number of beneficiaries who may be excluded or restricted, and it is not related to the land which happens to be the subject of the restriction.

33. I accept that the limitation on the power to exclude or restrict is expressed as a limitation on the number of beneficiaries who may be excluded or restricted. Plainly it would make no sense if there was no beneficiary left entitled to occupy land subject to a trust of land as a result of the exercise of the power under section 13. That is the force of the words '(but not all)'. But

---

[8] The facts of *Barclay* v *Barclay* [1970] 2 QB 677 provide a possible example: the testator's son was in occupation (he had lived with the testator), but the testator intended that the land be sold and that the beneficiaries (including the son) should share the proceeds.

if an estate consisting of adjoining properties, Blackacre and Whiteacre, was held subject to a trust of land and A and B were entitled to occupy the estate, it would be very surprising if the trustees were not able under section 13 to exclude or restrict B's entitlement to occupy Blackacre and at the same time to exclude or restrict A's entitlement to occupy Whiteacre, thereby leaving A alone entitled to occupy Blackacre and B Whiteacre. So also I do not see why, in relation to a single building which lends itself to physical partition, the trustees could not exclude or restrict one beneficiary's entitlement to occupy one part and at the same time exclude or restrict the other beneficiary's entitlement to occupy the other part. Each part is land subject to a trust of land and the beneficiaries are entitled to occupy that part until the entitlement of a beneficiary is excluded or restricted by the exercise of the power under section 13. So construed section 13(1) seems to me to make good sense and to provide a useful power which trustees might well wish to exercise in appropriate circumstances so as to be even-handed between beneficiaries. In contrast, I can see no good reason why Parliament should want to confine the trustees to the all or nothing approach urged by Mr Berry.

Comment

(1) Why did the suggested split cause difficulty?

(2) How was this difficulty avoided? Was any other interpretation of s 13 viable?

B. Spouses, civil partners, cohabitants and associated persons

An initial point is that the Civil Partnership Act 2004 recognises same-sex partnerships and gives them the same effect as marriage. The details lie outside property law, but the following extract identifies the principal points.

Extract 12.2.5

Civil Partnership Act 2004, ss 1, 2

1.—(1) A civil partnership is a relationship between two people of the same sex ('civil partners')—

(a) which is formed when they register as civil partners of each other . . .

(3) A civil partnership ends only on death, dissolution or annulment.

2.—(1) For the purposes of section 1, two people are to be regarded as having registered as civil partners of each other once each of them has signed the civil partnership document—

(a) at the invitation of, and in the presence of, a civil partnership registrar, and

(b) in the presence of each other and two witnesses.

Comment

(1) When civil partners are given rights, this is sometimes by amendment of the existing legislation (as in the following Extract from the Family Law Act 1996) and sometimes by direct provision in the Civil Partnership Act.

(2) Same sex couples can now marry: Marriage (Same Sex Couples) Act 2013.

A number of occupation rights are conferred by the Family Law Act 1996, some of which overlap the provisions in TLATA. The details lie more in family law than property law, but we will see that the Family Law Act both confers rights of occupation and authorises the regulation of occupation (whatever the source of rights to occupy).

Extract 12.2.6

Family Law Act 1996, ss 30, 33, 36

30.—(1) This section applies if—
- (a) one spouse or civil partner ('A') is entitled to occupy a dwelling-house by virtue of—
  - (i)   a beneficial estate or interest or contract; or
  - (ii) any enactment giving A the right to remain in occupation; and
- (b) the other spouse or civil partner ('B') is not so entitled.

(2) Subject to the provisions of this Part, B has the following rights ('home rights')—
- (a) if in occupation, a right not to be evicted or excluded from the dwelling-house or any part of it by A except with the leave of the court given by an order under section 33;
- (b) if not in occupation, a right with the leave of the court so given to enter into and occupy the dwelling-house.

33.—(1) If—
- (a) a person ('the person entitled')—
  - (i)   is entitled to occupy a dwelling-house by virtue of a beneficial estate or interest or contract or by virtue of any enactment giving him the right to remain in occupation, or
  - (ii) has home rights in relation to a dwelling-house, and
- (b) the dwelling-house—
  - (i)   is or at any time has been the home of the person entitled and of another person with whom he is associated, or
  - (ii) was at any time intended by the person entitled and any such other person to be their home,

the person entitled may apply to the court for an order containing any of the provisions specified in subsections (3), (4) and (5).

(3) An order under this section may—
- (a) enforce the applicant's entitlement to remain in occupation as against the other person ('the respondent');
- (b) require the respondent to permit the applicant to enter and remain in the dwelling-house or part of the dwelling-house;
- (c) regulate the occupation of the dwelling-house by either or both parties;
- (f) require the respondent to leave the dwelling-house or part of the dwelling-house; . . .

(6) In deciding whether to exercise its powers under subsection (3) and (if so) in what manner, the court shall have regard to all the circumstances including—
- (a) the housing needs and housing resources of each of the parties and of any relevant child;
- (b) the financial resources of each of the parties;
- (c) the likely effect of any order, or of any decision by the court not to exercise its powers under subsection (3), on the health, safety or well-being of the parties and of any relevant child; and
- (d) the conduct of the parties in relation to each other and otherwise.

(7) If it appears to the court that the applicant or any relevant child is likely to suffer significant harm attributable to conduct of the respondent if an order under this section containing one or more of the provisions mentioned in subsection (3) is not made, the court shall make the order unless it appears to it that—
- (a) the respondent or any relevant child is likely to suffer significant harm if the order is made; and
- (b) the harm likely to be suffered by the respondent or child in that event is as great as, or greater than, the harm attributable to conduct of the respondent which is likely to be suffered by the applicant or child if the order is not made.

(10)   An order under this section may, in so far as it has continuing effect, be made for a specified period, until the occurrence of a specified event or until further order.

36.—(1)   This section applies if—
  (a)   one cohabitant or former cohabitant is entitled to occupy a dwelling-house by virtue of a beneficial estate or interest or contract or by virtue of any enactment giving him the right to remain in occupation;
  (b)   the other cohabitant or former cohabitant is not so entitled; and
  (c)   that dwelling-house is the home in which they cohabit or a home in which they at any time cohabited or intended to cohabit.

(2)   The cohabitant or former cohabitant not so entitled may apply to the court for an order under this section against the other cohabitant or former cohabitant ('the respondent').

[The section contains provisions similar to s 33(3), (6) and (7). However, the relevant circumstances are wider than under s 33(6): they include 'the nature of the parties' relationship and in particular the level of commitment involved in it' and 'the length of time during which they have cohabited'.]

(10)   An order under this section must be limited so as to have effect for a specified period not exceeding six months, but may be extended on one occasion for a further specified period not exceeding six months.

Comment

(1) The extracts are limited to the most significant provisions in these sections.

(2) Section 33 refers to 'associated' persons. This term is widely defined by s 62(2) and includes married couples, civil partners, cohabitants, those living in the same household, those who 'have or have had an intimate personal relationship with each other which is or was of significant duration', relatives and parents and children.

(3) Section 36 applies to cohabitants, defined by s 62(1) as 'two persons who are neither married to each other nor civil partners of each other but are living together as husband and wife or as if they were civil partners'.

(4) Other significant sections include s 31 (proprietary status of home rights); s 35 (actions between former spouses and civil partners); and s 40 (conditions which may be imposed on applicants).

It will be seen that s 30 confers rights of occupation, whereas s 33 regulates rights of occupation. Section 36 is something of a hybrid in that it permits the court to make orders in favour of a person who otherwise would have no right to occupy. It is important to note that the protection given by s 36 is weaker than where there is a right of occupation. How is this apparent from the extracts?

Of these provisions, it is s 33 which overlaps with the regulation of occupation by TLATA, s 13. The stress in the Family Law Act on the financial needs and resources of the parties is not replicated in TLATA. If an action is brought under TLATA, s 14 (which enables the courts to regulate trustees' decisions, for example under s 13), is the court limited to the narrower criteria in TLATA? Where s 33 applies, should it operate to the exclusion of TLATA, s 14?[9]

[9] Compare the position regarding sale: p 418 below.

C. Rent and other financial adjustments

(i) Payments for past occupation

We now move to the financial consequences of occupation. It is clear, of course, that the trustees (under TLATA, s 13) or the court (under s 14) may determine that an occupier should pay rent (in the form of a compensation payment).[10] Any such decision will settle the matter for the future. However, what is the position where no such decision has been made, but the facts are that one co-owner has been occupying the land? Can the court make a retrospective order under its power in s 14 to make 'such order . . . relating to the exercise by the trustees of any of their functions . . . as the court thinks fit'?

<hr>

Extract 12.2.7

<hr>

***Stack v Dowden* [2007] 2 AC 432**

BARONESS HALE: 93.   . . . both these parties have a right of occupation. Section 13(1) gives the trustees the power to exclude or restrict that entitlement, but under section 13(2) this power must be exercised reasonably. The trustees also have power under section 13(3) to impose conditions upon the occupier. These include, under section 13(5), paying any outgoings or expenses in respect of the land and under section 13(6) paying compensation to a person whose right to occupy has been excluded or restricted. Under section 14(2)(a), both trustees and beneficiaries can apply to the court for an order relating to the exercise of these functions. Under section 15(1), the matters to which the court must have regard in making its order include (a) the intentions of the person or person who created the trust, (b) the purposes for which the property subject to the trust is held, (c) the welfare of any minor who occupies or might reasonably be expected to occupy the property as his home, and (d) the interests of any secured creditor of any beneficiary. Under section 15(2), in a case such as this, the court must also have regard to the circumstances and wishes of each of the beneficiaries who would otherwise be entitled to occupy the property.

94.   These statutory powers replaced the old doctrines of equitable accounting under which a beneficiary who remained in occupation might be required to pay an occupation rent to a beneficiary who was excluded from the property. The criteria laid down in the statute should be applied, rather than in the cases decided under the old law, although the results may often be the same . . .

LORD NEUBERGER: 150.   The court's power to order payment to a beneficiary, excluded from property he would otherwise be entitled to occupy, by the beneficiary who retains occupation, is now governed by sections 12 to 15 of the Trusts of Land and Appointment of Trustees Act 1996, having been formerly equitable in origin. However, I think that it would be a rare case where the statutory principles would produce a different result from that which would have resulted from the equitable principles.

151.   The 1996 Act appears to me to apply here in this way. The trustees, Ms Dowden and Mr Stack, agreed pursuant to section 13(1) of the 1996 Act (through the consent order of 11 April 2003 and not seeking to disturb the status quo after it expired) that Mr Stack would be excluded from the house. Accordingly, they could have agreed pursuant to section 13(3) and (6)(a) that Ms Dowden would pay 'compensation' to Mr Stack for his exclusion. They initially agreed that in the order of 11 April 2003 but, once it expired, they could not agree whether to exercise that power. Accordingly, the decision whether to require compensation was a matter for the court under section 14.

<hr>

[10] But only if the payee's rights have been restricted under s 13.

Extract 12.2.8

Murphy v Gooch [2007] 2 FLR 934 (Court of Appeal)

LIGHTMAN J: 10. . . . At one time the prevalent practice appears to have been that a co-owner in sole occupation would only be required to give credit for an occupation rent if he had actually or constructively ousted the other co-owner or co-owners from the jointly owned property. But more recent authorities made plain that an occupation rent may be ordered in any case where this is necessary to do broad justice or equity between the parties: see Lawrence Collins J in Byford v Butler [2004] 1 FLR 56 at 65. Lawrence Collins J cited with approval the judgment of Millett J in the case of In Re Pavlou [1993] 1 WLR 1046 at 1050 C-D . . .

11. But after the date of the Judgment on the 25th April 2007 the House of Lords handed down its decision in the case of Stack v Dowden [2007] UK HL 17; [2007] 2 WLR 831. The principal issue before the House of Lords in that case was the approach to be adopted by the court in determining the respective beneficial interests of co-owners of land. But there also arose a subsidiary issue as to the applicable principles to be adopted on the taking of accounts between co-owners and (most particularly) in determining claims by a co-owner out of occupation for an occupation rent from a co-owner in occupation. The House of Lords in Stack v Dowden was unanimously of the view that the court's power to order payment to a co-owner of an occupation rent is no longer governed by the doctrine of equitable accounting but is instead governed by sections 12–15 (and in particular the statutory principles laid down in section 15) of the 1996 Act. The results may often be the same (see Baroness Hale in paragraphs 93–4 with whom three of the law lords agreed); indeed it may be that it would be a rare case when the equitable and statutory principles would produce a different result (see Lord Neuberger at paragraph 150). But the statutory principles must be applied.

14. Under the previous equitable doctrine the court was concerned only with considerations relevant to achieving a just result between the parties. The statutory innovation is section 15, which requires the court in determining all applications for an order under section 14 to include amongst the other matters to which it has regard: (1) in all cases (so far as applicable) the four matters referred to by Baroness Hale; (2) in the case of applications relating to the exercise by trustees of the powers conferred by section 13 the circumstances and wishes of each of the beneficiaries who is (or apart from any previous exercise by the trustees would be) entitled to occupy the land under section 12; and (3) in case of any other application (other than one relating to the conveyance of land to beneficiaries absolutely entitled) the circumstances and wishes of any beneficiaries of full age entitled to an interest in possession. The wider ambit of relevant considerations means that the task of the court must now be, not merely to do justice between the parties, but to do justice between the parties with due regard to the relevant statutory considerations and in particular (where applicable) the welfare of the minor, the interests of secured creditors and the circumstances and wishes of the beneficiaries specified.

Comment

(1) In Stack v Dowden, the majority (agreeing with Baroness Hale) held that no payment should be made. Lord Neuberger dissented. Does his analysis of the legal principles differ from that of Baroness Hale?

(2) What difference does it make that TLATA, ss 12–15 are today applied?

(3) Though it is not clear from the dicta, Stack was dealing only with payments to be made after the court order. However, Murphy applied Stack (without further discussion) to payments for occupation predating the court order. Is that an obvious conclusion?

The above cases concern beneficiaries with rights to occupy. However, not every case will be covered by this. In particular, pre-Stack cases enabled a trustee in bankruptcy to claim the value of occupation (half the rental value, if they had equal shares) from the bankrupt's co-owner.

Extract 12.2.9

French v Barcham [2009] 1 WLR 1124

BLACKBURNE J: 18.   I do not accept that sections 12 to 15 of the 1996 Act provide an exhaustive regime for compensation for exclusion of a beneficiary from occupation of property held subject to a trust of land. An essential prerequisite of the power to award compensation under section 13(6) is the entitlement under section 12 of the beneficiary claiming the compensation to occupy land, ie the right of that beneficiary to occupy the land at any time by reason of that interest. What triggers the award of compensation is the exclusion or restriction of that right of occupation. Where, as is common ground, a person such as a trustee in bankruptcy who is entitled for the benefit of the bankrupt's creditors to an interest in possession of land subject to such a trust has no such right of occupation (and neither do the creditors), there is no scope for the operation of section 13. I do not therefore accept that, because Mr Barcham's trustee in bankruptcy has had no statutory right of occupation (a matter which, given the terms of section 12(2), Mr Davies readily conceded), Mrs Barcham was not liable to be charged an occupation rent (or, if one prefers so to describe it, equitable compensation) for her occupation of the property from the time that Mr Barcham's beneficial interest in the property vested in his trustee in bankruptcy.

19.   I do not consider that anything said by the House of Lords in *Stack* v *Dowden* [2007] 2 AC 432 leads to a different view of the scope of those provisions. That case was principally concerned with the criteria for the determination of the property rights of a cohabiting couple in the home which they had occupied . . .

20.   Finally, I do not accept Mr Learmonth's submission that it would make nonsense of the statutory regime contained in the 1996 Act if the regime were not exhaustive of the entitlement to compensation for exclusion from occupation. As worded the power to award compensation under section 13(6) is only exercisable as a condition to be imposed on the occupying beneficiary in relation to his occupation of the property in question. See section 13(3). It appears to look at the matter prospectively in the context of the occupying beneficiary's continued occupation. It is not difficult, especially if that view of section 13(6) is correct, to envisage cases of exclusion where both beneficiaries had a right of occupation yet where the statutory regime would not seem to be applicable. Where the scheme applies, it must be applied. But where it plainly does not I do not see why the party who is not in occupation of the land in question should be denied any compensation at all if recourse to the court's equitable jurisdiction would justly compensate him.

Comment

The occupier (Mrs Barcham) had to account for half the letting value. Is the reasoning likely to apply to others than trustees in bankruptcy?

Prior to *Stack*, accounting issues usually arose where the parties had been living together but the relationship had broken down and one had left. The following extract identifies the standard approach.

Extract 12.2.10

Suttill v Graham [1977] 1 WLR 819

STAMP LJ: . . . [A] beneficiary entitled to an equal share in equity of property of which he is a trustee, and which he himself occupied, is to be charged with at least an occupation rent; so that if as here he seeks to charge his co-beneficiary trustee with half the outgoings, he should be charged with half the occupation rent.

That is not precisely the way in which such a situation has been approached in the cases to which attention has been called by counsel on behalf of the husband. But in *Leake (formerly*

Bruzzi) v *Bruzzi* [1974] 1 WLR 1528 this court arrived at a similar conclusion by regarding the mortgage interest paid by the husband while in possession as something equivalent to rent or payment for use and occupation. That will normally produce a fair result and save costs; and where, as here, the husband in possession does not submit to be charged with an occupation rent, it must be wrong that he should seek to charge the wife with half the mortgage interest which he has paid while living in the property rent free and resisting a sale of the property.

Comment

(1) Is a rough and ready balance between rent and mortgage instalments the best way of dealing with such problems? Is it appropriate for all cases?

(2) Will this approach survive *Stack v Dowden*? Note also the dicta in *Jones v Kernott* [2012] 1 AC 776 (quoted in Extract 8.7.1), especially for situations where there has been a prolonged period of occupation.

One frequently cited case is *Jacobs* v *Seward*,[11] in which one of two tenants in common of a field complained that the other had made hay on the land and taken the hay away. Lord Hatherley LC was clear that 'So long as a tenant in common is only exercising lawfully the rights he has as tenant in common, no action can lie against him by his co-tenant. Now it is perfectly lawful for a tenant in common to make hay . . .'. The principles apply to joint tenancies in exactly the same way.[12]

Although the earlier position was that only ouster of the claimant (or rent receipts from tenants) would give rise to a duty to account, a more broadly based jurisdiction has been accepted in recent decades. Blackburne J said in *French v Barcham*:[13]

> The essential point, in my view, is that when on inquiry it would be unreasonable, looking at the matter practically, to expect the co-owner who is not in occupation to exercise his right as a co-owner to take occupation of the property, for example because of the nature of the property or the identity and relationship to each other of the co-owners, it would normally be fair or equitable to charge the occupying co-owner an occupation rent.

As we have seen, this was applied so that the trustee in bankruptcy of one co-owner could claim an occupation rent from the other co-owner.

Take a different example. Suppose that A and B have concurrent beneficial interests in land held as an investment under a trust, but that the trust permits the trustees (in specified circumstances) to allow a beneficiary to occupy. If A is allowed to occupy, can and should he be charged with an occupation rent?

(ii) Payments for improvements

Extract 12.2.11

Leigh v Dickeson (1884) 15 QBD 60

COTTON LJ: . . . As to the claim for improvements, it has been urged that no tenant in common is entitled to execute improvements upon the property held in common, and then to charge his co-tenant in common with the cost. This seems to me the true view, and I need not further

---

[11] (1872) LR 5 HL 464 at p 474.
[12] *Re Pavlou* [1993] 1 WLR 1046.
[13] [2009] 1 WLR 1124 at [34]; see also *Murphy*, Extract 12.2.8 above.

discuss the question as to improvements. As to the question of repairs, it is to be observed that when two persons are under a common obligation, one of them can recover from the other the amount expended in discharge or fulfilment of the common obligation; but that is not the position of affairs here: one tenant in common cannot charge another with the cost of repairs without a request, and in the present case it is impossible even to imply a request . . . [In] a suit for a partition it is usual to have an inquiry as to those expenses of which nothing could be recovered so long as the parties enjoyed their property in common; when it is desired to put an end to that state of things, it is then necessary to consider what has been expended in improvements or repairs: the property held in common has been increased in value by the improvements and repairs; and whether the property is divided or sold by the decree of the Court, one party cannot take the increase in value, without making an allowance for what has been expended in order to obtain that increased value; in fact, the execution of the repairs and improvements is adopted and sanctioned by accepting the increased value. There is, therefore, a mode by which money expended by one tenant in common for repairs can be recovered, but the procedure is confined to suits for partition.

Comment

(1) Sale is the modern equivalent to partition: the same principles apply to sale. Does it make sense to have a rule disallowing claims for improvements, but yet to bring them into reckoning on sale?

(2) When a claim for improvements is allowed, the value of any sole occupation must be brought into account, even where no such payment would otherwise be due.[14]

We should consider the application of these principles to cohabiting co-owners. Can a claim for improvements be made if the improvements were effected whilst they were still living together? Jonathan Parker LJ has stated:[15]

> I agree with Judge Behrens in *Clarke* v *Harlowe* [[2007] 1 FLR 1] that in the ordinary cohabitation case it is open to the court to infer from the fact of cohabitation that during the period of cohabitation it was the common intention of the parties that neither should thereafter have to account to the other in respect of expenditure incurred by the other on the property during that period for their joint benefit. Whether the court draws that inference in the given case will of course depend on the facts of that case.

Why might it be sensible to draw such an inference? Is the question affected by *Stack* v *Dowden*?

Rather similar to improvements is the payment of capital outstanding on a mortgage. Does the payer receive credit for this?

Extract 12.2.12

Leake v *Bruzzi* [1974] 1 WLR 1528

STEPHENSON LJ: . . . In giving the first judgment in this court in *Cracknell* v *Cracknell* [1971] P 356 Lord Denning MR stated that in that case . . . the wife had left the house of her own accord; and he stated that where the position was different and where she had been driven out of the

---

[14] *Att-Gen* v *Magdalen College, Oxford* (1854) 18 Beav 223 at p 255 (52 ER 88 at p 100) (point not taken on appeal: 6 HLC 189 (10 ER 1267)); *Williams* v *Williams* (1899) 81 LT NS 163.

[15] *Wilcox* v *Tait* [2007] 2 FLR 871 at [66].

house by the conduct of the husband it would be wrong for the expelling party (to call him that) to be given any credit for his mortgage repayments . . .

It seems unfortunate if the conduct of the parties, perhaps including the allegations that the husband made about adultery on the wife's part which were not proved or persisted in, have to be considered . . . We do not have to say whether there may not be cases in which the husband should be given no credit for any mortgage repayments such as the husband has made in this case since the wife left the matrimonial home. But my conclusion is that the wife should give the husband credit for half that part of the mortgage repayments which he has made in respect of capital . . .

Comment

(1) Should the conduct of the payer in 'driving out' the claimant be material?

(2) Remember that payment of mortgage instalments will generally be taken as offsetting compensation due for sole occupation: the bulk of such payments will be interest.

3. Management of the land

Not surprisingly, the primary responsibility for managing the land falls upon the trustees. However, as will become apparent, there are significant checks and balances. The beneficiaries are given a role to play in many cases, extending to full management where there has been delegation by the trustees. Equally importantly, the court has a wide power to review decisions by trustees.

Extract 12.3.1

Trusts of Land and Appointment of Trustees Act 1996, ss 6, 8

6.—(1)   For the purpose of exercising their functions as trustees, the trustees of land have in relation to the land subject to the trust all the powers of an absolute owner.

(3)   The trustees of land have power to acquire land under the power conferred by section 8 of the Trustee Act 2000.

(5)   In exercising the powers conferred by this section trustees shall have regard to the rights of the beneficiaries.

(6)   The powers conferred by this section shall not be exercised in contravention of, or of any order made in pursuance of, any other enactment or any rule of law or equity.

(9)   The duty of care under section 1 of the Trustee Act 2000 applies to trustees of land when exercising the powers conferred by this section.

8.—(1)   Sections 6 and 7 do not apply in the case of a trust of land created by a disposition in so far as provision to the effect that they do not apply is made by the disposition.

Comment

(1) Previous legislation listed specific powers available to trustees. Is it dangerous to confer powers in the general form found in s 6?

(2) Is it implicit in s 6(5) that trustees can exercise powers so as defeat rights of beneficiaries? If so, is this sensible or consistent with normal equitable principles? Can you think of examples where the exercise of powers might defeat rights? The effect of s 6(5) on purchasers is considered below.[16]

---

[16] See p 447.

(3) Section 8(1) represents a significant policy change. Since the nineteenth century, the law has striven to ensure that land subject to a trust can always be sold and managed by a small number of trustees: statute conferred powers to deal with the land and struck down attempts to exclude them. This policy reached its zenith in the 1925 legislation. It is, then, remarkable that s 8(1) permits powers (including sale) to be excluded. What justification might there be for this? Is the freedom afforded to settlors to be welcomed as a basic liberty to do with one's land as one thinks fit, or condemned as an invitation to inefficient land management?

(4) Can powers outside ss 6 and 7 (for example, delegation in s 9) be excluded?

(5) If powers are excluded, is there any way in which a desired transaction can be implemented?[17]

A. Sale

The way in which powers are exercised, circumscribed and controlled will be considered within the context of sale – sale has been in issue in the great majority of the cases.

(i) Consent requirements

Extract 12.3.2

Trusts of Land and Appointment of Trustees Act 1996, ss 8, 10

8.—(2) If the disposition creating such a trust makes provision requiring any consent to be obtained to the exercise of any power conferred by section 6 or 7, the power may not be exercised without that consent.

10.—(1) If a disposition creating a trust of land requires the consent of more than two persons to the exercise by the trustees of any function relating to the land, the consent of any two of them to the exercise of the function is sufficient in favour of a purchaser.

(3) Where at any time a person whose consent is expressed by a disposition creating a trust of land to be required to the exercise by the trustees of any function relating to the land is not of full age—

    (a) his consent is not, in favour of a purchaser, required to the exercise of the function, but

    (b) the trustees shall obtain the consent of a parent who has parental responsibility for him (within the meaning of the Children Act 1989) or of a guardian of his.

Comment

Section 8(2) ensures that purchasers may be affected by consent requirements, but useful protection is given by s 10. The court has explicit power under s 14 to authorise sale where a necessary consent cannot be achieved. In what circumstances are the courts likely to exercise this power?

A danger for purchasers (and trustees) was that consent requirements might sometimes be implied. We shall see later[18] that purchasers are protected against unregistered or (for unregistered land) undiscovered consent requirements.

---

[17] See Watt [1997] Conv 263.
[18] See pp 446–449 below.

In *Re Herklots' WT*,[19] the plaintiff had a right to take a house in part satisfaction of his third share, operative when a life interest terminated. The trustees proposed to sell the house, which would have the effect of defeating this right of the plaintiff. Ungoed-Thomas J had no hesitation in holding that the testatrix 'could not have intended that her intentions should be defeated by providing that the house . . . could be sold without the plaintiff's consent'. Today, could it be argued today that consent requirements must be expressly imposed to fall within s 8(2)?

(ii) Consultation requirements

Extract 12.3.3

Trusts of Land and Appointment of Trustees Act 1996, s 11

11.—(1)   The trustees of land shall in the exercise of any function relating to land subject to the trust—
  (a) so far as practicable, consult the beneficiaries of full age and beneficially entitled to an interest in possession in the land, and
  (b) so far as consistent with the general interest of the trust, give effect to the wishes of those beneficiaries, or (in case of dispute) of the majority (according to the value of their combined interests).
  (2)   Subsection (1) does not apply—
  (a) in relation to a trust created by a disposition in so far as provision that it does not apply is made by the disposition,
  (b) in relation to a trust created or arising under a will made before the commencement of this Act, or
  (c) in relation to the exercise of the power mentioned in section 6(2).

Comment

(1) Section 6(2) enables the trustees to transfer the legal estate to the beneficiaries (if all absolutely entitled, and of full age and capacity).

(2) The old law had very similar provisions, though not applying to express trusts. These attracted very little attention in the cases. Why should this have been? Are there any reasons to suppose that s 11 will play a more prominent role?

(iii) The decision to sell

Subject to specific points such as consent requirements and consultation, the decision whether or not to sell land is subject to the normal principles governing trustees' powers.

Extract 12.3.4

Tempest v Lord Camoys (1882) 21 Ch D 571

The two trustees differed as to whether a power to purchase land should be exercised.

CHITTY J: . . . The result therefore is that I should not be at liberty to control the exercise of this power, if the trustees proposed jointly to exercise it, unless I saw that there was a case of bad faith, which I say on these facts cannot be maintained before me. And it is impossible for me to hold that I have in those circumstances any right to direct the trustees to exercise this power

---

[19] [1964] 2 All ER 66 at p 71.

which is in their absolute discretion. Where one trustee refuses or declines to exercise the power, the power cannot be exercised at all . . .

Comment

(1) Chitty J was upheld by the Court of Appeal. The unanimity requirement is also seen in more recent cases such as *Hammersmith and Fulham LBC v Monk*[20] and *Hounslow LBC v Pilling.*[21]

(2) In the modern law, if the trustees are divided the starting point is that there is no sale: the power to sell has not been exercised. However, TLATA, s 14 confers on the court a wide jurisdiction to oversee trusts of land and review decisions by trustees. As will be seen below, sale may well be ordered if the trustees are divided.

(iv) Court applications

Many disputes involving concurrent interests can be resolved only by the court. As the same persons are usually both trustees and beneficiaries, they have to agree before any power can be exercised. Although the courts are traditionally loath to interfere with trustees' discretions,[22] there has long been jurisdiction as regards concurrent interests. Where there are no independent trustees (very common for concurrent interests), the courts have been ready to step in.

Extract 12.3.5

Trusts of Land and Appointment of Trustees Act 1996, s 14

14.—(1) Any person who is a trustee of land or has an interest in property subject to a trust of land may make an application to the court for an order under this section.

(2) On an application for an order under this section the court may make any such order—

(a) relating to the exercise by the trustees of any of their functions (including an order relieving them of any obligation to obtain the consent of, or to consult, any person in connection with the exercise of any of their functions), or

(b) declaring the nature or extent of a person's interest in property subject to the trust,

as the court thinks fit.

Comment

(1) Which of the following persons can apply? A trustee; a beneficiary; an unsecured creditor; the trustee in bankruptcy of a beneficiary or trustee; a secured creditor (mortgagee); a person who has contracted to buy the land from the trustees.

(2) Note the reference to the 'functions' of the trustees, though this term is not defined by TLATA.[23] What might it mean?

(3) There are certain things a trustee cannot do. Examples are refusing to recognise the right of a beneficiary to occupy,[24] or selling when the power of sale has been restricted by

---

[20] [1992] 1 AC 478; see also *Crawley BC v Ure* [1996] QB 13.
[21] [1993] 1 WLR 1242.
[22] Pettit, *Equity and the Law of Trusts* (12th ed), p 488.
[23] Though ss 6–9 are headed 'Functions of trustees of land', this is of limited use. Section 13 decisions (occupation) are outside this heading, but are assumed by s 15(2) to be 'functions'. Peter Gibson LJ in *Notting Hill Housing Trust v Brackley* [2002] HLR 212 at [15] describes functions as 'the exercise of a power or a duty'.
[24] Assuming there is no jurisdiction under TLATA, s 13, to limit the right.

the trust. Does the court have jurisdiction to disregard the limits on the trustees' powers in these cases? Is it relevant that s 14(2) expressly confers jurisdiction to relieve against consent or consultation requirements?

(4) Does s 14 confer jurisdiction over property in the trust other than land? Or over discretions which are not property related, such as the discretionary distribution of income?

(v) Exercising the court's jurisdiction

Before TLATA, there was no statutory provision relating to how the jurisdiction should be exercised. As will be seen, the courts fashioned effective guidelines based upon the purposes of the parties. Today, we must start with the legislation.

Extract 12.3.6

Trusts of Land and Appointment of Trustees Act 1996, s 15

15.—(1) The matters to which the court is to have regard in determining an application for an order under section 14 include—
 (a) the intentions of the person or persons (if any) who created the trust,
 (b) the purposes for which the property subject to the trust is held,
 (c) the welfare of any minor who occupies or might reasonably be expected to occupy any land subject to the trust as his home, and
 (d) the interests of any secured creditor of any beneficiary.
 (2) In the case of an application relating to the exercise in relation to any land of the powers conferred on the trustees by section 13, the matters to which the court is to have regard also include the circumstances and wishes of each of the beneficiaries who is (or apart from any previous exercise by the trustees of those powers would be) entitled to occupy the land under section 12.
 (3) In the case of any other application, other than one relating to the exercise of the power mentioned in section 6(2), the matters to which the court is to have regard also include the circumstances and wishes of any beneficiaries of full age and entitled to an interest in possession in property subject to the trust or (in case of dispute) of the majority (according to the value of their combined interests).

Comment

(1) The wishes of the beneficiaries with interests in possession (s 15(2), (3)) had no counterpart in the previous law. The new provisions can, however, be linked with the requirement that trustees should consult such beneficiaries and take their views into account. How useful are the wishes of the beneficiaries likely to be where there are concurrent interests? It would be dangerous to assume that the interests of these beneficiaries are always to be preferred to those of remaindermen or infants in successive interest trusts: all the section does is to list (not exclusively) matters to be taken into account.

(2) The words 'other application' in s 15(3) were interpreted by Neuberger J in *Mortgage Corpn* v *Shaire*[25] as meaning apart from s 15(2), rather than apart from s 15(1) and (2) together. Is this the natural interpretation of the words? Why was Neuberger J keen to reach the conclusion he did?

The main focus of the pre-1996 cases was on the purposes for which the land was bought: see now s 15(1)(a), (b). The cases are likely to remain a guide as to how TLATA will be

[25] [2001] Ch 743 at p 761.

applied. Accordingly, we will first turn to these cases. In considering them, we will need to consider how far TLATA introduces new principles which may affect them.

Extract 12.3.7

Jones v *Challenger* [1961] 1 QB 176

Following divorce, the former wife sought sale of the family home.

DEVLIN LJ: . . . At the front of his argument on behalf of the wife Mr ap Robert put *In re Mayo*.[i] In this case Simonds J said:[ii] 'The trust for sale will prevail, unless all three trustees agree in exercising the power to postpone.' If that dictum governs this case, Mr ap Robert must succeed. But he felt a difficulty in pushing his argument to this extent because of what was said by Lord Greene MR in *In re Buchanan-Wollaston's Conveyance*,[iii] where he laid down the principle more widely, and said[iv] that the court must ask itself 'whether or not the person applying for execution of the trust for sale is a person whose voice should be allowed to prevail'.

The apparent difference between these two dicta is, I think, explained when the different facts in the two cases are considered. *In re Mayo* was a simple uncomplicated case of a trust for sale of freehold property, where the beneficiaries were brother and sister, and where there was no suggestion that either of them were intended to or even wished to occupy the property. Simonds J was applying the simple and fundamental principle that in a trust for sale there is a duty to sell and a power to postpone; and, accordingly, one trustee may call upon the others to perform the duty, but all must be agreed if they are to exercise the power.

But this simple principle cannot prevail where the trust itself or the circumstances in which it was made show that there was a secondary or collateral object besides that of sale. Simonds J, in his judgment in *In re Mayo*, said that if there were mala fides, the position would be different. If it be not mala fides, it is at any rate wrong and inequitable for one of the parties to the trust to invoke the letter of the trust in order to defeat one of its purposes, whether that purpose be written or unwritten, and the court will not permit it. In *In re Buchanan-Wollaston's Conveyance* four owners, who each had separate but neighbouring properties, combined to buy a piece of land which they desired to keep as an open space. The land was conveyed to them as joint tenants and consequently a statutory trust for sale came into existence by virtue of section 35 of the Law of Property Act, 1925. The parties then entered into a covenant in which they agreed in effect to preserve the land as an open space. One of the parties subsequently sold his property and then applied against the opposition of the others to have the piece of land sold. The application was refused and it is plain from the judgment that in such circumstances the court has a complete discretion to do what is right and proper, and will not allow the voice of the man who is in breach of his obligation to prevail.

. . .

Bull v *Bull*[v] is a case in which the joint occupation was not matrimonial. The house was owned jointly by a mother and son but the son had provided the greater part of the purchase price. The son gave his mother notice to quit, but this court held that as a tenant in common she could not be ejected. Denning LJ said that the son could apply under section 30 [TLATA, s 14], and the court, in order that there might be a sale with vacant possession, could turn the mother out if it was right and proper to do so. I think that this dictum must be considered on the footing that the house was bought for the purpose of providing a home for mother and son and that, as the mother was still residing there, that purpose had not been brought to an end.

I see no inconsistency between [four cases, including *Bull* v *Bull*] and *In re Mayo*, in which no collateral purpose was manifest. There is, as I have said, something akin to mala fides if one trustee tries to defeat a collateral object in the trust by arbitrarily insisting on the duty of sale. He should have good grounds for doing so and, therefore, the court will inquire whether, in all the circumstances, it is right and proper to order the sale.

In the case we have to consider, the house was acquired as the matrimonial home. That was the purpose of the joint tenancy and, for so long as that purpose was still alive, I think that the right test to be applied would be that in *In re Buchanan-Wollaston's Conveyance*. But with the end of the marriage, that purpose was dissolved and the primacy of the duty to sell was restored. No doubt there is still a discretion. If the husband . . . was prepared to buy out the wife's interest, it might be proper to allow it, but he has not accepted a suggestion that terms of that sort should be made. In these circumstances, there is no way in which the discretion can properly be exercised except by an order to sell, because, since they cannot now both enjoy occupation of the property, that is the only way whereby the beneficiaries can derive equal benefit from their investment, which is the primary object of the trust.

It is said that it is hard on the husband that he should have to give up the house which it was his wife's choice and not his to abandon. So it is. But wherever there is a joint occupation, whether it is matrimonial or otherwise, and it is brought to an end, it may involve hardship and inconvenience on the person who would have preferred it to go on.

[i] [1943] Ch 302; 59 TLR 395; [1943] 2 All ER 440.
[ii] [1943] Ch 302, 304.
[iii] [1939] Ch 738; 55 TLR 604; [1939] 2 All ER 302.
[iv] [1939] Ch 738, 747.
[v] [1955] 1 QB 234; [1955] 2 WLR 78; [1955] 1 All ER 253.

Comment

(1) *Jones* v *Challenger* was the leading case prior to TLATA, demonstrating the importance of the purpose behind the purchase. Can the approach of Devlin LJ be seen as emasculating the obligation to sell, so that the question whether there should be a sale is only marginally affected by there being a trust for sale?

(2) In the modern law, the simple trust of land provides only a power to sell; disagreement between the trustees no longer points towards sale. In the light of this, is *Jones* v *Challenger* a reliable guide as to when sale will be ordered under trusts of land?

(3) The earlier case of *Re Mayo* demonstrated the importance of the obligation to sell (in a trust for sale) where there is no purpose as regards the use of the land. This could arise where successive interests are created or land is purchased as an investment, though nearly every joint purchase of land will involve some purpose. Can *Re Mayo* still be used as an indicator of the result where there is no purpose? Similarly, could it be relevant where the purpose has come to an end?

Perhaps the most difficult point is that, in very many cases, there is not just one purpose. Rather, there are a number of purposes for which the property has been bought. A variation on this theme is that a purpose may remain capable of substantial fulfilment. A purchase of a family home provides the best example. The purpose will usually be to provide a home for the two spouses (or partners) and their children, not just the two of them. It may be argued that this purpose can still be substantially fulfilled despite the departure of one of them. The next two cases illustrate these points.

Extract 12.3.8

Bedson v Bedson [1965] 2 QB 666

A shop was acquired for the husband's drapery business, with living accommodation above it. The husband paid the full price, but the property was conveyed to husband and wife as beneficial joint tenants.

LORD DENNING MR: . . . Applying these principles, we have here a case where the house was acquired for the joint purposes of husband and wife as a married couple: the first floor as the matrimonial home for the family to occupy; the ground floor as the business where husband and wife were to work so as to provide for the family. In considering whether an order for sale should be made, the court must undoubtedly have regard to those purposes. It will not allow one party to defeat them, or either of them, by arbitrarily insisting on a sale. In the words of Devlin LJ in *Jones* v *Challenger*,[i] 'it is at any rate wrong and inequitable for one of the parties to the trust to invoke the letter of the trust in order to defeat one of its purposes, whether that purpose be written or unwritten, and the court will not permit it'. If we were to allow the wife here to insist on a sale, it would enable her to defeat both the contemplated purposes. On the one hand, to destroy the matrimonial home and thus remove any chance of the family coming together there again; and, on the other hand, to destroy the business by means of which the husband is still providing for himself and his children. The wife demanded that this be done. The county court judge recorded the argument on her behalf in these words: 'The wife's solicitor argued that nevertheless the choice of language adopted by the conveyancer (which can have meant very little to husband or wife) is such that I am inescapably bound to hold that as from the signing of the document the wife was fully entitled in law to determine the joint tenancy unilaterally by deserting her husband, and thus to achieve his ruin by demanding that the business and property be sold up and one half of the proceeds paid to her.' The county court judge rejected this view. So do I. The wife is not entitled to invoke the letter of the trust in order to perpetuate such an injustice. Equity can and will step in to prevent it. The court can look at the purposes for which this property was acquired: and finding that a sale would defeat those purposes, the court can refuse to order it.

[i] [1961] 1 QB 176, 181.

Comment

(1) The court (Russell LJ dissenting on this point) ordered the husband to pay a weekly sum as compensation.

(2) Is the analysis of Lord Denning MR entirely compatible with *Jones* v *Challenger*?

Extract 12.3.9

Re Evers' Trust [1980] 1 WLR 1327

An unmarried couple bought a house to live in with their child and the woman's two sons from her earlier marriage. Their relationship subsequently broke down.

ORMROD LJ: . . . The irresistible inference from these facts is that, as the judge found, they purchased this property as a family home for themselves and the three children. It is difficult to imagine that the mother, then wholly responsible for two children, and partly for the third, would have invested nearly all her capital in the purchase of this property if it was not to be available to her as a home for the children for the indefinite future. It is inconceivable that the father, when he agreed to this joint adventure, could have thought otherwise, or contemplated the possibility of an early sale without the consent of the mother. The underlying purpose of the trust was, therefore, to provide a home for all five of them for the indefinite future . . .

It was further argued that the father ought to be allowed to 'take his money out' or 'to realise his investment'. In point of fact, his investment amounted to less than one-fifth of the purchase price of the property, and was smaller than the mother's investment. The major part of the purchase price was provided by the mortgagees, and the mother is prepared to accept full responsibility for paying the interest on the mortgage, and keeping up the capital repayments. The father has a secure home with his mother. There is no evidence that he has any need to realise his investment. It is an excellent one, combining complete security with considerable capital appreciation in money terms. His share is now said to be worth about £5,000, i.e., it has more than doubled in value in two years. On the other hand, a sale of the property now would put the mother into a very difficult position because she cannot raise the finance to rehouse herself or meet the cost of borrowing money at present rates. So there is no justification for ordering a sale at the present time.

For these reasons the judge was right not to order an immediate sale . . . But circumstances may change unpredictably. It may not be appropriate to order a sale when the child reaches 16 years – a purely arbitrary date – or it may become appropriate to do so much sooner, for example on the mother's remarriage, or on it becoming financially possible for her to buy the father out . . .

Comment

(1) The case provides a good example of the application of purpose principles to an unmarried couple.

(2) Is it safe to conclude that the court would not order sale while the purpose of providing a home for the children is capable of being fulfilled?

(3) One way of resolving the dilemma is by the occupier's buying out the other party. This is attractive as providing a clean break between the parties, though often the money will not be available to achieve this. Conversely, there may be cases where the property, less the mortgage, has a negative value. Should this affect the outcome?

(4) Today, the interests of children are listed by s 15 as a relevant consideration.

As indicated above, these cases may remain influential. However, two important points must be remembered. The first is that (save where there is a trust for sale) the trust of land no longer involves any preference for sale. This may be particularly important where there is no purpose or a purpose has come to an end. The second point is that s 15 merely lists matters for the court to take into account: whilst these are wider than recognised before 1996, no one of them is determinative. It must not be assumed that, for example, the existence of a purpose is conclusive that there will not be a sale. Apart from the welcome clarification of the position of children, s 15 also adds the interests of secured creditors. These are considered later in this chapter.[26]

The role of the earlier authorities was considered by Neuberger J in *Mortgage Corpn* v *Shaire* in the light of these (and other) factors. He came to the following conclusion:[27]

A difficult question . . . is the extent to which the old authorities are of assistance, and it is no surprise to find differing views expressed in the two textbooks from which I have quoted. On the one hand, to throw over all the wealth of learning and thought given by so many eminent judges to the problem which is raised on an application for sale of a house where competing interests exist seems somewhat arrogant and possibly rash. On the other hand, where one has concluded that the law has changed in a significant respect so that the court's discretion is significantly less fettered than it was, there are obvious dangers in relying on authorities which proceeded on the basis that the court's discretion was more fettered than it now is. I think it would be wrong to throw over all the earlier cases without paying them any regard. However, they have to be treated with caution, in light of the change in the law, and in many cases they are unlikely to be of great, let alone decisive, assistance.

---

[26] See pp 429–435.
[27] [2001] Ch 743 at p 761: see also Extract 12.3.20 below.

This appears to accord the earlier authorities rather less significance than one might have expected. However, the context of *Shaire* (sale requested by a secured creditor of a beneficiary) was one in which there was a particularly strong case for departing from the earlier cases. In other contexts, how far can one rely on *Shaire* to claim that the earlier authorities are out of date?

The position of children under TLATA has not been subject to sustained analysis. However, the following dicta indicate approaches that the courts may take.

First National Bank plc v *Achampong*,[28] Blackburne J in the Court of Appeal:

> 65.   While it is relevant to consider the interests of the infant grandchildren in occupation of the property, it is difficult to attach much if any weight to their position in the absence of any evidence as to how their welfare may be adversely affected if an order for sale is now made. It is for the person who resists an order for sale in reliance on section 15(1)(c) to adduce the relevant evidence.

White v *White*,[29] Thorpe LJ:

> 14.   [Counsel criticised] the manner in which the judge had dealt with the father's primary submission, namely that the welfare of the children demanded deferral. In his judgment, whilst he understandably recorded at page 10 that the consequences and risks for the children was the consideration that had given him the greatest cause for concern, he thereafter did no more than record the mother's response that in her view the children would and could adapt, and that sharing a bedroom, if need be, would be no hardship to them. The judge simply made no findings in relation to that response and did not explain how he had in the end reassured himself against that greatest concern.
>
> 15.   . . . it must be implicit in the judgment that the basis of the judge's reassurance was the clear finding that an order for sale would not preclude the father from down-sizing to a three bedroom property in the same locality, enabling the girls to stay at the same school.

[The order for sale was upheld.]

Neither of these cases indicates that the interests of children will routinely sway the decision. When would the interests of children be likely to be a stronger factor? *Edwards* v *Lloyds TSB Bank plc*[30] (Extract 12.3.21 below) may offer more hope, though it will be seen that the case for immediate sale was relatively weak.

(vi) Interplay between s 14 and family law jurisdiction

Extract 12.3.10

Matrimonial Causes Act 1973, ss 24, 25

24.—(1)   On granting a decree of divorce, a decree of nullity of marriage or a decree of judicial separation or at any time thereafter (whether, in the case of a decree of divorce, or of nullity of marriage, before or after the decree is made absolute), the court may make any one or more of the following orders, that is to say—

> (a)   an order that a party to the marriage shall transfer to the other party, to any child of the family or to such person as may be specified in the order for the benefit of such a child such property as may be so specified, being property to which the first-mentioned party is entitled, either in possession or reversion;

---

[28]   [2004] 1 FCR 18.
[29]   [2004] 2 FLR 321.
[30]   [2005] 1 FCR 139. See also, in the bankruptcy context, *Barca v Mears* [2005] 2 FLR 1 (Extract 12.3.17 below).

    (b) an order that a settlement of such property as may be so specified, being property to which a party to the marriage is so entitled, be made to the satisfaction of the court for the benefit of the other party to the marriage and of the children of the family or either or any of them;

. . .

25.—(1) It shall be the duty of the court in deciding whether to exercise its powers under section 23, 24 or 24A above and, if so, in what manner, to have regard to all the circumstances of the case, first consideration being given to the welfare while a minor of any child of the family who has not attained the age of eighteen.

(2) As regards the exercise of the powers of the court under section 23(1)(a), (b) or (c), 24 or 24A above in relation to a party to the marriage, the court shall in particular have regard to the following matters—

    (a) the income, earning capacity, property and other financial resources which each of the parties to the marriage has or is likely to have in the foreseeable future, including in the case of earning capacity any increase in that capacity which it would in the opinion of the court be reasonable to expect a party to the marriage to take steps to acquire;

    (b) the financial needs, obligations and responsibilities which each of the parties to the marriage has or is likely to have in the foreseeable future;

    (c) the standard of living enjoyed by the family before the breakdown of the marriage;

    (d) the age of each party to the marriage and the duration of the marriage;

    (e) any physical or mental disability of either of the parties to the marriage;

    (f) the contributions which each of the parties has made or is likely in the foreseeable future to make to the welfare of the family, including any contribution by looking after the home or caring for the family;

    (g) the conduct of each of the parties, if that conduct is such that it would in the opinion of the court be inequitable to disregard it;

    (h) in the case of proceedings for divorce or nullity of marriage, the value to each of the parties to the marriage of any benefit (for example, a pension) which, by reason of the dissolution or annulment of the marriage, that party will lose the chance of acquiring.

Comment

(1) This will apply whether or not the property is jointly owned. In this chapter we are, of course, interested in jointly owned property.

(2) Remember that this applies only to marriage. Disputes between unmarried couples can be resolved only under the s 14 jurisdiction,[31] though the courts may strive to reach similar results.[32]

(3) Equivalent provision is made for civil partners by the Civil Partnership Act 2004, Sched 5.

It is plain that s 24 confers a very wide discretion upon the court. As the criteria in s 25 demonstrate, this discretion is not circumscribed by normal property principles. An obvious question is as to how the s 24 discretion applies to disputes which could also lead to s 14 applications.

---

[31] Subject to the power under the Children Act 1989, Sched 1, para 1(2)(d)(e), to order settlements and transfers of property for the benefit of children.

[32] *Re Evers' Trust* [1980] 1 WLR 1327.

Extract 12.3.11

Williams v *Williams* **[1976] Ch 278**

LORD DENNING MR: [Having described the *Jones* v *Challenger* approach:] I must say that that approach is now outdated. When judges are dealing with the matrimonial home, they nowadays have great regard to the fact that the house is bought as a home in which the family is to be brought up. It is not treated as property to be sold nor as an investment to be realised for cash. That was emphasised by this court in the recent case of *Browne (formerly Pritchard)* v *Pritchard* [1975] 1 WLR 1366. The court, in executing the trust should regard the primary object as being to provide a home and not a sale. Steps should be taken to preserve it as a home for the remaining partner and children, but giving the outgoing partner such compensation, by way of a charge or being bought out, as is reasonable in the circumstances.

It seems to me that in this case the judge was in error in applying the old approach. He did not give proper effect to the modern view, which is to have regard to the needs of the family as a whole before a sale is ordered. We have here the wife and the four sons still in the house. The youngest son is only 13 years of age and still at school. It would not be proper at this stage to order the sale of the house, unless it were shown that alternative accommodation could be provided at a cheaper rate, and some capital released. That has not been shown here.

The truth is that the approach to these cases has been transformed since the Matrimonial Proceedings and Property Act 1970 and the Matrimonial Causes Act 1973 which have given the power to the court after a divorce to order the transfer of property. In exercising any discretion under section 30 of the Law of Property Act 1925, those Acts must be taken into account. The discretion should be exercised on the principles stated by this court in *Jackson* v *Jackson* [1971] 1 WLR 1539, 1543.

I would add this: An application about a matrimonial home should not be restricted to section 30 of the Law of Property Act 1925. In view of the wide powers of transfer and adjustment which are available under the new matrimonial property legislation it seems to me that the applications should be made to the Family Division under the relevant provisions. If taken out in another division, they should be transferred to a judge of the Family Division.

Comment

(1) TLATA makes fresh provision for trusts of land, with clearer elucidation of relevant factors in s 15. Does this render the approach of Lord Denning MR obsolete?

(2) Though the Court of Appeal adopted a similar approach in *Miller Smith* v *Miller Smith* [2010] 1 FLR 1402, the facts justified sale under TLATA in order to avoid delays in the matrimonial jurisdiction.

Although there is no similar property transfer provision for unmarried couples, occupation disputes can fall within s 33 of the Family Law Act 1996. We have already seen[33] that there could be an argument that s 33 provides the more appropriate basis for resolving occupation disputes. Given that sale will almost inevitably involve one party giving up occupation, might this also apply to sale applications involving unmarried couples?

(vii) Bankruptcy of a co-owner

On bankruptcy, the property of a co-owner is vested in the trustee in bankruptcy. It is usual for the trustee in bankruptcy to seek sale of the property, in order to realise the value

---

[33] See p 401 above.

of the bankrupt's share for the benefit of the creditors. It is quite clear that the trustee in bankruptcy can apply to the court under s 14. However, two special factors come into play. First, the Matrimonial Causes Act jurisdiction cannot be brought into play against the trustee in bankruptcy:[34] property principles therefore dominate. Secondly, the normal s 15 criteria for sale are inoperative (s 15(4)). Instead, the court has to operate within the terms of the Insolvency Act 1986.

Extract 12.3.12

Insolvency Act 1986, ss 335A, 283A

335A.—(1) Any application by a trustee of a bankrupt's estate under section 14 of the Trusts of Land and Appointment of Trustees Act 1996 (powers of court in relation to trusts of land) for an order under that section for the sale of land shall be made to the court having jurisdiction in relation to the bankruptcy.

(2) On such an application the court shall make such order as it thinks just and reasonable having regard to—

(a) the interests of the bankrupt's creditors;

(b) where the application is made in respect of land which includes a dwelling-house which is or has been the home of the bankrupt or the bankrupt's spouse or former spouse—

(i) the conduct of the spouse or former spouse, so far as contributing to the bankruptcy,

(ii) the needs and financial resources of the spouse or former spouse, and

(iii) the needs of any children; and

(c) all the circumstances of the case other than the needs of the bankrupt.

(3) Where such an application is made after the end of the period of one year beginning with the first vesting under Chapter IV of this Part of the bankrupt's estate in a trustee, the court shall assume, unless the circumstances of the case are exceptional, that the interests of the bankrupt's creditors outweigh all other considerations.

283A.—(1) This section applies where property comprised in the bankrupt's estate consists of an interest in a dwelling-house which at the date of the bankruptcy was the sole or principal residence of—

(a) the bankrupt,

(b) the bankrupt's spouse or civil partner, or

(c) a former spouse or former civil partner of the bankrupt.

(2) At the end of the period of three years beginning with the date of the bankruptcy the interest mentioned in subsection (1) shall—

(a) cease to be comprised in the bankrupt's estate, and

(b) vest in the bankrupt (without conveyance, assignment or transfer).

(3) Subsection (2) shall not apply if during the period mentioned in that subsection—

. . .

(b) the trustee applies for an order for sale in respect of the dwelling-house,

(6) The court may substitute for the period of three years mentioned in subsection (2) a longer period—

(a) in prescribed circumstances, and

(b) in such other circumstances as the court thinks appropriate.

---

[34] *Re Holliday* [1981] Ch 405 at p 419.

Comment

(1) Section 337 makes provision where children are living with the bankrupt, designed to ensure that the children receive similar protection.

(2) Although s 335A was inserted by TLATA, the general structure of the law is little changed from that originally enacted by the Insolvency Act 1986.

(3) Section 283A was inserted by the Enterprise Act 2002 and is intended to ensure that those who become bankrupt can emerge from that status within a reasonable period. What effect might it have on applications for sale (in the light of the following cases)?

The general structure of these provisions is to give the court a limited discretion. Within the first year, it is probably safe to assume that spouses and children (but not other cohabitants) will usually be safe from eviction. The cases reveal that actions for possession are often brought some time after bankruptcy, so the first year protection is likely to have limited practical effect. Much more important is the provision in s 335A(3) that the interests of the creditors shall prevail after one year unless the circumstances of the case are 'exceptional'. As is shown in the following case (decided on the pre-Insolvency Act 1986 law), this was intended to mirror the previous law as developed by the courts. Accordingly, the earlier cases remain vitally important.

Extract 12.3.13

Re Citro [1991] Ch 142

NOURSE LJ: . . . In a series of bankruptcy decisions relating to matrimonial homes subsequent to *Jones* v *Challenger* it has been held that the interests of the husband's creditors ought usually to prevail over the interests of the wife and any children and, with one exception, *In re Holliday (A Bankrupt), Ex parte Trustee of the Property of the Bankrupt* v *Holliday* [1981] Ch 405, a sale within a short period has invariably been ordered. It has also been assumed that no distinction ought to be made between a case where the property is still being enjoyed as the matrimonial home and one where it is not.

. . .

I now come to *In re Holliday* [1981] Ch 405 which, as I have said, is the only reported bankruptcy decision in which a sale within a short period has not been ordered. It is also the only previous case in which the bankruptcy decisions have been considered by this court. [There were divorce proceedings] . . . On or shortly before 3 March 1976 the wife gave notice of her intention to bring on her application for ancillary relief, whereupon, on that same day, the husband filed his own bankruptcy petition, asking for immediate adjudication . . .

. . . In the course of stating the facts, Buckley LJ said, at p 422, that the value of the equity of redemption in the matrimonial home might be taken to be of the order of £26,500 . . . [The] debts added up to about £6,500 and about £7,500 was needed in order fully to discharge the obligations and expenses under the bankruptcy . . . Buckley LJ . . . continued, at p 424:

> 'Of course, the creditors are entitled to payment as soon as the debtor is in a position to pay them. They are entitled to payment forthwith; they have an unassailable right to be paid out of the assets of the debtor. But in my view, when one of those assets is an undivided share in land in respect of which the debtor's right to an immediate sale is not an absolute right, that is an asset in the bankruptcy which is liable to be affected by the interest of any other party interested in that land, and if there are reasons which seem to the court to be good reasons for saying that the trust for sale of the land should not be immediately enforced, then that is an asset of the bankruptcy which is not immediately available because it cannot be immediately realised for the benefit of the creditors.'

He concluded that the house should not be sold, without the consent of the wife or pursuant to an order of the court, before 1 July 1985, some five years in the future.

Sir David Cairns agreed that in all the circumstances of the case the voice of the wife, on behalf of herself and the children, should prevail to the extent that the sale of the house should be deferred for a substantial period. He continued, at p 425:

'I reach that view because I am satisfied that it would at present be very difficult, if not impossible, for the wife to secure another suitable home for the family in or near Thorpe Bay; because it would be upsetting for the children's education if they had to move far away from their present schools, even if it were practicable, having regard to the wife's means, to find an alternative home at some more distant place; because it is highly unlikely that postpone-ment of the payment of the debts would cause any great hardship to any of the creditors; and because none of the creditors thought fit themselves to present a bankruptcy petition and it is quite impossible to know whether any one of them would have done so if the debtor had not himself presented such a petition.'

In referring to the earlier cases, he said that the trustee had succeeded there because no sufficiently substantial case of hardship of defendants had been established.

Finally, there is *In re Lowrie (A Bankrupt)* [1981] 3 All ER 353, another case where the husband and wife were living in the matrimonial home. The husband having been adjudicated bankrupt in 1979, his trustee applied to the county court for an order for sale, which order was made but suspended for 30 months. The trustee appealed successfully to the Divisional Court in Bankruptcy, who ordered a sale within a short period. In giving the first judgment, Walton J said, at p 355:

'One must always look at the whole of the circumstances of the case, and in exceptional circumstances there is no doubt that the trustee's voice will not be allowed to prevail in equity and the sale will not be ordered. A brilliant example of just such a situation is to be found in *In re Holliday (A Bankrupt)* . . . where the petition in bankruptcy had been presented by the husband himself as a tactical move, and quite clearly as a tactical move, to avoid a transfer of property order in favour of his wife, or ex-wife, at a time when no creditors what-soever were pressing and he was in a position in the course of a year or so out of a very good income to discharge whatever debts he had. He had gone off leaving the wife in the matrimonial home, which was the subject matter of the application, with responsibility for all the children on her own. One can scarcely, I think, imagine a more exceptional set of facts and the court gave effect to those exceptional facts.'

. . . In my view Walton J, in describing the circumstances in which the trustee's voice will not prevail as 'exceptional', stated a correct test. Alternatively, he might have described them as 'special', which to my mind means exactly the same thing.

The broad effect of these authorities can be summarised as follows. Where a spouse who has a beneficial interest in the matrimonial home has become bankrupt under debts which can-not be paid without the realisation of that interest, the voice of the creditors will usually prevail over the voice of the other spouse and a sale of the property ordered within a short period. The voice of the other spouse will only prevail in exceptional circumstances. No distinction is to be made between a case where the property is still being enjoyed as the matrimonial home and one where it is not.

What then are exceptional circumstances? As the cases show, it is not uncommon for a wife with young children to be faced with eviction in circumstances where the realisation of her bene-ficial interest will not produce enough to buy a comparable home in the same neighbourhood, or indeed elsewhere. And, if she has to move elsewhere, there may be problems over schooling and so forth. Such circumstances, while engendering a natural sympathy in all who hear of them, cannot be described as exceptional. They are the melancholy consequences of debt and improvidence with which every civilised society has been familiar. It was only in *In re Holliday* [1981] Ch 405 that they helped the wife's voice to prevail, and then only, as I believe, because of one special feature of that case. One of the reasons for the decision given by Sir David Cairns was that it was highly unlikely that postponement of payment of the debts would cause any great hardship to any of the creditors, a matter of which Buckley LJ no doubt took account as well . . . It must indeed be exceptional for creditors in a bankruptcy to receive 100p in the £ plus statutory interest in full and the passage of years before they do so does not make it less exceptional. On the other hand, without that special feature, I cannot myself see how the circumstances in *In re Holliday* could fairly have been treated as exceptional . . . I would not myself have regarded it as an exceptional circumstance that the husband had presented his own petition, even 'as a tactical move'. That was not something of the creditors' choosing and could not fairly have been held against them. I do not say that in other cases there might not be other exceptional circumstances. They must be identified if and when they arise.

. . .

Finally, I refer to section 336 [now s 335A] of the Insolvency Act 1986 which, although it does not apply to either of these cases, will apply to such cases in the future. In subsection (5) of that section the court is required, in the circumstances there mentioned, to 'assume, unless the circumstances of the case are exceptional, that the interests of the bankrupt's creditors outweigh all other considerations'. I have no doubt that that section was intended to apply the same test as that which has been evolved in the previous bankruptcy decisions . . .

Re Citro provides some guidance as to those rare cases in which the circumstances will be found exceptional. The following dicta may also be helpful.

Extract 12.3.14

Re Bailey [1977] 1 WLR 278

WALTON J: . . . Mr Crystal, for the trustee in bankruptcy, asks the court to give wider directions to trustees in bankruptcy throughout the country as to the position where there are children, but that, it seems to me, is equally something which this court cannot possibly do, because the situation must vary enormously from family to family. He, himself, instanced a case where, for example, a house had been specially adapted to suit the needs of a handicapped child, where there are obviously special circumstances; so special that, undoubtedly, this court would hesitate long before making an immediate order for sale. Further than that one cannot go, because one does not know what the countervailing hardship on the other side might be at the time when the matter comes for decision. One does not know whether there would be a likelihood of creditors being paid in full, what they would have to pay by way of interest for any borrowing they may, themselves, have to make to fill the gap until they get their money, and so forth . . .

Extract 12.3.15

Judd v *Brown* [1998] 2 FLR 360

HARMAN J: . . . In the present case the exceptional circumstance affects Josephine [the bankrupt's wife]. She has very recently – I think in December 1996 – been diagnosed as suffering from ovarian cancer and has undergone extensive surgery. She is undergoing a course of chemotherapy and the oncologist concerned with her case states that it is essential to avoid all stress upon Josephine so that she may better respond to treatment. The course is expected to continue over the next 5 or 6 months according to the oncologist's letter of 7 January 1997 which is in evidence.

Josephine's illness, for which everyone must feel deep sympathy, plainly creates difficulties of a very different character from such difficulties as obtaining substitute accommodation or arranging for children's schooling which are foreseeable and long-term conditions. This event must have been sudden, unforeseeable, of very recent occurrence, of gravity and is directly affected by the orders now sought. Although cancer in various forms attacks many people yet I think that as a matter of normal language people would say that a sudden and serious attack was an exceptional circumstance in any individual's life. When recovery from the attack is directly related to the orders sought it is, in my judgment, what is properly to be described as an exceptional reason for refusing the orders. If the occurrence of life-threatening illness is not an exceptional event I find it difficult to know what such an event can be. In this case the oncologist's view of the importance of security to his patient's possible recovery seems to me to reinforce the relevance of Josephine's illness. Further, the fact that a comparatively short time will enable matters to be resolved, it is to be hoped by a happy outcome, differentiates this particular case on its facts from a case of some person who suffers a long-term illness of indeterminate duration.

Comment

(1) Harman J refused merely to suspend sale for, say, eight months during the chemotherapy treatment: such a threat hanging over Josephine would increase the stress which the court sought to avoid.

(2) Why should unexpected events be exceptional? Just as children may require housing security for effective schooling, will not every family encounter illness and death sooner or later?

(3) Other cases include *Re Raval (a bankrupt)*[35] (sale postponed for a further year to allow accommodation to be found for a paranoid schizophrenic with three children) and *Re Haghighat*[36] (sale postponed for three years to allow local authority provision for a seriously disabled child).

It remains to consider the question why the law should give such prominence to the claims of creditors. Their claims look particularly weak when debts are incurred after the house has been purchased: they have chosen to extend credit to a person already committed to the family home. It is instructive that in *Re Citro* Sir George Waller dissented and, despite concurring, Bingham LJ regretted the conclusion. Consider the Report which led to the enactment of the Insolvency Act 1986.

Extract 12.3.16

Cork Committee on Insolvency Law and Practice (1982) Cmnd 8558

THE FAMILY HOME

1114.   The house in which a debtor is living with his wife and family (or, more often, the residual value of such a house after the repayment of the mortgage debt) is frequently the major asset of a consumer debtor and may also be the major asset of a sole or partnership trader.

1116.   Eviction from the family home therefore may be a disaster not only to the debtor himself (whose actions may have led to it) but also to those who are living there as his dependants who may not, and often do not, have any legal or beneficial rights in the property which they can enforce.

[35] [1998] 2 FLR 718.
[36] [2009] 1 FLR 1271.

1118.   It would be clearly wrong to allow a debtor or his family to continue to live in a lavish style at the expense of the debtor's creditors for an extended period. Nevertheless considerable personal hardship can be caused to the debtor's family by a sudden or premature eviction, and we believe it to be consonant with present social attitudes to alleviate the personal hardships of those who are dependant on the debtor but not responsible for his insolvency, if this can be achieved by delaying for an acceptable time the sale of the family home. We propose therefore to delay, but not to cancel, enforcement of the creditors' rights.

1119.   Trustees have usually acted with humanity both in the manner and in the timing of any sale of the family home. If the home is not over-lavish for the future living standard of the family, arrangements can often be made for the likely value to the creditors to be provided without a sale . . .

1120.   Nevertheless we consider that any new Insolvency Act should confer on the Court a specific power to postpone a trustee's rights of possession and sale of the family home. In exercising this power the Court should have particular regard to the welfare of any children of the family and of any adult members of the family who are ailing or elderly (see Law Commission Third Report at page 49). Giving this power to the Court will, we hope and expect, serve to support the natural inclination of the usually sympathetic trustee, and to protect the debtor's family in those cases where lack of sympathy with, or anger at, the debtor produces unfortunate and undeserved consequences for his family.

1121.   Where there are dependants, the Court should not order an immediate sale unless satisfied that no avoidable hardship to them will be caused by the sale of the family home. That is not to say that application need be made to the Court in every case; once the correct principles have been established, we believe that in only a very small minority of cases will the Court be concerned.

1122.   When an application does come before the Court, we consider that the Court must have wide discretion to enable it to make whatever order may be just and equitable in the great variety of circumstances that may arise. While the Court will first consider the dependants – and the greater their vulnerability the greater will be the protection needed – creditors' rights should be postponed only in order to prevent injury to the welfare of those dependants; not to preserve for them any particular standard of life.

1123.   No two cases will be alike; the Court must therefore have complete discretion to do what seems to it to be appropriate. Such guidelines as can be given must of necessity be in the most general terms and, indeed, little more than an indication of the factors for consideration. While some of us have considered that there should be a statutory limit on the length of time for which a postponement could be ordered, all of us are agreed that, in practice, any very lengthy postponement should be rare. The majority of us have concluded that the Court's powers should not be limited in duration. In the reported cases, both under the matrimonial legislation and (more rarely) under the bankruptcy law, much importance has been attached to the ages, welfare and educational prospects of the children.

1129.   In balancing the potential hardships involved in the sale of the family home against the interests of the creditors, the Court will give primary consideration to the welfare of dependant children, to the circumstances of the wife, and to the situation of dependant parents who are resident in the family dwelling.

Comment

(1) How far is the Insolvency Act 1986 consistent with these recommendations? See Cretney (1991) 107 LQR 177.

(2) Are there convincing reasons for saying that the interests of creditors should prevail (whether or not after the first year)?

(3) Is it relevant that mortgagees can sell mortgaged land if the borrower is unable pay mortgage instalments, without any special protection for partners or children?

Extract 12.3.17

Barca v *Mears* [2005] 2 FLR 1 (Ch D)

It was argued that a son's special educational needs were relevant so that sale should be refused.

STRAUSS QC: 32.   Nevertheless, I do not think that the view taken by the Deputy Registrar can be faulted on the basis that the law is as stated in *re Citro*. It is true that the 'special needs' aspect of the matter is a feature which was not present in this case, but Lorenzo's problems cannot be said to be extreme. Further, unlike *re Citro*, this is not a case in which there would be any question of his having to leave his present school, since he would be able to live in his mother's home, if necessary throughout the week. But for one submission made by Mr Barca, I would have had no hesitation in dismissing this appeal.

33.   However, at paragraph 29 of his Draft Skeleton Argument, Mr Barca invokes the European Convention on Human Rights. He submits that the Deputy Registrar failed to take account of his or his son's right to family life, home and privacy, stating that in the 8 year period since he became bankrupt his son had grown to know him as his father and that his right to family life, home and privacy were important aspects of his development. He submits at paragraph 29.4 that 'insolvency legislation in this area is particularly brutal and contrary to the average concept of fundamental freedoms and rights'. Mr Barca further raised the point in the course of oral argument and, particularly in the light of the view expressed by Bingham LJ in *re Citro*, I think that it is a point of some importance . . .

37.   Mr Gibbon submitted, in my view correctly, that where a court considers that a statutory provision, as interpreted before the Convention became part of English law, is incompatible with the Convention, it should seek to re-interpret the relevant provisions so as to achieve compatibility: only if this is not possible should a court consider granting a declaration of incompatibility . . .

38.   Mr Gibbon made the following further submissions, which I also accept:—

(1)   The right to 'respect' for private and family life and the home is not absolute. The state must have regard 'to the fair balance that has to be struck between the general interest of the community and the interests of the individual, the search for which balance is inherent in the whole Convention': *Cossey* v *UK* (1990) 13 EHRR 622 para 37.

(2)   What is 'necessary in a democratic society' requires an assessment of 'whether the interference complained of corresponded to a pressing social need, whether it was proportionate to the legitimate aim pursued, [and] whether the reasons given by the national authorities to justify it are relevant and sufficient': *Sunday Times* v *UK* (1979) 2 EHRR 245 at 277–8.

(3)   This proportionality test is satisfied if:

  (a)   the legislative objective is sufficiently important to justify the limitation on the fundamental right;

  (b)   the measures designed to meet the legislative objective are rationally connected with it; and

  (c)   the means used to impair the right or freedom are no more than is necessary to accomplish the legitimate objective.

See *Germany* v *Council of the European Union* [1995] ECR-I-3723 at 3755–6 and *de Freitas* v *Permanent Secretary of Ministry of Agriculture, Fisheries, Lands and Housing* [1998] 3 WLR 675, a decision relating to the Constitution of Antigua and Barbuda.

39.   Clearly, in many or perhaps most cases, the sale of a bankrupt's property in accordance with bankruptcy law will be justifiable on the basis that it is necessary to protect the rights of others, namely the creditors, and will not be a breach of the Convention. Nevertheless, it does seem to me to be questionable whether the narrow approach as to what may be 'exceptional circumstances' adopted in *re Citro*, is consistent with the Convention. It requires the court to adopt an almost universal rule, which prefers the property rights of the bankrupt's creditors to the property and/or personal rights of third parties, members of his family, who owe the creditors nothing. I think that there is considerable force in what is said by Ms Deborah Rook in *Property Law and Human Rights* at pp 203–5 to which Mr Gibbon very fairly referred me:

'It is arguable that, in some circumstances, [s 335A(3)] may result in an infringement of Article 8. The mortgagor's partner and children have the right to respect for their home and family life under Article 8 even though they may have no proprietary interest in the house . . . therefore it is possible that the presumption of sale in s 335A and the way that the courts have interpreted it, so that in the majority of cases an innocent partner and the children are evicted from the home, violates Convention rights . . .

The eviction of the family from their home, an event that naturally ensues from the operation of the presumption of sale in s 335A, could be considered to be an infringement of the right to respect of the home and family life under Article 8 if the presumption is given absolute priority without sufficient consideration being given to the Convention rights of the affected family. Allen [Mr T Allen in "The Human Rights Act (UK) and Property Law" in *Property and the Constitution*, Oxford, Hart Publishing, 1999 at p 163] observes that:

"As the law currently stands, the right to respect for family life and the home receives almost no consideration after the one year period. Whether such a strict limitation is compatible with the Convention is doubtful.". . .

. . . it may be that the courts, in applying s 335A . . . will need to adopt a more sympathetic approach to defining what constitutes "exceptional circumstances". If an immediate sale of the property would violate the family's rights under Article 8, the court may be required in compliance with its duty under s 3 of the HRA 1988 to adopt a broad interpretation of "exceptional circumstances" . . . to ensure the compatibility of this legislation with Convention rights.'

40.   In particular, it may be incompatible with Convention rights to follow the approach taken by the majority in *re Citro*, in drawing a distinction between what is exceptional, in the sense of being unusual, and what Nourse LJ refers to as the 'usual melancholy consequences' of a bankruptcy. This approach leads to the conclusion that, however disastrous the consequences may be to family life, if they are of the usual *kind* then they cannot be relied on under section 335A; they will qualify as 'exceptional' only if they are of an unusual kind, for example where a terminal illness is involved.

41.   It seems to me that a shift in emphasis in the interpretation of the statute may be necessary to achieve compatibility with the Convention. There is nothing in the wording of section 335A, or the corresponding wording of sections 336 and 337, to require an interpretation which excludes from the ambit of 'exceptional circumstances' cases in which the consequences of the bankruptcy are of the usual kind, but exceptionally severe. Nor is there anything in the wording to require a court to say that a case may not be exceptional, if it is one of the rare cases in which, on the facts, relatively slight loss which the creditors will suffer as a result of the postponement of the sale would be outweighed by disruption, even if of the usual kind, which will be caused in the lives of the bankrupt and his family. Indeed, on one view, this is what the Court of Appeal decided in *Re Holliday*.

42.   Thus it may be that, on a reconsideration of the sections in the light of the Convention, they are to be regarded as recognising that, in the general run of cases, the creditors' interests will outweigh all other interests, but leaving it open to a court to find that, on a proper consideration

of the facts of a particular case, it is one of the exceptional cases in which this proposition is not true. So interpreted, and without the possibly undue bias in favour of the creditors' property interests embodied in the pre-1998 case law, these sections would be compatible with the Convention.

43.   I do not need to reach a conclusion on this in the present case, because, even if this tentative view as to the proper approach to the interpretation of these sections is correct, I would still uphold the Deputy Registrar's decision on the facts of this case. . . . the creditors' interests must prevail:—

(a)   . . . The prejudice to the creditors would . . . be substantial.

(b)   Lorenzo's educational problems are not extreme, and there is no question of his having to move school even if Mr Barca's ability to help him were impaired.

(c)   It is unclear whether Mr Barca's ability to help Lorenzo will be impaired, or if so to what extent.

Comment

Would many cases be affected by the analysis of Strauss QC? See *National Westminster Bank plc* v *Rushmer* [2010] 2 FLR 362 at [50] for the position outside the bankruptcy context.

Contrast the approach of Peter Smith J in *Ford* v *Alexander* [2012] EWHC 266 (Ch); [2012] BPIR 528:

49.   It is clear that the circumstances of the case were extremely unusual. However in the context of section 335A in my view the requirements in sub section (2) and the change of emphasis in sub paragraph (3) do not infringe Article 8(2). They provide a necessary balance as between the rights of creditors and the respect for privacy and the home of the debtor. That balance serves the legitimate aim of protecting the rights and freedoms of others. I am therefore of the opinion that the requirements of section 335A satisfy the test of being necessary in a democratic society and are thus proportionate (see *McCann* v *United Kingdom* (App no 19009/04) and *Connors* v *United Kingdom* (App no 66746/01)). This was the conclusion in the pre *Pinnock* bankruptcy cases and I see no basis for coming to a different conclusion.

50.   For the same reasons I do not see that the decision of the Supreme Court in *Mayor and Burgess of London Borough of Hounslow* v *Powell & Ors* [2011] UKSC 8 offers any assistance. The checks and balances set out in section 335A in my view suggest a procedure that is proportionate and Article 8 adds nothing.

The judge rejected an argument that s 335A should be read as requiring proportionality rather than exceptional circumstances (or that exceptional should be interpreted in that way). To what extent, if at all, is *Ford* inconsistent with the approach of Strauss QC?

Extract 12.3.18

Insolvency Act 1986, s 313A

313A.—(1)   This section applies where—

(a)   property comprised in the bankrupt's estate consists of an interest in a dwelling-house which at the date of the bankruptcy was the sole or principal residence of—

(i)   the bankrupt,

(ii)   the bankrupt's spouse or civil partner, or

(iii)   a former spouse or former civil partner of the bankrupt, and

(b)   the trustee applies for an order for the sale of the property . . .

(2)   The court shall dismiss the application if the value of the interest is below the amount prescribed for the purposes of this subsection.

Comment

(1) The amount prescribed is £1,000 (after deducting mortgage loan and costs of sale).[37]

(2) How significant is this protection, added by the Enterprise Act 2002, likely to be?

(viii) The operation of s 14 as regards successors in title

The question to be considered here is whether a co-owner's successor in title is affected by a purpose which would have prevented the co-owner from obtaining an order for sale. One's initial instinct might be that the successor (including a mortgagee) should be in no better position than the selling co-owner.[38] However, the bankruptcy cases prior to the Insolvency Act 1986 used an analysis which treated the trustee in bankruptcy as a successor in title. In turn, some of the cases on successors in title have drawn upon the bankruptcy cases.

Extract 12.3.19

Abbey National plc v *Moss* [1994] 1 FLR 307

A mother transferred her house into the joint names of herself and her daughter, the purpose being to continue the use of the house as the mother's home (though the daughter also lived there with her family). The daughter mortgaged her interest to the plaintiff.[39] Following default by the daughter, the plaintiff sought sale.

PETER GIBSON LJ: It is to be observed that the reasoning of Nourse LJ [in *Re Citro*] expressly includes the proposition that the secondary purpose, viz that the property be occupied as the matrimonial home, can only exist while the spouses are both joint occupiers and also joint owners of the home, and this he founds on the fact that as a matter of property law, the basis of the husband's and the wife's joint occupation is their joint ownership of the beneficial interest in the home. It follows that Nourse LJ treats a case where the husband and wife are still living together in the matrimonial home but one of them becomes bankrupt as a case where the collateral purpose has come to an end. . . . It is entirely consistent with what seems to me to be the manifestly correct and principled proposition that where the collateral purpose has not come to an end the court will ordinarily not allow the trust for sale to defeat that purpose, even when there has been an assignment to another by an original party to that purpose. The assignee cannot normally be in a better position than the assignor. In the present case it is impossible to say that the collateral purpose, viz that Mrs Moss should continue to live in the property during her life, has come to an end by reason of Mrs Leto losing her beneficial interest through the mortgage, because the collateral purpose is wholly unaffected by that event. It would of course have been otherwise if the collateral purpose had been that she and Mrs Moss would live together in the property.

[Another] case was the earlier decision of this court in *Stott* v *Ratcliffe*, reported briefly in (1982) 126 Sol Jo 310 [in which one co-owner had died]. The court refused to order sale, both Lord Denning MR and Eveleigh LJ saying that the purpose of the trust was not completely fulfilled on the death of Mr Stott. In my judgment that decision too is entirely in line with the principles of *Jones* v *Challenger* in recognising that a subsisting collateral purpose will not be overridden by the trust for sale notwithstanding that the beneficial interest of one of the original

---

[37] SI 2004 No 547.

[38] The successor would, of course, be safe if he is a purchaser of a legal estate who is not bound by the other co-owner's interest.

[39] It appears that she forged a mortgage of the legal title; this took effect as a mortgage of her beneficial interest.

parties to that purpose has passed to another who is being kept out of the enjoyment both of the property and of the proceeds of sale.

. . . *Re Citro* only establishes that the collateral purpose will not be treated as subsisting when that purpose is to provide a matrimonial home and one of the parties ceases through bankruptcy or the like to own his share. It does not purport to apply where a different collateral purpose continues to subsist and where such purpose is not affected by the alienation by a party to that purpose of his share.

Comment

(1) In the normal case of co-ownership of a family home, will a successor in title be affected by the purpose? Is the reasoning persuasive?

(2) Why was the successor in title bound in *Moss*?

(3) The proposition that a purpose of joint occupation terminates on cesser of joint owner-ship (or on a mortgage of a beneficial interest) looks very artificial. Can it be defended?

(4) Since the Insolvency Act 1986, collateral purposes have not been relevant on bankruptcy. Does this affect the reasoning in *Moss*?

(5) Will a purpose survive the death of one of two occupying co-owners? Note that *Jones v Challenger*[40] assumes that the purpose terminates on the death of one.

In most cases, the mortgagor is one of the persons whose possession is intended. In these circumstances, the almost inevitable response of the courts pre-TLATA was to order sale unless there were 'exceptional circumstances' (the bankruptcy test). In *Bank of Baroda* v *Dhillon*,[41] the Court of Appeal rejected an argument that the defendant's overriding interest by virtue of actual occupation precluded an application for sale. Given that even the co-owner could have applied for sale, this was an optimistic argument!

However, a major problem in dealing with the cases in this area is to justify their use of analyses emanating from the bankruptcy cases. In particular, the use of the bankruptcy test of 'exceptional circumstances' outside the bankruptcy context becomes very difficult to explain. Remember also that purposes are not determinative of the outcome of a s 14 application; whilst very relevant, they are merely one of the factors the court should take into account.

The question of how to handle this material in the light of the fresh provision made by TLATA was considered in the next case.

Extract 12.3.20

Mortgage Corpn v Shaire [2001] Ch 743

NEUBERGER J: The question here is: ought I to make an order for sale of the house and, if not, what order ought I to make? . . .

Accordingly, there was, in relation to trusts for sale and before the 1996 Act came into force, no difference between the two types of case considered in *In re Citro (Domenico) (A Bankrupt)* [1991] Ch 142 [application by trustee in bankruptcy of a beneficiary] and *Lloyds Bank plc* v *Byrne & Byrne* [1993] 1 FLR 369 [application by secured creditor of a beneficiary]. The normal rule in such cases was that, save in exceptional circumstances, the wish of the person wanting

---

[40] [1961] 1 QB 176 at p 183; contrast *Stott v Ratcliffe* (1982) 126 SJ 310.
[41] [1998] 1 FLR 524.

the sale, be it a trustee in bankruptcy or a chargee, would prevail, and that the interests of children and families in occupation would be unlikely to prevail. These conclusions were applied in a number of cases at first instance, including *Barclays Bank plc v Hendricks* [1996] 1 FLR 258 (Laddie J) and *Zandfarid v Bank of Credit and Commerce International SA* [1996] 1 WLR 1420 (Jonathan Parker J).

However, trusts for sale and section 30 have now been effectively replaced by the 1996 Act. Section 1 of the 1996 Act has the effect of rendering trusts for sale obsolete, including those in existence on 1 January 1997, and replacing them with the less arcane and simpler trusts of land . . .

Two questions of principle have been canvassed. First, as a result of the 1996 Act, has the law, relating to the way in which the court will exercise its power to order a sale at the suit of a chargee of the interest of one of the owners of the beneficial interest in property, changed? In other words, does section 15 change the law from how it had been laid down in *In re Citro* [1991] Ch 142 and *Lloyds Bank plc v Byrne & Byrne* [1993] 1 FLR 369? Secondly, does section 15(3) apply in the present case?

The effect of the 1996 Act

To my mind, for a number of reasons, Mr Asif is correct in his submission on behalf of Mrs Shaire that section 15 has changed the law. First, there is the rather trite point that, if there was no intention to change the law, it is hard to see why Parliament has set out in section 15(2) and, indeed, on one view, section 15(3), the factors which have to be taken into account specifically, albeit not exclusively, when the court is asked to exercise its jurisdiction to order a sale.

Secondly, it is hard to reconcile the contention that Parliament intended to confirm the law as laid down in *Lloyds Bank plc v Byrne & Byrne* with the fact that, while the interest of a chargee is one of the four specified factors to be taken into account in section 15(1)(d), there is no suggestion that it is to be given any more importance than the interests of the children residing in the house: see section 15(1)(c). As is clear from the passage I have quoted from the judgment of Nourse LJ in *In re Citro* [1991] Ch 142, 157 as applied to a case such as this in light of *Lloyds Bank plc v Byrne & Byrne*, that would appear to represent a change in the law.

Thirdly, the very name 'trust for sale' and the law as it has been developed by the courts suggests that under the old law, in the absence of a strong reason to the contrary, the court should order sale. Nothing in the language of the new code as found in the 1996 Act supports that approach.

Fourthly, it is clear from the reasons in *Lloyds Bank plc v Byrne & Byrne*, and indeed the later two first instance cases to which I have referred, that the law, as developed under section 30 of the Law of Property Act 1925, was that the court should adopt precisely the same approach in a case where one of the co-owners was bankrupt (*In re Citro*) and a case where one of the co-owners had charged his interest (*Lloyds Bank plc v Byrne & Byrne*). It is quite clear that Parliament now considers that a different approach is appropriate in the two cases – compare section 15(2) and section 15(3) of the 1996 Act with section 15(4) and the new section 335A of the Insolvency Act 1986.

Fifthly, an indication from the Court of Appeal that the 1996 Act was intended to change the law is to be found in (an albeit plainly obiter) sentence in the judgment of Peter Gibson LJ in *Bankers Trust Co v Namdar* (unreported) 14 February 1997 . . .

Sixthly, the leading textbooks support the view that I have reached. In *Megarry & Wade, The Law of Real Property*, para 9–064, one finds:

'Although the authorities on the law prior to 1997 will therefore continue to provide guidance, the outcome will not in all cases be the same as it would have been under the previous law. This is because the legislation is much more specific as to the matters which a court is required to take into account . . .'

And in *Emmet on Title*, 19th ed looseleaf, vol 2, para 22–035:

'Cases decided on pre-1997 law may be disregarded as of little, if any, assistance . . . because the starting point . . . was necessarily a trust for sale implied or expressed as a conveyancing device enabling the convenient co-ownership of the property . . .'

Seventhly, the Law Commission report which gave rise to the 1996 Act, Transfer of Land, Trusts of Land (1989) (Law Com No 181), tends to support this view as well . . . In paragraph 12.9 of the report the Law Commission describe the aim as being to 'consolidate *and rationalise*' (emphasis added) the current approach. When commenting on the proposed equivalents of what are now section 15(2) and section 15(3) the Law Commission said, in footnote 143:

'Clearly, the terms of these guidelines may influence the exercise of the discretion in some way. For example, it may be that the courts' approach to creditors' interests will be altered by the framing of the guideline as to the welfare of children. If the welfare of children is seen as a factor to be considered independently of the beneficiaries' holdings, the courts may be less ready to order the sale of the home than they are at present.'

. . .

Eighthly, to put it at its lowest, it does not seem to me unlikely that the legislature intended to relax the fetters on the way in which the court exercised its discretion in cases such as *In re Citro* [1991] Ch 142 and *Lloyds Bank plc v Byrne & Byrne* [1993] 1 FLR 369, and so as to tip the balance somewhat more in favour of families and against banks and other chargees. Although the law under section 30 was clear following *In re Citro* and *Lloyds Bank plc v Byrne & Byrne*, there were indications of judicial dissatisfaction with the state of the law at that time. Although Bingham LJ agreed with Nourse LJ in *In re Citro*, he expressed, at p 161F, unhappiness with the result and Sir George Waller's dissatisfaction went so far as led him to dissent: see his judgment, at pp 161–163. Furthermore, there is a decision of the Court of Appeal in *Abbey National plc v Moss* [1994] 1 FLR 307 which suggests a desire for a new approach.

All these factors, to my mind, when taken together point very strongly to the conclusion that section 15 has changed the law. As a result of section 15, the court has greater flexibility than heretofore, as to how it exercises its jurisdiction on an application for an order for sale on facts such as those in *In re Citro* and *Lloyds Bank plc v Byrne & Byrne*. There are certain factors which must be taken into account: see section 15(1) and, subject to the next point, section 15(3). There may be other factors in a particular case which the court can, indeed should, take into account. Once the relevant factors to be taken into account have been identified, it is a matter for the court as to what weight to give to each factor in a particular case.

. . .

An order for sale?

Bearing in mind these conclusions as to the effect of the 1996 Act, ought I to make an order for sale? I consider, first, the matters to which I am specifically required to have regard in section 15(1) and section 15(3). So far as section 15(1)(a) is concerned, the house was acquired in 1987 as a home for Mr Fox, Mrs Shaire and Adam, and Mrs Shaire and Adam still live there and still want to live there. It is also true that Mrs Shaire has lived there since 1976, on her own since 1980. However, there is no evidence as to the intention of Mrs Shaire and Mr Fox as to what would happen to the house if Mr Fox died. Furthermore, Mr Fox changed the basis on which he held his interest when, albeit unknown to Mrs Shaire, he charged that interest first to FNB and then to TMC for a large sum to assist his business.

. . .

Secondly, there is section 15(1)(b). It is difficult to say for what purposes the house is held. So far as Mrs Shaire is concerned, it is primarily a home for her to live in, but also an asset as she has 75% of the beneficial interest. So far as TMC is concerned, it is partly security for the loan for which Mrs Shaire is liable, and it is an asset, as it has 25% of the beneficial interest which it is naturally anxious to sell to realise as much as it can from the mess it has got into through Mr Fox's dishonesty.

Section 15(1)(c) does not apply. Section 15(1)(d), concerned, as it is, with the interests of any secured creditor of any beneficiary, requires one to have regard to TMC's interest, which I have already described.

As to section 15(3), the major part of the beneficial interest is held, I have concluded, by Mrs Shaire and she obviously wishes to remain in occupation.

Having gone through the statutory required factors, I stand back to look at the position of the two parties. TMC does not want to be tied into a 25% equity in a property producing no income and with no certainty when it will be realised. Mrs Shaire is 48 and there is no reason to think that she will sell, let alone in the foreseeable future. TMC will also have no control over the state of the house or whether it is properly insured, save through the medium of the sub-rogated Chase mortgage which it currently has over Mrs Shaire's 75% interest. However, that mortgage could be redeemed at any time, for instance by Mrs Shaire remortgaging.

Thirdly, TMC points out that Mrs Shaire does not appear to need a house with three bedrooms, as she lives there alone with her son. If the house is sold, she will have between £105,000 and £145,000. Those figures are based on the value of the house; I currently have evidence of a value between £190,000 and £240,000.

Fourthly, TMC also contends that if Mrs Shaire stayed in the house she should have to pay not only the instalments on the Chase mortgage, but also a fair sum to compensate TMC for being kept out of any benefit from its quarter share in the house, and that, in light of the evidence she has given as to her means, she could not pay.

So far as Mrs Shaire's son, Adam, is concerned, he is earning and of age, and his interest, argues TMC (to my mind quite rightly), is not something which I should take into account.

So far as Mrs Shaire is concerned, she says, perfectly reasonably, that she does not want to leave the house. It has been her home since 1976 . . .

To my mind, for Mrs Shaire to have to leave her home of nearly a quarter of a century would be a real and significant hardship but not an enormous one. She would have a substantial sum that she could put towards a smaller home. Even if Adam continued to live with her, she would only need a two-bedroom house. On the other hand, I have no evidence as to what properties might be available for the sort of money which she would be able to pay. For TMC to be locked into a quarter of the equity in a property would be a significant disadvantage unless it had a proper return and a proper protection so far as insurance and repair is concerned.

It seems to me that if (a) TMC can be protected by sorting out the equitable interest providing for a proper return and ensuring that the house is repaired and insured and (b) Mrs Shaire can really pay a proper return, it would be right to refuse to make an order for possession and sale primarily because Mrs Shaire has a valid interest in remaining in the house and has a 75% interest in it, and because TMC is ultimately in the business of lending money on property in return for being paid interest.

What is suggested in relation to the 25% interest is either that Mrs Shaire is ordered to pay 3% per annum on the value of that 25% interest . . . or that a quarter of the rental value of the house based on the fair rent of the house . . . I do not find either course entirely satisfactory. It seems to me that the first course would be quite unfair on TMC . . . In any event, whichever of the two options one takes, TMC is not in the business of owning shares in property; it is in the business of lending on property.

An idea which attracts me is that put forward by Mr Lawrence on behalf of the solicitors, and accepted by Mr Harry, if there is no order for sale. This idea is that the house is valued at a specific figure (rather than the range I have mentioned) and that TMC is effectively taken out by having its equity converted into loan, and Mrs Shaire then has to pay interest on that loan. In my judgment, unless Mrs Shaire is in a position to agree that course and to meet the payments which that course would involve, I would not be prepared to refuse the order for sale. If she is prepared to agree that course and she is in a position to meet the repayments as and when they fall due, then I would be prepared to refuse an order for sale.

Comment

(1) Did the legislation justify departing from the results in the earlier cases?

(2) How many of the criteria influencing Neuberger J would operate outside the context of secured creditors' applications?

(3) The outcome in *Shaire* was an interesting compromise. Does it show the courts adopting a distinct pro-family analysis?

(4) Would *Abbey National plc* v *Moss* be differently decided today?

Shaire was quoted with approval by the Court of Appeal in *Bank of Ireland Home Mortgages Ltd* v *Bell*,[42] though it is revealing that it is quoted for the proposition that 'a powerful consideration is and ought to be whether the creditor is receiving proper recompense for being kept out of his money, repayment of which is overdue . . . In the present case it is plain that by refusing sale the judge has condemned the bank to go on waiting for its money with no prospect of recovery from Mr and Mrs Bell and with the debt increasing all the time, that debt already exceeding what could be realised on a sale. That seems to me to be very unfair to the bank.' In *Bell*, there was a large debt and the occupier's share was small, so the *Shaire* solution was not viable; sale was ordered.

Sale was also ordered by the Court of Appeal in *First National Bank plc* v *Achampong*,[43] employing the same analysis as in *Bell*. The case is principally of interest because the existence of children made no difference.

Extract 12.3.21

Edwards v *Lloyds TSB Bank plc* [2005] 1 FCR 139

PARK J: 29. . . . By way of comment on those factors [in s 15], the original intention was no doubt to provide a matrimonial home for the husband, Mrs Edwards and their children. In part that purpose has gone, because the marriage is over and the husband is no longer living in the house, but in part the purpose still survives, because the house is still the home for Mrs Edwards and the two children of the former marriage. A further factor, (c), is the welfare of any minor who occupies the property as his home. The two children are still minors, and they live in the house, so this factor is certainly relevant. Factor (d) is also relevant: 'the interests of any secured creditor of any beneficiary'. That brings into the evaluation the interests of the bank. Subsection (3) states that the court is also to have regard to the circumstances and wishes of any beneficiary of full age entitled to an interest in possession in the property. In this case that means that the court is to have regard to the circumstances and wishes of Mrs Edwards. Her wish is that the house should not be sold.

30.   I was referred to three recent decisions which considered the application of ss 14 and 15 in cases having some similarities to the case before me: *The Mortgage Corporation* v *Shaire* [2000] 1 FLR 973; *Bank of Ireland Home Mortgages Ltd* v *Bell* [2001] 2 FLR 809; and *First National Bank plc* v *Achampong* [2003] EWCA 487. In the first of those cases Neuberger J said

[42] [2001] 2 FLR 809 at p 816 (Peter Gibson LJ).
[43] [2004] 1 FCR 18; see also p 416 above.

that, in his opinion, ss 14 and 15 had to some extent changed the law. The court has a greater flexibility as to how it exercises its jurisdiction on an application for an order for sale. Having taken into account the factors identified in ss 15 and such other factors as arose, 'it is a matter for the court as to what weight to give to each factor in a particular case'. All three cases bring out the point that, if there is a creditor of a husband or wife and the creditor's interest is to be taken into account (as the bank's interest is in this case), it is unsatisfactory for the court simply to say that it declines to make any order for sale. In the *Bank of Ireland* case the Court of Appeal, reversing the decision of the first instance judge, said:

> 'In the present case it is plain that by refusing sale the judge has condemned the bank to go on waiting for its money with no prospect of recovery from Mr and Mrs Bell and with the debt increasing all the time, that debt already exceeding what could be realised on a sale.'

There are observations to a similar effect in the *Achampong* case. In *The Mortgage Corporation v Shaire* Neuberger J left it to the parties to try to agree terms between themselves, but he made it clear that, if Mrs Shaire would not agree to something which gave the bank a realistic prospect of recovering at least some of its money, he would simply make an order for sale.

31.   In this case the bank has applied for an order for sale, and Mrs Edwards has opposed the application. I must weigh up the various factors which are relevant and do the best I can to reach a balanced conclusion. I mention now two particular points on the facts of this case which were (I believe) not present in any of the three cases to which I was referred. First, if the house was sold now it is hard to see how Mrs Edwards could find the money to buy another smaller one. In the other cases it appears to have been different . . . If there was a sale and the husband's debt to the bank was taken out of half of the net proceeds before the balance was available to Mrs Edwards, I very much doubt that she would be able to find another house which she could afford to buy and which would be adequate to accommodate her and her children.

32.   Second, whereas in the other three cases it appears that the debt owed to the bank already exceeded the value of the interest over which the bank had an equitable charge, in the present case that is not so . . . the value of the bank's security (a 50% interest in the house) would be (if the entirety were sold) about £70,000. The husband's debt to the bank (£15,000 plus interest plus costs) is unlikely at present to be more than £40,000. It is true that interest is not currently being paid to the bank on the debt owed to it, but interest continues to accrue on the debt, and now and for some time to come the security will be sufficient to cover the increasing amount of the debt.

33.   In the circumstances I do not want to order an immediate sale, because I believe that that would be unacceptably severe in its consequences upon Mrs Edwards and her children. But equally I believe that I should make some order which, admittedly later rather than sooner, should enable the bank to recover its debt with accrued interest upon it. I intend to make an order along the following lines.

(i)   There be no order for an immediate sale of the house.

(ii)   However, there be an order for a postponed sale of the house.

(iii)   Subject to (iv) below, the sale should be postponed for five years. My thinking behind that period is that Mrs Edwards' younger child, her daughter, is now 13. In five years time she will not be a minor, and her interests will not be a factor which the court is required to take into account under factor (c) in section 15 . . .

(iv)   Either party may at any time apply to the court for my present order, and in particular the five years period prescribed in it, to be reviewed and, if the court thinks fit, varied . . .

(v)   In this sub-paragraph I indicate one provision which I do not propose to insert in the order. The order will not provide that, in the period until the house is sold, Mrs Edwards must pay the currently accruing interest to the bank . . . both because I think that it would be an excessive burden to place on her to require her to pay the interest in full period by period, and because of the feature which I described in paragraph 32 above, I will not impose any such requirement.

Comment

(1) Are the facts of *Edwards* materially different from the other cases?

(2) Would it be correct to conclude that creditors have nothing to fear from TLATA and the subsequent cases?

(3) Why does s 15 give protection to secured creditors but not to other successors in title?

B. Partition and termination of trusteeship

Partition consists of the physical splitting of the land between the co-owners. Originally, it was the natural response if either of the co-owners wished to terminate the co-ownership, but today it is rare. It would be ridiculous to split most normal houses into two halves.

Extract 12.3.22

Trusts of Land and Appointment of Trustees Act 1996, s 7

7.—(1)   The trustees of land may, where beneficiaries of full age are absolutely entitled in undivided shares to land subject to the trust, partition the land, or any part of it, and provide (by way of mortgage or otherwise) for the payment of any equality money.

(2)   The trustees shall give effect to any such partition by conveying the partitioned land in severalty (whether or not subject to any legal mortgage created for raising equality money), either absolutely or in trust, in accordance with the rights of those beneficiaries.

(3)   Before exercising their powers under subsection (2) the trustees shall obtain the consent of each of those beneficiaries.

Comment

(1) Why is s 7 limited to tenancies in common?

(2) If a beneficiary refuses to consent, can this be overridden by the court?

(3) Note that s 7 does not apply to successive interests, as the beneficiaries must be absolutely entitled. However, there is nothing to stop the trustees and beneficiaries (assuming that all the beneficiaries are identified and of full age) from agreeing to parcel out the land amongst the beneficiaries.

A rather different power is conferred on the trustees by s 6(2): they can end their trusteeship by transferring the land to the beneficiaries, provided they are of full age and absolutely entitled. This does not require the beneficiaries' consent, nor does it require them to be consulted.

C. Delegation

TLATA, s 9 permits trustees to delegate their powers to beneficiaries. This is considered in the following chapter.

4. Protecting purchasers: overreaching

The discussion in this chapter has so far considered the position of trustees and beneficiaries. Though an important role of the trust of land is to regulate these matters, the origins of the trust lay in the desire to promote the easy purchase of land. This is still a fundamental objective of the trust of land. It is imperative that the purchaser should be able to deal with a small number of people and not be concerned with beneficial interests, which may be fragmented between many beneficiaries. The former objective is aided by imposing a maximum of four trustees.[44] The principle of overreaching is crucial to avoiding problems with the beneficial interests. On sale, the beneficial interests are transferred from the land to the proceeds of sale. Instead of a share in 30, Acacia Avenue, the beneficiary has a share in £250,000 (the proceeds of sale).

Overreaching does not necessarily depend upon statutory provisions. Every time a trustee[45] disposes of property under a power, overreaching operates. What was significant about the legislation from the mid-nineteenth century onwards was that it introduced overreaching into all cases of successive and (later) concurrent ownership of land. Today, overreaching may be seen as consequential upon the unlimited powers conferred on trustees by TLATA, s 6. However, there are also provisions which spell out the overreaching principles in a little more detail.

Extract 12.4.1

Law of Property Act 1925, ss 2, 27

2.—(1)   A conveyance to a purchaser of a legal estate in land shall overreach any equitable interest or power affecting that estate, whether or not he has notice thereof, if—

> . . .

> (ii)   the conveyance is made by trustees of land and the equitable interest or power is at the date of the conveyance capable of being overreached by such trustees under the provisions of subsection (2) of this section or independently of that subsection, and the requirements of section 27 of this Act respecting the payment of capital money arising on such a conveyance are complied with;

. . .

27.—(1)   A purchaser of a legal estate from trustees of land shall not be concerned with the trusts affecting the land, the net income of the land or the proceeds of sale of the land whether or not those trusts are declared by the same instrument as that by which the trust of land is created.

(2)   Notwithstanding anything to the contrary in the instrument (if any) creating a trust of land or in any trust affecting the net proceeds of sale of the land if it is sold, the proceeds of sale or other capital money shall not be paid to or applied by the direction of fewer than two persons as trustees, except where the trustee is a trust corporation, but this subsection does not affect the right of a sole personal representative as such to give valid receipts for, or direct the application of, proceeds of sale or other capital money, nor, except where capital money arises on the transaction, render it necessary to have more than one trustee.

Comment

(1) Section 2(2) provides for extended overreaching powers where there is an 'ad hoc trust of land'. In brief, this enables overreaching of financial interests binding the trust (even if pre-dating it) where there are especially reliable trustees.[46] Similar trustees can act as single trustees within the exception to s 27(2).

---

[44]   Trustee Act 1925, s 34(2).

[45]   Or other person holding a power, such as a mortgagee.

[46]   Court approved or a trust corporation; Pettit, *Equity and the Law of Trusts* (12th ed), p 394. Companies formed to act as trustees and with substantial financial backing are included (SI 1975 No 1189).

(2) What interests fall within s 2(1)(ii): 'capable of being overreached . . . independently' of s 2(2)?

(3) Should purchasers who are not in good faith be protected? See *HSBC Bank plc v Dyche* [2010] 2 P&CR 58.

Extract 12.4.2

State Bank of India v *Sood* [1997] Ch 276

There were two trustees. They mortgaged trust land to secure existing debts owed by themselves and their companies. The question arose as to whether overreaching can take place where no capital money is received by the trustees.

PETER GIBSON LJ: . . . Before I turn to the statutory provisions, I would make a few general observations on overreaching. As is explained by Charles Harpum in his illuminating article, 'Overreaching, Trustees' Powers and the Reform of the 1925 Legislation' [1990] CLJ 277, overreaching is the process whereby existing interests are subordinated to a later interest or estate created pursuant to a trust or power. Mr Harpum arrived at that statement of the true nature of overreaching by a consideration of the effect of the exercise of powers of disposition in a settlement, referring to *Sugden on Powers*, 8th ed (1861), pp 482, 483. He argued cogently that a transaction made by a person within the dispositive powers conferred upon him will overreach equitable interests in the property the subject of the disposition, but ultra vires dispositions will not, and the transferee with notice will take the property subject to those interests. Mr Harpum expressed the view that the exercise intra vires of a power of disposition which does not give rise to any capital money, such as an exchange of land, overreaches just as much as a transaction which does. There is every reason to think that the draftsman of the 1925 property legislation fully appreciated the true nature of overreaching. A principal objective of the 1925 property legislation was to simplify conveyancing and the proof of title to land. To this end equitable interests were to be kept off the title to the legal estate and could be overreached on a conveyance to a purchaser who took free of them.

. . .

I accept that a novel and important point of law is raised by this appeal. Lending institutions regularly take security from businessmen in the form of a legal charge on property (which very frequently means that the matrimonial home is charged) to secure existing and future indebtedness, and very commonly that property will be registered land held by two registered proprietors on trust for sale with no restriction registered in respect of their power to transfer or mortgage that property. It was not suggested that it had ever been the practice of mortgagees to make inquiries of occupiers of the property as to any claimed rights. Yet if the third to seventh defendants are right, that is what the mortgagees must do if they are not to take subject to the beneficial interests of the occupiers.

It is remarkable that the point of law taken by those defendants does not appear to have arisen before in any reported case. We were taken by counsel to only two cases: *Williams & Glyn's Bank Ltd* v *Boland* [1979] Ch 312; [1981] AC 487 in the Court of Appeal and in the House of Lords and *City of London Building Society* v *Flegg* [1986] Ch 605; [1988] AC 54 in the Court of Appeal and in the House of Lords . . . In the present case the legal charge was not entered into to raise money for the discharge of an existing incumbrance nor was any money raised contemporaneously with the legal charge. No less surprising is the fact that counsel were not able to point to a single textbook for assistance or to any other academic writing, though the court drew counsel's attention to Mr Harpum's article to which I have already referred.

. . .

The crucial issue is the true construction of the final condition of section 2(1)(ii) relating to compliance with statutory requirements respecting the payment of capital money. There is no dispute that if capital money does arise under a conveyance by trustees for sale to a purchaser it must be paid to or applied as section 27(2) dictates. But for overreaching to occur, does capital money have to arise on and contemporaneously with the conveyance?

The judge appears to have assumed that there could be no overreaching if no capital money arose.

. . .

. . . Mr Crawford's [counsel for the bank] initial submission . . . [contended] that capital money arose whenever the Punjab National Bank advanced money, even if before the legal charge was executed. However, I cannot accept that what was done prior to the legal charge has any relevance to the condition that 'the statutory requirements respecting the payment of capital money arising under a disposition upon trust for sale are complied with.'. . .

Mr Crawford however had recourse to a further submission, adopting a point suggested by the court, that the relevant condition in section 2(1)(ii) should be construed as applying only to those cases where there was capital money arising under a disposition upon trust for sale, the statutory requirements of section 27(2) being simply irrelevant to a transaction under which no capital money arises. There are several types of conveyance to a purchaser (within the statutory meanings of those terms) other than a charge to secure existing and future debt which do not give rise to capital money, for example, an exchange or a lease not at a premium. Why should the legislature have intended to exclude such conveyances from having an overreaching effect?

. . .

A more substantial argument of policy advanced on behalf of the third to seventh defendants is that if overreaching occurs where no capital money arises, the beneficiaries' interests may be reduced by the conveyance leaving nothing to which the interests can attach by way of replace-ment save the equity of redemption, and that may be or become valueless. I see considerable force in this point, but I am not persuaded that it suffices to defeat what I see to be the policy of the legislation, to allow valid dispositions to overreach equitable interests. In my judgment on its true construction section 2(1)(ii) only requires compliance with the statutory requirements respecting the payment of capital money if capital money arises. Accordingly I would hold that capital money did not have to arise under the conveyance.

. . .

Much though I value the principle of overreaching as having aided the simplification of con-veyancing, I cannot pretend that I regard the resulting position in the present case as entirely satisfactory. The safeguard for beneficiaries under the existing legislation is largely limited to having two trustees or a trust corporation where capital money falls to be received. But that is no safeguard at all, as this case has shown, when no capital money is received on and con-temporaneously with the conveyance. Further, even when it is received by two trustees as in *City of London Building Society v Flegg* [1986] Ch 605; [1988] AC 54, it might be thought that beneficiaries in occupation are insufficiently protected. . . .

Comment

(1) Would the result have been the same if there had been a single trustee?

(2) There may be entirely proper transactions involving trust land without capital money arising. What examples could be given?

(3) On the facts, the bank thought that the trustees were charging their own property: normal and entirely proper conduct. What would the position have been if the bank had been aware of the trusts and hence of the breach of trust?

(4) In *National Westminster Bank plc* v *Malhan*,[47] Morritt V-C said 'I would conclude that the phrase in s 2(1) "capable of being overreached" refers to the terms and operation of Part I Law of Property Act 1925, not to the existence of the necessary power in the trustees to effect the disposition.' Is this a different analysis from that in *Sood*? Does it matter?

(5) Reform of overreaching is considered later in this section.

A. The need for two trustees

The requirement of two trustees is found in s 27(2) of the LPA, extracted above. The plain objective is to protect the beneficiaries against the possibility of a single trustee absconding with the money. In terms of establishing a balance between the need to protect the beneficiaries against fraud and the need to make the purchase of land as uncomplicated as possible, this requirement is a crucial aspect of the 1925 legislation. It must be asked to what extent it leaves the beneficiaries open to fraud or an undesired transaction, or, on the other hand, places the purchaser at risk. However, it is unlikely that any scheme could give full protection to both purchasers and beneficiaries in all cases.

Problems for purchasers arise where there is a single trustee, so that overreaching cannot take place. If the purchaser knows that there is a trust of land, then there is little difficulty in practice: the transaction will rarely proceed without a second trustee. Transfer of the property into joint names is, of course, an obvious signal that there is a trust of land. Much more problematic is the case where the purchaser is unaware of the trust. The most common example is where land is transferred to one person, but where a second person has a beneficial interest (giving rise to concurrent interests behind a trust of land) by virtue of contribution to the purchase price.[48] It is quite clear that a purchaser who pays the purchase money to a single trustee cannot take advantage of overreaching. The purchaser will be bound by the beneficial interest if it is either protected by an entry on the land register or constitutes an actual occupation overriding interest.[49] The overriding interest liability was established by the leading decision of the House of Lords in *Williams & Glyn's Bank Ltd* v *Boland*.[50]

This liability of a purchaser from a single trustee, as established by *Boland*, led to questions whether a purchaser from two trustees is bound by the interests of other beneficiaries in actual occupation.

Extract 12.4.3

City of London BS v *Flegg* [1988] AC 54

Husband and wife held land on trust for themselves and the wife's parents. All four occupied the house. The husband and wife, unknown to her parents, mortgaged the land to raise money for their own purposes.

LORD TEMPLEMAN: . . . The respondents resist the claim of the appellants to possession of Bleak House and rely on section 14 of the Law of Property Act 1925. Sections 27 and 28 of that

---

[47] [2004] EWHC 847 (Ch) at [42].
[48] *Gissing* v *Gissing* [1971] AC 886; see Chapter 8 above.
[49] Or, for unregistered land, there is notice: *Caunce* v *Caunce* [1969] 1 WLR 286; *Kingsnorth Finance Co Ltd* v *Tizard* [1986] 1 WLR 783.
[50] [1981] AC 487; see Extract 10.2.19 above.

Act which overreach the interests of the respondents under the trust for sale of Bleak House are to be found in Part I of the Act. Section 14 provides:

'This Part of this Act shall not prejudicially affect the interest of any person in possession or in actual occupation of land to which he may be entitled in right of such possession or occupation.'

The respondents were in actual occupation of Bleak House at the date of the legal charge. It is argued that their beneficial interests under the trust for sale were not overreached by the legal charge or that the respondents were entitled to remain in occupation after the legal charge and against the appellants despite the overreaching of their interests.

My Lords, the respondents were entitled to occupy Bleak House by virtue of their beneficial interests in Bleak House and its rents and profits pending the execution of the trust for sale. Their beneficial interests were overreached by the legal charge and were transferred to the equity of redemption held by the Maxwell-Browns and to the sum advanced by the appellants in consideration of the grant of the legal charge and received by the Maxwell-Browns. After the legal charge the respondents were only entitled to continue in occupation of Bleak House by virtue of their beneficial interests in the equity of redemption of Bleak House and that equity of redemption is subject to the right of the appellants as mortgagee to take possession. Sections 27 and 28 did not 'prejudicially' affect the interests of the respondents who were indeed prejudiced but by the subsequent failure of the trustees for sale to account to their beneficiaries for capital money received by the trustees. A beneficiary who is entitled to share in the proceeds of sale of land held on trust for sale relies on the trustees. Section 26(3) of the Act (as amended) [TLATA, s 11] requires trustees for sale to consult their beneficiaries and to give effect to the wishes of the majority of the beneficiaries 'but a purchaser shall not be concerned to see that the provisions of this subsection have been complied with'. If the argument for the respondents is correct, a purchaser from trustees for sale must ensure that a beneficiary in actual occupation is not only consulted but consents to the sale. Section 14 of the Law of Property Act 1925 is not apt to confer on a tenant in common of land held on trust for sale, who happens to be in occupation, rights which are different from and superior to the rights of tenants in common, who are not in occupation on the date when the interests of all tenants in common are overreached by a sale or mortgage by trustees for sale.

. . . The respondents claim to be entitled to overriding interests because they were in actual occupation of Bleak House on the date of the legal charge. But the interests of the respondents cannot at one and the same time be overreached and overridden and at the same time be overriding interests. The appellants cannot at one and the same time take free from all the interests of the respondents yet at the same time be subject to some of those interests. The right of the respondents to be and remain in actual occupation of Bleak House ceased when the respondents' interests were overreached by the legal charge save in so far as their rights were transferred to the equity of redemption. As persons interested under the trust for sale the respondents had no right to possession as against the appellants and the fact that the respondents were in actual occupation at the date of the legal charge did not create a new right or transfer an old right so as to make the right enforceable against the appellants.

One of the main objects of the legislation of 1925 was to effect a compromise between on the one hand the interests of the public in securing that land held in trust is freely marketable and, on the other hand, the interests of the beneficiaries in preserving their rights under the trusts. By the Settled Land Act 1925 a tenant for life may convey the settled land discharged from all the trusts powers and provisions of the settlement. By the Law of Property Act 1925 trustees for sale may convey land held on trust for sale discharged from the trusts affecting the proceeds of sale and rents and profits until sale. Under both forms of trust the protection and the only protection of the beneficiaries is that capital money must be paid to at least two trustees or a trust corporation. Section 14 of the Law of Property Act 1925 and section 70 of the Land Registration Act 1925 cannot have been intended to frustrate this compromise and to subject the purchaser to some beneficial interests but not others depending on the wayward-ness of actual occupation. The Court of Appeal took a different view, largely in reliance on the decision of this House in *Williams & Glyn's Bank Ltd v Boland* [1981] AC 487 . . . But in that case the interest of the wife was not overreached or overridden because the mortgagee advanced capital moneys to a sole trustee. If the wife's interest had been overreached by the mortgagee advancing capital moneys to two trustees there would have been nothing to justify the wife in remaining in occupation as against the mortgagee. There must be a combination of an interest which justifies continuing occupation plus actual occupation to constitute an overriding interest. Actual occupation is not an interest in itself.

LORD OLIVER: . . . My Lords, ever since *Boland's* case [1981] AC 487 it has been widely assumed by those called upon to advise banks and building societies that, so long as capital moneys arising from an exercise of their powers by trustees for sale holding on the statutory trusts have been paid in accordance with the statutory provisions to not less than two trustees or a trust corporation pursuant to the provisions of section 27 of the Law of Property Act 1925, a purchaser need not concern himself with the beneficial interest in the property even where one or more of the beneficiaries is or are in actual occupation of the property at the time of the transaction. That assumption was shared by the Law Commission in their report upon the implications of *Boland's* case presented to Parliament in August 1982, Property Law, The Implications of *Williams & Glyn's Bank Ltd v Boland* (Cmnd 8636), para 42. This appeal is, therefore, of very considerable importance not only to conveyancers but to anyone proposing to lend upon the security of property in respect of which there is any possibility of the existence of beneficial interests which have not been disclosed by the apparent absolute owner. If it be the case, as the Court of Appeal held, that the payment by the appellants in the instant case to two properly constituted trustees for sale, holding upon the statutory trusts, provides no sensible distinction from the ratio of the decision of this House in *Boland's* case, the legislative policy of the 1925 legislation of keeping the interests of beneficiaries behind the curtain and confining the investigation of title to the devolution of the legal estate will have been substantially reversed by judicial decision and financial institutions advancing money on the security of land will face hitherto unsuspected hazards, whether they are dealing with registered or unregistered land.

. . . The 1925 legislation achieved a measure of simplification by providing (in section 1(6) of the Law of Property Act 1925) that a legal estate should no longer be capable of subsisting or being created in an undivided share in land . . . The whole philosophy of the Act in relation to undivided shares was that a purchaser of the legal estate (which, by section 205(1)(xxi) includes a mortgagee) should not be concerned with the beneficial interests of the tenants in common which were shifted to the proceeds of sale. This is familiar material for conveyancers and it is unnecessary to do more than cite a few of the sections of the Act which have an immediate bearing on the problem raised by this appeal. Sections 34 and 36 deal with express limitations in undivided shares or to persons as joint tenants respectively but there is no section dealing specifically with the case where, as here, land becomes held beneficially for tenants in common by means of a resulting trust. Nevertheless, section 34(1) provides that an undivided share shall not be capable of being created except as provided by the Settled Land Act 1925 or as there-inafter mentioned and section 36(4) of the Settled Land Act 1925 provides in terms that an undivided share in land shall not be capable of being created except under a trust instrument or under the Law of Property Act 1925, and shall then only take effect behind a trust for sale. Having thus established the trust for sale as the conveyancing machinery through which effect is given to the interests of owners in undivided shares, those interests are, by virtue of the equitable doctrine of conversion, transferred to the proceeds of sale and the net rents and profits pending sale although, pending the exercise of the trustees' powers, they retain, by judicial construction, some of the incidents of the legal interests which they replaced. The Act, however, contains elaborate provisions for overreaching equitable interests and for exonerating purchasers from being concerned with them . . .

Thus far it is tolerably clear that the scheme of the Act is to enable a purchaser or mortgagee, so long as he pays the proceeds of sale or other capital moneys to not less than two trustees or to a trust corporation, to accept a conveyance or mortgage without reference at all to the beneficial interests of co-owners interested only in the proceeds of sale and rents and profits until sale, which are kept behind the curtain and do not require to be investigated. There are, however, a number of cases in which the question has arisen between beneficiary and trustee as to the rights of the beneficiary in occupation, either alone or in common with his or her co-beneficiary, of the trust property pending sale, particularly where the property has been purchased with a view to its being occupied, for instance, as the matrimonial home of the parties. In *Bull v Bull* [1955] 1 QB 234, where a mother and son had together purchased as their residence a house which had been conveyed into the son's name alone, the Court of Appeal upheld the decision of a county court judge who had dismissed the son's claim for possession . . . Denning LJ however went on to consider the way in which the mother was entitled to exercise her equitable interest in the following passage:

> 'The mother is entitled to rely on her equitable interest as tenant in common, which is preserved by two sections of the Law of Property Act 1925. The first is section 14 which provides that the Act "shall not prejudicially affect the interest of any person in possession or in actual occupation of land to which he may be entitled in right of such possession or occupation.". . .'

In the Court of Appeal in the instant case Dillon LJ followed and adopted this passage and held that, quite apart from the provisions of the Land Registration Act 1925, the respondents had an equitable interest in the property protected by occupation which took priority over the appellants' mortgage by virtue of section 14 of the Law of Property Act 1925. My Lords, the ambit of section 14 is a matter which has puzzled conveyancers ever since the Law of Property Act was enacted. It has been suggested that its purpose was to make it clear that the provisions of Part I were not prejudicially to affect the rights of occupiers of the land who either had or, by virtue of their occupation, were in the process of acquiring title by adverse possession. If so, the section seems unnecessary. Another suggestion canvassed during the course of the argument was that it might have been intended to preserve the right of, for instance, a statutory tenant under the Rent Acts whose status could quite properly be said to arise 'in right of' his occupation. For my part, I think that it is unnecessary for present purposes to seek to resolve the conundrum. What section 14 does not do, on any analysis, is to enlarge or add to whatever interest it is that the occupant has 'in right of his occupation' and in my judgment the argument that places reliance upon it in the instant case founds itself upon an assumption about the nature of the occupying co-owners' interest that cannot in fact be substantiated. The section cannot of itself create an interest which survives the execution of the trust under which it arises or answer the logically anterior question of what, if any, interest in the land is conferred by the possession or occupation. It is suggested in *Wolstenholme and Cherry's Conveyancing Statutes*, 13th ed (1972), vol 1, p 69, that section 14 was designed to preserve the principle, exemplified by *Hunt v Luck* [1902] 1 Ch 428, that a purchaser will have constructive notice of any rights reasonably discoverable from inspection of the property and, in particular, from inquiry of any occupier as to his interest and the terms on which he holds it. With that I respectfully agree. Leaving aside, however, the question whether the words 'in right of such possession or occupation' have, as the judge thought and as the appellants have argued before your Lordships, the effect of limiting the interests to which the section applies to those which are conferred by the preceding fact of possession or occupation or whether, as the Court of Appeal held in effect, they mean merely 'in respect of' or 'associated with' possession or occupation, the section cannot, in my judgment, have the effect of preserving, as equitable interests in the land, interests which are overreached by the exercise of the trustees' powers or of bringing onto the title which the purchaser from trustees for sale is required to investigate the equitable interest of every beneficiary who happens to be in occupation of the land. That would be to defeat the manifest purpose of the legislature in enacting the sections to which reference has already been made. Looking at the interest of the tenant in common in actual occupation and considering for the moment only the position in relation to unregistered land, one has, as it seems to me, to bear in mind always the distinction between his rights as against his co-beneficiaries or against the trustee or trustees in whom the legal estate is vested and his rights against a purchaser of the legal estate from the trustees for sale. His interest is overreached and the purchaser is absolved from inquiry only if the statutory requirements respecting the payment of capital money arising under a disposition upon trust for sale are complied with: sections 2(1)(ii) and 27. Until that occurs, he remains entitled to assert against the trustees and, indeed, against any purchaser from the trustees who has not complied with the statutory requirements all the incidents of his beneficial interest in the proceeds of sale of the property and in the net rents and profits until the sale. One of the incidents of that beneficial interest is, or may be according to the agreement between the beneficiaries or to the purpose for which the trust was originally created, the enjoyment of the property in specie either alone or concurrently with other beneficiaries. But the enjoyment in specie, whilst it may serve to give notice to third parties of the occupier's interest under the trust, is not a separate and severable right which can be regarded as, as it were, free standing. It is and has to be referable to the trust from which, and from which alone, it arises. It is the beneficial interest in the rents and profits pending sale that is the foundation of that enjoyment and there is nothing in the statute or in the cases – leaving aside, for the moment, the *Boland* case [1981] AC 487 which I shall have to come to a little later – to suggest that the enjoyment of the property in specie of itself confers some independent right which will survive the operation of the overreaching provisions of the Law of Property Act 1925. Indeed, the framers of that legislation would, I think, have been shocked and surprised to hear it asserted that a purchaser in proper form from the trustees of the statutory trusts was required to investigate the purposes for which the trust property had been acquired by the trustees or the terms of some private and unwritten agreement or understanding between the beneficiaries inter se or between one or more of the beneficiaries and the trustees. *Bull* v *Bull* [1955] 1 QB 234 was, of course, a case where the only question was whether a sole trustee was entitled to an order for possession against a beneficiary with a subsisting interest in the trust property who had been permitted to occupy it. In dealing with the occupying beneficiary's rights Denning LJ was at pains to say that the entitlement to retain possession which he held to exist was 'until the place is sold' . . .

[The] reason why a purchaser of the legal estate (whether by way of outright sale or by way or mortgage) from a single proprietor takes subject to the rights of the occupying beneficiary is not because section 14 of the Act confers upon the latter some interest in land which is incapable of being overreached but because, having constructive notice of the trust as a result of the beneficiary's occupation, he steps into the shoes of the vendor or mortgagor and takes the estate subject to the same equities as those to which it was subject in the latter's hands, those equities and their accompanying incidents not having been overreached by the sale under the provisions of section 2(1) and section 27 of the Act. Where the purchase has taken effect in accordance with those provisions, it is quite clear from the terms of the statute both that the purchaser, even with express notice, is not concerned with the beneficiary's interest in the proceeds of sale or the net rents and profits until sale and that that interest is overreached. The beneficiary's possession or occupation is no more than a method of enjoying in specie the rents and profits pending sale in which he is entitled to share. It derives from and is, as Mr Lindsay has graphically put it, fathered by the interests under the trust for sale. Once that goes, as it does on the execution of the trust for sale, then the foundation of the occupation goes and the beneficiary has no longer any 'interest . . . to which he may be entitled in right of such . . . occupation'.

Comment

(1) *Flegg* confirms the role of overreaching where there are two trustees. Apart from points based on the land registration legislation,[51] the parents' main argument was based on LPA, s 14. How convincing is the rebuttal of this argument?

(2) The speeches convey the impression that the conveyancers' world would fall apart if the result were different. Is this justified?

(3) Could overreaching be challenged on human rights grounds?[52]

B. Reform

Flegg and *Sood* are unusual examples of beneficiaries losing their interests because of the actions of two trustees. But equally troublesome is the idea that two trustees can decide whether the home of the beneficiaries can be sold, even if no financial loss will ensue.

Extract 12.4.4

Law Commission No 188: Overreaching: Beneficiaries in Occupation (footnotes omitted)

Change of circumstances

3.1   The 1925 legislation compromise between the need to protect beneficiaries under trusts of land and the demand for certainty and simplicity in conveyancing was satisfactory, and perhaps ideal, in the circumstances in which it was intended to operate. A purchaser from trustees could ignore the beneficial interests so long as he was careful to observe simple precautions in paying the price. This successfully hid the terms of the settlement 'behind the curtain'. Buying from trustees became as simple as buying from a single beneficial legal owner which it certainly had not been previously. At the same time, the financial interest of the beneficiary was safeguarded by transferring his claim to the proceeds of sale. So long as the trustees properly conducted the affairs of the settlement, it was not important to the beneficiary by what assets his interest was secured.

3.2   Doubts about these provisions arise now because, over the years, the patterns of land ownership and the use of settlements have changed. Although the rules with which we are concerned affect all types of real property, the changes relating to residential property are most significant. Since 1925, both the number of dwellings in England and Wales and the percentage of them which are owner-occupied have jumped dramatically. Couples have increasingly bought owner-occupied housing in their joint names, and this trend was accelerated by the decision in *Williams & Glyn's Bank Ltd* v *Boland*, following which lending institutions encouraged borrowers to buy jointly so that they, the institutions, had the advantage of the statutory overreaching rules. . . .

Protecting occupation of property

3.4   In our working paper we said, 'we are not in this exercise primarily concerned with protecting beneficiaries' financial interests. It is their prospect of enjoyment of the land itself and its loss where overreaching occurs upon which we wish to focus'. Some of those who responded

---

[51] Considered later in Lord Oliver's speech; see Extract 10.2.23 above.

[52] See Goymour in *The Impact of the UK Human Rights Act on Private Law* (ed Hoffmann), Chapter 12, pp 287–288 and 297–298.

ed with this view. One correspondent said, 'I do not think it right that people in actual
pation of property should be in peril of losing their home as a result of the overreaching
ss'. Another pointed out that 'almost all other occupiers [of residential property] have
rotection from arbitrary eviction'.

remain of the view that reform is required here. There are four main reasons. First,
sively financial protection given by the 1925 legislation is no longer appropriate for
s of their own homes; their real concern is often with the enjoyment of the property
ich will be lost after overreaching. Secondly, as the general understanding of many of
eficiaries with whom we are concerned is that they are joint owners, they should have
riate ownership rights. There is scant justification for the law giving preference to the
s of one joint owner over those of another, simply because the former was constituted
e of the legal estate. Thirdly, it is unsatisfactory that the consequences which a sale visits
a beneficiary in occupation are different depending whether the legal estate happens
ve been vested in one, or in more than one, person. Fourthly, it is difficult to defend the
ition where someone not married to the legal owner in actual occupation of their home, and
hich they own a share, has less right to remain there than a husband or wife without any
h ownership interest.

. . .

incipal recommendation

.1   We have concluded that the present protection of the interests of equitable owners in
occupation of property is, in some circumstances, inadequate. The owner of an equitable interest which carries a right of occupation is entitled to two distinct benefits: a right to the value of
the interest and that right to enjoy occupation. When the owner of a legal estate is in a similar
position, the law protects each right separately; if the owner opts to remain in possession, he
cannot be obliged to rely solely on the alternative financial right. The effect of overreaching is,
however, to oblige the equitable owner to surrender his occupation right in favour of his financial
one, without the chance to make a choice. We see no reason why equitable owners should be
at a disadvantage in this respect.

4.2   We are, however, conscious of the need to maintain arrangements which will not unduly
interfere with conveyancing. This leads us to place our emphasis on protecting the rights
of owners of equitable interests who are in actual occupation of the property. That very fact of
occupation can be used to alert prospective purchasers and mortgagees to the claims of the
equitable owners. It means that the protection of occupation rights does not extend to those
who, while they are entitled to occupy, are not currently exercising the right. While that means
that equitable owners will sometimes be at a disadvantage, when compared with legal owners,
it seems to us to be a reasonable compromise. It offers the right to continue in occupation, to
those who are already there, so it is likely to extend the new protection to those who most need
it, and of course protection extends to those who enter later.

Comment

(1) Is there a sufficiently serious problem to warrant intervention? Would the proposals
impose significant extra burdens on purchasers?

(2) The recommendations have not been accepted.[53]

53 (1998) 587 HL Deb WA213.

Extract 12.4.5

Harpum [1990] CLJ 277, *Cambridge Law Journal*, pp. 329–31,
© Cambridge University Press 1990

With the background of *Flegg* in mind, it is very easy to understand the thinking behi[nd]
proposals. It . . . But while the objective that trust beneficiaries in occupation should
sulted as to all dispositions of property is laudable, the means proposed by the Law Com
are heavy-handed and work injustice in other respects. Because the Commission is conc[e]
protect a beneficiary's 'prospect of enjoyment of the land itself' rather than his financial in[t]
it is mesmerised into thinking that the elevation of actual occupation almost into a right i[n]
is the panacea. This proposal to change the law on overreaching, considered in the cont[ext]
the Law Commission's other recommendations on trusts of land and registered land, is,
present writer's opinion, fundamentally flawed:

First, it strikes an unfair balance between those beneficiaries who are in actual occupa[tion]
and those who are not . . .

Secondly, it strikes an unfair balance between the beneficiary in actual occupation and [t]
purchaser by protecting the former at the expense of the latter. As the law presently stands, p[ur]
chasers are not concerned with beneficial interests which will be overreached on completion. [If]
the Law Commission's proposal is implemented, they will be. The Law Commission is confide[nt]
that conveyancers will come to terms with the greater demands that will be made upon them. Th[e]
Commission states somewhat disingenuously that 'We would not expect our recommendation[s]
to necessitate enquiries and inspections going beyond what is done at present'. Not only is tha[t]
statement untrue, but it misses the point. It is untrue, because at present purchasers know that
enquiries do not have to be made as to the beneficial rights of occupiers if payment is to be made
to two trustees. Therefore, under the Law Commission's proposals, purchasers will either be at
greater risk than at present (because solicitors will continue to trust vendors to disclose the rights
of occupiers) or they will have to bear the extra costs of the more extensive enquiries required.
If implemented, the Law Commission's proposals will mean the end of the curtain principle in
conveyancing, which was one of the keystones of the 1925 property legislation. The draftsman's
intention that the existence of trusts should be apparent from the face of the title will be finally
abandoned. Trusts will once again become a matter of title and a concern for purchasers.

Finally, the Law Commission has been forced to take the path of requiring the consent of
beneficiaries in actual occupation because it has failed to appreciate the basis on which overreaching rests. Overreaching is the necessary concomitant of a power of disposition. If the
trustees have no power to make a disposition, that disposition will not overreach. The present
writer believes that this principle could provide a far more effective means of securing the
objectives which the Law Commission seeks.

Comment

(1) Harpum proposes that powers of trustees (in particular, to grant second mortgages)
should be limited; this would have caught the facts in each of *Sood* and *Flegg*. Is this more
attractive than the Law Commission's proposals?

(2) It may be recalled that TLATA confers unlimited powers on trustees; this is inconsistent
with the thrust of Harpum's proposals. Does this invalidate his conclusions?

C. Protection against irregularities

One danger for a purchaser is that, despite the documents looking entirely in order, there may
be some breach of trust which enables the purchase to be challenged by the beneficiaries.
The legislation differentiates between unregistered and registered land.

(i) Unregistered land

Extract 12.4.6

Trusts of Land and Appointment of Trustees Act 1996, s 16

16.—(1) A purchaser of land which is or has been subject to a trust need not be concerned to see that any requirement imposed on the trustees by section 6(5), 7(3) or 11(1) has been complied with.

(2) Where—
  (a) trustees of land who convey land which (immediately before it is conveyed) is subject to the trust contravene section 6(6) or (8), but
  (b) the purchaser of the land from the trustees has no actual notice of the contravention, the contravention does not invalidate the conveyance.

(3) Where the powers of trustees of land are limited by virtue of section 8—
  (a) the trustees shall take all reasonable steps to bring the limitation to the notice of any purchaser of the land from them, but
  (b) the limitation does not invalidate any conveyance by the trustees to a purchaser who has no actual notice of the limitation.

(4) Where trustees of land convey land which (immediately before it is conveyed) is subject to the trust to persons believed by them to be beneficiaries absolutely entitled to the land under the trust and of full age and capacity—
  (a) the trustees shall execute a deed declaring that they are discharged from the trust in relation to that land, and
  (b) if they fail to do so, the court may make an order requiring them to do so.

(5) A purchaser of land to which a deed under subsection (4) relates is entitled to assume that, as from the date of the deed, the land is not subject to the trust unless he has actual notice that the trustees were mistaken in their belief that the land was conveyed to beneficiaries absolutely entitled to the land under the trust and of full age and capacity.

Comment

(1) Section 16(1) deals with failure to consider beneficiaries' rights (s 6(5)); failure to obtain consent to partition (s 7(3)); and failure to comply with consultation requirements (s 11(1)). Probably the most significant of these protections is that relating to consultation, though this mirrors the previous law.[54] It will be noted that there is, apparently, full protection for the purchaser as regards these irregularities. Unlike other irregularities considered in the Comments below, there is no exception for purchasers with actual notice.

(2) Section 16(2) provides protection against contravention of restrictions on trustees imposed by other legislation, provided there is no actual notice.

(3) The protection in s 16(3) is new. It concerns limitations on powers, including consent requirements.[55] Note that the purchaser is protected unless there is actual notice of the limitation; the trustees are under a duty to warn the purchaser. TLATA introduced the possibility of restricting powers; such restrictions constitute a novel problem for purchasers. However, it had always been possible to require consents and, in the past, a danger for purchasers was that a consent requirement might not be expressed in the documents of title. The protection is to be welcomed.

---

[54] LPA, s 26(3).
[55] We have seen that s 10 protects purchasers regarding multiple consent requirements and consents required from children: Extract 12.3.2 above.

(4) The problem dealt with by s 16(4) and (5) is that the documents may indicate to a purchaser that the trust has come to an end before the sale. This would be most obvious when the trustees transfer the land to an absolutely entitled beneficiary. Accordingly the purchaser will pay the purchase money to the beneficiary and therefore not to two trustees: there cannot be overreaching. The danger lies if the trust has not in fact ended. If the transfer contains a statement that the trustees are discharged (the 'deed of discharge'), then s 16(5) protects the purchaser, absent actual notice. This new protection[56] is to be welcomed.

The termination of a joint tenancy on the death of one of two joint tenants can also pose problems for purchasers. The trust will come to an end, but only if the equitable joint tenancy has not been severed; for the survivor to prove such a negative (no severance) to a purchaser is virtually impossible. On the death of a joint tenant (by far the most common termination of trusts of land), there is no transfer into which a deed of discharge can be inserted. Fortunately, there has long been legislation covering this situation.

Extract 12.4.7

Law of Property (Joint Tenants) Act 1964, s 1

1.—(1)   For the purposes of section 36(2) of the Law of Property Act 1925[i] . . . the survivor of two or more joint tenants shall, in favour of a purchaser of the legal estate, be deemed to be solely and beneficially interested if the conveyance includes a statement that he is so interested.

Provided that the foregoing provisions of this subsection shall not apply if, at any time before the date of the conveyance by the survivor—

    (a) a memorandum of severance (that is to say a note or memorandum signed by the joint tenants or one of them and recording that the joint tenancy was severed in equity on a date therein specified) had been endorsed on or annexed to the conveyance by virtue of which the legal estate was vested in the joint tenants; . . .

[i] 'Nothing in this Act affects the right of a survivor of joint tenants, who is solely and beneficially interested, to deal with his legal estate as if it were not held in trust.'

Comment

(1) A memorandum on the title deeds should be insisted upon whenever there is a severance. Otherwise the severance will not be binding on a purchaser from the survivor of the co-owners: the expectations of the first to die may be disappointed.

(2) It appears that actual notice will defeat a purchaser.[57]

---

[56] Modelled on the Settled Land Act 1925.
[57] *Grindal* v *Hooper* (1999) 96/48 LS Gaz 41; see Gravells [2000] Conv 461.

(ii) Registered land

Extract 12.4.8

Trusts of Land and Appointment of Trustees Act 1996, s 16(7);
Land Registration Act 2002, s 26

TLATA, s 16.—(7) This section does not apply to registered land.

LRA, s 26.—(1) Subject to subsection (2), a person's right to exercise owner's powers in relation to a registered estate or charge is to be taken to be free from any limitation affecting the validity of a disposition.
  (2) Subsection (1) does not apply to a limitation—
    (a) reflected by an entry in the register, or
    (b) imposed by, or under, this Act.
  (3) This section has effect only for the purpose of preventing the title of a disponee being questioned (and so does not affect the lawfulness of a disposition).

Comment

(1) The Law of Property (Joint Tenants) Act 1964 similarly exempts registered land.

(2) The reason for s 16(7) is not entirely clear. If there were no overriding interest and no entry on the register then all would agree that a registered disposition would be protected (so there is no need for s 16 protection). The point that troubled many people was that a beneficiary in actual occupation might be able to rely on the irregularity by virtue of having an overriding interest.[58]

(3) Most of these concerns were removed by the Land Registration Act 2002 (hereafter LRA), s 26.[59] How does this give greater protection than other land registration principles?

(4) LRA, s 26 protects against 'any limitation'. What sorts of limitations might the section apply to? Are there any irregularities which will fall outside these words? How do we treat the statutory requirement that purchase monies be paid to at least two trustees?

(5) Why do we have complex and varying provisions for unregistered land and a single broad provision for registered land? Which is preferable? What is the result if a purchaser of registered land is aware of an irregularity?

D. The effect and timing of overreaching

It is, of course, only interests under the trust which are overreached.[60] A separate point is that *Waller* v *Waller*[61] assumes that a purchaser who has merely contracted to purchase receives no protection in respect of the trustees' failure to consult. Is this pre-TLATA assumption compatible with the wording of s 16? Does it represent sound policy? Is it affected by LRA, s 26?

---

[58] For the scope of such irregularities, see Ferris and Battersby (2003) 119 LQR 94. *Birmingham Midshires Mortgage Services Ltd* v *Sabherwal* (1999) 80 P&CR 256 indicates that overreaching in registered land is not significantly affected by TLATA.

[59] Law Com No 271, paras 4.8–4.11.

[60] Though it has been seen (p 436 above) that the special ad hoc trust of land enables a wider range of interests (generally financial interests) to be overreached.

[61] [1967] 1 WLR 451; the result is readily defensible because of the separate objection that there was only one trustee.

5. Trusts for sale

It has already been seen[62] that express trusts for sale survive TLATA, though they are trusts of land and subject to all the provisions of the Act. We need to consider the significance of there being a trust for sale.

An initial point concerns the question whether the land must be sold.

Extract 12.5.1

Trusts of Land and Appointment of Trustees Act 1996, s 4

4.—(1)   In the case of every trust for sale of land created by a disposition there is to be implied, despite any provision to the contrary made by the disposition, a power for the trustees to postpone sale of the land; and the trustees are not liable in any way for postponing sale of the land, in the exercise of their discretion, for an indefinite period.

(2)   Subsection (1) applies to a trust whether it is created, or arises, before or after the commencement of this Act.

Comment

Given that s 8 permits a settlor to exclude other powers, why should the power to postpone sale be non-excludable?

The relevance of a trust for sale lies principally in what happens should the trustees be in disagreement. In such cases, the power to postpone has not been exercised and the land should be sold.[63] Is it material whether or not the same persons are both trustees and beneficiaries? A separate point is that it can be argued that using a trust for sale after 1996 is one way of making it clear to the trustees (and the court) that sale really is intended; they are likely to go along with the settlor's intention.

A quite different aspect of a trust for sale was that pre-1996 the courts treated the beneficial interests as being in money rather than in land: this doctrine of conversion treated the situation as if the trustees had already sold the land. Thus a reference to land in a statute or, say, a will might not include a beneficial interest under a trust for sale, though it was always a matter of interpretation. This was universally treated as very odd: few purchasers of a family home would consider that they had interests in money!

Extract 12.5.2

Trusts of Land and Appointment of Trustees Act 1996, s 3

3.—(1)   Where land is held by trustees subject to a trust for sale, the land is not to be regarded as personal property; and where personal property is subject to a trust for sale in order that the trustees may acquire land, the personal property is not to be regarded as land.

(2)   Subsection (1) does not apply to a trust created by a will if the testator died before the commencement of this Act.

(3)   Subject to that, subsection (1) applies to a trust whether it is created, or arises, before or after that commencement.

---

[62] Pages 391–392 above.
[63] *Re Mayo* [1943] Ch 302.

Comment

Trusts for sale will, presumably, be employed in the future only if sale is really intended. On this basis, is the abolition of conversion justified?

Further reading

Baker, A [2010] Conv 352: The judicial approach to 'exceptional circumstances': the impact of the Human Rights Act 1998.

Barnsley, D G [1998] CLJ 123: Co-owners' rights to occupy trust land.

Bright, S J [2009] Conv 378: Occupation rents and the Trusts of Land and Appointment of Trustees Act 1996: from property to welfare?

Ferris, G and Battersby, G (2003) 119 LQR 94: The general principles of overreaching and the modern legislative reforms, 1996–2002.

Fox, L (2005) 25 LS 201: Creditors and the concept of 'family home' – a functional analysis.

Gardner, S [2014] Conv 95: Material relief between ex-cohabitants 1: Liquidating beneficial interests otherwise than by sale.

13

Successive interests

This will be a brief chapter. In Chapter 3 we considered the types of interests which are recognised by the law and no more will be said on that matter. This chapter is mainly concerned with the legal regulation of successive interests. It has already been seen in Chapter 12 that the Trusts of Land and Appointment of Trustees Act 1996 (hereafter TLATA) applies to all post-1996 successive interests. Most of the provisions of that Act were investigated in that chapter and only those points which are of specific relevance to successive interests remain to be studied.

1. The rule against perpetuities

Before considering TLATA, a rather different form of regulation requires brief mention. The law has long restricted the creation of interests taking effect in the distant future.

Extract 13.1.1

Morris and Leach, *The Rule Against Perpetuities* (2nd ed) at pp 1–3, 13–17 (footnotes omitted)

WHAT THE RULE AGAINST PERPETUITIES IS AND IS NOT

The classic statement of the Rule against Perpetuities is that of Gray. It runs as follows:

> *No interest is good unless it must vest, if at all, not later than twenty-one years after some life in being at the creation of the interest.*

Much elaboration is needed to provide a solution for certain specific cases. But it is surprising how many cases are resolved by the foregoing sentence, plus only the following definition of the word 'vest':

   (a) A remainder is 'vested' when the persons to take it are ascertained and there is no condition precedent attached to the remainder other than the termination of the prior estates.

   (b) An executory interest (that is, an interest which cuts off a previous interest instead of following it when it has terminated) is not 'vested' until the time comes for taking possession.

   (c) Most important of all, a class gift is not 'vested' until the exact membership of the class has been determined; or, to put it differently, a class gift is still contingent if any more persons can become members of the class or if any present members can drop out of the class.

The Rule against Perpetuities is a rule invalidating interests which *vest* too remotely. Indeed, it is often called the rule against remoteness of vesting. Gray was never tired of insisting that this would have been a more suitable name for the Rule: much confusion, he thought, has resulted from the use of the more usual name.

. . .

3. RATIONALE OF THE RULE

The pressures which produced the Rule against Perpetuities are well known. They were family settlements which attempted to create by various devices the equivalent of an unbarrable entail in specific parcels of land . . . Long family settlements of land are now extremely rare, and those that exist are subject to the overriding statutory provision that 'the tenant for life may sell the settled land or any part thereof'. Under modern statutes like the Settled Land Act, 1925, and the Law of Property Act, 1925, there is always some person or some small number of persons who can sell the land, regardless of the future interests that may have been created in it, though the proceeds of sale may have to be held on the same trusts as the land. Why then do we need a Rule against Perpetuities today? Why should it not be scrapped as having served its purpose?

Before attempting to answer these questions we must be clear on two points. First, we must understand the reasons why the inalienability of land is considered harmful. Second, we must note once more that the Rule against Perpetuities is not primarily concerned with such inalienability.

Why is the inalienability of land considered harmful? The short answer is that it causes economic stagnation. If land is limited to A in fee, with a gift over to B in fee on the happening of a contingency, A can sell his interest, and B can sell his interest, but the trouble is that neither will be able to find a purchaser . . . Even if A and B combine together to sell the land, they will still have difficulty in doing so because they will be unable to agree about their proper shares in the purchase price . . . If A prefers not to sell his interest but to make a profit from the land, he has less incentive to do so than he would have if he were absolute owner. Thus it seems undeniable that, before the Settled Land Acts, the creation of future interests in land hindered its alienability and so made it less productive and tended to diminish national wealth . . .

But, as we have seen, the Rule is not satisfied by the fact that the interests are alienable. It applies although the land is vested in trustees on trust for sale. It applies to trusts of personalty although the trustees have power to change the investments. It has survived the modern statutes which make land freely alienable at all times. Whatever may have been the position in past centuries, it is plain that the modern Rule is primarily directed not against the inalienability of specific land but against the remote vesting of interests in a shifting fund.

Several reasons have been advanced for the continued existence of the Rule. We proceed to examine a few of them.

(1) It is sometimes said that the Rule prevents an undue concentration of wealth in the hands of a few. This may have been true in past times, but the existence of graduated income tax, surtax and death duties renders the Rule (if this is its sole object) quite unnecessary today.

(2) It is said that the Rule prevents capricious or eccentric dispositions. To some extent this is undoubtedly true. But if this is the sole object of the Rule, it is about as inefficient an instrument for the purpose as could well be devised . . . If the prevention of capricious testamentary dispositions is the sole object of the Rule, we ought to be able to devise some more efficient substitute.

(3) It is said to be socially desirable that the wealth of the world should be controlled by its living members and not by the dead. Few would dispute this as a general proposition: but it is not so clear how the Rule against Perpetuities tends to promote this result. Professor Simes gives two illustrations. First, he says that trustees cannot invest as freely as absolute owners can, and that if too much capital is tied up in private trusts, none will be available for financing new economic enterprises such as jet propulsion and atomic energy. To the present authors it seems rather far-fetched to suggest that we owe these marvels, even indirectly, to the Rule against Perpetuities . . .

(4) Another reason for the Rule suggested by Professor Simes seems to the present authors far more realistic. It is that 'the Rule against Perpetuities strikes a fair balance between

the desires of members of the present generation, and similar desires of succeeding generations, to do what they wish with the property which they enjoy'. It is a natural human desire to
provide for one's family in the foreseeable future. The difficulty is that if one generation is
allowed to create unlimited future interests in property, succeeding generations will receive the
property in a restricted state and thus be unable to indulge the same desire . . .

Extract 13.1.2

Law Commission CP 133: The Rules Against Perpetuities and Excessive Accumulations (footnotes omitted)

5.17   It may be argued in favour of abolition of the rule against perpetuities that the policy
functions of the rule are no longer important, that the rule is no longer essential to their fulfilment, that the rule is an unnecessary restriction on the free right to dispose of property or that
abolition of the rule would be justified by the simplification of the law relating to future interests
which would result. In this section we evaluate these arguments.

No need for a rule against perpetuities

5.18   As we have seen, the principal justifications for having a rule against perpetuities are to
restrict dead hand control and to promote alienability of property. But the relevance of these
objectives must be considered in the context of modern social conditions. The importance of
landed estates and family dynasties in English society has diminished compared with earlier
centuries, as ownership of property is now more widespread. Most individuals are likely to be
concerned that on their death they should benefit their immediate family and grandchildren
rather than considering future generations. Settlors contemplating the creation of trusts with
remote interests, following the abolition of the rule, would still face the tax and practical disadvantages of such dispositions, and practitioners of whom we made inquiries indicated that
they thought it unlikely that many would choose to ignore such advice in the context of family
settlements. If that is the case then it seems doubtful whether the economic benefits of alienability of property would be lost by abolition of the rule.

5.19   It must be considered whether there would be other economic effects of abolishing the
rule. One suggestion is that the growth of an economy may be stifled if large amounts of property are held on trust for long periods, and the rule against perpetuities plays a part in avoiding
this by requiring vesting to take place within a restricted period, and thus helping to promote
absolute ownership. The rationale behind the argument is that trustees of property subject to
contingent interests are prevented by their fiduciary position from taking actions involving the
degree of risk an absolute owner might consider appropriate, and therefore a lack of risk investment in the economy may develop. But the validity of this view seems limited . . .

5.20   One view, therefore, is that the desire to tie up property for excessively long periods was
a social evil of a bygone age, and that nowadays the absence of a rule against perpetuities
would have no harmful effect in terms of rendering property inalienable or allowing dead hand
control to be exerted to an unacceptable extent.

   . . .

Performance of functions by other rules of law

5.23   The case for abolition of the rule against perpetuities is strengthened if other rules of law
successfully perform the functions of curtailing dead hand control and ensuring the alienability
of property . . . [The Law Commission considers statutory powers of sale, taxation and variation
of trusts.]

Comment

(1) Note that TLATA permits settlors to exclude the power of sale. Does this affect the case for abolition?

(2) See also Maudsley, *The Modern Law of Perpetuities*, Chapter 9, and Deech (1984) OxJLS 454.

The Law Commission subsequently adopted the views of respondents to the Consultation Paper and recommends the retention of a perpetuities rule.

Extract 13.1.3

Law Commission No 251: The Rules Against Perpetuities and Excessive Accumulations (footnotes omitted)

2.25　[The majority of respondents] considered that the rule still fulfilled the function of controlling the power of one generation to dictate the devolution of property, that such a function remained an important one, and that no other rule of law was either sufficient to or as effective in achieving it. Some respondents considered that the abolition of the rule could have adverse economic consequences. There was a widespread view that, if the rule were abolished, settlors would undoubtedly create future interests which they could not under the present law. Indeed, this was supported by evidence from a number of firms of solicitors who had clients who wished to do just that.

Comment

It is proposed that the rule should apply only to successive and qualified (non-absolute) interests and therefore not to commercial transactions.

Extract 13.1.4

Perpetuities and Accumulations Act 2009

5.—(1)　The perpetuity period is 125 years (and no other period).

7.—(1)　Subsection (2) applies if (apart from this section and section 8) an estate or interest would be void on the ground that it might not become vested until too remote a time.
　(2)　In such a case—
　　(a)　until such time (if any) as it becomes established that the vesting must occur (if at all) after the end of the perpetuity period the estate or interest must be treated as if it were not subject to the rule against perpetuities, and
　　(b)　if it becomes so established, that does not affect the validity of anything previously done (whether by way of advancement, application of intermediate income or otherwise) in relation to the estate or interest.

Comment

(1) Note that there is no role for the old period of a life in being plus 21 years.

(2) The Law Commission observes that 'other factors, such as taxation, are likely in most cases to lead to the final vesting of property under a trust or settlement long before the end of the 125-year period.'[1]

(3) The wait and see principle (s 7) has operated since 1964.

---

[1] Paragraph 8.13.

2. The need for statutory regulation

Extract 13.2.1

Simpson, *A History of the Land Law* (2nd ed) at pp 239–240 (footnotes omitted)

. . . At common law a life tenant had severely limited powers. He was liable for waste; thus he was unable to cut timber, or open new mines, or plough up ancient meadow land; at the same time he was under no liability to prevent permissive waste, so that he could let the land fall into poor condition, with impunity. He could only alienate the land for his own life, so that he was quite unable to tap the full capital value of one part of the settled land even if he intended to apply the capital to develop the remainder. His own capital was frequently absorbed in paying extravagant portions, so that he had little left to devote to good management; the fact that his interest determined on his death did not encourage life tenants to invest their private moneys in settled land. To a great extent these disadvantages could be overcome by the insertion in settlements of clauses which conferred wider powers upon the life tenant. In Bridgeman's model conveyance the life tenant is made unimpeachable for waste, and during the eighteenth century the best-drawn settlements regularly enlarged the life tenant's powers. A precedent in Hayes's *Introduction to Conveyancing*, published in 1840, gives the life tenant a wide power of leasing, selling, and exchanging the settled land. But all too often such powers were not included, and in the nineteenth century there arose a widespread dissatisfaction with the effects of such ill-drawn settlements upon the welfare of settled land. The economic development of the country was being hindered by the prevalence of land which it was impossible to utilize fully, so that both the beneficiaries under strict settlements and the country at large suffered.

Comment

It may well be that the problems operated more as regards large estates and not as regards the everyday conveyancing of houses.[2]

3. The response of the 1925 legislation

Reforms commenced in the last quarter of the nineteenth century, culminating in the 1925 legislation. This provided a structure which, despite constant criticism, survived until TLATA.

Extract 13.3.1

Law Commission Working Paper No 94: Trusts of Land (footnotes omitted)

3.2   The following problems are those that arise because, at present, successive interests in land can be created either as settled land under the Settled Land Act 1925 or as interests behind a trust for sale. It has often been suggested that a dual system is unnecessary and that one system for successive interests would be sufficient. Originally the two systems performed different functions. The strict settlement, using combinations of life interests and entailed interests (which before 1926 could exist as legal estates), was intended to keep land within the ownership of a particular family. In many cases the tenant for life would occupy the land. The trust for sale was used either where a sale was actually intended, or where the land concerned was intended to be an investment, to be bought and sold as market conditions demanded, the tenant for life being paid the income from it. By the mid-19th century it was apparent that strict

---

[2] Anderson, *Lawyers and the Making of English Land Law 1832–1940*, pp 45, 78.

settlements caused difficulty in that, if the settlement was not well drafted, the powers of the tenant for life were too limited to enable the land to be managed properly, and however the settlement was drafted, sale of the land was extremely difficult as no person had the power to convey the fee simple. A series of reforming statutes culminating in the Settled Land Act 1925 increased the powers of the tenant for life and ensured that there was also some person able to convey the fee simple in the land. At the same time the Law of Property Act 1925, s 1 prevented life interests from existing as legal estates, so that all settlements had to take effect behind a trust. The effect of these reforms has been to remove many of the differences between the two systems of settlement. In either system the land can be sold and the strict settlement is no longer an effective method of keeping land in the family. The remaining differences centre on who makes the decisions with respect to the land. It is arguable that the differences are not sufficient to justify the continuing existence of two systems.

The dual structure has been swept away by TLATA, at least for settlements set up after the Act, so it is unnecessary to discuss either the details or the problems of the previous law. Suffice to say that the Settled Land Act 1925 provided an unduly complex structure which was unpopular and prone to cause error. More fundamentally, the giving of powers to the tenant for life, despite its origins in the role of the tenant for life in nineteenth-century settlements, fits uneasily with the intentions of many modern settlors. Meanwhile, the much more common trust for sale (with powers vested in the trustees) suffered from the drawbacks already encountered in the previous chapter.

4. The trust of land

All settlements created since TLATA take effect as trusts of land. This means that the land is managed by the trustees, who are given unlimited powers.

One particular feature of the trust of land is that s 8(1) permits the settlor to restrict the trustees' powers, including the power to sell the land.[3] Is it likely that many settlors will exercise their new freedom to exclude the power to sell?

The trust of land provisions considered in the previous chapter are, of course, applicable to successive interests. They will not be repeated in this chapter. Thought should, however, be given to the ways in which the different relationships involved in successive interests may influence the role and outcome of some of the rules. One example concerns rights of occupation: occupation will not be intended in a fair number of successive interest trusts (the land being held as an investment). The willingness of the court to exercise its s 14 discretion in relation to disputes as to sale may be influenced by the fact that in concurrent interests the feuding parties are likely to be both the beneficiaries and the trustees. Successive interests more commonly involve independent trustees, and the court may therefore be less likely to intervene, at least where the trustees are unanimous.

On the other hand, the duty imposed by s 11 to consult beneficiaries with interests in possession may be of principal significance for successive interest trusts. In concurrent interests, consultation is an arid exercise when the feuding parties are both trustees and beneficiaries. Another point in concurrent interests is that parties are quite likely to have the same size shares, thus cancelling each other out. These factors are less likely to apply in successive interest trusts. But how likely is it that the courts will in practice tell the trustees to give effect to the views of the life interest holder (or the majority of them)?

---

[3] Previously, the power of sale had been inviolate; see, e.g., Settled Land Act 1925, s 106.

5. Beneficiary control of management

Consultation provides, of course, one route to beneficiary control over management. Others can include making one or more beneficiaries trustees, whether or not alongside independent trustees, and requiring their consent for sale or other transactions.

However, one attraction of the old Settled Land Act settlement for some settlors was that the land was managed by the life tenant. Quite apart from the old dynastic form of settlement, this fits a trust in favour of the settlor's widow or widower for life. In a trust of the family home, the settlor may well wish the widow or widower to manage it. The idea of management by independent trustees might be very alien.

Extract 13.5.1

Trusts of Land and Appointment of Trustees Act 1996, ss 9, 9A

9.—(1) The trustees of land may, by power of attorney, delegate to any beneficiary or beneficiaries of full age and beneficially entitled to an interest in possession in land subject to the trust any of their functions as trustees which relate to the land.

(3) A power of attorney under subsection (1) shall be given by all the trustees jointly and (unless expressed to be irrevocable and to be given by way of security) may be revoked by any one or more of them . . .

(5) A delegation under subsection (1) may be for any period or indefinite.

(7) Beneficiaries to whom functions have been delegated under subsection (1) are, in relation to the exercise of the functions, in the same position as trustees (with the same duties and liabilities); but such beneficiaries shall not be regarded as trustees for any other purposes (including, in particular, the purposes of any enactment permitting the delegation of functions by trustees or imposing requirements relating to the payment of capital money).

9A.—(1) The duty of care under section 1 of the Trustee Act 2000 applies to trustees of land in deciding whether to delegate any of their functions under section 9.

(2) Subsection (3) applies if the trustees of land—

(a) delegate any of their functions under section 9, and

(b) the delegation is not irrevocable.

(3) While the delegation continues, the trustees—

(a) must keep the delegation under review,

(b) if circumstances make it appropriate to do so, must consider whether there is a need to exercise any power of intervention that they have, and

(c) if they consider that there is a need to exercise such a power, must do so.

(4) Power of intervention' includes—

(a) a power to give directions to the beneficiary;

(b) a power to revoke the delegation.

(5) The duty of care under section 1 of the 2000 Act applies to trustees in carrying out any duty under subsection (3).

(6) A trustee of land is not liable for any act or default of the beneficiary, or beneficiaries, unless the trustee fails to comply with the duty of care in deciding to delegate any of the trustees' functions under section 9 or in carrying out any duty under subsection (3).

Comment

(1) Does s 9 ensure that the wishes of the settlor are given effect to? Does the court discretion under s 14 provide a sufficient safeguard against recalcitrant trustees?

(2) Purchasers are provided protection in respect of unauthorised[4] or revoked[5] delegations of authority, provided that they are unaware of the problem. It might be added that a power of attorney requires a deed.[6]

(3) Section 9A (inserted by the Trustee Act 2000) makes fresh provision for trustees' duties of care. Does it impose necessary and sufficient controls?

Further reading

Gallanis, T P [2000] CLJ 284: The rules against perpetuities and the Law Commission's flawed philosophy.

Sparkes, P (1998) 12 *Trust Law International* 148: Perpetuities reform.

---

[4] TLATA, s 9(2).
[5] Powers of Attorney Act 1971, s 5.
[6] Powers of Attorney Act 1971, s 1, as amended by Law of Property (Miscellaneous Provisions) Act 1989, Sched 1, para 6.

14

Leases: requirements and types

Most people have a good idea of what a lease is. It is a way of giving a person rights to the enjoyment of land for a specified period, sometimes described as temporary property ownership. The contrast with freehold estates (life estates, in particular) is explained by Lawson and Rudden[1] as follows:

> The distinction between freehold and leasehold estates has a practical justification which has remained virtually the same from the thirteenth century to the present day. Leasehold estates have always been thought of on commercial lines. Persons have always been willing to invest in terms of years, whether by purchase, or by taking them as security of loans of money, or merely in order to secure possession of land for a guaranteed period as tenants of farms or shop premises. Long terms of as much as ninety-nine years have commonly been granted at low rents to persons who undertake to build on the land. On the other hand, although freehold interests other than the fee simple have a present actuarial value, they are not marketable to the same extent as leasehold interests; and certainly no one would at the present day give a life interest to a person with the intention that he should turn it into ready money. A life interest is meant to provide an annual income for an indefinite number of years . . .

This explains why leases, alongside fees simple, are recognised as legal estates by the Law of Property Act 1925 (hereafter LPA), s 1. Given that leases involve the use of land and can be sold to others who wish to use the land, it would be wholly inappropriate to allow them to be overreached in the manner of, for example, life interests.

As will be seen later in this chapter, not every tenancy requires a fixed period. Thus the law recognises tenancies at will, which either party can terminate at any time, and tenancies at sufferance, rather similar tenancies which arise if a tenant 'holds over' at the end of a lease. These are not really estates at all, rather relationships of landlord and tenant.

1. Requirements of leases

A. Certainty requirements: rent, commencement and length

It is unsurprising that leases require certainty regarding their fundamental elements. However, what is particularly interesting is that leases have developed specific rules which are more demanding than contractual certainty requirements.

Let us first consider rent. An initial question is whether rent is an essential component of a lease.

---

[1] *The Law of Property* (2nd ed), p 94.

Extract 14.1.1

Ashburn Anstalt v *Arnold* **[1989] Ch 1**

FOX LJ: ... In *Street* v *Mountford* [1985] AC 809 Lord Templeman, who gave the leading speech, regarded three hallmarks as decisive in favour of a tenancy of residential accommodation, namely exclusive possession, for a term, at a rent . . . As regards rent, Arnold & Co was not required to pay a rent under the provisions of clause 5, nor did it do so . . . We treat the case as one where no rent was payable. Did that prevent the provisions of clause 5 from creating a tenancy? We do not think so. We are unable to read Lord Templeman's speech in *Street* v *Mountford* as laying down a principle of 'no rent, no lease'. In the first place, that would be inconsistent with section 205(1)(xxvii) of the Law of Property Act 1925, which defines 'Term of years absolute' as 'a term of years (taking effect either in possession or in reversion whether or not at a rent) . . .' Secondly, it would be inconsistent with the judgment of Windeyer J in *Radaich* v *Smith* (1959) 101 CLR 209, 222, which was expressly approved by Lord Templeman in *Street* v *Mountford* . . .

In the circumstances I conclude that the reservation of a rent is not necessary for the creation of a tenancy. That conclusion involves no departure from Lord Templeman's proposition in *Street* v *Mountford*, at p 825:

> 'If exclusive possession at a rent for a term does not constitute a tenancy then the distinction between a contractual tenancy and a contractual licence of land becomes wholly unidentifiable.'

We are saying only that we do not think that Lord Templeman was stating the quite different proposition that you cannot have a tenancy without a rent.

Comment

(1) This has the support of other authorities.[2]

(2) How are the dicta in *Street* v *Mountford* distinguished?

(3) Longer leases are commonly granted in return for a capital sum. There may then be a nominal ('peppercorn') rent.

Most difficulties arise where the amount of the rent is not clearly stipulated: this is most commonly a problem in contracts for leases. In *King's Motors (Oxford) Ltd* v *Lax*,[3] Burgess V-C observed:

> The argument for uncertainty is that, as the rent was not agreed and was left to be agreed, unless the parties were – if you like to put it that way – to play the game together and agree, the contract is not enforceable and is void for uncertainty. In substance it amounts to no more than a contract to enter into a contract which is always given as the classic example of an agreement which is unenforceable.

However, an agreement which provides a formula whereby a rent can be determined is effective. Even such an uncertain formula as 'to be fixed having regard to the market value of the premises . . .' was held valid in *Brown* v *Gould*.[4]

---

[2] *Canadian Imperial Bank of Commerce* v *Bello* (1991) 64 P&CR 48; *Skipton BS* v *Clayton* (1993) 66 P&CR 223.
[3] [1970] 1 WLR 426 at p 428.
[4] [1972] Ch 53.

Extract 14.1.2

Corson v Rhuddlan BC (1990) 59 P&CR 185

There was an option to renew 'at a rent to be agreed ([not to] exceed the rent hereby reserved)'.

RALPH GIBSON LJ: . . . The second agreement [in *Foley* v *Classique Coaches Ltd*] provided that the defendants would purchase from the plaintiff all the petrol required by them 'at a price to be agreed by the parties in writing and from time to time'. This court, (Scrutton, Greer and Maugham LJJ) after consideration of the cases of *May and Butcher Ltd* and *Hillas & Co* v *Arcos*, held that a term must be implied in the agreement that the petrol supplied should be of reasonable quality and be sold at a reasonable price, and that, if any dispute arose as to what was a reasonable price, it was to be determined by arbitration under the arbitration clause. There was therefore:[i]

> 'an effective and enforceable contract although as to the future no definite price had been agreed with regard to the petrol.'

. . .

I would therefore hold that the matters relied upon by Mr Orr as excluding the possibility of implication of the fair rent term do not have the effect in law for which he contended. The task of the court, therefore, is to construe the option clause in the second lease in accordance with the approach of their Lordships in *Hillas & Co* v *Arcos*. It must be construed in the context of the entire transaction of which the second lease formed part. It is expressed in terms suitable and relevant to contractual right and obligation and not to the mere expression of a willingness at the end of the first term to negotiate, free of any legal obligation, for the grant of a new term. If it was intended to be no more than a statement that the landlords would negotiate, it was grossly misleading to anyone unfamiliar with the argument capable of being mounted upon the decision in the case of *King's Motors (Oxford) Ltd* v *Lax*, and it served no purpose whatever in a contractual document. If there was to be no obligation there was no need for or point in the definition of the time for service of notice for the exercise of the option . . . It is just and necessary to imply the provision for the rent to be a fair rent.

There is said to be authority in the way of taking that course. In *King's Motors (Oxford) Ltd* v *Lax* the option clause was contained in a seven-year lease of a petrol station and provided for a further term of seven years . . . It is, again, I think, not necessary for this court to decide whether the decision in the *Lax* case was correct because the provision for a maximum rent is, in my judgment, a material distinction. For my part, however, I incline to the view that it was, as Mr George submitted, wrongly decided, . . . A provision that the rent should be a fair rent could, I think, have been implied in the *Lax* case. I can see no risk of difficulty arising from such a conclusion. If parties intend an option clause to be no more than an indication that the landlord will be willing to consider a request for a new lease without obligation and on terms to be agreed, there is no difficulty in making that intention clear if there is thought to be any utility in including such a statement in the document.

[i] [1934] 2 KB 1 at p 10, per Scrutton LJ.

Comment

Is anything left of the rule that the rent must be certain? What happens if the agreement says nothing about rent at all (assuming that both parties intend that rent should be paid)?

It has long been a requirement that leases should have a certain beginning and a certain end. Turning to the beginning, one factor is that a lease may commence in the future: I can create a lease for five years commencing in a year's time. The tenant has a legal lease immediately, though of course no right to the land until the year has elapsed.

Extract 14.1.3

Law of Property Act 1925, s 149(3)

149.—(3)   A term, at a rent or granted in consideration of a fine, limited after the commencement of this Act to take effect more than twenty-one years from the date of the instrument purporting to create it, shall be void, and any contract made after such commencement to create such a term shall likewise be void . . .

Comment

(1) This provision has been held to invalidate contracts for leases only in so far as the lease, *at the time granted*, will take effect more than 21 years thereafter.[5] What is the effect of the following arrangements? A grants a lease to B to commence in 25 years' time. A contracts to grant a lease to C in 25 years' time. A contracts to grant a lease to D in 15 years' time, to commence ten years thereafter. A contracts to grant a lease to E in three years' time, to commence 22 years thereafter.

(2) Leases commonly contain provisions for renewal. What is the effect of s 149(3) on such provisions? Does this help to explain the differing results in the examples given above?

(3) Because future leases are difficult to discover, in registered land they have to be registered and cannot be overriding interests, regardless of their length.[6]

The fact that leases may commence in the future means that uncertainty may arise as to the date of commencement.

Extract 14.1.4

Harvey v Pratt **[1965] 1 WLR 1025**

LORD DENNING MR: The first point is this: the document does not specify any date from which the lease is to commence. It has been settled law for all my time that, in order to have a valid agreement for a lease, it is essential that it should appear, either in express terms or by reference to some writing which would make it certain, or by reasonable inference from the language used, on what day the term is to commence . . .

Mr Pearson has argued before us that there was an implied term that the lease should commence within a reasonable time. He says that this point was not considered in the earlier cases. He argues that on a sale of land there is an implied term that completion should be within a reasonable time; so why, he argues, should not there be the same with a lease? Why cannot there be an implied term that it should commence within a reasonable time?

I think the answer to that argument, however persuasive, is that the law is now settled on the point . . . It is settled beyond question that, in order for there to be a valid agreement for a lease, the essentials are not only for the parties to be determined, the property to be determined, the length of the term and the rent, but also the date of its commencement. This document does not contain it. It is not sufficient to say you can supply it by an implied term as to reasonable time.

DAVIES LJ: . . . In the case of a contract for the sale of freehold, the subject-matter is ascertained, namely, the land. In the case of an agreement for a lease, if the length of the term and the commencement of the term are not defined, then the subject of the agreement or contract is uncertain . . .

---

[5] *Re Strand & Savoy Properties Ltd* [1960] Ch 582.
[6] Land Registration Act 2002, s 27(2)(b)(ii), Sched 3, paras 1(b), 2(d). There is a relaxation for future leases taking effect within three months of grant.

Comment

(1) Is the contrast between the freehold and leasehold adequately explained by Davies LJ?[7] Is the duration of the term (the subject matter of the grant) affected by the time it commences?

(2) Is *Harvey* compatible with the approach taken in *Corson*?

In more recent years, however, greater difficulty has been experienced regarding the requirement of a certain end. The nature of a lease is that it must be for a certain maximum period and, unless its termination is clearly stated, this may not be satisfied.

Extract 14.1.5

Prudential Assurance Co Ltd v London Residuary Body [1992] 2 AC 386

By a 1930 agreement, land was leased until required for road widening.

LORD TEMPLEMAN: . . . Section 205(1)(xxvii) was in these terms:

> '"Term of years absolute" means a term of years . . . either certain or liable to determination by notice . . .'

The term expressed to be granted by the agreement in the present case does not fall within this definition.

Ancient authority, recognised by the Act of 1925, was applied in *Lace v Chantler* [1944] KB 368. A dwelling house was let at the rent of 16s 5d per week. Lord Greene MR (no less) said, at pp 370–371:

> 'Normally there could be no question that this was an ordinary weekly tenancy, duly determinable by a week's notice, but the parties in the rent-book agreed to a term which appears there expressed by the words "furnished for duration", which must mean the duration of the war. The question immediately arises whether a tenancy for the duration of the war creates a good leasehold interest. In my opinion, it does not. A term created by a leasehold tenancy agreement must be expressed either with certainty and specifically or by reference to something which can, at the time when the lease takes effect, be looked to as a certain ascertainment of what the term is meant to be. In the present case, when this tenancy agreement took effect, the term was completely uncertain. It was impossible to say how long the tenancy would last. Mr Sturge in his argument has maintained that such a lease would be valid, and that, even if the term is uncertain at its beginning when the lease takes effect, the fact that at some future time it will be rendered certain is sufficient to make it a good lease. In my opinion, that argument is not to be sustained . . .'

> . . .

When the agreement in the present case was made, it failed to grant an estate in the land. The tenant however entered into possession and paid the yearly rent of £30 reserved by the agreement. The tenant entering under a void lease became by virtue of possession and the payment of a yearly rent, a yearly tenant holding on the terms of the agreement so far as those terms were consistent with the yearly tenancy . . .

Now it is said that when in the present case the tenant entered pursuant to the agreement and paid a yearly rent he became a tenant from year to year on the terms of the agreement including clause 6 which prevents the landlord from giving notice to quit until the land is required for road widening. This submission would make a nonsense of the rule that a grant for an uncertain

---

[7] See also Megarry V-C in *Brown v Gould* [1972] Ch 53 at p 61.

term does not create a lease and would make nonsense of the concept of a tenancy from year to year because it is of the essence of a tenancy from year to year that both the landlord and the tenant shall be entitled to give notice determining the tenancy.

In *Doe d Warner* v *Browne* (1807) 8 East 165 there was an agreement to lease at a rent of £40 per annum and it was agreed that the landlord, W Warner, should not raise the rent nor turn out the tenant 'so long as the rent is duly paid quarterly, and he does not expose to sale or sell any article that may be injurious to W Warner in his business'. The tenant duly paid his rent and did not commit any breach of covenant. The landlord gave six months' notice and it was held that the notice was good . . .

Lawrence J said, at p 167:

'If this interest be not determinable so long as the tenant complies with the terms of the agreement, it would operate as an estate for life; which can only be created by deed . . . The notion of a tenancy from year to year, the lessor binding himself not to give notice to quit, which was once thrown out by Lord Mansfield, has been long exploded.'

. . .

My Lords, I consider that the principle in *Lace* v *Chantler* [1944] KB 368 reaffirming 500 years of judicial acceptance of the requirement that a term must be certain applies to all leases and tenancy agreements. A tenancy from year to year is saved from being uncertain because each party has power by notice to determine at the end of any year. The term continues until determined as if both parties made a new agreement at the end of each year for a new term for the ensuing year. A power for nobody to determine or for one party only to be able to determine is inconsistent with the concept of a term from year to year: see *Doe d Warner* v *Browne*, 8 East 165 and *Cheshire Lines Committee* v *Lewis & Co*, 50 LJQB 121 . . .

A lease can be made for five years subject to the tenant's right to determine if the war ends before the expiry of five years. A lease can be made from year to year subject to a fetter on the right of the landlord to determine the lease before the expiry of five years unless the war ends. Both leases are valid because they create a determinable certain term of five years. A lease might purport to be made for the duration of the war subject to the tenant's right to determine before the end of the war. A lease might be made from year to year subject to a fetter on the right of the landlord to determine the lease before the war ends. Both leases would be invalid because each purported to create an uncertain term. A term must either be certain or uncertain. It cannot be partly certain because the tenant can determine it at any time and partly uncertain because the landlord cannot determine it for an uncertain period. If the landlord does not grant and the tenant does not take a certain term the grant does not create a lease.

LORD BROWNE-WILKINSON: . . . It is difficult to think of a more unsatisfactory outcome or one further away from what the parties to the 1930 agreement can ever have contemplated. Certainly it was not a result their contract, if given effect to, could ever have produced. If the 1930 agreement had taken effect fully, there could never have come a time when the freehold to the remainder of No 263–265 would be left without a road frontage.

This bizarre outcome results from the application of an ancient and technical rule of law which requires the maximum duration of a term of years to be ascertainable from the outset. No one has produced any satisfactory rationale for the genesis of this rule. No one has been able to point to any useful purpose that it serves at the present day.

Comment

(1) Sparkes[8] writes: 'To relax the requirement of certainty would be to allow the creation by accident of an incumbrance against property of indefinite duration at what may become

[8] (1993) 109 LQR 93 at pp 112–113.

a derisory rent. The rule of certainty coupled with the available escape routes achieves surprisingly fair results.' Does this, or any other reasoning, counter Lord Browne-Wilkinson's criticisms?

(2) Lord Templeman demonstrates that a lease for an uncertain period can be made effective by the simple device of redrafting it as a lease for a certain period terminable on the uncertain event. Is this an argument for or against the certainty requirement as applied in *Prudential*? The result in *Lace* v *Chantler* was reversed by the Validation of War-time Leases Act 1944, providing for ten-year leases determinable on notice at the end of the war.

(3) How convincing is the explanation of periodic tenancies? As will be seen later in this chapter, a periodic tenancy is viewed as a single continuing tenancy, rather than as a succession of tenancies.

(4) If the lease in *Prudential* were to be valid, how would one distinguish it from a determinable fee simple? Might it be argued that the payment of rent, rather than a certain period, is today the principal distinguishing feature of leases?

Extract 14.1.6

Mexfield Housing Co-operative Ltd v *Berrisford* [2012] 1 AC 955

A monthly tenancy provided that the landlord could not terminate the tenancy whilst the tenant complied with the terms of the lease. It was held that this was inconsistent with the certain maximum duration rule.

LORD NEUBERGER:

Is such an arrangement capable of being a tenancy as a matter of law?
23.   I turn to the second issue, namely whether an arrangement, which can only come to an end by service of one month's notice by the tenant, or by the landlord invoking a right of determination on one or more of the grounds set out in clause 6, is capable, as a matter of law, of being a tenancy in accordance with its terms. Mr Wonnacott [counsel for the appellant tenant] accepts that it is not so capable. His concession is supported both by very old authority and by high modern authority.
24.   It seems to have been established for a long time that an agreement for an uncertain term cannot be a tenancy in the sense of being a term of years. In *Say* v *Smith* (1563) Plowd 269, 272, Anthony Brown J said that 'every contract sufficient to make a lease for years ought to have certainty in three limitations, viz in the commencement of the term, in the continuance of it, and in the end of it . . . and words in a lease, which don't make this appear, are but babble.'
25.   That is consistent with what was stated in Bracton's *De Legibus et Consuetudinibus Angliae*, written in the mid-thirteenth century . . . This statement was referred to with approval by Sir Edward Coke in Co Litt 42a (1628), and much the same is stated in *Brook's New Cases* (1554/5) pl 462 . . .
26.   Much more recently, in *Lace* v *Chantler* [1944] KB 368, the Court of Appeal held that a purported letting 'for the duration [of the Second World War]' could not take effect as 'a good tenancy for the duration of the war' as it was for an uncertain term, and that it was consequently ineffective. This decision was distinguished by a subsequent Court of Appeal in *Ashburn Anstalt* v *Arnold* [1989] Ch 1, where it was held that a right to occupy premises until the owner gave one quarter's notice certifying he needed the premises for redevelopment created a tenancy binding on third parties.
27.   Less than 20 years ago, the House of Lords approved and applied *Lace* [1944] KB 368, and disapproved and overruled *Ashburn* [1989] Ch 1 . . . The House of Lords held that this

arrangement was incapable of creating a tenancy, as it was for an uncertain, potentially perpetual, duration. Lord Templeman (with whom the other members of the House of Lords agreed, albeit with reluctance in most cases) said at [1992] 2 AC 386, 394F, that there had been '500 years of judicial acceptance of the requirement that a term must be certain applies to all leases and tenancy agreements'.

33.   Following the decision of the House of Lords in *Prudential* [1992] 2 AC 386, the law appeared clear in its effect, intellectually coherent in its analysis, and, in part, unsatisfactory in its practical consequences. The position appears to have been as follows. (i) An agreement for a term, whose maximum duration can be identified from the inception, can give rise to a valid tenancy; (ii) an agreement which gives rise to a periodic arrangement determinable by either party can also give rise to a valid tenancy; (iii) an agreement could not give rise to a tenancy as a matter of law if it was for a term whose maximum duration was uncertain at the inception; (iv) (a) a fetter on a right to serve notice to determine a periodic tenancy was ineffective if the fetter is to endure for an uncertain period, but (b) a fetter for a specified period could be valid.

34.   If we accept that that is indeed the law, then, subject to the point to which I next turn, the Agreement cannot take effect as a tenancy according to its terms. As the judgment of Lady Hale demonstrates (and as indeed the disquiet expressed by Lord Browne-Wilkinson and others in *Prudential* [1992] 2 AC 386 itself shows), the law is not in a satisfactory state. There is no apparent practical justification for holding that an agreement for a term of uncertain duration cannot give rise to a tenancy, or that a fetter of uncertain duration on the right to serve a notice to quit is invalid. There is therefore much to be said for changing the law, and overruling what may be called the certainty requirement, which was affirmed in *Prudential* [1992] 2 AC 386, on the ground that, in so far as it had any practical justification, that justification has long since gone, and, in so far as it is based on principle, the principle is not fundamental enough for the Supreme Court to be bound by it. It may be added that Lady Hale's Carrollian characterisation of the law on this topic is reinforced by the fact that the common law accepted perpetually renewable leases as valid: they have been converted into 2000-year terms by section 145 of the Law of Property Act 1922.

35.   However, I would not support jettisoning the certainty requirement, at any rate in this case. First, as the discussion earlier in this judgment shows, it does appear that for many centuries it has been regarded as fundamental to the concept of a term of years that it had a certain duration when it was created. It seems logical that the subsequent development of a term from year to year (ie a periodic tenancy) should carry with it a similar requirement, and the case law also seems to support this.

36.   Secondly, the 1925 Act appears to support this conclusion. Having stated in section 1(1) that only two estates can exist in land, a fee simple and a term of years, it then defines a term of years in section 205(1)(xxvii) as meaning 'a term of years . . . either certain or liable to determination by notice [or] re-entry'; as Lord Templeman said in *Prudential* [1992] 2 AC 386, 391B, this seems to underwrite the established common law position. The notion that the 1925 Act assumed that the certainty requirement existed appears to be supported by the terms of section 149(6). As explained more fully below, this provision effectively converts a life tenancy into a determinable term of 90 years. A tenancy for life is a term of uncertain duration, and it was a species of freehold estate prior to 1926, but, in the light of section 1 of the 1925 Act, if it was to retain its status as a legal estate, it could only be a term of years after that date. Presumably it was converted into a 90-year term because those responsible for drafting the 1925 Act thought it could not be a term of years otherwise.

37.   Thirdly, the certainty requirement was confirmed only some 20 years ago by the House of Lords. Fourthly, while not a very attractive point, there is the concern expressed by Lord Browne-Wilkinson, namely that to change the law in this field 'might upset long established titles' – [1992] 2 AC 386, 397A. Fifthly, at least where the purported grant is to an individual, as opposed to a company or corporation, the arrangement does in fact give rise to a valid tenancy,

as explained below. Finally, it has been no part of either party's case that the Agreement gave rise to a valid tenancy according to its terms (if, as I have concluded, it has the meaning for which Mr Wonnacott contends).

Would such a tenancy have been treated as a tenancy for life before 1926?

38. While Mr Wonnacott accepts that the arrangement contained in the Agreement would not be capable of constituting a tenancy in accordance with its terms, he contends that, at any rate before 1926, the arrangement would have been treated by the court as a tenancy for the life of Ms Berrisford, determinable before her death by her under clause 5, or by Mexfield under clause 6.

39. There is much authority to support the proposition that, before the 1925 Act came into force, an agreement for an uncertain term was treated as a tenancy for the life of the tenant, determinable before the tenant's death according to its terms. In Bracton (op cit) vol 3, p 50 (f176b), it will be recalled that the grant of an uncertain term was held to give rise to a 'free tenement', provided that the formalities had been complied with. The nature of this free tenement would appear to be a tenancy for the life of the grantee. That is clear from what was said in Littleton on *Tenures* (1481/2) vol 2, section 382 namely: '[I]f an abbot make a lease to a man, to have and to hold to him during the time that he is abbot . . . the lessee hath an estate for the term of his owne life: but this is on condition . . . that if the abbot resign, or be deposed, that then it shall be lawful for his successor to enter.'

40. In Co Litt vol 1, p 42a, it is similarly stated that if an estate is granted to a person until, inter alia, she marries, or so long as she pays £40 'or for any like incertaine term', 'the lessee hath in judgment of law an estate for life determinable if [the formalities of creation are satisfied]'. This passage was quoted and applied by North J in *In re Carne's Settled Estates* [1899] 1 Ch 324, 329 . . .

Is the agreement converted into a 90-year term by section 149(6)?

45. The next step in Mr Wonnacott's argument is that, given that the Agreement would have given rise to a tenancy for life prior to 1926, the effect of section 149(6) of the 1925 Act ('section 149(6)') is that the Agreement is now to be treated as a term of 90 years determinable on the death of Ms Berrisford, subject to the rights of determination in clauses 5 and 6.

49. Mr Gaunt contends that section 149(6) is concerned with tenancies which automatically end with the tenant's death, not with tenancies which can be determined on the tenant's death, and, in this case, the effect of clause 6(c) is that the tenancy can be determined, not that it automatically determines, on the tenant's death. I accept that section 149(6) only applies to tenancies which automatically determine on death, and I am prepared to assume that clause 6(c) can only be invoked by service of a notice. However, the argument misses the point, because the Agreement is (or would be in the absence of sections 1 and 149 of the 1925 Act) a tenancy for life, not because of the specific terms of, or circumstances described in, clause 6(c), but because it is treated as such by a well-established common law rule.

50. It is also suggested that section 149(6) does not apply to arrangements such as the Agreement which are determinable in circumstances other than the tenant's death – e.g. on the grounds set out in clause 6. I can see no reasons of principle for accepting that contention, and it appears to me that there are strong practical reasons for rejecting it . . .

53. The fact is that it was not argued in [*Lace* or *Prudential*] that the arrangement involved would have created a life tenancy as a matter of common law, and that, following section 149(6), such an arrangement would now give rise to a 90-year term, determinable on the tenant's death (and Mr Wonnacott was kind enough to point out that such an argument would not have assisted, and may even have harmed, the unsuccessful respondent's case in *Prudential* [1992] 2 AC 386). Some of the statements about the law by Lord Greene and Lord Templeman can now be seen

to be extravagant or inaccurately wide, but it is only fair to them to repeat that this was, at least in part, because the tenancy for life argument was not raised before them.

Ms Berrisford's alternative case in contract

58. This conclusion renders it unnecessary to consider two alternative arguments, which were raised by Mr Wonnacott, namely that (i) if the Agreement did not create a tenancy, it nonetheless gave rise to a binding personal contract between Mexfield and Ms Berrisford, which Ms Berrisford is entitled to enforce against Mexfield so long as it owns the premises, or (ii) if the Agreement created a periodic tenancy with an impermissible fetter on the right of the landlord to serve notice to quit, the fetter is nonetheless enforceable as against Mexfield so long as it is the owner of the premises.

59. However, having heard full submissions on those two arguments, I incline fairly strongly to the view that, if Ms Berrisford had failed in establishing that she had a subsisting tenancy of the premises, she would nonetheless have defeated Mexfield's claim for possession on the ground that she is entitled to enforce her contractual rights.

60. If the Agreement does not create a tenancy for technical reasons, namely because it purports to create an uncertain term, it is hard to see why, as a matter of principle, it should not be capable of taking effect as a contract, enforceable as between the parties personally, albeit not capable of binding their respective successors, as no interest in land or other proprietary interest would subsist.

61. The argument to the contrary rests in part on authority [Lord Greene in *Lace*; *Prudential*] and in part on principle . . .

62. It does not seem to me that the observations of Lord Greene, although they are strongly expressed views of a highly reputable judge, can withstand principled analysis. As Lord Templeman made clear in *Street* [1985] AC 809, while the parties' rights and obligations are primarily determined by what they have agreed, the legal characterisation of those rights is ultimately a matter of law. If the Agreement is incapable of giving rise to a tenancy for some old and technical rule of property law, I do not see why, as a matter of principle, that should render the Agreement invalid as a matter of contract.

63. The fact that the parties may have thought they were creating a tenancy is no reason for not holding that they have agreed a contractual licence any more than in *Street* [1985] AC 809, the fact that the parties clearly intended to create a licence precluded the court from holding that they had, as a matter of law, created a tenancy . . .

67. . . . Given that no question of statutory protection could arise, it seems to me far less likely that the parties would have intended a weekly tenancy determinable at any time on one month's notice than a licence which could only be determined pursuant to clauses 5 and 6.

69. That leaves Mr Wonnacott's further alternative argument, namely that, if Mexfield is right and there is a periodic tenancy, then, even if the fetter on the landlord's right to serve a notice to quit is objectionable in landlord and tenant law, it can be enforced as between the original parties as a matter of contract. That was the basis on which Wilson LJ felt able to find for Ms Berrisford in the Court of Appeal. I prefer to say nothing about that point . . .

LADY HALE: 94. . . . But it is not difficult to imagine circumstances in which the same analysis [lease for life] would apply but be very far from the intentions of the parties. And that analysis is not available where the tenant is a company or corporation. So there the court is unable to give effect to the undoubted intentions of the parties. Yet, as the Court pointed out in *Midland Railway*, it is always open to the parties to give effect to those intentions by granting a very long term of years, determinable earlier on the happening of the uncertain event. The law, it would seem, has no policy objection to such an arrangement, so it is difficult to see what policy objection it can have to upholding the arrangement to which the parties in fact came.

95. It is even more bizarre that, had the 'tenancy for life' analysis not been available, the conclusion might have been, not that this was a contractual tenancy enforceable as such as between the original parties, but that it was a contractual licence, also enforceable as such between the original parties. This, as I understand it, is the difference between English and Scots law. I do not understand that it makes any difference to the result.

96. As will be apparent, I entirely agree with the reasoning and conclusions reached by Lord Neuberger on the first question: does Ms Berrisford have a subsisting tenancy? For that reason, I do not think it necessary to express an opinion on the alternative case in contract. But it seems to me obvious that the consequence of our having reached the conclusions which we have on the first issue is to make the reconsideration of the decision in *Prudential*, whether by this Court or by Parliament, a matter of some urgency . . .

Comment

(1) It was a seven judge court. Though all delivered judgments, there was general agreement with Lord Neuberger's analysis.

(2) As is apparent from Lady Hale's judgment, the certainty rule was not well received. There are comments from several judges (taking a more sceptical approach than Lord Neuberger) that the rule is barely acceptable today. Would a future challenge to it in the Supreme Court be viable?

(3) The lease for life analysis provides an effective way to give effect to the intention of the parties. What flaws might it have? For s 149(6), see Extract 14.2.14 below.

(4) At [67], Lord Neuberger places stress on the intention of the parties in holding that there would have been a contractual licence rather than a monthly lease (shorn of the restraint on termination). Is this consistent with *Street v Mountford*?

(5) Should it be possible to use a contractual analysis if there is a monthly tenancy?

B. Exclusive possession

(i) Early developments

Exclusive possession has always been required for leases, but what counts as exclusive possession?

Extract 14.1.7

Daly v Edwardes (1900) 83 LT 548[9]

Did the right to run bars in a theatre constitute a lease?

RIGBY LJ: . . . No doubt the persons who had got a licence to sell refreshments had a perfect right to say to others, You must not come behind our bars because you will interfere with us, not because you would be a trespasser. They would say, whether to the lessee of the theatre, or to anybody else, You must not come here, because we have the right by contract to do everything that is required for serving refreshments, and we cannot do that effectually and properly if you come behind the bars. That is not treating them as trespassers on land. I cannot see that that was in their minds. I asked a question which probably was a very small matter, but it seemed to me not immaterial, 'Who lights the rooms', and it appears that the lessee of the

---

[9] Upheld (1901) 85 LT 650; see also *Clore v Theatrical Properties Ltd* [1936] 3 All ER 483.

theatre does so. That lighting probably would not involve much interference . . . I apprehend that if there had been any difficulty about the electric lights during the performance, it would have been the lessee of the theatre who would have been entitled to see that the lights were put right. At any rate, if any catastrophe had happened, it would be set right by him and not by the alleged lessees of these refreshment rooms. On the whole, I think that the proper conclusion is that Frank Warr and Co took no estate or interest in land, but that they were entitled, for all reasonable purposes, to consider themselves as having an exclusive licence to provide refreshments and all that follows from that privilege, and nothing else at all . . .

In the years after the Second World War, the Court of Appeal began to insist that exclusive possession did not always lead to a lease: in appropriate circumstances there would be a licence. In large measure, this was a consequence of the legislation protecting tenants. Landlords were keen not to have leases protected by the legislation. Though the courts, at least until the late 1970s, were reluctant to allow landlords to contract out of the protection accorded to tenants, there were some circumstances in which they were prepared to find licences. However, the tide turned in the 1980s.

(ii) *Street* v *Mountford*

<hr>

Extract 14.1.8

<hr>

Street v *Mountford* [1985] AC 809

LORD TEMPLEMAN: . . . The traditional view that the grant of exclusive possession for a term at a rent creates a tenancy is consistent with the elevation of a tenancy into an estate in land. The tenant possessing exclusive possession is able to exercise the rights of an owner of land, which is in the real sense his land albeit temporarily and subject to certain restrictions. A tenant armed with exclusive possession can keep out strangers and keep out the landlord unless the landlord is exercising limited rights reserved to him by the tenancy agreement to enter and view and repair. A licensee lacking exclusive possession can in no sense call the land his own and cannot be said to own any estate in the land. The licence does not create an estate in the land to which it relates but only makes an act lawful which would otherwise be unlawful.

On behalf of Mr Street his counsel, Mr Goodhart QC, relies on recent authorities which, he submits, demonstrate that an occupier granted exclusive possession for a term at a rent may nevertheless be a licensee . . .

My Lords, there is no doubt that the traditional distinction between a tenancy and a licence of land lay in the grant of land for a term at a rent with exclusive possession. In some cases it was not clear at first sight whether exclusive possession was in fact granted . . .

In the case of residential accommodation there is no difficulty in deciding whether the grant confers exclusive possession. An occupier of residential accommodation at a rent for a term is either a lodger or a tenant. The occupier is a lodger if the landlord provides attendance or services which require the landlord or his servants to exercise unrestricted access to and use of the premises. A lodger is entitled to live in the premises but cannot call the place his own. In *Allan* v *Liverpool Overseers* (1874) LR 9 QB 180, 191–192 Blackburn J said:

> 'A lodger in a house, although he has the exclusive use of rooms in the house, in the sense that nobody else is to be there, and though his goods are stowed there, yet he is not in exclusive occupation in that sense, because the landlord is there for the purpose of being able, as landlords commonly do in the case of lodgings, to have his own servants to look after the house and the furniture, and has retained to himself the occupation, though he has agreed to give the exclusive enjoyment of the occupation to the lodger.'

If on the other hand residential accommodation is granted for a term at a rent with exclusive possession, the landlord providing neither attendance nor services, the grant is a tenancy; any express reservation to the landlord of limited rights to enter and view the state of the premises and to repair and maintain the premises only serves to emphasise the fact that the grantee is entitled to exclusive possession and is a tenant. In the present case it is conceded that Mrs Mountford is entitled to exclusive possession and is not a lodger . . .

There can be no tenancy unless the occupier enjoys exclusive possession; but an occupier who enjoys exclusive possession is not necessarily a tenant. He may be owner in fee simple, a trespasser, a mortgagee in possession, an object of charity or a service occupier. To constitute a tenancy the occupier must be granted exclusive possession for a fixed or periodic term certain in consideration of a premium or periodical payments. The grant may be express, or may be inferred where the owner accepts weekly or other periodical payments from the occupier.

Occupation by service occupier may be eliminated. A service occupier is a servant who occupies his master's premises in order to perform his duties as a servant. In those circumstances the possession and occupation of the servant is treated as the possession and occupation of the master and the relationship of landlord and tenant is not created; see *Mayhew* v *Suttle* (1854) 4 El&Bl 347 . . .

The cases on which Mr Goodhart relies begin with *Booker* v *Palmer* [1942] 2 All ER 674. The owner of a cottage agreed to allow a friend to install an evacuee in the cottage rent free for the duration of the war. The Court of Appeal held that there was no intention on the part of the owner to enter into legal relationships with the evacuee . . .

In the present case, the agreement dated 7 March 1983 professed an intention by both parties to create a licence and their belief that they had in fact created a licence . . . Both parties enjoyed freedom to contract or not to contract and both parties exercised that freedom by contracting on the terms set forth in the written agreement and on no other terms. But the consequences in law of the agreement, once concluded, can only be determined by consideration of the effect of the agreement. If the agreement satisfied all the requirements of a tenancy, then the agreement produced a tenancy and the parties cannot alter the effect of the agreement by insisting that they only created a licence. The manufacture of a five-pronged implement for manual digging results in a fork even if the manufacturer, unfamiliar with the English language, insists that he intended to make and has made a spade.

It was also submitted that in deciding whether the agreement created a tenancy or a licence, the court should ignore the Rent Acts. If Mr Street has succeeded, where owners have failed these past 70 years, in driving a coach and horses through the Rent Acts, he must be left to enjoy the benefit of his ingenuity unless and until Parliament intervenes. I accept that the Rent Acts are irrelevant to the problem of determining the legal effect of the rights granted by the agreement. Like the professed intention of the parties, the Rent Acts cannot alter the effect of the agreement.

. . .

Errington v *Errington and Woods* [1952] 1 KB 290 concerned a contract by a father to allow his son to buy the father's house on payment of the instalments of the father's building society loan . . . Denning LJ continued, at pp 297–298:

'We have had many instances lately of occupiers in exclusive possession who have been held to be not tenants, but only licensees. When a requisitioning authority allowed people into possession at a weekly rent: . . . when a landlord told a tenant on his retirement that he could live in a cottage rent free for the rest of his days: . . . when a landlord, on the death of the widow of a statutory tenant, allowed her daughter to remain in possession, paying rent for six months: *Marcroft Wagons Ltd* v *Smith* [1951] 2 KB 496; when the owner of a shop allowed the manager to live in a flat above the shop, but did not require him to do so, and the value of the flat was taken into account at £1 a week in fixing his wages: . . . in each of those cases the occupier was held to be a licensee and not a tenant . . . The result of all these cases is that, although a person who is let into exclusive possession is prima facie to be considered a tenant, nevertheless he will not be held to be so if the circumstances negative any intention to create a tenancy. Words alone may not suffice. Parties cannot turn a tenancy into a licence merely by calling it one. But if the circumstances and the conduct of the parties show that all that was intended was that the occupier should be granted a personal privilege, with no interest in the land, he will be held to be a licensee only.'

In *Errington* v *Errington and Woods* [1952] 1 KB 290 and in the cases cited by Denning LJ at p 297 there were exceptional circumstances which negatived the prima facie intention to create a tenancy, notwithstanding that the occupier enjoyed exclusive occupation. The intention to create a tenancy was negatived if the parties did not intend to enter into legal relationships at all, or where the relationship between the parties was that of vendor and purchaser, master and service occupier, or where the owner, a requisitioning authority, had no power to grant a tenancy. These exceptional circumstances are not to be found in the present case where there has been the lawful, independent and voluntary grant of exclusive possession for a term at a rent.

If the observations of Denning LJ are applied to the facts of the present case it may fairly be said that the circumstances negative any intention to create a mere licence. Words alone do not suffice. Parties cannot turn a tenancy into a licence merely by calling it one. The circumstances and the conduct of the parties show that what was intended was that the occupier should be granted exclusive possession at a rent for a term with a corresponding interest in the land which created a tenancy.

. . .

In *Facchini* v *Bryson* [1952] 1 TLR 1386, an employer and his assistant entered into an agreement which, inter alia, allowed the assistant to occupy a house for a weekly payment on terms which conferred exclusive possession . . . Denning LJ referred to several cases including *Errington* v *Errington and Woods* and *Cobb* v *Lane* and said, at pp 1389–1390:

'In all the cases where an occupier has been held to be a licensee there has been something in the circumstances, such as a family arrangement, an act of friendship or generosity, or such like, to negative any intention to create a tenancy . . . In the present case, however, there are no special circumstances. It is a simple case where the employer let a man into occupation of a house in consequence of his employment at a weekly sum payable by him. The occupation has all the features of a service tenancy, and the parties cannot by the mere words of their contract turn it into something else. Their relationship is determined by the law and not by the label which they choose to put on it . . .'

The decision, which was thereafter binding on the Court of Appeal and on all lower courts, referred to the special circumstances which are capable of negativing an intention to create a tenancy and reaffirmed the principle that the professed intentions of the parties are irrelevant. The decision also indicated that in a simple case a grant of exclusive possession of residential accommodation for a weekly sum creates a tenancy.

. . .

In *Shell-Mex and BP Ltd* v *Manchester Garages Ltd* [1971] 1 WLR 612 the Court of Appeal after carefully examining an agreement whereby the defendant was allowed to use a petrol company's filling station for the purposes of selling petrol, came to the conclusion that the agreement did not grant exclusive possession to the defendant who was therefore a licensee . . .

In my opinion the agreement was only 'personal in its nature' and created 'a personal privilege' if the agreement did not confer the right to exclusive possession of the filling station. No other test for distinguishing between a contractual tenancy and a contractual licence appears to be understandable or workable.

. . .

In *Somma v Hazelhurst* [1978] 1 WLR 1014, a young unmarried couple H and S occupied a double bedsitting room for which they paid a weekly rent. The landlord did not provide services or attendance and the couple were not lodgers but tenants enjoying exclusive possession . . . The Court of Appeal were diverted from the correct inquiries by the fact that the landlord obliged H and S to enter into separate agreements and reserved power to determine each agreement separately. The landlord also insisted that the room should not in form be let to either H or S or to both H and S but that each should sign an agreement to share the room in common with such other persons as the landlord might from time to time nominate. The sham nature of this obligation would have been only slightly more obvious if H and S had been married or if the room had been furnished with a double bed instead of two single beds. If the landlord had served notice on H to leave and had required S to share the room with a strange man, the notice would only have been a disguised notice to quit on both H and S. The room was let and taken as residential accommodation with exclusive possession in order that H and S might live together in undisturbed quasi-connubial bliss making weekly payments. The agreements signed by H and S constituted the grant to H and S jointly of exclusive possession at a rent for a term for the purposes for which the room was taken and the agreement therefore created a tenancy. Although the Rent Acts must not be allowed to alter or influence the construction of an agreement, the court should, in my opinion, be astute to detect and frustrate sham devices and artificial transactions whose only object is to disguise the grant of a tenancy and to evade the Rent Acts. I would disapprove of the decision in this case that H and S were only licensees . . .

. . . My Lords, the only intention which is relevant is the intention demonstrated by the agreement to grant exclusive possession for a term at a rent. Sometimes it may be difficult to discover whether, on the true construction of an agreement, exclusive possession is conferred. Sometimes it may appear from the surrounding circumstances that there was no intention to create legal relationships. Sometimes it may appear from the surrounding circumstances that the right to exclusive possession is referable to a legal relationship other than a tenancy. Legal relationships to which the grant of exclusive possession might be referable and which would or might negative the grant of an estate or interest in the land include occupancy under a contract for the sale of the land, occupancy pursuant to a contract of employment or occupancy referable to the holding of an office. But where as in the present case the only circumstances are that residential accommodation is offered and accepted with exclusive possession for a term at a rent, the result is a tenancy.

The position was well summarised by Windeyer J sitting in the High Court of Australia in *Radaich v Smith* (1959) 101 CLR 209, 222, where he said:

> '. . . And he cannot be other than a tenant, because a legal right of exclusive possession is a tenancy and the creation of such a right is a demise. To say that a man who has by agreement with a landlord, a right of exclusive possession of land for a term is not a tenant is simply to contradict the first proposition by the second. A right of exclusive possession is secured by the right of a lessee to maintain ejectment and, after his entry, trespass . . .'

Comment

(1) The basis for the present law is to be found in this speech: specific aspects of it will be considered in the sections below.

(2) It is interesting that only four earlier decisions are overruled (*Somma* was one of them). Were the other earlier cases convincingly distinguished by Lord Templeman?

(3) How persuasive is the argument that the distinction between leases and licences becomes 'wholly unidentifiable' if exclusive possession is not conclusive? How compelling is the colourful analogy of spades and forks? Is it arguable that a licence is a generic category capable of comprising very different rights – a gardening tool?

(4) A general question is how far the courts normally force legal categories (contracts and trusts, for example) on to people who do not wish to enter them. Judging by the reasoning in *Street*, would parties be able to agree that a right capable of being an easement should be a licence? The Court of Appeal has had no problems in deciding that there can be a licence in such cases:[10] what does this tell us about the reasoning in *Street*?

(5) Lord Templeman stresses that the result is not based upon the Rent Acts. Is this credible?

(6) The earlier cases, and in particular Lord Denning, stressed that the parties could not turn a lease into a licence. What difference is there between the reasoning in these cases and that in *Street*?

Whatever the merits of its analysis, *Street* certainly represents the starting point for modern analyses of this area: it was resoundingly reaffirmed by the House of Lords in *AG Securities v Vaughan*.[11] As will be seen later, however, *AG Securities* places more stress on the policy of the legislation protecting tenants.

One point of interest is that *Street* has been applied to commercial tenancies,[12] where the statutory protection is weaker and the need to prevent contracting out of statutory protection is much less compelling.

Extract 14.1.9

National Car Parks Ltd v *Trinity Development Co (Banbury) Ltd* [2002] 2 P&CR 253

A question arose whether a right to operate a car park amounted to a licence.

ARDEN LJ: 26. ... The court must, of course, look at the substance but, as I see it, it does not follow from that that what the parties have said is totally irrelevant and to be disregarded. For my part, I would agree with the judge that some attention must be given to the terms which the parties have agreed. On the other hand it must be approached with healthy scepticism, particularly, for instance, if the parties' bargaining positions are asymmetrical.

28.   So the court must look to the substance and not to the form. But it may help, in determining what the substance was, to consider whether the parties expressed themselves in a particular way. Of course I bear in mind in *Street* v *Mountford* that the apparent effect of an agreement which, it was common ground, conferred exclusive possession on the occupier, was to create a tenancy on that ground. It would in my judgment be a strong thing for the law to disregard totally the parties' choice of wording and to do so would be inconsistent with the general principle of freedom of contract and the principle that documents should be interpreted as a whole. On the other hand, I agree with Mr Furber's submission that it does not give rise to any presumption. At most it is relevant as a pointer.

Comment

(1) Similarly, Jonathan Parker LJ has stated:[13]

> ... this was a contract negotiated between two substantial parties of equal bargaining power and with the benefit of full legal advice. Where the contract so negotiated contains not merely

---

[10] *IDC Group Ltd* v *Clark* (1992) 65 P&CR 179; Hill (1996) 16 LS 200 at pp 200–208.
[11] [1990] 1 AC 417; see Extract 14.1.22 below.
[12] *University of Reading* v *Johnson-Houghton* [1985] 2 EGLR 113; *Dellneed Ltd* v *Chin* (1986) 53 P&CR 172; *London & Associated Investment Trust plc* v *Calow* [1986] 2 EGLR 80; *Colchester BC* v *Smith* [1991] Ch 448 at p 484 (upheld [1992] Ch 421 on other grounds).
[13] *Clear Channel UK Ltd* v *Manchester City Council* [2006] L&TR 93 at [29].

a label but a clause which sets out in unequivocal terms the parties' intention as to its legal effect, I would in any event have taken some persuading that its true effect was directly contrary to that expressed intention.

The context was that of advertising hoardings, in which exclusive possession was not obvious.

(2) Would this analysis apply to residential agreements? Mummery LJ has said that:[14]

> . . . a rent-free arrangement for the exclusive use and occupation of premises would not create a tenancy, if the correct inference from the purpose of the arrangement and the surrounding circumstances was that there was no intention to create the landlord and tenant relationship between the parties.

(3) Does the cumulative effect of these cases reflect a movement against the approach in *Street* v *Mountford*?

(iii) Shams; lodgers

It will be recalled that *Street* castigated as a sham the provision in *Somma* that the occupiers should share with others the double bedsitting room: the reality was that it was suitable only for the two of them living as a couple. Subsequent cases adopted the following definition by Diplock LJ[15] of a sham:

> I apprehend that, if it has any meaning in law, it means acts done or documents executed by the parties to the 'sham' which are intended by them to give to third parties or to the court the appearance of creating between the parties legal rights and obligations different from the actual legal rights and obligations (if any) which the parties intend to create. But one thing, I think, is clear in legal principle, morality and the authorities . . . that for acts or documents to be a 'sham', with whatever legal consequences follow from this, all the parties thereto must have a common intention that the acts or documents are not to create the legal rights and obligations which they give the appearance of creating.

Extract 14.1.10

AG Securities v *Vaughan* [1990] 1 AC 417

LORD TEMPLEMAN: . . . It would have been more accurate and less liable to give rise to mis-understandings if [in *Street*] I had substituted the word 'pretence' for the references to 'sham devices' and 'artificial transactions'. *Street* v *Mountford* was not a case which involved a pretence concerning exclusive possession . . .

The fact that clause 16 was a pretence appears from its terms and from the negotiations. Clause 16 in terms conferred on Mr Antoniades [the landlord] and other persons the right to share the bedroom occupied by Mr Villiers and Miss Bridger. Clause 16 conferred power on Mr Antoniades to convert the sitting-room occupied by Mr Villiers and Miss Bridger into a bedroom which could be jointly occupied by Mr Villiers, Miss Bridger, Mr Antoniades and any person or persons nominated by Mr Antoniades. The facilities in the flat were not suitable for sharing between strangers. The flat, situated in an attic with a sloping roof, was too small for sharing between strangers . . . The addendum imposed on Mr Villiers and Miss Bridger sought to add plausibility to the pretence of sharing by forfeiting the right of Mr Villiers and Miss Bridger

---

[14] *Vesely* v *Levy* [2008] L&TR 153 at [49] (trustees allowed a friend of a beneficiary into possession). See also Extract 14.1.15 below.

[15] *Snook* v *London & West Riding Investments Ltd* [1967] 2 QB 786 at p 802.

to continue to occupy the flat if their double-bedded romance blossomed into wedding bells. Finally and significantly, Mr Antoniades never made any attempt to obtain increased income from the flat by exercising the powers which clause 16 purported to reserve to him. Clause 16 was only designed to disguise the grant of a tenancy and to contract out of the Rent Acts.

LORD OLIVER: . . . But though subsequent conduct is irrelevant as an aid to construction, it is certainly admissible as evidence on the question of whether the documents were or were not genuine documents giving effect to the parties' true intentions. Broadly what is said by Mr Colyer is that nobody acquainted with the circumstances in which the parties had come together and with the physical lay-out and size of the premises could seriously have imagined that the clauses in the licence which, on the face of them, contemplate the respondent and an apparently limitless number of other persons moving in to share the whole of the available accommodation, including the bedroom, with what, to all intents and purposes, was a married couple committed to paying £174 a month in advance, were anything other than a smoke-screen; and the fact the respondent, who might be assumed to want to make the maximum profit out of the premises, never sought to introduce anyone else is at least some indication that that is exactly what it was . . .

. . . I read [the judge's] finding that, 'the licences are artificial transactions designed to evade the Rent Acts' as a finding that they were sham documents designed to conceal the true nature of the transaction.

Comment

(1) *AG Securities* will be studied in more detail below[16] in the context of joint occupiers.

(2) What is the difference between sham and pretence?[17] Where does Lord Oliver stand on this issue?

Several cases have discussed shams in the context of purported lodging agreements.

Extract 14.1.11

Aslan v *Murphy* [1990] 1 WLR 766

LORD DONALDSON MR:

General principles

The status of a tenant is essentially different from that of a lodger and owners of property are free to make accommodation available on either basis. Which basis applies in any particular case depends upon what was the true bargain between the parties. It is the ascertainment of that true bargain which lies at the heart of the problem.

. . .

Exclusive or non-exclusive occupation

This is the touchstone by which the 'spade' of tenancy falls to be distinguished from the 'fork' of lodging. In this context it is necessary to consider the rights and duties of the person making the accommodation available ('the owner') and the rights of other occupiers. The occupier has in the end to be a tenant or a lodger. He cannot be both. But there is a spectrum of exclusivity

---

[16] See Extract 14.1.22.
[17] See Bright [2002] CLJ 146; McFarlane and Simpson in *Rationalizing Property, Equity and Trusts* (ed Getzler), Chapter 8.

ranging from the occupier of a detached property under a full repairing lease, who is without doubt a tenant, to the overnight occupier of a hotel bedroom who, however up-market the hotel, is without doubt a lodger. The dividing line – the sorting of the forks from the spades – will not necessarily or even usually depend upon a single factor, but upon a combination of factors.

Pretences

Quite apart from labelling, parties may succumb to the temptation to agree to pretend to have particular rights and duties which are not in fact any part of the true bargain. Prima facie, the parties must be taken to mean what they say, but given the pressures on both parties to pretend, albeit for different reasons, the courts would be acting unrealistically if they did not keep a weather eye open for pretences, taking due account of how the parties have acted in perform-ance of their apparent bargain. This identification and exposure of such pretences does not necessarily lead to the conclusion that their agreement is a sham, but only to the conclusion that the terms of the true bargain are not wholly the same as those of the bargain appearing on the face of the agreement. It is the true rather than the apparent bargain which determines the question 'tenant or lodger?'

. . .

Aslan v Murphy (No 1)

The defendant was the occupier of room 2A at 54, Redcliffe Gardens, London, SW10. It is a basement room measuring 4′3″ by 12′6″. He occupied this room under an agreement which recited:

> 'the licensor is not willing to grant the licensee exclusive possession of any part of the room hereinafter referred to [and] the licensee is anxious to secure the use of the room notwith-standing that such use be in common with the licensor and such other licensees or invitees as the licensor may permit . . .'

The introduction to the operative part of the agreement provided:

> 'By this licence the licensor licences the licensee to use (but not exclusively) all the furnished room . . . on each day between the hours of midnight and 10.30 a.m. and between noon and midnight, but at no other times . . .'

The judge was, of course, quite right to approach the matter on this basis that it is not a crime, nor is it contrary to public policy, for a property owner to license occupiers to occupy a property on terms which do not give rise to a tenancy. Where he went wrong was in considering whether the whole agreement was a sham and, having concluded that it was not, giving effect to its terms, i.e. taking it throughout at face value. What he should have done, and I am sure would have done if he had known of the House of Lords approach to the problem, was to consider whether the whole agreement was a sham and, if it was not, whether in the light of the factual situation the provisions for sharing the room and those depriving the defendant of the right to occupy it for 90 minutes out of each 24 hours were part of the true bargain between the parties or were pretences. Both provisions were wholly unrealistic and were clearly pretences.

In this court an attempt to uphold the judge's decision was made upon a different basis, namely, the landlord's right to retain the keys . . . Provisions as to keys are often relied upon in support of the contention that an occupier is a lodger rather than a tenant. Thus in *Duke* v *Wynne*, to which we turn next, the agreement required the occupier 'not to interfere with or change the locks on any part of the premises, [or] give the key to any other than an authorised occupier of the premises'. Provisions as to keys, if not a pretence which they often are, do not have any magic in themselves. It is not a requirement of a tenancy that the occupier shall have exclusive possession of the keys to the property. What matters is what underlies the provisions as to keys. Why does the owner want a key, want to prevent keys being issued to the friends of the occupier or want to prevent the lock being changed?

A landlord may well need a key in order that he may be able to enter quickly in the event of emergency: fire, burst pipes or whatever. He may need a key to enable him or those authorised by him to read meters or to do repairs which are his responsibility. None of these underlying reasons would of themselves indicate that the true bargain between the parties was such that the occupier was in law a lodger. On the other hand, if the true bargain is that the owner will provide genuine services which can only be provided by having keys, such as frequent cleaning, daily bed-making, the provision of clean linen at regular intervals and the like, there are materials from which it is possible to infer that the occupier is a lodger rather than a tenant. But the inference arises not from the provisions as to keys, but from the reason why those provisions formed part of the bargain . . .

Duke v *Wynne* . . .

. . .

Were the defendants tenants or lodgers? Unlike the facts in *Aslan* v *Murphy (No 1)* it would have been possible for them to have shared the house with another occupant. There were three bedrooms. One could have been used by the defendants, one by the children and the third, which was a very small room, by a lodger. However, the evidence did not disclose any immediate intention on the part of the plaintiff to make such an arrangement and she never in fact did so. Meanwhile, the defendants in fact occupied the whole house. In cases such as this the court has to determine whether the true bargain is that the occupiers are entitled to exclusive possession of the premises, unless and until the owner requires them to share, or whether the true bargain is that their entitlement is only to their share in the right to occupy, although, as there is currently no other occupant, it will be impracticable and unreasonable to seek to prevent their de facto occupation of the whole premises. If the former is the case and, for the time being, they have an entitlement to exclusive occupation, they are tenants and their status cannot at some future date be unilaterally converted into that of lodgers by the owner requiring them to share their occupation: *Antoniades* v *Villiers* [1990] AC 417. If the latter is the case, they never achieve the status of tenants.

In the instant appeal it is quite clear that the true bargain was that the defendants should be entitled to exclusive occupation unless and until the plaintiff wanted to exercise her right to authorise someone else to move in as a lodger and she never suggested that this was a serious possibility . . .

But the situation could have been different. If the plaintiff had determined to have two couples as lodgers, she might not have been able to find them simultaneously. The first couple might have de facto occupation of the whole house meanwhile, but could not have claimed to be tenants since the plaintiff would de jure herself have been a co-occupier until the second pair of lodgers arrived. Applying the test of what was the true bargain between the parties, the court would have wanted to know what steps (if any) were being taken by the owner to fill the vacancy. If the owner was not actively seeking another occupant, it would be inherently more likely that the first couple were *entitled* to [exclusive] possession of the whole in the meanwhile and so were tenants.

Comment

(1) Does the possession of keys have any significance?

(2) Why was there a lease in *Duke* v *Wynne*? Is this an example of a pretence?

Following *Street*, many potential landlords were tempted to make their occupiers lodgers. While terms designed artificially to deny exclusive possession are clearly ineffective, genuine lodger transactions are effective as licences. But how onerous must the landlord's obligations be in order to succeed in circumventing *Street*?

Extract 14.1.12

Markou v *Da Silvaesa* (1986) 52 P&CR 204

RALPH GIBSON LJ: . . . This agreement requires the landlord to provide attendance and services for the licensee but – and I shall return to this point later in this judgment – the obligation to provide attendance and services is not conclusive that the occupier is a licensee: provision of the attendance or services must, as set out in Lord Templeman's speech, require the landlord or his servants to exercise unrestricted access to and use of the premises . . . Clause 9 of the agreement does not specify the extent or frequency of the attendance or services to be provided, and this is an aspect of the written agreement upon which all these appellants have relied in submitting that the agreement by itself could not be shown to require 'unrestricted' access to and over the premises. The task of the court in applying the principles laid down in *Street* v *Mountford* is not that of applying the words of a statute. I take the meaning of the word 'unrestricted' in this context to be primarily concerned with the landlord's need to go into and out of the lodger's rooms at the convenience of the landlord and without the lodger being there to let the landlord in. The amount and frequency of the attendance and services agreed to be provided are relevant but the question to be answered is whether, in all the circumstances, having regard to the landlord's obligations, it is clear that the landlord requires unrestricted access and has reserved the right to exercise such access in order to look after the house and the furniture. Where an agreement describes attendance and services, as in this case, without specifying the extent or frequency of them, the court may and, as I think, should treat the agreement as imposing upon the landlord an obligation to provide the attendance and services to an extent and frequency and standard which are in all the circumstances reasonable. Such a standard upon the material before the learned judge in this appeal could not be regarded as either extensive or elaborate; it would be of the order of removing rubbish daily or at least every other day, cleaning once a week and laundering sheets fortnightly . . .

. . . If it should appear to the court, after consideration of all the evidence, that, from the making of the agreement, and with reference to an earlier agreement in similar terms between Mr Silvaesa and the landlords, no cleaning of the flat by the landlord had been carried out or offered, and that the laundering of bed linen and removal of rubbish had been carried out without exercise of or need for any right of access to the room, then it might be open to the court to conclude that the true agreement between the parties did not require unrestricted access to and use of the premises by the landlord so as to cause these appellants to be lodgers and not tenants . . .

Comment

(1) Can a landlord avoid *Street* by accepting minimal obligations?

(2) In *Markou*, summary judgment in favour of the landlord was refused. This was partly because other terms in the agreement (especially those providing for vacating the flat for 90 minutes each day) were shams: this cast doubts on the status of all the provisions. It provides an example of bad provisions infecting an agreement which might otherwise seem impregnable.

Extract 14.1.13

Huwyler v *Ruddy* (1995) 28 HLR 550

PETER GIBSON LJ: . . . It will be noted that the agreement was in respect of 'the room' in flat 7 . . . Services were provided in the form of laundry of bed linen and cleaning the room. An estimate was given of the time occupied in performing the cleaning service, and that was found to be 20 minutes per week.

The plaintiff's brother who at one time had a room in the flat was the person who performed that service. He would clean the room at a time which was not inconvenient to the defendant and would remove the rubbish and produce the clean linen. All the rooms had locks on the door and we were told that the defendant had a key right from the start for his room, but so did the plaintiff's brother who was, therefore, able to enter the room to perform the cleaning services which I have indicated.

. . .

The judge found that the services which had been provided wound down gradually. In 1990 the defendant wrote a letter to Camden Council complaining of the rent that he was required to pay. By then, the rent had been increased to £65 per week, apparently because of the Community Charge, and the defendant pointed out that he was no longer obtaining services that he had originally obtained from the plaintiff. The judge found that subsequently there was a discussion between the defendant and the plaintiff's brother and what the judge called a *modus vivendi* was reached between them that the defendant would do his own cleaning.

. . .

Mr Carrott [counsel for the defendant] drew attention to one sentence in the speech of Lord Templeman at page 818A where this was said:

'The occupier is a lodger if the landlord provides attendance or services which require the landlord or his servants to exercise unrestricted access to and use of the premises.'

Mr Carrott submitted that the judge should have made an express finding as to unrestricted access. I do not agree. For my part I do not regard that statement by Lord Templeman as meaning that it is only where the landlord provides attendance or services requiring the landlord to exercise unrestricted access that the occupier is a lodger . . .

In the present case, if one looks at the rights and obligations of the defendant and the plaintiff in relation to room A, it seems to me that, as the judge said about the obligation to provide services to the defendant, the plaintiff was obliged to be able to get into room A as and when necessary, although obviously he respected the privacy of the defendant. In my judgment the plaintiff, by his obligation to provide service in the form of cleaning, did have unrestricted access in the sense indicated. Of course, if the purpose of the access was so trivial as to make the obligation a sham, then the Court could disregard such right and obligation. But I cannot see how that could be said of the obligation in the present case.

. . .

[On the winding down and eventual cesser of services:] Thus the judge was saying that, as a matter of contractual entitlement, there was only a forbearance by the defendant in requiring the performance of the services, and that was a matter which was agreed with the plaintiff. But it does not follow (and the judge is certainly not implying) that the defendant could not have insisted on the resumption of the services. It seems to me that there is no reason why, at any stage, he could not have asked that the contractual services be resumed.

When we are considering whether or not there is an agreement or a licence, in my judgment we must look at the contractual position between the parties. I respectfully agree with the judge that as a matter of contract, therefore, the position did not change either when the defendant moved to room C or subsequently when the *modus vivendi* was reached.

Comment

(1) Would Lord Templeman have approved of this result?

(2) Are the analyses of unrestricted access in *Markou* and *Huwyler* the same?

(3) Is the stress on contractual entitlement in *Huwyler* consistent with *Aslan*?

Similar principles have been applied in relation to hostel accommodation.

Extract 14.1.14

Westminster City Council v *Clarke* [1992] 2 AC 288

In the discharge of their statutory duties, the council ran a hostel for the homeless.

LORD TEMPLEMAN: . . . From the point of view of the council the grant of exclusive possession would be inconsistent with the purposes for which the council provided the accommodation at Cambridge Street. It was in the interests of Mr Clarke and each of the occupiers of the hostel that the council should retain possession of each room. If one room became uninhabitable another room could be shared between two occupiers. If one room became unsuitable for an occupier he could be moved elsewhere. If the occupier of one room became a nuisance he could be compelled to move to another room where his actions might be less troublesome to his neighbours. If the occupier of a room had exclusive possession he could prevent the council from entering the room save for the purpose of protecting the council's interests and not for the purpose of supervising and controlling the conduct of the occupier in his interests. If the occupier of a room had exclusive possession he could not be obliged to comply with the terms and the conditions of occupation. Mr Clarke could not, for example, be obliged to comply with the directions of the warden or to exclude visitors or to comply with any of the other conditions of occupation which are designed to help Mr Clarke and the other occupiers of the hostel and to enable the hostel to be conducted in an efficient and harmonious manner . . . In the circumstances of the present case I consider that the council legitimately and effectively retained for themselves possession of room E and that Mr Clarke was only a licensee with rights corresponding to the rights of a lodger. In reaching this conclusion I take into account the object of the council, namely the provision of accommodation for vulnerable homeless persons, the necessity for the council to retain possession of all the rooms in order to make and administer arrangements for the suitable accommodation of all the occupiers and the need for the council to retain possession of every room not only in the interests of the council as the owners of the terrace but also for the purpose of providing for the occupiers supervision and assistance. For many obvious reasons it was highly undesirable for the council to grant to any occupier of a room exclusive possession which obstructed the use by the council of all the rooms of the hostel in the interests of every occupier . . .

This is a very special case which depends on the peculiar nature of the hostel maintained by the council, the use of the hostel by the council, the totality, immediacy, and objectives of the powers exercisable by the council and the restrictions imposed on Mr Clarke. The decision in this case will not allow a landlord, private or public, to free himself from the Rent Acts or from the restrictions of a secure tenancy merely by adopting or adapting the language of the licence to occupy.

Comment

How does this fit with Lord Templeman's dictum in *Street* that the occupier of residential premises will be either a tenant or a lodger?

The application of *Street* to public sector landlords was confirmed by Lord Hoffmann in *Bruton* v *London & Quadrant Housing Trust*:[18]

> Mr Henderson, who appeared for the trust, submitted that there were 'special circumstances' in this case which enabled one to construe the agreement as a licence despite the presence of all the characteristics identified in *Street* v *Mountford* [1985] AC 809. These circumstances were that the trust was a responsible landlord performing socially valuable functions, it had agreed with the council not to grant tenancies, Mr Bruton had agreed that he was not to have a tenancy and the trust had no estate out of which it could grant one.

---

[18] [2000] 1 AC 406 at p 414.

In my opinion none of these circumstances can make an agreement to grant exclusive possession something other than a tenancy. The character of the landlord is irrelevant because although the Rent Acts and other Landlord and Tenant Acts do make distinctions between different kinds of landlords, it is not by saying that what would be a tenancy if granted by one landlord will be something else if granted by another.

Extract 14.1.15

Camden LBC v Shortlife Community Housing Ltd (1992) 25 HLR 330

MILLETT J: . . . Did the parties intend SCH to be granted a legal right to exclusive possession of any of the flats? Their professed intention, plainly demonstrated by the terms of the documents, was that it should not. Any right to exclusive possession was clearly and unequivocally excluded. Unless the parties' professed intention differed from their true intention, or failed to reflect 'the true substance of the real transaction', this is conclusive . . .

There were sound reasons for the Council not granting SCH exclusive possession of the flats. Indeed, the suggestion that it did intend such a grant has something of an air of unreality. The flats were council flats due for imminent demolition or rehabilitation. They had only recently been vacated by council tenants to enable the works to be undertaken. The Council was making interim arrangements. In the short time for which the flats were to be made available to the homeless, it obviously did not intend them to be occupied by tenants; if it did it would not have gone to the trouble of decanting its existing tenants. It was not intending merely to replace one kind of tenant by another. It was recovering possession of part of its housing stock which was due for renewal; and rather than leave properties empty or occupied by squatters, it was making them available for short-term occupancy by persons in housing need, but, without divesting itself of the right to possession which it had only just resumed. The only alternative courses of action which the Council contemplated were to leave the properties empty or to suffer them to be occupied by squatters. That alone indicates its determination to retain possession in itself.

Comment

(1) Is the stress on the legitimate needs of the landlord consistent with *Street*?

(2) Would the result have been the same if there had been a private landlord?

Next, a point on terminology should be considered.

Extract 14.1.16

Hill (1989) 52 MLR 408 at p 410 (footnotes omitted)

In principle there is an important difference between 'exclusive possession' and 'exclusive occupation': exclusive possession is determined by reference to the parties' rights, whereas exclusive occupation is a question of fact. The significance of the distinction can be illustrated by a simple example: a lodger will often have exclusive occupation of the room which he occupies, but he does not enjoy the right to exclusive possession since the owner 'provides attendance or services which require the landlord or his servant to exercise unrestricted access to and use of the premises'. It is for this reason that a lodger is not a tenant.

In recent years there has been a regrettable tendency for some judges to use the expressions exclusive possession and exclusive occupation interchangeably. For example, Lord Templeman, having clearly stated in *Street* v *Mountford* that exclusive possession is a prerequisite of a tenancy, employs the phrase exclusive occupation throughout his speech in *AG Securities* v

Vaughan and *Antoniades v Villiers*. For the most part such variations in terminology do not signify intentional changes of substance, and opportunities for reaching incorrect results are limited since occupation and possession will often go hand in hand. However, the potential for incorrect analysis is serious, as Lord Templeman's speech in *Antoniades v Villiers* reveals.

Comment

(1) The interchanging of the terms is apparent in many of the cases: it is unsafe to draw conclusions from the language used.

(2) The lodger cases can of course be explained quite neatly by the absence of exclusive possession. Given that they clearly give rise to licences, does it matter whether we use the language of exclusive occupation?

A final issue in this section concerns a specific problem for shams. Suppose A leases land to B in order that it can be enjoyed by C. The reason for the lease to B (normally a company) is to take advantage of an exemption whereby the statutory protection of tenants is inapplicable. The question, unlike in the other cases in this section, is not whether there is a lease or a licence, but whether the underlying reality of possession by C should be recognised by treating the situation as if A had leased directly to C.

Extract 14.1.17

Hilton v Plustitle Ltd [1989] 1 WLR 149

CROOM-JOHNSON LJ: . . . In the present case the judge found as a fact that it was the intention of both parties, with all knowledge of what this involved, that the flat should be let to the company and not to Miss Rose personally. This finding has not been challenged. Directing himself in accordance with the law as stated by Diplock LJ in the *Snook* case, he held that this transaction was not a sham. We do not find it possible to fault this reasoning.

. . .

Mr Walter has relied on the decision in *Gisborne v Burton* [1988] 3 WLR 921. The Court of Appeal (Dillon and Russell LJJ, Ralph Gibson LJ dissenting) held that the head lease to the wife was a sham and that the subtenant was in reality the tenant and he was entitled to the protection of the Agricultural Holdings Acts, notwithstanding that he had fully understood that the whole purpose of the transaction was to avoid his having such security.

Dillon LJ dealt with the facts as being analogous to those in *Johnson v Moreton* [1980] AC 37. In *Johnson's* case the agricultural tenant had entered into a covenant not to serve a counter-notice under the Agricultural Holdings Act 1948. The House of Lords held that to allow such a covenant to be effective would be contrary to public interest as defeating the purpose for which the Act had been passed. It was not possible for tenants to contract out of the protection which Parliament had intended that they should have. The covenant was therefore unenforceable. Dillon LJ compared *Gisborne's* case with *Johnson's* case. He concluded that the inclusion of the landlord's wife in the series of leases had the effect at the highest of making her

> 'a mere nominee or agent of [the husband] to grant a tenancy to [Mr Burton], and what actually happened was that [the husband] granted such a tenancy': [1988] 3 WLR 921, 928

. . . Dillon LJ also took into account the recent tax cases based on *W T Ramsay Ltd v Inland Revenue Commissioners* [1982] AC 300, such as *Furniss v Dawson* [1984] AC 474, where it was stated that the fiscal consequences of a series of transactions should be examined. Dillon LJ said, at p 927:

'It seems to me that a similar principle must be applicable wherever there is a pre-ordained series of transactions which is intended to avoid some mandatory statutory provision, even if not of a fiscal nature. You must look at the effect of the scheme as a whole . . .'

It was in applying that test that Dillon LJ concluded that the landlord's wife had been only the agent of the landlord.

. . .

In the present case, the company was not the plaintiff's agent. It was the only tenant to whom he was prepared to let the property, and the covenants in the lease were perfectly capable of being complied with by the company through its nominee, Miss Rose, and enforced against the company by the plaintiff. Unlike *Street* v *Mountford* the transaction did represent the true position . . .

We conclude that if the facts are consistent with the purported transaction, we see no reason why, by analogy with *Gisborne's* case, public policy should override the transaction which was deliberately intended to avoid, but not evade, the Rent Acts . . .

Comment

(1) Could this be viewed as a pretence within *Street*?

(2) Despite criticism,[19] the decision has the support of the Court of Appeal in *Belvedere Court Management Ltd* v *Frogmore Developments Ltd*:[20]

> There was no element of pretence, as there was in *Gisborne* v *Burton* [1989] QB 390. The parties were not doing one thing and saying another. I would also accept the judge's view that the Atherton leases were an artificial device intended to circumvent a result the Act would otherwise have brought about. But . . . I am not for my part satisfied that in the field of real property the principles in *Ramsay* and *Furniss* entitle the court simply to ignore or override apparently effective transactions which on their face confer an interest in land on the transferee. Many transactions between group companies may be artificial.

(3) The taxation cases have more recently been analysed as being based on statutory interpretation,[21] which makes it more difficult to apply them in the leases context.

(iv) Exceptional categories

The courts have been resistant to creating new categories beyond those listed by Lord Templeman in *Street*, not even recognising an exception for short-term possession given under statutory duties to the homeless.[22] The House of Lords has held in *Bruton* v *London & Quadrant Housing Trust*[23] that there will still be a lease even though the landlord does not have an estate in the land. This controversial aspect of *Bruton* is considered in the following chapter.

(a) Purchasers in possession prior to completion

The question here is whether the purchaser is a tenant at will[24] or a licensee (as stated by Denning LJ in *Errington*). Our first case links this category with a more general description of the exceptional categories.

---

[19] Sparkes (1989) 52 MLR 557; Bright (1991) 11 OxJLS 136, but cf [2002] CLJ 146.

[20] [1997] QB 858 at p 876.

[21] *Barclays Mercantile Business Finance Ltd* v *Mawson* [2005] 1 AC 684.

[22] *Family Housing Association* v *Jones* [1990] 1 WLR 779, approved (with some regret) in *Bruton* v *London & Quadrant Housing Trust* [2000] 1 AC 406 at pp 410, 412, 414: see p 482 above.

[23] [2000] 1 AC 406; Extract 15.1.6 below. See also Extract 14.2.13 below, as regards tenancies by estoppel.

[24] *Doe d Tomes* v *Chamberlaine* (1839) 5 M&W 14 (151 ER 7); *Wheeler* v *Mercer* [1957] AC 416 at p 425.

Extract 14.1.18

Ramnarace v *Lutchman* [2001] 1 WLR 1651 (PC)

LORD MILLETT: 16. A tenancy at will is of indefinite duration, but in all other respects it shares the characteristics of a tenancy. As Lord Templeman observed [in *Street* v *Mountford*] [1985] AC 809, 818, there can be no tenancy unless the occupier enjoys exclusive possession; but the converse is not necessarily true. An occupier who enjoys exclusive possession is not necessarily a tenant. He may be the freehold owner, a trespasser, a mortgagee in possession, an object of charity or a service occupier. Exclusive possession of land may be referable to a legal relationship other than a tenancy or to the absence of any legal relationship at all. A purchaser who is allowed into possession before completion and an occupier who remains in possession pending the exercise of an option each has in equity an immediate interest in the land to which his possession is ancillary. They are not tenants at will: see *Essex Plan Ltd* v *Broadminster* (1988) 56 P&CR 353, 356 per Hoffmann J.

17. A person cannot be a tenant at will where it appears from the surrounding circumstances that there was no intention to create legal relations. A tenancy is a legal relationship; it cannot be created by a transaction which is not intended to create legal relations. This provides a principled rationalisation of the statement of Denning LJ in *Facchini* v *Bryson* [1952] 1 TLR 1386, 1389 on which the Court of Appeal relied in the present case. Before an occupier who is in exclusive occupation of land can be treated as holding under a licence and not a tenancy there must be something in the circumstances such as a family arrangement, an act of friendship or generosity or suchlike, to negative any intention to create legal relations.

18. . . . But a tenancy at will commonly arises where a person is allowed into possession while the parties negotiate the terms of a lease or purchase. He has no interest in the land to which his possession can be referred, and if in exclusive and rent-free possession is a tenant at will. In *Hagee (London) Ltd* v *AB Erikson and Larson* [1976] QB 209, 217 Scarman LJ described this as one of the 'classic circumstances' in which a tenancy at will arose.

Comment

(1) What is the relationship between tenancies at will and licences?

(2) It appears that a person negotiating a sale or lease will, if allowed into possession, be a tenant at will. If the negotiations are concluded, there will be a licence until the sale or lease is completed. What reasons are there for this contrast? Does it make sense?

(b) Owners, mortgagees and trespassers

Generally speaking, these categories are not controversial and cause little difficulty. However, questions can arise as to whether a person who enters as a trespasser has subsequently been accepted as a tenant.

Extract 14.1.19

Westminster City Council v *Basson* (1990) 62 P&CR 57

The defendant entered as the lover of the tenant, who had since left the premises.

MUSTILL LJ: . . . I now return to the letter of September 27, 1985, which has been the focal point of this appeal. As has been recorded, it begins with the words,

> 'I refer to your unlawful occupation of the above accommodation and confirm that legal proceedings have been instigated for the recovery of vacant possession of the dwelling.'

These words are plainly inconsistent with any notion that the appellant was in occupation of the premises with the consent of the council. It is however argued by Mr Macpherson on her behalf that the effect of that first paragraph is nullified by what followed. I need not read it again, but Mr Macpherson submits that we here find the office making administrative arrangements in advance for the payment of monetary consideration labelled 'Use and Occupation charges'. That expression is an accurate description of sums paid in respect of a tenancy. It is not apt terminology, so the submission goes, for amounts payable by a trespasser. Thus, it is submitted, the letter must have been intended to communicate the consent of the Westminster Council to the appellant's continued occupation of the premises. Accordingly we have present all three indicia of a tenancy, recognised in *Street* v *Mountford*, namely the grant of permission to occupy, exclusive occupation and regular payment referrable to that occupation.

That argument would have had at least something to commend it if the letter had not begun in the way which I have described and if it had not ended with the words:

'In making the payments as Use and Occupation Charges this arrangement is not intended as the creation of a tenancy or a Licence akin to a tenancy in any way whatsoever.'

. . . The council was saying this:

'We desire you to vacate the premises. We trust that you will do so voluntarily. If not we shall take steps to remove you. Meanwhile we are not going to let you remain there free of charge and to make sure that we are paid we shall expect to receive payment at the stated rate in the stated manner until we succeed in regaining possession.'

Speaking for myself, I feel no doubt that this letter is entirely inconsistent with the proposition that the appellant was remaining in the council premises with the consent of the council.

Comment

(1) This was unaffected by the subsequent issue of a rent book and assessment of a claim for rent rebate, Mustill LJ observing that 'these merely show that one department of the council was not fully aware of what was happening in the other departments'. Is this being unduly generous to the council?

(2) There were numerous cases on 'tolerated trespassers' in public sector housing, where a tenancy had been terminated but the tenant not evicted. Fortunately, this odd and trouble-some category no longer exists.[25]

(c) Service occupiers

Extract 14.1.20

Norris v *Checksfield* [1991] 1 WLR 1241

WOOLF LJ: . . . Mr Zeidman submitted that an employee can be a licensee, although his occupation of the premises is not *necessary* for the purposes of the employment, if he is genuinely *required* to occupy the premises for the *better performance* of his duties. In my judgment this submission accurately reflects the law . . .

As Mr Seaward correctly submitted, it would not suffice if the occupation was a 'fringe benefit' or merely an inducement to encourage the employee to work better. Unless the occupation fulfilled this test, the fact that the employee had exclusive possession and paid rent would almost inevitably establish a service tenancy: see generally *Street* v *Mountford* [1985] AC 809 and *AG Securities* v *Vaughan* [1990] 1 AC 417, 459, *per* Lord Templeman.

---

[25] Housing and Regeneration Act 2008, s 299 and Sched 11; *Knowsley Housing Trust* v *White* [2009] AC 636.

. . . In my judgment it would not be sensible, unless compelled to do so, to restrict an employer's ability to grant a licence to situations where the employment which would be benefited by the employee taking up occupation commenced simultaneously with or prior to the occupation of the premises. There may be many circumstances where it would be desirable for the employee to take up occupation before the relevant work commenced . . . If for some reason it becomes apparent that the employee is not going to be able to fulfil the requirements of that employment within a reasonable time, then the position may be different . . .

Comment

The cases before *Street* revealed some loosening of the requirements. It now seems that the law has reverted to its original state.[26]

(d) An object of charity

The cases discussed in *Street* provide good examples of this category.

Extract 14.1.21

Colchester BC v Smith [1991] Ch 448

On the termination of a lease, renewal was refused but the occupier was allowed to continue to occupy the land (together with other land) rent free until the end of the year.

FERRIS J: . . . Although in this case the council did, in my judgment, grant exclusive possession to Mr Tillson it did not do so at a rent and only in a limited sense can it be said to have done so for a term. In my view the rejection of Mr Tillson's implied offer to pay a reasonable rent, the expression of the transaction in terms of non-objection to continued occupation as distinct from grant, the insistence that Mr Tillson must occupy at his own risk and must give up possession at short notice if the land were required for other purposes, all point towards this being an exceptional transaction, not intended to give rise to legal obligations on either side.

Comment

(1) Ferris J's decision was upheld on other grounds in the Court of Appeal.[27]

(2) Is this really a case of charity?

(3) Would it suffice to prove that the rent is deliberately well below market levels?[28]

(4) Would it suffice if a charity charges no rent to beneficiaries of the charity, but instead charges them for maintenance and services?[29]

(v) Joint occupiers

Frequently, houses and flats are occupied by two or more persons. There is no difficulty in finding that the occupiers jointly enjoy exclusive possession where there is an arrangement for them to live together and jointly to be responsible for the rent. At the other end of the spectrum, there may be occupiers not living together, where the landlord leaves it up to them to decide who shall use which rooms; typically, they will not each be responsible for the entire rent.

---

[26] *See Royal Philanthropic Society v County* [1985] 2 EGLR 109.
[27] [1992] Ch 421.
[28] *See Royal Philanthropic Society v County* [1985] 2 EGLR 109 (landlord was occupier's employer).
[29] *Gray v Taylor* [1998] 1 WLR 1093 (almshouses).

Extract 14.1.22

AG Securities v *Vaughan* [1990] 1 AC 417

AG Securities, the first of two linked appeals, had facts similar to the second situation outlined above. The second appeal, *Antoniades* v *Villiers*, was closer to the first.

LORD TEMPLEMAN: . . . Parties to an agreement cannot contract out of the Rent Acts; if they were able to do so the Acts would be a dead letter because in a state of housing shortage a person seeking residential accommodation may agree to anything to obtain shelter . . . Since parties to an agreement cannot contract out of the Rent Acts, the grant of a tenancy to two persons jointly cannot be concealed, accidentally or by design, by the creation of two documents in the form of licences. Two persons seeking residential accommodation may sign any number of documents in order to obtain joint shelter. In considering one or more documents for the purpose of deciding whether a tenancy has been created, the court must consider the surrounding circumstances including any relationship between the prospective occupiers, the course of negotiations and the nature and extent of the accommodation and the intended and actual mode of occupation of the accommodation. If the owner of a one-bedroomed flat granted a licence to a husband to occupy the flat provided he shared the flat with his wife and nobody else and granted a similar licence to the wife provided she shared the flat with the husband and nobody else, the court would be bound to consider the effect of both documents together. If the licence to the husband required him to pay a licence fee of £50 per month and the licence to the wife required her to pay a further licence fee of £50 per month, the two documents read together in the light of the property to be occupied and the obvious intended mode of occupation would confer exclusive occupation on the husband and wife jointly and a tenancy at the rent of £100.

. . .

Where residential accommodation is occupied by two or more persons the occupiers may be licensees or tenants of the whole or each occupier may be a separate tenant of part. In the present appeals the only question raised is whether the occupiers are licensees or tenants of the whole.

In the first appeal under consideration the company entered into four separate agreements with four separate persons between 1982 and 1985. The agreements were in the same form save that the periodical sum payable under one agreement did not correspond to the sum payable pursuant to any other agreement. The company was not bound to make agreements in the same form or to require any payment . . . Under the standard form agreement the company did not retain power to allocate the four bedrooms but delegated this power to the occupiers for the time being. If the occupiers had failed to allocate the bedrooms the company would have been obliged to terminate one or more of the agreements. The respondents claim that they are joint tenants of the flat. No single respondent claims to be a tenant of a bedroom.

The Court of Appeal, . . . (Fox and Mustill LJJ, Sir George Waller dissenting), concluded that the four respondents were jointly entitled to exclusive occupation of the flat. I am unable to agree. If a landlord who owns a three-bedroom flat enters into three separate independent tenancies with three independent tenants each of whom is entitled to one bedroom and to share the common parts, then the three tenants, if they agree, can exclude anyone else from the flat. But they do not enjoy exclusive occupation of the flat jointly under the terms of their tenancies. In the present case, if the four respondents had been jointly entitled to exclusive occupation of the flat then, on the death of one of the respondents, the remaining three would be entitled to joint and exclusive occupation of the flat. But, in fact, on the death of one respondent the remaining three would not be entitled to joint and exclusive occupation of the flat. They could not exclude a fourth person nominated by the company. I would allow the appeal.

In the first appeal the four agreements were independent of one another. In the second appeal the two agreements were interdependent. Both would have been signed or neither. The two agreements must therefore be read together. Mr Villiers and Miss Bridger applied to rent the flat jointly and sought and enjoyed joint and exclusive occupation of the whole of the flat. They shared the rights and the obligations imposed by the terms of their occupation. They acquired joint and exclusive occupation of the flat in consideration of periodical payments and they therefore acquired a tenancy jointly. Mr Antoniades required each of them, Mr Villiers and Miss Bridger, to agree to pay one half of each aggregate periodical payment, but this circumstance cannot convert a tenancy into a licence. A tenancy remains a tenancy even though the landlord may choose to require each of two joint tenants to agree expressly to pay one half of the rent. The tenancy conferred on Mr Villiers and Miss Bridger the right to occupy the whole flat as their dwelling. Clause 16 reserved to Mr Antoniades the power at any time to go into occupation of the flat jointly with Mr Villiers and Miss Bridger. The exercise of that power would at common law put an end to the exclusive occupation of the flat by Mr Villiers and Miss Bridger, terminate the tenancy of Mr Villiers and Miss Bridger, and convert Mr Villiers and Miss Bridger into licensees. But the powers reserved to Mr Antoniades by clause 16 cannot be lawfully exercised because they are inconsistent with the provisions of the Rent Acts.

. . .

In *Hadjiloucas* v *Crean* [1988] 1 WLR 1006, two single ladies applied to take a two-roomed flat with kitchen and bathroom. Each signed an agreement to pay £260 per month to share the use of the flat with one other person. The two ladies moved into the flat and enjoyed exclusive occupation. In terms, if the agreement of one lady was terminated, the owner could require the other to share the flat with a stranger. The judge in the county court decided that the agreements only created licences. The Court of Appeal ordered a retrial in order that all the facts might be investigated. Since, however, the two ladies applied for and enjoyed exclusive occupation unless and until one of their agreements was terminated, the ladies acquired a tenancy protected by the Rent Acts. The reservation to the owner of the right at common law to require one of the ladies to share the flat with a stranger was a pretence.

LORD OLIVER: . . . The facts in [*AG Securities*] are startlingly different from those in the case of *Antoniades* . . . It is the purpose and intention of both parties to each agreement that it should confer an individual right on the licensee named, that he should be liable only for the payment which he had undertaken, and that his agreement should be capable of termination without reference to the agreements with other persons occupying the flat. The judge found that the agreements were not shams and that each of the four occupants had arrived independently of one another and not as a group . . . The only questions are those of the effect of each agreement *vis-à-vis* the individual licensee and whether the agreements collectively had the effect of creating a joint tenancy among the occupants of the premises for the time being by virtue of their having between them exclusive possession of the premises.

. . . But if the licence agreement is what it purports to be, that is to say, merely an agreement for permissive enjoyment as the invitee of the landlord, then each shares the use of the premises with other invitees of the same landlord. The landlord is not excluded for he continues to enjoy the premises through his invitees, even though he may for the time being have precluded himself by contract with each from withdrawing the invitation. Secondly, the fact that under each agreement an individual has the privilege of user and occupation for a term which overlaps the term of user and occupation of other persons in the premises, does not create a single indivisible term of occupation for all four consisting of an amalgam of the individual overlapping periods. Thirdly, there is no single sum of money payable in respect of use and occupation. Each person is individually liable for the amount which he has agreed, which may differ in practice from the amounts paid by all or some of the others.

. . . For my part, I agree with the dissenting judgment of Sir George Waller in finding no unity of interest, no unity of title, certainly no unity of time and, as I think, no unity of possession. I find it impossible to say that the agreements entered into with the respondents created either individually or collectively a single tenancy either of the entire flat or of any part of it.

Comment

(1) Other passages relating to shams and pretences have already been quoted.[30] *Street* and *AG Securities* are the two leading cases on leases and licences. Are there differences in the ways the two cases approach this area? How does *AG Securities* fit with Lord Templeman's statement in *Street* that occupiers of residential property are either lodgers or tenants?

(2) Hill[31] comments, 'If the court had found that clause 16 was genuine, the occupiers would have been licensees . . . they would not have had a right to exclusive possession', finding Lord Templeman's analysis 'bizarre' and 'unorthodox'. Is this criticism justified?

(3) Why does the law distinguish between the occupiers in *AG Securities* and *Antoniades*? Is it simply that the reality of *Antoniades* was that there was a joint agreement with the two occupiers (looking behind the form of the documents), whereas in *AG Securities* there were four independent agreements?

(4) Lord Templeman discusses *Hadjiloucas*, which is an interesting case as the occupiers were friends rather than living together as man and wife. The facts reveal that one of the friends had left and been replaced by another person. Is Lord Templeman's analysis consistent with the facts? How relevant is it that each of the friends was liable for the entire rent?

(5) Lord Oliver notes the four unities which are essential for there to be a joint tenancy. This is pursued in the next case.

Extract 14.1.23

Mikeover Ltd v Brady [1989] 3 All ER 618

Two occupiers living together were each liable for half the rent.

SLADE LJ: . . . The decision in *Street* v *Mountford* [1985] 2 All ER 289, [1985] AC 809 establishes that the enjoyment by one person of exclusive occupation of premises for a term in consideration of periodical payments creates a tenancy save in exceptional circumstances not relevant to this appeal: see *Antoniades* v *Villiers* [1988] 3 All ER 1058 at 1065, [1988] 3 WLR 1205 at 1212 per Lord Templeman. Similarly, as the last-mentioned decision illustrates, the enjoyment by more than one person of joint exclusive occupation of premises for the same term in consideration of periodical payments is capable of creating a joint tenancy.

It is, however, well settled that four unities must be present for the creation of a joint tenancy, namely the unities of possession, interest, title and time: see Megarry and Wade *The Law of Real Property* (5th edn, 1984) pp 419–422 . . . The dispute concerns unity of interest. The general principle, as stated in *Megarry and Wade* p 240, is:

> 'The interest of each joint tenant is the same in extent, nature and duration, for in theory of law they hold but one estate.'

'Interest' in this context must, in our judgment, include the bundle of rights and obligations representing that interest. The difficulty, from the defendant's point of view, is that the two agreements, instead of imposing a joint liability on him and Miss Guile to pay a deposit of £80 and monthly payments of £173.32, on their face imposed on each of them individual and separate obligations to pay only a deposit of £40 and monthly payments of only £86.66. On the face of it, the absence of joint obligations of payment [is] inconsistent with the existence of a joint tenancy.

---

[30] See Extract 14.1.10 above.
[31] (1989) 52 MLR 408 at pp 410–411. *Parkins* v *Westminster CC* (1997) 30 HLR 894 holds that a genuine sharing term creates a licence, even if initially there is only one occupant.

Counsel for the defendant sought to meet this difficulty in three ways. First, he contended that the two agreements were, as he put it, 'interdependent' and must be read together. When so read, he submitted, they should be construed as placing on the two parties joint obligations. However, it seems to us quite impossible to rewrite the two agreements in this manner as a matter of construction . . .

Next counsel for the defendant, as we understood him, contended that, in so far as the two agreements purported to render each of the defendant and Miss Guile merely individually liable for the payment of a deposit of £40 and monthly payments of £86.66, they were 'shams'. The true intention of the parties, he submitted, to be inferred from all the circumstances, was that they should be jointly liable to make monthly payments of £173.32 and to pay a deposit of £80 (to the return of which they should be jointly entitled in due course).

In this context, the subsequent conduct of the parties is admissible in evidence, not for the purpose of construing the agreements but on the question whether the documents were or were not genuine documents giving effect to the parties' true intentions: see *Antoniades v Villiers* [1988] 3 All ER 1058 at 1072, [1988] 3 WLR 1205 at 1221 per Lord Oliver.

However, the onus of proving a sham falls on the defendant and, in our judgment, the parties' subsequent conduct affords no support, or at least no sufficient support, to his case in this respect . . . During the period of joint occupation, monthly payments had been made in the sum of £173.32. The judge, however, found that there was nothing significant in this point. As he put it:

> 'Miss Guile had a bank account; the defendant did not. The money was sent by cheque by post. It was a matter of convenience for everybody for Miss Guile to pay by cheque and send the cheque by post to the plaintiffs and recoup herself from the defendant for his share of the money paid out. It was merely a matter of convenience that Miss Guile paid the money due in that way.'

> . . .

In our judgment, in so far as the judge was addressing his mind to the question of the payment of the deposit and the monthly sums, he was amply justified in his finding that there was no sham . . .

Counsel for the defendant, as his last line of defence, submitted that even on this footing the defendant and Miss Guile were in law capable of being (and were in fact) joint tenants. In this context he invoked the authority of a dictum of Lord Templeman in *Antoniades v Villiers* [1988] 3 All ER 1058 at 1066, [1988] 3 WLR 1205 at 1214 where he said:

> 'Mr Antoniades required each of them, Mr Villiers and Miss Bridger, to agree to pay one-half of each aggregate periodical payment, but this circumstance cannot convert a tenancy into a licence. A tenancy remains a tenancy even though the landlord may choose to require each of two joint tenants to agree expressly to pay one-half of the rent.'

Lord Templeman was saying this in the context of two agreements which he regarded as shams. With great respect, however, if he was intending to say that a joint tenancy can exist even though the supposed joint tenants are not jointly liable for the whole rent, the weight of authority appears to go the other way. In *Antoniades v Villiers* [1988] 3 All ER 1058 at 1073, [1988] 3 WLR 1205 at 1222 Lord Oliver said:

> 'If the real transaction was, as the judge found, one under which the appellants became joint tenants with exclusive possession, on the footing that the two agreements are to be construed together, then it would follow that they were together jointly and severally responsible for the whole rent. It would equally follow that they could effectively exclude the respondent and his nominees.'

> . . .

On these authorities, it appears to us that unity of interest imports the existence of joint rights and joint obligations. We therefore conclude that the provisions for payment contained in these two agreements (which were genuinely intended to impose and did impose on each party an obligation to pay no more than the sums reserved to the plaintiffs by his or her separate agreement) were incapable in law of creating a joint tenancy, because the monetary obligations of the two parties were not joint obligations and there was accordingly no complete unity of interest. It follows that there was no joint tenancy. Since inter se Miss Guile and the defendant had no power to exclude each other from occupation of any part of the premises, it also follows that their respective several rights can never have been greater than those of licensees during the period of their joint occupation . . .

Comment

(1) Is this result consistent with what was said about separate obligations in *AG Securities*?

(2) Does unity of interest require joint obligations?

(3) Is this a green light for those who wish to avoid creating a lease?

(4) Why cannot it be argued that there is a tenancy in common if one of the unities is missing?

Our last case in this section returns to the *AG Securities* type of case. Where is the line drawn between separate and interdependent arrangements?

Extract 14.1.24

Stribling v Wickham **[1989] 2 EGLR 35**

PARKER LJ: . . . True it is that the original three agreements were entered into at the same time, as were renewals, but each of the three defendants first entered into his agreement at a different time and in different circumstances. True it is that all were friends, but there is nothing odd in friends sharing on a licence basis which leaves each of them free to leave on short notice, which imposes on each the duty to pay only a share of the total amount which the landlord wishes to receive, which enables the owner to remove one who had become unsatisfactory and, if necessary, to put in his own selected sharer or sharers. No doubt he would not exercise the reserved right if the occupants tendered someone compatible to them and acceptable to him, for harmony is clearly best achieved if all occupants know and like each other . . .

Comment

(1) The agreements were held to be licences.

(2) Can this case be distinguished from *Hadjiloucas*, discussed in *AG Securities*?

(vi) At a rent for a term

In *Street*, Lord Templeman mentioned this as a requirement for a lease. It has already been seen that rent does not appear to be strictly necessary: *Ashburn Anstalt v Arnold.*[32] On the other hand, the requirement that there be a term has been confirmed as a requirement of a lease by *Prudential Assurance Co Ltd v London Residuary Body.*[33]

However, a tenancy at will can exist where there is no rent and no term and periodic tenancies can last for an indefinite time. These tenancies will be investigated later in this chapter.

---

[32] [1989] Ch 1; see Extract 14.1.1 above.
[33] [1992] 2 AC 386; see Extract 14.1.5 above.

2. Types of leases

A. Term of years absolute

The lease for a term of years is the standard form of tenancy: the period may be as short or as long as the parties stipulate. Remember that, as observed above, the maximum duration must be certain.

B. Periodic tenancies

We have already seen that the essence of a periodic tenancy is that it may continue indefinitely: from month to month or from year to year, for example. It is a legal estate and, because the period is invariably less than three years, does not require writing regardless of how long the tenancy actually lasts.

Extract 14.2.1

Hammersmith and Fulham LBC v Monk [1992] 1 AC 478

Could one of two joint periodic tenants serve notice so as to determine the tenancy?

LORD BRIDGE: . . . For a large part of this century there have been many categories of tenancy of property occupied for agricultural, residential and commercial purposes where the legislature has intervened to confer upon tenants extra-contractual rights entitling them to continue in occupation without the consent of the landlord, either after the expiry of a contractual lease for a fixed term or after notice to quit given by the landlord to determine a contractual periodic tenancy. It is primarily in relation to joint tenancies in these categories that the question whether or not notice to quit given by one of the joint tenants can determine the tenancy is of practical importance, particularly where, as in the instant case, the effect of the determination will be to deprive the other joint tenant of statutory protection. This may appear an untoward result and may consequently provoke a certain reluctance to hold that the law can permit one of two joint tenants unilaterally to deprive his co-tenant of 'rights' which both are equally entitled to enjoy. But the statutory consequences are in truth of no relevance to the question which your Lordships have to decide. That question is whether, at common law, a contractual periodic tenancy granted to two or more joint tenants is incapable of termination by a tenant's notice to quit unless it is served with the concurrence of all the joint tenants. That is the proposition which the appellant must establish in order to succeed.

As a matter of principle I see no reason why this question should receive any different answer in the context of the contractual relationship of landlord and tenant than that which it would receive in any other contractual context. If A and B contract with C on terms which are to continue in operation for one year in the first place and thereafter from year to year unless determined by notice at the end of the first or any subsequent year, neither A nor B has bound himself contractually for longer than one year. To hold that A could not determine the contract at the end of any year without the concurrence of B and vice versa would presuppose that each had assumed a potentially irrevocable contractual obligation for the duration of their joint lives, which, whatever the nature of the contractual obligations undertaken, would be such an improbable intention to impute to the parties that nothing less than the clearest express contractual language would suffice to manifest it . . .

Thus the application of ordinary contractual principles leads me to expect that a periodic tenancy granted to two or more joint tenants must be terminable at common law by an appropriate notice to quit given by any one of them whether or not the others are prepared to concur . . .

[After quoting *Blackstone's Commentaries*, Book II (1766), ch 9, pp 145–147:] Hence, from the earliest times a yearly tenancy has been an estate which continued only so long as it was the will of both parties that it should continue, albeit that either party could only signify his unwillingness that the tenancy should continue beyond the end of any year by giving the appropriate advance notice to that effect. Applying this principle to the case of a yearly tenancy where either the lessor's or the lessee's interest is held jointly by two or more parties, logic seems to me to dictate the conclusion that the will of all the joint parties is necessary to the continuance of the interest.

In *Doe d Aslin* v *Summersett* (1830) 1 B&Ad 135, the freehold interest in land let on a yearly tenancy was vested jointly in four executors of a will to whom the land had been jointly devised. Three only of the executors gave notice to the tenant to quit. It was held by the Court of King's Bench that the notice was effective to determine the tenancy. Delivering the judgment, Lord Tenterden CJ said, at pp 140–141:

'Upon a joint demise by joint tenants upon a tenancy from year to year, the true character of the tenancy is this, not that the tenant holds of each the share of each so long as he and each shall please, but that he holds the *whole* of *all* so long as he *and all* shall please; and as soon as any one of the joint tenants gives a notice to quit, he effectually puts an end to *that* tenancy; the tenant has a right upon such a notice to give up *the whole*, . . .'

. . .

There are three principal strands in the argument advanced for the appellant. First, reliance is placed on the judgment in *Gandy* v *Jubber* (1865) 9 B&S 15, for the proposition that a tenancy from year to year, however long it continues, is a single term, not a series of separate lettings . . . The passage relied on reads, at p 18:

'. . . the true nature of such a tenancy is that it is a lease for two years certain, and that every year after it is a springing interest arising upon the first contract and parcel of it, so that if the lessee occupies for a number of years, these years by computation from time past, make an entire lease for so many years, and that after the commencement of each new year it becomes an entire lease certain for the years past and also for the year so entered on, and that it is not a reletting at the commencement of the third and subsequent years. We think this is the true nature of a tenancy from year to year created by express words, and that there is not in contemplation of law a recommencing or reletting at the beginning of each year.'

It must follow from this principle, Mr Reid submits, that the determination of a periodic tenancy by notice is in all respects analogous to the determination of a lease for a fixed term in the exercise of a break clause, which in the case of joint lessees clearly requires the concurrence of all. But reference to the passage from *Bacon's Abridgment*, 7th ed, vol IV, p 839, on which the reasoning is founded shows that this analogy is not valid . . . Thus the fact that the law regards a tenancy from year to year which has continued for a number of years, considered retrospectively, as a single term in no way affects the principle that continuation beyond the end of each year depends on the will of the parties that it should continue or that, considered prospectively, the tenancy continues no further than the parties have already impliedly agreed upon by their omission to serve notice to quit.

[The second submission was based upon the trust imposed by the LPA.]

Finally, it is said that all positive dealings with a joint tenancy require the concurrence of all joint tenants if they are to be effective. Thus, a single joint tenant cannot exercise a break clause in a lease, surrender the term, make a disclaimer, exercise an option to renew the term or apply for relief from forfeiture. All these positive acts which joint tenants must concur in performing are said to afford analogies with the service of notice to determine a periodic tenancy which is likewise a positive act. But this is to confuse the form with the substance. The action of giving notice to determine a periodic tenancy is in form positive; but both on authority and on the principle so aptly summed up in the pithy Scottish phrase 'tacit relocation' the substance of the matter is that it is by his omission to give notice of termination that each party signifies the necessary positive assent to the extension of the term for a further period.

For all these reasons I agree with the Court of Appeal that, unless the terms of the tenancy agreement otherwise provide, notice to quit given by one joint tenant without the concurrence of any other joint tenant is effective to determine a periodic tenancy.

Comment

(1) The appellant's arguments, despite being unsuccessful in *Monk*, reveal much of the nature of periodic tenancies. Can they be regarded as a series of individual tenancies?

(2) Is it consistent with the nature of periodic tenancies to say that 'it is by his omission to give notice of termination that each party signifies the necessary positive assent to the extension of the term'?

(3) How appropriate is the contract-based analysis employed by Lord Bridge?

(4) The practical consequences of *Monk* are generally thought to be unfortunate and the Law Commission has proposed that a joint tenant of a residential tenancy should be able to give notice to leave the joint tenancy without terminating the lease.[34]

A human rights challenge to the ability of public sector landlords to evict the remaining joint tenant in such cases was rejected by a majority of the House of Lords in *Harrow LBC v Qazi*.[35] However, this was not the last word on the point. There are two bases upon which human rights may be relevant. The first is that the decision by the local authority landlord to take possession may fall foul of the Article 8 right of respect for the home. This was held by the European Court of Human Rights in *McCann v UK*[36] and we saw in Chapter 2 that the Supreme Court in *Manchester City Council v Pinnock*[37] overruled *Qazi*. Though there must be scope for issues of proportionality to be considered in all cases, this does not mean that the landlord's claim is bound to fail.

The following Extract concerns the second way in which human rights have been employed: a direct challenge on the rule in *Monk*.

Extract 14.2.2

Sims v Dacorum BC [2014] UKSC 63; [2014] 3 WLR 1600

LORD NEUBERGER: 5. Accordingly, following the reasoning in *Monk*, Dacorum contends that the secure tenancy granted to Mr and Mrs Sims has come to an end, and Mr Sims must vacate the house. *Monk* was decided before the Human Rights Act 1998 was enacted, and, now that it has come into force, Mr Sims contends that his rights (a) to respect for his home under article 8 of the European Convention on Human Rights and/or (b) peacefully to enjoy his possessions under article 1 of the first protocol to the Convention ('A1P1') would be wrongly infringed if Dacorum's claim succeeds. Accordingly, he contends that the decision, or the effect of the decision, in *Monk* should now be reconsidered.

---

[34] Law Com No 297, paras 2.44, 4.12.
[35] [2004] 1 AC 983.
[36] [2008] 28 EG 114.
[37] [2011] 2 AC 104; Extract 2.3.1 above.

14. A1P1 provides, inter alia, that everyone is entitled to 'peaceful enjoyment of his possessions', and that nobody should be 'deprived of his possessions except in the public interest and subject to conditions provided for by law'.

15. The property which Mr Sims owned and of which he complains to have been wrongly deprived, whether one characterises it as the tenancy or an interest in the tenancy, was acquired by him on terms that (i) it would be lost if a notice to quit was served by Mrs Sims (clause 100), and (ii) if that occurred, Dacorum could decide to permit him to stay in the house or find other accommodation for him (clause 101). The property was lost as a result of Mrs Sims serving a notice to quit, and Dacorum did consider whether to let Mr Sims remain, as he requested, and decided not to let him do so. Given that Mr Sims was deprived of his property in circumstances, and in a way, which was specifically provided for in the agreement which created it, his A1P1 claim is plainly very hard to sustain. The point was well put in the written case of Mr Chamberlain QC on behalf of the Secretary of State: 'the loss of [Mr Sims's] property right is the result of a bargain that he himself made'. . . .

17. Clause 100 is consistent with a common law principle which is not now attacked, and its effect is anyway mitigated by clause 101. Further, it is not an unreasonable provision, in that someone's interest has to suffer when one of two joint periodic tenants serves a notice to quit. If the result is not as decided in *Monk*, either the tenant who served the notice is forced to remain a tenant against her will, or the landlord is landed with one tenant instead of two, which means less security – and, in a case such as the present, a family property occupied by a single person. Just as a joint tenant in Mr Sims's position can claim that the outcome determined as correct in *Monk* is harsh, so could a joint tenant in Mrs Sims's position or a landlord in Dacorum's position contend that either of the alternative outcomes is harsh.

21. So far as Mr Sims's case on article 8 is concerned, there is no doubt but that he was entitled to raise the question of the proportionality of Dacorum's pursuit of the claim for possession of the house in the light of *Pinnock v Manchester City Council* [2010] UKSC 45, [2011] 2 AC 104 and *Hounslow LBC v Powell* [2011] UKSC 8, [2011] 2 AC 186, as explained by Lord Hodge in *R (CN) v Lewisham LBC* [2014] UKSC 62, paras 58–60 and 63. However, in this case, that point gets Mr Sims nowhere. As I have already indicated in paras 18 and 19 of this judgment, the Deputy District Judge carefully considered that question, and, in relation to Mr Sims's case on article 8, she came to the conclusion that Dacorum's 'careful decision-making process amply accorded with article 8.1 [and] that the decision that the Council made was one to which it could reasonably have come'. She then said that '[h]aving reviewed all the relevant factors myself, in my judgment it is lawful and proportionate to make an order for possession in this case'. Again, I consider that this was plainly correct.

22. In these circumstances, Mr Arden argued that the service of the notice to quit by Mrs Sims was itself a violation of Mr Sims's article 8 rights because it put in jeopardy his right to remain in his home. The fact that the service of the notice to quit put Mr Sims's right to stay in his home at risk does not mean that it therefore operated as an infringement of his right to respect for his home. No judgment of the Strasbourg court begins to justify such a proposition. Mrs Sims had the right to serve the notice, and, as already observed, the service of such a notice and its consequences were specifically covered by the agreement which gave Mr Sims the right to occupy the house as his home in the first place (see clauses 100 and 101).

23. I accept that the effect of the service of the notice to quit was to put at risk Mr Sims's enjoyment of his home. I also accept that different considerations may very well apply for article 8 purposes to Mr Sims, who is at risk of losing what has been his family home for many years, from those considerations that apply to temporarily housed homeless people who are at risk of losing their temporary accommodation as in *R (CN) v Lewisham*. However, I do not consider that that undermines the point that full respect for Mr Sims's article 8 rights was accorded by the facts that (i) his tenancy was determined in accordance with its contractual terms to which he had agreed in clause 100 of the tenancy agreement, (ii) he was entitled to the benefit

of clause 101 of his tenancy agreement, (iii) under the Protection from Eviction Act 1977, he could not be evicted without a court order, and (iv) the court would have to be satisfied that Dacorum was entitled to evict him as a matter of domestic law, and (v) the court could not make such an order without permitting him to raise a claim that it would be disproportionate to evict him, in accordance with the reasoning in *Pinnock* and *Powell*.

Comment

(1) The A1P1 analysis may be linked to that in *Horsham Properties Group Ltd* v *Clark* [2009] 1 WLR 1255 (Extract 21.4.33 below).

(2) Would there have been a stronger human rights argument if the agreement had not included clause 100, so that the Council simply relied upon *Monk*?

(i) Creation

Although periodic tenancies can be created expressly, the principal point of interest is as to when they will be implied. Traditionally,[38] the courts implied a periodic tenancy from the payment of rent, particularly where there was a failure to grant a legal lease (usually because of the absence of a deed) or the tenant held over on the ending of a lease.

Extract 14.2.3

Javad v *Aqil* [1991] 1 WLR 1007

NICHOLLS LJ: . . . As already foreshadowed, the sole issue on this appeal is whether the tenant went into occupation as a tenant at will or as a quarterly tenant. This is the sole issue, because the parties have pleaded and presented their cases in this way . . .

Much of the argument before us was directed at the legal consequence which follows from proof of possession and payment of rent by reference to a quarterly period. For the tenant it was submitted that proof of those facts raises a presumption in favour of a periodic tenancy which can only be rebutted, and the occupant be held to be a tenant at will, by an express agreement to that effect. Alternatively, this presumption is not rebutted by the fact that the grant of a lease is under discussion, in a case where a substantial sum has been paid over as rent in advance . . .

I cannot accept the tenant's submissions. They are contrary both to principle and to authority. I shall consider first the position in principle. A tenancy, or lease, is an interest in land. With exceptions immaterial for present purposes, a tenancy springs from a consensual arrangement between two parties: one person grants to another the right to possession of land for a lesser term than he, the grantor, has in the land. The extent of the right thus granted and accepted depends primarily upon the intention of the parties.

As with other consensually-based arrangements, parties frequently proceed with an arrangement whereby one person takes possession of another's land for payment without having agreed or directed their minds to one or more fundamental aspects of their transaction. In such cases the law, where appropriate, has to step in and fill the gaps in a way which is sensible and reasonable. The law will imply, from what was agreed and all the surrounding circumstances, the terms the parties are to be taken to have intended to apply. Thus if one party permits another to go into possession of his land on payment of a rent of so much per week or month, failing more the inference sensibly and reasonably to be drawn is that the parties intended that there should be a weekly or monthly tenancy. Likewise, if one party permits another to remain in possession after the expiration of his tenancy. But I emphasise the qualification 'failing more'. Frequently there will be more. Indeed, nowadays there normally will be other material surrounding circumstances. The simple situation is unlikely to arise often, not least because of the extent to which statute

---

[38] See, e.g., *Thomas* v *Packer* (1857) 1 H&N 669 (156 ER 1370).

has intervened in landlord–tenant relationships. Where there is more than the simple situation, the inference sensibly and reasonably to be drawn will depend upon a fair consideration of all the circumstances, of which the payment of rent on a periodical basis is only one, albeit a very important one. This is so, however large or small may be the amount of the payment.

To this I add one observation, having in mind the facts of the present case. Where parties are negotiating the terms of a proposed lease, and the prospective tenant is let into possession or permitted to remain in possession in advance of, and in anticipation of, terms being agreed, the fact that the parties have not yet agreed terms will be a factor to be taken into account in ascertaining their intention. It will often be a weighty factor. Frequently in such cases a sum called 'rent' is paid at once in accordance with the terms of the proposed lease: for example, quarterly in advance. But, depending on all the circumstances, parties are not to be supposed thereby to have agreed that the prospective tenant shall be a quarterly tenant. They cannot sensibly be taken to have agreed that he shall have a periodic tenancy, with all the consequences flowing from that, at a time when they are still not agreed about the terms on which the prospective tenant shall have possession under the proposed lease, and when he has been permitted to go into possession or remain in possession merely as an interim measure in the expectation that all will be regulated and regularised in due course when terms are agreed and a formal lease granted.

. . .

[In] *Longrigg, Burrough & Trounson* v *Smith*, 251 EG 847 . . . Ormrod LJ observed, at p 849:

'The old common law presumption of a tenancy from the payment and acceptance of a sum in the nature of rent dies very hard. But I think the authorities make it quite clear that in these days of statutory controls over the landlord's rights of possession, this presumption is unsound and no longer holds. The question now is a purely open question; it is simply: is it right and proper to infer from all the circumstances of the case, including the payments, that the parties had reached an agreement for a tenancy? I think it does not now go any further than that . . . The question is whether the proper inference from all the circumstances is that the parties had agreed upon a new tenancy . . .'

Ormrod LJ's statement of the relevant question does not differ from what I have sought to set out above. The thrust of his trenchant observation, that the authorities make it clear that the 'presumption is unsound and no longer holds', was, if I understand him aright, that the circumstances in which the presumption will operate will seldom, if ever, arise in present day conditions. Whether the correct view is that, having regard to the statutory controls, the so-called 'old common law presumption' no longer exists, or is that the cases in which it will operate in practice are very few and far between, seems to me to be a peculiarly arid issue on which it is not necessary to express an opinion. At the end of the day it will always be for him who asserts he enjoys an interest in another's land to make good his claim.

Comment

(1) Is there ever a presumption of a periodic tenancy today?

(2) When are periodic tenancies likely to be implied today?

(3) *Javad* involved the taking of possession before negotiations had been completed. Would the result be the same if a tenant holds over (paying rent) after a lease has come to an end? See *Barclays Wealth Trustees (Jersey) Ltd* v *Erimus Housing Ltd* [2014] 2 P&CR 85 (negotiations in progress concerning renewing the lease).

(ii) Terms

Given that most periodic tenancies are implied, many questions have arisen concerning their terms. What is the relevant period? In *Adler v Blackman*,[39] Somervell LJ stated:

---

[39] [1953] 1 QB 146 at pp 149–150.

[I]t will be noted that the rent as expressed in the agreement was so much per week. The decided cases, when a yearly tenancy has been implied, are cases where the rent is stated as a rent per year, though, of course, such a rent may be payable half-yearly, quarterly, monthly, or, in one of the reported cases, weekly.

... But in a case like the present, where the rent is expressed to be per week, I think when the fixed period has come to an end one should not presume anything but a weekly tenancy, namely, a tenancy for the period in respect of which the rent is expressed.

Is this a sensible distinction?

Periodic tenancies have frequently been found when a term of years is void for want of a deed, or else when the term has come to an end. What covenants in the lease should be implied into the periodic tenancy?

Extract 14.2.4

Martin v *Smith* (1874) LR 9 Ex 50

A void seven-year lease contained a covenant to undertake painting in the seventh year.

KELLY CB: ... It is now clearly settled that when a tenant enters under an agreement for a term which is void at law, he is liable as a tenant from year to year, on all the terms of the agreement applicable to a yearly tenancy ... The question, then, is whether the term of the agreement that the tenant should paint during the last year of the term of seven years is applicable to a tenancy from year to year which has, in fact, continued during the whole of that period; and it appears to me that, although during that period the defendant was only tenant from year to year, and his tenancy might at any time have been determined by a half year's notice to quit, yet his occupying under the agreement amounted to a promise that, if he should continue to occupy for the entire term, he would perform what was by the agreement to be performed in the last year of that period.

Comment

Which of the following terms in a void lease would you expect to be implied into a periodic tenancy? A covenant to put in repair? Covenants regulating the use of the premises? Forfeiture clauses? A covenant requiring payment of a capital sum (premium) at the beginning of the lease?

(iii) Termination

Extract 14.2.5

Queen's Club Gardens Estates Ltd v *Bignell* [1924] 1 KB 117

LUSH J: [T]here are two points to be considered – namely: first, what length of notice to quit must a landlord or tenant give to determine a weekly tenancy; second, whether the notice to quit must expire at the end of the weekly term or may expire during the currency of that term?

With regard to the first point – namely, what ought the length of the notice to quit to be – several possible answers have been suggested. ... Several cases have decided that a reasonable notice is all that is necessary. I cannot bring myself to accept that view. A notice to quit which was expressed to be to quit at the end of a reasonable time would clearly not be a good notice because it would not be definite or certain. Again, if a landlord or tenant gave a notice to quit on such and such a date, no one would know whether it was a valid notice until some jury or other tribunal had found that it was in fact reasonable, because in the absence of such a finding even reasonable people might take different views as to whether it was in the circumstances a reasonable notice to quit. The tendency of modern decisions, however, has been to define a reasonable notice to quit as being a week's notice. That in my opinion is the proper view . . .

The second point – namely, whether the notice to quit must expire at the end of a current week, or may be made to expire on any day the landlord or tenant chooses to fix – is of a more serious character . . . With great respect to two of my learned brethren who have recently decided this question in a way which is contrary to my opinion, I think the true view is that in any periodic tenancy, whether it be yearly, quarterly, monthly, or weekly, the notice to quit must expire at the end of the current period. It has been clearly settled, as is admitted, that in the cases of a yearly tenancy and a quarterly tenancy the notice to quit must expire at the end of the current period, and that in either of those cases it would be bad if it were made to expire in the middle of that period . . .

. . . If the party who desires to give notice is doubtful as to the day on which the period expires, he can make sure that the notice will be valid by adding the words that are given in the common form of notice to quit to the effect that if the date mentioned is not the real date on which the period expires, then the notice to quit is to expire on the proper day of expiry next after the expiration of the current period.

Comment

(1) For yearly tenancies, six months' notice is required,[40] while the full period is necessary for shorter periodic tenancies.

(2) Is there any good reason why the notice has to take effect at the end of a period?

(3) If the landlord of, say, a monthly tenancy does not know when the period ends, what notice should be given and when will it be effective?

(4) The parties may, of course, make express provision for notice.

C. Tenancy at will

The tenancy at will is not so much an estate as a relationship between landlord and tenant: there is no period for which the tenant is entitled to the land.

Extract 14.2.6

Wheeler v Mercer **[1957] AC 416**

VISCOUNT SIMONDS: . . . It may, I think, be truly said that, since a tenant at will is regarded at law as being in possession by his own will and at the will, express or implied, of his landlord, he is a tenant by their mutual agreement, and the agreement may therefore be called a tenancy agreement. He is distinguished from a tenant at sufferance in that such a tenant is said to be in possession without either the agreement or disagreement of the landlord . . . A tenancy at will, though called a tenancy, is unlike any other tenancy except a tenancy at sufferance, to which it is next-of-kin. It has been properly described as a personal relation between the landlord and his tenant: it is determined by the death of either of them or by any one of a variety of acts, even by an involuntary alienation, which would not affect the subsistence of any other tenancy.

The tenancy at will has fallen out of favour in recent decades.

---

[40] See, e.g., *Jones* v *Mills* (1861) 10 CBNS 788 at p 799 (142 ER 664 at p 668).

Extract 14.2.7

Errington v Errington [1952] 1 KB 290

Occupation was permitted in return for payment of mortgage instalments, with a promise to transfer the fee simple when the mortgage had been paid off.

DENNING LJ: . . . The relationship of the parties is open to three possible legal constructions: (i) That the couple were tenants at will paying no rent. That is what the judge thought they were. He said that, in this case, just as in *Lynes* v *Snaith*,[i] the defendant 'was in exclusive possession and was therefore not a mere licensee but in the position of a tenant at will'. But in my opinion it is of the essence of a tenancy at will that it should be determinable by either party on demand, and it is quite clear that the relationship of these parties was not so determinable. The father could not eject the couple as long as they paid the instalments regularly to the building society. It was therefore not a tenancy at will . . . (iii) That the couple were licensees, having a permissive occupation short of a tenancy, but with a contractual right, or at any rate, an equitable right to remain so long as they paid the instalments, which would grow into a good equitable title to the house itself as soon as the mortgage was paid. This is, I think, the right view of the relationship of the parties.

[i] [1899] 1 QB 486.

Comment

(1) Could it be argued that, collateral to the tenancy at will, there is a contractual obligation not to give notice?[41] This contractual obligation would be analogous to the equitable lease which can exist alongside a tenancy at will or periodic tenancy. Might this conflict with certainty requirements?

(2) See also *Ramnarace* v *Lutchman*[42] on the effect of possession where there are negotiations or a contract.

Where there is no contractual setting, a very different approach has been adopted to deny a tenancy at will. In cases such as *Facchini* v *Bryson*,[43] Denning LJ referred to 'circumstances, such as a family arrangement, an act of friendship or generosity, or such like, [which] negative any intention to create a tenancy', and this was seized upon by Lord Templeman in *Street* as a basis upon which to explain the earlier cases favouring licences. How does this fit the analysis in *Wheeler* v *Mercer*? In *Street*, why did not Lord Templeman restore the original scope of tenancies at will?

D. Tenancy at sufferance

These tenancies do not play a prominent role in the modern law and little needs to be said. They occur when a tenant holds over at the end of a lease, but without the landlord's permission (which would result in a tenancy at will or a periodic tenancy) or direct prohibition (which would result in trespass). They are similar to the tenancy at will, but with the possibility of penal rent obligations.[44]

---

[41] See Hargreaves (1953) 69 LQR 466.
[42] [2001] 1 WLR 1651; Extract 14.1.18 above.
[43] [1952] 1 TLR 1386.
[44] Megarry and Wade, *The Law of Real Property* (8th ed), paras 17–110 et seq.

E. Equitable leases

It was seen earlier (see Chapter 5)[45] that an agreement for a lease will be implied where a lease is void for failure to comply with formality requirements. Subject to there being writing which satisfies the Law of Property (Miscellaneous Provisions) Act 1989, s 2, this agreement will then constitute an equitable lease. The result was that frequently there would be a tenancy at will or (more likely) a periodic tenancy at law, but that equity would recognise a lease for the full intended term. This equitable lease would be used to prevent the enforcement of any termination of the legal tenancy.[46]

Extract 14.2.8

Walsh v Lonsdale (1882) 21 Ch D 9

Could a landlord under an agreement for a lease exercise the legal remedy of distress (seizure of the tenant's goods) for rent due under the agreement?

JESSEL MR: . . . The question is one of some nicety. There is an agreement for a lease under which possession has been given. Now since the Judicature Act the possession is held under the agreement. There are not two estates as there were formerly, one estate at common law by reason of the payment of the rent from year to year, and an estate in equity under the agreement. There is only one Court, and the equity rules prevail in it. The tenant holds under an agreement for a lease. He holds, therefore, under the same terms in equity as if a lease had been granted, it being a case in which both parties admit that relief is capable of being given by specific performance. That being so, he cannot complain of the exercise by the landlord of the same rights as the landlord would have had if a lease had been granted. On the other hand, he is protected in the same way as if a lease had been granted; he cannot be turned out by six months' notice as a tenant from year to year. He has a right to say, 'I have a lease in equity, and you can only re-enter if I have committed such a breach of covenant as would if a lease had been granted have entitled you to re-enter according to the terms of a proper proviso for re-entry.' That being so, it appears to me that being a lessee in equity he cannot complain of the exercise of the right of distress merely because the actual parchment has not been signed and sealed.

Comment

Distress was abolished by the Tribunals, Courts and Enforcement Act 2007, with a replacement remedy for commercial leases.[47]

A common examination question is whether an agreement for a lease is as good as a legal lease.

Extract 14.2.9

Manchester Brewery Co v Coombs [1901] 2 Ch 608

FARWELL J: . . . Although it has been suggested that the decision in *Walsh v Lonsdale*[i] takes away all differences between the legal and equitable estate, it, of course, does nothing of the sort, and the limits of its applicability are really somewhat narrow. It applies only to cases where there is a contract to transfer a legal title, and an act has to be justified or an action maintained

---

[45] See p 134 above.
[46] *Browne* v *Warner* (1808) 14 Ves 156, 409 (33 ER 480, 578).
[47] See p 566 below.

by force of the legal title to which such contract relates. It involves two questions: (1) Is there a contract of which specific performance can be obtained? (2) If Yes, will the title acquired by such specific performance justify at law the act complained of, or support at law the action in question? It is to be treated as though before the Judicature Acts there had been, first, a suit in equity for specific performance, and then an action at law between the same parties; and the doctrine is applicable only in those cases where specific performance can be obtained between the same parties in the same court, and at the same time as the subsequent legal question falls to be determined . . . It is not necessary to call in aid this doctrine in matters that are purely equitable; its existence is due entirely to the divergence of legal and equitable rights between the same parties, nor does it affect the rights of third parties.

[i] 21 Ch D 9.

Extract 14.2.10

Maitland, *Equity* (2nd ed) at p 158 (footnotes omitted)

. . . I have heard remarks upon *Walsh* v *Lonsdale* which seemed to imply that since the Judicature Act an agreement for a lease is in all respects as good as a lease. Now Jessel certainly did not say this, and to say it would certainly be untrue. An agreement for a lease is not equal to a lease. An equitable right is not equivalent to a legal right; between the contracting parties an agreement for a lease may be as good as a lease; just so between the contracting parties an agreement for the sale of land may serve as well as a completed sale and conveyance. But introduce the third party and then you will see the difference. I take a lease; my lessor then sells the land to X; notice or no notice my lease is good against X. I take a mere agreement for a lease, and the person who has agreed to grant the lease then sells and conveys to Y, who has no notice of my merely equitable right. Y is not bound to grant me a lease.

Comment

(1) How do these last two Extracts fit with what was said in *Walsh* v *Lonsdale*?

(2) One difficult area for the application of this material has been the running of covenants. (This is discussed in Chapter 16.[48])

(3) When, if at all, might a periodic tenancy, existing alongside an equitable lease, have any significance today?

(4) It should be remembered that certain statutory provisions apply only to legal leases.[49]

These Extracts come from a century ago. The following dictum of Lord Browne-Wilkinson is representative of much modern thinking:[50]

> There are many proprietary rights, apart from trusts, which are only enforceable in equity. For example, an agreement for a lease under which the tenant has entered is normally said to be as good as a lease, since under such an agreement equity treats the lease as having been granted and the 'lessee' as having a proprietary interest enforceable against the whole world except the bona fide purchaser for value without notice . . .

[48] See p 600 below.
[49] Both land charges and land registration contain explicit examples. Another less obvious example is LPA, s 62 (implication of easements).
[50] *Tinsley* v *Milligan* [1994] 1 AC 340 at pp 370–371. However, it would be wrong to think that the differences between law and equity have been eradicated: Baker (1977) 93 LQR 529. Also contrast *Scott* v *Southern Pacific Mortgages Ltd* [2014] 3 WLR 1163, p 133 above.

In my judgment to draw such distinctions between property rights enforceable at law and those which require the intervention of equity would be surprising. More than 100 years has elapsed since the administration of law and equity became fused. The reality of the matter is that, in 1993, English law has one single law of property made up of legal and equitable interests.

Is this approach, which goes on to recognise that legal and equitable rights may have differing incidents, likely to have any practical impact on the law relating to equitable leases?

A related question concerns the availability of specific performance. Particular problems have arisen where specific performance is barred by the tenant's breach of the terms of the lease.

Extract 14.2.11

Swain v Ayres (1888) 21 QBD 289

LORD ESHER MR: . . . The distinction between law and equity is now abolished in the sense that the same Court is to give effect to both, and that, when the doctrines of law and equity conflict, the latter are to prevail. I should therefore be disposed to say that, when there is such a state of things that a Court of Equity would compel specific performance of an agreement for a lease by the execution of a lease, both in the Equity and Common Law Divisions the case ought to be treated as if such a lease had been granted and was actually in existence. There would then be the equivalent of a lease, that is to say, the lease of which equity would compel the execution in specific performance of the agreement. That is a very different thing from saying that, where equity would not compel specific performance by the execution of a lease, the lease of which equity would not decree execution is to be considered in equity as existing. That contention seems to me quite untenable. It seems to me quite impossible to say that equity would consider a lease in existence, though it would not grant specific performance by decreeing execution of a lease. Such a contention seems to me to make the doctrine of equity on the subject self-contradictory.

Comment

This has proved difficult in the context of relief against forfeiture. Today (unlike at the time of *Swain*) the relief legislation explicitly includes agreements for leases[51] and it would be very odd if relief could be given and yet the tenant fails because of refusal of specific performance. It seems that this danger will be avoided today.[52]

F. Tenancies by estoppel

The tenancy by estoppel operates where the landlord has no (or insufficient) title to the land when a lease is granted.

---

[51] See, e.g., LPA, s 146(5)(a).
[52] Woodfall, *Landlord and Tenant*, para 17.125; *Sport Internationaal Bussum BV v Inter-Footwear Ltd* [1984] 1 WLR 776 at p 790.

Extract 14.2.12

Industrial Properties (Barton Hill) Ltd v *AEI Ltd* [1977] QB 580

LORD DENNING MR: . . . If a landlord lets a tenant into possession under a lease, then, so long as the tenant remains in possession *undisturbed by any adverse claim* – then the tenant cannot dispute the landlord's title. Suppose the tenant (not having been disturbed) goes out of possession and the landlord sues the tenant on the covenant for rent or for breach of covenant to repair or to yield up in repair. The tenant cannot say to the landlord: 'You are not the true owner of the property.' Likewise, if the landlord, on the tenant's holding over, sues him for possession or for use and occupation or mesne profits, the tenant cannot defend himself by saying: 'The property does not belong to you, but to another.'

But if the tenant is disturbed *by being evicted by title paramount or the equivalent* of it, then he can dispute the landlord's title . . .

Short of eviction by title paramount, or its equivalent, however, the tenant is estopped from denying the title of the landlord . . . This is manifestly correct: for, without an adverse claim, it would mean that the tenant would be enabled to keep the property without paying any rent to anybody or performing any covenants. That cannot be right.

Comment

(1) Are third parties, particularly purchasers of the fee simple, affected by tenancies by estoppel?

(2) This passage deals with whether the tenant can object to the landlord's title. Similarly, the landlord cannot rely on his own lack of title to deny liability to the tenant.

(3) Do the rules on tenancies by estoppel produce fairness to each of the landlord and tenant?

Extract 14.2.13

Bruton v *London & Quadrant Housing Trust* [2000] 1 AC 406

LORD HOFFMANN: . . . Secondly, I think that Millett LJ may have been misled by the ancient phrase 'tenancy by estoppel' into thinking that it described an agreement which would not otherwise be a lease or tenancy but which was treated as being one by virtue of an estoppel. In fact, as the authorities show, it is not the estoppel which creates the tenancy, but the tenancy which creates the estoppel. The estoppel arises when one or other of the parties wants to deny one of the ordinary incidents or obligations of the tenancy on the ground that the landlord had no legal estate. The basis of the estoppel is that having entered into an agreement which constitutes a lease or tenancy, he cannot repudiate that incident or obligation. So in *Morton* v *Woods* (1869) LR 4 QB 293, a factory owner granted a second mortgage to a bank to secure advances. But the mortgagor had no legal estate, having conveyed it to the first mortgagee, and therefore could not confer one upon the second mortgagee. As additional security, the borrower 'attorned tenant' to the second mortgagee, that is to say, acknowledged a relationship of landlord and tenant between them . . . The Court of Queen's Bench held that the mortgagor was estopped from denying the bank's legal title [as landlord]. Kelly CB said, at p 304:

> 'it is the creation of the tenancy, or the estoppel, which arises from the creation of the relation of landlord and tenant by agreement between the parties, that makes the actual legal estate unnecessary to support the distress . . .'

Thus it is the fact that the agreement between the parties constitutes a tenancy that gives rise to an estoppel and not the other way round. It therefore seems to me that the question of tenancy by estoppel does not arise in this case. The issue is simply whether the agreement is a tenancy. It is not whether either party is entitled to deny some obligation or incident of the tenancy on the ground that the trust had no title.

Comment

(1) What point is being made by Lord Hoffmann in this passage?

(2) Is there such a legal entity as a tenancy by estoppel?

(3) *Bruton* will be further considered in the following chapter.[53]

G. Special cases

(i) Leases for life

Extract 14.2.14

Law of Property Act 1925, s 149(6)

149.—(6) Any lease or underlease, at a rent, or in consideration of a fine, for life or lives or for any term of years determinable with life or lives, or on the marriage of the lessee, or any contract therefor . . . shall take effect as a lease, underlease or contract therefor, for a term of ninety years determinable after the death or marriage (as the case may be) of the original lessee, or of the survivor of the original lessees, by at least one month's notice in writing given to determine the same . . .

Comment

(1) Note that this structure ensures a certain maximum duration. It was discussed and applied by the Supreme Court in *Mexfield Housing Co-operative Ltd* v *Berrisford* [2012] 1 AC 955 (Extract 14.1.6 above).

(2) What happens if there is no rent or fine (capital payment)? Why is one of them required?

(3) Why does the provision extend to grants and contracts for a *term of years determinable on* death or marriage? What is the effect of a lease 'to Jenny for five years or until she earlier marries'?

(ii) Perpetually renewable leases

The setting here is that a lease may contain a covenant for its renewal at the tenant's request. If the renewed lease also contains such a covenant, then there is the prospect of leases stretching into the indefinite future.

Extract 14.2.15

Law of Property Act 1922, Sched 15, para 5

5.   A grant, after the commencement of this Act, of a term, subterm, or other leasehold interest with a covenant or obligation for perpetual renewal, which would have been valid if this Part of this Act had not been passed, shall (subject to the express provisions of this Act) take effect as a demise for a term of two thousand years or in the case of a subdemise for a term less in duration

---

[53] Extract 15.1.6 below.

by one day than the term out of which it is derived, to commence from the date fixed for the commencement of the term, subterm, or other interest, and in every case free from any obligation for renewal or for payment of any fines, fees, costs, or other money in respect of renewal.

Extract 14.2.16

Caerphilly Concrete Products Ltd v Owen [1972] 1 WLR 372

RUSSELL LJ: . . . The approach to the question whether a lease is perpetually renewable is not in doubt. The language used must plainly lead to that result: though the fact that an argument is capable of being sustained at some length against that result does not of course suffice. As a matter of history, when a covenant by a lessor conferred a right to renewal of the lease, the new grant to contain the same or the like covenants and provisos as were contained in the lease, the courts refused to give literal effect to that language, which if taken literally would mean that the second lease would contain the same covenant (or option) to renew, totidem verbis, and so on perpetually. The reference to the same covenants was construed as not including the option covenant itself. This limited the tenant's right to one renewal. In order therefore to make it plain that the covenants to be contained in the second lease (to be granted under the exercise of the option to renew) were to include also the covenant to renew, draftsmen were accustomed to insert phrases such as 'including this covenant', so as to achieve a perpetually renewable lease. As I have indicated, if they did not do this, the second lease would not contain any option clause.

SACHS LJ: . . . Already 20 years ago judicial unease at having to determine [the parties'] intentions in cases of the instant type by a blinkered approach is reflected in the judgments in *Parkus* v *Greenwood*, both at first instance [1950] Ch 33 and on appeal [1950] Ch 644. At first instance it fell to Harman J to discuss the decision reached in *Green* v *Palmer* [1944] Ch 328 . . . In his judgment at p 37 Harman J not unnaturally said of that earlier case: 'That was an instance of a six monthly furnished tenancy and the improbability that the parties had thought of creating a 2,000 years term was very high.' He made a similar observation with regard to the lease he was himself considering, which was for three years with a renewal covenant for a further three years phrased in a way that accorded with the formula . . .

The judicial unease of 1950 is, so far as I am concerned, by now increased by two factors. First, more and more leases over the two succeeding decades have tended to come from pens not fully trained in the art of conveyancing. Secondly, over the same period the value of the pound sterling has been decreasing rapidly, thus making it even more unlikely that a man of business in the course of a normal transaction would knowingly part 'for ever' with his rights over land in return for a static rent . . .

Comment

(1) The court held that it was bound to find a perpetually renewable lease on the wording of the lease.

(2) Given the concerns expressed by Sachs LJ, does the law require reform?

(iii) Discontinuous leases

Entitlement under a lease need not be continuous. Thus there can be a lease for the first week in May each year for ten years: this constitutes one lease rather than ten. How might this be of significance?[54]

---

[54] See *Cottage Holiday Associates Ltd* v *Customs & Excise Commissioners* [1983] QB 735 (LPA, s 149(3)).

Further reading

Bright, S (1993) 13 LS 38: Uncertainty in leases: is it a vice?

Bright, S [2002] CLJ 146: Avoiding tenancy legislation: sham and contracting out revisited.

Gardner, S (1987) 7 OxJLS 60: Equity, estate contracts and the Judicature Acts: *Walsh* v *Lonsdale* revisited.

Hill, J (1996) 16 LS 200: Intention and the creation of property rights: are leases different?

McFarlane, B and Simpson, E F (2003) 'Tackling avoidance' in *Rationalizing Property, Equity and Trusts*, ed. J Getzler, OUP Oxford, Chapter 8.

Sparkes, P (1993) 109 LQR 93: Certainty of leasehold terms.

15

Leases: obligations and remedies

Leases invariably impose obligations on the parties. Rent is virtually always payable; restrictions on the use of the premises and duties to repair provide other obvious examples. In this chapter, we will consider those obligations which are implied by legislation (generally for short leases of residential property) or the courts. There is much detailed law in this area, especially regarding repair and the state of the premises; only the principal rules and provisions will be covered.

We will also consider how obligations are enforced. Forfeiture of the lease for breach by the tenant is an important topic and takes up the second half of the chapter.

1. The operation of contract principles

Leases rules have evolved over many centuries and have become well established in the process. Much contract analysis, in comparison, is relatively recent. It is unsurprising that some of the leases rules are different from modern contract theory. Yet there is no difficulty in viewing leases as contracts: the landlord agrees with the tenant that the latter should enjoy the premises for a certain period in return for a rent (or capital payment, usually called a premium). Can we dump the old leases rules in favour of contract principles?

Sometimes, contract rules operate alongside traditional lease analyses. This may be said of *Hammersmith and Fulham LBC* v *Monk*,[1] in which we have seen that contract principles were employed to explain the termination of jointly held periodic tenancies. In the following case, obligations relating to access to leasehold flats were in issue. The background is that the common law, as will be seen later, very rarely imposes repairing obligations.

Extract 15.1.1

Liverpool City Council v *Irwin* [1977] AC 239

LORD CROSS: . . . One starts with the general principle that the law does not impose on a servient owner any liability to keep the servient property in repair for the benefit of the owner of an easement. If I let you a house on my land with a right of way to it over my property and the surface of the way is in need of repair you cannot call on me to repair it if I have not expressly agreed to do so . . . I see no reason why the same principle should not be applicable when the owner of a house lets part of an upper storey in it to a single tenant . . . But must it follow that the same principle must be applied to the case where a landlord lets off parts of his property to a number of different tenants retaining in his ownership 'common parts' – halls, staircases, corridors and so on – which are used by all the tenants? I think that it would be contrary to common sense to press the general principle so far. In such a case I think that the implication should be

---

[1] [1992] 1 AC 478; Extract 14.2.1 above.

the other way and that, instead of the landlord being under no obligation to keep the common parts in repair and such facilities as lifts and chutes in working order unless he has expressly contracted to do so, he should – at all events in the case of ordinary commercial lettings – be under some obligation to keep the common parts in repair and the facilities in working order unless he has expressly excluded any such obligation.

LORD SALMON: . . . Clearly, there was a contractual relationship between the tenants and the council with legal obligations on both sides. Those of the tenants are meticulously spelt out in the council's printed form which mentions none of the council's obligations. But legal obligations can be implied as well as expressed.

Comment

This needs to be considered together with the material later in this chapter on repairing obligations. In so far as obligations to repair are not normally implied into leases, does *Irwin* run counter to orthodox analysis?

More interesting are cases where the leases rules differ from contract rules. One controversial question has been whether frustration can apply to leases.

Extract 15.1.2

National Carriers Ltd v *Panalpina (Northern) Ltd* [1981] AC 675

LORD WILBERFORCE: . . . To place leases of land beyond a firm line of exclusion seems to involve anomalies, to invite fine distinctions, or at least to produce perplexities. How, for example, is one to deal with agreement for leases? . . .

Two arguments only by way of principle have been suggested. The first is that a lease is more than a contract: it conveys an estate in land. This must be linked to the fact that the English law of frustration, unlike its continental counterparts, requires, when it applies, not merely adjustment of the contract, but its termination. But this argument, by itself, is incomplete as a justification for denying that frustration is possible. The argument must continue by a proposition that an estate in land once granted cannot be divested – which, as Viscount Simon LC pointed out in the *Cricklewood* case [1945] AC 221, 229, begs the whole question.

. . .

In the second place, if the argument is to have any reality, it must be possible to say that frustration of leases cannot occur because in any event the tenant will have that which he bargained for, namely, the leasehold estate. Certainly this may be so in many cases – let us say most cases. Examples are *London and Northern Estates Co* v *Schlesinger* [1916] 1 KB 20, where what was frustrated (viz the right of personal occupation) was not at the root of the contract, and requisitioning cases, for example, *Whitehall Court Ltd* v *Ettlinger* [1920] 1 KB 680, where again the tenant was left with something he could use. But there may also be cases where this is not so. A man may desire possession and use of land or buildings for, and only for, some purpose in view and mutually contemplated. Why is it an answer, when he claims that this purpose is 'frustrated', to say that he has an estate if that estate is unusable and unsaleable? In such a case the lease, or the conferring of an estate, is a subsidiary means to an end, not an aim or end of itself. This possible situation is figured, in fact, by Viscount Simon LC in the *Cricklewood* case [1945] AC 221, 229.

The second argument of principle is that on a lease the risk passes to the lessee, as on a sale it passes to the purchaser (see *per* Lord Goddard in the *Cricklewood* case). But the two situations are not parallel. Whether the risk – or any risk – passes to the lessee depends on the terms of the lease: it is not uncommon, indeed, for some risks – of fire or destruction – to be specifically allocated . . .

To provide examples, as of a 999 year lease during which a frustrating event occurs, or of those in decided cases (see above), to show that in such cases frustration will not occur, is insufficient as argument. These examples may be correct: they may cover most, at least most normal, cases. But the proposition is that there can be no case outside them and that I am unable to accept.

LORD SIMON: . . . the law should if possible be founded on comprehensive principles: compartmentalism, particularly if producing anomaly, leads to the injustice of different results in fundamentally analogous circumstances. To deny the extension of the doctrine of frustration to leaseholds produces a number of undesirable anomalies. It is true that theoretically it would create an anomalous distinction between the conveyance of a freehold interest and of a leasehold of, say, 999 years. But it would be only in exceptional circumstances that a lease for as long as 999 years would in fact be susceptible of frustration. On the other hand, to deny the application of the doctrine would create an anomalous distinction between the charter of a ship by demise . . . and a demise of land . . . Then there would be the distinction between a lease and other chattel interests – say, under a hire-purchase agreement. But most striking of all is the fact that the doctrine of frustration undoubtedly applies to a licence to occupy land: see, for example, *Krell* v *Henry* [1903] 2 KB 740 and the other Coronation cases . . . I am clearly of opinion that the balance of anomaly indicates that the doctrine of frustration should be applied to a lease.

Comment

(1) Lord Russell disagreed. Are there good reasons for leases having special rules?

(2) Lack of access for 20 months out of a ten-year lease was held not to constitute frustration on the facts. What might suffice?

Termination of leases for breach by tenants has been the subject of detailed leases rules over many years, it normally being essential for the lease to contain a forfeiture clause and, as will be seen later in this chapter, forfeiture is subject to extensive statutory and court control.

Extract 15.1.3

Progressive Mailing House Pty Ltd v *Tabali Pty Ltd*
(1985) 157 CLR 17 (High Court of Australia)

MASON J: . . . Repudiation or fundamental breach of a lease involves considerations which are not present in the case of an ordinary contract. First, the lease vests an estate or interest in land in the lessee and a complex relationship between the parties centres upon that interest in property. Secondly, this relationship has been shaped historically in very large measure by the law of property, though in recent times the relationship has been refined and developed by means of contractual arrangements. Thus, traditionally at common law a breach of a covenant by a lessee, even breach of the covenant to pay rent, conferred no right on the lessor to re-enter unless the lease reserved a right of re-entry . . .

These incidents of the law of landlord and tenant indicate that mere breaches of covenant on the part of the lessee do not amount to a repudiation or fundamental breach. Indeed, it is of some significance that the instances in which courts have held that a lessee has repudiated his lease are cases in which the lessee has abandoned possession of the leased property. But too much should not be made of this as very few cases of repudiation by lessees have come before the courts. I would therefore specifically reject the appellant's submission that abandonment of possession is necessary to constitute a case of repudiation by a lessee.

DEANE J: . . . The rationale of [the earlier] approach was the perceived inappropriateness of those contractual doctrines to a leasehold estate viewed as analogous to a form of feudal tenure. On the other hand, the general trend in this century, particularly in relation to leases of urban premises, has been away from the type of lease which can realistically be so viewed. It has been towards the lease, at a commercial rental and for a shorter term, framed in the language of executory promises of widening content and diminishing relevance to the actual demise. It is apparent that the special rules of property law regarding chattels real are inadequate as the exclusive determinant of rights and liabilities under such modern leases. That being so, it has become necessary for courts to look somewhat more critically at the rational basis and justification of the traditional assumption that leases generally were beyond the reach of fundamental doctrines of the law of contract.

The actual application to leasehold interests of the common law doctrines of frustration and termination for fundamental breach involves some unresolved questions which are best left to be considered on a case by case basis whereby adequate attention can be focussed on particular problems which might be overlooked in any effort at judicial codification. One cannot however ignore the fact that the clear trend of common law authority is to deny any general immunity of contractual leases from the operation of those doctrines of contract law . . .

Extract 15.1.4

Hussein v Mehlman [1992] 2 EGLR 87 (County Court)

Could a lease be terminated by the landlord's repudiatory breach?

ASSISTANT RECORDER SEDLEY QC: . . . Although a contract of letting, whether for a term of years certain or for a periodic 'springing' term, differs from other contracts in creating an estate in land, it is nevertheless a contract: see *United Scientific Holdings Ltd* v *Burnley Borough Council* [1978] AC 904, at pp 929E, 935B, 944B, 947B–C, 956F–H, 962A and 963H–964B, approving *C H Bailey Ltd* v *Memorial Enterprises Ltd* [1974] 1 WLR 728; and, most recently, *Hammersmith and Fulham London Borough Council* v *Monk* [1991] 3 WLR 1144, at pp 1147C, G, and 1156C, G–H. Since, in the ordinary way, any contract may be brought to an end by one party's repudiatory conduct, the question to be answered is whether a contract of letting is an exception to the rule.

In *C H Bailey Ltd* v *Memorial Enterprises Ltd* at p 732C, Lord Denning MR said:

'It is time to get away from the medieval concept of rent. That appears from a passage in *Holdsworth, A History of English Law*, vol VII (1900), p 262 . . . in modern law, rent is not conceived of as a thing, but rather as a payment which a tenant is bound by his contract to make to his landlord for the use of the land.

The time and manner of the payment is to be ascertained according to the true construction of the contract, and not by reference to out-dated relics of medieval law.'

. . .

It seems clear, then, that, although the modern law of landlord and tenant has not made obsolete the availability of distress for rent or the concept of an estate in land arising out of the relationship, these are no longer the foundation of the relationship but are its incidents: its foundation is the contract to pay money or give other consideration in return for the exclusive right to occupy land. (It may or may not be that the rent-free tenancy is an anomaly in this context, but that rare species cannot swim very far against the tide of the general law.)

The anchor by which Mr Russen, in his able argument, seeks to secure his client's boat against this tide is the decision of the Court of Appeal in *Total Oil Great Britain Ltd* v *Thompson Garages (Biggin Hill) Ltd* [1972] 1 QB 318 . . .

Lord Denning held that the covenant was not severable from the rest of the lease and went on at p 324A:

'The second point is: what is the effect of the repudiation by the oil company which was accepted by the dealer? Does it put an end to the lease? I think not. A lease is a demise. It conveys an interest in land. It does not come to an end like an ordinary contract on repudiation and acceptance. There is no authority on the point, but there is one case which points that way. It is *Leighton's Investment Trust Ltd* v *Cricklewood Property & Investment Trust Ltd* [1943] KB 493 . . . [1945] AC 221. Lord Russell of Killowen and Lord Goddard at pp 234 and 244 were both of opinion that frustration does not bring a lease to an end. Nor I think does repudiation and acceptance.'

. . .

The *Total Oil* decision, at its fullest, is therefore to be found in the judgment of Lord Denning. If it stood by itself it would, at this level, be binding authority for the proposition that because of the special character of a demise of land a lease is not terminable by frustration nor, therefore, by repudiation and acceptance.

However, since the *Total Oil* case was decided in 1971, both the major and the minor premises upon which Lord Denning's second holding was based appear to have been destroyed by decisions of the House of Lords. As I have already indicated, the major premise that a lease of land is in its essence different from other contracts has been overset, in particular by the decision of the House of Lords in *United Scientific Holdings Ltd* v *Burnley Borough Council*. The minor premise that a lease cannot be determined by frustration has been overset by the decision of the House of Lords in *National Carriers Ltd* v *Panalpina (Northern) Ltd* [1981] AC 675 . . .

This reasoning [in *Panalpina*], it seems to me, not only takes away the minor premise of the *Total Oil* judgment but has fundamental implications for its major premise: it continues the process, to which I have referred, of assimilating leases to other contracts . . .

Very recently the Court of Appeal has held, apparently without argument to the contrary and without any citation of authority, that a tenancy agreement which one party is induced to enter into by the fraud of the other can be rescinded at the innocent party's election: *Killick* v *Roberts* [1991] 4 All ER 289, at p 292d. This seems another step down the same road.

. . .

I recognise that the proposition that a contract of tenancy can be repudiated like any other contract has a number of important implications, which it is not appropriate to explore on the facts of this case. For example, if the obligation to pay rent is as fundamental as the obligation to keep the house habitable, it will follow that a default in rent payments is a repudiatory act on the tenant's part. That this may follow is not, however, a reason for going back on what appears to me to be the inexorable effect of binding authority . . .

Comment

(1) Is it satisfactory to apply contract principles without understanding the 'important implications' which may follow?[2]

(2) It is traditionally thought that covenants in leases are independent: either party can enforce covenants even though they are in breach of their own obligations.[3] Do the recent developments cast doubt on these rules?

---

[2] Sedley QC did say that statutory controls over forfeiture by the landlord would apply.
[3] *Melville* v *Grapelodge Developments Ltd* (1978) 39 P&CR 179 (landlord suing); *Taylor* v *Webb* [1937] 2 KB 283 at p 290 (tenant suing).

Extract 15.1.5

Reichman v Beveridge [2007] 1 P&R 358

L sued T for rent. T argued that L should have mitigated his loss by forfeiting the lease and reletting the premises.

LLOYD LJ: 11.   There is no doubt that, where a party to a lease seeks to recover damages from the other for breach of covenant under the lease, the rules about mitigation of loss will apply.

12.   However, Mr Gauntlett [counsel for T] seeks to go further than that, and to establish that the same rule applies even if the landlord does not terminate the lease for breach of the tenant's covenants, but merely sues for each instalment of rent as it falls due . . .

[*White & Carter (Councils) Ltd* v *McGregor* [1962] A.C. 413 is discussed.]

17.   There is, therefore, a very limited category of cases in which, although the innocent party to a contract has not accepted a repudiation by the other party, and although the innocent party is able to continue to perform all his obligations under the contract despite the absence of co-operation from the other party, nevertheless the court will not allow the innocent party to enforce his full contractual right to maintain the contract in force and sue for the contract price. The characteristics of such cases are that an election to keep the contract alive would be wholly unreasonable and that damages would be an adequate remedy, or that the landlord would have no legitimate interest in making such an election. Mr Gauntlett seeks to establish that a case where the tenant has not only failed to pay rent and all other sums due under the lease, but has also abandoned the demised premises is, or may be, within this category of cases.

Would damages be an adequate remedy for the landlord?

18.   Mr Gauntlett's proposition has to be that, if the landlord terminates the tenancy and takes steps to relet, and if the sums payable to him as a result are less than those that would have been payable during the period of the lease after the date on which he took possession, he can recover that loss by way of damages from the tenant. Otherwise damages would not be an adequate remedy for the loss caused, as compared with the landlord's position if he held the tenant to the lease and sued for the rent as it fell due.

19.   Once the landlord has taken possession he cannot recover rent under the lease. The question is whether he can recover damages for the loss of the future rent, which would have to be on the basis that it was loss caused by the tenant's breach of contract. There is no English case which decides that the landlord can recover damages of this kind. There is at least one English decision to the contrary, but it is of some antiquity. In Canada and Australia, however, the highest courts have decided that such damages can be recovered.

26.   Moreover, the actual decision in *Walls* v *Atcheson* [(1826) 11 Moore CP and Exch Reports 379] is authority for the proposition that . . . a landlord cannot recover damages from the tenant for loss of rent after he has re-entered so as to bring the lease to an end, though it is fair to say that it was not argued on the basis of acceptance of the tenant's repudiation and damages for that breach of contract. There is no English authority which decides otherwise, despite the developments in Canada and Australia which I have described. *Woodfall on Landlord and Tenant*, at para 17.315, suggests that a landlord may accept a tenant's repudiation and sue for loss of future rent, but the authorities cited are those which I have mentioned from Canada and Australia. It does not seem to me that this is a correct statement of English law as it now stands on this point.

30.   The important point is whether it could be said that a landlord was acting wholly unreasonably in failing to take steps to find an alternative tenant to whom to let in place of the defaulting tenant, rather than leaving the lease in place and suing for the rent as it falls due. That is to be considered against the background of the rights and obligations under the lease. If the lease remains in force, the landlord is entitled to the rent and other sums falling due . . .

31.   Another factor of practical relevance is that it would almost always be open to the tenant under the terms of the lease (as in the present case) to seek to find an assignee or sub-tenant and to ask the landlord's consent to the assignment or underletting. Of course the tenant might face practical and economic problems in this respect. If the current rent is higher than the market rent, it would be difficult to find an assignee . . . Nevertheless, it seems to me that it would be difficult to describe the landlord's position as wholly unreasonable if it took the line that the tenant, whose default created the problem, should bear the burden of finding a solution, in circumstances in which the lease allows the tenant to do so, with an obligation on the landlord not unreasonably to refuse consent to such a proposal.

Conclusion

39.   Mr Gauntlett urged on us a modern approach to the relationship between landlord and tenant, focussing on principles of contract law, and a policy approach which would not leave premises empty, after the tenants had abandoned them and while the landlord waited for the end of the lease, so as to avoid the waste of useful space and to ensure that property is put to beneficial use. As to the latter factor, if there is enough demand for the space, the market rent may exceed that payable under the lease in which case the landlord will no doubt terminate the lease and re-let at a profit. Equally, the tenant can attempt to find an assignee or sub-tenant to use the premises; it is not only the landlord who can take steps to fill the space.

40.   Leaving aside policy issues of that kind, it seems to me that Mr Gauntlett's submissions fail to take account of the present state of English law as to the consequences of the premature termination of a tenancy, or of the very limited scope for the intervention of equity as explained in *White & Carter* and subsequent cases . . .

42.   . . . I do not decide whether or not repudiation plays any, and if so what, part in the English law of landlord and tenant. That is not directly in issue before us, and it would be wrong to decide it unnecessarily. There is, however, no case in English law that shows that a landlord can recover damages from a former tenant in respect of loss of future rent after termination, and there is at least one case which decides that he cannot. In those circumstances, either damages are not an adequate remedy for the landlord, or at least the landlord would be acting reasonably in taking the view that he should not terminate the lease because he may well not be able to recover such damages. In principle, moreover, if the landlord chooses to regard it as up to the tenant to propose an assignee, sub-tenant or, if he wishes, a substitute tenant under a new tenancy, rather than take the initiative himself, that is not unreasonable, still less wholly unreasonable.

Comment

(1) Considerable stress is placed on *White & Carter* for the proposition that L was entitled to maintain the lease in being and sue for rent, unless L was acting 'wholly unreasonably'.

(2) Was Lloyd LJ justified in concluding that L could not claim rent after terminating the lease? Should Commonwealth cases such as *Progressive Mailing* (which was discussed) have been given greater weight than *Walls* v *Atcheson*?

(3) Would the result have been different if L had been able to sue for rent after termination?

Extract 15.1.6

Bruton v *London & Quadrant Housing Trust* [2000] 1 AC 406

The 'landlord' held only a licence. Could the landlord grant a lease attracting statutory repairing obligations?

LORD HOFFMANN: [Having held that there were no 'special circumstances' taking the case outside *Street* v *Mountford*:] My Lords, in my opinion, that is the end of the matter. But the Court of Appeal did not stop at that point. In the leading majority judgment, Millett LJ said [1998] QB 834, 845 that an agreement could not be a lease unless it had a further characteristic, namely that it created a legal estate in the land which 'binds the whole world'. If, as in this case, the grantor had no legal estate, the agreement could not create one and therefore did not qualify as a lease. The only exception was the case in which the grantor was estopped from denying that he could not create a legal estate. In that case, a 'tenancy by estoppel' came into existence. But an estoppel depended upon the grantor having purported to grant a lease and in this case the trust had not done so. It had made it clear that it was only purporting to grant a licence.

My Lords, I hope that this summary does justice to the closely reasoned judgment of Millett LJ. But I fear that I must respectfully differ at three critical steps in the argument.

First, the term 'lease' or 'tenancy' describes a relationship between two parties who are designated landlord and tenant. It is not concerned with the question of whether the agreement creates an estate or other proprietary interest which may be binding upon third parties. A lease may, and usually does, create a proprietary interest called a leasehold estate or, technically, a 'term of years absolute'. This will depend upon whether the landlord had an interest out of which he could grant it. Nemo dat quod non habet. But it is the fact that the agreement is a lease which creates the proprietary interest. It is putting the cart before the horse to say that whether the agreement is a lease depends upon whether it creates a proprietary interest.

. . .

It seems to me that Denning LJ [in *Lewisham Borough Council* v *Roberts* [1949] 2 KB 608] was focusing on the question of whether the Crown could create a legal interest in the land which would be binding upon third parties and said, correctly, that the Crown could not create such an interest without having an estate of its own. It is true that he said the Crown could not 'grant a lease' and this could be read to mean that the absence of a legal estate prevented the Crown from entering into the relationship of landlord and tenant. But I do not think that this is what he had in mind. In any case, the Crown in that case could not have validly entered into such a relationship because it would have been ultra vires its statutory powers under the Emergency Powers (Defence) Act 1939: see *Minister of Agriculture and Fisheries* v *Matthews* [1950] 1 KB 148.

Millett LJ, at p 846, distinguished *Family Housing Association* v *Jones* [1990] 1 WLR 779, where, as I have said, the facts were very similar to those in the present case, on the ground that 'the fact that the grantor had no title was not referred to in argument or the judgments'. In my opinion this is easily explained by the fact that the grantor's title or lack of title was irrelevant to the issue in the case.

. . .

Thirdly, I cannot agree that there is no inconsistency between what the trust purported to do and its denial of the existence of a tenancy. This seems to me to fly in the face of *Street* v *Mountford* [1985] AC 809. In my opinion, the trust plainly did purport to grant a tenancy. It entered into an agreement on terms which constituted a tenancy. It may have agreed with Mr Bruton to say that it was not a tenancy. But the parties cannot contract out of the Rent Acts or other landlord and tenant statutes by such devices. Nor in my view can they be used by a landlord to avoid being estopped from denying that he entered into the agreement he actually made.

Comment

(1) The second 'critical step' concerned tenancies by estoppel and has already been quoted.[4]

---

[4] Extract 14.2.13 above.

(2) What would be the consequences of such a 'contractual' lease?

(3) In the Court of Appeal, the debate was whether a tenancy by estoppel existed. Is this a preferable way of characterising the issue in *Bruton*?

(4) What is the role of *Bruton* in the debate as to the application of contractual principles to leases?

The nature of the *Bruton* lease has been considered by the House of Lords.

Extract 15.1.7

Kay v Lambeth LBC [2006] 2 AC 465

Lambeth gave a licence to LQHT. There was a *Bruton* lease by LQHT to Kay, the appellants. LQHT surrendered their licence and were granted a lease (the effect of that lease is not discussed in the extract).

LORD SCOTT: 138. . . . But, it is said, it was not open to LQHT to surrender the tenancies that, as *Bruton* had held, LQHT had granted to the appellants. So, the argument proceeds, the appellants' *Bruton* tenancies must have survived the surrender by LQHT of its 1986 licence and have become, in the scintilla temporis between the surrender of the licence and the grant of the 1995 lease, tenancies held directly of Lambeth. Lambeth thereby became, and has remained, bound by the tenancies . . .

143.   But the *Mellor* v *Watkins* [(1874) LR 9 QB 400] principle and the *Pennell* v *Payne* [[1995] QB 192] principle can have no relevance to a case in which a tenancy has been granted by someone without any estate in the land in question. The *Bruton* tenancies are all of that character. LQHT was, when it granted the *Bruton* tenancies, merely a licensee of Lambeth. The tenancies were not granted by Lambeth and were not carved by LQHT out of any estate that Lambeth had granted to LQHT. They were not derivative estates. LQHT, prior to the grant of the 1995 lease, had no estate in the land. It merely had a contractual licence. In these circumstances the *Mellor* v *Watkins* point that the intermediate landlord cannot by a consensual surrender give away an interest that belongs to a sub-tenant has no substance. True it is that LQHT could not by a surrender of its licence give away or prejudice the rights of the *Bruton* tenants against itself, LQHT. But these rights never were enforceable against Lambeth. Once the LQHT licence had been terminated the appellants were trespassers as against Lambeth.

Comment

(1) For the effect of a surrender of a head *tenancy* on a sub-tenancy (the *Mellor* v *Watkins* principle), see Extracts 16.1.2 and 16.1.3 below.

(2) Lord Scott proceeds to describe Kay's lease as a '"non-estate" tenancy'. Is it acceptable to say that there can be a lease or tenancy without there being an estate?

(3) If the licence could not have been terminated save by breach of contract (in fact it was terminable on three months' notice), why should LQHT be able to defeat the rights of the defendant tenants? This question needs to be considered in conjunction with the law regarding contractual licences (studied in Chapter 18).

(4) Other arguments, especially that the licensees acted as agents for Lambeth, also failed in the Court of Appeal: [2005] QB 352. Human rights aspects of *Kay* have been overruled (see Extract 2.3.1 above).

(5) In *Mexfield Housing Co-operative Ltd* v *Berrisford* [2012] 1 AC 955 at [65], Lord Neuberger states that *Bruton* 'was about relativity of title which is the traditional bedrock

of English land law'. This idea is developed by Roberts [2012] Conv 87. How does relativity of title apply to *Bruton*? Is it a convincing analysis?

2. The landlord's covenant for quiet enjoyment; non-derogation from grant

Unless there is an express covenant, a covenant for quiet enjoyment is implied into every lease.

Extract 15.2.1

Southwark LBC v Mills [2001] 1 AC 1

Tenants sued their landlords because the normal activities of their neighbours in an elderly block of flats were clearly audible; the soundproofing was agreed to be far short of modern building regulations standards.

LORD HOFFMANN: . . . Neither tenancy agreement contains any warranty on the part of the landlord that the flat has sound insulation or is in any other way fit to live in. Nor does the law imply any such warranty. This is a fundamental principle of the English law of landlord and tenant . . .

. . . In *McNerny v Lambeth London Borough Council* (1988) 21 HLR 188, 194 Dillon LJ said that . . . it was . . . not for the courts to create liabilities which Parliament had not thought fit to enact. Taylor LJ spoke to the same effect. This seems to me to show a proper sensitivity to the limits of permissible judicial creativity and to be no more than constitutional propriety requires. In 1996 the Law Commission, in its report Landlord and Tenant: Responsibility for State and Condition of Property (1996) (Law Com No 238) recommended, at p 169, para 11.16, that a statutory warranty that a dwelling house is fit for human habitation should be implied into any lease for less than seven years. The Commission also recommended, at p 171, paras 11.28– 11.29, that the criteria for determining whether a dwelling house was fit for human habitation should be those listed in section 604 of the Housing Act 1985, as amended. These include such matters as dampness, adequate provision for lighting, heating and ventilation, facilities for cooking and effective drains. But they contain no mention of sound insulation. The Commission recorded, at p 51, para 4.44, that sound insulation was a factor which had been suggested for inclusion in the fitness standard but made no recommendation.

. . .

A third statutory technique is to prevent the creation of substandard housing in the first place. This is achieved by the requirement that new buildings and conversions should conform to standards laid down in building regulations. Local authorities have had power to make such regulations or byelaws since the middle of the last century . . . The Building Regulations 1985 (SI 1985/1065) contained for the first time a requirement that walls and floors which separate one dwelling from another should resist the transmission of airborne and impact sound: see Part E of Schedule 1 to the Regulations. Similar provisions are now contained in the Building Regulations 1991 (SI 1991/2768). But the regulations apply only to buildings erected or con- verted after they came into force. They are of no assistance to the appellants.

In the absence of any modern statutory remedy which covers their complaint, the appellants have attempted to fill the gap by pressing into service two ancient common law actions. They are the action on the covenant for quiet enjoyment and the action of nuisance. My Lords, I naturally accept that if the present case falls squarely within the scope of either of these actions, the appellants must succeed. But if the question is whether the common law should be devel- oped or extended to cover them, your Lordships must in my opinion have regard to the fact that

Parliament has dealt extensively with the problem of substandard housing over many years but so far declined to impose an obligation to install soundproofing in existing dwellings. No doubt Parliament had regard to the financial burden which this would impose upon local authority and private landlords. Like the Court of Appeal in *McNerny* v *Lambeth London Borough Council* 21 HLR 188, 194, I think that in a field such as housing law, which is very much a matter for the allocation of resources in accordance with democratically determined priorities, the development of the common law should not get out of step with legislative policy.

I shall consider first the covenant for quiet enjoyment . . . Clause B4 of Ms Baxter's agreement says: 'The council shall not interfere with the tenants' rights to quiet enjoyment of the premises during the continuance of the tenancy.' Read literally, these words would seem very apt. The flat is not quiet and the tenant is not enjoying it. But the words cannot be read literally. The covenant has a very long history. It has been expressed or implied in conveyances and leases of English land for centuries. It comes from a time when, in a conveyancing context, the words 'quiet enjoyment' had a technical meaning different from what they would today signify to a non-lawyer who was unacquainted with their history. So in *Jenkins* v *Jackson* (1888) 40 ChD 71, 74 Kekewich J felt obliged to point out that the word 'quietly' in the covenant:

'does not mean undisturbed by noise. When a man is quietly in possession it has nothing whatever to do with noise . . . "Peaceably and quietly" means without interference – without interruption of the possession.'

. . .

The covenant for quiet enjoyment is therefore a covenant that the tenant's lawful possession of the land will not be substantially interfered with by the acts of the lessor or those lawfully claiming under him. For present purposes, two points about the covenant should be noticed. First, there must be a substantial interference with the tenant's possession. This means his ability to use it in an ordinary lawful way. The covenant cannot be elevated into a warranty that the land is fit to be used for some special purpose: see *Dennett* v *Atherton* (1872) LR 7 QB 316. On the other hand, it is a question of fact and degree whether the tenant's ordinary use of the premises has been substantially interfered with. In *Sanderson* v *Berwick-upon-Tweed Corpn* (1884) 13 QBD 547 the flooding of a substantial area of agricultural land by water discharged from neighbouring land occupied by another tenant of the same landlord was held to be a breach of the covenant. In *Kenny* v *Preen* [1963] 1 QB 499 a landlord's threats to evict the tenant, accompanied by repeated shouting and knocking on her door, was held to be a breach. . . . For my part, . . . I do not see why, in principle, regular excessive noise cannot constitute a substantial interference with the ordinary enjoyment of the premises . . . The fact that the appellants complain of noise is therefore not in itself a reason why their actions should fail.

There is however another feature of the covenant which presents the appellants with a much greater difficulty. It is prospective in its nature: see *Norton on Deeds*, 2nd ed (1928), pp 612–613. It is a covenant that the tenant's lawful possession *will* not be interfered with by the landlord or anyone claiming under him. The covenant does not apply to things done before the grant of the tenancy, even though they may have continuing consequences for the tenant . . . [In] *Spoor* v *Green* (1874) LR 9 Ex 99 the plaintiff bought land and built houses upon it. The houses were damaged by subsidence caused by underground mining which had taken place before the sale. The Court of Exchequer held that there was no breach of the covenant for quiet enjoyment which had been given by the vendor . . .

The tenant takes the property not only in the physical condition in which he finds it but also subject to the uses which the parties must have contemplated would be made of the parts retained by the landlord. *Anderson* v *Oppenheimer* (1880) 5 QBD 602, in which it was contemplated that the cistern would be used to contain water, demonstrates this proposition. An even more pertinent case is *Lyttelton Times Co Ltd* v *Warners Ltd* [1907] AC 476. The plaintiffs owned a hotel in Christchurch, New Zealand, next to the premises in which the defendants operated a printing press. They made an agreement under which the defendants would rebuild their premises and grant a lease of the upper floors to the plaintiffs for use as additional hotel bedrooms. Unfortunately the noise and vibrations of the press beneath caused substantial inconvenience to the occupants of the bedrooms. The plaintiffs claimed an injunction to restrain the defendants from working their press. They said that the defendants knew that they intended to use the premises as bedrooms and were under an implied obligation not to interfere with their convenient use. But Lord Loreburn LC, giving the advice of the Privy Council, said that the plaintiffs also knew that the defendants intended to use their premises for printing. He went on, at p 481:

> 'When it is a question of what shall be implied from the contract, it is proper to ascertain what in fact was the purpose, or what were the purposes, to which both intended the land to be put, and having found that, both should be held to all that was implied in this common intention . . . if it be true that neither has done or asks to do anything which was not contemplated by both, neither can have any right against the other.'

If one stands back from the technicalities of the law of landlord and tenant and construes the tenancy agreement in accordance with ordinary contractual principles, I think that one reaches the same conclusion. In the grant of a tenancy it is fundamental to the common understanding of the parties, objectively determined, that the landlord gives no implied warranty as to the condition or fitness of the premises. Caveat lessee. It would be entirely inconsistent with this common understanding if the covenant for quiet enjoyment were interpreted to create liability for disturbance or inconvenience or any other damage attributable to the condition of the premises. Secondly, the lease must be construed against the background facts which would reasonably have been known to the parties at the time it was granted. The tenant in *Anderson v Oppenheimer* (1880) 5 QBD 602 must be taken to have known that the building had a water system and that the landlord would therefore keep the cistern supplied with water. The hotel owners in *Lyttelton Times Co Ltd* v *Warners Ltd* [1907] AC 476 must be taken to have known that the lessor of their bedrooms would be operating a printing press downstairs. They did not realise that the noise and vibrations would be a problem, but that was because of the way in which the premises had been constructed. On that point the landlord gave no warranty. Against this background, the lease could not be construed as entitling the tenant to close down the landlord's business.

LORD MILLETT: . . . My Lords, these appeals illuminate a problem of considerable social importance. No one, least of all the two councils concerned, would wish anyone to live in the conditions to which the tenants in these appeals are exposed. For the future, building regulations will ensure that new constructions and conversions have adequate sound insulation. But the huge stock of pre-war residential properties presents an intractable problem. Local authorities have limited resources, and have to decide on their priorities. Many of their older properties admit damp and are barely fit for human habitation. Southwark London Borough Council has estimated that it would cost £1.271 billion to bring its existing housing stock up to acceptable modern standards. Its budget for 1998–1999 for major housing schemes was under £55m. The average cost of installing sound installation in the flats in Casino Avenue is £8,000 per flat. There are 34 similar flats in the estate, so that the total cost would be about £272,000. The borough-wide cost could be of the order of £37m. The relevant local residents' association has considered that the installation of sound insulation is not a priority need.

These cases raise issues of priority in the allocation of resources. Such issues must be resolved by the democratic process, national and local. The judges are not equipped to resolve them. All that we can do is to say that there is nothing in the relevant tenancy agreements or current legislation, or in the common law, which would enable the tenants to obtain redress through the courts.

Comment

(1) A claim based on nuisance was also rejected.

(2) What is meant by 'quiet enjoyment'?

(3) What connection does the covenant have with (i) nuisance and (ii) repairing liability?

(4) Does the House of Lords place too much stress on the practical implications of holding that there is liability?

(5) Why is the covenant 'prospective in nature'? What is the significance of this?

Abusive conduct by landlords has frequently troubled the courts, as can be seen by the following extract.

Extract 15.2.2

Drane v Evangelou [1978] 1 WLR 455

LORD DENNING MR: . . . Counsel for the defendant submitted that [the] claim was for breach of a covenant for quiet enjoyment. He cited a passage from *Woodfall on Landlord and Tenant*, 27th ed (1968), para 1338: 'Since the claim is in contract, punitive or exemplary damages cannot be awarded.' The judge at once said: 'What about trespass? Does the claim not lie in trespass?' Counsel for the defendant urged that trespass was not pleaded. The judge then said: 'The facts are alleged sufficiently so it does not matter what label you put upon it.' The judge was right. The plaintiff in the particulars of claim gave details saying that three men broke the door, removed the plaintiff's belongings, bolted the door from the inside: and so forth. Those facts were clearly sufficient to warrant a claim for trespass . . .

Comment

The court upheld an award of £1,000 exemplary damages. This is significant because financial loss is frequently small in these cases.

A wide range of statutory controls exist which are directed towards such conduct by landlords, or at least can be applied to such cases.

Extract 15.2.3

Criminal Law Act 1977, s 6

6.—(1) Subject to the following provisions of this section, any person who, without lawful authority, uses or threatens violence for the purpose of securing entry into any premises for himself or for any other person is guilty of an offence, provided that—
  (a) there is someone present on those premises at the time who is opposed to the entry which the violence is intended to secure; and
  (b) the person using or threatening the violence knows that that is the case.
  (1A) Subsection (1) above does not apply to a person who is a displaced residential occupier . . .
  (2) Subject to subsection (1A) above, the fact that a person has any interest in or right to possession or occupation of any premises shall not for the purposes of subsection (1) above constitute lawful authority for the use or threat of violence by him or anyone else for the purpose of securing his entry into those premises.

Extract 15.2.4

Protection from Eviction Act 1977, s 1

1.—(2) If any person unlawfully deprives the residential occupier of any premises of his occupation of the premises or any part thereof, or attempts to do so, he shall be guilty of an offence unless he proves that he believed, and had reasonable cause to believe, that the residential occupier had ceased to reside in the premises.

(3) If any person with intent to cause the residential occupier of any premises—

(a)   to give up the occupation of the premises or any part thereof; or

(b)   to refrain from exercising any right or pursuing any remedy in respect of the premises or part thereof;

does acts likely to interfere with the peace or comfort of the residential occupier or members of his household, or persistently withdraws or withholds services reasonably required for the occupation of the premises as a residence he shall be guilty of an offence.

Comment

(1) It is important to note that the simple enforcement of one's proprietary rights does not confer a defence.

(2) Section 1(3A)–(3C) of the Protection from Eviction Act 1977 extends liability to cases where the landlord 'knows or has reasonable cause to believe that the conduct is likely to cause' the giving up of occupation.

Extract 15.2.5

Housing Act 1988, ss 27–28

27.—(1) This section applies if, at any time after 9th June 1988, a landlord (in this section referred to as 'the landlord in default') or any person acting on behalf of the landlord in default unlawfully deprives the residential occupier of any premises of his occupation of the whole or part of the premises.

(2) This section also applies if, at any time after 9th June 1988, a landlord (in this section referred to as 'the landlord in default') or any person acting on behalf of the landlord in default—

(a)   attempts unlawfully to deprive the residential occupier of any premises of his occupation of the whole or part of the premises, or

(b)   knowing or having reasonable cause to believe that the conduct is likely to cause the residential occupier of any premises—

(i)   to give up his occupation of the premises or any part thereof, or

(ii)   to refrain from exercising any right or pursuing any remedy in respect of the premises or any part thereof,

does acts likely to interfere with the peace or comfort of the residential occupier or members of his household, or persistently withdraws or withholds services reasonably required for the occupation of the premises as a residence,

and, as a result, the residential occupier gives up his occupation of the premises as a residence.

(3) Subject to the following provisions of this section, where this section applies, the landlord in default shall, by virtue of this section, be liable to pay to the former residential occupier, in respect of his loss of the right to occupy the premises in question as his residence, damages assessed on the basis set out in section 28 below.

(8) . . . it shall be a defence for the defendant to prove that he believed, and had reasonable cause to believe—

(a)   that the residential occupier had ceased to reside in the premises in question . . . ; or

    (b)   that, where the liability would otherwise arise by virtue only of the doing of acts or the withdrawal or withholding of services, he had reasonable grounds for doing the acts or withdrawing or withholding the services in question.

    28.—(1)   The basis for the assessment of damages referred to in section 27(3) above is the difference in value, determined as at the time immediately before the residential occupier ceased to occupy the premises in question as his residence, between—

    (a)   the value of the interest of the landlord in default determined on the assumption that the residential occupier continues to have the same right to occupy the premises as before that time; and

    (b)   the value of that interest determined on the assumption that the residential occupier has ceased to have that right.

Comment

(1) This civil remedy has been very significant because the value of leased residential premises may be very much below the vacant possession value. One early case involved an award of £31,000.[5] Now that statutory protection of tenants has diminished, the remedy will be less important.

(2) Damages may be reduced on account of the occupier's conduct or the unreasonable refusal of an offer to reinstate the occupier.

(3) The Protection from Harassment Act 1997 provides both civil and criminal remedies for harassment, save by reasonable conduct. Injunctions may be awarded and damages 'for (among other things) any anxiety caused by the harassment and any financial loss'. Does this legislation add anything to tenants' protection?

The principle that a grantor may not derogate from his grant sometimes ensures that the leased property can be used as intended. Such situations may not readily fit within covenants for quiet enjoyment.

Extract 15.2.6

Harmer v *Jumbil (Nigeria) Tin Areas Ltd* [1921] 1 Ch 200

A tenant took a lease of land for use as an explosives magazine, both parties being aware that explosives licences would require there to be no buildings within a certain radius. Could the landlord build on adjacent retained land within that radius?

WARRINGTON LJ: The question is whether the principle that a grantor cannot be allowed to derogate from his own grant is applicable under the facts of the present case . . .

    The principle is now well settled, and I propose, in explanation of it, to read one or two passages from the judgment of Parker J in *Browne* v *Flower*.[i] . . . What the learned judge said was this: 'The plaintiffs next relied on the maxim that no one can be allowed to derogate from his own grant. This maxim is generally quoted as explaining certain implications which may arise from the fact that, or the circumstances under which, an owner of land grants or demises part of it, retaining the remainder in his own hands. The real difficulty is in each case to ascertain how far such implications extend . . . But the implications usually explained by the maxim that no one can derogate from his own grant do not stop short with easements. Under certain circumstances there will be implied on the part of the grantor or lessor obligations which restrict the user of the land retained by him further than can be explained by the implication of any

---

[5] *Tagro* v *Cafane* [1991] 1 WLR 378.

easement known to the law. Thus, if the grant or demise be made for a particular purpose, the grantor or lessor comes under an obligation not to use the land retained by him in such a way as to render the land granted or demised unfit or materially less fit for the particular purpose for which the grant or demise was made.' Now it is under that branch that the circumstances of the present case fall.

. . . But it is contended that, when it is laid down that the lessor is under an obligation not to render the demised premises unfit for the purpose for which they were demised, all that is thereby meant is that he must not do anything which renders them physically unfit.

Undoubtedly this is the first case in which this particular question has arisen, but for myself I confess that I can see no reason why the principle should be limited in the way contended for by the defendants. The premises have become unfit for the purpose for which they were demised, and this because it is no longer legal for the plaintiff to use them for that purpose by reason of the acts of the defendants . . .

[i] [1911] 1 Ch 219, 224, 225.

Useful as the doctrine is, the reports are full of cases where it has not been applied.

Extract 15.2.7

Birmingham, Dudley & District Banking Company v Ross (1888) 38 Ch D 295

The defendant was developing an area and leased part of it. Could the lessee prevent the development of nearby plots which reduced the light to the leased land?

COTTON LJ: . . . It is very true that when a man grants a house, he grants that which is necessary for the existence of that house, and it might have been a serious question here if it had been shewn that the interference with the light was of such a character as entirely to prevent the house of the Plaintiffs being used as a house. But that was not the case made . . .

. . . it is, in my opinion, impossible to imply an obligation on the corporation not to let their land in any way for building otherwise than for erecting such building as was on it at the time; and if we cannot do that I cannot see how any line can be drawn as to the obligation they undertook as regards building; because, unless we say that they undertook an obligation not to put any building higher than that which then existed, I cannot see where we can impose any obligation or fix any line as to the height to which buildings might be put.

Extract 15.2.8

Port v Griffith [1938] 1 All ER 295

The defendant landlord retained shops, close to the leased premises. Could the defendant permit their use in a manner which would compete with the tenant's business?

LUXMOORE J: [In *Browne v Flower*,[i] Parker J] states, at p 227:

'It is quite reasonable for a purchaser to assume that a vendor who sells land for a particular purpose will not do anything to prevent its being used for that purpose, but it would be utterly unreasonable to assume that the vendor was undertaking restrictive obligations which would prevent his using land retained by him for any lawful purpose whatsoever merely because his so doing might affect the amenities of the property he had sold. After all, a purchaser can always bargain for those rights which he deems indispensable to his comfort.'

Applying what was said by Parker, J, to the facts of the present case, the question to be determined appears to be: Has the letting by the defendants to Fisher of Shops Nos 4 and 5 rendered the plaintiff's Shop No 3 unfit, or materially less fit, to be used for the purposes for which it was demised?

The presence of a trade rival in premises next door to those occupied by the trader may, or may not, be a detriment to any particular business. I do not think that I should be justified in saying that the presence of a trade rival next door must of necessity be a detriment, but, whatever the view may be, the presence of a trade rival next door does not render the premises on which the trader is carrying on his business unfit for that purpose, although it may incidentally reduce the profit ratio to be earned in that business . . .

[i] [1911] 1 Ch 219.

Comment

(1) When will the non-derogation principle apply?

(2) Does it add much to covenants for quiet enjoyment? Could the two be seen as manifestations of the same underlying principle?[6]

(3) Could *Port* v *Griffith* be distinguished in the case of a highly specialised shop?[7]

3. Repairing obligations

Traditionally the common law imposed repairing obligations on neither landlord nor tenant: it was up to them to specify any duties. This is reflected in the following dictum of Lord Campbell CJ in *Gott* v *Gandy*:[8]

It is clear to my mind that, though, in the absence of an express contract, a tenant from year to year is not bound to do substantial repairs, yet, in the absence of an express contract, he has no right to compel his landlord to do them.

More recently, *Liverpool City Council* v *Irwin*[9] has shown how covenants may sometimes be implied into leases.

Extract 15.3.1

Duke of Westminster v *Guild* [1985] QB 688

The tenant had the right to use a drain under the landlord's land. Was the landlord bound to repair it?

SLADE LJ: . . . The present case is in our judgment distinguishable from *Liverpool City Council* v *Irwin* [1977] AC 239 in at least two material respects. First there is a formal lease which, on the face of it, represents the apparently complete bargain between the parties. Secondly, this present case is not in our opinion a type of landlord–tenant situation, which gives rise to special considerations, such as the case of a high-rise building in multiple occupation, where the essential means of access to the unit are retained in the landlord's occupation, thus making it appropriate for the court to imply any particular term as a legal incident of the contract.

Accordingly, for the purpose of considering whether the suggested contractual obligation falls to be implied in the present case, we can see no justification for applying a test more favourable to the defendant than the test applicable to the construction of any ordinary commercial lease of unfurnished premises or land which does not fall into a special category such as was referred to by Lord Wilberforce or Lord Cross of Chelsea.

---

[6] As suggested by Lindley LJ in *Robinson* v *Kilvert* (1889) 41 Ch D 88 at p 95.
[7] *Oceanic Village Ltd* v *Shirayma Shokussan Co Ltd* [2001] L&TR 478 (London Aquarium shop).
[8] (1853) 2 El&Bl 845 at p 847 (118 ER 984 at p 985).
[9] [1977] AC 239; Extract 15.1.1 above.

. . .

Perhaps it would have been sensible or even reasonable for the defendant on entering into the lease to exact an express covenant by the plaintiffs to do these repairs. But he did not do so and we find it impossible to presume an intention on the part of all parties to the lease that such a covenant should be included. An obligation of this nature cannot in our judgment properly be added to the lease by a process of implication.

<hr>

Extract 15.3.2

Barrett v *Lounova (1982) Ltd* [1990] 1 QB 348

<hr>

The lease required the tenant to undertake interior repairs, but was silent as to the exterior.

KERR LJ: [After citing cases including *Irwin* and *Guild*:] So it follows that a repairing obligation upon the landlord can clearly arise as a matter of implication. But that leaves the question already mentioned, which I find difficult and on the borderline, whether the terms and circumstances of this particular lease enable such an implication to be made. . . . In my view the clue lies in what Slade LJ referred to as a 'correlative obligation', in this case one which is correlative to the express covenant by the tenant to keep the inside and fixtures in good repair, order and condition.

The considerations which lead me to that conclusion are the following. It is obvious, as shown by this case itself, that sooner or later the covenant imposed on the tenant in respect of the inside can no longer be complied with unless the outside has been kept in repair . . . In my view it is therefore necessary, as a matter of business efficacy to make this agreement workable, that an obligation to keep the outside in repair must be imposed on someone. For myself, I would reject the persuasive submission of Mr Pryor on behalf of the landlord, that both parties may have thought that in practice the landlord – or possibly the tenant – would do the necessary repairs, so that no problem would arise. In my view that is not a businesslike construction of a tenancy agreement.

Accordingly, on the basis that an obligation to keep the outside in a proper state of repair must be imposed on someone, three answers are possible.

First, that the tenant is obliged to keep the outside in repair as well as the inside, at any rate to such extent as may be necessary to enable him to perform his covenant. I would reject that as being unbusinesslike and unrealistic. In the case of a tenancy of this nature, which was to become a monthly tenancy after one year, the rent being paid weekly, it is clearly unrealistic to conclude that this could have been the common intention . . .

The second solution would be the implication of a joint obligation on both parties to keep the outside in good repair. I reject that as being obviously unworkable and I do not think that Mr Pryor really suggested the contrary.

That leaves one with the third solution, an implied obligation on the landlord. In my view this is the only solution which makes business sense. The recorder reached the same conclusion by following much the same route, and I agree with him.

Comment

(1) Why was a duty to repair implied when earlier cases might have suggested otherwise?

(2) In many respects the most interesting aspect of *Barrett* is that the court rejects a position where no party is under a duty to repair. This does look different from the previous law. P F Smith has written[10] that 'At first sight, the Court of Appeal have denied

<hr>

[10] [1988] Conv 448 at p 449; contrast his later views [2003] Conv 112 at pp 117–118.

the existence of a general rule of no liability on the part of the landlord to do repairs.' How revolutionary is *Barrett*?

Extract 15.3.3

Adami v Lincoln Grange Management Ltd (1997) 30 HLR 982 (CA)

As in *Barrett*, interior repairing obligations were imposed on tenants.

SIR JOHN VINELOTT: . . . In the context of a lease for a term of some 260 years at a nominal rent granted by a corporate lessor originally incorporated as a management company, in which shares are held by the lessees of all the maisonettes and flats comprised in the development and which contains detailed provisions governing the repair of the individual maisonettes and flats, the levying of a service charge to meet the costs of the maintenance of the community land and for insurance to be effected and maintained at the expense of the lessees to cover damage from any catastrophe affecting a block as a whole so far as reasonably foreseeable, it is, in my judgment, impossible to presume an intention that the cost of maintaining the structure of each block should fall on the lessor . . .

[After considering the solutions discussed in *Barrett*:] In the context of a lease for over 260 years at a nominal rent containing the elaborate provisions which I have summarised, there is another possibility, namely that neither would be under an obligation to make good defects in the structure of the block arising otherwise than from the insured risks and that such defects would be dealt with, if the situation arose, by co-operation between the lessees all of whom, as I have said, are shareholders in Lincoln Grange Management Ltd and Lincoln Grange Management Ltd in its capacity as lessor and manager.

The decision of the Court of Appeal in *Barrett v Lounova* is, of course, binding on this court. However, in my judgment it must be taken as decided upon the special facts of that case and no principle can be discerned which requires the implication of an obligation on the part of the lessor to keep the structure of the block in good repair . . .

Comment

How much damage to *Barrett* has been inflicted?

A. Obligations on tenants

Traditionally, duties were expressed in terms of the ancient rules relating to waste, but this 'is a somewhat archaic subject, now seldom mentioned'.[11]

Extract 15.3.4

Warren v Keen [1954] 1 QB 15

DENNING LJ: . . . Apart from express contract, a tenant owes no duty to the landlord to keep the premises in repair. The only duty of the tenant is to use the premises in a husbandlike, or what is the same thing, a tenantlike manner . . . It can, I think, best be shown by some illustrations. The tenant must take proper care of the place. He must, if he is going away for the winter, turn off the water and empty the boiler. He must clean the chimneys, when necessary, and also the windows. He must mend the electric light when it fuses. He must unstop the sink when it is blocked by his waste. In short, he must do the little jobs about the place which a reasonable tenant would do. In addition, he must, of course, not damage the house, wilfully or negligently; and he must see that his family and guests do not damage it: and if they do, he must repair it.

---

[11] *Mancetter Developments Ltd v Garmanson Ltd* [1986] QB 1212 at p 1218.

But apart from such things, if the house falls into disrepair through fair wear and tear or lapse of time, or for any reason not caused by him, then the tenant is not liable to repair it.

Comment

Warren involved a weekly tenancy. Should these standards vary according to the length of the lease and whether or not residential premises are involved?

B. Obligations on landlords

(i) Fitness for habitation

Extract 15.3.5

Smith v *Marrable* (1843) 11 M&W 5 (152 ER 693)

Liability was found when a house was infested with bugs.

LORD ABINGER CB: . . . A man who lets a ready-furnished house surely does so under the implied condition or obligation – call it which you will – that the house is in a fit state to be inhabited. Suppose, instead of the particular nuisance which existed in this case, the tenant discovered the fact – unknown perhaps to the landlord – that lodgers had previously quitted the house in consequence of having ascertained that a person had recently died in it of plague or scarlet fever; would not the law imply that he ought not to be compelled to stay in it? . . .

Comment

How does this fit with ideas of *caveat emptor*? Can it be argued that tenants should ensure that premises fit their requirements?

Extract 15.3.6

Hart v *Windsor* (1843) 12 M&W 68 (152 ER 1114)

Could an obligation be implied into an unfurnished tenancy?

PARKE B: . . . It appears, therefore, to us to be clear upon the old authorities, that there is no implied warranty on a lease of a house, or of land, that it is, or shall be, reasonably fit for habitation or cultivation. . . .
    . . . *Smith* v *Marrable* . . . was the case of a demise of a ready-furnished house for a temporary residence at a watering-place. It was not a lease of real estate merely . . .
    We are all of opinion, for these reasons, that there is no contract, still less a condition, implied by law on the demise of real property only, that it is fit for the purpose for which it is let. The principles of the common law do not warrant such a position; and though, in the case of a dwelling-house taken for habitation, there is no apparent injustice in inferring a contract of this nature, the same rule must apply to land taken for other purposes – for building upon, or for cultivation; and there would be no limit to the inconvenience which would ensue. It is much better to leave the parties in every case to protect their interests themselves, by proper stipulations, and if they really mean a lease to be void by reason of any unfitness in the subject for the purpose intended, they should express that meaning.

Comment

How damaging is this to the reasoning in *Smith* v *Marrable*?

Extract 15.3.7

Sarson v Roberts [1895] 2 QB 395

KAY LJ: . . . The cases have gone to this extent, that when a person hires a furnished house there is an implied condition that it shall be fit to live in at the time of the hiring. It is easy to see how that comes about, because the landlord, knowing the purpose of the tenant in hiring the house, must be taken to warrant that the house he is letting shall be reasonably fit for the purpose for which it is hired. To extend this warranty so as to make it apply to the condition of the house during the tenancy is not, to my mind, reasonable. The condition is that at the time of letting the premises they are in such a state that the tenant can take them. It is no defence on the part of the landlord to an action for breach of the condition that he did not know that the premises were otherwise than fit for occupation, because he could ascertain, and ought to have known. If the condition is extended, so as to apply if the premises become insanitary during the term, the landlord would be in a different position. He may be at a distance and know nothing as to the state of the house, or it may become insanitary from causes over which he has had no power or control. The rule at best is extremely artificial, because it does not extend to unfurnished lodgings; and I am certainly not inclined to extend it beyond the decision in *Smith* v *Marrable*.[i]

[i] 11 M&W 5; 12 LJ (Ex) 223.

Comment

How convincing is this restriction to the initial grant?

(ii) Statutory duties

Particularly for short residential tenancies, the common law position has long been regarded as unsatisfactory. There are two principal provisions, both originating before the current 1985 legislation.

Extract 15.3.8

Landlord and Tenant Act 1985, ss 8, 10–13

8.—(1) In a contract to which this section applies for the letting of a house for human habitation there is implied, notwithstanding any stipulation to the contrary—

    (a) a condition that the house is fit for human habitation at the commencement of the tenancy, and

    (b) an undertaking that the house will be kept by the landlord fit for human habitation during the tenancy.

10.—In determining for the purposes of this Act whether a house is unfit for human habitation, regard shall be had to its condition in respect of the following matters—

repair,
stability,
freedom from damp,
internal arrangement,
natural lighting,
ventilation,
water supply,
drainage and sanitary conveniences,
facilities for preparation and cooking of food and for the disposal of waste water;

and the house shall be regarded as unfit for human habitation if, and only if, it is so far defective in one or more of those matters that it is not reasonably suitable for occupation in that condition.

11.—(1)   In a lease to which this section applies (as to which, see sections 13 and 14) there is implied a covenant by the lessor—

(a)   to keep in repair the structure and exterior of the dwelling-house (including drains, gutters and external pipes),

(b)   to keep in repair and proper working order the installations in the dwelling-house for the supply of water, gas and electricity and for sanitation (including basins, sinks, baths and sanitary conveniences, but not other fixtures, fittings and appliances for making use of the supply of water, gas or electricity), and

(c)   to keep in repair and proper working order the installations in the dwelling-house for space heating and heating water.

(1A)   If a lease to which this section applies is a lease of a dwelling-house which forms part only of a building, then, subject to subsection (1B), the covenant implied by subsection (1) shall have effect as if—

(a)   the reference in paragraph (a) of that subsection to the dwelling-house included a reference to any part of the building in which the lessor has an estate or interest; and

(b)   any reference in paragraphs (b) and (c) of that subsection to an installation in the dwelling-house included a reference to an installation which, directly or indirectly, serves the dwelling-house and which either—

(i)   forms part of any part of a building in which the lessor has an estate or interest; or

(ii)   is owned by the lessor or under his control.

(3)   In determining the standard of repair required by the lessor's repairing covenant, regard shall be had to the age, character of the dwelling-house and the locality in which it is situated.

(4)   A covenant by the lessee for the repair of the premises is of no effect so far as it relates to the matters mentioned in subsection (1)(a) to (c), except so far as it imposes on the lessee any of the requirements mentioned in subsection (2)(a) or (c).

(5)   The reference in subsection (4) to a covenant by the lessee for the repair of the premises includes a covenant—

(a)   to put in repair or deliver up in repair,

(b)   to paint, point or render,

(c)   to pay money in lieu of repairs by the lessee, or

(d)   to pay money on account of repairs by the lessor.

(6)   In a case in which the lessor's repairing covenant is implied there is also implied a covenant by the lessee that the lessor, or any person authorised by him in writing, may at reasonable times of the day and on giving 24 hours' notice in writing to the occupier, enter the premises comprised in the lease for the purpose of viewing their condition and state of repair.

12.—(1)   A covenant or agreement, whether contained in a lease to which section 11 applies or in an agreement collateral to such a lease, is void in so far as it purports—

(a)   to exclude or limit the obligations of the lessor or the immunities of the lessee under that section, or

(b)   to authorise any forfeiture or impose on the lessee any penalty, disability or obligation in the event of his enforcing or relying upon those obligations or immunities, unless the inclusion of the provision was authorised by the county court.

13.—(1)   Section 11 (repairing obligations) applies to a lease of a dwelling-house granted on or after 24th October 1961 for a term of less than seven years.

(1A)   Section 11 also applies to a lease of a dwelling-house in England granted on or after the day on which section 166 of the Localism Act 2011 came into force which is—

    (a) a secure tenancy for a fixed term of seven years or more granted by a person within section 80(1) of the Housing Act 1985 (secure tenancies: the landlord condition), or

    (b) an assured tenancy for a fixed term of seven years or more that—

        (i)   is not a shared ownership lease, and

        (ii) is granted by a private registered provider of social housing.

Comment

(1) Section 8 applies to leases with a rent not exceeding £52 (£80 in London). This much criticised restriction (the figures date back to 1957) means that the section virtually never applies today. Section 10 lists criteria for establishing fitness for habitation.

(2) The s 11 duty is significant, though it is important to note the specific statutory obligations. For example, does the legislation apply to (i) a central heating unit? (ii) a fitted gas fire? (iii) a free-standing electric heater? (iv) failure to provide any heating? (v) an electric cooker as a fitted unit in the kitchen? (vi) damage to plaster?[12]

Particular difficulties have arisen in applying the duty (whether under the legislation or an express covenant) to keep in repair. If the ceiling collapses, it is easy to say that it must be repaired. But, to take a common problem in recent decades, what happens if the house or flat suffers from excessive condensation? Typically, the problem is that premises suffer from a design defect, rather than failure of some component. Can the tenant complain that premises are not up to present standards?

Extract 15.3.9

Ravenseft Properties Ltd v Davstone (Holdings) Ltd [1980] QB 12

Stone cladding in a dangerous state had to be replaced by the tenant (of a block of flats) under a repairing covenant. Was the tenant obliged to pay for inserting expansion joints, the absence of which had caused the problem?

FORBES J: . . . The true test is, as the cases show, that it is always a question of degree whether that which the tenant is being asked to do can properly be described as repair, or whether on the contrary it would involve giving back to the landlord a wholly different thing from that which he demised.

    In deciding this question, the proportion which the cost of the disputed work bears to the value or cost of the whole premises, may sometimes be helpful as a guide . . . I accept Mr Clark's estimate that the cost [of inserting the joints] would have been in the region of £5,000. The total cost of the remedial works was around £55,000 . . . For comparison, the cost of building a structure of this kind in 1973 would have been in the region of £3 million, or rather more. I find myself wholly unable to accept that the cost of inserting these joints could possibly be regarded as a substantial part of the cost of the repairs, much less a substantial part of the value or cost of the building. Mr Colyer urges me not to consider cost and that may, perhaps, in some circumstances, be right. He argues that the result of carrying out this improvement is to give back to the landlord a safe building instead of a dangerous one and this means the premises now are of a wholly different character . . . I cannot accept this. The expansion joints form but a trivial part of this whole building and looking at it as a question of degree, I do not consider that they amount to such a change in the character of the building as to take them out of the ambit of the covenant to repair.

---

[12] *Grand v Gill* [2011] 1 WLR 2253 (the issue being whether plaster is part of the 'structure').

. . . By [the time of repair] it was proper engineering practice to see that such expansion joints were included, and it would have been dangerous not to include them. In no realistic sense, therefore, could it be said that there was any other possible way of reinstating this cladding than by providing the expansion joints which were, in fact, provided.

Comment

Did the tenant have a good point that the landlord was going to get a building back which was better than when leased?

Extract 15.3.10

Quick v *Taff Ely BC* [1986] QB 809

Tenants complained of condensation, which caused damage to contents and decorations.

DILLON LJ: [The judge's] ultimate reasoning seems to me to be on the following lines viz: (1) recent authorities such as *Ravenseft Properties Ltd* v *Davstone (Holdings) Ltd* [1980] QB 12 and *Elmcroft Developments Ltd* v *Tankersley-Sawyer* (1984) 270 EG 140 show that works of repair under a repairing covenant, whether by a landlord or a tenant, may require the remedying of an inherent defect in a building; (2) the authorities also show that it is a question of degree whether works which remedy an inherent defect in a building may not be so extensive as to amount to an improvement or renewal of the whole which is beyond the concept of repair; (3) in the present case the replacement of windows and the provision of insulation for the lintels does not amount to such an improvement or renewal of the whole; (4) therefore, the replacement of the windows and provision of the insulation to alleviate an inherent defect is a repair which the council is bound to carry out under the repairing covenant.

But, with every respect to the judge, this reasoning begs the important question. It assumes that any work to eradicate an inherent defect in a building must be a work of repair, which the relevant party is bound to carry out if, as a matter of degree, it does not amount to a renewal or improvement of the building. In effect, it assumes the broad proposition urged on us by Mr Blom-Cooper for the plaintiff that anything defective or inherently inefficient for living in or ineffective to provide the conditions of ordinary habitation is in disrepair. But that does not follow from the decisions in *Ravenseft's* case [1980] QB 12 and *Elmcroft's* case, 270 EG 140 that works of repair *may* require the remedying of an inherent defect.

Mr Blom-Cooper's proposition has very far-reaching implications indeed . . . The construction of the covenant must be the same whether it is implied as a local authority's covenant in a tenancy of a council house or is expressly included as a tenant's or landlord's covenant in a private lease which is outside section 32.[i] A tenant under such a lease who had entered into such a repairing covenant would, no doubt, realise, if he suffered from problems of condensation in his house, that he could not compel the landlord to do anything about those problems. But I apprehend that the tenant would be startled to be told – as must follow from Judge Francis's decision – that the landlord has the right to compel him, the tenant, to put in new windows. If the reasoning is valid, where is the process to stop? . . . if the judge's reasoning was correct, it would seem that, if the point had been properly pleaded early enough, the plaintiff might have compelled the council to put in a radiator system of heating.

In my judgment, the key factor in the present case is that disrepair is related to the physical condition of whatever has to be repaired, and not to questions of lack of amenity or inefficiency. I find helpful the observation of Atkin LJ in *Anstruther-Gough-Calthorpe* v *McOscar* [1924] 1 KB 716, 734 that repair 'connotes the idea of making good damage so as to leave the subject so far as possible as though it had not been damaged'. Where decorative repair is in question one must look for damage to the decorations but where, as here, the obligation is merely to keep the structure and exterior of the house in repair, the covenant will only come into operation where there has been damage to the structure and exterior which requires to be made good.

If there is such damage caused by an unsuspected inherent defect, then it may be necessary to cure the defect, and thus to some extent improve without wholly renewing the property as the only practicable way of making good the damage to the subject matter of the repairing covenant. That, as I read the case, was the basis of the decision in *Ravenseft* [1980] QB 12 . . .
. . .

In the present case the liability of the council was to keep the structure and exterior of the house in repair – not the decorations. Though there is ample evidence of damage to the decorations and to bedding, clothing and other fabrics, evidence of damage to the subject matter of the covenant, the structure and exterior of the house, is far to seek. Though the condensation comes about from the effect of the warm atmosphere in the rooms on the cold surfaces of the walls and windows, there is no evidence at all of physical damage to the walls – as opposed to the decorations – or the windows.

There is indeed evidence of physical damage in the way of rot in parts of the wooden surrounds of some of the windows but (a) that can be sufficiently cured by replacing the defective lengths of wood and (b) it was palpably not the rot in the wooden surrounds which caused damage to the bedding, clothes and fabrics in the house, and the rot in the wooden surrounds cannot have contributed very much to the general inconvenience of living in the house for which the judge awarded general damages.

[i] Now s 11 of the Landlord and Tenant Act 1985.

Comment

(1) This involved a landlord's obligation. How convincing is it to rely on the application of the same principles to tenants' covenants?

(2) Is the result in *Quick* consistent with the purposes of the legislation?

Extract 15.3.11

Stent v Monmouth DC (1987) 54 P&CR 193

STOCKER LJ: . . . [I]f the only defect in the door was that it did not perform its primary function of keeping out the rain, and the door was otherwise undamaged and in a condition which it or its predecessors had been at the time of the letting, then it seems to me, on the authorities of *Quick* and *Aquarius*, this cannot amount to a defect for the purpose of a repairing covenant even though, as it seems to me in layman's terms, that a door which does not keep out the rain is a defective door, and one which is in need of some form of repair or modification or replacement . . .

In this case, however, the factual position is that the damage [to the door] undoubtedly did occur . . . Accordingly, applying the reasoning of this court from the cases cited, and in particular *Ravenseft Properties Ltd* v *Davstone (Holdings) Ltd* and *Elmcroft Developments Ltd* v *Tankersley-Sawyer*, the former having been specifically approved by this court, in my judgment the replacement of the wooden door by a self-sealing aluminium door was a mode of repair which a sensible person would have adopted; and the same reasoning applies if for the word 'sensible' there is substituted some such word as 'practicable' or 'necessary' . . .

Accordingly, in my view and upon those authorities, in this case the repair carried out in 1983 by the installation of a purpose-built, self-sealing aluminium door was one of the methods which could have been adopted much earlier, and which in my view should have been adopted. Of course, it does not follow that the self-sealing door is the only sensible way in which that object could be achieved. There may well have been others, but in my view the obligation under the covenant in this case was one which called upon the appellants to carry out repairs which not only effected the repair of the manifestly damaged parts but also achieved the object of rendering it unnecessary in the future for the continual repair of this door . . .

Comment

(1) The defendant was liable for damage (mainly to carpets) caused by the ingress of water before 1983.

(2) Is *Stent* any more generous than the earlier cases?

When there is a breach of a repairing obligation, damages may be claimed for consequential damage to property or injury to the person of the tenant. However, such claims often face a somewhat unexpected hurdle.

Extract 15.3.12

O'Brien v *Robinson* [1973] AC 912

A ceiling collapsed on the plaintiff and his wife.

LORD MORRIS: . . . On the one hand, it has been said that it would be wholly unreasonable to make a lessor liable for failing to remedy a defect of which he was unaware. So the liability to repair is one that arises only upon notice that there is a need to repair. Where by contract between lessor and lessee there has been a covenant to keep in repair the parties must have intended that the obligation of the lessor would only arise if the lessor had notice of want of repair and a condition or stipulation to that effect should be imported into the contract. The lessee in occupation would be in the best position to know of any state of disrepair. On the other hand, it has been said that if a lessor chooses or is required to covenant to keep premises in repair then there is an absolute obligation upon him. Alternatively, even if ordinarily there is no obligation on the part of a lessor until he is told by his lessee of a need for repair, a lessee can only give notice of any condition of which he is aware and accordingly cannot give notice of some unknown or unseen condition or latent defect: if, in these circumstances, the lessee suffers injury by reason of the premises not being in repair liability should rest upon the lessor.

. . . even if there is a right of entry for the purpose of viewing the condition of the premises it has been argued that frequent visits by a lessor would not be expected or desired and in order to acquire knowledge of any want of repair a lessor would in fact be dependent largely upon receiving information from his lessee.

It may here be stated that in the present case the learned judge held that the second appellant was not a tenant. As a consequence of this any liability of the respondent to her would have to be established in reliance upon the provisions of section 4 of the Occupiers' Liability Act 1957.[i]

In the case of *Morgan* v *Liverpool Corporation* [1927] 2 KB 131 one basis of claim was that there had been a failure to perform the statutory undertaking that the house would be 'kept in all respects reasonably fit for human habitation'. As I have shown, there was at that date a statutory right in a landlord to enter for the purposes of inspection. The accident which gave rise to the claim was that when the upper portion of a window was being opened one of the cords of the window sash broke with the result that the top part of the window slipped down and caught and injured the plaintiff's hand . . . The Court of Appeal held that the landlord was not liable and that any liability was conditional upon his having been given notice of any defects even though they were latent ones and that this result was not affected by the fact that the landlord had a right to enter in order to inspect . . .

Then in *McCarrick* v *Liverpool Corporation* [1947] AC 219 the question whether *Morgan's* case was correctly decided was presented for consideration in this House. The tenant's wife had fallen by reason of the defective condition of two stone steps leading from the kitchen to the back kitchen . . . No notice of want of repair was given to the landlords. They had the statutory right of entry to view the state of the premises. The defects would appear to have been patent. The tenant could therefore be aware of them: so also could the landlords have been had they exercised their right of entry. It was argued that *Morgan's* case was wrongly decided, that the Housing Act 1936 contained no provision requiring notice, that the duty imposed on a landlord by the Act (particularly as he was given a right of entry to inspect) was absolute and was analogous to that imposed on a factory occupier by the Factory Acts, and that the effect of the legislation should not be minimised or neutralised by introducing notions inspired by the old law.

Very important questions of principle were therefore raised. The significant previous authorities were considered. It was held that the decision in *Morgan's* case was correct. Lord Thankerton said that the effect of section 2 (1) of the Act of 1936 was to incorporate the prescribed condition in the contract so that it became an integral part of it and the statutory origin of the condition did not differentiate it, in any question of construction, from any of the conventional stipulations in the contract: it followed, therefore, that a condition as to notice of the material defect (established by a long line of authority) fell to be implied. Lord Porter said that, whatever view might have been taken of the section if no previous history lay behind it, it had to be remembered that similar provisions in earlier Acts had been interpreted as only requiring the landlord to repair after notice: he considered that it was too late to re-interpret its meaning . . .

. . . The question does, however, arise whether the decision of this House in *McCarrick's* case governs the present appeal which concerns a latent defect.

. . . *Morgan's* case must, I think, be regarded as a case in which the defect was latent even though some defects in a window sash-cord might be visible . . . In my view, these and other parts of the judgment of Atkin LJ were based on the reasoning that it is only when defects (though previously latent or invisible) become patent and are made known to the landlord that his liability to repair arises. Furthermore, it seems to me that both the words of Lord Simonds and his reasoning in *McCarrick's* case show that a landlord's obligation to take action only arises when he has notice of a defect. He will not have notice if no one knows that there is a defect.

The question does not now arise for express decision as to whether a landlord's obligation to repair will arise not only when he receives notice from his tenant of a defect but also if he receives such notice *aliunde* or if he has knowledge of it . . . The purpose of a notice is to impart knowledge that the moment for action under a covenant to repair has or may have arisen. If a lessor who is under an obligation to keep premises in repair acquires knowledge that there is a state of disrepair which may be dangerous, then, even if such knowledge is not shared by the lessee, I would consider that there arises an obligation on the part of the lessor to take appropriate action.

[i] Now Defective Premises Act 1972, s 4; Extract 15.3.17 below.

Comment

(1) Is the result justified by the constraints of authority or the proper interpretation of the implied terms?

(2) Should latent and patent defects be distinguished?

(3) Where the defect occurs on land outside the lease, should the reasoning in *O'Brien* protect the landlord who is unaware of the defect?[13]

The *O'Brien* analysis has not been well received. Thus Lord Donaldson MR stated:[14]

---

[13] *British Telecommunications plc v Sun Life Assurance Society plc* [1996] Ch 69 holds that the landlord receives no protection; P F Smith [1996] Conv 59.

[14] *McGreal v Wake* [1984] 1 EGLR 42 at p 43.

It is, as we think, unfortunate that the House of Lords felt impelled in *O'Brien* v *Robinson* [1973] AC 912 to hold that liability under this covenant only arises when the landlord learns, or perhaps is put on inquiry, that there is a need for such repairs, because such a construction penalises the conscientious landlord and rewards the absentee. Furthermore a covenant to 'keep in repair' would appear to be much more onerous than one to 'repair on notice' . . .

Fortunately, *O'Brien* has been largely bypassed by statutory developments, as we will see below.[15]

C. Enforcing repairing obligations

Generally speaking the normal contractual remedies are available. However, some qualifications need to be considered. As regards actions by the landlord, the fear has been that landlords may be making a profit or imposing unfair pressures on tenants. The Landlord and Tenant Act 1927, s 18, provides that damages during the lease are limited to 'the amount (if any) by which the value of the reversion . . . is diminished owing to the breach' and that, on termination of the lease, no damages are available if the premises are to be pulled down. There are further restrictions which will be considered in the forfeiture setting: see Leasehold Property (Repairs) Act 1938.[16]

The remedy of specific performance has given rise to controversy. Longstanding authority was against landlords' use of this remedy.

Extract 15.3.13

Jeune v *Queens Cross Properties Ltd* [1974] Ch 97

The tenant sought specific performance against the landlord.

PENNYCUICK V-C: . . . Now, on the face of it, in common sense and justice, it seems perfectly clear that this is the appropriate relief. The defendant's repairing covenant requires it to maintain, repair and renew the structure, including the external walls. A mandatory order upon the defendant to reinstate the balcony is a much more convenient order than an award of damages leaving it to the individual plaintiffs to do the work. There is nothing burdensome or unfair in the order sought.

My only pre-occupation in this matter has been in regard to a principle which I am told is stated in some textbooks to the effect that specific performance will never be ordered of repairing covenants in a lease. So far as the general law is concerned, apart from a repairing covenant in a lease, it appears perfectly clear that in an appropriate case the court will decree specific performance of an agreement to build if certain conditions are satisfied . . .

Now [*Hill* v *Barclay* (1810) 16 Ves Jun 402] is, I think, an authority laying down the principle that a landlord cannot obtain against his tenant an order for specific performance of a covenant to repair. It does not however apply to a landlord's covenant to repair . . .

Counsel for the plaintiffs has looked through various textbooks on the law of landlord and tenant and assures me that – although *Hill* v *Barclay*, 16 Ves 402, is repeatedly cited – there is no other authority in point.

. . . I cannot myself see any reason in principle, why, in an appropriate case, an order should not be made against a landlord to do some specific work pursuant to his covenant to repair. Obviously, it is a jurisdiction which should be carefully exercised.

[15] See Extract 15.3.17.
[16] See Extract 15.4.22 below.

Comment

Section 17 of the Landlord and Tenant Act 1985 explicitly permits specific performance against landlords in non-business[17] tenancies.

Extract 15.3.14

Rainbow Estates Ltd v Tokenhold Ltd **[1999] Ch 64 (Ch D)**

Could specific performance be awarded against a tenant?

LAWRENCE COLLINS QC: [After citing *Jeune* and subsequent cases:] In my judgment, a modern law of remedies requires specific performance of a tenant's repairing covenant to be available in appropriate circumstances, and there are no constraints of principle or binding authority against the availability of the remedy. First, even if want of mutuality were any longer a decisive factor (which it is not) the availability of the remedy against the tenant would restore mutuality as against the landlord. Second, the problems of defining the work and the need for supervision can be overcome by ensuring that there is sufficient definition of what has to be done in order to comply with the order of the court . . .

   Subject to the overriding need to avoid injustice or oppression, the remedy should be available when damages are not an adequate remedy or, in the more modern formulation, when specific performance is the appropriate remedy. This will be particularly important if there is substantial difficulty in the way of the landlord effecting repairs: the landlord may not have a right of access to the property to effect necessary repairs, since (in the absence of contrary agreement) a landlord has no right to enter the premises, and the condition of the premises may be deteriorating.

   . . .

   It follows that not only is there a need for great caution in granting the remedy against a tenant, but also that it will be a rare case in which the remedy of specific performance will be the appropriate one: in the case of commercial leases, the landlord will normally have the right to forfeit or to enter and do the repairs at the expense of the tenant; in residential leases, the landlord will normally have the right to forfeit in appropriate cases.

Comment

(1) *Hill* v *Barclay* was explained as based upon want of mutuality. Was this analysis properly open to a judge of first instance?

(2) It was observed that the protection accorded to tenants by the Leasehold Property (Repairs) Act 1938 would not apply to specific performance claims. However, the court could consider similar criteria in deciding whether to award specific performance.

Failure by landlords to repair has caused longstanding difficulties in the provision of appropriate remedies. *Melville* v *Grapelodge Developments Ltd*[18] saw an argument that the tenant could withhold rent. Neill J responded as follows:

> I am also satisfied that there is no sound basis for the defendants' argument that their obligation to pay rent was suspended because of the plaintiffs' breach of the undertaking. By the lease dated March 21, the defendants undertook an obligation to pay rent in accordance with the terms of the lease, and in my view the obligation was not removed or altered by any breach by the plaintiffs of the undertaking . . .

---

[17] For definition, see s 32.
[18] (1978) 39 P&CR 179.

Extract 15.3.15

British Anzani (Felixstowe) Ltd v *International Marine Management (UK) Ltd* [1980] QB 137

FORBES J: . . . Mr Harman's next point, and it is an important one, is that there can be no set off, equitable or otherwise, against rent . . .

On a consideration of these cases it seems to me that *Taylor* v *Beal*, Cro Eliz 222, is authority for the proposition that there are at least two sets of circumstances in which at common law there can be a set off against rent, one where the tenant expends money on repairs to the demised premises which the landlord has covenanted to carry out, but in breach has failed to do so (at any rate where the breach significantly affects the use of the premises), and the other where the tenant has paid money at the request of the landlord in respect of some obligation of the landlord connected with the land demised. To this proposition there must be added two riders. First, that as the landlord's obligation to repair premises demised does not arise until the tenant has notified him of want of repair, such notification must have been given before the set off can arise; and secondly that the set off must be for a sum which is not to be regarded as unliquidated damages . . . The latest expression of opinion about this matter is in *Lee-Parker* v *Izzet* [1971] 1 WLR 1688 . . . Goff J discussed the principle of *Taylor* v *Beal* and he said, at p 1693:

> 'I do not think this is bound up with technical rules of set off. It is an ancient common law right. I therefore declare that so far as the repairs are within the express or implied covenants of the landlord, the third and fourth defendants are entitled to recoup themselves out of future rents and defend any action for payment thereof . . .'

. . .

Then Mr Harman argues that rent is something special, that it is invested with something almost in the nature of an aura. He says rent issues out of the land. It is a debt due which has attached to it many special rights such as the right to distrain and the right of forfeiture, without previously serving a notice under section 146 of the Law of Property Act 1925. These two rights, he argues, are unique examples of self-help remedies which it is not surprising ought not to be interfered with by any set off . . .

A consideration of all these cases leads me to the conclusion that except in cases of distress or replevin equity has never refused to interfere to protect a tenant whose landlord was bringing proceedings based on non-payment of rent, if the tenant had a bona fide cross-claim for unliquidated damages against the landlord, provided that he was not covered by an existing common law remedy and that the ordinary rules pertaining to equitable set off were obeyed. I referred to these earlier in this judgment and they are as succinctly put by Parker J in *The Teno* [1977] 2 Lloyd's Rep 289, 297:

> '. . . where the cross-claim not only arises out of the same contract as the claim but is so directly connected with it that it would be manifestly unjust to allow the claimant to recover without taking into account the cross-claim there is a right of set off in equity of an unliquidated claim.'

. . .

While I am satisfied that it is proper in principle to allow that a cross-claim could be effective as an equitable set off against a claim for rent, it by no means follows that such a defence is available in all circumstances. The important qualification is that the equity must impeach the title to the legal demand, or in other words go to the very foundation of the landlord's claim. This seems to me to involve consideration of the proposition that the tenant's cross-claim must at least arise under the lease itself, or directly from the relationship of landlord and tenant created by the lease.

Comment

(1) *Melville* reached the same conclusion (the decisions were virtually contemporaneous), but was less fully reasoned.

(2) Is it safe to advise a tenant not to pay rent if the landlord has failed to repair?

A wide range of other remedies is available, ranging from local authority powers in cases of statutory nuisances and disrepair to appointment of receivers and control over excessive management charges on tenants. Space does not permit consideration of these remedies, though local authority notices requiring remedial work for premises unfit for human habitation or in disrepair (with power to undertake the work at the landlord's expense) can be quite significant. The Commonhold and Leasehold Reform Act 2002 (hereafter CLRA) enables long leaseholders (essentially with leases exceeding 21 years) to require management to be transferred to an RTM company which they control. There are a number of rules that have to be satisfied, but perhaps the most interesting point is that it is not necessary to show any breach by L: this is a free-standing right accorded to tenants.

D. Liability for personal injuries

In this section, we will consider the landlord's liability, whether or not there is a breach of a repairing obligation. One point is quite clear: in the case of breach, the landlord is liable to the tenant.

Extract 15.3.16

McNerny v *Lambeth LB* (1988) 21 HLR 188

It was claimed that excess moisture and condensation damaged property and caused ill health.

DILLON LJ: . . . The third alternative was that the claim was put as a claim for damages in negligence and that is the claim which alone has been pursued in this court. It is said that the council was in breach of a duty to take reasonable care in all the circumstances. One asks at this point: reasonable care in what respects or to what end, because it is necessary to define what duty is said to be in question. I had difficulty myself at times in following Mr Kershaw's formulation of the duty and unless it has been formulated it is hard to consider whether it exists in law. It must go wider than the duty under the repairing covenant if it is to avail the plaintiff in the conditions of this case where the repairing covenant does not apply because there is no relevant disrepair.

. . .

The judge decided that there was no such duty in law and he held that he was bound to reach that conclusion by the decision of the House of Lords in the case of *Cavalier* v *Pope* [1906] AC 428. The principle upheld in that case is summarised quite shortly in a paragraph in the speech of Lord MacNaghten at p 430 where he said this:

'The facts are not in dispute. The law laid down by the Court of Common Pleas in the passage quoted by the Master of the Rolls from the judgment of Erle CJ in *Robbins* v *Jones* is beyond question: "A landlord who lets a house in a dangerous state is not liable to the tenant's customers or guests for accidents happening during the term: for, fraud apart, there is no law against letting a tumble-down house; and the tenant's remedy is upon his contract, if any."'

Robbins v *Jones* was decided in 1863. It is reported in 15 CB (NS) 221 . . .

Since the development of the law of negligence in *Donoghue* v *Stevenson* [1932] AC 562 there has been considerable criticism of *Cavalier* v *Pope*, and suggestions have been made that the law stated in *Cavalier* v *Pope* and the preceding authorities has been overtaken by the development of the law of negligence in *Donoghue* v *Stevenson* and the cases on negligence which have followed from that . . .

There are certain qualifications to *Cavalier* v *Pope* which are now well established. One is that it does not apply to a furnished letting. I will come back to that later. The second is that it does not apply where the landlord was the builder of the dwelling-house and the building was built negligently. The fact that the builder was also the owner and landlord of the site does not cancel his negligence qua builder. That emerges from the well-known decision of the House of Lords in *Anns* v *Merton London Borough Council* [1978] AC 728, and it is particularly decided in *Rimmer* v *Liverpool City Council* [[1985] QB 1] . . .

In the present case, however, even if the landlords' predecessor as local authority and housing authority was responsible for the building of the block of flats in Muller Road in the first place, there is no evidence of negligence when they were built, or that the building was not entirely in accordance with the technology and standards of the times. That leaves, therefore, the case of what has been called the 'bare landlord' – the landlord who was not the negligent builder of the premises and who has let them by an unfurnished letting.

The judge in the court below treated the present case as a case of a 'bare landlord' and it is conceded in argument by Mr Kershaw for the plaintiff that this is indeed such a case. But in such a case, so far as this court is concerned, the decision in *Cavalier* v *Pope* stands and is binding . . .

There is an alternative approach to this appeal which, in my judgment, leads to the same result. Even if the court is not bound by *Cavalier* v *Pope*, should the court interfere to raise a new duty at common law not heretofore recognised or is that a matter for Parliament? This is an area where Parliament has intervened to prescribe the duties for landlords that Parliament thinks appropriate. It is a field of importance in relation to social policy and also affects the finances of local authorities very considerably. It is concerned generally with housing those less advantaged.

. . . I can see force in the argument that if a furnished house must be fit for the purposes for which it is let, so a house or flat let unfurnished, albeit newly decorated, to a tenant who is expected to move in immediately, and may be moving in the case of local authority housing from really bad housing conditions, should be fit for the purposes for which it is let . . . But in my judgment it is for Parliament and not for the courts to introduce such a development into the law.

Comment

(1) The lack of disrepair (under the repairing covenant) rested on the *Quick* test.

(2) How convincing are the reasons for not recognising a duty of care?

(3) The statutory intervention mentioned by Dillon LJ is found in the following extract.

Extract 15.3.17

Defective Premises Act 1972, s 4

4.—(1) Where premises are let under a tenancy which puts on the landlord an obligation to the tenant for the maintenance or repair of the premises, the landlord owes to all persons who might reasonably be expected to be affected by defects in the state of the premises a duty to take such care as is reasonable in all the circumstances to see that they are reasonably safe from personal injury or from damage to their property caused by a relevant defect.

(2)   The said duty is owed if the landlord knows (whether as the result of being notified by the tenant or otherwise) or if he ought in all the circumstances to have known of the relevant defect.

(3)   In this section 'relevant defect' means a defect in the state of the premises existing at or after the material time and arising from, or continuing because of, an act or omission by the landlord which constitutes or would if he had had notice of the defect, have constituted a failure by him to carry out his obligation to the tenant for the maintenance or repair of the premises . . .

(4)   Where premises are let under a tenancy which expressly or impliedly gives the landlord the right to enter the premises to carry out any description of maintenance or repair of the premises, then, as from the time when he first is, or by notice or otherwise can put himself, in a position to exercise the right and so long as he is or can put himself in that position, he shall be treated for the purposes of subsections (1) to (3) above (but for no other purpose) as if he were under an obligation to the tenant for that description of maintenance or repair of the premises; but the landlord shall not owe the tenant any duty by virtue of this subsection in respect of any defect in the state of the premises arising from, or continuing because of, a failure to carry out an obligation expressly imposed on the tenant by the tenancy.

Comment

(1) Why was this was not applicable in *McNerny*?

(2) When might a tenant be able to sue under s 4, but not otherwise?[19]

(3) It had been doubted whether anybody other than the tenant could recover for breach of a duty to repair, but these doubts are swept aside by s 4.

(4) Does this deny any significance to *O'Brien* v *Robinson* (Extract 15.3.12 above)?

E. Reform

Extract 15.3.18

Law Commission No 238: Responsibility for State and Conditions of Property (some footnotes omitted)

7.7   . . . [W]e propose that there should be a statutory repairing obligation that applies by way of default where and to the extent that the parties have not made provision for repairs. This would take the form of two implied covenants [on the part of the landlord] that could be freely excluded or modified. The first would relate to the premises let and the second to the common parts and to any other property under the landlord's control which might affect the enjoyment of the premises let. The purpose of these default covenants would not be to impose on the parties any minimum standard of repair, but to encourage parties who are negotiating the terms of a lease to consider the issue of repairs and then to make express provision in the lease for them . . .

[For dwelling houses]
8.34   We set out in the following paragraphs our proposals for a new implied covenant by a landlord that he will ensure both at the time when the premises are let and throughout the term that the premises are fit for human habitation. It will apply to certain leases granted for a term of less than seven years . . .

---

[19] See *Sykes* v *Harry* [2001] QB 1014 for the situation where the landlord does not have notice of the defect.

[As regards tenants' obligations]

10.33   We can see little point in retaining the present law, which blends in an uncertain amalgam principles of both tort[i] and contract law. Any reform must provide one cause of action that applies to leases, periodic tenancies, tenancies at will and sufferance, and licences alike. That cause of action must be available whether the occupation in question is contractual or not. Consistently with our general approach to the relationship of landlord and tenant in this report, the obligations which we propose should operate by way of a default so that the parties are free to modify or exclude them. There must be certainty not only as to the relationships to which these obligations apply, but also as to their content.

10.34   In formulating our recommendations we have revisited earlier proposals made by the Commission on this subject. Our proposals are in two parts. First, we recommend the abolition of the application of the law of waste to tenancies and licences. Secondly, we propose by way of replacement, the creation of an implied obligation on the part of tenants and licensees to take reasonable care of the property which they occupy.

[i] And two torts at that – waste and trespass.

Comment

The Law Commission would retain the statutory repairing obligations for short leases of dwelling-houses. The proposals are endorsed by Law Com No 297 (2006).

4. Forfeiture

Forfeiture clauses are almost invariably inserted into leases.

Extract 15.4.1

Billson v Residential Apartments Ltd [1992] 1 AC 494

LORD TEMPLEMAN: . . . By the common law, when a tenant commits a breach of covenant and the lease contains a proviso for forfeiture, the landlord at his option may either waive the breach or determine the lease. In order to exercise his option to determine the lease the landlord must either re-enter the premises in conformity with the proviso or must issue and serve a writ claiming possession. The bringing of an action to recover possession is equivalent to an entry for the forfeiture . . .

Before the intervention of Parliament, if a landlord forfeited by entering into possession or by issuing and serving a writ for possession, equity could relieve the tenant against forfeiture but only in cases under the general principles of equity whereby a party may be relieved from the consequences of fraud, accident or mistake or in cases where the breach of covenant entitling the landlord to forfeit was a breach of the covenant for payment of rent.

. . .

In 1881 Parliament interfered to supplement equity and to enable any tenant to be relieved from forfeiture. The need for such intervention was and is manifest because otherwise a tenant who had paid a large premium for a 999-year lease at a low rent could lose his asset by a breach of covenant which was remediable or which caused the landlord no damage. The forfeiture of any lease, however short, may unjustly enrich the landlord at the expense of the tenant. In creating a power to relieve against forfeiture for breach of covenant Parliament protected the landlord by conferring on the court a wide discretion to grant relief on terms or to refuse relief altogether. In practice this discretion is exercised with the object of ensuring that the landlord is not substantially prejudiced or damaged by the revival of the lease.

. . .

Section 146(1) [Law of Property Act 1925] prevents the landlord from enforcing a right of re-entry or forfeiture by action or otherwise so that the landlord cannot determine the lease by issuing and serving a writ or by re-entering the premises until the tenant has failed within a reasonable time to remedy the breach and make reasonable compensation. Section 146(2) enables the tenant to apply to the court for relief where the landlord 'is proceeding, by action or otherwise' to enforce his right of re-entry or forfeiture. If the landlord 'is proceeding' to determine the lease by issuing and serving a writ, the tenant may apply for relief after the writ has been served. If the landlord 'is proceeding' to determine the lease by re-entering into possession, the tenant may apply for relief after the landlord has re-entered.

Comment

(1) *Billson* involved relief after peaceable re-entry and will be further studied in that setting.[20]

(2) It is easy to lose sight of the point that it is the landlord's decision which forfeits, not the court order. Indeed, the tenant in possession pending court proceedings is not there under the lease (if relief is refused) and so is not liable to pay the stipulated rent. The position has been described by Lord Neuberger[21] as 'anomalous and archaic'; the Law Commission has proposed changing this, so that forfeiture will be effected by the court order.[22]

Peaceable re-entry may take place simply by changing the locks so that the tenant cannot get in. As we will see later, *Billson* removes much of its attraction; in any event, it runs the risk of breach of the criminal law. The use of violence or threats of violence falls foul of the Criminal Law Act 1977, s 6.[23]

Extract 15.4.2

Protection from Eviction Act 1977, ss 2, 3, 5

2.—Where any premises are let as a dwelling on a lease which is subject to a right of re-entry or forfeiture it shall not be lawful to enforce that right otherwise than by proceedings in the court while any person is lawfully residing in the premises or part of them.

3.—(1)   Where any premises have been let as a dwelling under a tenancy which is neither a statutorily protected tenancy nor an excluded tenancy and—
  (a) the tenancy (in this section referred to as the former tenancy) has come to an end, but
  (b) the occupier continues to reside in the premises or part of them,
it shall not be lawful for the owner to enforce against the occupier, otherwise than by proceedings in the court, his right to recover possession of the premises.

5.—(1)   Subject to subsection (1B) below no notice by a landlord or a tenant to quit any premises let (whether before or after the commencement of this Act) as a dwelling shall be valid unless—
  (a) it is in writing and contains such information as may be prescribed, and
  (b) it is given not less than four weeks before the date on which it is to take effect.

---

[20] Extract 15.4.16 below.
[21] *Knowsley Housing Trust* v *White* [2009] 1 AC 636 at [81].
[22] Law Com No 303, p 566 below.
[23] Extract 15.2.3 above.

Comment

(1) Would re-entry in breach of these provisions be effective?[24]

(2) This legislation effectively precludes peaceable re-entry of dwelling-houses. The sole exception is where the tenant has voluntarily left the house.

A. Protection for residential tenants

Extract 15.4.3

Commonhold and Leasehold Reform (DETR) (2000) Cm 4843, section 4.6

3.   However, unscrupulous landlords have still been able to exploit leaseholders' fears about the costs of legal proceedings and the prospect of losing their homes in order to secure payment of unreasonable charges, often in relation to minor or non-existent breaches of covenants. Formal notices of intended forfeiture proceedings under section 146 of the Law of Property Act 1925 are often phrased in intimidating terms.

5.   The Government therefore considers that there is a need to prevent the commencement of forfeiture proceedings until the facts of the matter have been determined.

10.   The Government considers that in order to prevent abuse, proceedings leading to possession or forfeiture should be separated from proceedings to determine facts. It therefore proposes an extension of the principle of section 81 of the Housing Act 1996 (see paragraph 2). This would apply to all disputes relating to breaches of covenants other than a failure to pay ground rent, and would prevent the issue of section 146 notices before the facts have been determined.

12.   Where service charges were outstanding, it would be open to the landlord or leaseholders to apply to a LVT [leasehold valuation tribunal] for a determination that the sum claimed is reasonable and lawfully due . . .

OTHER BREACHES

14.   In addition to non-payment of sums due under a lease, landlords are also able to take forfeiture action in respect of any breaches of covenant or condition by the leaseholder under his or her lease. Common examples of such conditions are a requirement for the leaseholder to obtain the landlord's consent before carrying out structural alterations or a ban on the leaseholder keeping a pet. As in the case of non-payment, we consider it important that a landlord should be required to substantiate any allegation of a breach before taking formal forfeiture action. (This would not, however, prevent a landlord seeking an injunction to stop or remedy the breach in an emergency situation.)

Extract 15.4.4

Commonhold and Leasehold Reform Act 2002, ss 166–168, 171

166.—(1)   A tenant under a long lease of a dwelling is not liable to make a payment of rent under the lease unless the landlord has given him a notice relating to the payment; and the date on which he is liable to make the payment is that specified in the notice.

---

[24] See *Belgravia Property Investment and Development Co Ltd* v *Webb* [2002] L&TR 481.

(3)   The date on which the tenant is liable to make the payment must not be—
  (a)   either less than 30 days or more than 60 days after the day on which the notice is given, or
  (b)   before that on which he would have been liable to make it in accordance with the lease.

167.—(1)   A landlord under a long lease of a dwelling may not exercise a right of re-entry or forfeiture for failure by a tenant to pay an amount consisting of rent, service charges or administration charges (or a combination of them) ('the unpaid amount') unless the unpaid amount—
  (a)   exceeds the prescribed sum, or
  (b)   consists of or includes an amount which has been payable for more than a prescribed period.
(2)   The sum prescribed under subsection (1)(a) must not exceed £500.

168.—(1)   A landlord under a long lease of a dwelling may not serve a notice under section 146(1) of the Law of Property Act 1925 (c. 20) (restriction on forfeiture) in respect of a breach by a tenant of a covenant or condition in the lease unless subsection (2) is satisfied.
(2)   This subsection is satisfied if—
  (a)   it has been finally determined on an application under subsection (4) that the breach has occurred,
  (b)   the tenant has admitted the breach, or
  (c)   a court in any proceedings, or an arbitral tribunal in proceedings pursuant to a post-dispute arbitration agreement, has finally determined that the breach has occurred.
(3)   But a notice may not be served by virtue of subsection (2)(a) or (c) until after the end of the period of 14 days beginning with the day after that on which the final determination is made.
(4)   A landlord under a long lease of a dwelling may make an application to a leasehold valuation tribunal for a determination that a breach of a covenant or condition in the lease has occurred.

171.—(1)   The appropriate national authority may by regulations prescribe requirements which must be met before a right of re-entry or forfeiture may be exercised in relation to a breach of a covenant or condition in a long lease of an unmortgaged dwelling.

Comment

(1) These extracts are highly selective: much more detail is contained in the legislation. Long leases are, generally speaking, those exceeding 21 years. The prescribed sum for s 167 is £350 and the prescribed period is three years: SI 2004 No 3086.

(2) Control over service charges (often a source of disputes) is found in the Housing Act 1996, amended by CLRA. This requires a leasehold valuation tribunal determination prior to forfeiture.

(3) The wording of s 171 is opaque as to its intended role. It is designed to allow further protection for vulnerable tenants who face the risk of losing a valuable lease because of inaction on their part. Why is it restricted to unmortgaged dwellings?

(4) The DETR paper observes 'In practice, forfeiture rarely occurs.' Why, then, are these new provisions necessary?

(5) Are the provisions likely to be effective in avoiding forfeiture (or the threat of forfeiture) in all but very serious and deliberate breaches?

B. Waiver

As Lord Templeman stated in *Billson*, the landlord has a choice whether or not to forfeit. Once a decision not to forfeit is communicated, this waives the breach; thereafter, forfeiture cannot be based upon it. What conduct will be deemed to constitute waiver?

Extract 15.4.5

Central Estates (Belgravia) Ltd v *Woolgar (No 2)* [1972] 1 WLR 1048

LORD DENNING MR: . . . The first point is whether or no the landlords waived the forfeiture by accepting rent. The dates are these: The landlords by their agents knew of the conviction [for keeping a brothel in the house] on July 23, 1970. That is the important date of knowledge. The partner instructed the clerks in his office to put a tab on the ledgers so as to make sure they did not accept any rent after knowing of this conviction . . . Something went amiss in the office . . . In . . . the middle of September 1970, the landlords' agents, through their office, sent out a demand for the £10 quarter's rent, which was falling due on September 29, 1970. The tenant, on September 22, 1970, paid that £10 . . .

. . . [I]f it is sought to say that an existing lease *continues in existence* by waiver of forfeiture, then the intention of the parties does not matter. It is sufficient if there is an unequivocal act done by the landlord which recognises the existence of the lease after having knowledge of the ground of forfeiture. The law was well stated by Parker J in *Matthews* v *Smallwood* [1910] 1 Ch 777, 786, which was accepted by this court in *Oak Property Co Ltd* v *Chapman* [1947] KB 886, 898:

> 'It is also, I think, reasonably clear upon the cases that whether the act, coupled with the knowledge, constitutes a waiver is a question which the law decides, and therefore it is not open to a lessor who has knowledge of the breach to say "I will treat the tenancy as existing, and I will receive the rent, or I will take advantage of my power as landlord to distrain; but I tell you that all I shall do will be without prejudice to my right to re-enter, which I intend to reserve." That is a position which he is not entitled to take up. If, knowing of the breach, he does distrain, or does receive the rent, then by law he waives the breach, and nothing which he can say by way of protest against the law will avail him anything.'

. . .

So we have simply to ask: Was this rent demanded and accepted by the landlords' agents with knowledge of the breach? It does not matter that they did not intend to waive. The very fact that they accepted the rent with the knowledge constitutes the waiver. The position here is quite plain. The agents, who had full authority to manage these properties on behalf of the landlords, did demand and accept the rent with full knowledge . . .

I know that the judge found that the agents had no intention to waive, and finds also that the tenant knew they had no intention to waive. That seems to me to make no difference. The law says that if the agents stated in terms: 'We do not intend to waive', it would not have availed them. If an express statement does not avail a landlord, nor does an implied one. So it does not avail the landlords here.

Comment

Is there any justification for allowing waiver when the tenant knows that the landlord did not intend to waive?

Extract 15.4.6

Re A Debtor [1995] 1 WLR 1127

On 16 December, landlords claimed rent (payable in advance) due on 1 September and 1 December (neither payment was made). The judge held that the claim for rent waived the September breach and this was not challenged.

RATTEE J: . . . The judge went on to hold that to claim the rent due on 1 December, even after the right to re-enter had arisen 14 days after 1 December, was in no way inconsistent with an exercise of the right of re-entry which arose once that rent had been unpaid for 14 days. The right of re-entry reserved by the lease is, in the usual way, expressed to be without prejudice to the landlord's right of action in respect of any antecedent breach of covenant by the tenant. Thus, a re-entry for non-payment of rent within the permitted 14 days leaves unaffected the landlord's right to recover the unpaid rent and is not inconsistent with an exercise of the latter right.

There is of course ample authority for the obvious proposition that a demand for or acceptance of rent accrued due after a breach of covenant by the tenant is inconsistent with, and therefore waives, the landlord's right to forfeit the lease for that breach because such demand or acceptance is a recognition that the lease has continued after the breach . . . However, in my judgment, the same reasoning cannot apply to a demand for or acceptance of rent accrued due on or before the relevant breach. As is recognised by the terms of the right of re-entry itself in this case, there is nothing inconsistent between forfeiting the lease and demanding or accepting rent accrued due before the right to forfeiture arose . . .

Comment

Why is a distinction drawn between the September and December rent liability?

The impact of the waiver rules is much less significant for continuing breaches (such as improper use of the premises or failure to repair), as the landlord can rely on the breach after the waiver.[25]

C. Relief: non-payment of rent

Relief against forfeiture is complicated because of the many different rules applicable. Three points must be borne in mind. First, there is a distinction between rent and non-rent breaches. Second, relief is sometimes equitable and sometimes statutory. Lastly, different statutory provisions apply in the county court and High Court, though the former has unlimited jurisdiction in forfeiture and relief actions.[26]

Extract 15.4.7

Common Law Procedure Act 1852, ss 210, 212

210.—In all cases between landlord and tenant, as often as it shall happen that one half year's rent shall be in arrear, and the landlord or lessor, to whom the same is due, hath right by law to re-enter for the non-payment thereof, such landlord or lessor shall and may, without any formal demand or re-entry, serve a writ in ejectment for the recovery of the demised premises . . . ; and in case the lessee or his assignee, or other person claiming or deriving under the said

---

[25] LPA, s 148.
[26] High Court and County Courts Jurisdiction Order 1991 (SI 1991 No 724), art 2.

lease, shall permit and suffer judgment to be had and recovered on such trial in ejectment, and execution to be executed thereon, without paying the rent and arrears, together with full costs, and without proceeding for relief in equity within six months after such execution executed, then and in such case the said lessee, his assignee, and all other persons claiming and deriving under the said lease, shall be barred and foreclosed from all relief or remedy in law or equity, . . .

212.—If the tenant or his assignee do or shall, at any time before the trial in such ejectment, pay or tender to the lessor or landlord, his executors or administrators, or his or their attorney in that cause, or pay into the court where the same cause is depending, all the rent and arrears, together with the costs, then and in such case all further proceedings on the said ejectment shall cease and be discontinued [without any new lease].

Extract 15.4.8

County Courts Act 1984, ss 138, 139

138.—(1) This section has effect where a lessor is proceeding by action in a county court (being an action in which the county court has jurisdiction) to enforce against a lessee a right of re-entry or forfeiture in respect of any land for non-payment of rent.

(2) If the lessee pays into court or to the lessor not less than 5 clear days before the return day all the rent in arrear and the costs of the action, the action shall cease, and the lessee shall hold the land according to the lease without any new lease.

(3) If—

    (a) the action does not cease under subsection (2); and

    (b) the court at the trial is satisfied that the lessor is entitled to enforce the right of re-entry or forfeiture,

the court shall order possession of the land to be given to the lessor at the expiration of such period, not being less than 4 weeks from the date of the order, as the court thinks fit, unless within that period the lessee pays into court or to the lessor all the rent in arrear and the costs of the action.

(4) The court may extend the period specified under subsection (3) at any time before possession of the land is recovered in pursuance of the order under that subsection.

(7) If the lessee does not—

    (a) within the period specified in the order; or

    (b) within that period as extended under subsection (4),

    pay into court or to the lessor—

        (i) all the rent in arrear; and

        (ii) the costs of the action,

the order shall be enforceable in the prescribed manner and so long as the order remains unreversed the lessee shall, subject to subsections (8) and (9A), be barred from all relief.

(9A) Where the lessor recovers possession of the land at any time after the making of the order under subsection (3) (whether as a result of the enforcement of the order or otherwise) the lessee may, at any time within six months from the date on which the lessor recovers possession, apply to the court for relief; and on any such application the court may, if it thinks fit, grant to the lessee such relief, subject to such terms and conditions, as it thinks fit.

139.—(1) In a case where section 138 has effect, if—

    (a) one-half-year's rent is in arrear at the time of the commencement of the action; and

    (b) the lessor has a right to re-enter for non-payment of that rent; and . . .

the service of the summons in the action in the prescribed manner shall stand in lieu of a demand and re-entry.

(2) Where a lessor has enforced against a lessee, by re-entry without action, a right of re-entry or forfeiture as respects any land for non-payment of rent, the lessee may at any time within six

months from the date on which the lessor re-entered apply to the county court for relief, and on any such application the court may, if it thinks fit, grant to the lessee such relief as the High Court could have granted.

(i) Formal demands

The archaic rules on formal demands (the demand must be made before sunset on the day the rent is due) are limited by ss 210 and 139. In any event, leases invariably exclude the need for formal demands.

(ii) Relief before trial

Sections 212 and 138 provide an absolute right to relief if the rent is paid before the judgment is operative. Note that s 212 applies only where s 210 operates.[27] What is the significance of this?

(iii) Other relief

Extract 15.4.9

Gill v *Lewis* [1956] 2 QB 1

JENKINS LJ: . . . Section 210 provides (to put it shortly) that a landlord is to have a right to re-enter when there is a half-year's rent in arrear; and then it goes on to stipulate that any claim to relief (under what was then purely the old equitable jurisdiction) which a tenant desires to make must be made within six months after execution of the judgment in respect of which relief is sought. It therefore sets a time limit on the equitable jurisdiction to which I understand a tenant could formerly appeal at any distance of time . . .

. . . By way of illustration of the manner in which the jurisdiction to grant relief from forfeiture for non-payment of rent has been exercised by the courts Mr Grundy referred us to *Stanhope* v *Haworth*,[i] in which an order had been made for possession for non-payment of rent, and the premises were a colliery. Relief was applied for towards the end of the period of six months allowed by section 210 of the Act of 1852. It was held that the parties had so altered their position in the meantime that it would be inequitable to grant relief. It appears that in the meantime the landlord had let other people into possession and had made arrangements with them for the working of the colliery, and a considerable amount of money had been spent on the footing that the lease was at an end . . .

. . . So that case shows that where parties have altered their position in the meantime, and in particular where the rights of third parties have intervened, relief ought not to be granted where the effect of it would be to defeat the new rights of third parties or be unfair to the landlord having regard to the way in which he has altered his position.

. . .

As to the conclusion of the whole matter, in my view, save in exceptional circumstances, the function of the court in exercising this equitable jurisdiction is to grant relief when all that is due for rent and costs has been paid up, and (in general) to disregard any other causes of complaint that the landlord may have against the tenant. The question is whether, provided all is paid up, the landlord will not have been fully compensated; and the view taken by the court is that if he gets the whole of his rent and costs, then he has got all he is entitled to so far as rent is concerned, and extraneous matters of breach of covenant, and so forth, are, generally speaking, irrelevant.

---

[i] (1886) 3 TLR 34.

---

[27] *Standard Pattern Co Ltd* v *Ivey* [1962] Ch 432, criticised by Megarry (1962) 78 LQR 168.

Comment

Neither the poor payment record of the tenant nor a conviction for an isolated indecent assault committed on the premises sufficed to deny relief.[28] Is the law too generous towards tenants in these circumstances? Should a landlord have to put up with tenants who consistently fail to pay rent until the very last minute for relief?

When may equitable relief operate where ss 210 and 138 do not? Should the courts award relief where more than six months have elapsed since re-entry?[29]

The next case considers the terms upon which relief is given.

Extract 15.4.10

Bland v *Ingrams Estates Ltd* (No 2) [2002] Ch 177

Questions arose against the background that in 1996, following forfeiture, the landlord had leased the land to Mr and Mrs Uddin.

CHADWICK LJ: 12. I turn now to the terms upon which relief from forfeiture should be granted. The principles are not, I think, in doubt. First, the proviso for re-entry on non-payment of rent is treated in equity as a security for the rent: see *Howard* v *Fanshawe* [1895] 2 Ch 581, 588. Accordingly, relief will normally be granted upon terms that the arrears of rent and any costs properly associated with the re-entry are discharged: . . .

13.   Second, the effect of an order granting relief from forfeiture is to restore the lease for all purposes; the original lease continues as if there had been no interruption by re-entry: see *Dendy* v *Evans* [1910] 1 KB 263, 269, 270 and *Driscoll* v *Church Comrs for England* [1957] 1 QB 330, 340, 344, 348. The consequence, in the present case, of the grant of relief from the forfeiture of the 1994 lease will be that the 1996 lease takes effect as a lease of the reversion. As from 29 April 1996 Mr and Mrs Uddin will have been the persons immediately entitled in reversion on the determination of the 1994 lease. They will have been interposed as intermediate landlord between Mr and Mrs Beer and Ingrams Estates.

14.   Third, the object of the court when granting relief is to put the lessor (as well as the lessee) back in the position in which he would have been if there had been no forfeiture: see *Egerton* v *Jones* [1939] 2 KB 702, 706. It is this principle which underlies the practice of requiring the applicant, as a term of relief, to pay the costs properly incurred by the lessor in connection with the re-entry and the proceedings for relief. Accordingly, the applicant will normally be required to pay the lessor's costs of the forfeiture proceedings, save in so far as those costs have been increased by the lessor's opposition to the grant of relief, upon appropriate terms: . . .

15.   Fourth – and by way of further application of the principles (1) that, on relief being granted, the lease is restored for all purposes and (2) that the object of the court is to put the lessor back into the position in which he would have been if there had been no forfeiture – the court must take into account the fact (if it be so) that the lease contains a provision for rent review at a date between the date of forfeiture and the date of relief. The lessor is not to be denied the benefit of any increased rent which would have resulted from the operation of the rent review provisions during the period prior to the grant of relief from forfeiture: see *Soteri* v *Psylides* [1991] 1 EGLR 138, 140.

Comment

(1) Following relief, what is the relationship between the forfeited lease and the Uddins' lease?

(2) Applying the principles stated by Chadwick LJ, how should the following be treated: (i) arrears of rent; (ii) the prospect of additional rent under rent review provisions (not

---

[28] Contrast *Test Valley* BC v *Minilec Engineering Ltd* [2005] 2 EGLR 113.
[29] *Thatcher* v *CH Pearce & Sons (Contractors) Ltd* [1968] 1 WLR 748.

activated following forfeiture); (iii) the value of the land for the period the tenant had been out of possession?

(3) The Uddins had constructive notice of the right to relief. Would the analysis be different if the landlord's title had been registered?

(iv) Sub-tenants and mortgagees

Forfeiture automatically terminates any sublease or mortgage.[30] It is, therefore, most important that holders of these interests can seek relief. Equity permitted this, and they also fall within s 210 and, by implication, ss 212[31] and 138.[32]

However, the Law of Property Act 1925 (hereafter LPA) s 146(4) provides the most commonly used route for relief for sub-tenants and mortgagees and, indeed, probably ousts the old equitable jurisdiction. This will be considered in the following section.[33]

Recent cases have considered the position of equitable chargees. They have been held to be outside both the High Court's jurisdiction and s 146(4).[34] However, all is not lost. Relief may be claimed in the county court (we have noted that it has unlimited jurisdiction)[35] and the chargee can in any event assert the tenant's right to relief by joining the tenant.[36]

D. Relief: non-rent breaches

Extract 15.4.11

Law of Property Act 1925, s 146

146.—(1) A right of re-entry or forfeiture under any proviso or stipulation in a lease for a breach of any covenant or condition in the lease shall not be enforceable, by action or otherwise, unless and until the lessor serves on the lessee a notice—

    (a) specifying the particular breach complained of; and

    (b) if the breach is capable of remedy, requiring the lessee to remedy the breach; and

    (c) in any case, requiring the lessee to make compensation in money for the breach;

and the lessee fails, within a reasonable time thereafter, to remedy the breach, if it is capable of remedy, and to make reasonable compensation in money, to the satisfaction of the lessor, for the breach.

    (2) Where a lessor is proceeding, by action or otherwise, to enforce such a right of re-entry or forfeiture, the lessee may, in the lessor's action, if any, or in any action brought by himself, apply to the court for relief; and the court may grant or refuse relief, as the court, having regard to the proceedings and conduct of the parties under the foregoing provisions of this section, and to all the other circumstances, thinks fit . . .

    (5) For the purposes of this section—

        (a) 'Lease' includes an original or derivative under-lease; also an agreement for a lease where the lessee has become entitled to have his lease granted; also a grant at a fee farm rent, or securing a rent by condition;

        . . .

---

[30] *Great Western Railway Co* v *Smith* (1875) Ch D 235; *Dewar* v *Goodman* [1909] AC 72.
[31] *Doe d Wyatt* v *Byron* (1845) 1 CB 624 (135 ER 685).
[32] *United Dominions Trust Ltd* v *Shellpoint Trustees Ltd* [1993] 4 All ER 310.
[33] See p 559.
[34] *Bland* v *Ingrams Estates Ltd* [2001] Ch 767 (for s 146(4), see [60]).
[35] *Croydon (Unique) Ltd* v *Wright* [2001] Ch 318.
[36] *Bland* v *Ingrams Estates Ltd* [2001] Ch 767.

(7)   For the purposes of this section a lease limited to continue as long only as the lessee abstains from committing a breach of covenant shall be and take effect as a lease to continue for any longer term for which it could subsist, but determinable by a proviso for re-entry on such a breach . . .

(11)   This section does not, save as otherwise mentioned, affect the law relating to re-entry or forfeiture or relief in case of non-payment of rent.

(12)   This section has effect notwithstanding any stipulation to the contrary.

(13)   The county court has jurisdiction under this section.

Comment

It is important to note that there are two reliefs here. First, there is a *right* to relief where the breach is remedied within a reasonable period and, second, in all cases the court may in its discretion grant relief.

(i) The notice

Extract 15.4.12

Rugby School (Governors) v *Tannahill* [1935] 1 KB 87

GREER LJ: . . . The material facts are that, some time before the notice was served, the defendant had been knowingly and actively permitting the house to be used as a brothel, and I have little doubt she had been receiving profits in respect of this immoral business. The covenant, the breach of which is complained of, expressly forbids the tenant to permit the premises to be used for such a purpose . . . It is conceded that in the notice given by the plaintiffs the defendant was not required to remedy the breach, nor was she required to make compensation in money in respect thereof. Mr Fearnley-Whittingstall contends that in view of these omissions the proceedings to recover possession fail *ab initio*.

The first point is, whether this particular breach is capable of remedy. In my judgment MacKinnon J was right in coming to the conclusion that it was not. I think perhaps he went further than was really necessary for the decision of this case in holding that a breach of any negative covenant – the doing of that which is forbidden – can never be capable of remedy. It is unnecessary to decide the point on this appeal; but in some cases where the immediate ceasing of that which is complained of, together with an undertaking against any further breach, it might be said that the breach was capable of remedy. This particular breach, however – conducting the premises, or permitting them to be conducted, as a house of ill-fame – is one which in my judgment was not remedied by merely stopping this user. I cannot conceive how a breach of this kind can be remedied. The result of committing the breach would be known all over the neighbourhood and seriously affect the value of the premises. Even a money payment together with the cessation of the improper use of the house could not be a remedy. Taking the view as I do that this breach was incapable of remedy, it was unnecessary to require in the notice that the defendant should remedy the breach.

The further question is whether the absence of any statement in the notice requiring compensation in money in respect of the breach is fatal to the validity of the notice. As to that, the decision of the Court of Appeal in *Lock* v *Pearce*[i] binds us to hold that the plaintiffs were under no obligation to require compensation in money . . . Lindley LJ there used these words:[ii] '. . . Supposing the lessor does not want compensation, is the notice to be held bad because he does not ask for it? There is no sense in that . . .'

[i] [1893] 2 Ch 271.
[ii] [1893] 2 Ch 279.

Comment

It is well settled that compensation need not be claimed unless desired, but the question of remediability (especially of negative covenants) has proved very difficult.

Extract 15.4.13

Glass v Kencakes Ltd [1966] 1 QB 611

PAULL J: . . . The question before me therefore resolves itself into a question which can be simply stated, but which I have found very difficult to decide. I would state it in these words: where the covenant, the breach of which is complained of, is a covenant that premises shall only be used in a certain manner and that covenant is broken by a sub-tenant of the lessee, is it capable of remedy by the lessee where the user which constitutes the breach is in fact an immoral user but where the lessee does not know that there is any such or any breach and the circumstances are such that the lessee has no reason to suppose that any, and in particular any such, breach has been or is being committed by the sub-tenant? . . .

In *Rugby School (Governors)* v *Tannahill*[i] Mackinnon J,[ii] in the court below, had held that a breach of any negative covenant is not capable of remedy. You cannot put back the past and undo that which has been done. As Harman LJ pointed out in *Hoffman v Fineberg*,[iii] such a solution would render the provisions of section 146 of the Law of Property Act, 1925, easy to apply. The Court of Appeal, however, took a different view. Greer LJ[iv] did not go further than to say that while he had no hesitation in saying that permitting a house to be used as a brothel was incapable of remedy, Mackinnon J had gone further than was really necessary for the decision and that it was unnecessary to decide whether Mackinnon J was right or not. Maugham LJ,[v] however, went somewhat further and used words which I need not quote, but which Harman LJ in the later case said[vi] (and in my judgment rightly said) meant that Maugham LJ rejected the wideness of Mackinnon J's statement and left the matter an uncharted sea.

While there can be no doubt but that the *Rugby School* case held that permitting the use of premises for immoral or illegal purposes is incapable of remedy, it does not follow that the court held that a mere breach of user carried out by a sub-tenant of the lessee, of which breach the lessee does not and cannot reasonably know, renders the lessee's breach incapable of remedy even if the breach involved immoral user of the premises. As Mr Littman pointed out, if such is the position it would follow that the freeholder of a large block of flats could terminate the long lease of a lessee of the whole block merely because, however careful the lessee had been, one of the large number of tenants did in fact use a flat for the purpose of prostitution for even one night and force the lessee to go to the expense of claiming relief, a claim which, on one argument of Mr Bagnall, the court would not grant in fact once there had been immoral user of the premises.
. . .

On the other hand, it may be said that if one considers damage to premises it does not matter who has used the premises for the immoral purpose, although again it would seem to me that it may well be that both the Lord Justices had in mind a situation where it became known in the neighbourhood that the same person who had committed the breach was still going on in occupation and that the premises might well be so used again.

. . . I think the following propositions may be stated: (1) The mere fact that the breach complained of is a breach of user by a sub-tenant contrary to a covenant in the lease does not render the breach incapable of remedy. If one of the tenants of these flats in Queensway had, unknown to the defendants, carried on a small business of dressmaking in the flats, I would hold without hesitation that the breach was capable of remedy so far as the defendants are concerned, but it may be that the remedy would have to consist not only of stopping the tenant from carrying on that business but of bringing an action for forfeiture, it being then left to the court to decide whether the particular tenant should be granted relief. (2) The fact that the business user involves immorality does not in itself render the breach incapable of remedy, provided that the lessees neither knew of nor had any reason to know of the fact that the flat was being so used. The remedy in such a case, however, must involve not only that immediate steps are taken to stop such a user so soon as the user is known, but that an action for forfeiture of the sub-tenant's lease must be started within a reasonable time . . . (3) It does not follow that such a breach is always capable of remedy. All the circumstances must be taken into consideration. For example, if the notice is not the first notice which has had to be served, or if there are particularly revolting circumstances attaching to the user, or great publicity, then it might well be that the slate could not be wiped clean, or, to use another phrase, the damage to the property might be so great as to render the breach incapable of remedy.

[i] [1935] 1 KB 87; 51 TLR 84, CA.
[ii] [1934] 1 KB 695, 700, 701.
[iii] [1949] Ch 245, 254; [1948] 1 All ER 592, 596.
[iv] [1935] 1 KB 87, 90, 91.
[v] *Ibid* 92.
[vi] [1949] Ch 245, 255.

Comment

(1) Is this result compatible with the 'stigma' analysis of *Rugby School*?

(2) How convincing is the argument that any other result would permit the forfeiture of a lease because of a minor breach by one of many sublessees?

Extract 15.4.14

Expert Clothing Service & Sales Ltd v *Hillgate House Ltd* [1986] Ch 340

SLADE LJ: . . . First, [counsel for the plaintiffs] pointed out that (as is common ground) the first defendant's failure to build by 28 September 1982 was a 'once and for all' breach of the relevant covenant, and not a continuing breach . . . He submitted that the breach of a covenant such as this, which can only be broken once, is *ex hypothesi* in no case capable of remedy.

Some superficial support for this conclusion is perhaps to be found in the judgments in *Scala House & District Property Co Ltd* v *Forbes* [1974] QB 575, in which the Court of Appeal held that the breach of a covenant not to assign, underlet or part with possession was not a breach capable of remedy within the meaning of section 146(1). In the course of his judgment, Russell LJ, having referred to the relevant breach, said, at p 585:

> 'If it is capable of remedy, and is remedied in reasonable time, the lessor is unable to prove that a condition precedent to his ability to seek to forfeit by action or otherwise has been fulfilled. Here at once is a problem. An unlawful subletting is a breach once and for all. The subterm has been created.'

Russell LJ then turned to the authorities, including the *Rugby School* case [1935] 1 KB 87, as to which he made these comments, at p 585:

> 'this court expressed the view that breach of negative covenants might be capable of remedy, but not this one, on the ground that the stigma attaching to the premises would not be removed by mere cesser of the immoral user. I observe that it does not appear to have been considered whether the breach in that case was incapable of remedy on another ground, viz: that the wrongful user had ceased before the section 146 notice.'

After his review of the authorities, Russell LJ continued, at p 588:

> '. . . If a user in breach has ceased before the section 146 notice (quite apart from the stigma cases) then either it is incapable of remedy and after notice there is nothing in the way of a

writ: or the cesser of use has somehow deprived the lessor of his ability to seek to forfeit though he has done nothing to waive the breach, a situation in law which I find extremely difficult to spell out of section 146.'

But whatever might be the position in user breach cases, Russell LJ concluded that a breach by an unlawful subletting is not capable of remedy at all . . .

It might well be regarded as anomalous if the once and for all breach of a negative covenant not to sublet were to be regarded as 'capable of remedy' within section 146, provided that the unlawful subtenancy was still current at the date of the section 146 notice, but (as Russell LJ considered) were not to be regarded as 'capable of remedy' if the unlawful subtenancy had been determined at that date . . .

However, in the *Scala House* case [1974] QB 575 this court was addressing its mind solely to the once and for all breach of a negative covenant. No corresponding anomaly arises if the once and for all breach of a positive covenant is treated as capable of remedy. While the *Scala House* decision is, of course, authority binding on this court for the proposition that the breach of a negative covenant not to assign, underlet or part with possession is never 'capable of remedy', it is not, in my judgment, authority for the proposition that the once and for all breach of a positive covenant is never capable of remedy.

Mr Neuberger, on behalf of the defendants, did not feel able to go so far as to support the view of MacKinnon J that the breach of a positive covenant is *always* capable of remedy. He accepted, for example, that the breach of a covenant to insure might be incapable of remedy at a time when the premises had already been burnt down . . .

Nevertheless, I would, for my part, accept Mr Neuberger's submission that the breach of a positive covenant (whether it be a continuing breach or a once and for all breach) will ordinarily be capable of remedy. As Bristow J pointed out in the course of argument, the concept of capability of remedy for the purpose of section 146 must surely be directed to the question whether the harm that has been done to the landlord by the relevant breach is for practicable purposes capable of being retrieved. In the ordinary case, the breach of a promise to do something by a certain time can for practical purposes be remedied by the thing being done, even out of time.

Comment

(1) Why is a distinction drawn between continuing and 'once and for all' breaches?

(2) What was the reasoning in *Scala*? Is it convincing?

(3) How is *Scala* distinguished? Is the reasoning of Slade LJ consistent with the ideas underpinning *Scala*?

Extract 15.4.15

Savva v *Hussein* (1996) 73 P&CR 150

Tenants committed quite minor breaches of covenants not to make alterations to the premises.

STAUGHTON LJ: . . . It is established law in this court that the breach of a covenant not to assign without consent cannot be remedied. That was decided in *Scala House & District Property Co Ltd* v *Forbes*.[i] Even then relief from forfeiture was granted, so that may not be of any great consequence.

In my judgment, except in a case of breach of a covenant not to assign without consent, the question is: whether the remedy referred to is the process of restoring the situation to what it would have been if the covenant had never been broken, or whether it is sufficient that the mischief resulting from a breach of the covenant can be removed. When something has been done without consent, it is not possible to restore the matter wholly to the situation which it was in before the breach. The moving finger writes and cannot be recalled. That is not to my mind what is meant by a remedy, it is a remedy if the mischief caused by the breach can be removed. In the case of a covenant not to make alterations without consent or not to display signs without consent, if there is a breach of that, the mischief can be removed by removing the signs or restoring the property to the state it was in before the alterations.

ⁱ [1974] QB 575.

Comment

(1) Is any of the reasoning in *Scala* left? How can the actual result in *Scala* be justified today?

(2) When, if at all, will a breach not be remediable?

(3) *Savva* demonstrates the triumph of the analysis in *Glass*. Does it represent good policy to have a wide interpretation of remediability?

(4) The Law Commission's proposals for reform of forfeiture involve the court's having a discretion as to forfeiture in all cases.[37]

Somewhat more recently, Neuberger LJ[38] has held a covenant against parting with or sharing possession remediable, observing of *Scala*:

> First, it was only concerned with underletting; secondly, the reasoning of the leading judgment in the case is, at least in part, demonstrably fallacious and inconsistent with common sense and many other authorities; thirdly, it has been overtaken and marginalised by *Expert Clothing* and *Savva*; fourthly, there is no reason of logic or principle why the reasoning or conclusion in *Scala House* should be extended to apply to a breach which falls short of creating a legal interest.

(ii) The position after the notice

This was described by Slade LJ in *Expert Clothing*[39] as follows:

> An important purpose of the section 146 procedure is to give even tenants who have hitherto lacked the will or the means to comply with their obligations one last chance to summon up that will or find the necessary means before the landlord re-enters. In considering what 'reasonable time' to allow the defendants, the plaintiffs, in serving their section 146 notice, would, in my opinion, have been entitled to take into account the fact that the defendants already had enjoyed 15 months in which to fulfil their contractual obligations to reconstruct and to subject the defendants to a correspondingly tight timetable running from the date of service of the notice . . . However, I think they were not entitled to say, in effect: 'We are not going to allow you any time at all to remedy the breach, because you have had so long to do the work already.'

Where the breach is not remedied within a reasonable time,[40] the court still possesses a discretion to award relief. Naturally, the significance of the breach for the landlord will be weighed against the potential loss of a valuable asset in the hands of the tenant. An important point is that, once possession has been taken under the court order, it is too late to claim relief.[41] This is different from the position regarding rent. Can this difference be justified?

---

[37] Law Com No 303.
[38] *Akici* v *LR Butlin Ltd* [2006] 1 WLR 201 at [74].
[39] [1986] Ch 340 at p 358.
[40] Likely to be three months for repairs: *Bhojwani* v *Kingsley Investment Trust Ltd* [1992] 2 EGLR 70 at p 73.
[41] *Quilter* v *Mapleson* (1882) 9 QBD 672; confirmed by *Billson* v *Residential Apartments Ltd* [1992] 1 AC 494 at pp 538, 542.

(iii) Peaceable re-entry

It has been seen that it may be possible for a landlord to forfeit by peaceable re-entry, without any court order. Does the tenant have any right to relief after such re-entry?

Extract 15.4.16

Billson v Residential Apartments Ltd **[1992] 1 AC 494**

The first quotation is taken from a dissenting Court of Appeal judgment.

NICHOLLS LJ: [The lack of a power to give relief] leads to a wholly unacceptable conclusion. Take this very case. A landlord serves a section 146 notice, which is not complied with. So the landlord is entitled to forfeit the lease. According to the argument of the landlords in the present case, if the landlord chooses to effect the forfeiture by forcing his way into the premises, he is in a better position than if he had applied to the court for an order for possession. Had he applied to the court, the tenant would have applied for relief from forfeiture and the court would have granted relief if it was equitable to do so. But if he takes the law into his own hands, and without further warning to the tenant re-takes possession of the leased property, no application for relief from forfeiture can then be made. The court is powerless. The landlord is secure, even if he used physical force to obtain entry, provided he is careful to see that no one is actually on the property at the time and provided the premises are not let as a dwelling.

That cannot be right. Such a conclusion would be an incitement to all landlords to re-enter forcibly whenever they can do so. That would amount to the courts granting a charter for forcible entry . . . But the lawyers would also have to advise landlords that, in the case of non-residential property, they should keep watch on the property. They should do this surreptitiously, so as not to alert their tenants to what they have in mind. They should then enter, by force if necessary, once they see that the coast is clear and there is no one on the property . . . The stronger the tenant's claim for relief, the more important it would be for the landlord to keep away from the court and to pounce on the property, in the evening or at the weekend, and change the locks and then sit back secure in the knowledge that the forfeiture is complete and that is an end of the matter.

. . . The policy of the law is to discourage self-help when confrontation and a breach of the peace are likely to follow. If a tenant, who is in breach of covenant, will not quit but persists in carrying on his business despite the landlord's right of re-entry, the proper course for a responsible landlord is to invoke the due process of law and seek an order for possession from the court.

LORD TEMPLEMAN: The tenant may apply for relief where the landlord is 'proceeding, by action or otherwise' to enforce his rights. The tenant may apply for relief where the landlord is 'proceeding' by action and also where the landlord is proceeding 'otherwise' than by action. This can only mean that the tenant may apply for relief where the landlord is proceeding to forfeit by re-entry after the expiry of a section 146 notice. If re-entry bars relief, the right of the tenant to apply for relief where the landlord is proceeding otherwise than by action is substantially inoperative and the words 'or otherwise' in section 146(2) have no application. In my opinion those words must have been included because Parliament intended that a tenant should be able to obtain relief against a landlord whether the landlord has asserted his rights by a writ or by re-entering. It is said that a tenant served with a section 146 notice could during and after the expiration of the notice apply for relief under section 146(2) but if he fails to do so he is at the mercy of the landlord who decides to re-enter and whose rights are therefore, it is said, quite unaffected by the provisions of section 146(2) designed to relieve tenants from the consequences of breach of covenant. In my opinion the ambiguous words 'is proceeding' can mean 'proceeds' and should not be construed so as to produce the result that a tenant served with a section 146 notice can only ensure that he will be able to apply for relief if he does so before he knows whether or not the landlord intends to proceed at all or whether, if the landlord decides to proceed, he will issue and serve a writ or will attempt to re-enter.

When a tenant receives a section 146 notice he will not know whether the landlord can be persuaded that there is no breach or persuaded to accept in due course that any breach has been remedied and that he has been offered adequate and satisfactory compensation or whether the landlord will seek to determine the lease by issuing and serving a writ or will seek to determine the lease by re-entering the premises. The tenant will not wish to institute proceedings seeking relief from forfeiture if those proceedings will be aggressive and hostile and may be premature and unnecessary . . .

The right conferred by section 146(2) on a tenant to apply for relief against forfeiture may without violence to the language, be construed as a right to apply 'where a lessor proceeds, by action or otherwise' to enforce a right of re-entry. So construed, section 146(2) enables the tenant to apply for relief whenever and however the landlord claims that the lease has been determined for breach of covenant. I have no doubt that this was the object and intention and is the effect of section 146.

. . .

We were informed that the researches of counsel had not disclosed any reported case in which a landlord has forfeited by re-entry and then successfully denied the right of the tenant to apply for relief.

The landlords or their advisers, perhaps incensed by the activities of the tenants in the present case, conceived and carried out a dawn raid which fortunately did not result in bloodshed. Since the decision of the Court of Appeal in the instant case there has been a proliferation of section 146 notices followed by pressure on tenants to surrender on terms favourable to the landlord. If this appeal were not allowed, the only safe advice for a tenant would be to issue proceedings for relief against forfeiture as soon as a section 146 notice is received at a time when the tenant cannot know whether relief will be necessary. A tenant ignorant of the development in the law pioneered by the landlords in the present case will be at the mercy of an aggressive landlord. The conclusions which I have reached will not entail these consequences and will not again involve Parliament in correcting judicial constructions of statute by further legislation.

Comment

(1) It is easy to see the desirability of relief being available, but is the decision justified by the wording of the legislation?

(2) Does this decision preclude any risk of a human rights challenge to peaceable re-entry?[42]

(3) In the Court of Appeal, the majority held that the statutory code in s 146 ousted any equitable relief.[43] Equitable relief was not argued in the House of Lords.

(iv) Sub-tenants and mortgagees

Most applications are made under the LPA, s 146(4), quoted below, but this involves a new lease rather than the continuation of the existing lease as occurs under s 146(1) or (2).

Extract 15.4.17

Escalus Properties Ltd v *Robinson* **[1996] QB 231**

If relief under the LPA, s 146(4) were obtained, compensation for the use of the land for the period until relief would be payable. This greatly exceeded the rent which would be payable if s 146(2) relief was ordered (the rent payable under the terms of the lease).

---

[42] See Bruce (2000) 150 NLJ 462.
[43] See Extract 15.4.19 below.

NOURSE LJ: . . . It is well established that the effect of an order for relief under section 146(2) is to restore the lease as if it had never been forfeited, and with it any underlease: see the decision of this court in *Dendy v Evans* [1910] 1 KB 263. That is what is meant when it is said that relief is granted retrospectively. But where relief is granted under section 146(4) it can only be granted as from the date of the order granting it . . .

The rival contentions as to section 146(2) and (4) are, shortly stated, as follows. Relying on the definition of 'lessee' in subsection (5)(b) and the decision in *United Dominions Trust Ltd* v *Shellpoint Trustees Ltd* [1993] 4 All ER 310, the mortgagee contends that it is entitled to apply for and obtain relief under subsection (2), with the same results as under section 138(9A) and (9B) of the County Courts Act 1984. In answer, the landlord, relying on authorities not cited in the *United Dominions Trust* case, in particular the decision of this court in *Nind v Nineteenth Century Building Society* [1894] 2 QB 226, contends that an underlessee cannot be granted relief under subsection (2), but only under subsection (4), and that in any event, as a matter of discretion, the mortgagee ought to be granted relief under subsection (4) . . .

It is clear that the definition of 'lessee' in section 146(5)(b) of the Act of 1925 is wider than that in section 14(3) of the Act of 1881. Instead of including merely an original underlessee, a derivative underlessee and the heirs, executors, administrators and assigns of a lessee, it now includes 'the persons deriving title under a lessee' . . . They must include not only those who acquire the lessee's own estate but also those who acquire a lesser estate by way of subdemise . . .

If therefore the definition of 'lessee' in section 146(5)(b) is applied to 'the lessee' in section 146(2), it is seen that where a lessor is proceeding to enforce a right of forfeiture under section 146(1) an underlessee, no less than the lessee himself, may apply to the court for relief. It is no longer permissible, as a matter of construction, to restrict the class of applicants to those who are in privity of contract or estate with the lessor. Such a construction would fail to give full effect to subsection (5)(b) . . .

From his very great experience in these matters Mr Neuberger has told us that it has never before been suggested that an underlessee can obtain relief under section 146(2). Had I not heard the full and careful arguments on these appeals, I too would have assumed the suggestion to be ill-founded. But on reflection I do not think it surprising that Parliament should have brought about the result I now believe it has.

Comment

When will it be appropriate to grant relief under s 146(2) so as to continue the existing lease? How relevant should it be that the head tenant would not be entitled to relief, perhaps because of his immoral use of another part of the premises held under the head lease?

Extract 15.4.18

Law of Property Act 1925, s 146(4)

146.—(4)   Where a lessor is proceeding by action or otherwise to enforce a right of re-entry or forfeiture under any covenant, proviso, or stipulation in a lease, or for non-payment of rent, the court may, on application by any person claiming as under-lessee any estate or interest in the property comprised in the lease or any part thereof, either in the lessor's action (if any) or in any action brought by such person for that purpose, make an order vesting, for the whole term of the lease or any less term, the property comprised in the lease or any part thereof in any person entitled as under-lessee to any estate or interest in such property upon such conditions as to execution of any deed or other document, payment of rent, costs, expenses, damages, compensation, giving security, or otherwise, as the court in the circumstances of each case may think fit, but in no case shall any such under-lessee be entitled to require a lease to be granted to him for any longer term than he had under his original sublease.

Comment

(1) This also applies to mortgagees.[44]

(2) Unlike the rest of s 146, subsection (4) applies to all breaches, not just non-rent breaches.

(3) As with s 146(2), relief cannot be claimed once the landlord has taken possession under a court order. This provides a distinct trap for mortgagees, who might be unaware of the circumstances until it is too late.[45] However, there may be jurisdiction to set aside the forfeiture order in such circumstances.[46]

Our next question is whether there is any equitable right to relief. This is particularly important if possession has been taken under a court order.

Extract 15.4.19

Billson v Residential Apartments Ltd [1992] 1 AC 494 (CA)

SIR NICOLAS BROWNE-WILKINSON V-C: . . . From the early 19th century until *Shiloh Spinners Ltd* v *Harding* [1973] AC 691 it was thought that the court had no inherent jurisdiction to grant relief from forfeiture for 'wilful' breach of covenant other than the covenant to pay rent or some other specified sum of money. This is a point of central importance in the present case. The decision in *Shiloh Spinners* disclosed, retrospectively, that the view so held for 150 years had been erroneous. The court had originally had an inherent jurisdiction to relieve in such cases (though such jurisdiction was to be exercised with great caution). However, the House of Lords recognised that, in certain areas, such inherent jurisdiction might have been implicitly removed by Parliament in conferring on the court statutory powers of relief.

In *Shiloh Spinners* it was argued that, although the covenant and forfeiture provision there in question did not arise as between landlord and tenant, the statutory provisions for relief from forfeiture as between landlord and tenant contained in section 146 of the Law of Property Act 1925 and its predecessors had impliedly removed the whole equitable jurisdiction to relieve in such cases. The House of Lords rejected this argument. After mentioning some of the statutes dealing with relief in cases between landlord and tenant, Lord Wilberforce said, at p 725:

> 'In my opinion where the courts have established a general principle of law or equity, and the legislature steps in with particular legislation in a particular area, it must, unless showing a contrary intention, be taken to have left cases outside that area where they were under the influence of the general law . . .'

The question therefore is whether the legislature has stepped into the area of relief against forfeiture for wilful breach of covenant (other than to pay rent) as between landlord and tenant so as to have excluded the old equitable jurisdiction to relieve in that area.

. . . I have reluctantly come to the conclusion that the inherent equitable jurisdiction as between landlord and tenant to relieve from forfeiture for wilful breach of covenant (other than a covenant for the payment of rent) has been extinguished by reason of Parliament having legislated comprehensively in that field.

Comment

(1) This decision was in the context of peaceable re-entry and the availability of s 146(2) relief for tenants. The problems with peaceable re-entry (before the successful appeal to the

---

[44] *Grand Junction Co Ltd* v *Bates* [1954] 2 QB 160.
[45] *Egerton* v *Jones* [1939] 2 KB 702.
[46] *Rexhaven Ltd* v *Nurse* (1995) 28 HLR 241.

House of Lords on statutory relief) explain Sir Nicolas Browne-Wilkinson's reluctance. How is the argument for equitable jurisdiction affected by the House of Lords decision?

(2) Does the logic of the decision exclude any equitable jurisdiction as regards sub-tenants and mortgagees, for whom provision is made by s 146(4)? Would this apply to rent breaches as well as non-rent breaches?

So far, we have been considering when there is jurisdiction to grant relief. When relief is granted, questions arise as to what conditions to impose.

Extract 15.4.20

Chatham Empire Theatre (1955) Ltd v *Ultrans Ltd* [1961] 1 WLR 817

The defendants held a sublease of a cinema.

SALMON J: . . . Mr Goodall argued that the defendants should be granted relief against forfeiture only if they pay the whole of the rent outstanding at the date of the issue of the writ in respect of the cinema, the theatre, the car park and the restaurant premises, that is to say, all the premises comprised in the head lease. He bases that contention on the well-known principle which is alluded to by Joyce J in *London Bridge Buildings Co* v *Thomson*[i] and by Lord Greene MR in *Egerton* v *Jones*[ii] that in a case of relief against forfeiture the plaintiffs are entitled to be put back into the position that they would have been in if the forfeiture had not occurred. There is no doubt about that principle, and no question arises where a tenant is applying for relief against forfeiture in an action by his landlord. In this case, however, the question is how that principle applies – and it does obviously apply – when a sub-lessee of a part of the premises is claiming relief against forfeiture; is the landlord entitled to be put back in the same position as he was in before the forfeiture qua the whole of the premises in the head lease or only in respect of the premises of which the sub-lessee is in possession?

. . .

In my judgment it is clearly equitable that the landlord should be put in the same position as he was in before the forfeiture qua that part of the property, namely, the cinema, let to the defendants. In my judgment the defendants ought to be required, as a condition of obtaining relief, to pay £585 plus an element for the premium and not the whole of the £2,730. One can envisage a case in which a block of property comprising a large number of shops and other premises is let to one corporation for £30,000 a year. The corporation then sublet the separate shops to various small shopkeepers at perhaps £300 a year each . . . If Mr Goodall's contention is correct, the apparently wide discretion conferred by subsection (4) of section 146 is so limited that the court could not grant relief to the small shopkeeper unless he paid the £15,000 rent in arrear [for half a year] in respect of the whole block . . . I can certainly conceive of cases where it would be quite wrong to give a sub-lessee relief on this basis; great hardship could be caused to the head lessor if granting relief to one or two of many sub-tenants would make it impossible for him to deal with the premises as a whole. Every case must be considered on its own facts.

[i] (1903) 89 LT 50.
[ii] [1939] 2 KB 702; 55 TLR 1089; [1939] 3 All ER 889, CA.

Comment

Why was such relief appropriate in *Chatham*? Why should a landlord be forced to deal with his property in parts, rather than as a single unit as in the head lease?

Extract 15.4.21

Ewart v *Fryer* [1901] 1 Ch 499

ROMER LJ: ... I think that the section gives the most ample discretion to the Court ... That section did not, to my mind, of necessity contemplate that the terms of the original lease should be kept alive, either all or any of them, though, no doubt, speaking generally, regard would be had to them, and most of them probably would be kept alive in the new lease that had to be fixed as between the original lessor and the underlessee; but, as a matter of fact, it is not necessary that in the new lease there should be inserted any term of the original lease. The section is perfectly general. For example, the Court is not bound to give to the lessee the whole of the term of his underlease. Probably it generally would do so, but it is not bound of necessity to do it. It is bound to have regard to the words at the end of the section, and not to give him a longer term than the term of his underlease ... It does not follow that the rent must of necessity be either the rent fixed by the original lease or the rent fixed by the underlease. It is to be such a rent as will do justice between the parties under the circumstances. For example, it would clearly be inequitable in some cases to say that the rent must of necessity be the rent of the original lease. Take the case where the original lease was at a rent of 50*l* and the underlease at a rent of 150*l* – would it be equitable that, because of the forfeiture of the original lease at the instance of the original lessor, and the abolition of the original rent, the underlessee at a rent of 150*l* should be entitled to say, 'Now I ought to have the rent in my lease reduced from 150*l* to 50*l*'? To my mind, clearly not. It must not be forgotten, as I have already said, that when the underlessee comes to the Court for assistance he does so on the footing that the original lessee's rights are gone in favour of the original lessor.

Neither would it be fair in every case to fix the terms of the new lease by reference to the terms of the underlease. Take a case where the original lease was at a rent of 150*l* and the underlease at a rent of 50*l*: clearly it would be unfair in that case to fix the rent by reference to the rent of the underlease. The landlord should not be obliged to give up his rent of 150*l* in exchange for the lesser rent of 50*l*. ... If the underlessee is by his new lease in substantially no worse a position than that which he occupied before the forfeiture, he certainly cannot complain.

Comment

Why does the law favour the result that the landlord, but never the tenant, may be better off?

(v) Repairing covenants

Extract 15.4.22

Leasehold Property (Repairs) Act 1938, s 1

1.—(1) Where a lessor serves on a lessee under subsection (1) of section one hundred and forty-six of the Law of Property Act, 1925, a notice that relates to a breach of a covenant or agreement to keep or put in repair during the currency of the lease all or any of the property comprised in the lease and at the date of the service of the notice three years or more of the term of the lease remain unexpired, the lessee may within twenty-eight days from that date serve on the lessor a counter-notice to the effect that he claims the benefit of this Act.

(2) A right to damages for a breach of such a covenant as aforesaid shall not be enforceable by action commenced at any time at which three years or more of the term of the lease remain unexpired unless the lessor has served on the lessee not less than one month before the commencement of the action such a notice ...

(3)   Where a counter-notice is served by a lessee under this section, then, notwithstanding anything in any enactment or rule of law, no proceedings, by action or otherwise, shall be taken by the lessor for the enforcement of any right of re-entry or forfeiture under any proviso or stipulation in the lease for breach of the covenant or agreement in question, or for damages for breach thereof, otherwise than with the leave of the court.

(5)   Leave for the purposes of this section shall not be given unless the lessor proves—

    (a)   that the immediate remedying of the breach in question is requisite for preventing substantial diminution in the value of his reversion, or that the value thereof has been substantially diminished by the breach;

    (b)   that the immediate remedying of the breach is required for giving effect in relation to the premises to the purposes of any enactment . . . ;

    . . .

    (d)   that the breach can be immediately remedied at an expense that is relatively small in comparison with the much greater expense that would probably be occasioned by postponement of the necessary work; or

    (e)   special circumstances which in the opinion of the court, render it just and equitable that leave should be given.

Extract 15.4.23

Sidnell v *Wilson* **[1966] 2 QB 67**

LORD DENNING MR: . . . That Act was passed shortly before the war because of a great mischief prevalent at that time. Unscrupulous people used to buy up the reversion of leases, and then bring pressure to bear on the tenants by an exaggerated list of dilapidations . . . The effect of a counternotice is that the landlord cannot proceed to forfeit the premises or to claim damages *unless he has the leave of the court* . . .

Let me say at once that in the great majority of dilapidation cases when there is want of repair during the term, leave will not be given: for in most cases the reversion is not diminished much in value by the breach. But this case is out of the ordinary. It is clear that, if the breach which the landlord alleges is established, the value of the reversion has been substantially diminished. Dry rot has invaded the premises . . . The landlord does, therefore, bring himself within section 1(5)(a), provided always that he is right in saying that the tenant was in breach.

Extract 15.4.24

SEDAC Investments Ltd v *Tanner* **[1982] 1 WLR 1342 (Ch D)**

MICHAEL WHEELER QC: . . . The whole scheme of section 1 of the Act of 1938 appears to commence with – and to hinge upon – the service of a valid lessor's section 146 notice: and if, therefore, I am right in holding that a section 146 notice, to be effective, must be served *before* the breach is remedied, I am forced to the conclusion that in a case such as the present, where the lessor remedied the breach before attempting to serve a notice under section 146(1), he has thereby put it out of his power to serve a valid section 146 notice at all, with the result that he has deprived the lessee of his right to serve a counter-notice: and the consequence of this seems inevitably to be that the court has no jurisdiction to give the lessor leave to commence proceedings for damages because that jurisdiction arises, as I have already indicated, only when (and because) the lessee has served a valid counter-notice.

I frankly confess that I have reached this conclusion with surprise and regret; surprise, because the scheme . . . appears to make no provision whatsoever for the situation where the consequences of the breach of the repairing covenant require (or might reasonably be thought to require) urgent attention and where, for example, the lessor takes immediate remedial action either of his own volition or, perhaps, because the lessee is unable or unwilling to take the necessary action sufficiently promptly; regret, because I can see no reason why, in such circumstances, the lessor should (as I have felt bound to hold) be unable to apply to the court for leave to commence proceedings for damages . . .

I see no merit in the argument that by remedying the breach himself the lessor has thereby prevented the lessee from doing so, possibly at less cost. That is a point which might well be argued in the action for damages itself . . .

Comment

(1) How should the legislation have been drafted?

(2) The following case shows how to mitigate the effects of *SEDAC*.

Extract 15.4.25

Jervis v Harris [1996] Ch 195

MILLETT LJ: . . . The question, therefore, is whether the landlord's right to enter the property, effect the repairs himself and then claim [under a clause in the lease] to recover the cost of doing so from the tenant is a claim for damages for breach of a covenant by the tenant 'to keep or put in repair during the currency of the lease all or any of the property comprised in the lease'.

. . .

The short answer to the question is that the tenant's liability to reimburse the landlord for his expenditure on repairs is not a liability in damages for breach of his repairing covenant [at] all. The landlord's claim sounds in debt not damages; and it is not a claim to compensation for breach of the tenant's covenant to repair, but for reimbursement of sums actually spent by the landlord in carrying out repairs himself. I shall expand on each of these distinctions in turn.

The law of contract draws a clear distinction between a claim for payment of a debt and a claim for damages for breach of contract . . .

Moreover, the landlord's monetary claim under such a clause is not a claim for compensation for loss suffered by him by reason of the tenant's failure to repair but for reimbursement of expenditure which he incurred in order to avoid such loss. The difference is one of substance. The loss which the landlord suffers by reason of the tenant's failure to repair is the diminution of the value of his interest in the property . . .

But a clause such as clause 2(10) works very differently. It enables the landlord to take remedial action himself to avoid any loss consequent on the tenant's failure to repair. Once the landlord has carried out the repairs himself, the value of his interest in the property is restored. The work of repair enures to the benefit of the tenant as well as the landlord. The landlord is out of pocket, but that is because he has carried out repairs, not because the property is in disrepair.

. . .

In my view, every consideration points in the same direction, that it was not the intention of Parliament to put obstacles in the way of a landlord whose object is to secure that necessary repairs are carried out, preferably at the expense of the tenant, but if necessary at his own.

Comment

(1) Was the court justified in not applying the legislation?

(2) Does this result leave the tenant exposed to some of the dangers which the legislation was designed to protect against? What is the optimal solution for cases of this nature?

E. Reform

The Law Commission has issued several reports,[47] which would amend many of the rules detailed above. Peaceable re-entry will disappear, though replaced by a 'summary termination notice' for straightforward cases. Otherwise, as mentioned above, forfeiture would be by order of the court. Waiver rules would be abolished and subsumed within the court's discretion. The s 146 notice would disappear and, with it, rights to relief: in future a tenant default notice would be required in all cases and relief would be discretionary. Clearer provision would be made for sub-tenants and mortgagees.

5. Distress and commercial rent arrears recovery

Distress was the ancient remedy of seizing goods on the premises to cover unpaid rent; the goods could be sold. It was abolished by the Tribunals, Courts and Enforcement Act 2007 and replaced (for commercial tenancies only) by a new scheme for commercial rent arrears recovery. The worst problems of the previous law are countered by requiring notice to be given and allowing the tenant to ask the court to intervene.

Further reading

Elliott, D W (1964) 80 LQR 244: Non-derogation from grant.

Harwood, M (2000) 20 LS 503: Leases: are they still not really real?

Lower, M [2010] Conv 38: The Bruton tenancy.

Morgan, J (2009) 'Leases: Property, contract or more?' in *Modern Studies in Property Law*, Vol 5, ed. M Dixon, Chapter 17.

Reynolds, J I (1974) 37 MLR 377: Statutory covenants of fitness and repair: social legislation and the judges.

Roberts, N [2012] Conv 87: The Bruton tenancy: a matter of relativity.

Smith, P F [2003] Conv 112: Disrepair and unfitness revisited.

Tromans, S [1986] Conv 187: Forfeiture of leases: relief for underlessees and holders of other derivative interests.

---

[47] Most recently, Law Com No 303.

16

Leases: parties and the running of covenants

1. Introduction

Covenants in leases are very important, as the last chapter demonstrates. Both landlord and tenant may well assign their estates during the lease, especially where the lease is for an extended period. It comes as no surprise that a landlord may choose to sell the freehold reversion: it is a valuable asset. The tenant may also wish to assign the lease. It would be possible to surrender the lease to the landlord, but one or both parties may prefer that the lease should continue and that an assignee should have possession under it. There is then the obvious question as to how far covenants in the lease can be enforced after the reversion and the lease are assigned. Outside the leases context, the benefit of covenants can generally be assigned, but it is exceptional for their burden to bind successors in title.

The relationship between the parties may be shown by Figure 16.1, in which the lease has been assigned to A^L and the freehold reversion to A^R.

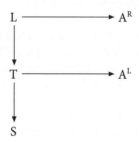

Figure 16.1

Extract 16.1.1

City of London Corporation v Fell [1994] 1 AC 458

LORD TEMPLEMAN: . . . At common law, after an assignment, the benefit of a covenant by the original landlord which touches and concerns the land runs with the term granted by the lease. The burden of a covenant by the original tenant which touches and concerns the land also runs with the term: see *Spencer's Case* (1583) 5 Co Rep 16a.

By statute, the benefit of a covenant by the original tenant which touches and concerns the land runs with the reversion . . .

By statute, the burden of a covenant by the original landlord which touches and concerns the land also runs with the reversion . . .

The principle that the benefit and burden of covenants in a lease which touch and concern the land run with the term and with the reversion is necessary for the effective operation of the law of landlord and tenant. Common law, and statute following the common law, recognise two forms of legal estate in land, a fee simple absolute in possession and a term of years absolute: see section 1 of the Act of 1925. Common law, and statute following the common law, were faced with the problem of rendering effective the obligations under a lease which might endure for a period of 999 years or more beyond the control of any covenantor. The solution was to annex to the term and the reversion the benefit and burden of covenants which touch and concern the land. The covenants having been annexed, every legal owner of the term granted by the lease and every legal owner of the reversion from time to time holds his estate with the benefit of and subject to the covenants which touch and concern the land. The system of leasehold tenure requires that the obligations in the lease shall be enforceable throughout the term, whether those obligations are affirmative or negative. The owner of a reversion must be able to enforce the positive covenants to pay rent and keep in repair against an assignee who in turn must be able to enforce any positive covenants entered into by the original landlord. Common law retained the ancient rule that the burden of a covenant does not run with the land of the covenantor except in the case of a lease, but even that rule was radically modified by equity so far as negative covenants were concerned: see *Tulk* v *Moxhay* (1848) 2 Ph 774.

. . . Nourse LJ neatly summarised the position when he said in an impeccable judgment [1993] QB 589, 604:

> 'The contractual obligations which touch and concern the land having become imprinted on the estate, the tenancy is capable of existence as a species of property independently of the contract.'

. . . The assignee is not liable for a breach of covenant committed after the assignee has himself in turn assigned the lease because once he has assigned over he has ceased to be the owner of the term to which the covenants are annexed.

Figure 16.1 also shows a sublease (or underlease) to S: a lease is carved out of T's lease. Suppose the lease to T was for ten years at a rent of £20,000 pa. The sublease might be on very different terms: for two years at £30,000 pa rent, for example. Unlike the position between L (or A^R) and A^L, there is no landlord and tenant relationship between L (or A^R) and S: we say that there is no *privity of estate* between them. This means that they cannot sue each other on the covenants. This explains the result in legal terminology, but why should the sub-tenant not be liable on the covenants when the assignee is liable?

Subleases are liable to be defeated if the head lease comes to an end; a consequence of being carved out of the head lease. The general rules were expressed very clearly by Simon Brown LJ in *Pennell* v *Payne*:[1]

> At common law, the general rule is that, when the head tenancy comes to an end, any subtenancy derived out of it also automatically and simultaneously comes to an end. This general rule applies without question when the head tenancy comes to an end by effluxion of time, by a landlord's notice to quit, or by forfeiture. It is equally beyond question that the general rule does not apply in cases of surrender and merger.

---

[1] [1995] QB 192 at p 197.

Extract 16.1.2

St Marylebone Property Co Ltd v Fairweather [1963] AC 510

LORD DENNING: . . . At common law, if a leaseholder made an underlease and afterwards surrendered his term to the freeholder, then the freeholder could not evict the underlessee during the term of the underlease: see *Pleasant (Lessee of Hayton)* v *Benson*.[i] But this was not because there was any assignment from surrenderor to surrenderee. It is clear that, upon the surrender, the head term was determined altogether . . . Under [sections 139 and 150 of the Law of Property Act, 1925], on a surrender of the head lease, an underlessee becomes a direct tenant of the freeholder on the terms of his underlease. So that the surrender does operate as if it were an assignment of the surrenderor's interest . . . The question may be asked: why did the common law on a surrender protect the under-lessee from eviction? The answer is to be found in Coke upon Littleton II, p 338b, where it is said that 'having regard to the parties to the surrender, the estate is absolutely drowned . . . But having regard to strangers, who were not parties or privies thereunto, lest by a voluntary surrender they may receive prejudice touching any right or interest they had before the surrender, the estate surrendered hath in consideration of law a continuance.' This passage applies in favour of an underlessee so as to protect him from eviction during the term of his underlease . . .

[i] (1811) 14 East 234.

Extract 16.1.3

Barrett v Morgan [2000] 2 AC 264

The landlords served a notice to terminate a periodic tenancy. The tenants agreed not to serve a counter-notice under the Agricultural Holdings Act 1986, which could have protected them. What was the effect of this on a subtenancy?

LORD MILLETT: The question for decision, therefore, is whether the fact that the notices to quit were served by the freeholders pursuant to an agreement or understanding in that behalf with the head tenants deprived them of the effect which they would have had if they had been served without any prior agreement or understanding.

The Court of Appeal held that it did. They observed that a subtenancy is not determined by the surrender of the head tenancy and, while they recognised that the head tenancy had not in fact been surrendered, they treated a notice to quit given by a landlord by prior arrangement with the tenant as tantamount to a surrender because both transactions are consensual. As Sir Richard Scott V-C put it, at p 1117:

> 'It is unilateral notices to quit that destroy subtenancies; it is unilateral acts determining the head-tenancies that destroy subtenancies. Consensual acts done by arrangement between landlord and tenant do not, in my opinion, do so.'

Now this is, with respect, a very curious doctrine. If correct, it means that a person cannot achieve with consent what he could achieve without it. It also means that parties whose interests happen to coincide must take care not to discuss the matter beforehand or risk failing to achieve together what either could achieve on his own. One would suppose that, if a person is entitled to achieve a particular result by unilateral action on his part without the consent of another party, he can achieve that result whether or not he obtains the consent of that party. I think that the Court of Appeal confused two different senses in which a transaction may be said to be consensual. Some transactions (and a surrender of a tenancy is one of them) are consensual in the sense that they are dependent for their effectiveness on the consent of some other party. Other transactions (such as the determination of a tenancy by notice to quit) are effective whether or not the other party gives his consent to it. If such consent is forthcoming, the transaction may no doubt be described as consensual; but that does not alter the fact that its effectiveness does not depend on consent.

I propose first to consider the question as a matter of principle and then to review the principal authorities on which the Court of Appeal relied for their conclusion.

A lease or tenancy for a fixed term comes to an end by effluxion of time on the date fixed for its determination. A periodic tenancy comes to an end on the expiry of a notice to quit served by the landlord on the tenant or by the tenant on the landlord. As Lord Hoffmann explained in *Newlon Housing Trust* v *Alsulaimen* [1999] 1 AC 313, 317, it also comes to an end by effluxion of time. In each case the tenancy is determined in accordance with its terms. By granting and accepting a periodic tenancy with provision, express or implied, for its determination by notice to quit, the parties have agreed at the outset on the manner of its termination. The parties and their successors in title, including those who derive title under them, are bound by their agreement.

A lease or tenancy may also be surrendered at any time by the tenant to his immediate landlord. A surrender is simply an assurance by which a lesser estate is yielded up to the greater, and the term is usually applied to the giving up of a lease or tenancy before its expiration. If a tenant surrenders his tenancy to his immediate landlord, who accepts the surrender, the tenancy is absorbed by the landlord's reversion and is extinguished by operation of law.

. . .

On its surrender the tenancy is brought to end prematurely at a time and in a manner not provided for by the terms of the tenancy agreement. In this respect it differs from the case where a tenancy is determined by notice to quit. It is because the landlord or his predecessor in title has not, by granting the tenancy, previously agreed that the tenant should have the right to surrender the tenancy prematurely that the landlord's consent is necessary.

. . .

Although a person such as a subtenant having a derivative interest may benefit by the surrender and consequent extinguishment of the estate out of which his interest is derived, he cannot be prejudiced by it. It is a general and salutary principle of law that a person cannot be adversely affected by an agreement or arrangement to which he is not a party. So far as he is concerned, it is res inter alios acta . . .

This account is sufficient to demonstrate that there are major differences in the way in which a tenancy is brought to an end by surrender and the way in which the head tenancy was brought to an end by the arrangements in the present case.

First, when a tenancy is surrendered it is brought to an end prematurely otherwise than at the time and in the manner stipulated by the tenancy agreement. When it is determined by notice to quit it is determined in accordance with the provisions of the tenancy agreement and at a time and in the manner previously agreed between the parties or their predecessors in title.

Secondly, the landlord or his predecessor in title has not agreed in advance to accept the premature determination of the tenancy by surrender, and accordingly a surrender is ineffective without his consent. But by granting and accepting a periodic tenancy the parties or their predecessors in title have agreed in advance that the tenancy should be terminable by notice to quit served by either party on the other, and accordingly no further consent is necessary whether or not it is forthcoming in fact.

Thirdly, a subtenant holds a derivative title which cannot be prejudiced by the surrender of the head tenancy from which it is derived or any other agreement between the parties to the head tenancy which is later than the creation of his subtenancy. His title is, however, precarious, for it cannot survive the natural termination of the head tenancy in accordance with its terms agreed before his subtenancy was created.

Fourthly, when the head tenancy is surrendered, it is treated as continuing until its natural termination so far as this is necessary to support the derivative interest of the subtenant. That is all that is meant by saying that 'the estate . . . hath . . . a continuance'. But when it is determined by notice to quit, it has come to the end of its natural life. There is no further period remaining during which the tenancy can have continuance.

In my opinion, this is sufficient to demonstrate that the arrangements in the present case were not tantamount to but very different in character from a surrender . . .

Comment

(1) Was the Court of Appeal justified in its use of consensual agreements in the *Barrett* context?

(2) Does the law draw the most appropriate distinctions as to which subleases survive the termination of the head lease? What justification is there for their ever doing so?

(3) Suppose L and T wish a future sublease to S to survive termination of the lease. Does principle suggest that the lease can provide for this?[2]

Further issues concerning subleases, in particular how to distinguish them from assignments and exceptional cases where L can enforce covenants against S, will be considered later in this chapter.

A final, but very important, introductory point is that the operation of covenants was amended and put on a statutory footing by the Landlord and Tenant (Covenants) Act 1995 (hereafter the 1995 Act). The core principles as outlined in this introduction are largely unaffected, though there is no longer any requirement that covenants 'touch and concern' the land. The scheme established by the 1995 Act applies only to leases entered into after 1995 ('new tenancies'), though we shall see that a few changes do extend to old leases. It follows that for decades, or longer, there will be many thousands of leases to which the previous law applies; this chapter will therefore deal with both old and new tenancies. A question to be considered, once the Act has been studied, is whether there is good reason for all of its provisions not applying to old tenancies.

2. Assignment and subletting

Before looking at the rules as to when covenants run, more needs to be said regarding two topics. The first is the distinction between assignment and subletting; the second relates to restrictions in a lease on assigning and subletting. We will also consider concurrent leases (two leases entered into by the same landlord over the same property).

A. Assignment or sublease?

If the transaction is to be for a shorter period than the lease then it can take effect only as a sublease: it is plain that T is not parting with the entirety of the lease. More difficult is the question whether a transaction for as long as the lease can take effect as a sublease or whether it must take effect as an assignment.

---

[2] See *PW & Co v Milton Gate Investments Ltd* [2004] Ch 142.

Extract 16.2.1

Milmo v Carreras [1946] KB 306

LORD GREENE MR: . . . We have had a very interesting and careful argument from Mr Granville Sharp, who has referred us to a number of authorities bearing on the question of what is the effect of a document purporting to be a sub-lease, which, in fact, purports to create a sub-term equal in point of time, or greater in point of time, than the residue of the head term. There have been many cases in which the effect of such a document has been considered, and a controversy has existed as to whether such a document must be described as an assignment, or whether it can properly be described as a sub-lease . . . For the purposes of this case, I think it is sufficient to say that, in accordance with a very ancient and established rule, where a lessee, by a document in the form of a sub-lease, divests himself of everything that he has got (which he must necessarily do if he is transferring to his so-called sub-lessee an estate as great as, or purporting to be greater than, his own) he from that moment is a stranger to the land, in the sense that the relationship of landlord and tenant, in respect of tenure, cannot any longer exist between him and the so-called sub-lessee. That relationship must depend on privity of estate. I myself find it impossible to conceive of a relationship of landlord and tenant which has not got that essential element of tenure in it, and that implies that the tenant holds of his landlord, and he can only do that if the landlord has a reversion.

Comment

(1) The effect of the decision can be avoided by the simple device of subletting for the length of the lease less (say) ten days.

(2) How convincing is Lord Greene MR's reasoning?

(3) If an intended subletting takes effect as an assignment, is this likely to cause problems for the parties?

(4) The Law Commission has proposed amending this principle for residential tenancies.[3]

The rule is relaxed where the head tenancy is a periodic tenancy, the nature of which is that it is capable of lasting indefinitely. Thus Pollock CB in *Oxley v James*[4] said:

> . . . It is clear that, if a tenant from year to year demises for a term of years, and the original tenancy from year to year lasts beyond that term, such a demise is not an assignment, but there is a reversion, on which covenant may be maintained.

Is there adequate justification for distinguishing periodic tenancies from those for terms of years where it is confidently expected that the term will be extended?

B. Restrictions on assigning and subletting

Leases almost invariably contain restrictions on T's power to assign and sublet. It is uncommon for a lease to contain an absolute bar on assignment and subletting. Normally, it is provided that L must consent. Why are such restrictions inserted? Why are absolute bars unusual?

---

[3] Law Com 297, para 6.17.
[4] (1844) 13 M&W 209 at p 214 (153 ER 87 at p 89).

Old Grovebury Manor Farm Ltd v W Seymour Plant Sales & Hire Ltd (No 2) [1979] 1 WLR 1397 (CA)

A lease was assigned without L's consent, which was required by the lease.

LORD RUSSELL OF KILLOWEN: . . . It is, I think, at the heart of the argument of counsel for the plaintiff that somehow this was not a valid assignment. He said, 'Well; it is effective and valid as between the assignor and assignee but not as between the lessor and the original lessee.' I am afraid that I am wholly unable to accept that. It is the fact, of course, that the assignment was in breach of covenant, but all that means is that there is an occasion offered to the lessor to forfeit the lease and put an end to it. It is of the nature of the creation of a term of years that the owner of the term is capable of dealing with it as a piece of property . . .

Comment

(1) Can choses in action be assigned if assignment is prohibited by the contract? Why should leases be assignable in such circumstances?

(2) Although the assignment is effective, the breach of covenant may trigger a forfeiture of the lease. Should the notice of forfeiture be served on T or A^L (the issue in *Old Grovebury*)?

(3) How does this fit with land registration principles?

Landlord and Tenant Act 1927, s 19

19.—(1) In all leases whether made before or after the commencement of this Act containing a covenant condition or agreement against assigning, underletting, charging or parting with the possession of demised premises or any part thereof without licence or consent, such covenant condition or agreement shall, notwithstanding any express provision to the contrary, be deemed to be subject—

    (a) to a proviso to the effect that such licence or consent is not to be unreasonably withheld, but this proviso does not preclude the right of the landlord to require payment of a reasonable sum in respect of any legal or other expenses incurred in connection with such licence or consent; . . .

  (1A) Where the landlord and the tenant under a qualifying lease have entered into an agreement specifying for the purposes of this subsection—

    (a) any circumstances in which the landlord may withhold his licence or consent to an assignment of the demised premises or any part of them, or

    (b) any conditions subject to which any such licence or consent may be granted,

    then the landlord—

      (i) shall not be regarded as unreasonably withholding his licence or consent to any such assignment if he withholds it on the ground (and it is the case) that any such circumstances exist, and

     (ii) if he gives such licence or consent subject to any such conditions, shall not be regarded as giving it subject to unreasonable conditions;

. . .

Comment

Section 19(1A) was added by the 1995 Act (only new tenancies are qualifying leases) as a counterweight to the limiting of the liability of T after assignment (discussed later in this chapter).[5] In particular, s 19(1A) enables L to provide that consent will not be given unless T guarantees A[L]'s performance of the covenants (in so far as that is permitted by the 1995 Act). Could it operate as a significant restriction upon the protection originally accorded by s 19?

Section 19 does not apply to absolute prohibitions. These include not only covenants which prohibit assignment in any circumstances, but also provisions which prohibit assignments unless certain conditions are satisfied.[6] Does this give landlords a too easy way of avoiding the need to prove reasonableness?

Extract 16.2.4

Landlord and Tenant Act 1988, ss 1, 4

1.—(3)   Where there is served on the person who may consent to a proposed transaction a written application by the tenant for consent to the transaction, he owes a duty to the tenant within a reasonable time—

    (a)   to give consent, except in a case where it is reasonable not to give consent,

    (b)   to serve on the tenant written notice of his decision whether or not to give consent specifying in addition—

        (i)   if the consent is given subject to conditions, the conditions,

        (ii)   if the consent is withheld, the reasons for withholding it.

    (4)   Giving consent subject to any condition that is not a reasonable condition does not satisfy the duty under subsection (3)(a) above.

    (6)   It is for the person who owed any duty under subsection (3) above—

    (a)   if he gave consent and the question arises whether he gave it within a reasonable time, to show that he did,

    (b)   if he gave consent subject to any condition and the question arises whether the condition was a reasonable condition, to show that it was,

    (c)   if he did not give consent and the question arises whether it was reasonable for him not to do so, to show that it was reasonable,

and, if the question arises whether he served notice under that subsection within a reasonable time, to show that he did.

4.—A claim that a person has broken any duty under this Act may be made the subject of civil proceedings in like manner as any other claim in tort for breach of statutory duty.

Extract 16.2.5

Norwich Union Life Insurance Society v *Shopmoor Ltd* [1999] 1 WLR 531

Could L justify failure to consent on the assignee's financial standing, despite earlier asking no questions about it?

SIR RICHARD SCOTT V-C: . . . The [1988] Act was intended to remedy the state of affairs in which a landlord, by his dilatory failure to respond to an application for consent to an assignment or to subletting, could cause substantial financial damage to the tenant without the tenant having any remedy for that damage. A tenant might lose a valuable property transaction because of the landlord's failure to deal expeditiously with the application for consent. It is clear that it was an intention of the Act to remedy that state of affairs . . .

---

[5] See pp 591–594 below.
[6] *Crestfort Ltd* v *Tesco Stores Ltd* [2005] L&TR 413.

In my judgment, however, the Act of 1988 has altered the law in this respect. It has done so by necessary implication, although not explicitly. The landlord has a statutory duty to the tenant within a reasonable time to give consent, except in a case where it is reasonable not to give consent. In judging whether it is reasonable not to give consent, the position must, in my view, be tested by reference to the state of affairs at the expiry of the reasonable time. If, at that time, the landlord has raised no point and there is no point outstanding which could constitute a reasonable ground for refusal of consent, then it seems to me that the landlord's duty is positively, as expressed by section 1(3), to give consent. The question whether the case is one 'Where it is reasonable not to give consent' ought, in my judgment, to be tested by reference to the point at which the reasonable time for dealing with the application has expired. If at that point it cannot be shown that it is reasonable for the landlord not to give consent, then the statutory duty of the landlord is to give consent, the court can so declare and the tenant can, in my judgment, proceed on the footing that the assignment in question would not constitute breach of a covenant not to assign without consent.

Comment

How significant is *Shopmoor* likely to be in the conduct of applications for consent? Would orally expressed reasons suffice? See *Footwear Corporation Ltd* v *Amplight Properties Ltd* [1999] 1 WLR 551.

Extract 16.2.6

Go West Ltd v *Spigarolo* [2003] QB 1140 (CA)

L refused consent. Could L thereafter, still within a reasonable time, change that decision and give consent subject to conditions?

MUNBY J: 31.   The problem arises because, as the 1988 Act has been drafted, it is not of itself, on the expressed words of the Act, a breach of statutory duty for a landlord to refuse consent unreasonably. As Mr Dutton pointed out – and this is what gives his argument some initial plausibility – the *only* statutory duties imposed on a landlord by section 1(3) of the Act are: (i) under section 1(3)(a) the 'duty . . . within a reasonable time . . . to give consent, except in a case where it is reasonable not to give consent', and (ii) under section 1(3)(b) the 'duty . . . within a reasonable time . . . to serve on the tenant written notice of his decision whether or not to give consent'.

32.   So it follows, said Mr Dutton [counsel for L], that the only possible breaches of statutory duty are failures within a reasonable time either to 'give consent' (assuming, that is, that it is not reasonable to refuse consent) or to 'serve . . . written notice of his decision' in the proper form; that it is not, of itself, a breach of statutory duty to refuse consent; that it is not, in particular, a breach of statutory duty to refuse consent before a reasonable time has elapsed; that a refusal of consent amounts to a breach of statutory duty only once a reasonable time has elapsed; and that in consequence the judge erred in law in holding that the landlords on 30 May 2001 'were in breach of their duty' under the 1988 Act.

33.   However plausible this argument may appear at first blush, in my judgment it is simply wrong.

34.   In the first place it is based on a fallacy, namely that there is some objectively ascertainable 'reasonable time' which exists independently of and is not affected by the landlord's refusal of consent.

36.   . . . Assume that the tenant makes his application on day J; the landlord responds with a proper request for information on day K; the tenant could and should have responded by day L but delays until day M. In such circumstances the tenant may not be able to say that the reasonable time has expired on day N, as it would if he had responded on day L. The landlord, depending on the circumstances (for example the volume of material supplied by the tenant

which he and his advisers have to assimilate), may be able to demonstrate that he needs more time, say until day O.

38.   So I agree entirely with Mr Dutton when he suggested in argument that what is a reasonable time cannot necessarily be determined when the tenant makes his application: one has to assess the question of what was a reasonable time as at the end of the period starting with the tenant's application. But that, with all respect to Mr Dutton, merely demonstrates the essential flaw in his submissions. If in the one case the reasonable time is lengthened because of the tenant's behaviour, why should it not be reduced in another case because of the landlord's behaviour?

39.   This leads on to the second point. In one important sense the 'reasonable time' requirement in section 1(3) is there to protect the tenant: the landlord must perform his duty 'within a reasonable time'. But in another and equally important sense it is there to protect the landlord: the landlord is given a reasonable time within which to do what the 1988 Act requires of him. Moreover, the 'reasonable time' referred to in section 1(3) is the time within which the *landlord* has to do something, not the time within which the tenant has to do anything. In other words, and as section 1(3) makes clear, the 'reasonable time' is the time reasonably required by the *landlord* to do the things which the Act requires of him.

40.   But once the landlord has done what the 1988 Act requires of him – in particular, once the landlord has served written notice in accordance with section 1(3)(b) of the Act – there is nothing left for him to do. He therefore does not require any further time. So, in my judgment, he cannot assert that the reasonable time he requires has not yet elapsed. By taking the final step that has to be taken within the reasonable time allowed by the Act the landlord himself necessarily brings that time to an end.

Comment

(1) *Norwich Union* is approved.

(2) Is the balance of convenience in favour of the arguments of L or of T?

How long is a reasonable period? Compare the following dicta. The first are from *Go West*.[7]

It may be that the reasonable time referred to in section 1(3) will sometimes have to be measured in weeks rather than days; but even in complicated cases, it should in my view be measured in weeks rather than months.

Subsequently, Carnwath LJ held:[8]

20.   ... the Judge was too ready, in my view, to categorise this as an uncomplicated transaction capable of summary treatment. Indeed, his view of the relative simplicity of the issue sits oddly with the overall effect of his judgment, which was that Riverland, even with the assistance of experienced legal advisers, arrived at the wrong answer and thereby incurred a lawsuit involving a claim of some £3m ... the transaction ... contained the unusual feature of a very substantial reverse premium, equating in financial terms to the bulk of the contractual rent over the remainder of the term. This was no doubt dictated by the market conditions, but it raised unusual legal and estate management issues which merited serious consideration.

21.   ... In my view, whatever earlier discussions there had been, Riverland was entitled to adequate time following receipt of the completed application to consider the serious financial and legal implications of a refusal with its advisers, and if necessary to report to the relevant Board. In

---

[7] At [73].
[8] *NCR Ltd v Riverland Portfolio No 1 Ltd* [2005] 2 P&CR 463.

the absence of special exceptional circumstances, a period of less than three weeks (particularly in the holiday period) cannot in my view be categorised as inherently unreasonable for that process.

23.   . . . it is in neither side's interests, at least where a refusal is being contemplated, for the decision to be rushed. The lessor is properly concerned to protect himself against the possible consequences of a finding of unreasonableness, while the lessee's primary objective is to achieve an underletting, rather than an uncertain cause of action under the Act.

Does a clear picture emerge as to how quickly decisions need to be taken?

Extract 16.2.7

International Drilling Fluids Ltd v *Louisville Investments (Uxbridge) Ltd* [1986] Ch 513

BALCOMBE LJ: . . . From the authorities I deduce the following propositions of law.

(1)   The purpose of a covenant against assignment without the consent of the landlord, such consent not to be unreasonably withheld, is to protect the lessor from having his premises used or occupied in an undesirable way, or by an undesirable tenant or assignee: *per* A L Smith LJ in *Bates* v *Donaldson* [1896] 2 QB 241, 247, approved by all the members of the Court of Appeal in *Houlder Brothers & Co Ltd* v *Gibbs* [1925] Ch 575.

(2)   As a corollary to the first proposition, a landlord is not entitled to refuse his consent to an assignment on grounds which have nothing whatever to do with the relationship of landlord and tenant in regard to the subject matter of the lease: see *Houlder Brothers & Co Ltd* v *Gibbs*, a decision which (despite some criticism) is binding on this court: *Bickel* v *Duke of Westminster* [1977] QB 517 . . .

(3)   The onus of proving that consent has been unreasonably withheld is on the tenant . . .

(4)   It is not necessary for the landlord to prove that the conclusions which led him to refuse consent were justified, if they were conclusions which might be reached by a reasonable man in the circumstances: *Pimms Ltd* v *Tallow Chandlers Company* [1964] 2 QB 547, 564.

(5)   It may be reasonable for the landlord to refuse his consent to an assignment on the ground of the purpose for which the proposed assignee intends to use the premises, even though that purpose is not forbidden by the lease: see *Bates* v *Donaldson* [1896] 2 QB 241, 244.

(6)   There is a divergence of authority on the question, in considering whether the landlord's refusal of consent is reasonable, whether it is permissible to have regard to the consequences to the tenant if consent to the proposed assignment is withheld . . .

In a recent decision of this court, *Leeward Securities Ltd* v *Lilyheath Properties Ltd* (1983) 271 EG 279 concerning a sub-letting which would attract the protection of the Rent Act, both Oliver LJ and O'Connor LJ made it clear in their judgments that they could envisage circumstances in which it might be unreasonable to refuse consent to an underletting, if the result would be that there was no way in which the tenant (the sub-landlord) could reasonably exploit the premises except by creating a tenancy to which the Rent Act protection would apply, and which inevitably would affect the value of the landlord's reversion . . .

But in my judgment a proper reconciliation of those two streams of authority can be achieved by saying that while a landlord need usually only consider his own relevant interests, there may be cases where there is such a disproportion between the benefit to the landlord and the detriment to the tenant if the landlord withholds his consent to an assignment that it is unreasonable for the landlord to refuse consent.

(7)   Subject to the propositions set out above, it is in each case a question of fact, depending upon all the circumstances, whether the landlord's consent to an assignment is being unreasonably withheld: see *Bickel* v *Duke of Westminster* [1977] QB 517, 524, and *West Layton Ltd* v *Ford* [1979] QB 593, 604, 606–607.

Comment

(1) The detriment to T was that it was virtually impossible to assign the lease save on the basis proposed, which involved 'serviced office' use: that is, providing office facilities for other organisations rather than for the tenant. Such use was not precluded by the lease, but might make it more difficult to sell the reversion. Given that such sale was not contemplated, refusal of consent was held unreasonable.

(2) Are any of the propositions affected by the 1988 legislation?[9]

A recurrent question is whether grounds for refusal are indeed collateral to the relationship of landlord and tenant. The next case involves refusal of permission on grounds of good estate management of a building, in which the leased flat was situated.

Extract 16.2.8

Bromley Park Garden Estates Ltd v *Moss* [1982] 1 WLR 1019

CUMMING-BRUCE LJ: . . . The reason given throughout the correspondence by Mr Broomfield on behalf of the plaintiffs was that it was the plaintiffs' policy not to permit assignments of residential tenancies. They required surrender instead . . .

The reason described by Mr Broomfield in evidence, and accepted by the judge as his ground for decision, was wholly extraneous to the intention of the parties to the contract when the covenant was granted and accepted. That reason cannot be relied upon merely because it would suit the landlords' investment plans, or their purpose in obtaining from Miss Wynn-Higgins the surrender of her lease. It may well enhance the financial interests of the landlord to obtain a single tenant holding the whole building on a full repairing covenant with long-term capital advantage when they put the building upon the market, but that intention and policy is entirely outside the intention to be imputed to the parties at the time of the granting of the lease to Brown or the assignment to Miss Wynn-Higgins . . .

DUNN LJ: . . . *West Layton Ltd* v *Ford* [1979] QB 593 shows that in considering whether the landlords' refusal of consent is unreasonable, the court should look first at the covenant in the context of the lease and ascertain the purpose of the covenant in that context. If the refusal of the landlord was designed to achieve that purpose then it may not be unreasonable, even in the case of a respectable and responsible assignee; but if the refusal is designed to achieve some collateral purpose wholly unconnected with the terms of the lease, as in *Houlder Brothers & Co Ltd* v *Gibbs* [1925] Ch 575, and as in the present case, then that would be unreasonable, even though the purpose was in accordance with good estate management.

Comment

(1) Is this a justified use of the collateral grounds test, given that the case concerns a purpose relating to the building of which the leased premises formed part?

(2) Both judges stress the purpose of the covenant. Does this simply reward good drafting, which may ensure that virtually any factor may be taken into account?

One specific issue, raised in many cases a few decades ago, is whether L can take into account the fact that the lease, in the hands of the assignee, will attract statutory protection.

---

[9] Note *Air India* v *Balabel* [1993] 2 EGLR 66.

This was a particularly significant issue in the days when that protection was being extended by legislation. In *West Layton Ltd* v *Ford*,[10] Roskill LJ upheld a refusal:

> It seems to me that the effect of the request which this landlord has had made to him by the tenant is to invite him to agree to alter the nature of the property which was being let from commercial property, namely, a butcher's shop with residential accommodation above, to property which would be let on a multiple tenancy – by which I mean to more tenants or lessees than one, because there will be not only the tenancy of the shop but also the separate sub-tenancy upstairs of the residential accommodation, which would be a tenancy attracting Rent Act protection.

Extract 16.2.9

Ashworth Frazer Ltd v *Gloucester City Council* [2001] 1 WLR 2180

The House of Lords held that it will normally be reasonable to refuse consent if it is reasonably believed that the assignee will act in breach of covenant.

LORD RODGER: 71.   [It was argued that, if there were assignment, the] landlord would therefore be in the same position, neither better nor worse, to enforce the user covenant. As an analysis of the landlord's legal position that is undoubtedly correct. But the reality is that a reasonable landlord could well look at the matter more broadly and see that his position would be significantly altered by the assignment. It is one thing to have a tenant who complies with the user covenant in the lease and against whom there is no need to take steps to enforce the covenant. It is quite another to have a new tenant who does not comply with, or who challenges the interpretation of, the user covenant and against whom the landlord might need to take steps to enforce it or to contest the tenant's interpretation, with all the inconvenience and potential cost involved. It is also a different thing to have a new tenant who intends to apply to the Lands Tribunal under section 84 of the Law of Property Act 1925 to discharge or modify the user covenant. Again the landlord would face the prospect of becoming embroiled in legal proceedings. If they occurred, all or any of these matters would make a huge practical difference to the landlord. So the prospect that one or other of them will probably happen is one which a reasonable landlord must be entitled at least to take into account when asked to consent to the assignment of a lease.

Comment

(1) This is the most recent leading case. It may be seen as allowing greater flexibility, also reflected in Lord Bingham's statement that 'the landlord's obligation is to show that his conduct was reasonable, not that it was right or justifiable'. Do these analyses tilt the balance too far in the landlord's favour?

(2) Should a breach prior to assignment automatically justify refusal of consent? A recent case is *Singh* v *Dhanji* [2014] EWCA Civ 414.

C. Concurrent leases

A final and very different point concerns the effect of L's entering into a lease with T and then a second lease with T2. We are not here concerned with any competition between T and T2 for possession: the parties recognise that T will have possession. What the second lease does is to transfer L's rights to T2 for the duration of the second lease. The effect of the two leases is illustrated in Figure 16.2.

[10] [1979] QB 593 at p 605.

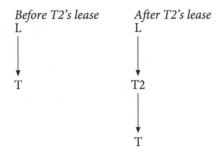

Figure 16.2

T2 can collect rent and enforce covenants. Figure 16.2 presents the position as if there were a sublease, although there is of course no such thing. How does the situation differ from that of an actual sublease?

3. Enforcing covenants after assignment

A. Privity of estate: general rules

Extract 16.3.1

Landlord and Tenant (Covenants) Act 1995, s 3

3.—(1)   The benefit and burden of all landlord and tenant covenants of a tenancy—
  (a)   shall be annexed and incident to the whole, and to each and every part, of the premises demised by the tenancy and of the reversion in them, and
  (b)   shall in accordance with this section pass on an assignment of the whole or any part of those premises or of the reversion in them.
  (2)   Where the assignment is by the tenant under the tenancy, then as from the assignment the assignee—
  (a)   becomes bound by the tenant covenants of the tenancy except to the extent that—
    (i)   immediately before the assignment they did not bind the assignor, or
    (ii)   they fall to be complied with in relation to any demised premises not comprised in the assignment; and
  (b)   becomes entitled to the benefit of the landlord covenants of the tenancy except to the extent that they fall to be complied with in relation to any such premises.
  (3)   Where the assignment is by the landlord under the tenancy, then as from the assignment the assignee—
  (a)   becomes bound by the landlord covenants of the tenancy except to the extent that—
    (i)   immediately before the assignment they did not bind the assignor, or
    (ii)   they fall to be complied with in relation to any demised premises not comprised in the assignment; and
  (b)   becomes entitled to the benefit of the tenant covenants of the tenancy except to the extent that they fall to be complied with in relation to any such premises.

Comment

It will be seen that these rules have a similar effect to privity of estate in old tenancies. More detailed points will be considered in the remainder of this chapter.

Old tenancies

The running of the covenants has been regulated by statute and common law since the sixteenth century.

Extract 16.3.2

Law of Property Act 1925, ss 141, 142

141.—(1) Rent reserved by a lease, and the benefit of every covenant or provision therein contained, having reference to the subject-matter thereof, and on the lessee's part to be observed or performed, and every condition of re-entry and other condition therein contained, shall be annexed and incident to and shall go with the reversionary estate in the land, or in any part thereof, immediately expectant on the term granted by the lease . . .

142.—(1) The obligation under a condition or of a covenant entered into by a lessor with reference to the subject-matter of the lease shall, if and as far as the lessor has power to bind the reversionary estate immediately expectant on the term granted by the lease, be annexed and incident to and shall go with that reversionary estate, or the several parts thereof, notwithstanding severance of that reversionary estate, and may be taken advantage of and enforced by the person in whom the term is from time to time vested . . .

Extract 16.3.3

Spencer's Case (1583) 5 Co Rep 16a (77 ER 72)

6. If lessee for years covenants to repair the houses during the term, it shall bind all others as a thing which is appurtenant, and goeth with the land in whose hands soever the term shall come . . . And if the law should not be such, great prejudice might accrue to him; and reason requires, that they, who shall take benefit of such covenant when the lessor makes it with the lessee, should on the other side be bound by the like covenants when the lessee makes it with the lessor.

B. Which covenants run?

The requirement of touching and concerning (or having 'reference to the subject matter' of the tenancy) applies in old tenancies and is discussed below. Very different provision is made by the 1995 Act.

Extract 16.3.4

Landlord and Tenant (Covenants) Act 1995, ss 2, 3, 4, 28

2.—(1) This Act applies to a landlord covenant or a tenant covenant of a tenancy—
  (a) whether or not the covenant has reference to the subject matter of the tenancy, and
  (b) whether the covenant is express, implied or imposed by law . . .

3.—(6) Nothing in this section shall operate—
  (a) in the case of a covenant which (in whatever terms) is expressed to be personal to any person, to make the covenant enforceable by or (as the case may be) against any other person; or
  (b) to make a covenant enforceable against any person if, apart from this section, it would not be enforceable against him by reason of its not having been registered under the Land Registration Act 1925 or the Land Charges Act 1972.

4.—The benefit of a landlord's right of re-entry under a tenancy—

    (a)   shall be annexed and incident to the whole, and to each and every part, of the reversion in the premises demised by the tenancy, and

    (b)   shall pass on an assignment of the whole or any part of the reversion in those premises.

28.—(1)   In this Act (unless the context otherwise requires)—

'landlord' and 'tenant', in relation to a tenancy, mean the person for the time being entitled to the reversion expectant on the term of the tenancy and the person so entitled to that term respectively; 'landlord covenant', in relation to a tenancy, means a covenant falling to be complied with by the landlord of premises demised by the tenancy;

   . . .

'tenant covenant', in relation to a tenancy, means a covenant falling to be complied with by the tenant of premises demised by the tenancy.

Comment

(1) Other parts of s 3 were quoted in Extract 16.3.1 above.

(2) The running of rights of re-entry (s 4) replicates the position for old leases, though there was some doubt whether the broken covenant itself had to touch and concern.[11]

(3) Freehold covenants still must touch and concern.[12] Can the more relaxed rule for leasehold covenants be justified?

Extract 16.3.5

BHP Petroleum Great Britain Ltd v *Chesterfield Ltd* [2002] Ch 194

The question arose whether a covenant expressed to be personal to the landlord was a landlord covenant.

JONATHAN PARKER LJ: 46.   Mr Lewison, for Chesterfield, submits that the agreement is a 'collateral agreement', and that the obligations in question constitute a 'landlord covenant', within the definitions of those expressions in section 28(1) of the 1995 Act. Accordingly, he submits, by virtue of section 3(1) of the 1995 Act the burden of those obligations passed to Chesterfield (Neathouse) Ltd on the transfer of the reversion, notwithstanding that the obligations are expressed to be personal to Chesterfield: . . .

47.   Mr Lewison submits that the effect of the judge's decision is to reinstate the distinction between covenants which 'touch and concern' the land demised on the one hand, and personal covenants on the other: a distinction which Parliament, on the recommendation of the Law Commission, set out to abolish when it passed the 1995 Act.

59.   The crux, as we see it, is the definition of 'landlord' in section 28(1) as meaning 'the person *for the time being* entitled to the reversion expectant on the term of the tenancy'. (My emphasis.) We find it impossible to read that definition as meaning only the original landlord. In agreement with the judge [2001] 3 WLR 277, 286, para 22 we consider that those words clearly connote the person who may *from time to time* be entitled to the reversion on the tenancy. It follows that, transposing that definition into the definition of the expression 'landlord covenant', what one has is an obligation 'falling to be complied with by [the person who may from time to time be entitled to the reversion on the tenancy]'. An obligation which (that is to say, the burden of which) is personal to the original landlord is, by definition, not such an obligation, since it does not fall to be performed by the person who may from time to time be entitled to the reversion on the tenancy.

---

[11] Any such requirement was questioned by the House of Lords in *Shiloh Spinners Ltd* v *Harding* [1973] AC 691 at p 717.

[12] See p 710 below.

61.   With respect to Mr Lewison, Chesterfield's argument on the 1995 Act issue seems to us to be based on the fallacy that there is a direct antithesis between a personal covenant (that is to say a covenant which is personal in the sense that the burden of it is expressed to be personal to the covenantor) on the one hand and a covenant which 'touches and concerns', or which relates to, the land on the other. As Mr Barnes correctly submits, there is no such direct antithesis. A covenant which relates to the land may nevertheless be expressed to be personal to one or other or both of the parties to it. That is a matter for the contracting parties.

62.   Nor can we see anything in the 1995 Act to fetter the freedom of contracting parties to place a contractual limit on the transmissibility of the benefit or burden of obligations under a tenancy. On the contrary, that no such fetter was intended by Parliament is clearly demonstrated, in our judgment, by section 3(6)(a) (quoted earlier).

Comment

(1) The technical issue in the case was whether s 8 of the 1995 Act (Extract 16.3.17 below) applied. That section relates to the liability of L after assignment to A^R.

(2) Both the analysis in *BHP* and s 3(6)(a) mean (separately) that such a covenant will not bind assignees. Does this mean that one of them is redundant? Is the scope of the *BHP* analysis and s 3(6)(a) the same? Is their effect (assuming that they apply) the same?

(3) The decision was approved by the House of Lords in *London Diocesan Fund* v *Phithwa* [2005] 1 WLR 3956.

(4) How real is the danger that touching and concerning may be returning to the modern law? If the court considers that it makes most sense if the covenant doesn't bind assignees, how much scope is there for reaching that result? Consider this example. Suppose there is a lease of a field, in which the tenant covenants to keep his adjoining house (not leased) in repair. Is an assignee of the lease of the field bound by the covenant? Does it make any difference if the assignee has also acquired the house?

(5) Unsurprisingly, Neuberger J has held that a covenant can be a landlord covenant even if it does not relate to the reversion of the leased land.[13] The context was a landlord's covenant not to compete on adjoining land.

There is also an exemption, found in s 3(2), (3), for covenants which affect another part of the leased land. Thus if T takes a lease of a field and a house, covenanting to keep the house in repair, an assignee from T of the field will not be bound by the covenant.

Some covenants constitute separate proprietary interests (options to renew the lease or purchase the reversion are examples, as are restrictive covenants). One characteristic of proprietary interests is that they may have to be registered, though there is a statutory exception for most restrictive covenants. For unregistered land, *Taylors Fashions Ltd* v *Liverpool Victoria Trustees Co Ltd*[14] held that failure to register prevents the running of renewal covenants under privity of estate. However, the landlord's title will normally be registered and the interest will be enforceable either as an overriding interest (leases not exceeding seven years) or because it is protected by notice (as part of the registration of the lease). Might the holding in *Taylors Fashions* be affected by s 3 of the 1995 Act (see Extract 16.3.1 above)?

---

[13] *Oceanic Village Ltd* v *United Attractions Ltd* [2000] Ch 234 at p 244.

[14] [1982] QB 133 at pp 142–143.

Old tenancies

The covenant must 'touch and concern' the land, or in the language of the Law of Property Act 1925 (hereafter LPA), ss 141 and 142, have 'reference to the subject-matter' of the lease. It is important to note that this requires more than that the covenant must not be personal to a specific individual. A well-known example of a covenant which does not touch and concern is an option for T to purchase the freehold. Such an option is clearly not personal in nature.

The core principles are to be found in two cases, one nineteenth-century and one from the 1990s.

Extract 16.3.6

Congleton Corporation v *Pattison* (1808) 10 East 130 (103 ER 725)

T covenanted not to employ those from outside the parish.

BAYLEY J: . . . [I]n order to bind the assignee the covenant must either affect the land itself during the term, such as those which regard the mode of occupation; or it must be such as per se, and not merely from collateral circumstances, affect the value of the land at the end of the term. Covenants to restrain the exercise of particular trades in houses fall within the first class: they affect the mode in which the property is to be enjoyed during the term . . . But here the state of the premises will be the same at the end of the term, whether the parish be more or less burdened with poor. I agree that the value of the reversion will not be so much if the poor's rate on the land be increased; but that burden would be increased by a collateral circumstance; and where the value of the reversion is only altered by collateral circumstances, the covenant will not bind the assignee of the land . . .

Comment

A covenant not to employ a certain person has been held to touch and concern,[15] on the basis that the use of the premises (a licensed restaurant) might be affected by his involvement. Is this a sensible or principled distinction?

Extract 16.3.7

P & A Swift Investments v *Combined English Stores Group plc* [1989] AC 632

LORD OLIVER: . . . The meaning of those words 'per se, and not merely from collateral circumstances' has been the subject matter of a certain amount of judicial consideration and the judgment of Sir Nicolas Browne-Wilkinson V-C in *Kumar* v *Dunning* [1989] QB 193 . . . contains a careful and helpful review of the authorities . . .

The Vice-Chancellor stated his conclusion, at p 204:

'From these authorities I collect two things. First, that the acid test whether or not a benefit is collateral is that laid down by Best J, namely, is the covenant beneficial to the owner for the time being of the covenantee's land, and to no one else? Secondly, a covenant simply to pay a sum of money, whether by way of insurance premium, compensation or damages, is a covenant capable of touching and concerning the land provided that the existence of the covenant, and the right to payment thereunder, affects the value of the land in whomsoever it is vested for the time being.'

. . .

---

[15] *Lewin* v *American & Colonial Distributors Ltd* [1945] Ch 225.

Formulations of definitive tests are always dangerous, but it seems to me that, without claiming to expound an exhaustive guide, the following provides a satisfactory working test for whether, in any given case, a covenant touches and concerns the land: (1) the covenant benefits only the reversioner for time being, and if separated from the reversion ceases to be of benefit to the covenantee; (2) the covenant affects the nature, quality, mode of user or value of the land of the reversioner; (3) the covenant is not expressed to be personal (that is to say neither being given only to a specific reversioner nor in respect of the obligations only of a specific tenant); (4) the fact that a covenant is to pay a sum of money will not prevent it from touching and concerning the land so long as the three foregoing conditions are satisfied and the covenant is connected with something to be done on to or in relation to the land.

Comment

(1) A good example of a covenant to pay money which touches and concerns is a covenant to maintain fire insurance, where there is an obligation to rebuild in the case of fire.[16]

(2) *Swift* involved the liability of T's guarantor to A^R. It did not therefore involve privity of estate and the principles it articulates may not always be easily applied where there is a lease.

Extract 16.3.8

Caerns Motor Services Ltd v *Texaco Ltd* [1994] 1 WLR 1249 (Ch D)

Did a covenant to sell only L's petrol touch and concern?

JUDGE PAUL BAKER QC: . . . As I indicated, their Lordships [in *Swift*] there were not dealing with a case of the correct application of section 141 of the Law of Property Act 1925, which, to my mind, is the starting point of the investigation. When we have travelled through that, it will be found that the test [in *Swift*] does apply and gives a satisfactory result in this case. It is not right, in my judgment, to start using that test where their Lordships have said, in both cases, that the section is not applicable in the circumstances they had to deal with. Of course the inquiry is the same. It is still an inquiry as to whether the relevant covenant touches and concerns the land, but one has to approach it differently, in my judgment, according to whether one is applying section 141 or whether one is looking at covenants where there is no privity of estate. One reason why one has to do that is because the application of section 141 and its predecessor has been encrusted with many authorities which one has to look at before considering and applying a test which has been devised for the other class of case.

So I accept the defendants' submissions in this sense: there is really only one question here, whether the covenants relating to the supply of petrol touch and concern the land, or have 'reference to the subject matter' to use the statutory language, within the meaning of section 141 of the Law of Property Act 1925.

The tie certainly affects the mode in which the land is used. We also start with this, that the reversion on this lease is assignable. Normally a set of tenant's covenants have relation to the subject matter, the leased property. There may be exceptions and one may be able to identify among the tenant's covenants some that do not, but in the main one starts with a set of tenant's covenants all having relation to the subject matter.

There have been cited to me a number of cases relating the brewer's tie in relation to the supply of beer to public houses. There is such an obvious analogy there that no one has doubted that one can get useful guidance out of those cases when one comes to deal with the petrol cases. The leading case, behind which there is no point in going, is *Clegg* v *Hands* (1890) 44 Ch D 503, a decision of the Court of Appeal. That is a case of brewer's tie. That case shows that a covenant of this sort can 'touch and concern the land' . . .

---

[16] *Vernon* v *Smith* (1821) 5 B&Ald 1 (106 ER 1094).

Comment

(1) The problem lies in the extent to which Lord Oliver's tests reflect the first part of Bayley J's analysis: 'affect the land itself during the term, such as those which regard the mode of occupation'. Lord Oliver's tests relate far more to the effect on the reversion.

(2) Covenants relating to the use of the land originated in ensuring an appropriate use for the land. In cases such as *Caerns*, they operate so as to benefit L's business which is only collaterally related to the land. Should such covenants touch and concern?

L may also enter into covenants designed to benefit T's business. In contrast to T's covenant in *Caerns*, such covenants do not have a direct effect on the leased land.

Extract 16.3.9

Kumar v Dunning [1989] QB 193

SIR NICOLAS BROWNE-WILKINSON V-C: . . . In *Thomas v Hayward* (1869) LR 4 Ex 311 a covenant by the lessor of a public house not to use adjoining land for the sale of liquor was held not to touch and concern the land because its value to the tenant was collateral: it related to the business he carried on, not to the land itself. The decision was a hard one and is to be treated as authority for no more than that a covenant the value of which is wholly dependent on the use of the land for a specific business is collateral.

Next Mr Blackburne relied on *Dewar v Goodman* [1909] AC 72. In that case, a head lease contained a covenant by the head lessee to repair all buildings erected on the land, which numbered some 211 in total. The head lessee granted an underlease of two of the houses and covenanted with the underlessee to perform the covenants in the head lease so far as they related to premises not comprised in the underlease. The plaintiff was the assignee of the under-lease: the defendant was the assignee of the head lease. Because of a breach of the covenant to repair in the head lease, the freeholder forfeited the head lease and ejected the plaintiff. The plaintiff sued the defendant for damages for breach of the lessor's covenant to perform the covenants in the underlease. The House of Lords held that the covenant to perform the covenants in the head lease did not touch and concern the land in the underlease because it did not require anything to be done on the land demised: the covenant related to the buildings other than those contained in the underlease. Surprisingly, there is little discussion of the second limb of the test in *Congleton Corporation v Pattison* (1808) 10 East 130, i.e., that it is sufficient if the covenant per se affects the value of the land even though this does not involve doing anything on the land of the covenantee itself. Even more surprisingly, although both cases were decided within months of each other and the argument and decision in the House of Lords in *Dewar v Goodman* [1909] AC 72 was given after the argument in the House of Lords in *Dyson v Forster* [1909] AC 98, in neither case is the other referred to, although Lord Loreburn LC was party to both decisions.

I find the two cases very difficult, if not impossible, to reconcile. The performance of the covenant by the head lessee in *Dewar v Goodman* [1909] AC 72 was manifestly of value to the underlessee for the time being and to no one else. Yet this point is not dealt with in the judgment . . . If, as I suspect, the two decisions are in fact irreconcilable, I am free to choose between them. I prefer to follow *Dyson v Forster* which gives effect to the second limb in the *Congleton* test, 10 East 130, 138 (which everyone has treated as the true basic test) whereas *Dewar v Goodman* appears to ignore the second limb completely.

Comment

(1) We have seen that *Kumar* was approved by the House of Lords in *Swift*.

(2) Apart from insurance payments and rent, what other payments might touch and concern?

A pair of somewhat similar covenants have given rise to especial difficulty: options for T to renew the lease and to purchase the reversion. Romer LJ discussed them as follows:[17]

> [An option to purchase] is not a provision for the continuance of the term, like a covenant to renew, which has been held to run with the reversion, though the fact that a covenant to renew should be held to run with the land has by many been considered as an anomaly, which it is too late now to question, though it is difficult to justify. An option to purchase is not a provision for the shortening of the term of the lease, like a notice to determine or a power of re-entry, though the result of the option, if exercised, would or might be to destroy the tenancy. It is, to our minds, concerned with something wholly outside the relation of landlord and tenant . . .

C. Breaches committed after assignment

The question here is whether T and A^L can be made liable if, for example, $A2^L$ fails to pay rent (see Figure 16.3). The liability of L for A^R's breaches raises similar problems, but has not been so troublesome in practice. It is separately dealt with towards the end of this section.

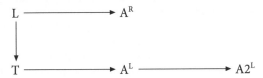

Figure 16.3

(i) Privity of estate

Extract 16.3.10

Landlord and Tenant (Covenants) Act 1995, ss 5, 11

5.—(1)   This section applies where a tenant assigns premises demised to him under a tenancy.

(2)   If the tenant assigns the whole of the premises demised to him, he—

   (a)   is released from the tenant covenants of the tenancy, and

   (b)   ceases to be entitled to the benefit of the landlord covenants of the tenancy,

as from the assignment.

11.—(1)   This section provides for the operation of sections 5 to 10 in relation to assignments in breach of a covenant of a tenancy or assignments by operation of law ('excluded assignments').

(2)   In the case of an excluded assignment subsection (2) or (3) of section 5—

   (a)   shall not have the effect mentioned in that subsection in relation to the tenant as from that assignment, but

   (b)   shall have that effect as from the next assignment (if any) of the premises assigned by him which is not an excluded assignment.

Comment

(1) The s 5 protection for tenants also applies to assignees.[18]

(2) We will see that s 5 replicates the previous position regarding privity of estate. The major significance of s 5 lies in the context of T's contractual liability. This is considered later in this section.

---

[17] *Woodall v Clifton* [1905] 2 Ch 257 at p 279.
[18] A tenant is defined by s 28 (Extract 16.3.4 above) so as to mean the person entitled to the lease for the time being.

(3) Section 11 is plainly intended to ensure that (for excluded assignments) T and A^L remain liable after their respective assignments. What is the basis of such liability? Is there any provision in the Act which says that there is liability after assignment?[19]

(4) Why should excluded assignments be treated differently?

Old tenancies

Extract 16.3.11

Onslow v Corrie (1817) 2 Madd 330 (56 ER 357)

Was A^L liable following a further assignment to A2^L?

PLUMER V-C: . . . Why is the assignee liable to the landlord? Because of the *privity of estate*. The original lessee is liable in respect of the *privity of contract*. The liability of an assignee of a lease begins and ends with his character of assignee. In him there is no personal confidence by the lessor. Ever since the case of *Pitcher* v *Toovey*,[i] it has been held that by an assignment, an assignee exonerates himself from all claims in respect of rent, even though he assigns to a beggar. An assignee may, whenever he pleases, assign again; and the moment he divests himself of the character of assignee, he also shakes off his liability for rent. It is very different as to the original lessee, for he in all cases before the late Act remained liable to his covenant to pay the rent notwithstanding his assignment, and whoever might be the assignee; but an assignee is only liable by privity of estate, which ceases when he ceases to be assignee, and loses that character . . .

[i] Carthew 177; S C 1 Salk 81; 4 Mod 71; and 2 Ventr 228, and S C by the name of *Toovey* v *Pitcher*; 3 Lev 295, and 1 Show 340. *Le Caux* v *Nash*, Str 1221, and see *Chancellor* v *Poole*, Dougl 764, and *Adell* v *Wake*, 3 Compt N P 394. These cases established the law; but see 1 Ventr 329, 331. T Raym 303; T Jones, 109, *contra*.

Comment

The risk of an impecunious assignee is mitigated by the fact that leases invariably provide that L must consent to the assignment. An unauthorised assignment by A^L will be a breach of covenant rendering A^L liable for damages. Under the 1995 Act, it will be an excluded assignment with the result that A^L will be liable under s 5.

(ii) Contractual liability: original landlord and tenant

The contractual liability of the original tenant (mentioned in the extract from *Onslow* v *Corrie*) was the most controversial aspect of covenant liability. Unsurprisingly therefore, it is the area most changed by the 1995 Act. In order to understand the need for change, we need first to understand how the law operated before the 1995 Act.

(a) The development of the law up to the 1995 Act

When T takes a lease from L, T's covenants are construed so as to make T contractually liable on the covenants for the entire duration of the lease. We need to ask why this approach was taken by the courts and whether it is justified in the context of modern leases.

This contractual liability was much criticised in the economic depression of the late 1980s and early 1990s. A significant number of tenants became insolvent and the position was made worse because rental levels had dropped sharply: L would not be inclined to

---

[19] As will be seen below, prior to the 1995 Act T usually had contractual liability after assignment. It would be less common for A^L to have contractual liability.

forfeit when there was no prospect of re-letting the premises at the old rent. The result was that firms which had assigned premises many years earlier were faced with rent demands out of the blue. To add insult to injury, they were sometimes charged rent at a far higher rate from that stipulated in the original lease.

Extract 16.3.12

Friends' Provident Life Office v British Railways Board [1996] 1 All ER 336

A^L negotiated a change in the covenants (in A^L's favour); at the same time the rent was significantly increased.

BELDAM LJ: . . . Before the recorder the lessor argued that the lessee was bound by the covenants contained in the lease as varied by the deed of variation, basing its contention on the decision of Harman J in *Centrovincial Estates plc v Bulk Storage Ltd* (1983) 46 P&CR 393 and two later cases . . . In particular, the lessor founded its argument on the statement of Harman J that—

> 'the basic answer which any real property lawyer would give to a question about an assignee's power to deal with a tenancy interest is that each assignee is the owner of the whole estate and can deal with it so as to alter it or its terms. The estate as so altered then binds the original tenant, because the assignee has been put into the shoes of the original tenant and can do all such acts as the original tenant could have done.' (See 46 P&CR 393 at 396.)

Harman J supported this statement of the law by passages taken from the judgments of this court in *Baynton v Morgan* (1888) 22 QBD 74 at 77–78, 80–81 and 83.

. . .

Apart from the passage in the judgment of Harman J in *Centrovincial Estates plc v Bulk Storage Ltd* (1983) 46 P&CR 393 at 396 referred to by the recorder in his judgment and the other cases based upon this dictum, there is no authority to support so radical a departure from the generally accepted view that [the change could not make T liable] . . .

[He quoted from Nourse LJ and Lord Templeman in *City of London Corp v Fell* [1993] QB 589, [1994] 1 AC 458:] These two judgments reassert with added emphasis the conventional distinction between the contractual liability of the lessee under his personal covenants and the liability of the assignee for the obligations of the covenants 'imprinted' on the legal estate. In principle therefore it is difficult to see how obligations accepted by the lessee in his contract with the lessor can be varied or increased by a subsequent agreement made by the lessor with the assignee. Relying on the judgments in *Baynton v Morgan* (1888) 22 QBD 74 for the general proposition that the assignee of a lease was empowered by the assignment to do anything that the original lessee could have done, Harman J in *Centrovincial Estates* appears to have concluded that the rights and obligations of the parties privy to the contract could be altered and made more onerous by agreement between the parties privy to the estate.

But the judges in *Baynton v Morgan* did not decide this. The question was not before them and it is clear from the judgments that if it had been the court would have been likely to decide the contrary. What the judges did decide was that the assignee of the lease had by the assignment been put into the position of lessee and in that character was authorised to vary the estate by surrender of part of the holding without such variation amounting to surrender and regrant of the term and thus without affecting the liability of the original lessee under his covenants. Harman J was in my view correct in his assertion that an assignee's power to deal with a tenancy interest is as the owner of the whole estate who can deal with it so as to alter it or its terms, but in error in adding:

> 'The estate as so altered then binds the original tenant, because the assignee has been put into the shoes of the original tenant and can do all such acts as the original tenant could have done.' (See *Centrovincial Estates plc v Bulk Storage Ltd* (1983) 46 P&CR 393 at 396.)

. . .

SIR CHRISTOPHER SLADE: ... I derive from this note [McLoughlin [1984] Conv 443] the following propositions.

(1)   The assignment of a lease does not destroy the privity of contract which exists between the landlord and the original tenant; in the result, the original tenant remains liable on all his covenants contained in the original lease, notwithstanding the assignment.

(2)   If the contract embodied in the original lease itself provides for some variation in the future of the obligations to be performed by the tenant (e.g. by a rent review clause), the original tenant may be bound to perform the obligations as so varied, even though the variations occur after the assignment of the lease – this will depend on the construction of the relevant covenant(s) in the original lease.

(3)   The actual decision in *Centrovincial Estates* is justifiable on ground (2) above ...

(4)   If, on the other hand, an assignee of the lease by arrangement with the landlord agrees to undertake some obligation not contemplated by the contract contained in the original lease, the estate may be altered, but the variation does not affect the obligations of the original tenant ...

These four propositions are, in my opinion, correct in law and the present case falls within the fourth of them.

Comment

When will a variation increase T's liability? Would a review of the rent under a rent review clause suffice? Would an extension of the lease under an option held by the tenant suffice? Would other extensions of the lease suffice?

Friends' Provident rejected the proposition that the variation constituted a new lease, thereby terminating T's contractual liability. A similar argument is that T is acting as surety and that therefore any alteration releases T's guarantee liability. Many years before *Friends' Provident*, Lord Esher MR had responded:[20]

> The true answer to this contention seems to me to be that this is not a contract of guarantee. We must construe this contract, which is in writing, in accordance with its terms. There is not a word in it about a guarantee. It is a direct promise that certain sums of money shall be paid as rent on certain days during a certain period.

Extract 16.3.13

Law Commission No 174: Landlord and Tenant Law: Privity of Contract and Estate (footnotes omitted)

3.1   In Part III of the Working Paper, we identified the following criticisms of the present law:

(a)   It is intrinsically unfair that anyone should bear burdens under a contract in respect of which they derive no benefit and over which they have no control: contractual obligations undertaken in a lease should only regulate relations between current owners with interests in the property.

(b)   When a demand is made under the continuing liability of the original tenant it will often not only be unexpected, but beyond the means of the former tenant; there is no logical way in which a former tenant who does understand that there is a contingent liability can estimate its amount.

(c)   A single lease can contain some covenants of which the burden automatically passes to an assignee, by privity of estate, and others of which the burden does not pass automatically. This contrast in a single document, which is not apparent from its wording, is unsatisfactory ...

---

[20] *Baynton v Morgan* (1888) 22 QBD 74 at p 77.

(d) Many laymen do not realise that the original parties have a continuing liability and most leases do not make it clear on their face.

(e) Where a lease contains a rent review clause, the original tenant's liability, under privity of contract, normally extends to payment of the higher rents after revision. For this reason, privity of contract sometimes results in the original tenant having a greater liability than he understood he was assuming. While this may merely reflect the increased value of the premises, it can cast on a former tenant a burden resulting from an increased value from which he has derived no benefit.

(f) Landlords who are in practice the main beneficiaries of the privity of contract principle are unduly protected. They have the ability to enforce obligations undertaken by tenants by action against both the original tenant and the current tenant, as well as, in many cases, against intermediate assignees who enter into direct covenants with the landlord before taking their assignments. This makes the principle one-sided, and unreasonably multiplies the remedies available to landlords.

(g) Original tenants against whom covenants are enforced after they have assigned the lease are not adequately protected, nor do they have adequate means of reimbursement. They are not released even if the tenant in possession agrees materially to vary the extent of the liability, they are not entitled to notice of default and they have no right to take back possession of the property. Former tenants are therefore often deprived of the opportunity to limit their liability by taking prompt remedial action. Faced with demands they must meet, they are often unable even to have recourse to the property to recoup any losses . . .

3.3 Against these criticisms we pointed out that continuing liability of the original parties to leases is a matter of contract. They are free to vary the normal rule. This is sometimes done, but not frequently. Some feel that a heavy burden lies on those who propose any further restriction on freedom of contract, but others question whether there is any true freedom here because there is widely thought to be an inequality of bargaining power between landlords and tenants, favouring landlords.

Comment

Paragraph 3.1 contains strong arguments, but are they sufficiently strong to justify interfering with freedom of contract? It should be noted that contractual liability has arisen only in commercial leases. Though theoretically applicable to residential leases, it has never been significant in that context.

(b) Tenant protection under the 1995 Act

The most important point is that s 5 of the 1995 Act (Extract 16.3.10 above) ousts contractual liability: 'If the tenant assigns the whole of the premises demised to him, he . . . is released from the tenant covenants of the tenancy'. Just as the assignor has no privity of estate liability for subsequent breaches, neither is there privity of contract liability. As will be seen below, s 25 prohibits contracting out of the effect of s 5. Prior to the Act, L commonly entered into a contract with A^L so that A^L's liability would be similar to the contractual liability of T. Is this consistent with s 5?

The s 5 protection is subject to two qualifications. We have already seen[21] that s 11 excludes cases where the assignment is in breach of covenant or by operation of law. Much more important are authorised guarantee arrangements.

---

[21] See Extract 16.3.10 above.

Extract 16.3.14

Landlord and Tenant (Covenants) Act 1995, s 16

16.—(1)   Where on an assignment a tenant is to any extent released from a tenant covenant of a tenancy by virtue of this Act ('the relevant covenant'), nothing in this Act (and in particular section 25) shall preclude him from entering into an authorised guarantee agreement with respect to the performance of that covenant by the assignee.

(2)   For the purposes of this section an agreement is an authorised guarantee agreement if—

    (a)   under it the tenant guarantees the performance of the relevant covenant to any extent by the assignee; and

    (b)   it is entered into in the circumstances set out in subsection (3); and

    (c)   its provisions conform with subsections (4) and (5).

(3)   Those circumstances are as follows—

    (a)   by virtue of a covenant against assignment (whether absolute or qualified) the assignment cannot be effected without the consent of the landlord under the tenancy or some other person;

    (b)   any such consent is given subject to a condition (lawfully imposed) that the tenant is to enter into an agreement guaranteeing the performance of the covenant by the assignee; and

    (c)   the agreement is entered into by the tenant in pursuance of that condition.

(4)   An agreement is not an authorised guarantee agreement to the extent that it purports—

    (a)   to impose on the tenant any requirement to guarantee in any way the performance of the relevant covenant by any person other than the assignee; or

    (b)   to impose on the tenant any liability, restriction or other requirement (of whatever nature) in relation to any time after the assignee is released from that covenant by virtue of this Act.

(5)   Subject to subsection (4), an authorised guarantee agreement may—

    (a)   impose on the tenant any liability as sole or principal debtor in respect of any obligation owed by the assignee under the relevant covenant;

    (b)   impose on the tenant liabilities as guarantor in respect of the assignee's performance of that covenant which are no more onerous than those to which he would be subject in the event of his being liable as sole or principal debtor in respect of any obligation owed by the assignee under that covenant;

    (c)   require the tenant, in the event of the tenancy assigned by him being disclaimed, to enter into a new tenancy of the premises comprised in the assignment—

        (i)   whose term expires not later than the term of the tenancy assigned by the tenant, and

        (ii)   whose tenant covenants are no more onerous than those of that tenancy;

    (d)   make provision incidental or supplementary to any provision made by virtue of any of paragraphs (a) to (c).

Comment

(1) The vital point to note is that this guarantee is limited to the duration of the immediate assignment. Why is this? Note that, on a subsequent assignment, A^L (then the assignor) may be required to enter into an authorised guarantee agreement.

(2) The operation of this provision needs to be considered together with s 19(1A) of the Landlord and Tenant Act 1927[22] on the giving of consent to assignments. How common are authorised guarantee agreements likely to be?

---

[22] See Extract 16.2.3 above.

The above provisions apply (as do most provisions in the Act) only to new tenancies. However, contractual liability was thought so troublesome that three more specific protections apply both to new tenancies and old tenancies.[23]

Extract 16.3.15

Landlord and Tenant (Covenants) Act 1995, ss 17–19

17.—(1) This section applies where a person ('the former tenant') is as a result of an assignment no longer a tenant under a tenancy but—

    (a) (in the case of a tenancy which is a new tenancy) he has under an authorised guarantee agreement guaranteed the performance by his assignee of a tenant covenant of the tenancy under which any fixed charge is payable; or

    (b) (in the case of any tenancy) he remains bound by such a covenant.

(2) The former tenant shall not be liable . . . to pay any amount in respect of any fixed charge payable under the covenant unless, within the period of six months beginning with the date when the charge becomes due, the landlord serves on the former tenant a notice informing him—

    (a) that the charge is now due; and

    (b) that in respect of the charge the landlord intends to recover from the former tenant such amount as is specified in the notice and (where payable) interest calculated on such basis as is so specified.

(4) Where the landlord has duly served a notice under subsection (2) or (3), the amount (exclusive of interest) which the former tenant or (as the case may be) the guarantor is liable to pay in respect of the fixed charge in question shall not exceed the amount specified in the notice . . .

18.—(1) This section applies where a person ('the former tenant') is as a result of an assignment no longer a tenant under a tenancy . . .

(2) The former tenant shall not be liable under the agreement or (as the case may be) the covenant to pay any amount in respect of the covenant to the extent that the amount is referable to any relevant variation of the tenant covenants of the tenancy effected after the assignment.

(4) For the purposes of this section a variation of the tenant covenants of a tenancy is a 'relevant variation' if either—

    (a) the landlord has, at the time of the variation, an absolute right to refuse to allow it; or

    (b) the landlord would have had such a right if the variation had been sought by the former tenant immediately before the assignment by him but, between the time of that assignment and the time of the variation, the tenant covenants of the tenancy have been so varied as to deprive the landlord of such a right.

19.—(1) Where in respect of any tenancy ('the relevant tenancy') any person ('the claimant') makes full payment of an amount which he has been duly required to pay in accordance with section 17, together with any interest payable, he shall be entitled (subject to and in accordance with this section) to have the landlord under that tenancy grant him an overriding lease of the premises demised by the tenancy.

(2) For the purposes of this section 'overriding lease' means a tenancy of the reversion expectant on the relevant tenancy which—

    (a) is granted for a term equal to the remainder of the term of the relevant tenancy plus three days or the longest period (less than three days) that will not wholly displace the landlord's reversionary interest expectant on the relevant tenancy, as the case may require; and

---

[23] 1995 Act, s 1(2).

(b) (subject to subsections (3) and (4) and to any modifications agreed to by the claimant and the landlord) otherwise contains the same covenants as the relevant tenancy, as they have effect immediately before the grant of the lease.

(7) The landlord shall not be under any obligation to grant an overriding lease of the demised premises under this section at a time when the relevant tenancy has been determined . . .

Comment

(1) For new tenancies (where the assignor is protected by s 5), when will these added protections be important?

(2) Section 17 applies in particular to rent and service charge liability.

(3) For the purposes of s 18, what is a variation? Does it include the operation of a rent review clause, or a provision for renewal of the lease? Suppose L has a right to extend the term of the lease. Would its exercise be a relevant variation?

(4) Does *Friends' Provident* (Extract 16.3.12 above) provide greater protection to T than s 18?[24]

(5) An overriding lease is a form of concurrent lease. What is its attraction for T?

(6) Taking these provisions together, do they ensure that T is unlikely to be liable for more than six months' rent?

The requirement in s 17 to give notice has given rise to one unanticipated problem. Suppose that rent is being paid, but a rent review is in progress. If (as is common) the rent review could be retrospective to more than six months before it is finalised, should a s 17 notice be served?[25] Does the legislation point one way or another? As a matter of sound legal policy, should a notice be required?

(c) Anti-avoidance

The statutory provisions protecting assignors against liability after assignment deliberately interfere with freedom of contract. Their intended effect could be thwarted if the parties could contract out of the provisions.

Extract 16.3.16

Landlord and Tenant (Covenants) Act 1995, s 25

25.—(1) Any agreement relating to a tenancy is void to the extent that—
(a) it would apart from this section have effect to exclude, modify or otherwise frustrate the operation of any provision of this Act, or . . .

Comment

(1) Note that s 25 is not limited to protecting the effect of ss 5 and 17–19, though this is its most significant function. It has been litigated in the context of the assignment of the reversion (Extract 16.3.18 below).

(2) Can the parties (whether in the lease or guarantee agreement) specify that liability under an authorised guarantee agreement is wider than s 16 provides for?

---

[24] Bridge [1996] CLJ 313 at p 335.
[25] *Scottish and Newcastle plc* v *Raguz* [2008] 1 WLR 2494 held such a notice unnecessary.

(3) The section also catches fresh guarantees by guarantors, save by being a party to an authorised guarantee agreement: *K/S Victoria Street* v *House of Fraser (Stores Management) Ltd.*[26]

(iii) Assignment of the reversion

Contractual liability may apply as much to L as to T, though it is much less significant in practice.

Extract 16.3.17

Landlord and Tenant (Covenants) Act 1995, ss 6, 8

6.—(1)   This section applies where a landlord assigns the reversion in premises of which he is the landlord under a tenancy.

(2)   If the landlord assigns the reversion in the whole of the premises of which he is the landlord—

   (a)   he may apply to be released from the landlord covenants of the tenancy in accordance with section 8; and

   (b)   if he is so released from all of those covenants, he ceases to be entitled to the benefit of the tenant covenants of the tenancy as from the assignment.

8.—(1)   For the purposes of section 6 or 7 an application for the release of a covenant to any extent is made by serving on the tenant, either before or within the period of four weeks beginning with the date of the assignment in question, a notice informing him of—

   (a)   the proposed assignment or (as the case may be) the fact that the assignment has taken place, and

   (b)   the request for the covenant to be released to that extent.

(2)   Where an application for the release of a covenant is made in accordance with subsection (1), the covenant is released to the extent mentioned in the notice if—

   (a)   the tenant does not, within the period of four weeks beginning with the day on which the notice is served, serve on the landlord or former landlord a notice in writing objecting to the release, or

   (b)   the tenant does so serve such a notice but the court, on the application of the landlord or former landlord, makes a declaration that it is reasonable for the covenant to be so released, or

   (c)   the tenant serves on the landlord or former landlord a notice in writing consenting to the release and, if he has previously served a notice objecting to it, stating that that notice is withdrawn.

Comment

(1) Why are these provisions more complex than s 5 for tenants?

(2) If L is not released on an assignment, s 7 permits the s 8 procedure to be activated on a subsequent assignment of the reversion.

(3) The application of s 8 was central to *BHP Petroleum Great Britain Ltd* v *Chesterfield Ltd*,[27] in which the tenant had failed to serve a counternotice.

---

[26] [2012] Ch 497, the principles are summarised at [53]; for release of guarantors, see s 24.
[27] [2002] Ch 194; Extract 16.3.5 above.

Extract 16.3.18

London Diocesan Fund v *Phithwa* [2005] 1 WLR 3956

A lease provided for the landlord not to be liable after assignment, bypassing the s 8 procedure.

LORD NICHOLLS: 10. . . . One of the principal mischiefs the Act was intended to remedy was that, as the law stood, the original tenant of a lease remained liable for performance of the tenant's covenants throughout the entire duration of the lease. A tenant might part with his lease and many years later find himself liable for substantial amounts of unpaid rent, perhaps much increased under rent review provisions, and for the cost of making good extensive dilapidations. 11.   This was considered unfair. This potential liability was not widely understood by tenants, and it could lead to hardship. Section 5 of the Act remedied this defect in the law . . . 12.   Section 6 contains a corresponding provision for the benefit of landlords in respect of landlord covenants, but this provision is not so far-reaching in its effect. Unlike the automatic release of tenant covenants brought about by assignment of the whole of the demised premises, assignment of the reversion in the whole of the demised premises does not automatically relieve the landlord from his liability under the landlord covenants. The Law Commission considered the new provision regarding landlord covenants could not mirror precisely the position regarding tenant covenants. Tenants rarely, if ever, have a right to give or withhold consent to dispositions by their landlord. Moreover, there was less need for radical change with landlord covenants because landlords undertake far fewer obligations than tenants, and landlords may not be troubled by the prospect of continuing responsibility: see para 4.16 of its report. 13.   So sections 6 to 8 of the Act provide a landlord with a means which may result in his being released from the landlord covenants but will not necessarily do so . . . 14.   These statutory provisions might readily be stultified if the parties to a lease could exclude their operation. In particular, the provision for automatic release of tenant covenants on assignment of a lease would be a weak instrument if it were open to a landlord to provide that the original tenant's contractual liability should continue for the whole term notwithstanding section 5. So the Act, in section 25, enacts a comprehensive anti-avoidance provision . . . But does this agreement 'frustrate the operation' of any provision of the Act? That is the key question. 16.   . . . Sections 5 to 8 are relieving provisions. They are intended to benefit tenants, or landlords, as the case may be. That is their purpose. That is how they are meant to operate. These sections introduced a means, which cannot be ousted, whereby in certain circumstances, without the agreement of the other party, a tenant or landlord can be released from a liability he has assumed. The object of the legislation was that on lawful assignment of a tenancy or reversion, and irrespective of the terms of the tenancy, the tenant or the landlord should have an exit route from his future liabilities. This route should be available in accordance with the statutory provisions. 17.   Thus the mischief at which the statute was aimed was the *absence* in practice of any such exit route. Consistently with this the legislation was not intended to close any *other* exit route already open to the parties: in particular, that by agreement their liability could be curtailed from the outset or later released or waived. The possibility that by agreement the parties may limit their liability in this way was not, it seems, perceived as having unfair consequences in practice, even though landlords normally have greater bargaining power than tenants. So there was no call for legislation to exclude the parties' capacity to make such an agreement, ending their liability in circumstances other than those provided in the Act. 18.   Section 25 is of course to be interpreted generously, so as to ensure the operation of the Act is not frustrated, either directly or indirectly. But there is nothing in the language or scheme of the Act to suggest the statute was intended to exclude the parties' ability to limit liability under their covenants from the outset in whatever way they may agree. An agreed limitation of this nature does not impinge upon the operation of the statutory provisions.

21.   Nor do the events in this case exemplify a loophole in the Act Parliament cannot have intended. The risks involved were not obscure or concealed. They were evident on the face of the subleases. The sublessees were to pay up-front a capitalised rent for the whole term of the subleases. But clause 6 enabled Avonridge to shake off all its landlord obligations at will. Any competent conveyancer would, or should, have warned the sublessees of the risks, clearly and forcefully.

Comment

(1) Lord Walker dissented. How convincing are the reasons why s 25 did not apply? See Dixon [2006] Conv 79.

(2) Is the argument that a competent conveyancer should have warned the sub-lessees consistent with the policy of the legislation?

(iv) Recovery in respect of contractual liability

Suppose T has been held liable to L. Can T recover from A^L or (where relevant) a subsequent assignee of the lease? When T is liable, this is almost inevitably because the present tenant is insolvent.

In new tenancies, T will normally be liable only under an authorised guarantee agreement. Because liability is as guarantor; this necessarily means that the current tenant (A^L) has the primary liability and can be sued by T.

Old tenancies

As regards current tenants, a similar conclusion is reached.[28] However, T may wish to claim against A^L when $A2^L$ has become insolvent.

Extract 16.3.19

Land Registration Act 2002, Sched 12, para 20

20 (2)   The transferee covenants with the transferor that during the residue of the term granted by the registered lease the transferee and the persons deriving title under him will—
   (a)   pay the rent reserved by the lease,
   (b)   comply with the covenants and conditions contained in the lease, and
   (c)   keep the transferor and the persons deriving title under him indemnified against all actions, expenses and claims on account of any failure to comply with paragraphs (a) and (b).

(5)   This paragraph does not apply to a lease which is a new tenancy for the purposes of section 1 of the Landlord and Tenant (Covenants) Act 1995 (c. 30).

Comment

(1) For unregistered land, similar covenants are implied: LPA, s 77(1)(C).

(2) These provisions establish that the immediate assignee (whether or not the current tenant) can be sued by the assignor. Is this liability affected by the tenant protection provisions of the 1995 Act?

(3) Why should para 20 not apply to new tenancies?

---

[28]   *Moule v Garrett* (1872) LR 7 Ex 101.

D. Breaches committed before assignment

(i) Obligations

Extract 16.3.20

Landlord and Tenant (Covenants) Act 1995, s 23

23.—(1)   Where as a result of an assignment a person becomes, by virtue of this Act, bound by or entitled to the benefit of a covenant, he shall not by virtue of this Act have any liability or rights under the covenant in relation to any time falling before the assignment.

(2)   Subsection (1) does not preclude any such rights being expressly assigned to the person in question.

(3)   Where as a result of an assignment a person becomes, by virtue of this Act, entitled to a right of re-entry contained in a tenancy, that right shall be exercisable in relation to any breach of a covenant of the tenancy occurring before the assignment as in relation to one occurring thereafter, unless by reason of any waiver or release it was not so exercisable immediately before the assignment.

Comment

This makes it perfectly clear that the assignee has no liability for breaches before the assignment. The assignor (T or L) remains liable. This replicates the position prior to the 1995 Act. The position regarding continuing breaches (failure to repair provides a good example) is explained by the following words of Jenkins LJ:[29]

> An assignee of a term . . . is, of course, liable for the disrepair of the premises as they stand when he takes over, so far as their then state of disrepair falls within the scope of the tenant's repairing covenants, but particular breaches committed before the assignment to him, as distinct from the state of the premises when he takes over, are matters, generally speaking, with which he is not concerned.

(ii) Rights to sue

The position regarding rights to sue is similarly governed by s 23 of the 1995 Act. The assignee has no claim in relation to pre-assignment breaches. The most common application of this is where there are arrears of rent when L assigns to A^R. Subject to any express assignment, only L can claim the arrears. Does it make sense that A^R can claim forfeiture (see s 23(3)) but not damages?

Old tenancies

Although most cases involve rent arrears at the time of assignment of the reversion, the leading case involves T's covenant to repair. Who can claim them, L or A^R?

Extract 16.3.21

***Re King* [1963] Ch 459**

UPJOHN LJ: . . . I turn, then, to a consideration of the meaning of section 141 and construe the language used in its ordinary and natural meaning, which seems to me quite plain and clear. To illustrate this, consider the case of a lease containing a covenant to build a house according to certain detailed specifications before a certain day. Let me suppose that after that certain day

---

[29] *Granada Theatres Ltd* v *Freehold Investment (Leytonstone) Ltd* [1959] Ch 592 at p 606.

the then lessor assigns the benefit of the reversion to an assignee, and at the time of the assignment the lessee has failed to perform the covenant to build. Who can sue the lessee for breach of covenant? It seems to me clear that the assignee alone can sue. Upon the assignment the benefit of every covenant on the lessee's part to be observed and performed is annexed and incident to and goes with the reversionary estate. The benefit of that covenant to build, therefore, passed; as it had been broken, the right to sue also passed as part of the benefit of the covenant and, incidentally, also the right to re-enter, if that has not been waived . . . Suppose the right to sue for breach of that covenant did not pass, and that right remained in the assignor, then the assignee would take the lease without the benefit of that covenant and he could never enforce it. So he has not got the benefit of every covenant contained in the lease and the words of the section are not satisfied. That cannot be right . . . Of course, the assignor and assignee can always agree that the benefit of the covenant shall not pass, in which case the assignor can still sue, if necessary, in the name of the assignee.

Comment

(1) This has been held to apply to rent arrears: *London & County (A & D) Ltd v Wilfred Sportsman Ltd.*[30]

(2) Bearing in mind the arguments in *Re King*, can the solution in s 23 be justified?

A similar question is whether T or A^L can sue in respect of L's breaches before the assignment of the lease.

Extract 16.3.22

City & Metropolitan Properties Ltd v Greycroft Ltd [1987] 1 WLR 1085 (Ch D)

MOWBRAY QC: . . . Both [the tenant's] liability and the benefit of the landlord's covenants run with the lease at common law by privity of estate under *Spencer's Case* (1583) 5 Co Rep 16a: see *Smith's Leading Cases*, 13th ed (1929), vol 1, p 51. There is a close analogy between the two. I take the view that, by this analogy, the landlord's liability to the tenant for existing breaches survives the assignment of the lease, in the same way as the tenant's liability to the landlord.

. . . [Counsel] pointed out that the Court of Appeal has held section 141(1) to make a statutory transfer of the whole benefit of a tenant's covenant to an assignee of the reversion: *In re King, decd* [1963] Ch 459 and *London and County (A & D) Ltd v Wilfred Sportsman Ltd* [1971] Ch 764. He asked me to apply that principle by analogy to an assignment of the lease.

It is not possible to apply those decisions. They turned on words corresponding to the first part of section 142(1), 'shall . . . be annexed and incident to and shall go with that reversionary estate . . .'. The middle passage of section 142(1) is quite different. It does not say that the right to take advantage of the landlord's covenants is annexed or incident to the term, or 'shall go with' it, the graphic phrase specially relied on by Diplock LJ in *In re King, decd* [1963] Ch 459, 497 . . .

Comment

(1) How convincing is the argument that T should be able to sue for pre-assignment breaches by L as he or she is liable for pre-assignment breaches of the tenant's covenants?

(2) The contrast with *Re King* is remarkable. Is it justified by s 142? (See Extract 16.3.2 for ss 141 and 142.)

(3) The approach in *Greycroft* is, of course, that adopted by s 23 for new tenancies.

[30] [1971] Ch 764.

E. Equitable leases and equitable assignments

We will deal first with old tenancies, as this is the context in which problems may arise.

Old tenancies

The question is whether the normal rules relating to the running of covenants apply to equitable leases. Contractual liability is the same, but does liability under privity of estate apply?

Extract 16.3.23

Purchase v Lichfield Brewery Co [1915] 1 KB 184

Was the assignee (by way of mortgage) of an equitable lease liable on the covenants?

LUSH J: . . . The only point which the county court judge decided was that the present case was governed by *Williams* v *Bosanquet*.[i] In my view that case does not apply. The lease in question there was under seal. It was assigned by deed to mortgagees. That was a valid assignment . . . In this case there was no lease under seal. No term was created as between lessor and lessee. Therefore the question decided in *Williams* v *Bosanquet* does not arise in this case. Consequently the judgment of the county court judge cannot stand on the grounds on which he has based it.

. . . It does not follow from *Walsh* v *Lonsdale*[ii] that a Court of Equity would decree specific performance against mere mortgagees who only took an assignment by way of security. In my opinion it would leave the parties to their position at law. Accordingly the matter stands thus: A tenant under an agreement, whose only title to call himself a lessee depends on his right to specific performance of the agreement, assigns his right to assignees. The assignees never had a term vested in them because no term was ever created; therefore there was never privity of estate. They never went into possession or were recognized by the landlord; therefore there was never privity of contract. It is impossible that specific performance of a contract can be decreed against a person with whom there is neither privity of contract nor privity of estate. Therefore these assignees are not liable to perform the terms of the agreement and this appeal must be allowed.

[i] 1 Brod&B 238.
[ii] 21 Ch D 9.

Comment

Since the 1925 legislation, a mortgage of a legal lease can take effect only as a sublease (or legal charge), not as an assignment.[31]

Extract 16.3.24

Boyer v Warbey [1953] 1 QB 234

DENNING LJ: . . . Seeing that the agreement touched and concerned the thing demised, it ran with the land so as to bind the assignee, the tenant, as soon as he entered into possession. I know that before the Judicature Act, 1873, it was said that the doctrine of covenants running with the land only applied to covenants under seal and not to agreements under hand: see *Elliott* v *Johnson*.[i] But since the fusion of law and equity, the position is different. The distinction between agreements under hand and covenants under seal has been largely obliterated. There

---

[31] See p 736 below.

is no valid reason nowadays why the doctrine of covenants running with the land – or with the reversion – should not apply equally to agreements under hand as to covenants under seal; and I think we should so hold, not only in the case of agreements for more than three years which need the intervention of equity to perfect them, but also in the case of agreements for three years or less which do not.

[i] (1868) LR 2 QB 120.

Comment

(1) Part of the reasoning in *Purchase* is that specific performance is not available against the assignee. How, if at all, does Denning LJ counter this reasoning? Are equitable leases most properly regarded as contracts for leases or as equitable versions of legal leases? Can any such distinction sensibly be drawn?

(2) *Boyer* v *Warbey* stands as the most recent authority and complements modern trends to limit differences between legal and equitable rights.[32] Although *Boyer* is not directly supported by other decisions, the *Purchase* line of cases was fairly weak in terms of number of cases, authority and reasoning.

Even if covenants in equitable leases do not run, there are several ways in which an assignee may be made liable. Clearly, possession cannot be insisted upon without obser-vance of the covenants, and it may also be possible to imply a contract with the assignee.[33]

On the assignment of the reversion, the running of covenants has always been based on statute. Sections 141 and 142 of the LPA have been interpreted so as to apply to equitable leases.[34]

Let us turn to equitable assignments of legal leases. Such assignments usually exist where a contract to assign has not been followed by a deed of assignment.

Extract 16.3.25

Cox v *Bishop* (1857) 8 De GM&G 815 (44 ER 604)

TURNER LJ: . . . If, on the other hand, these Defendants [equitable assignees] are not at law liable to the Plaintiffs, what are the grounds alleged by this bill upon which they are in equity to be made liable? Simply that they have contracted to purchase interests in the lease and have been in possession. The contracts to purchase, however, are not contracts with the Plaintiffs, and there is nothing in the bill to shew that the Plaintiffs are in any manner entitled to the bene-fit of those contracts, and if the Defendants are liable by virtue of their possession, the liability, as I apprehend is to be enforced at law and not in equity . . .

These considerations seem to me to prove, if proof be wanted, that the relation of landlord and tenant is a legal and not an equitable relation, and this view of the case seems to me to introduce another and not unimportant consideration. Where persons enter into contracts, they must surely be assumed to contract with reference to the rights and liabilities incident to the subject-matter of the contract. Must not these Defendants, therefore, when they agreed to take and purchase interests in this lease, be taken to have understood that, as between them and the landlord, they would not become liable until the lease was assigned to them? Can this Court extend and alter their contract, and hold them to be so liable before the assignment is made? Upon these grounds I think that, upon principle, this bill cannot be maintained.

[32] See, e.g., *Tinsley* v *Milligan* [1994] 1 AC 340 at pp 370–371, quoted at p 504 above.
[33] For details, see R J Smith [1978] CLJ 98 at pp 105–111.
[34] *Cole* v *Kelly* [1920] 2 KB 106; *Rye* v *Purcell* [1926] 1 KB 446 at p 452.

Comment

(1) The authority in favour of this is much more convincing than the authority in favour of the *Purchase* approach to equitable leases.

(2) To what extent do equitable leases and equitable assignments raise different legal issues? Could the reasoning in *Boyer* v *Warbey* be used to attack *Cox* v *Bishop*? Is it relevant that after an equitable assignment the assignor will remain liable to L under privity of estate?

As with equitable leases, it may be possible to circumvent the absence of liability. In particular, it may be possible to argue that L's consent to the assignment is based upon the assignment being legal: when L accepts rent from A^L, this gives rise to an estoppel whereby A^L cannot deny that there is a legal assignment.[35]

New tenancies

All these problems are swept away. Section 28(1) of the 1995 Act defines tenancies and assignments so as to include agreements for tenancies and equitable assignments. But *Lankester & Son Ltd* v *Rennie* [2014] EWCA 1515 at [25] doubts (not citing s 28) whether the 1995 Act applies to equitable assignments. Consider also this example: T contracts to assign to A^L in a month's time. The assignment is never executed, although A^L goes into possession. Is T liable for the rent after the date of the contract, after a month's time or after A^L goes into possession?

4. Subleases

As seen earlier in this chapter, L and S are not in privity of estate and so cannot enforce covenants against each other. However, it certainly does not follow that S can ignore the covenants in the head lease with impunity. Breach of those covenants is likely to trigger a forfeiture which will destroy the sublease. The terms of the sublease will normally oblige S to comply with most of the covenants (except payment of rent and, sometimes, repairing obligations) in the head lease, though L cannot enforce S's covenant with T.[36] Could L rely on the Contracts (Rights of Third Parties) Act 1999?[37]

In the case of restrictive covenants in the head lease, nevertheless, L can sue S regardless of the terms of the sublease.

Extract 16.4.1

***Hall* v *Ewin* (1887) 37 Ch D 74**

COTTON LJ: . . . The Defendant *Ewin*, who was himself an under-lessee, granted an underlease to *McNeff*, in which there was a covenant that he could not exercise any noisome or offensive trade or business without the consent in writing of *Ewin*. If the Plaintiffs had shewn that *Ewin* had granted this underlease for the purpose of its being used for an offensive trade or had granted a written license to *McNeff* so to use it, he would have acted in a way inconsistent with the covenants in the original lease, and I should have had no hesitation in granting an injunction against him; but he has done nothing of the kind, and the case made against him is that by standing by and allowing the house to be used for the exhibition of wild beasts, he has acted

---

[35] *Rodenhurst Estates Ltd* v *WH Barnes Ltd* [1936] 2 All ER 3.
[36] *Amsprop Trading Ltd* v *Harris Distribution Ltd* [1997] 1 WLR 1025; see Extract 20.1.4 below.
[37] Extract 20.1.5 below.

in violation of the covenant. I give no opinion whether the Plaintiff would have had a right of action against him if he had been bound in law by the covenant. There is no doubt that under the principle of *Tulk* v *Moxhay*,[i] if a man had actually done anything in contravention of the covenants of which he had notice, the Court would grant an injunction. As I understand *Tulk* v *Moxhay*, the principle there laid down was that if a man bought an underlease, although he was not bound in law by the restrictive covenants of the original lease, yet if he purchased with notice of those covenants the Court of Chancery could not allow him to use the land in contravention of the covenants. That is a sound principle. If a man buys land subject to a restrictive covenant, he regulates the price accordingly, and it would be contrary to equity to allow him to use the land in contravention of the restriction. But here the Plaintiff does not seek to restrain *Ewin* from using the house in a particular way, or from doing something which will enable the tenant so to use it, but to compel him to bring an action against his tenant who is in possession of the house.

[i] 2 Ph 774.

Comment

Restrictive covenants can be enforced regardless of privity of estate, as will be seen in Chapter 20. It is well established that there must be land benefited by the covenant. How is this satisfied in the case of a sublease, assuming that L does not have any adjoining land?

Extract 16.4.2

Landlord and Tenant (Covenants) Act 1995, s 3(5)

3.—(5) Any landlord or tenant covenant of a tenancy which is restrictive of the user of land shall, as well as being capable of enforcement against an assignee, be capable of being enforced against any other person who is the owner or occupier of any demised premises to which the covenant relates, even though there is no express provision in the tenancy to that effect.

Comment

The principal provisions of s 3 concern the liability of assignees. What is the intended role of s 3(5): to replace the common law, to codify it while leaving the equitable principles unaffected or something else?

Extract 16.4.3

Hemingway Securities Ltd v *Dunraven Ltd* (1994) 71 P&CR 30

Was a covenant not to sublet binding on a sub-lessee?

JACOB J: . . . I should say that the plaintiffs put their case also on the doctrine of *Tulk* v *Moxhay*. They say here is a restrictive covenant; it is well settled that a restrictive covenant for the benefit of the landlords' reversion counts for the purposes for the doctrine of *Tulk* v *Moxhay*; the restrictive covenant accordingly runs with the land; it accordingly binds the second defendants; they are acting in breach of it and, therefore, again, an injunction to compel them to stop acting in breach of it and in effect to gain a mandatory injunction should be granted.

Again, I do not see the answer to this way of putting the plaintiff's case. It was suggested that a covenant against alienation is not a restrictive covenant for the purposes of the *Tulk* v *Moxhay* doctrine. That doctrine was limited to covenants in respect of the mode of user of property. No direct authority was cited to that effect and I do not see why, in principle, it should be so . . .

Comment

(1) The use of restrictive covenants for this type of promise is considered in Chapter 20;[38] it will be seen that this application of restrictive covenants is highly controversial. It is significant in the leases context because it has the potential to bypass protections available to tenants.

(2) Does the *Hemingway* covenant fall within the words 'restrictive of the user' in s 3(5)? Does it matter?

Lastly, in a commercial lease S may be liable to pay rent directly to L if there are arrears of rent under the head lease and notice is given by L;[39] this is the counterpart of S's statutory freedom from the remedy of commercial rent arrears recovery (previously distress) for rent due from T.

Further reading

Bridge, S [1996] CLJ 313: Former tenants, future liabilities and the privity of contract principle: the Landlord and Tenant (Covenants) Act 1995.

Clarke, A [1996] CLP Pt 1, pp 97–114 [on the Landlord and Tenant (Covenants) Act 1995].

Fancourt, T [2006] Conv 37: Licences to assign: another turn of the screw?

---

[38] See p 713 below.
[39] Tribunals, Courts and Enforcement Act 2007, ss 81–84.

17

Commonhold

Commonhold is a twenty-first century area of property law.[1] It provides a management structure appropriate for groups of properties such as flats, where there is interdependency between the individual units and usually with common areas which need to be managed. Despite the term 'commonhold', it is not a new tenure or estate. Rather, it is based on the freehold fee simple, though some of its incidents differ from normal freehold rules. Especially with blocks of flats, their interdependency on matters of repair makes it essential to have obligations which run with the land. Running of the burden of positive covenants is not recognised in freehold land. This led to leases being used for such developments. Today, commonhold allows the use of freeholds. However, the scheme does far more than allow positive covenants to run; it provides a comprehensive structure for the management of the land involved.

The Commonhold and Leasehold Reform Act 2002 (hereafter CLRA) has produced a new and complex statutory area; it is necessary to study a textbook or periodical literature to get a feel for its operation. This chapter will include the principal statutory provisions and give some guidance as regards the major issues.

First, however, we should note some of the basic principles. The fee simple of the individual units will be vested in individual owners. Although a fee simple is involved, special rules and obligations operate. The common parts (stairs, roadways, roofs provide obvious examples) are vested in the commonhold association (CA). The CA, a company controlled by the unit-holders, both administers the common parts and oversees the individual units (the latter may involve, for example, taking out insurance policies and ensuring that unit-holders comply with their obligations). The commonhold community statement (CCS) is a vitally important document which will establish the roles and duties of the CA and unit-holders. Naturally, it may vary greatly from one development to another.

1. Becoming commonhold land

An initial observation is that commonhold is available either when a development is first undertaken (before units are sold) or for existing developments.

---

[1] Clarke [2002] Conv 349 provides a useful critical analysis.

Extract 17.1.1

**Commonhold and Leasehold Reform Act 2002, ss 1–3;
Commonhold Regulations 2004, reg 3**

1.—(1) Land is commonhold land if—
    (a) the freehold estate in the land is registered as a freehold estate in commonhold land,
    (b) the land is specified in the memorandum of association of a commonhold association as the land in relation to which the association is to exercise functions, and
    (c) a commonhold community statement makes provision for rights and duties of the commonhold association and unit-holders (whether or not the statement has come into force).

2.—(1) The Registrar shall register a freehold estate in land as a freehold estate in commonhold land if—
    (a) the registered freeholder of the land makes an application under this section, and
    (b) no part of the land is already commonhold land.

3.—(1) An application under section 2 may not be made in respect of a freehold estate in land without the consent of anyone who—
    (a) is the registered proprietor of the freehold estate in the whole or part of the land,
    (b) is the registered proprietor of a leasehold estate in the whole or part of the land granted for a term of more than than [sic] 21 years,
    (c) is the registered proprietor of a charge over the whole or part of the land, or
    (d) falls within any other class of person which may be prescribed.

Reg 3. (1) An application under section 2 may not be made in respect of a freehold estate in land without the consent of anyone who is—
    (d) subject to paragraph (2), the holder of a lease granted for a term of not more than 21 years which will be extinguished by virtue of section 7(3)(d) or 9(3)(f).
  (2) An application under section 2 may be made without the consent of a person who would otherwise be required to consent by virtue of paragraph (1)(d) if—
    (a) the person is entitled to the grant of a term of years absolute—
      (i) of the same premises as are comprised in the extinguished lease;
      (ii) on the same terms as the extinguished lease, except to the extent necessary to comply with the Act and these Regulations and excluding any terms that are spent;
      (iii) at the same rent as the rent payable under, and including the same provisions for rent review as were included in, the extinguished lease as at the date on which it will be extinguished;
      (iv) for a term equivalent to the unexpired term of the lease which will be extinguished; and
      (v) to take effect immediately after the lease is extinguished by virtue of section 7(3)(d) or 9(3)(f).

Comment

(1) Section 1 reflects some of the basic principles of the commonhold system.

(2) The requirements for consent in s 3 are crucial. In a new development, this should not be problematic. It should be noted, however, that charges over the common parts are extinguished (CLRA, s 28(3)) and any chargee will need to take this into account. In existing developments, every unit-holder within the relevant development[2] has to consent.

---

[2] Nor can this be avoided by excluding particular flats from the commonhold. CLRA, Sched 2, para 1 requires all the units beneath the commonhold to be within the commonhold: it prohibits flying freehold commonhold schemes.

For larger developments, this will almost certainly mean that conversion to commonhold is not feasible:[3] 'The Government recognises that this is a very high hurdle and that it may effectively make it impossible for the majority of long leasehold developments to convert to commonhold. However, it is of the essence of commonhold that all the unit-holders should be members of the commonhold association with the same rights and duties as between themselves and the association.'

(3) It is important to note that commonhold is a form of landholding for freeholders: it is not available to tenants. This will not normally be a problem for new developments, given that the developer will usually have the fee simple. Existing developments will invariably involve the unit-holders having leases (a result of the inadequacy of the rules for running of covenants in freehold land). If it is desired to bring an existing development within commonhold, it will first be necessary for the tenants to acquire the freehold by the enfranchisement procedure (itself eased, for leases over 21 years, by CLRA).

(4) Reg 3 refers to entitlement to a replacement lease. Such leases are authorised by reg 11(2).

(5) Many flats are held by tenants paying a full market rent. Does commonhold provide a useful structure for these flats, whether the development is a new or existing one?

We can now turn to the effect of registration as commonhold.

Extract 17.1.2

Commonhold and Leasehold Reform Act 2002, ss 7, 9

7.—(1) This section applies where—
   (a) a freehold estate in land is registered as a freehold estate in commonhold land in pursuance of an application under section 2, and
   (b) the application is not accompanied by a statement under section 9(1)(b).
   (2) On registration—
   (a) the applicant shall continue to be registered as the proprietor of the freehold estate in the commonhold land, and
   (b) the rights and duties conferred and imposed by the commonhold community statement shall not come into force (subject to section 8(2)(b)).
   (3) Where after registration a person other than the applicant becomes entitled to be registered as the proprietor of the freehold estate in one or more, but not all, of the commonhold units—
   (a) the commonhold association shall be entitled to be registered as the proprietor of the freehold estate in the common parts,
   (b) the Registrar shall register the commonhold association in accordance with paragraph (a) (without an application being made),
   (c) the rights and duties conferred and imposed by the commonhold community statement shall come into force, and
   (d) any lease of the whole or part of the commonhold land shall be extinguished by virtue of this section.

---

[3] *Commonhold and Leasehold Reform* (DETR) (2000) Cm 4843, para 2.2.3.

(4) For the purpose of subsection (3)(d) 'lease' means a lease which—
    (a) is granted for any term, and
    (b) is granted before the commonhold association becomes entitled to be registered as the proprietor of the freehold estate in the common parts.

9.—(1) This section applies in relation to a freehold estate in commonhold land if—
    (a) it is registered as a freehold estate in commonhold land in pursuance of an application under section 2, and
    (b) the application is accompanied by a statement by the applicant requesting that this section should apply.

(2) A statement under subsection (1)(b) must include a list of the commonhold units giving in relation to each one the prescribed details of the proposed initial unit-holder or joint unit-holders.

(3) On registration—
    (a) the commonhold association shall be entitled to be registered as the proprietor of the freehold estate in the common parts,
    (b) a person specified by virtue of subsection (2) as the initial unit-holder of a commonhold unit shall be entitled to be registered as the proprietor of the freehold estate in the unit,
    (c) a person specified by virtue of subsection (2) as an initial joint unit-holder of a commonhold unit shall be entitled to be registered as one of the proprietors of the freehold estate in the unit,
    (d) the Registrar shall make entries in the register to reflect paragraphs (a) to (c) (without applications being made),
    (e) the rights and duties conferred and imposed by the commonhold community statement shall come into force, and
    (f) any lease of the whole or part of the commonhold land shall be extinguished by virtue of this section.

(4) For the purpose of subsection (3)(f) 'lease' means a lease which—
    (a) is granted for any term, and
    (b) is granted before the commonhold association becomes entitled to be registered as the proprietor of the freehold estate in the common parts.

Comment

(1) Section 7 operates where the commonhold is set up before the units are sold off. It comes fully into force when the first unit is sold off. Section 8 (not quoted) makes provision for this 'transitional period'.

(2) It is clear from these sections that the unit-holders have legal fees simple. Commonhold is not a new tenure or estate. However, we shall see that the incidents of this fee simple are very special.

(3) Note the effect of the commonhold as terminating existing leases; it needs to be considered in the context of the principles quoted above regarding consent. How may this justified? Note that s 17 permits leases of units to be created subsequently (subject to a limit of seven years for residential units)[4] and that s 10 provides for compensation to be paid to tenants who had not consented to the commonhold.

---

[4] Commonhold Regulations 2004, reg 11.

2. Commonhold association and commonhold community statement

Extensive provision is made by the legislation. We will consider a small proportion of it.

Extract 17.2.1

Commonhold and Leasehold Reform Act 2002, Sched 3, paras 7, 10, 13; ss 36, 31–32, 38

7   A person is entitled to be entered in the register of members of a commonhold association if he becomes the unit-holder of a commonhold unit in relation to which the association exercises functions . . .

10   A person may not become a member of a commonhold association otherwise than by virtue of a provision of this Schedule. Where a member of a commonhold association ceases to be a unit-holder or joint unit-holder of a commonhold unit in relation to which the association exercises functions—

    (a) he shall cease to be a member of the commonhold association, but

    (b) paragraph (a) does not affect any right or liability already acquired or incurred in respect of a matter relating to a time when he was a unit-holder or joint unit-holder.

13   A member of a commonhold association may resign by notice in writing to the association if (and only if) he is a member by virtue of paragraph 5 or 6 of this Schedule (and not also by virtue of any other paragraph).

36.—(1)   This section applies in relation to any provision of this Part (a 'voting provision') which refers to the passing of a resolution by a commonhold association.

(2)   A voting provision is satisfied only if every member is given an opportunity to vote in accordance with any relevant provision of the memorandum or articles of association or the commonhold community statement.

31.—(1)   A commonhold community statement is a document which makes provision in relation to specified land for—

    (a) the rights and duties of the commonhold association, and

    (b) the rights and duties of the unit-holders.

(2)   A commonhold community statement must be in the prescribed form.

(3)   A commonhold community statement may—

    (a) impose a duty on the commonhold association;

    (b) impose a duty on a unit-holder;

    (c) make provision about the taking of decisions in connection with the management of the commonhold or any other matter concerning it.

(4)   Subsection (3) is subject to—

    (a) any provision made by or by virtue of this Part, and

    (b) any provision of the memorandum or articles of the commonhold association.

(5)   In subsection (3)(a) and (b) 'duty' includes, in particular, a duty—

    (a) to pay money;

    (b) to undertake works;

    (c) to grant access;

    (d) to give notice;

    (e) to refrain from entering into transactions of a specified kind in relation to a commonhold unit;

    (f) to refrain from using the whole or part of a commonhold unit for a specified purpose or for anything other than a specified purpose;

    (g) to refrain from undertaking works (including alterations) of a specified kind;

    (h) to refrain from causing nuisance or annoyance;

    (i) to refrain from specified behaviour;

    (j) to indemnify the commonhold association or a unit-holder in respect of costs arising from the breach of a statutory requirement.

(6) Provision in a commonhold community statement imposing a duty to pay money (whether in pursuance of subsection (5)(a) or any other provision made by or by virtue of this Part) may include provision for the payment of interest in the case of late payment.

(7) A duty conferred by a commonhold community statement on a commonhold association or a unit-holder shall not require any other formality.

(8) A commonhold community statement may not provide for the transfer or loss of an interest in land on the occurrence or non-occurrence of a specified event.

(9) Provision made by a commonhold community statement shall be of no effect to the extent that—

    (a) it is prohibited by virtue of section 32,

    (b) it is inconsistent with any provision made by or by virtue of this Part,

    (c) it is inconsistent with anything which is treated as included in the statement by virtue of section 32, or

    (d) it is inconsistent with the memorandum or articles of association of the commonhold association.

32.—(1) Regulations shall make provision about the content of a commonhold community statement.

38.—(1) A commonhold community statement must make provision—

    (a) requiring the directors of the commonhold association to make an annual estimate of the income required to be raised from unit-holders to meet the expenses of the association,

    (b) enabling the directors of the commonhold association to make estimates from time to time of income required to be raised from unit-holders in addition to the annual estimate,

    (c) specifying the percentage of any estimate made under paragraph (a) or (b) which is to be allocated to each unit,

    (d) requiring each unit-holder to make payments in respect of the percentage of any estimate which is allocated to his unit, and

. . .

(2) For the purpose of subsection (1)(c)—

    (a) the percentages allocated by a commonhold community statement to the commonhold units must amount in aggregate to 100;

    (b) a commonhold community statement may specify 0% in relation to a unit.

Comment

(1) The provisions relating to the CA indicate that it must be controlled by the unit-holders. In practice, most management decisions will be taken by a committee of management. How confident can one be that the quality of management will be superior to the much criticised management by landlords? Do individual unit-holders have anything to fear from the new system?

(2) The provisions in s 31 provide a good idea as to the sort of provisions that are included in the CCS. For details of compulsory provisions, see Commonhold Regulations 2004, reg 15 and Sched 3.

(3) What is the significance of s 31(8)? Might it mean that powers to compel compliance with obligations lack teeth?

(4) The provisions of s 38 are crucial. For the average CA, the only source of income will be the unit-holders and it is essential that funds are raised on a clear basis.

3. Common parts

Extract 17.3.1

Commonhold and Leasehold Reform Act 2002, ss 25–29

25.—(1) In this Part 'common parts' in relation to a commonhold means every part of the commonhold which is not for the time being a commonhold unit in accordance with the commonhold community statement.

(2) A commonhold community statement may make provision in respect of a specified part of the common parts (a 'limited use area') restricting—
  (a) the classes of person who may use it;
  (b) the kind of use to which it may be put.
. . .

26.—A commonhold community statement must make provision—
  (a) regulating the use of the common parts;
  (b) requiring the commonhold association to insure the common parts;
  (c) requiring the commonhold association to repair and maintain the common parts.

27.—(1) Nothing in a commonhold community statement shall prevent or restrict—
  (a) the transfer by the commonhold association of its freehold estate in any part of the common parts, or
  (b) the creation by the commonhold association of an interest in any part of the common parts.
(2) In this section 'interest' does not include—
  (a) a charge, or
  (b) an interest which arises by virtue of a charge.

28.—(1) It shall not be possible to create a charge over common parts.
(3) Where by virtue of section 7 or 9 a commonhold association is registered as the proprietor of common parts, a charge which relates wholly or partly to the common parts shall be extinguished by virtue of this subsection to the extent that it relates to the common parts.
. . .

29.—(1) Section 28 shall not apply in relation to a legal mortgage if the creation of the mortgage is approved by a resolution of the commonhold association.
(2) A resolution for the purposes of subsection (1) must be passed—
  (a) before the mortgage is created, and
  (b) unanimously.

Comment

(1) These provisions also illustrate the role of the CA.

(2) Why should there be general power to transfer, but not charge, common parts? When is a charge possible?

4. Units

The control over units is established by the CCS, which we have already considered. Both restrictive and positive obligations are permitted by ss 31 and 38 (Extract 17.2.1). Normally, of course, positive covenants in freehold land do not bind purchasers.

Extract 17.4.1

Commonhold and Leasehold Reform Act 2002, ss 14, 16, 35

14.–(1)   A commonhold community statement must make provision regulating the use of commonhold units.

(2)   A commonhold community statement must make provision imposing duties in respect of the insurance, repair and maintenance of each commonhold unit.

(3)   A duty under subsection (2) may be imposed on the commonhold association or the unit-holder.

16.–(1)   A right or duty conferred or imposed—
    (a)   by a commonhold community statement, or
    (b)   in accordance with section 20,
shall affect a new unit-holder in the same way as it affected the former unit-holder.

(2)   A former unit-holder shall not incur a liability or acquire a right—
    (a)   under or by virtue of the commonhold community statement, or
    (b)   by virtue of anything done in accordance with section 20.

35.–(1)   The directors of a commonhold association shall exercise their powers so as to permit or facilitate so far as possible—
    (a)   the exercise by each unit-holder of his rights, and
    (b)   the enjoyment by each unit-holder of the freehold estate in his unit.

(2)   The directors of a commonhold association shall, in particular, use any right, power or procedure conferred or created by virtue of section 37 for the purpose of preventing, remedying or curtailing a failure on the part of a unit-holder to comply with a requirement or duty imposed on him by virtue of the commonhold community statement or a provision of this Part.

(3)   But in respect of a particular failure on the part of a unit-holder (the 'defaulter') the directors of a commonhold association—
    (a)   need not take action if they reasonably think that inaction is in the best interests of establishing or maintaining harmonious relationships between all the unit-holders, and that it will not cause any unit-holder (other than the defaulter) significant loss or significant disadvantage, and
    (b)   shall have regard to the desirability of using arbitration, mediation or conciliation procedures (including referral under a scheme approved under section 42) instead of legal proceedings wherever possible.

Comment

(1) Why is provision for the duties in s 14(2) mandatory? What might be a sensible allocation of responsibility as between unit-holders and CA?

(2) Section 16 provides authority for the crucial principle that purchasers of units are bound by obligations, whether restrictive or positive. Enforcement is dealt with by the CCS, para 4.11 (Commonhold Regulations 2004, Sched 3). Enforcement by other unit-holders is permitted, though subject to provisions designed to encourage dispute resolution and involvement by the CA.

(3) The management role of the CA is emphasised by s 35. Is it likely to avoid strained relationships between individual unit-holders and CA?

A rather different element concerns the freedom of the unit-holder to deal with the unit: is it more restricted than a normal freehold?

Extract 17.4.2

Commonhold and Leasehold Reform Act 2002, ss 15, 17–18, 20–22

15.—(1) In this Part a reference to the transfer of a commonhold unit is a reference to the transfer of a unit-holder's freehold estate in a unit to another person—
    (a) whether or not for consideration,
    (b) whether or not subject to any reservation or other terms, and
    (c) whether or not by operation of law.
(2) A commonhold community statement may not prevent or restrict the transfer of a commonhold unit.
. . .

17.—(1) It shall not be possible to create a term of years absolute in a residential commonhold unit unless the term satisfies prescribed conditions.
(2) The conditions may relate to—
    (a) length;
    (b) the circumstances in which the term is granted;
    (c) any other matter.
. . .

18.—An instrument or agreement which creates a term of years absolute in a commonhold unit which is not residential (within the meaning of section 17) shall have effect subject to any provision of the commonhold community statement.

20.—(1) A commonhold community statement may not prevent or restrict the creation, grant or transfer by a unit-holder of—
    (a) an interest in the whole or part of his unit, or
    (b) a charge over his unit.
(2) Subsection (1) is subject to sections 17 to 19 (which impose restrictions about leases).
(3) It shall not be possible to create an interest of a prescribed kind in a commonhold unit unless the commonhold association—
    (a) is a party to the creation of the interest, or
    (b) consents in writing to the creation of the interest.
(4) A commonhold association may act as described in subsection (3)(a) or (b) only if—
    (a) the association passes a resolution to take the action, and
    (b) at least 75% of those who vote on the resolution vote in favour.
(6) In this section 'interest' does not include—
    (a) a charge, or
    (b) an interest which arises by virtue of a charge.

21.—(1) It shall not be possible to create an interest in part only of a commonhold unit.
(2) But subsection (1) shall not prevent—
    (a) the creation of a term of years absolute in part only of a residential commonhold unit where the term satisfies prescribed conditions,
    (b) the creation of a term of years absolute in part only of a non-residential commonhold unit, or

(c) the transfer of the freehold estate in part only of a commonhold unit where the commonhold association consents in writing to the transfer.

(9) Where the freehold interest in part only of a commonhold unit is transferred, the part transferred—

(a) becomes a new commonhold unit by virtue of this subsection, or

. . .

22.—(1) It shall not be possible to create a charge over part only of an interest in a commonhold unit.

Comment

(1) The inability to limit transfers represents a contrast to the position in most leases. Are there circumstances in which this might be thought a disadvantage of commonholds?

(2) Why are there limits on the power to lease residential units? Leases up to seven years are permitted: Commonhold Regulations 2004, reg 11.

(3) For other interests (apart from charges), the individual CCS must be consulted (no limits are included in the Commonhold Regulations 2004).

(4) Why are there special rules relating to part-units? Do they strike the right balance?

(5) Considering these provisions as a whole, do they provide an unduly restrictive control over units? Should commonhold be treated as a new form of tenure, rather than an application of freehold?

5. The use of commonhold

Extract 17.5.1

Law Commission CP 186: Easements, Covenants and Profits à Prendre (footnotes omitted)

11.4 Since the Commonhold and Leasehold Reform Act 2002 and the commonhold regulations came into force, there has been a low level of take up. As at 20 February 2008 only 14 commonholds had been registered. We understand that the Ministry of Justice considers this to be disappointing and that it will be consulting on ways to improve the commonhold legislation and to promote the take up of commonhold in due course.

Comment

(1) Why has the take-up of commonhold (which came into effect in 2004) been so slow? Does it indicate fundamental flaws in the scheme?

(2) In 2006, it had been announced that commonhold would be used for a very large development.[5]

---

[5] Driscoll (2006) 168 PLJ 3; Baker (2006) 10 L&T Rev 70.

Further reading

Clarke, D [2002] Conv 349: The enactment of commonhold: problems, principles and perspectives.

Roberts, N [2002] Conv 341: Commonhold: a new property term – but no property in a term?

Smith, P F [2004] Conv 194: The purity of commonholds.

van der Merwe, C G and Smith, P (2005) 'Commonhold – a critical appraisal', in *Modern Studies in Property Law*, Vol 3, ed. E. Cooke, Chapter 11.

Part IV
Other interests in land

18

Licences

Licences pose very different problems than other rights and interests covered by this book. Most interests in land can be defined with precision, as a result of decisions spanning many years. Licences, on the other hand, cannot be so clearly defined. The essential point is that they constitute a residual category. Permissions to do acts in relation to land constitute licences in so far as they do *not* amount to estates (freehold or leasehold) or interests such as easements. That is not to say that every arrangement relating to land constitutes a potential licence. Exceptions are readily found, for example, in security interests such as mortgages and in covenants obliging the covenantor to act, or desist from acting.

Even more troublesome is the fundamental question whether licences deserve any place at all in a book on property law. The traditional view, still persuasive, is that licences amount to no more than personal rights between the licensor and licensee which do not affect purchasers. The following dictum of Vaughan CJ[1] is frequently cited: 'A dispensation or license properly passeth no interest, nor alters or transfers property in any thing, but only makes an action lawful, which without it had been unlawful.' If this still represents the law, then arguably property law should be no more concerned about licences than about any other personal contract which relates to land. However, since the mid-twentieth century there has been a struggle between this traditional view and new developments which have sought to accord proprietary status to at least some licences.

It has been observed that licences encompass a broad range of rights. Some are very close to normal proprietary interests. Indeed, many of the cases concern rights which would be interests if only the appropriate formalities (deed or writing) had been employed. This is especially significant for estoppel licences. Other licences may be to do acts which would otherwise constitute a trespass or nuisance and often appear to be further away from traditional proprietary categories. However, the cases do not generally distinguish between the substance of the rights claimed as licences. Instead, they concentrate upon the different ways in which the law recognises the licence: contract, estoppel, constructive trust. At some stage, thought needs to be given to the question whether we should, for example, distinguish licences to reside on land from other licences. It might be argued that residential licences are more likely to be informally created by those who are unaware of proprietary categories and formalities rules. They are also of especial importance to the parties, the right to respect for a home being recognised as a basic human right.[2] Is this a promising avenue for development?

The weakest form of licence is the bare licence: a bare permission to exercise the licence. Here, the law is very much as stated by Vaughan CJ in 1673. At the other end of the spectrum,

---

[1] *Thomas v Sorrell* (1673) Vaugh 330 at p 351 (124 ER 1098 at p 1109).
[2] European Convention on Human Rights, Art 8.

a licence may be attached to a conventional property interest. Thus a right to fish (a proprietary interest: a profit) requires a licence to enter the relevant land in order to fish. Here the licence partakes of the nature of the property interest. As will be seen, the precise limits of this apparently obvious principle are highly contentious. Other licences will be created by contract. The willingness of the courts to enforce such contracts has led to arguments that these licences could be proprietary. Some licences (including bare licences) may be relied upon by the licensee in such a way as to give rise to an estoppel. Such estoppels may well bind purchasers and provide one of the strongest arguments for proprietary status. Unconscionable conduct on the part of purchasers may give rise to a constructive trust and this forms another area for analysis. We will now turn to these forms of recognition of licences, though no more will be said about bare licences.

1. Forms of licences

A. Licences coupled with an interest

The basic idea that such licences bind purchasers in the same manner as the proprietary interest to which it is coupled (such as a profit) is uncontroversial. Somewhat more difficult, but convenient and well supported by authority,[3] is the proposition that an interest in a chattel on the land suffices.

Extract 18.1.1

Hurst v *Picture Theatres Ltd* [1915] 1 KB 1

The plaintiff, who had bought a ticket, had been ejected from a cinema. In order to maintain an action for trespass, he had to show a right to remain on the premises. The defendant cinema owner claimed a right to remove ticket holders.

BUCKLEY LJ: . . . The proposition is based upon the well-known decision in *Wood* v *Leadbitter*.[i] Let me at the outset say what *Wood* v *Leadbitter* seems to me to have decided. It affirmed that a mere licence, whether or not it be under seal, by which I mean a licence not coupled with an interest or a grant whether it be under seal or not, is revocable. It affirmed also that if there be a licence coupled with an interest or coupled with a grant, it is not, or at any rate in general is not, revocable. For those two propositions, I read these two sentences from the case of *Wood* v *Leadbitter*.[ii] 'A mere licence is revocable; but that which is called a licence is often something more than a licence; it often comprises or is connected with a grant, and then the party who has given it cannot in general revoke it, so as to defeat his grant, to which it was incident. It may further be observed, that a licence under seal (provided it be a mere licence) is as revocable as a licence by parol; and, on the other hand, a licence by parol, coupled with a grant, is as irrevocable as a licence by deed, provided only that the grant is of a nature capable of being made by parol.' Those are propositions with which, as it seems to me, no one quarrels or can quarrel. *Wood* v *Leadbitter* rested, I think, upon one of two grounds – I will indicate them both – but I think it was the second of those which I am going to mention. The first ground is that the man who bought his ticket for the race meeting had not obtained any grant of the right to come during the currency of the meeting to see any particular spectacle from its commencement to its termination. If that were the ground, it would, I think, be erroneous. I conceive he had the

---

[3] *James Jones & Sons Ltd* v *Earl of Tankerville* [1909] 2 Ch 440.

right to see what was to be seen during the days covered by his ticket. But I do not think that was the ground on which the Court decided it. They decided it upon the ground, which will be found at p 842 and onwards, that no incorporeal inheritance affecting land can be created or transferred otherwise than by deed, a proposition which was discussed with some elaboration in the course of the judgment. What Alderson B was saying there was: this man has got no deed; he has got nothing under seal; he has therefore not got a grant; he cannot in this Court be heard to say he is a grantee, and because he is not a grantee he is a mere licensee, and being a mere licensee (whether it is under seal or not under seal does not make any difference) the licence is revocable.

Let me for a moment discuss this present case upon the footing that *Wood v Leadbitter* stands as good law at this date. I am going to say presently that to my mind it does not, but suppose it does stand as good law at this date. What is the grant in this case? The plaintiff in the present action paid his money to enjoy the sight of a particular spectacle. He was anxious to go into a picture theatre to see a series of views or pictures during, I suppose, an hour or a couple of hours. That which was granted to him was the right to enjoy looking at a spectacle, to attend a performance from its beginning to its end. That which was called the licence, the right to go upon the premises, was only something granted to him for the purpose of enabling him to have that which had been granted him, namely, the right to see. He could not see the performance unless he went into the building. His right to go into the building was something given to him in order to enable him to have the benefit of that which had been granted to him, namely, the right to hear the opera, or see the theatrical performance, or see the moving pictures as was the case here. So that here there was a licence coupled with a grant. If so, *Wood v Leadbitter* does not stand in the way at all. A licence coupled with a grant is not revocable; *Wood v Leadbitter* affirmed as much.

[i] 13 M&W 838.
[ii] 13 M&W at p 844.

In *Hounslow LBC v Twickenham Garden Developments Ltd*,[4] Megarry J noted that there is some support for the approach taken in *Hurst* and then observed:

> If for this purpose 'interest' is not confined to an interest in land or in chattels on the land, what does it extend to? If a right to attend a creditor's meeting or to see a cinema performance suffices to constitute an interest, can it be said that the right and duty to do works on land fall short of being an interest? I cannot see why it should. Yet if this be so, it is not easy to see any fair stopping place in what amounts to an interest, short of any legitimate reason for being on the land.
>
> [In later summarising the position] I feel great doubt whether the word 'interest' means anything more than an interest in property, though it matters not whether that property is real or personal, or legal or equitable. Today, with contractual licences recognised as being capable of being made irrevocable in their own right, there is no need to torture the word 'interest' into embracing miscellaneous collections of rights.

Comment

(1) Is the licence coupled with an interest analysis properly applied by *Hurst*?

(2) Buckley LJ also relied upon the Judicature Acts, in a passage quoted below.[5] This contract-based analysis, rather than that based on a licence coupled with a grant, has dominated thinking in more recent cases.

[4] [1971] Ch 233, pp 244, 254.
[5] Extract 18.1.4.

B. Contractual licences

Much of the interest in the past half century has been directed towards the question whether contractual licences bind purchasers. However, a logically prior question concerns the extent to which contractual licences can be revoked by the licensor. If the licensor can revoke them, then there can be no question of their binding purchasers. Accordingly, we will need to look at the position between licensor and licensee as well as the position of purchasers.

An initial question, however, is whether there is a contractual licence in the first place. This is largely a matter of contract law, but arrangements regarding the family home have caused particular problems.

Dicta of Lord Denning MR in two cases may be compared.

Extract 18.1.2

Tanner v Tanner [1975] 1 WLR 1346

The defendant, who had recently given birth to twins of which the plaintiff was the father, gave up her flat to move to accommodation provided by the plaintiff.

LORD DENNING MR: . . . It is said that they were only licensees – bare licensees – under a licence revocable at will: and that the plaintiff was entitled in law to turn her and the twins out on a moment's notice . . . She had given up her flat where she was protected by the Rent Acts – at least in regard to rent and it may be in regard also to security of tenure. She had given it up at his instance so as to be able the better to bring up the children. It is impossible to suppose that in that situation she and the babies were bare licensees whom he could turn out at a moment's notice. The plaintiff recognised this when he offered to pay the defendant £4,000 to get her out. What was then their legal position? She herself said in evidence: 'The house was supposed to be ours until the children left school.' It seems to me that enables an inference to be drawn, namely, that in all the circumstances it is to be implied that she had a licence – a contractual licence – to have accommodation in the house for herself and the children so long as they were of school age and the accommodation was reasonably required for her and the children. There was, it is true, no express contract to that effect, but the circumstances are such that the court should imply a contract by the plaintiff – or, if need be, impose the equivalent of a contract by him – whereby they were entitled to have the use of the house as their home until the girls had finished school . . .

Extract 18.1.3

Hardwick v Johnson [1978] 1 WLR 683

A married couple were licensees of the husband's mother. They agreed to make payments which in due course would pay off the mortgage, but their financial situation was such that few payments were in fact made. After the husband left the house, the mother sought possession.

LORD DENNING MR: . . . So we have to consider once more the law about family arrangements. In the well-known case of *Balfour v Balfour* [1919] 2 KB 571, 579, Atkin LJ said that family arrangements made between husband and wife 'are not contracts . . . because the parties did not intend that they should be attended by legal consequences'. Similarly, family arrangements between parent and child are often not contracts which bind them: see *Jones v Padavatton* [1969] 1 WLR 328. Nevertheless these family arrangements do have legal consequences: and, time and time again, the courts are called upon to determine what is the true legal relationship resulting from them . . . The court has to look at all the circumstances and spell out the legal relationship. The court will pronounce in favour of a tenancy or a licence, a loan or a gift, or a trust – according to which of these legal relationships is most fitting in the situation which has arisen: and will find the terms of that relationship according to what reason and justice require . . .

Of all these suggestions, I think the most fitting is a personal licence. The occupation of the house was clearly personal to this young couple. It was a personal privilege creating a licence such as we have often had: see *Errington* v *Errington and Woods* [1952] 1 KB 290. I do not think it could properly be called a contractual licence because it is difficult to say that this family arrangement was a contract. *Balfour* v *Balfour* [1919] 2 KB 571 is authority for saying there was no contract. I should have thought it was more in the nature of an equitable licence of which the court has to spell out the terms.

Comment

(1) Roskill and Browne LJJ preferred to rely on a contractual licence in *Hardwick*, though all the judges agreed that the mother's claim failed.

(2) Which approach in these cases best fits contractual principles?

(3) In *Hardwick*, Lord Denning MR relies upon a 'personal licence'. What is this? How could the licensor be prevented from revoking it?

(i) Licensor and licensee

We can now turn to the question whether a contractual licence can be revoked by the licensor.

Extract 18.1.4

Hurst v *Picture Theatres Ltd* [1915] 1 KB 1

BUCKLEY LJ: . . . So far I have been treating it as if *Wood* v *Leadbitter* were law as now administered in every Court. Let us see how that matter stands. *Wood* v *Leadbitter* was a case decided in a Court of law before the Judicature Act; it was a case to be decided, therefore, simply upon the principles which are applicable in a Court of law as distinguished from a Court of Equity.

. . .

The position of matters now is that the Court is bound under the Judicature Act to give effect to equitable doctrines. The question we have to consider is whether, having regard to equitable considerations, *Wood* v *Leadbitter* is now law, meaning that *Wood* v *Leadbitter* is a decision which can be applied in its integrity in a Court which is bound to give effect to equitable considerations. In my opinion, it is not . . .

There is another way in which the matter may be put. If there be a licence with an agreement not to revoke the licence, that, if given for value, is an enforceable right. If the facts here are, as I think they are, that the licence was a licence to enter the building and see the spectacle from its commencement until its termination, then there was included in that contract a contract not to revoke the licence until the play had run to its termination. It was then a breach of contract to revoke the obligation not to revoke the licence, and for that the decision in *Kerrison* v *Smith*[i] is an authority.

PHILLIMORE LJ (dissenting): [After referring to the Judicature Act:] In other words, the man has the estate which equity thinks he ought to have. That has no bearing on the question if there is no estate, and no interest in land given by the document relied on. Assume, therefore, that there was a contract, and assume that the purported revocation was a breach of the contract, and assume that of which I am not certain, that equity would give specific performance of such a contract, still specific performance does not necessarily put the man before he has got specific performance in the legal possession which he gets after he has got specific performance. It does in the case of interests in land because the interest in land now is the interest which he had in equity before. But it does not necessarily do so with regard to interests arising by reason of a contract . . . Collins J in *Kerrison* v *Smith* puts it in this way: 'It was conceded that the grantor has a right to revoke a licence, but the point set up by the plaintiff, that there was a contract, for the breach of which the plaintiff was entitled to recover damages, was never properly dealt with. There appears to be no case in which the point has been specifically raised and decided, as to whether there is a right to maintain an action for breach of contract, if a licence is revoked, although there is a right to revoke the licence, but on principle it seems to me that the two rights are compatible with one another.' That is to say the licence can be revoked, in which case the man becomes a trespasser if he stays on, but nevertheless there may be a contract for which the man may recover damages.

[i] [1897] 2 QB 445.

Comment

As between licensor and licensee, should it be relevant whether or not the contract is for an interest in land? How potent is the maxim that equity treats as done what ought to be done?

Extract 18.1.5

Winter Garden Theatre (London) Ltd v *Millenium Productions Ltd*
[1946] 1 All ER 678

LORD GREENE MR: . . . The next question which I must mention is this. The respondents have purported to determine the licence. If I have correctly construed the contract their doing so was a breach of contract. It may well be that, in the old days, that would only have given rise to a right to sue for damages. The licence would have stood revoked, but after the expiration of what was the appropriate period of grace the licensees would have been trespassers and could have been expelled, and their right would have been to sue for damages for breach of contract, as was said in *Kerrison* v *Smith*.[i] But the matter requires to be considered further, because the power of equity to grant an injunction to restrain a breach of contract is, of course, a power exercisable in any court. The general rule is that, before equity will grant such an injunction, there must be, on the construction of the contract, a negative clause express or implied. In the present case it seems to me that the grant of an option which, if I am right, is an irrevocable option, must imply a negative undertaking by the licensor not to revoke it. That being so, in my opinion, such a contract could be enforced in equity by an injunction. Then the question would arise, at what time can equity interfere? If the licensor were threatening to revoke, equity, I apprehend, would grant an injunction to restrain him from carrying out that threat. But supposing he has in fact purported to revoke, is equity then to say: 'We are now powerless. We cannot stop you from doing anything to carry into effect your wrongful revocation?' I apprehend not. I apprehend equity would say: 'You have revoked and the licensee had no opportunity of stopping you doing so by an injunction; but what the court of equity can do is to prevent you from carrying that revocation into effect and restrain you from doing anything under it.' In the present case, nothing has been done. The appellants are still there. I can see no reason at all why, on general principles, equity should not interfere to restrain the licensors from acting upon the purported revocation, that revocation being, as I consider, a breach of contract.

[i] [1897] 2 QB 445; 30 Digest 512, *1675*; 66 LJQB 762; 77 LT 344.

Comment

(1) The decision was reversed on its facts by the House of Lords,[6] but Viscount Simon LC approved the result of *Hurst* on contractual grounds and Lord Uthwatt agreed with Lord Greene MR's analysis.

(2) Why need one refer to a negative undertaking not to revoke? Is this anything more than an undertaking not to break the contract?

Extract 18.1.6

Hounslow LBC v *Twickenham Garden Developments Ltd* [1971] Ch 233

The plaintiff licensor sought to evict the defendant building contractor; there was a dispute as to whether the defendant was in breach of the building contract.

MEGARRY J: . . . Quite apart, then, from the question whether the contractor has a licence coupled with an interest, there is the question whether the contractor has a contractual licence which either expressly or by implication is subject to a negative obligation by the borough not to revoke it. If this is so, then, on the law laid down by the Court of Appeal, equity would interfere to prevent the borough from revoking the licence or, if it had been revoked, from acting on the revocation. A fortiori, equity would refuse to grant the borough an injunction to enforce the revocation.

Now in this case the contract is one for the execution of specified works on the site during a specified period which is still running. The contract confers on each party specified rights on specified events to determine the employment of the contractor under the contract. In those circumstances, I think that there must be at least an implied negative obligation of the borough not to revoke any licence (otherwise than in accordance with the contract) while the period is still running, just as in *Hurst* v *Picture Theatres Ltd* [1915] 1 KB 1 there was an implied negative obligation not to revoke the licence until the performance had concluded: see at pp 10, 13, per Buckley and Kennedy LJJ.

. . . The case of building operations is really a fortiori a cinema performance, because it must be obvious to all from the outset that far more is involved in the building contractor moving his equipment on to a site, hiring his labour, making his sub-contracts and so on, and then in putting a stop to all operations, than is involved in a member of a cinema audience going in, sitting down and then getting up and leaving . . .

There is a further consideration of some importance. This is not a case in which the issue is merely one of damages, as in *Wood* v *Leadbitter*, *Hurst* v *Picture Theatres Ltd* or *Cowell* v *Rosehill Racecourse Co Ltd* [(1937) 56 CLR 605]. The borough is seeking equitable relief, namely, an injunction to expel what on one view may be a trespasser and on another view may be someone with a contractual right to remain; and on the latter view the borough is asking the court to assist it in breaking its contract. I do not think that the court will do this.

Comment

Should it make any difference whether it is the licensor or licensee who is seeking a remedy?

Extract 18.1.7

Evershed (1954) 70 LQR 326 at pp 333, 337–338

Now *Hurst's* case was the case of a licence to see a single performance of a film. And even the longest modern film would not have given Hurst time to get an injunction from a Chancery judge

---

[6] [1948] AC 173.

and return with his order to the cinema before the end of the showing. In other words, whatever the theory, equity in practice could not intervene in time. It was that fact which influenced so strongly Lord Justice Phillimore in his dissenting judgment; for he thought that, until equity had in some way intervened, the legal right remained unaffected, and therefore, that the licence was effectively revoked. You will find in the *Winter Garden* case a remarkable passage in the judgment in the Court of Appeal of Lord Greene, my distinguished predecessor, a passage to which I will refer later. He was of the opinion that *Hurst's* case was rightly decided because the theoretical availability of the equitable remedy sufficed to render the revocation of the licence 'ineffective' and so to make good Hurst's claim.

[After considering the judgments of the High Court of Australia in *Cowell* v *Rosehill Racecourse Co Ltd* (1937) 56 CLR 605:] Now let me try to put to you as briefly as I can the argument of the majority of the court [in *Cowell*] for rejecting the plaintiff's claim, and for rejecting also the validity of the English decision in *Hurst's* case.

In the first place it was said – and forcibly said – that the view of the majority in our Court of Appeal was founded on the view that the man who took a ticket to attend a race meeting – or a performance at the cinema – thereby acquired some interest in the land on which the races were held or the film exhibited. This (said the Australian judges) was a heresy. Is it suggested (said Sir John Latham CJ) that, if 50,000 people pay for tickets to watch a football match, there are created 50,000 interests in land – or, alternatively, 50,000 easements? And if it be the latter, then the easements would be of a novel and peculiar kind since, though there would be in every case a servient tenement, there would be a dominant tenement in none. In other words, the easements would be easements in gross of a kind hitherto unknown to the law. On similar lines, the Australian judges were able effectively to attack so much of the judgments of the majority in the Court of Appeal (Buckley and Kennedy LJJ) as had appeared to rest on the point made of the absence of a seal in *Wood's* case; for (as they observed) the absence of a seal was only relevant (if at all) in relation to the question of proprietary interests. A licence of this kind, if effectively revocable, is none the less revocable if given under seal. I am bound to say, for my part, that I think much of the language of the majority of judges in *Hurst's* case in the Court of Appeal is open to the criticism made against them, the criticism that they thought too much in terms of a proprietary interest of some kind emerging from the grant of licence. But I think also that that was not the end of the matter. Nor, indeed, did the Australian judges. For they went on to consider whether, apart from the emergence of any such proprietary right, there was still to be discerned a sufficient equity to give Cowell his remedy. They said not. They accepted the view that it did not matter that a plaintiff in the situation of Cowell or Hurst would not in the circumstances obviously be able to go to a court of equity and get an injunction in time to make his contractual right practically effective. Further, they accepted the view that, if equity would have intervened (given time) and would have granted an 'unconditional' injunction, then the effect would have been to prevent the defendants in equity from setting up the defence of an 'effectively' revoked licence. That much is common ground. But what they said was that, even if there had been time, equity could not and would not grant an injunction – or at least an injunction, without conditions, to restrain a breach of the contractual promise in the licence. The right to go upon the racecourse must (they said) have in any case been hedged round by a complex series of conditions and rules (for example, so as to enable the licensor to eject, in case of disturbances, sudden dangers, and the like) apart from the obviously implied obligation of the licensee not to misbehave himself. And they also denied the existence of any clear implication of a negative kind, on the licensor's part, not to revoke the licence, so long as the licensee did properly behave himself – or not to revoke it save on the happening of some events capable (though implicit) of plain statement. Finally, they said, in answer to the contention that the defendants were pleading their own wrongful act, that there was no precedent for such a contention where the alleged wrongful act was the assertion of the unquestioned legal right of revocation . . .

Comment

(1) Should it be relevant that no equitable remedy had been obtained before the eviction of the licensee in *Hurst*?

(2) Evershed observes that the High Court of Australia viewed *Hurst* 'as a clear legal mis-apprehension and as a sentimental heresy'. Can this criticism be rebutted?

(3) The Australian view is that equity would not normally give a remedy to contractual licensees, at least as regards entertainment contracts. Is this a convincing viewpoint?

(4) What would the Australian view be towards building contracts?[7] Would the High Court of Australia have approved of the decision in *Hounslow*?

(ii) Purchaser and licensee

The earlier twentieth-century cases provide Court of Appeal and House of Lords authority for the proposition that licences do not bind purchasers.[8] However, these cases pre-dated *Winter Garden Theatre* and the modern recognition that contractual licences can be enforced in equity against the licensor.

Extract 18.1.8

Errington v *Errington* [1952] 1 KB 290

The licensor permitted his son and daughter-in-law to live in a house, paying the mortgage, with a promise that the house would be theirs when the mortgage was paid off.

DENNING LJ: . . . Law and equity have been fused for nearly 80 years, and since 1948 it has been clear that, as a result of the fusion, a licensor will not be permitted to eject a licensee in breach of a contract to allow him to remain: see *Winter Garden Theatre, London* v *Millenium Productions Ltd*,[i] per Lord Greene, and in the House of Lords per Lord Simon; nor in breach of a promise on which the licensee has acted, even though he gave no value for it: see *Foster* v *Robinson*,[ii] where Sir Raymond Evershed MR said that as a result of the oral arrangement to let the man stay, he was entitled as licensee to occupy the premises without any payment of rent for the rest of his days. This infusion of equity means that contractual licences now have a force and validity of their own and cannot be revoked in breach of the contract. Neither the licensor nor anyone who claims through him can disregard the contract except a purchaser for value without notice.

[i] [1946] 1 All ER 678, 680; [1948] AC 173, 191.
[ii] [1951] 1 KB 149, 156.

Extract 18.1.9

National Provincial Bank Ltd v *Ainsworth* [1965] AC 1175

The case involved a claim by a deserted wife to remain in occupation (the deserted wife's equity). Such a claim was recognised to be good as against the husband, but could it bind purchasers?

LORD WILBERFORCE: . . . Early in the development of the doctrine it was perceived that the deserted wife's right could not be classified as an equitable interest in land (see *Thompson* v

---

[7] See *Graham H Roberts Pty Ltd* v *Maurbeth Investments Pty Ltd* [1974] 1 NSWLR 93.
[8] *Clore* v *Theatrical Properties Ltd* [1936] 3 All ER 483; *King* v *David Allen & Sons, Billposting, Ltd* [1916] 2 AC 54.

Earthy[i] *per* Roxburgh J). This appears to me to have been inevitable and correct, and it should have led to the conclusion that the wife's right was not binding on third parties. But, instead, it was sought to describe it as an 'equity' which as such could be binding on assignees of the husband. In the authorities, the word is used in several senses and for several purposes. Sometimes it is used as referring merely to the exercise of an equitable remedy, such as a remedy by injunction: the thought seems to have been that since the courts will interfere by injunction to prevent interference with or departure from a right, that gives to the proprietor of the right something which is capable of binding not only the other party but his assignees, or successors, provided of course that they have notice of the right. In this form the argument is clearly fallacious. The fact that a contractual right can be specifically performed, or its breach prevented by injunction, does not mean that the right is any the less of a personal character or that a purchaser with notice is bound by it: what is relevant is the nature of the right, not the remedy which exists for its enforcement. Before your Lordships the argument was not put in this form. It was said that the wife's right was an equitable claim, binding on the husband's conscience, and that consistently with what has been decided in relation to such matters as restrictive covenants, it should be held to be binding on the conscience of a 'purchaser' with notice . . .

In my opinion, this line of argument is but a revival of a fallacy that, because an obligation binds a man's conscience, it therefore becomes binding on the consciences of those who take from him with notice of the obligation. But this has been decisively rejected, not only in relation to covenants (enforceable by specific performance) entered into by the predecessor of the purchaser whom it is sought to bind (*London & South Western Railway Co* v *Gomm*[ii] – I refer to the judgment of Lindley LJ) but in the law of restrictive covenants to which an appeal by way of analogy was made.

[i] [1951] 2 KB 596.
[ii] (1882) 20 Ch D 562, 587, CA.

Comment

(1) The link between the deserted wife's equity and contractual licences existed because earlier deserted wife's equity cases had relied upon *Errington*. Although the House of Lords expressly did not reject *Errington*, that case plainly cannot be justified on the reasoning that an equitable remedy is available.

(2) Does Denning LJ in *Errington* offer any explanation for why the purchaser was bound? The 'purchaser' was the successor in title under the licensor's will. Should this be relevant?

(3) There was little hard authority after *Errington*, though there were some dicta (mainly of Lord Denning MR!) and assumptions that purchasers were bound.

Extract 18.1.10

Ashburn Anstalt v *Arnold* **[1989] Ch 1**

FOX LJ: . . . It is Arnold & Co's case that even if the 1973 agreement created no tenancy after 28 February 1973, so that its occupancy thereafter is that of a contractual licensee only, its rights are nevertheless binding upon a purchaser for value with notice of the licence. Lord Templeman in *Street* v *Mountford* [1985] AC 809, 814 said:

> 'A licence in connection with land while entitling the licensee to use the land for the purposes authorised by the licence does not create an estate in the land.'

That was not challenged on behalf of Arnold & Co, but it was said that a contractual licence does give rise to an interest (as opposed to an estate) in the land; we must assume for this purpose that the rights are of sufficiently certain duration to be capable of subsisting as an interest in land. If they are not, the point does not arise. The question then is whether Arnold & Co's proposition is correct in law. Until comparatively recently it would, we think, have been rejected. As long ago as 1674, in *Thomas* v *Sorrell* (1674) Vaugh 330, 351, Vaughan CJ said:

'A dispensation or licence properly passeth no interest, nor alters or transfers property in any thing, but only makes an action lawful, which without it had been unlawful.'

A number of cases in this century support that view.

. . .

The next case is *King* v *David Allen and Sons (Billposting) Ltd* [1916] 2 AC 54 . . . Earl Loreburn said, at p 62:

'. . . But we must look at the document itself, and it seems to me that it does not create any interest in the land at all; it merely amounts to a promise on the part of Mr King that he would allow the other party to the contract to use the wall for advertising purposes, and there was an implied undertaking that he would not disable himself from carrying out his contract.'

. . .

We are unable to reconcile the approach of the House of Lords in *King* v *David Allen* with the submission, on behalf of Arnold & Co, that a mere contractual licence is an interest in land binding on a purchaser with notice. The two front of house rights cases to which we have referred are to the same effect.

The next case of consequence is *Clore* v *Theatrical Properties Ltd* [1936] 3 All ER 483, which was again concerned with front of house rights. The agreement provided:

'the lessor does hereby demise and grant unto the lessee the free and exclusive use of all the refreshment rooms . . . of the theatre . . . for the purpose only of the supply to and accommodation of the visitors to the theatre and for no other purpose . . .'

The definition clause provided that the terms 'lessor' and 'lessee' should include their executors, administrators and assigns. The assignee of the lessor sought to prevent an assignee of the lessee from exercising any of the rights under the agreement. It was held that the agreement was not a lease but a licence, and was not binding upon a third party. The court, as we read the judgments, regarded the case as falling within the examples of *Daly* v *Edwardes*, 83 LT 548 and *Frank Warr & Co Ltd* v *London County Council* [1904] 1 KB 713. The licensee had sought to rely upon *De Mattos* v *Gibson* (1859) 4 De G&J 276 and *Lord Strathcona Steamship Co Ltd* v *Dominion Coal Co Ltd* [1926] AC 108. That was not accepted. Lord Wright MR regarded these authorities as confined to charterparties and said, at p 491: 'I do not think that a personal covenant as in the present case can be binding on a third party with notice . . .'

Down to this point we do not think that there is any serious doubt as to the law. A mere contractual licence to occupy land is not binding on a purchaser of the land even though he has notice of the licence.

We come now to a case which is of central importance on the present issue. That is *Errington* v *Errington and Woods* [1952] 1 KB 290 . . .

It is not in doubt that the actual decision was correct. It could be justified on one of three grounds. (i) There was a contract to convey the house on completion of the payments giving rise to an equitable interest in the form of an estate contract which would be binding on the widow: see *Megarry & Wade, The Law of Real Property*, 5th ed (1984), p 806. The widow was not a purchaser for value. (ii) The daughter-in-law had changed her position in reliance upon a representation binding on the widow as a privy of the representor: see *Spencer Bower and Turner, Estoppel by Representation*, 3rd ed (1977), p 123. (iii) The payment of the instalments by the son or the daughter-in-law gave rise to direct proprietary interests by way of constructive trust, though it is true that, until *Gissing* v *Gissing* [1971] AC 886, the law relating to constructive trusts in this field was not much considered.

Accordingly, it does not appear to have been necessary, in order to produce a just result, to have accepted the broad principle stated, at p 299, in the passage which we have quoted, that 'Neither the licensor nor anyone who claims through him can disregard the contract except a purchaser for value without notice.' That statement itself is not supported by any citation of authority, and indeed we do not think it could have been supported on the authorities. None of the cases prior to *Errington* v *Errington and Woods* to which we have referred, except *Thomas* v *Sorrell*, Vaugh 330, is mentioned in the judgments and it does not appear that any was cited.

The decision of the House of Lords in *Winter Gardens Theatre (London) Ltd* v *Millennium Productions Ltd* [1948] AC 173 does not advance the matter. It was the first occasion on which a licensee was held entitled to an injunction restraining the licensor from revoking a licence in breach of contract. The case was concerned with contract only. In our view it is not an authority for the proposition that a contractual licence creates an interest in land capable of binding third parties.

[Other cases, including *Ainsworth*, are considered.]

These cases were the subject of consideration by Goff J in *In re Solomon, A Bankrupt, Ex parte Trustees of the Property of the Bankrupt* v *Solomon* [1967] Ch 573. Goff J concluded that the wife in that case was not a contractual licensee, and accordingly he did not have to decide which authority he should follow. But he expressed a preference for the reasoning of Russell LJ in the *Hastings Car Mart* case [1964] Ch 665 and was hesitant to recognise the existence of a new species of equitable right.

It is convenient to pause at this point because, although there are later cases in what may be regarded as this series, there is none in which a contractual licence is held to bind a third party in the absence of a finding that the third party took the land as a constructive trustee. It is therefore appropriate to review how the law stands, or ought to stand, in the absence of such a finding.

Young v *Bristol Aeroplane Co Ltd* [1944] KB 718 establishes the familiar rule that this court is bound to follow its own decisions save that (relevantly to this case) it is entitled and bound to decide which of two conflicting decisions of its own it will follow, and it is bound to refuse to follow a decision of its own which, though not expressly overruled, cannot in its opinion stand with a decision of the House of Lords.

It must, we think, be very doubtful whether this court's decision in *Errington* v *Errington and Woods* [1952] 1 KB 290 is consistent with its earlier decisions in *Daly* v *Edwardes*, 83 LT 548; *Frank Warr & Co* v *London County Council* [1904] 1 KB 713 and *Clore* v *Theatrical Properties Ltd* [1936] 3 All ER 483. That decision cannot be said to be in conflict with any later decision of the House of Lords, because the House expressly left the effect of a contractual licence open in the *Hastings Car Mart* case [*Ainsworth*]. But there must be very real doubts whether *Errington* can be reconciled with the earlier decisions of the House of Lords in *Edwardes* v *Barrington*, 85 LT 650, and *King* v *David Allen and Sons (Billposting) Ltd* [1916] 2 AC 54. It would seem that we must follow those cases or choose between the two lines of authority. It is not, however, necessary to consider those alternative courses in detail, since in our judgment the House of Lords cases, whether or not as a matter of strict precedent they conclude this question, state the correct principle which we should follow.

Our reasons for reaching this conclusion are based upon essentially the same reasons as those given by Russell LJ in the *Hastings Car Mart* case [1964] Ch 665, 697 and by Professor Wade in the article, 'Licences and Third Parties' (1952) 68 LQR 337, to which Russell LJ refers. Before *Errington* the law appears to have been clear and well understood. It rested on an important and intelligible distinction between contractual obligations which gave rise to no estate or interest in the land and proprietary rights which, by definition, did. The far-reaching statement of principle in *Errington* was not supported by authority, not necessary for the decision of the case and *per incuriam* in the sense that it was made without reference to authorities which, if they would not have compelled, would surely have persuaded the court to adopt a different ratio. Of course, the law must be free to develop. But as a response to problems which had arisen, the *Errington* rule (without more) was neither practically necessary nor theoretically convincing. By contrast, the finding on appropriate facts of a constructive trust may well be regarded as a beneficial adaptation of old rules to new situations.

Comment

(1) The case was actually decided on the basis that there was a lease; that aspect of the case was overruled by *Prudential Assurance Co Ltd v London Residuary Body*.[9] Does this affect the authority of *Ashburn Anstalt* regarding licences?

(2) Fox LJ does not consider the dicta in earlier cases (not all of which were cited) which are supportive of *Errington*. Should these have affected his decision? Does their omission materially weaken the authority of his judgment?

(3) Subsequent cases have adopted the *Ashburn Anstalt* analysis of licences.[10]

(4) Could the Land Registration Act 2002 (hereafter LRA), s 116 (Extract 1.3.4 above) affect this analysis?

(5) The use of constructive trusts and estoppel is considered below.

It is sometimes said[11] that the proviso to s 4(1) of the Law of Property Act 1925 precludes the development of new equitable interests such as contractual licences. It reads:

> Provided that, after the commencement of this Act (and save as hereinafter expressly enacted), an equitable interest in land shall only be capable of being validly created in any case in which an equivalent equitable interest in property real or personal could have been validly created before such commencement.

Are there other ways in which this proviso can be interpreted?

C. Constructive trusts

Any form of licence may be protected by a constructive trust, but it has most often been discussed and applied in the context of contractual licences.

Extract 18.1.11

Binions v Evans [1972] Ch 359

The defendant had a contractual licence from her deceased husband's former employers. The employers sold the land to the plaintiffs, but subject to the licence and with a reduction in the purchase price.

LORD DENNING MR: . . . Suppose, however, that the defendant did not have an equitable interest at the outset, nevertheless it is quite plain that she obtained one afterwards when the

---

[9] [1992] 2 AC 386.

[10] Cases include *IDC Group Ltd v Clark* [1992] 1 EGLR 187 (Sir Nicolas Browne-Wilkinson V-C at first instance; upheld 65 P&CR 179); *Canadian Imperial Bank of Commerce v Bello* (1991) 64 P&CR 48; *Nationwide Anglia BS v Ahmed & Balakrishnan* (1995) 70 P&CR 381; *Lloyd v Dugdale* [2002] 2 P&CR 167 at [52].

[11] *Hanchett-Stamford v Att-Gen* [2009] Ch 173 at [31]; Briggs [1983] Conv 285 at pp 290–291.

Tredegar Estate sold the cottage. They stipulated with the plaintiffs that they were to take the house 'subject to' the defendant's rights under the agreement. They supplied the plaintiffs with a copy of the contract: and the plaintiffs paid less because of her right to stay there. In these circumstances, this court will impose on the plaintiffs a constructive trust for her benefit: for the simple reason that it would be utterly inequitable for the plaintiffs to turn the defendant out contrary to the stipulation subject to which they took the premises. That seems to me clear from the important decision of *Bannister* v *Bannister* [1948] 2 All ER 133, which was applied by the judge, and which I gladly follow.

This imposing of a constructive trust is entirely in accord with the precepts of equity. As Cardozo J once put it: 'A constructive trust is the formula through which the conscience of equity finds expression', see *Beatty* v *Guggenheim Exploration Co* (1919) 225 NY 380, 386: or, as Lord Diplock put it quite recently in *Gissing* v *Gissing* [1971] AC 886, 905, a constructive trust is created 'whenever the trustee has so conducted himself that it would be inequitable to allow him to deny to the cestui que trust a beneficial interest in the land acquired'.

I know that there are some who have doubted whether a contractual licensee has any protection against a purchaser, even one who takes with full notice. We were referred in this connection to Professor Wade's article Licences and Third Parties in (1952) 68 LQR 337, and to the judgment of Goff J in *In re Solomon, A Bankrupt, Ex parte Trustee of the Property of the Bankrupt* v *Solomon* [1967] Ch 573. None of these doubts can prevail, however, when the situation gives rise to a constructive trust.

Comment

(1) The imposition of these constructive trusts was considered earlier (see Chapter 6).[12] Lord Denning MR (in further dicta in *Binions*) indicated that such constructive trusts would be readily imposed in favour of occupiers. Although *Ashburn Anstalt* approved the decision in *Binions*, the circumstances in which a constructive trust would be appropriate were strictly limited. It will be necessary for the purchaser to promise to respect the licence. In particular, this will not automatically be satisfied by purchasing 'subject to' the licence: these words might well be intended to protect the vendor against complaints by the purchaser.

(2) It had been suggested in some earlier cases that a constructive trust would be imposed upon the licensor, thereby providing a basis for binding purchasers.[13] This was rejected by *Ashburn Anstalt*; promises by purchasers provide the sole route to constructive trusts in the licences context.

(3) It was observed above that constructive trusts have been most commonly encountered where there is a contractual licence, rather than other forms of licences. Is there any explanation for this?

The nature of the constructive trust also requires some thought. Is it a proprietary right which can bind subsequent purchasers?[14] In other words, would a purchaser from the plaintiffs in *Binions* have been bound? One point is clear: a fresh undertaking to respect the licence could give rise to a fresh constructive trust.

---

[12] See pp 179 et seq. For *Ashburn Anstalt*, see Extract 6.2.11.
[13] *DHN Food Distributors Ltd* v *Tower Hamlets LBC* [1976] 1 WLR 852; *Re Sharpe* [1980] 1 WLR 219.
[14] In registered land, the licensee would usually have an overriding interest by virtue of actual occupation.

Extract 18.1.12

Chattey v *Farndale Holdings Inc* (1996) 75 P&CR 298

PWD was held to be subject to a constructive trust. PWD charged the land to BBL, who sold the land to Farndale. Was Farndale subject to a constructive trust?

MORRITT LJ (rejecting the claim): In my view the crucial distinction between [*Lyus* v *Prowsa* [1982] 1 WLR 1044] and this is the finding that the trust was also imposed on the second defendants by the terms of their contract. There is no finding in this case that there is imposed on Farndale a constructive trust similar to that which the judge found to be imposed on PWD.

. . .

In my view these observations [in *Ashburn Anstalt* v *Arnold*] apply as much to the position of the second defendant in *Lyus* v *Prowsa* as to Farndale in this case. The fact that they had notice of the prior contracts or obligations was insufficient to impose an obligation on them and unless there was such an obligation it could not be a fraud on their part to rely on the provisions of the Land Registration Act 1925 as conferring on them an unincumbered title.

Comment

(1) While this appears to be authority that subsequent purchasers are not affected, is it really based upon the protection of Farndale under the land registration provisions? In other words, is the case saying that any constructive trust binding on PWD fails against Farndale because it is neither protected on the register nor an overriding interest?[15] Whether the constructive trust does not bind purchasers or the problem was that it was unprotected, the result either way is that a fresh constructive trust would have to be imposed.

(2) The court approved the analysis of Blackburne J at first instance, who had held that BBL were not bound even though they were equitable chargees and so could not take advantage of failure to protect the claim. Does this presuppose that a fresh constructive trust is always required before a subsequent purchaser can be bound?

(3) One observation in the licences context (*Chattey* was not a licences case) is that it would seem odd for a contractual licence protected by a purchaser's promise (the constructive trust) to bind purchasers when the licensee's promise does not. Can there be constructive trusts which do not bind purchasers?

If constructive trusts giving effect to licences bind purchasers, a question needs to be asked regarding express trusts. Can the licensor and licensee set up an express trust so as to give effect to a licence and argue that the trust binds purchasers? If purchasers are bound in these cases, what impact does this have upon the law's insistence (seen in *Ainsworth* and *Ashburn Anstalt*) on a finite list of proprietary interests? We normally think of beneficial interests under trusts as fitting into normal proprietary categories (estates, easements, etc.), but is this essential? How do purpose trusts fit in?

D. Estoppel licences

Estoppel claims were investigated earlier (see Chapter 7), where it was seen that expectations encouraged or acquiesced in by the owner will give rise to an equity if the claimant

---

[15] On the facts, there was no actual occupation.

relies on them to his or her detriment. The connection with licences can arise in three ways. First, most estoppel claims involve expectations of normal property interests such as the fee simple or an easement. However, mistake or lack of formalities precludes the property interest from existing. Until the court gives a remedy, the claimant can usually have no more than a licence. However, the estoppel protects the proprietary expectation rather than the licence. Indeed, it would be just as effective if the claimant had not entered the land and had never become a licensee (though such facts would be exceptional).

The second and third connections are more relevant to this chapter: the expectation may be as to a licence or, even where the expectation is of a normal property right, the court may order a licence as the remedy. The courts have applied estoppel in both these types of situation, without distinguishing them from other estoppel cases.[16] This is not surprising, but the most interesting question is whether these estoppel licences bind purchasers. There are in fact very few cases involving such estoppel licences and purchasers, but they appear to assume that purchasers are bound in the same way as for other estoppels.[17] This receives particularly interesting support from *Ashburn Anstalt v Arnold*,[18] as it has been seen that the court suggested that *Errington v Errington*[19] could have been decided on estoppel grounds. Yet Lord Scott has recently said[20] that 'The estoppel becomes a "proprietary" estoppel – a sub-species of a "promissory" estoppel – if the right claimed is a proprietary right, usually a right to or over land . . .'. This was not in the context of licences, but might it suggest that estoppel licences are not proprietary?

As recognised by the Law Commission, a distinction must be drawn between cases where the purchase is before the court determines the remedy and those after the award of the remedy.[21] Before the remedy is granted, the discretion as to remedy must be considered. Whether or not a licence is the subject of the expectation, we do not know at the time of purchase whether the court will give a licence or a conventional property interest as a remedy. We have seen that, for registered land, LRA, s 116 ensures that purchasers are bound.[22] McFarlane[23] argues to the contrary and urges that non-proprietary rights (such as licences) should not be capable of binding purchasers even though protected by estoppel. In many ways this is a persuasive argument, but it is difficult to reconcile with most present thinking, with the approach of the Law Commission and with LRA, s 116. Insofar as McFarlane suggests that non-proprietary remedies would not affect purchasers, is it consistent with Lord Scott's recent dicta quoted above? Separately, how are those dicta to be reconciled with s 116?

Once the court has ordered a licence as a remedy, the position seems very different. It then seems more difficult to avoid the question whether that licence binds a purchaser. However, examples of purchasers after remedy (whether a licence or conventional property interest) are very few.

---

[16] *Plimmer v Mayor of Wellington* (1884) 9 App Cas 699; *Inwards v Baker* [1965] 2 QB 29; *Williams v Staite* [1979] Ch 291; *Coombes v Smith* [1986] 1 WLR 808 (claim failed); *Greasley v Cooke* [1980] 1 WLR 1306; *Bostock v Bryant* (1990) 61 P&CR 23 (claim failed); *Matharu v Matharu* (1994) 68 P&CR 93; *Maharaj v Chand* [1986] AC 898.

[17] *Inwards v Baker* [1965] 2 QB 29 (before remedy given); *Williams v Staite* [1979] Ch 291 (after remedy given).

[18] [1989] Ch 1.

[19] [1952] 1 KB 290.

[20] *Cobbe v Yeoman's Row Management Ltd* [2008] 1 WLR 1752 at [15].

[21] Law Com No 254, para 3.35.

[22] Extract 7.3.1 above.

[23] [2003] CLJ 661.

Extract 18.1.13

Maharaj v Chand [1986] AC 898

PRIVY COUNCIL: . . . The present case fairly satisfies the requirements. On Rooney J's findings, at the time of the acquisition of the land and the building of the house the plaintiff represented to the defendant that it would be a permanent home for her and her children. Indeed the representation was that she would be treated as living there as his wife. In reasonable reliance on the representation she acted to her detriment by giving up the flat . . .

In these circumstances it would plainly be inequitable for the plaintiff to evict her. It is right to hold that as against him she has in effect permission to reside permanently in the house, on the basis that the children may be with her for as long as they need a home. As has already been noted, it is a personal right not amounting to a property interest diminishing the rights of the plaintiff's lessor and mortgagee.

Comment

(1) Legislation in Fiji prevented the creation of a proprietary interest. Accordingly, for an estoppel to operate, it was necessary for the remedy to be non-proprietary and the claim was limited to a personal licence. In these circumstances, is *Maharaj* authority for the proposition that all licences awarded as remedies are non-proprietary? If so, how would this fit with property principles generally?

(2) There is some authority suggesting that purchasers are bound by the estoppel licence,[24] but the question never appears to have been fully discussed.

(3) Is this affected by LRA, s 116?

E. Contractual and estoppel licences: the links

It has been seen that it is pretty clear that contractual licences are not proprietary interests binding purchasers, whereas estoppel licences will usually bind purchasers (at least before a remedy is granted). Can such a distinction be justified? Normally, one thinks of estoppel claims as being weaker, in legal terms, than contractual claims, so it is surprising that their proprietary effect may be greater. Is it easier to prove detriment for estoppel than consideration for contract?

We should also note that the remedy in estoppel lies within the court's discretion. At first sight, the lack of certainty regarding remedy would appear to provide a strong argument against proprietary status. Could it, on the other hand, be used to urge the opposite? Given the discretion, is it possible to draw a distinction between estoppel licences and estoppels protecting proprietary claims?[25] It might be that estoppel licences have fastened onto the coat-tails of other estoppel claims.

Let us assume that estoppel licences can bind purchasers. Does this mean that estoppel can be employed to ensure that a contractual licence binds a purchaser (assuming sufficient detriment for estoppel)? There seems to be no difficulty in asserting that estoppels can be used to enforce promises.[26] The question has not received much attention in the cases, though it is revealing that, as was seen above, *Ashburn Anstalt* thought that *Errington* v *Errington* could have been decided on estoppel grounds.[27]

---

[24] *Williams* v *Staite* [1979] Ch 291; *Pascoe* v *Turner* [1979] 1 WLR 431.
[25] This would not be relevant after the court has given a remedy (the issue in *Maharaj*).
[26] See especially *Thorner* v *Major* [2009] 1 WLR 776 (Extract 7.1.5 above).
[27] But why was estoppel not relied upon in *Ashburn Anstalt* itself?

Extract 18.1.14

Lloyds Bank plc v Carrick [1996] 4 All ER 630

An estate contract failed as against a purchaser because it had not been registered as a land charge. It was argued that, as a result of detrimental reliance, it could be enforced as an estoppel, for which registration would not be a problem.

MORRITT LJ: . . . In my judgment the claim of Mrs Carrick fails on a number of grounds. First, as in the case of the constructive trust, I do not see how there is any room for the application of the principles of proprietary estoppel when at the time of the relevant expenditure there was already a bare trust arising in consequence of an enforceable contract to the same effect as the interest sought pursuant to the proprietary estoppel. As the evidence showed Mrs Carrick knew of the need for a conveyance and was content that it should be deferred. Thus at the time that she paid the price and committed herself to the expenditure on the subsequent improvements she believed, rightly, that she was spending the money in respect of her own property, albeit under an uncompleted contract. In this respect I see no relevant distinction between this case and that of *Western Fish Products Ltd* v *Penwith DC* [[1981] 2 All ER 204].

Second, this is not a case in which the expectations of Mrs Carrick have been defeated by Mr Carrick seeking to resile from the position he had encouraged her to expect. As far as he is concerned he has always accepted that she had contracted to buy the maisonette and had paid the price in full. As against him the contract is still binding and enforceable . . .

Third, it was common ground that the right arising from a proprietary estoppel cannot exceed that which the party sought to be estopped encouraged the other to believe that she had or would acquire. The party sought to be estopped is Mr Carrick. In so far as he encouraged Mrs Carrick to believe that she was or would become the beneficial owner of the maisonette there is no further right to be obtained for she was, and, subject to the charge, still is. But counsel for Mrs Carrick submits that Mr Carrick went further and encouraged her in the belief that she was or would become the legal owner of the maisonette. Apart from the facts that this was never alleged in the defence of Mrs Carrick nor explored in evidence at the trial I do not think that it could avail Mrs Carrick. Section 4(6) of the 1972 [Land Charges] Act invalidates, as against the bank, any unregistered contract by the estate owner for the conveyance of the legal estate. It cannot be unconscionable for the bank to rely on the non-registration of the contract. I do not see how it could be right to confer on Mrs Carrick indirectly, and by means of a proprietary estoppel binding on the bank, that which Parliament prevented her from obtaining directly by the contract it has declared to be void. To avoid any future misunderstanding I would emphasise that there was and is a valid and enforceable contract as against the vendor. Accordingly this case is quite unlike those which may become more prevalent where there is no contract at all, not because there was no agreement but because the agreement was not in writing as now required by s 2 of the Law of Property (Miscellaneous Provisions) Act 1989.

In my judgment, the claim based on proprietary estoppel fails. In the circumstances it is unnecessary to consider further the submission of counsel for the bank to the effect that a proprietary estoppel cannot give rise to an interest in land capable of binding successors in title. This interesting argument will have to await another day, though it is hard to see how in this court it can surmount the hurdle constituted by the decision of this court in *E R Ives Investments Ltd* v *High* [1967] 1 All ER 504, [1967] 2 QB 379.

Comment

(1) In *ER Ives Investment Ltd* v *High*,[28] an equitable easement was void for non-registration. Nevertheless, an estoppel claim succeeded in the Court of Appeal. Can this be reconciled

---

[28] [1967] 2 QB 379 (see Extract 7.4.1 above for the benefit and burden analysis also relied upon).

with *Carrick*? Note that in *Ives* the reliance was after the land had been sold once, but before a subsequent sale to the plaintiffs. Is this a material factor?

(2) *Carrick* does not, of course, involve a licence. Could *Carrick* be used to assert that a court will not permit reliance on an estoppel when there is already a contractual licence?

(3) In neither *Ives* nor *Carrick* was the detriment the same as the contractual consideration. Assuming that contract and estoppel can overlap, should an estoppel be recognised where the contractual consideration constitutes the detriment?

F. Other analyses

There may be other methods of enforcing licences, even as against purchasers. They may not involve conventional property analyses, but produce much the same result as if there were a proprietary interest. The constructive trust, already considered, provides an excellent example, as does the benefit and burden doctrine. Another possibility, which may initially seem surprising in the property setting, is that the economic torts may apply. This is most likely where there is a contractual licence.

Extract 18.1.15

Esso Petroleum Co Ltd v Kingswood Motors (Addlestone) Ltd [1974] QB 142

Esso sought to enforce a solus tie (relating to the sale of petrol) against purchasers who had purchased in breach of the terms of the solus tie.

BRIDGE J: . . . But Mr Christie's interesting submission on this part of the case is that, if I go to a line of authority stemming from the well-known decision in *Tulk* v *Moxhay* (1848) 2 Ph 774 and if I go in particular to the decision of the Court of Appeal in *London County Council* v *Allen* [1914] 3 KB 642, I find that the law, as a matter of policy, has stopped short at enforcing the obligations undertaken by a landowner in relation to anything to be done on the land he owns against a successor in title to that landowner, except in the cases in which such enforcement can be based on the equitable principle in *Tulk* v *Moxhay*, 2 Ph 774; and one requirement for the application of that principle is that the covenantee seeking such enforcement retains land which is capable of being benefited by the obligations sought to be enforced. He submits that if the doctrine relied on by Esso, that courts can deploy all their powers against those tortfeasors who conspire to induce breaches of contract, is applied in the way in which Esso ask for it to be applied in this case, that doctrine will come into head-on collision with the other doctrine restricting the court's power, once the land has changed hands, to enforce against the new owner any obligation deriving from contractual covenants entered into by the former owner. Mr Christie says also that the exercise of the court's powers as sought, would contravene the policy embodied in the Land Charges Act 1925 and the Land Registration Act 1925 – the policy of the legislature that only registered interests and overriding interests are binding on a purchaser. I hope I have fairly summarised the way in which the argument is put.

In my judgment the answer to it is that those doctrines really never meet at all because they are concerned with two entirely different things. The *Tulk* v *Moxhay*, 2 Ph 774 line of cases is not, as it seems to me, remotely concerned with the tort of conspiracy to induce breaches of contract, and I can see no reason whatever why the powers of the court to act against tortfeasors who bring about breaches of contract by other persons should be limited in the way suggested simply because the breach of contract which the conspirators have succeeded in inducing is one which involves a transfer of title to land. Pertinently and helpfully, Mr Wood draws an analogy between the power of which he seeks the exercise in this case and other situations in which the court's powers are deployed against persons in general in a way which may involve the transfer of land, as in actions for specific performance or for rectification of the consequences of mistake or fraud. As it was put by Mr Brodie, who also intervened to assist me on this part of the argument, I am not asked to enforce an equitable doctrine which makes some party not privy to a contract nevertheless liable in certain circumstances to perform that contract. I am asked to enforce the personal liability incurred by a tortfeasor to undo the consequences of his tort which could have been restrained before it was committed. In a proper case, I ask myself: what reason can there be in principle why the tortfeasor should not be ordered to undo that which he has done?

Comment

(1) This liability is in the context of covenants. Could similar reasoning apply to licences?

(2) How well does *Kingswood* fit with conventional property analyses? It should be remembered that the economic torts generally require the tortfeasor (purchaser, in the land context) to be aware of the contract, so the rules are very different from those governing interests in land.

(3) Compare the role of personal obligations in the registration context, discussed earlier (see p 321 above).

It is thought possible to place a restriction on the register which will make it difficult to sell land free from a positive covenant, despite the fact that positive covenants do not bind purchasers.[29] There is some authority[30] that a similar analysis can be used as regards licences – ensuring that a transfer cannot be registered unless the purchaser agrees with the licensee to respect the licence.

2. Creation and transfer of licences

Little need be said under this heading. If, as seems likely, licences are not proprietary interests, then no formalities are required for their creation: an oral contract, for example, would suffice. A slightly more difficult question is whether the benefit of licences can be transferred.

The circumstances of very many cases will be such that the licence will be personal to the licensee, especially in the context of the family home. The licence in *Binions* v *Evans*,[31] for example, was personal to the widow and clearly could not be assigned. However, many licences are not inherently personal, an example being the 'front of the house' rights in *Clore* v *Theatrical Properties Ltd*.[32] The Court of Appeal accepted that the benefit of those rights could be assigned.

Proprietary status is centrally concerned with the question whether the burden of the licence runs so as to bind successors in title: this has already been discussed. If the benefit of a licence is personal to the licensee, is this an argument against proprietary status?

---

[29] See p 318 above.
[30] *Donington Park Leisure Ltd* v *Wheatcroft & Son Ltd* [2006] EWHC 904 (Ch) at [45].
[31] [1972] Ch 359; see Extract 18.1.11 above.
[32] [1936] 3 All ER 483.

3. The relationship constituted by the licence

Licences can be infinitely various: the relationship between licensor and licensee will vary according to the terms of each licence. The single question discussed in this section is whether a licensee can bring actions in trespass and nuisance. These actions will be particularly important if persons other than the licensor interfere with the licence. We are not here concerned with purchasers, but with others who interfere without any interest in the land justifying such action.

The conventional view is that neither trespass nor nuisance is available to the licensee and that this constitutes a real difference between licences and proprietary interests such as leases and easements.[33] However, *National Provincial Bank Ltd* v *Ainsworth*[34] supports the availability of trespass for licensees in possession (or, at least, exclusive possession).

Extract 18.3.1

Manchester Airport plc v *Dutton* [2000] QB 133

A licensee who had not entered the land sought to evict trespassers.

CHADWICK LJ (dissenting): . . . That passage [in *Allan* v *Liverpool Overseers* (1874) LR 9 QB 180], as it seems to me, provides clear authority for the proposition that an action for ejectment – the forerunner of the present action for recovery of land – as well as an action for trespass can only be brought by a person who is in possession or who has a right to be in possession. Further, that possession is synonymous, in this context, with exclusive occupation – that is to say occupation (or a right to occupy) to the exclusion of all others, including the owner or other person with superior title (save in so far as he has reserved a right to enter).

. . .

A tenant or a licensee who was in actual possession – that is to say, in occupation in circumstances in which he had exclusive possession in fact – could maintain an action for trespass against intruders; but that is because he relied on the fact of his possession and not on his title.

The licence in the present case, as it seems to me, is a clear example of a personal permission to enter the land and use it for some stipulated purpose. In my view, it would be contrary to what Windeyer J described as 'long-established law' to hold that it conferred on the airport authority rights to bring an action in rem for possession of the land to which it relates.

LAWS LJ: But if the airport company, were it in actual occupation and control of the site, could obtain an order for possession against the trespassers, why may it not obtain such an order before it enters into occupation, so as to evict the trespassers and enjoy the licence granted to it? As I understand it, the principal objection to the grant of such relief is that it would amount to an ejectment, and ejectment is a remedy available only to a party with title to or estate in the land; which as a mere licensee the airport company plainly lacks. It is clear that this was the old law . . .

However, in this I hear the rattle of mediaeval chains. Why was ejectment only available to a claimant with title? The answer, as it seems to me, lies in the nature of the remedy before the passing of the Common Law Procedure Act 1852 (15 & 16 Vict. c. 76) . . .

In my judgment the old learning demonstrates only that the remedy of ejectment was simply not concerned with the potential rights of a licensee: a legal creature who, probably, rarely engaged the attention of the courts before 1852 or for some time thereafter . . . But I think there is a logical mistake in the notion that because ejectment was only available to estate owners,

---

[33] *Hill* v *Tupper* (1863) 2 H&C 121 (159 ER 51) (trespass).
[34] [1965] AC 1175 at p 1232.

possession cannot be available to licensees who do not enjoy de facto occupation. The mistake inheres in this: if the action for ejectment was by definition concerned *only* with the rights of estate owners, it is necessarily silent upon the question, what relief might be available to a licensee. The limited and specific nature of ejectment means only that it was not available to a licensee; it does not imply the further proposition that *no* remedy by way of possession can now be granted to a licensee not in occupation. Nowadays there is no distinct remedy of ejectment; a plaintiff sues for an order of possession, whether he is himself in occupation or not. The proposition that a plaintiff not in occupation may only obtain the remedy if he is an estate owner assumes that he must bring himself within the old law of ejectment. I think it is a false assumption.

I would hold that the court today has ample power to grant a remedy to a licensee which will protect but not exceed his legal rights granted by the licence. If, as here, that requires an order for possession, the spectre of history (which, in the true tradition of the common law, ought to be a friendly ghost) does not stand in the way. The law of ejectment has no voice in the question; it cannot speak beyond its own limits. Cases such as *Radaich v Smith*, 101 CLR 209 and *Street v Mountford* [1985] AC 809 were concerned with the distinction between licence and tenancy, which is not in question here.

In my judgment the true principle is that a licensee not in occupation may claim possession against a trespasser if that is a necessary remedy to vindicate and give effect to such rights of occupation as by contract with his licensor he enjoys. This is the same principle as allows a licensee who is in de facto possession to evict a trespasser. There is no respectable distinction, in law or logic, between the two situations. An estate owner may seek an order whether he is in possession or not. So, in my judgment, may a licensee, if other things are equal. In both cases, the plaintiff's remedy is strictly limited to what is required to make good his legal right. The principle applies although the licensee has no right to exclude the licensor himself. Elementarily he cannot exclude any occupier who, by contract or estate, has a claim to possession equal or superior to his own. Obviously, however, that will not avail a bare trespasser.

In this whole debate, as regards the law of remedies in the end I see no significance as a matter of principle in any distinction drawn between a plaintiff whose right to occupy the land in question arises from title and one whose right arises only from contract. In every case the question must be, what is the reach of the right, and whether it is shown that the defendant's acts violate its enjoyment. If they do, and (as here) an order for possession is the only practical remedy, the remedy should be granted. Otherwise the law is powerless to correct a proved or admitted wrongdoing; and that would be unjust and disreputable. The underlying principle is in the Latin maxim (for which I make no apology), 'ubi jus, ibi sit remedium'.

Comment

(1) Which analysis is most closely attuned to legal principles?[35] Leaving aside the earlier cases, which best fits the modern law?

(2) Should it make any difference if the licence merely allowed access?[36]

Extract 18.3.2

Hunter v Canary Wharf Ltd [1997] AC 655

Canary Wharf Tower interfered with television reception. Amongst the plaintiffs complaining about this, there were many without a proprietary interest, including spouses and children.

---

[35] Lord Neuberger MR recognised the controversy in *Mayor of London v Hall* [2011] 1 WLR 504 at [26]–[27], but did not need to pronounce upon it.

[36] See *Countryside Residential (North Thames) Ltd v A Child* (2000) 81 P&CR 10.

LORD GOFF: . . . It follows that, on the authorities as they stand, an action in private nuisance will only lie at the suit of a person who has a right to the land affected. Ordinarily, such a person can only sue if he has the right to exclusive possession of the land, such as a freeholder or tenant in possession, or even a licensee with exclusive possession. Exceptionally however, as *Foster* v *Warblington Urban District Council* shows, this category may include a person in actual possession who has no right to be there; and in any event a reversioner can sue in so far as his reversionary interest is affected. But a mere licensee on the land has no right to sue.

. . .

Moreover, any such departure from the established law on this subject, such as that adopted by the Court of Appeal in the present case, faces the problem of defining the category of persons who would have the right to sue. The Court of Appeal adopted the not easily identifiable category of those who have a 'substantial link' with the land, regarding a person who occupied the premises 'as a home' as having a sufficient link for this purpose. But who is to be included in this category? It was plainly intended to include husbands and wives, or partners, and their children, and even other relatives living with them. But is the category also to include the lodger upstairs, or the au pair girl or resident nurse caring for an invalid who makes her home in the house while she works there? If the latter, it seems strange that the category should not extend to include places where people work as well as places where they live, where nuisances such as noise can be just as unpleasant or distracting. In any event, the extension of the tort in this way would transform it from a tort to land into a tort to the person, in which damages could be recovered in respect of something less serious than personal injury and the criteria for liability were founded not upon negligence but upon striking a balance between the interests of neighbours in the use of their land. This is, in my opinion, not an acceptable way in which to develop the law.

Comment

Lord Hope said very much the same, though Lord Hoffmann might place more stress on proprietary status than exclusive possession. Lord Cooke dissented.

How well protected are licensees today? Are there sound reasons why licensees protected by contract or estoppel should not be able to bring actions in trespass and nuisance unless they are in exclusive possession?

Further reading

Battersby, G [1991] Conv 36: Contractual and estoppel licences as proprietary interests in land.

Baughen, S (1994) 14 LS 147: Estoppels over land and third parties: an open question?

Briggs, A [1983] Conv 285: Contractual licences: a reply.

McFarlane, B [2003] CLJ 661: Proprietary estoppel and third parties after the Land Registration Act 2002.

19

Easements and profits

Easements and profits form one of the best known categories of interests in another person's land. A feature of most profits and every easement is that there are two plots of land involved: the benefited (dominant) land and the burdened (servient) land. The major issues to be considered in relation to easements and profits are, first, what rights fall within these categories and, second, the ways in which they are implied or arise from long user (prescription).

Before going into these issues, it is worth remembering that some other legal categories cover very similar ground. A brief summary of these categories must suffice. Restrictive covenants (the principal focus of Chapter 20) are very similar rights involving two plots of land. A promise not to use land in a certain way (examples are not to build on it, or not to use it for business purposes) will constitute a restrictive covenant. As will be seen below,[1] the courts are reluctant to recognise new easements which are restrictive of what the servient owner can do (as opposed to permitting the dominant owner to do something). There are good reasons for this, including the desire to avoid the generous rules for the creation of easements and to apply the statutory provisions permitting the variation or discharge of out-of-date restrictive covenants. Another category consists of certain natural rights which benefit all land; some of these are virtually identical to easements. The best example is the right of support: the right that excavations on neighbouring land should not cause the collapse of your land. This right is limited because it does not protect buildings on the land, save where the land would have subsided even if not built upon. An easement of support, by contrast, may protect buildings. As an easement, it must have been created by the servient owner.

Lastly, easements and profits must be held for the benefit of the dominant land or (for profits only) an individual. Rights in favour of a fluctuating group of people, most commonly the inhabitants of a particular locality, do not qualify. Nevertheless, these last rights may exist by way of custom. This is an archaic area: user since 1189 must have been feasible. Profits cannot be acquired by fluctuating groups in this way, but the courts have displayed a high level of inventiveness in recognising long use. Thus a Crown grant may be implied, regardless of the chances of such a grant being infinitesimally small. The area illustrates the desire of the courts to cloak long-established practice with some degree of legal protection.

The Law Commission issued a report on easements and covenants in 2011.[2] It is not proposed to codify or reform the entirety of easements (and profits). Instead, often significant reforms are proposed for specific areas. Accordingly, the proposals will be covered as the relevant areas are covered.

---

[1] See p 653.
[2] Law Com No 327: Making Land Work: Easements, Covenants and Profits à Prendre.

1. What can be an easement or a profit?

A. Profits

The essence of a profit is the right to take something from another person's land, examples being game, fish, turf, minerals and grazing by animals. Our interest in profits lies not so much in the specifics of these rights, but the fact that profits can exist in favour of individuals (in gross) as well as in favour of land (appurtenant, or 'in a que estate').

Extract 19.1.1

Lord Chesterfield v *Harris* [1908] 2 Ch 397

BUCKLEY LJ: . . . Now, upon the evidence before us, there is no doubt that for about three centuries freeholders of these five parishes or townships, that is, in the same position as the present defendants, have notoriously and publicly asserted, and have exercised *nec per vim nec clam nec precario*, the right of fishing which the defendants claim in their defence to this action. . . . The question is whether the right which is claimed is one which is recognized by the law. What is the nature and extent of the right? It is claimed not as a right in gross, but as appurtenant, or annexed to, the ownership of a freehold tenement, whether land or house – a profit à prendre by prescription in a que estate. Further, it is a right to take that profit in the soil of another without stint. Each of the possessors of the right (and their number is indefinite) may appropriate out of the waters of the Wye along the stretch in question as many fish as he can catch for the purpose either of consumption or of sale. There is no limitation in reference to the nature or extent of his freehold tenement or the wants of its occupants. Can such a claim be supported in law . . . [i] Can there be a prescription for a profit à prendre, in the form of a common of fishery *in alieno solo*, without stint? The general rule of law as to rights of profit à prendre in a que estate seems to be clear. In my opinion it has been correctly stated that no profit to be enjoyed over or taken from land can be made appurtenant to land unless it is accessorial to the enjoyment of the land in relation to which it is claimed. A claim by one landowner to enter upon his neighbour's land and cut down trees and sell them is a claim of a profit à prendre in gross, and cannot be made appurtenant to land, as it is in no wise accessorial to the enjoyment of an estate; but a claim to cut down thorns and firewood to burn in the dwelling-house of the claimant is a profit à prendre accessorial to the enjoyment of the dwelling-house and may be made appurtenant thereto, so as to give to mere occupiers thereof for the time being a right to the privileges . . . The reason of the rule may, I suppose, be twofold. In the first place, the fact of the appendancy of the right to the tenement points naturally to the maintenance of some relation, in the exercise of the right, between the extent of that exercise and the nature of that tenement and the requirements of its enjoyment. And, in the second place, if the exercise were without stint, it might result in the exercise of his right by one of the commoners becoming the destruction of the rights of the other commoners and, where the right belongs to the grantor in common with the grantees, of the grantor himself also, as for example if all the turf were cut and taken away, or all the wood in the servient tenement were cut and taken away.

[i] 7 App Cas 633.

Comment

(1) Why was custom not possible?

(2) How do profits (in gross or appurtenant) pass to successors to the original holder?

(3) Note that it is frequently difficult to prove prescription of a right in gross: one cannot automatically rely on use by predecessors in title.

(4) Are you convinced by the reasons for denying appurtenant profits without stint?

B. Easements

There are many cases illustrating the limits on what can be an easement. The standard tests are found in our first case.

Extract 19.1.2

Re Ellenborough Park [1956] Ch 131

EVERSHED MR: The substantial question raised in this appeal is whether the respondent, or those whom he has been appointed to represent, being the owners of certain houses fronting upon, or, in some few cases, adjacent to, the garden or park known as Ellenborough Park in Weston-super-Mare, have any right known to the law, and now enforceable by them against the owners of the park, to the use and enjoyment of the park to the extent and in the manner later more precisely defined . . .

The substantial question in the case . . . is one of considerable interest and importance. It is clear from our brief recital of the facts that, if the house owners are now entitled to an enforceable right in respect of the use and enjoyment of Ellenborough Park, that right must have the character and quality of an easement as understood by, and known to, our law. It has, therefore, been necessary for us to consider carefully the qualities and characteristics of easements, and, for such purpose, to look back into the history of that category of incorporeal rights in the development of English real property law . . .

But it can be said at once that, with the possible exception of the first, none of [four cases considered] constitutes or involves a direct decision upon the question now before us: and although the existence of gardens surrounded by houses, the owners or occupiers of which enjoy in practice the amenities of the gardens, is a well-known feature of town development throughout the country, no other case appears to have come before the courts in which the validity of the rights in fact enjoyed in the gardens has ever been tested.

. . .

But, before we proceed to those matters of fact, it will be proper, as a foundation for all that follows in this judgment, to attempt a brief account of the emergence in the course of the history of our law, of the rights known to us as 'easements', and thereafter, so far as relevant for present purposes, to formulate what can now be taken to be the essential qualities of those rights. For the former purpose we cannot do better than cite a considerable passage from the late Sir William Holdsworth's *Historical Introduction to the Land Law* (Clarendon Press, 1927, p 265). The author states: 'Both the term "easement" and the thing itself were known to the mediaeval common law. At the latter part of the sixteenth century it was described in Kitchin's book on courts, and defined in the later editions of the "Termes de la Ley".' After stating the definition and observing its obvious defects from the point of view of modern law, Sir William proceeds:

> 'But these defects in the definition are instructive, because they indicate that the law as to easements was as yet rudimentary.
>
> It was still rudimentary when Blackstone wrote. In fact, right down to the beginning of the nineteenth century, there was but little authority on many parts of this subject. Gale, writing in 1839, said: "The difficulties which arise from the abstruseness and refinements incident to the subject have been increased by the comparatively small number of decided cases affording matter for defining and systematising this branch of the law. Upon some points indeed there is no authority at all in English law."
>
> The industrial revolution, which caused the growth of large towns and manufacturing industries, naturally brought into prominence such easements as ways, watercourses, light, and support; and so Gale's book became the starting-point of the modern law, which rests largely upon comparatively recent decisions.

But, though the law of easements is comparatively modern, some of its rules have ancient roots. There is a basis of Roman rules introduced into English law by Bracton, and acclimatized by Coke . . . The law, as thus developed, sufficed for the needs of the country in the eighteenth century. But, as it was no longer sufficient for the new economic needs of the nineteenth century, an expansion and an elaboration of this branch of the law became necessary. It was expanded and elaborated partly on the basis of the old rules, which had been evolved by the working of the assize of nuisance, and its successor the action on the case; partly by the help of Bracton's Roman rules and partly, as Gale's book shows, by the help of the Roman rules taken from the Digest, which he frequently and continuously uses to illustrate and to supplement the existing rules of law.'

The reference to Sir E Coke we take to be a reference to *Coke upon Littleton*, citations from which and criticisms of which will be found, for example, in *Gale on Easements*, 12th ed, p 305.

The passage which we have read from Sir William Holdsworth sufficiently serves to explain the appearance and the prominence of Roman dicta in the English law of easements, commonly called, indeed, by the Latin name of 'servitudes': and it may well be possible that Farwell J's rejection of the jus spatiandi as a legal right by English law was derived in part from its similar rejection by the law of Rome . . . It by no means follows that the kind of right which is here in question, arising out of a method of urban development that would not have been known to Roman lawyers, can in any case be said to fall within its scope. And, in any event, its validity must depend, in our judgment, upon a consideration of the qualities which must now be attributed to all easements by the law relating to easements as it has now developed in England.

For the purposes of the argument before us Mr Cross and Mr Goff were content to adopt, as correct, the four characteristics formulated in Dr Cheshire's *Modern Real Property*, 7th ed, pp 456 et seq. They are (1) there must be a dominant and a servient tenement: (2) an easement must 'accommodate' the dominant tenement: (3) dominant and servient owners must be different persons, and (4) a right over land cannot amount to an easement, unless it is capable of forming the subject-matter of a grant.

The four characteristics stated by Dr Cheshire correspond with the qualities discussed by Gale in his second chapter, sections 2, 5, 3, and 6 and 8 respectively. Two of the four may be disregarded for present purposes, namely, the first and the third. If the garden or park is, as it is alleged to be, the servient tenement in the present case, then it is undoubtedly distinct from the alleged dominant tenements, namely, the freeholds of the several houses whose owners claim to exercise the rights. It is equally clear that if these lands respectively constitute the servient and dominant tenements then they are owned by different persons. The argument in the case is found, accordingly, to turn upon the meaning and application to the circumstances of the present case of the second and fourth conditions; that is, first, whether the alleged easement can be said in truth to 'accommodate' the dominant tenement – in other words, whether there exists the required 'connexion' between the one and the other: and, secondly, whether the right alleged is 'capable of forming the subject-matter of a grant'. The exact significance of this fourth and last condition is, at first sight perhaps, not entirely clear. As between the original parties to the 'grant', it is not in doubt that rights of this kind would be capable of taking effect by way of contract or licence. But for the purposes of the present case, as the arguments made clear, the cognate questions involved under this condition are: whether the rights purported to be given are expressed in terms of too wide and vague a character; whether, if and so far as effective, such rights would amount to rights of joint occupation or would substantially deprive the park owners of proprietorship or legal possession; whether, if and so far as effective, such rights constitute mere rights of recreation, possessing no quality of utility or benefit; and on such grounds cannot qualify as easements.

. . .

Can it be said, then, of the right of full enjoyment of the park in question, which was granted by the conveyance of December 23, 1864, and which, for reasons already given, was, in our view, intended to be annexed to the property conveyed to Mr Porter, that it accommodated and served that property? It is clear that the right did, in some degree, enhance the value of the property, and this consideration cannot be dismissed as wholly irrelevant. It is, of course, a point to be noted; but we agree with Mr Cross's submission that it is in no way decisive of the problem; it is not sufficient to show that the right increased the value of the property conveyed, unless it is also shown that it was connected with the normal enjoyment of that property. It appears to us that the question whether or not this connexion exists is primarily one of fact, and depends largely on the nature of the alleged dominant tenement and the nature of the right granted. As to the former, it was in the contemplation of the parties to the conveyance of 1864 that the property conveyed should be used for residential and not commercial purposes. That appears from the conveyance itself, and the covenant by the purchaser already quoted, that the dwelling-house, etc., which he bound himself to build should not 'be occupied or used as an open or exposed shop or for any purpose of trade or commerce other than a lodging-house or private school or seminary' without the vendor's written consent. Since it is stated in paragraph 4 of Mr Rendell's affidavit in support of the summons, and has been conceded that all the conveyances of plots for building purposes fronting or near Ellenborough Park were as regards (inter alia) user substantially the same as the conveyance of 1864, the inevitable inference is that the houses, which were to be built upon the plots, were to constitute a residential estate. As appears from the map, the houses, which were built upon the plots around and near to Ellenborough Park, varied in size, some being large detached houses and others smaller and either semi-detached or in a row. We have already stated that the purchasers of all the plots, which actually abutted on the park, were granted the right to enjoy the use of it, as were also the purchasers of some of the plots which, although not fronting upon the park, were only a short distance away from it. As to the nature of the right granted, the conveyance of 1864 shows that the park was to be kept and maintained as a pleasure ground or ornamental garden, and that it was contemplated that it should at all times be kept in good order and condition and well stocked with plants and shrubs; and the vendors covenanted that they would not at any time thereafter erect or permit to be erected any dwelling-house or other building (except a grotto, bower, summer-house, flower-stand, fountain, music-stand or other ornamental erection) within or on any part of the pleasure ground. On these facts Mr Cross submitted that the requisite connexion between the right to use the park and the normal enjoyment of the houses which were built around it or near it had not been established. He likened the position to a right granted to the purchaser of a house to use the Zoological Gardens free of charge or to attend Lord's Cricket Ground without payment. Such a right would undoubtedly, he said, increase the value of the property conveyed but could not run with it at law as an easement, because there was no sufficient nexus between the enjoyment of the right and the use of the house. It is probably true, we think, that in neither of Mr Cross's illustrations would the supposed right constitute an easement, for it would be wholly extraneous to, and independent of, the use of a house as a house, namely, as a place in which the householder and his family live and make their home; and it is for this reason that the analogy which Mr Cross sought to establish between his illustrations and the present case cannot, in our opinion, be supported. A much closer analogy, as it seems to us, is the case of a man selling the freehold of part of his house and granting to the purchaser, his heirs and assigns, the right, appurtenant to such part, to use the garden in common with the vendor and his assigns. In such a case, the test of connexion, or accommodation, would be amply satisfied; for just as the use of a garden undoubtedly enhances, and is connected with, the normal enjoyment of the house to which it belongs, so also would the right granted, in the case supposed, be closely connected with the use and enjoyment of the part of the premises sold. Such, we think, is in substance the position in the present case. The park became a communal garden for the benefit and enjoyment of those whose houses adjoined it or were in its close proximity. Its flower beds, lawns and walks were calculated to afford all the amenities which it is the purpose of the garden of a house to provide; and, apart from the fact that these amenities extended to a number of householders, instead of being confined to one (which on this aspect of the case is immaterial), we can see no difference in principle between Ellenborough Park and a garden in the ordinary signification of that word. It is the collective garden of the neighbouring houses, to whose use it was dedicated by the owners of the estate and as such amply satisfied, in our judgment, the requirement of connexion with the dominant tenements to which it is appurtenant. The result is not affected by the circumstance that the right to the park is in this case enjoyed by some few houses which are not immediately fronting on the park. The test for present purposes, no doubt, is that the park should constitute in a real and intelligible sense the garden (albeit the communal garden) of the houses to which its enjoyment is annexed. But we think that the test is satisfied as regards these few neighbouring, though not adjacent, houses. We think that the extension of the right of enjoyment to these few houses does not negative the presence of the necessary 'nexus' between the subject-matter enjoyed and the premises to which the enjoyment is expressed to belong.

Mr Cross referred us to, and to some extent relied upon, *Hill* v *Tupper*,[i] but in our opinion there is nothing in that case contrary to the view which we have expressed. In that case, the owner of land adjoining a canal was granted the exclusive right to let boats out for hire on the canal. He did so and then sought to restrain a similar activity by a neighbouring landowner. He sought to establish that his grant constituted an easement but failed. Pollock CB said in his judgment:[ii] 'It is not competent to create rights unconnected with the use and enjoyment of land, and annex them to it so as to constitute a property in the grantee.' It is clear that what the plaintiff was trying to do was to set up, under the guise of an easement, a monopoly which had no normal connexion with the ordinary use of his land, but which was merely an independent business enterprise. So far from the right claimed sub-serving or accommodating the land, the land was but a convenient incident to the exercise of the right.

For the reasons which we have stated, we are unable to accept the contention that the right to the full enjoyment of Ellenborough Park fails in limine to qualify as a legal easement for want of the necessary connexion between its enjoyment and the use of the properties comprised in the conveyance of 1864, and in the other relevant conveyances.

We turn next to Dr Cheshire's fourth condition for an easement – that the right must be capable of forming the subject-matter of a grant. As we have earlier stated, satisfaction of the condition in the present case depends on a consideration of the questions whether the right conferred is too wide and vague, whether it is inconsistent with the proprietorship or possession of the alleged servient owners, and whether it is a mere right of recreation without utility or benefit.

To the first of these questions the interpretation which we have given to the typical deed provides, in our judgment, the answer; for we have construed the right conferred as being both well defined and commonly understood. In these essential respects the right may be said to be distinct from the indefinite and unregulated privilege which, we think, would ordinarily be understood by the Latin term 'jus spatiandi', a privilege of wandering at will over all and every part of another's field or park, and which, though easily intelligible as the subject-matter of a personal licence, is something substantially different from the subject-matter of the grant in question, namely, the provision for a limited number of houses in a uniform crescent of one single large but private garden.

Our interpretation of the deed also provides, we think, the answer to the second question; for the right conferred no more amounts to a joint occupation of the park with its owners, no more excludes the proprietorship or possession of the latter, than a right of way granted through a passage, or than the use by the public of the gardens of Lincoln's Inn Fields (to take one of our former examples) amount to joint occupation of that garden with the London County Council, or involve an inconsistency with the possession or proprietorship of the council as lessees. It is conceded that, in any event, the plaintiff owners of the park are entitled to cut the timber growing on the park and to retain its proceeds. We have said that in our judgment, under the deed, the flowers and shrubs grown in the garden are equally the park owners' property. We see nothing repugnant to a man's proprietorship or possession of a piece of land that he should decide to make it and maintain it as an ornamental garden, and should grant rights to a limited number of other persons to come into it for the enjoyment of its amenities.

. . .

The third of the questions embraced in Dr Cheshire's fourth condition rests primarily on a proposition stated in Theobald's *The Law of Land*, 2nd ed (1929), at p 263, where it is said that an easement 'must be a right of utility and benefit and not one of mere recreation and amusement'. It does not appear that a proposition in similar terms is stated by Gale . . .

. . . [In *Mounsey* v *Ismay*[iii]] Baron Martin considered, without deciding, the question whether an easement of the kind claimed could in any case exist as an easement in gross: and proceeded as follows:

> 'But, however this may be, we are of opinion that to bring the right within the term "easement" in the second section (of the Prescription Act) it must be one analogous to that of a right of way which precedes it and a right of watercourse which follows it, and must be a right of utility and benefit and not one of mere recreation and amusement.'

The words which we have quoted were used in reference to a claim for a right to conduct horse races and, in our judgment, the formula adopted by Theobald should be read in the light of that circumstance. In any case, if the proposition be well-founded, we do not think that the right to use a garden of the character with which we are concerned in this case can be called one of mere recreation and amusement, as those words were used by Martin B. No doubt a garden is a pleasure – on high authority, it is the purest of pleasures – but, in our judgment, it is not a right having no quality either of utility or benefit as those words should be understood. The right here in suit is, for reasons already given, one appurtenant to the surrounding houses as such, and constitutes a beneficial attribute of residence in a house as ordinarily understood. Its use for the purposes, not only of exercise and rest but also for such domestic purposes as were suggested in argument – for example, for taking out small children in perambulators or otherwise – is not fairly to be described as one of mere recreation or amusement, and is clearly beneficial to the premises to which it is attached. If Baron Martin's test is applied, the right in suit is, in point of utility, fairly analogous to a right of way passing over fields to, say, the railway station, which would be none the less a good right, even though it provided a longer route to the objective. We think, therefore, that the statement of Baron Martin must at least be confined to exclusion of rights to indulge in such recreations as were in question in the case before him, horse racing or perhaps playing games, and has no application to the facts of the present case.

As appears from what has been stated earlier, the right to the full enjoyment of Ellenborough Park, which was granted by the 1864 and other relevant conveyances, was, in substance, no more than a right to use the park as a garden in the way in which gardens are commonly used. In a sense, no doubt, such a right includes something of a jus spatiandi, inasmuch as it involves the principle of wandering at will round each part of the garden, except of course, such parts as comprise flower beds, or are laid out for some other purpose, which renders walking impossible or unsuitable. We doubt, nevertheless, whether the right to use and enjoy a garden in this manner can with accuracy be said to constitute a mere jus spatiandi. Wandering at large is of the essence of such a right and constitutes the main purpose for which it exists. A private garden, on the other hand, is an attribute of the ordinary enjoyment of the residence to which it is attached, and the right of wandering in it is but one method of enjoying it. On the assumption, however, that the right now in question does constitute a jus spatiandi, or that it is analogous thereto, it becomes necessary to consider whether the right, which is in question in these proceedings, is, for that reason, incapable of ranking in law as an easement.

Farwell J twice indicated that in his opinion the jus spatiandi is an interest which is not known to our law; and we think it is true to say that this principle has been widely accepted in the profession without sufficient regard being had, perhaps, to the exact language in which Farwell J expressed himself or the circumstances in which his view of the matter was propounded . . .

It will be noted that in both of these cases the judge said that a jus spatiandi is 'not known to our law' and the question arises as to what precisely he meant by using that phrase. He may have meant: (a) that it was unknown to our law, because it found no place in the Roman law of servitudes; (b) that it was repugnant to the ownership of land that other persons should have rights of user over the whole of it; (c) that the law will not recognize rights to use a servient tenement for the purposes of mere recreation and pleasure; or (d) that such rights are too vague and uncertain to be capable of definition. Which of these meanings the judge had in mind it is difficult to know; and indeed, he may have had some other meaning. If, however, one attributes to the phrase 'not known to the law' its ordinary signification, namely, that it was a right which our law had refused to recognize, it is clear, we think, that he would at least have expressed himself in less general terms had his attention been drawn to *Duncan* v *Louch*[iv] . . .

. . .

[We] agree with Danckwerts J in regarding *Duncan* v *Louch* as being a direct authority in the defendants' favour. It has never, so far as we are aware, been since questioned, and we think it should, in the present case, be followed.

[i] (1863) 2 H&C 121.
[ii] *Ibid.* 127.
[iii] 3 H&C 486.
[iv] 6 QB 904.

Comment

(1) What are the 'four characteristics' of easements? What is meant by 'capable of forming the subject-matter of a grant'?

(2) What is a *jus spatiandi*? Why is its status as an easement in doubt?

(3) Would the courts recognise the right to sunbathe on a lakeside shore owned by the servient owner? Or the right, shared by a number of houses, to use a swimming pool?[3]

The continuing vitality of easements is reflected in the following dicta of Lord Shaw in the Privy Council, recognising an easement of storage:[4]

> The law must adapt itself to the conditions of modern society and trade, and there is nothing in the purposes for which the easement is claimed inconsistent in principle with a right of easement as such. This principle is of general application, and was so treated in the House of Lords in *Dyce* v *Hay* ((1852) 1 Macq 305) by Lord St Leonards LC, who observed: 'The category of servitudes and easements must alter and expand with the changes that take place in the circumstances of mankind.'

More difficulty may be encountered where a business is benefited by a supposed easement, as shown by the following two well-known cases.

[3] See also p 653 below.
[4] *Attorney-Gen of Southern Nigeria* v *John Holt & Co (Liverpool) Ltd* [1915] AC 599 at p 617.

Extract 19.1.3

Hill v *Tupper* (1863) 2 H&C 121 (159 ER 51)

The plaintiff, who held a lease of a small area of land bordering a canal, was given the sole and exclusive right to put pleasure boats on it. He claimed that this right was infringed when the defendant, the owner of an inn bordering the canal, also put boats on it.

POLLOCK CB: After the very full argument which has taken place, I do not think it necessary to assign any other reason for our decision, than that the case of *Ackroyd* v *Smith* (10 CB 164) expressly decided that it is not competent to create rights unconnected with the use and enjoyment of land, and annex them to it so as to constitute a property in the grantee. This grant merely operates as a licence or covenant on the part of the grantors, and is binding on them as between themselves and the grantee, but gives him no right of action in his own name for any infringement of the supposed exclusive right. It is argued that, as the owner of an estate may grant a right to cut turves, or to fish or hunt, there is no reason why he may not grant such a right as that now claimed by the plaintiff. The answer is, that the law will not allow it. So the law will not permit the owner of an estate to grant it alternately to his heirs male and heirs female. A new species of incorporeal hereditament cannot be created at the will and pleasure of the owner of property; but he must be content to accept the estate and the right to dispose of it subject to the law as settled by decisions or controlled by act of parliament. A grantor may bind himself by covenant to allow any right he pleases over his property, but he cannot annex to it a new incident, so as to enable the grantee to sue in his own name for an infringement of such a limited right as that now claimed.

Extract 19.1.4

Moody v *Steggles* (1879) 12 Ch D 261

The plaintiff owned the 'Grosvenor Arms', a public house set back from a main road down a narrow side street. From the main road, it was obscured by the defendant's house. The plaintiff claimed an easement to put a sign advertising the 'Grosvenor Arms' on the defendant's house.

FRY J: . . . The next point taken on behalf of the Defendants is this: It is said that the easement in question relates, not to the tenement, but to the business of the occupant of the tenement, and that therefore I cannot tie the easement to the house. It appears to me that that argument is of too refined a nature to prevail, and for this reason, that the house can only be used by an occupant, and that the occupant only uses the house for the business which he pursues, and therefore in some manner (direct or indirect) an easement is more or less connected with the mode in which the occupant of the house uses it. To illustrate this by the cases which have been cited. The easement which was upheld in *Wood* v *Hewett*[i] was to have a hatch in another man's soil. The hatch was only useful to the tenement so long as the plaintiff occupied it as a miller. Therefore, in that sense, the easement was connected with the business of the occupant. So in *Lancaster* v *Eve*[ii] the easement was to have a pile fixed in the waterway of the *Thames*, which was useful so long only as the occupant of the plaintiff's premises used them for the purposes of a wharf. Similarly in *Hoare* v *Metropolitan Board of Works*,[iii] which is still more like the present case, the easement was to have a signboard supported by a pole fixed into the common, an easement which could be useful only so long as the occupant used the house for some purpose which rendered an invitation to the public desirable. I think, therefore, that that argument also fails.

[i] 8 QB 913.
[ii] 5 CB (NS) 717.
[iii] Law Rep 9 QB 296.

Comment

(1) *Moody* v *Steggles* makes it very clear that easements can benefit businesses. Furthermore, it has already been seen that new examples of easements are recognised. Why, then, was there not a valid easement in *Hill* v *Tupper*?

(2) In *Hill* v *Tupper*, could the defendant (owner of the inn) have been granted an easement to put boats on the canal? How would such a claim differ from that made by the plaintiff?[5]

In addition to the criteria considered in *Re Ellenborough Park*, three other factors need to be considered.

(i) No positive obligations

The nature of an easement is a right to do something on a neighbour's land or (less commonly) to prevent the neighbour from doing something. An easement cannot take the form of an obligation imposed on a neighbour (this would be a positive covenant). This rule seems impregnable as a general principle, the only question being how far it applies.

The sole exception generally recognised is the easement of fencing, sometimes called a quasi-easement.

Extract 19.1.5

Crow v *Wood* [1971] 1 QB 77

LORD DENNING MR: . . . The question is, therefore, whether a right to have a fence or wall kept in repair is a right which is capable of being granted by law. I think it is because it is in the nature of an easement. It is not an easement strictly so called because it involves the servient owner in the expenditure of money. It was described by Gale [*Easements*, 11th ed (1932), p 432] as a 'spurious kind of easement'. But it has been treated in practice by the courts as being an easement. Professor Glanville Williams on *Liability for Animals* (1939), says, at p 209: 'If we put aside these questions of theory and turn to the practice of the courts, there seems to be little doubt that fencing is an easement.' In *Jones* v *Price* [1965] 2 QB 618, 633, Willmer LJ said: 'It is clear that a right to require the owner of adjoining land to keep the boundary fence in repair is a right which the law will recognise as a quasi-easement.' Diplock LJ, at p 639, points out that it is a right of such a nature that it can be acquired by prescription which imports that it lies in grant, for prescription rests on a presumed grant.

It seems to me that it is now sufficiently established – or at any rate, if not established hitherto, we should now declare – that a right to have your neighbour keep up the fences is a right in the nature of an easement which is capable of being granted by law so as to run with the land and to be binding on successors. It is a right which lies in grant and is of such a nature that it can pass under section 62 of the Law of Property Act, 1925.

Comment

(1) Why should the law make an exception for fencing? How relevant is it that the servient land bordered common land on which sheep grazed? Might *Crow* v *Wood* lead to flexibility in other contexts?

(2) The Law Commission[6] recommends that no new such rights should be permitted: they could (if express) take effect as land obligations.

---

[5] See *P&S Platt Ltd* v *Crouch* [2004] 1 P&CR 242.
[6] Law Com No 327, para 5.94.

Extract 19.1.6

Rance v *Elvin* (1985) 50 P&CR 9

The plaintiff claimed an easement for the uninterrupted passage of fresh water through pipes on the defendant Malcway's land. The supply (which was to both the plaintiff's and the defendant's land) was metered; Malcway would be charged by the water company, with a right to recoup payments from the plaintiff for his share.

BROWNE-WILKINSON LJ: . . . [Counsel] submits that the positive obligation which the judge held to be fatal to the plaintiff's claim relates not to an easement for the passage of the water through the pipes, but to the right to receive a supply of water in the pipes at all, a right which he does not now claim. Mr Rattee made what to my mind is a crucial distinction between two distinct types of right, *viz*: (a) a right to a supply of water; and (b) a right to the uninterrupted passage of any water that may come into the pipes under Malcway's land.

The plaintiff is now claiming only the right of type (b). Then, says Mr Rattee, the positive obligation to pay water charges which the judge found to be fatal to the plaintiff's claim is not an incident of the right of type (b): such obligation relates only to the supply of the water by the water company to the meter. If someone (be it Malcway or someone else) pays for such supply and water gets into the private water system, Malcway is not entitled to stop such supply passing through the system. Such a right to the free and uninterrupted passage and running of water through the pipes on the property in 1977 is exactly the right granted by the 1977 conveyance and is a classic example of an easement. Malcway is entitled at any time to refuse to pay for the supply of water through the meter, but in that event the plaintiff would be free to make his own arrangement with the water company.

Mr Cullen, for Malcway, submits that this analysis of the right granted is over-refined. He says that the reality of the case is, as the judge found, that the plaintiff is actually claiming a right to the supply of the water which he is in fact using and that therefore the easement claimed is a composite easement both to the supply of the water and to the passage of the water through the pipes. Therefore, as the judge held, the easement claimed does impose the indirect positive obligation on Malcway to pay for the water consumed on the alleged dominant tenement, Chantry Farm House.

In my judgment, Mr Rattee's submissions are correct. Looking first at the 1977 conveyance itself, the right granted is a right simply to the passage of water and no more. It does not purport to confer any right to insist on someone else ensuring the presence of water in the pipes. However, if water in fact reaches the private pipe system under Malcway's land by any means whatever, there is appurtenant to Chantry Farm House a right that such water shall be permitted to pass through the pipes to Chantry Farm. No positive obligation is imposed on Malcway by such right to the passage of water supplied by another. It is the classic form of an easement of passage. Malcway cannot do any physical act interrupting the passage of such water without being liable for an actionable interference. On the other hand, Malcway is under no obligation to ensure that any water does in fact reach the private water system.

The matter can be illustrated by considering what would have been the position if there had originally been no meter through which the water passed from the main into the pipes. There could not in my judgment have been any question but that Chantry Farm House was entitled to an easement for the passage of such water. If thereafter a meter had been installed by Seabrook or Malcway in order to obtain a supply of water for its own purposes, that could not have defeated the easement to the passage of the water to Chantry Farm House. The obligation to pay for such supply would arise not from the existence of the easement for the passage of water, but from the arrangements made by Malcway for the supply of water to the private system. Similarly, given the express grant of an easement in the 1977 conveyance, I cannot see that it makes any difference what arrangements for the supply of water had been made by Seabrook before 1977 and continued thereafter by Seabrook and Malcway.

Comment

(1) Is the obligation in *Rance* v *Elvin* truly negative when the servient owner has the choice of either paying for the water or having his own supply cut off?

(2) The cost element was relatively low in *Rance* v *Elvin*. Could there be an easement for the supply of hot water from the servient owner's central heating unit, when the supply heats both plots of land? Note that *Duffy* v *Lamb*[7] accepts the application of *Rance* v *Elvin* to the supply of electricity.

(3) Positive obligations may of course be enforced as contractual terms (subject to privity of contract) or, as in *Liverpool CC* v *Irwin*,[8] as leasehold covenants. In the latter case, they will bind purchasers.

Limits to *Rance* may be seen in the following dicta of Lord Scott:[9]

> I doubt whether the grant of a right to use a neighbour's swimming pool could ever qualify as a servitude. The grantor, the swimming pool owner, would be under no obligation to keep the pool full of water and the grantee would be in no position to fill it if the grantor chose not to do so.

Can this to be reconciled with *Rance*?

The rejection of positive obligations helps explain why the servient owner is under no obligation to do acts such as repairing rights of way.

(ii) No new negative easements

Some negative easements are recognised: the clearest and best-known example is the right to light. This is a right that the servient owner shall not build in such a way as to diminish light below that 'required for the ordinary purposes of inhabitancy or business'.[10]

Extract 19.1.7

Phipps v Pears [1965] 1 QB 76

LORD DENNING MR: . . . The case, so put, raises the question whether there is a right known to the law to be protected – by your neighbour's house – from the weather. Is there an easement of protection?

There are two kinds of easements known to the law: positive easements, such as a right of way, which give the owner of land *a right himself to do something* on or to his neighbour's land: and negative easements, such as a right of light, which gives him *a right to stop his neighbour doing something* on his (the neighbour's) own land. The right of support does not fall neatly into either category. It seems in some way to partake of the nature of a positive easement rather than a negative easement. The one building, by its weight, exerts a thrust, not only downwards, but also sideways on to the adjoining building or the adjoining land, and is thus doing something to the neighbour's land, exerting a thrust on it, see *Dalton v Angus*,[i] *per* Lord Selborne LC.[ii] But a right to protection from the weather (if it exists) is entirely negative. It is a right to stop your neighbour pulling down his own house. Seeing that it is a negative easement, it must be looked at with caution. Because the law has been very chary of creating any new negative easements.

---

[7] (1997) 75 P&CR 364; the servient owner paid for the electricity and charged the dominant owner.
[8] [1977] AC 239.
[9] *Moncrieff* v *Jamieson* [2007] 1 WLR 2620 at [47].
[10] *Colls* v *Home & Colonial Stores Ltd* [1904] AC 179 at p 204; see p 696 below.

Take this simple instance: Suppose you have a fine view from your house. You have enjoyed the view for many years. It adds greatly to the value of your house. But if your neighbour chooses to despoil it, by building up and blocking it, you have no redress. There is no such right known to the law as a right to a prospect or view, see *Bland* v *Moseley*[iii] cited by Lord Coke in *Aldred's* case.[iv] The only way in which you can keep the view from your house is to get your neighbour to make a covenant with you that he will not build so as to block your view. Such a covenant is binding on him by virtue of the contract. It is also binding in equity on anyone who buys the land from him with notice of the covenant. But it is not binding on a purchaser who has no notice of it, see *Leech* v *Schweder*.[v]

Take next this instance from the last century. A man built a windmill. The winds blew freely on the sails for thirty years working the mill. Then his neighbour built a schoolhouse only 25 yards away which cut off the winds. It was held that the miller had no remedy: for the right to wind and air, coming in an undefined channel, is not a right known to the law, see *Webb* v *Bird*.[vi] The only way in which the miller could protect himself was by getting his neighbour to enter into a covenant.

The reason underlying these instances is that if such an easement were to be permitted, it would unduly restrict your neighbour in his enjoyment of his own land. It would hamper legitimate development, see *Dalton* v *Angus*,[vii] *per* Lord Blackburn.[viii] Likewise here, if we were to stop a man pulling down his house, we would put a brake on desirable improvement. Every man is entitled to pull down his house if he likes. If it exposes your house to the weather, that is your misfortune. It is no wrong on his part. Likewise every man is entitled to cut down his trees if he likes, even if it leaves you without shelter from the wind or shade from the sun; see the decision of the Master of the Rolls in Ireland in *Cochrane* v *Verner*.[ix] There is no such easement known to the law as an easement to be protected from the weather.

[i]   (1881) 6 App Cas 740, HL.
[ii]   *Ibid.* 793.
[iii]   (1587) cited in 9 Co Rep 58a.
[iv]   (1610) 9 Co Rep 57b.
[v]   (1874) 9 Ch App 463.
[vi]   (1861) 10 CBNS 268; (1862) 13 CBNS 841.
[vii]   (1881) 6 App Cas 740.
[viii]   *Ibid.* 824.
[ix]   (1895) 29 ILT 571.

Comment

(1) Are the reasons given by Lord Denning for not recognising new negative easements convincing? Are there any other reasons?

(2) Do you regard the easement of support as positive or negative? What about the right to use drains under the servient land, or the supply of water in *Rance* v *Elvin*?

(3) Most potential negative easements may exist as restrictive covenants. This overlap was noted by the Law Commission:[11]

> For the future, attempts to create negative easements expressly will give rise to land obligations if the requirements of clause 1 of the draft Bill are met; but all four negative easements will continue to be able to arise by implication or prescription, which meets consultees' concerns.

Is it problematic that these rights will sometimes be land obligations and sometimes easements?

[11]   Law Com No 327, para 5.99.

(iii) No claim to possession

This factor may be viewed as an attempt to distinguish easements from claims which are better seen as a fee simple or a lease. Our first case provides the basis for modern thinking in this area.

Extract 19.1.8

Copeland v Greenhalf [1952] Ch 488

A wheelwright claimed an easement to store vehicles on an eight foot wide part of a strip of land, itself varying in width between 15 and 35 feet.

UPJOHN J: . . . I think that the right claimed goes wholly outside any normal idea of an easement, that is, the right of the owner or the occupier of a dominant tenement over a servient tenement. This claim (to which no closely related authority has been referred to me) really amounts to a claim to a joint user of the land by the defendant. Practically, the defendant is claiming the whole beneficial user of the strip of land on the south-east side of the track there; he can leave as many or as few lorries there as he likes for as long as he likes; he may enter on it by himself, his servants and agents to do repair work thereon. In my judgment, that is not a claim which can be established as an easement. It is virtually a claim to possession of the servient tenement, if necessary to the exclusion of the owner; or, at any rate, to a joint user, and no authority has been cited to me which would justify the conclusion that a right of this wide and undefined nature can be the proper subject-matter of an easement. It seems to me that to succeed, this claim must amount to a successful claim of possession by reason of long adverse possession.

Many easements involve some element of interference with the possession and enjoyment of the servient land. The next two cases provide good illustrations of how such rights can still be easements.

Extract 19.1.9

Miller v Emcer Products Ltd [1956] Ch 304

A lease of office premises granted the right to use lavatories in another part of the building.

ROMER LJ: . . . In my judgment the right had all the requisite characteristics of an easement. There is no doubt as to what were intended to be the dominant and servient tenements respectively, and the right was appurtenant to the former and calculated to enhance its beneficial use and enjoyment. It is true that during the times when the dominant owner exercised the right, the owner of the servient tenement would be excluded, but this in greater or less degree is a common feature of many easements (for example, rights of way) and does not amount to such an ouster of the servient owner's rights as was held by Upjohn J to be incompatible with a legal easement in *Copeland v Greenhalf*.[i] No case precisely in point on this issue was brought to our attention, but the right to use a lavatory is not dissimilar, I think, to the right to use a neighbour's kitchen for washing, the validity of which as an easement was assumed without question in *Heywood v Mallalieu*.[ii]

[i] [1952] Ch 488; [1952] 1 TLR 786; [1952] 1 All ER 809.
[ii] (1883) 25 Ch D 357.

Extract 19.1.10

Ward v Kirkland [1967] Ch 194

A wall of the plaintiff's cottage was built on the boundary with the defendant's land. Maintenance required access from the defendant's land; could such a right of access constitute an easement?

UNGOED-THOMAS J: . . . The plaintiff claims the right to maintain the wall as an easement to which he is entitled. The first question which has been raised is whether such a right is capable of being an easement. At first impression, certainly, it has the four qualities essential to an easement. . . . The objection which is taken to such a right as this constituting an easement is that, so it is said, it would amount to an exclusion of the servient owner from possession of his land.

. . .

The facts of this case, and the kind of right to maintain, which would involve – as the evidence establishes – no more even for the purposes of window-cleaning than monthly visits to the property, are very far removed from the facts in *Copeland* v *Greenhalf*.[i] It was submitted, however, that such a right would in effect exclude the defendant from the use of part of the farmyard next to the cottage, or interfere substantially with such use. It is quite clear, of course, that the farmyard could be used right up to the cottage wall, but the user could not be such as to destroy the right or any easement to maintain which might exist. Similar considerations arise even in cases of rights of way, because the owner of the servient tenement cannot exercise his property rights in such a way as to defeat the easement which exists over it. I for my part find no difficulty in coming to the conclusion that such a right as is claimed here is not a right that would be defeated upon the ground that it would amount to the possession or joint possession of part of the defendant's property, being that part over which the plaintiff would be exercising his right to maintain his wall.

[i] [1952] Ch 488.

Comment

It is clear that, in these cases, the servient owner is prevented from the normal full use of the land. Why is this not an objection?

Parking of cars has formed the basis of several recent cases. The entire area was reviewed in the House of Lords in *Moncrieff* v *Jamieson*.[12] The case is difficult to assess because it is a Scottish case (the two Scots Law Lords chose to say nothing about the English cases) and the claim was nothing like as extensive as that in, for example, *Copeland* v *Greenhalf*. The dicta are, accordingly, obiter.

Extract 19.1.11

Moncrieff v Jamieson [2007] 1 WLR 2620

A servitude (easement) to park cars was claimed, in circumstances where there was an express right of access by car. Our interest in the case lies in the discussion of the right to park, rather than whether such a right should be implied.

LORD SCOTT:
The right to park as a servitude
47. It is convenient to start with the question whether a servitudal right to park appurtenant to some identifiable dominant land, i.e. a right in rem and not simply a contractual right, is recognised by law. In my opinion there should be no doubt that it is and, if there is any such doubt, that doubt should be now dispelled. I can see no reason in principle, subject to a few qualifications, why any right of limited use of the land of a neighbour that is of its nature of benefit to the dominant land and its owners from time to time should not be capable of being created as a servitudal right in rem appurtenant to the dominant land: see *Gale on Easements*, 17th ed (2002), para 1–35. An essential qualification of the above stated proposition, a qualification that

[12] [2007] 1 WLR 2620.

I would derive from the all-important civiliter principle, is that the right must be such that a reasonable use thereof by the owner of the dominant land would not be inconsistent with the beneficial ownership of the servient land by the servient owner. I must later examine the so-called 'ouster' principle, the principle which, it is said, prevents the creation of a servitude if the servitude contended for would prevent any reasonable use being made of the servient land, and some of the authorities relating to that principle. To the extent, however, that the 'ouster' principle is asserting that a servitude must not be inconsistent with the continued beneficial ownership of the servient land by the servient owner, I would unreservedly accept it. If, for example, the nature of the purported servitude were to place the dominant owner in such occupation of the servient land as to bar the servient owner from possession or control of the land I would find it very difficult to accept that the right could constitute a servitude. An express grant of such a right might be construed as a grant of the fee simple (see per Lopes LJ in *Reilly* v *Booth* (1890) 44 Ch D 12, 26) or might be construed as the grant of a contractual licence, but I do not as at present advised see how it could be the grant of a servitude . . .

'Deprivation of ownership'
54.   It has been argued that the rights of parking claimed by the pursuers in respect of the pink land deprive the defenders of any reasonable use of that land, are therefore inconsistent with their ownership of the pink land and should not be recognised as servitudal rights in rem that can bind them and their successors in title. This is the so-called 'ouster' principle to which I have already referred . . . Every servitude or easement will bar some ordinary use of the servient land. For example, a right of way prevents all manner of ordinary uses of the land over which the road passes. The servient owner cannot plough up the road. He cannot grow cabbages on it or use it for basketball practice. A viaduct carrying water across the servient land to the dominant land will prevent the same things. Every servitude prevents any use of the servient land, whether ordinary or otherwise, that would interfere with the reasonable exercise of the servitude. There will always be some such use that is prevented . . .
55.   In *Wright* v *Macadam* [1949] 2 KB 744, the Court of Appeal had to consider whether the right to use a coal shed could exist as an easement and held that it could: see per Jenkins LJ, at p 752. It has been suggested that the case may have turned on whether the claimant had sole use of the coal shed, but it is difficult to see any difference in principle between a case in which the dominant owner has sole use of a patch of ground for storage purposes, e.g. a coal shed, and a case in which the dominant owner is the only user of a strip of road for access purposes or of a viaduct for the passage of water. Sole user, as a concept, is quite different from, and fundamentally inferior to, exclusive possession. Sole use of a coal shed for the storage of coal does not prevent the servient owner from using the shed for any purposes of his own that do not interfere with the dominant owner's reasonable use for the storage of coal. The dominant owner entitled to a servitude of way or for the passage of water along a viaduct does not have possession of the land over which the road or the viaduct passes. If the coal shed door had been locked with only the dominant owner possessing a key and entry by the servient owner barred, so that the dominant owner would have been in possession and control of the shed, I would have regarded it as arguable that the right granted was inconsistent with the servient owner's ownership and inconsistent with the nature of a servitude or an easement. But sole use for a limited purpose is not, in my opinion, inconsistent with the servient owner's retention of possession and control or inconsistent with the nature of an easement. This conclusion is supported by Lord Evershed MR's remarks in *In re Ellenborough Park* [1956] Ch 131, 176 where the issue was whether the right to use a communal garden could take effect as an easement. He said that:

'the right conferred no more amounts to a joint occupation of the park with its owners, no more excludes the proprietorship or possession of the latter, than a right of way granted through a passage, or than the use by the public of the gardens of Lincoln's Inn Fields . . . amount to joint occupation of that garden with the London County Council, or involve an inconsistency with the possession or proprietorship of the council as lessees.'

56.   *Copeland* v *Greenhalf* [1952] Ch 488, a case that goes the other way, was a case in which a prescriptive easement to use a strip of land by the side of a private roadway for depositing vehicles and for other purposes connected with a wheelwright's business had been claimed. Upjohn J, at p 498, rejected the claim on the ground that:

'Practically, the defendant is claiming the whole beneficial user of the strip of land . . . It is virtually a claim to possession of the servient tenement, if necessary to the exclusion of the owner . . .'

There may be arguments as to whether the facts of the case justified those remarks but, for my part, I would accept that if they did Upjohn J was right to reject the easement claim and to require the defendant, if he was to succeed in resisting the plaintiff's claim to remove him from the land, to establish a title by adverse possession.

57.   It has often been commented that *Wright* v *Macadam* was not cited to Upjohn J and the possible inconsistency between the two cases was addressed by Judge Paul Baker QC in *London & Blenheim Estates Ltd* v *Ladbroke Retail Parks Ltd* [1992] 1 WLR 1278 where a right of parking had been claimed. He commented, at p 1286, that the question whether the right to park that had been claimed was consistent with the nature of an easement was one of degree: 'A small coal shed in a large property is one thing. The exclusive use of a large part of the alleged servient tenement is another.' I think, with respect, that this attempt to reconcile the two authorities was addressing the wrong point. The servient land in relation to a servitude or easement is surely the land over which the servitude or easement is enjoyed, not the totality of the surrounding land of which the servient owner happens to be the owner . . .

58.   As to the right to park and the 'ouster' objection, Sir Robert Megarry V-C in *Newman* v *Jones* (unreported), 22 March 1982, a case concerning the right of lessees of a block of 14 flats to park in the grounds of the block, said: 'I feel no hesitation in holding that a right for a landowner to park a car anywhere in a defined area is capable of existing as an easement.' But Judge Paul Baker QC in the *London & Blenheim Estates* case [1992] 1 WLR 1278 formulated, and the Court of Appeal in *Batchelor* v *Marlow* [2003] 1 WLR 764 applied, a test that disqualified the right to park from existing as an easement if (per Judge Paul Baker QC):

'the right granted in relation to the area over which it is to be exercisable is such that it would leave the servient owner without any reasonable use of his land, whether for parking or anything else . . .'

In *Batchelor* v *Marlow* Tuckey LJ posed the question, at p 768:

'Does an exclusive right to park six cars for $9^{1}/_{2}$ hours every day of the working week leave the plaintiff without any reasonable use of his land, whether for parking or anything else?'

and gave the answer that:

'[The plaintiff's] right to use his land is curtailed altogether for intermittent periods throughout the week. Such a restriction would, I think, make his ownership of the land illusory.'

For that reason the Court of Appeal rejected the claim to a prescriptive easement to park the six cars for the period mentioned.

59.   In my respectful opinion the test formulated in the *London & Blenheim Estates* case [1992] 1 WLR 1278 and applied by the Court of Appeal in *Batchelor* v *Marlow* [2003] 1 WLR 764, a test that would reject the claim to an easement if its exercise would leave the servient owner with no 'reasonable use' to which he could put the servient land, needs some qualification. It is

impossible to assert that there would be no use that could be made by an owner of land over which he had granted parking rights. He could, for example, build above or under the parking area. He could place advertising hoardings on the walls. Other possible uses can be conjured up. And by what yardstick is it to be decided whether the residual uses of the servient land available to its owner are 'reasonable' or sufficient to save his ownership from being 'illusory'? It is not the uncertainty of the test that, in my opinion, is the main problem. It is the test itself. I do not see why a landowner should not grant rights of a servitudal character over his land to any extent that he wishes. The claim in *Batchelor* v *Marlow* for an easement to park cars was a prescriptive claim based on over 20 years of that use of the strip of land. There is no difference between the characteristics of an easement that can be acquired by grant and the characteristics of an easement that can be acquired by prescription. If an easement can be created by grant it can be acquired by prescription and I can think of no reason why, if an area of land can accommodate nine cars, the owner of the land should not grant an easement to park nine cars on the land. The servient owner would remain the owner of the land and in possession and control of it. The dominant owner would have the right to station up to nine cars there and, of course, to have access to his nine cars. How could it be said that the law would recognise an easement allowing the dominant owner to park five cars or six or seven or eight but not nine? I would, for my part, reject the test that asks whether the servient owner is left with any reasonable use of his land, and substitute for it a test which asks whether the servient owner retains possession and, subject to the reasonable exercise of the right in question, control of the servient land.

LORD NEUBERGER: 139. . . . If the right to park a vehicle in an area that can hold 20 vehicles is capable of being a servitude or an easement, then it would logically follow that the same conclusion should apply to an area that can hold two vehicles. On that basis, it can be said to be somewhat contrary to common sense that the arrangement is debarred from being a servitude or an easement simply because the parties have chosen to identify a precise space in the area, over which the right is to be exercised, and the space is just big enough to hold the vehicle. Also, presumably on the pursuers' case, such a right would indeed be capable of being a servitude or an easement if the servient owner had the right to change the location of the precise space within the area from time to time.

140.   At least as at present advised, I am not satisfied that a right is prevented from being a servitude or an easement simply because the right granted would involve the servient owner being effectively excluded from the property. In this connection, the Privy Council in *Attorney General of Southern Nigeria* v *John Holt & Co (Liverpool) Ltd* [1915] AC 599, 617 appears to have held that a right to store materials on land could be an easement although it involved the dominant owner enjoying an 'exclusive' right to enjoy the property concerned. Citing *Dyce* v *Hay* in support, the Privy Council immediately went on to observe that, in considering arguments as to whether a right could be an easement 'The law must adapt itself to the conditions of modern society and trade'. Further, the Court of Appeal in *Wright* v *Macadam* [1949] 2 KB 744 held that an apparently exclusive right to store coal in a small shed was capable of being an easement. Neither case was cited to Upjohn J in *Copeland* v *Greenhalf*.

143.   Accordingly, I see considerable force in the views expressed by Lord Scott in paras 57 and 59 of his opinion, to the effect that a right can be an easement notwithstanding that the dominant owner effectively enjoys exclusive occupation, on the basis that the essential requirement is that the servient owner retains possession and control. If that were the right test, then it seems likely that *Batchelor* v *Marlow* [2003] 1 WLR 764 was wrongly decided. However, unless it is necessary to decide the point to dispose of this appeal, I consider that it would be dangerous to try and identify degree of ouster is required to disqualify a right from constituting a servitude or easement, given the very limited argument your Lordships have received on the topic.

144.   As I have mentioned, there are a number of cases which can be said to support the approach of the Court of Appeal in *Batchelor* v *Marlow*, although it may be possible to distinguish

them. The point does not appear to be settled in Australia: see the difference of opinion in the recent case *White* v *Betalli* [2007] NSWCA 243. I am also concerned that, if we were unconditionally to suggest that exclusion of the servient owner from occupation, as opposed to possession, would not of itself be enough to prevent a right from being an easement, it might lead to unexpected consequences or difficulties which have not been explored in argument in this case. Thus, if the right to park a vehicle in a one-vehicle space can be an easement, it may be hard to justify an effectively exclusive right to store any material not being an easement, which could be said to lead to the logical conclusion that an occupational licence should constitute an interest in land.

Comment

(1) Lord Mance chose not to express an opinion on these questions. How great is the authority of Lord Scott's judgment?[13]

(2) Why does Lord Neuberger not express a final conclusion? Are his reasons convincing?

(3) When considering whether a right is too extensive to be recognised as an easement, should we look at the specific area over which it is exercised or the entire plot owned by the servient owner?

(4) Both judges are critical of the analysis in *Batchelor* v *Marlow*. Why should an easement be recognised if the servient owner is left with no reasonable use for the land?

(5) When, if ever, would a right be too extensive to qualify as an easement? Can the result in *Copeland* v *Greenhalf* still be justified?

The Law Commission[14] has considered this area:

> We conclude therefore that while an easement must not grant exclusive possession, the ouster principle should be abolished. An easement that stops short of exclusive possession, even if it deprives the owner of much of the use of his land, or indeed of all reasonable use of it, is valid. The effect of this would be to reverse, for the future, the decision in *Batchelor* v *Marlow*, for example, and therefore to validate a potentially wide range of parking easements.

Does this produce the same result as that espoused by Lord Scott?

Extract 19.1.12

Kettel v *Bloomfold Ltd* [2012] EWHC 1422 (Ch); [2014] L&TR 514

HHJ DAVID COOKE: 21.   There is no doubt that an easement for parking can exist, but it seems to me that notwithstanding the agreement between counsel I must address the question whether I am precluded by *Batchelor* v *Marlow* from finding that an easement exists in this case. . . .

22.   I do not believe that an easement is excluded, essentially for the same reason as given by HHJ Purle QC in *Virdi*,[f] that the rights exercisable by the defendant over the space cannot be said in the circumstances of this case to leave him with no reasonable use of the land and so make his ownership of it illusory.

23.   I approach this from the starting point that the defendant may do anything that a freeholder could normally do, except to the extent that it is excluded by the terms of the right granted in the lease, i.e. except to the extent that it would be inconsistent with the express right

---

[13] In *Polo Woods Foundation* v *Shelton-Agar* [2010] 1 All ER 539 at [121], Warren J considered that *Batchelor* remains binding on lower courts; see also *Kettel* v *Bloomfold Ltd* [2012] L&TR 514 at [12].

[14] Law Com No 327, para 3.208.

to park a car, together with any terms to be implied as a normal matter of construction. Thus the defendant may pass on foot or by vehicle across the space freely if there is no vehicle parked on it for the time being or avoiding one that is. He may authorise others to do likewise (and has done so in the other estate leases). He may choose, change and repair the surface, keep it clean and remove obstructions (and is obliged to do so in providing the Services). He may lay pipes or other service media under it, as he may wish to do for the benefit of the estate buildings. He may in principle build above it (as is proposed under the crash deck scheme) or provide overhead projections such as wires.

[i] *Virdi* v *Chana* [2008] EWHC 2901 (Ch).

Comment

Does this differ significantly in its result from what Lord Scott had argued? Is it consistent with the outcome in *Batchelor*?

2. The creation and transfer of easements and profits

A. Implied easements

Unlike most other property interests, easements[15] are very often implied into transfers. This occurs where an owner of land sells part of it. The parties may not provide for rights of way, access for repairs, rights to use drains or rights to light. Nevertheless, the law often (many argue too often) steps in to imply such easements. This nearly always operates in favour of the purchaser (implied grant); relatively rarely in favour of the seller (implied reservation).

This greater generosity in favour of a purchaser leads to questions as to which of two transfers comes first. If O sells part of his land to P and then the remainder to Q, it follows that P may have implied rights over the land which O retains (implied grant) and which is now owned by Q. On the other hand, O is unlikely to have implied rights over P (implied reservation) and therefore it is unlikely that any rights exist which can be passed on to Q. Note that when O sells to Q it is too late to imply rights over land now owned by P: as a matter of basic principle, O cannot create rights over land owned by somebody else. However, where the sales to P and Q are in substance contemporaneous the law treats each as if it were the first. Thus both P and Q could take advantage of the more generous implied grant rules. This was clearly held by Buckley LJ in *White* v *Taylor (No 2)*,[16] where the various sales took place by auction on the same day. It was stressed that: 'Each purchaser must be taken to have known the vendor was at the same time selling the other lots to the other purchasers upon the terms of the conditions of sale.'

Extract 19.2.1

Wheeldon v Burrows (1879) 12 Ch D 31

THESIGER LJ: [After rejecting any general rule in favour of implied reservation:] One other point remains, and that I shall dispose of in a very few words. It is said that, even supposing the maxims which I have stated to be correct, this case is an exception which comes within the rule

---

[15] Profits can be implied in similar ways, although this would change under the Law Commission's proposals (Law Com No 327, para 3.9). The great majority of the cases involve easements.
[16] [1969] 1 Ch 160.

laid down in *Swansborough v Coventry*[i] and *Compton v Richards*,[ii] namely, that, although the land and houses were not in fact conveyed at the same time, they were conveyances made as part and parcel of one intended sale by auction. It seems to me that that proposition cannot be supported for one moment. We start here with an absolute conveyance in January, 1876. What right have we to look back to any previous contract or to any previous arrangement between the parties? If it had been the case of an ordinary contract, and there had been parol negotiations, it is well-established law that you cannot look to those parol negotiations in order to put any construction upon the document which the parties entered into for the purpose of avoiding any dispute as to what might be their intentions in the bargain made between them. The same rule of law applies, and even more strongly in the case of a conveyance, which alone must regulate the rights of the parties. In the cases which have been cited the conveyances were founded upon transactions which in Equity were equivalent to conveyances between the parties at the time when the transactions were entered into, and those transactions were entered into at the same moment of time and as part and parcel of one transaction. There may be, and there is, according to *Swansborough v Coventry*, another exception to the rule which I have mentioned; but here the sale by auction was abortive as regards the Defendant's property. There was a conveyance in January of the Plaintiff's property without any reservation, and there was no contract of purchase on the part of the Defendant until more than a month after that conveyance had been complete. I believe I am expressing the view of the other members of the Court when I say that it appears to the Court that under such circumstances there is no exception to the general rule.

[i] 9 Bing 305.
[ii] 1 Price 27.

Comment

(1) Why did the contemporaneous sales rule not apply?

(2) Note that the stress is on the time of contract rather than conveyance.

(3) Sales are invariably made subject to contract, the binding contract being entered into several weeks later. Which is the relevant time: agreement subject to contract or formal contract?

(4) Suppose that A puts two adjoining properties in the hands of an estate agent for sale (not by auction). One is sold almost immediately, the other after a delay of three weeks. Are these sales contemporaneous? Might the rule be one of contemporaneous marketing rather than contemporaneous sale?

(i) Implied reservation

Extract 19.2.2

Wheeldon v Burrows (1879) 12 Ch D 31

The defendant claimed, by implied reservation, a right to light.

THESIGER LJ: . . . We have had a considerable number of cases cited to us, and out of them I think that two propositions may be stated as what I may call the general rules governing cases of this kind. The first of these rules is, that on the grant by the owner of a tenement of part of that tenement as it is then used and enjoyed, there will pass to the grantee all those continuous and apparent easements (by which, of course, I mean *quasi* easements), or, in other words, all those easements which are necessary to the reasonable enjoyment of the property granted, and which have been and are at the time of the grant used by the owners of the entirety for the benefit of the part granted. The second proposition is that, if the grantor intends to reserve any right over the tenement granted, it is his duty to reserve it expressly in the grant. Those are the general rules governing cases of this kind, but the second of those rules is subject to certain exceptions. One of those exceptions is the well-known exception which attaches to cases of what are called ways of necessity; and I do not dispute for a moment that there may be, and probably are, certain other exceptions, to which I shall refer before I close my observations upon this case.

Both of the general rules which I have mentioned are founded upon a maxim which is as well established by authority as it is consonant to reason and common sense, viz, that a grantor shall not derogate from his grant. It has been argued before us that there is no distinction between what has been called an implied grant and what is attempted to be established under the name of an implied reservation; and that such a distinction between the implied grant and the implied reservation is a mere modern invention, and one which runs contrary, not only to the general practice upon which land has been bought and sold for a considerable time, but also to authorities which are said to be clear and distinct upon the matter. So far, however, from that distinction being one which was laid down for the first time by and which is to be attributed to Lord *Westbury* in *Suffield* v *Brown*,[i] it appears to me that it has existed almost as far back as we can trace the law upon the subject . . .

i 4 DJ&S 185.

Comment

Although it involved an implied reservation claim, *Wheeldon* v *Burrows* is commonly cited for the rules on implied grant; it will be considered further in that context below.

As was made clear by Thesiger LJ, implied reservation is sometimes possible. We will consider easements of necessity (the most common case), but another example is where there are reciprocal rights as between the two tenements.[17]

The next case considers the basis of easements of necessity.

Extract 19.2.3

Nickerson v Barraclough [1981] Ch 426

BRIGHTMAN LJ: . . . In this court we have heard a great deal of argument about ways of necessity – what is their basis, how they can be acquired and whether they can be lost. With the utmost respect to the Vice-Chancellor, I have come to the conclusion that the doctrine of way of necessity is not founded upon public policy at all but upon an implication from the circumstances. I accept that there are reported cases, and textbooks, in which public policy is suggested as a possible foundation of the doctrine, but such a suggestion is not, in my opinion, correct. It is well established that a way of necessity is never found to exist except in association with a grant of land: see *Proctor* v *Hodgson* (1855) 10 Exch 824, where it was held that land acquired by escheat got no way of necessity; and *Wilkes* v *Greenway* (1890) 6 TLR 449, where land acquired by prescription got no way of necessity. If a way of necessity were based upon public policy, I see no reason why land acquired by escheat or by prescription should be excluded. Furthermore, there would seem to be no particular reason to father the doctrine of way of necessity upon public policy when implication is such an obvious and convenient

---

17 *Richards* v *Rose* (1853) 9 Exch 218 (156 ER 93), approved in *Wheeldon* v *Burrows*.

candidate for paternity. There is an Australian case, *North Sydney Printing Pty Ltd* v *Sabemo Investment Corporation Pty Ltd* [1971] 2 NSWLR 150, where that conclusion was reached. Furthermore, I cannot accept that public policy can play any part at all in the construction of an instrument; in construing a document the court is endeavouring to ascertain the expressed intention of the parties. Public policy may require the court to frustrate that intention where the contract is against public policy, but in my view public policy cannot help the court to ascertain what that intention was. So I reach the view that a way of necessity is not founded upon public policy; that considerations of public policy cannot influence the construction of the 1906 conveyance . . .

Comment

Why does it matter whether easements of necessity are based upon public policy or implication?

Extract 19.2.4

Union Lighterage Co v *London Graving Dock Co* [1902] 2 Ch 557

Tie-rods on the plaintiff's land held in place the wooden walls of the appellant's dock.

STIRLING LJ: . . . The appellants did not dispute that there is no express reservation in the conveyance to the plaintiffs, but they contended that the easement claimed by the defendants is an 'easement of necessity' within the recognised exception to the second rule. Now, in the passages cited the expressions 'ways of necessity' and 'easements of necessity' are used in contrast with the other expressions, 'easements which are necessary to the reasonable enjoyment of the property granted', and 'easements . . . necessary to the reasonable enjoyment of the property conveyed', and the word 'necessity' in the former expressions has plainly a narrower meaning than the word 'necessary' in the latter.

In my opinion an easement of necessity, such as is referred to, means an easement without which the property retained cannot be used at all, and not one merely necessary to the reasonable enjoyment of that property. In *Wheeldon* v *Burrows*,[i] the lights which were the subject of decision were certainly reasonably necessary to the enjoyment of the property retained, which was a workshop, yet there was held to be no reservation of it. So here it may be that the tie-rods which pass through the plaintiffs' property are reasonably necessary to the enjoyment of the defendants' dock in its present condition; but the dock is capable of use without them, and I think that there cannot be implied any reservation in respect of them.

[i] 12 Ch D 31.

Comment

(1) Vaughan Williams LJ dissented, but on a different point.

(2) The strict approach adopted by Stirling LJ means that it is difficult to prove an easement of necessity unless the land is landlocked. Might there be other easements which satisfy Stirling LJ's requirements?[18]

Alongside this strict approach, there is a more generous analysis based upon the joint intention of the parties as to the use of the land.

---

[18] Cf *Walby* v *Walby* [2013] 1 EGLR 111 at [32] (drainage rights).

Extract 19.2.5

***Wong* v *Beaumont Property Trust Ltd* [1965] 1 QB 173**

LORD DENNING MR: The plaintiff is the tenant of a Chinese restaurant in Exeter called the 'Chopstick'. It is situated underground below Nos 83 and 84, Queen Street, Exeter. He has a kitchen there where he cooks the food. It is so badly ventilated, however, that it is necessary to have an air duct so as to take the used air up to the roof. This duct will have to be fixed on to the back wall of the building which belongs to the landlords . . .

. . . The public health inspector says it is absolutely essential, if the business is to be carried on at all, that this ventilation duct should be put in. But the landlords object . . .

The question is: Has the plaintiff a right to put up this duct without the landlords' consent? If he is to have any right at all, it must be by way of easement and not merely by way of implied contract. He is not the original lessee, nor are the defendants the original lessors. Each is a successor in title. As between them, a right of this kind, if it exists at all, must be by way of an easement. In particular, an easement of necessity. The law on the matter was stated by Lord Parker of Waddington in *Pwllbach Colliery Co Ltd* v *Woodman*,[i] where he said,[ii] omitting immaterial words, 'The law will readily imply the grant or reservation of such easements as may be necessary to give effect to the common intention of the parties to a grant of real property, with reference to the manner or purposes in and for which the land granted . . . is to be used. But it is essential for this purpose that the parties should intend that the subject of the grant . . . should be used in some definite and particular manner. It is not enough that the subject of the grant . . . should be intended to be used in a manner which may or may not involve this definite and particular use.' That is the principle which underlies all easements of necessity. If you go back to Rolle's Abridgment you will find it stated in this way:[iii] If I have a field inclosed by my own land on all sides, and I alien this close to another, he shall have a way to this close over my land, as incident to the grant; for otherwise he cannot have any benefit by the grant.

I would apply those principles here. Here was the grant of a lease to the lessee for the very purpose of carrying on a restaurant business. It was to be a popular restaurant, and it was to be developed and extended. There was a covenant not to cause any nuisance; and to control and eliminate all smells; and to comply with the Food Hygiene Regulations. That was 'a definite and particular manner' in which the business had to be conducted. It could not be carried on in that manner at all unless a ventilation system was installed by a duct of this kind. In these circumstances it seems to me that, if the business is to be carried on at all – if, in the words of Rolle's Abridgment,[iv] the lessee is to 'have any benefit by the grant' at all – he must of necessity be able to put a ventilation duct up the wall.

[i] [1915] AC 634; 31 TLR 271, HL(E).
[ii] [1915] AC 634, 646.
[iii] 2 Rol Abr 60, pl 17, 18; 1 Saund (1871 ed) 570; see *Gale on Easements*, 13th ed, p 98.
[iv] 2 Rol Abr 60, pl 17, 18.

Comment

(1) In *Wong*, the implication operated in favour of the grantee. However, such implications also operate in favour of the grantor (reservation). One well-known example is *Lyttelton Times Co Ltd* v *Warners Ltd*.[19] Are such reservations likely to be more difficult to prove?

(2) Both *Wong* and *Lyttelton Times* involved leases. Is this merely a coincidence?

(3) Would this principle allow connection to mains utilities (water, electricity, gas) on the vendor's land, where land is sold for residential building? See *Donovan* v *Rana* [2014] 1 P&CR 374.

[19] [1907] AC 476 (PC), though note the cautious response of Scrutton LJ in *Aldridge* v *Wright* [1929] 2 KB 115 at pp 155–156.

(ii) Implied grants: the rule in *Wheeldon* v *Burrows*

Extract 19.2.6

Wheeldon v *Burrows* (1879) 12 Ch D 31

THESIGER LJ: . . . on the grant by the owner of a tenement of part of that tenement as it is then used and enjoyed, there will pass to the grantee all those continuous and apparent easements (by which, of course, I mean *quasi* easements), or, in other words, all those easements which are necessary to the reasonable enjoyment of the property granted, and which have been and are at the time of the grant used by the owners of the entirety for the benefit of the part granted.

. . . in the case of a grant you may imply a grant of such continuous and apparent easements or such easements as are necessary to the reasonable enjoyment of the property conveyed, and have in fact been enjoyed during the unity of ownership . . .

Comment

(1) What does Thesiger LJ mean by a *quasi*-easement?

(2) Note that continuous and apparent easements are equated ('or, in other words') with those necessary for the reasonable enjoyment of the land. Does this make sense?

The relationship between the two tests will be considered below, but a historical analysis helps explain the wording of the rule, if not its meaning today: Simpson (1967) 83 LQR 240:

> . . . Well before Gale's book was published there was authority for the view that a grantee would take easements of necessity (the paradigm example being a way to a land-locked tenement). There was, however, some doubt as to quite what 'necessity' meant in this context, as there still is. Now one technique for improving the lot of the grantee was to extend the concept of an easement of necessity so that it would include easements *'reasonably necessary'* to the enjoyment of the land granted. Had Gale never written his book it is probable that this would have been the way in which the doctrine of implied grant developed. But Gale superimposed upon this potential line of development his civilian doctrine of *destination*, expressed in terms of 'continuous and apparent' easements . . . Willes, the first editor of Gale, picked up the idea that his author's doctrine as to 'continuous and apparent' easements only applied to 'necessary' easements, and turned to the English cases for illumination as to what 'necessity' meant . . .
>
> This ingenious attempt to produce a synthesis between common law and civilian doctrine lies behind Thesiger LJ's uncertainties in *Wheeldon* v *Burrows* . . .

In considering the rule in *Wheeldon* v *Burrows*, a number of issues need to be addressed. The first concerns the meaning of 'continuous and apparent' and the second that of 'necessary for reasonable enjoyment'. A third issue, already alluded to, is the relationship between the two tests. These issues, naturally enough, cannot be considered in isolation from each other. An obvious point is that if both tests have to be satisfied, the courts may be prepared to take a more relaxed approach in deciding what is necessary for reasonable enjoyment.

Extract 19.2.7

Borman v *Griffith* [1930] 1 Ch 493

The plaintiff agreed to take a lease of a former gardener's lodge in a large park. There was access by a rear track to the lodge, but the plaintiff sought a right of way over the main drive which passed the lodge. This had previously been used as an access and was the only viable access for the heavy vehicles involved with the plaintiff's poultry business.

MAUGHAM J: . . . The plaintiff being entitled to specific performance, the Court would decide that he must be given all such rights of way as, according to the doctrine of the Court in regard to implied grants, would pass upon a conveyance or a demise. In my view, the principles laid down in such cases as *Wheeldon v Burrows*;[i] *Brown v Alabaster*;[ii] and *Nicholls v Nicholls*[iii] are applicable. Without going through all those cases in detail, I may state the principle as follows – namely, that where, as in the present case, two properties belonging to a single owner and about to be granted are separated by a common road, or where a plainly visible road exists over the one for the apparent use of the other, and that road is necessary for the reasonable enjoyment of the property, a right to use the road will pass with the quasi-dominant tenement, unless by the terms of the contract that right is excluded: and in my opinion, if the present position were that the plaintiff was claiming against the lessor specific performance of the agreement of October 10, 1923, he would be entitled to be given a right of way for all reasonable purposes along the drive, including the part that passes the farm on the way to the orchard.

It is true that the easement, or, rather, quasi-easement, is not continuous. But the authorities are sufficient to show that a grantor of property, in circumstances where an obvious, i.e., visible and made road is necessary for the reasonable enjoyment of the property by the grantee, must be taken prima facie to have intended to grant a right to use it.

[i] 12 Ch D 31.
[ii] 37 Ch D 490.
[iii] 81 LT 811.

Comment

(1) Note that the rule is here applied to a contract for a lease. In so far as the rule is based upon the principle that a grantor should not derogate from his grant, is this defensible?

(2) The requirement that the right be continuous is practically negated. At most, the requirement is that the easement is continuously apparent. How many easements are continuous? Is there any point in requiring continuous use?

(3) Suppose there are drains running under the grantor's land. Is a right to use these drains continuous and apparent?[20]

(4) Such a second access would never be impliedly reserved as an easement of necessity: the case provides a good example of the broader scope of implied grants under the rule in *Wheeldon v Burrows*.

Extract 19.2.8

Ward v Kirkland [1967] Ch 194

The passage extracted above[21] shows how the plaintiff claimed an easement to go on the defendant's land in order to maintain a cottage wall.

UNGOED-THOMAS LJ: . . . First, then, implication of law. Did the right to maintain the wall pass as an easement on the occasion of the conveyance in 1928 by the rector as common owner of the farm and the cottage? The source of the law on this subject is *Wheeldon v Burrows*[i] [the relevant passages are quoted]. Reading that passage on its own, on first impression, it would appear that the 'easements which are necessary to the reasonable enjoyment of the property conveyed' might be a separate class from 'continuous and apparent easements'. It has been

[20] *Pyer v Carter* (1851) 1 H&N 916 (156 ER 1472); *Schwann v Cotton* [1916] 2 Ch 120 (upheld at p 459).
[21] Extract 19.1.10.

recognised that there is some difficulty in these descriptions, to which I have referred, of the easements which come within the ambit of the doctrine of *Wheeldon* v *Burrows*. It has been suggested that perhaps the 'easements necessary to the reasonable enjoyment of the property conveyed' might refer to negative easements, whereas what we are concerned with here is positive easements. However that may be, I understand that there is no case in which positive easements which are not 'continuous and apparent' have been held to come within the doctrine of *Wheeldon* v *Burrows*. Here, there has certainly been continuous user, in the sense that the right has been in fact used whenever the need arose. But the words 'continuous and apparent' seem to be directed to there being on the servient tenement a feature which would be seen on inspection and which is neither transitory nor intermittent; for example, drains, paths, as contrasted with the bowsprits of ships overhanging a piece of land.

Here, it is conceded that it was only possible or practicable for the occupiers of the cottage to maintain the boundary wall by going onto the defendant's property as claimed in this case. That would be obvious on an inspection of the properties. But here there was no feature on the defendant's property designed or appropriate for such maintenance. The question is whether that requirement is necessary. If it is not necessary, then there are no clearly defined limits to the area of user; and if the easement extends to maintain the whole wall, as it must, then there could be no interference with that easement and therefore no building in the yard along that wall.

Professor Cheshire, in his book on Real Property, says[ii] that

'The two words "continuous" and "apparent" must be read together and understood as pointing to an easement which is accompanied by some obvious and permanent mark on the land itself, or at least by some mark which will be disclosed by a careful inspection of the premises.'

Then he gives instances, and says:[iii]

'A right of way is not necessarily such a quasi-easement as will pass under the rule in *Wheeldon* v *Burrows*. To do so it must be apparent. There is no difficulty where there is a definite made road over the quasi-servient tenement to and for the apparent use of the quasi-dominant tenement. Such will clearly pass upon a severance of the common tenement. But the existence of a formed road is not essential, and if there are other indicia which show that the road was being used at the time of the grant for the benefit of the quasi-dominant tenement and that it is necessary for the reasonable enjoyment of that tenement, it will pass to a purchaser of the latter.'

It seems to me that in the absence of a continuous and apparent feature designed or appropriate for the exercise of the easement on the servient tenement, there is not a continuous and apparent easement within the requirements of *Wheeldon* v *Burrows* in the case of alleged positive easements. I, therefore, come to the conclusion that the easement claimed was not created by implication of law.

[i] (1878) 12 Ch D 31, CA.
[ii] *Modern Real Property*, 9th ed (1962), p 468.
[iii] *Ibid*. 469.

Comment

(1) Anybody inspecting the premises would conclude that the dominant land could be maintained only by access from the neighbouring land. Is it defensible to insist upon some feature on the servient land?

(2) An easement was nevertheless implied under s 62 of the Law of Property Act 1925 (hereafter LPA), discussed below.

(3) In the absence of an easement, access for maintenance is dealt with by the Access to Neighbouring Land Act 1992.

Extract 19.2.9

Wheeler v *JJ Saunders Ltd* [1996] Ch 19

The plaintiffs claimed a right of way over the defendant's land. When the plaintiffs bought the dominant land, there were two access routes, but no express grant. The defendants barred one of the access routes which ran over their land.

STAUGHTON LJ: . . . Even to a novice in the law of easements, it seems clear that the class of easements implied in favour of a grantee is wider than easements of necessity. The question is how much wider? There are other authorities on the topic, including the decision of the House of Lords in *Sovmots Investments Ltd* v *Secretary of State for the Environment* [1979] AC 144, 168, where Lord Wilberforce said, quoting from *Wheeldon* v *Burrows*, 12 Ch D 31:

> '"easements . . . necessary to the reasonable enjoyment of the property granted, and *which have been and are at the time of the grant used* by the owners of the entirety for the benefit of the part granted" (see *per* Thesiger LJ, at p 49, my emphasis).'

One does not want to chop words over fine, and even if it were open to us to seek to improve on what was said by Lord Wilberforce, I would follow that passage as it stands.

For my part I do not consider that the south entrance was necessary for the reasonable enjoyment of Kingdown Farm House. The east entrance would do just as well. It was said to be four inches or 10 centimetres narrower than the south entrance. That was not critical. The gate at the south entrance, which was usually shut, shows to my mind that it was not the main entrance and was probably only used on rare occasions. I would therefore hold, differing from the judge, that Dr and Mrs Wheeler acquired no right of way through the south entrance.

PETER GIBSON LJ: . . . That proposition [in *Wheeldon* v *Burrows*] was said to be a general rule, founded on the maxim that the grantor should not derogate from his grant; but the grantor by the terms of his grant can always exclude the rule. It is perhaps surprising that so important a matter as a right of way should be capable of being granted merely by implication in a modern conveyance, but Thesiger LJ's proposition has been accepted as correctly stating the law and cannot now be doubted.

There have been some doubts as to whether the requirement that the easement should be continuous and apparent is an alternative to the requirement that the easement be necessary for the reasonable enjoyment of the property granted: see *Megarry & Wade, The Law of Real Property*, 5th ed (1984), pp 862–863. But to my mind it is tolerably clear from Thesiger LJ's introduction of the test of necessity by the words 'or, in other words' that he was treating the first requirement as synonymous with the second. It is plain that the test of what is necessary for the reasonable enjoyment of land is not the same as the test for a way of necessity and in *Cheshire and Burn's Modern Law of Real Property*, 15th ed (1994), p 541, note 14 'necessary' is said to indicate that the way 'conduces to the reasonable enjoyment of the property'.

Ferris J, in refusing an interlocutory injunction for the demolition of the wall erected by the defendant to bar the southern exit from the yard of Kingdown Farm House, said that there was 'considerable doubt that the use of the southern access way falls within the requirement for necessity'. But he appeared to be giving the word 'necessity' its normal meaning rather than the special meaning which it has for the purposes of the rule in *Wheeldon* v *Burrows*. The judge said that the requirement of necessity meant 'simply that reasonable use of the property cannot be had without the easement', and that 'the entrance on to the B3371 can properly be regarded as a front entrance to that property and the others as secondary or back entrances'. I am not able to say that the judge erred when he found that the front entrance was necessary for the reasonable enjoyment of the property on the evidence before him.

Comment

(1) Sir John May agreed with Staughton LJ and accordingly no easement was implied.

(2) Secondary accesses are frequently claimed under the rule in *Wheeldon* v *Burrows*. One standard case is where terraced houses have their principal access at the front and a secondary access to their rear gardens from a track running across the bottoms of the gardens. It is likely that such secondary access will be implied as an easement.[22] Against this background, how defensible is the result in *Wheeler*?

(3) Do these cases assist in deciding whether both tests (continuous and apparent; necessary for reasonable enjoyment) must be satisfied? What policy should the law adopt in this respect?

A final point to note is that the rule is subject to contrary intention. One particularly important question is how far exclusion of an easement from the contract will prevent any implication into the conveyance.

Extract 19.2.10

Squarey v *Harris-Smith* (1981) 42 P&CR 118

According to the Law Society's 1934 Conditions of Sale, there was no entitlement to a right of way. Apart from this, a right of way would have been implied into the conveyance.

OLIVER LJ: . . . The point is not, curiously, mentioned in Judge Stock's judgment but it is common ground that it was argued below and Mr Byrt very fairly concedes that the condition, having been incorporated, must be given its full status as a contractual term and cannot just be ignored because it is one of a number of printed conditions which the parties may well not actually have read.

Mr Wakefield argues that the clause is apt in its terms, and is indeed designed, to oust both the rule in *Wheeldon* v *Burrows* and section 62 of the Law of Property Act 1925, and Mr Byrt's first point is that this is not, in fact, the right construction of the condition.

I confess to having been somewhat surprised that a condition of this nature should have formed part of the common form Conditions of Sale for many years without the fact having attracted some attention either in textbooks or reported decisions. Nevertheless, on looking into the matter, I think for my part that it is really unarguable that, as a matter of construction, it does not have the effect which Mr Wakefield claims for it and such researches as I have been able to carry out into conveyancing textbooks indicates that it was drafted with this object in mind.

It has, as it seems to me, a dual effect. First, it ousts from the contract any implication of any right under the *Wheeldon* v *Burrows* doctrine which might interfere with the vendor's free use of his own land, and the range of possible rights that do not have that effect must be a very limited one. Secondly, it enables the vendor to insist, if he wishes to do so, upon the exclusion from the *conveyance* of the general words which are implied under section 62.

In my judgment, therefore, the condition must be fatal to any claim under *Wheeldon* v *Burrows*. That is a conclusion at which I regret being compelled to arrive but I see no escape from it.

Mr Byrt's answer is the same as that given by Mr Henty in the court below – namely, that since the vendor did not in fact insist upon an exclusion in the conveyance as he was entitled to, the right claimed, although excluded from the *contract*, was not excluded from the conveyance. But I cannot accept that, for my part. A right claimed under *Wheeldon* v *Burrows* is, it seems to

---

[22] *Brown* v *Alabaster* (1887) 37 Ch D 490; *Hansford* v *Jago* [1921] 1 Ch 322.

me, a right which is claimed by implication and I do not, for my part, see how there can be an implication of a term which is expressly excluded by the contract pursuant to which the conveyance is executed.

Comment

(1) Is it satisfactory that a standard term, which in all probability has never been considered by either party, should have this effect?

(2) The current Standard Conditions of Sale do not make provision for easements.

What happens if the contract provides for terms to be reserved, but the conveyance is silent? In *Holaw (470) Ltd* v *Stockton Estates Ltd*,[23] Neuberger J provided guidance:

> ... What [the defendant] does contend is that, properly construed, the LS [Law Society] Condition merely gave CIS a right to insist that the transfer contained any rights contemplated by the LS Condition ...
>
> I have reached the conclusion that the defendant's case on this issue should be rejected. On the face of it, the LS Condition represents an unequivocal agreement between the parties to Kenyon's contract as to what the conveyance or transfer executed pursuant to its terms should include. As a matter of ordinary language, an agreement between parties that a particular conveyance or transfer 'shall contain' certain reservations in favour of one party does not merely confer a right on that party to ask for such reservations to be included: it represents a bilateral agreement between the parties that they will be included. [It would be otherwise if the Condition] is expressed in terms of giving the vendor an option ...

Comment

(1) Does this distinction place too much stress on fine differences in wording?

(2) Is *Holaw* consistent with the analysis and result in *Squarey*?

(iii) Implied grants under the general words: LPA, s 62

Extract 19.2.11

Law of Property Act 1925, s 62

62.—(1) A conveyance of land shall be deemed to include and shall by virtue of this Act operate to convey, with the land, all buildings, erections, fixtures, commons, hedges, ditches, fences, ways, waters, watercourses, liberties, privileges, easements, rights, and advantages whatsoever, appertaining or reputed to appertain to the land or any part thereof, or, at the time of conveyance, demised, occupied, or enjoyed with, or reputed or known as part or parcel of or appurtenant to the land or any part thereof.

Extract 19.2.12

International Tea Stores Co v Hobbs [1903] 2 Ch 165

The plaintiff bought the dominant tenement from the defendant. Previously, he had been the defendant's tenant of the same premises. He had used a secondary access through the defendant's yard during business hours when the yard was open. Was an easement to use this secondary access implied into the conveyance?

---

[23] (2000) 81 P&CR 404 at pp 413–414.

FARWELL J: . . . The real truth is that you do not consider the question of title to use, but the question of fact of user; you have to inquire whether the way has in fact been used, not under what title has it been used, although you must of course take into consideration all the circumstances of the case, as appears from the *Birmingham Banking Co's Case*[i] and *Godwin v Schweppes, Limited*.[ii]

Further, with regard to this question of the materiality of the licence, I have the decision in *Kay v Oxley*[iii] that the licence is immaterial. Blackburn J says:[iv] 'I do not think it necessary to consider whether or not that parol licence, which was given by the defendant, to use the road, was revocable; or whether an action might not have been maintained for obstructing the tenant in doing that which he had a parol licence to do; or whether an action of trespass could have been brought against the tenant for using that road. I do not think it material to decide that. The licence was not in fact revoked.' He therefore, as I understand him, treats the only relevant question as being: Was the way in fact enjoyed at the date of the conveyance? If so, the fact that it was enjoyed under a licence which had not been revoked was immaterial. If it had been enjoyed without any licence at all for a number of years, although no prescriptive right had been or could have been acquired, still it was in fact enjoyed. It is in each case a question of fact to be determined on the circumstances of the case whether it has, or has not, been enjoyed within the meaning of the statute.

[i] 38 Ch D 295.
[ii] [1902] 1 Ch 926, 933.
[iii] LR 10 QB 360.
[iv] *Ibid*. 368.

Comment

(1) This case established that s 62 does much more than pass the benefit of existing easements. Where the circumstances show a use which could be an easement (despite no act of creation as an easement), the section transmutes it into a permanent legal easement. What is there in the wording of s 62 which justifies this result?

(2) Section 62 is immensely powerful. Whenever the owner of the land has permitted (or not prevented) something which is of the nature of an easement, a subsequent conveyance or lease will ensure that it cannot be revoked.

Extract 19.2.13

Green v Ashco Horticultural Ltd [1966] 1 WLR 889

CROSS J: . . . It is said that [at] the date of the present lease, the third lease, [the plaintiff] was in fact using this passageway, the court and the back door for the conveyance of goods, which were unloaded from his lorry or from the delivery lorries in the passageway, and that until shortly before the lease he was using also his small delivery van in the same way. He says that the question whether or not what he was doing was being done by the express consent of the defendants' predecessors, W C Billings & Sons Ltd (hereinafter referred to as 'Billings Ltd'), is as a matter of law irrelevant.

Looking at the matter for a moment apart from authority, one might have thought that in a case of this sort the question whether or not there was an express licence by the landlord for the doing of the acts in question was a highly relevant matter. If the owner of two properties, one of which is in lease, allows the tenant to make use of the adjoining property in hand in a certain way without protest or the grant of any express consent the tenant may well be justified in thinking when his lease is renewed that he is to have under the renewed lease an automatic right to do on the adjoining property what the landlord previously knew he was doing and did not require him to obtain any express licence to do. On the other hand, if he has had to obtain an express licence to do the acts in question, one might think that he could hardly expect to get a right to go on doing the acts under the new lease without a further express permission. But, be that as it may, it is clear that the law is otherwise. In *International Tea Stores Co v Hobbs*,[i] the facts of which are strikingly similar to the facts here, Farwell J decided that for the purpose of the operation of the section in the Conveyancing Act, 1881, which corresponded to the present section of the Law of Property Act, 1925, it made no difference whatever whether the consent of the landlord was tacit or express; and that decision was approved by the Court of Appeal in *Wright v Macadam*.[ii] Indeed, in a recently reported case, *Ward v Kirkland*,[iii] Ungoed-Thomas J said (I think by way of dictum, having regard to his findings of fact) that it makes no difference whether the express consent was given to endure for a period of time or was asked for and given every time the right was exercised; and given the principle laid down in *Hobbs'* case,[iv] it is difficult to see any logical distinction between an express consent to last over a period and an express consent to each separate act of user. I share the doubts expressed by Tucker LJ in *Wright v Macadam*[v] as to the justice of the law in this regard. But there it is; there is no doubt what the law is.

But, as Farwell J pointed out in *Hobbs'* case[vi] and Jenkins LJ repeated in *Wright v Macadam*,[vii] there are two sets of circumstances which may prevent section 62 from operating. In the first place, the section can only operate if the kind of user relied on could have been the subject of a grant of a legal right; and secondly, the section will not operate if at the time of the conveyance or lease in question it was, or should have been, apparent to the grantee or lessee that the enjoyment which he claims to have been converted into a right by the section was only temporary. I do not think that the second qualification on the general rule has any application here. Green ought perhaps to have realised – perhaps, indeed, he did – that Billings Ltd were consenting to his doing what he was doing only because of their personal regard for him, and that they would not necessarily be so considerate to a successor in title. But he had no reason to think that so long as he was tenant things would not be allowed to go on as before. But the first qualification on the general rule appears to me to place an insuperable obstacle in the plaintiff's way. On the facts as I find them, the consent which Billings Ltd gave to Green using the back entrance was always subject to the exigencies of their own business and the requirements of the tenants of their garages. They were prepared to let Green use the back entrance if and when it was not inconvenient to them and their tenants. If it was inconvenient they told him so; and for the time being he had to desist from using the bank [sic] entrance. But a purported grant of a right of way for such periods as the servient owner may permit one to use it would not confer any legal right at all . . . Green would be getting under section 62 a larger legal easement than the privilege which he was in fact enjoying. There is nothing in *Hobbs'* case[viii] which forces me to arrive at so unjust a result.

[i] [1903] 2 Ch 165.
[ii] [1949] 2 KB 744; [1949] 2 All ER 565, CA.
[iii] [1966] 1 WLR 601; [1966] 1 All ER 609.
[iv] [1903] 2 Ch 165.
[v] [1949] 2 KB 744 at 754/755.
[vi] [1903] 2 Ch 165.
[vii] [1949] 2 KB 744 at 751.
[viii] [1903] 2 Ch 165.

Comment

(1) The doubts expressed by Cross J about the justice of these cases are interesting. In *Wright v Macadam* [1949] 2 KB 744, Tucker LJ said: 'The result is that the defendant, through his act of kindness in allowing this lady to use the coal shed, is probably now a wiser man, and I may perhaps regret that the decision in this case may tend to discourage landlords from acts of kindness to their tenants. But there it is: that is the law.'

(2) Is it satisfactory that neighbourly conduct should be penalised in this way? Are there arguments for leaving the section in its present form?

Extract 19.2.14

Goldberg v *Edwards* [1950] Ch 247

The defendants leased an annex to their house, used for business, to the plaintiffs. Six months before the lease was executed in July, the plaintiffs entered into possession and were allowed access through the front door of the house, though there was a separate side access to the annex.

EVERSHED MR: [Having held that a right of access for customers was 'expressly limited to such time as the landlord should occupy the house herself' and therefore outside s 62:] That leaves only the personal right. As I have indicated, my main difficulty has been in deciding whether that was similarly limited or limited in some other way so as not properly to be capable of being annexed to the subject-matter of the demise. Having regard to his judgment, I think that I am bound to regard the view of the judge as having been that, in contradistinction to the other rights, it was intended to be something which the plaintiffs should enjoy qua lessees during the term of the demise, though it should not be enjoyed by their servants, workmen or any other persons with their authority. Therefore, I think, to quote Jenkins LJ in the recent case of *Wright* v *Macadam*:[i] 'It is a right or easement of a kind which could be readily included in a lease or conveyance by the insertion of appropriate words in the parcels.' What those would be I will state later, because, in the view which I take, it is necessary to see that the injunction or declaration to which the plaintiffs may be entitled is properly formulated.

. . . On the hypothesis of fact which I am making, the privilege granted here was not tempo-rary, like, for instance, a temporary right of light when it is obvious that buildings shortly to be erected will obscure it. The present privilege is in some ways indeed not dissimilar to that which in *Wright* v *Macadam* was held to be covered by s 62, namely, a privilege for the tenant to use a shed for storing her coal. I therefore think that, if the right which I have defined was one which was being enjoyed at the time of the conveyance, it is covered by s 62.

. . . I am anxious to guard myself from saying that rights, which were purely personal in the strict sense of that word, would necessarily in every case be covered by s 62. I base myself on the view that the right here given, though limited to the lessees, was given to them qua lessees; and, as such, it seems to me, it is covered by the principle of *Wright* v *Macadam* and by s 62. The Vice-Chancellor was of the opinion that the right date to consider was January 18. With all respect to him, I have come to a different conclusion: I think that the words 'at the time of con-veyance' apply to no other date than July 10. I do not find that result startling or surprising, where a landlord chooses to let his tenant in six months before the grant of a lease and allows him to exercise certain privileges. He can always protect himself, if he wants to, by the terms of the lease. Further, it has to be assumed that the terms of the bargain are intended to be in accordance with the rights or privileges which the tenant is allowed to enjoy in fact. Therefore, I do not feel that there is any difficulty in the way of my construction. On the other hand, there might be considerable difficulty in the way of the opposite view where, as sometimes happens, especially in the case of building agreements, a tenant may be let into possession long before the relevant lease, on the understanding that he does a great deal of work himself.

In my judgment the right of the plaintiffs, and it is the only right which they have established, is a right in themselves alone as lessees, and not in their servants or workmen or persons authorized by them, to pass through the defined passage to and from their works. That right, I think, should be exercised only during reasonable business hours.

[i] [1949] 2 KB 744, 752.

Comment

(1) The Court of Appeal also held that the right was not necessary for the reasonable enjoy-ment of the land. The case therefore provides an example of the broader application of

s 62. In so far as the rule in *Wheeldon* v *Burrows* is based, ultimately, upon the intentions of the parties, does this make the application of s 62 indefensible?

(2) No easement under s 62 would have arisen but for the interval between the plaintiff's entering into occupation and the formal entry into a lease. What advice would you give to landlords to avoid the result in *Goldberg* v *Edwards*?

(3) Stress was placed upon the fact that the permission was personal to the tenant and did not extend to other people. Why should the nature of the permission be relevant? In fact, the plaintiff's employees and visitors had been using the front door. It was conceded that this did not give rise to an easement, because permission for this had been for a limited period which had terminated when the landlord ceased to occupy the house. Is this consistent with *International Tea Stores Co* v *Hobbs*?

For s 62 to apply, does the use of the claimed right need to be continuous up to the time of the grant? Two cases may be contrasted.

Extract 19.2.15

Green v *Ashco Horticultural Ltd* [1966] 1 WLR 889

A right of way was claimed, based in part on access by a van.

CROSS J: . . . In fact, as I have said, Green disposed of his van in 1958 . . . I do not think it would be right to dismiss the alternative claim, so far as concerns Green's small van, simply on the ground that he had no such van at the date of the grant of the present lease. One ought not, I think, in a case like this to confine oneself to a single moment of time – when possibly there might have been no user at all. One ought to look at a reasonable period of time before the grant in question in order to see whether there was anything over that period which could be called a pattern of regular user in any particular way or ways. Here, if one looks at the evidence over the whole period from 1931 to 1959, there is no doubt that there was regular user by this small delivery van. Although he disposed of this van in 1958, it was not clear in 1959 that he would never get another one . . .

Extract 19.2.16

Le Strange v *Pettefar* (1939) 161 LT 300

LUXMOORE LJ: . . . it is clear that under the section the material time to be considered is the date of the lease – *i.e.*, the 16th September, 1937. Now whatever may be the position with regard to the defendant's earlier enjoyment of his so-called right, the plaintiff had made it plain before the 16th September, 1937, that he was disputing the existence of any such right when the lease was granted. There was a considerable correspondence with regard to the matter; it is sufficient to refer to the letter of the 14th July, 1937, from the plaintiff's solicitor to the defendant. The defendant answered this letter on the 15th July, saying in effect that he had enjoyed the alleged right without interruption for over twenty years. Admittedly there was at this date no legal right to use the old metalled surface in the way claimed by the defendant. At the highest, any such user by the defendant was permissive. The plaintiff was entitled to withdraw his permission at any time before any new lease was granted. The plaintiff in no way resiled from the position set out in his solicitor's letter of the 14th July, 1937. I have no hesitation in holding that at the date when the lease of the 16th September, 1937, was granted to the defendant no such right as is claimed by him was enjoyed with or appertained to or was reputed to appertain to or was known as part or parcel of the land thereby demised, for if it had ever been enjoyed, it was enjoyed by permission or sufferance. The permission was in express terms revoked and the defendant had no expectation of the continuance of the so-called right after the grant of the new lease.

Comment

(1) Suppose that in *Le Strange* the land had been leased to a third party, rather than to the occupier. Would s 62 have applied? Is it possible to articulate a principle which reconciles *Green* and *Le Strange*?

(2) As one would expect, the law relating to the rule in *Wheeldon* v *Burrows* is similar.[24]

These cases demonstrate the very wide effect of s 62. However, *Borman* v *Griffith*[25] established that s 62 does not apply to contracts. If the contract is silent, it follows that there is no right to a conveyance with s 62 easements and the vendor can insist upon expressly excluding s 62 from the conveyance.[26] Nevertheless, Maugham J in *Borman* was able to imply a contractual right under the rule in *Wheeldon* v *Burrows*.

What is the outcome if there is evidence that the implication of a s 62 easement would be contrary to the intentions of the parties?

Extract 19.2.17

Clark v *Barnes* [1929] 2 Ch 368

Buyer and seller agreed that the contract should not include the right of way now claimed by the buyer.

LUXMOORE J: [It] is necessary to consider the second question which is raised in the action; and that is the question whether the plaintiff is entitled to rectification of the conveyance or not. That depends on whether there has been a mutual mistake between the parties in the terms in which the conveyance has been executed. As I have already pointed out, the contract itself does not include any provision which will entitle the defendant to claim to have such a right of way as he claims, granted to him. The question then is, is the plaintiff entitled to have words inserted in the deed of conveyance, to limit the operation of the Law of Property Act, 1925, s 62; and to prevent the grant of such a right of way by implication? It is plain that if this point had been raised before the conveyance had been executed and the court had been asked to determine what the form of the conveyance would be, such a limitation would undoubtedly have been inserted, and on this ground the plaintiff is entitled to have the conveyance rectified. Further I am satisfied that it was not intended to grant any such right of way. This conclusion depends entirely on the view which I have taken of the evidence of what happened when the agreement was entered into . . .

In those circumstances I think the plaintiff is entitled to succeed in his claim to have the conveyance rectified by the insertion of proper words to prevent the implication of a right of way under the Law of Property Act, 1925, s 62.

Comment

(1) We have seen that s 62 does not imply easements into contracts. If the contract is silent, it follows that there is always a right to exclude the operation of s 62 from the conveyance. Does this mean that there could be rectification in cases such as *Goldberg* v *Edwards*?

---

[24] *Costagliola* v *English* (1969) 210 EG 1425.
[25] [1930] 1 Ch 493; Extract 19.2.7 above.
[26] *Re Peck & The School Board for London* [1893] 2 Ch 315.

(2) Section 62(4) provides that 'This section applies only if and as far as a contrary intention is not expressed in the conveyance.' Could this have been relied upon in *Clark* v *Barnes* as an alternative basis for the decision?

(iv) Diversity of occupation: *Wheeldon* v *Burrows* and LPA, s 62 compared

As discussed above, the potential scope of s 62 is immense. However, the cases establish an important condition for its application.

Extract 19.2.18

Long v *Gowlett* [1923] 2 Ch 177

SARGANT J: . . . The defendant says, and says truly, that during the common ownership and occupation by Nichols and his widow of the defendant's land (or Lot 1) and of the plaintiff's land (or Lot 2) the common owner and occupier was accustomed, when occasion arose, to proceed from the south bank within Lot 1 to the south bank within Lot 2, and to repair the south bank and cut weeds within the limits of Lot 2. And on these facts it is contended for the defendant that this constituted a 'privilege easement right or advantage' over or in relation to Lot 2, which at the time of the conveyance was occupied or enjoyed with Lot 1; and accordingly, that this advantage passed to the defendant by virtue of the express words of the sub-section as included in the conveyance by virtue of the statute. The argument is not based in any way on the existence of any continuous and apparent easement existing over Lot 2 in favour of Lot 1; indeed, any such claim would be incompatible with the evidence, which clearly establishes that there was no defined way at all along the south bank. The claim is founded upon there having been a statutory introduction into the conveyance to the defendant of words equivalent to or identical with those either expressly contained or statutorily introduced in the corresponding conveyances in such cases as *James* v *Plant*;[i] *Watts* v *Kelson*;[ii] *Bayley* v *Great Western Ry Co*;[iii] and *White* v *Williams*.[iv]

It is, therefore, necessary for the purpose of dealing with the matter on this footing to consider whether, during the common ownership and occupation of Lot 1 and Lot 2 by Mr Nichols and his widow, and therefore at the date of the conveyance, there was a 'privilege, easement, right or advantage' of the kind now claimed, which can properly be said to have been 'demised, occupied or enjoyed' with Lot 1 over Lot 2. It is very difficult to see how this can have been the case. No doubt the common owner and occupier did in fact repair the bank of Lot 2, and cut the weeds there; and no doubt also this repair and cutting would enure not solely for the benefit of Lot 2 (which comprised, amongst other things, a lawn tennis court), so as to prevent its being flooded, but also and very likely to a greater extent for the benefit of Lot 1. But there is nothing to indicate that the acts done on Lot 2 were done otherwise than in the course of the ownership and occupation of Lot 2, or that they were by way of using a 'privilege, easement or advantage' over Lot 2 in connection with Lot 1. The common owner and occupier of Whiteacre and Blackacre may in fact use Blackacre as an alternative and more convenient method of communication between Whiteacre and a neighbouring village. But it has never been held, and would I think be contrary to principle to hold, that (in default of there being a made road over Blackacre forming a continuous and apparent means of communication) a sale and conveyance of Whiteacre alone would carry a right to pass over Blackacre in the same way in which the common owner had been accustomed to pass. As it seems to me, in order that there may be a 'privilege, easement or advantage' enjoyed with Whiteacre over Blackacre so as to pass under the statute, there must be something done on Blackacre not due to or comprehended within the general rights of an occupying owner of Blackacre, but of such a nature that it is attributable to a privilege, easement, right or advantage, however precarious, which arises out of the ownership or occupation of Whiteacre, altogether apart from the ownership or occupation of Blackacre. And it is difficult to see how, when there is a common ownership of both Whiteacre and Blackacre, there can be any such relationship between the two closes as (apart from the case of continuous and apparent easements or that of a way of necessity) would be necessary to create a 'privilege, easement, right or advantage' within the words of s 6, sub-s 2, of the statute. For this purpose it would seem that there must be some diversity of ownership or occupation of the two closes sufficient to refer the act or acts relied on not to mere occupying ownership, but to some advantage or privilege (however far short of a legal right) attaching to the owner or occupier of Whiteacre as such and de facto exercised over Blackacre . . .

[i] 4 Ad&E 749.
[ii] LR 6 Ch 166.
[iii] 26 Ch D 434.
[iv] [1922] 1 KB 727.

A similar analysis is adopted by Lord Wilberforce in *Sovmots Investments Ltd* v *SSE*:[27]

> Equally, section 62 does not fit this case. The reason is that when land is under one ownership one cannot speak in any intelligible sense of rights, or privileges, or easements being exercised over one part for the benefit of another. Whatever the owner does, he does as owner and, until a separation occurs, of ownership or at least of occupation, the condition for the existence of rights, etc., does not exist: see *Bolton* v *Bolton* (1879) 11 Ch D 968, 970 *per* Fry J and *Long* v *Gowlett* [1923] 2 Ch 177, 189, 198, in my opinion a correct decision.

Comment

(1) Is Lord Wilberforce more or less guarded than Sargant J?

(2) How can the wording of s 62 justify the requirement of diversity?

(3) Lord Wilberforce refers to when 'a separation occurs, of ownership or at least of occupation'. In the present context, are we concerned with diversity of occupation or of ownership?

(4) Is it satisfactory that the rule in *Wheeldon* v *Burrows* should apply where there is no such diversity?

Extract 19.2.19

Kent v *Kavanagh* [2007] Ch 1

The case involved claims to easements on the enfranchisement of a lease (into a fee simple). The rules on enfranchisement are not of interest to us, but there are dicta on both *Wheeldon* v *Burrows* and s 62.

CHADWICK LJ: 43. The two propositions which, together, comprise the rule (or rules) in *Wheeldon* v *Burrows* are confined, in their application, to cases in which, by reason of the conveyance (or lease), land formerly in common ownership ceases to be owned by the same person. It is in cases of that nature that, in order to give effect to what must be taken to be the common intention of the grantor and the grantee, the conveyance (or lease) will operate as a grant (for the benefit of the land conveyed) of such easements over the land retained by the grantor as are necessary to the reasonable enjoyment of the land conveyed. But, because the principle is founded on the common intention of the parties, the easements necessary to the reasonable enjoyment of the land conveyed are those which reflect (and, following separation of ownership, are needed to give effect to) the use and enjoyment of the land conveyed at the

---

[27] [1979] AC 144 at p 169; Harpum (1977) 41 Conv 415, (1979) 43 Conv 113; P Smith (1978) 42 Conv 449.

time of the conveyance and while that land and the retained land were in the common ownership of the grantor.

44.   It is necessary to ask how far either of the two propositions which Thesiger LJ identified
in *Wheeldon* v *Burrows* can have any application in a case where, at the time of the conveyance,
the land conveyed and the land retained, although in common ownership, were not in common
occupation. In particular, can either of the two propositions have any application where the land
conveyed was occupied by a tenant holding under a lease from the common owner. Assuming,
for the moment, that the land is not conveyed to the tenant, there are, of course, two distinct
questions: (i) what easements over the retained land pass with the conveyance of the freehold
and (ii) what easements are reserved out of the land conveyed for the benefit of the retained
land. The rights of the tenant over the land retained; and the rights of the grantor (as owner of
the land retained) over the land held under the lease are unaffected by the conveyance. Prima
facie, those rights will depend on the terms of the lease – but may include rights which passed
to the tenant under the first rule in *Wheeldon* v *Burrows* when the lease was granted.

45.   In the absence of an express grant, the answer to the first of those questions – what
easements over the retained land pass with the conveyance of the freehold – turns, as it seems
to me, not on any application of the first rule in *Wheeldon* v *Burrows* but on the operation of
section 62 of the Law of Property Act 1925. Under section 62 a conveyance of land operates
to convey with the land 'all . . . ways . . . easements, rights, and advantages whatsoever, appertaining or reputed to appertain to the land . . . or, at the time of conveyance, demised . . . or
enjoyed with . . . the land'. I can see no reason why those words are not apt to convey, with the
freehold, rights of way over the retained land which are, at the time of the conveyance, enjoyed
by the tenant in occupation of the land conveyed. For my part, I find that analysis more
attractive than one which relies upon the first rule in *Wheeldon* v *Burrows*. It seems to me an
unnecessary and artificial construct to hold that the grantor, as common owner and the landlord
of the land conveyed, is himself using the rights over the retained land which his tenant enjoys
under the lease.

46.   In reaching that conclusion I have had regard to the observations of Lord Wilberforce in
the *Sovmots* appeal [1979] AC 144, 169 [quoted above].

    As Lord Wilberforce pointed out, there can be no sensible concept of rights over one part of
land for the benefit of another part while the two parts are in common ownership and occupation. But, once there is a separation of occupation (because part of land in common ownership
is held by a tenant under a lease) there is no conceptual difficulty. There may well be rights over
the untenanted part of the land for the benefit of the tenanted part. If there are, those rights are
within the wide compass of section 62 of the 1925 Act.

Comment

Kent indicates that *Wheeldon* v *Burrows* does not apply if there is prior diversity of occupation. Does this fit well with the principles explaining *Wheeldon*? Does it matter?

Notwithstanding these cases, there has been controversy as to whether s 62 applies if,
despite absence of diversity of occupation, the easement is continuous and apparent. In
P&S Platt Ltd v *Crouch*,[28] Peter Gibson LJ had observed (prior to *Kent*):

> The rights were continuous and apparent, and so it matters not that prior to the sale of the hotel
> there was no prior diversity of occupation of the dominant and servient tenancies. Accordingly,
> I reach the conclusion that s 62 operated to convert the rights into full easements . . .

---

[28] [2004] 1 P&CR 242 at [42]; see also Longmore LJ at [59]. *Platt* is supported by *Alford* v *Hannaford* [2011]
EWCA Civ 1099 at [36].

Extract 19.2.20

Wood v *Waddington* [2014] EWHC 1358 (Ch)

MORGAN J: 132.   . . . It may be that a test of 'continuous and apparent' is not an improvement on the statutory wording of 'enjoyed with'. The reference to an easement being 'continuous and apparent' appears to be taken from the case law dealing with the implication of easements: see *Wheeldon* v *Burrows* (1879) 12 Ch D 31 (to which I refer below). However, in that context, the phrase 'continuous and apparent' does not stand alone as it operates in conjunction with a requirement that the right claimed is necessary for the reasonable enjoyment of the land conveyed. . . .

(8) Conclusions as to the operation of section 62
133.   I will now summarise my understanding of the legal position. There is no absolute rule that a right of way cannot be claimed under section 62 where there has not been diversity of occupation before the relevant conveyance. The ultimate question is whether the advantage in question was, on the facts, 'enjoyed with' the land conveyed. Those words require two things to be shown. The advantage must have been 'enjoyed' in the period before the conveyance. Further, the advantage must have been enjoyed 'with' the land conveyed so that, after the conveyance, it will be appurtenant to the land conveyed as the dominant tenement. For these purposes, a consideration of how the advantage was actually used and whether it was apparently for the benefit of the land conveyed and apparently a burden on the land retained will be of great importance. The cases on the general words before the 1881 Act show, for example, that where there was a driveway leading across the land retained to serve the land conveyed it is possible to hold that the advantage of the use of the driveway was enjoyed with the land conveyed. I do not suggest that this example is the only possible case where a right of way would pass under the general words.

Comment

Is this consistent with *Long*, *Sovmots* and *Kent*? If *Platt* is correct, what role is left for *Wheeldon* v *Burrows*?

(v) Reform

Extract 19.2.21

Law Com CP 186: Easements, Covenants and Profits à Prendre
Law Com No 327: Making Land Work: Easements, Covenants and Profits à Prendre

[Distinguishing implied grant and implied reservation]
[Consultation Paper] 4.49   Many years may have elapsed, and many transfers of the relevant benefited and burdened lands may have taken place, before the existence or scope of an easement becomes an issue. It will then be necessary for the parties to the dispute to look back to the conveyance or other transaction which it is claimed gave rise to the easement in the first place. This may involve unravelling numerous and complex subsequent transfers of the relevant land. From the point of view of a successor in title seeking an implied easement, it is a matter of chance whether it turns out that the claim is for implied grant or implied reservation. Yet it remains the case that the party whose claim is based on implied grant is in a better position than the party who discovers that it will be necessary to prove an implied reservation.

[Report] 3.29   . . . The vast majority of consultees were in favour of this change. Implication serves a useful purpose where there has been inadvertence or mistake, and such things befall disponors as much as disponees.

3.30   We recommend that in determining whether an easement should be implied, it should not be material whether the easement would take effect by grant or by reservation.

[LPA, s 62]

[Report] 3.59   In the Consultation Paper we noted that section 62 is a trap for the unwary, as well as being uncertain in its effect and in the extent to which it overlaps with *Wheeldon* v *Burrows*. There have been numerous expressions of dissatisfaction with the section's trans-formation of precarious rights into legal interests. It may prevent important rights from being lost; but it does so only when the facts fit a particular pattern, and it may equally preserve unimportant arrangements, converting a friendly permission into a valuable property right, contrary to the intention of the 'grantor'. Because it operates subject to expressed contrary intention, well-drafted contracts provide for its exclusion, either in whole or as regards certain rights such as light.

3.61   Consultees generally supported our proposal. The potentially unexpected effects of section 62 were regarded as unwelcome; particular dangers were highlighted in the context of rights to light. The Chancery Bar Association said:

> [The creative effect] of section 62 is capricious and has led to pernicious results where the creation of a legal easement was clearly not intended, but was not properly excluded.

3.64   We recommend that section 62 of the Law of Property Act 1925 shall no longer operate to transform precarious benefits into legal easements or profits on a conveyance of land.

[On a replacement test]

3.32   We take the view that a single statutory test for implication is required, to replace the existing group of methods. The Consultation Paper set out alternative tests, derived from the current law, which could be employed to determine whether an easement is to be implied. It offered consultees the option of an approach based upon ascertaining the actual intentions of the parties; or an approach based upon a set of presumptions which would apply in each transaction. . . . A third option offered to consultees was a single rule based on what is neces-sary for the reasonable use of the land – by which, we explained, we meant a more generous test than the current law of easements of necessity. Finally, we discussed a test based upon the contractual rules of implication.

3.33   While there was almost unanimous consensus among consultees that reform was appropriate, there was a divergence of opinion as to how best to achieve this.

3.35   We have also concluded that a contractual test would be unacceptable, being alien to the context of a property right. Terms may be implied into a contract on the basis of a group of alternative tests, generally described as necessity, business efficacy and the 'officious bystander' test. Our Advisory Board members in particular felt that the introduction of an unfamiliar test in this context would add to uncertainty . . .

3.36   Reform of the law of implication of easements will not, of course, have any impact upon the contractual rules for implication. There may be occasions when the contractual rules will be successfully pleaded so as to imply a term into a land contract, to the effect that a particular easement would be granted; specific performance could then be sought to enforce that term. We are not aware of cases where this has been attempted, but it would always remain a pos-sibility, perhaps in unusual circumstances.

3.37   There was some support for an intention-based test. But more consultees expressed concern about the evidential difficulties to which such a test would give rise – a view which we think has merit. The difficulties would be considerable, and would become more pronounced over time and with changes of ownership. The test would be impracticable where the disposi-tion was by will.

3.40   We also reject an approach based on the presumption that certain rights were intended. We see no merit in presuming an intention that can then be rebutted – so that what is eventually implied, or not implied, may bear no relationship to what is actually needed to make the land viable. And while consultees did, on the whole, prefer an approach based upon presumptions to one based upon the parties' actual intentions, the responses highlighted the difficulty in settling a list of presumptions.

3.42 A test of what is necessary for the reasonable use of the land attracted significant support from consultees, and we have come to the conclusion that this is the most appropriate principle upon which to base the implication of easements. It is an objective test, which does not depend upon the state of mind of the parties nor upon factual details such as whether or not a quasi-easement is visible. It is likely to encompass all those cases where the implication of an easement is of practical importance.

3.43 The wording 'necessary for the reasonable use of the land' derives from the American Restatement, which provides some useful commentary. In order to assist parties and the courts in determining whether that test has been passed, we have also concluded that it would be useful for the test to be accompanied by a non-exclusive list of factors that a court is to bear in mind in assessing what is necessary for the reasonable use of land. In formulating that list of factors we have had in mind the current law and the elements within it that consultees regard as important, and also the sort of practical problems that tend to arise on the ground.

3.45 We recommend that an easement shall be implied as a term of a disposition where it is necessary for the reasonable use of the land at that date, bearing in mind:

(1) the use of the land at the time of the grant;

(2) the presence on the servient land of any relevant physical features;

(3) any intention for the future use of the land, known to both parties at the time of the grant;

(4) so far as relevant, the available routes for the easement sought; and

(5) the potential interference with the servient land or inconvenience to the servient owner.

3.47 Our recommended test would replace all the other methods of implication in the current law.

3.48 The factors we have listed can be seen to replicate the most useful and practical features of the current law, particularly in their focus on the physical characteristics of land and the intentions of the parties for future use . . .

Comment

(1) Are there convincing reasons for rejecting the long-standing distinction between grant and reservation?

(2) The rejection of the effect of s 62 would be welcomed by many. Is it relevant that standard forms of contract (used by buyers and sellers of land) make no general attempt to restrict its operation (other than as regards rights to light)?

(3) Would the new test constitute a significant change in comparison with *Wheeldon* v *Burrows* (as it applies to implied grant)?

B. Prescription

The courts have long sought to cloak long-standing practice with legal rights. This is one of the reasons why adverse possession is recognised. In the easements context, the result has been that 20 years' exercise may give rise to a legal easement (or profit) provided that it is exercised 'as of right'.

(i) Forms of prescription

First it should be noted that there are three forms of prescription. Common law prescription and lost modern grant are described in the following case.

Extract 19.2.22

Simmons v Dobson [1991] 1 WLR 720

FOX LJ: . . . I come then to the contention that the plaintiff succeeds on the basis of lost modern grant. That doctrine arises from the inadequacies of common law prescription. At common law, acquisition of a prescriptive right depended upon the claimant establishing (amongst other things) the requisite period of user. Thus, common law prescription was based upon a presumed grant. The grant would be presumed only where the appropriate user had continued from time immemorial. That was fixed as the year 1189; that date originated in a mediaeval statute. It was usually impossible to satisfy that test. Accordingly, the courts held that if user 'as of right' for 20 years or more was established, continued user since 1189 would be presumed. That was satisfactory as far as it went, but there were gaps. In particular the presumption of immemorial user could be rebutted by showing that, at some time since 1189, the right did not exist. For example, an easement of light could not be claimed in respect of a house built after 1189.

It was because of the unsatisfactory nature of common law prescription that the doctrine of lost modern grant was introduced. It was judge-made. The doctrine presumed from long usage that an easement had, in fact, been granted since 1189 but the grant had got lost. The form which the doctrine took was, initially, that juries were told that from user during living memory, or even during 20 years, they could presume a lost grant. After a time the jury were recommended to make that finding and finally they were directed to do so. Nobody believed that there ever was a grant. But it was a convenient and workable fiction. The doctrine was ultimately approved by the House of Lords in *Dalton* v *Henry Angus & Co* (1881) 6 App Cas 740.

Comment

(1) To what extent is lost modern grant more useful than common law prescription?

(2) Is it to be applauded or regretted that the law employs fictions to justify prescription?

The Prescription Act 1832 provides the third route to prescription. It is too complex for full analysis, but its essence is that prescription results from user for the last 20 years. It avoids the pitfalls in common law prescription and the fictions in lost modern grant, but the requirement that it must be the *last* 20 years' user (s 4: 'the period next before some suit or action . . .') has meant that it has not superseded the older forms of prescription.[29] It is a common feature of prescription claims that the dispute is brought to a head by the servient owner preventing the exercise of the claimed right. It is obvious that this interruption of the user cannot be allowed to oust the Act in all cases, otherwise it would virtually never apply! Section 4 provides as follows:

> . . . no act or other matter shall be deemed to be an interruption, within the meaning of this statute, unless the same shall have been or shall be submitted to or acquiesced in for one year after the party interrupted shall have had or shall have notice thereof . . .

Extract 19.2.23

Davies v Du Paver [1953] 1 QB 184

In May, the servient owner began to block the claimed easement with a fence. The plaintiff objected and his solicitors wrote a series of letters on his behalf over the next two months. The fence was completed early in August, but proceedings were not commenced until late September in the following year.

---

[29] It must also be continuous; see *Hollins* v *Verney* (1884) 13 Ch D 304.

MORRIS LJ: . . . The fence was completed on August 9. Could it be said that the plaintiff had submitted to, or acquiesced in, the existence of the fence by that date? Having regard to the events that had happened, and to the correspondence, I would have thought, had it been for me to decide this question of fact, that the answer would be in the negative. The parties were breathing fury on each side of a newly erected fence. Could it be said that the challenging protests of the plaintiff must, as the August days passed, be deemed to have signified nothing, and that his former claims and assertions should be regarded as supplanted by submission and acquiescence? As time went by, it might well be that silence and inaction could be interpreted as submission or acquiescence. But the date when submission or acquiescence begins must be determined as a question of fact, having regard to all the circumstances. Had there been a beginning by January 1, 1951, or by December 1, 1950, or by November 1, 1950? These are all questions of fact. Unless it is held that there was submission or acquiescence by September 27, 1950, there would not be a period of one year. The judge referred to *Glover* v *Coleman*[i] and stated: 'On the evidence I hold that neither of the plaintiffs submitted to or acquiesced in the interruption.' This was a finding of fact which the judge was, in my view, entitled to make, and accordingly I consider that the first submission fails.

SINGLETON LJ (dissenting): . . . The acceptance of any such argument would mean the substitution of a reasonable time for the period of one year in s 4 of the Act. That would never do. I agree that it is a question of fact which has to be decided, and the question is: Was there submission to the interruption for one year? That question, I consider, must be answered in the affirmative, though there were protests and objections beforehand.

[i] LR 10 CP 108.

Comment

(1) Which judgment more accurately reflects the wording of the section and the policy of the law?

(2) Would Singleton LJ ever accept an extension of the one-year period?

(ii) Requirements for all forms of prescription

Recent claims to public rights (especially village and town greens) provide some assistance in establishing the nature of use 'as of right'.

Extract 19.2.24

R (Lewis) v *Redcar and Cleveland BC (No 2)* [2010] 2 AC 70

It was objected that the claimants to a town green (the 'residents') had shown deference to golfers in respect of a golf course over which the right was claimed.

LORD WALKER: 36.   . . . But I have great difficulty in seeing how a reasonable owner would have concluded that the residents were not asserting a right to take recreation on the disputed land, simply because they normally showed civility (or, in the inspector's word, deference) towards members of the golf club who were out playing golf. It is not as if the residents took to their heels and vacated the land whenever they saw a golfer . . . But courteous and sensible though they were (with occasional exceptions) the fact remains that they were regularly, in large numbers, crossing the fairways as well as walking on the rough, and often (it seems) failing to clear up after their dogs when they defecated. A reasonably alert owner of the land could not have failed to recognise that this user was the assertion of a right and would mature into an established right unless the owner took action to stop it.

The following cases show that certain factors will be fatal to a use being as of right.

Extract 19.2.25

Sturges v *Bridgman* (1879) 11 Ch D 852

The defendant confectioner had for years created noise while pounding materials. This did not bother his neighbour, the plaintiff doctor, until the plaintiff built a consulting room close to the source of the noise. The defendant claimed a prescriptive right to pound materials.

THESIGER LJ: . . . Here then arises the objection to the acquisition by the Defendant of any easement. That which was done by him was in its nature such that it could not be physically interrupted; it could not at the same time be put a stop to by action. Can user which is neither preventible nor actionable found an easement? We think not. The question, so far as regards this particular easement claimed, is the same question whether the Defendant endeavours to assert his right by Common Law or under the *Prescription Act*. That Act fixes periods for the acquisition of easements, but, except in regard to the particular easement of light, or in regard to certain matters which are immaterial to the present inquiry, it does not alter the character of easements, or of the user or enjoyment by which they are acquired. This being so, the laws governing the acquisition of easements by user stands thus: Consent or acquiescence of the owner of the servient tenement lies at the root of prescription, and of the fiction of a lost grant, and hence the acts or user, which go to the proof of either the one or the other, must be, in the language of the civil law, *nec vi nec clam nec precario*; for a man cannot, as a general rule, be said to consent to or acquiesce in the acquisition by his neighbour of an easement through an enjoyment of which he has no knowledge, actual or constructive, or which he contests and endeavours to interrupt, or which he temporarily licenses. It is a mere extension of the same notion, or rather it is a principle into which by strict analysis it may be resolved, to hold, that an enjoyment which a man cannot prevent raises no presumption of consent or acquiescence.

Comment

(1) The reference to 'consent or acquiescence' is reminiscent of estoppel. How far is prescription similar to proprietary estoppel?

(2) Questions have recently been raised as to whether the law recognises an easement by prescription to create noise, largely because of uncertainty and varying noise levels. However, the Supreme Court has confirmed that such prescription is possible: *Lawrence* v *Fen Tigers Ltd* [2014] AC 822 (see especially [33]–[34] and [37]).

It is unusual for prescriptive rights to be asserted by force (*vi*), though use in the face of contrary instructions will also fail.[30] Illegal use was also said to preclude prescription, but this must be reviewed following the decision of the House of Lords in *Bakewell Management Co Ltd* v *Brandwood*.[31] The context was that of rights over commons, where use without the owner's consent is illegal. To deny prescription on this basis was thought unreasonable. In the words of Lord Scott at [47],

> In my opinion, if an easement over land can be lawfully granted by the landowner the easement can be acquired either by prescription under section 2 of the 1832 Act or by the fiction of lost modern grant whether the use relied on is illegal in the criminal sense or merely in the tortious sense. I can see no valid reason of public policy to bar that acquisition.

It is more common to assert that the user was not open (*clam*).

---

[30] *Taylor* v *Betterment Properties (Weymouth) Ltd* [2012] 2 P&CR 32 provides a recent example (claim to a public right); an appeal on other points was dismissed [2014] AC 1072.
[31] [2004] 2 AC 519.

Extract 19.2.26

Hollins v *Verney* (1884) 13 Ch D 304

LINDLEY LJ: . . . Moreover, as the enjoyment which is pointed out by the statute is an enjoyment which is open as well as of right, it seems to follow that no actual user can be sufficient to satisfy the statute, unless during the whole of the statutory term (whether acts of user be proved in each year or not) the user is enough at any rate to carry to the mind of a reasonable person who is in possession of the servient tenement, the fact that a continuous right to enjoyment is being asserted, and ought to be resisted if such right is not recognised, and if resistance to it is intended.

Comment

This test was used to deny prescription where access for cutting wood had been exercised at 12-yearly intervals.

As the following case demonstrates, permission (*precario*) plainly defeats prescription. Difficult issues can still arise.

Extract 19.2.27

Gaved v *Martyn* (1865) 19 CBNS 732 (144 ER 974)

WILLES J: . . . A plaintiff who is seeking to establish an enjoyment for the statutable period of twenty years, must, – with this exception, that he need not satisfy the jury of the fact of there having been a lost grant, or that the enjoyment commenced before the time of legal memory, – make out that his enjoyment has been under a claim of right. And I apprehend it would clearly be competent, in answer to such a claim, to shew that the enjoyment originated under an agreement with the tenant or owner of the servient tenement, and therefore was precarious and not as of right: and, upon proof of that fact, it would be for the jury to say whether the tenant of the dominant tenement had not continued the enjoyment in pursuance of a similar agreement, and whether it was not precarious . . .

One difficult question is how far permission covers all future use by the claimant. Cotton LJ has stated:[32]

> . . . you must see whether the acts have been done as of right, that is to say, not secretly, not as acts of violence, not under permission from time to time given by the person on whose soil the acts were done. I say 'from time to time given', not that it should necessarily be yearly, but from time to time during the period the exercise during which is said to establish the right . . .

Comment

In what circumstances will a consent not govern the period of user? Would it be relevant that the servient land is sold after consent is given? Does consent relate to the full 20 years relied upon, or is it fatal if there has been consent for any part of that 20 years?

A rather different question is whether permission can be implied from the servient owner's conduct.

---

[32] *Earl de la Warr* v *Miles* (1881) 17 Ch D 535 at p 596.

Extract 19.2.28

Mills v *Silver* [1991] Ch 271

DILLON LJ: . . . I turn now to the judge's point on tolerance. The question is whether the judge has correctly directed himself in law. To put it another way, did the tolerance of the successive servient owners – James Price until 1970 and in his case tolerance out of good neighbourliness and because the use was too insignificant to matter to him or cause him any inconvenience – of such vehicular use of the disputed track as there was in Joe Phillips' time preclude a prescriptive right being acquired, even though no express permission was ever granted to Joe Phillips and no reservations as to his use of the disputed track with vehicles were ever communicated to him by anyone.

The topic of tolerance has bulked fairly large in recent decisions of this court dealing with claims to prescriptive rights, since the decision in *Alfred F Beckett Ltd* v *Lyons* [1967] Ch 449. If passages in successive judgments are taken on their own out of context and added together, it would be easy to say, as, with all respect, it seems to me that the judge did in the present case, that there is an established principle of law that no prescriptive right can be acquired if the user by the dominant owner of the servient tenement in the particular manner for the appropriate number of years has been tolerated without objection by the servient owner. But there cannot be any such principle of law because it is, with rights of way, fundamentally inconsistent with the whole notion of acquisition of rights by prescription. It is difficult to see how, if there is such a principle, there could ever be a prescriptive right of way. It follows that the various passages in the judgments in question cannot be taken on their own out of context. If each case is looked at on its own and regarded as a whole, none lays down any such far-reaching principle. In my judgment, the judge in the present case has misapplied the authorities, by taking passages out of context, and misdirected himself in arriving at the supposed principle of law which he has sought to apply.

STOCKER LJ: . . . The judge seems to have based his decision in part on the proposition that 'toleration' of a user is insufficient to establish a user as of right. It seems to me implicit from the terms of his judgment that he considered that there was a distinction between 'toleration' and 'acquiescence' for the purpose of establishing a right of way by prescription or a lost modern grant, even if the facts concerning the nature and extent of the user might otherwise have supported an easement of a right of way over the disputed track. The validity of this conclusion is one of the issues which arise on this appeal.

The question whether or not there has been over the relevant period such use of a disputed right of way as to give rise to the conclusion that the owner of the servient tenement acquiesced in it so as to give rise to a presumption of a lost modern grant and thus to justify the existence of the right as an enforceable easement is a matter which inevitably involves retrospective conclusions from the evidence related to a long period of time. To draw a distinction between 'acquiescence' on the one hand and 'toleration' on the other seems to me an impossible exercise unless the word 'toleration' is used simply as a convenient label to apply to factual situations where the user claimed, as of right, was too casual or trivial to give rise to any legal obligation or where the user is to be explained on the basis of permission or consent. The terms 'acquiescence' and 'toleration' are not wholly synonymous, but are sufficiently nearly so as to convey virtually the same meaning. Thus the *Shorter Oxford Dictionary* states as one of the meanings of 'acquiesce' as being 'to agree tacitly to, or concur in' and one of the meanings of 'tolerate' is 'to allow [to] exist, or to be done or practised, without authoritative interference or molestation'. Without more it seems to me that no general principle of law can be derived from the cases cited since broadly speaking the two words mean the same thing.

Comment

(1) How strong is the argument that a friendly landowner should not be bound by prescription merely by not objecting to a user doing no harm? Does the case encourage legalistic attitudes on the part of neighbours?

(2) Is this analogous to principles applied in adverse possession?[33]

(iii) Prescription where there is a lease

Extract 19.2.29

Simmons v *Dobson* [1991] 1 WLR 720

FOX LJ: . . . Now in relation to common law prescription generally, user had to be by or on behalf of a fee simple owner against a fee simple owner. An easement can be granted expressly by a tenant for life or tenant for years so as to bind their respective limited interests, but such rights cannot be acquired by prescription: see *Wheaton* v *Maple & Co* [1893] 3 Ch 48 and *Kilgour* v *Gaddes* [1904] 1 KB 457. Thus Lindley LJ in the former case said [1893] 3 Ch 48, 63:

> 'The whole theory of prescription at common law is against presuming any grant or covenant not to interrupt, by or with any one except an owner in fee. A right claimed by prescription must be claimed as appendant or appurtenant to land, and not as annexed to it for a term of years.'

In *Kilgour* v *Gaddes* [1904] 1 KB 457 that was cited with approval by Collins MR, at p 465 . . .

It is common ground that at all material times the fee simple of numbers 151 and 153 has been vested in the same person.

Against that background I take the view that, as a matter of authority, it is established that one tenant cannot acquire an easement by prescription at common law against another tenant holding under the same landlord. The position is, I think, the same in relation to section 2 of the Prescription Act 1832 . . .

What we are concerned with here is neither common law prescription strictly so called nor a claim under the Prescription Act 1832 but a claim based on the lost modern grant doctrine. The question is whether the restrictive rule as to prescription by and against leaseholders applies to cases of lost modern grant.

In terms of practicalities, it is difficult to see if one were starting from scratch that there is serious objection to leaseholders prescribing against each other for the duration of their limited interests (but it has to be said that to introduce such a rule retrospectively now could affect what were hitherto bought and sold as clear titles). And, as Mr Vickers says, in a modern, urban situation it is hard to see why two householders on one side of the street should be able to prescribe for easements against each other's land because each holds in fee simple while on the other side of the street one leaseholder under the residue of a 999-year lease can for 20 years or more walk along a path at the back of his neighbour's garden (also held on a long lease) without acquiring any rights in respect thereof. That, however, is the way the law has gone in England . . .

While, therefore, there appears to be no case which directly decides that there can be no lost modern grant by or to a person who owns a lesser estate than the fee, the dicta are to the contrary and are very strong and of long standing. I take them to represent settled law. I should mention for completeness that the law in Ireland has gone the other way: *Flynn* v *Harte* [1913] 2 IR 322 and *Tallon* v *Ennis* [1937] IR 549.

---

[33]   See p 91 et seq above.

As to any departure from that state of the law, there are, I think difficulties of principle. It is clear that common law prescription and prescription under the Act of 1832 are, as a matter of decision, not available by or to owners of less estates than the fee. Lost modern grant is merely a form of common law prescription. It is based upon a fiction which was designed to meet, and did meet, a particular problem. It would, I think, be anomalous to extend the fiction further by departure, in relation to lost modern grant, from the fundamental principle of common law prescription referred to by Lindley LJ.

Comment

(1) Why is prescription against tenants impossible? Note that Lord Millett[34] has doubted whether the rules would survive review by the Supreme Court. Can a tenant obtain a right by prescription against a fee simple owner?

(2) *Simmons* v *Dobson* extended the no-prescription rule from common law and statutory prescription to lost modern grant, supported by dicta rather than direct decision. Was this extension appropriate?

(3) The Law Commission (Law Com No 327, para 3.148) considered that amendment would require complex drafting and might give rise to problems; no reform was recommended. Does this make review by the Supreme Court more or less likely?

(iv) Reform

Extract 19.2.30

Law Reform Committee, 14th Report (1966) Cmnd 3100

ABOLITION OR IMPROVEMENT?

30. It is clear from the foregoing statement of the existing position that the law of prescription is unsatisfactory, uncertain and out of date, and that it needs extensive reform. The first and most important question for consideration, then, is whether any system of prescription should be preserved, or whether, subject to suitable transitional arrangements, prescription should be abolished and easements should in the future be capable of being created only by grant. If abolition is desirable, the only further question is what transitional provisions are necessary. If, on the other hand, prescription is to be preserved in some form, we must consider how far the law should be reformed.

. . .

Recommendation in favour of abolition

32. By a small majority we have decided to recommend that, subject to the necessary transitional arrangements, the prescriptive acquisition of easements should be abolished. We would not replace prescription by any other method of acquisition, except for rights of support which we discuss separately later in this report . . . The main considerations which have persuaded the majority to favour abolition are, briefly, that there is little, if any, moral justification for the acquisition of easements by prescription, a process which either involves an intention to get something for nothing or, where there is no intention to acquire any right, is purely accidental. Moreover, the user which eventually develops into a full-blown legal right, enjoyable not only by

---

[34] *China Field Ltd* v *Appeal Tribunal (Buildings)* [2009] 5 HKC 231 (Hong Kong Final Court of Appeal); Merry [2010] Conv 176.

the dominant owner himself but also by his successors in title for ever, may well have originated in the servient owner's neighbourly wish to give a facility to some particular individual, or (perhaps even more commonly) to give a facility on the understanding, unfortunately unexpressed in words or at least unprovable, that it may be withdrawn if a major change of circumstances ever comes about.

33. There is no reason why a person who wishes to acquire an easement over someone else's land should not adopt the straightforward course of asking for it . . . Moreover, if easements could be acquired only by written grant, many of the doubts about the precise nature and extent of the easement would, we hope, disappear. In the absence of a grant, there does seem to be considerable difficulty in finding a formula which will not do injustice to a servient owner by rendering him liable to have far more extensive rights imposed on him than he could be said to have recognised by acquiescence . . .

34. There are also arguments in favour of abolition based as much on practical convenience as on any general theory. It will not be very long now – comparatively speaking, at least – before compulsory registration of title to land on sale will become universal throughout the country, and the aim here should be for the register to be, as far as possible, a true mirror of the title. No doubt this ideal can never be absolutely achieved, but easements arising from prescription certainly constitute one of the most troublesome of the 'over-riding interests' which bind the land without being registered . . .

35. Moreover, if a servient owner is to be liable to be saddled with easements created by prescription, then the law ought to provide him with some simple and cheap method of protecting himself against what may otherwise be imposed upon him by the passage of time . . .

36. We do not consider that it is necessary or appropriate for the same legal rules to apply to the acquisition of easements by prolonged enjoyment as apply to the acquisition of title to land by adverse possession. Certainty of title to land is a social need and occupation of land which has long been unchallenged should not be disturbed. Moreover, a squatter's occupation of land is sufficiently notorious to invite preventive action. There is no comparable need to establish easements, and user even 'as of right' may be insidious. The creation of easements, which may limit the use or development of the servient land, should not be encouraged. No serious hardship would result if in future, subject to appropriate transitional safeguards, no easement could be acquired by prescription.

Minority view in favour of retention

38. The arguments which in the view of the minority can be used against the considerations urged in favour of abolition in the preceding paragraphs of this report are—

 (a) Many of the unsatisfactory characteristics of the existing law in the field of prescription can be remedied by the simplifications and amendments discussed later in this report and do not call for the abolition of prescription.

 (b) There is no less moral justification for the acquisition of easements by prescription than there is for obtaining a title to land by adverse possession: to represent prescription as a process of 'easement stealing' is to ignore the fact that it involves open enjoyment over a long period in the assertion of a right, and that it is a process designed to give legal recognition and validity to a state of affairs of long standing, in which successive servient owners may have acquiesced.

 (c) The dominant owner for the time being is not in most cases a person who wishes to acquire an easement, but a person who believes or assumes that he is entitled to an easement . . .

 (d) In spite of the differences between adverse possession and prescription, the same fundamental considerations apply to them . . .

 (e) It should not be assumed that the doctrine is only called in aid where there has in fact been no grant . . .

Extract 19.2.31

Law Commission CP 186: Easements, Covenants and Profits à Prendre (footnotes omitted)

4.180   Long use has always been recognised as giving rise to beliefs or expectations in relation to land that ought to be protected on the basis of security of possession and utility. There are a number of examples of the utility of prescription. Prescription performs the useful function of saving landowners from the consequences of a failure to grant or reserve easements expressly. In some cases, the landowner would have a remedy in negligence against the solicitor or other conveyancer responsible for the problem which has come to light. In other cases, particularly where the error happened some time ago, such a remedy may not be viable. However, irrespective of the availability of a remedy in negligence, it seems to us that where the parties have clearly proceeded for some considerable time on the basis that rights exist and may be exercised, it may be just and reasonable for the court to recognise those rights.

4.181   Claimants rarely set out deliberately to acquire an easement by long use; they much more frequently believe or assume that they are entitled to an easement. Although it is not necessary that it do so, this belief may have induced the purchase of, or the expenditure of money upon, the dominant land. Abolition of prescription without replacement could lead to a situation where landowners mistakenly believe that they are entitled to an easement and use the land accordingly. In these circumstances, the land would be being used in a way which is not reflected on the register or recognised outside it.

4.182   Finally, and most importantly, prescription recognises the fact that land is a social resource, in that it cannot be utilised without the co-operation of neighbouring landowners. Neighbouring landowners, to varying degrees, rely on one another for rights of access, drainage, support, and water. In many cases co-operation between neighbouring landowners is regulated through legal instruments and informal arrangements. However, there will always remain cases where reliance on one's neighbour is entirely unregulated and may have occurred for a substantial period of time. In such circumstances there is an arguable case for clothing the user with legal right.

4.183   We therefore do not currently consider that outright abolition of prescriptive acquisition is desirable. Prescription plays a useful residual role, ensuring that long use is recognised as a legal interest binding upon the owners of servient land.

Extract 19.2.32

Law Commission No 327: Making Land Work: Easements, Covenants and Profits à Prendre (footnotes omitted)

3.79   However, consultees strongly favoured the retention of prescription. We asked in the Consultation Paper whether the current law of prescription should be abolished without replacement, and most consultees said no. They believed that it still serves a useful purpose. We also note that abolition may lead to unforeseen problems; a number of jurisdictions that have abolished both prescription and implication have had to introduce new statutory methods for providing important easements that have been inadvertently omitted from land transfers.

3.80   So we do not recommend the abolition of prescription.

3.81   We asked in the Consultation Paper if prescription might be abolished for negative easements only, on the basis that such easements are in any event an anomaly in the law, and that prescription for such rights (particularly light) gives rise to disproportionate practical problems. The views of consultees varied widely on that question, but again there was no consensus in favour of abolition. Caution was urged particularly about rights to light, which of course are a very important factor in the context of urban development. We do not therefore recommend the abolition of prescription for negative easements.

3.83 We asked in the Consultation Paper whether proprietary estoppel could fulfil the role of prescription, and consultees were almost unanimous that it could not. We agree . . .

3.94 We take the view that acquiescence is a way of describing what is required for prescription. It is not the same as permission (which of course must be absent), but is rather a state of tolerance, where the use is carried out openly, and the servient owner does not object, but does not actively permit. The idea of knowledge, or of opportunity for knowledge, is built into the idea that the use is not secret, and acquiescence is part of our understanding of the requirements for prescription. Neither has to be proved as a separate element in the claim.

3.123 We recommend that:

(1) an easement will arise by prescription on completion of 20 years' continuous qualifying use;

(2) qualifying use shall be use without force, without stealth and without permission; and

(3) qualifying use shall not be use which is contrary to the criminal law, unless such use can be rendered lawful by the dispensation of the servient owner.

Comment

(1) How convincing are the arguments for abolition? Is the approach of the Law Commission in these proposals consistent with the great restriction of adverse possession by the Land Registration Act 2002?

(2) Might it be argued that easements typically provide greater benefit for the dominant land than burdens for the servient land and therefore that they should be encouraged as far as possible?

(3) To what extent is the proposal of the Law Commission different from the present methods of prescription? Note that prescription would not apply to profits.

3. The relationship constituted by easements and profits

There are huge numbers of cases dealing with the extent of rights under easements and the duties on dominant and servient owners. They are largely related to the specific circumstances of each case and, in particular, the terms of the grant. This section is limited to a few central principles.

Extract 19.3.1

***White* v *Grand Hotel, Eastbourne Ltd* [1913] 1 Ch 113**

The dominant land was converted from a private residence into a garage for a hotel; drivers of guests' cars resided in the garage.

COZENS-HARDY MR: . . . The plaintiffs' main point was this: they said that the right of way, which was granted under circumstances which I shall state hereafter, was limited in its nature; that it was only a right of way for what I may call domestic purposes as distinct from trade purposes; and that it was only for such use as could reasonably be expected to be in the contemplation of the parties at the time when the defendants' house, St Vincent Lodge, was a private residence, and ought not to be altered now that St Vincent Lodge is turned into a garage. We heard that point fully argued by counsel for the appellants and we have come to the conclusion that there is no ground for limiting the right of way in the manner suggested. It is not a right of way claimed by prescription. It is a right of way claimed under a grant, and, that being so, the only thing that the Court has to do is to construe the grant; and unless there is some limitation to be found in the grant, in the nature of the width of the road or something of that kind, full effect must be given to the grant, and we cannot consider the subsequent user as in any way sufficient to cut down the generality of the grant.

Extract 19.3.2

McAdams Homes Ltd v *Robinson* (2005) 1 P&CR 520

A bakery enjoyed an implied easement of drainage. What was the effect on this easement when the bakery was demolished and replaced by two houses? It seemed probable that there would be a five-fold increase in foul water flow.

NEUBERGER LJ: 20. The question that arises in the present case can be expressed in the following more general way. Where an easement is granted by implication on the sale of a property, which is used for a particular purpose at the time of the conveyance, what are the principles governing the extent to which the easement can still be enjoyed by the owner of that property if he changes its use and/or constructs buildings on it? In order to answer that question, assistance can be found from a number of authorities cited to us.

21. Neither party challenged the correctness of these authorities, although many of them are concerned with easements other than drainage. Some circumspection must be engaged when applying the reasoning in those authorities, both generally and in relation to this case. One is here concerned with an implied grant. Accordingly much may depend on the particular facts of the case. Further, the answer may depend on the nature of easement, as not all points applicable to one type of easement will necessarily be applicable to another . . .

22. I should also mention that many of the cases to which we have been referred were concerned with easements arising by prescription, as opposed to easements arising by implication, as in this case. In my judgment, at least in the great majority of cases, there should be little difference in the principles applicable to the two types of case . . . In each type of case, the easement does not come into existence by an express agreement, whose effect can then be construed by the court . . . In each case the existence, nature and extent of the deemed grant must depend on the circumstances existing at the date of the grant.

23. I now turn to consider the cases which have been cited to us, and the principles which can be derived from them.

24. First, where the dominant land (*i.e.*, the property benefiting from the easement) is used for a particular purpose at the time an easement is created, an increase, even if substantial, in the intensity of that use, resulting in a concomitant increase in the use of the easement, cannot of itself be objected to by the servient owner . . .

27. Secondly, excessive use of an easement by the dominant land will render the dominant owner liable in nuisance. The law is stated thus, in the present, 17th, edition of *Gale on Easements* at para 6–90:

> 'If the dominant owner makes excessive use of the right of drainage by discharging more matter than the system is designed to cope with, thus causing flooding of the servient land, he will be liable in nuisance. What amounts to excessive use depends on the grant construed in the light of the circumstances surrounding its creation which may include the capacity of an existing system or the size of the buildings on the dominant land at the date of grant.'

29. . . . where there is a change in the use of, or the erection of new buildings on, the dominant land, without having any effect on the nature or extent of the use of the easement, the change, however, radical, will not affect the right of the dominant owner to use the easement. In *Lutrell's Case* (1601) 4 Co Rep 86a, a prescriptive right to a watercourse was not lost by the dominant owner demolishing two ancient fulling mills and erecting in their place two new corn grinding mills. The Exchequer Chamber held at 87a that the dominant owner 'might alter the mill into what nature of a mill he pleased, provided always that no prejudice should thereby arise, either by diverting or stopping of the water, as it was before . . .'.

31. . . . In [*Atwood* v *Bovis Homes Ltd* [2001] Ch 371], the dominant land, which had at all times been used for agricultural purposes, had a prescriptive right to drain surface water over

neighbouring land. Notwithstanding that the proposed change in the dominant land, namely a development to a housing estate, would be very substantial, I held that the right could still be enjoyed and would not be lost. This was because the dominant owner, through the medium of a water drainage scheme, was going to ensure that the quantum of surface water passing over the neighbouring land would remain wholly unaffected by this radical development.

33.   These cases appear to me to rest on the proposition that the servient owner is ultimately more concerned with an alteration in the nature or extent of the enjoyment of the easement over his land, rather than with a change in the nature or extent of the use of the dominant land. The use of the dominant land will determine the character and extent of the enjoyment of the easement, and a change in the use may obviously lead to an alteration in that enjoyment. However, where the change in the use of the dominant land does not lead to such an alteration, there is no basis for concluding that the easement cannot continue to be enjoyed in connection with the dominant land.

49.   The issue before the judge was whether the drainage easement, impliedly granted in 1982 at a time when the dominant land was used as a bakery, could continue to be enjoyed following the redevelopment of the dominant land for the purpose of two residential houses.

50.   The authorities discussed above appear to me to indicate that that issue should have been determined by answering two questions. Those questions are:

(i)   whether the development of the dominant land, i.e. the site, represented a 'radical change in the character' or a 'change in the identity' of the site . . . as opposed to a mere change or intensification in the use of the site . . . ;

(ii)   whether the use of the site as redeveloped would result in a substantial increase or alteration in the burden on the servient land, ie the cottage . . .

54.   I readily acknowledge that there are two unsatisfactory features of the approach embodied in the two questions I have identified as requiring to be answered in a case such as this. First, as already mentioned, the various cases to which we have been referred are not entirely consistent and clear. However, I believe that the two questions represent a principled, consistent and coherent basis for determining the issue. Further, to put it at its lowest, it does not seem to me that the way in which any of the judgments in the cases have been expressed is inconsistent with the approach which I have suggested.

55.   The second potentially unsatisfactory feature of the approach I have suggested is that both questions could be said to involve an exercise which, in many circumstances, may have a rather uncertain outcome. What may appear to be 'a radical change in character' to one judge could easily appear differently to another judge; equally, one judge may consider a particular increase in the burden on the servient land to be 'substantial', whereas another judge may not. It is, perhaps, inevitable that the questions have to be expressed in this rather generalised way, because each case will very much turn on its own facts . . .

58.   In my judgment, the combination of structural change, involving the destruction of the one building on the site and its replacement by two other buildings, and change of use, from purely industrial to purely residential, meant that the judge's conclusion that there was a radical change in the character of the site was one he was entitled to reach.

Comment

(1) Should different principles apply to express easements? Is Neuberger LJ justified in treating implied and prescriptive easements in the same way?

(2) Is the test propounded (a) sensible and (b) reasonably straightforward to apply?

One particular problem is where a right of way is used for access through the dominant land to further land.

Extract 19.3.3

Harris v *Flower* (1904) 74 LJ Ch 127

The dominant owner built a factory on land which was partly the dominant land ('pink land') and partly other land ('white land').

VAUGHAN-WILLIAMS LJ: . . . The reason of it is that a right of way of this sort restricts the owner of the dominant tenement to the legitimate user of his right; and the Court will not allow that which is in its nature a burthen on the owner of the servient tenement to be increased without his consent and beyond the terms of the grant. I do not know that it makes any difference whether the right of way arises by prescription or grant. The burthen imposed on the servient tenement must not be increased by allowing the owner of the dominant tenement to make a use of the way in excess of the grant. There can be no doubt in the present case that, if this building is used as a factory, a heavy and frequent traffic will arise which has not arisen before. This particular burthen could not have arisen without the user of the white land as well as of the pink. It is not a mere case of user of the pink land, with some usual offices on the white land connected with the buildings on the pink land. The whole object of this scheme is to include the profitable user of the white land as well as of the pink, and I think the access is to be used for the very purpose of enabling the white land to be used profitably as well as the pink, and I think we ought under these circumstances to restrain this user.

Extract 19.3.4

Bracewell v *Appleby* [1975] Ch 408

The dominant land was a house accessed by a private right of way. The owner bought further land ('blue land'), whose only access was through the dominant land. He built an extra house partly on the dominant land and partly on the blue land. Could the right of way be used for access, through the dominant land, to the new house?

GRAHAM J: . . . Mr Jackson's sheet-anchor, *Harris* v *Flower*, 74 LJ Ch 127, justifies his assertion that the grant of access to no 3 does not enable the defendant to establish that he has a right to extend his right of way to the blue land to which it is not appurtenant, thereby in practice doubling the burden on the servient tenements of the plaintiffs because there are now two houses and families using Hill Road from no 3 instead of one as before. The words of Romer LJ were, at p 132:

> 'If a right of way be granted for the enjoyment of Close A, the grantee, because he owns or acquires Close B, cannot use the way in substance for passing over Close A to Close B.'

The circumstances in that case and in the present case are parallel and in my judgment the principles of *Harris* v *Flower*, as expressed above by Romer LJ, govern this case. His words are quoted in *Gale, Easements*, 14th ed (1972), p 282 and it does not appear that there has ever been any criticism of them as not expressing accurately the true legal position.

Comment

(1) It appears that most of the new house was on the blue land. Would it be different if the blue land constituted the garden of the new house (perhaps 60% of the overall plot on which the new house stood) or if only a small part of the house was built on the blue land?

(2) Suppose that building materials for the new house were stored on the dominant land. Does this justify using the right of way to deliver them? Contrast *Williams* v *James*[35] and *Skull* v *Glenister*.[36]

(3) Land adjacent to a house is used for car parking. Can a right of way for the house be used for access to the car parking area?[37] Should it make any difference whether access is through the dominant land?

The Law Commission[38] originally saw the problems as severe enough to justify rejection of *Harris* v *Flower*. However, their final report recognises that rejection would be both controversial and likely to cause problems: the proposal has been dropped.

Rights to light have spawned much litigation.

Extract 19.3.5

Allen v *Greenwood* [1980] Ch 119

BUCKLEY LJ: . . . The authority which must now be regarded as the leading case on this topic is undoubtedly the decision of the House of Lords in *Colls* v *Home and Colonial Stores Ltd* [1904] AC 179, from which I think the following formulation of the principle can be distilled: the amount of light to which a dominant owner is entitled under a prescriptive claim is sufficient light, according to ordinary notions, for the comfortable or beneficial use of the building in question, again according to ordinary notions, for such purposes as would constitute normal uses of a building of its particular character. If the building be a dwelling house, the measure must be related to reasonable standards of comfort as a dwelling house. If it be a warehouse, a shop or a factory, the measure must be related to reasonable standards of comfort or beneficial use (for comfort may not be the most appropriate test in the case of such a building) as a warehouse, a shop or a factory as the case may be. These may very probably differ from the standards which would apply to a dwelling house. If the building be a greenhouse, the measure must, in my opinion, be related to its reasonably satisfactory use as a greenhouse.

In the present case the plaintiffs have not used their greenhouse otherwise than for such purposes as a domestic greenhouse would normally be used – purposes for which domestic greenhouses have been used for many generations. Accordingly, no question arises of their claiming an amount of light which would be extraordinary for a greenhouse. It is true that the satisfactory use of a greenhouse may require a freer access of light than a room in a dwelling house, just as the comfortable use of a dwelling house may require more light than the satisfactory use of a warehouse; but this, in my view, is of no significance. It would, in my judgment, and with deference to those who have suggested otherwise, be ridiculous to say that a greenhouse had enough light because a man could read a newspaper there with reasonable comfort. A north light may be very good for an artist's studio and may do very well for a sitting room in a dwelling house, but may be quite inadequate for a greenhouse.

Comment

There are many cases on rights to light, mostly implied or prescriptive. Do advances in artificial lighting since *Colls* v *Home & Colonial Stores Ltd* justify a different approach to this area?[39]

---

[35] (1867) LR 2 CP 577.

[36] (1864) 16 CBNS 81 (143 ER 1055).

[37] See *Das* v *Linden Mews Ltd* [2003] 2 P&CR 58; *Wall* v *Collins* [2007] Ch 390.

[38] Law Com CP 186, para 5.70; Law Com No 327, para 2.70.

[39] Rights to light are considered in Law Com No 356 (dropping a proposal that prescription should cease to apply).

4. Termination of easements and profits

The dominant and servient owners can of course agree to termination, subject to the normal formalities being satisfied. Slightly more special is the rule that termination occurs if there is unity of both ownership and possession in the same person. If one of the plots is later sold, both vendor and purchaser need to remember that old easements are not automatically resuscitated, though they may be implied on the principles already discussed.

Problems have arisen where a tenant holds an easement. Suppose that the tenant acquires the freehold, does the merger of the lease into the freehold (so that the lease terminates) mean that the easement also terminates?

Extract 19.4.1

Wall v *Collins* [2007] Ch 390

CARNWATH LJ: 13. The premise of the judge's reasoning was that the right of way was 'attached to the lease', and accordingly that when the lease was extinguished by merger, the right was lost. That approach was based on a passage from *Sara, Boundaries and Easements*, 3rd ed (2002), para 12.18:

> 'a person cannot grant an easement for an estate greater than that which he holds in the property and . . . a person cannot take an easement for an estate greater than that which he holds in the [dominant] tenement. This means that if the [grantee] is a lessee at the time of the grant, but subsequently becomes the freeholder, the easement should cease to exist since the leasehold estate to which it attached has merged in the freehold.'

In my view, the first part of that passage does not bear the interpretation the judge put on it, and the second is, with respect, wrong.

14. As to the scope of the right granted in 1911, it is clear that Mr Hurst could neither grant the benefit, nor accept the burden, of a right in excess of his then 999-year interest in each property. To that extent the judge's conclusion that the right granted at that stage could not benefit or burden the freehold reversion, in which Mr Hurst had no interest, is clearly right. I do not read the first part of the passage in *Sara* as intended to say more than that.

15. That is not the same as saying that the right was 'attached to' the leasehold interest. An easement must be appurtenant to a dominant tenement, but not necessarily to any particular interest for the time being. Thus for example the 1925 Act provides that a legal easement may be created for the equivalent of a freehold interest, or for an interest 'equivalent to . . . a term of years absolute': section 1(2)(a). In the latter case, there is nothing to suggest that an easement for a term of years has to be attached to a leasehold interest of equivalent duration. All that matters is that the grantee has an interest at least co-extensive with the period of the easement . . .

16. It follows, in my view, that merger of the lease into a larger interest in the dominant tenement is not in itself fatal to the continued existence of the easement, for the period for which it was granted. The dominant tenement remains unchanged and there is no legal impediment to the continued enjoyment of the easement by the occupier for the time being of that tenement.

18. Mr Foster accepted, as I understand him, that in respect of the servient tenement, the merger of the leasehold with the freehold would not remove the burden of the easement, at least for the period of the original lease. This seems right as a matter of common sense. The owner of a servient tenement should not be able to escape the burden of an easement by dealings to which those interested in the dominant tenement are not parties. Equally, as a matter of common sense, it is difficult to see why a lessee should be worse off, so far as concerns an easement annexed to the land, merely because he has acquired a larger interest in the dominant tenement.

Comment

(1) Note that it was a 999 year lease: one can see why the court was reluctant to see the easement disappear on merger with a freehold which had virtually no economic significance.

(2) The decision has received criticism (Ward [2007] Conv 464), but also some support (Lyall [2010] Conv 300). Is the reasoning of Carnwath LJ persuasive?

(3) The Law Commission[40] would reverse the decision, but provide a simple procedure for electing that the easement should continue. Is there a danger that such an election might be overlooked, especially for non-express easements?

Abandonment provides a form of termination that is rarely encountered for other interests. The approach is well summarised by Buckley LJ:[41]

> To establish abandonment of an easement the conduct of the dominant owner must, in our judgment, have been such as to make it clear that he had at the relevant time a firm intention that neither he nor any successor in title of his should thereafter make use of the easement . . . Abandonment is not, we think, to be lightly inferred. Owners of property do not normally wish to divest themselves of it unless it is to their advantage to do so, notwithstanding that they may have no present use for it.

Two cases are commonly cited to show the working of abandonment.

Extract 19.4.2

Moore v *Rawson* (1824) 3 B&C 332 (107 ER 756)

ABBOTT CJ: I am of opinion that the plaintiff is not entitled to maintain this action. It appears that many years ago the former owner of his premises had the enjoyment of light and air by means of certain windows in a wall of his house. Upon the site of this wall he built a blank wall without any windows. Things continued in this state for seventeen years. The defendant, in the interim, erected a building opposite the plaintiff's blank wall, and then the plaintiff opened a window in that which had continued for so long a period a blank wall without windows, and he now complains that that window is darkened by the buildings which the defendant so erected. It seems to me that, if a person entitled to ancient lights pulls down his house and erects a blank wall in the place of a wall in which there had been windows, and suffers that blank wall to remain for a considerable period of time, it lies upon him at least to shew, that at the time when he so erected the blank wall, and thus apparently abandoned the windows which gave light and air to the house, that was not a perpetual, but a temporary abandonment of the enjoyment; and that he intended to resume the enjoyment of those advantages within a reasonable period of time. I think that the burthen of shewing that lies on the party who has discontinued the use of the light. By building the blank wall, he may have induced another person to become the purchaser of the adjoining ground for building purposes, and it would be most unjust that he should after-wards prevent such a person from carrying those purposes into effect. For these reasons I am of opinion, that the rule for a nonsuit must be made absolute.

BAYLEY J: The right to light, air, or water, is acquired by enjoyment, and will, as it seems to me, continue so long as the party either continues that enjoyment or shews an intention to continue it. In this case the former owner of the plaintiff's premises had acquired a right to the enjoyment of the light; but he chose to relinquish that enjoyment, and to erect a blank wall instead of one in which there were formerly windows. At that time he ceased to enjoy the light in the mode in

---

[40] Law Com No 327, para 3.255.
[41] *Gotobed* v *Pridmore* (1970) 217 EG 759 (as quoted in *Williams* v *Usherwood* (1981) 45 P&CR 235 at p 256).

which he had used to do, and his right ceased with it. Suppose that, instead of doing that, he had pulled down the house and buildings, and converted the land into a garden, and continued so to use it for a period of seventeen years; and another person had been induced by such conduct to buy the adjoining ground for the purposes of building. It would be most unjust to allow the person who had so converted his land into garden ground, to prevent the other from building upon the adjoining land which he had, under such circumstances, been induced to purchase for that purpose . . .

HOLROYD J: I am of the same opinion. I think, however, that the right acquired by the enjoyment of the light, continued no longer than the existence of the thing itself in respect of which the party had the right of enjoyment; I mean the house with the windows; when the house and the windows were destroyed by his own act, the right which he had in respect of them was also extinguished. If, indeed, at the time when he pulled the house down, he had intimated his intention of rebuilding it, the right would not then have been destroyed with the house . . .

LITTLEDALE J: . . . It is said, however, that as he can only acquire the right by twenty years' enjoyment, it ought not to be lost without disuse for the same period; and that as enjoyment for such a length of time is necessary to found a presumption of a grant, there must be a similar non-user, to raise a presumption of a release. And this reasoning, perhaps, may apply to a right of common or of way. But there is a material difference between the mode of acquiring such rights and a right to light and air. The latter is acquired by mere occupancy; the former can only be acquired by user, accompanied with the consent of the owner of the land; for a way over the lands of another can only be lawfully used, in the first instance, with the consent, express or implied, of the owner . . . The right, therefore, is acquired by mere occupancy, and ought to cease when the person who so acquired it discontinues the occupancy. If, therefore, as in this case, the party who has acquired the right once ceases to make use of the light and air which he had appropriated to his own use, without shewing any intention to resume the enjoyment, he must be taken to have abandoned the right. I am of opinion, that as the right is acquired by mere user, it may be lost by non-user . . .

Comment

(1) Two principal elements emerge: the conduct of the dominant owner and the reliance (building) by the servient owner. Do the judgments show these to be cumulative or alternative elements of abandonment?[42]

(2) Is it appropriate to distinguish different forms of easements? The next case involves a right of way.

Extract 19.4.3

Cook v Mayor & Corporation of Bath (1868) LR 6 Eq 177

MALINS V-C: The most important question raised in this case is, whether the fact that the Plaintiff, or one of his predecessors, closed this back-door, and allowed it to remain so closed for at least thirty years, and only re-opened it about four years since, must be considered as an abandonment of the right of way claimed.

The law on this point is not entirely free from difficulty, but I understand the principle applicable to it to be as follows: – A right of way or a right to light may be abandoned, and it is always a question of fact to be ascertained by a jury, or by the Court, from the surrounding circumstances, whether the act amounts to an abandonment, or was intended as such. If in this case the Defendants had commenced building before this back-door had been re-opened, I should have been of opinion that the Plaintiff had, by allowing it so to remain closed, led them

---

[42] See Davis [1995] Conv 291; *Crossley & Sons Ltd* v *Lightowler* (1867) LR 2 Ch App 478.

into incurring expense, and therefore could not prevent their acting on the impression that he intended to abandon his right.

In *Moore* v *Rawson*,[i] a very valuable case, . . . *Abbott*, CJ, in the Court of Queen's Bench, held that the Plaintiff could not maintain an action, and directed a nonsuit; but it is clear that if there had been no buildings erected before the expiration of seventeen years, the Plaintiff might have resumed his windows, and acquired a new right of action against the Defendants. The same principle was laid down by *Erle*, J, in *Stokoe* v *Singers*;[ii] and in *Ward* v *Ward*;[iii] *Pollock*, CB, and *Alderson*, B, held that mere non-user of a way did not, in the absence of the acquisition of rights by other parties in consequence of it, amount to an abandonment; but only raised the inference that there had been no occasion to use it; and in *Crossley* v *Lightowler*[iv] Vice-Chancellor *Wood* laid down the law in the same way.

That is my view in this case; and this house having been erected with a back-door leading into the lane, conferred on the owner as much right to use the back-door as he had to use the front-door. It is clear that if this door had remained open the whole time, although during the whole time there had only existed the right without any exercise of it, still there would have been a continuing right unless some other parties had acquired adverse rights, which would have been prejudiced by the renewed exercise of the right.

[i] 3 B&C 332.
[ii] 8 E&B 31.
[iii] 7 Ex 838.
[iv] Law Rep 3 Eq 279.

Comment

(1) The 'closed' door had been bricked up.

(2) Can a right of way ever be abandoned without reliance by the servient owner?[43]

(3) Given that use of a claimed right is recognised by prescription, should not non-use be similarly recognised? Is the balance between prescription and abandonment affected if we consider negative easements, such as rights to light?

(4) The Law Commission proposes a presumption of abandonment after 20 years. Why should a presumption be applied here, when it has no role for prescription?

Further reading

Baker, A [2012] Conv 37: Recreational privileges as easements: law and policy.

Bridge, S (2005) 'Prescriptive acquisition of easements: abolition or reform?' in *Modern Studies in Property Law*, Vol 3, (ed) E Cooke, Chapter 1.

Davis, C [1995] Conv 291: Abandonment of an easement: is it a question of intention only?

Dawson, I and Dunn, A (1998) 18 LS 510: Negative easements – a crumb of analysis.

Harpum, C (1979) 43 Conv 113: *Long* v *Gowlett*: a strong fortress.

Spark, G [2012] Conv 6: Easements of parking and storage: are easements non-possessory interests in land?

Sturley, M F (1980) 96 LQR 557: Easements in gross.

Tee, L [1998] Conv 115: Metamorphoses and section 62 of the Law of Property Act 1925.

Turner, P G [2012] Conv 19: Prescription by and against lessees.

[43] See *Swan* v *Sinclair* [1924] 1 Ch 254 and *Williams* v *Usherwood* (1981) 45 P&CR 235.

20
Covenants

Covenants are obligations entered into by deed. As such, they may appear to be more part of contract law than property law. However, they may involve promises by holders of interests in land and operate in favour of holders of interests in land. This brings them much closer to the property context. We will consider positive covenants, which involve positive obligations to act, and restrictive covenants, which involve promises not to do something. Our concern will be with two questions. First, does the burden of a covenant run so as to bind a purchaser from the covenantor? This is the principal hallmark of a proprietary interest. Second, does the benefit of a covenant run so as to benefit a purchaser from the covenantee? The burden of positive covenants does not normally run and this has rendered the law inadequate to deal with the need of modern property owners, especially as regards flats. This led to a new area of law, commonhold (which was dealt with in Chapter 17). A final introductory comment is that covenants between landlord and tenant are governed by special rules (these were discussed in Chapter 16).

1. Positive covenants

A. Running of the burden

The following case illustrates the approach of the law towards permitting the running of the burden and, more generally, creating new interests in land.

Extract 20.1.1

***Keppell v Bailey* (1834) 2 My&K 517 (39 ER 1042)**

LORD BROUGHAM LC: . . . Consider the question first upon principle. There are certain known incidents to property and its enjoyment; among others, certain burthens where with it may be affected, or rights which may be created and enjoyed over it by parties other than the owner; all which incidents are recognised by the law . . . But it must not therefore be supposed that incidents of a novel kind can be devised and attached to property at the fancy or caprice of any owner. It is clearly inconvenient both to the science of the law and to the public weal that such a latitude should be given. There can be no harm in allowing the fullest latitude to men in binding themselves and their representatives, that is, their assets real and personal, to answer in damages for breach of their obligations. This tends to no mischief, and is a reasonable liberty to bestow; but great detriment would arise and much confusion of rights if parties were allowed to invent new modes of holding and enjoying real property, and to impress upon their lands and tenements a peculiar character, which should follow them into all hands, however remote. Every close, every messuage, might thus be held in a several fashion; and it would hardly be possible to know what rights the acquisition of any parcel conferred, or what obligations it imposed . . .

The difference is obviously very great between such a case as this and the case of covenants in a lease, whereby the demised premises are affected with certain rights in favour of the lessor. The lessor or his assignees continue in the reversion while the term lasts. The estate is not out of them, although the possession is in the lessee or his assigns. It is not at all inconsistent with the nature of property that certain things should be reserved to the reversioners all the while the term continues; it is only something taken out of the demise, some exception to the temporary surrender of the enjoyment; it is only that they retain, more or less partially, the use of what was wholly used by them before the demise, and what will again be wholly used by them when that demise is at an end . . .

That covenants are not *legal* proprietary interests was confirmed by the Court of Appeal in *Austerberry* v *Oldham Corporation*[1] and has never been seriously questioned in more recent years. As will be seen later in this chapter, it has been accepted for over a century and a half that the burden of restrictive covenants can run in equity. Attempts to extend this rule to positive covenants have been consistently rejected, most recently by the House of Lords in *Rhone* v *Stephens*.[2]

There is one context in which the rules are especially inconvenient: flats. The nature of flats is that it is necessary to have obligations regarding repairs and maintenance, both of the individual flats and of the premises as a whole. One consequence of this is that, instead of a sale of the freehold of individual flats, a long lease is almost invariably used (unless commonhold is employed). The tenant pays a capital sum (premium) and a small or nominal rent. As the extract from *Keppell* v *Bailey* shows, this enables the covenants, both positive and restrictive, to be enforced between the landlord and tenant and their assignees. Assuming that the parties are content with a leasehold relationship, does this solve the problems of the running of covenants in flats?

The doctrine of benefit and burden (that a person cannot take advantage of an agreement without accepting a burden attached to that benefit) has already been discussed;[3] it could be very important in the covenants context. However, the restrictions imposed by *Rhone* v *Stephens*[4] mean that one must be able to show that the covenant is reciprocal to a right which the covenantor's successor in title wishes to enjoy. How extensive is the scope for draftsmen to make the doctrine apply by explicitly linking the positive covenant to a benefit enjoyed by the covenantor?

Other methods of circumventing the positive covenants rules include:

(1) Chains of covenants, whereby the covenantor requires a later purchaser to comply with the original covenant. The covenantor remains liable on the original covenant after sale and the fresh covenant is some protection against the risks faced by the covenantor. It is a purely contractual approach: the original covenantee is not a party to the fresh covenant. It is the only method (other than the use of leases for flats) to be widely employed.

(2) Requiring the covenantee's consent before sale, aimed at getting a fresh covenant between the covenantee and the new purchaser (most effective in registered land; p 313 above).

(3) Granting a long lease, almost immediately converted into a fee simple under statutory provisions which permit the continued enforcement of covenants.

(4) Linking the covenant to a rentcharge.

---

[1] (1885) 29 Ch D 750; see also Law of Property Act 1925 (hereafter LPA), s 1.
[2] [1994] 2 AC 310; Extract 20.2.2 below.
[3] See p 217 above.
[4] [1994] 2 AC 310 (Extract 7.4.3 above).

The Law Commission[5] has concluded that, 'None of these methods is therefore ideal; they can all be made to work but only indirectly, with unnecessary cost and risk and, in the case of indemnity chains, only for a limited, and uncertain, period.' Is this conclusion justified, or are they sufficiently flexible so as to avoid any need for further reform of this area of law?

B. Running of the benefit

It is not surprising that the benefit of covenants can pass to purchasers from the covenantee. After all, the assignment of the benefit of any non-personal contract is possible. However, covenants relating to land possess two advantages. The first is historical: before the Judicature Acts 1873–75, assignments generally could not take effect at law, whereas the benefit of covenants relating to land has always been able to pass at law. More significantly, the benefit can pass without express assignment.

Extract 20.1.2

***Smith and Snipes Hall Farm Ltd* v *River Douglas Catchment Board* [1949] 2 KB 500**

The defendants covenanted to improve and maintain river banks, in favour of the plaintiffs' predecessors in title.

TUCKER LJ: . . . It is said for the defendants that the benefit of the covenant does not run with the land . . . Further, it is contended that such a covenant must by the terms of the deed in which it is contained relate to some specific parcel of land, the precise extent and situation of which can be identified by reference to the deed alone. It is first necessary to ascertain from the deed that the covenant is one which 'touches or concerns' the land, that is, it must either affect the land as regards mode of occupation, or it must be such as per se, and not merely from collateral circumstances, affects the value of the land, and it must then be shown that it was the intention of the parties that the benefit thereof should run with the land . . . In my view the language of the deed satisfies both tests.

. . .

In this state of the authorities it seems clear, despite some dicta tending to the contrary view, that such a covenant if it runs with the land is binding on the covenantor though a mere stranger, and that this point will not avail the defendant board. As to the requirement that the deed containing the covenant must expressly identify the particular land to be benefited, no authority was cited to us and in the absence of such authority I can see no valid reason why the maxim 'Id certum est quod certum reddi potest' ['A matter is certain if it can be made certain.'] should not apply, so as to make admissible extrinsic evidence to prove the extent and situation of the lands of the respective land owners . . .

Comment

(1) As will be seen later,[6] more demanding rules were developed for restrictive covenants.

(2) A separate problem was that it had been thought that the claimant had to possess the same estate as the covenantee. In *Smith and Snipes*, this could have caused difficulty because one of the claimants was a lessee. The Court of Appeal held that this old rule was abrogated by LPA, s 78.[7]

We can now turn to the effect of LPA, s 56 on the running of covenants.

---

[5] Law Com No 327, para 5.27.
[6] See p 714 below.
[7] For s 78, see pp 714–720 below. This ruling was confirmed by *Williams* v *Unit Construction Co Ltd* (1955) 19 Conv NS 262.

Extract 20.1.3

Law of Property Act 1925, s 56

56.—(1) A person may take an immediate or other interest in land or other property, or the benefit of any condition, right of entry, covenant or agreement over or respecting land or other property, although he may not be named as a party to the conveyance or other instrument.

As will be seen, two issues emerge. First, does the section enable identifiable third parties to sue on a covenant? In the covenants context, these third parties are usually the holders of adjoining land which is benefited by the covenant. The second issue is whether it permits future successors in title (whether from the covenantor or a third party who can sue) to bring actions on the covenant.

Extract 20.1.4

Amsprop Trading Ltd v Harris Distribution Ltd [1997] 1 WLR 1025

A head landlord attempted to sue on a covenant between his tenant and a sub-lessee.

NEUBERGER J: . . . If one construes section 56 as widely as the words allow, one might conclude that it:

> '[left] the courts free, in cases respecting property, to go back to the old common law, whereby a third party can sue on a contract made expressly for his benefit; and rid also of the old rule about deeds inter partes.'

These are the words of Denning LJ in *Drive Yourself Hire Co (London) Ltd* v *Strutt* [1954] 1 QB 250, 274 which summarise the conclusion that he reached.

However, I consider that the view cannot stand in light of the reasoning of the House of Lords in *Beswick* v *Beswick* [1968] AC 58. In that case Lord Upjohn discussed the history and ambit of section 56 in some detail, at pp 102–107. Although he described his views as 'obiter and tentative', at p 105G, he cited with approval, at p 106, the view of Simonds J in *White* v *Bijou Mansions Ltd* [1937] Ch 610, 625:

> 'under section 56 . . . only that person can call it in aid who, although not named as a party to the conveyance or other instrument, is yet a person to whom that conveyance or other instrument purports to grant some thing or with which some agreement or covenant is purported to be made.'

Lord Pearce took the same view, and indeed expressly agreed with Lord Upjohn, at pp 92–94. Lord Guest, at p 87B, was 'not satisfied' that the limitations put on section 56 by Simonds J could be justified, but the extent of his disagreement is unclear. The views of Lord Reid and Lord Hodson appear to be somewhat more equivocal. However, Lord Hodson's agreement, at p 80C, with the judgment of Crossman J in *In re Foster, decd; Hudson* v *Foster* [1938] 3 All ER 357 (cited by Lord Pearce, at pp 93–94, from which it can be seen that Crossman J agreed with Simonds J) appears to me to show that Lord Hodson also agreed with Lord Upjohn. Lord Reid's observations, at p 74E–F, and his quotation of, and reference to, the view of Simonds J on p 75 coupled with his disagreement, at p 76A, with the view of Denning LJ that *In re Miller's Agreement; Uniacke* v *Attorney-General* [1947] Ch 615 (where Wynn-Parry J quoted and approved the views of Simonds and Crossman JJ) was wrongly decided manifest at least an inclination towards the same view of Lord Upjohn.

    . . .

I consider that the ambit of section 56 is accurately summarised in *Megarry and Wade*, p 763:

> 'The true aim of section 56 seems to be not to allow the third party to sue on a contract merely because it is made for his benefit; the contract must purport to be made *with* him. Just as, under the first part of the section, a person cannot benefit by conveyance unless it purports to be made *to* him (as grantee), so he cannot benefit by a covenant which does not purport to be made *with* him (as covenantee).'

Comment

(1) Note that the action was not brought on the leasehold covenants rules. Why was this?

(2) Given the difference of opinion in *Beswick v Beswick*, how definitive is the ruling of Neuberger J?

Turning to the effect of s 56 on successors in title, the position is somewhat clearer. Although Denning LJ was prepared to rely on the section to enable successors in title to sue in *Smith and Snipes*, the better view is that it has no role to play in this area. It has been accepted since *Kelsey v Dodd*[8] in 1881 that 'you could not covenant with a non-existent person'. However, once a third party has the benefit of a covenant by virtue of s 56, successors in title may be able to sue on the principles stated by Tucker LJ in *Smith and Snipes*.

Extract 20.1.5

Contracts (Rights of Third Parties) Act 1999, s 1

1.—(1) Subject to the provisions of this Act, a person who is not a party to a contract (a 'third party') may in his own right enforce a term of the contract if—

(a) the contract expressly provides that he may, or

(b) subject to subsection (2), the term purports to confer a benefit on him.

(2) Subsection (1)(b) does not apply if on a proper construction of the contract it appears that the parties did not intend the term to be enforceable by the third party.

(3) The third party must be expressly identified in the contract by name, as a member of a class or as answering a particular description but need not be in existence when the contract is entered into.

Comment

(1) To what extent, if at all, is this wider than s 56 for covenants and contracts relating to land? Note that the 1999 Act places some qualifications upon the third party right: these may make it less attractive than a right under s 56.

(2) How might the 1999 Act affect the operation of chains of covenants[9] entered into on the sale of the burdened land?

(3) Does subsection (3) provide a useful new route for the running of the benefit of covenants?

---

[8] 52 LJ Ch 34 at p 39, approved by the Court of Appeal in *Grant v Edmondson* [1931] 1 Ch 1 at p 27.
[9] See p 702 above.

2. Restrictive covenants

Extract 20.2.1

Tulk v *Moxhay* (1848) 2 Ph 774 (41 ER 1143)

LORD COTTENHAM LC (without calling upon the other side): That this Court has jurisdiction to enforce a contract between the owner of land and his neighbour purchasing a part of it, that the latter shall either use or abstain from using the land purchased in a particular way, is what I never knew disputed. Here there is no question about the contract: the owner of certain houses in the square sells the land adjoining, with a covenant from the purchaser not to use it for any other purpose than as a square garden. And it is now contended, not that the vendee could violate that contract, but that he might sell the piece of land, and that the purchaser from him may violate it without this Court having any power to interfere. If that were so, it would be impossible for an owner of land to sell part of it without incurring the risk of rendering what he retains worthless. It is said that, the covenant being one which does not run with the land, this Court cannot enforce it; but the question is, not whether the covenant runs with the land, but whether a party shall be permitted to use the land in a manner inconsistent with the contract entered into by his vendor, and with notice of which he purchased. Of course, the price would be affected by the covenant, and nothing could be more inequitable than that the original purchaser should be able to sell the property the next day for a greater price, in consideration of the assignee being allowed to escape from the liability which he had himself undertaken.

That the question does not depend upon whether the covenant runs with the land is evident from this, that if there was a mere agreement and no covenant, this Court would enforce it against a party purchasing with notice of it; for if an equity is attached to the property by the owner, no one purchasing with notice of that equity can stand in a different situation from the party from whom he purchased . . .

Comment

(1) What is it about restrictive covenants which justifies their enforcement against purchasers?

(2) The idea that equitable remedies bind purchasers was roundly rejected by the House of Lords in *National Provincial Bank Ltd* v *Ainsworth*:[10] it is necessary to possess an interest in land.

A. The limitation to restrictive covenants

Extract 20.2.2

Rhone v *Stephens* [1994] 2 AC 310

The roof of a house extended over the adjoining cottage. The owner of both house and cottage sold the cottage, covenanting to keep the roof in repair. Both house and cottage were subsequently sold.

LORD TEMPLEMAN: . . . My Lords, equity supplements but does not contradict the common law. When freehold land is conveyed without restriction, the conveyance confers on the purchaser the right to do with the land as he pleases provided that he does not interfere with the rights of others or infringe statutory restrictions. The conveyance may however impose restrictions

---

[10] [1965] AC 1175; Extract 18.1.9 above.

which, in favour of the covenantee, deprive the purchaser of some of the rights inherent in the ownership of unrestricted land. In *Tulk* v *Moxhay* (1848) 2 Ph 774, a purchaser of land covenanted that no buildings would be erected on Leicester Square. A subsequent purchaser of Leicester Square was restrained from building. The conveyance to the original purchaser deprived him and every subsequent purchaser taking with notice of the covenant of the right, otherwise part and parcel of the freehold, to develop the square by the construction of buildings. Equity does not contradict the common law by enforcing a restrictive covenant against a successor in title of the covenantor but prevents the successor from exercising a right which he never acquired. Equity did not allow the owner of Leicester Square to build because the owner never acquired the right to build without the consent of the persons (if any) from time to time entitled to the benefit of the covenant against building . . .

Equity can thus prevent or punish the breach of a negative covenant which restricts the user of land or the exercise of other rights in connection with land. Restrictive covenants deprive an owner of a right which he could otherwise exercise. Equity cannot compel an owner to comply with a positive covenant entered into by his predecessors in title without flatly contradicting the common law rule that a person cannot be made liable upon a contract unless he was a party to it. Enforcement of a positive covenant lies in contract; a positive covenant compels an owner to exercise his rights. Enforcement of a negative covenant lies in property; a negative covenant deprives the owner of a right over property. As Lord Cottenham LC said in *Tulk* v *Moxhay*, at p 778: 'if an equity is attached to the property by the owner, no one purchasing with notice of that equity can stand in a different situation from the party from whom he purchased'.

Following *Tulk* v *Moxhay* there was some suggestion that any covenant affecting land was enforceable in equity provided that the owner of the land had notice of the covenant prior to his purchase . . .

These . . . cases did not survive the decision of the Court of Appeal in *Haywood* v *Brunswick Permanent Benefit Building Society* (1881) 8 QBD 403. In that case land had been conveyed in consideration of a rent charge and a covenant to build and repair buildings; a mortgagee of the land was held not to be liable on the covenant either at law or in equity although the mortgagee had notice of the covenant. Brett LJ said, at p 408, that *Tulk* v *Moxhay*:

'decided that an assignee taking land subject to a certain class of covenants is bound by such covenants if he has notice of them, and that the class of covenants comprehended within the rule is that covenants restricting the mode of using the land only will be enforced. It may be also, but it is not necessary to decide here, that all covenants also which impose such a burden on the land as can be enforced against the land would be enforced . . . it is said that if we decide for the defendants we shall have to overrule *Cooke* v *Chilcott*, 3 Ch D 694. If that case was decided on the equitable doctrine of notice, I think we ought to overrule it.'

. . .

In *London and South Western Railway Co* v *Gomm* (1882) 20 Ch D 562 an option to purchase land on the happening of an uncertain event was held to be void for remoteness. It was argued that the covenant was enforceable in equity. Jessel MR said, at pp 582–583:

'With regard to the argument founded on *Tulk* v *Moxhay*, 2 Ph 774, that case was very much considered by the Court of Appeal at Westminster in *Haywood* v *Brunswick Permanent Benefit Building Society*, 8 QBD 403, and the court there decided that they would not extend the doctrine of *Tulk* v *Moxhay* to affirmative covenants, compelling a man to lay out money or do any other act of what I may call an active character, but that it was to be confined to restrictive covenants. Of course that authority would be binding upon us if we did not agree to it, but I most cordially accede to it. I think that we ought not to extend the doctrine of *Tulk* v *Moxhay* in the way suggested here. The doctrine of that case . . . appears to me to be either an extension in equity of the doctrine of *Spencer's Case*, 5 Co Rep 16a to another line of cases, or else an extension in equity of the doctrine of negative easements; . . .'

. . .

In the *Austerberry* case, 29 Ch D 750 the owners of a site of a road covenanted that they and their successors in title would make the road and keep it in repair. The road was sold to the defendants and it was held that the repair covenant could not be enforced against them. Cotton LJ said, at pp 773–774:

'undoubtedly, where there is a restrictive covenant, the burden and benefit of which do not run at law, courts of equity restrain anyone who takes the property with notice of that covenant from using it in a way inconsistent with the covenant. But here the covenant which is attempted to be insisted upon on this appeal is a covenant to lay out money in doing certain work upon this land; and, that being so . . . that is not a covenant which a court of equity will enforce: it will not enforce a covenant not running at law when it is sought to enforce that covenant in such a way as to require the successors in title of the covenantor to spend money, and in that way to undertake a burden upon themselves . . .'

. . .

For over 100 years it has been clear and accepted law that equity will enforce negative covenants against freehold land but has no power to enforce positive covenants against successors in title of the land. To enforce a positive covenant would be to enforce a personal obligation against a person who has not covenanted. To enforce negative covenants is only to treat the land as subject to a restriction.

Mr Munby, who argued the appeal persuasively on behalf of the plaintiffs, referred to an article by Professor Sir William Wade [1972 B] CLJ 157 and other articles in which the present state of the law is subjected to severe criticism. In 1965 a report by a committee appointed by the Lord Chancellor and under the chairmanship of Lord Wilberforce, the Report of the Committee on Positive Covenants Affecting Land (1965) (Cmnd 2719), referred to difficulties caused by the decision in the *Austerberry* case and recommended legislation to provide that positive covenants which relate to the use of land and are intended to benefit specified other land should run with the land. The Law Commission published on 5 July 1971 Working Paper No 36 in which the present law on positive rights was described as being illogical, uncertain, incomplete and inflexible. The Law Commission Report on Transfer of Land (1984) (Law Com 127) (HC 201) . . . made recommendations for the reform of the law relating to positive and restrictive obligations and submitted a draft Bill for that purpose. Nothing has been done.

In these circumstances your Lordships were invited to overrule the decision of the Court of Appeal in the *Austerberry* case. To do so would destroy the distinction between law and equity and to convert the rule of equity into a rule of notice. It is plain from the articles, reports and papers to which we were referred that judicial legislation to overrule the *Austerberry* case would create a number of difficulties, anomalies and uncertainties and affect the rights and liabilities of people who have for over 100 years bought and sold land in the knowledge, imparted at an elementary stage to every student of the law of real property, that positive covenants, affecting freehold land are not directly enforceable except against the original covenantor. Parliamentary legislation to deal with the decision in the *Austerberry* case would require careful consideration of the consequences. Moreover, experience with leasehold tenure where positive covenants are enforceable by virtue of privity of estate has demonstrated that social injustice can be caused by logic. Parliament was obliged to intervene to prevent tenants losing their homes and being saddled with the costs of restoring to their original glory buildings which had languished through wars and economic depression for exactly 99 years.

Mr Munby submitted that the decision in the *Austerberry* case had been reversed remarkably but unremarked by section 79 of the Law of Property Act 1925 which, so far as material, provides:

'(1) A covenant relating to any land of a covenantor or capable of being bound by him, shall, unless a contrary intention is expressed, be deemed to be made by the covenantor on behalf of himself, his successors in title and the persons deriving title under him or them, and, subject as aforesaid, shall have effect as if such successors and other persons were expressed . . .'

This provision has always been regarded as intended to remove conveyancing difficulties with regard to the form of covenants and to make it unnecessary to refer to successors in title. A similar provision relating to the benefit of covenants is to be found in section 78 of the Act of 1925. In *Smith and Snipes Hall Farm Ltd* v *River Douglas Catchment Board* [1949] 2 KB 500, followed in *Williams* v *Unit Construction Co Ltd* (1951) 19 Conv (NS) 262, it was held by the Court of Appeal that section 78 of the Act of 1925 had the effect of making the benefit of positive covenants run with the land. Without casting any doubt on those long standing decisions I do not consider that it follows that section 79 of the Act of 1925 had the corresponding effect of making the burden of positive covenants run with the land. In *Jones* v *Price* [1965] 2 QB 618, 633, Willmer LJ repeated that: 'a covenant to perform positive acts . . . is not one the burden of which runs with the land so as to bind the successors in title of the covenantor: see *Austerberry* v *Oldham Corporation*.'

In *Sefton* v *Tophams Ltd* [1967] 1 AC 50, 73, 81, Lord Upjohn and Lord Wilberforce stated that section 79 of the Law of Property Act 1925 does not have the effect of causing covenants to run with the land. Finally, in *Federated Homes Ltd* v *Mill Lodge Properties Ltd* [1980] 1 WLR 594, 605–606, Brightman J referred to the authorities on section 78 of the Act of 1925 and said that: 'Section 79, in my view, involves quite different considerations and I do not think that it provides a helpful analogy.'

Comment

(1) How well does *Rhone* fit with the decision and judgment in *Tulk* v *Moxhay* itself?

(2) *Gomm* describes the doctrine of *Tulk* v *Moxhay* as 'an extension in equity of the doctrine of *Spencer's Case* [the running of covenants in leases] . . . or else an extension in equity of the doctrine of negative easements'. How accurate and useful is this observation?

(3) To what extent is the analysis of Lord Templeman justified by arguments from principle, from pragmatism or from overwhelming authority? See Gardner [1995] CLJ 60 at pp 63–67.

(4) How strong is the argument based upon LPA, s 79? Section 78 is considered below.[11]

(5) Note the Law Commission's proposals: Extracts 20.4.1 and 20.4.2 below.

A consequential question concerns the test for deciding whether a covenant is positive: a useful test is whether the covenantor must 'put his hand into his pocket'.[12] In *Tulk* v *Moxhay*, the covenant was to 'keep and maintain the said piece of ground and square garden . . . in its then form, and in sufficient and proper repair as a square garden and pleasure ground, in an open state and uncovered with any buildings'. Megarry J provides some help for such 'mixed' covenants in *Shepherd Homes Ltd* v *Sandham (No 2)* [1971] 1 WLR 1062:

> . . . First, the question is not whether a covenant is negative in wording but whether it is negative in substance. This, indeed, is implicit in *Tulk* v *Moxhay* (1848) 2 Ph 774 itself; and in reply to a question Mr Mervyn Davies accepted that his argument involved an assault on that case. That assault seems to me to be contrary to many other decisions and dicta, and to the whole approach of equity in these matters; and to that, when so much water has flowed under the bridges, I shall give no countenance. Second, what is worded or set out in the instrument as a single covenant may give rise to more obligations than one; and if one obligation is positive, that is no reason why another obligation should not be negative, and be enforced as such . . .

---

[11] See p 714.
[12] Cotton LJ in *Haywood* v *Brunswick Permanent Benefit BS* (1881) 8 QBD 403 at p 409.

B. The requirement of a dominant tenement

Extract 20.2.3

London CC v *Allen* [1914] 3 KB 642

BUCKLEY LJ: . . . The reasoning of Lord Cottenham's judgment in *Tulk* v *Moxhay*[i] is that if an owner of land sells part of it reserving the rest, and takes from his purchaser a covenant that the purchaser shall use or abstain from using the land purchased in a particular way, that covenant (being one for the protection of the land reserved) is enforceable against a subpurchaser with notice. The reason given is that, if that were not so, it would be impossible for an owner of land to sell part of it without incurring the risk of rendering what he retains worthless. If the vendor has retained no land which can be protected by the restrictive covenant, the basis of the reasoning of the judgment is swept away. In *Haywood* v *Brunswick Permanent Benefit Building Society*[ii] the Court of Appeal declined to extend the doctrine of *Tulk* v *Moxhay* to covenants other than restrictive covenants. They rejected the doctrine that, inasmuch as the defendants took the land with notice of the covenants, they were bound in equity to perform them. That therefore is not the principle upon which the equitable doctrine rests. In the present case we are asked to extend the doctrine of *Tulk* v *Moxhay* so as to affirm that a restrictive covenant can be enforced against a derivative owner taking with notice by a person who never has had or who does not retain any land to be protected by the restrictive covenant in question. In my opinion the doctrine does not extend to that case. The doctrine is that a covenant not running with the land, but being a negative covenant entered into by an owner of land with an adjoining owner, binds the land in equity and is enforceable against a derivative owner taking with notice. The doctrine ceases to be applicable when the person seeking to enforce the covenant against the derivative owner has no land to be protected by the negative covenant. The fact of notice is in that case irrelevant.

[i] 2 Ph 774.
[ii] (1881) 8 QBD 403.

Comment

(1) Buckley LJ stressed that the *Gomm* analysis required (whether on the analogy of *Spencer's Case* or of easements) a property interest in the covenantee.

(2) Are the reasons for limiting *Tulk* v *Moxhay* convincing?

(3) The limitation has proved inconvenient in some cases and statute has introduced some relaxations, in particular for certain public bodies as covenantees (Housing Act 1985, s 609 applies to local housing authorities).

(4) The dominant land need not be a separate plot. Thus the landlord's reversion suffices for a restrictive covenant by a tenant.[13] Why would a landlord seek to rely on a restrictive covenant rather than on the rules for leasehold covenants?

C. Touching and concerning the dominant tenement

It comes as no surprise that there must not only be a dominant tenement but that it must be 'touched and concerned' by the covenant. *Rogers* v *Hosegood*[14] employed the test that it

---

[13] *Hall* v *Ewin* (1887) 37 Ch D 74.
[14] [1900] 2 Ch 388 at p 395 (Farwell J, upheld by the Court of Appeal).

'must either affect the land as regards mode of occupation, or it must be such as per se, and not merely from collateral circumstances, affects the value of the land'.

Two issues may be considered. The first is how far a large estate can be benefited by a covenant which is entered into regarding a relatively small adjoining plot.

Extract 20.2.4

Wrotham Park Estate Co Ltd v *Parkside Homes Ltd* [1974] 1 WLR 798

BRIGHTMAN J: . . . Wilberforce J in *Marten* v *Flight Refuelling Ltd* [1962] Ch 115 dealing with a covenant restricting land to agricultural user said, at p 136:

> 'If an owner of land, on selling part of it, thinks fit to impose a restriction on user, and the restriction was imposed for the purpose of benefiting the land retained, the court would normally assume that it is capable of doing so. There might, of course, be exceptional cases where the covenant was on the face of it taken capriciously or not bona fide, but a covenant taken by the owner of an agricultural estate not to use a sold-off portion for other than agricultural purposes could hardly fall within either of these categories.'

> . . .

> . . . There can be obvious cases where a restrictive covenant clearly is, or clearly is not, of benefit to an estate. Between these two extremes there is inevitably an area where the benefit to the estate is a matter of personal opinion, where responsible and reasonable persons can have divergent views sincerely and reasonably held. In my judgment, in such cases, it is not for the court to pronounce which is the correct view. I think that the court can only decide whether a particular view is one which can reasonably be held.

> If a restriction is bargained for at the time of sale with the intention of giving the vendor a protection which he desires for the land he retains, and the restriction is expressed to be imposed for the benefit of the estate so that both sides are apparently accepting that the restriction is of value to the retained land, I think that the validity of the restriction should be upheld so long as an estate owner may reasonably take the view that the restriction remains of value to his estate, and that the restriction should not be discarded merely because others may reasonably argue that the restriction is spent . . .

Comment

(1) A stricter approach had been taken earlier by Clauson J in *Re Ballard's Conveyance*,[15] but this seems to have been overtaken by the later cases.

(2) Today, nearly all covenants are taken for the benefit of 'each and every part' of the dominant land.[16] It follows that the question of touching and concerning must be considered in relation to the part involved in the case. Suppose that the covenantee sells a small part of the benefited land, half a mile away from the burdened land. The courts might well hold that such a far part of an estate is not benefited.[17] Is any scope left for the generous approach adopted in *Wrotham Park*?

The second issue concerns the nature of the covenant. Nearly all restrictive covenants relate to the way in which the land can be used, preventing building or business use being

---

[15] [1937] Ch 473.
[16] *Federated Homes Ltd* v *Mill Lodge Properties Ltd* [1980] 1 WLR 594, Extract 20.2.9 below.
[17] This would be relevant if that far part had been sold to the claimant.

obvious examples. Subject to restraint of trade rules, it seems clear that a covenant can benefit a trade on the dominant land by excluding competition.[18]

It is unusual for it to be doubted whether covenants of this nature benefit the dominant land, but the following case indicates limits.

Extract 20.2.5

Cosmichome Ltd v *Southampton City Council* [2013] EWHC 1378 (Ch); [2013] 1 WLR 2436

A covenant restricted use to BBC use and use for broadcasting.

SIR WILLIAM BLACKBURNE: 22. Mr Coppel submitted that the restrictive covenant secures the presence of a well-known public, national broadcaster on a major, centrally-located parcel of land adjacent to the Council's Civic Centre and the Council's other arts-based sites and that it does so for the purpose of its use as a broadcasting centre. . . .

26. Given the varied nature of the land uses in the immediate vicinity it is hard to suppose that the restrictive covenant, confining the use of the Site effectively to BBC use as a broadcasting centre, can have any material impact on the nature, quality or amenity of the adjoining Council-owned land. . . . Even less likely is the idea that any such change of use or identity of the user could adversely affect the values of any of those areas.

27. If it had been the case that the BBC Building acts as a magnet, drawing members of the public into the Cultural Quarter to enjoy the various facilities available to them in the Council-owned area of the Quarter (for example, in the Mayflower Theatre or the Gantry Arts Centre), it might plausibly be suggested that the restriction impacts favourably on the value and amenity of those other facilities. But that is most certainly not the case. It appears that the BBC Building is not open to the public in the sense that, say, a museum or an arts centre or a public library is.

32. I can well understand the wish of the Council to have and retain a national institution as publicly well-known as the BBC as an occupant of one of its city centre sites and, better still, in close proximity to the Civic Centre, Guildhall and various present or intended cultural facilities in the Cultural Quarter. But I am quite unable to see how in any real sense that presence impacts upon either the nature of the Council-owned land in the immediate vicinity, or its quality, amenity, or value. . . .

36. In the light of this review of the relevant evidence I conclude that the restrictive covenant cannot be said to have benefited the Council's adjoining or adjacent land when it was imposed in 1989 and it does not do so now. Moreover, the balance of the evidence strongly suggests that the reason for its imposition was twofold: to seek thereby to maintain the BBC at the Site and to serve as the lever for extracting a payment if and when the BBC should seek to have it removed and go elsewhere. As such it is in the nature of a money payment obligation rather than a restrictive covenant properly so called. It is not intended to protect or preserve the amenity or value of the Council's adjacent land. . . .

Comment

(1) Could one distinguish between BBC use and broadcasting use?

(2) Does the case adopt too financial an approach to benefit?

(3) It is not uncommon for covenants to be intended to provide control for the covenantee over the use of land or to provide a way of extracting a share of profits if the use changes. To what extent does *Cosmichome* limit the use of covenants for these purposes?

Negative covenants can take very different forms. Contrast the following dicta.

---

[18] See, e.g., *Newton Abbot Co-operative Society Ltd* v *Williamson & Treadgold Ltd* [1952] Ch 286; *Re Royal Victoria Pavilion, Ramsgate* [1961] Ch 581 and *Williams* v *Kiley* [2003] 1 EGLR 46.

Extract 20.2.6

Shepherd Homes Ltd v Sandham (No 2) [1971] 1 WLR 1062

MEGARRY J: . . . A covenant may relate to land and be negative in nature, and yet not be of such a nature that the burden will run with the land in equity; for the nature of the covenant may not be such that it could benefit any other land. Thus the burden of a covenant conferring a right of pre-emption or imposing other restrictions on dispositions would normally, I imagine, be incapable of running with the land under the doctrine of *Tulk* v *Moxhay*, 2 Ph 774, and so might some trade or professional restrictions imposed to protect a business or profession rather than the land . . .

Extract 20.2.7

Hemingway Securities Ltd v Dunraven Ltd (1994) 71 P&CR 30

A landlord sought to enforce against a sub-tenant a covenant restricting assignment.

JACOB J: . . . It was suggested that a covenant against alienation is not a restrictive covenant for the purposes of the *Tulk* v *Moxhay* doctrine. That doctrine was limited to covenants in respect of the mode of user of property. No direct authority was cited to that effect and I do not see why, in principle, it should be so. One can have covenants subject to the doctrine not to build things without showing plans first; covenants against multiple occupation; and I do not see why this particular restrictive covenant against alienation should be treated differently.

Extract 20.2.8

University of East London v Barking and Dagenham LBC [2005] Ch 354

LIGHTMAN J: 28. . . . The right of pre-emption as a form of estate contract accordingly has not created an interest in land. In the alternative it has been suggested that a right of pre-emption (in particular if framed as a restrictive covenant) operates in law as a restrictive covenant. The argument proceeds that, since the grant of the right of pre-emption impliedly imposes on the grantor a negative obligation not to part with the land so as to frustrate the right, a right of pre-emption may be capable of binding successors in title as a restrictive covenant, if it obeys the rules for such covenants, including the rule that the covenant must be for the protection of adjacent land of the covenantee: see e.g. *Barnsley's Land Options*, 3rd ed (1998), pp 165 and 184–186 and *Megarry & Wade, The Law of Real Property*, 6th ed (2000), p 685, para 12–063. This suggestion appears dubious, for a restrictive covenant is concerned with restricting the use of land, and not with restraints on alienation. Certainly the pre-emption covenant in this case is not a restrictive covenant though it forms an integral part of a single scheme together with the user and approval covenants.

Comment

(1) Doubts were also expressed by Russell LJ in *Caldy Manor Estate Ltd* v *Farrell*,[19] though *Hemingway* was applied in *Test Valley BC* v *Minilec Engineering Ltd* [2005] 2 EGLR 113. When *Hemingway* was later cited to Lightman J in *Crestfort Ltd* v *Tesco Stores Ltd*,[20] he left the question open. Which is the preferable approach?

(2) Rights of pre-emption (which involve an obligation to sell) were not recognised as property rights until the Land Registration Act 2002, s 115. Does this suggest that they should be distinguished from other forms of restraints on alienation?

---

[19] [1974] 1 WLR 1303 at p 1307.
[20] [2005] L&TR 413 at [58].

D. The running of the benefit

A particular feature of restrictive covenants is the development of rules for the passing of the benefit. In other areas of land law where there is benefited land (easements; positive covenants), this has not caused difficulty. Unfortunately, the same cannot be said of restrictive covenants. There are three ways in which the benefit may pass: annexation, assignment and schemes of development.

(i) Annexation

Annexation is the permanent linking of the benefit to the land. The effect of annexation is explained by the Court of Appeal in *Rogers v Hosegood*[21] as follows:

> [W]hen the benefit has been once clearly annexed to one piece of land, it passes by assignment of that land, and may be said to run with it, in contemplation as well of equity as of law, without proof of special bargain or representation on the assignment. In such a case it runs, not because the conscience of either party is affected, but because the purchaser has bought something which inhered in or was annexed to the land bought.

Annexation plainly has a powerful effect. However, by the late 1970s two major problems had emerged. The first was that annexation required some provision in the document linking the covenant to the land and identifying it.[22] The second, which was the cause of much litigation, was that annexation was presumed to be to the whole of the land. It followed that a purchaser of part of the land was unable to rely on the annexation.[23] This could be avoided if the annexation were to each and every part of the land.[24]

Extract 20.2.9

Federated Homes Ltd v Mill Lodge Properties Ltd **[1980] 1 WLR 594**

BRIGHTMAN LJ: . . . In my judgment the benefit of this covenant was annexed to the retained land, and I think that this is a consequence of section 78 of the Act of 1925, which reads:

'(1) A covenant relating to any land of the covenantee shall be deemed to be made with the covenantee and his successors in title and the persons deriving title under him or them, and shall have effect as if such successors and other persons were expressed. For the purposes of this subsection in connexion with covenants restrictive of the user of land "successors in title" shall be deemed to include the owners and occupiers for the time being of the land of the covenantee intended to be benefited . . .'

Mr Price submitted that there were three possible views about section 78. One view, which he described as 'the orthodox view' hitherto held, is that it is merely a statutory shorthand for reducing the length of legal documents. A second view, which was the one that Mr Price was inclined to place in the forefront of his argument, is that the section only applies, or at any rate only achieves annexation, when the land intended to be benefited is signified in the document by express words or necessary implication as the intended beneficiary of the covenant. A third

---

[21] [1900] 2 Ch 388.

[22] *Renals v Cowlishaw* (1878) 9 Ch D 125; (1879) 11 Ch D 866; *Reid v Bickerstaff* [1909] 2 Ch 305. Wade argues ([1972B] CLJ 157 at pp 168–169) that *Marten v Flight Refuelling Ltd* [1962] Ch 115 permits annexation to be implied from the surrounding circumstances, but this is rejected by over *J Sainsbury plc v Enfield LBC* [1989] 1 WLR 590; see also Ryder (1972) 36 Conv 20.

[23] An assignment might rescue the purchaser: *Russell v Archdale* [1964] Ch 38.

[24] *Marquess of Zetland v Driver* [1939] Ch 1.

view is that the section applies if the covenant in fact touches and concerns the land of the covenantee, whether that be gleaned from the document itself or from evidence outside the document.

For myself, I reject the narrowest interpretation of section 78, the supposed orthodox view, which seems to me to fly in the face of the wording of the section. Before I express my reasons I will say that I do not find it necessary to choose between the second and third views because, in my opinion, this covenant relates to land of the covenantee on either interpretation of section 78. Clause 5 (iv) shows clearly that the covenant is for the protection of the retained land and that land is described in clause 2 as 'any adjoining or adjacent property retained by the vendor'. This formulation is sufficient for annexation purposes: see *Rogers* v *Hosegood* [1900] 2 Ch 388.

. . .

The first point to notice about section 78(1) is that the wording is significantly different from the wording of its predecessor section 58(1) of the Conveyancing Act 1881. The distinction is underlined by section 78(2), which applies section 78(1) only to covenants made after the commencement of the Act. Section 58(1) of the Act of 1881 did not include the covenantee's successors in title or persons deriving title under him or them, or the owner or occupiers for the time being of the land of the covenantee intended to be benefited. The section was confined, in relation to realty, to the covenantee, his heirs and assigns, words which suggest a more limited scope of operation than is found in section 78.

If, as the language of section 78 implies, a covenant relating to land which is restrictive of the user thereof is enforceable at the suit of (1) a successor in title of the covenantee, (2) a person deriving title under the covenantee or under his successors in title, and (3) the owner or occupier of the land intended to be benefited by the covenant, it must, in my view, follow that the covenant runs with the land, because ex hypothesi every successor in title to the land, every derivative proprietor of the land and every other owner and occupier has a right by statute to the covenant. In other words, if the condition precedent of section 78 is satisfied – that is to say, there exists a covenant which touches and concerns the land of the covenantee – that covenant runs with the land for the benefit of his successors in title, persons deriving title under him or them and other owners and occupiers.

This approach to section 78 has been advocated by distinguished textbook writers; see Dr Radcliffe's article 'Some Problems of the Law Relating to Restrictive Covenants' (1941) 57 LQR 203, Professor Wade's article, 'Covenants – A Broad and Reasonable View' and the apt cross-heading 'What is wrong with section 78?' [1972B] CLJ 151, 171, and *Megarry and Wade, The Law of Real Property*, 4th ed (1975), p 764. Counsel pointed out to us that the fourth edition of *Megarry and Wade* indicates a change of mind on this topic since the third edition.

Although the section does not seem to have been extensively used in the course of argument in this type of case, the construction of section 78 which appeals to me appears to be consistent with at least two cases decided in this court. The first is *Smith and Snipes Hall Farm Ltd* v *River Douglas Catchment Board* [1949] 2 KB 500 . . . The two important points are that the agreement was not expressed to be for the benefit of the landowner's successors in title; and there was no assignment of the benefit of the agreement in favour of the second plaintiff, the tenant. In reliance, as I understand the case, upon section 78 of the Act of 1925, it was held that the second plaintiff was entitled to sue the catchment board for damages for breach of the agreement. It seems to me that that conclusion can only have been reached on the basis that section 78 had the effect of causing the benefit of the agreement to run with the land so as to be capable of being sued upon by the tenant.

The other case, *Williams* v *Unit Construction Co Ltd* (unreported in the usual series of law reports but fully set out in 19 Conveyancer 262), was decided by this court in 1951 . . .

We were referred to observations in the speeches of Lord Upjohn and Lord Wilberforce in *Sefton* v *Tophams Ltd* [1967] 1 AC 50, 73 and 81, to the effect that section 79 of the Act of 1925, relating to the burden of covenants, achieved no more than the introduction of statutory shorthand into the drafting of covenants. Section 79, in my view, involves quite different considerations and I do not think that it provides a helpful analogy.

It was suggested by Mr Price that, if this covenant ought to be read as enuring for the benefit of the retained land, it should be read as enuring only for the benefit of the retained land as a whole and not for the benefit of every part of it; with the apparent result that there is no annexation of the benefit to a part of the retained land when any severance takes place . . .

I find the idea of the annexation of a covenant to the whole of the land but not to a part of it a difficult conception fully to grasp. I can understand that a covenantee may expressly or by necessary implication retain the benefit of a covenant wholly under his own control, so that the benefit will not pass unless the covenantee chooses to assign; but I would have thought, if the benefit of a covenant is, on a proper construction of a document, annexed to the land, prima facie it is annexed to every part thereof, unless the contrary clearly appears. It is difficult to see how this court can have reached its decision in *Williams* v *Unit Construction Co Ltd*, 19 Conveyancer 262, unless this is right. The covenant was, by inference, annexed to every part of the land and not merely to the whole, because it will be recalled that the plaintiff was a tenant of only one of the four houses which had the benefit of the covenant.

. . .

In the end, I come to the conclusion that section 78 of the Law of Property Act 1925 caused the benefit of the restrictive covenant in question to run with the red land and therefore to be annexed to it, with the result that the plaintiff is able to enforce the covenant against Mill Lodge, not only in its capacity as owner of the green land, but also in its capacity as owner of the red land.

Comment

(1) Central to the case is the novel use of s 78, with the rejection of its previous interpretation as a word-saving provision. This has been vigorously criticised by Newsom (1981) 97 LQR 32, both on grounds of authority and because it 'destroys the whole basis' of titles accepted under conveyancers' understanding of the law. How cogent are these criticisms today?

(2) It has subsequently been confirmed that the earlier statutory provisions did not have the effect of statutory annexation.[25]

(3) It is interesting that the cases relied upon by Brightman LJ are principally positive covenant cases. Is this surprising?

(4) The preference for annexation to each and every part is a very important part of the decision. In so far as this departs from the law as previously applied in the courts, is it to be welcomed or criticised? Is there any reason why the covenantee might prefer annexation to the whole?

Extract 20.2.10

Crest Nicholson Residential (South) Ltd v *McAllister* [2004] 1 WLR 2409

CHADWICK LJ: 29. It is clear that the court approached the question of annexation in the *Federated Homes* case [1980] 1 WLR 594 on the basis that the density covenant was taken for the benefit of retained land which could be identified in the 1971 conveyance . . .

---

[25] *J Sainsbury plc* v *Enfield LBC* [1989] 1 WLR 590.

30.   The decision of this court in the *Federated Homes* case leaves open the question whether section 78 of the 1925 Act only effects annexation when the land intended to be benefited is described in the instrument itself (by express words or necessary implication, albeit that it may be necessary to have regard to evidence outside the document fully to identify that land) or whether it is enough that it can be shown, from evidence wholly outside the document, that the covenant does in fact touch and concern land of the covenantee which can be identified.

31.   It is clear from Brightman LJ's reference in the *Federated Homes* case [1980] 1 WLR 594, 604C–G to *Rogers* v *Hosegood* [1900] 2 Ch 388 that it is sufficient for the conveyance to describe the land intended to be benefited in terms which enable it to be identified from other evidence. In *Rogers* v *Hosegood* the covenant was given for the benefit of the vendors, their heirs and assigns 'and others claiming under them to all or any of their lands adjoining or near to the' premises conveyed . . .

32.   The question left open in the *Federated Homes* case [1980] 1 WLR 594 had, I think, already been answered in the judgment of this court in *Marquess of Zetland* v *Driver* [1939] Ch 1, a decision not cited in the *Federated Homes* case. The applicable principles were restated in the following passage, at pp 7–8:

> 'Covenants restricting the user of land imposed by a vendor upon a sale fall into three classes: (i) covenants imposed by the vendor for his own benefit; (ii) covenants imposed by the vendor as owner of other land, of which that sold formed a part, and intended to protect or benefit the unsold land; and (iii) covenants imposed by a vendor upon a sale of land to various purchasers who are intended mutually to enjoy the benefit of and be bound by the covenants: *Osborne* v *Bradley* [1903] 2 Ch 446, 450. Covenants of the first class are personal to the vendor and enforceable by him alone unless expressly assigned by him. Covenants of the second class . . . can only be validly imposed if they comply with certain conditions. Firstly, they must be negative covenants . . . Secondly, the covenant must be one that touches or concerns the land, by which is meant that it must be imposed for the benefit or to enhance the value of the land retained by the vendor or some part of it, and no such covenant can ever be imposed if the sale comprises the whole of the vendor's land . . . Thirdly, *the land which is intended to be benefited must be so defined as to be easily ascertainable*, and the fact that the covenant is imposed for the benefit of that particular land should be stated in the conveyance and the persons or the class of persons entitled to enforce it. The fact that the benefit of the covenant is not intended to pass to all persons into whose hands the unsold land may come is not objectionable so long as the class of persons intended to have the benefit of the covenant is clearly defined.' (Emphasis added.)

33.   In its later decision in the *Federated Homes* case [1980] 1 WLR 594 this court held that the provisions of section 78 of the 1925 Act had made it unnecessary to state, in the conveyance, that the covenant was to be enforceable by persons deriving title under the covenantee or under his successors in title and the owner or occupier of the land intended to be benefited, or that the covenant was to run with the land intended to be benefited; but there is nothing in that case which suggests that it is no longer necessary that the land which is intended to be benefited should be so defined that it is easily ascertainable. In my view, that requirement, identified in *Marquess of Zetland* v *Driver* [1939] Ch 1 remains a necessary condition for annexation.

34.   . . . It is obviously desirable that a purchaser of land burdened with a restrictive covenant should be able not only to ascertain, by inspection of the entries on the relevant register, that the land is so burdened, but also to ascertain the land for which the benefit of the covenant was taken – so that he can identify who can enforce the covenant. That latter object is achieved if the land which is intended to be benefited is defined in the instrument so as to be easily ascertainable. To require a purchaser of land burdened with a restrictive covenant, but where the land for the benefit of which the covenant was taken is not described in the instrument, to make inquiries as to what (if any) land the original covenantee retained at the time of the

conveyance and what (if any) of that retained land the covenant did, or might have 'touched and concerned' would be oppressive. It must be kept in mind that (as in the present case) the time at which the enforceability of the covenant becomes an issue may be long after the date of the instrument by which it was imposed.

37. To my mind, the decision in *Marquess of Zetland* v *Driver* [1939] Ch 1 goes much of the way to answer a second question which this court did not need to address in the *Federated Homes* case [1980] 1 WLR 594: whether the effect of the section 78 of the Law of Property Act 1925 is displaced by a contrary intention manifested in the instrument itself. But that question was addressed, specifically, in *Roake* v *Chadha* [1984] 1 WLR 40, to which I now turn.

39. It was accepted on behalf the plaintiffs [in *Roake*] that the express words of the covenant appeared to exclude annexation. It was accepted, also, that their case could not be advanced on the basis of a building scheme. But it was said that, nevertheless, the covenant imposed by the transfer of 4 April 1934 had become annexed to the land then forming part of the Sudbury Court Estate and subsequently conveyed out of that estate by the transfers of 28 May 1934 and 22 March 1935 by the operation of section 78 of the 1925 Act. Reliance was placed on the contrast between the language of section 78 and section 79 (burden of covenants relating to land) of that Act. Section 79(1) is in these terms:

'A covenant relating to any land of a covenantor or capable of being bound by him, shall, *unless a contrary intention is expressed*, be deemed to be made by the covenantor on behalf of himself his successors in title and the persons deriving title under him or them, and, *subject as aforesaid*, shall have effect as if such successors and other persons were expressed.' (Emphasis added.)

It was pointed out, correctly, that the words which I have emphasised are not found in section 78(1) of the Act. So, it was said, the legislature must have intended the provisions of section 78 (benefit of covenants relating to land) to be mandatory; it must have intended that those provisions could not be excluded by a contrary intention, however clearly expressed.

40. Judge Paul Baker QC, sitting as a judge of the High Court, rejected that submission. After analysing the judgment of Brightman LJ in *Federated Homes Ltd* v *Mill Lodge Properties Ltd* [1980] 1 WLR 594, and pointing out that no reason of policy had been suggested to explain why section 78 of the 1925 Act should be mandatory, the judge said [1984] 1 WLR 40, 46:

'I am thus far from satisfied that section 78 has the mandatory operation which [counsel] claimed for it. But if one accepts that it is not subject to a contrary intention, I do not consider that it has the effect of annexing the benefit of the covenant in each and every case irrespective of the other express terms of the covenant. I note that Brightman LJ in the *Federated Homes* case did not go so far as that, for he said, at p 606: "I find the idea of the annexation of a covenant to the whole of the land but not to a part of it a difficult conception fully to grasp. I can understand that a covenantee may expressly or by necessary implication retain the benefit of a covenant wholly under his own control, so that the benefit will not pass unless the covenantee chooses to assign; but I would have thought, if the benefit of a covenant is, on a proper construction of a document, annexed to the land, prima facie it is annexed to every part thereof, unless the contrary clearly appears." So at least in some circumstances Brightman LJ is considering that despite section 78 the benefit may be retained and not pass or be annexed to and run with land. In this connection, I was also referred by [counsel for the defendants] to *Elphinstone's Covenants Affecting Land* (1946), p 17, where it is said in a footnote: "but it is thought that, as a covenant must be construed as a whole, the court would give due effect to words excluding or modifying the operation of this section . . ." The true position as I see it is that even where a covenant is deemed to be made with successors in title as section 78 requires, one still has to construe the covenant as a whole to see whether the benefit of the covenant is annexed. Where one finds, as in the

Federated Homes case, the covenant is not qualified in any way, annexation may be readily inferred; but where, as in the present case, it is expressly provided: "this covenant shall not enure for the benefit of any owner or subsequent purchaser of any part of the vendor's Sudbury Court Estate at Wembley unless the benefit of this covenant shall be expressly assigned . . ." one cannot just ignore these words. One may not be able to exclude the operation of the section in widening the range of the covenantees, but one has to consider the covenant as a whole to determine its true effect. When one does that, then it seems to me that the answer is plain and in my judgment the benefit was not annexed. That is giving full weight to both the statute in force and also what is already there in the covenant.'

41.   I respectfully agree, first, that it is impossible to identify any reason of policy why a covenantor should not, by express words, be entitled to limit the scope of the obligation which he is undertaking; nor why a covenantee should not be able to accept a covenant for his own benefit on terms that the benefit does not pass automatically to all those to whom he sells on parts of his retained land. As Brightman LJ pointed out, in the passage cited by Judge Paul Baker QC, a developer who is selling off land in lots might well want to retain the benefit of a building restriction under his own control. Where, as in *Roake v Chadha* [1984] 1 WLR 40 and the present case, development land is sold off in plots without imposing a building scheme, it seems to me very likely that the developer will wish to retain exclusive power to give or withhold consent to a modification or relaxation of a restriction on building which he imposes on each purchaser; unfettered by the need to obtain the consent of every subsequent purchaser to whom (after imposing the covenant) he has sold off other plots on the development land. I can see no reason why, if original covenantor and covenantee make clear their mutual intention in that respect, the legislature should wish to prevent effect being given to that intention.

42.   Second, it is important to keep in mind that, for the purposes of its application to restrictive covenants – which is the context in which this question arises where neither of the parties to the dispute were, themselves, party to the instrument imposing the covenant or express assignees of the benefit of the covenant – section 78 of the 1925 Act defines 'successors in title' as the owners and occupiers for the time being *of the land of the covenantee intended to be benefited*. In a case where the parties to the instrument make clear their intention that land retained by the covenantee at the time of the conveyance effected by the transfer is to have the benefit of the covenant only for so long as it continues to be in the ownership of the original covenantee, and not after it has been sold on by the original covenantee – unless the benefit of the covenant is expressly assigned to the new owner – *the land of the covenantee intended to be benefited* is identified by the instrument as (i) so much of the retained land as from time to time has not been sold off by the original covenantee and (ii) so much of the retained land as has been sold off with the benefit of an express assignment, but as not including (iii) so much of the land as has been sold off without the benefit of an express assignment. I agree with the judge in *Roake v Chadha* [1984] 1 WLR 40 that, in such a case, it is possible to give full effect to the statute and to the terms of the covenant.

43.   This approach to section 78 of the 1925 Act provides, as it seems to me, the answer to the question why, if the legislature did not intend to distinguish between the effect of section 78 (mandatory) and the effect of section 79 (subject to contrary intention), it did not include the words 'unless a contrary intention is expressed' in the first of those sections. The answer is that it did not need to. The qualification 'subject to contrary intention' is implicit in the definition of 'successors in title' which appears in section 78(1); that is the effect of the words 'the land of the covenantee intended to be benefited'. If the terms in which the covenant is imposed show – as they did in *Marquess of Zetland v Driver* [1939] Ch 1 and in *Roake v Chadha* [1984] 1 WLR 40 – that the land of the covenantee intended to be benefited does not include land which may subsequently be sold off by the original covenantee in circumstances where (at the time of that subsequent sale) there is no express assignment of the benefit of the covenant, then the owners

and occupiers of the land sold off in those circumstances are not 'owners and occupiers for the time being of the land of the covenantee intended to be benefited'; and so are not 'successors in title' of the original covenantee for the purposes of section 78(1) in its application to covenants restrictive of the user of land.

44.   By contrast, the definition of 'successors in title' for the purposes of section 79(1) appears in subsection (2) of that section: 'the owners and occupiers for the time being of *such* land'. In that context 'such land' means 'any land of a covenantor or capable of being bound by him [to which the covenant relates].' The counterpart in section 79 of 'land of the covenantee intended to be benefited' (in section 78(1)) is 'such land'. 'Such land' in that context means the land referred to in section 79(1); that is to say 'any land of a covenantor or capable of being bound by him'. But section 79(1) imposes two qualifications; (i) the land must be land to which the covenant relates and (ii) there must be no expression of contrary intention. The section could, perhaps, have described the land as 'land of the covenantor (or capable of being bound by him) intended to be burdened'. But the effect would have been the same. If the parties did not intend that land, burdened while in the ownership of the covenantor, should continue to be subject to the burden in hands of his successors (or some of his successors), they could say so. On a true analysis there is no difference in treatment in the two sections. There is a difference in the drafting technique used to achieve the same substantive result . . .

Comment

(1) Does *Marquess of Zetland* provide such an easy answer as Chadwick LJ thought to the question left open in *Federated Homes*?

(2) Just how significant is statutory annexation after *Crest Nicholson*?

(3) Does the reasoning in *Crest Nicholson* support the argument that the rules for the passing of the benefit of positive covenants may be more relaxed than those for restrictive covenants?

(4) Is a convincing explanation given by Chadwick LJ as to why contrary intention suffices to exclude statutory annexation, given that s 78 (unlike s 79) makes no reference to contrary intention? Why might the parties want to prevent annexation?

(5) It has been seen[26] that *Rhone v Stephens* denied that s 79 (passing of the burden) had a similar effect to s 78 (passing the benefit). Is this distinction between the two sections justified? Is the question affected by *Crest Nicholson*?

Etherton J has recently stated:[27]

> In my judgment, it is not necessary as a matter of law that, in addition to showing that the coven-ants relate to and 'touch and concern' the retained land, and that the retained land can be easily be ascertained from the conveyance and admissible extrinsic evidence, the defendants must also show an intention that the retained land should benefit from the covenants . . .

Is this a natural consequence of the *Federated Homes* approach to s 78 (as Etherton J thought) or an unfortunate qualification on *Crest Nicholson*?

(ii) Assignment

After *Federated Homes*, even as limited by *Crest Nicholson*, it will be relatively unusual to have to rely on assignment. Accordingly, this area can be considered briefly. Most

---

[26] Extract 20.2.2 above.
[27] *Mohammadzadeh v Joseph* [2008] 1 P&CR 107.

non-personal contractual rights can, of course, be assigned. In the restrictive covenant context, the question is how far the proprietary context limits the normal contractual principles.

Extract 20.2.11

Re Union of London & Smith's Bank Ltd's Conveyance, Miles v Easter [1933] Ch 611

ROMER LJ: . . . It is plain, however, from these and other cases, and notably that of *Renals* v *Cowlishaw*,[i] that if the restrictive covenant be taken not merely for some personal purpose or object of the vendor, but for the benefit of some other land of his in the sense that it would enable him to dispose of that land to greater advantage, the covenant, though not annexed to such land so as to run with any part of it, may be enforced against an assignee of the covenantor taking with notice, both by the covenantee and by persons to whom the benefit of such covenant has been assigned, subject however to certain conditions. In the first place, the 'other land' must be land that is capable of being benefited by the covenant – otherwise it would be impossible to infer that the object of the covenant was to enable the vendor to dispose of his land to greater advantage. In the next place, this land must be 'ascertainable' or 'certain', to use the words of Romer and Scrutton LJJ respectively . . . In the third place, the covenant cannot be enforced by the covenantee against an assign of the purchaser after the covenantee has parted with the whole of his land.

This last point was decided, and in our opinion rightly decided, by Sargant J in *Chambers* v *Randall*.[ii] As pointed out by that learned judge, the covenant having been entered into to enable the covenantee to dispose of his property to advantage, that result will in fact have been obtained when all that property has been disposed of. There is therefore no longer any reason why the Court should extend to him the benefit of the equitable doctrine of *Tulk* v *Moxhay*.[iii] That is only done when it is sought to enforce the covenant in connection with the enjoyment of land that the covenant was intended to protect. But it was also held by Sargant J in the same case, and in our opinion rightly held, that although on a sale of the whole or part of the property intended to be protected by the covenant the right to enforce the covenant may be expressly assigned to the purchaser, such an assignment will be ineffective if made at a later date when the covenantee has parted with the whole of his land . . . To hold [otherwise] would be to treat the covenant as having been obtained, not only for the purpose of enabling the covenantee to dispose of his land to the best advantage, but also for the purpose of enabling him to dispose of the benefit of the covenant to the best advantage.

[i] 9 Ch D 125.
[ii] [1923] 1 Ch 149.
[iii] 2 Ph 774.

Comment

Is there sufficient reason for denying assignment after the covenantee has sold all the benefited land?

A number of further points regarding assignment should be noted:

(1) Unlike express annexation, the benefited land can be identified from the surrounding circumstances and need not be identified by the covenant itself.[28]

---

[28] *Newton Abbot Co-operative Society Ltd* v *Williamson & Treadgold Ltd* [1952] Ch 286.

(2) It seems probable that the assignment has to be repeated on each sale of the land: there is no doctrine of 'delayed annexation' on an initial assignment.[29]

Can LPA, s 62 be used to imply an assignment?

Extract 20.2.12

Roake v Chadha **[1984] 1 WLR 40 (Ch D)**

JUDGE PAUL BAKER QC: . . . I must now turn to the alternative argument of the plaintiffs based on section 62 of the Law of Property Act 1925. This argument is directed to the conveyances or transfers conveying the alleged benefited land to the predecessors of the plaintiffs, and ultimately to the respective plaintiffs themselves. In each of these transfers, so I am prepared to assume, there is to be implied the general words of section 62 of the Act of 1925:

> '(1) A conveyance of land shall be deemed to include and shall by virtue of this Act operate to convey, with the land, all buildings, erections, fixtures, commons, hedges, ditches, fences, ways, waters, watercourses, liberties, privileges, easements, rights, and advantages whatsoever, appertaining or reputed to appertain to the land . . .'

. . .

The argument is that the benefit of the covenant contained in the original transfer to the predecessor of the defendants, William Lambert, was carried by the words 'rights and advantages whatsoever appertaining or reputed to appertain to the land, or any part thereof'. It seems an argument on these lines was accepted by Mr John Mills QC, the deputy judge who gave the decision at first instance in the *Federated Homes* case [1980] 1 WLR 594, but I have not seen it, and so cannot comment on it. The proposition now contended for is not a new one. In *Rogers v Hosegood* [1900] 2 Ch 388, it was similarly put forward as an alternative argument to an argument based on annexation . . . Farwell J sitting in the Chancery Division, said, at p 398:

> 'It is not necessary for me to determine whether the benefit of the covenants would pass under the general words to which I have referred above, if such covenants did not run with the land. If they are not in fact annexed to the land, it may well be that the right to sue thereon cannot be said to belong, or be reputed to belong, thereto; but I express no final opinion on this point.'

In the Court of Appeal the point was canvassed in argument but not referred to in the judgment of the court, which was given by Collins LJ.

In the present case, the covenant in terms precludes the benefit passing unless it is expressly assigned. That being so, as it seems to me, it is not a right 'appertaining or reputed to appertain' to land within the meaning of section 62 of the Law of Property Act 1925. As to whether the benefit of a covenant not annexed can ever pass under section 62, I share the doubts of Farwell J. Mr Henty suggested – and there may well be something in this – that the rights referred to in section 62 are confined to legal rights rather than equitable rights which the benefit of restrictive covenants is. But again I place it on construction. It cannot be described as a right appertaining or reputed to appertain to land when the terms of the covenant itself would seem to indicate, or indicates, to be the opposite.

---

[29] *Re Pinewood Estate, Farnborough* [1958] Ch 280; apparently supported by *Emile Elias & Co Ltd v Pine Groves Ltd* [1993] 1 WLR 305 at p 309 (PC). Note the criticism of Hayton (1971) 87 LQR 539 at pp 565–567; *Cygnet Healthcare Ltd* v *Greenswan Consultants Ltd* [2009] EWHC 1318 (Ch) at [14] may support delayed annexation.

Comment

(1) Could s 62 ever apply to restrictive covenants?

(2) The *Roake* analysis is supported by *Kumar v Dunning*.[30]

(iii) Schemes of development

It is common for there to be a scheme of development of an area of land such that identical covenants are imposed on all purchasers. If the circumstances fit within the requirements for such schemes then the land is bound by a 'local law'. The most obvious consequence is that the benefit passes without any need for annexation or assignment, though this is less significant after *Federated Homes*. Other consequences will be considered in due course, but first we must consider the requirements for a scheme to be recognised.

Extract 20.2.13

Elliston v Reacher [1908] 2 Ch 374

PARKER LJ: [It] must be proved (1) that both the plaintiffs and defendants derive title under a common vendor; (2) that previously to selling the lands to which the plaintiffs and defendants are respectively entitled the vendor laid out his estate, or a defined portion thereof (including the lands purchased by the plaintiffs and defendants respectively), for sale in lots subject to restrictions intended to be imposed on all the lots, and which, though varying in details as to particular lots, are consistent and consistent only with some general scheme of development; (3) that these restrictions were intended by the common vendor to be and were for the benefit of all the lots intended to be sold, whether or not they were also intended to be and were for the benefit of other land retained by the vendor; and (4) that both the plaintiffs and the defendants, or their predecessors in title, purchased their lots from the common vendor upon the footing that the restrictions subject to which the purchases were made were to enure for the benefit of the other lots included in the general scheme whether or not they were also to enure for the benefit of other lands retained by the vendors . . . I may observe, with reference to the third point, that the vendor's object in imposing the restrictions must in general be gathered from all the circumstances of the case, including in particular the nature of the restrictions. If a general observance of the restrictions is in fact calculated to enhance the values of the several lots offered for sale, it is an easy inference that the vendor intended the restrictions to be for the benefit of all the lots, even though he might retain other land the value of which might be similarly enhanced, for a vendor may naturally be expected to aim at obtaining the highest possible price for his land. Further, if the first three points be established, the fourth point may readily be inferred, provided the purchasers have notice of the facts involved in the three first points; but if the purchaser purchases in ignorance of any material part of those facts, it would be difficult, if not impossible, to establish the fourth point.

Extract 20.2.14

Baxter v Four Oaks Properties Ltd [1965] Ch 816

CROSS J: . . . The defendants naturally rely on Parker J's second requirement and argue that as Lord Clanrikarde did not lay out the part of his estate which faced Lichfield Road in lots before he began to sell it off, there could be no enforceable building scheme here, even though Lord Clanrikarde and the purchasers from him may have thought that there was.

---

[30] [1989] QB 193, Sir Nicolas Browne-Wilkinson V-C at p 198.

It is, however, to be observed that *Elliston* v *Reacher*[i] was not a case in which there was direct evidence afforded by the execution of the deed of mutual covenant that the parties in fact intended a building scheme. The question was whether one could properly infer that intention in all the circumstances. In such a case, no doubt the fact that the common vendor did not divide his estate into lots before beginning to sell it is an argument against there having been intention on his part and on the part of the various purchasers that there should be a building scheme, because it is, perhaps, prima facie unlikely that a purchaser of a plot intends to enter into obligations to an unknown number of subsequent purchasers. But I cannot believe that Parker J was intending to lay down that the fact that the common vendor did not bind himself to sell off the defined area to which the common law was to apply in lots of any particular size but proposed to sell off parcels of various sizes according to the requirement of the various purchasers must, as a matter of law, preclude the court from giving effect to a clearly proved intention that the purchasers were to have rights inter se to enforce the provisions of the common law.

[i] [1908] 2 Ch 374.

Comment

This approach was adopted by *Re Dolphin's Conveyance*,[31] in which there was no common vendor because the original vendor had died during the sales. Stamp J stressed that the basis of the approach lies in the common intention and common interest of the parties. This relaxation of the *Elliston* v *Reacher* test has enabled schemes to be more readily found.

Despite these recent cases, it would be a mistake to assume that it is easy to prove a scheme of development. In *Re Dolphin's Conveyance* itself, Stamp J observed that it is 'trite law' that it is not enough that conveyances of plots contain the same covenants: some element of mutuality must be shown. The decision of the Privy Council in *Emile Elias & Co Ltd* v *Pine Groves Ltd*[32] demonstrates that the *Elliston* v *Reacher* tests will still be applied where the reciprocity (the common intention and common interest) does not overtly appear from the covenant. In particular, it was stressed that it will be difficult to find a scheme if the covenants imposed are not identical.

Turning now to the effect of schemes, one very important element is that land retained by the developer within the scheme will be bound by the covenants. This has been well explained by Megarry J:[33]

Perhaps I may go back to first principles and try to summarise the matter in my own way. The most straightforward case is where A owns the entire estate and, having laid it out, himself sells individual lots to individual purchasers who enter into the covenants of the scheme. As soon as he sells a lot to the first purchaser, B, the scheme crystallises. Not only is B bound in respect of his lot to A, for the benefit of the remainder of the estate, but also A is bound, in respect of the remainder of the estate, to B, for the benefit of B's plot. It may be noted that while B is bound by the express covenants that he entered into, A may well have entered into no express covenants with B; and yet the concept of a scheme of development requires that A shall be treated as having impliedly bound himself by the provisions of the scheme. If A then sells another plot to C, C is taking part of the land that has already been subjected to the scheme in favour of B, and the covenants that he enters into are treated as being made for the benefit not only of A's remaining land but also of B's plot.

[31] [1970] Ch 654, especially at p 663.
[32] [1993] 1 WLR 305.
[33] *Brunner* v *Greenslade* [1971] Ch 993 at p 1003.

As well as easing the enforcement of covenants as between purchasers, this stops the seller from having a change of plan and using unsold plots in a manner inconsistent with the covenants.[34]

A very different point concerns the termination of restrictive covenants, specifically when two plots within the scheme become owned by the same person. On the analogy of easements, one would expect the covenant to terminate as between these plots.

Extract 20.2.15

Texaco Antilles Ltd v *Kernochan* [1973] AC 609 (PC)

PRIVY COUNCIL: . . . It is no doubt true that if the restrictions in question exist simply for the mutual benefit of two adjoining properties and both those properties are bought by one man the restrictions will automatically come to an end and will not revive on a subsequent severance unless the common owner then recreates them. But their Lordships cannot see that it follows from this that if a number of people agree that the area covered by all their properties shall be subject to a 'local law' the provisions of which shall be enforceable by any owner for the time being of any part against any other owner and the whole area has never at any time come into common ownership an action by one owner of a part against another owner of a part must fail if it can be shown that both parts were either at the inception of the scheme or at any time subsequently in common ownership. The view which their Lordships favour is supported by dicta of Sir H H Cozens-Hardy MR in *Elliston* v *Reacher* [1908] 2 Ch 665, 673 and of Simonds J in *Lawrence* v *South County Freeholds Ltd* [1939] Ch 656, 677–683, but at the time when this case was heard by the Court of Appeal there was no decision on the point. Subsequently, however, in *Brunner* v *Greenslade* [1971] Ch 993 which raised the point, Megarry J followed those dicta. The appellants submitted that his decision was wrong but in their Lordships' view it was right.

Comment

In any event, other property owners within the scheme could still enforce the covenants. A different ruling would have resulted in rather strange 'pockets of unenforceability' within the scheme.

(iv) Conclusions

Even after *Federated Homes*, the passing of the benefit appears unduly complex. In particular, one may query whether annexation and assignment play any useful role today. As has been argued,[35] much of the problem may lie in the confusion of proprietary and contractual ideas underpinning annexation and assignment.

Federated Homes means that annexation will operate in many cases, subject to a contrary intention. Following *Crest Nicholson*, however, the rules place emphasis upon identifying the benefited land. That this fulfils some useful purpose is indicated by the fact that identification would be essential for registered land under the Law Commission proposals.[36] Why, if at all, does the covenantor (or a successor in title) need to know what land is benefited? Are the needs of the covenantors and successors in title satisfied by the identification rules in *Rogers* v *Hosegood* (see *Crest Nicholson*, Extract 20.2.10 at [31])? Is there any justification for applying a stricter rule than is found in easements?

---

[34] As attempted in *Hudson* v *Cripps* [1896] 1 Ch 265.
[35] See especially Hayton (1971) 87 LQR 539.
[36] Law Com No 327, para 5.60, Extract 20.4.2 below.

Turning to assignment, two specific elements should be noted. First, there is no need for the covenant to identify the benefited land and, secondly, the covenantor (or a successor in title) will usually be unaware that an assignment has taken place. To what extent do these elements cause problems for those who wish to develop their land in possible breach of a restrictive covenant? How far is it adequate to insist that we are concerned with nothing more than the assignment of the benefit of a contract, so that limiting the right to assign cannot be justified?

Lastly, it should be considered whether the Contracts (Rights of Third Parties) Act 1999, Extract 20.1.5 above, may provide an alternative route for the running of the benefit of covenants. If so, would this add anything to the current annexation rules?

E. Modification

Extract 20.2.16

Law of Property Act 1925, s 84

84.—(1)   The Upper Tribunal shall (without prejudice to any concurrent jurisdiction of the court) have power from time to time, on the application of any person interested in any freehold land affected by any restriction arising under covenant or otherwise as to the user thereof or the building thereon, by order wholly or partially to discharge or modify any such restriction on being satisfied—

> (a) that by reason of changes in the character of the property or the neighbourhood or other circumstances of the case which the Upper Tribunal may deem material, the restriction ought to be deemed obsolete; or
>
> (aa) that in a case falling within subsection (1A) below the continued existence thereof would impede some reasonable user of the land for public or private purposes or, as the case may be, would unless modified so impede such user; or
>
> (b) that the persons of full age and capacity for the time being or from time to time entitled to the benefit of the restriction, whether in respect of estates in fee simple or any lesser estates or interests in the property to which the benefit of the restriction is annexed, have agreed, either expressly or by implication, by their acts or omissions, to the same being discharged or modified; or
>
> (c) that the proposed discharge or modification will not injure the persons entitled to the benefit of the restriction:

. . .

(1A)   Subsection (1)(aa) above authorises the discharge or modification of a restriction by reference to its impeding some reasonable user of land in any case in which the Upper Tribunal is satisfied that the restriction, in impeding that user, either—

> (a) does not secure to persons entitled to the benefit of it any practical benefits of substantial value or advantage to them; or
>
> (b) is contrary to the public interest;

and that money will be an adequate compensation for loss or disadvantage (if any) which any such person will suffer from the discharge or modification.

Comment

Compensation may be ordered in favour of the holder of the restrictive covenant.

One issue in considering the role of s 84 is the impact of the planning permission system. At one time, it was thought that this might render restrictive covenants redundant. By the 1960s, this had been disproved.

Extract 20.2.17

Law Commission No 11: Restrictive Covenants

18. . . . From the individual's point of view control by private covenant has obvious advantages over planning control, in that it can cover matters of important detail with which a planning authority would not be concerned and the procedure of enforcement is available to a person who is entitled to the benefit of the covenant and is aggrieved by a breach, instead of depending upon the planning authority's decision to act.

19. We conclude that, notwithstanding the broad control now exercised by planning authorities in matters such as density of building and use of land, privately imposed restrictions will continue to have a useful part to play, complementary to that of planning controls . . .

Comment

Re Martin's Application[37] shows that the grant of planning permission does not mean that the covenant should necessarily be modified so as allow the development.

Extract 20.2.18

Law Commission No 327: Making Land Work: Easements, Covenants and Profits à Prendre (footnotes omitted)

7.30 We pointed out in the Consultation Paper that there have been calls for some years now for the extension of the Lands Chamber's jurisdiction so as to enable it to make orders for the discharge and modification of easements. This was a recommendation of the Law Reform Committee, in its Fourteenth Report, as well as a proposal made in the 1971 Law Commission Working Paper on Appurtenant Rights. The lack of such an extended jurisdiction has been the subject of adverse comment by the courts. We noted that a number of other countries have introduced such a jurisdiction, whether for their courts or for a tribunal.

7.32 Consultees supported that change, and we recommend it below. However, our recommendation extends only to easements and profits created after implementation of reform; to extend the jurisdiction to interests already in existence would risk contravening Article 1 of the First Protocol to the European Convention on Human Rights and Fundamental Freedoms . . .

7.34 Positive land obligations are, as we have commented, potentially more onerous than restrictive ones, and we have taken it as essential that if positive obligations are to be able to bind land, it must be possible to apply for them to be discharged or modified. Consultees agreed, and we so recommend.

7.60 We recommend that the Lands Chamber of the Upper Tribunal should only modify an easement or profit if it is satisfied that the modified interest will not be materially less convenient to the benefited owner and will be no more burdensome to the land affected.

7.69 We recommend that the Lands Chamber of the Upper Tribunal should have the power to modify or discharge a positive land obligation if, as a result of changes in circumstances, performance of the obligation has ceased to be reasonably practicable or has become unreasonably expensive when compared with the benefit that it confers.

Comment

(1) We will see later that a new category of land obligations is proposed for both restrictive and positive obligations (Extracts 20.4.1 and 20.4.2).

---

[37] (1988) 57 P&CR 119.

(2) The Law Commission is not pursuing an original proposal to redraft the grounds for an application regarding restrictive covenants.

(3) Why are special rules required for easements and positive obligations?

The following extract provides a more targeted example of a power to modify.

Extract 20.2.19

Housing Act 1985, s 610

610.—(1)   The local housing authority or a person interested in any premises may apply to the county court where—

    (a) owing to changes in the character of the neighbourhood in which the premises are situated, they cannot readily be let as a single dwelling-house but could readily be let for occupation if converted into two or more dwelling-houses, or

    (b) planning permission has been granted . . . for the use of the premises as converted into two or more separate dwelling-houses instead of as a single dwelling-house,

and the conversion is prohibited or restricted by the provisions of the lease of the premises, or by a restrictive covenant affecting the premises, or otherwise.

(2)   The court may, after giving any person interested an opportunity of being heard, vary the terms of the lease or other instrument imposing the prohibition or restriction, subject to such conditions and upon such terms as the court may think just.

3. Enforcement of covenants

Positive covenants do not normally give rise to difficulty: damages will usually be a straightforward and adequate remedy. Restrictive covenants are more problematic. Invariably, the claimant wishes to prevent the conduct in breach of the covenant. An injunction is fairly readily granted so far as prospective breaches are concerned. However, in many cases the defendant will have commenced building in breach of the covenant and an injunctive remedy would either force demolition of the building or preclude its use.

The principles applicable to remedies arise not only in the covenant context, but also where there is a trespass or interference with an easement. This doesn't mean that they will necessarily be applied in an identical manner in the various contexts.

Extract 20.3.1

Lawrence v *Fen Tigers Ltd* [2014] UKSC 13; [2014] 2 WLR 433

Questions arose concerning remedies for noise amounting to a nuisance.

LORD NEUBERGER: 101.   Where a claimant has established that the defendant's activities constitute a nuisance, *prima facie* the remedy to which she is entitled (in addition to damages for past nuisance) is an injunction to restrain the defendant from committing such nuisance in the future; of course, the precise form of any injunction will depend very much on the facts of the particular case. However, ever since Lord Cairns' Act (the Chancery Amendment Act 1858 (21 & 22 Vict c 27)), the court has had power to award damages instead of an injunction in any case, including a case of nuisance – see now section 50 of the Senior Courts Act 1981. . . .

102.   The question which arises is what, if any, principles govern the exercise of the court's jurisdiction to award damages instead of an injunction. The case which is probably most frequently cited on the question is *Shelfer* v *City of London Electric Lighting Co* [1895] 1 Ch 287 . . .

104.   A L Smith LJ said at 322–323, in a frequently cited passage:

> '[A] person by committing a wrongful act (whether it be a public company for public purposes or a private individual) is not thereby entitled to ask the court to sanction his doing so by purchasing his neighbour's rights, by assessing damages in that behalf, leaving his neighbour with the nuisance, or his lights dimmed, as the case may be. In such cases the well known rule is not to accede to the application, but to grant the injunction sought, for the plaintiff's legal right has been invaded, and he is prima facie entitled to an injunction.
> There are, however, cases in which this rule may be relaxed, and in which damages may be awarded in substitution . . . In my opinion, it may be stated as a good working rule that – (1) If the injury to the plaintiff's legal rights is small, (2) And is one which is capable of being estimated in money, (3) And is one which can be adequately compensated by a small money payment, (4) And the case is one in which it would be oppressive to the defendant to grant an injunction – then damages in substitution for an injunction may be given.'

110.   In more recent times, the Court of Appeal seems to have assumed that the approach of Lindley and A L Smith LJJ in *Shelfer* represents the law, and indeed that the four tests suggested by A L Smith LJ are normally to be applied, so that, unless all four tests are satisfied, there was no jurisdiction to refuse an injunction. . . .

119.   . . . It seems to me that (i) an almost mechanical application of A L Smith LJ's four tests, and (ii) an approach which involves damages being awarded only in 'very exceptional circumstances', are each simply wrong in principle, and give rise to a serious risk of going wrong in practice . . .

120.   The court's power to award damages in lieu of an injunction involves a classic exercise of discretion, which should not, as a matter of principle, be fettered, particularly in the very constrained way in which the Court of Appeal has suggested . . . And, as a matter of practical fairness, each case is likely to be so fact-sensitive that any firm guidance is likely to do more harm than good. . . .

121.   . . . it is only right to acknowledge that this does not prevent the courts from laying down rules as to what factors can, and cannot, be taken into account by a judge when deciding whether to exercise his discretion to award damages in lieu. Indeed, it is appropriate to give as much guidance as possible so as to ensure that, while the discretion is not fettered, its manner of exercise is as predictable as possible. I would accept that the *prima facie* position is that an injunction should be granted, so the legal burden is on the defendant to show why it should not. . . .

123.   Where does that leave A L Smith LJ's four tests? While the application of any such series of tests cannot be mechanical, I would adopt a modified version of the view expressed by Romer LJ in *Fishenden* 153 LT 128, 141. First, the application of the four tests must not be such as 'to be a fetter on the exercise of the court's discretion'. Secondly, it would, in the absence of additional relevant circumstances pointing the other way, normally be right to refuse an injunction if those four tests were satisfied. Thirdly, the fact that those tests are not all satisfied does not mean that an injunction should be granted.

124.   As for the second problem, that of public interest, I find it hard to see how there could be any circumstances in which it arose and could not, as a matter of law, be a relevant factor. . . . The fact that a defendant's business may have to shut down if an injunction is granted should, it seems to me, obviously be a relevant fact, and it is hard to see why relevance should not extend to the fact that a number of the defendant's employees would lose their livelihood, although in many cases that may well not be sufficient to justify the refusal of an injunction. Equally, I do not see why the court should not be entitled to have regard to the fact that many other neighbours in addition to the claimant are badly affected by the nuisance as a factor in favour of granting an injunction.

Comment

(1) Lords Sumption, Mance, Clarke and Carnwath agreed that *Shelfer* applied tests that were too inclined to lead to injunctive relief, though there were disagreements as to how the law should develop.

(2) How is this likely to impact on breaches of restrictive covenants?

When damages are awarded under Lord Cairns' Act, how are they to be assessed? The reduction in the value of the claimant's land may be small, but the claimant usually seeks a proportion of the defendant's profit, based upon what the claimant might have received as consideration for giving permission for the development.

Extract 20.3.2

Jaggard v *Sawyer* [1995] 1 WLR 269

It was established that the defendant had no right of access over the plaintiff's land to a newly built house. The situation was treated as analogous to the house's having been built in breach of a restrictive covenant.

MILLETT LJ: . . . Having decided to refuse an injunction and to award the plaintiff damages instead, the judge had to consider the measure of damages. He based them on her share of the amount which, in his opinion, the plaintiff and the other residents of Ashleigh Avenue could reasonably have demanded as the price of waiving their rights. In this he applied the measure of damages which had been adopted by Brightman J in *Wrotham Park Estate Co Ltd* v *Parkside Homes Ltd* [1974] 1 WLR 798, a case which has frequently been followed. It would not be necessary to consider this matter further but for the fact that in the recent case in this court of *Surrey County Council* v *Bredero Homes Ltd* [1993] 1 WLR 1361 doubts were expressed as to the basis on which this measure of damages could be justified and whether it was consistent with the reasoning of Lord Wilberforce in *Johnson* v *Agnew* [1980] AC 367. It is, therefore, necessary to examine those cases further.

. . .

[After examining those cases:] Accordingly I am of opinion that the judge was not precluded by the decision of the House of Lords in *Johnson* v *Agnew* from adopting the measure of damages which he did. It is, however, necessary to notice the observations of Steyn LJ in *Surrey County Council* v *Bredero Homes Ltd* [1993] 1 WLR 1361, 1369:

> 'In my view *Wrotham Park Estate Co Ltd* v *Parkside Homes Ltd* [1974] 1 WLR 798 is only defensible on the basis of the third or restitutionary principle . . . The plaintiffs' argument that the *Wrotham Park* case can be justified on the basis of a loss of bargaining opportunity is a fiction.'

I find these remarks puzzling. It is plain from his judgment in the *Wrotham Park* case that Brightman J's approach was compensatory, not restitutionary. He sought to measure the damages by reference to what the plaintiff had lost, not by reference to what the defendant had gained. He did not award the plaintiff the profit which the defendant had made by the breach, but the amount which he judged the plaintiff might have obtained as the price of giving its consent. The amount of the profit which the defendant expected to make was a relevant factor in that assessment, but that was all.

Both the *Wrotham Park* and *Bredero Homes* cases (unlike the present) were concerned with a single past breach of covenant, so that the measure of damages at common law and under the Act was the same. Prima facie the measure of damages in either case for breach of a covenant not to build a house on neighbouring land is the diminution in the value of the plaintiff's land occasioned by the breach. One element in the value of the plaintiff's land immediately before the breach is attributable to his ability to obtain an injunction to prevent the building. Clearly a defendant who wished to build would pay for the release of the covenant, but only so long as the court could still protect it by the grant of an injunction. The proviso is important. It is the ability to claim an injunction which gives the benefit of the covenant much of its value. If the plaintiff delays proceedings until it is no longer possible for him to obtain an injunction, he destroys his own bargaining position and devalues his right. The unavailability of the remedy of injunction at one and the same time deprives the court of jurisdiction to award damages under the Act and removes the basis for awarding substantial damages at common law. For this reason, I take the view that damages can be awarded at common law in accordance with the approach adopted in the *Wrotham Park* case, but in practice only in the circumstances in which they could also be awarded under the Act.

Comment

(1) How does Millett LJ justify the *Wrotham Park* measure of damages?[38] Is the justification convincing? Are there alternative approaches?

(2) Is the analysis in *Lawrence* as to when injunctive relief is available likely to impact on the damages available?

(3) In *Lawrence*, it was left open whether the *Jaggard* approach could apply to nuisance (different views were expressed). The general application of principles allowing for the claimant to recover a share of the defendant's benefit must be doubted.

4. Reform

Extract 20.4.1

Law Commission CP 186: Easements, Covenants and Profits à Prendre (footnotes omitted)

[Easements and covenants]

15.26   The Law Commission considered the reform of easements, profits appurtenant and covenants in its 1971 Working Paper, Transfer of Land: Appurtenant Rights. It suggested specific reforms relating to these areas of law and it also proposed their amalgamation and reclassification . . .

15.30   Where the 1971 model and our proposals differ in substance is that the reclassification proposed in 1971 would require legislative codification of the law. We do not consider that codification (which would involve drafting comprehensive and detailed legislation) is a necessary or a proportionate response to the problems encountered in this area of the law. Both easements and profits are well-recognised property interests. As we are not proposing fundamentally to alter the characteristics of such rights, we see little policy justification for renaming them and codifying the law relating to them. Reclassification for its own sake is futile, and is likely only to promote litigation as parties contend that particular rights should fall within one category rather than another.

[Positive covenants and Land Obligations]

7.39   The benefit of a positive covenant can run at law. However, the greatest and clearest deficiency in the law of positive covenants is that the burden of a positive covenant does not

---

[38] In *Attorney-Gen v Blake* [2001] 1 AC 268 at p 281, Lord Nicholls approves the 'damages for loss of a bargaining opportunity' analysis.

run so as to bind successors in title of the covenantor, either at law or in equity. Such devices as are available to circumvent this rule are complex and insufficiently comprehensive. As a result, it is not possible to bind successors in title of the burdened land to a simple positive obligation, such as to keep trees pruned to below a certain height or to maintain a boundary wall.

7.45   We consider it to be a defect that the burden of a positive covenant entered into between nearby landowners does not run with the land of the covenantor. This contrasts with the position of covenants between landlord and tenant where it is possible to enforce both positive and restrictive covenants between successors in title as well as the original parties to the lease, due to the doctrine of privity of estate . . .

7.74   It could be argued that the law should simply be amended to allow positive covenants to run with the land, without reforming the law of restrictive covenants. In 1984, the Law Commission . . . concluded that it would not be possible for the law of restrictive covenants to remain unchanged. Nor could the law of restrictive covenants be retained and simply expanded, so as to embrace positive covenants. This remains the case today for the following reasons:

(1)   Positive covenants demand a legal regime which is different in fundamental respects to that which currently applies to restrictive covenants. For example:

  (a)   A smaller class of persons should be bound by a positive covenant than a restrictive covenant. This is because positive covenants require action to be taken and that action may be burdensome and expensive. It would be inappropriate, for example, if a weekly tenant of the burdened land became liable to perform a positive covenant to erect and maintain a costly sea wall. By contrast, the owner of any interest, however small, in the burdened land is bound to observe a restrictive covenant. This is as it should be, because a restrictive covenant requires people merely to refrain from doing the specified thing.

    . . .

(2)   Since a new legal regime would have to be created for positive covenants, it would not be right to reproduce in that regime the serious incidental faults which beset the law of restrictive covenants . . .

(3)   It would be inconsistent to leave two separate and different regimes, one markedly inferior to the other, governing two legal entities (positive and restrictive covenants) which ought in any rational system of law to be conceptually the same.

7.79   We provisionally propose:

(3)   that there should be a new legislative scheme of Land Obligations to govern the future use and enforcement of positive and restrictive obligations.

<hr>

Extract 20.4.2

<hr>

**Law Commission No 327: Making Land Work: Easements,
Covenants and Profits à Prendre (footnotes omitted)**

The Law Commission accepts the arguments in the Consultation Paper for making the burden of positive obligations run (noting that the existence of workarounds such as chains of covenants shows both the practical need for and the acceptance of such an outcome). It proposes a new scheme covering both restrictive and positive obligations.

5.63   We have concluded that we should recommend the reform of positive obligations. But along with that must go recommendations about safeguards, in order to minimise practical and economic risk. We have not favoured the approach adopted in some jurisdictions of having a list of permissible positive obligations; but we have taken the view that careful definition, a touch and concern requirement, the ability to register the benefit of the obligation (rather than just the burden) and the facility to have burdens discharged or modified are all important elements of reform.

5.69   We recommend that the owner of an estate in land shall be able to create positive and negative obligations that will be able to take effect (subject to the formal requirements for the creation of legal interests) as legal interests appurtenant to another estate in land, and therefore as registrable interests pursuant to the Land Registration Act 2002, provided that:

(1)   the benefit of the obligation touches and concerns the benefited land;

(2)   the obligation is either:

   (a)   an obligation not to do something on the burdened land;

   (b)   an obligation to do something on the burdened land or on the boundary (or any structure or feature that is treated as marking or lying on the boundary) of the burdened and benefited land; or

   (c)   an obligation to make a payment in return for the performance of an obligation of the kind mentioned in paragraph (b); and

(3)   the obligation is not made between lessor and lessee and relating to the demised premises.

5.70   We recommend that for the future, covenants made by the owner of an estate in land and that satisfy the conditions set out above shall take effect, not as promises and not in accordance with the current law relating to restrictive covenants, but as legal interests in the burdened land, appurtenant to the benefited estate in land.

5.71   These two recommendations work together, both enabling the creation of obligations as interests and ensuring that future covenants take effect as such interests, and indeed as legal interests when the formal requirements for their creation are met. That means that in terms of drafting, there is freedom – but no compulsion – for conveyancers to draft restrictive covenants as they currently do. There is no requirement to use any particular form of words, provided that the obligation imposed meets the requirements for a valid land obligation in the draft Bill.

5.72   Technically, these new obligations are akin to the land obligations of the 1984 recommendations and to the new legal interest that we proposed in the Consultation Paper, and 'land obligations' is the most natural of the available labels for them. This is neither the scheme recommended in 1984 nor, in much of its detail, the scheme provisionally proposed in the Consultation Paper. What we recommend here is a much simpler arrangement and one that involves far more continuity with the current law. Yet it is clearly a scheme that provides for obligations to take effect as legal interests, and the word 'obligation' is important. As will be seen, the word plays an important role in the draft Bill.

5.89   We recommend that following the implementation of reform it should no longer be possible to create freehold covenants enforceable under *Tulk* v *Moxhay*.

6.50   Land Registry will not, as things stand, register a right of way without a plan, or a description sufficiently precise to enable the delineation of the route on a title plan or an accurate verbal description for inclusion on the register. Similarly, an application for registration of a land obligation would require an indication of the extent of the benefited and burdened land except where these are, respectively, co-extensive with a registered title.

6.51   Accordingly, we see no need to recommend a statutory requirement for a plan. The statutory requirements for the creation of a legal land obligation should be the same, in fact, as those for the creation of a legal easement. The formal creation requirements follow without further provision from the background law, in particular section 52 of the Law of Property Act 1925 and sections 2 and 27 of the Land Registration Act 2002 . . .

6.62   We recommend that land obligations, whether restrictive or positive, should be incapable of creation by implication or prescription, and that section 62 of the Law of Property Act 1925 should not operate so as to create a land obligation or to convert one from a leasehold to a freehold interest.

6.83   We recommend that provided that title to the benefited and burdened land is registered, the fact that they are in common ownership and possession shall not prevent the creation or existence of land obligations.

6.98   We recommend that the benefit of a land obligation shall be appurtenant to the estate in land for the benefit of which it is imposed and shall therefore be transmitted with that estate and to any estates (but not to interests) derived out of it.

6.115   We recommend that the burden of a positive land obligation be transmitted:

(1)   to estates derived out of a burdened estate which confer a right to immediate possession of the burdened land, in accordance with the normal priority rules, save that the burden of a positive obligation shall not pass to a lease for seven years or less; and

(2)   to mortgagees when they come into possession of a burdened estate.

6.116   We recommend that where a landlord and a tenant are both burdened by a positive land obligation, the landlord shall be liable to the tenant if the tenant suffers loss as a result of the landlord's breach of the obligation unless the parties expressly provide otherwise in the relevant lease.

Comment

(1) Is there a good case for amalgamating easements and covenants?

(2) Is the case for the running of the burden of obligations made out? Are there any restrictions on what may be put into a land obligation?

(3) What will be the fate of the existing rules on the transmission of the benefit? Will there be any scope for schemes of development?

Further reading

Gardner, S (1982) 98 LQR 279: The proprietary effect of contractual obligations under *Tulk* v *Moxhay* and *De Mattos* v *Gibson*.

Hayton, D J (1971) 87 LQR 539: Restrictive covenants as property interests.

Martin, J [1996] Conv 329: Remedies for breach of restrictive covenants.

Newsom, G H (1981) 97 LQR 32: Universal annexation?

Turano, L [2000] Conv 377: Intention, interpretation and the 'mystery' of section 79 of the Law of Property Act 1925. ER Rep 9.

21

Mortgages

In this chapter, we encounter the use of land for a quite different purpose: security for a loan (or other obligation). Mortgages are extremely common in the everyday purchase of a family home: few people have enough money to be able to afford to purchase a house outright. However, mortgages may secure any form of loan, one example being a loan to a business. Land is generally very good security. It is unlikely to disappear or be destroyed,[1] and its value is more stable than, for example, shares. As a result, loans secured on land are likely to attract lower rates of interest: the risks in the event of default on loan repayments are reduced.

The traditional essence of a mortgage lies in the transfer of a property interest to the mortgagee (the lender). Before the 1925 legislation, this would normally be the legal fee simple. The mortgagor (the borrower) would retain an equity of redemption: the right to recover the property on repayment of the loan. This approach has two principal drawbacks. Mortgagors normally regard themselves as owning the property. Although this is ensured in economic terms by the equity of redemption, it can seem odd that ownership is vested in the mortgagee. It can also lead to complexity in the title: the fee simple is transferred to the mortgagee and then re-transferred on repayment of the loan.

1. Forms of mortgage

Extract 21.1.1

Law of Property Act 1925, ss 85, 87, 88

85.—(1) A mortgage of an estate in fee simple shall only be capable of being effected at law either by a demise for a term of years absolute, subject to a provision for cesser on redemption, or by a charge by deed expressed to be by way of legal mortgage:

Provided that a first mortgagee shall have the same right to the possession of documents as if his security included the fee simple.

(2) Any purported conveyance of an estate in fee simple by way of mortgage made after the commencement of this Act shall (to the extent of the estate of the mortgagor) operate as a demise of the land to the mortgagee for a term of years absolute, without impeachment for waste, but subject to cesser on redemption, in manner following, namely:—

    (a) A first or only mortgagee shall take a term of three thousand years from the date of the mortgage:
        . . .

and, in this subsection, any such purported conveyance as aforesaid includes an absolute conveyance with a deed of defeasance and any other assurance which, but for this subsection, would operate in effect to vest the fee simple in a mortgagee subject to redemption.

---

[1] Insurance can cover dangers such as fire.

87.—(1)   Where a legal mortgage of land is created by a charge by deed expressed to be by way of legal mortgage, the mortgagee shall have the same protection, powers and remedies (including the right to take proceedings to obtain possession from the occupiers and the persons in receipt of rents and profits, or any of them) as if—

> (a)   where the mortgage is a mortgage of an estate in fee simple, a mortgage term for three thousand years without impeachment of waste had been thereby created in favour of the mortgagee; . . .

88.—(1)   Where an estate in fee simple has been mortgaged by the creation of a term of years absolute limited thereout or by a charge by way of legal mortgage and the mortgagee sells under his statutory or express power of sale—

> (a)   the conveyance by him shall operate to vest in the purchaser the fee simple in the land conveyed subject to any legal mortgage having priority to the mortgage in right of which the sale is made and to any money thereby secured . . .

(2)   Where any such mortgagee obtains an order for foreclosure absolute, the order shall operate to vest the fee simple in him . . .

Comment

(1) Similarly, mortgages of leases take effect by way of sublease (or legal charge) rather than assignment: s 86.

(2) Virtually all modern mortgages take effect as legal charges. For registered land, this is the only form of legal mortgage since the Land Registration Act 2002; s 85(2) is disapplied.

(3) The legislation ensures that the position of the mortgagee is not prejudiced by not possessing the fee simple. Foreclosure is the termination of the equity of redemption by court order. As will be seen later, it is rare today.

(4) Can second mortgages (when a mortgagor executes a second mortgage, usually to secure an additional loan) constitute legal interests today?

The mortgagee enjoys a mixture of remedies based on a 3,000-year lease and specific rights conferred by the legislation (or the individual mortgage). These remedies, particularly possession and sale, will be considered in detail later. However, it must be queried whether the modern form of mortgage (even in its guise as legal charge) reflects the needs and expectations of the parties. How much of an improvement is it on the pre-1925 law?

So far, we have been considering legal mortgages, but the role of equity must also be considered.

Extract 21.1.2

Law Commission No 204: Transfer of Land: Land Mortgages
(footnotes omitted)

Equitable charge

2.12   Equitable charges can be created consensually over any legal or equitable interest in land. The charge must be made in writing but no other formality or particular form of words is necessary: the only requirement is that the parties demonstrate an intention to make the property 'liable, or specially appropriated, to the discharge of a debt or some other obligation'. There is a clear theoretical distinction between an equitable mortgage and an equitable charge, and they are different in effect, although often confused in practice. We return to this point in paragraph 2.14 below.

Reduction in number of types of security

2.13   Whilst this proliferation of types of security interests in land is historically explicable, we are satisfied that it no longer serves any useful purpose. As far as legal mortgages are concerned, it is difficult to justify the continued existence of the mortgage by demise, given that it is no longer used in practice and has the same effect in law as the charge by way of legal mortgage. The problem with equitable security interests in a legal estate is rather different. The principle underlying the equitable mortgage of a legal estate is the rule in *Walsh* v *Lonsdale*, a general property law principle which applies to mortgages in precisely the same way as it applies to fees simple, leases and easements. Nevertheless, if the equitable charge is included, it does mean that there are at least three, and possibly four, ways of taking an informal security over a legal estate. Whilst there are small differences in effect between these different types of equitable security, there is no apparent difference in function: none seems to fulfil a function that could not be fulfilled by any one of the others . . .

Removal of the distinction between mortgages and charges

2.14   A mortgage is conceptually different from a charge: a mortgage involves some degree of transfer of the mortgaged property to the mortgagee, with a provision for re-transfer on repayment of the loan, whereas a charge merely gives the chargee a right of recourse to the charged property as security for the loan. However, in English law the distinction is blurred and the terms are often used interchangeably, sometimes as if they were synonymous and sometimes as if one was a generic term including the other. The confusion is exacerbated by uncertainty over the correct classification of the mortgage by demise and the charge by way of legal mortgage. The mortgage by demise is technically a mortgage, in that it involves the grant of a substantial legal estate to the mortgagee. However, equitable restriction of the mortgagee's ownership-type rights has resulted in it acquiring a close resemblance to a charge. The charge by way of legal mortgage is in name and form a charge, but in substance it is the same as the mortgage by demise.

. . .

3.1   It is central to our proposal for the creation of a new kind of mortgage that the attributes of the mortgage should be expressly defined by statute, rather than defined by reference to pre-existing forms of mortgage or by analogy to any other legal relationship. It is therefore necessary to consider what interest in the mortgaged property a mortgagee ought to have under the new mortgage, whether formal or informal. It is also important that our reform should bring together in a single enactment the rules which govern the relationship between mortgagor and mortgagee. This will be particularly useful in commercial transactions. In such cases the parties often wish to negotiate detailed terms to fit the particular circumstances, and that makes essential a knowledge of the parameters which the law lays down.

3.2   The guiding principle we have adopted in defining the nature of the new mortgage is that the only function of the mortgaged property is to provide security for the performance of the mortgagor's payment obligations. It follows from this that the nature and extent of the mortgagee's interest ought to be dictated by the need to preserve the value of the security and, where necessary, to enforce it.

Comment

(1) What is the difference between legal and equitable mortgages?

(2) Buckley LJ said this of equitable charges: '. . . property is expressly or constructively made liable, or specially appropriated, to the discharge of a debt or some other obligation, and confers on the chargee a right of realisation by judicial process, that is to say, by the

appointment of a receiver or an order for sale'.[2] What is the difference between equitable mortgages and equitable charges?

(3) What improvements would the Law Commission's proposals make? Are they needed?[3]

2. Creation of mortgages

By and large, the normal formalities for the creation of legal and equitable interests apply. However, there are two specific points to consider. The first concerns the operation of ss 85 and 86 when there is an absolute conveyance, but there is proof from surrounding circumstances that it was intended to operate as security for a loan.

Extract 21.2.1

Grangeside Properties Ltd v *Collingwoods Securities Ltd* [1964] 1 WLR 139

HARMAN LJ: . . . Now the argument Mr Blundell advanced . . . was that the assignment here [of a lease] was not expressed to be by way of mortgage. He argued that [s 86(1)] means that if the assignment is expressed to be by way of mortgage, the subsection will operate, but if it is not so expressed, it will not. The other view is that 'by way of mortgage' means being in fact by way of mortgage, and though this was by way of mortgage and though it was expressed to be an assignment, it would operate as a sub-demise. Mr Blundell goes on to argue that it does not operate under section 86(1) as an absolute assignment because none of the parties intended it so to do and therefore the judge . . . was justified in ignoring it. In my judgment that is wholly wrong. Section 86(2) cannot have intended to alter the ancient law, which had always been, that Chancery would treat as a mortgage that which was intended to be a conveyance by way of security between A and B. Once a mortgage, always a mortgage and nothing but a mortgage, has been a principle for centuries. 'By way of mortgage' must mean that which is in fact intended as a mortgage . . . It could not be that section 86(2) is intended to sweep away the view of the law which had always been that if you proved the thing was a mortgage, equity would allow you to have your equity of redemption to redeem on payment of the mortgage money, interest and costs. In my view this document did operate, although expressed as an absolute assignment, by way of sub-demise.

Comment

(1) What circumstances might show that an apparently absolute conveyance is in fact a mortgage?

(2) How does *Grangeside* operate if title is registered and the apparent transferee (mortgagee) is registered as proprietor of the fee simple?

(3) *HSBC Bank plc* v *Dyche* [2010] 2 P&CR 58 employed a common intention constructive trust analysis for a registered title – the mortgagee held on trust for the mortgagor. This avoids the effect of the 2002 Act (this was not cited, nor was *Grangeside*). However, could there be problems in introducing a trust of land analysis, including overreaching, into a mortgage context?

The second point concerns the formalities required for equitable mortgages. Equity had long treated the deposit of title deeds with a lender as an equitable mortgage. The following

---

[2] *Swiss Bank Corporation* v *Lloyds Bank Ltd* [1982] AC 584 at p 595.
[3] They are not being implemented: (1998) 588 HL Deb WA213.

extract considers the impact of the stricter requirements of writing introduced by s 2 of the Law of Property (Miscellaneous Provisions) Act 1989.[4]

Extract 21.2.2

United Bank of Kuwait plc v *Sahib* [1997] Ch 107

PETER GIBSON LJ: . . . The effect of section 2 of the Act of 1989 is, therefore, that a contract for a mortgage of or charge on any interest in land or in the proceeds of sale of land can only be made in writing and only if the written document incorporates all the terms which the parties have expressly agreed and is signed by or on behalf of each party. In the present case it is not suggested that there is any such written document.

Mr Pymont argued before the judge and before us that it was unnecessary for Sogenal to rely on any contract . . . He relied on the rule which has operated since *Russel* v *Russel* (1783) 1 Bro CC 269 to which I referred at the beginning of this judgment. He did not dispute that the basis of the rule, as expounded in the authorities, is that the court infers an agreement to mortgage in the absence of contrary evidence.

On this part of the case the judge expressed his conclusion in a way which is in my opinion entirely correct, ante, p 126D–G:

'Whether or not the enforcement of the agreement which is to be inferred or presumed from the deposit of title deeds was properly to be regarded as an example of the operation of the doctrine of part performance, as Lord Selborne LC suggested in *Maddison* v *Alderson* (1883) 8 App Cas 467, or as a sui generis exception to the Statute of Frauds 1677 which was outside the proper scope of that doctrine – in that the act of part performance relied upon was not the act of the mortgagee who was seeking to enforce the agreement – there can, in my view, be no doubt that the courts have, consistently, treated the rule that a deposit of title deeds for the purpose of securing a debt operates, without more, as an equitable mortgage or charge as contract-based, and have regarded the deposit as a fact which enabled the contract to be enforced notwithstanding the absence of evidence sufficient to satisfy the Statute of Frauds . . .'

I would emphasise the essential contractual foundation of the rule as demonstrated in the authorities. The deposit by way of security is treated both as prima facie evidence of a contract to mortgage and as part performance of that contract . . .

Mr Pymont made seven submissions as to why section 2 of the Act of 1989 did not apply to a deposit of title deeds.

(1) He submitted that there is nothing in the Act of 1989 which expressly or by necessary implication repeals the provisions of the Act of 1925 and later legislation recognising and extending the scope of a security by deposit of title deeds . . .

He drew attention to the fact that some commentators have concluded from this that section 2 was not intended to repeal the rule relating to the creation of security by deposit of title deeds: see *Snell's Equity*, 29th ed (1990), p 445, *Cheshire and Burn's Modern Law of Real Property*, 15th ed (1994), p 679 and Bently and Coughlan, 'Informal dealings with land after section 2' (1990) 10 LS 325, 341.

I differ with reluctance from such distinguished property lawyers, but I am not persuaded that their views on this point are correct . . .

The new formalities required by section 2 govern the validity of all dispositions of interests in land. I cannot see that the references relied on by Mr Pymont in the earlier legislation can displace what otherwise is the plain meaning and effect of section 2 on contracts in whatever form to mortgage land.

[4] The legislation is considered at pp 117–133 above.

(2) Mr Pymont pointed to the fact that there is nothing in the Law Commission's report which initiated the reforms effected by the Act of 1989 to suggest that security by deposit of title deeds was intended to be affected or was even considered.

... But the intention of the Law Commission to include in its proposals contracts to grant mortgages was made plain (see paragraph 4.3 of the report) ... In any event, if the wording of section 2 is clear, as I think it is, the absence from the Law Commission's report of a reference to security by deposit of title deeds cannot alter the section's effect.

...

(4) Mr Pymont then said that the rule that a deposit of title deeds by way of security creates a mortgage is not dependent on any actual contract between the parties ...

I accept that there need not be an express contract between the depositor of the title deeds and the person with whom they are deposited for an equitable mortgage to arise (subject to section 2). But I have already stated why it is clear from the authorities that the deposit is treated as rebuttable evidence of a contract to mortgage ...

(5) ... To the extent that part performance is an essential part of the rationale of the creation of an equitable mortgage by the deposit of title deeds, that too is inconsistent with the new philosophy of the Act of 1989 ...

Comment

(1) Was there adequate justification for overturning the long-standing recognition of mortgages by deposit of title deeds?

(2) What must a mortgagee do to ensure that a valid mortgage is created? Does the simple possession of the title deeds confer any protection? Is there any equivalent for registered land?

(3) The creation of equitable charges requires writing by the chargor: LPA s 53(1)(a). Might this be used to avoid the more demanding requirement of the 1989 Act that both parties must sign? See *Kinane* v *Mackie-Conteh* [2005] WTLR 345 at [35].

It may be possible to rely on estoppel to avoid the requirements of writing. In *Kinane* v *Mackie-Conteh*,[5] Arden LJ said:

> Thus, the requirement that the defendant encouraged (or allowed) the claimant to believe that he would acquire an interest in land may (depending on the facts) consist in the defendant encouraging the claimant (by words or conduct) to believe that the agreement for the disposition of an interest in land (here a security interest) was valid and binding ... the requirement that the defendant encouraged or permitted the claimant in his erroneous belief is not satisfied simply by the admission of the invalid agreement in evidence. In this sort of case, the claimant has to show that the defendant represented to the claimant, by his words or conduct, including conduct in the provision or delivery of the agreement, that the agreement created an enforceable obligation.

3. Vitiating factors

The mortgaging of homes to secure another person's debts has posed many problems in recent decades. Most common has been a mortgage given by a wife to secure a loan to her husband's business. There is a danger, of course, that the mortgagor will not understand the significance of what he or she is doing and that the borrower (frequently desperate to

---

[5] [2005] WTLR 345 at [28]–[29]; Extract 5.2.14 above. It was seen in Chapter 5 that the application of estoppel in the context of the 1989 Act is controversial.

get the loan) will exert fraud, misrepresentation or undue influence. A detailed review of vitiating factors lies more within contract than property law and will not be undertaken. However, their impact upon the mortgagee is important for property law.

At one time it seemed as if mortgagees might owe duties to mortgagors based upon inequality of bargaining power. However, this analysis has been rejected by the House of Lords[6] and today it is essential to concentrate upon the conduct of the person whose loan is to be secured. There are two major House of Lords decisions (*O'Brien* in 1993 and *Etridge* in 2001) and these will form the basis of our study. The major emphasis will be on the lengthy *Etridge* decision, as this adjusts the *O'Brien* analysis in the light of a torrent of intervening litigation.

Extract 21.3.1

Barclays Bank plc v O'Brien [1994] 1 AC 180

LORD BROWNE-WILKINSON:

Policy considerations

The large number of cases of this type coming before the courts in recent years reflects the rapid changes in social attitudes and the distribution of wealth which have recently occurred. Wealth is now more widely spread. Moreover a high proportion of privately owned wealth is invested in the matrimonial home. Because of the recognition by society of the equality of the sexes, the majority of matrimonial homes are now in the joint names of both spouses. Therefore in order to raise finance for the business enterprises of one or other of the spouses, the jointly owned home has become a main source of security. The provision of such security requires the consent of both spouses.

In parallel with these financial developments, society's recognition of the equality of the sexes has led to a rejection of the concept that the wife is subservient to the husband in the management of the family's finances. A number of the authorities reflect an unwillingness in the court to perpetuate law based on this outmoded concept. Yet, as Scott LJ in the Court of Appeal rightly points out [1993] QB 109, 139, although the concept of the ignorant wife leaving all financial decisions to the husband is outmoded, the practice does not yet coincide with the ideal. In a substantial proportion of marriages it is still the husband who has the business experience and the wife is willing to follow his advice without bringing a truly independent mind and will to bear on financial decisions. The number of recent cases in this field shows that in practice many wives are still subjected to, and yield to, undue influence by their husbands. Such wives can reasonably look to the law for some protection when their husbands have abused the trust and confidence reposed in them.

On the other hand, it is important to keep a sense of balance in approaching these cases. It is easy to allow sympathy for the wife who is threatened with the loss of her home at the suit of a rich bank to obscure an important public interest viz, the need to ensure that the wealth currently tied up in the matrimonial home does not become economically sterile. If the rights secured to wives by the law renders vulnerable loans granted on the security of matrimonial homes, institutions will be unwilling to accept such security, thereby reducing the flow of loan capital to business enterprises. It is therefore essential that a law designed to protect the vulnerable does not render the matrimonial home unacceptable as security to financial institutions.

. . .

---

[6] *National Westminster Bank plc v Morgan* [1985] AC 686.

Undue influence

A person who has been induced to enter into a transaction by the undue influence of another ('the wrongdoer') is entitled to set that transaction aside as against the wrongdoer. Such undue influence is either actual or presumed. In *Bank of Credit and Commerce International SA v Aboody* [1990] 1 QB 923, 953, the Court of Appeal helpfully adopted the following classification.

Class 1: Actual undue influence
In these cases it is necessary for the claimant to prove affirmatively that the wrongdoer exerted undue influence on the complainant to enter into the particular transaction which is impugned.

Class 2: Presumed undue influence
In these cases the complainant only has to show, in the first instance, that there was a relationship of trust and confidence between the complainant and the wrongdoer of such a nature that it is fair to presume that the wrongdoer abused that relationship in procuring the complainant to enter into the impugned transaction. In Class 2 cases therefore there is no need to produce evidence that actual undue influence was exerted in relation to the particular transaction impugned . . . Such a confidential relationship can be established in two ways, viz,

Class 2(A)
Certain relationships (for example solicitor and client, medical advisor and patient) as a matter of law raise the presumption that undue influence has been exercised.

Class 2(B)
Even if there is no relationship falling within Class 2(A), if the complainant proves the de facto existence of a relationship under which the complainant generally reposed trust and confidence in the wrongdoer, the existence of such relationship raises the presumption of undue influence . . .

An invalidating tendency?

Although there is no Class 2(A) presumption of undue influence as between husband and wife, it should be emphasised that in any particular case a wife may well be able to demonstrate that de facto she did leave decisions on financial affairs to her husband thereby bringing herself within Class 2(B) . . .

Undue influence, misrepresentation and third parties

Up to this point I have been considering the right of a claimant wife to set aside a transaction as against the wrongdoing husband when the transaction has been procured by his undue influence. But in surety cases the decisive question is whether the claimant wife can set aside the transaction, not against the wrongdoing husband, but against the creditor bank. Of course, if the wrongdoing husband is acting as agent for the creditor bank in obtaining the surety from the wife, the creditor will be fixed with the wrongdoing of its own agent and the surety contract can be set aside as against the creditor. Apart from this, if the creditor bank has notice, actual or constructive, of the undue influence exercised by the husband (and consequentially of the wife's equity to set aside the transaction) the creditor will take subject to that equity and the wife can set aside the transaction against the creditor (albeit a purchaser for value) as well as against the husband: see *Bainbrigge* v *Browne* (1881) 18 Ch D 188 and *Bank of Credit and Commerce International SA* v *Aboody* [1990] 1 QB 923, 973 . . .

Conclusions

(a) Wives

[After rejecting any 'special equity' protecting wives] In my judgment, if the doctrine of notice is properly applied, there is no need for the introduction of a special equity in these types of cases. A wife who has been induced to stand as a surety for her husband's debts by his undue influence, misrepresentation or some other legal wrong has an equity as against him to set aside that transaction. Under the ordinary principles of equity, her right to set aside that transaction will be enforceable against third parties (e.g. against a creditor) if either the husband was acting as the third party's agent or the third party had actual or constructive notice of the facts giving rise to her equity. Although there may be cases where, without artificiality, it can properly be held that the husband was acting as the agent of the creditor in procuring the wife to stand as surety, such cases will be of very rare occurrence. The key to the problem is to identify the circumstances in which the creditor will be taken to have had notice of the wife's equity to set aside the transaction.

The doctrine of notice lies at the heart of equity. Given that there are two innocent parties, each enjoying rights, the earlier right prevails against the later right if the acquirer of the later right knows of the earlier right (actual notice) or would have discovered it had he taken proper steps (constructive notice). In particular, if the party asserting that he takes free of the earlier rights of another knows of certain facts which put him on inquiry as to the possible existence of the rights of that other and he fails to make such inquiry or take such other steps as are reasonable to verify whether such earlier right does or does not exist, he will have constructive notice of the earlier right and take subject to it. Therefore where a wife has agreed to stand surety for her husband's debts as a result of undue influence or misrepresentation, the creditor will take subject to the wife's equity to set aside the transaction if the circumstances are such as to put the creditor on inquiry as to the circumstances in which she agreed to stand surety.

. . .

Therefore in my judgment a creditor is put on inquiry when a wife offers to stand surety for her husband's debts by the combination of two factors: (a) the transaction is on its face not to the financial advantage of the wife; and (b) there is a substantial risk in transactions of that kind that, in procuring the wife to act as surety, the husband has committed a legal or equitable wrong that entitles the wife to set aside the transaction.

It follows that unless the creditor who is put on inquiry takes reasonable steps to satisfy himself that the wife's agreement to stand surety has been properly obtained, the creditor will have constructive notice of the wife's rights.

What, then are the reasonable steps which the creditor should take to ensure that it does not have constructive notice of the wife's rights, if any? Normally the reasonable steps necessary to avoid being fixed with constructive notice consist of making inquiry of the person who may have the earlier right (i.e. the wife) to see whether such right is asserted. It is plainly impossible to require of banks and other financial institutions that they should inquire of one spouse whether he or she has been unduly influenced or misled by the other. But in my judgment the creditor, in order to avoid being fixed with constructive notice, can reasonably be expected to take steps to bring home to the wife the risk she is running by standing as surety and to advise her to take independent advice. As to past transactions, it will depend on the facts of each case whether the steps taken by the creditor satisfy this test. However for the future in my judgment a creditor will have satisfied these requirements if it insists that the wife attend a private meeting (in the absence of the husband) with a representative of the creditor at which she is told of the extent of her liability as surety, warned of the risk she is running and urged to take independent legal advice . . .

(b) Other persons

I have hitherto dealt only with the position where a wife stands surety for her husband's debts. But in my judgment the same principles are applicable to all other cases where there is an emotional relationship between cohabitees.

Comment

(1) Are there other approaches which could be used to protect sureties (the wife in *O'Brien*)?

(2) Does the law maintain a satisfactory balance between the needs of mortgagees and home-owners?

(3) The *O'Brien* analysis has not been followed in Australia, where the unconscionability of the mortgagee's conduct has been used as a basis for attacking the mortgage.[7]

Following *O'Brien*, problems arose with many of its component parts (finding undue influence, imputing notice to the lender, consequences of being put on inquiry). In particular, banks almost invariably did not give advice, but relied on certificates by solicitors that the wife had been advised. The solicitor was commonly the husband's solicitor and sometimes the lender's.

Extract 21.3.2

Royal Bank of Scotland plc v Etridge (No 2) [2002] 2 AC 773

LORD NICHOLLS:

Undue influence

11. Even this test [whether one party has reposed sufficient trust and confidence in the other] is not comprehensive. The principle is not confined to cases of abuse of trust and confidence. It also includes, for instance, cases where a vulnerable person has been exploited. Indeed, there is no single touchstone for determining whether the principle is applicable. Several expressions have been used in an endeavour to encapsulate the essence: trust and confidence, reliance, dependence or vulnerability on the one hand and ascendancy, domination or control on the other. None of these descriptions is perfect. None is all embracing. Each has its proper place.

12. In *CIBC Mortgages plc v Pitt* [1994] 1 AC 200 your Lordships' House decided that in cases of undue influence disadvantage is not a necessary ingredient of the cause of action. It is not essential that the transaction should be disadvantageous to the pressurised or influenced person, either in financial terms or in any other way . . .

Burden of proof and presumptions

13. Whether a transaction was brought about by the exercise of undue influence is a question of fact. Here, as elsewhere, the general principle is that he who asserts a wrong has been committed must prove it . . .

14. Proof that the complainant placed trust and confidence in the other party in relation to the management of the complainant's financial affairs, coupled with a transaction which calls for explanation, will normally be sufficient, failing satisfactory evidence to the contrary, to discharge the burden of proof . . .

---

[7] *Garcia v National Australia Bank Ltd* (1998) 155 ALR 614, especially at p 625; Gardner (1999) 115 LQR 1.

18.   The evidential presumption discussed above is to be distinguished sharply from a different form of presumption which arises in some cases. The law has adopted a sternly protective attitude towards certain types of relationship in which one party acquires influence over another who is vulnerable and dependent and where, moreover, substantial gifts by the influenced or vulnerable person are not normally to be expected. Examples of relationships within this special class are parent and child, guardian and ward, trustee and beneficiary, solicitor and client, and medical adviser and patient. In these cases the law presumes, irrebuttably, that one party had influence over the other. The complainant need not prove he actually reposed trust and confidence in the other party. It is sufficient for him to prove the existence of the type of relationship.
19.   It is now well established that husband and wife is not one of the relationships to which this latter principle applies . . . Although there is no presumption, the court will nevertheless note, as a matter of fact, the opportunities for abuse which flow from a wife's confidence in her husband. The court will take this into account with all the other evidence in the case. Where there is evidence that a husband has taken unfair advantage of his influence over his wife, or her confidence in him, 'it is not difficult for the wife to establish her title to relief': see *In re Lloyds Bank Ltd; Bomze and Lederman* v *Bomze* [1931] 1 Ch 289, 302, per Maugham J.

Independent advice

20.   Proof that the complainant received advice from a third party before entering into the impugned transaction is one of the matters a court takes into account when weighing all the evidence . . . But a person may understand fully the implications of a proposed transaction, for instance, a substantial gift, and yet still be acting under the undue influence of another. Proof of outside advice does not, of itself, necessarily show that the subsequent completion of the transaction was free from the exercise of undue influence. Whether it will be proper to infer that outside advice had an emancipating effect, so that the transaction was not brought about by the exercise of undue influence, is a question of fact to be decided having regard to all the evidence in the case.

Manifest disadvantage

21.   As already noted, there are two prerequisites to the evidential shift in the burden of proof from the complainant to the other party. First, that the complainant reposed trust and confidence in the other party, or the other party acquired ascendancy over the complainant. Second, that the transaction is not readily explicable by the relationship of the parties.
22.   Lindley LJ summarised this second prerequisite in the leading authority of *Allcard* v *Skinner* 36 Ch D 145, . . . at p 185 'But if the gift is so large as not to be reasonably accounted for on the ground of friendship, relationship, charity, or other ordinary motives on which ordinary men act, the burden is upon the donee to support the gift. . . .
26.   Lord Scarman [in *National Westminster Bank plc* v *Morgan* [1985] AC 686] attached the label 'manifest disadvantage' to this second ingredient necessary to raise the presumption. This label has been causing difficulty. It may be apt enough when applied to straightforward transactions such as a substantial gift or a sale at an undervalue. But experience has now shown that this expression can give rise to misunderstanding. The label is being understood and applied in a way which does not accord with the meaning intended by Lord Scarman, its originator.
27.   The problem has arisen in the context of wives guaranteeing payment of their husband's business debts. In recent years judge after judge has grappled with the baffling question whether a wife's guarantee of her husband's bank overdraft, together with a charge on her share of the matrimonial home, was a transaction manifestly to her disadvantage.
28.   In a narrow sense, such a transaction plainly ('manifestly') is disadvantageous to the wife. She undertakes a serious financial obligation, and in return she personally receives nothing. But that would be to take an unrealistically blinkered view of such a transaction. Unlike the

relationship of solicitor and client or medical adviser and patient, in the case of husband and wife there are inherent reasons why such a transaction may well be for her benefit. Ordinarily, the fortunes of husband and wife are bound up together. If the husband's business is the source of the family income, the wife has a lively interest in doing what she can to support the business. A wife's affection and self-interest run hand-in-hand in inclining her to join with her husband in charging the matrimonial home, usually a jointly-owned asset, to obtain the financial facilities needed by the business. The finance may be needed to start a new business, or expand a promising business, or rescue an ailing business.

29.   Which, then, is the correct approach to adopt in deciding whether a transaction is disadvantageous to the wife: the narrow approach, or the wider approach? The answer is neither. The answer lies in discarding a label which gives rise to this sort of ambiguity. The better approach is to adhere more directly to the test outlined by Lindley LJ in *Allcard* v *Skinner* 36 Ch D 145, and adopted by Lord Scarman in *National Westminster Bank plc* v *Morgan* [1985] AC 686, in the passages I have cited.

30.   I return to husband and wife cases. I do not think that, in the ordinary course, a guarantee of the character I have mentioned is to be regarded as a transaction which, failing proof to the contrary, is explicable only on the basis that it has been procured by the exercise of undue influence by the husband. Wives frequently enter into such transactions. There are good and sufficient reasons why they are willing to do so, despite the risks involved for them and their families. They may be enthusiastic. They may not. They may be less optimistic than their husbands about the prospects of the husbands' businesses. They may be anxious, perhaps exceedingly so. But this is a far cry from saying that such transactions as a class are to be regarded as prima facie evidence of the exercise of undue influence by husbands.

31.   I have emphasised the phrase 'in the ordinary course'. There will be cases where a wife's signature of a guarantee or a charge of her share in the matrimonial home does call for explanation. Nothing I have said above is directed at such a case.

The complainant and third parties: suretyship transactions

38.   The jurisprudential route by which the House reached its conclusion in *O'Brien's* case has attracted criticism from some commentators. It has been said to involve artificiality and thereby create uncertainty in the law. I must first consider this criticism. In the ordinary course a bank which takes a guarantee security from the wife of its customer will be altogether ignorant of any undue influence the customer may have exercised in order to secure the wife's concurrence. In *O'Brien* Lord Browne-Wilkinson prayed in aid the doctrine of constructive notice. In circumstances he identified, a creditor is put on inquiry. When that is so, the creditor 'will have constructive notice of the wife's rights' unless the creditor takes reasonable steps to satisfy himself that the wife's agreement to stand surety has been properly obtained: see [1994] 1 AC 180, 196.

39.   Lord Browne-Wilkinson would be the first to recognise this is not a conventional use of the equitable concept of constructive notice. The traditional use of this concept concerns the circumstances in which a transferee of property who acquires a legal estate from a transferor with a defective title may nonetheless obtain a good title, that is, a better title than the transferor had. That is not the present case. The bank acquires its charge from the wife, and there is nothing wrong with her title to her share of the matrimonial home. The transferor wife is seeking to resile from the very transaction she entered into with the bank, on the ground that her apparent consent was procured by the undue influence or other misconduct, such as misrepresentation, of a third party (her husband). She is seeking to set aside her contract of guarantee and, with it, the charge she gave to the bank.

41.   There is a further respect in which *O'Brien* departed from conventional concepts Traditionally, a person is deemed to have notice (that is, he has 'constructive' notice) of a prior right when he does not actually know of it but would have learned of it had he made the requisite inquiries. A purchaser will be treated as having constructive notice of all that a reasonably prudent purchaser

would have discovered. In the present type of case, the steps a bank is required to take, lest it have constructive notice that the wife's concurrence was procured improperly by her husband, do not consist of making inquiries. Rather, *O'Brien* envisages that the steps taken by the bank will reduce, or even eliminate, the risk of the wife entering into the transaction under any misapprehension or as a result of undue influence by her husband. The steps are not concerned to discover whether the wife has been wronged by her husband in this way. The steps are concerned to minimise the risk that such a wrong may be committed.

42.   These novelties do not point to the conclusion that the decision of this House in *O'Brien* is leading the law astray . . .

The threshold: when the bank is put on inquiry

44.   In *O'Brien* the House considered the circumstances in which a bank, or other creditor, is 'put on inquiry'. Strictly this is a misnomer. As already noted, a bank is not required to make inquiries. But it will be convenient to use the terminology which has now become accepted in this context. The House set a low level for the threshold which must be crossed before a bank is put on inquiry. For practical reasons the level is set much lower than is required to satisfy a court that, failing contrary evidence, the court may infer that the transaction was procured by undue influence . . . In my view, this passage [in *O'Brien*], read in context, is to be taken to mean, quite simply, that a bank is put on inquiry whenever a wife offers to stand surety for her husband's debts.

48.   As to the type of transactions where a bank is put on inquiry, the case where a wife becomes surety for her husband's debts is, in this context, a straightforward case. The bank is put on inquiry. On the other side of the line is the case where money is being advanced, or has been advanced, to husband and wife jointly. In such a case the bank is not put on inquiry, unless the bank is aware the loan is being made for the husband's purposes, as distinct from their joint purposes. That was decided in *CIBC Mortgages plc v Pitt* [1994] 1 AC 200.

49.   Less clear-cut is the case where the wife becomes surety for the debts of a company whose shares are held by her and her husband. Her shareholding may be nominal, or she may have a minority shareholding or an equal shareholding with her husband. In my view the bank is put on inquiry in such cases, even when the wife is a director or secretary of the company. Such cases cannot be equated with joint loans. The shareholding interests, and the identity of the directors, are not a reliable guide to the identity of the persons who actually have the conduct of the company's business.

The steps a bank should take

50.   The principal area of controversy on these appeals concerns the steps a bank should take when it has been put on inquiry. In *O'Brien* [1994] 1 AC 180, 196–197 Lord Browne-Wilkinson said that a bank can reasonably be expected to take steps to bring home to the wife the risk she is running by standing as surety and to advise her to take independent advice . . .

51.   The practice of the banks involved in the present cases, and it seems reasonable to assume this is the practice of banks generally, is not to have a private meeting with the wife. Nor do the banks themselves take any other steps to bring home to the wife the risk she is running. This has continued to be the practice since the decision in *O'Brien's* case. Banks consider they would stand to lose more than they would gain by holding a private meeting with the wife. They are, apparently, unwilling to assume the responsibility of advising the wife at such a meeting. Instead, the banking practice remains, as before, that in general the bank requires a wife to seek legal advice. The bank seeks written confirmation from a solicitor that he has explained the nature and effect of the documents to the wife.

52.   Many of the difficulties which have arisen in the present cases stem from serious deficiencies, or alleged deficiencies, in the quality of the legal advice given to the wives . . . On behalf

of the wives it has been submitted that under the current practice the legal advice is often perfunctory in the extreme and, further, that everyone, including the banks, knows this. Independent legal advice is a fiction. The system is a charade. In practice it provides little or no protection for a wife who is under a misapprehension about the risks involved or who is being coerced into signing. She may not even know the present state of her husband's indebtedness.

53. My Lords, it is plainly neither desirable nor practicable that banks should be required to attempt to discover for themselves whether a wife's consent is being procured by the exercise of undue influence of her husband. This is not a step the banks should be expected to take. Nor, further, is it desirable or practicable that banks should be expected to insist on confirmation from a solicitor that the solicitor has satisfied himself that the wife's consent has not been procured by undue influence. As already noted, the circumstances in which banks are put on inquiry are extremely wide. They embrace every case where a wife is entering into a suretyship transaction in respect of her husband's debts. Many, if not most, wives would be understandably outraged by having to respond to the sort of questioning which would be appropriate before a responsible solicitor could give such a confirmation. In any event, solicitors are not equipped to carry out such an exercise in any really worthwhile way, and they will usually lack the necessary materials. Moreover, the legal costs involved, which would inevitably fall on the husband who is seeking financial assistance from the bank, would be substantial. To require such an intrusive, inconclusive and expensive exercise in every case would be an altogether disproportionate response to the need to protect those cases, presumably a small minority, where a wife is being wronged.

55. . . . It seems to me that, provided a suitable alternative is available, banks ought not to be compelled to take this course [advising the wife, as required by *O'Brien*]. Their reasons for not wishing to hold a personal meeting are understandable. Commonly, when a bank seeks to enforce a security provided by a customer, it is met with a defence based on assurances alleged to have been given orally by a branch manager at an earlier stage: that the bank would continue to support the business, that the bank would not call in its loan, and so forth. Lengthy litigation ensues. Sometimes the allegations prove to be well-founded, sometimes not. Banks are concerned to avoid the prospect of similar litigation which would arise in guarantee cases if they were to adopt a practice of holding a meeting with a wife at which the bank's representative would explain the proposed guarantee transaction. It is not unreasonable for the banks to prefer that this task should be undertaken by an independent legal adviser.

56. I shall return later to the steps a bank should take when it follows this course. Suffice to say, these steps, together with advice from a solicitor acting for the wife, ought to provide the substance of the protection which *O'Brien* intended a wife should have. Ordinarily it will be reasonable that a bank should be able to rely upon confirmation from a solicitor, acting for the wife, that he has advised the wife appropriately.

57. The position will be otherwise if the bank knows that the solicitor has not duly advised the wife or, I would add, if the bank knows facts from which it ought to have realised that the wife has not received the appropriate advice. In such circumstances the bank will proceed at its own risk.

The content of the legal advice

61. Thus, in the present type of case it is not for the solicitor to veto the transaction by declining to confirm to the bank that he has explained the documents to the wife and the risks she is taking upon herself. If the solicitor considers the transaction is not in the wife's best interests, he will give reasoned advice to the wife to that effect. But at the end of the day the decision on whether to proceed is the decision of the client, not the solicitor. A wife is not to be precluded from entering into a financially unwise transaction if, for her own reasons, she wishes to do so.

62. That is the general rule. There may, of course, be exceptional circumstances where it is glaringly obvious that the wife is being grievously wronged. In such a case the solicitor should decline to act further . . .

63.   In *Royal Bank of Scotland plc* v *Etridge (No 2)* [1998] 4 All ER 705, 722, para 49, the Court of Appeal said that if the transaction is 'one into which no competent solicitor could properly advise the wife to enter', the availability of legal advice is insufficient to avoid the bank being fixed with constructive notice. It follows from the views expressed above that I am unable to agree with the Court of Appeal on this point.

64.   . . . In the type of case now under consideration the relevant retainer stems from the bank's concern to receive confirmation from the solicitor that, in short, the solicitor has brought home to the wife the risks involved in the proposed transaction. As a first step the solicitor will need to explain to the wife the purpose for which he has become involved at all. He should explain that, should it ever become necessary, the bank will rely upon his involvement to counter any suggestion that the wife was overborne by her husband or that she did not properly understand the implications of the transaction. The solicitor will need to obtain confirmation from the wife that she wishes him to act for her in the matter and to advise her on the legal and practical implications of the proposed transaction.

65.   When an instruction to this effect is forthcoming, the content of the advice required from a solicitor before giving the confirmation sought by the bank will, inevitably, depend upon the circumstances of the case. Typically, the advice a solicitor can be expected to give should cover the following matters as the core minimum. (1) He will need to explain the nature of the documents and the practical consequences these will have for the wife if she signs them. She could lose her home if her husband's business does not prosper. Her home may be her only substantial asset, as well as the family's home. She could be made bankrupt. (2) He will need to point out the seriousness of the risks involved. The wife should be told the purpose of the proposed new facility, the amount and principal terms of the new facility, and that the bank might increase the amount of the facility, or change its terms, or grant a new facility, without reference to her. She should be told the amount of her liability under her guarantee. The solicitor should discuss the wife's financial means, including her understanding of the value of the property being charged. The solicitor should discuss whether the wife or her husband has any other assets out of which repayment could be made if the husband's business should fail. These matters are relevant to the seriousness of the risks involved. (3) The solicitor will need to state clearly that the wife has a choice. The decision is hers and hers alone. Explanation of the choice facing the wife will call for some discussion of the present financial position, including the amount of the husband's present indebtedness, and the amount of his current overdraft facility. (4) The solicitor should check whether the wife wishes to proceed. She should be asked whether she is content that the solicitor should write to the bank confirming he has explained to her the nature of the documents and the practical implications they may have for her, or whether, for instance, she would prefer him to negotiate with the bank on the terms of the transaction. Matters for negotiation could include the sequence in which the various securities will be called upon or a specific or lower limit to her liabilities. The solicitor should not give any confirmation to the bank without the wife's authority.

66.   The solicitor's discussion with the wife should take place at a face-to-face meeting, in the absence of the husband. It goes without saying that the solicitor's explanations should be couched in suitably non-technical language. It also goes without saying that the solicitor's task is an important one. It is not a formality.

67.   The solicitor should obtain from the bank any information he needs. If the bank fails for any reason to provide information requested by the solicitor, the solicitor should decline to provide the confirmation sought by the bank.

Independent advice

69.   I turn next to the much-vexed question whether the solicitor advising the wife must act for the wife alone. Or, at the very least, the solicitor must not act for the husband or the bank in the current transaction save in a wholly ministerial capacity, such as carrying out conveyancing

formalities or supervising the execution of documents and witnessing signatures. Commonly, in practice, the solicitor advising the wife will be the solicitor acting also for her husband either in the particular transaction or generally.

72. [A] balancing exercise is called for. Some features point in one direction, others in the opposite direction. Factors favouring the need for the solicitor to act for the wife alone include the following. Sometimes a wife may be inhibited in discussion with a solicitor who is also acting for the husband or whose main client is the husband. This occurred in *Banco Exterior Internacional v Mann* [1995] 1 All ER 936: see the finding of the judge, at p 941F–G. Sometimes a solicitor whose main client is the husband may not, in practice, give the same single-minded attention to the wife's position as would a solicitor acting solely for the wife. Her interests may rank lower in the solicitor's scale of priorities, perhaps unconsciously, than the interests of the husband. Instances of incompetent advice, or worse, which have come before the court might perhaps be less likely to recur if a solicitor were instructed to act for the wife alone and gave advice solely to her. As a matter of general understanding, independent advice would suggest that the solicitor should not be acting in the same transaction for the person who, if there is any undue influence, is the source of that influence.

73. The contrary view is that the solicitor may also act for the husband or the bank, provided the solicitor is satisfied that this is in the wife's best interests and satisfied also that this will not give rise to any conflicts of duty or interest. The principal factors favouring this approach are as follows. A requirement that a wife should receive advice from a solicitor acting solely for her will frequently add significantly to the legal costs. Sometimes a wife will be happier to be advised by a family solicitor known to her than by a complete stranger. Sometimes a solicitor who knows both husband and wife and their histories will be better placed to advise than a solicitor who is a complete stranger.

74. In my view, overall the latter factors are more weighty than the former. The advantages attendant upon the employment of a solicitor acting solely for the wife do not justify the additional expense this would involve for the husband. When accepting instructions to advise the wife the solicitor assumes responsibilities directly to her, both at law and professionally. These duties, and this is central to the reasoning on this point, are owed to the wife alone . . . If he decides to accept instructions, his assumption of legal and professional responsibilities to her ought, in the ordinary course of things, to provide sufficient assurance that he will give the requisite advice fully, carefully and conscientiously. Especially so, now that the nature of the advice called for has been clarified. If at any stage the solicitor becomes concerned that there is a real risk that other interests or duties may inhibit his advice to the wife he must cease to act for her.

Obtaining the solicitor's confirmation

79. . . . (1) . . . Since the bank is looking for its protection to legal advice given to the wife by a solicitor who, in this respect, is acting solely for her, I consider the bank should take steps to check *directly with the wife* the name of the solicitor she wishes to act for her. To this end, in future the bank should communicate directly with the wife, informing her that for its own protection it will require written confirmation from a solicitor, acting for her, to the effect that the solicitor has fully explained to her the nature of the documents and the practical implications they will have for her. She should be told that the purpose of this requirement is that thereafter she should not be able to dispute she is legally bound by the documents once she has signed them. She should be asked to nominate a solicitor whom she is willing to instruct to advise her, separately from her husband, and act for her in giving the necessary confirmation to the bank. She should be told that, if she wishes, the solicitor may be the same solicitor as is acting for her husband in the transaction. If a solicitor is already acting for the husband and the wife, she

should be asked whether she would prefer that a different solicitor should act for her regarding the bank's requirement for confirmation from a solicitor.

The bank should not proceed with the transaction until it has received an appropriate response directly from the wife.

(2)   Representatives of the bank are likely to have a much better picture of the husband's financial affairs than the solicitor. If the bank is not willing to undertake the task of explanation itself, the bank must provide the solicitor with the financial information he needs for this purpose. Accordingly it should become routine practice for banks, if relying on confirmation from a solicitor for their protection, to send to the solicitor the necessary financial information. What is required must depend on the facts of the case. Ordinarily this will include information on the purpose for which the proposed new facility has been requested, the current amount of the husband's indebtedness, the amount of his current overdraft facility, and the amount and terms of any new facility . . .

(3)   Exceptionally there may be a case where the bank believes or suspects that the wife has been misled by her husband or is not entering into the transaction of her own free will. If such a case occurs the bank must inform the wife's solicitors of the facts giving rise to its belief or suspicion.

. . .

A wider principle

82.   . . . In the *O'Brien* case the House was concerned with formulating a fair and practical solution to problems occurring when a creditor obtains a security from a guarantor whose sexual relationship with the debtor gives rise to a heightened risk of undue influence. But the law does not regard sexual relationships as standing in some special category of their own so far as undue influence is concerned . . . [*Burch*, Extract 21.3.3 below, is considered.]

84.   The crucially important question raised by this wider application of the *O'Brien* principle concerns the circumstances which will put a bank on inquiry. A bank is put on inquiry whenever a wife stands as surety for her husband's debts . . .

86.   But the law cannot stop at this point, with banks on inquiry only in cases where the debtor and guarantor have a sexual relationship or the relationship is one where the law presumes the existence of trust and confidence. That would be an arbitrary boundary, and the law has already moved beyond this . . .

87.   These considerations point forcibly to the conclusion that there is no rational cut-off point, with certain types of relationship being susceptible to the *O'Brien* principle and others not. Further, if a bank is not to be required to evaluate the extent to which its customer has influence over a proposed guarantor, the only practical way forward is to regard banks as 'put on inquiry' in every case where the relationship between the surety and the debtor is non-commercial . . .

89.   By the decisions of this House in *O'Brien* and the Court of Appeal in *Credit Lyonnais Bank Nederland NV* v *Burch* [1997] 1 All ER 144, English law has taken its first strides in the development of some such general principle. It is a workable principle. It is also simple, coherent and eminently desirable. I venture to think this is the way the law is moving, and should continue to move . . .

LORD HOBHOUSE: 107.   In agreement with what I understand to be the view of your Lordships, I consider that the so-called class 2(B) presumption should not be adopted. It is not a useful forensic tool. The wife or other person alleging that the relevant agreement or charge is not enforceable must prove her case . . .

108.   . . . There are arguments which would favour a higher threshold [for putting the lender on inquiry]. It would enable a more positive approach to be taken to the response. It would avoid calling for a response when the level of risk did not really justify it. But the advantage of this low

threshold is that it assists banks to put in place procedures which do not require an exercise of judgment by their officials and I accept Lord Nicholls's affirmation of the low threshold. This, however, is not to say that banks are at liberty to close their eyes to evidence of higher levels of risk or fail to respond appropriately to higher risks of which they have notice.

LORD SCOTT: 173. ... the fact that the solicitor is acting also for the bank in arranging for completion of the security does not, in my opinion, alter the answers ... The solicitor's role in acting for the bank is essentially administrative. He must see that the security document is validly executed and, if necessary, see to its registration. If there are documents of title to whose custody the bank, as chargee, is entitled, the solicitor will usually have to obtain them and hold them to the bank's order. But he has no consultative role vis-à-vis the bank. His duties to the bank do not, in my opinion, in the least prejudice his suitability to advise the wife.

174. ... If there is some particular reason known to the bank for suspecting undue influence or other impropriety by the husband, then, in my view, the bank should insist on advice being given to the wife by a solicitor independent of the husband (see Lord Browne-Wilkinson in *O'Brien*, at p 197).

Comment – general; undue influence

(1) All the Lords agreed with Lord Nicholls; Lords Hobhouse and Scott also delivered full speeches.

(2) Lord Scott expresses similar views to Lord Hobhouse regarding class 2(B) presumptions. Does Lord Nicholls agree?

(3) Is there any modern role for a requirement of manifest disadvantage?

(4) Following *Etridge*, will it be easier or more difficult to prove undue influence?

(5) If a relationship involving trust and confidence is shown, should it be a sufficient vitiating factor that the borrower fails to tell the mortgagor (his wife) that he was intending to leave her?[8]

Comment – imputing notice

(1) The House of Lords had previously noted that notice was not being used in its traditional sense.[9] Does it matter?

(2) How readily is notice imputed when the mortgagor or surety is a family member? Is it different in other contexts? Should it be?

Comment – consequences of being put on inquiry

(1) Was it appropriate to depart from the *O'Brien* requirement that the lender should advise the surety or mortgagor?

(2) Does the lender have anything to fear from the rules laid down in *Etridge*?

(3) Before *Etridge*, the fear was expressed that banks were offloading risks on to solicitors. Does the House of Lords establish an appropriate balance?

(4) Very detailed rules are laid down. What is the result if they are not followed? Suppose, for example, that the wife is fully and properly advised by her husband's solicitor and she

---

[8] *Hewett v First Plus Financial Group plc* [2010] 2 FLR 177 (stressing a duty of 'candour and fairness').
[9] *Barclays Bank plc v Boulter* [1999] 1 WLR 1919.

chose to ask that solicitor for advice. Would it be material if the lender had contacted neither wife nor solicitor?[10]

(5) Can legal advice be given by (i) the borrower's solicitor; (ii) the lender's solicitor? How can the outcome be justified?

(6) One problem is that undue influence may be so invasive that even impartial legal advice is ignored by a surety.[11] Is this danger adequately protected against? What happens if the solicitor believes that undue influence has in fact been exercised?

(7) Leaving aside the risk just mentioned, can one be confident that wives and other sureties will in fact be fully and accurately advised?

(8) Who takes the risk if inappropriate advice is given by the solicitor? Why?

The next case involves very different circumstances: a mortgage by an employee.

Extract 21.3.3

Credit Lyonnais Bank Nederland NV v Burch [1997] 1 All ER 144

The employee's mortgage covered an additional £20,000 loan to the employer. As was common in bank mortgages, it contained an all-monies clause, whereby the total indebtedness of the employer was secured.

NOURSE LJ: . . . Under the terms of the legal charge, Miss Burch was required not simply to pledge her home as security for the £20,000 extension; she was required to pledge it without limit. Worse than that, she was required to enter into a personal covenant guaranteeing not simply repayment of the additional £20,000, nor even repayment up to the new limit of £270,000; she was required to guarantee without limit repayment of all API's borrowings from the bank, present and future and of whatever kind, together with interest, commission, charges, legal and other costs, charges and expenses . . .

A case based on an unconscionable bargain not having been made below, a decision of this court cannot be rested on that ground. But the unconscionability of the transaction remains of direct materiality to the case based on undue influence. Since it was so manifestly disadvantageous to Miss Burch, the bank could not be said to have taken reasonable steps to avoid being fixed with constructive notice of Mr Pelosi's undue influence over her when neither the potential extent of her liability had been explained to her nor had she received independent advice.

As to the first of those requirements, I agree with the recorder that it was not enough for Miss Burch to be told repeatedly that the mortgage was unlimited in time and amount. She could not assess the significance of that without being told of the extent of API's current borrowings and the current limit.

MILLETT LJ: . . . It is an extreme case. The transaction was not merely to the manifest disadvantage of Miss Burch; it was one which, in the traditional phrase, 'shocks the conscience of the court'. Miss Burch committed herself to a personal liability far beyond her slender means,

---

[10] The risks are illustrated by *National Westminster Bank plc v Amin* [2002] 1 FLR 735 (solicitor not shown to be acting for the surety) and *UCB Corporate Services Ltd v Williams* [2003] 1 P&CR 168 (honest belief that the wife was advised by a solicitor provided no protection, even though there was such advice). See also *Lloyds TSB Bank v Holdgate* [2003] HLR 335.

[11] Lord Nicholls at [20]. In *Steeples v Lea* (1997) 76 P&CR 157, Millett LJ stated at p 160: 'The stronger the influence which is exerted, the greater the determination of the party influenced to do what the influencer wants; the greater the determination produced by the influence the less the ability of the party influenced to heed warnings or to take sensible advice.'

risking the loss of her home and personal bankruptcy, and obtained nothing in return beyond a relatively small and possibly temporary increase in the overdraft facility available to her employer, a company in which she had no financial interest. The transaction gives rise to grave suspicion. It cries aloud for an explanation.

. . .

In the present case the only relationship between Mr Pelosi (and his company) on the one hand and Miss Burch on the other which has been proved (and of which the bank had any knowledge) was that of employer and junior employee. That is not a relationship within class 2A. At the same time, it is clearly one which is capable of developing into a relationship of trust and confidence with the attendant risk of abuse, particularly in the case of a small business where the parties are accustomed to work closely together.

. . .

The bank submitted that in the absence of evidence that there was a sexual or emotional tie between Mr Pelosi and Miss Burch the facts were insufficient to justify the judge's finding that there was a relationship of confidence between them; and that, in the absence of evidence that the bank was aware of such a tie between Mr Pelosi and Miss Burch, the facts known to the bank were insufficient to fix it with notice of the existence of a relationship of trust and confidence between them. I do not accept this. The presence of a sexual or emotional tie would at least make the transaction explicable . . . Her livelihood and that of her family would no doubt depend on the success of the business; and a refusal to entertain her husband's importunity might put at risk the marital relationship as well as the continued prosperity of herself and her family. Similar considerations would no doubt influence a cohabitee and her adviser.

. . .

The bank submitted that it had discharged its duty to Miss Burch by urging her to obtain independent legal advice. This does not accurately reflect the legal position. The bank owed no duty to Miss Burch. If it urged Miss Burch to take independent legal advice, this was for its own protection. If it had not had cause to suspect that Miss Burch's agreement to enter into the transaction might have been improperly obtained, it would have had no need to encourage her to take legal advice. Since it did have cause to suspect it, it could not avoid the consequences unless two conditions were satisfied: (i) it must have taken reasonable steps to allay any such suspicion; and (ii) the result of the steps which it took must be such as would reasonably allay any such suspicion.

The bank urged Miss Burch to obtain independent legal advice. In a letter obviously written at the instance of Mr Pelosi and after consultation with him, she declined to do so. The bank had taken all reasonable steps open to it to allay any suspicion it might have had that Miss Burch's agreement to the transaction had been procured by the exercise of undue influence on the part of Mr Pelosi. But what followed could not reasonably have allayed any such suspicion; on the contrary, it should have confirmed it.

That is sufficient to dispose of this appeal, but I should not be taken to accept that it would necessarily have made any difference even if Miss Burch had entered into the transaction after taking independent legal advice. Such advice is neither always necessary nor always sufficient. It is not a panacea. The result does not depend mechanically on the presence or absence of legal advice. I think that there has been some misunderstanding of the role which the obtaining of independent legal advice plays in these cases.

. . . If she does [obtain independent legal advice], and enters into the transaction none-theless, the third party will usually escape the consequences of notice. This is because he is normally entitled to assume that the solicitor has discharged his duty and that the complainant has followed his advice. But he cannot make any such assumption if he knows or ought to know that it is false.

. . . [The bank] must have known that no competent solicitor could advise her to enter into a guarantee in the terms she did. He would be bound to inquire, of the bank if necessary, of the reason why it required additional security. Having discovered that it was to enable the limit of the company's overdraft to be increased from £250,000 to £270,000, he would be bound to advise Miss Burch that an unlimited guarantee was unnecessary and inappropriate for this purpose, and that, if she felt that she must accommodate Mr Pelosi's wishes, she should offer a limited guarantee with a limit of £20,000 . . .

Comment

(1) Could the mortgage be challenged as an unconscionable bargain, as Nourse LJ suggested?

(2) All-monies clauses are now inconsistent with the Code of Banking Practice, at least as regards sureties.

(3) Are the dicta about the effect of legal advice (if it had been given) consistent with *Etridge*?

Suppose a charge is voidable. What is the effect of this on a replacement charge, which is not by itself affected by undue influence (or other vitiating factor)?

Extract 21.3.4

Yorkshire Bank plc v *Tinsley* [2004] 1 WLR 2380

A wife's charge was voidable. Following marriage breakdown, the relevant property was sold and the wife acquired a new property. She was required to enter into a replacement charge in favour of the original chargee.

LONGMORE LJ: 17.   As far as I am aware, this is the first case in which this court has had to consider the enforceability of a subsequent mortgage in the circumstance of an earlier voidable mortgage. So it is sensible to consider the question as a matter of principle.

PRINCIPLE

18.   It would be natural to expect that if, without more, an obligation incurred between two or three parties is legally ineffective in any way, any new obligation arising out of the release of such earlier obligation would be legally ineffective in a similar way. It may not be easy to find authority for such a broad proposition but, in principle 'nothing will come of nothing', as King Lear observed . . .

19.   So also, in my judgment, it must be for undue influence. If a mortgage or guarantee is voidable for undue influence as against a husband and against a bank, a replacement mortgage, even if undue influence is not operative at the time of such replacement, will itself be voidable, at any rate if the replacement mortgage is taken out as a condition of discharging an earlier voidable mortgage. This should be the case even if there is a new contract rather than a mere variation of an old contract.

21.   Of course, if a replacement or substitute mortgage is made with a different lender, that different lender cannot be deemed to be aware of matters of which the first lender is deemed to be aware. But if the lender is the same there is no reason why the constructive notice should invariably be deemed to have disappeared when the earlier mortgage is discharged. Mr Hall Taylor's submission that on a remortgage the charge should only be voidable if the bank is actually (rather than constructively) aware of the undue influence has no support in the jurisprudence, and such voidability would seldom arise in practice on the facts.

PETER GIBSON LJ: 35.   I would be reluctant to reach a decision which would cause significant practical difficulties for lenders in property transactions, but I am not persuaded that we are doing any such thing in allowing this appeal. It is rightly not suggested that a lender should be put on inquiry about previous transactions to which the lender is not a party. But if the same lender was the mortgagee in the prior voidable mortgage and requires the discharge of the prior mortgage and the grant to it of a new mortgage, I can see no sufficient objection to holding the new mortgage taken in substitution for the earlier mortgage also to be voidable. The lender should know from its own records whether or not it protected itself in the earlier mortgage transaction.

Comment

When will a replacement charge be free of the original vitiating factor?

A quite separate point concerns the likely outcome in these cases. The property is usually jointly owned with the debtor. Can the debtor be sued and be made bankrupt?

Extract 21.3.5

Alliance and Leicester plc v *Slayford* (2000) 33 HLR 743

PETER GIBSON LJ: 20. . . . As every textbook on real property or mortgages makes clear, a mortgagee has a number of remedies all designed to enforce payment of what is due to him under the mortgage, which may be pursued concurrently as soon as the mortgagor is in default or successively, until payment in full is recovered or the mortgagee acts in a way which amounts to an election . . . I would add that it would not help mortgagors, mortgagees or the courts if mortgagors had to claim and pursue to judgment all its possible claims at one and the same time. Mortgagees usually only go for possession initially and pursue other remedies later if they have to, and that practice is entirely sensible and to the advantage of all concerned.

22.   The judge thought it plain that the pursuit by the Bank of a money claim with a view to bankrupting Mr Slayford was an impermissible attempt to achieve by the back door what could not be achieved by the front door and flouted the possession order. Mr Marsden sought to uphold the judge on this . . .

23.   Mr Marsden accepts that this is not a case where an unsuccessful party is making a collateral attack on an earlier decision. Nor is it a case where a mortgagee has misled the mortgagor about further proceedings. When he was asked whether there were any authorities which supported his submissions, Mr Marsden was unable to show us any. Unfortunately the judge was not shown authorities which point in a different direction. In *Zandfarid* v *BCCI* [1996] 1 WLR 1420 a mortgagee bank sought to obtain possession of the matrimonial home of the mortgagors. The mortgagor wife raised a defence on the basis of *Barclays Bank* v *O'Brien* [1994] 1 AC 180 and, on an application under RSC Ord. 88 by the mortgagee, possession was refused. The mortgagee served statutory demands on the mortgagors and when they were not met, it petitioned for the bankruptcy of the mortgagors, giving up its security. The mortgagors claimed that the mortgagee, in commencing bankruptcy proceedings, was seeking to circumvent the wife's equity. They argued that it should not be allowed to obtain an order for sale by the back door and called the bankruptcy petition an abuse of process as being issued for an indirect purpose, the enforcement of the security by an order for sale of the matrimonial home.

25.   . . . Millett LJ, with whom Rose LJ agreed, describes the wife's claim as completely unarguable. He pointed out that success by the wife on her defence to the possession proceedings would still leave the mortgagee a secured creditor of the husband with a valid and enforceable charge over his interest in the matrimonial home, though it would have no claim against the wife or her interest. He said that the mortgagor [should read 'mortgagee'] would have three possible courses of action open to it. The first was that it could apply to the court for an order for possession and sale under section 30 [Law of Property Act 1925; now Trusts of Land and Appointment of Trustees Act 1996, s 14], making the wife a party so that she might raise whatever defence she might choose. Second, as a judgment creditor of the husband it could

apply for a charging order. Third it could do what it did, giving up its security and bringing bankruptcy proceedings against the husband. He said that the wife was not prejudiced: 'If she is evicted as a result of the bank's application under section 30 . . . she will be evicted . . . because, unhappily, she is married to a judgment debtor who cannot satisfy the judgment debt except out of the proceeds of sale of his interest in the property.'

28. I do not intend to take up time with the citation of further authority, as the position in law seems to me to be abundantly clear: there is no abuse of process in a mortgagee, who has been met with a successful *O'Brien* type defence taken by the wife of the mortgagor, merely choosing to pursue his remedies against the mortgagor by suing on the personal covenant with a view as an unsecured creditor to bankrupting him, even though this may lead to an application by the trustee in bankruptcy for the sale of the property in which the wife has an equitable interest.

Comment

(1) What will the likely outcome be as regards the surety (the wife in *Slayford*)?

(2) This is in the context of an *O'Brien* claim. Might bankruptcy be attractive to secured lenders in other contexts?

4. The relationship created by the mortgage

A. Rules protecting the mortgagor

(i) The right to redeem

The right to redeem (to free the land from the mortgage by paying off the loan) is crucial to every mortgage. Equity will imply it if the agreement is silent as to redemption, as in *Grangeside*.[12] Nearly all mortgages provide for a time at which there is a contractual right to redeem: this is the legal right to redeem, traditionally set at six months. After this time, the equitable right to redeem kicks in, so that redemption is not limited by the contractual provisions. In modern mortgages, it is more usual to provide the real time at which repayment is intended, with the result that redemption is likely to operate under the contract rather than the equitable right to redeem.

Problems may arise where the contract postpones redemption for many years.

Extract 21.4.1

Knightsbridge Estates Trust Ltd v *Byrne* [1939] Ch 441

Redemption was postponed for 40 years.

SIR WILFRID GREENE MR: . . . It was not contended that a provision in a mortgage deed making the mortgage irredeemable for a period of years is necessarily void. The argument was that such a period must be a 'reasonable' one, and it was said that the period in the present case was an unreasonable one by reason merely of its length. This argument was not the one accepted by the learned judge.

Now an argument such as this requires the closest scrutiny, for, if it is correct, it means that an agreement made between two competent parties, acting under expert advice and presumably knowing their own business best, is one which the law forbids them to make upon the ground that it is not 'reasonable' . . . A decision to that effect would, in our view, involve an unjustified interference with the freedom of business men to enter into agreements best suited

[12] Extract 21.2.1 above.

to their interests and would impose upon them a test of 'reasonableness' laid down by the Courts without reference to the business realities of the case.

... the respondents were, when the negotiations began, desirous of obtaining for themselves two advantages: (1) a reduction in the rate of interest, (2) the right to repay the mortgage moneys by instalments spread over a long period of years ... The sum involved was a very large one, and the length of the period over which the instalments were spread is to be considered with reference to this fact ... The resulting agreement was a commercial agreement between two important corporations experienced in such matters, and has none of the features of an oppressive bargain where the borrower is at the mercy of an unscrupulous lender ...

But in our opinion the proposition that a postponement of the contractual right of redemption is only permissible for a 'reasonable' time is not well-founded. Such a postponement is not properly described as a clog on the equity of redemption, since it is concerned with the contractual right to redeem. It is indisputable that any provision which hampers redemption after the contractual date for redemption has passed will not be permitted. Further, it is undoubtedly true to say that a right of redemption is a necessary element in a mortgage transaction, and consequently that, where the contractual right of redemption is illusory, equity will grant relief by allowing redemption. This was the point in the case of *Fairclough* v *Swan Brewery Co*[i] ...

Moreover, equity may give relief against contractual terms in a mortgage transaction if they are oppressive or unconscionable, and in deciding whether or not a particular transaction falls within this category the length of time for which the contractual right to redeem is postponed may well be an important consideration. In the present case no question of this kind was or could have been raised.

But equity does not reform mortgage transactions because they are unreasonable. It is concerned to see two things – one that the essential requirements of a mortgage transaction are observed, and the other that oppressive or unconscionable terms are not enforced. Subject to this, it does not, in our opinion, interfere.

[i] [1912] AC 565.

Comment

(1) The decision was upheld in the House of Lords on other grounds: [1940] AC 613.

(2) Is it a matter of concern that the mortgagor cannot redeem for 40 years?

Extract 21.4.2

Fairclough v *Swan Brewery Co Ltd* [1912] AC 565

A mortgage of a 20-year lease could not be redeemed until six weeks before its termination.

PRIVY COUNCIL: Is there any difference between forbidding redemption and permitting it, if the permission be a mere pretence? Here the provision for redemption is nugatory. The incumbrance on the lease the subject of the mortgage according to the letter of the bargain falls to be discharged before the lease terminates, but at a time when it is on the very point of expiring, when redemption can be of no advantage to the mortgagor even if he should be so fortunate as to get his deeds back before the actual termination of the lease. For all practical purposes this mortgage is irredeemable. It was obviously meant to be irredeemable.

Comment

(1) Given that the mortgagor invariably retains occupation, why should the law bother if redemption is postponed in this way?

(2) The effect of the decision may be to penalise borrowers by restricting the use of such leases as security for medium-term mortgages. Why?

(ii) Clogs and fetters on the right to redeem

Much trouble has been caused by terms which in some way impede the right of the mortgagor to redeem the property free of the provisions of the mortgage. One blatant example
is a mortgagee's option to purchase the property.

Extract 21.4.3

Samuel v Jarrah Timber & Wood Paving Corporation Ltd **[1904] AC 323**

LORD MACNAGHTEN: . . . In the Court of Appeal the question was treated as governed by the
principle, of which *Noakes v Rice*[i] is a recent example, that on redemption the mortgagor is
entitled to have the thing mortgaged restored to him unaffected by any condition or stipulation
which formed part of the mortgage transaction.

That principle, I think, is perfectly sound. But, in my opinion, the question here depends
rather upon the rule that a mortgagee is not allowed at the time of the loan to enter into a contract for the purchase of the mortgaged property.

This latter rule, I think, is founded on sentiment rather than on principle. It seems to have had
its origin in the desire of the Court of Chancery to protect embarrassed landowners from imposition and oppression. And it was invented, I should suppose, in order to obviate the necessity of
inquiry and investigation in cases where suspicion may be probable and proof difficult . . .

Speaking for myself, I should not be sorry if your Lordships could see your way to modify it
so as to prevent its being used as a means of evading a fair bargain come to between persons
dealing at arms' length and negotiating on equal terms. The directors of a trading company in
search of financial assistance are certainly in a very different position from that of an impecunious landowner in the toils of a crafty money-lender. At the same time I quite feel the difficulty
of interfering with any rule that has prevailed so long, and I am not prepared to differ from the
conclusion at which the Court of Appeal has arrived.

[i] [1902] AC 24.

Comment

Given what Lord Macnaghten says, is the rule anything more than an unfortunate and
anachronistic relic of the past?

Extract 21.4.4

Lewis v Frank Love Ltd **[1961] 1 WLR 261**

An option was contained in a separate but contemporaneous document.

PLOWMAN J: . . . It was argued by Mr Settle for the defendants that the doctrine of clog on
the equity does not apply where the clog was not imposed as part of the original mortgage
transaction . . .

A number of cases on the principles which apply to questions of clogging the equity were
cited, and the first to which I should refer is *Reeve v Lisle*.[i] I refer to this case because, to my
mind, it establishes, first of all, that what has to be looked at in the case of a mortgage transaction is the substance of the matter and not the form in which the bargain is carried out. Lord
Halsbury LC said:[ii] 'The view of the Court of Appeal, who had all the facts before them (and
I do not propose to question the view which they have taken of these documents read together),
is this, that the later transaction was entirely separate . . .'

Lord Halsbury is there stating that it is not enough merely to look at the documents
themselves for the purpose of discovering what the true transaction is, but that the object and
purpose with which the documents were entered into must be inquired into. Applying that to

the present case, it seems to me that the object and purpose with which these documents were entered into was as part of a bargain whereby the plaintiff was to get a loan of £6,500, and the defendants were to get an option to purchase part of his property.

. . . it seems to me clear that one of the terms on which the defendants were prepared to advance the sum of £6,500 was that they should obtain an option to purchase part of the plaintiff's land. If that is so, it follows from what Lord Lindley was there saying [in *Samuel*] that the doctrine of clogging the equity applies to that transaction; and if the doctrine of clogging the equity does apply, it is, I should have thought, beyond argument that the option to purchase was in fact a clog on the equity because, of course, if it is exercised it will prevent the plaintiff from getting back the piece of land to which it applies.

[i] [1902] AC 461; 18 TLR 767, HL.
[ii] [1902] AC 461, 463.

Comment

(1) When will an option in a separate document be valid? Should it be relevant that loans can often be called in by the lender at any time?

(2) *Lewis* was approved by the Court of Appeal in *Jones* v *Morgan*, though Lord Phillips MR observed that 'the doctrine of a clog on the equity of redemption is, so it seems to me, an appendix to our law which no longer serves a useful purpose and would be better excised'.[13] Can anything be said in its favour?

(3) The option rules are heavily qualified by the application of the principles in *Kreglinger* v *New Patagonia Meat and Cold Storage Co Ltd* [1914] AC 25 (Extract 21.4.9 below). This will be considered after *Kreglinger*.

Most clogs and fetters relate not to the ability to redeem, but to the state of the mortgaged property after redemption.

Extract 21.4.5

Biggs v *Hoddinott* [1898] 2 Ch 307

CHITTY LJ: The mortgage here is a mortgage of a public-house for a time certain by publicans to a brewer, effected in the usual way, and it contains a covenant by the mortgagors during the continuance of the security to take all their beer from the mortgagee, and a covenant by the mortgagee to supply it. It is contended that the covenant by the mortgagors is void in equity. The first objection I have to make is that it in no way affects the equity of redemption, for it is not stipulated that damages for breach of the covenant shall be covered by the security, and redemption takes place quite independently of the covenant; so this is not a case where the right to redeem is affected . . . It has been contended that the principle is established by the authorities that a mortgagee shall not stipulate for any collateral advantage to himself. I think the cases only establish that the mortgagee shall not impose on the mortgagor an unconscionable or oppressive bargain.

Comment

This firmly establishes that collateral benefits (i.e. in addition to interest) are enforceable while the mortgage continues.

[13] [2002] 1 EGLR 125 at [86].

Extract 21.4.6

Santley v *Wilde* **[1899] 2 Ch 474**

A lease for ten years of a theatre was mortgaged. Given the weakness of such a security, the parties agreed on a loan for five years, with the mortgagee entitled to a third of the profits of underleases for the full ten years.

LINDLEY MR: . . . Any provision inserted to prevent redemption on payment or performance of the debt or obligation for which the security was given is what is meant by a clog or fetter on the equity of redemption and is therefore void . . . The Courts of Equity have fought for years to maintain the doctrine that a security is redeemable. But when and under what circumstances? On the performance of the obligation for which it was given. If the obligation is the payment of a debt, the security is redeemable on the payment of that debt. That, in my opinion, is the true principle applicable to the cases, and that is what is meant when it is said there must not be any clog or fetter on the equity of redemption. If so, this mortgage has no clog or fetter at all . . .

. . .

That means that this lease is granted or assigned by the mortgagor to the mortgagee as security not only for the payment of the 2000*l* and interest, but also for the payment of the one-third of the net profit rents to the end of the term. If I am right in the principle which I have laid down, that does not clog the right of redemption upon the performance of the obligation for which the security was given. That is the nature of the transaction, and the good sense of it.

Comment

As will be seen from the following cases, the relatively liberal views of Lindley MR proved the catalyst for controversy.

Extract 21.4.7

Noakes & Co Ltd v *Rice* **[1902] AC 24**

The mortgage contained a solus tie similar to that in *Biggs*, save that it did not cease on redemption.

LORD DAVEY: The third doctrine . . . might be expressed in this form: Once a mortgage always a mortgage and nothing but a mortgage. The meaning of that is that the mortgagee shall not make any stipulation which will prevent a mortgagor, who has paid principal, interest, and costs, from getting back his mortgaged property in the condition in which he parted with it . . . When the mortgage is paid off the security is at an end, and, as the mortgagee is no longer kept out of his money, the remuneration to him for the use of his money is also at an end. I confess I should have decided the case of *Santley* v *Wilde*[i] differently from the way in which it was dealt with in the Court of Appeal. After the payment of principal and interest, and everything which had become payable up to the date of redemption, the property in that case remained charged with the payment to the mortgagee of one-third share of the profits, and the stipulation to that effect should, I think, have been held to be a clog or fetter on the right to redeem. The principle is this – that a mortgage must not be converted into something else; and when once you come to the conclusion that a stipulation for the benefit of the mortgagee is part of the mortgage transaction, it is but part of his security, and necessarily comes to an end on the payment off of the loan.

[i] [1899] 2 Ch 474.

Comment

(1) Is *Santley* inconsistent with principle?

(2) If the House of Lords had not adopted this approach, would this have left mortgagors significantly unprotected?

(3) Is it unthinkable that interest should be payable after redemption? What if no interest is payable for the first two years of the mortgage but instead for two years after redemption?

Extract 21.4.8

Bradley v *Carritt* [1903] AC 253

A mortgage of tea shares required the mortgagor to use his best endeavours to ensure the employment (before and after redemption) of the mortgagee as tea broker to the company.

LORD MACNAGHTEN: . . . That stipulation [in *Santley*] was, as it seems to me, unquestionably part of the mortgage transaction . . . That seems to me to be a very far-reaching decision. It reduces the rule that a mortgage cannot be made irredeemable to a dead letter. You have only to tack on some stipulation, such as men of business might well agree to if there were no mortgage, and the thing is done . . .

But it may be said . . . that, putting aside the case of *Santley* v *Wilde*,[i] there is no case to be found in the books from the earliest times to the present day in which a mortgagee after redemption ever attempted to keep on foot the benefit of any collateral stipulation which was part and parcel of the mortgage transaction . . .

My Lords, it seems to me to be playing with words to say that on redemption these shares came back to Mr Bradley no worse than they were when he mortgaged them. If I part with property owing to a temporary necessity and the property is returned to me afterwards, do I get it back just as it was when it comes enveloped in an atmosphere of danger which was not present when I parted with it? Is it none the worse? Is its usefulness to me unimpaired if it now requires delicate handling and cautious treatment to prevent its becoming a source of mischief to its owner? Mr Bradley could not have safely sold or mortgaged any of these shares when he got them back. True, their value to a purchaser or a mortgagee would be just the same . . . My Lords, I do not think it is necessary that there should be any hold upon the property, direct or indirect. I think, as I ventured to say in *Noakes* v *Rice*,[ii] that equity will not permit any device or contrivance designed or calculated to prevent or impede redemption.

LORD LINDLEY (dissenting): . . . Clause 4 in no way fetters the right to redeem, nor obstructs the mortgagor in the practical exercise of that right, or of the use or enjoyment of his shares when he gets them back. He can then do what he likes with them, free from all control by the mortgagee. How it can be said that clause 4 clogs the equity of redemption or infringes the rule, once a mortgage always a mortgage, passes my comprehension . . .

I cannot bring myself to believe that it is part of the law of this country that mortgagors and mortgagees cannot make what bargains they like with each other so long as such bargains are not inconsistent with the right of the mortgagor to redeem the property mortgaged by discharging the debt or obligation to secure which the mortgage was effected.

[i] [1899] 2 Ch 474.
[ii] [1902] AC 24.

Comment

(1) The majority was 3:2.

(2) What is the point of disagreement? Whose analysis is the more convincing?

(3) How would Lord Lindley explain the result in *Noakes*?

(4) Should it be possible to argue that the promise affects the mortgagor personally rather than the land?

Extract 21.4.9

Kreglinger v New Patagonia Meat and Cold Storage Co Ltd
[1914] AC 25

A right of pre-emption over mortgaged skins was challenged.

VISCOUNT HALDANE LC: . . . What is vital in the appeal now under consideration is to classify accurately the transaction between the parties. What we have to do is to ascertain from scrutiny of the circumstances whether there has really been an attempt to effect a mortgage with a provision preventing redemption of what was pledged merely as security for payment of the amount of the debt and any charges besides that may legitimately be added . . . We are considering the simple question of what is the effect on the right to redeem of having inserted into the formal instrument signed when the money was borrowed an ordinary commercial contract for the sale of skins extending over a period. It appears that it was the intention of the parties that the grant of the security should not affect the power to enter into such a contract, either with strangers or with the appellants, and if so I am unable to see how the equity of redemption is affected. No doubt it is the fact that on redemption the respondents will not get back their business as free from obligation as it was before the date of the security. But that may well be because outside the security and consistently with its terms there was a contemporaneous but collateral contract, contained in the same document as constituted the security, but in substance independent of it. If it was the intention of the parties, as I think it was, to enter into this contract as a condition of the respondents getting their advance, I know no reason either in morals or in equity which ought to prevent this intention from being left to have its effect . . . In *Noakes & Co v Rice*[i] . . . the House held that . . . a covenant by the mortgagor to buy the beer of the mortgagee after redemption of the public-house mortgaged was really a term of the mortgage and was inoperative as being, not merely a collateral agreement, but in truth a restriction on the right to get back the security free from the terms of the mortgage. That was the case of the mortgage of a specific property. The decision that the transaction was what it was held to be is at all events readily intelligible . . . The decision [in *Bradley*] was a striking one. It was not unanimous, for Lord Lindley dissented from the conclusions of Lord Macnaghten and Lord Davey. It is binding on your Lordships in any case in which the transaction is really of the same kind, although it does not follow that all the dicta in the judgments of those of your Lordships' House who were in a majority must be taken as of binding authority. And it certainly cannot, in my opinion, be taken as authoritatively laying down that the mere circumstance that after redemption the property redeemed may not, as the result of some bargain made at the time of the mortgage, be in the same condition as it was before that time, is conclusive against the validity of that bargain. To render it invalid the bargain must, when its substance is examined, turn out to have formed part of the terms of the mortgage and to have really cut down a true right of redemption. I think that the tendency of recent decisions has been to lay undue stress on the letter of the principle which limits the jurisdiction of equity in setting aside contracts. The origin and reason of the principle ought, as I have already said, to be kept steadily in view in applying it to fresh cases. There appears to me to have grown up a tendency to look to the letter rather than to the spirit of the doctrine. The true view is, I think, that judges ought in this kind of jurisdiction to proceed cautiously, and to bear in mind the real reasons which have led Courts of Equity to insist on the free right to redeem and the limits within which the purpose of the rule ought to confine its scope . . .

Speaking for myself, and notwithstanding the high authority of Lord Davey, I think that the tendency of Lord Lindley's conclusion is the one which is most consonant with principle, and I see no valid reason why this House should not act in accordance with it in the case now under consideration.

[i] [1902] AC 24.

Comment

(1) The triumph of Lord Lindley's approach is apparent. How is it reconciled with the earlier decisions?

(2) The essence of the analysis appears to be that of a collateral contract. Does this fit contractual notions of collateral contracts? Is it anything more than a legal fig leaf hiding a change in legal analysis?

(3) Apart from options, there has been very little subsequent litigation on clogs and fetters. What conclusions might be drawn from this?

Lord Parker employed an analysis which asked whether the right should be seen as repugnant to the right to redeem. Glanville Williams[14] criticised this, saying that:

'though in some respects progressive, [it] did not rid equity of the obscurantist approach involved in the doctrine of repugnancy . . . Lord Parker considered it possible to imply a term contrary to the express terms, and then to hold the express terms void for repugnancy to the term so implied . . . There is no logical contradiction between (a) an option to purchase and (b) a proviso for redemption if the option be not exercised.'

If this criticism is valid, is there any other way of explaining the strict rules regarding options?

Extract 21.4.10

Warnborough Ltd v *Garmite Ltd* [2003] EWCA Civ 1544

Warnborough sold land to Garmite, leaving the purchase money on mortgage. At the same time, Garmite gave Warnborough an option to repurchase the land for the original sale price. Warnborough was accordingly the mortgagee and the grantee of the option.

JONATHAN PARKER LJ: 1. The issue on this appeal is whether an option to purchase real property is unenforceable on the ground that it is, in the archaic – and arcane – language of the old courts of Chancery, 'a clog on the equity of redemption' of the grantor of the option in circumstances where, at the same time as the grant of the option, the grantee sold the property to the grantor leaving the purchase price outstanding as a loan secured on the property. For present purposes, the expression 'clog on the equity of redemption' means an objectionable restriction on the rights of a borrower who has mortgaged his property as security for the debt.
33. [Counsel for Garmite] submits that the facts of the instant case are to be distinguished from the facts in *Kreglinger*, where a right of pre-emption granted to a mortgagee to purchase the mortgagor's products at market value was held not to constitute a 'clog'. He points out that in the instant case the price of £130,000 payable under the First Option represents . . . approximately one third of the current market value of the Property.
34. Mr Galway-Cooper also referred us to Law Commission Report 204 (Transfer of Land – Land Mortgages), published in November 1991, and to Law Commission Working Paper 99 (Land Mortgages), published in 1986, which refer to the 'clogs' rule and make recommendations designed to clarify and rationalise the law in that area. He relies in particular on the description of the 'clogs' rule in the Working Paper (paragraph 3.33) as 'inflexible'.
37. Mr Paul Teverson (for Warnborough), in his written skeleton argument, accepts that a mortgagee cannot, as a term of the mortgage, stipulate for an option to purchase the mortgaged property. However, he submits that so far as the First Option is concerned it was a term of the bargain between Warnborough as vendor and Garmite as purchaser that the entire

---

[14] (1944) 60 LQR 190 at p 191.

purchase price should be left outstanding secured on the Property, and that Warnborough should have an option to repurchase the Property if certain specified conditions were met. He submits that it is of the greatest significance that Warnborough was selling its own property, and that the deputy judge appears to have attached no weight to this factor.

38. He submits, relying on *Kreglinger*, that the correct characterisation of the transaction is critical; and that, in the words of Lord Haldane LC in that case . . . , the transaction in the instant case cannot be characterised as 'one of mortgage simply'.

The relevant authorities

42. As long ago as the beginning of the last century [*Samuel v Jarrah*; Extract 21.4.3 above], the origins and rationale of the principle that an option to purchase mortgaged property granted at the same time as the mortgage constitutes a 'clog' on the borrower's equity of redemption and is accordingly unenforceable were already regarded by the House of Lords as obscure.

50. The following comments can, I think, fairly be made on the above extracts from the judgments of their Lordships in *Samuel v Jarrah*. In the first place, none of their Lordships expressed any enthusiasm for the rule, at least in its application to an option to purchase entered into contemporaneously with a mortgage; and Lords Halsbury and Macnaghten viewed it with positive distaste, in so far as it operated to strike down a fair commercial bargain freely negotiated on equal terms between parties who knew what they were doing. Secondly, both Lord Macnaghten and Lord Lindley regarded the relevant question as being whether or not the option fell to be characterised as a term of the loan: i.e. in the words of Lord Lindley, 'What is the true nature of [the] agreement?' Thirdly, both their Lordships treated that question as primarily one of fact.

69. [After quoting extensively from *Kreglinger*] Thus, in *Kreglinger* their Lordships adopted the same approach as that of Lords Macnaghten and Lindley in *Samuel v Jarrah* in addressing the question whether the relevant transaction was in substance one of mortgage, and in answering that question by reference to the parties' intentions as gathered from all the circumstances.

Conclusions

72. In the light of the authorities to which I have referred, it has to be accepted that the 'unruly dog' is still alive (although one might perhaps reasonably expect its venerable age to inhibit it from straying too far or too often from its kennel); and that however desirable an appendectomy might be thought to be, no such relieving operation has as yet been carried out. Indeed, Mr Teverson did not seek to contend otherwise.

73. That said, it is in my judgment glaringly clear from the authorities that the mere fact that, contemporaneously with the grant of a mortgage over his property, the mortgagor grants the mortgagee an option to purchase the property does no more than raise the question whether the rule against 'clogs' applies: it does not begin to answer that question. As has been said over and over again in the authorities, in order to answer that question the court has to look at the 'substance' of the transaction in question: in other words, to inquire as to the true nature of the bargain which the parties have made. To do that, the court examines all the circumstances, with the assistance of oral evidence if necessary.

76. Although it would clearly not be appropriate to attempt to lay down any absolute rule, it does seem to me that where the option to purchase which is sought to be challenged as a 'clog' is granted against the background of a sale of the property by the grantee of the option, as owner of the property, to the grantor for a price which is to be left outstanding on mortgage, there must be a very strong likelihood that, on an examination of all the circumstances, the court will conclude, as it did in *Davies v Chamberlain*, that the substance of the transaction is one of sale and purchase and not one of mortgage. At all events, if one is limited to a consideration of only the bare transaction documents (as we have been) that seems to me to be the provisional

conclusion to which they point. On the face of the transaction documents (and leaving aside any other factor) to describe the sale as 'incidental' to the loan seems to me, with respect to Mr Galway-Cooper, to turn the transaction completely on its head.

83. I would therefore allow Warnborough's appeal . . .

Comment

(1) The analysis was confirmed in a subsequent hearing in the same case.[15]

(2) *Warnborough* needs to be considered together with the cases on options discussed above (Extracts 21.4.3–21.4.4). Could the result be justified by the principles established in those cases?

(3) Is it still appropriate to regard options as representing a special category?

(4) It is easy to see that the option in *Warnborough* is more accurately viewed as part of the sale arrangement rather than as part of the mortgage. If that is required for the collateral contract analysis in *Kreglinger* to operate, then this might well limit the scope of *Kreglinger*. Would this be a fair reading of *Warnborough*?

(iii) Restraint of trade

Solus ties, as found in *Biggs* and *Noakes*, may give rise to questions of public policy, though the details of restraint of trade lie outside the scope of this book.

Extract 21.4.11

Esso Petroleum Co Ltd v *Harper's Garage (Stourport) Ltd* [1968] AC 269

LORD REID: . . . It is true that it would be an innovation to hold that ordinary negative covenants preventing the use of a particular site for trading of all kinds or of a particular kind are within the scope of the doctrine of restraint of trade. I do not think they are. Restraint of trade appears to me to imply that a man contracts to give up some freedom which otherwise he would have had. A person buying or leasing land had no previous right to be there at all, let alone to trade there, and when he takes possession of that land subject to a negative restrictive covenant he gives up no right or freedom which he previously had. I think that the 'tied house' cases might be explained in this way . . .

LORD WILBERFORCE: . . . These authorities then establish, and to that extent I have no desire to question them, that as part of a transaction of mortgage, it is permissible, so far as the rules of equity are concerned, both to postpone the date of repayment and, at any rate during the period of the loan, to tie the mortgagor to purchase exclusively the products of the mortgagee. Such an arrangement would fall fairly within the principle I have earlier suggested, as coming within a recognised and accepted category of transactions, in precisely the same manner as a lease. But just as provisions contained in a lease, affecting the lessees' (or lessors') liberty of trade, which pass beyond what is normally found in and ancillary to this type of transaction and enter upon the field of regulation of the parties' trading activities, may fall to be tested as possible restraints of trade, so, in my opinion, may those in a mortgage. The mere designation of a transaction as a mortgage, however true, does not ipso facto protect the entire contents of the arrangements from examination, however fettering of trade these arrangements may be. If their purpose and nature is found not to be ancillary to the lending of money upon security, as, for example, to make the lending more profitable or safer, but some quite independent

---

[15] [2007] 1 P&CR 34.

purpose, they may and should be independently scrutinised. This scrutiny is called for in the present case: for it is clear, upon consideration of the mortgage both taken by itself and in its relation to the solus agreement which shortly preceded it, that so far from the tie being ancillary to a predominant transaction of lending money, the mortgage, as was the solus agreement, was entered into as part of a plan, designed by Esso, to tie the Corner Garage to its products for as long as possible.

Comment

(1) The postponement of redemption, as well as the tie, was struck down. It appears that ties for up to five years will be held reasonable and therefore valid.

(2) When, if at all, will a longer tie in a mortgage be enforceable?

(3) The decision is also important for solus ties in leasehold and freehold covenants.

(iv) Unfair terms

As seen in many of the above cases, unfair and unconscionable terms are liable to be struck down, though *Knightsbridge*[16] emphasised that mere unreasonableness is insufficient.

Extract 21.4.12

Multiservice Bookbinding Ltd v *Marden* [1979] Ch 84

A mortgage tied the capital and interest to the value of the Swiss franc. Devaluation of the pound resulted in repayment of £63,000 being required to discharge a £36,000 loan, even after capital repayments of £24,000.

BROWNE-WILKINSON J: . . . I turn then to the question whether the mortgage is unconscionable or unreasonable. The plaintiffs' starting point on this aspect of the case is a submission that a lender on mortgage is only entitled to repayment of principal, interest and costs. If the lender additionally stipulates for a premium or other collateral advantage the court will not enforce such additional stipulation unless it is reasonable. Then it is submitted that clause 6, providing for the payment of the Swiss franc uplift in addition to the nominal amount of capital and interest, is a premium which in all the circumstances is unreasonable. Alternatively it is said that the terms of the mortgage taken together are unreasonable. In my judgment the argument so advanced is based on a false premise. Since the repeal of the usury laws there has been no general principle that collateral advantages in mortgages have to be 'reasonable' . . .

I have dealt with these authorities at some length because the sheet anchor of Mr Nugee's argument, that mere unreasonableness is sufficient to invalidate a stipulation, is the use of the word 'unreasonable' by Goff J in *Cityland and Property (Holdings) Ltd* v *Dabrah* [1968] Ch 166. In that case the plaintiff company was the freehold owner of a house of which the defendant had been the tenant for 11 years. His lease expired and the plaintiff company sold the freehold to him for £3,500, of which the defendant paid £600 in cash and the balance of £2,900 was left by the plaintiff company on mortgage. The mortgage was in unusual terms in that it contained simply a covenant to pay, by instalments, the sum of £4,553, that is to say, a premium of 57% over the sum advanced. No explanation was given as to what this premium represented. The defendant defaulted in paying his instalments after only one year, and the plaintiff was seeking to enforce his security for the full sum of £4,553 less payments actually made. Not surprisingly Goff J refused to permit this on the grounds that the excess over £2,900 was an unlawful premium. Bearing in mind the relative strength of lender and borrower, the size of

---

[16] See Extract 21.4.1 above.

the premium and the lack of any explanation or justification for it, the premium in that case was unconscionable and oppressive. The difficulty arises from a passage in the judgment [employing an 'unreasonable' test] . . . There are other passages in the judgment where Goff J seems to treat the words 'unreasonable' and 'unconscionable' as being interchangeable. But in that case it was unnecessary for him to distinguish between the two concepts, since on either test the premium was unenforceable. I do not think that Goff J intended to cut down the obvious effect of the *Kreglinger* case [1914] AC 25 in any way. Moreover, the decision of the Court of Appeal in *Knightsbridge Estates Trust Ltd v Byrne* [1939] Ch 441 was not cited to him.

I therefore approach the second point on the basis that, in order to be freed from the necessity to comply with all the terms of the mortgage, the plaintiffs must show that the bargain, or some of its terms, was unfair and unconscionable: it is not enough to show that, in the eyes of the court, it was unreasonable. In my judgment a bargain cannot be unfair and unconscionable unless one of the parties to it has imposed the objectionable terms in a morally reprehensible manner, that is to say, in a way which affects his conscience.

The classic example of an unconscionable bargain is where advantage has been taken of a young, inexperienced or ignorant person to introduce a term which no sensible well-advised person or party would have accepted. But I do not think the categories of unconscionable bargains are limited: the court can and should intervene where a bargain has been procured by unfair means.

. . . considering the mortgage bargain as a whole, in my judgment there was no great inequality of bargaining power as between the plaintiffs and the defendant. The plaintiff company was a small but prosperous company in need of cash to enable it to expand . . . The defendant is not a professional moneylender and there is no evidence of any sharp practice of any kind by him. The borrowers were represented by independent solicitors of repute. Therefore the background does not give rise to any pre-supposition that the defendant took an unfair advantage of the plaintiffs.

. . . if it were relevant I would be of the view that the terms were unreasonable judged by the standards which the court would adopt if it had to settle the terms of a mortgage. In particular I consider that it was unreasonable both for the debt to be inflation proofed by reference to the Swiss franc and at the same time to provide for a rate of interest 2% above bank rate – a rate which reflects at least in part the unstable state of the pound sterling. On top of this interest on the whole sum advanced was to be paid throughout the term. The defendant made a hard bargain. But the test is not reasonableness.

Comment

(1) What were the crucial differences between *Cityland* and *Multiservice*?

(2) Does equity normally interfere in contracts in this manner? Could it be argued either that today there is no justification for any special tenderness towards mortgagors, or (at the opposite extreme) that the test ought to be one of reasonableness?

(3) Is there any likelihood of challenges to variable interest rates being successful?[17]

If the mortgagor is legally advised, then it will be difficult to challenge the transaction:[18]

But it is for a solicitor to advise the naïve, the trusting or the unbusinesslike in their dealings with the more astute. In such a case the client relies on the solicitor to protect his interests; and, if the solicitor is competent and fulfils his role, the imbalance which would otherwise exist by reason of

[17] See *Paragon Finance plc v Nash* [2002] 1 WLR 685 on implied terms as to reasonableness; also *Paragon Finance plc v Pender* [2005] 1 WLR 3412 at [119]–[120].

[18] Chadwick LJ in *Jones v Morgan* [2002] 1 EGLR 125 at [40].

the client's naïveté, trust and lack of business experience is redressed. The parties meet on equal terms, at least in that respect.

Alongside equity, two statutory controls may be noted.

Extract 21.4.13

Consumer Credit Act 1974, ss 140A, 140C

140A.—(1)   The court may make an order under section 140B in connection with a credit agreement if it determines that the relationship between the creditor and the debtor arising out of the agreement (or the agreement taken with any related agreement) is unfair to the debtor because of one or more of the following—

- (a)   any of the terms of the agreement or of any related agreement;
- (b)   the way in which the creditor has exercised or enforced any of his rights under the agreement or any related agreement;
- (c)   any other thing done (or not done) by, or on behalf of, the creditor (either before or after the making of the agreement or any related agreement).

(2)   In deciding whether to make a determination under this section the court shall have regard to all matters it thinks relevant (including matters relating to the creditor and matters relating to the debtor).

140C.—(1)   In this section and in sections 140A and 140B 'credit agreement' means any agreement between an individual (the 'debtor') and any other person (the 'creditor') by which the creditor provides the debtor with credit of any amount.

Comment

(1) Section 140B confers wide powers on the court, including powers to alter the terms of the agreement and to require the repayment of sums already paid by the debtor.

(2) These provisions were inserted by the Consumer Credit Act 2006, replacing an 'extortionate' test, which was satisfied if the required payments were 'grossly exorbitant'.

(3) Under the previous law, high interest rates were upheld where the lender faced a high risk of default and other lenders were reluctant to lend.[19] On the other hand, inflated charges (combined with high interest rates) have been struck down.[20] Would the 2006 changes affect the outcome of these cases?

(4) How should one treat the argument that some borrowers are such bad risks that loans should not be made to them?

Extract 21.4.14

Unfair Terms in Consumer Contracts Regulations 1999[21]

4.   (1)   These Regulations apply in relation to unfair terms in contracts concluded between a seller or a supplier and a consumer.

5.   (1)   A contractual term which has not been individually negotiated shall be regarded as unfair if, contrary to the requirement of good faith, it causes a significant imbalance in the parties' rights and obligations arising under the contract, to the detriment of the consumer.

[19]   One example is *Davies* v *Directloans Ltd* [1986] 1 WLR 823.
[20]   *Castle Phillips Finance Co Ltd* v *Williams* [1986] CCLR 13; applied in *Castle Phillips Co Ltd* v *Wilkinson* [1992] CCLR 83.
[21]   SI 1999 No 2083.

(2)   A term shall always be regarded as not having been individually negotiated where it has been drafted in advance and the consumer has therefore not been able to influence the substance of the term.

. . .

6.   (1)   Without prejudice to regulation 12, the unfairness of a contractual term shall be assessed, taking into account the nature of the goods or services for which the contract was concluded and by referring, at the time of conclusion of the contract, to all the circumstances attending the conclusion of the contract and to all the other terms of the contract or of another contract on which it is dependent.

(2)   In so far as it is in plain intelligible language, the assessment of fairness of a term shall not relate—

> (a)   to the definition of the main subject matter of the contract, or
> (b)   to the adequacy of the price or remuneration, as against the goods or services supplied in exchange.

8.   (1)   An unfair term in a contract concluded with a consumer by a seller or supplier shall not be binding on the consumer.

(2)   The contract shall continue to bind the parties if it is capable of continuing in existence without the unfair term.

Comment

(1) The application of the Regulations to land transactions is confirmed by *R (Khatun)* v *Newham LBC.*[22]

(2) What, if anything, is the significance for mortgages of the exclusion of the 'adequacy of the price or remuneration'?[23]

(3) Do the Regulations add anything to the other controls over unfair terms?

(4) These Extracts relate to controls over specific mortgage terms. It is important to add that there is more general control over lenders and the terms they employ; this is briefly described in Extract 21.4.34 in the context of sale.

B. Rights and remedies of the mortgagee

(i) Foreclosure

Once the legal date for redemption has passed, the mortgagee can apply to the court to terminate the equitable right to redeem. The mortgagee ends up as owner of the property.

Extract 21.4.15

Campbell v *Holyland* (1877) 7 Ch D 166

JESSEL MR: . . . Courts of Equity interfered with actual contract to this extent, by saying there was a paramount intention that the estate should be security, and that the mortgage money should be debt; and they gave relief in the shape of redemption on that principle. Of course that would lead, and did lead, to this inconvenience, that even when the mortgagor was not willing to redeem, the mortgagee could not sell or deal with the estate as his own, and to remedy that

---

[22] [2005] 1 QB 37.
[23] See *Director General of Fair Trading* v *First National Bank plc* [2002] 1 AC 481. This extends to charges levied on borrowers: *Office of Fair Trading* v *Abbey National plc* [2009] 1 AC 696.

inconvenience the practice of bringing a foreclosure suit was adopted, by which a mortgagee was entitled to call on the mortgagor to redeem within a certain time, under penalty of losing the right of redemption. In that foreclosure suit the Court made various orders – interim orders fixing a time for payment of the money – and at last there came the final order which was called foreclosure absolute, that is, in form, that the mortgagor should not be allowed to redeem at all; but it was form only, just as the original deed was form only; for the Courts of Equity soon decided that, notwithstanding the form of that order, they would after that order allow the mortgagor to redeem . . .

Under what circumstances that discretion should be exercised is quite another matter. The mortgagee had a right to deal with an estate acquired under foreclosure absolute the day after he acquired it; but he knew perfectly well that there might be circumstances to entitle the mortgagor to redeem, and everybody buying the estate from a mortgagee who merely acquired a title under such an order was considered to have the same knowledge, namely, that the estate might be taken away from him by the exercise, not of a capricious discretion, but of a judicial discretion by the Court of Equity which had made the order.

. . .

Then it is said you must not interfere against purchasers. As I have already explained, there are purchasers and purchasers. If the purchaser buys a freehold estate in possession after the lapse of a considerable time from the order of foreclosure absolute, with no notice of any extraneous circumstances which would induce the Court to interfere, I for one should decline to interfere with such a title as that; but if the purchaser bought the estate within twenty-four hours after the foreclosure absolute, and with notice of the fact that it was of much greater value than the amount of the mortgage debt, is it to be supposed that a Court of Equity would listen to the contention of such a purchaser that he ought not to be interfered with?

Comment

(1) Foreclosure still applies even though the mortgagor today retains the legal fee simple: LPA, s 88(2), Extract 21.1.1 above.

(2) The mortgagor is normally allowed six months before the foreclosure is made 'absolute'.

(3) Normally, any purchaser will have a registered title today. Will the purchaser receive additional protection from land registration principles?

Foreclosure is very rare today; the normal remedy following default is sale, under powers discussed below. The court has jurisdiction to order sale whenever foreclosure is sought.[24] A further factor makes foreclosure unattractive to mortgagees: any excess of the debt over the value of the land cannot be recovered from the mortgagor once the mortgagee has sold the land.[25] Are there any circumstances in which foreclosure might be of use today?[26]

(ii) Possession

Because the mortgagee has a long lease (or similar rights, if a legal charge) there is a right to possession. In practice, possession is rarely taken save in cases of default in payment of mortgage interest, and then as a prelude to sale by the mortgagee. What other reasons might induce a mortgagee to take possession, bearing in mind that the mortgagee must account for profits made?

---

[24] LPA, s 91(1).
[25] *Lockhart* v *Hardy* (1846) 9 Beav 349 (50 ER 378); *Rudge* v *Richens* (1873) LR 8 CP 358. The reasoning is based on the mortgagor's entitlement to redeem if repayment of the secured loan is required.
[26] Law Com No 204, para 7.27, recommended its abolition.

(a) The mortgagor's possession

The mortgagor almost invariably retains possession: this is obvious for the everyday mortgage of family homes. It is most strange that there is no general principle explaining this possession. Unless the mortgage deed confers rights of possession on the mortgagor, reliance is simply placed upon mortgagees not exercising their rights to possession.

Extract 21.4.16

Esso Petroleum Co Ltd v *Alstonbridge Properties Ltd* [1975] 1 WLR 1474

WALTON J: . . . This claim is resisted . . . upon the grounds (i) that a term ought to be implied in the present mortgage that the mortgagee is not to be entitled to possession unless the mortgagor defaults; (ii) that if such an implication is made, the mortgagee only becomes entitled to possession so long as the mortgagor is in default, and that if the mortgagor corrects any default . . . the mortgagee thereafter loses all rights to possession once again. I think this is a matter where one has got to go back to first principles. I accept that the court will be ready to find an implied term in an instalment mortgage that the mortgagor is to be entitled to remain in possession against the mortgagee until he makes default in payment of one of the instalments. But there must be something upon which to hang such a conclusion in the mortgage other than the mere fact that it is an instalment mortgage. Thus, for example, in *Birmingham Citizens Permanent Building Society* v *Caunt* [1962] Ch 883 the terms of clause 6 of the mortgage [which entitled the mortgagee to possess on default] readily enabled the implication to be made. I can find nothing in the present mortgage which would enable the court to make any such implication here . . .

Even if I had been able to make any such implication, it could only be an implication until some default by the borrower, and this default quite clearly took place when the instalments were unpaid. I do not think that there is any such general doctrine as that for which Mr Lightman contends, that if the mortgagor after default then tenders the arrears the implication that he is entitled to possession revives . . .

Comment

(1) Many modern mortgages do confer an express right to possess until default.

(2) Should mortgagors' rights to possession revive if arrears are paid off?

(b) Jurisdiction to postpone possession

Extract 21.4.17

Birmingham Citizens Permanent BS v *Caunt* [1962] Ch 883

RUSSELL J: . . . Harman J has referred to the right to possession in terms which I adopt. In *Alliance Perpetual Building Society* v *Belrum Investments Ltd*[i] he said:[ii] '. . . It is usually designed to enable the mortgagees to exercise their power of sale, which can only be done with advantage if vacant possession can be offered. It has nothing to do with the enforcement of the mortgage debt, or with foreclosure. Possession is a remedy to which a mortgagee is entitled as of right against the mortgagor, whether the principal or interest be due or not, unless there is some special clause in the mortgage excluding it . . .'

. . . Finally, in *Four-Maids Ltd* v *Dudley Marshall (Properties) Ltd*,[iii] he said: 'I said there, and I repeat now,' – he is referring to the cases which I have just been quoting from – 'that the right of the mortgagee to possession in the absence of some contract has nothing to do with default on the part of the mortgagor. The mortgagee may go into possession before the ink is dry on the mortgage unless there is something in the contract, express or by implication, whereby he

become payable immediately the mortgage is executed is a case where the mortgagor is entitled to defer payment. That is a submission which I find is impossible to accept.

Comment

(1) Why are bank overdraft mortgages different? Does it make good practical sense to distinguish them from other mortgages?

(2) It will be seen later that the courts are now prepared to treat the intended life of the mortgage as the 'reasonable period' for which possession can be postponed. This means that it is less necessary to rely on s 8: the problems identified in *Clark* evaporate away. What impact does this have on bank overdraft mortgages?

Endowment mortgages were very common some years ago and, unsurprisingly, the Court of Appeal in *Bank of Scotland* v *Grimes*[28] held them to be within s 8. This was despite the money not being due until the policy matures. Is there any inconsistency between *Habib* and *Grimes*? If so, does it matter?

A quite different problem concerns the position where there is no default, or default has been remedied.

Extract 21.4.23

Western Bank Ltd v *Schindler* [1977] Ch 1

BUCKLEY LJ: . . . I have been very much puzzled during the argument about the proper interpretation of section 36. If subsection (1) is read literally, the conditional clause introduced by the words 'if it appears to the court' (which I shall refer to as 'the conditional clause') appears to restrict the operation of the section to cases in which some sum is due or some default has taken place and remains unremedied when the application comes before the court. This, however, seems to me to lead to a ridiculous result . . . A defaulting mortgagor would therefore be in a better position than one not in default . . . I cannot believe that Parliament can have intended this irrational and unfair result. I must therefore investigate whether the section is capable of some other construction.

Mr Lightman, in the course of his ingenious and helpful argument, has suggested that section 36 by inference abrogates a mortgagee's right to possession when there is no sum due and no subsisting default on the part of the mortgagor under the mortgage. I feel unable to accept this suggestion. Section 36 is an enabling section which empowers the court to inhibit the mortgagee's right to take possession. It confers a discretionary power on the court to achieve this result. It is, in my judgment, impossible to spell out of it a positive abrogation of an important property right, and, moreover, an abrogation of it only in particular circumstances.

I think, however, that the section is capable of interpretation in a way which makes it applicable to a case in which a mortgagee seeks possession when no sum is due and no other default is subsisting under the mortgage. I can see no reason why the legislature should confer the discretionary power on the court when the mortgagor is in default, but should not do so when he is not in default. The manifest unfairness, as I think, of such a position seems to me a strong ground for believing that it must have been Parliament's intention to confer the power, default or no default, notwithstanding the ineptness of the language of the section to achieve this result. The only part of the section which appears to contradict such an intention is the conditional clause. This can only apply when the mortgagor is in arrear with some payment or is otherwise in default. It would be very natural for Parliament to provide that, where the mortgagor is in arrear or otherwise in default, the discretionary power should not be used to

[28] [1985] QB 1179, followed in *Royal Bank of Scotland plc v Miller* [2002] QB 255.

prevent the mortgagee from taking immediate possession unless the court were satisfied that there was a genuine likelihood of the mortgagor being able to put himself right within a reasonable time. On this approach, the conditional clause operates as a restriction on the court's free exercise of discretion . . . Although the language of the section is certainly inartistic to achieve this result and interpreting it in this way may involve some violence to the language (not, in my view, very great), nevertheless I think that, when the section is read as a whole in the context of the subject matter and particularly having regard to the arbitrary unfairness of the literal construction, it is possible to spell this meaning out of the words used . . .

GOFF LJ (dissenting on this point): It seems to me that there are only two courses open to the court; the one preferred by Buckley LJ and Scarman LJ to construe the clause as conferring a discretion in all cases, reading the conditional clause merely as a qualification on that discretion in the case of unpaid money due or other default; the other to construe the section literally and face whatever anomalies or absurdities that produces. For my part, with all respect, I think the latter is the correct course. It is, in my judgment, inescapable that the result of their construction is that the section operates as a positive enactment disentitling the mortgagee to exercise his proprietary right to take possession save on showing some cause other than the mere existence of his right as legal owner. That is perhaps less startling than saying that the right is wholly abrogated save upon default, but in my view it comes very near to it . . . It is one thing to grant an adjournment to enable something specific to be done, such as is contemplated by the conditional clause. It is altogether different to grant an adjournment to see if some act, event or failure may occur which will entitle the mortgagee to exercise a right which at the time of the adjournment he does not possess, since ex hypothesi he is not entitled to exercise his proprietary right save on due cause being shown.

On the other hand, the anomalies and absurdities said to flow from the literal construction may be more apparent than real, because of the equitable liability to account on the footing of wilful default. Where there has never been any default, or where the court has allowed time for it to be remedied, which has been done, the mortgagee will not ordinarily be in a position to exercise any power of sale . . .

Comment

(1) The facts were most unusual because interest was not technically due until redemption. The court was unanimous in ordering possession; interest was not being paid and the mortgagor had defaulted on premiums on an endowment life policy.

(2) Does Goff LJ adequately rebut the argument that his interpretation is 'ridiculous'?

(3) Difficulty also arose concerning the length of the postponement. The approach taken in our next case (*Norgan*) renders this less significant today.

(d) The exercise of the statutory discretion

A common feature of possession cases is that substantial arrears have built up by the time of the court hearing. Even if current payments can be afforded (perhaps by social security payments), payment of the arrears is likely to be a challenge. It is crucially important to determine the period over which arrears have to be paid.

Extract 21.4.24

Cheltenham & Gloucester BS v Norgan [1996] 1 WLR 343

WAITE LJ: . . . The judge's statement that in the experience of his court 'a period of 2 to 4 years is the maximum that will normally be allowed' as reasonable for the purposes of section 36(2) accords with the comment in *The Supreme Court Practice 1995*, vol 1, para 88/5/9 . . .

The opposing arguments which Mr Croally and Mr Waters have developed in their helpful written and oral submissions are as follows. Mr Croally contends that there is a primary assumption that a reasonable period is the term of the mortgage, and for that he relies on the dicta already cited from *First Middlesbrough Trading & Mortgage Co Ltd v Cunningham* (1974) 28 P&CR 69 and *Western Bank Ltd v Schindler* [1977] Ch 1. That assumption is reinforced, he says, in the present case by the fact that there is sufficient equity to protect the mortgagee's eventual entitlement to repayment of the principal debt in full in 2008, that the mortgagor has deposed on affidavit to budgeting proposals under which (with the help she now receives from the Department of Social Security) there is a reasonable prospect of her being able to pay off the arrears in full by the expiry of the mortgage term, and that such a proposal would accord with the policy declared on the face of the CML statement. Mr Waters contends that such an approach takes too narrow a view of the court's discretion. The delaying powers under section 36 represent a substantial interference with the contractual right which the parties have themselves freely negotiated, namely the right of the mortgagee to repayment in full of the whole mortgage debt as soon as a default occurs . . . Given the number of these cases which come before the courts every day, it would lead, so Mr Waters submits, to unnecessary cost and delay if in every case the court was required to undertake the sort of detailed inquiry which would be necessary if one is to weigh to a nicety the effect on the one hand upon the lender of having to submit to a phasing of repayment of arrears over the whole remaining term of the mortgage and the ability on the other hand of the mortgagor to maintain such payments . . .

Conclusion

There is no doubt that Mr Waters's argument has strong pragmatic advantages . . . Nevertheless, although I would not go quite so far with Mr Croally as to say it should be an 'assumption', it does seem to me that the logic and spirit of the legislation require, especially in cases where the parties are proceeding under arrangements such as those reflected in the CML statement, that the court should take as its starting-point the full term of the mortgage and pose at the outset the question: 'Would it be possible for the mortgagor to maintain payment-off of the arrears by instalments over that period?'

. . . I would acknowledge, also, that this approach will be liable to demand a more detailed analysis of present figures and future projections than it may have been customary for the courts to undertake until now. There is likely to be a greater need to require of mortgagors that they should furnish the court with a detailed 'budget' of the kind that has been supplied by the mortgagor in her affidavit in the present case . . . There may also be cases, as Mr Waters points out, in which it is less obvious than in this case that the mortgagee is adequately secured – and detailed evidence, if necessary by experts, may be required to see if and when the lender's security will become liable to be put at risk as a result of imposing postponement of payments in arrear. Problems such as these – which I suspect will arise only rarely in practice although they will undeniably be daunting when they do arise – should not, however, be allowed, in my judgment, to stand in the way of giving effect to the clearly intended scheme of the legislation.

There is another factor which, to my mind, weighs strongly in favour of adopting the full term of the mortgage as the starting-point for calculating a 'reasonable period' for payment of arrears. It is prompted by experience in this very case. The parties have been before the court with depressing frequency over the years on applications to enforce, or further to suspend, the warrant of possession, while Mrs Norgan and her husband have struggled, sometimes with success and sometimes without, to meet whatever commitment was currently approved by the court. Cheltenham has (in exercise of its power to do so under the terms of the mortgage) added to its security the costs it has incurred in connection with all these attendances . . . It is an experience which brings home the disadvantages which both lender and borrower are liable to suffer if frequent attendance before the court becomes necessary as a result of multiple applications under section 36 of the Act of 1970 – to say nothing of the heavy inroads made upon court hearing time. One advantage of taking the period most favourable to the mortgagor at the outset is that if his or her hopes of repayment prove to be ill-founded and the new instalments initially ordered as a condition of suspension are not maintained but themselves fall into arrear, the mortgagee can be heard with justice to say that the mortgagor has had his chance, and that the section 36 powers (although of course capable in theory of being exercised again and again) should not be employed repeatedly to compel a lending institution which has already suffered interruption of the regular flow of interest to which it was entitled under the express terms of the mortgage to accept assurances of future payment from a borrower in whom it has lost confidence.

Comment

(1) Given that the legislation was primarily intended to cover short-term payment problems arising from ill-health or unemployment, is this the 'clearly intended' result?

(2) Despite *Norgan*, the Ministry of Justice has said (CP55/09, para 55) that the 'normal practice appears to be that arrears are likely to be spread over two to four years'. In *Bank of Scotland plc v Zinda* [2012] 1 WLR 728, there was a postponement of 9½ years when 23 years were left (the length of postponement was not in issue).

(3) As Waite LJ comments, many cases involve repeated failure to comply with court orders. Is the approach of *Norgan* likely to make the position of such mortgagors better or worse?

(4) How relevant should the CML (Council of Mortgage Lenders) policy be?

Extract 21.4.25

First National Bank plc v *Syed* [1991] 2 All ER 250

DILLON LJ: . . . It cannot be proper, with a view ostensibly to clearing the arrears within a reasonable period, to make an order for payments which the defendants cannot afford and have no foreseeable prospects of being able to afford within a reasonable time. Equally it cannot be proper, under these sections, to make an order for payments which the defendants can afford if those will not be enough to pay off the arrears within a reasonable period and also to cover the current instalments.

In this court, however, Miss Smith has directed attention to a different power which applies because the credit agreement is a regulated agreement under the 1974 [Consumer Credit] Act. It is a regulated agreement because . . . the lender, the plaintiff, was not a local authority, building society or other body exempted by s 16 of the 1974 Act.

The remedy available in these circumstances is that of a time order under s 129 of the 1974 Act. That section provides, so far as relevant:

'(1) If it appears to the court just to do so . . . (c) in an action brought by a creditor . . . to enforce a regulated agreement or any security, or recover possession of any . . . land to which a regulated agreement relates, the court may make an order under this section (a "time order"). (2) A time order shall provide for one or both of the following, as the court considers just—(a) the payment by the debtor . . . of any sum owed under a regulated agreement or a security by such instalments, payable at such times, as the court, having regard to the means of the debtor . . . considers reasonable . . .'

. . .

Under this section, then, the court is empowered to order payment by instalments which are reasonable having regard to the means of the debtor. But the court can only exercise the power if it appears, or is considered, just to do so. But consideration of what is just does not exclude consideration of the creditor's position; it is not limited to the debtor's position. I cannot think that it is just, in the circumstances of this case, . . . to require the plaintiff to accept the instalments the defendants can afford, when those will be too little even to keep down the accruing interest on the defendants' account.

Moreover the remedy of a time order under the section would seem to be directed at rescheduling the whole of the indebtedness under the regulated agreement, the principal which has become presently payable as a result of default as well as the arrears and current interest; but I can see no prospect whatsoever of the defendants being able to make any repayment of the principal without a sale of the property.

Comment

Time orders are principally important for extending the period for payment. Given the substantial length of most mortgages, such orders are unlikely to achieve much, quite apart from being limited to regulated agreements.[29]

A very different type of case is where the mortgagor intends to sell the property and thereby pay off the mortgage. This may provide a defence even under *Caunt*. It has the advantages that a better price may be obtained than under a forced mortgagee's sale and (less meritoriously) that a prolonged period of marketing will postpone the evil day when possession finally has to be given up.[30]

Extract 21.4.26

National & Provincial BS v Lloyd [1996] 1 All ER 630

A mortgage included four barns.

NEILL LJ: . . . The first submission, made on behalf of the society, was that the authorities established that an order for possession of mortgaged property should only be deferred to allow a mortgagor time to sell such property where the prospects of an early sale were best served by allowing a mortgagor time and, furthermore, the authorities established that any such deferment should be short.

It is true that both at common law (see the decision of Russell J in *Caunt's* case to which Sir John Pennycuick referred in *Markham*'s case) and in the passages to which I have referred in the more recent cases since the enactment of s 36 of the 1970 Act, it has been said that in the case of the sale of mortgaged property the adjournment or suspension which will be allowed will only be allowed if a sale will take place within a short period of time. Speaking for myself, however, I do not understand that there is any rule of law to this effect. Accordingly, if there were, in a hypothetical case, clear evidence that the completion of the sale of a property, perhaps by piecemeal disposal, could take place in six or nine months or even a year, I see no reason why a court could not come to the conclusion in the exercise of its discretion under the two sections that, to use the words of the section, 'the mortgagor [was] likely to be able within a reasonable period to pay any sums due under the mortgage'. The question of a 'reasonable period' would be a question for the court in the individual case.

Comment

(1) It was held that there was insufficient evidence that the mortgage debt would be covered by the sales.

(2) The court considered that the lapse of time since default (1992) was relevant. Why should it be?

---

[29] See also *Southern & District Finance plc v Barnes* (1995) 27 HLR 691.
[30] See *Cheltenham & Gloucester plc v Krausz* [1997] 1 WLR 1558; Extract 21.4.43 below.

Extract 21.4.27

Bristol & West BS v *Ellis* (1996) 73 P&CR 158

AULD LJ: . . . The instinct of the courts in determining a reasonable period for this purpose seems to have been to adopt the common law approach before the 1970 Act, see *Birmingham Citizens Permanent Building Society* v *Caunt*,[i] of fixing on a 'short' period . . .

Mr Duggan, on behalf of the building society sought to extract from [*Lloyd*] a principle that a year is about the maximum period that a court could consider reasonable for this purpose. Whilst that may be a likely maximum in many cases, I do not read Neill LJ's words as establishing it as a rule of law or as a matter of general guidance. It all depends on the individual circumstances of each case, though the important factors in most are likely to be the extent to which the mortgage debt and arrears are secured by the value of the property and the effect of time on that security.

Where the property is already on the market and there is some indication of delay on the part of the mortgagor, it may be that a short period of suspension of only a few months would be reasonable (see, *e.g. Clothier*[ii]). Where there is likely to be considerable delay in selling the property and/or its value is close to the total of the mortgage debt and arrears so that the mortgagee is at risk as to the adequacy of the security, immediate possession or only a short period of suspension may be reasonable. Where there has already been considerable delay in realising a sale of the property and/or the likely sale proceeds are unlikely to cover the mortgage debt and arrears or there is simply no sufficient evidence as to sale value, the normal order would be for immediate possession . . .

. . . As to the time of sale, all that the district judge had was her statement in her affidavit that she anticipated selling within three to five years when her children completed their education. As to value, the evidence was not compelling: two estate agents' estimates of between £80,000 and £85,000 as against the redemption figure at the time of just over £77,000 plus costs . . . the total figure of indebtedness is now about £70,000 . . . Given the inevitable uncertainty as to the movement of property values over the next few years and the reserve with which the courts should approach estate agents' estimates of sale prices (see *Clothier*[iii]) no court could be sanguine about the adequacy, now or continuing over that period, of the property as a security for the mortgage debt and arrears. In my view, the evidence was simply insufficient to entitle the district judge to contemplate, behind the order he made, a likelihood that the house would or could be sold at a price sufficient to discharge Mrs Ellis's overall debt to Bristol & West within any reasonable period, and certainly not one of up to three to five years.

[i] [1962] Ch 883, *per* Russell J.
[ii] *Target Home Loans Ltd* v *Clothier* [1994] 1 All ER 439, CA.
[iii] [1994] 1 All ER 439 at 445, *per* Nolan LJ.

Comment

(1) Is this approach generous or harsh? When is it likely to aid mortgagors?

(2) In *Clothier*, Nolan LJ had observed that estate agents 'would win by a distance any competition between members of different professions for optimism'.

Extract 21.4.28

Cheltenham & Gloucester BS plc v *Booker* [1997] 1 FLR 311

Can the mortgagor retain possession while the mortgagee arranges sale?

MILLETT LJ: . . . If the court is satisfied:
(a) that possession will not be required by the mortgagee pending completion of the sale but only by the purchasers on completion;

(b) that the presence of the mortgagor pending completion will enhance, or at least not depress, the sale price;

(c) that the mortgagor will co-operate in the sale by showing prospective purchasers round the property and so forth; and

(d) that he will give possession to the purchaser on completion,

it seems to me that there is no reason in principle why the court should accede to a mortgagee's insistence that immediate possession prior to the sale should be given to him.

However, while the jurisdiction exists, experience shows that these conditions are seldom likely to be satisfied. Accordingly, in my judgment, the jurisdiction should be sparingly exercised, and then exercised only with great caution. If the conditions which I have mentioned exist, the court is likely to entrust the conduct of the sale to the mortgagor. There is an inherent illogicality in entrusting conduct of the sale to the mortgagee and yet leaving the mortgagor in possession pending completion unless the mortgagee has agreed to this course. The obtaining of possession with a view to giving it to the purchaser is part of the necessary arrangements for sale. In my opinion the party having conduct of the sale ought normally to have the right to decide when it is desirable for him to obtain possession from those in occupation in order to enable the sale to be effectively carried through.

As the plaintiffs observe, . . . if the contractual obligation to give vacant possession, which the mortgagee will wish to assume in order to obtain the best price reasonably obtainable, is separated from the ability to give immediate vacant possession, the mortgagee is put at risk of being in breach of contract through circumstances beyond his control. Moreover, if the conduct of the sale is given to the mortgagee, any prospective purchaser will become aware prior to exchange of contracts that the property is being sold by a mortgagee who has not yet obtained vacant possession. The risk that the borrower will not vacate the property on completion will become apparent and the purchaser may be deterred from proceeding. He will also be aware that the sale is a forced sale, so that the advantage of achieving a better price through continued owner occupation is unlikely to be realised.

Comment

Is it likely that a mortgagor will ever be allowed to keep possession while the mortgagee sells?

A rather different statutory protection is given to tenants of mortgagors by the Mortgage Repossessions (Protection of Tenants etc) Act 2010. This is limited to postponing possession for no more than two months.

Financial problems in recent years have concentrated minds on the risk of large numbers of possession claims against owner-occupiers. This has led to non-statutory controls over possession claims.

Extract 21.4.29

Pre-Action Protocol for Possession Claims based on Mortgage or Home Purchase Plan Arrears in Respect of Residential Property[31]

1 Preamble

1.1

This Protocol describes the behaviour the court will normally expect of the parties prior to the start of a possession claim within the scope of paragraph 3.1 below.

---

[31] http://www.justice.gov.uk/courts/procedure-rules/civil/protocol/prot_mha

1.2
This Protocol does not alter the parties' rights and obligations.

1.3
It is in the interests of the parties that mortgage payments or payments under home purchase plans are made promptly and that difficulties are resolved wherever possible without court proceedings. However in some cases an order for possession may be in the interest of both the lender and the borrower.

2 Aims

2.1
The aims of this Protocol are to—
   (1)   ensure that a lender or home purchase plan provider (in this Protocol collectively referred to as 'the lender') and a borrower or home purchase plan customer (in this Protocol collectively referred to as 'the borrower') act fairly and reasonably with each other in resolving any matter concerning mortgage or home purchase plan arrears; and
   (2)   encourage more pre-action contact between the lender and the borrower in an effort to seek agreement between the parties, and where this cannot be reached, to enable efficient use of the court's time and resources.

2.2
Where either party is required to communicate and provide information to the other, reasonable steps should be taken to do so in a way that is clear, fair and not misleading. If the lender is aware that the borrower may have difficulties in reading or understanding the information provided, the lender should take reasonable steps to ensure that information is communicated in a way that the borrower can understand.

5 Initial contact and provision of information

5.1
Where the borrower falls into arrears the lender must provide the borrower with—
(1)   where appropriate, the required regulatory information sheet or the National Homelessness Advice Service booklet on mortgage arrears; and
(2)   information concerning the amount of arrears which should include—
      (a)   the total amount of the arrears;
      (b)   the total outstanding of the mortgage or the home purchase plan; and
      (c)   whether interest or charges will be added, and if so and where appropriate, details or an estimate of the interest or charges that may be payable.

5.2
The parties must take all reasonable steps to discuss with each other, or their representatives, the cause of the arrears, the borrower's financial circumstances and proposals for repayment of the arrears (see 7.1). For example, parties should consider whether the causes of the arrears are temporary or long term and whether the borrower may be able to pay the arrears in a reasonable time.

5.3
The lender must advise the borrower to make early contact with the housing department of the borrower's Local Authority and, should, where necessary, refer the borrower to appropriate sources of independent debt advice.

5.5

The lender must respond promptly to any proposal for payment made by the borrower. If the lender does not agree to such a proposal it should give reasons in writing to the borrower within 10 business days of the proposal.

5.6

If the lender submits a proposal for payment, the borrower must be given a reasonable period of time in which to consider such proposals. The lender must set out the proposal in sufficient detail to enable the borrower to understand the implications of the proposal.

5.7

If the borrower fails to comply with an agreement, the lender should warn the borrower, by giving the borrower 15 business days notice in writing, of its intention to start a possession claim unless the borrower remedies the breach in the agreement.

6 Postponing the start of a possession claim

6.1

A lender must consider not starting a possession claim for mortgage arrears where the borrower can demonstrate to the lender that the borrower has—
    (1)   submitted a claim to—
        (a)   the Department for Works and Pensions (DWP) for Support for Mortgage Interest (SMI); or
        (b)   an insurer under a mortgage payment protection policy; or
        (c)   a participating local authority for support under a Mortgage Rescue Scheme,
    and has provided all the evidence required to process a claim;
    (2)   a reasonable expectation of eligibility for payment from the DWP or from the insurer or support from the local authority; and
    (3)   an ability to pay a mortgage instalment not covered by a claim to the DWP or the insurer in relation to a claim under paragraph 6.1(1)(a) or (b).

6.2

If a borrower can demonstrate that reasonable steps have been or will be taken to market the property at an appropriate price in accordance with reasonable professional advice, the lender must consider postponing starting a possession claim. The borrower must continue to take all reasonable steps actively to market the property where the lender has agreed to postpone starting a possession claim.

7 Further matters to consider before starting a possession claim

Starting a possession claim should normally be a last resort and such a claim must not normally be started unless all other reasonable attempts to resolve the position have failed. The parties should consider whether, given the individual circumstances of the borrower and the form of the agreement, it is reasonable and appropriate to do one or more of the following—
    (1)   extend the term of the mortgage;
    (2)   change the type of mortgage;
    (3)   defer payment of interest due under the mortgage;
    (4)   capitalise the arrears; or
    (5)   make use of any Government forbearance initiatives in which the lender chooses to participate.

Comment

(1) Would the application of the Protocol affect the outcome of any of the cases previously considered?

(2) What might happen if a lender were to ignore the Protocol?

(e) Duties of the mortgagee in possession

It has been observed that the mortgagor is nearly always in possession. It is perfectly clear that the mortgagee, who receives interest on the loan, cannot also retain the financial benefits of possession.

Extract 21.4.30

White v City of London Brewery Co (1889) 42 Ch D 237

Mortgagee brewers took possession of a public house and let it as a tied house. Substantial profits were made from the supply of beer to the tenant.

COTTON LJ: . . . The great contention was that the mortgagor was entitled to the profits made by the mortgagees as brewers in supplying the mortgaged property, which was a public-house, with their own beer . . .

In my opinion the profits of the brewers from supplying beer . . . are not profits of the mortgaged hereditaments, they are profits of the brewers' business, which is not in any way carried on upon the mortgaged premises. I know of no authority, and Mr Cozens-Hardy can give me none, that a mortgagee is bound to account for any profits thus made. There was a suggestion that the mortgagee was in some respects in the same position as a trustee, but that was not pressed. As regards certain matters no doubt a mortgagee is liable to the same obligations and restrictions as a trustee, but he is not a trustee, and there is no authority to shew that if a mortgagee of a public-house who is a brewer supplies the public-house with his beer, he is liable to account for the profits he makes by so supplying it.

Comment

Because it was let as a tied house, the rent was lower. The mortgagee had to account for the reduction, as well as the rent actually received. However, these figures were dwarfed by the brewing profits.

(iii) Sale and other statutory powers

The legislation confers a number of powers on mortgagees, though only sale will be considered in any depth. Sale is by far the most common remedy to recover the mortgage debt on default. In financial terms, it is fair to mortgagors as they receive any surplus over the sums owing. It might be noted that many mortgages make explicit provision for sale and other powers.

(a) When is there a power of sale?

Extract 21.4.31

Law of Property Act 1925, ss 101, 103, 104

101.—(1) A mortgagee, where the mortgage is made by deed, shall, by virtue of this Act, have the following powers . . . :

(i) A power, when the mortgage money has become due, to sell, or to concur with any other person in selling, the mortgaged property, or any part thereof, either subject to prior charges or not, and either together or in lots, by public auction or by private contract . . . ; and

(ii) A power, at any time after the date of the mortgage deed, to insure . . . ; and

(iii) A power, when the mortgage money has become due, to appoint a receiver of the income of the mortgaged property . . .

103.—A mortgagee shall not exercise the power of sale conferred by this Act unless and until—

(i) Notice requiring payment of the mortgage money has been served on the mortgagor or one of two or more mortgagors, and default has been made in payment of the mortgage money, or of part thereof for three months after such service; or

(ii) Some interest under the mortgage is in arrear and unpaid for two months after becoming due; or

(iii) There has been a breach of some [other] provision contained in the mortgage deed . . .

104.—(1) A mortgagee exercising the power of sale conferred by this Act shall have power, by deed, to convey the property sold, for such estate and interest therein as he is by this Act authorised to sell or convey or may be the subject of the mortgage, freed from all estates, interests, and rights to which the mortgage has priority, but subject to all estates, interests, and rights which have priority to the mortgage.

(2) Where a conveyance is made in exercise of the power of sale conferred by this Act, or any enactment replaced by this Act, the title of the purchaser shall not be impeachable on the ground—

(a) that no case had arisen to authorise the sale; or

(b) that due notice was not given; or

(c) where the mortgage is made after the commencement of this Act, that leave of the court, when so required, was not obtained; or

(d) whether the mortgage was made before or after such commencement, that the power was otherwise improperly or irregularly exercised;

and a purchaser is not, either before or on conveyance, concerned to see or inquire whether a case has arisen to authorise the sale, or due notice has been given, or the power is otherwise properly and regularly exercised; but any person damnified by an unauthorised, or improper, or irregular exercise of the power shall have his remedy in damages against the person exercising the power.

Comment

(1) The phrase 'has become due' in s 101 applies very readily to the traditional six-month mortgage. Its application to modern mortgages is less straightforward when repayment of capital is postponed for many years. However, it is not unusual for mortgages to provide, *for the purposes of s 101*, that the capital becomes due after six months.

(2) Receivers are useful where the property produces income (usually rent) and the mortgagee wishes to avoid the mortgagor's getting and dissipating it. Receivers are deemed to be agents of the mortgagor (s 109(2)).

(3) Section 104(1) is most important when there are successive mortgages on the same property. If the second of three mortgagees sells,[32] what is the effect on the other two mortgagees and the mortgagor?

---

[32] Possession of the title deeds by the first mortgagee makes such sales of unregistered land difficult.

It is generally said that s 101 governs when the power arises and s 103 when it is exercisable. If it has not arisen, there is simply no power to sell. Once it has arisen, however, purchasers are protected by s 104 against irregularities in its exercise: we do not want to involve them in questions such as how long interest has been in arrears. Cotton LJ considered the position where there is actual knowledge of an irregularity:

> I think that if the purchaser knew as a fact that those things which ought to be done, had not been done, she cannot be allowed to say that the sale was regular: she cannot be allowed to say that the sale was properly made in exercise of the power, if she knew that the three months which were required had not passed.[33]

Extract 21.4.32

Land Registration Act 2002, s 52

52. —(1)   Subject to any entry in the register to the contrary, the proprietor of a registered charge is to be taken to have, in relation to the property subject to the charge, the powers of disposition conferred by law on the owner of a legal mortgage.

(2)   Subsection (1) has effect only for the purpose of preventing the title of a disponee being questioned (and so does not affect the lawfulness of a disposition).

Comment

(1) This is similar to Land Registration Act 2002, s 26 (Extract 12.4.8 above), which protects those dealing with registered proprietors.

(2) Apart from LRA s 52, the powers of disposition conferred by the 2002 Act relate to dealing with the charge, not the estate charged.[34] It follows that powers of disposition as regards the fee simple (or other charged estate) must be as found in s 101. It has been held that s 101 confers a power of sale even if the charge is not registered (so that it takes effect only in equity): *Swift 1st Ltd* v *Colin* [2012] Ch 206.

(3) As intended by the Law Commission, this clearly protects purchasers against any limitation on the s 101 powers. The Law Commission also states:[35] 'if a chargee's power of disposition has not arisen at all – as where the legal date for redemption has been postponed for many years – a disponee will obtain a good title in the absence of anything on the register to indicate some limitation on those powers.' Does the wording of s 52 justify this proposition?

(4) How does this affect the dicta of Cotton LJ, quoted above, regarding purchasers who are aware of the irregularity?

Extract 21.4.33

Horsham Properties Group Ltd v *Clark* [2009] 1 WLR 1255

When the mortgagors defaulted, the mortgagees sold the land without first taking possession. The purchaser now sought possession, as the sale overreached the mortgagors' interests.

---

[33] *Selwyn* v *Garfit* (1888) 38 Ch D 273 at p 283.
[34] See s 23(2): 'Owner's powers in relation to a registered charge consist of – (a) power to make a disposition of any kind permitted by the general law in relation to an interest of that description . . .'
[35] Law Com No 271, para 7.8.

BRIGGS J: 1. . . . The main issue which I have to decide, which has potentially wide-ranging implications, is whether section 101 of the Law of Property Act 1925 ('the LPA'), construed as it and its predecessors have been since 1860, infringes the [Human Rights] Convention rights of mortgagors (and residential mortgagors in particular) by permitting mortgagees to overreach the mortgagor's rights in relation to the mortgaged property by selling it out of court, without first obtaining a court order for possession, or an order for sale.

8. . . . [The mortgagor] sensibly acknowledged that the traditional (pre-Human Rights Act) understanding of the relationship between section 101 of the LPA and section 36 of the Administration of Justice Act 1970 ('section 36') enabled a mortgagee to sell without seeking a court order permitting him to do so, and enabled a purchaser from the mortgagee to obtain possession . . .

25. [The mortgagor relied on Article 1 of the First Protocol (A1FP): protection against deprivation of possessions.] I have no difficulty in concluding that Miss Beech's share in the equity of redemption in relation to the Property was a 'possession' . . .

27. Miss Williams submitted that the application of that analysis to the present case engaged A1FP because Miss Beech's rights in relation to the Property had been taken away by the exercise of GMAC's statutory power of sale, conferred not by private contact, but by section 101 . . .

35. My primary reason for [concluding that A1FP is not engaged] is that section 101 serves to implement rather than override the private bargain between mortgagor and mortgagee. As I have described, its history, going back to 1860, is that it supplies a convenient power of sale out of court to mortgagees in substitution for the parties having (as they routinely did before 1860) to spell out such a power in every legal mortgage. It is in substance a form of conveyancing shorthand designed to implement the ordinary expectations of mortgagors and mortgagees while reducing the costs and delays of conveyancing. Far from overriding the parties' private bargain, . . . it implements and gives effect to it . . .

36. Furthermore, all the statutory powers in section 101 are expressed to be subject to contrary intention. Section 101(4) . . . demonstrates that section 101 serves rather than overrides the parties' bargain. It is in my judgment as far removed from the concept of State intervention into private rights through overriding legislation, which lies behind A1FP, as it is possible for legislation to get. It is neither rigid, arbitrary or discriminatory, and its effect is not only apparent on the face of section 101, but (in the present case) spelt out in terms in the Mortgage itself . . .

42. That is, on Miss Williams' eminently sensible concessions, sufficient to determine the case against Miss Beech . . .

43. The second question is whether any supposed deprivation of possessions constituted by a mortgagee's sale out of court without first obtaining a court order for possession is justified in the public interest. In this respect Miss Williams relied with some force upon the way in which in practice such a sale circumvents the court's discretion to relieve the mortgagor from having to give up possession of a dwelling house under section 36 of the Administration of Justice Act 1970. She submitted that the court's discretion under section 36 was typically responsive (albeit before the event) to the requirement imposed by A1FP for a proportionate balance to be struck as between private property and public interest . . .

44. In my judgment, any deprivation of possession constituted by the exercise by a mortgagee of its powers under section 101 of the Law of Property Act after a relevant default by the mortgagor is justified in the public interest, and requires no case-by-case exercise of a proportionality discretion by the court, for the following reasons. First, it reflects the bargain habitually drawn between mortgagors and mortgagees for nearly 200 years, in which the ability of a mortgagee to sell the property offered as a security without having to go to court has been identified as a central and essential aspect of the security necessarily to be provided if substantial property based secured lending is to be available at affordable rates of interest. That it is in the public interest that property buyers and owners should be able to obtain lending for that purpose can

hardly be open to doubt, even if the loan-to-value ratios at which it has recently become possible have now become a matter of controversy.

45.   Secondly, I am bound by the decision of the Court of Appeal in *Ropaigealach* [see p 774
above] to conclude that there was no wider policy behind section 36 of the Administration of
Justice Act 1970 than to put back what the courts had shortly before taken away, namely a
discretion to stay or adjourn proceedings for possession, triggered only where the mortgagee
considered it necessary or appropriate to go to court in the first place. The question whether
any wider policy ought to be implemented wherever steps taken by a mortgagee to realise its
security are likely to lead to the obtaining of possession is a matter for Parliament, and upon
which Parliament has yet, so far as I can ascertain, to form any view. It would be quite wrong
for the courts in a vigorous and imaginative interpretation of the Human Rights Convention to
make that policy, as it were, on the hoof.

Comment

(1) Is this analysis of the relationship between A1FP and LPA, s 101 justified? See also *Sims
v Dacorum BC* [2014] UKSC 63; [2014] 3 WLR 1600, Extract 14.2.2 above.

(2) Is it acceptable that overreaching can take place so as to bypass the restrictions on
taking possession?

(3) It will be seen below that reasonable care must be taken to obtain a proper price on sale.
It is very likely that selling without vacant possession (as the mortgagors are still there) will
attract a much reduced price, regardless of how much care is taken. In these circumstances,
could the mortgagee be liable for not obtaining a proper price?

(4) The unsuccessful human rights argument prompts the question whether Article 8
could be employed by the partner or children of the mortgagor to challenge possession
and sale.[36]

Extract 21.4.34

Mortgages: Power of Sale and Residential Property
(Ministry of Justice CP55/09)[37]

13.   *Horsham* did not change the law in this area. In addition, the mortgage in question in
Horsham was a buy to let mortgage, under the terms of which the borrowers were not permitted
to live in the property themselves. Further, the borrowers continued to live in the property for a
substantial period of time without making payments. This was not a case of a mortgage taken
out for the purpose of funding an owner-occupied family home.

22.   As mentioned, our proposals only relate to *residential owner-occupier mortgages*: This is
not a defined legal term . . . We exclude buy to let mortgages because they are commercial
investments in property . . .

65.   The CML has released a statement on behalf of all of its members that they will not move
to sell a residential property in which the customer is resident and the loan is non-commercial
without first obtaining a court order for possession. Information from lending industry stakeholders indicates that even prior to this statement, the practice was never used in residential
owner-occupier situations. After checking with advice sector stakeholders, the courts, and the
media, the MoJ has not found any cases where this has occurred on a non-commercial loan.
One reason for this may be that in most cases, we imagine that the buyer of a property from a
lender will require vacant possession or a sitting tenant. Buying subject to the occupation of

---

[36] See Nield and Hopkins (2013) 33 LS 431.

[37] http://webarchive.nationalarchives.gov.uk/ and http://www.justice.gov.uk/about/docs/mortgages-power-sale.pdf

even a trespasser requires a willingness to go to court and recover possession before any enjoyment or income can be had from the property.

66.   Mortgages are generally created as part of a financial services transaction. The majority (first-charge residential mortgages) are regulated by the FSA. FSA regulation imposes a number of outcome-focused requirements on first charge mortgage lenders. At a high level there are a number of principles which all regulated firms must satisfy, including the principle that they treat their customers fairly. Targeted conduct of business requirements support this objective through, for example, requiring lenders to:

- Have in place a policy for ensuring the fair treatment of borrowers in payment difficulties;
- Make all reasonable efforts to reach an agreement with customers regarding any shortfall so that repossession is an action of last resort;
- Make early contact with customers in payment difficulty and provide information about their options, including signposting the availability of independent advice sources, and;
- Provide customers with regular information about accounts in arrears and any charges that are being applied.

67.   In November 2008 FSA wrote to the heads of all lending institutions in the UK, stating that if lenders were to employ the power of sale in situations where a court order for possession would have been denied, the FSA would be inclined to view such actions as unfair practices.

68.   Second and subsequent mortgages are regulated by the OFT under consumer credit legislation. The OFT is responsible for enforcing its regulations.

70.   Notwithstanding the apparent lack of use – or indeed intention to use – the power of sale as a means of avoiding the court protections available in relation to the exercise of the right to possession, the possibility of the use of a power of sale in this way still seems to be a cause for concern. From this perspective, the present law provides potential for abuse by a lender of its rights. Critics of the present position point to the apparent imbalance between the protections available in possession proceedings before the court and the apparent freedom for lenders in relation to the power of sale.

79.   Like the *Horsham* case, *Ropaigealach* illustrates a remedy that is available to lenders without the involvement of the courts, and as such it is subject to the potential criticism that it leaves borrowers inadequately protected. Also as with *Horsham*, lending industry stakeholders have stated that it is extremely rare to see the right to possession exercised in this way, and that where mistakes are made, in practice lenders will usually return the keys to the borrower.

116.   In this chapter we summarise our provisional proposal that a lender's power of sale in relation to a residential owner-occupier mortgage should only be exercisable by agreement with the borrower or by order of the court.

117.   We propose that, in the absence of agreement, the exercise of the power of sale should only be considered to be authorised by the court either where an order for possession exists, or where the court makes an order for sale using the same criteria as it does for granting an order for possession. . . .

118.   We do not propose any special treatment for abandoned properties. Where a property is abandoned and the borrower cannot be contacted we propose that a lender will need a court order in order to sell the property. We welcome views on this proposal and the potential scope of its impact.

119.   Nor do we propose to make any special provision for unilateral 'handing in the keys'. As the power of sale may be exercised by agreement, where the borrower hands over the keys because he or she has reached an agreement with the lender, (or the lender accepts a unilateral 'handing in' of keys), this would mean there is no requirement for a court order.

120.   The proposal will apply to residential owner-occupier mortgages. A mortgage falls within this category when it is a mortgage to finance the purchase of a property in which the borrower intends to live. This is the classic example of the home-owner mortgage. This includes mortgages

to secure loans to finance the building of a home for occupation by the borrower or its improvement. It does not include loans secured on the family home to secure financing for a business or investment venture, perhaps linked to a business account overdraft.

122. A loan for mixed purposes must be outside the scope of the new provision. However, the mere inclusion of an obligation to repay costs and expenses to the lender should not tip a mortgage from one category to another.

Comment

(1) Is there any real problem resulting from *Horsham*?

(2) Would the proposed reforms achieve anything? Do they leave mortgagors of houses with inadequate protection?

One specific question concerns the effect of a contract to sell.

Extract 21.4.35

Waring v *London & Manchester Assurance Co Ltd* [1935] Ch 311

CROSSMAN J: . . . If, before the date of the contract, the plaintiff had tendered the principal with interest and costs, or had paid it into Court in proceedings, then, if the company had continued to take steps to enter into a contract for sale, or had purported to do so, the plaintiff would, in my opinion, have been entitled to an injunction restraining it from doing so . . . Counsel for the plaintiff, who has argued the case most excellently, submitted that, notwithstanding that the company exercised its power of sale by entering into the contract, the plaintiff's equity of redemption has not been extinguished, as there has been no completion by conveyance, and that, pending completion, the plaintiff is still entitled to redeem, that is, to have the property reconveyed to him on payment of principal, interest, and costs . . . In my judgment, s 101 of that Act, which gives to a mortgagee power to sell the mortgaged property, is perfectly clear, and means that the mortgagee has power to sell out and out, by private contract or by auction, and subsequently to complete by conveyance; and the power to sell is, I think, a power by selling to bind the mortgagor. If that were not so, the extraordinary result would follow that every purchaser from a mortgagee would, in effect, be getting a conditional contract liable at any time to be set aside by the mortgagor's coming in and paying the principal, interest, and costs. Such a result would make it impossible for a mortgagee, in the ordinary course of events, to sell unless he was in a position to promise that completion should take place immediately . . .

. . . Sect 104, sub-s 2, upon which also counsel for the plaintiff relied, does not seem to me to affect the question at all. Its purpose is simply to protect the purchaser and to make it unnecessary for him, pending completion and during investigation of title, to ascertain whether the power of sale has become exercisable. Of course, if the purchaser becomes aware, during that period, of any facts showing that the power of sale is not exercisable, or that there is some impropriety in the sale, then, in my judgment, he gets no good title on taking the conveyance.

Comment

If the power is truly exercised on contract, why should awareness of an irregularity, arising between contract and conveyance, be relevant?

Duke v *Robson*[38] held that the mortgagee's power of sale was unaffected by a mortgagor's prior contract to sell the land. How does this fit with the legislation and the cases? Does it

---

[38] [1973] 1 WLR 267.

represent sound policy?[39] Such cases will be rare, because normally only the party in possession will be able to find a person willing to buy.

(b) Duties owed by the mortgagee

Extract 21.4.36

Cuckmere Brick Co Ltd v *Mutual Finance Ltd* [1971] Ch 949

Auctioneers failed to advertise the existence of planning permission for the land.

SALMON LJ: . . . It is well settled that a mortgagee is not a trustee of the power of sale for the mortgagor. Once the power has accrued, the mortgagee is entitled to exercise it for his own purposes whenever he chooses to do so. It matters not that the moment may be unpropitious and that by waiting a higher price could be obtained. He has the right to realise his security by turning it into money when he likes. Nor, in my view, is there anything to prevent a mortgagee from accepting the best bid he can get at an auction, even though the auction is badly attended and the bidding exceptionally low. Providing none of those adverse factors is due to any fault of the mortgagee, he can do as he likes. If the mortgagee's interests, as he sees them, conflict with those of the mortgagor, the mortgagee can give preference to his own interests, which of course he could not do were he a trustee of the power of sale for the mortgagor.

Mr Vinelott contends that the mortgagee's sole obligation to the mortgagor in relation to a sale is to act in good faith . . .

It is impossible to pretend that the state of the authorities on this branch of the law is entirely satisfactory. There are some dicta which suggest that unless a mortgagee acts in bad faith he is safe. His only obligation to the mortgagor is not to cheat him. There are other dicta which suggest that in addition to the duty of acting in good faith, the mortgagee is under a duty to take reasonable care to obtain whatever is the true market value of the mortgaged property at the moment he chooses to sell it: compare, for example, *Kennedy* v *de Trafford* [1896] 1 Ch 762; [1897] AC 180 with *Tomlin* v *Luce* (1889) 43 Ch D 191, 194.

The proposition that the mortgagee owes both duties, in my judgment, represents the true view of the law. Approaching the matter first of all on principle, it is to be observed that if the sale yields a surplus over the amount owed under the mortgage, the mortgagee holds this surplus in trust for the mortgagor. If the sale shows a deficiency, the mortgagor has to make it good out of his own pocket. The mortgagor is vitally affected by the result of the sale but its preparation and conduct is left entirely in the hands of the mortgagee. The proximity between them could scarcely be closer. Surely they are 'neighbours'. Given that the power of sale is for the benefit of the mortgagee and that he is entitled to choose the moment to sell which suits him, it would be strange indeed if he were under no legal obligation to take reasonable care to obtain what I call the true market value at the date of the sale. Some of the textbooks refer to the 'proper price', others to the 'best price' . . . I prefer to call it 'the true market value'.

. . .

The only other matter that remains to be considered is Mr Vinelott's submission that even if the defendants were under a duty to take reasonable precautions, they discharged that duty by going to reputable auctioneers and estate agents and leaving the sale in their hands. Mr Vinelott submits that the defendants are not responsible for any blunder which their agents may have committed. That submission certainly cannot be squared with Cotton LJ's judgment in *Tomlin* v *Luce* (1889) 43 Ch D 191. I do not think, however, that it is necessary for me to express any concluded view upon it.

---

[39] The Law Commission would allow damages to the mortgagor if the mortgagee had acted unreasonably: Law Com No 204, paras 7.16 et seq.

Comment

(1) The court split on whether the duty had been broken; the majority held it had.

(2) What was the basis for imposing the duty? Is the duty overly onerous on mortgagees, or is the freedom given to them too great?

Extract 21.4.37

Parker-Tweedale v *Dunbar Bank plc* [1991] Ch 12

Trust property was mortgaged, the plaintiff being a beneficiary under the trust. Could the plaintiff sue under *Cuckmere Brick*?

NOURSE LJ: . . . This reference [in *Cuckmere Brick*] to 'neighbours' has enabled the plaintiff to argue that the duty is owed to all those who are within the neighbourhood principle; i.e., to adapt the words of Lord Atkin, to all persons who are so closely and directly affected by the sale that the mortgagee ought reasonably to have them in contemplation as being so affected when he is directing his mind to the sale . . .

In my respectful opinion it is both unnecessary and confusing for the duties owed by a mortgagee to the mortgagor and the surety, if there is one, to be expressed in terms of the tort of negligence. The authorities which were considered in the careful judgments of this court in *Cuckmere Brick Co Ltd* v *Mutual Finance Ltd* [1971] Ch 949 demonstrate that the duty owed by the mortgagee to the mortgagor was recognised by equity as arising out of the particular relationship between them . . .

Once it is recognised that the duty owed by the mortgagee to the mortgagor arises out of the particular relationship between them, it is readily apparent that there is no warrant for extending its scope so as to include a beneficiary or beneficiaries under a trust of which the mortgagor is the trustee.

Extract 21.4.38

Downsview Nominees Ltd v *First City Corporation Ltd* [1993] AC 295

PRIVY COUNCIL: . . . Several centuries ago equity evolved principles for the enforcement of mortgages and the protection of borrowers. The most basic principles were, first, that a mortgage is security for the repayment of a debt and, secondly, that a security for repayment of a debt is only a mortgage. From these principles flowed two rules, first, that powers conferred on a mortgagee must be exercised in good faith for the purpose of obtaining repayment and secondly that, subject to the first rule, powers conferred on a mortgagee may be exercised although the consequences may be disadvantageous to the borrower . . .

The general duty of care said to be owed by a mortgagee to subsequent encumbrancers and the mortgagor in negligence is inconsistent with the right of the mortgagee and the duties which the courts applying equitable principles have imposed on the mortgagee . . . If a mortgagee exercises his power of sale in good faith for the purpose of protecting his security, he is not liable to the mortgagor even though he might have obtained a higher price and even though the terms might be regarded as disadvantageous to the mortgagor. *Cuckmere Brick Co Ltd* v *Mutual Finance Ltd* [1971] Ch 949 is Court of Appeal authority for the proposition that, if the mortgagee decides to sell, he must take reasonable care to obtain a proper price but is no authority for any wider proposition . . . The duties imposed by equity on a mortgagee and on a receiver and manager would be quite unnecessary if there existed a general duty in negligence to take reasonable care in the exercise of powers and to take reasonable care in dealing with the assets of the mortgagor company.

Comment

These last two cases approve *Cuckmere Brick* but clarify the basis of the duty. Does it matter what that basis is?

(c) The timing of sale

As stated in *Cuckmere Brick*, the mortgagee can choose when to sell. In the words of Chitty J in *Farrar v Farrars Ltd*:[40]

> He is bound to sell fairly, and to take reasonable steps to obtain a proper price; but he may proceed to a forced sale for the purpose of paying the mortgage debt ... The mortgagor has no right after the power has arisen to insist that the mortgagee shall wait for better times before selling ... The mortgagee has a right to obtain payment of his debt through the exercise of his power when it has arisen, without regard to the then existing condition of the market. He cannot be required to run any risk in postponing the sale, or to speculate for the mortgagor's benefit.

Subsequently, there were some suggestions that the mortgagee may not have an entirely free hand.[41] However, the courts have restored the mortgagee's freedom to decide on the timing.

Extract 21.4.39

Silven Properties Ltd v Royal Bank of Scotland plc [2004] 1 WLR 997 (CA)

LIGHTMAN J: 4. ... The relevant complaint made by the claimants at the trial in respect of these sales was that the receivers were under a duty not to sell the properties as they were. Instead they were under a duty before selling, in order to obtain the best price obtainable, to pursue planning applications for the development of the properties and (in the case of two of the properties, which were vacant or partially vacant, but in respect of which there were negotiations for grant of leases) to proceed with the grant of leases, and to defer a sale until these goals were achieved ...

5. The issue of law raised on this appeal is of some considerable practical importance. Earlier authorities have expressed the view that the duties of receivers appointed by mortgagees are the same as the duties of the mortgagees themselves in respect of the sale of mortgaged property and that mortgagees do not have the duties for which the claimants contend.

13. A mortgagee has no duty at any time to exercise his powers as mortgagee to sell, to take possession or to appoint a receiver and preserve the security or its value or to realise his security. He is entitled to remain totally passive. If the mortgagee takes possession, he becomes the manager of the charged property: see *Kendle v Melsom* (1998) 193 CLR 46, 64 (High Court of Australia). He thereby assumes a duty to take reasonable care of the property secured: see *Downsview Nominees Ltd v First City Corpn Ltd* [1993] AC 295, 315a, per Lord Templeman; and this requires him to be active in protecting and exploiting the security, maximising the return, but without taking undue risks: see *Palk v Mortgage Services Funding plc* [1993] Ch 330, 338a, per Sir Donald Nicholls V-C.

14. A mortgagee 'is not a trustee of the power of sale for the mortgagor'. This time-honoured expression can be traced back at least as far as Sir George Jessel MR in *Nash v Eads* (1880) 25 SJ 95. In default of provision to the contrary in the mortgage, the power is conferred upon the mortgagee by way of bargain by the mortgagor for his own benefit and he has an unfettered discretion to sell when he likes to achieve repayment of the debt which he is owed: see

---

[40] (1888) 40 Ch D 395 at p 398.
[41] *Standard Chartered Bank Ltd v Walker* [1982] 1 WLR 1410 at p 1415 (Lord Denning MR); *Palk v Mortgage Services Funding plc* [1993] Ch 330 at p 338 (Sir Donald Nicholls V-C).

Cuckmere Brick Co Ltd v *Mutual Finance Ltd* [1971] Ch 949, 969g. A mortgagee is at all times free to consult his own interests alone whether and when to exercise his power of sale. The most recent authoritative restatement of this principle is to be found in *Raja* v *Austin Gray* [2003] 1 EGLR 91, 96, para 59, per Peter Gibson LJ. The mortgagee's decision is not constrained by reason of the fact that the exercise or non-exercise of the power will occasion loss or damage to the mortgagor: see *China and South Sea Bank Ltd* v *Tan Soon Gin (alias George Tan)* [1990] 1 AC 536. It does not matter that the time may be unpropitious and that by waiting a higher price could be obtained: he is not bound to postpone in the hope of obtaining a better price: see *Tse Kwong Lam* v *Wong Chit Sen* [1983] 1 WLR 1349, 1355b.

15. The claimants contend that a mortgagee is not entitled to ignore the fact that a short delay might result in a higher price. For this purpose they rely on certain obiter dicta of Lord Denning MR in *Standard Chartered Bank* v *Walker* [1982] 1 WLR 1410, 1415g–h, 1416a. The mortgagee in that case, having obtained insufficient on the sale at auction of the property charged to recover the sum secured, applied for summary judgment against the mortgagor for that sum. The mortgagor resisted the application alleging that the mortgagee had sold at an undervalue on a variety of grounds one of which was that the sale took place at the wrong time of year. The Court of Appeal gave the mortgagor leave to defend on the ground that there was an arguable case that the sale had been negligently handled. It was common ground in that case that a mortgagee can choose his own time for sale: see Fox LJ, at p 1418f–g. Lord Denning MR accepted that there were dicta to this effect, but added that he did not think that this meant that the mortgagee could sell at the worst possible moment and that it was at least arguable that in choosing the time he must exercise a reasonable degree of care. The view expressed by Lord Denning MR cannot stand with the later authorities to which we have referred and which state quite categorically that the mortgagee is under no such duty of care to the mortgagor in respect of the timing of a sale and can act in his own interests in deciding whether and when he should exercise his power of sale.

16. The mortgagee is entitled to sell the mortgaged property as it is. He is under no obligation to improve it or increase its value. There is no obligation to take any such pre-marketing steps to increase the value of the property as is suggested by the claimants. The claimants submitted that this principle could not stand with the decision of the Privy Council in *McHugh* v *Union Bank of Canada* [1913] AC 299. Lord Moulton in that case, at p 312, held that, if a mortgagee does proceed with a sale of property which is unsaleable as it stands, a duty of care may be imposed on him when taking the necessary steps to render the mortgaged property saleable. The mortgage in that case was of horses, which the mortgagee needed to drive to market if he was to sell them. The mortgagee was held to owe to the mortgagor a duty to take proper care of them whilst driving them to market. The duty imposed on the mortgagee was to take care to preserve, not increase, the value of the security. The decision accordingly affords no support for the claimants' case.

17. The mortgagee is free (in his own interest as well as that of the mortgagor) to investigate whether and how he can 'unlock' the potential for an increase in value of the property mortgaged (e.g. by an application for planning permission or the grant of a lease) and indeed (going further) he can proceed with such an application or grant. But he is likewise free at any time to halt his efforts and proceed instead immediately with a sale. By commencing on this path the mortgagee does not in any way preclude himself from calling a halt at will: he does not assume any such obligation of care to the mortgagor in respect of its continuance as the claimants contend. If however the mortgagee is to seek to charge to the mortgagor the costs of the exercise which he has undertaken of obtaining planning permission or a lessee, subject to any applicable terms of the mortgage, the mortgagee may only be entitled to do so if he acted reasonably in incurring those costs and fairly balanced the costs of the exercise against the potential benefits taking fully into account the possibility that he might at any moment 'pull the plug' on these efforts and the consequences for the mortgagor if he did so.

Comment

(1) Is there anything to be said for the approach of Lord Denning MR that sale should not take place at 'the worst possible time' (where this would require delay for a matter of weeks or a month or two)?

(2) One can understand why onerous obligations are not imposed on mortgagees. However, should they not be under an obligation to undertake inexpensive and quickly undertaken work which any reasonable property owner would undertake before selling? Clearing rubbish from the property could be one simple example.

(3) A somewhat different point is that the power of sale is not properly exercised if none of the reasons is to recover the secured debt: *Meretz Investments NV v ACP Ltd.*[42] In the possession context, compare *Quennell* v *Maltby* [1979] 1 WLR 318, Extract 21.4.18 above.

(d) The destination of the proceeds of sale

Extract 21.4.40

Law of Property Act 1925, s 105

105.—The money which is received by the mortgagee, arising from the sale, after discharge of prior incumbrances to which the sale is not made subject, if any, or after payment into court under this Act of a sum to meet any prior incumbrance, shall be held by him in trust to be applied by him, first, in payment of all costs, charges, and expenses properly incurred by him as incident to the sale or any attempted sale, or otherwise; and secondly, in discharge of the mortgage money, interest, and costs, and other money, if any, due under the mortgage; and the residue of the money so received shall be paid to the person entitled to the mortgaged property, or authorised to give receipts for the proceeds of the sale thereof.

Comment

Suppose that R's land is mortgaged to A for a £25,000 loan, then to B for £100,000 and then to C for £10,000. B sells the land to P for £150,000. What should B do with the proceeds?

(e) The court's jurisdiction to order sale

Extract 21.4.41

Law of Property Act 1925, s 91(2)

91.—(2)   In any action, whether for foreclosure, or for redemption, or for sale, or for the raising and payment in any manner of mortgage money, the court, on the request of the mortgagee, or of any person interested either in the mortgage money or in the right of redemption, and, notwithstanding that—
  (a)   any other person dissents; or
  (b)   the mortgagee or any person so interested does not appear in the action;
and without allowing any time for redemption or for payment of any mortgage money, may direct a sale of the mortgaged property, on such terms as it thinks fit, including the deposit in court of a reasonable sum fixed by the court to meet the expenses of sale and to secure performance of the terms.

---

[42] [2007] Ch 197 at [300]–[314]; not considered on appeal [2008] Ch 244.

Comment

Traditionally, sale has been ordered in foreclosure actions and when exceptional circumstances require sale, as where a power of sale has been defectively drafted.[43]

Extract 21.4.42

Palk v Mortgage Services Funding plc [1993] Ch 330

Following default, the mortgagee wished to take possession and lease the property, waiting until the property market improved to sell (the loan exceeded the value of the property). The mortgagor wished to sell immediately in order to minimise liability.

SIR DONALD NICHOLLS V-C: Underlying the present case is not merely a disagreement between a mortgagor and a mortgagee about the likely future trend of house prices. I suspect that probably another feature is a difference in their attitudes towards taking risks. We were told that Mortgage Services has many properties in a similar situation and that this case raises an important question of principle for the company. A substantial lender may be prepared to take risks that would be imprudent for a householder with limited financial resources.

There is also the further feature that the interests of the mortgagor and the mortgagee do not march hand in hand in all respects. The security afforded by the house is not the only remedy possessed by Mortgage Services: the company also has a personal claim against Mrs Palk. If the property market does not improve as Mortgage Services hopes, and so the shortfall ultimately becomes larger than it is now, the company can have recourse against Mrs Palk for the increased shortfall. Hence, it is said, Mortgage Services is intent on speculating at Mrs Palk's expense . . .

The thrust of Mortgage Services' answer is that, in exchange for the loan, it acquired a security and several remedies. The company may choose which remedy it wishes to pursue and when, so long as it acts in good faith and not for some collateral purpose. It may choose the time of sale, however disadvantageous this may be for the mortgagor. If it decides to sell, it must exercise reasonable care to obtain the proper market value, but it is under no duty to exercise its power of sale. Mr Lightman relied on the observations of Lord Templeman in *China and South Sea Bank Ltd v Tan Soon Gin (alias George Tan)* [1990] 1 AC 536, 545:

> 'If the creditor chose to exercise his power of sale over the mortgaged security he must sell for the current market value but the creditor must decide in his own interest if and when he should sell.'

Thus, he submitted, if the mortgagee decides to postpone a sale indefinitely, there is no occasion for the court to intervene . . .

A duty to be fair

. . .

For present purposes it is sufficient to note that, quite apart from section 91(2), there is a legal framework which imposes some constraints of fairness on a mortgagee who is exercising his remedies over his security.

In the present case Mortgage Services is exercising its rights over the house . . . If the situation had been that the rental would exceed or equal or at least approach the interest she would save if the house were sold, it might have been reasonable for the company to decide to postpone the sale and to let the house for the time being. In the long run property prices can be expected to recover, so postponing the sale would be in the company's interest and would

---

[43] *Twentieth Century Banking Corporation Ltd v Wilkinson* [1977] Ch 99.

be unlikely to be prejudicial to Mrs Palk. That is not the situation. Mortgage Services intends to let the property, despite the income shortfall: the rentals to be credited to Mrs Palk will fall significantly short of the interest she would save if the house were sold. This is an important feature of this case. Unless good fortune shines on the parties, she is bound to suffer financially by a postponement of the sale . . .

However, and this is my second observation on the mortgagees' argument, whether in these circumstances Mortgage Services is in breach of any duty it owes to Mrs Palk is not a crucial question on this appeal, for this reason: an exercise by the court of its statutory power to direct a sale even against the wishes of Mortgage Services is not dependent on there first having been a breach of duty by the company. The discretion given to the court by section 91(2) is not hedged about with preconditions . . . That Mortgage Services is not, or may not be, in breach of any duty it owes Mrs Palk is only one of the circumstances to be taken into account.

The court's discretion

I turn therefore to the question of discretion. As to this, the features which strike me most forcibly are, first, the unfairness of Mrs Palk being compelled to participate in and underwrite the risk Mortgage Services wishes to take . . . The second notable feature is that the primary objective of the company can be achieved without Mrs Palk being compelled to become an unwilling risk-taker. If Mortgage Services takes over the property at current market value, it can obtain for itself the benefit of any improvement in house prices. This result would strike a fair balance between the interests of the parties.

Section 91(2) gives the court a discretion in wide terms. The discretion is unfettered. It can be exercised at any time. Self-evidently, in exercising that power the court will have due regard to the interests of all concerned. The court will act judicially. But it cannot be right that the court should decline to exercise the power if the consequence will be manifest unfairness.

In my view this is a case in which a sale should be directed even though there will be a deficiency. It is just and equitable to order a sale because otherwise unfairness and injustice will follow.

Comment

(1) Much is made of the point that the risk is being placed on Mrs Palk. Is this convincing when there is no evidence that she would be able to pay present or future arrears?

(2) Is it correct that the exercise of discretion is not related to breach of duty by the mortgagors?

(3) *Palk* was followed by Jacob J in *Polonski* v *Lloyds Bank Mortgages Ltd*,[44] in which the mortgagor simply wished to move home: 'a perfectly legitimate exercise of her undoubted right to live where she wants'. Is this a significant extension of *Palk*?

Where the value of the house exceeds the debt, mortgagors rarely encounter any difficulty in selling and paying off the mortgage. But what is the position if there is negative equity and the mortgagee is seeking possession?

Extract 21.4.43

Cheltenham & Gloucester plc v *Krausz* [1997] 1 WLR 1558

PHILLIPS LJ: . . . In *Palk's* case the issue was simply whether or not the property should be sold. No issue arose as to the terms on which it should be sold. As to that matter, section 91(2) empowers the court to direct a sale 'on such terms as it thinks fit' . . .

[44] [1998] 1 FLR 896 at p 899.

Barrett v Halifax Building Society (1995) 28 HLR 634 marks the next development in this area of the law, and one which demonstrates the importance of the present appeal. In that case the plaintiffs had mortgaged their home and then defaulted on their repayment obligations. The situation was one of negative equity – the mortgage debt substantially exceeded the value of their home . . . By the time that [the mortgagors'] action came on for hearing they had negotiated a sale of the property, subject to contract. They sought an order that they be permitted to proceed with that sale and to remain in possession until completion . . . The mortgagees resisted the order sought. They did not contend that they would be able to obtain a better price but urged that if the sale went ahead it would break their established policy not to permit borrowers with negative equity themselves to conduct the sale of their property without also at the same time making proposals for the repayment of any resulting deficit. The judge held that this was not a material circumstance which he ought to take into account when exercising his discretion . . . He proceeded to grant the plaintiffs the order that they sought . . .

The consequences of the procedure followed in *Barrett's* case appear to me to be far reaching. In any case in which there is negative equity it will be open to the mortgagor to resist an order for possession on the ground that he wishes to obtain a better price by remaining in possession and selling the property himself. In not every case will the primary motive for such an application be the wish to obtain a better price than that which the mortgagee is likely to obtain on a forced sale. Often the mortgagor will be anxious to postpone for as long as possible the evil day when he has to leave his home. This court has ample experience of hopeless applications for leave to appeal against possession orders designed to achieve just that end. There will be a danger, if the mortgagee does not obtain possession, that the mortgagor will delay the realisation of the property by seeking too high a price, or deliberately procrastinating on completion . . . For these reasons it seems to me that the procedure followed and the decision reached in the *Barrett* case tend fundamentally to undermine the value of the mortgagee's entitlement to possession . . .

Before the decision in *Palk's* case it seemed that section 36 of the Act of 1970 and section 91 of the Act of 1925 were complementary. An application under section 91 would only be contemplated where the proceeds of sale were expected to exceed the mortgage debt. In these circumstances section 36 gave the court the power to suspend possession in order to enable an application for sale under section 91 to be made. It is, however, quite clear that section 36 does not empower the court to suspend possession in order to permit the mortgagor to sell the mortgaged premises where the proceeds of sale will not suffice to discharge the mortgage debt, unless of course other funds will be available to the mortgagor to make up the shortfall. A mortgagor seeking relief in the circumstances of *Palk's* case is thus unable to invoke any statutory power to suspend the mortgagee's right to enter into possession.

. . .

In my judgment the very specific delimitation of the power given by section 36 makes it clear that the legislature did not intend that the court should have any wider jurisdiction to curtail the mortgagee's right to possession. That right enables the mortgagee to exercise his power of sale in the manner he chooses and in the confidence that he can offer a purchaser vacant possession . . .

MILLETT LJ: . . . [*Palk*] does not support the making of [a sale] order where the mortgagee is taking active steps to obtain possession and enforce its security by sale. Still less does it support the giving of the conduct of the sale to the mortgagor in a case where there is negative equity, so that it is the mortgagee who is likely to have the greater incentive to obtain the best price and the quickest sale. Both these steps were taken in *Barrett v Halifax Building Society*, 28 HLR 634. I have serious doubt whether that case was rightly decided . . .

Comment

(1) How significant a qualification upon *Palk* is this decision?

(2) Could it be argued that the court underplays the s 91(2) jurisdiction, under which it can be ordered that the conduct of the sale be undertaken by the mortgagor?[45]

(3) In *Barrett*, the mortgagor had negotiated a sale and it was not argued that the price was too low. Is there any real justification for Millett LJ's criticism of the decision? Is it ever wise for a prospective purchaser from the mortgagor to proceed with the purchase if it is discovered that there is negative equity?

Further reading

Bamforth, N [1996] CLP Pt 2, pages 207–244: Lord Macnaghten's puzzle: the mortgage of real property in English law.

Brown, S [2007] Conv 316: The Consumer Credit Act 2006: real additional mortgagor protection?

Nield, S and Hopkins, N (2013) 33 LS 431: Human rights and mortgage repossession: beyond property law using Article 8.

Rudden, B (1961) 25 Conv 278: Mortgagee's right to possession.

Thompson, M (2003) 'Mortgages and undue influence', in *Modern Studies in Property Law*, Vol 2, ed. E Cooke, Chapter 7.

Watt, G (2007) 'The lie of the land: mortgage law as legal fiction', in *Modern Studies in Property Law*, Vol 4, ed. E Cooke, Chapter 4.

Whitehouse, L (1997) 'The right to possession: the need for substantive reform', in *The Reform of Property Law*, eds. P Jackson and D Wilde, Chapter 9.

[45] See Dixon (1998) 18 LS 279.

Index